AF207892

FRENCH PAINTING

1830-1920

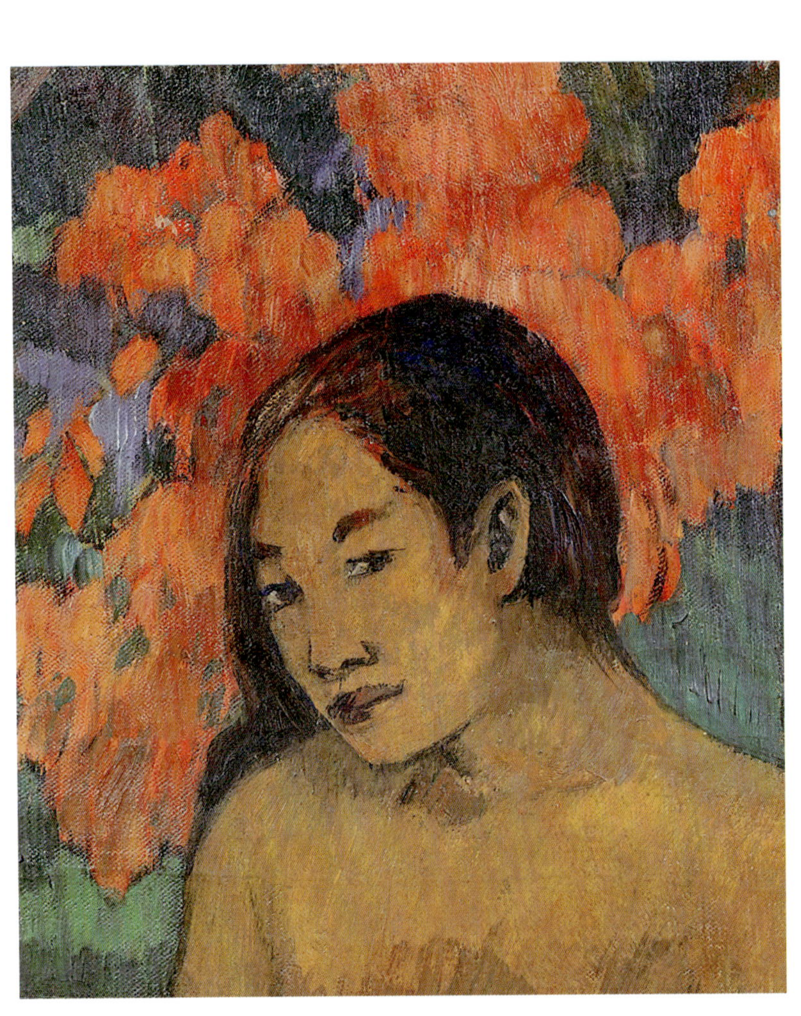

VALENTIN GRIVET

FRENCH PAINTING
LA PEINTURE FRANÇAISE
FRANZÖSISCHE MALEREI
LA PINTURA FRANCESA
PINTURA FRANCESA
FRANSE SCHILDERKUNST

1830-1920

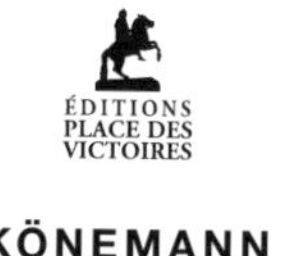

ÉDITIONS
PLACE DES
VICTOIRES

KÖNEMANN

Contents

Sommaire

Inhalt

Índice

Indice

Inhoud

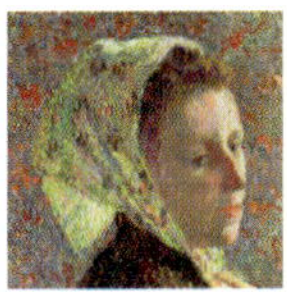

6 Introductory remarks
Introduction
Einleitung
Introducción
Introdução
Inleiding

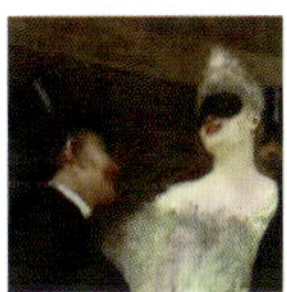

10 The Belle époque
La Belle Époque
Die Belle Époque
La Belle Époque
A Belle Époque
De Belle Époque

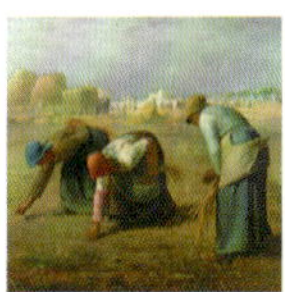

56 Naturalism
Le naturalisme
Der Naturalismus
Naturalismo
Naturalismo
Naturalisme

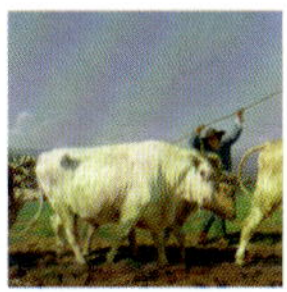

98 The Realism
Le réalisme
Der Realismus
El Realismo
O Realismo
Realisme

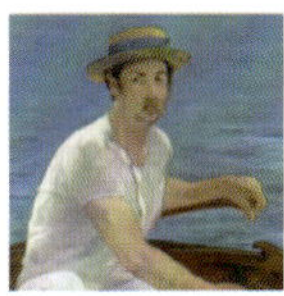

154 The Forerunners of Impressionism
Les précurseurs de l'impressionnisme
Die Vorläufer des Impressionismus
Les Precursores del Impresionismo
O Provisório do Impressionismo
De Voorloper van het Impressionisme

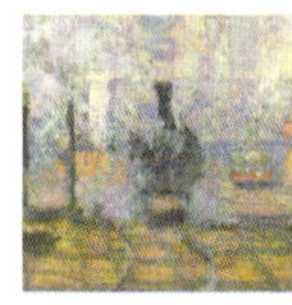

194 Impressionism
L'impressionnisme
Der Impressionismus
Impresionismo
Impressionismo
Impressionisme

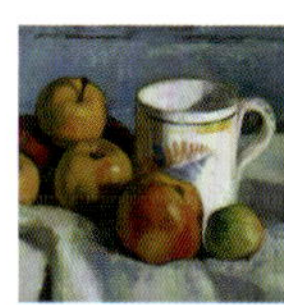

308 Post-Impressionism
Le postimpressionnisme
Der Postimpressionismus
Postimpresionismo
Pós-Impressionismo
Postimpressionisme

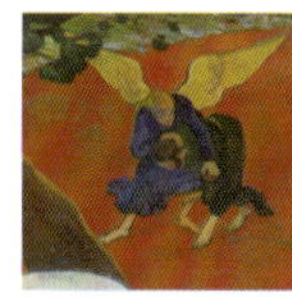

370 Paul Gauguin and the Nabis
Paul Gauguin et les Nabis
Paul Gauguin und die Nabis
Paul Gauguin y los Nabis
Paul Gauguin e o Nabis
Paul Gauguin en de Nabis

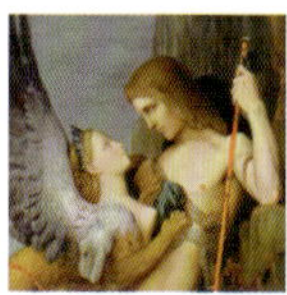

464 Symbolism
Le symbolisme
Der Symbolismus
Simbolismo
Símbologia
Symbolisme

502 Index

Introductory remarks

Academic Art, Naturalism, Realism, Impressionism, Neo-Impressionism, Divisionism, Synthetism, Symbolism - in the history of art, style designations serve to order things. It is a chronological sequence that provides continuity, but is usually characterized by breaks and overlaps. Style designations are therefore always an artificially created division. The work of many painters - and this applies especially to the 19th century - is characterized by several currents. Thus Henri Gervex or Jean Béraud not only belonged to academic art but also to the style of the Belle Époque, and even Henri Fantin-Latour, who first turned to realism and later to symbolism, can hardly be assigned to a concrete style.

The time span covered in this book is relatively short. It stretches from the middle of the 19th century to the first years of the following century - a time marked by great social, political, technical and

Introduction

Académisme, art pompier, naturalisme, réalisme, impressionnisme, néo-impressionnisme, divisionnisme, synthétisme, symbolisme… les classifications chères à l'histoire de l'art ont le mérite de clarifier les choses en proposant une chronologie, faite de continuités, de ruptures, d'influences croisées. Mais cette succession de mouvements, de courants, d'écoles, est un découpage par essence artificiel. Car certains peintres – et cela s'annonce particulièrement vrai pour le XIXe siècle –, peuvent être assimilés, selon les périodes de leur œuvre, à plusieurs tendances. À titre d'exemple, des peintres comme Henri Gervex ou Jean Béraud appartiennent autant à l'art académique qu'au style de la Belle Époque, et l'inclassable Henri Fantin-Latour, l'ami de Manet et des futurs impressionnistes, a produit des œuvres réalistes avant de basculer dans le symbolisme.

Einleitung

Akademische Kunst, Naturalismus, Realismus, Impressionismus, Neoimpressionismus, Divisionismus, Synthetismus, Symbolismus – Stilbezeichnungen dienen in der Kunstgeschichte dazu, den Dingen eine Ordnung zu geben, einen chronologischen Ablauf, der Kontinuität vorgibt, in der Regel aber durch Brüche und sich kreuzende Einflüsse gekennzeichnet ist. Stilbezeichnungen sind deshalb immer eine künstlich geschaffene Einteilung. Das Werk vieler Maler – und dies gilt insbesondere für das 19. Jh. – ist in mehreren Strömungen verwurzelt. So gehören Henri Gervex oder Jean Béraud nicht nur der Akademischen Kunst sondern gleichzeitig dem Stil der Belle Époque an, und auch Henri Fantin-Latour, der sich zuerst dem Realismus und später dem Symbolismus zuwandte, lässt sich kaum einem konkreten Stil zuordnen.

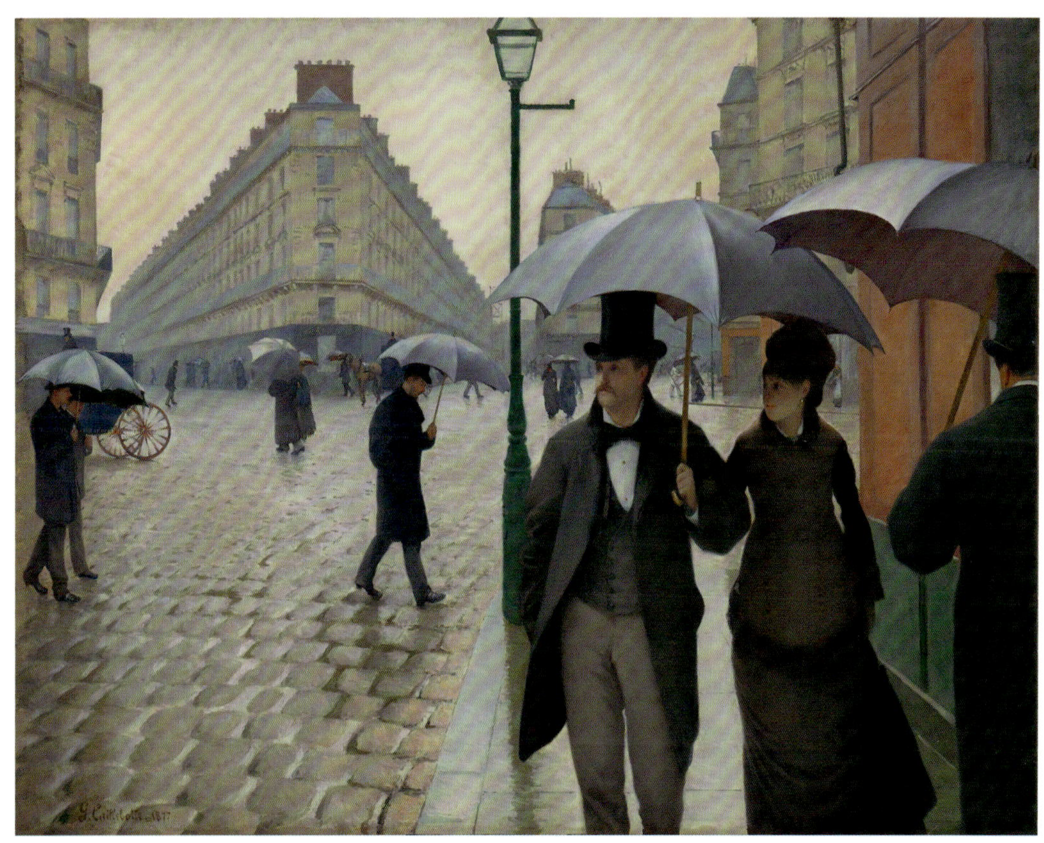

Introducción

Arte Académico, Naturalismo, Realismo, Impresionismo, Neo-Impresionismo, Divisionismo, Sintetismo, Simbolismo - en la historia del arte, las designaciones de estilo sirven para ordenar las cosas. Es una secuencia cronológica que proporciona continuidad, pero que generalmente se caracteriza por rupturas y superposiciones. Por lo tanto, las denominaciones de estilo son siempre una división creada artificialmente. La obra de muchos pintores -y esto se aplica especialmente al siglo XIX- se caracteriza por varias corrientes. Así, Henri Gervex o Jean Béraud no sólo pertenecían al arte académico, sino también al estilo de la Belle Époque, e incluso Henri Fantin-Latour, que primero se dedicó al realismo y después al simbolismo, por lo que difícilmente puede ser asignado a un estilo concreto.

El período de tiempo cubierto en este libro es relativamente corto. Se extiende desde mediados del siglo XIX hasta los primeros años del siglo siguiente,

Introdução

Arte Acadêmica, Naturalismo, Realismo, Impressionismo, Neoimpressionismo, Divisionismo, Sintetismo, Simbolismo - na história da arte, designações de estilo servem para ordenar coisas. É uma sequência cronológica que proporciona continuidade, mas é geralmente caracterizada por quebras e sobreposições. As designações de estilo são, portanto, sempre uma divisão criada artificialmente. O trabalho de muitos pintores - e isto aplica-se especialmente ao século XIX - é caracterizado por várias correntes. Assim, Henri Gervex ou Jean Béraud não só pertenciam à arte acadêmica, mas também ao estilo da Belle Époque, e mesmo Henri Fantin-Latour, que primeiro recorreu ao realismo e depois ao simbolismo, dificilmente pode ser atribuído a um estilo concreto. O período de tempo coberto neste livro é relativamente curto. Estende-se desde meados do século XIX até aos primeiros anos do século seguinte - uma época marcada por grandes mudanças sociais, políticas, técnicas e

Inleiding

Academische kunst, naturalisme, realisme, impressionisme, neo-impressionisme, divisionisme, synthetisme, symbolisme: in de kunstgeschiedenis dienen stijlbenamingen om een ordening aan te brengen. Het is een chronologisch verloop dat continuïteit suggereert, maar meestal gekenmerkt wordt door onderbrekingen en overlappingen. Stijlbenamingen zijn daarom altijd een kunstmatige indeling. Het werk van veel schilders – en dit geldt vooral voor de 19e eeuw – wordt gekenmerkt door verschillende stromingen. Zo vertegenwoordigden Henri Gervex en Jean Béraud niet alleen de academische kunst, maar ook de stijl van de belle époque, en zelfs Henri Fantin-Latour, die zich eerst tot het realisme en later tot het symbolisme wendde, laat zich moeilijk bij één concrete stijl indelen.

De tijdspanne die in dit boek wordt behandeld, is relatief kort en loopt van het midden van de 19e eeuw tot de eerste jaren van de volgende eeuw. Het is een tijd

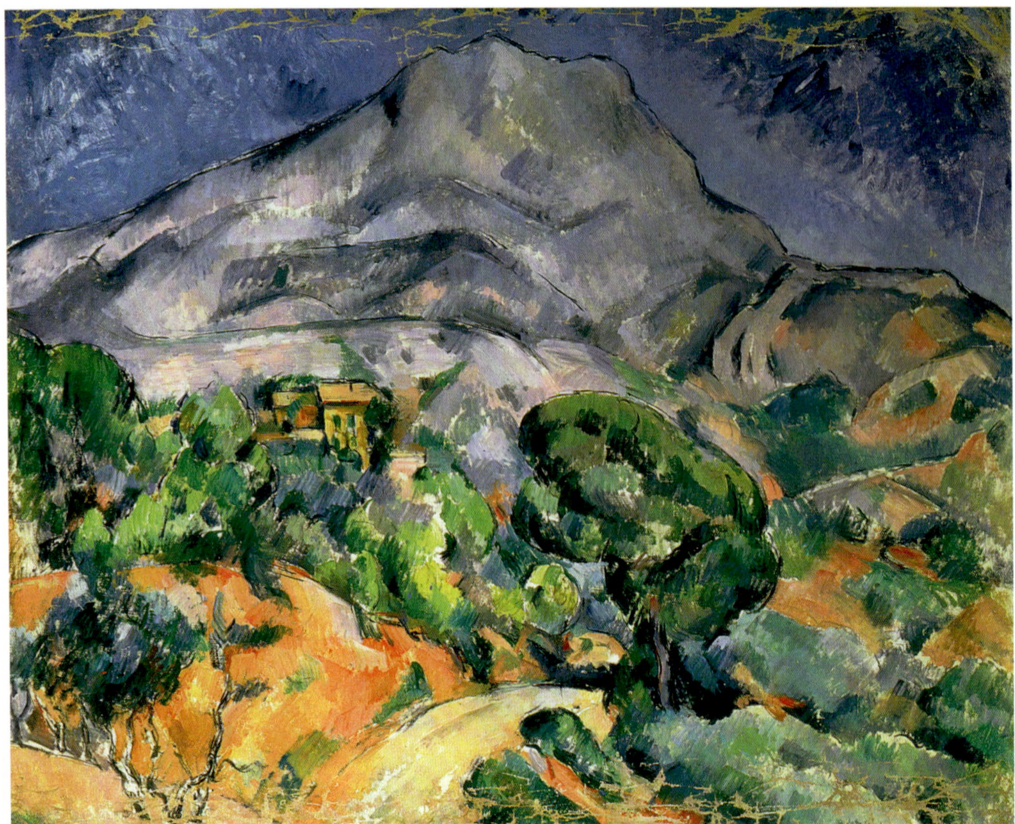

Mont Sainte-Victoire

Route devant la montagne
Sainte-Victoire

Straße vor dem Gebirge
Sainte-Victoire

Carretera frente a las
montañas Sainte-Victoire

Estrada em frente às
montanhas Sainte-Victoire

Weg voor de Mont
Sainte-Victoire

PAUL CÉZANNE (1839-1906)
1898-1902, Oil on canvas/
Huile sur toile,
78 × 99 cm, State Hermitage
Museum, St. Petersburg

urban changes. From the realistic paintings of
Gustave Courbet to the Impressionist movement
to the Nabis group of artists, the development
of painting during this period is enormous.
Jean-Baptiste Camille Corot, Claude Monet,
Edgar Degas, Gustave Caillebotte, Paul Gauguin,
Henri de Toulouse-Lautrec, Paul Cézanne
and Pierre Bonnard all contributed their share
to the path to modernism. The history of French
painting, illustrated by more than 400 works,
unfolds in eight chronologically and thematically
structured chapters. The artists represented
will not only be presented with their most
important paintings, but also with their lesser
known ones. This provides insights into all
facets of their work.

La période étudiée au fil de ces pages est relativement
courte. Elle se déploie entre le milieu du XIXe siècle
et le début du siècle suivant, une époque traversée
par de profondes mutations, sociales, politiques,
techniques, urbaines… Des premiers succès réalistes
de Gustave Courbet aux compositions stylisées des
Nabis, en passant par l'aventure des impressionnistes,
le chemin parcouru par les peintres est considérable.
Jean-Baptiste Camille Corot, Claude Monet,
Edgar Degas, Gustave Caillebotte, Paul Gauguin,
Henri de Toulouse-Lautrec, Paul Cézanne,
Pierre Bonnard… ont tous posé une pierre à l'édifice
de la modernité. Scandé en huit chapitres à la fois
thématiques et chronologiques, ce livre déroule une
histoire de la peinture française, à travers une sélection
de plus de quatre cent cinquante œuvres. Pour chacun
des artistes représentés, le parti pris a été de réunir les
chefs-d'œuvre incontournables, mais aussi de proposer
des tableaux moins connus, qui mettent en lumière
d'autres facettes de leurs recherches.

Die in diesem Werk behandelte Zeitspanne ist
relativ kurz. Sie erstreckt sich von der Mitte des
19. Jahrhunderts bis in die ersten Jahre des darauf
folgenden – eine Zeit, die geprägt war von großen
sozialen, politischen, technischen und urbanen
Veränderungen. Angefangen bei den realistischen
Gemälden von Gustave Courbet über die Bewegung der
Impressionisten bis hin zur Künstlergruppe der Nabis
– die Entwicklung, die die Malerei während dieser Zeit
durchläuft, ist enorm. Jean-Baptiste Camille Corot,
Claude Monet, Edgar Degas, Gustave Caillebotte,
Paul Gauguin, Henri de Toulouse-Lautrec, Paul Cézanne
oder Pierre Bonnard trugen alle ihren Teil zum Weg in
die Moderne bei. In acht chronologisch und thematisch
aufgebauten Kapiteln entfaltet sich die Geschichte der
französischen Malerei, die von mehr als 400 Werken
bebildert wird. Die vertretenen Künstler werden dabei
nicht nur anhand ihrer wichtigsten Gemälde vorgestellt,
sondern auch durch ihre weniger bekannten. So ergeben
sich Einblicke in alle Facetten ihres Schaffens.

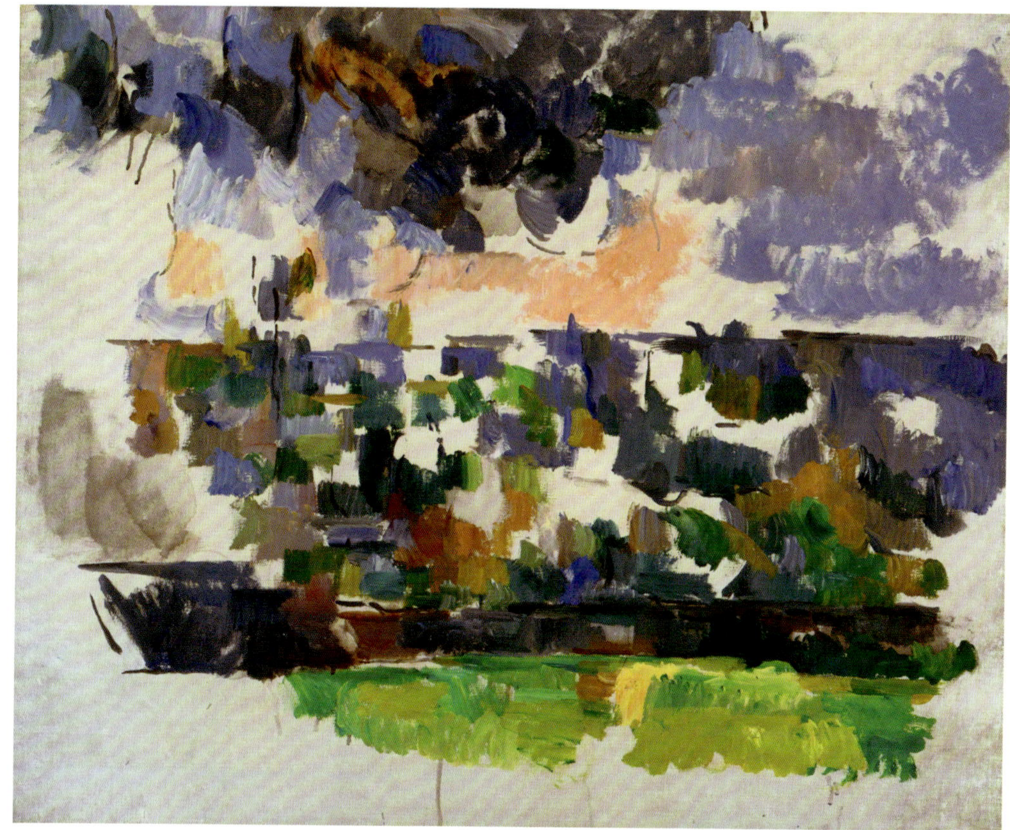

una época marcada por grandes cambios sociales, políticos, técnicos y urbanos. Desde las pinturas realistas de Gustave Courbet hasta el movimiento impresionista y el grupo de artistas Nabis, el desarrollo de la pintura durante este período es enorme. Jean-Baptiste Camille Corot, Claude Monet, Edgar Degas, Gustave Caillebotte, Paul Gauguin, Henri de Toulouse-Lautrec, Paul Cézanne y Pierre Bonnard contribuyeron con su aportación al camino del modernismo. La historia de la pintura francesa, ilustrada por más de 400 obras, se desarrolla en ocho capítulos cronológica y temáticamente estructurados. Los artistas representados no sólo serán presentados con sus pinturas más importantes, sino también con las menos conocidas. Esto proporciona una visión de todas las facetas de su trabajo.

urbanas. Das pinturas realistas de Gustave Courbet ao movimento impressionista ao grupo de artistas Nabis, o desenvolvimento da pintura durante este período é enorme. Jean-Baptiste Camille Corot, Claude Monet, Edgar Degas, Gustave Caillebotte, Paul Gauguin, Henri de Toulouse-Lautrec, Paul Cézanne e Pierre Bonnard contribuíram para o caminho do modernismo. A história da pintura francesa, ilustrada por mais de 400 obras, desdobra-se em oito capítulos cronológica e tematicamente estruturados. Os artistas representados não só serão apresentados com suas pinturas mais importantes, mas também com as menos conhecidas. Isso fornece insights sobre todas as facetas de seu trabalho.

die gekenmerkt wordt door grote maatschappelijke, politieke, technische en stedelijke veranderingen. Van de realistische schilderijen van Gustave Courbet tot de beweging van het impressionisme en de kunst van de Nabis, de ontwikkeling die de schilderkunst in deze periode onderging, was enorm. Jean-Baptiste Camille Corot, Claude Monet, Edgar Degas, Gustave Caillebotte, Paul Gauguin, Henri de Toulouse-Lautrec, Paul Cézanne en Pierre Bonnard hielpen allemaal mee aan het effenen van het pad naar de moderne kunst. De geschiedenis van de Franse schilderkunst, geïllustreerd met meer dan 400 werken, ontvouwt zich in acht chronologisch en thematisch opgebouwde hoofdstukken. De vertegenwoordigde kunstenaars worden daarbij niet alleen met hun belangrijkste schilderijen, maar ook met hun minder bekende schilderijen voorgesteld. Dat geeft een beter inzicht in alle facetten van hun werk.

The Belle époque

La Belle Époque

Die Belle époque

La Belle époque

A Belle époque

De Belle époque

The Belle Époque

As a synonym for technical and social progress, the Belle Époque describes the period between the 1870s and the outbreak of the First World War. At the time of the second industrial revolution, the image of Paris was transformed by the large-scale transformations of the urban planner Georges Eugène Haussmann. The bourgeoisie satisfied its hunger for distraction and pleasure in the lively atmosphere of the capital, which had become a true flagship of modernity. The works in this chapter all date from the last decades of the 19th century. Their creators set themselves the task of bringing Paris' atmosphere and charm to life on the canvas. James Tissot, Jean Béraud, Paul-Albert Besnard or Henri Gervex captured the transformation of the cityscape, the enjoyment of pleasures and the customs of the time in a realistic style, with precise strokes and often with bright colors. In addition to their aesthetic qualities, these paintings have a documentary value - they draw a portrait of

La Belle Époque

Synonyme de progrès techniques et d'avancées sociales, la Belle Époque couvre une large période qui s'étend entre les années 1870 et le début de la Première Guerre mondiale. À l'heure de la deuxième révolution industrielle, Paris est en pleine mutation, au fil des campagnes d'urbanisation engagées par Georges Eugène Haussmann. Avide de plaisirs et de sorties, la bourgeoisie profite alors de la vie animée de la capitale, devenue une véritable vitrine de la modernité. L'iconographie retenue pour ce premier chapitre se concentre exclusivement sur les dernières décennies du XIXe siècle. Elle réunit les principaux tableaux de peintres qui se sont appliqués à restituer l'atmosphère et les charmes de Paris. Dans un style réaliste, au tracé précis et aux couleurs souvent éclatantes, James Tissot, Jean Béraud, Paul-Albert Besnard ou Henri Gervex témoignent du paysage urbain transformé, des divertissements, des mœurs. Au-delà de leurs indéniables qualités esthétiques, leurs œuvres ont

Die Belle Époque

Als Synonym für technischen und sozialen Fortschritt bezeichnet die Belle Époque die Zeitspanne zwischen den 1870er-Jahren und dem Ausbruch des Ersten Weltkrieges. Zur Zeit der zweiten industriellen Revolution wandelt sich das Gesicht Paris durch die groß angelegten Umgestaltungen des Stadtplaners Georges Eugène Haussmann. Das Bürgertum stillt seinen Hunger nach Zerstreuung und Vergnügen an der belebten Atmosphäre der Hauptstadt, die zu einem wahren Aushängeschild der Moderne geworden ist. Die Werke dieses Kapitels stammen alle aus den letzten Jahrzehnten des 19. Jahrhunderts. Ihre Erschaffer machten es sich zur Aufgabe, die Atmosphäre und den Charme Paris auf der Leinwand zum Leben zu erwecken. In einem realistischen Stil, mit präzisem Strich und häufig mit leuchtenden Farben halten James Tissot, Jean Béraud, Paul-Albert Besnard oder Henri Gervex die Verwandlung des Stadtbilds, die Freuden des Vergnügens und die Bräuche der Zeit fest. Neben ihren

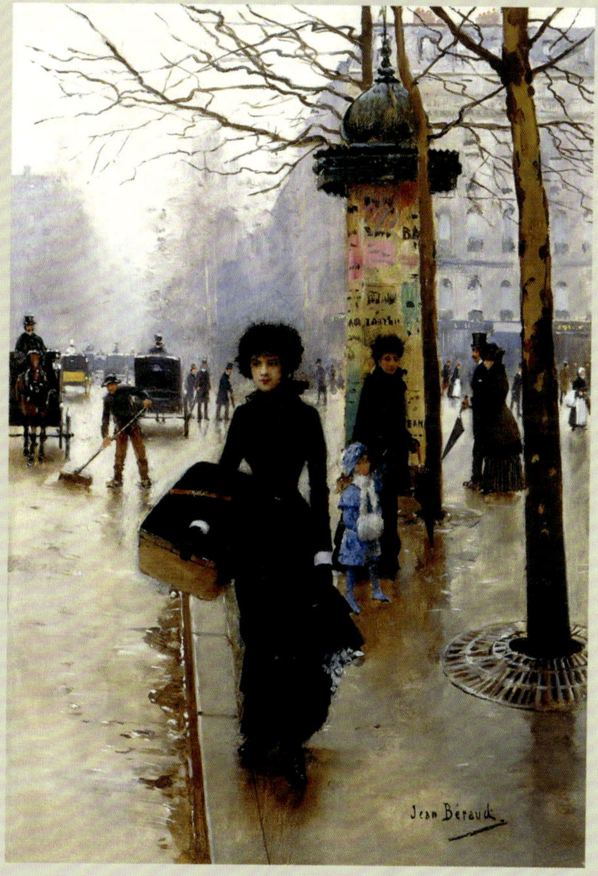

La Belle Époque

Sinónimo de progreso técnico y social, la Belle Époque describe el período comprendido entre la década de 1870 y el estallido de la Primera Guerra Mundial. En el momento de la segunda revolución industrial, la imagen de París fue transformada por las grandes transformaciones del urbanista Georges Eugène Haussmann. La burguesía satisface su hambre de distracción y placer en el ambiente animado de la capital, que se ha convertido en un verdadero buque insignia de la modernidad.

Todas las obras de este capítulo datan de las últimas décadas del siglo XIX. Sus creadores se propusieron la tarea de dar vida a la atmósfera y el encanto de París en el lienzo. James Tissot, Jean Béraud, Paul-Albert Besnard o Henri Gervex captan la transformación del paisaje urbano, los placeres del placer y las costumbres de la época en un estilo realista, con trazos precisos y a menudo con colores vivos. Además de sus cualidades estéticas, estas pinturas tienen un valor

A Belle Époque

Sinônimo de progresso técnico e social, a Belle Époque descreve o período entre a década de 1870 e o início da Primeira Guerra Mundial. Na época da segunda revolução industrial, a imagem de Paris foi transformada pelas transformações em grande escala do urbanista Georges Eugène Haussmann. A burguesia satisfaz a sua fome de distração e prazer na atmosfera animada da capital, que se tornou uma verdadeira bandeira da modernidade.

As obras deste capítulo datam todas das últimas décadas do século XIX. Seus criadores se propuseram a tarefa de dar vida à atmosfera e ao charme de Paris na tela. James Tissot, Jean Béraud, Paul-Albert Besnard ou Henri Gervex capturam a transformação da paisagem urbana, os prazeres do prazer e os costumes da época num estilo realista, com traços precisos e muitas vezes com cores vivas. Para além das suas qualidades estéticas, estas pinturas têm um valor documental - desenham um retrato de toda

De belle Époque

Als synoniem voor technische en maatschappelijk vooruitgang markeert de belle époque de periode tussen de jaren 1870 en het uitbreken van de Eerste Wereldoorlog. Ten tijde van de tweede industriële revolutie veranderde de aanblik van Parijs door de grootschalige vernieuwingen door de stedenbouwkundige Georges Eugène Haussmann. De burgerij bevredigde haar honger naar afleiding en plezier in de levendige sfeer van de hoofdstad, die tot een heus vlaggenschip van de moderniteit was uitgegroeid.

De werken in dit hoofdstuk dateren allemaal van de laatste decennia van de 19e eeuw. De makers ervan stelden zichzelf tot doel de sfeer en charme van Parijs tot leven te brengen op het doek. James Tissot, Jean Béraud, Paul-Albert Besnard en Henri Gervex legden de transformatie van het stadslandschap, de geneugten van het amusement en de gewoonten van die tijd vast in een realistische stijl, met precieze penseelstreken en

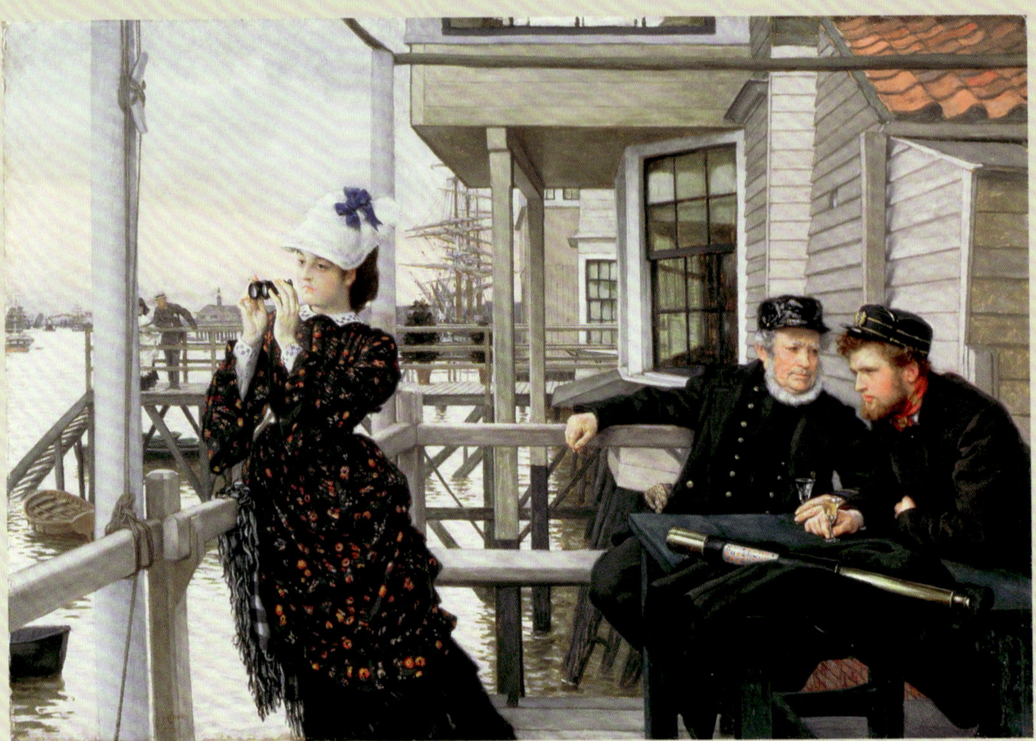

an entire epoch. Unfortunately, the majority of these painters are no longer adequately appreciated today. Some of them were even forgotten in the shadow of the Impressionists. The following pages invite you to rediscover them and their paintings, which tell of night-time pleasures in cafés and bars, the fashionable festivals and balls, the big boulevards or the Parisian women in their long dresses. But the painters of the Belle Époque also understood intimate interiors, such as the return after a ball, men smoking cigars in muted salons or women dedicating themselves to the daily activities in their apartments. James Tissot and Jacques-Émile Blanche created unique portraits of the most important figures in art, entertainment and literature, including Marcel Proust.

une valeur documentaire, et dessinent le portrait d'une époque. La plupart de ces artistes sont aujourd'hui injustement mésestimés, certains même oubliés, relégués à l'ombre de leurs illustres contemporains impressionnistes. L'occasion est donnée ici de les redécouvrir, aux travers de compositions séduisantes, qui mettent en scène les Parisiennes en robes longues, la vie nocturne des brasseries et des cafés, les fêtes mondaines, les bals, les spectacles sur les grands boulevards. Les peintres de la Belle Époque multiplient également les scènes d'intérieurs, retours de soirées, hommes fumant le cigare dans des salons feutrés, ou femmes s'adonnant à des activités du quotidien dans leur appartement. Le portrait n'est pas oublié, sous le pinceau de James Tissot et de Jacques-Émile Blanche, qui immortalisa quelques-unes des plus grandes figures des arts, du spectacle et de la littérature, dont Paul Valéry et l'incontournable Marcel Proust.

ästhetischen Qualitäten besitzen diese Gemälde einen dokumentarischen Wert – sie zeichnen das Porträt einer ganzen Epoche. Der Großteil ihrer Maler wird heute leider nicht mehr angemessen gewürdigt. Einige von ihnen gerieten im Schatten der Impressionisten sogar in Vergessenheit. Die folgenden Seiten laden dazu ein, sie und ihre Gemälde wiederzuentdecken, die vom nächtlichen Vergnügen in Cafés und Bars, den mondänen Festen und Bällen, den großen Boulevards oder den Pariserinnen in ihren langen Kleidern zeugen. Die Maler der Belle Époque verstanden sich aber auch auf intime Interieurs, wie die Rückkehr nach einem Ball, Zigarre rauchende Männer in gedämpften Salons oder Frauen, die sich den täglichen Beschäftigungen in ihrer Wohnung widmen. Durch die Pinsel von James Tissot und Jacques-Émile Blanche entstehen einmalige Porträts, die die wichtigsten Persönlichkeiten der Kunst, der Unterhaltung und der Literatur festhalten, darunter Marcel Proust.

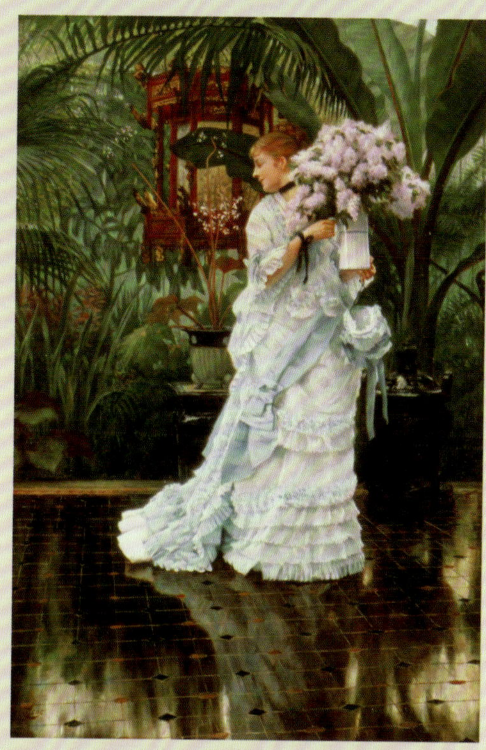

documental: dibujan un retrato de toda una época. Desafortunadamente, la mayoría de sus pintores ya no son apreciados como deberían serlo hoy en día. Algunos de ellos fueron incluso olvidados a la sombra de los impresionistas. Las siguientes páginas le invitan a redescubrir sus cuadros, que hablan de los placeres nocturnos en cafés y bares, de las fiestas y bailes de moda, de los grandes bulevares o de las mujeres parisinas con sus largos vestidos. Pero los pintores de la Belle Époque también comprendían los interiores íntimos, como el regreso después de un baile, los hombres fumando puros en salones apagados o las mujeres dedicándose a las actividades diarias en sus apartamentos. James Tissot y Jacques-Émile Blanche crearon retratos únicos de las figuras más importantes del arte, el entretenimiento y la literatura, incluido el novelista Marcel Proust.

uma época. Infelizmente, a maioria dos seus pintores já não são adequadamente apreciados hoje em dia. Alguns deles foram mesmo esquecidos à sombra dos Impressionistas. As páginas seguintes convidam você a redescobrir ela e suas pinturas, que contam os prazeres noturnos em cafés e bares, os festivais e bailes da moda, as grandes avenidas ou as mulheres parisienses em seus longos vestidos. Mas os pintores da Belle Époque também compreendiam interiores íntimos, como o regresso depois de um baile, homens fumando charutos em salões silenciosos ou mulheres dedicando-se às atividades diárias em seus apartamentos. James Tissot e Jacques-Émile Blanche criaram retratos únicos das figuras mais importantes da arte, entretenimento e literatura, incluindo Marcel Proust.

vaak met heldere kleuren. Naast esthetische kwaliteiten bezitten deze schilderijen een documentaire waarde – ze tekenen het portret van een heel tijdperk. Helaas krijgen de meeste van deze schilders tegenwoordig niet meer de waardering die ze verdienen. Sommigen raakten zelfs vergeten in de schaduw van de impressionisten. De volgende pagina's nodigen u uit om deze schilders en hun schilderijen, die vertellen over nachtelijke genoegens in cafés en bars, mondaine feesten en bals, de grote boulevards en Parijse vrouwen in hun lange jurken, opnieuw te ontdekken. De schilders van de belle époque wisten echter ook wel raad met intieme interieurs, zoals de terugkeer na een bal, sigaren rokende mannen in gedempte salons of vrouwen die hun dagelijkse dingen doen in hun huis. James Tissot en Jacques-Émile Blanche schilderden unieke portretten van de belangrijkste persoonlijkheden uit de kunst, amusementswereld en literatuur, onder wie Marcel Proust.

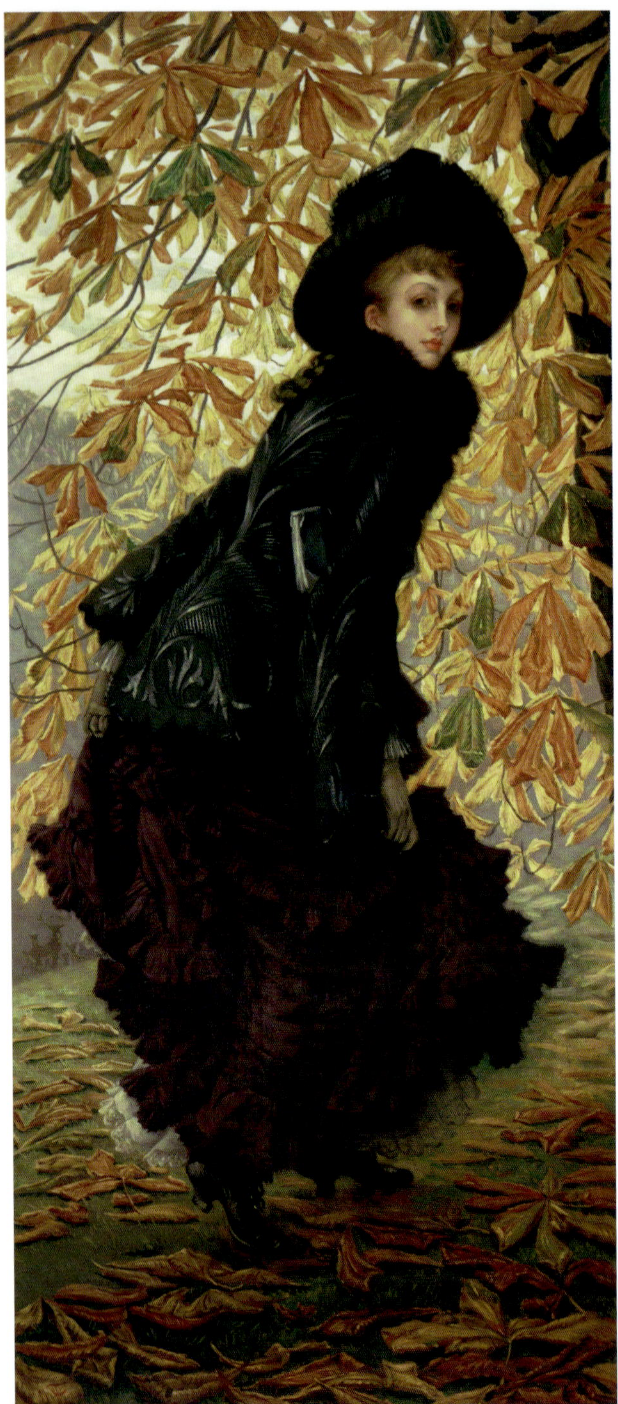

October

Tissot painted Kathleen Newton in the midst of colorful autumn leaves that allow only fragments of the sky and the ground to shine through. His lover and muse died tragically of tuberculosis in 1882.

Octobre

Dans un décor de feuilles dorées d'automne où n'apparaît qu'un fragment de ciel et d'herbe, Tissot a peint Kathleen Newton, sa compagne et muse, qui sera tragiquement emportée par la tuberculose en 1882.

Oktober

Tissot malt Kathleen Newton inmitten bunter Herbstblätter, die nur Fragmente des Himmels und des Bodens durchscheinen lassen. Seine Geliebte und Muse verstarb 1882 tragisch an Tuberkulose.

Octubre

Tissot pinta a Kathleen Newton en medio de coloridas hojas otoñales que sólo dejan pasar fragmentos del cielo y del suelo. Su amante y musa murió trágicamente de tuberculosis en 1882.

Outubro

A Tissot pinta Kathleen Newton no meio de folhas de outono coloridas que permitem que apenas fragmentos do céu e da terra brilhem. O seu amante e musa morreram tragicamente de tuberculose em 1882.

Oktober

Tissot schilderde Kathleen Newton te midden van kleurrijke herfstbladeren die slechts stukjes van de lucht en de grond laten doorschemeren. Zijn geliefde en muze stierf in 1882 op tragische wijze aan tuberculose.

JAMES TISSOT (1836-1902)

1877, Oil on canvas/Huile sur toile,
116,8 × 53,3 cm,
Musée des Beaux-Arts, Montréal

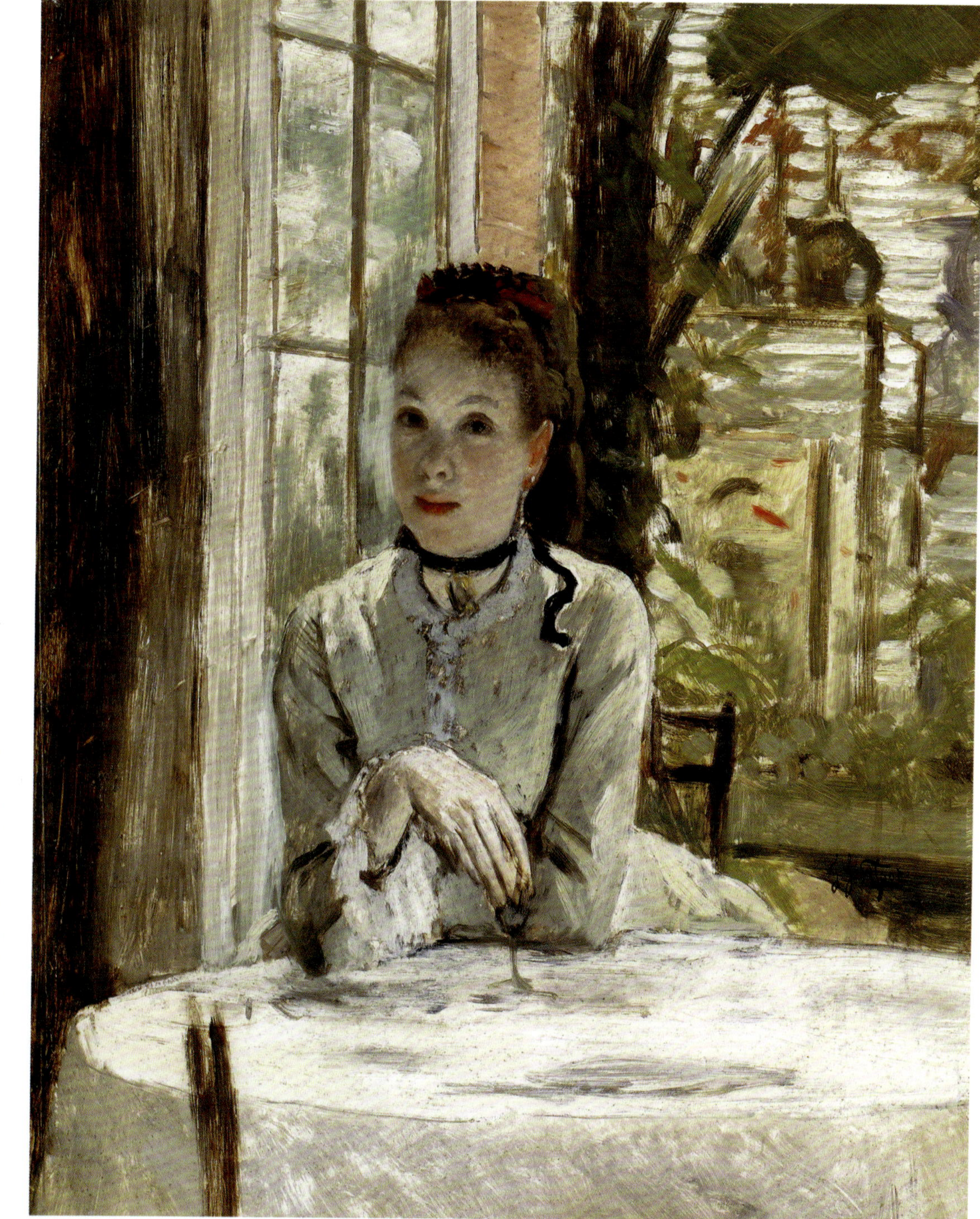

A Woman in an
Elegant Interior

Femme dans un
élégant intérieur

Frau in einem
eleganten
Interieur

Mujer en un
interior elegante

Mulher num
interior elegante

Vrouw in een
elegant interieur

JAMES TISSOT
(1836-1902)

Oil on canvas/
Huile sur toile,
40,5 × 31,7 cm,
Private collection

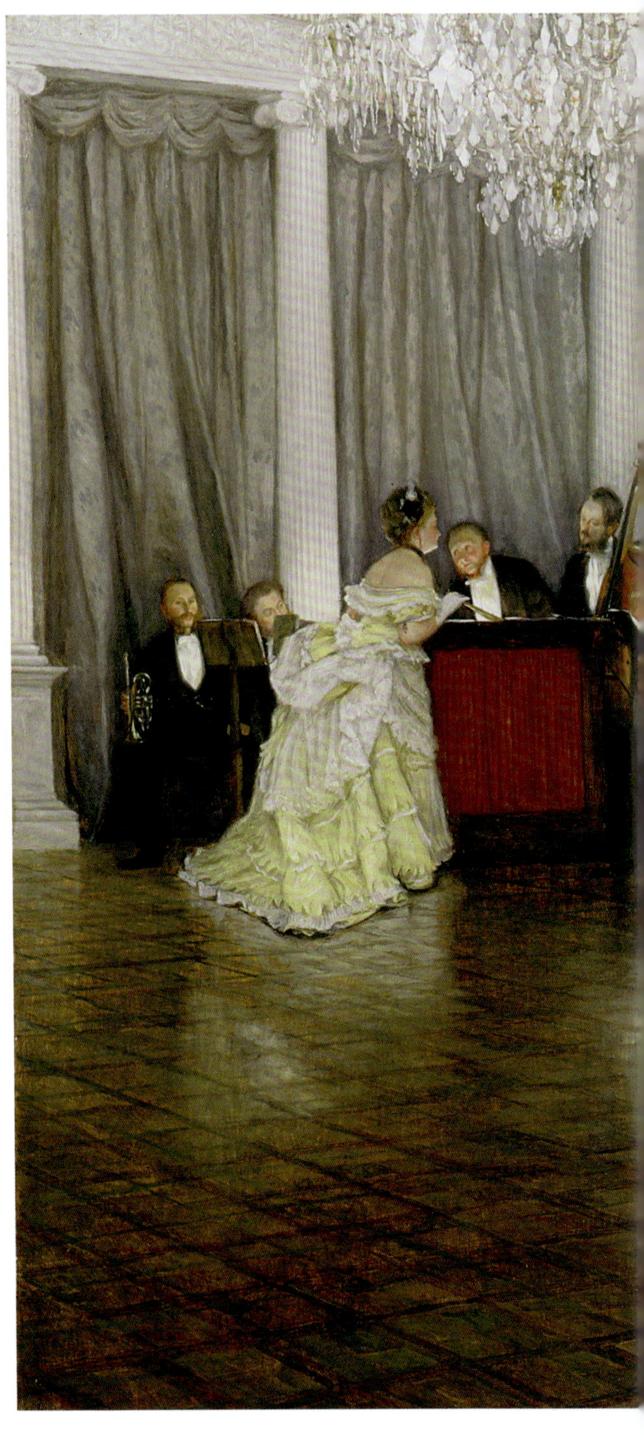

Too Early

Trop tôt

Zu früh

Demasiado pronto

Muito cedo

Te vroeg

JAMES TISSOT (1836-1902)

1873, Oil on canvas/Huile sur toile,
71 × 102 cm, Guildhall Art Gallery, London

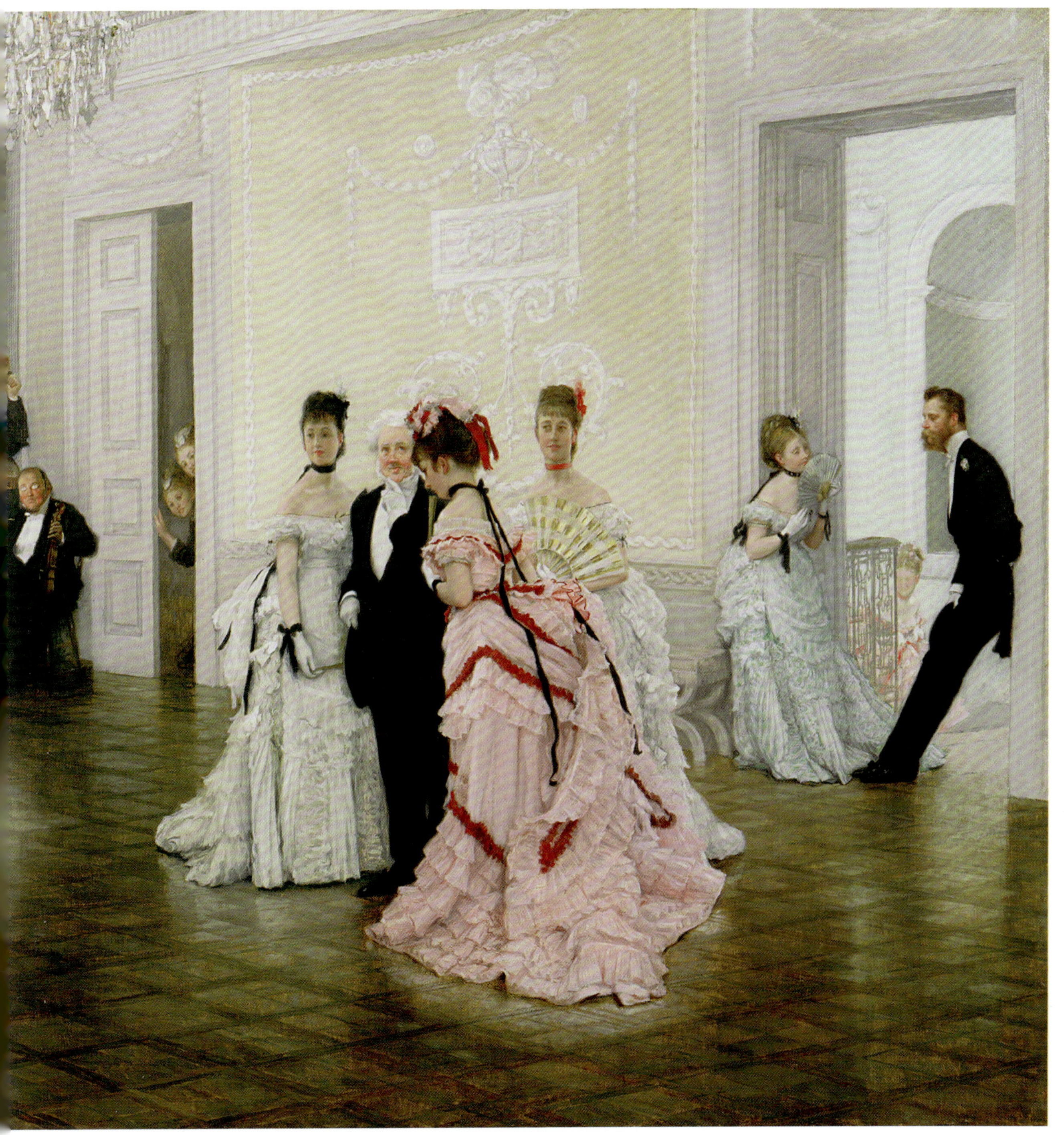

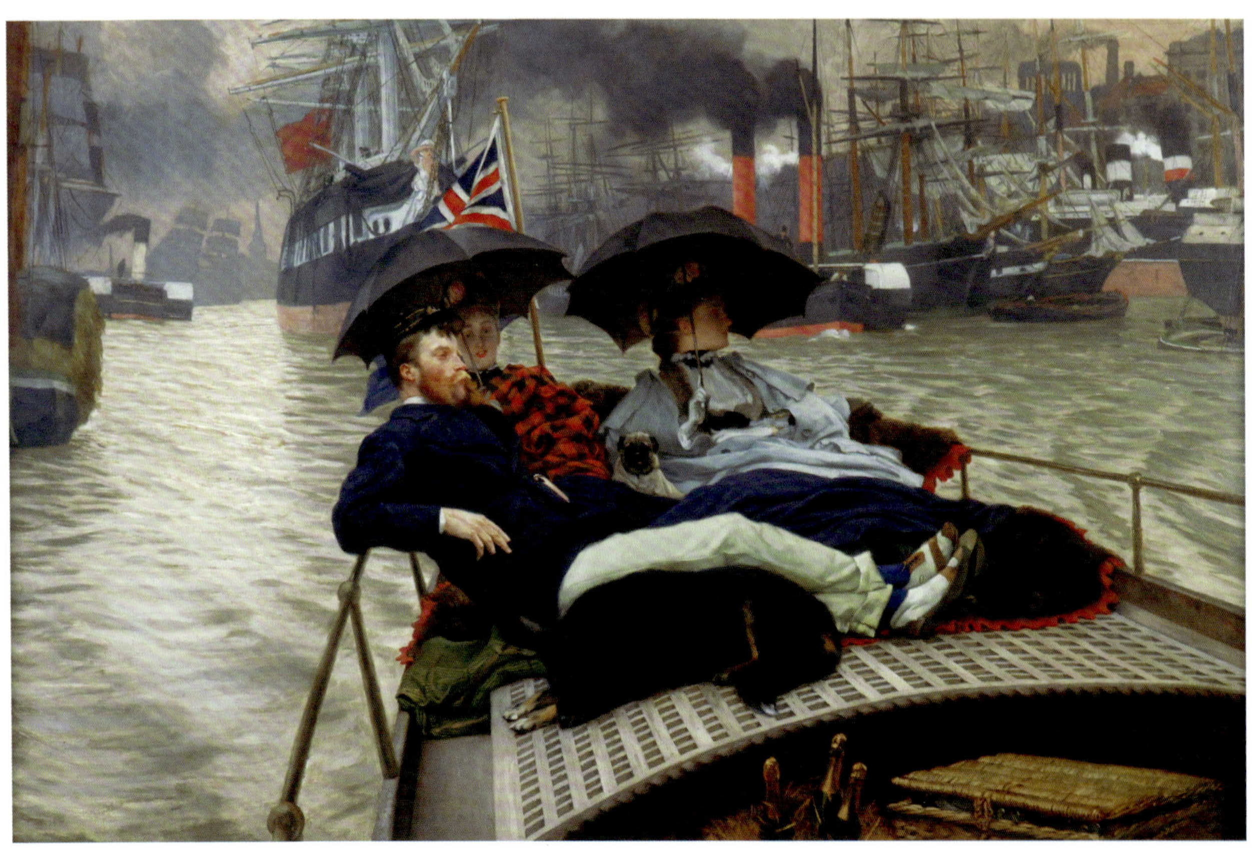

The Thames

Sur la Tamise

Die Themse

En el Támesis

O Tamisa

Op de Theems

JAMES TISSOT (1836-1902)

c. 1876, Oil on canvas/
Huile sur toile, 72,5 × 118 cm,
The Hepworth Wakefield, Wakefield

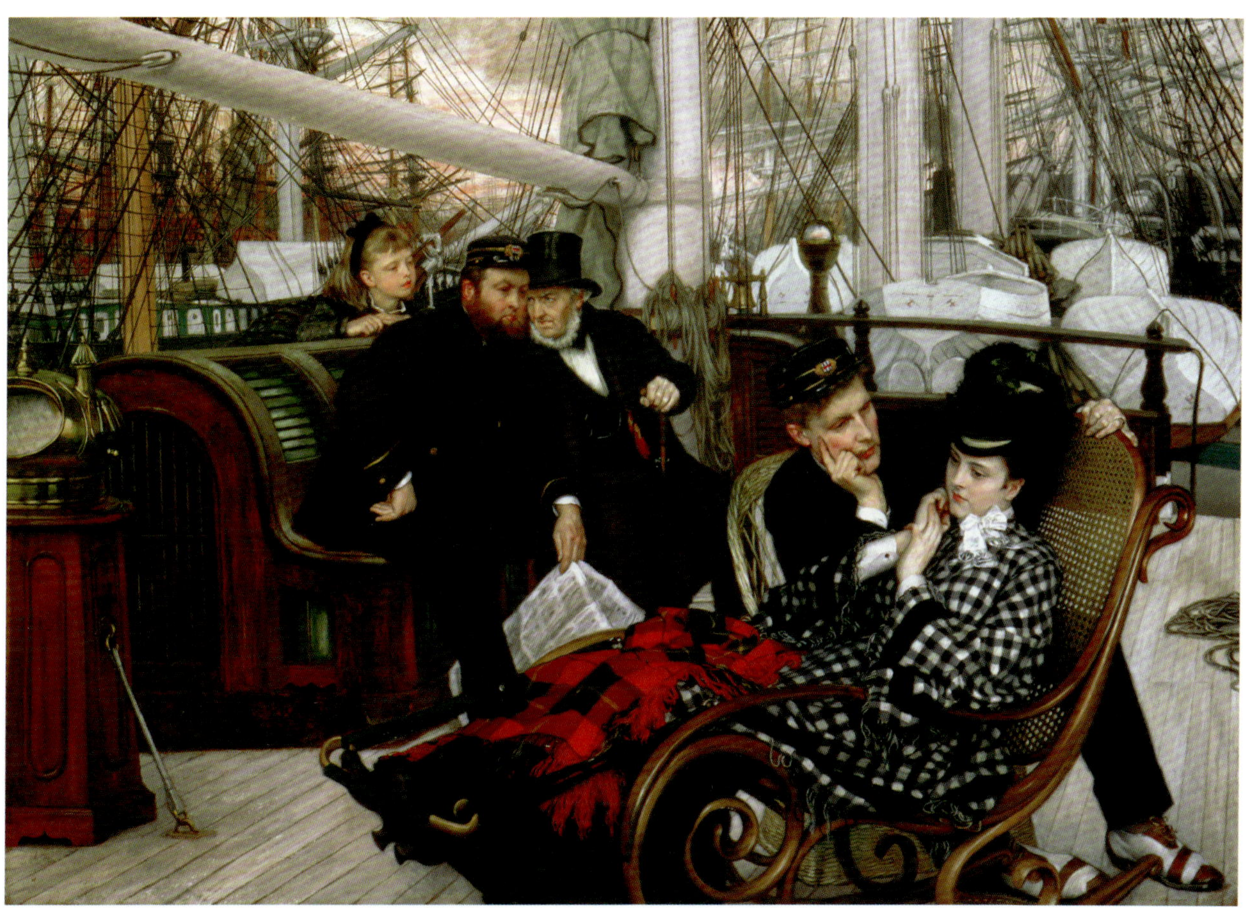

The Last Evening

The scene takes place on a ship the night before departure. The relationships between the persons seem to be multilayered. Two men and a child in the background observe the couple in the foreground, absorbed in themselves.

Le Dernier Soir

La scène se déroule sur un paquebot, la veille du départ. La relation entre les personnages est ambiguë. Qui sont les deux hommes et l'enfant à l'arrière-plan qui observent le couple en pleine confidence ?

Der letzte Abend

Die Szene spielt auf einem Schiff am Abend vor der Abfahrt. Die Beziehungen der Personen scheinen vielschichtig. Zwei Männer und ein Kind im Hintergrund beobachten das in sich selbst vertiefte Paar im Vordergrund.

La última noche

La escena tiene lugar en un barco la noche anterior a la salida. Las relaciones entre las personas parecen ser de varios niveles. Dos hombres y un niño en el fondo observan a la pareja en primer plano, absortos en sí mismos.

A última noite

A cena acontece num navio na noite anterior à partida. As relações entre as pessoas parecem ser multifacetadas. Dois homens e uma criança ao fundo observam o casal em primeiro plano, absorvidos em si mesmos.

De laatste avond

Het tafereel speelt zich af op een schip op de avond van vertrek. De relaties tussen de personen ogen gelaagd. Twee mannen en een kind op de achtergrond observeren het in zichzelf opgaande paar op de voorgrond.

JAMES TISSOT (1836-1902)

1873, Oil on canvas/Huile sur toile, 72 × 103 cm, Guildhall Art Gallery, London

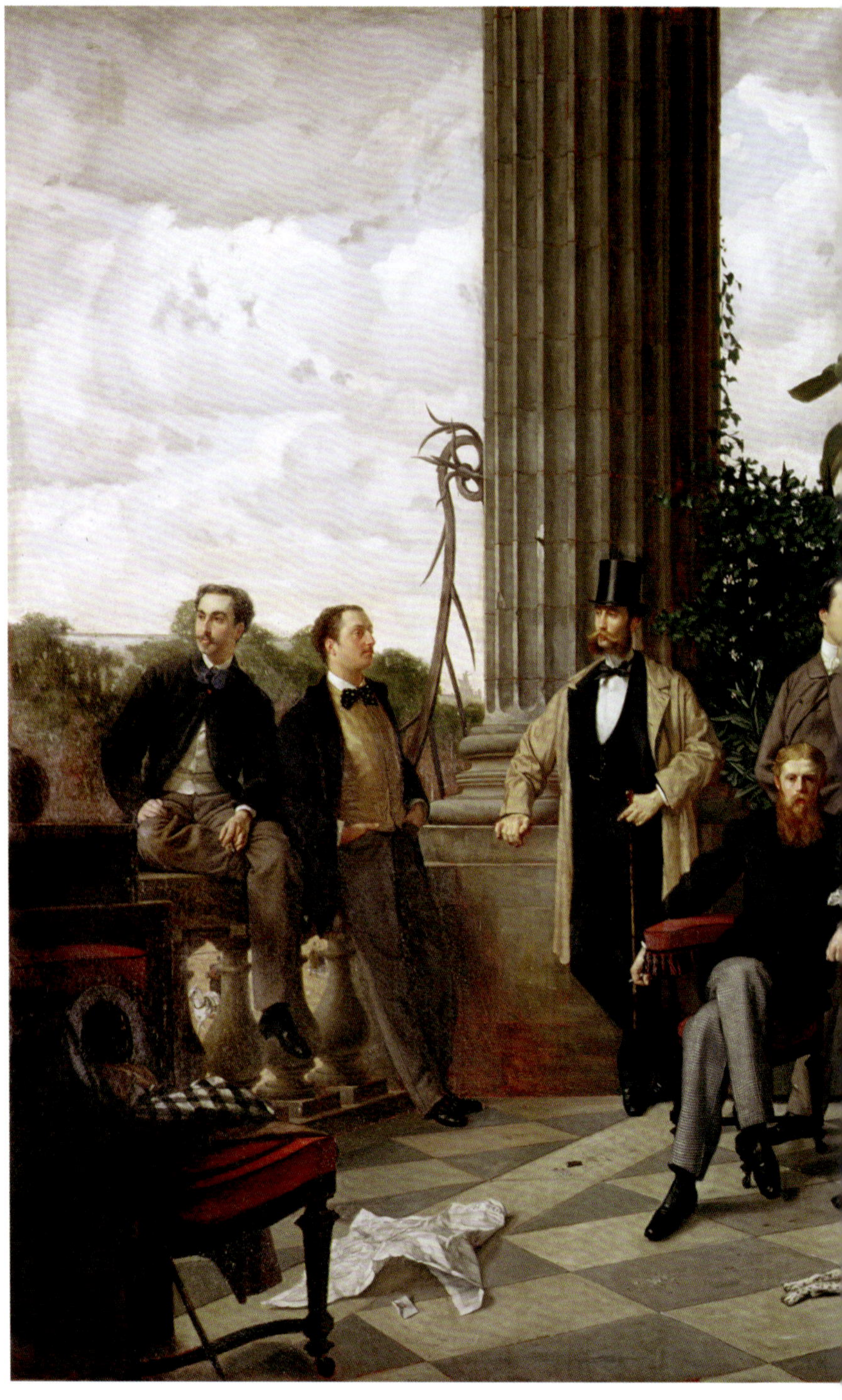

The Circle of the Rue Royale, Paris

Le Cercle de la rue Royale, Paris

Der Cercle de la rue Royale

Le Cercle de la rue Royale, París

O Cercle de la rue Royale

Le cercle de la Rue Royale

JAMES TISSOT (1836–1902)
1868, Oil on canvas/Huile sur toile,
175 × 281 cm, Musée d'Orsay, Paris

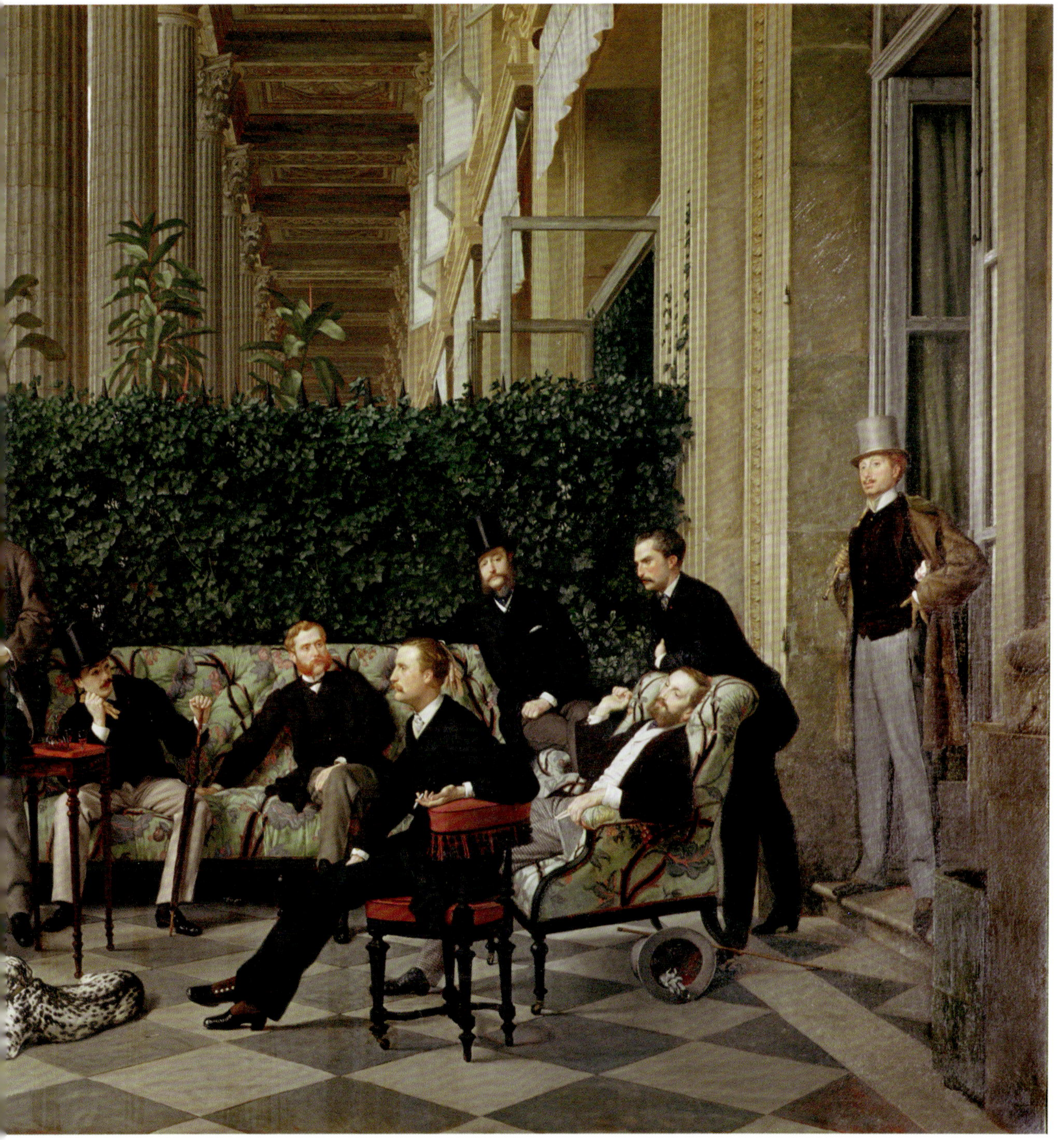

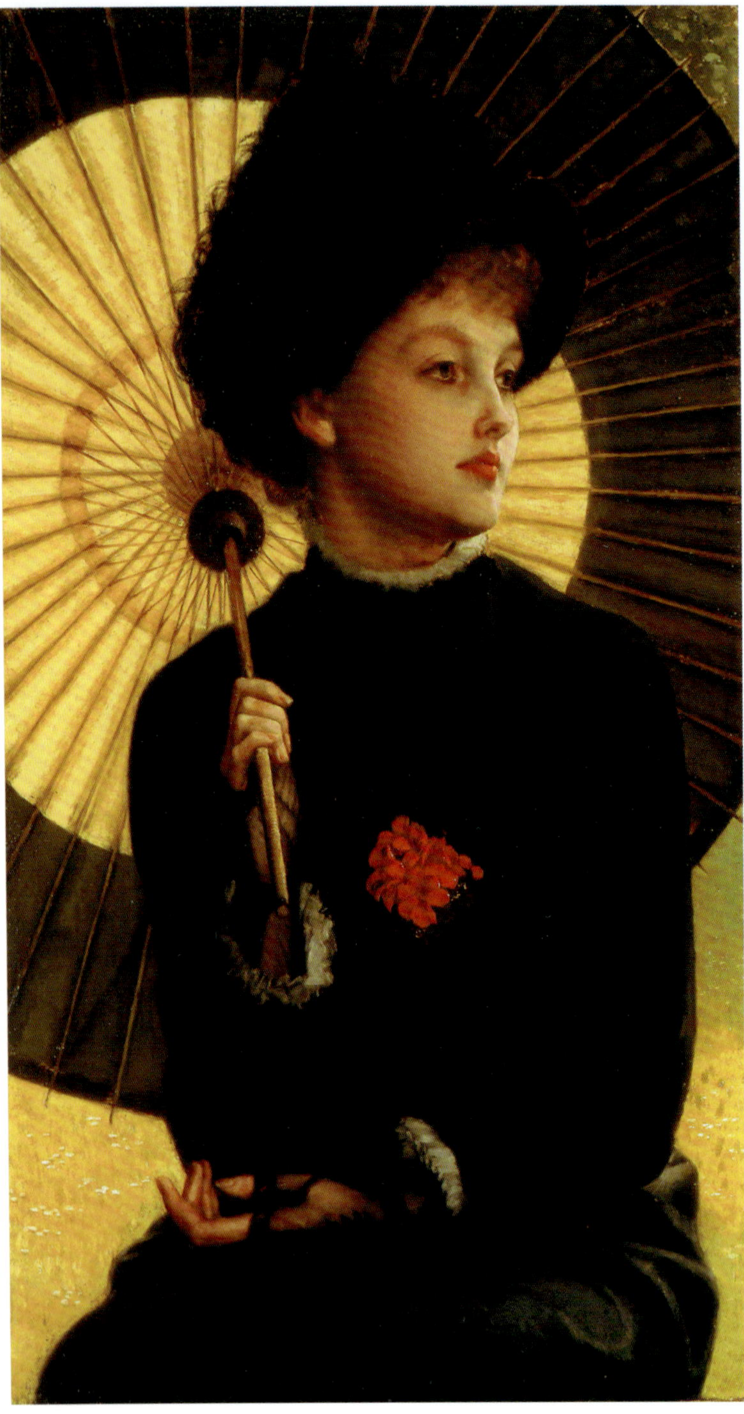

The Lady with the Parasol or Summer

La Dame à l'ombrelle (Kathleen Newton)

Die Dame mit dem Sonnenschirm *oder* Sommer

La dama de la sombrilla (Kathleen Newton)

A senhora com o guarda-sol ou o verão

De zomer *of* Dame met parasol

JAMES TISSOT (1836-1902)

1878-80, Oil on canvas/Huile sur toile,
142 × 54 cm, Private collection

Portrait of Mrs. Kathleen Newton
in a red dress and black bonnet

Kathleen Newton also sat as a model for this motif. Tissot demonstrates his flawless technique, which is reflected in the perfectly executed facial features and the elaboration of the jewelry and fabrics.

Portrait de Mrs. Kathleen Newton
en robe rouge et bonnet noir

Kathleen Newton a posé pour ce portrait mélancolique, où l'artiste fait preuve d'une technique irréprochable, tant dans la pureté des traits du visage que dans le traitement des détails, bijoux ou étoffes.

Bildnis der Kathleen Newton in einem
roten Kleid und schwarzen Hut

Auch für dieses Motiv saß Kathleen Newton Modell. Tissot stellt seine makellose Technik unter Beweis, die sich in den perfekt ausgeführten Gesichtszügen und der Herausarbeitung des Schmucks und der Stoffe zeigt.

Retrato de Kathleen Newton con
vestido rojo y sombrero negro

Kathleen Newton también se sentó como modelo para este motivo. Tissot demuestra su técnica impecable, que se refleja en la perfecta ejecución de los rasgos faciales y en la elaboración de las joyas y tejidos.

Retrato de Kathleen Newton em
vestido vermelho e chapéu preto

Kathleen Newton também se sentou como modelo para este motivo. A Tissot comprova a sua técnica impecável, que se reflecte nas características faciais perfeitamente executadas e na elaboração das jóias e tecidos.

Portret van Kathleen Newton in een
rode jurk en zwarte hoed

Kathleen Newton zat ook model voor dit werk. Tissot bewees hier zijn onberispelijke techniek, die zichtbaar is in de perfect uitgevoerde gelaatstrekken en de uitwerking van de sieraden en stoffen.

JAMES TISSOT (1836-1902)

1880, Oil on canvas/Huile sur toile,
58,4 × 45,7 cm, Private collection

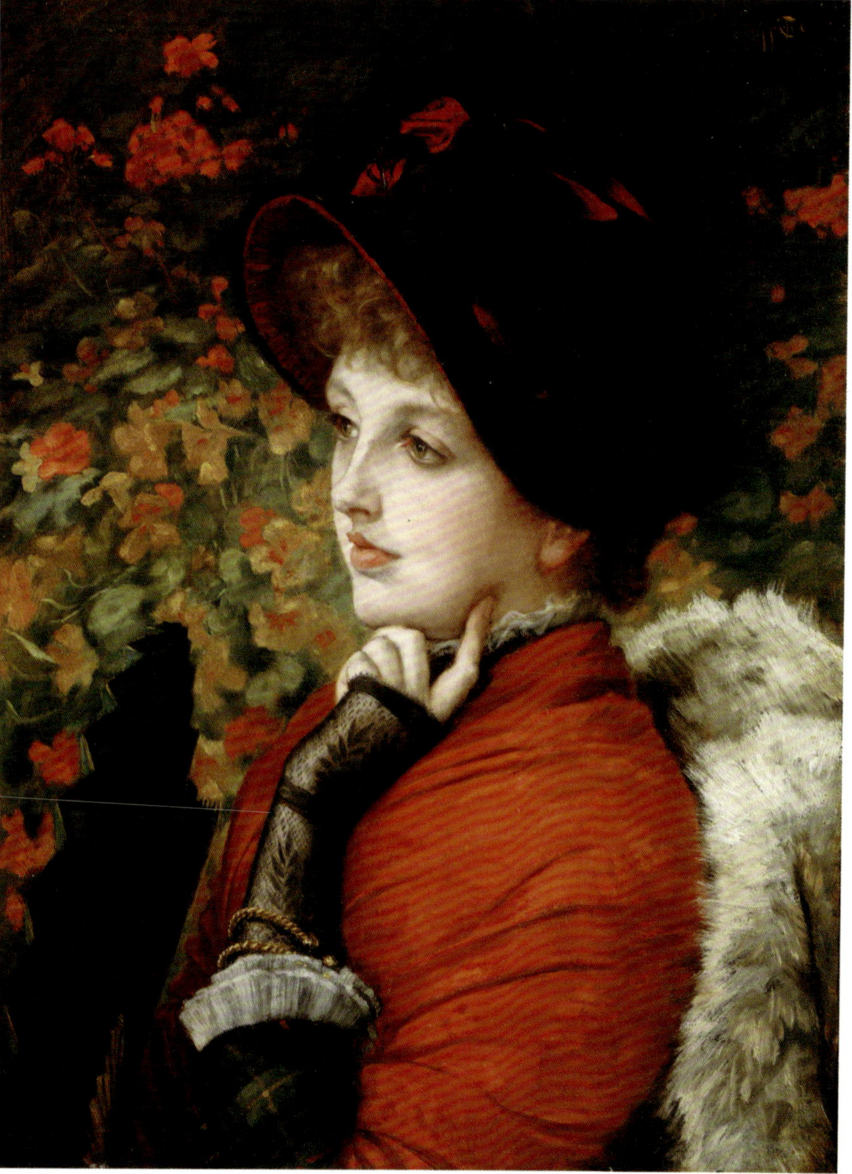

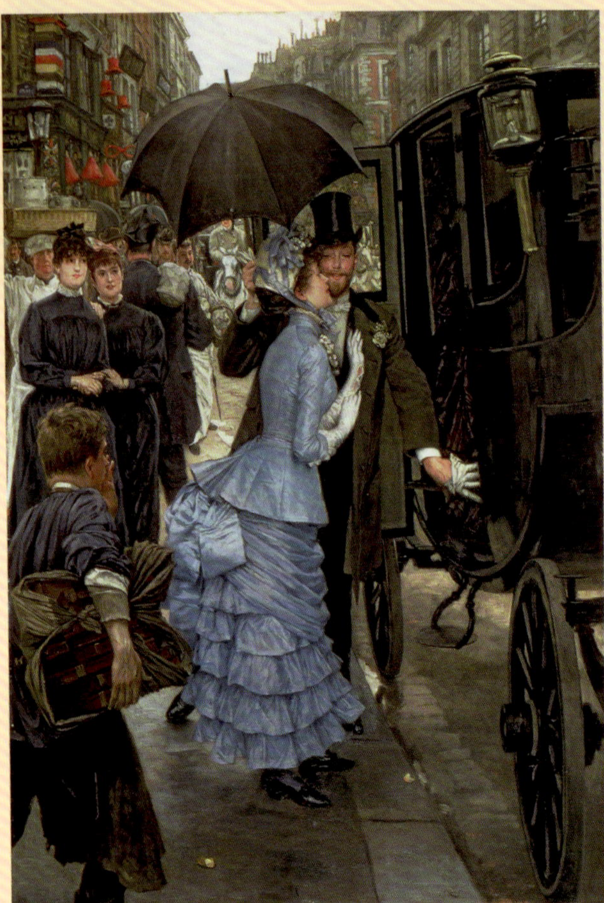

The Bridesmaid

La Demoiselle d'honneur

Die Brautjungfer

La dama de honor

A dama de honra

Het bruidsmeisje

JAMES TISSOT (1836-1902)

1883-85, Oil on canvas/
Huile sur toile, 147,3 × 101,6 cm,
Leeds Museums and Galleries, Leeds

JAMES TISSOT

James Tissot (1836-1902), born in Nantes, is remembered by posterity for his sophisticated portraits. However, he also created motifs inspired by the Middle Ages, historical paintings and - towards the end of his life after returning from a pilgrimage to Palestine - some religious works. He spent his career between Paris and London, where he settled in 1871 and quickly enjoyed great success. He rejected the invitation of his friend Edgar Degas to take part in the first Impressionist group exhibition in 1874. During the Second Empire in France and the Victorian Age in England, his realistic style and precise illustrations made him a portraitist of Parisian and London society. Women are his most common motifs. With great care he depicted not only faces but also dresses, coats, hats and veils.

JAMES TISSOT

Né à Nantes, James Tissot (1836-1902) est un peintre éclectique, dont la postérité n'a retenu qu'une seule catégorie d'œuvres : les peintures mondaines. Il a pourtant réalisé des scènes d'inspiration médiévale, une poignée de tableaux à sujets historiques, et à la fin de sa vie – de retour d'un pèlerinage en Palestine –, quelques toiles religieuses. L'artiste fait carrière entre Paris et Londres, où il s'installe en 1871 et jouit, très rapidement, d'un succès considérable. Malgré l'invitation de son ami Edgar Degas, Tissot refusera de participer à la première exposition du groupe des peintres impressionnistes en 1874. Fidèle à un style réaliste au dessin précis, il devient le portraitiste de l'élégance parisienne sous le Second Empire, et celui de la haute société londonienne à l'époque victorienne. Les femmes occupent l'essentiel de ses compositions. Tissot porte la même attention aux traits du visage qu'au rendu des robes, manteaux, chapeaux et éventails.

JAMES TISSOT

Der in Nantes geborene James Tissot (1836–1902) ist der Nachwelt vor allem wegen seiner mondänen Porträts in Erinnerung geblieben. Er schuf aber auch Motive, die vom Mittelalter inspiriert waren, Historiengemälde und – gegen Ende seines Lebens nach der Rückkehr von einer Pilgerfahrt nach Palästina – einige religiöse Werke. Seine Karriere verbrachte er zwischen Paris und London, wo er sich 1871 niederlässt und schnell große Erfolge feiert. Die Einladung seines Freundes Edgar Degas, 1874 an der ersten Gruppenausstellung der Impressionisten teilzunehmen, schlägt er aus. Während des Zweiten Kaiserreichs in Frankreich und dem Viktorianischen Zeitalter in England steigt er mit seinem realistischen Stil und präzisen Abbildungen zum Porträtisten der Pariser und Londoner Gesellschaft auf. Frauen sind seine häufigsten Motive. Mit großer Sorgfalt bildet er nicht nur Gesichter, sondern auch Kleider, Mäntel, Hütte und Schleier ab.

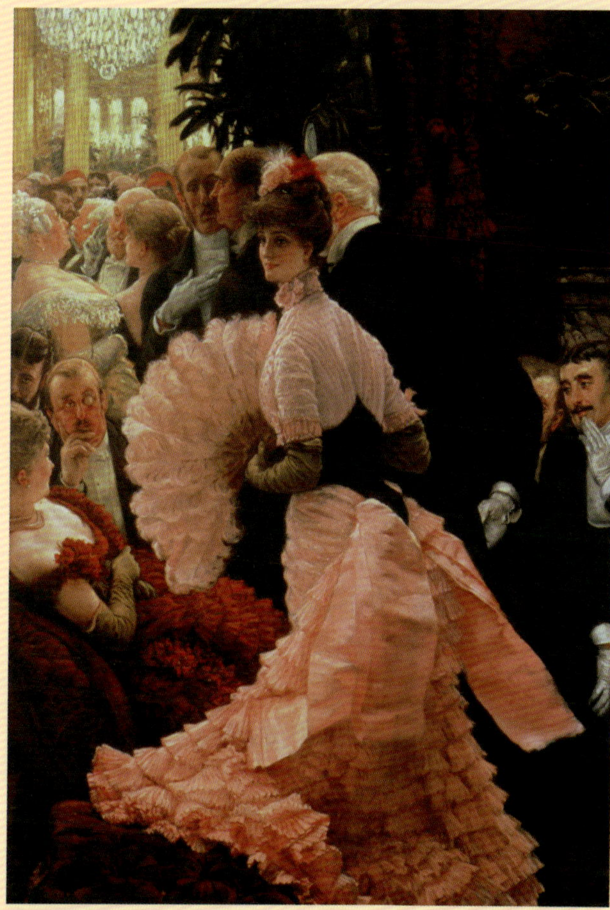

JAMES TISSOT (1836-1902)

1883-85, Oil on canvas/Huile sur toile, 142,24 × 101,6 cm,
Albright Knox Art Gallery, Buffalo

JAMES TISSOT

James Tissot (1836-1902), nacido en Nantes, es
recordado por la posteridad por sus sofisticados
retratos. Sin embargo, también creó motivos inspirados
en la Edad Media, pinturas históricas y, hacia el final
de su vida después de regresar de una peregrinación
por Palestina, algunas obras religiosas. Pasó su carrera
entre París y Londres, donde se estableció en 1871 y
rápidamente tuvo un gran éxito. Rechazó la invitación
de su amigo Edgar Degas para participar en la primera
exposición colectiva impresionista de 1874. Durante el
Segundo Imperio en Francia y la Edad Victoriana en
Inglaterra, su estilo realista y sus ilustraciones precisas
lo convirtieron en un retratista de la sociedad parisina y
londinense. Las mujeres son sus motivos más comunes.
Con mucho cuidado, no sólo muestra rostros, sino
también vestidos, abrigos, sombreros y velos.

JAMES TISSOT

James Tissot (1836-1902), nascido em Nantes,
é lembrado pela posteridade por seus retratos
sofisticados. No entanto, ele também criou motivos
inspirados na Idade Média, pinturas históricas
e - no final de sua vida depois de retornar de uma
peregrinação à Palestina - algumas obras religiosas.
Ele passou sua carreira entre Paris e Londres, onde
se estabeleceu em 1871 e rapidamente teve grande
sucesso. Ele rejeitou o convite de seu amigo Edgar
Degas para participar da primeira exposição coletiva
impressionista em 1874. Durante o Segundo Império
na França e a Era Vitoriana na Inglaterra, seu estilo
realista e ilustrações precisas fizeram dele um retratista
da sociedade parisiense e londrina. As mulheres são
os seus motivos mais comuns. Com muito cuidado,
ele retrata não apenas rostos, mas também vestidos,
casacos, chapéus e véus.

JAMES TISSOT

De in Nantes geboren James Tissot (1836-1902) is
bij latere generaties vooral bekend gebleven door
zijn mondaine portretten. Maar hij schilderde
ook middeleeuws geïnspireerde onderwerpen,
historiestukken en – tegen het einde van zijn leven, na
zijn terugkeer van een pelgrimstocht naar Palestina
– enkele religieuze werken. Hij bracht zijn werkende
leven door tussen Parijs en Londen, waar hij zich in
1871 vestigde en al snel veel succes had. Hij sloeg de
uitnodiging van zijn vriend Edgar Degas om deel te
nemen aan de eerste groepstentoonstelling van de
impressionisten in 1874 af. Tijdens het Tweede Keizerrijk
in Frankrijk en de victoriaanse tijd in Engeland maakte
hij met zijn realistische stijl en precieze afbeeldingen
carrière als portretschilder van de hoge kringen in Parijs
en Londen. Vrouwen schilderde hij het meest. Uiterst
zorgvuldig schilderde hij niet alleen gezichten, maar ook
jurken, jassen, hoeden en sluiers.

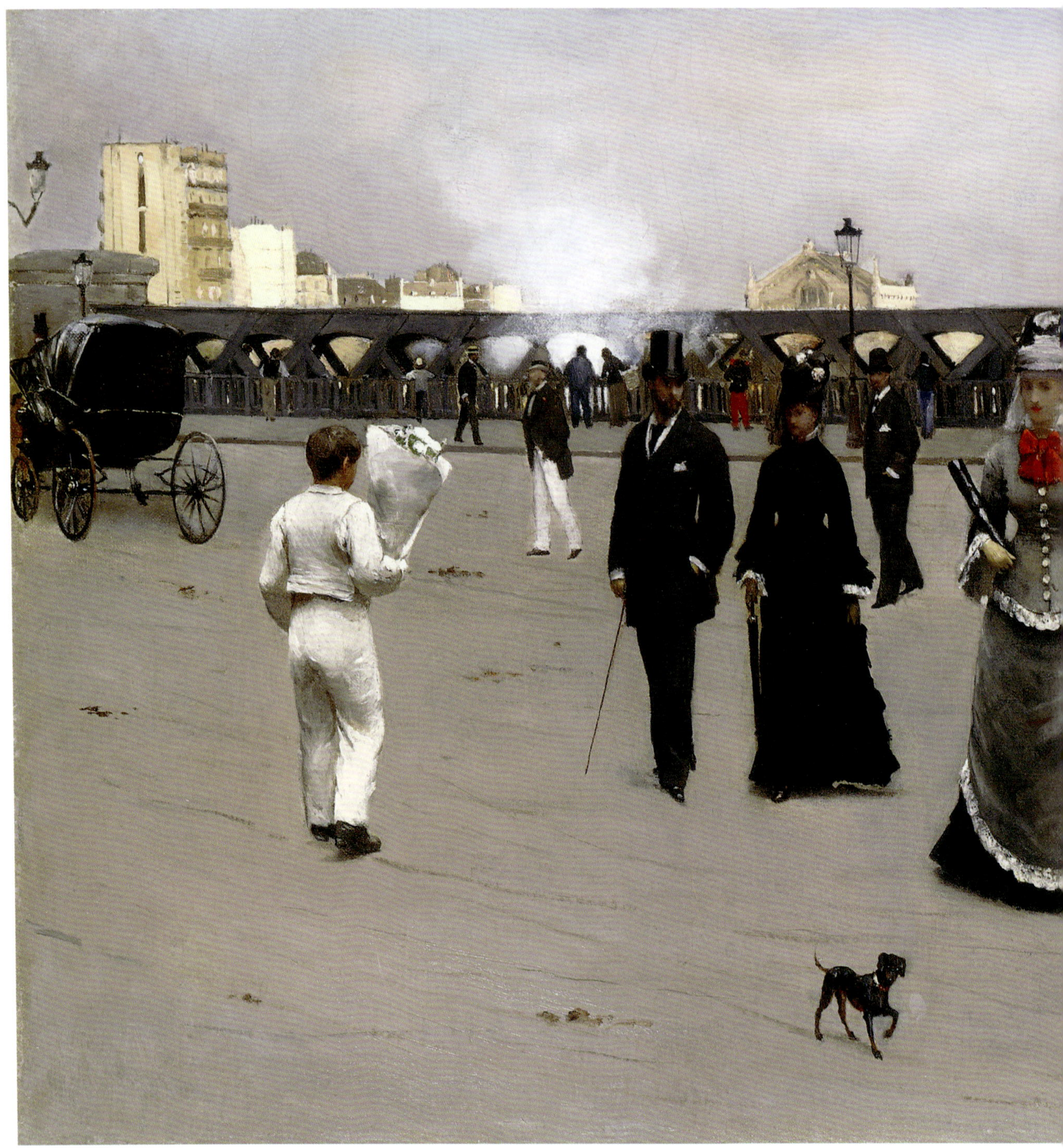

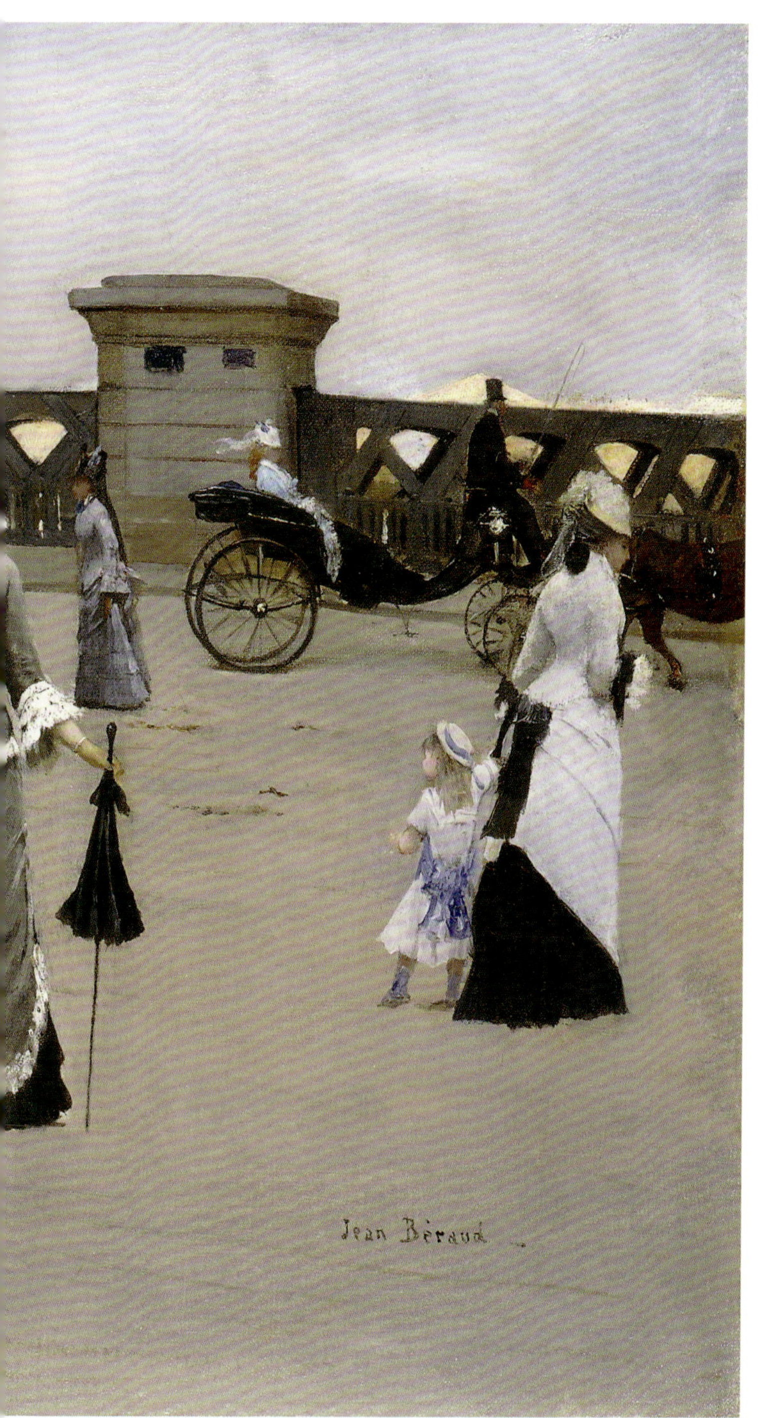

Le Pont de l'Europe

Shortly before Gustave Caillebotte immortalized the Paris Bridge in his paintings, Béraud painted a picture in classical style. It shows a cityscape reminding us of the pleasures of strolling.

La Place et le Pont de l'Europe

Peint peu avant le tableau de Gustave Caillebotte immortalisant le même pont de Paris, le tableau de Béraud est de facture plus classique : un paysage urbain placé sous le signe des plaisirs de la promenade.

Der Place und Pont de l'Europe

Kurz bevor Gustave Caillebotte die Pariser Brücke in seinen Gemälden verewigt, malt Béraud ein Bild klassischer Machart. Es zeigt eine Stadtlandschaft, die an die Freuden des Flanierens erinnert.

La plaza y el Puente de Europa

Poco antes de que Gustave Caillebotte inmortalizara el puente de París en sus pinturas, Béraud pintó un cuadro de estilo clásico. Muestra un paisaje urbano que recuerda a los placeres del paseo.

The Place and Pont de l'Europe

Pouco antes de Gustave Caillebotte imortalizar a Ponte de Paris em suas pinturas, Béraud pintou um quadro de estilo clássico. Mostra uma paisagem urbana reminiscente dos prazeres de passear.

Place en Pont de l'Europe

Kort voordat Gustave Caillebotte de Parijse brug in zijn schilderijen vereeuwigde, schilderde Béraud dit doek in klassieke stijl. Het toont een stadslandschap dat de geneugten van het flaneren in herinnering brengt.

JEAN BÉRAUD (1849-1935)

c. 1875-78, Oil on canvas/Huile sur toile, 18,3 × 73,7 cm,
Private collection

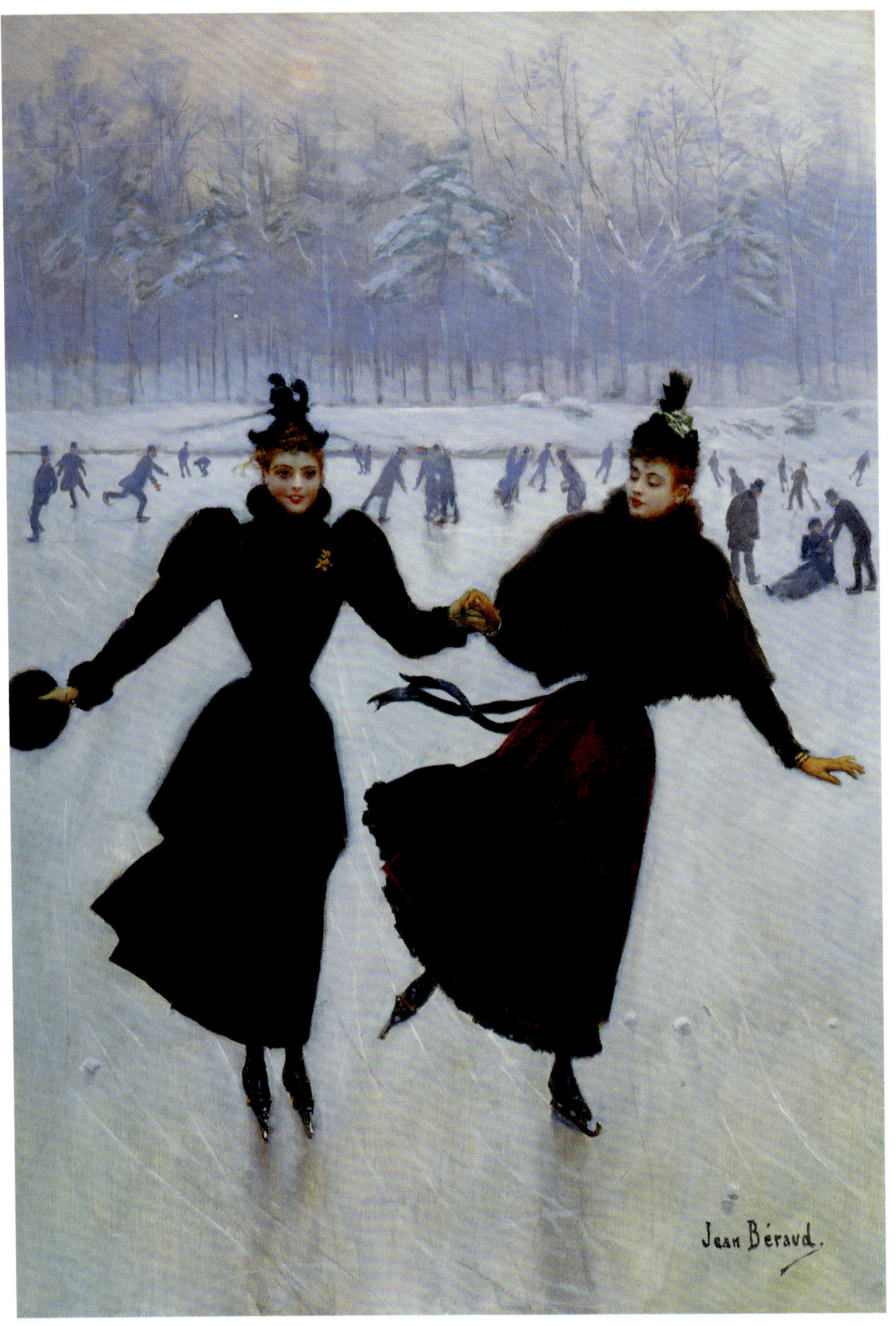

The Skaters

Les Patineuses

Die Schlittschuhläuferinnen

Las patinadoras

Os patinadores de gelo

De schaatsters

JEAN BÉRAUD (1849-1935)
1888, Oil on canvas/Huile sur toile,
60 × 42 cm, Private collection

Outside the Opera, Paris

Aux abords de l'Opéra, Paris

Vor der Pariser Oper

Frente a la Ópera de París

Em frente à Ópera de Paris

Voor de Opera in Parijs

JEAN BÉRAUD (1849-1935)
1879, Oil on canvas/
Huile sur toile, Private collection

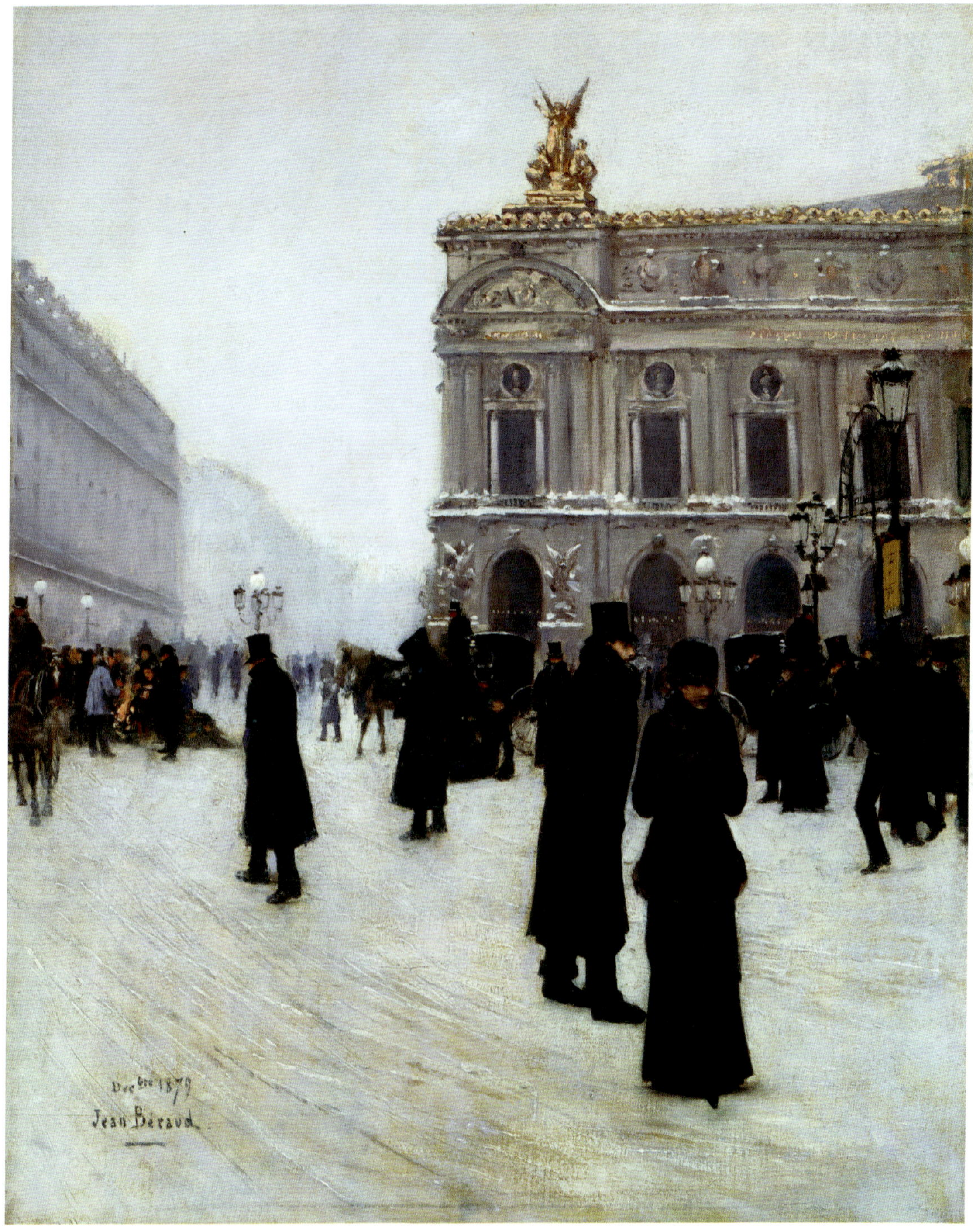

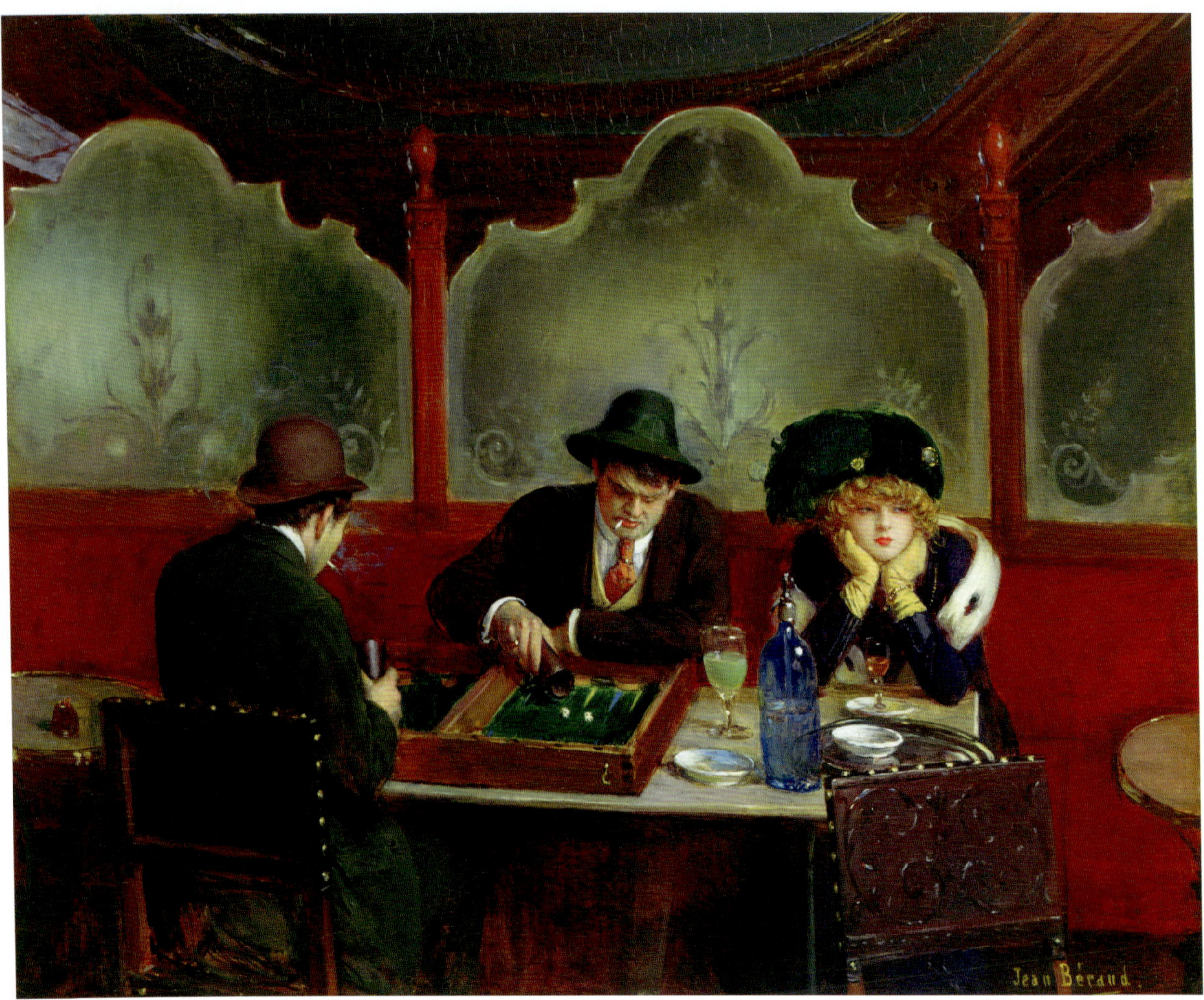

The Backgammon Players

Les Joueurs de jacquet backgammon

Backgammon in einem Café

Los jugadores de Backgammon

Backgammon num Café

De backgammonspelers

JEAN BÉRAUD (1849-1935)
n.d., Oil on panel/Huile sur panneau,
58,4 × 72,4 cm, Private collection

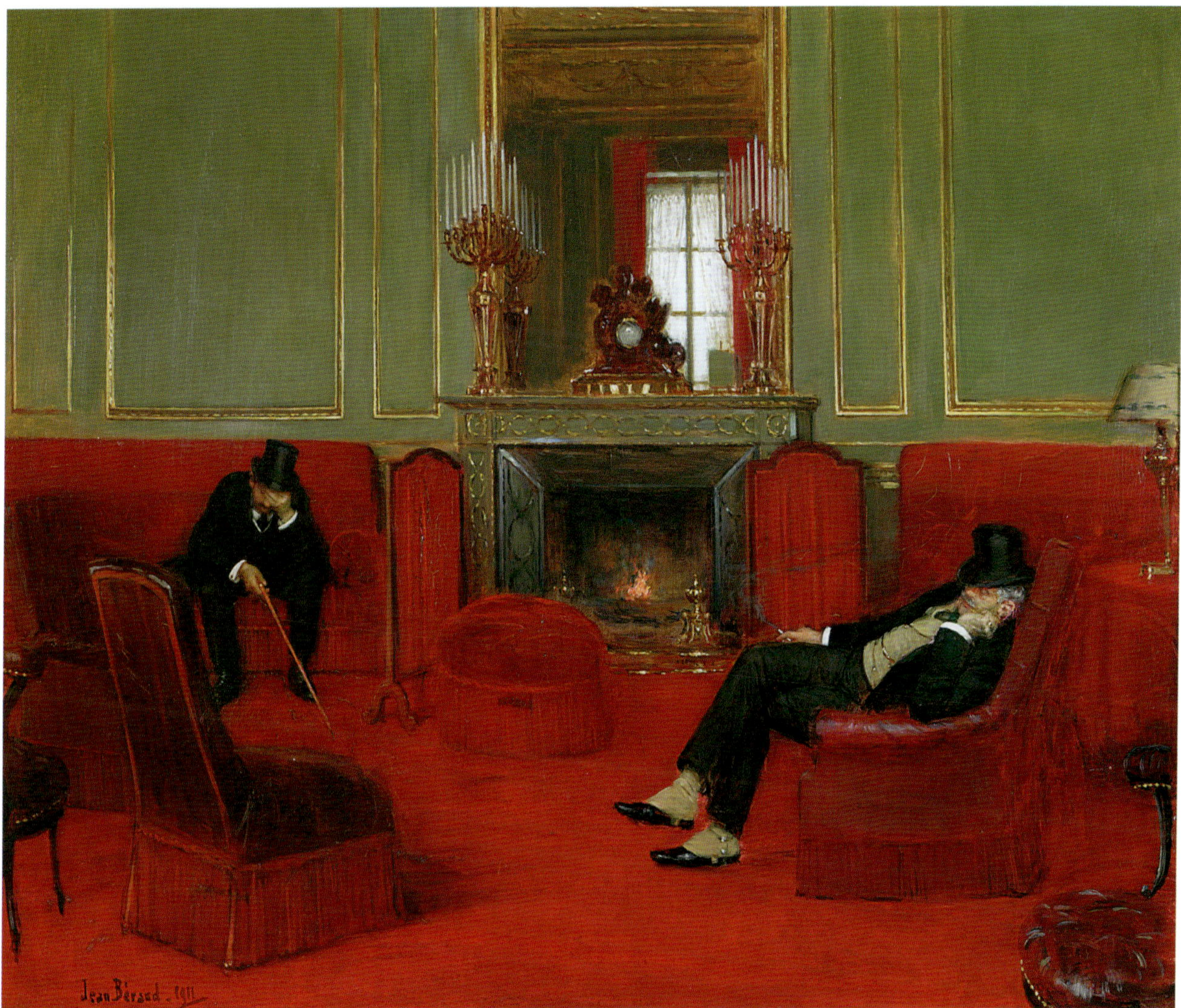

The Club

Béraud painted not only animated views, but also calm scenes. The two sleepy men are at the centre of a composition structured by color, in which the green and the red divide the painting.

Le Cercle

Peintre des scènes animées, Béraud excelle aussi à rendre des atmosphères feutrées. Les deux hommes assoupis sont placés dans une composition structurée par la couleur, le vert et le rouge qui partagent le tableau.

JEAN BÉRAUD (1849-1935)
1911, Oil on canvas/Huile sur toile, 61 × 73,5 cm, Musée d'Orsay, Paris

Der Klub

Béraud malt nicht nur belebte Ansichten, sondern auch ruhige Szenen. Die zwei schläfrigen Männer stehen im Zentrum einer durch Farbe strukturierten Komposition, in der das Grün und das Rot das Gemälde teilen.

El Club

Béraud pinta no sólo vistas animadas, sino también escenas tranquilas. Los dos hombres dormidos están en el centro de una composición estructurada por colores, en la que el verde y el rojo dividen el cuadro.

O Clube

Béraud pinta não só vistas animadas, mas também cenas calmas. Os dois homens sonolentos estão no centro de uma composição estruturada pela cor, na qual o verde e o vermelho dividem a pintura.

De club

Béraud schilderde niet alleen levendige, maar ook rustige taferelen. De twee slaperige mannen staan centraal in deze door kleuren opgebouwde compositie, waarin het groen en rood het schilderij in tweeën delen.

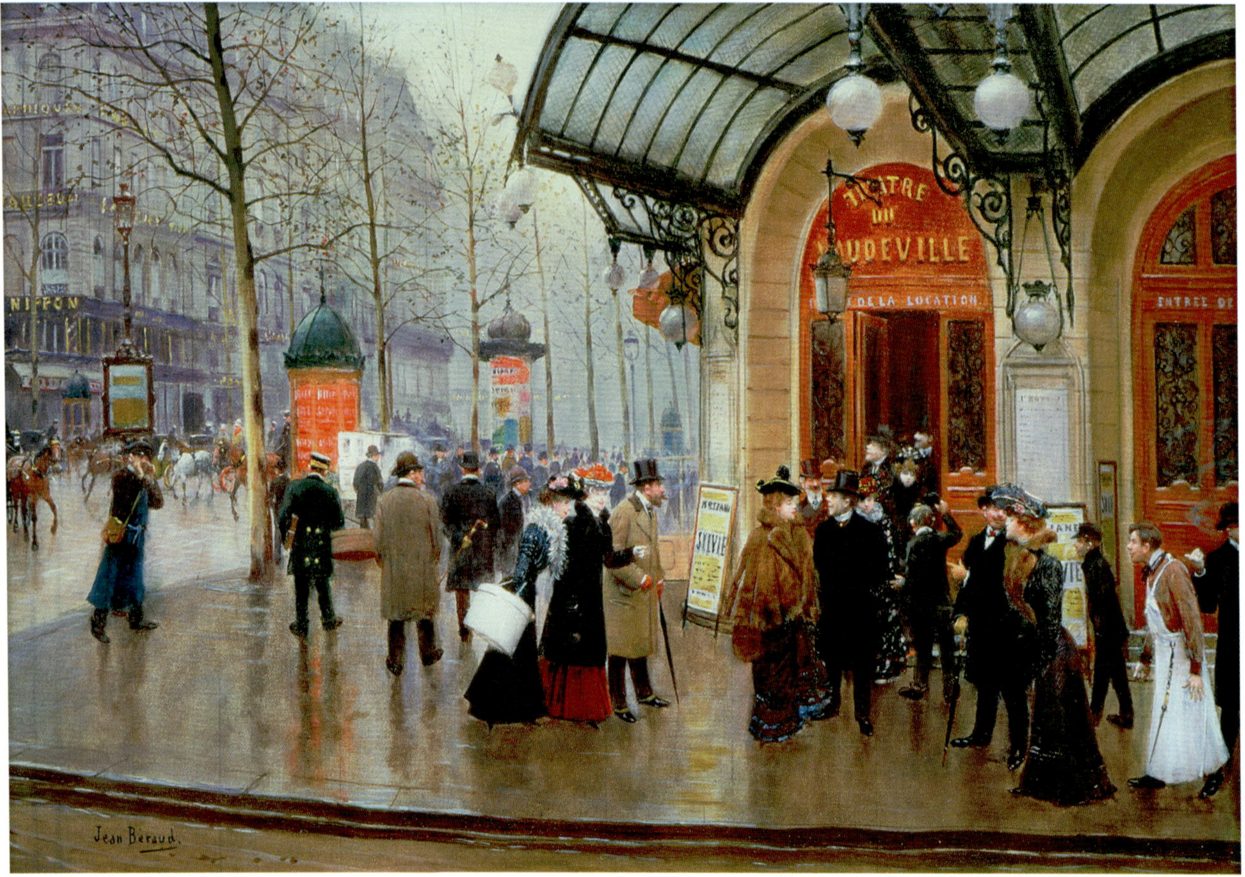

Outside the Vaudeville Theatre, Paris

Even on the busy sidewalks of the capital there was a real spectacle before and after the performances. The Théâtre de Vaudeville, which no longer exists, was located on the Boulevard des Capucines.

Devant le théâtre du Vaudeville, Paris

Le spectacle n'est pas seulement dans la salle, mais aussi sur les trottoirs grouillants de la capitale, avant ou après la représentation. Le théâtre du Vaudeville, disparu, se situait boulevard des Capucines.

JEAN BÉRAUD (1849-1935)

n. d ., Oil on canvas/Huile sur toile, Private collection

Vor dem Théâtre de Vaudeville in Paris

Auch auf den belebten Bürgersteigen der Hauptstadt bot sich vor und nach den Vorstellungen ein wahres Schauspiel dar. Das heute verschwundene Théâtre de Vaudeville befand sich auf dem Boulevard des Capucines.

Frente al Teatro de Vaudeville de París

Incluso en las concurridas aceras de la capital hubo un verdadero espectáculo antes y después de las actuaciones. El Teatro de Vaudeville, hoy desaparecido, estaba situado en el Boulevard des Capucines.

Em frente ao Théâtre de Vaudeville em Paris

Mesmo nas calçadas movimentadas da capital havia um verdadeiro espetáculo antes e depois das apresentações. O Théâtre de Vaudeville, que hoje desapareceu, estava localizado na Boulevard des Capucines.

Voor het Théâtre de Vaudeville in Parijs

Ook op de drukke trottoirs van de hoofdstad speelde zich voor en na de voorstellingen een levendig schouwspel af. Het Théâtre de Vaudeville, dat niet meer bestaat, stond aan de Boulevard des Capucines.

The Box by the Stalls

Die Loge im Théâtre des Variétés

A caixa no Théâtre des Variétés

La Baignoire, au théâtre des Variétés

El palco del Théâtre des Variétés

De loge van het Théâtre des Variétés

JEAN BÉRAUD (1849-1935)

1883, Oil on canvas/Huile sur toile, 49 × 40,5 cm, Musée Carnavalet, Paris

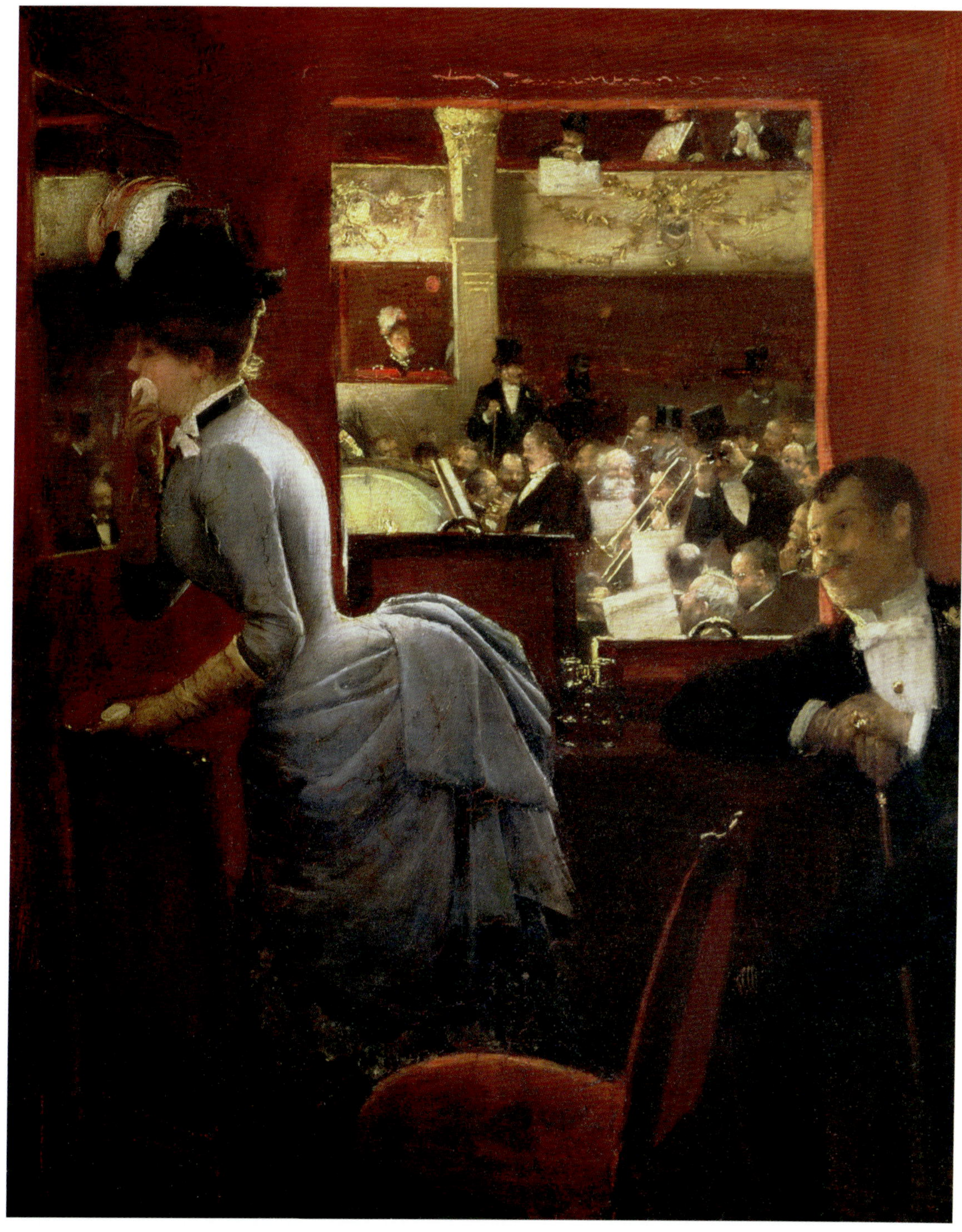

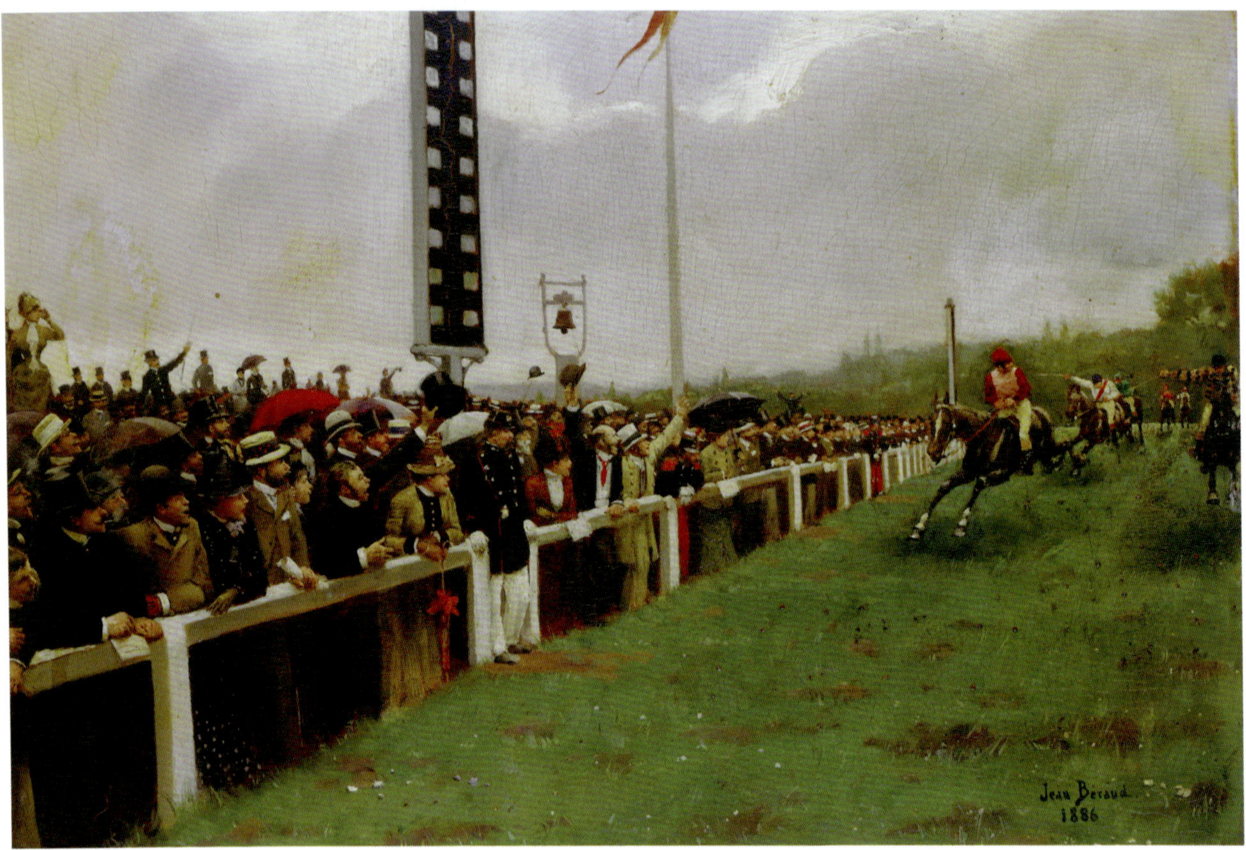

Horse racing in Longchamp

In the diagonally divided, contemporary composition, Béraud focused on the enthusiastic spectators who crowd behind the barriers. The horses are pushed into the background.

Course à Longchamp, l'arrivée au poteau

Dans une composition très moderne régie par une diagonale dynamique, Béraud s'intéresse davantage à l'exaltation qu'exerce la course sur le public massé derrière les barrières, qu'aux chevaux eux-mêmes.

Pferderennen in Longchamp

In der diagonal aufgeteilten, zeitgenössischen Komposition legt Béraud den Fokus auf die begeisterten Zuschauer, die sich hinter den Absperrungen drängen. Die Pferde rücken dabei in den Hintergrund.

Carreras de caballos en Longchamp

En una composición muy moderna gobernada por una diagonal dinámica, a Béraud le interesa más la emoción del público detrás de las vallas que los propios caballos.

Corridas de cavalos em Longchamp

Na composição contemporânea e diagonalmente dividida, Béraud concentra-se nos espectadores entusiastas que se aglomeram por detrás das barreiras. Os cavalos são empurrados para o fundo.

Paardenrennen in Longchamp

In de diagonaal verdeelde, eigentijdse compositie richtte Béraud zich op de enthousiaste toeschouwers achter de hekken. De paarden verdwijnen daardoor naar de achtergrond.

JEAN BÉRAUD (1849-1935)

1886, Oil on canvas/Huile sur toile, 38 × 55 cm, Musée Carnavalet, Paris

Un Figaro de rêve

JEAN BÉRAUD (1849-1935)

c. 1875, Oil on canvas/
Huile sur toile,
25,5 × 54,3 cm,
Private collection

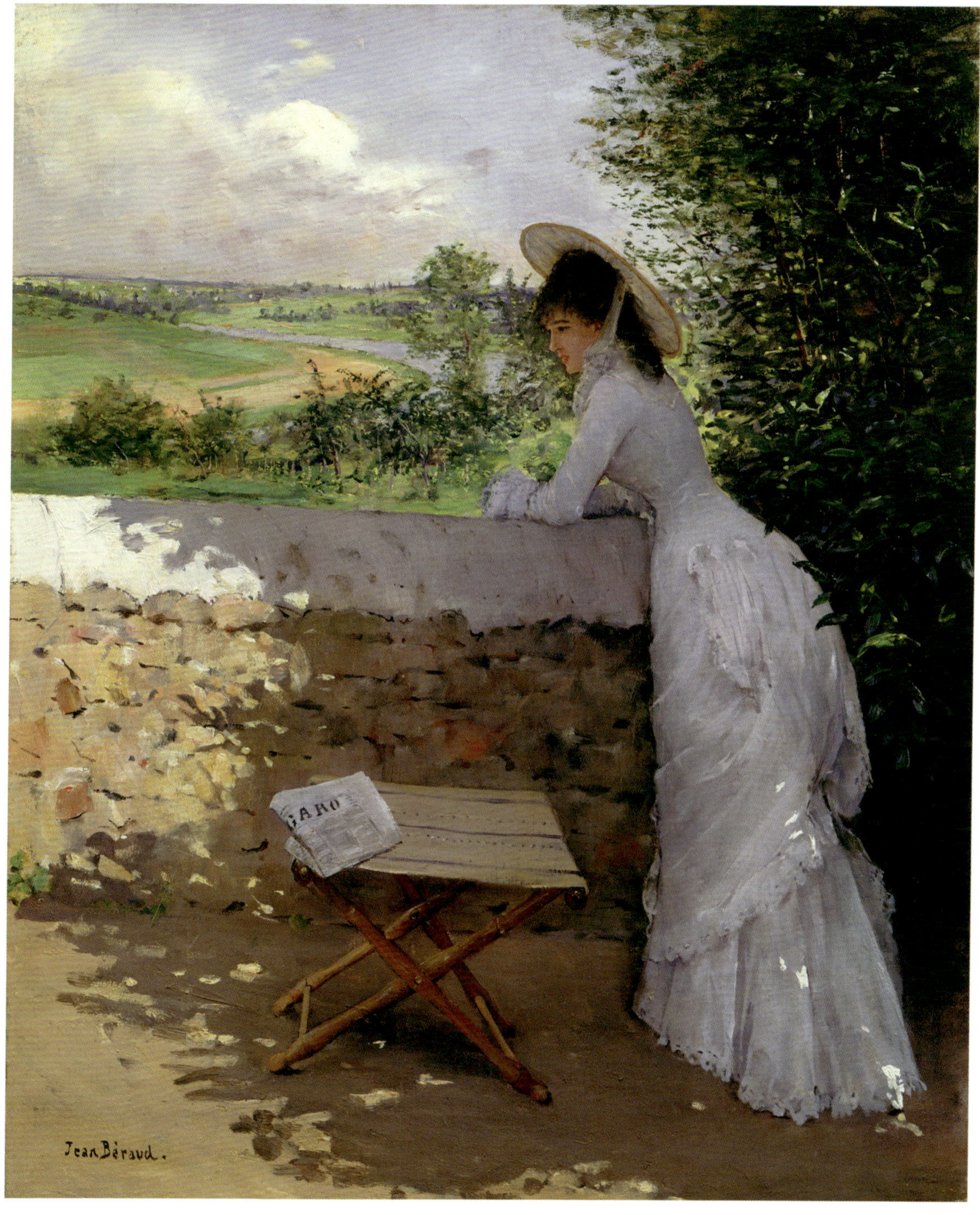

Jean Béraud.

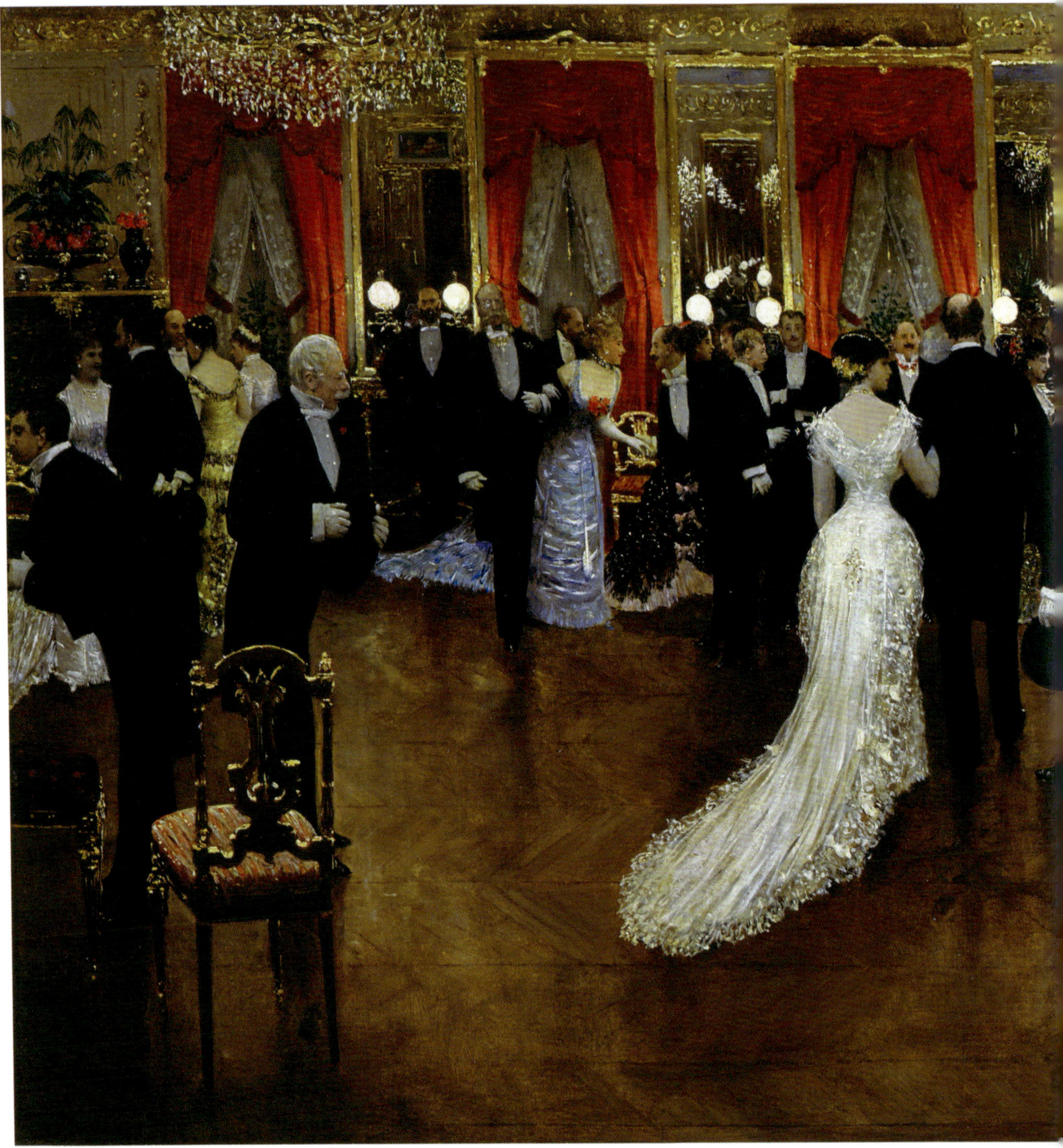

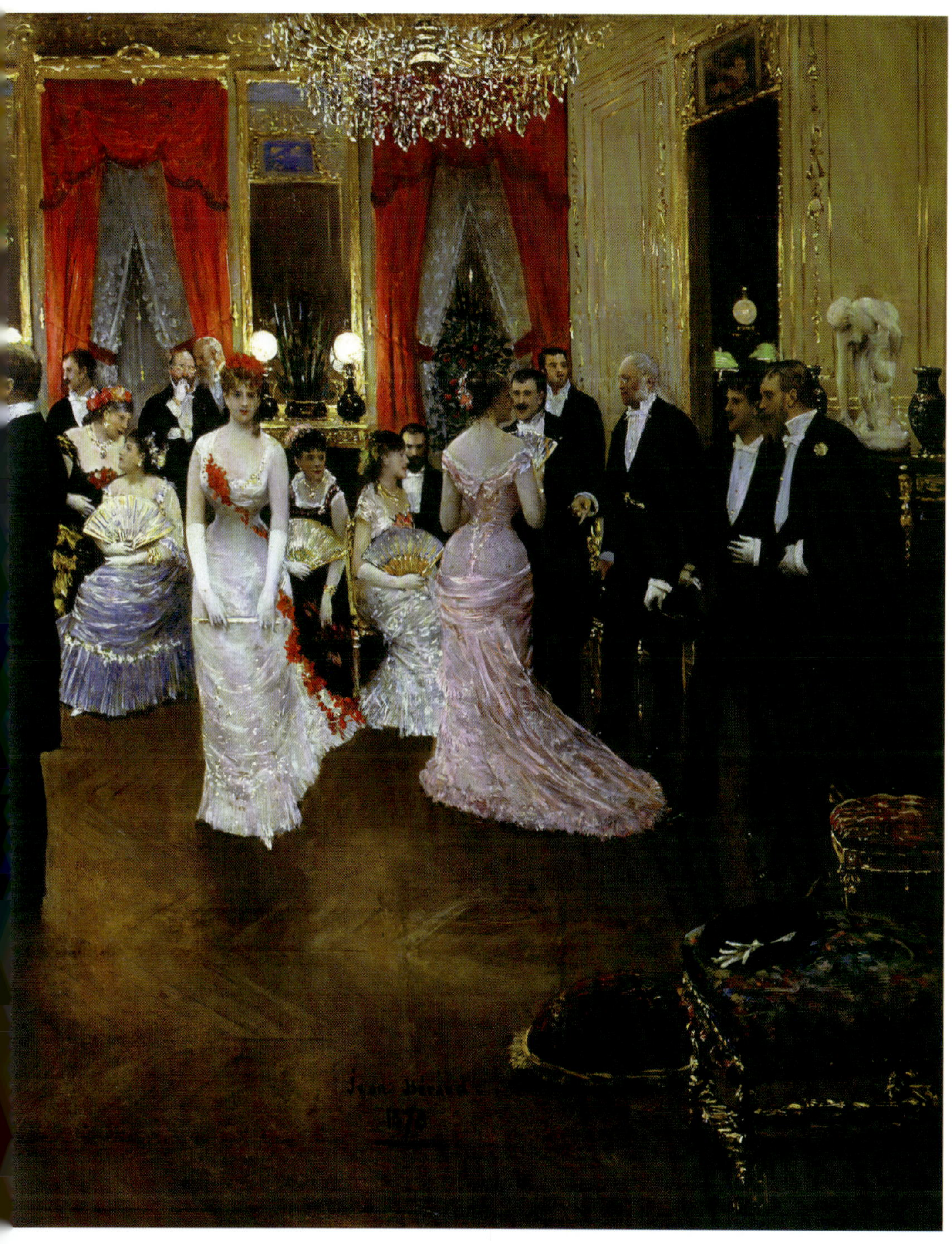

A Soirée

Une soirée

Soirée

Velada

Soirée

Soirée

JEAN BÉRAUD (1849-1935)
1878, Oil on canvas/
Huile sur toile, 65 × 117 cm,
Musée d'Orsay, Paris

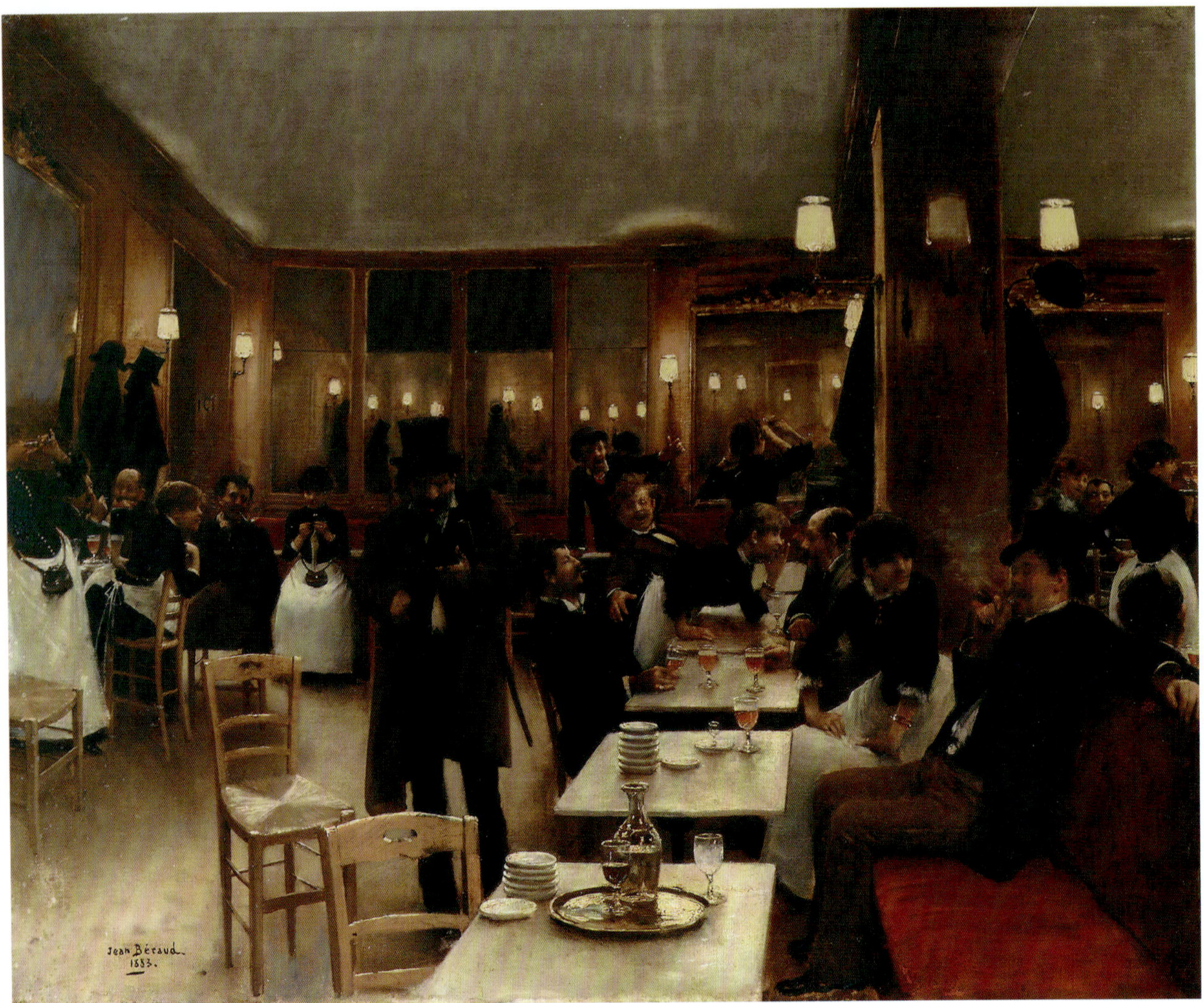

The Brasserie

La Brasserie

Die Brasserie

La Brasserie

A Brasserie

De Brasserie

JEAN BÉRAUD (1849-1935)
1883, Oil on canvas/Huile sur toile,
65,5 × 81,4 cm, Private collection

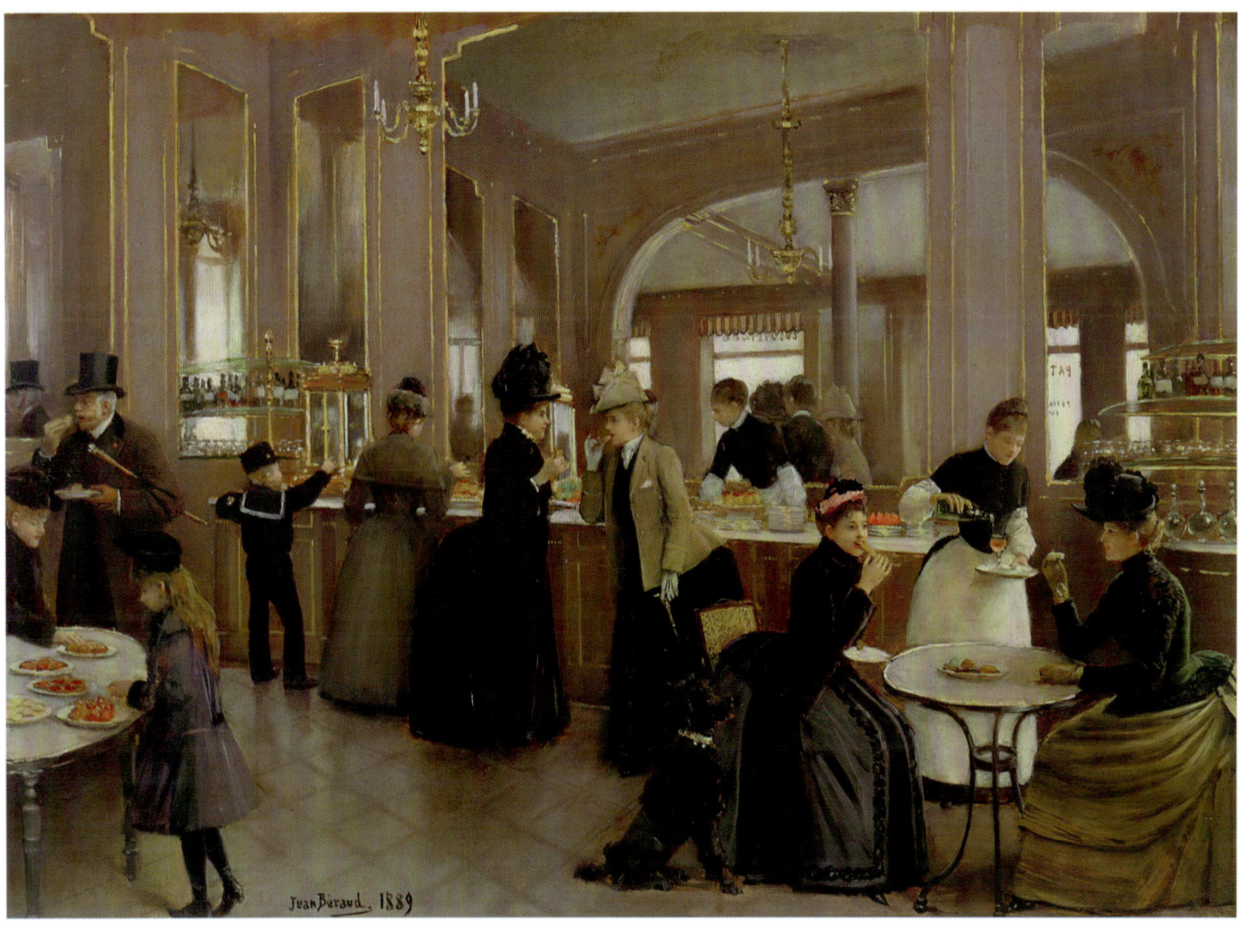

La Pâtisserie Gloppe

The elegant paneling and large mirrors made the Gloppe Pâtisserie café on the roundabout of the Champs-Élysées a chic and popular meeting place for the bourgeoisie towards the end of the 19th century.

La Pâtisserie Gloppe

Orné d'élégantes boiseries et de grands miroirs, le salon de thé de la pâtisserie Gloppe, au rond-point des Champs-Élysées, était un lieu chic très prisé de la bourgeoisie de la fin du XIXe siècle.

JEAN BÉRAUD (1849-1935)

1889, Oil on canvas/Huile sur toile, 38 × 53 cm, Musée Carnavalet, Paris

La pâtisserie Gloppe

Die eleganten Vertäfelungen und großen Spiegel machten das Café der Pâtisserie Gloppe am Kreisverkehr der Champs-Élysées zu einem schicken und beliebten Treffpunkt des Bürgertums gegen Ende des 19. Jahrhunderts.

La Pastelería Gloppe

Los elegantes paneles y los grandes espejos hicieron del café Gloppe Pâtisserie, situado en la rotonda de los Campos Elíseos, un lugar de encuentro elegante y popular para la burguesía de finales del siglo XIX.

La pâtisserie Gloppe

O revestimento elegante e os grandes espelhos fizeram do café Gloppe Pâtisserie na rotunda dos Champs-Élysées um ponto de encontro chique e popular para a burguesia no final do século XIX.

La pâtisserie Gloppe

De elegante lambrisering en de grote spiegels maakten Pâtisserie Gloppe op de rotonde van de Champs-Élysées eind 19e eeuw tot een chic en populair trefpunt voor de bourgeoisie.

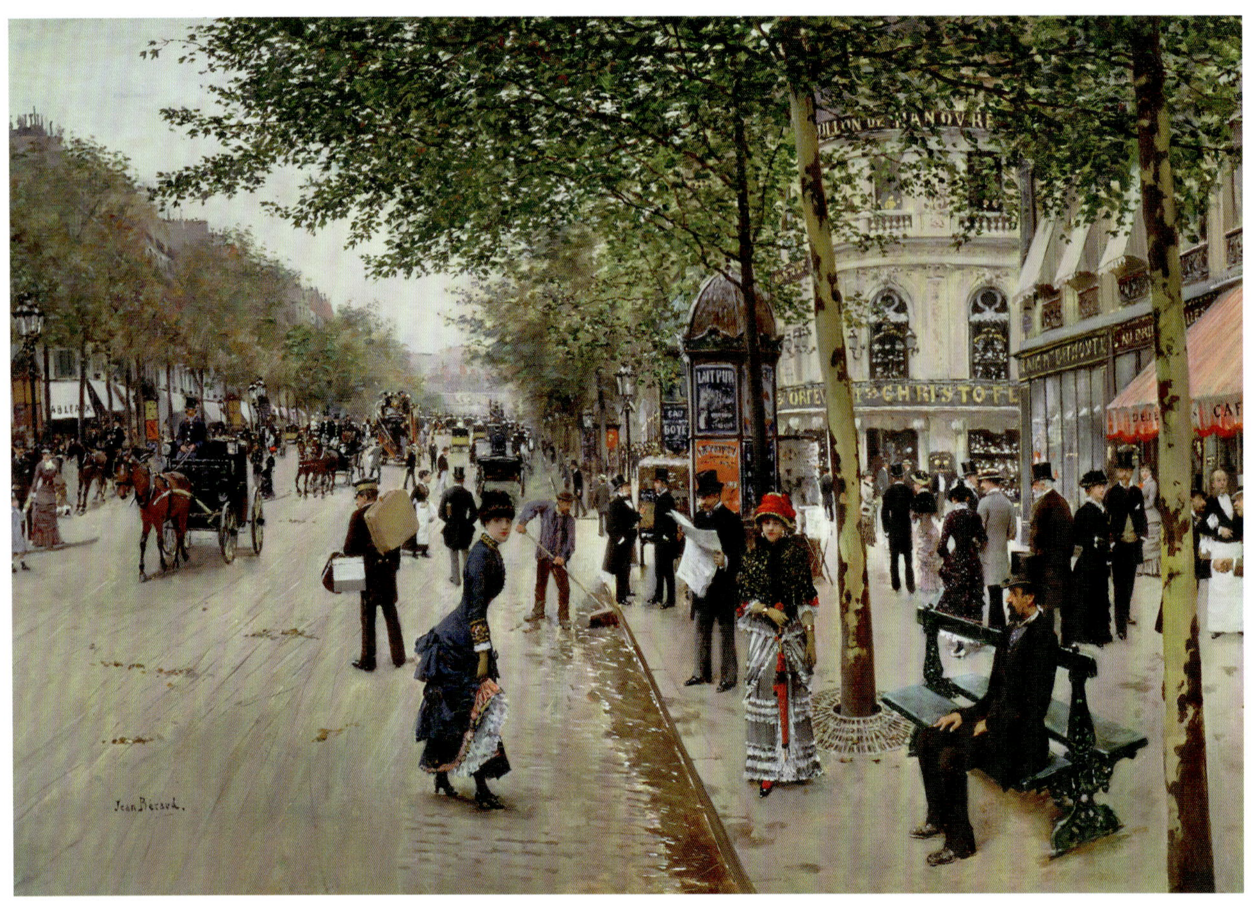

Boulevard des Capucines

JEAN BÉRAUD (1849-1935)

1896, Oil on canvas/Huile sur toile,

50,8 x 73 cm, Private collection

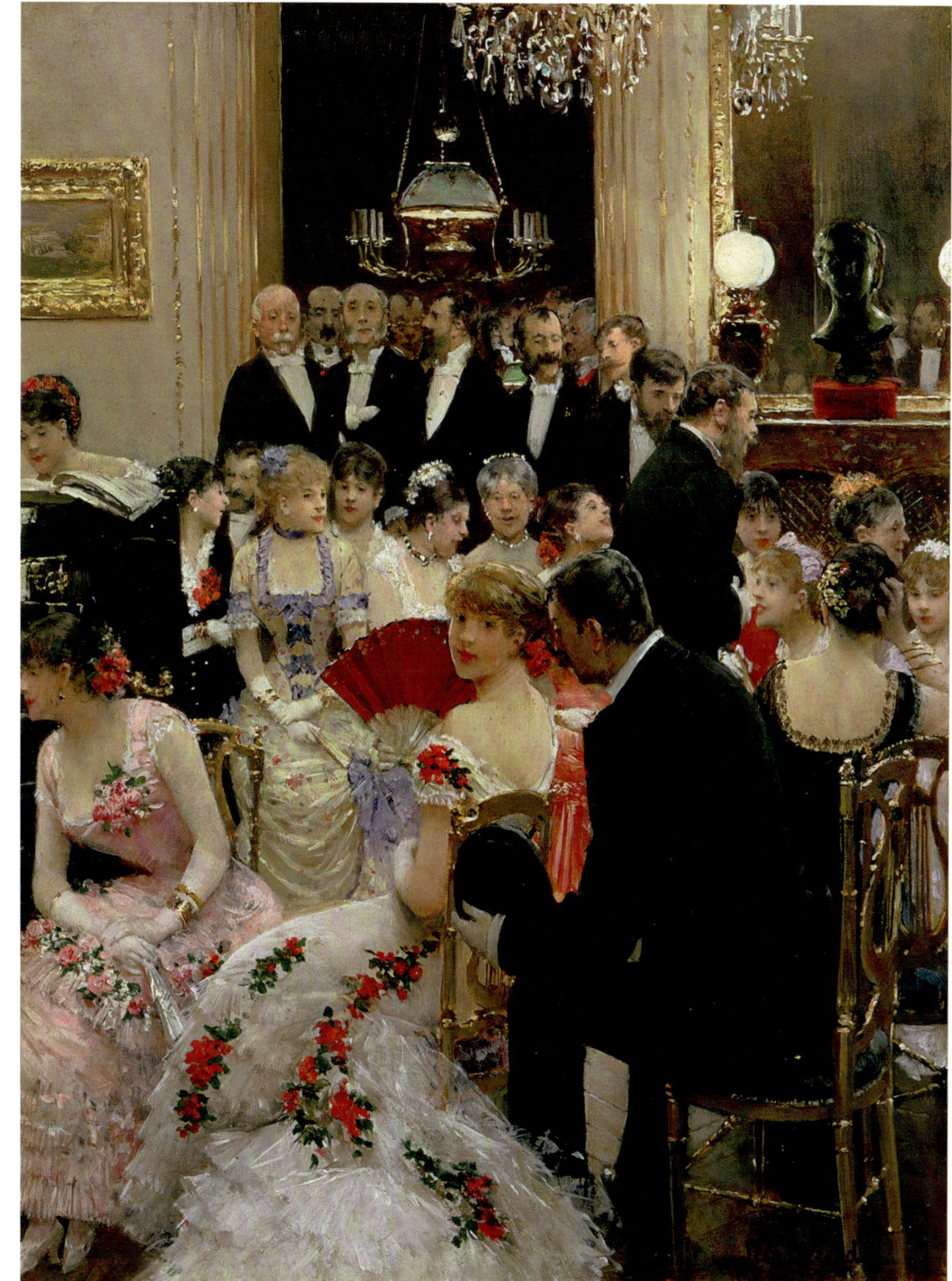

The Soiree

La Soirée

Die Abendgesellschaft

La velada

A festa da noite

De soirée

JEAN BÉRAUD (1849-1935)
c. 1880, Oil on canvas/
Huile sur toile, 35 × 27 cm,
Musée Carnavalet, Paris

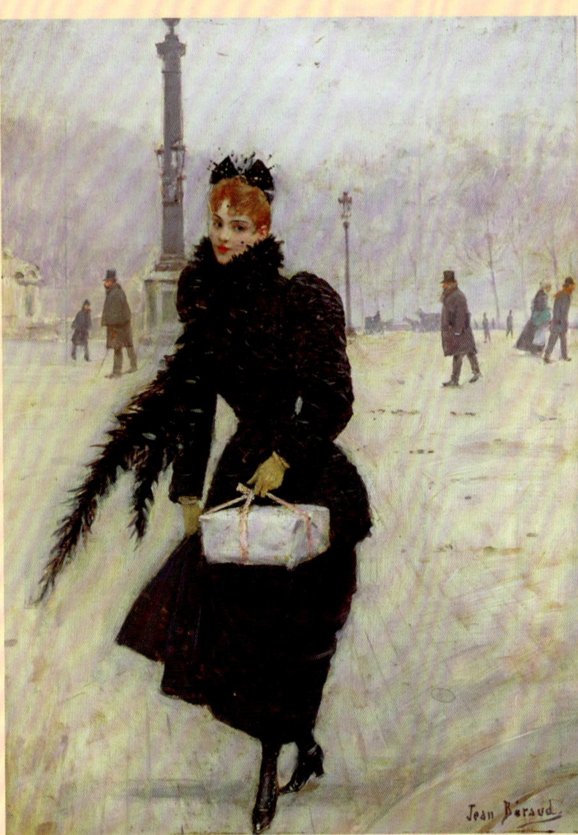

Parisian woman, Place de la Concorde

Parisienne sur la place de la Concorde

Pariserin, Place de la Concorde

Parisina, Place de la Concorde

Parisiense, Place de la Concorde

Parisienne, Place de la Concorde

JEAN BÉRAUD (1849-1935)

c. 1885, Oil on canvas/Huile sur toile, 47,7 × 39,8 cm, Musée Carnavalet, Paris

JEAN BÉRAUD

Jean Béraud (1849-1935) was one of the most important chroniclers of Parisian life towards the end of the 19th century. The son of a sculptor, he studied at the École des Beaux-Arts in Paris, in the studio of the painter Léon Bonnat. The painting *After the Funeral* became his first great success at the salon. He quickly developed into a popular bourgeois painter at the time of the Third Republic. His motifs repeatedly show animated views of the capital, day and night. He painted intimate genre paintings as well as group and individual portraits, inspired by everyday life, he was fascinated above all by the simple professions, the shops (*La Pâtisserie Gloppe*) and the cafés. But his work was also devoted to lesser-known subjects, such as public and political meetings or work in editorial offices (*The Newsroom of the Journal des Débats*). In addition, he created some outstanding religious paintings, which have fallen into oblivion in the shadow of his Paris motifs.

JEAN BÉRAUD

Il est l'un des grands chroniqueurs de la vie parisienne de la fin du XIXᵉ siècle. Fils de sculpteur, Jean Béraud (1849-1935) a débuté son apprentissage d'artiste à l'École nationale des beaux-arts de Paris, dans l'atelier du peintre académique Léon Bonnat. *Le Retour de l'enterrement*, en 1876, est son premier franc succès sur les cimaises du Salon. Il devient rapidement un peintre très apprécié de la bourgeoisie de la IIIᵉ République, et multiplie à l'envi les vues animées de la capitale, de jour ou de nuit, les scènes de genre intimistes, et les portraits individuels ou de groupes. Jean Béraud puise son inspiration dans la vie quotidienne, s'appliquant à mettre en valeur les petits métiers, les commerces (*La Pâtisserie Gloppe*) et les cafés. Il s'intéresse aussi à des sujets plus rarement traités, comme les réunions publiques et politiques, ou les salles de rédaction (*La Salle de rédaction du* Journal des débats). On lui doit également quelques surprenantes toiles religieuses, aujourd'hui oubliées, éclipsées par les tableaux parisiens qui ont fait sa réputation.

JEAN BÉRAUD

Jean Béraud (1849-1935) war einer der wichtigsten Chronisten des Pariser Lebens gegen Ende des 19. Jahrhunderts. Der Sohn eines Bildhauers lässt sich an der École des Beaux-Arts in Paris ausbilden, im Atelier des Malers Léon Bonnat. Das Gemälde *Der Heimweg von der Beerdigung* wird zu seinem erst großen Erfolg auf dem Salon. Schnell entwickelt er sich zu einem beliebten Maler des Bürgertums zur Zeit der Dritten Republik. Seine Motive zeigen immer wieder belebte Ansichten der Hauptstadt, am Tag und in der Nacht. Er malt intime Genrebilder sowie Gruppen- und Einzelporträts, für die er sich vom alltäglichen Leben inspirieren lässt, an dem ihm vor allem die kleinen Berufe, die Geschäfte (*La Pâtisserie Gloppe*) und die Cafés faszinieren. Er widmet sich aber auch weniger verbreiteten Sujets, wie öffentlichen und politischen Versammlungen oder der Arbeit in Redaktionsräumen (*Redaktionsbüro des Journal des débats*). Darüber hinaus schafft er einige herausragende religiöse Gemälde, die im Schatten seiner Paris-Motive, heute in Vergessenheit geraten sind.

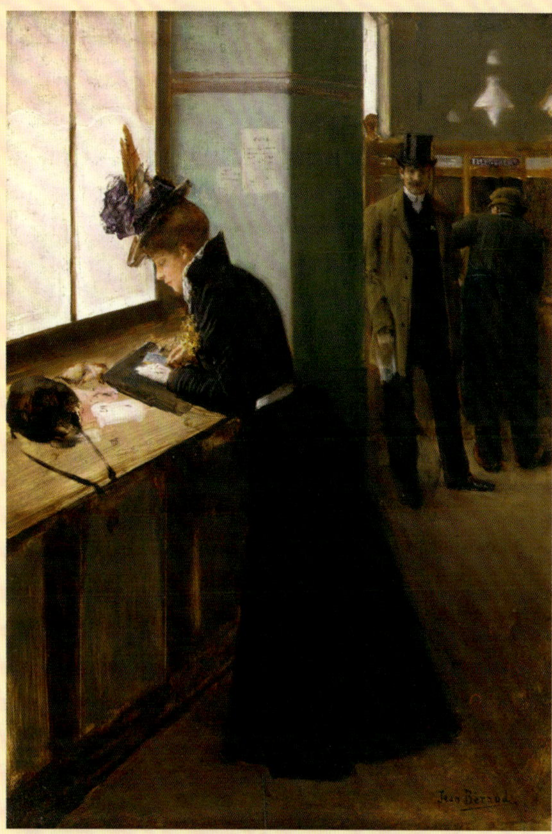

JEAN BÉRAUD

Jean Béraud (1849-1935) fue uno de los cronistas más importantes de la vida parisina a finales del siglo XIX. Hijo de un escultor, estudió en la École des Beaux-Arts de París, en el estudio del pintor Léon Bonnat. El cuadro *De regreso del funeral* se convierte en su primer gran éxito en el salón. Rápidamente se convirtió en un pintor popular burgués en la época de la Tercera República. Sus motivos muestran repetidamente vistas animadas de la capital, tanto de día como de noche. Pinta cuadros íntimos de género, así como retratos de grupo e individuales, inspirados en la vida cotidiana, que le fascinan sobre todo en las profesiones sencillas, las tiendas (*La Pâtisserie Gloppe*) y los cafés. Pero también se dedica a temas menos conocidos, como las reuniones públicas y políticas o el trabajo en las redacciones (*La sala de redacción*). Además, creó algunas pinturas religiosas destacadas, que han caído en el olvido a la sombra de sus motivos parisinos.

JEAN BÉRAUD

Jean Béraud (1849-1935) foi um dos mais importantes cronistas da vida parisiense no final do século XIX. Filho de um escultor, estudou na École des Beaux-Arts de Paris, no estúdio do pintor Léon Bonnat. A pintura *O caminho de casa do funeral* tornase o seu primeiro grande sucesso no salão. Ele rapidamente se tornou um pintor burguês popular na época da Terceira República. Os seus motivos mostram repetidamente vistas animadas da capital, dia e noite. Ele pinta pinturas de gênero íntimo, assim como retratos de grupo e individuais, inspirados na vida cotidiana, que o fascinam sobretudo nas profissões simples, nas lojas (*La Pâtisserie Gloppe*) e nos cafés. Mas também é dedicado a temas menos conhecidos, como reuniões públicas e políticas ou trabalho em redações (*Redação do Journal des débats*). Além disso, ele criou algumas pinturas religiosas pendentes, que caíram no esquecimento na sombra de seus motivos de Paris.

JEAN BÉRAUD

Jean Béraud (1849-1935) was een van de belangrijkste chroniqueurs van het Parijse leven van eind 19e eeuw. Deze zoon van een beeldhouwer studeerde aan de École des Beaux-Arts in Parijs, in het atelier van de schilder Léon Bonnat. Het schilderij *Op de terugweg van de begrafenis* wordt zijn eerste grote succes op de Salon. Ten tijde van de Derde Republiek werd hij al snel zeer geliefd bij de bourgeoisie. Zijn werken tonen steeds opnieuw levendige gezichten op de hoofdstad, overdag en 's nachts. Hij schilderde zowel intieme genrestukken als individuele en groepsportretten, waarvoor hij zich liet inspireren door het dagelijks leven. Daarbij vond hij vooral de eenvoudige beroepen, winkels (*La Pâtisserie Gloppe*) en cafés fascinerend. Maar hij hield zich ook bezig met minder bekende onderwerpen, zoals publieke en politieke bijeenkomsten of het werk op redacties (*De redactie van het Journal des débats*). Daarnaast maakte hij enkele opvallende religieuze schilderijen, die, overschaduwd door zijn Parijse motieven, tegenwoordig in de vergetelheid zijn geraakt.

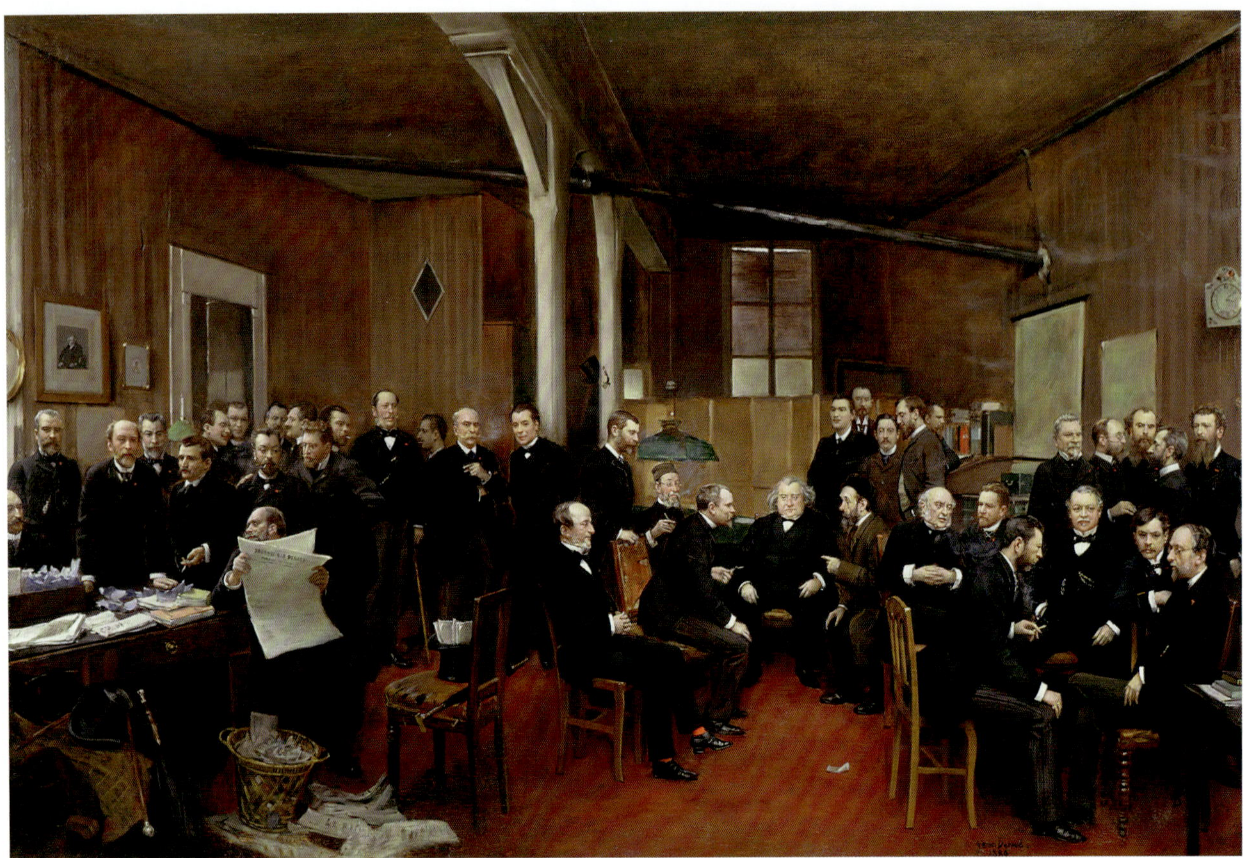

The Newsroom of the *Journal des Débats*

La Salle de rédaction du *Journal des débats*

Redaktionsbüro des *Journal des débats*

Redacción del *Journal des débats*

Redacção do *Journal des débats*

De redactie van het *Journal des débats*

JEAN BÉRAUD (1849-1935)

1889, Oil on canvas/Huile sur toile, 98 × 151 cm, Musée d'Orsay, Paris

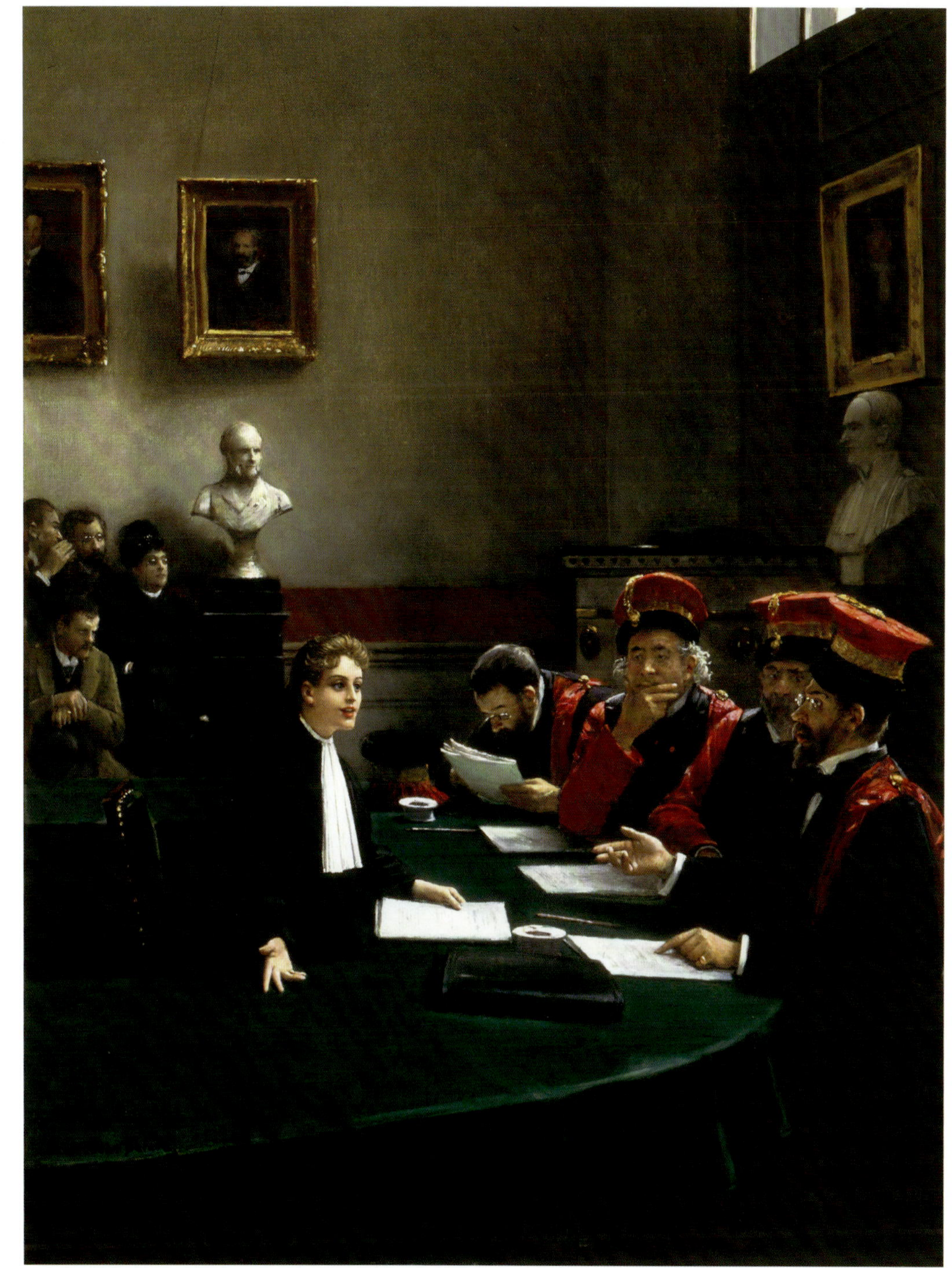

The Doctoral Jury of
Jeanne Chauvin

Le Jury de thèse de
Jeanne Chauvin

Die Doktorandenjury
von Jeanne Chauvin

El Jurado Doctoral
de Jeanne Chauvin

O Júri de Doutoramento
de Jeanne Chauvin

De Doctorale Jury
van Jeanne Chauvin

JEAN BÉRAUD (1849-1935)

c. 1900, Oil on canvas/
Huile sur toile,
63,5 × 48,3 cm,
Private collection

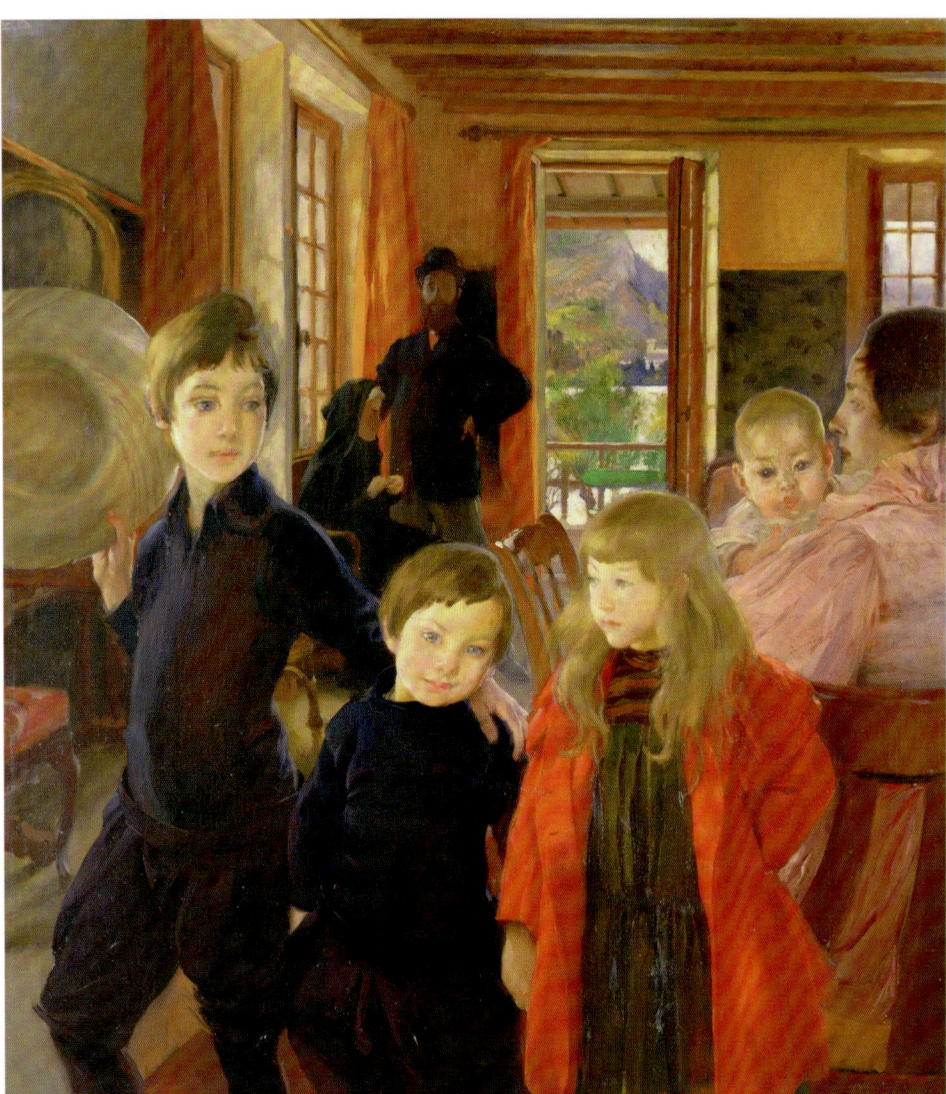

The Artist's Family

Albert Besnard painted his wife and four children in the living room in their house in Talloires, Haute-Savoie. In the background he can be seen next to his mother-in-law.

La famille de l'artiste

Albert Besnard immortalise sa femme et ses quatre enfants dans le salon de leur propriété de Talloires, en Haute-Savoie. Il s'est lui-même représenté à l'arrière-plan, en compagnie de sa belle-mère.

Die Familie des Künstlers

Albert Besnard malte seine Frau und vier Kinder in der Umgebung ihres Wohnzimmers in ihrem Haus in Talloires im Département Haute-Savoie. Im Hintergrund ist er neben seiner Schwiegermutter zu sehen.

La familia del artista

Albert Besnard pintó a su esposa y a sus cuatro hijos en el salón de su casa en Talloires, Haute-Savoie. En el fondo se le puede ver junto a su suegra.

A família do artista

Albert Besnard pintou sua esposa e quatro filhos ao redor de sua sala de estar em sua casa em Talloires, Haute-Savoie. No fundo, ele pode ser visto ao lado da sogra.

De familie van de schilder

Albert Besnard schilderde zijn vrouw en vier kinderen in de woonkamer van hun huis in Talloires, Haute-Savoie. Op de achtergrond is hijzelf te zien naast zijn schoonmoeder.

ALBERT BESNARD (1849-1934)

1890, Oil on canvas/Huile sur toile, 132 × 120,5 cm, Musée d'Orsay, Paris

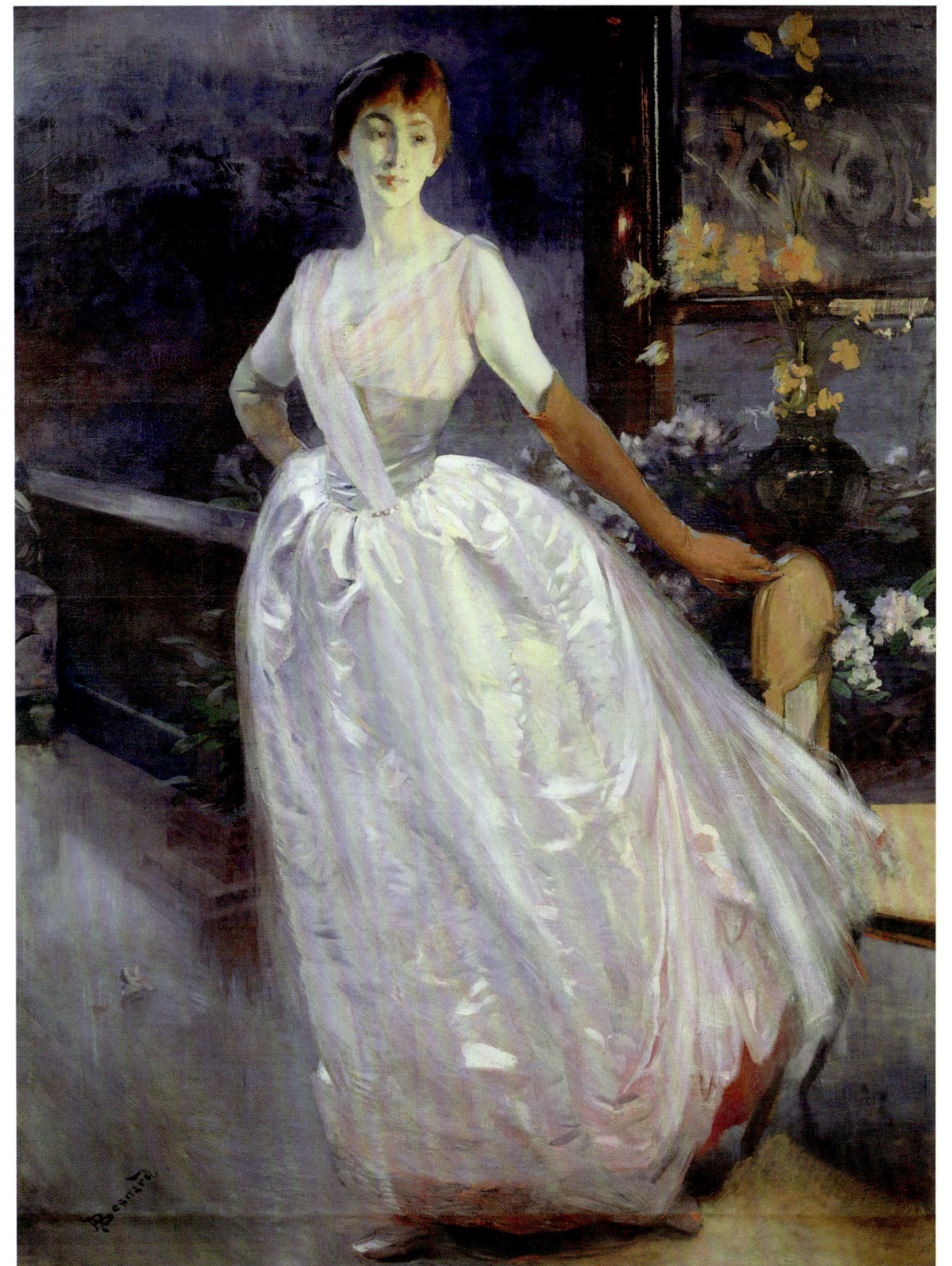

Madame Roger Jourdain

ALBERT BESNARD
(1849-1934)
1886, Oil on canvas/
Huile sur toile,
199 × 150,5 cm,
Musée d'Orsay, Paris

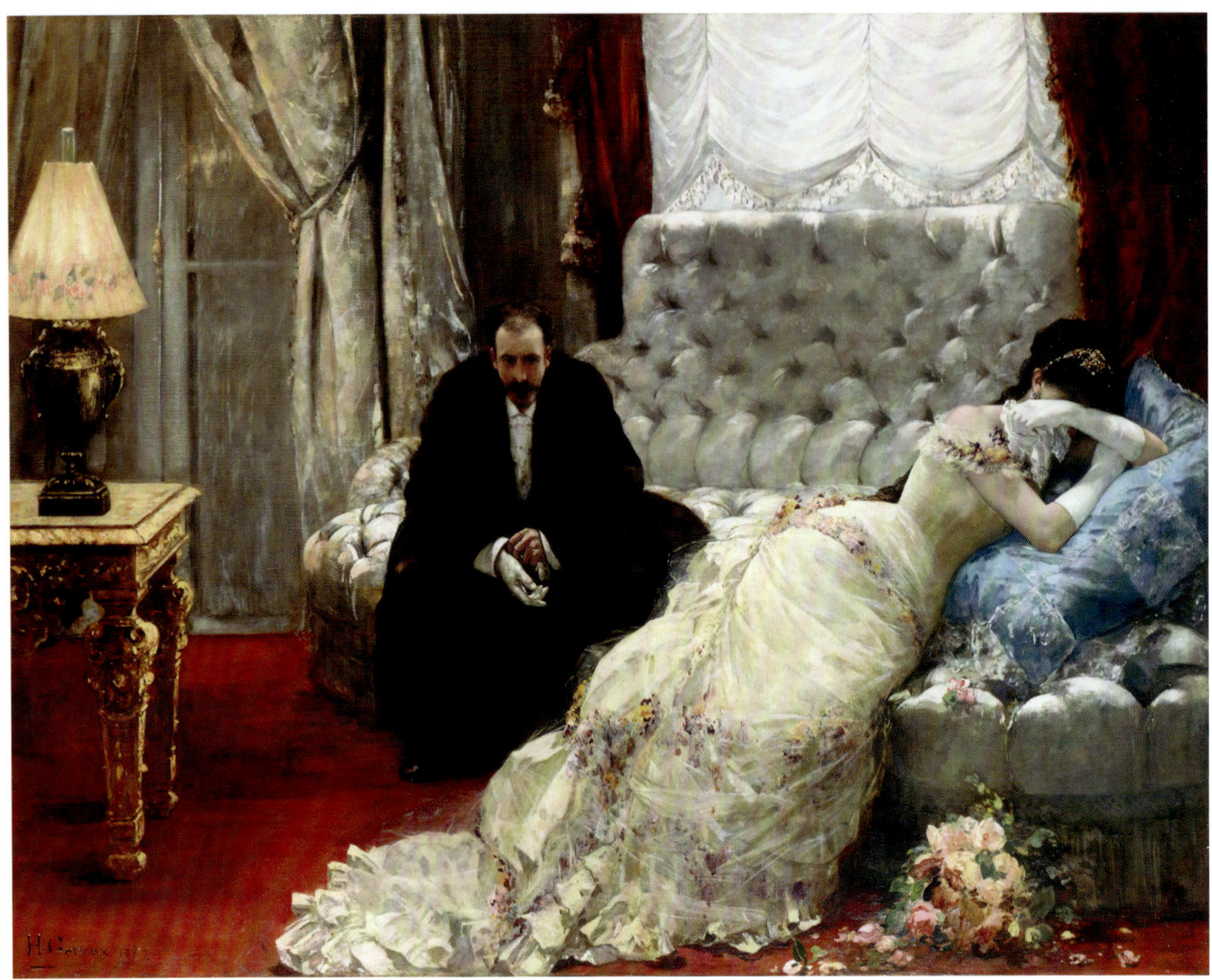

Return from the Ball

Retour du bal

Rückkehr vom Ball

De vuelta del baile

Retorno de bola

Terugkeer na het bal

HENRI GERVEX (1852-1929)
1885, Oil on canvas/Huile sur toile,
66 × 81,2 cm,
Private collection

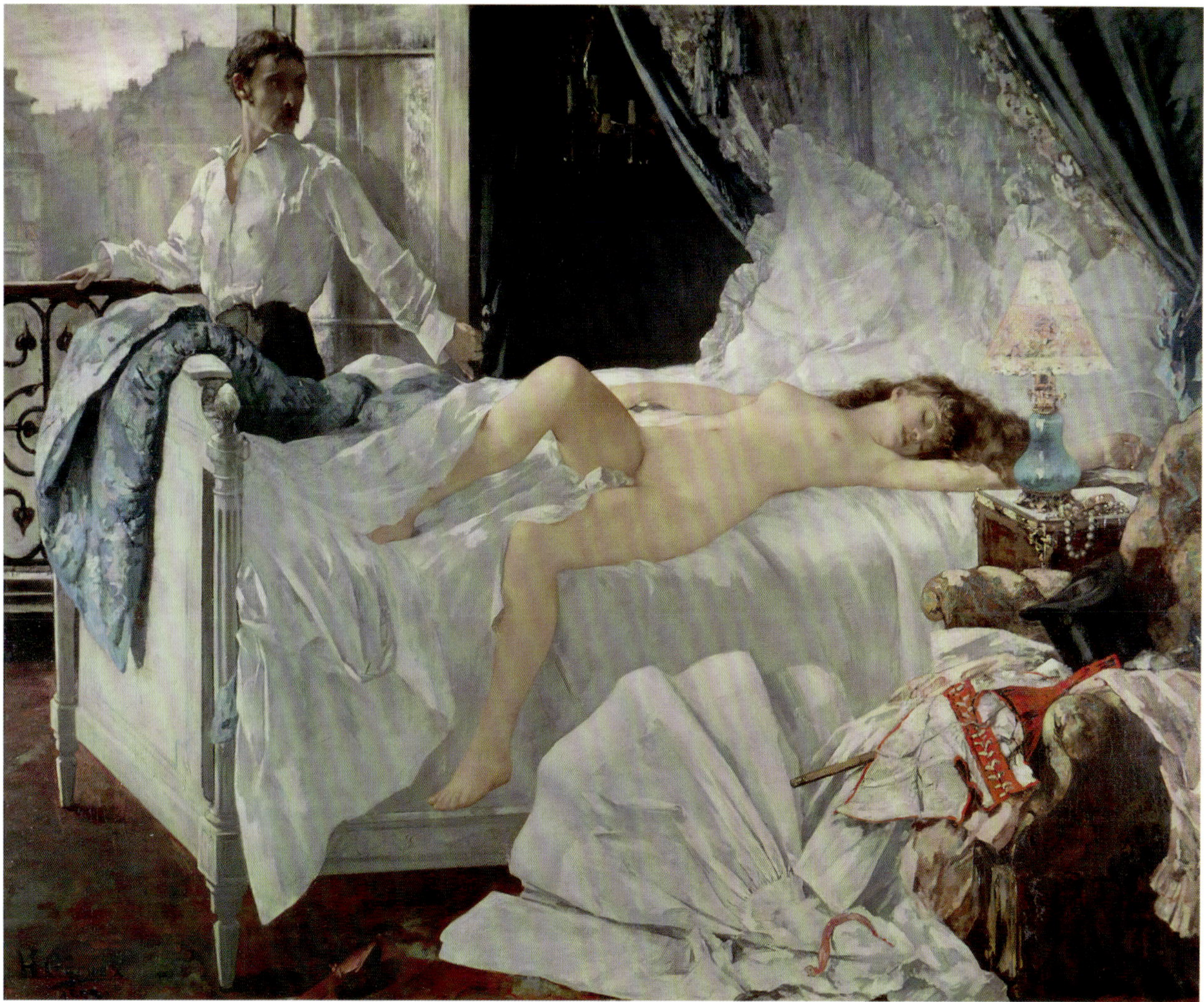

Rolla

The work is based on a poem by Alfred de Musset from 1833. A young, impoverished bourgeois turns his attention to the sleeping prostitute Marie - shortly before he poisons himself.

Rolla

Le peintre s'inspire d'un poème d'Alfred de Musset de 1833. Le regard tourné vers Marie, une prostituée endormie, un jeune bourgeois ruiné et dépravé s'apprête à se suicider en avalant du poison.

Rolla

Das Werk basiert auf einem Gedicht von Alfred de Musset aus dem Jahr 1833. Ein junger, verarmter Bourgeois richtet seinen Blick auf die schlafende Prostituierte Marie – kurz bevor er sich selbst vergiftet.

Rolla

La obra se basa en un poema de Alfred de Musset de 1833, en el que un joven burgués empobrecido presta atención a la prostituta dormida Marie, poco antes de envenenarse a sí mismo.

Rolla

A obra é baseada em um poema de Alfred de Musset de 1833. Um jovem burguês empobrecido volta sua atenção para a prostituta adormecida Marie - pouco antes de se envenenar.

Rolla

Het werk is gebaseerd op een gedicht van Alfred de Musset uit 1833. Een jonge, verarmde burger richt zijn blik op de slapende prostituee Marie, vlak voordat hij zichzelf vergiftigt.

HENRI GERVEX (1852-1929)

1878, Oil on canvas/Huile sur toile, 175,5 × 222 cm, Musée des Beaux-Arts, Bordeaux

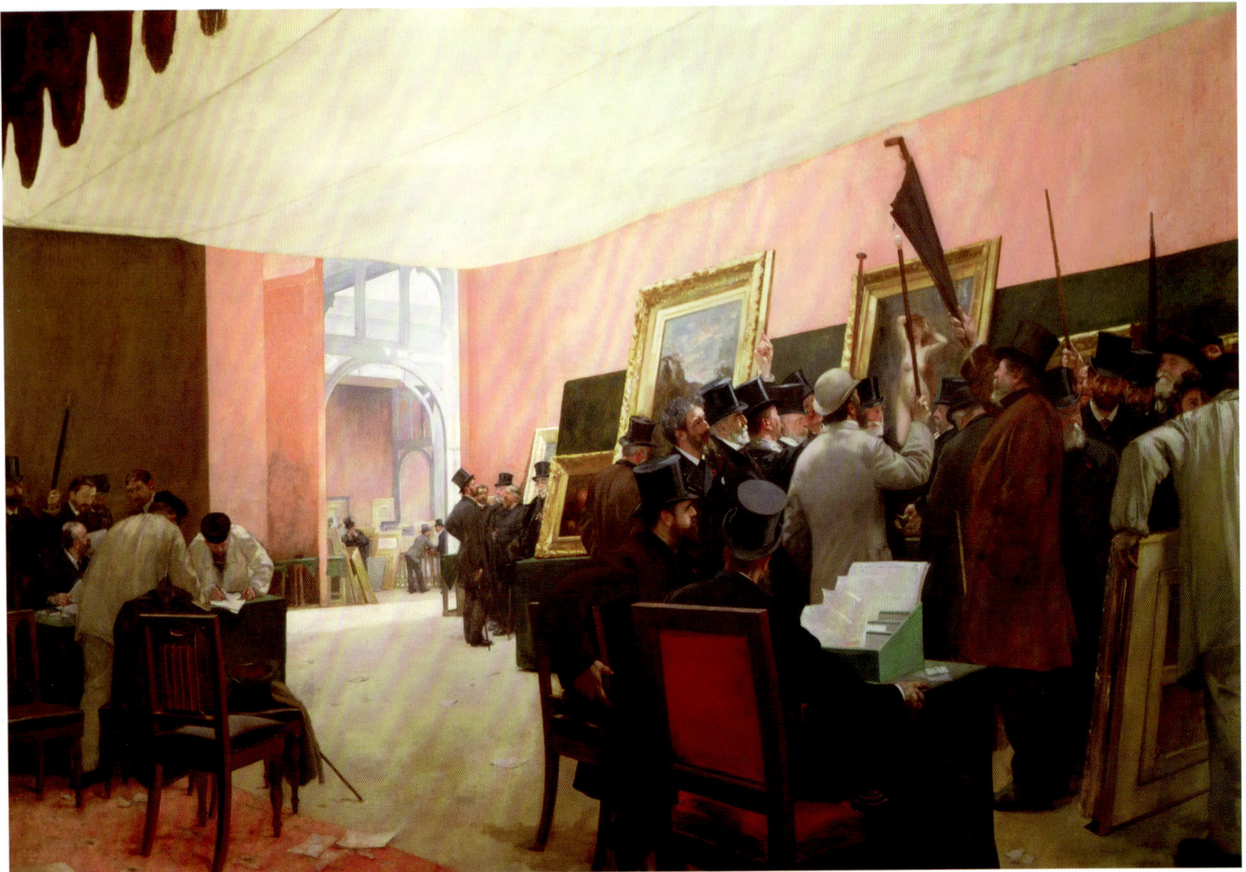

A Meeting of the Judges of the Salon des Artistes Francais

Although the salon played an important role in the everyday life of the artist, illustrations of the processes behind the scenes are rare. On the first floor of the Palais de l'Industrie, the jury examined every single painting.

Une séance du jury de peinture

Si le Salon revêt une importance considérable à l'époque pour les artistes, il est rare d'en voir les coulisses. Le jury examine chaque peinture, dans une salle du premier étage du palais de l'Industrie.

HENRI GERVEX (1852-1929)
Before 1885, Oil on canvas/Huile sur toile, 300 × 419,5 cm, Musée d'Orsay, Paris

Jury der Académie des Beaux-Arts

Obwohl der Salon eine bedeutende Rolle im Künstleralltag einnahm, sind Abbildungen der Vorgänge hinter den Kulissen rar. Im ersten Stock des Palais de l'Industrie begutachtete die Jury jedes einzelne Gemälde.

Jurado de la Academia de Bellas Artes

Aunque el salón jugó un papel importante en la vida cotidiana del artista, las ilustraciones de los procesos entre bastidores son raras. En la primera planta del Palais de l'Industrie, el jurado examinó cada uno de los cuadros.

Júri da Académie des Beaux-Arts

Embora o salão tenha desempenhado um papel importante na vida cotidiana do artista, são raras as ilustrações dos processos nos bastidores. No primeiro andar do Palais de l'Industrie, o júri examinou todos os quadros.

Bijeenkomst van de schilderjury

Hoewel de Salon een belangrijke rol speelde in het leven van kunstenaars, zijn schilderijen van het reilen en zeilen achter de schermen zeldzaam. Op de eerste verdieping van het Palais de l'Industrie beoordeelde de jury elk schilderij.

Before the Operation
or Doctor Péan
Teaching his Discovery
of the Compression
of Blood Vessels at
Saint-Louis Hospital

Avant l'opération *ou*
Le Docteur Péan
enseignant à l'hôpital
Saint-Louis sa découverte
du pincement
des vaisseaux

Vor der Operation *oder*
Doktor Péan lehrt im
Krankenhaus Saint-
Louis seine Technik
des Abklemmens
der Blutgefässe

Antes de la operación *o*
el Doctor Péan enseñando
en el hospital Saint-Louis
su técnica de sujeción de
los vasos sanguíneos

Antes da operação *ou*
o Doutor Péan ensina no
hospital Saint-Louis a sua
técnica de pinçamento
dos vasos sanguíneos

Voor de operatie *of*
Dokter Péan laat in
het ziekenhuis van
Saint-Louis de techniek
van het bloedvaten
afklemmen zien

HENRI GERVEX (1852-1929)
1887, Oil on canvas/
Huile sur toile,
242 × 188 cm,
Musée d'Orsay, Paris

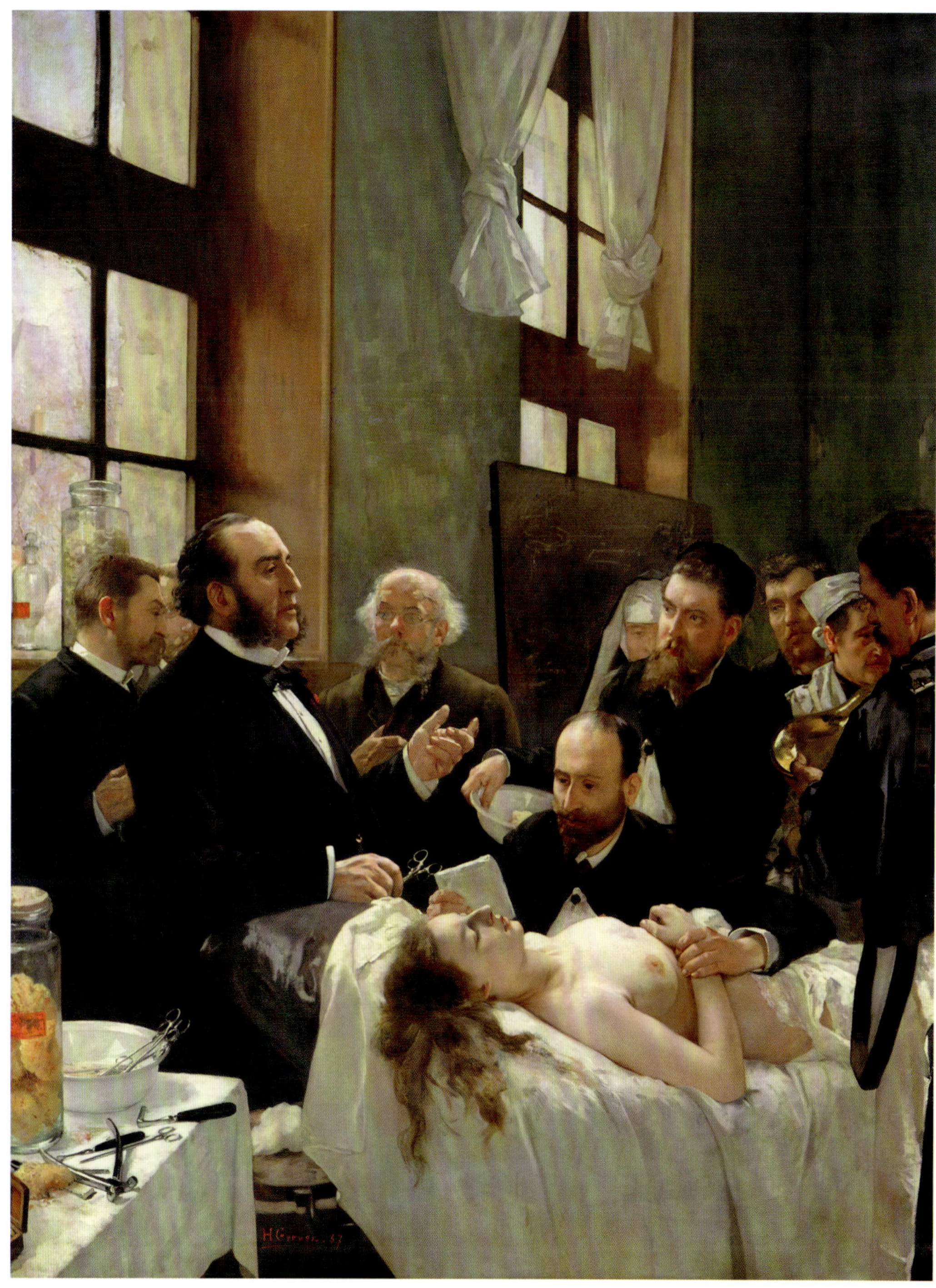

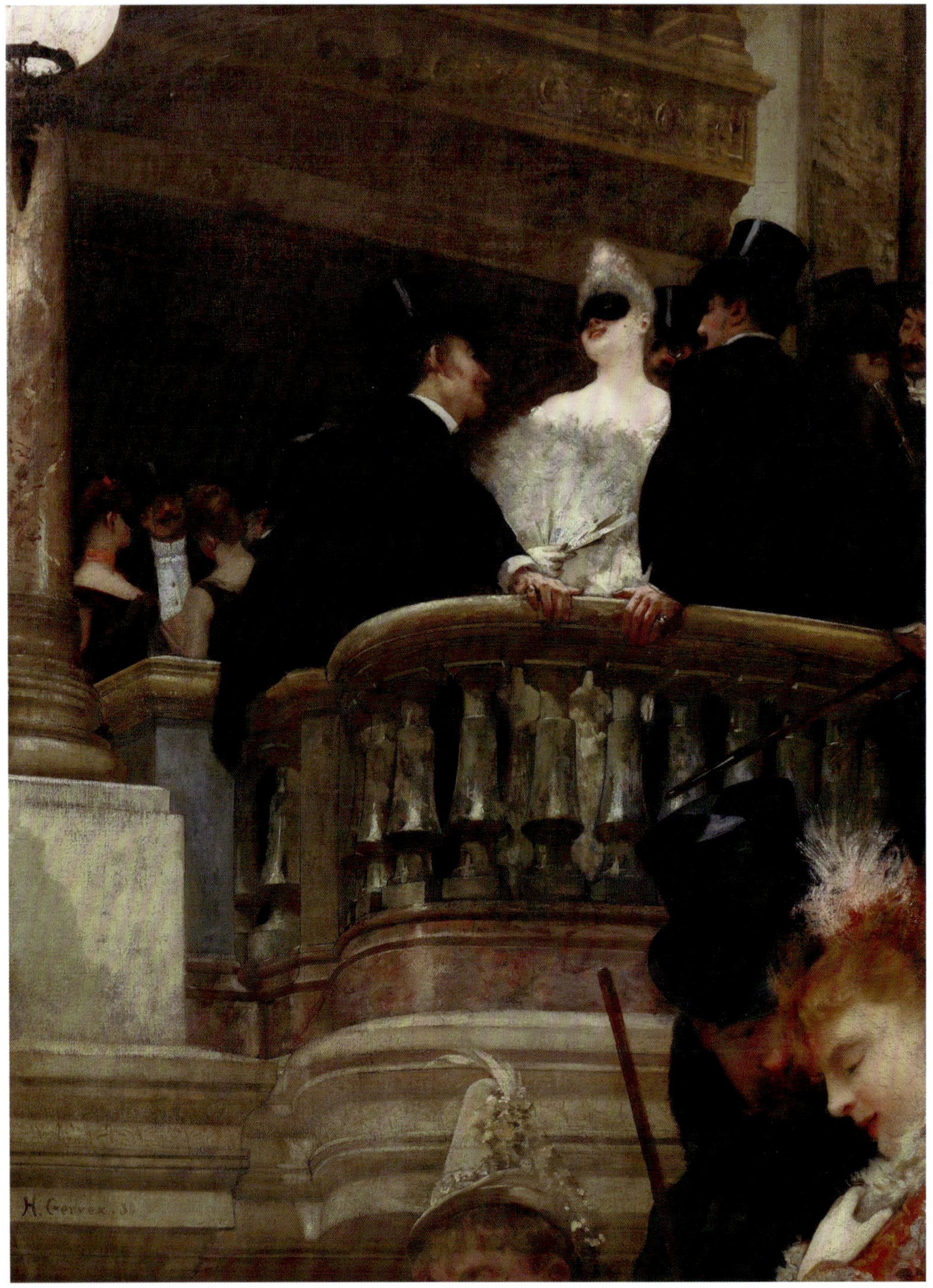

Masked Ball at the Opera

Le Bal de l'Opéra

Maskenball in der Oper

Baile de Máscaras
en la Ópera

Baile Mascarado na Ópera

Gemaskerd bal in de Opera

HENRI GERVEX (1852-1929)
1886, Oil on canvas/
Huile sur toile, 85 × 63 cm,
Musée d'Orsay, Paris

Study for a portrait of Tsar Nicholas II (1868-1918)

In 1898 Gervex stayed in Russia for the second time. He painted his work *The Coronation of Nicholas II*, which he showed at the World Exhibition in 1900, and several portraits of the Tsar, including this study..

Étude pour un portrait du tsar Nicolas II (1868-1918)

En 1898, Gervex se rend pour la deuxième fois en Russie. Il peint le *Couronnement de Nicolas II*, envoyé à l'Exposition universelle de 1900, et un ensemble de portraits du tsar, dont cette délicate esquisse.

Studie für ein Porträt des Zaren Nikolaus II. (1868-1918)

1898 hält sich Gervex zum zweiten Mal in Russland auf. Er malt sein Werk *Die Krönung Nikolaus II.*, das er auf der Weltausstellung im Jahr 1900 zeigt, und mehrere Porträts des Zaren, darunter diese Studie.

Estudio para un retrato del zar Nicolás II (1868-1918)

En 1898 Gervex se queda en Rusia por segunda vez. Pintó su obra *La coronación de Nicolás II*, que expuso en la Exposición Universal de 1900, y varios retratos del zar, incluido este estudio.

Estudo para um retrato do czar Nicolau II (1868-1918)

Em 1898 Gervex fica na Rússia pela segunda vez. Ele pintou sua obra *A Coroação de Nicolau II*, que ele mostrou na Exposição Mundial em 1900, e vários retratos do czar, incluindo este estudo.

Studie voor een portret van tsaar Nicolaas II (1868-1918)

In 1898 verbleef Gervex voor de tweede keer in Rusland. Hij schilderde *De kroning van Nicolaas II*, dat hij op de Wereldtentoonstelling van 1900 toonde, en enkele portretten van de tsaar, waaronder deze studie.

HENRI GERVEX (1852-1929)

1898, Oil on canvas/Huile sur toile, 70 × 56 cm, Private collection

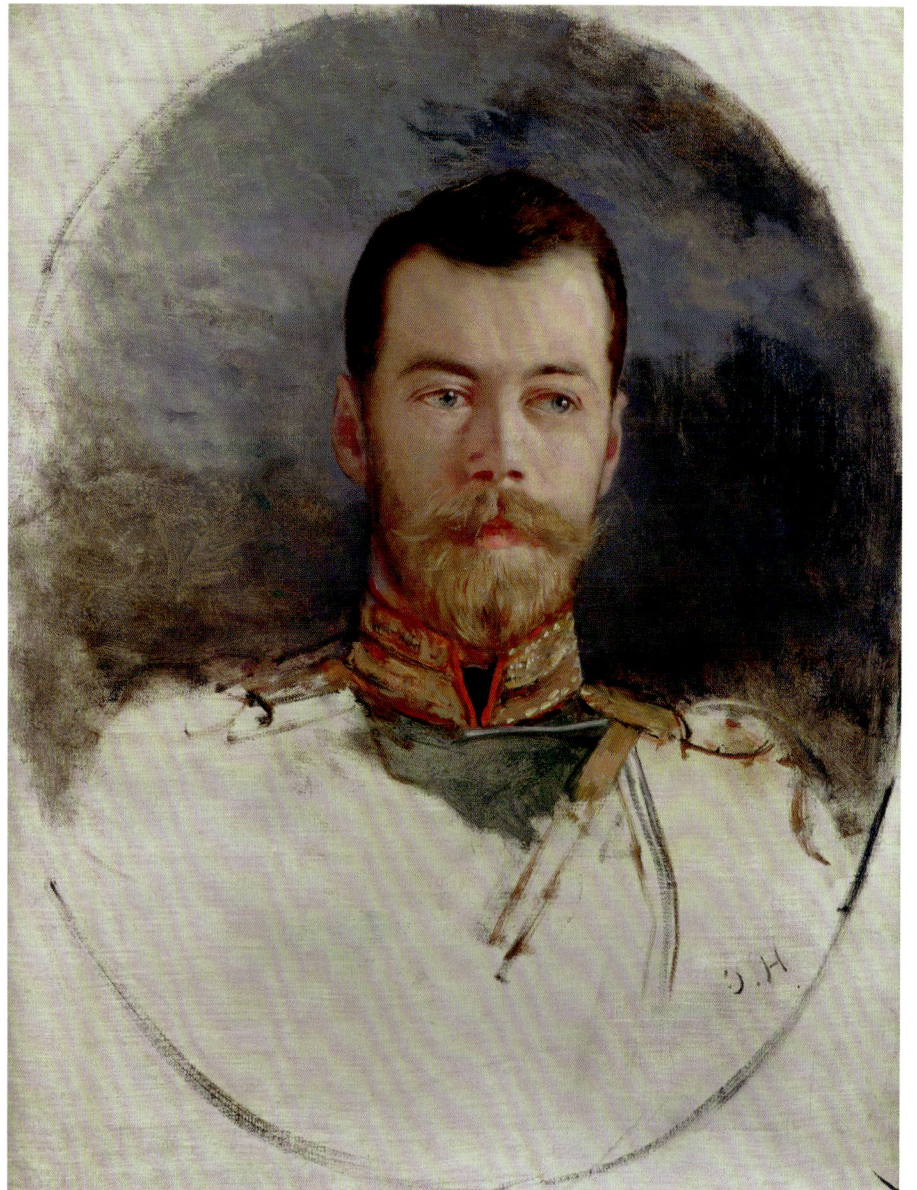

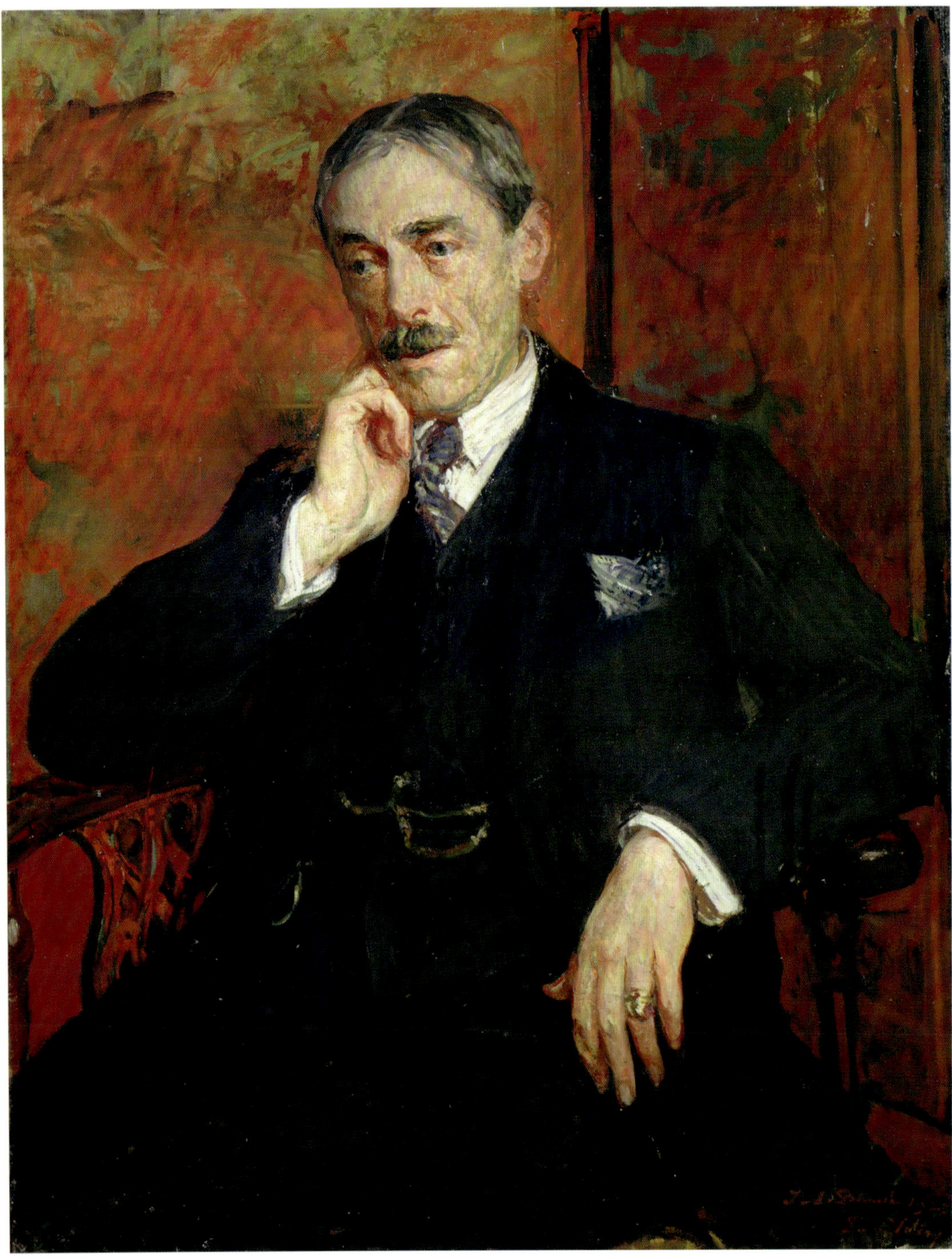

Paul Valéry
(1871-1945)

**JACQUES-
ÉMILE BLANCHE**
(1861-1942)

1928, Oil on canvas/
Huile sur toile,
90 × 75 cm,
Musée des Beaux-Arts,
Rouen

Portrait of Marcel Proust

As a portraitist of the glamorous Paris, Blanche immortalized numerous writers and artists. Proust was only 21 years old when he paints him. The writer was to keep the painting until his death.

Portrait de Marcel Proust

Peintre mondain, Blanche a immortalisé les figures de la vie littéraire et artistique de son époque. Hiératique, le teint blafard, Proust a ici 21 ans. L'écrivain conservera ce portrait jusqu'à sa mort.

Porträt von Marcel Proust

Als Porträtist des mondänen Paris verewigte Blanche zahlreiche Schriftsteller und Künstler. Proust ist gerade mal 21 Jahre alt, als er ihn malt. Der Schriftsteller wird das Gemälde bis zu seinem Tod behalten.

Retrato de Marcel Proust

Como retratista del glamoroso París, Blanche inmortalizó a numerosos escritores y artistas. Proust sólo tiene 21 años cuando lo pinta. El escritor conservará el cuadro hasta su muerte.

Retrato de Marcel Proust

Como retratadora da glamorosa Paris, Blanche imortalizou numerosos escritores e artistas. O Proust só tem 21 anos quando o pinta. O escritor ficará com o quadro até à sua morte.

Portret van Marcel Proust

Als portretschilder van het mondaine Parijs vereeuwigde Blanche talrijke schrijvers en kunstenaars. Proust was pas 21 jaar toen Blanche dit werk schilderde. De schrijver zou het houden tot zijn dood.

JACQUES-ÉMILE BLANCHE (1861-1942)

1892, Oil on canvas/Huile sur toile, 73,5 × 60,5 cm, Musée d'Orsay, Paris

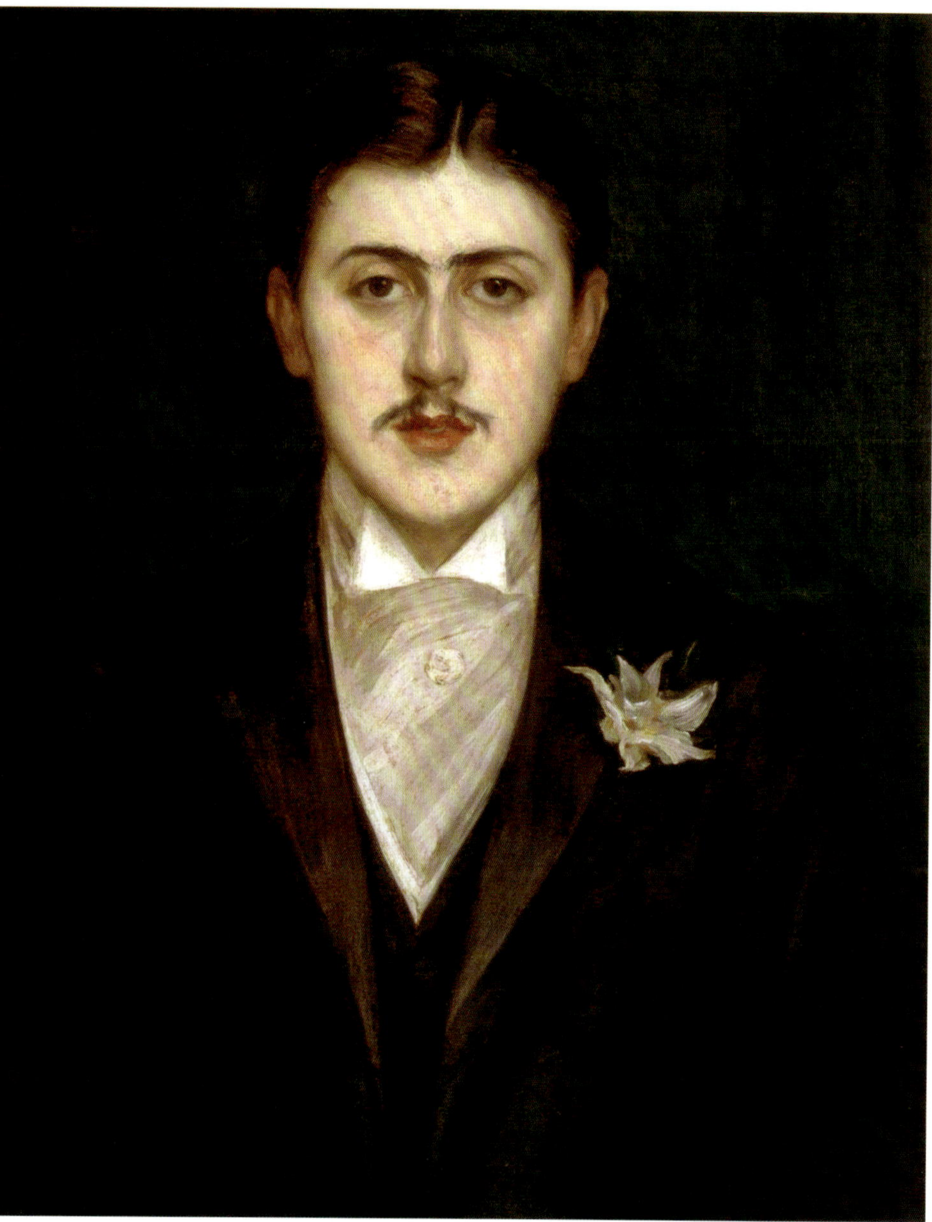

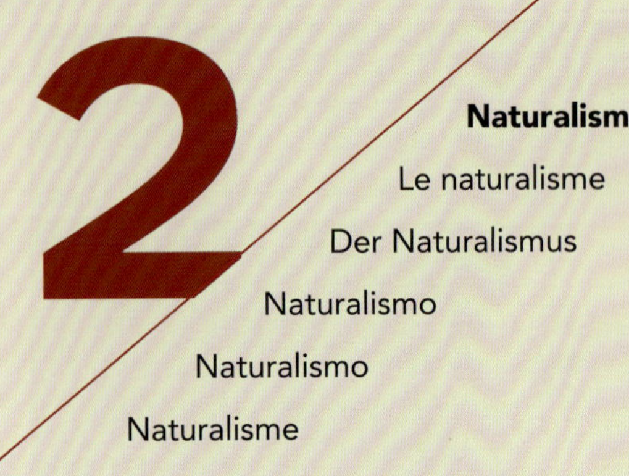

Naturalism

Le naturalisme

Der Naturalismus

Naturalismo

Naturalismo

Naturalisme

Naturalism

From the 1830s and 1840s, paintings that paid homage
to the beauty of nature became popular - in their
original appearance and not as an idealized image.
Landscape painting developed into a genre of its own
and took its place in the world of painting. Green areas,
the banks of the Seine, forests and clearings, but also
the sea offered artists new motifs. Jean-Baptiste Camille
Corot played a decisive role in the development of the
genre. He traveled through Italy and was inspired by the
Campagna Romana (*Tivoli, The Gardens of Villa d'Este*).
Sometimes his works still bear witness to classicism -
when they are decorated with small mythological scenes
(*The Dance of the Nymphs*). In most cases, however, he
devoted himself exclusively to nature.
His examples were followed by Narcisse Diaz de
la Peña, Théodore Rousseau and Charles-François
Daubigny. As members of the Barbizon School, they
made landscape painting their passion. They left the
studio to work outdoors, creating hundreds of paintings

Le naturalisme

Dès les années 1830-1840, un goût nouveau s'affirme
pour des toiles célébrant les beautés de la nature,
observée simplement pour ce qu'elle est. La place
accordée au paysage est de plus en plus importante,
et va devenir un sujet à part entière. La campagne
verdoyante, les rives de la Seine, les forêts, les clairières,
mais aussi les bords de mer, offrent aux artistes de
nouveaux sujets. Jean-Baptiste Camille Corot joue un
rôle décisif dans cette évolution. Il a voyagé en Italie,
observé les paysages de la région de Rome (*Tivoli, les
jardins de la villa d'Este [Italie]*). Ses œuvres conservent
parfois une part de classicisme, lorsqu'elles sont
agrémentées de petites scènes mythologiques (*La Danse
des nymphes*). Mais dans la majorité des cas, elles sont
entièrement dévolues à la nature.
Dans son sillage, Narcisse Diaz de la Peña, Théodore
Rousseau, Charles-François Daubigny… vont aller
encore plus loin. Assimilés au groupe de l'école de
Barbizon, ces peintres se passionnent pour le paysage

Der Naturalismus

Ab den 1830er- und 1840er-Jahren werden Gemälde
populär, die die Schönheit der Natur huldigen – in ihrer
ursprünglichen Erscheinung und nicht als idealisiertes
Abbild. Die Landschaftsmalerei entwickelt sich zu
einem eigenen Genre und nimmt ihren festen Platz in
der Welt der Malerei ein. Grüne Landstriche, die Ufer
der Seine, Wälder und Lichtungen aber auch das Meer
bieten sich den Künstlern als neue Motive an. Eine
entscheidende Rolle in der Entwicklung des Genres
spielt Jean-Baptiste Camille Corot. Er bereist Italien
und lässt sich von der Campagna Romana inspirieren
(*Tivoli, Die Gärten der Villa d'Este*). Manchmal zeugen
seine Werke noch vom Klassizismus – wenn sie mit
kleinen mythologischen Szenen ausgeschmückt sind
(*Tanz der Nymphen*). In den meisten Fällen widmet er
sich jedoch ausschließlich der Natur.
Seinem Beispiel folgen Narcisse Diaz de la Peña,
Théodore Rousseau oder Charles-François Daubigny.
Als Angehörige der Schule von Barbizon machen sie die

JEAN-BAPTISTE CAMILLE COROT (1796-1875)
1871, Oil on canvas/Huile sur toile, 105 × 74,6 cm,
Minneapolis Institute of Arts, Minneapolis

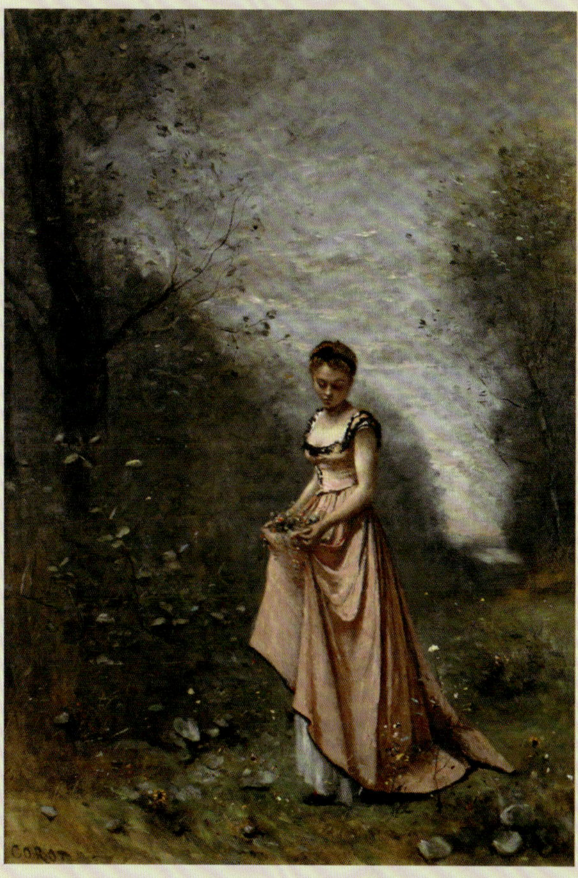

Naturalismo

A partir de los años 1830 y 1840, las pinturas que rindieron homenaje a la belleza de la naturaleza se hicieron populares - en su apariencia original y no como una imagen idealizada. La pintura paisajística se convirtió en un género propio y ocupó su lugar en el mundo de la pintura. Las zonas verdes, las orillas del Sena, los bosques y los claros, pero también el mar ofrecen a los artistas nuevos motivos. Jean-Baptiste Camille Corot juega un papel decisivo en el desarrollo del género. Viaja por Italia y se inspira en la Campagna Romana (*Tivoli, Los Jardines de Villa d'Este*). A veces, sus obras siguen siendo testigos del clasicismo, cuando están decoradas con pequeñas escenas mitológicas (*La danza de las Ninfas*). En la mayoría de los casos, sin embargo, se dedica exclusivamente a la naturaleza. Sus ejemplos son seguidos por Narcisse Diaz de la Peña, Théodore Rousseau y Charles-François Daubigny. Como miembros de la Escuela Barbizon, hacen de la pintura de paisajes su pasión. Salen del

Naturalismo

A partir das décadas de 1830 e 1840, pinturas que homenageiam a beleza da natureza tornaram-se populares - em sua aparência original e não como uma imagem idealizada. A pintura paisagística desenvolveu-se num género próprio e tomou o seu lugar no mundo da pintura. Áreas verdes, as margens do Sena, florestas e clareiras, mas também o mar oferece aos artistas novos motivos. Jean-Baptiste Camille Corot desempenha um papel decisivo no desenvolvimento do género. Viaja pela Itália e é inspirado na Campagna Romana (*Tivoli, Os Jardins da Villa d'Este*). Por vezes, as suas obras ainda testemunham o classicismo - quando são decoradas com pequenas cenas mitológicas (*Dança das Ninfas*). Na maioria dos casos, porém, ele se dedica exclusivamente à natureza.

Seus exemplos são seguidos por Narcisse Diaz de la Peña, Théodore Rousseau e Charles-François Daubigny. Como membros da Escola Barbizon, fazem da pintura paisagística a sua paixão. Eles saem do estúdio para

Naturalisme

Vanaf de jaren 1830 en 1840 werden schilderijen die een eerbetoon brachten aan de schoonheid van de natuur populair – in haar oorspronkelijke vorm en niet als een geïdealiseerd beeld. De landschapsschilderkunst ontwikkelde zich tot een genre op zich en kreeg een plaats in de wereld van de schilderkunst. Groene landstreken, de oevers van de Seine, bossen en open plekken, maar ook de zee boden kunstenaars nieuwe onderwerpen. Jean-Baptiste Camille Corot speelde een beslissende rol in de ontwikkeling van het genre. Hij reisde door Italië en liet zich inspireren door de campagna Romana (*Tivoli, tuinen van de Villa d'Este*). Soms vertoonden zijn werken nog sporen van het classicisme – als ze zijn versierd met kleine mythologische scènes (*De dans van de nimfen*). In de meeste gevallen wijdde hij zich echter volledig aan de natuur.

Zijn voorbeeld werd gevolgd door Narcisse Diaz de la Peña, Théodore Rousseau en Charles-François Daubigny. Als leden van de school van Barbizon maakten ze van de landschapsschilderkunst hun

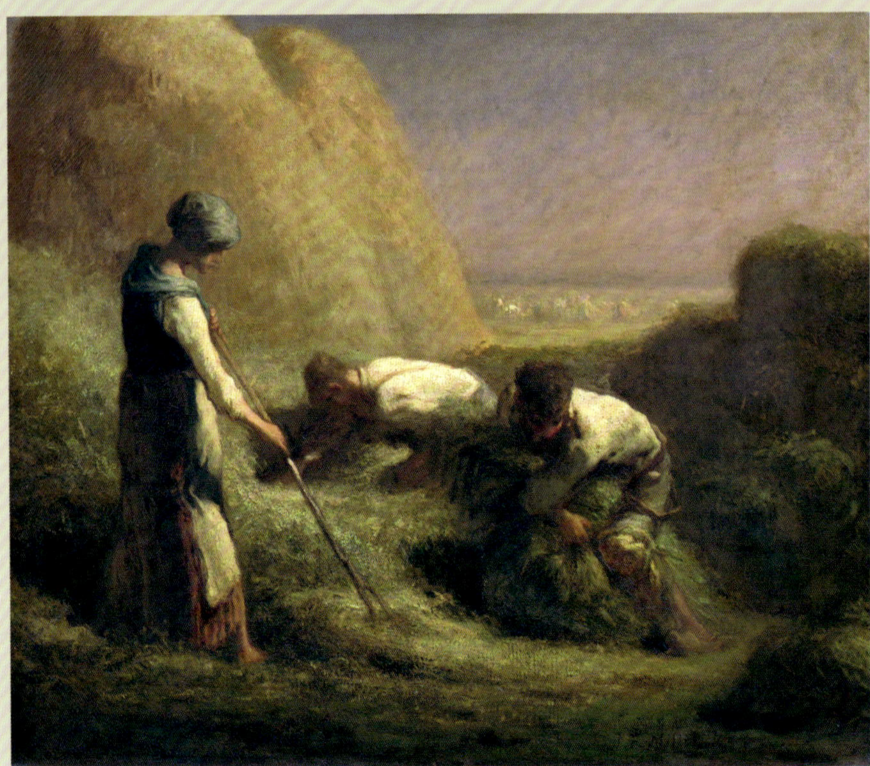

The Hay Trussers

Les Botteleurs de foin

Die Heubinder

Los gavilladores

A pasta de feno

De hooibinders

JEAN-FRANÇOIS MILLET (1814-1875)
c. 1850/51, Oil on canvas/Huile sur toile,
56 × 65 cm, Musée du Louvre, Paris

with countless variations of color, light and views of the surrounding nature. But also figurative representations were depictd in Naturalism. Corot created remarkable portraits (*Dreamer at the Fountain, The Woman with the Pearl*), while Jean-François Millet became famous for his paintings of field work and rural life. Corn pickers, sowers and shepherds populate his melancholic scenes in the morning or evening light, which are immersed in a mystical silence (*The Angelus*). From the 1870s onwards, the work of these artists inspired the future Impressionists, who incorporated the style into their paintings.

jusqu'à l'obsession. Ils sortent de l'atelier et travaillent en plein air, produisant des centaines d'œuvres qui sont autant de variations de couleurs, de lumière, de points de vue sur ce qui les entoure. Mais le naturalisme n'exclut pas pour autant les personnages. Jean-Baptiste Camille Corot a produit de remarquables tableaux de figures (*La Rêveuse à la fontaine, La Femme à la perle…*), et Jean-François Millet s'affirme comme le peintre des travaux des champs et de la vie paysanne. Représentés aux premières lueurs du matin comme au crépuscule, glaneurs, semeurs et gardiens de moutons peuplent des tableaux empreints de mélancolie, baignés d'un silence mystique (*L'Angélus*). Les recherches de tous ces artistes trouveront un écho et un prolongement dans la peinture des futurs impressionnistes, à l'aube des années 1870.

Landschaftsmalerei zu ihrer Passion. Sie verlassen das Atelier, um im Freien zu arbeiten und schaffen dabei Hunderte Gemälde mit unzähligen Variationen der Farben, des Lichts und der Ansichten der sie umgebenden Natur. Aber auch figürliche Darstellungen sind im Naturalismus vertreten. Jean-Baptiste Corot schuf bemerkenswerte Porträts (*Die Träumende am Brunnen, Die Frau mit der Perle*), während Jean-François Millet mit seinen Gemälden der Feldarbeit und des Landlebens bekannt wird. Ährenleser, Sämänner und Schafhirten bevölkern seine melancholischen Szenen im Morgen- oder Abendlicht, die in eine mystische Stille getaucht sind (*Beim Angelusläuten*). Das Wirken dieser Künstler wird ab den 1870er-Jahren die zukünftigen Impressionisten inspirieren, die den Stil in ihrer Gemälde einfließen lassen.

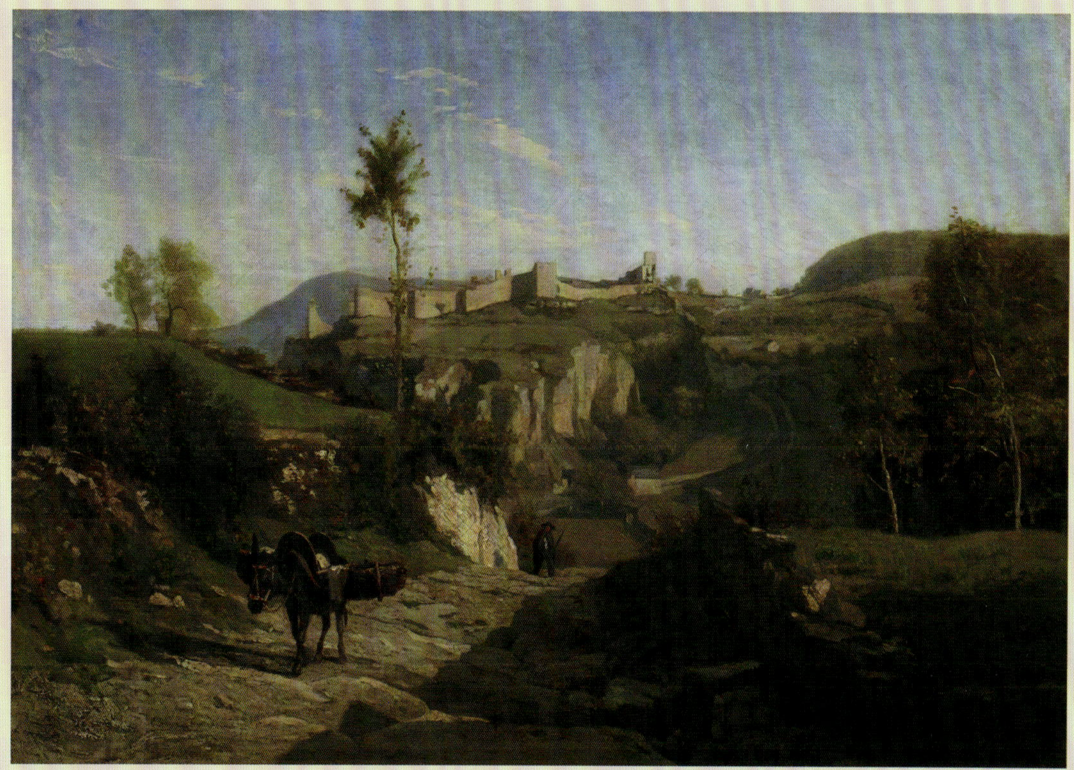

estudio para trabajar al aire libre, creando cientos de pinturas con innumerables variaciones de color, luz y vistas de la naturaleza circundante. Pero también las representaciones figurativas están representadas en el naturalismo. Corot creó retratos notables (*El soñador en la fuente, La mujer con la perla*), mientras que Jean-François Millet se hizo famoso por sus pinturas sobre el trabajo de campo y la vida rural. Cosechadores de maíz, sembradores y pastores pueblan sus escenas melancólicas a la luz de la mañana o de la noche, inmersas en un silencio místico (*El Ángelus*). A partir de la década de 1870, el trabajo de estos artistas inspirará a los futuros impresionistas, que incorporaron el estilo en sus pinturas.

trabalhar ao ar livre, criando centenas de pinturas com inúmeras variações de cor, luz e vistas da natureza circundante. Mas também as representações figurativas estão representadas no Naturalismo. Corot criou retratos notáveis (*O Sonhador na Fonte, A Mulher com a Pérola*), enquanto Jean-François Millet se tornou famoso por suas pinturas de campo e vida rural. Orelhas de colhedores de milho, semeadores e pastores povoam suas cenas melancólicas de manhã ou à noite, imersas em um silêncio místico (*No Anel do Angelus*). A partir da década de 1870, o trabalho destes artistas irá inspirar os futuros impressionistas, que incorporaram o estilo em suas pinturas.

passie. Ze verlieten het atelier om buiten te werken en maakten honderden schilderijen met ontelbare variaties in kleur, licht en uitzicht op de omliggende natuur. Maar ook figuratieve voorstellingen zijn in het naturalisme vertegenwoordigd. Corot maakte opmerkelijke portretten (*Droomster bij de fontein, De vrouw met de parel*), terwijl Jean-François Millet beroemd werd met zijn schilderijen over het werken en leven op het platteland. Arenleessters, zaaiers en herders bevolken zijn melancholieke taferelen in het ochtend- of avondlicht, die zijn ondergedompeld in een mystieke stilte (*Het angelus*). Vanaf de jaren 1870 zou het werk van deze schilders een inspiratiebron zijn voor de toekomstige impressionisten, die de stijl in hun schilderijen verwerkten.

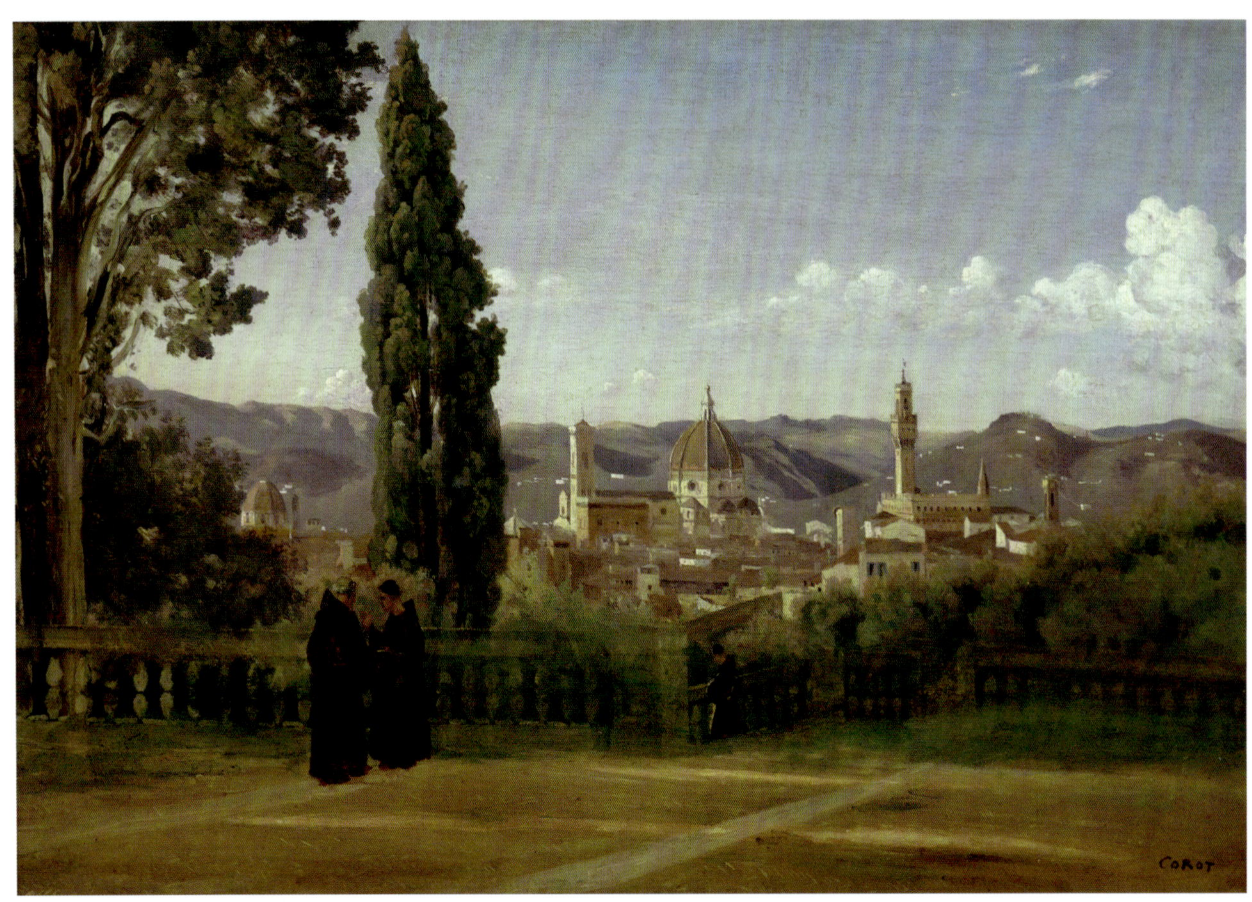

View of Florence from the Boboli Gardens

Vue de Florence depuis le jardin de Boboli

Florenz von den Boboli-Gärten aus

Florencia desde los Jardines de Boboli

Florença dos Jardins de Boboli

Gezicht op Florence vanuit de Boboli-tuinen

JEAN-BAPTISTE CAMILLE COROT (1796-1875)

c. 1835-40, Oil on canvas/Huile sur toile, 51 × 73,5 cm,
Musée du Louvre, Paris

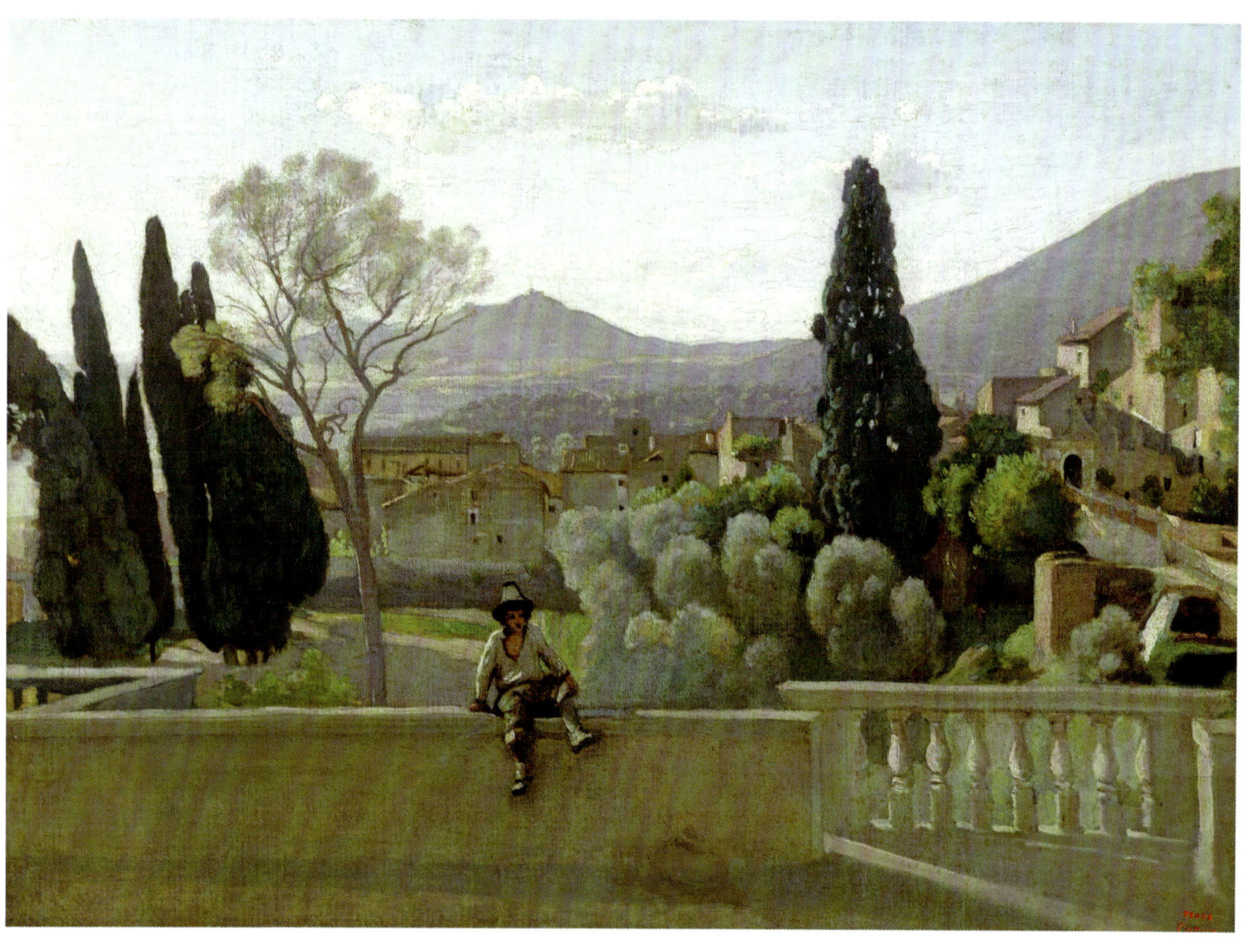

The Gardens of Villa d'Este, Tivoli

The actual motif is the landscape, but Corot used figures to illustrate the scale. At the same time, he created a foreground that increases depth and perspective.

Tivoli, les jardins de la villa d'Este

Si le paysage est bien le sujet principal du tableau, la figure solitaire permet d'en donner l'échelle, et d'animer la toile, en créant un premier plan qui renforce l'effet de profondeur et de perspective.

JEAN-BAPTISTE CAMILLE COROT (1796-1875)

1843, Oil on canvas/Huile sur toile, 43 × 61 cm, Musée du Louvre, Paris

Tivoli, Die Gärten der Villa d'Este

Das eigentliche Motiv ist die Landschaft. Corot nutzte aber Figuren zur Verdeutlichung des Maßstabs. Gleichzeitig erzeugt er einen Vordergrund, mit der die Tiefenwirkung und Perspektive steigert.

Tivoli, los jardines de Villa d'Este

Si el paisaje es el tema principal del cuadro, la figura solitaria permite escalarlo y animar el lienzo, creando un primer plano que refuerza el efecto de profundidad y perspectiva.

Tivoli, Os jardins de Villa d'Este

O motivo real é a paisagem. Mas Corot usou figuras para ilustrar a escala. Ao mesmo tempo, cria um primeiro plano que aumenta a profundidade e a perspectiva.

Tivoli, tuinen van de Villa d'Este

Het eigenlijke onderwerp is het landschap. Maar Corot gebruikte figuren om de afmetingen duidelijk te maken. Tegelijkertijd creëerde hij een voorgrond die de diepte en het perspectief vergroot.

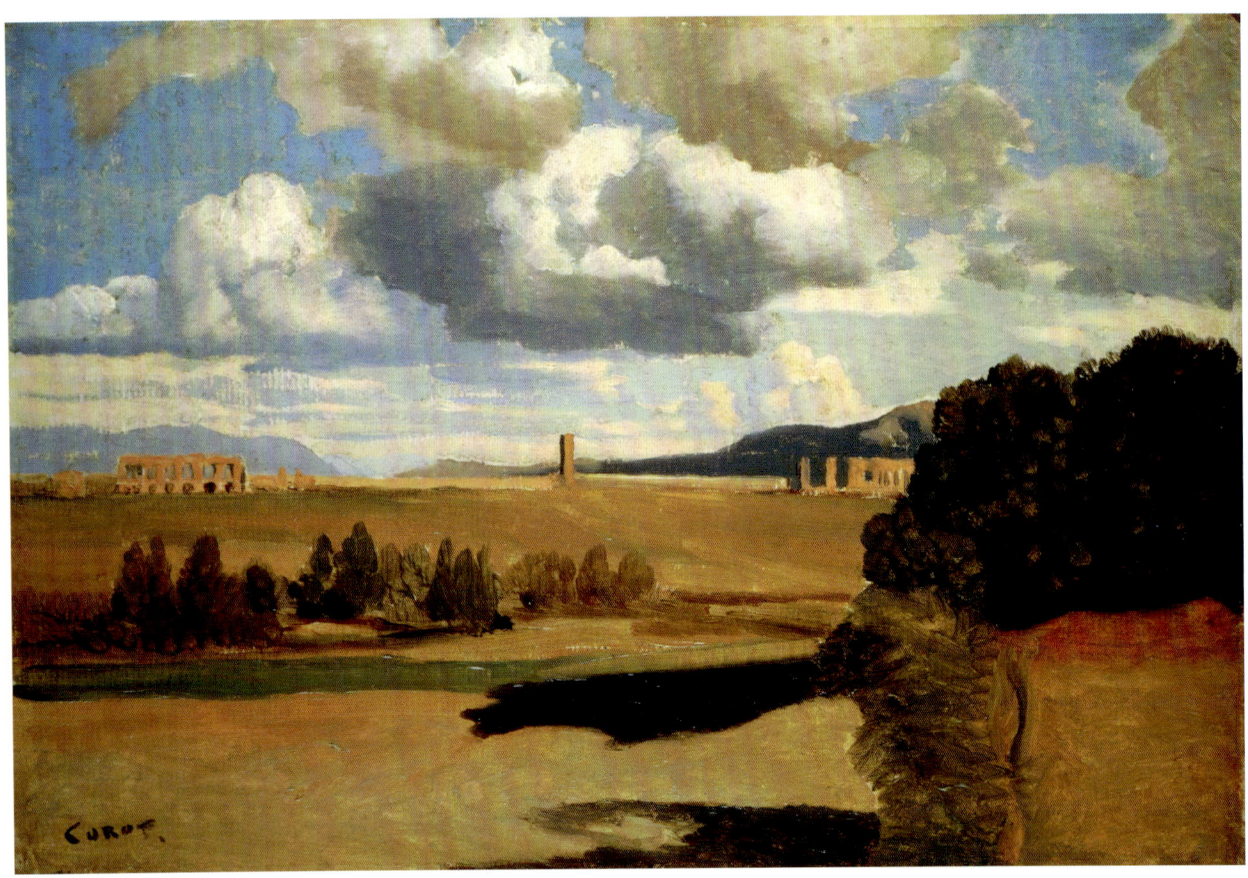

The Roman Campagna with the Claudian Aqueduct

Campagne romaine avec l'aqueduc Claudio

Campagna Romana mit dem Aquädukt Claudio

Campagna Romana con el acueducto Claudio

Campagna Romana com o aqueduto Claudio

Campagna Romana met het aquaduct van Claudius

JEAN-BAPTISTE CAMILLE COROT (1796-1875)

c. 1826, Oil on paper on canvas/Huile sur papier posé sur toile, 22,8 × 34 cm, The National Gallery, London

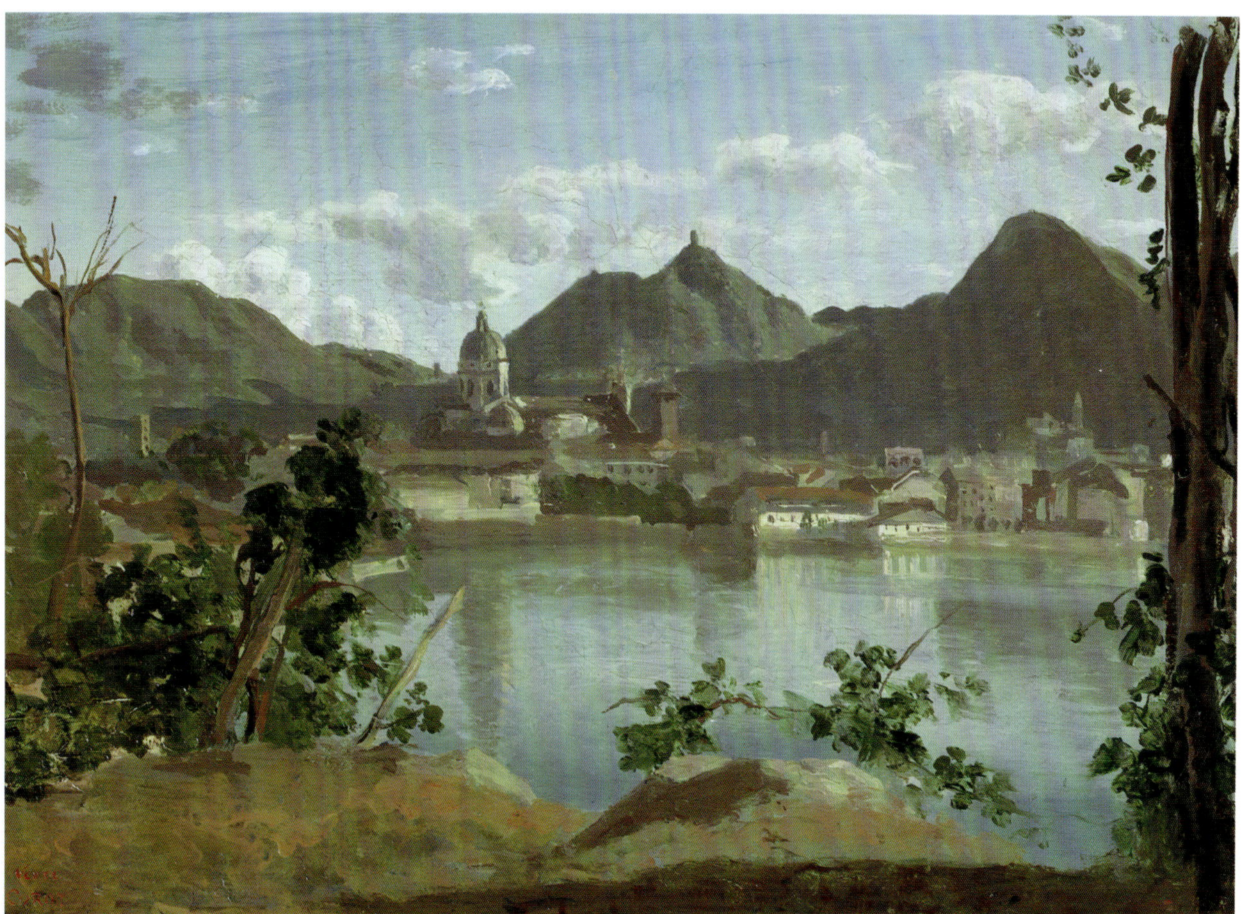

The Town and Lake Como

La Ville et le Lac de Côme

Stadt und See von Como

Ciudad y lago de Como

Cidade e lago de Como

Stad en meer van Como

JEAN-BAPTISTE CAMILLE COROT (1796-1875)

1834, Oil on canvas/Huile sur toile, 29,5 × 42 cm, Private collection

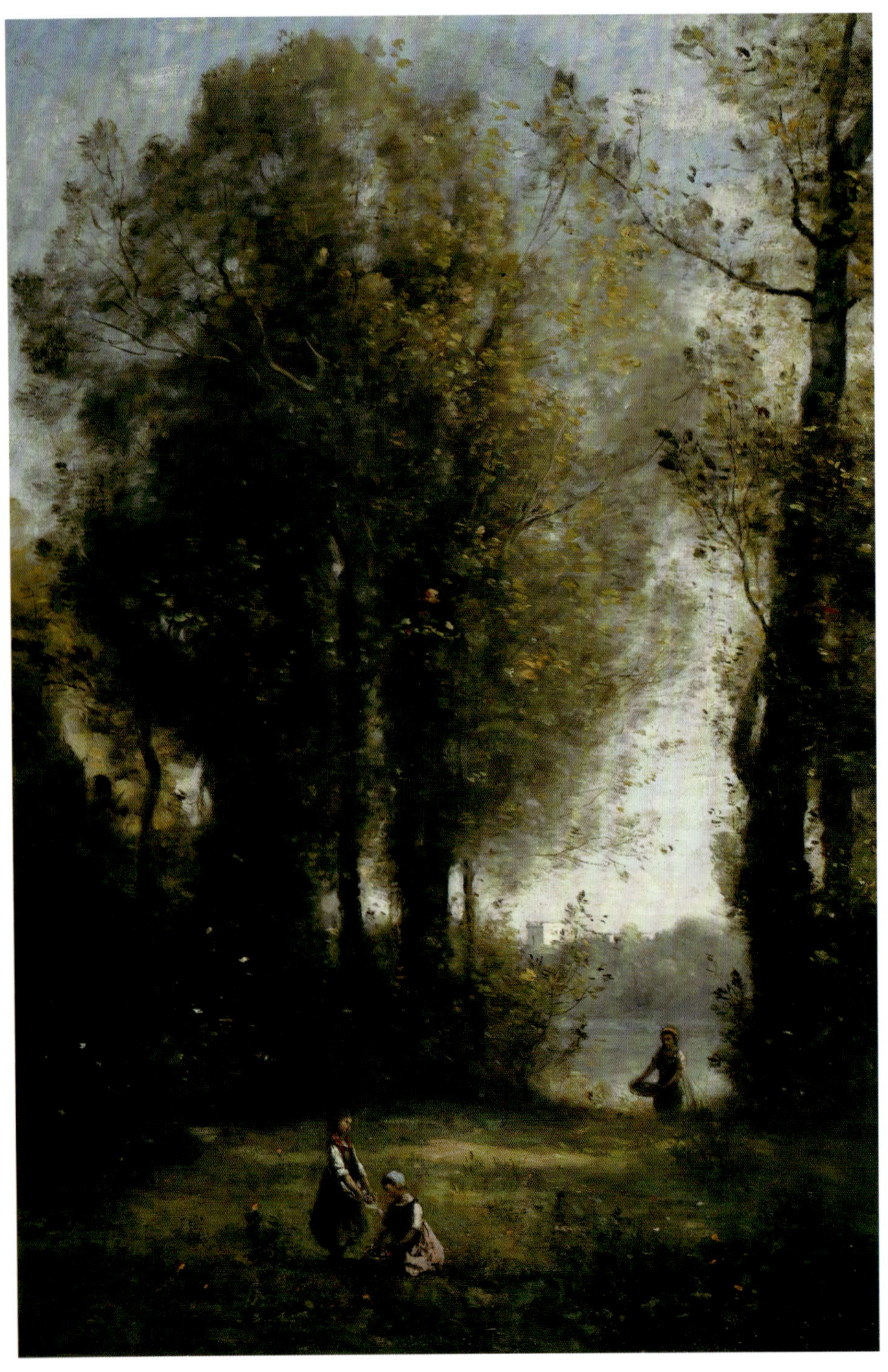

Picking Daisies

La Cueillette des marguerites

Beim Gänseblümchenpflücken

Recogiendo margaritas

Ao apanhar margaridas

Madeliefjes plukken

JEAN-BAPTISTE CAMILLE COROT (1796-1875)

c. 1865-70, Oil on canvas/Huile sur toile, 71,8 × 48,5 cm, Private collection

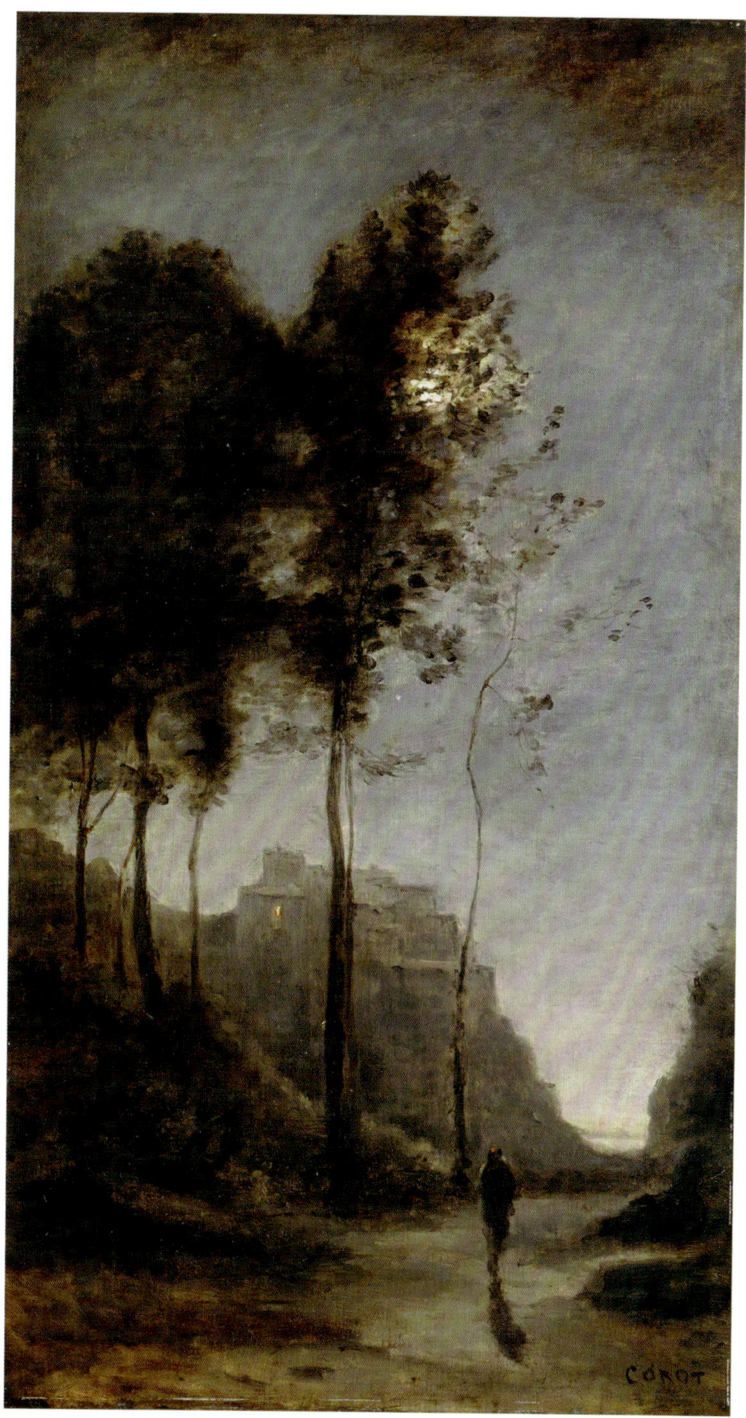

Moonlight on the Edge of a Gulf

Clair de lune au bord d'un golfe

Mondschein über einer Bucht

Luz de luna sobre una bahía

Luar sobre uma baía

Maanlicht boven een baai

JEAN-BAPTISTE CAMILLE COROT (1796-1875)

1858, Oil on canvas/Huile sur toile,
63,5 × 35,6 cm, Private collection

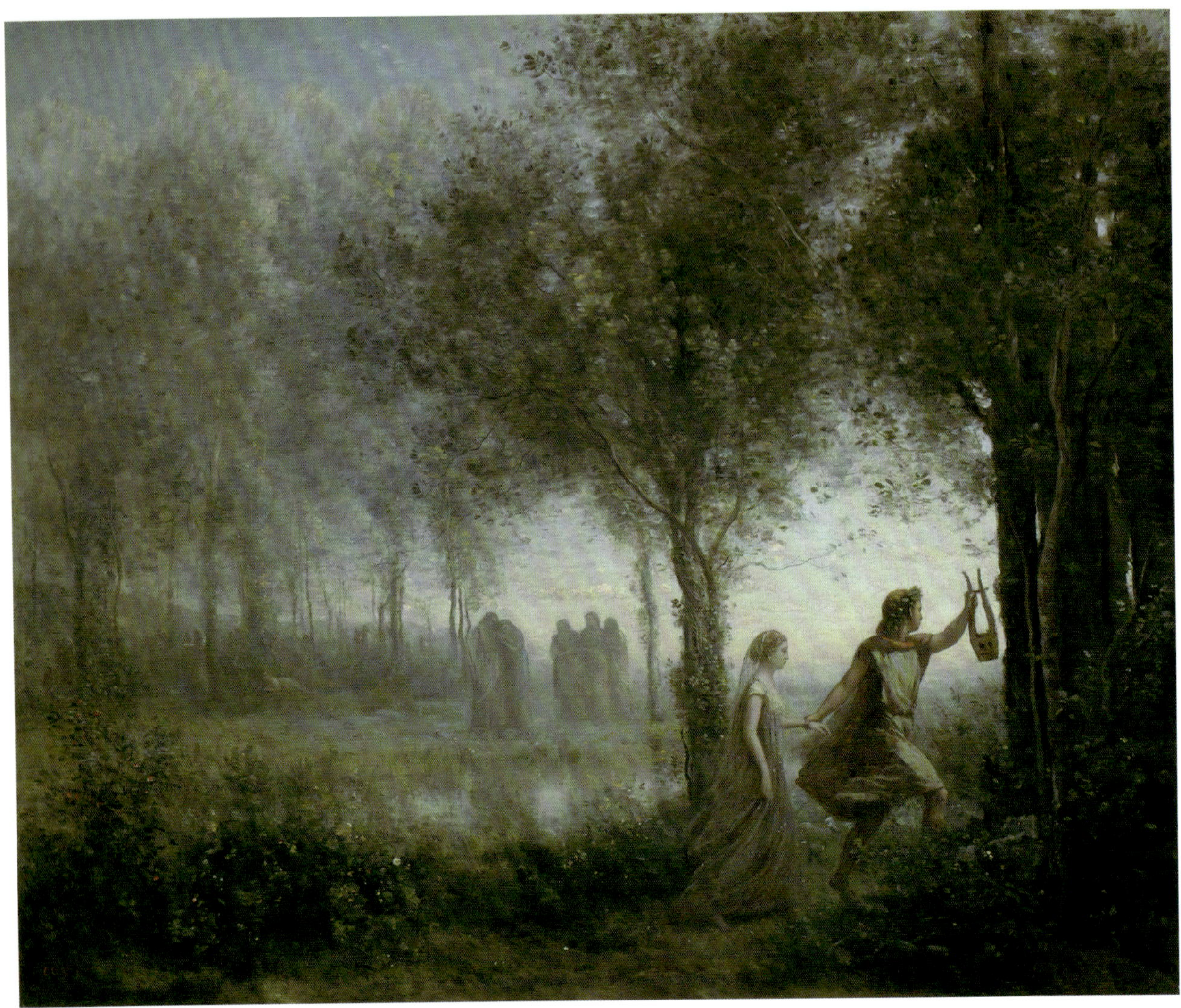

Orpheus Leading Eurydice from the Underworld

Orphée ramenant Eurydice des Enfers

Orpheus geleitet Eurydike aus der Unterwelt

Orfeo conduciendo a Eurídice fuera del inframundo

Orfeu lidera Eurídice do Submundo

Orpheus leidt Eurydice uit de onderwereld

JEAN-BAPTISTE CAMILLE COROT (1796-1875)

1861, Oil on canvas/Huile sur toile,

112,3 × 137,1 cm,

Museum of Fine Arts, Houston

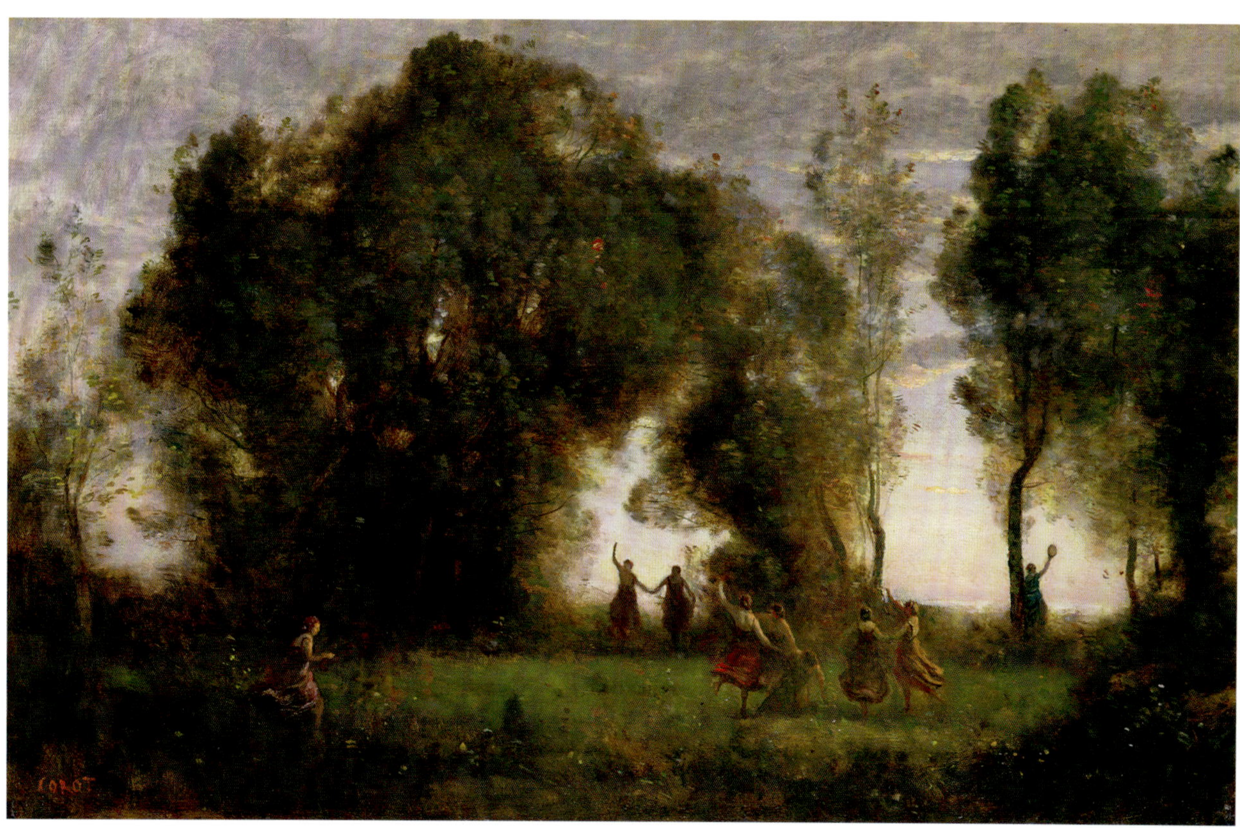

The Dance of the Nymphs

The subject is influenced by classicism. Yet it testifies to Corot's interest in the beauty of nature. The nymphs seem to move on a stage consisting of a green backdrop.

Une matinée *ou* La Danse des nymphes

Par le sujet de la toile, Corot s'inscrit dans un certain classicisme, tout en affirmant son intérêt pour les beautés de la nature. Les nymphes semblent évoluer sur une scène, dans un théâtre de verdure.

Der Tanz der Nymphen

Das Sujet ist klassizistisch beeinflusst. Dennoch zeugt es von Corots Interesse für die Schönheit der Natur. Die Nymphen scheinen sich auf einer Bühne zu bewegen, die aus einer grünen Kulisse besteht.

La Danza de las Ninfas

El sujeto está influenciado por el clasicismo. Sin embargo, es un testimonio del interés de Corot por la belleza de la naturaleza. Las ninfas parecen moverse en un escenario que consiste en un fondo verde.

A Dança das Ninfas

O tema é influenciado pelo classicismo. Mas testemunha o interesse de Corot pela beleza da natureza. As ninfas parecem mover-se num palco que consiste num pano de fundo verde.

De dans van de nimfen

Het onderwerp is classicistisch beïnvloed. Toch getuigt het van Corots interesse in de schoonheid van de natuur. De nimfen lijken zich te bewegen op een podium in een theater van groen.

JEAN-BAPTISTE CAMILLE COROT (1796-1875)

c. 1860, Oil on canvas/Huile sur toile, 48,1 × 77,2 cm, Musée d'Orsay, Paris

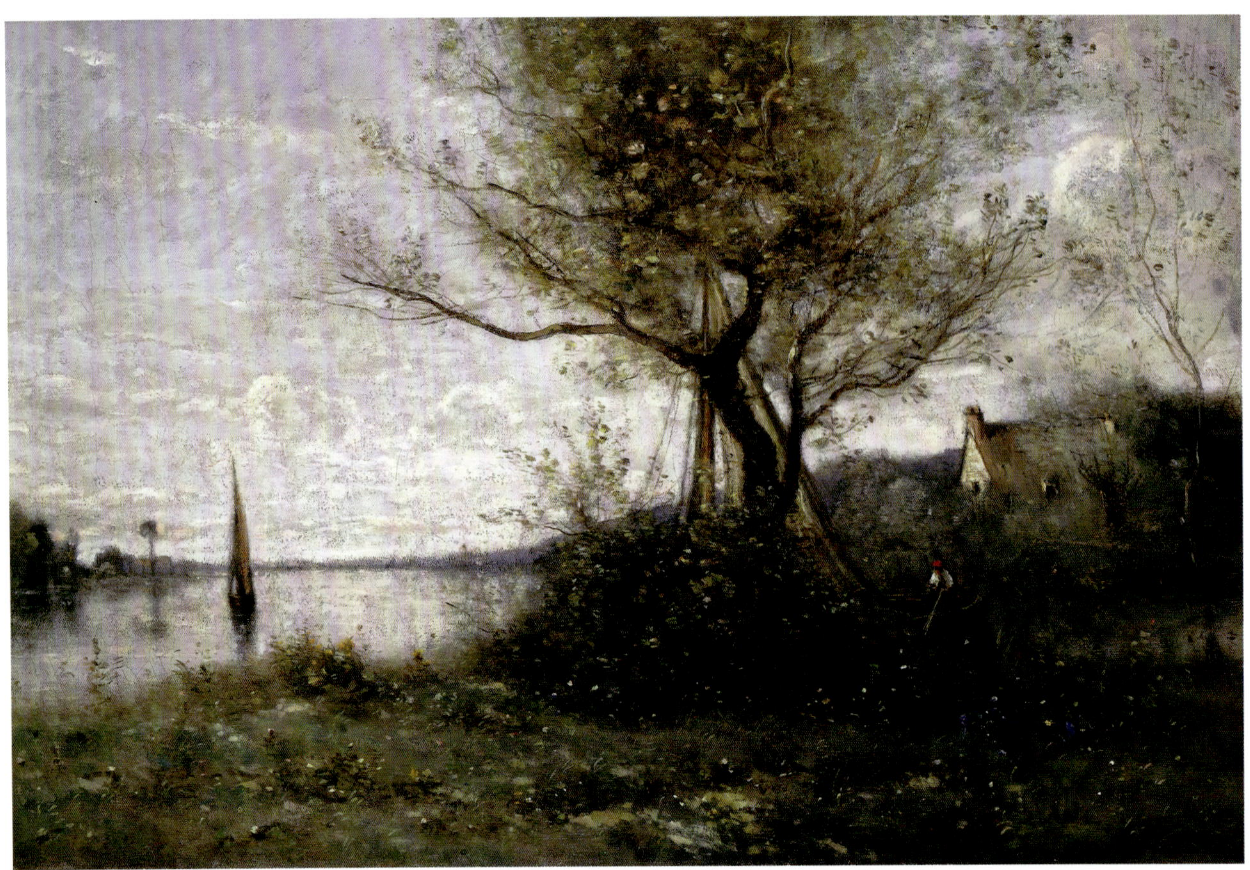

Boat at the Edge of an Island

Bateau aux abords d'une île

Boot am Ufer einer Insel

Barco en la orilla de una isla

Barco na costa de uma ilha

Boot voor de oever van een eiland

JEAN-BAPTISTE CAMILLE COROT (1796-1875)

Oil on canvas/Huile sur toile, 49,5 × 74 cm, Private collection

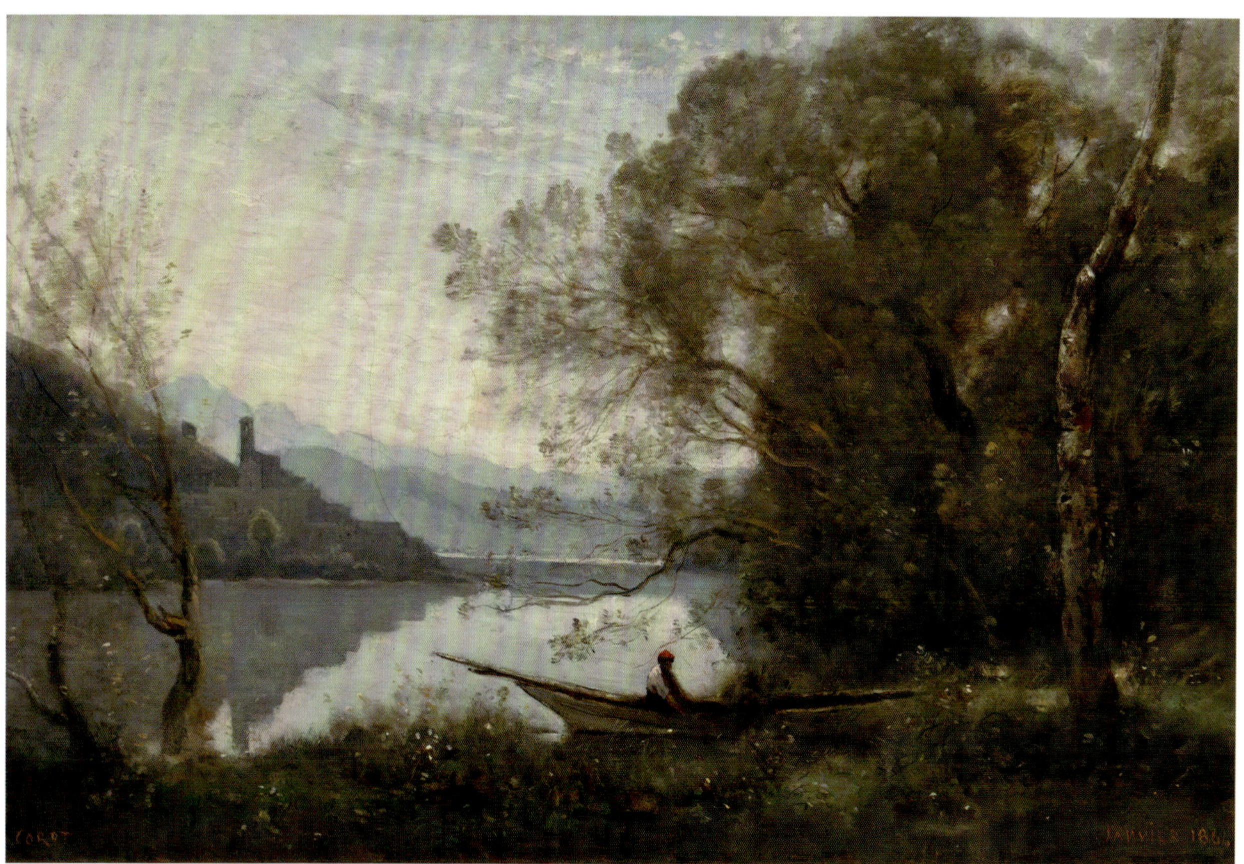

The Moored Boatman: Souvenir of an Italian Lake

Le Batelier amarré : souvenir d'un lac italien

Vor Anker liegender Schiffer, Erinnerungen an einen italienischen See

Patrón anclado, recuerdos de un lago italiano

Capitão ancorado, memórias de um lago italiano

Voor anker liggende schipper, herinneringen aan een Italiaans meer

JEAN-BAPTISTE CAMILLE COROT (1796-1875)

1861, Oil on canvas/Huile sur toile, 60,96 × 90,17 cm, National Gallery of Art, Washington

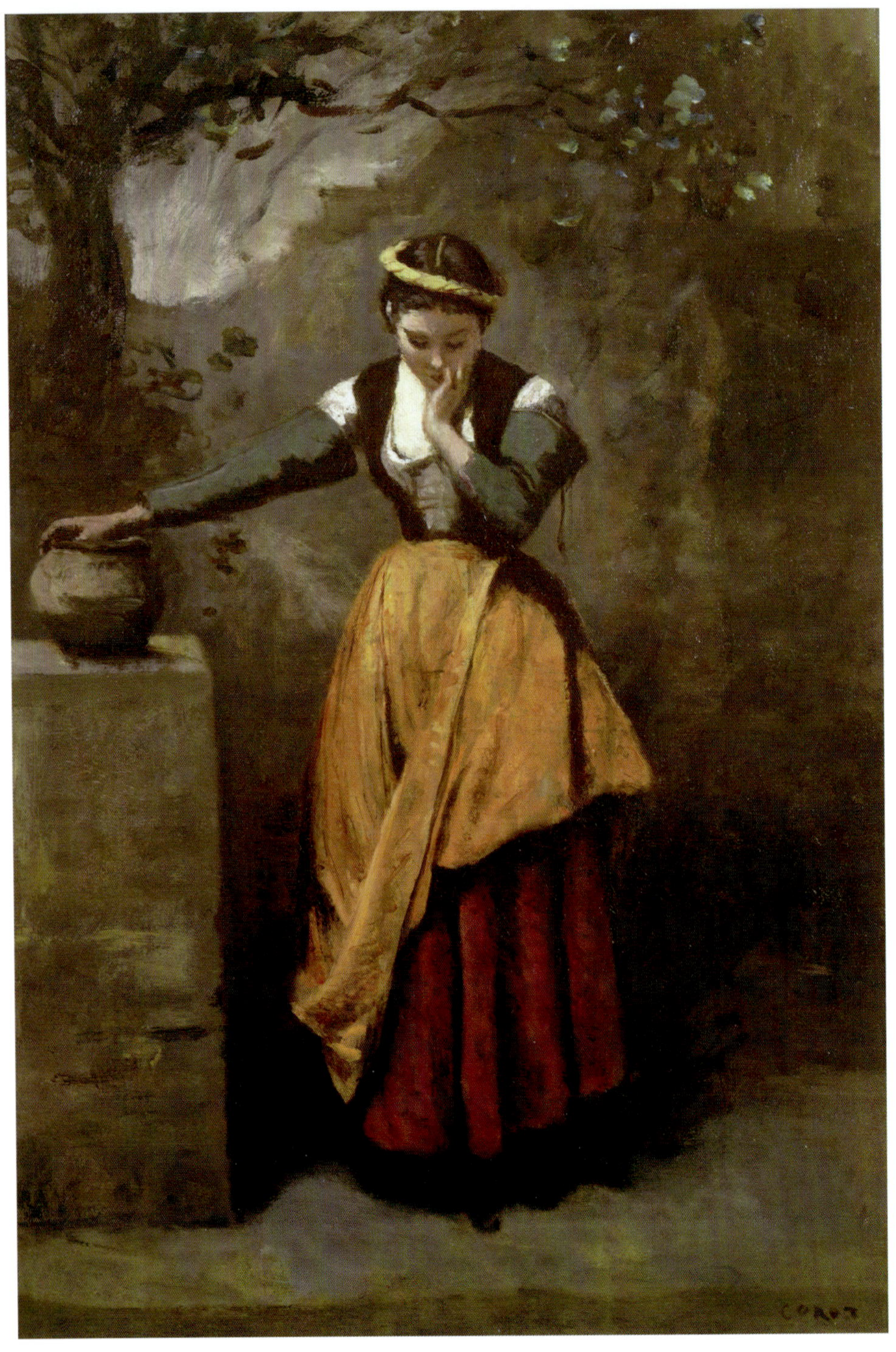

Dreamer at the Fountain

La Rêveuse à la fontaine

Die Träumende am Brunnen

Soñadora en la fuente

O sonhador na fonte

Droomster bij de fontein

JEAN-BAPTISTE CAMILLE COROT (1796-1875)

c. 1860-70, Oil on canvas/Huile sur toile,
64,5 × 44,2 cm, Private collection

Young Woman at the Well

Corot is primarily known for his landscapes. His portraits are among his more personal works. He never exhibited them in public, but only showed them to his friends in his studio.

Jeune femme au puits

Corot est célèbre pour ses paysages, moins pour ses tableaux de figures. Ces derniers constituent la part la plus intime de son œuvre. Il ne les exposait pas, mais les montrait à ses amis dans son atelier.

Junge Frau am Brunnen

Corot ist in erster Linie für seine Landschaften bekannt. Seine Porträts zählen zu seinen persönlicheren Werken. Er stellt sie nie öffentlich aus, sondern zeigt sie nur seinen Freunden im Atelier.

Mujer joven en el pozo

Corot es conocido principalmente por sus paisajes. Sus retratos se encuentran entre sus obras más personales. Nunca las exhibe en público, sino que sólo se las muestra a sus amigos en su estudio.

Jovem mulher na fonte

Corot é conhecida principalmente pelas suas paisagens. Os seus retratos estão entre as suas obras mais pessoais. Ele nunca os expõe em público, mas só os mostra aos seus amigos no seu estúdio.

Jonge vrouw bij de bron

Corot staat vooral bekend om zijn landschappen. Zijn portretten behoren tot de meer persoonlijke werken. Hij exposeerde ze nooit in het openbaar, maar toonde ze alleen in het atelier aan zijn vrienden.

JEAN-BAPTISTE CAMILLE COROT (1796-1875)
1865-70, Oil on canvas/Huile sur toile,
65 × 40 cm, Musée d'Art et d'Histoire, Genève

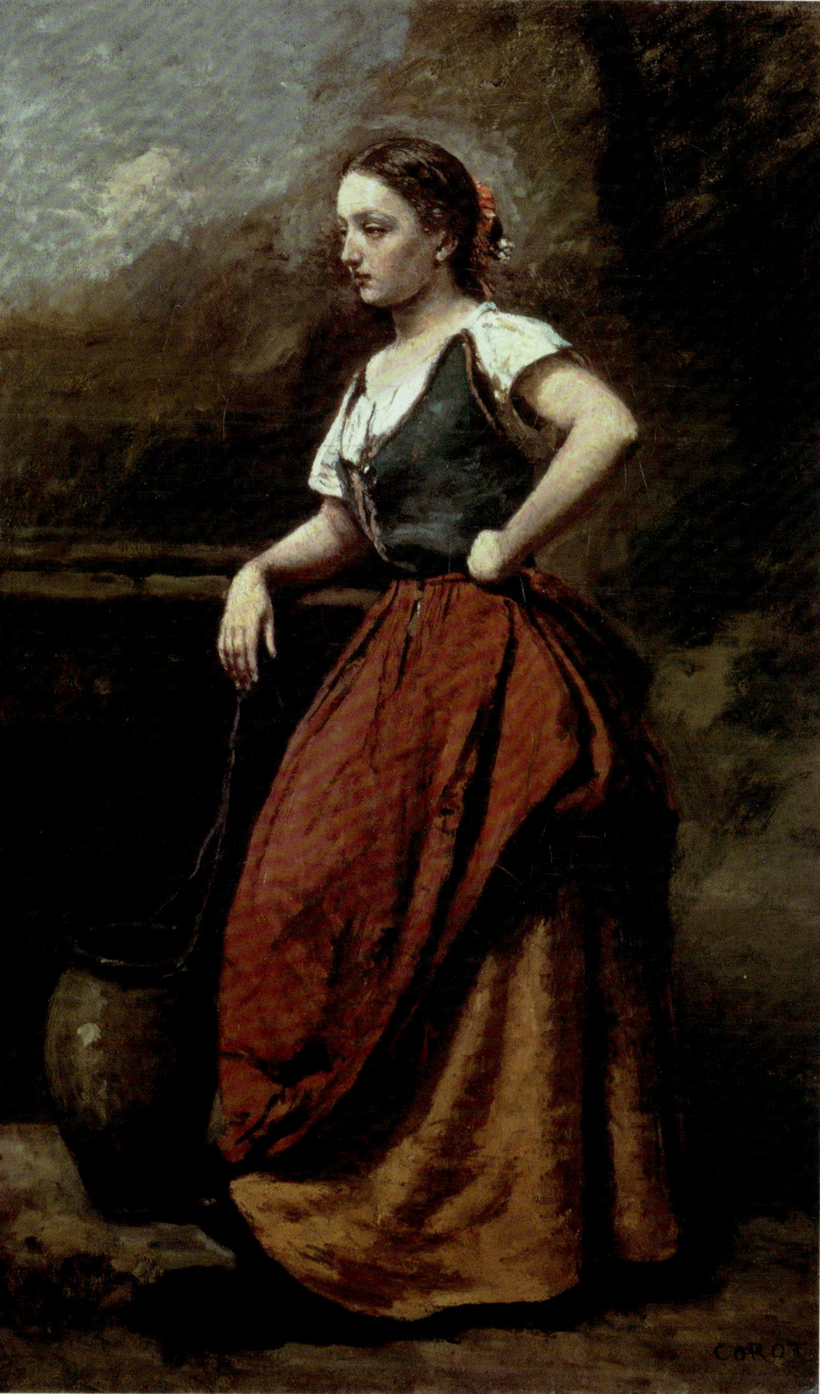

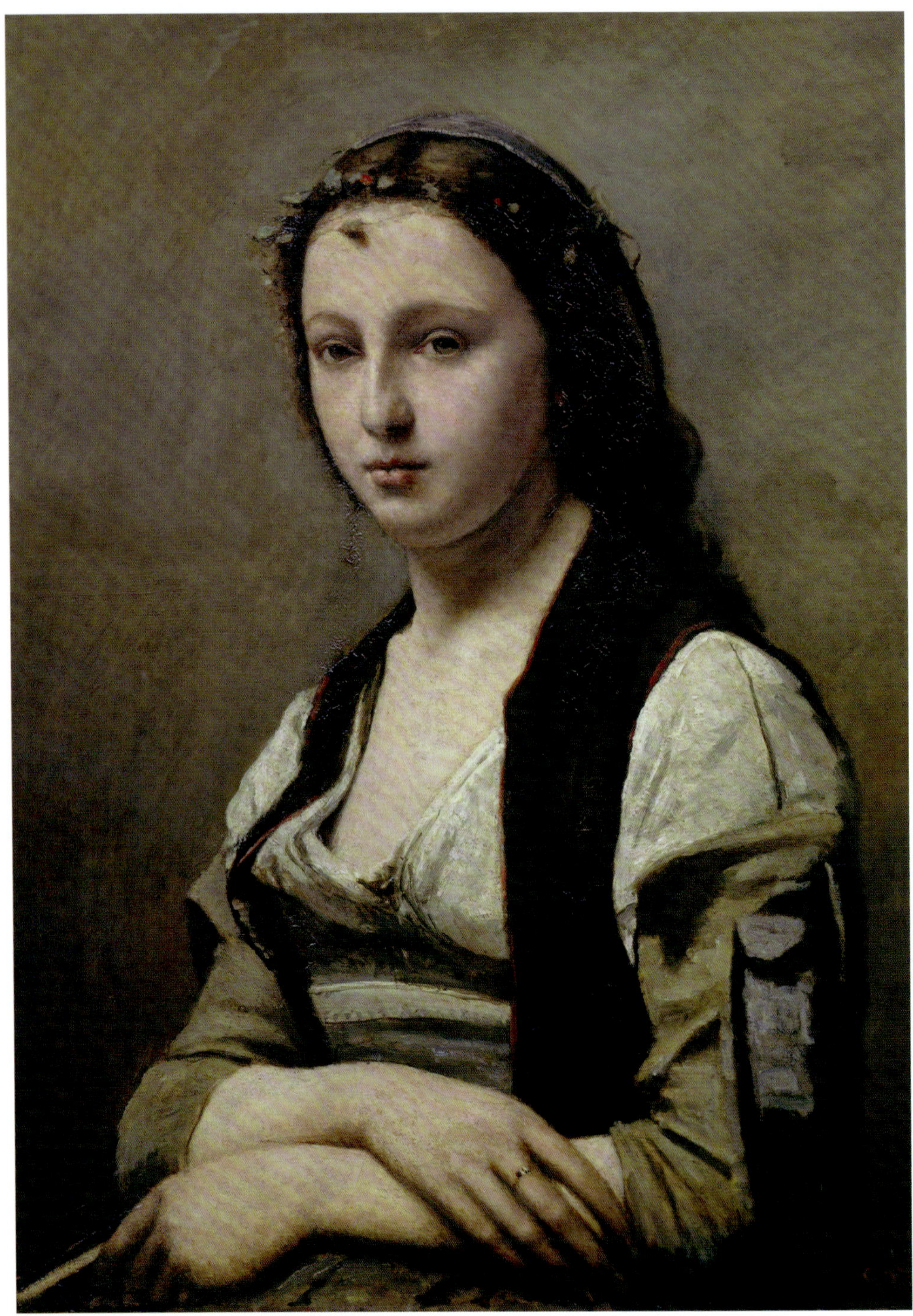

The Woman with the Pearl

La Femme à la perle

Die Frau mit der Perle

Mujer con una perla

A mulher com a pérola

De vrouw met de parel

JEAN-BAPTISTE CAMILLE COROT
(1796-1875)

c. 1868-70, Oil on canvas/Huile sur toile,
70 × 55 cm, Musée du Louvre, Paris

Forest of Fontainebleau, Autumn

Forêt de Fontainebleau, automne

Der Wald von Fontainebleau im Herbst

El bosque de Fontainebleau en otoño

A floresta de Fontainebleau no Outono

Bos van Fontainebleau in de herfst

NARCISSE DIAZ DE LA PEÑA (1807-1876)

1871, Oil on wood/Huile sur bois, 78 × 64,7 cm,
Walters Art Museum, Baltimore

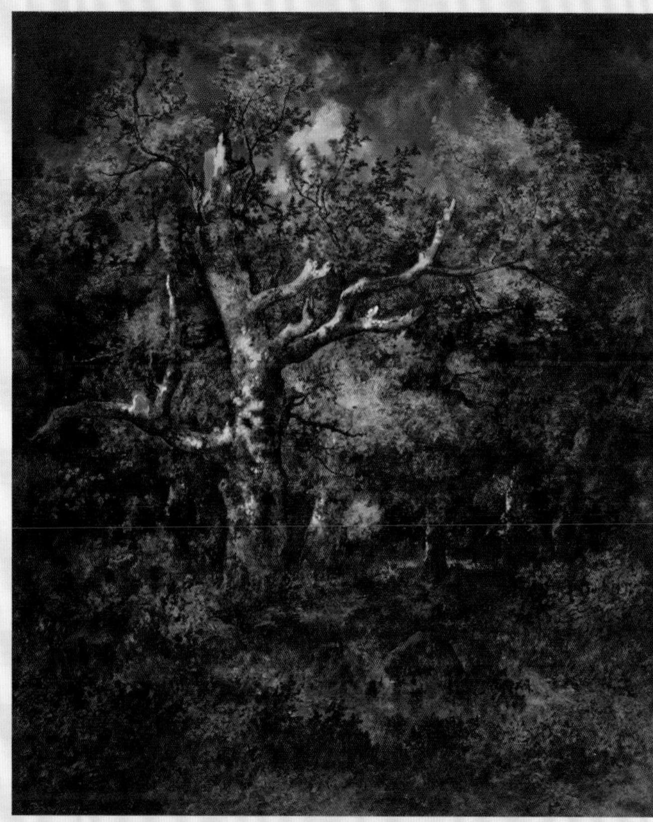

La escuela de Barbizon

De 1830 a 1875, Barbizon, un pueblo al borde del
bosque de Fontainebleau, se convirtió en un lugar de
encuentro para los artistas que querían pintar al aire
libre, una práctica favorecida desde la década de 1840
por el desarrollo de los tubos de pintura. A partir de
1849, la conexión ferroviaria París-Melun simplificó
la accesibilidad. Muchos pintores viven en el albergue
de la pareja Ganne, que ahora alberga el Museo de la
Escuela Barbizon. Nunca se vieron a sí mismos como
una "escuela" clásica, sino como un grupo de artistas
con una pasión común: la naturaleza como motivo.
Jean-Baptiste Camille Corot -uno de los primeros
en Fontainebleau- y Jean-François Millet, Charles
Daubigny, Théodore Rousseau, Jules Dupré y Narcisse
Diaz de la Peña instalan sus caballetes en el bosque o en
los claros. Como admiradores de la pintura holandesa
del siglo XVII, e inspirados por los paisajes ingleses
de John Constable, influyeron en los impresionistas
posteriores.

A escola de Barbizon

De 1830 a 1875, Barbizon, uma aldeia à beira da floresta
de Fontainebleau, tornou-se um ponto de encontro para
artistas que queriam pintar ao ar livre - uma prática
favorecida a partir de 1840 pelo desenvolvimento de
tubos de tinta. A partir de 1849, a conexão ferroviária
Paris-Melun simplificou a acessibilidade. Muitos
pintores vivem no albergue do casal Ganne, que agora
abriga o Museu da Escola Barbizon. Nunca se viram
como uma "escola" clássica, mas sim como um grupo
de artistas com uma paixão comum: a natureza como
motivo. Jean-Baptiste Camille Corot - um dos primeiros
em Fontainebleau - e Jean-François Millet, Charles
Daubigny, Théodore Rousseau, Jules Dupré e Narcisse
Diaz de la Peña montam os seus cavalete na floresta ou
em clareiras. Como admiradores da pintura holandesa
do século 17, e inspirados pelas paisagens inglesas
de John Constable, eles foram para influenciar os
impressionistas mais tarde.

De school van Barbizon

Tussen 1830 en 1875 was Barbizon, een dorp aan de rand
van het bos van Fontainebleau, een ontmoetingsplaats
voor kunstenaars die buiten wilden schilderen — een
praktijk die vanaf 1840 werd bevorderd door de
ontwikkeling van verftubes. Vanaf 1849 maakte de
treinverbinding tussen Parijs en Melun de plaats beter
bereikbaar. Veel schilders verbleven in de herberg van
het echtpaar Ganne, die nu het museum van de school
van Barbizon huisvest. De kunstenaars beschouwden
zichzelf nooit als een klassieke 'school', maar eerder als
een groep kunstenaars met een gemeenschappelijke
passie: de natuur als onderwerp. Jean-Baptiste Camille
Corot — een van de eerste in Fontainebleau — en Jean-
François Millet, Charles Daubigny, Théodore Rousseau,
Jules Dupré en Narcisse Diaz de la Peña zetten hun ezel
op in het bos of op open plekken. Als bewonderaars
van de 17e-eeuwse Nederlandse schilderkunst en
geïnspireerd door de Engelse landschappen van
John Constable zouden zij de latere impressionisten
beïnvloeden.

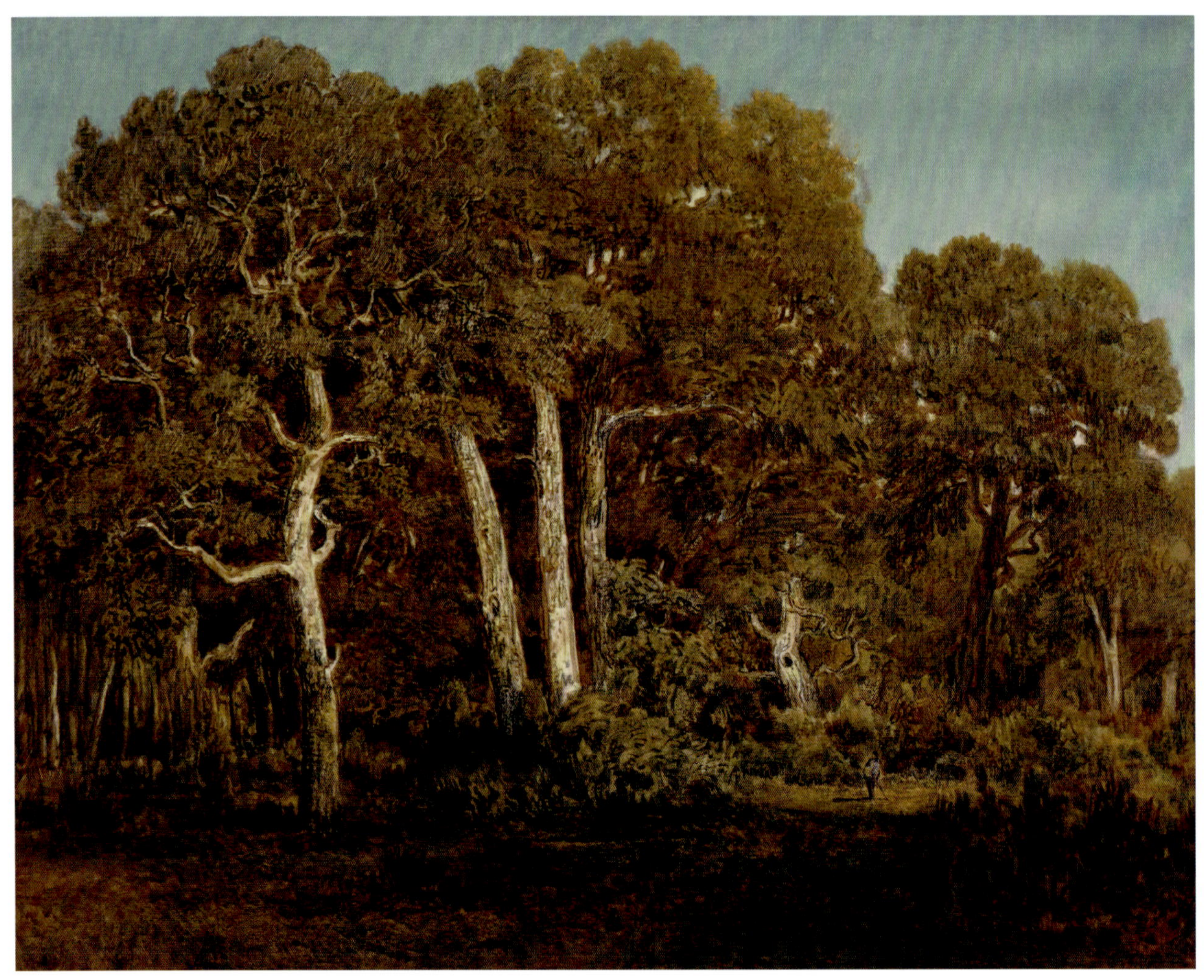

The Great Oaks of Old Bas-Bréau

Le Grand Chêne du vieux Bas-Bréau

Die große Eiche des alten Bas-Bréau

El gran roble del viejo Bas-Bréau

O grande carvalho do velho Bas-Bréau

De grote eiken van het oude Bas-Bréau

THÉODORE ROUSSEAU (1812-1867)

1864, Oil on canvas/Huile sur toile, 90,2 × 116,8 cm, Museum of Fine Arts, Houston

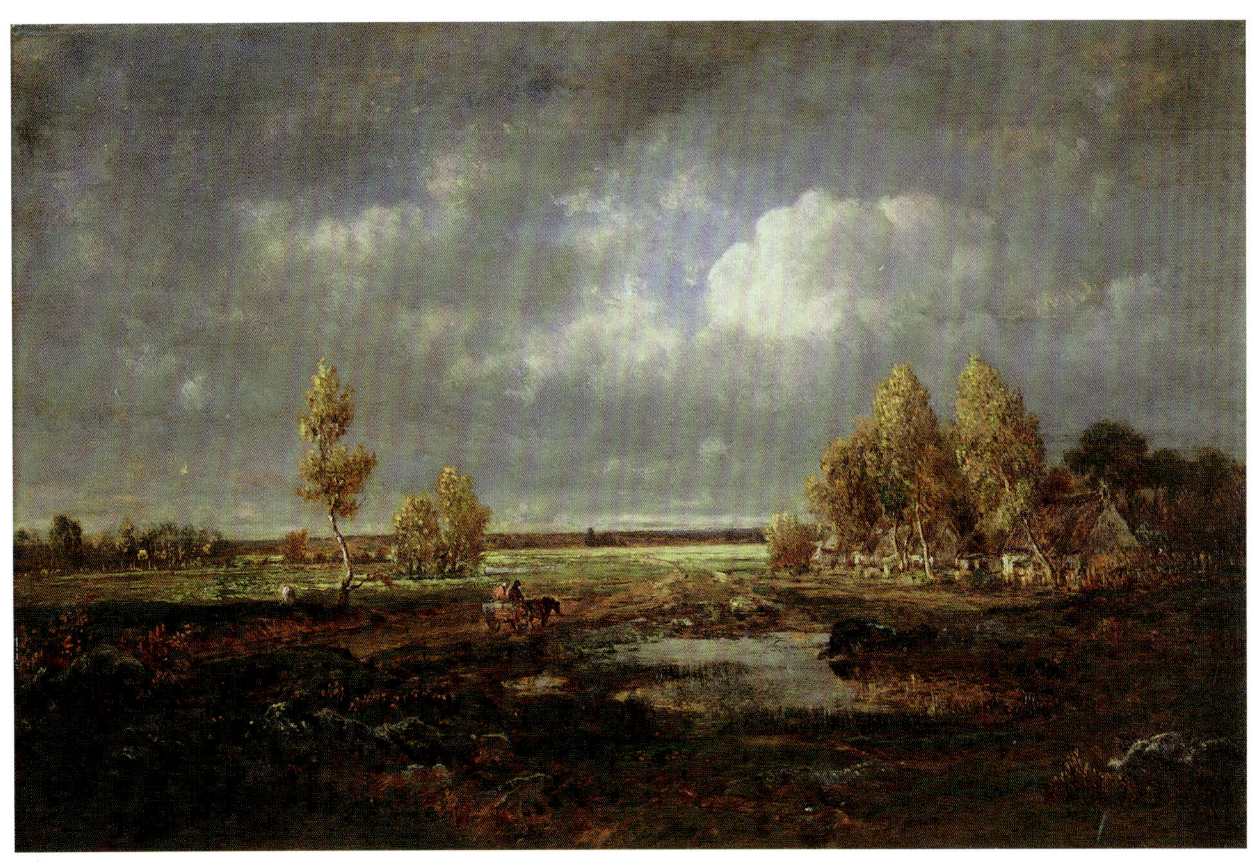

The Pond near the Road, Farm in Le Berry

La Mare près de la route, ferme dans le Berry

Der Teich neben der Straße, Bauernhof im Berry

El estanque junto a la carretera, granja en Berry

A lagoa ao lado da estrada, fazenda em Berry

De vijver naast de weg, boerderij in Le Berry

THÉODORE ROUSSEAU (1812-1867)

c. 1845-48, Oil on canvas/Huile sur toile, 34,5 × 53,5 cm, Musée d'Orsay, Paris

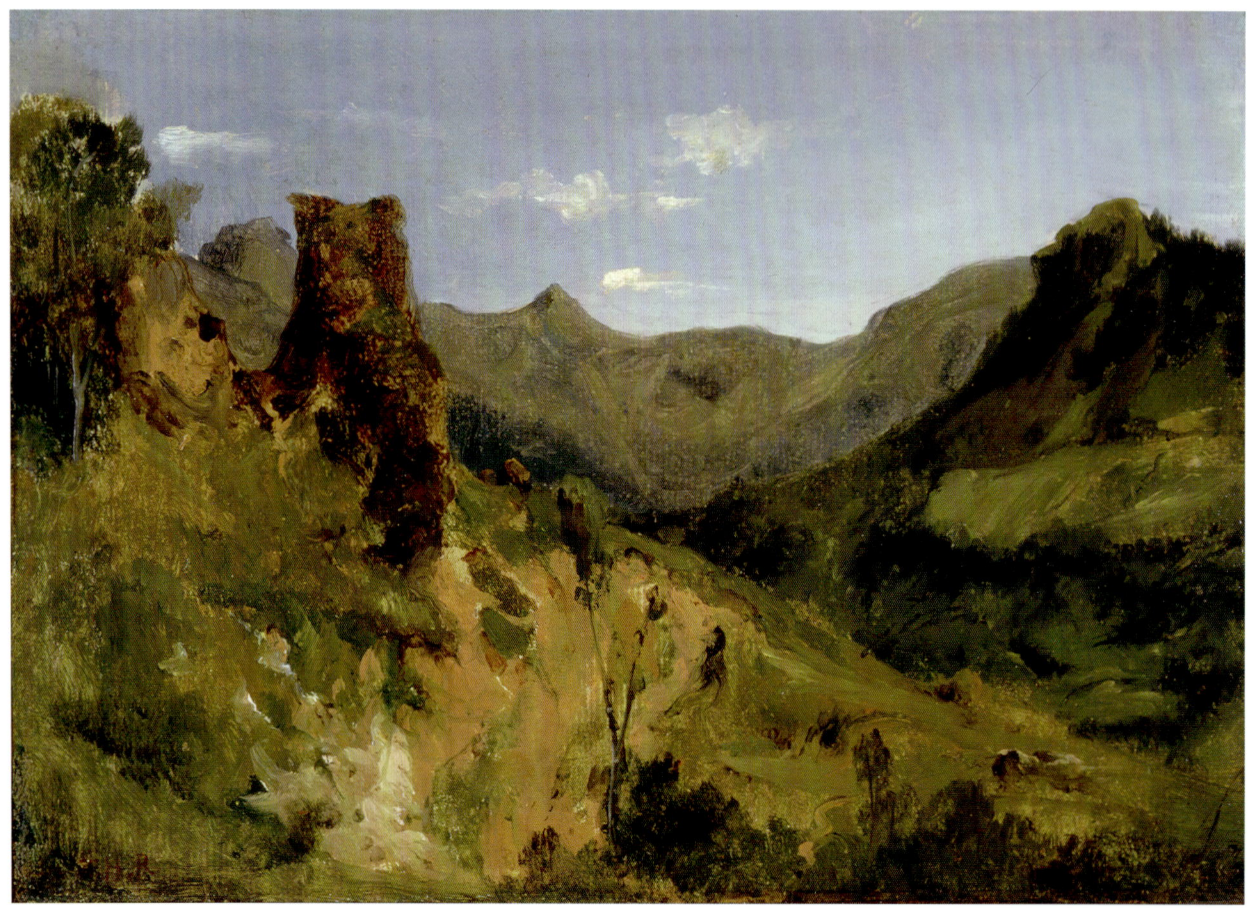

Valley in the Auvergne Mountains

Théodore Rousseau was a passionate landscape painter.
As a prominent representative of the Barbizon School, he
traveled through the Vendée, the Alps and the Auvergne,
where he made numerous paintings and sketches.

Vallée dans la montagne auvergnate

Tout l'œuvre de Théodore Rousseau s'articule autour
du paysage. Figure majeure de l'école de Barbizon, il a
également voyagé et multiplié tableaux et esquisses en
Vendée, dans les Alpes ou en Auvergne.

Tal in den Bergen der Auvergne

Théodore Rousseau war ein passionierter Landschaftsmaler.
Als prominenter Vertreter der Schule von Barbizon bereist
er das Vendée, die Alpen und die Auvergne, wo zahlreiche
Gemälde und Skizzen entstehen.

Valle en las montañas de Auvernia

Théodore Rousseau era un apasionado paisajista. Como
destacado representante de la Escuela Barbizon, viajó por
la Vendée, los Alpes y Auvernia, donde realizó numerosas
pinturas y bocetos.

Vale nas montanhas de Auvergne

Théodore Rousseau era um pintor paisagista apaixonado.
Como representante proeminente da Escola Barbizon,
viajou pela Vendée, pelos Alpes e pela Auvergne, onde fez
inúmeras pinturas e esboços.

Dal in de bergen van de Auvergne

Théodore Rousseau was een gepassioneerd
landschapsschilder. Als prominente vertegenwoordiger van
de school van Barbizon reisde hij door de Vendée, de Alpen
en de Auvergne, waar hij talrijke schilderijen en schetsen
maakte.

THÉODORE ROUSSEAU (1812-1867)

1830, Oil on paper mounted on canvas/ Huile sur papier marouflé sur toile, 21,9 × 31,1 cm, Saint-Louis Art Museum, St. Louis

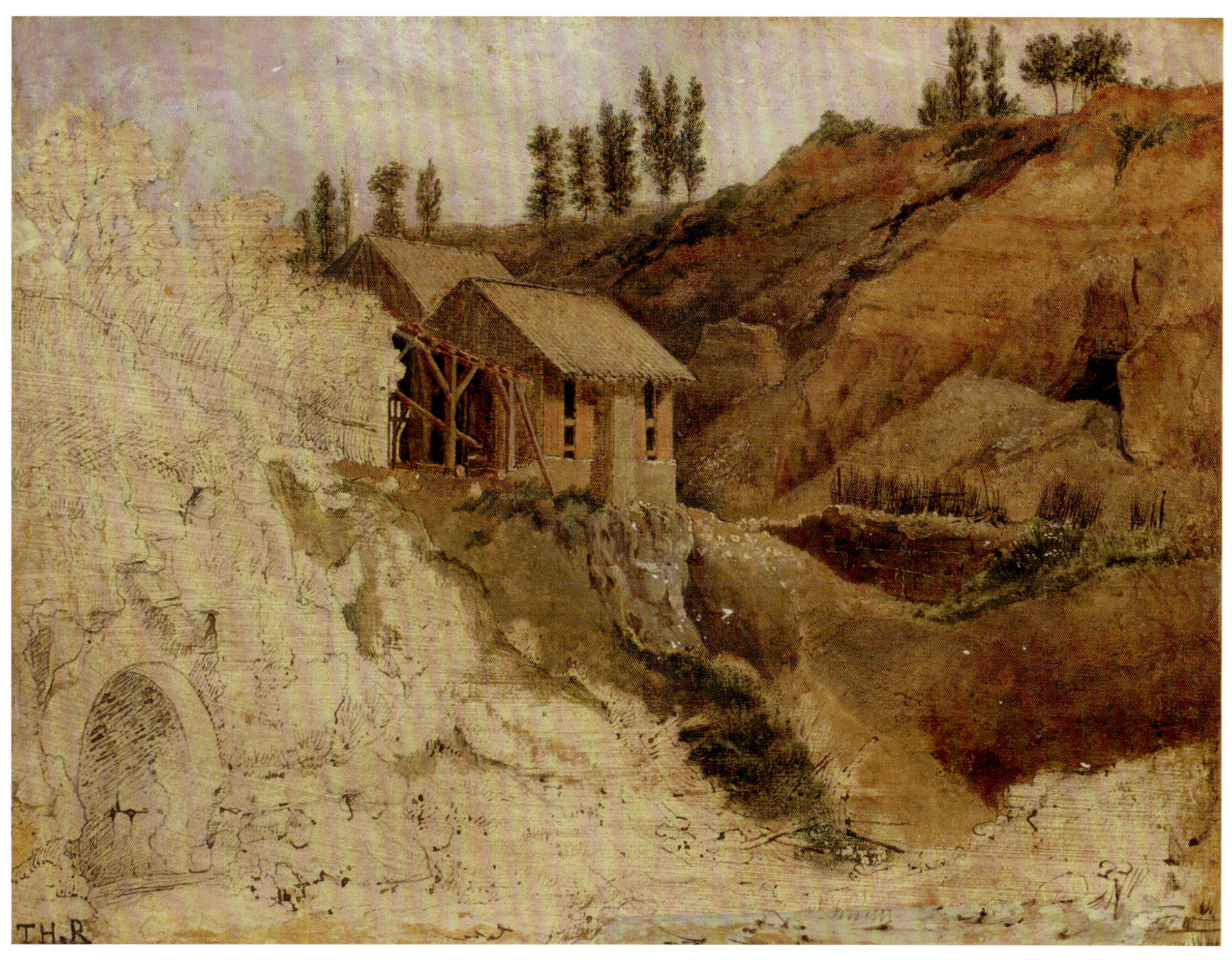

A Quarry

Une carrière

Ein Steinbruch

Una cantera

Uma pedreira

Een steengroeve

THÉODORE ROUSSEAU (1812-1867)

1827, Oil on paper/Huile sur papier,

30 × 40,2 cm,

Museum voor Schone Kunsten, Gent

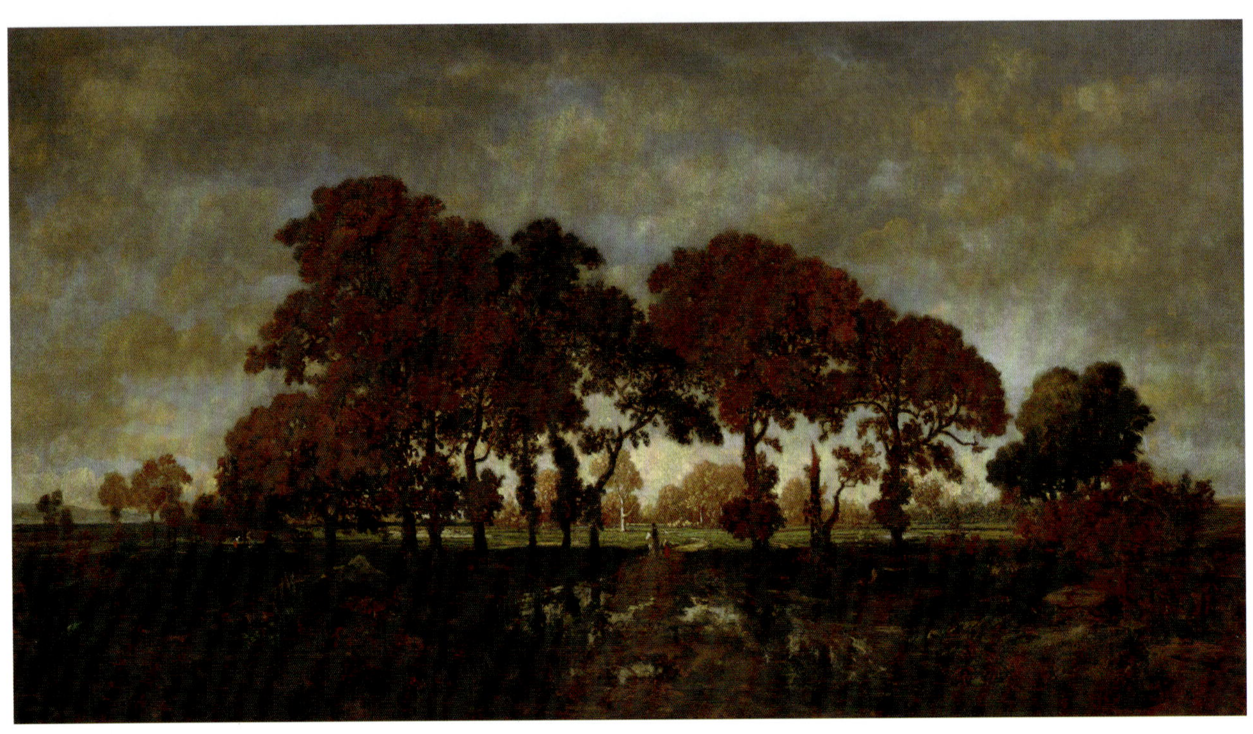

After the Rain

Après la pluie

Nach dem Regen

Después de la lluvia

Depois da chuva

Na de regen

THÉODORE ROUSSEAU (1812-1867)

c. 1850, Oil on canvas/Huile sur toile, 78,74 × 146,05 cm, National Gallery of Art, Washington

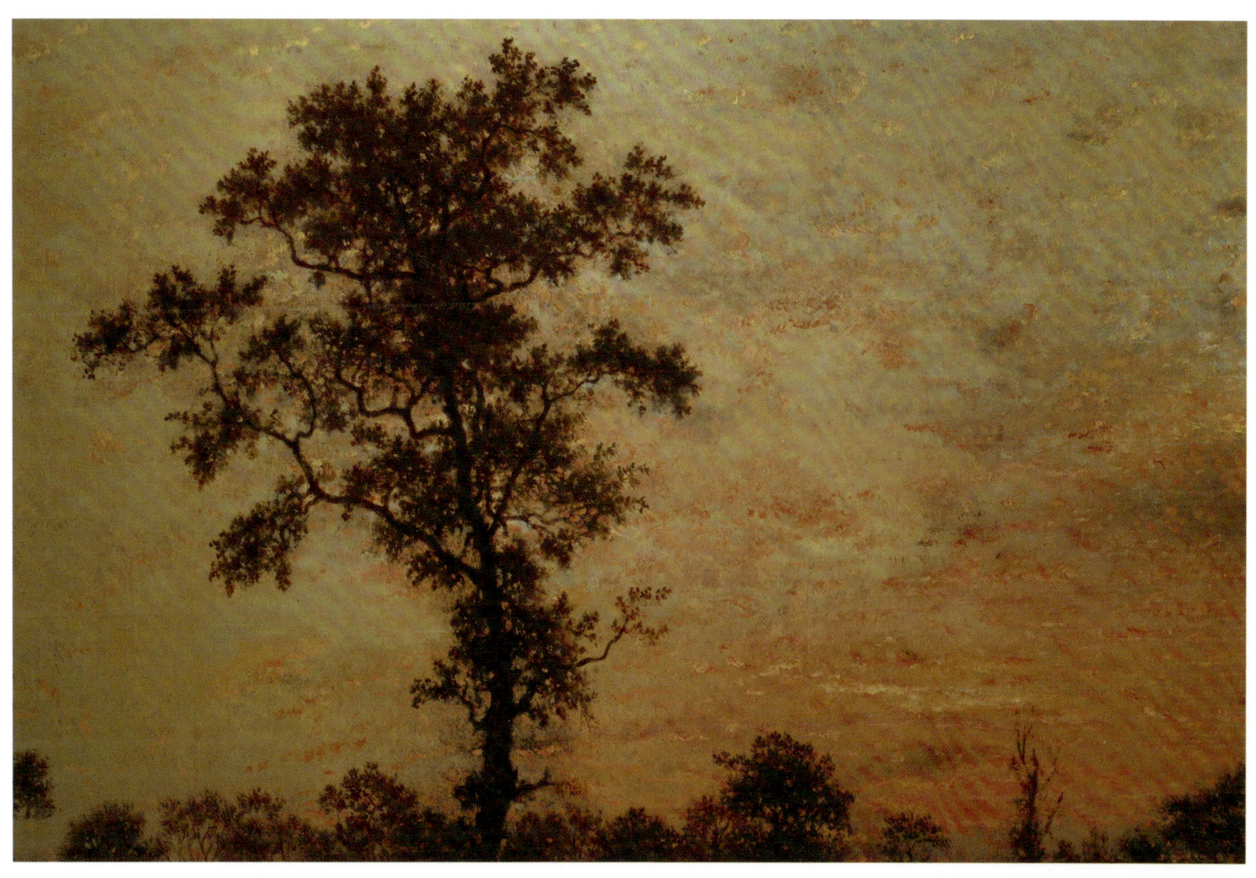

Edge of the Forest, Sun Setting

Lisière de forêt, soleil couchant

Sonnenuntergang am Waldrand

Atardecer al borde del bosque

Pôr-do-sol à beira da floresta

Zonsondergang aan de rand van het bos

THÉODORE ROUSSEAU (1812-1867)

c. 1845/46, Oil on canvas/Huile sur toile, 68,58 × 91,44 cm, Los Angeles County Museum of Art, Los Angeles

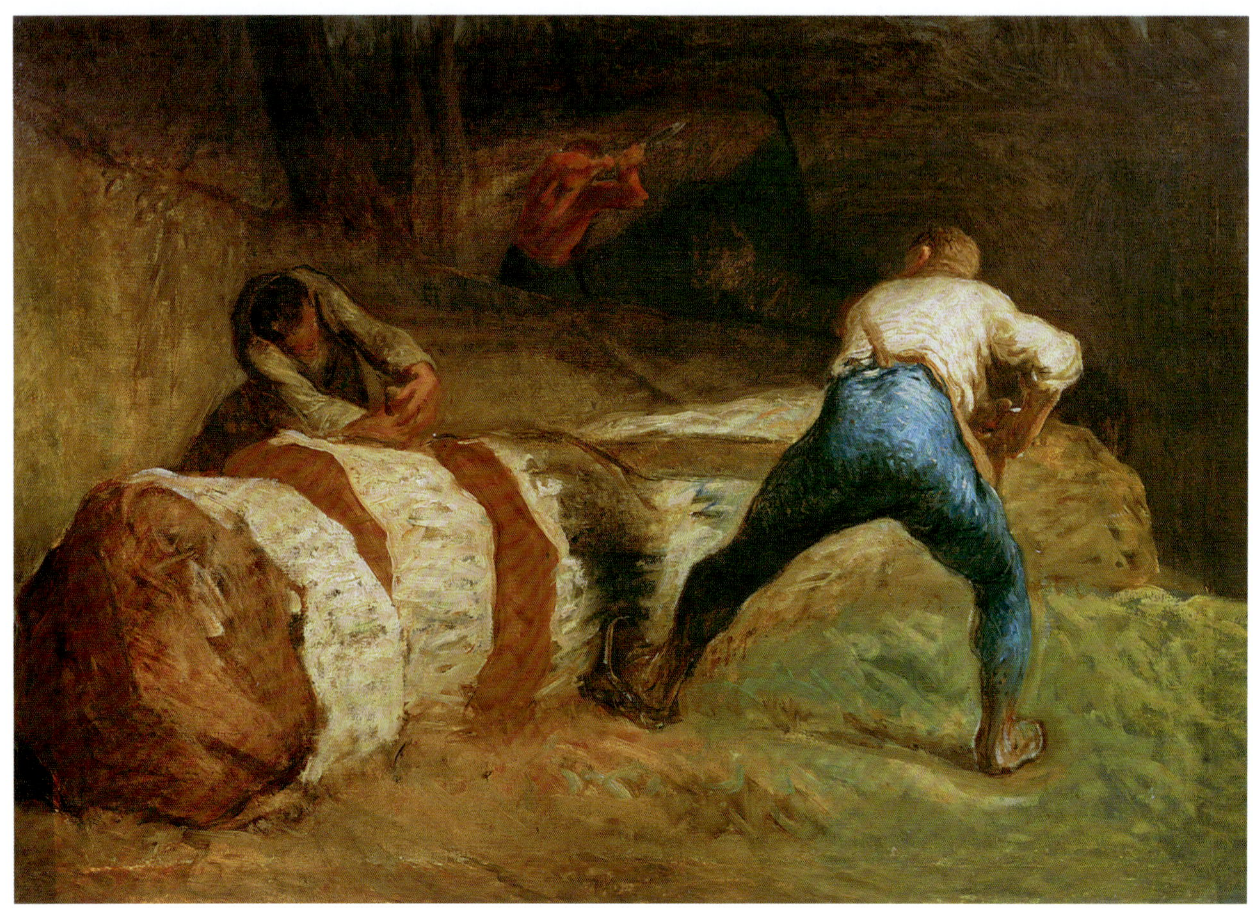

The Wood Sawyers

Les Bûcherons

Waldarbeiter beim Holzsägen

Los leñadores

Trabalhador florestal serrando madeira

De houtzagers

JEAN-FRANÇOIS MILLET (1814-1875)

c. 1850-52, Oil on canvas/Huile sur toile,
57 × 81 cm, Victoria & Albert Museum, London

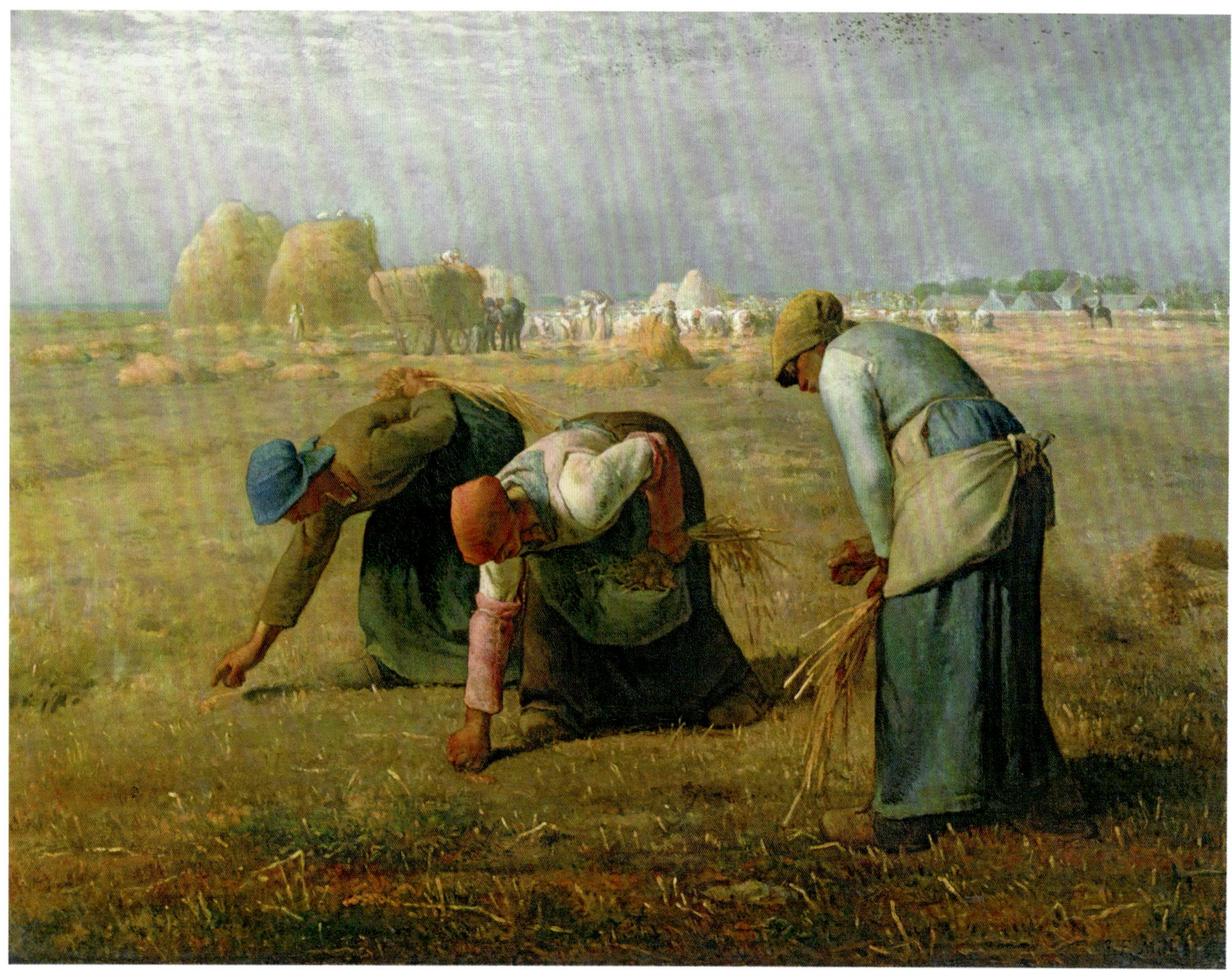

The Gleaners

Millet devoted himself to rural motifs. The picture is the result of a ten-year study of female gleaners. Shortly before sunset, three women are bending down to pick up the last ears of corn.

Les Glaneuses

Millet est le peintre de la vie paysanne. Ce tableau couronne dix ans de recherches autour du thème des glaneuses. Courbées, trois femmes ramassent les épis oubliés par la moisson, avant le coucher du soleil.

Die Ährenleserinnen

Millet widmete sich bäuerlichen Motiven. Das Bild ist das Ergebnis einer zehn Jahre währenden Studie über Ährenleserinnen. Kurz vor Sonnenuntergang sammeln drei gebückte Frauen die letzten Ähren auf.

Las espigadoras

Millet se dedicó a los motivos rurales. La imagen es el resultado de un estudio de diez años de duración sobre las espigadoras. Poco antes de la puesta del sol, tres mujeres encorvadas recogen las últimas mazorcas de maíz.

Os leitores de orelha

O Millet dedicou-se a motivos rurais. O quadro é o resultado de um estudo de dez anos com mulheres orelheiras. Pouco antes do pôr-do-sol, três mulheres dobradas apanham as últimas espigas de milho.

De arenleessters

Millet schilderde boerenmotieven. Dit schilderij is het resultaat van een tienjarige studie naar arenleessters. Kort voor zonsondergang pikken drie gebukte vrouwen de laatste korenaren op.

JEAN-FRANÇOIS MILLET (1814-1875)

1857, Oil on canvas/Huile sur toile, 83,5 × 110 cm, Musée d'Orsay, Paris

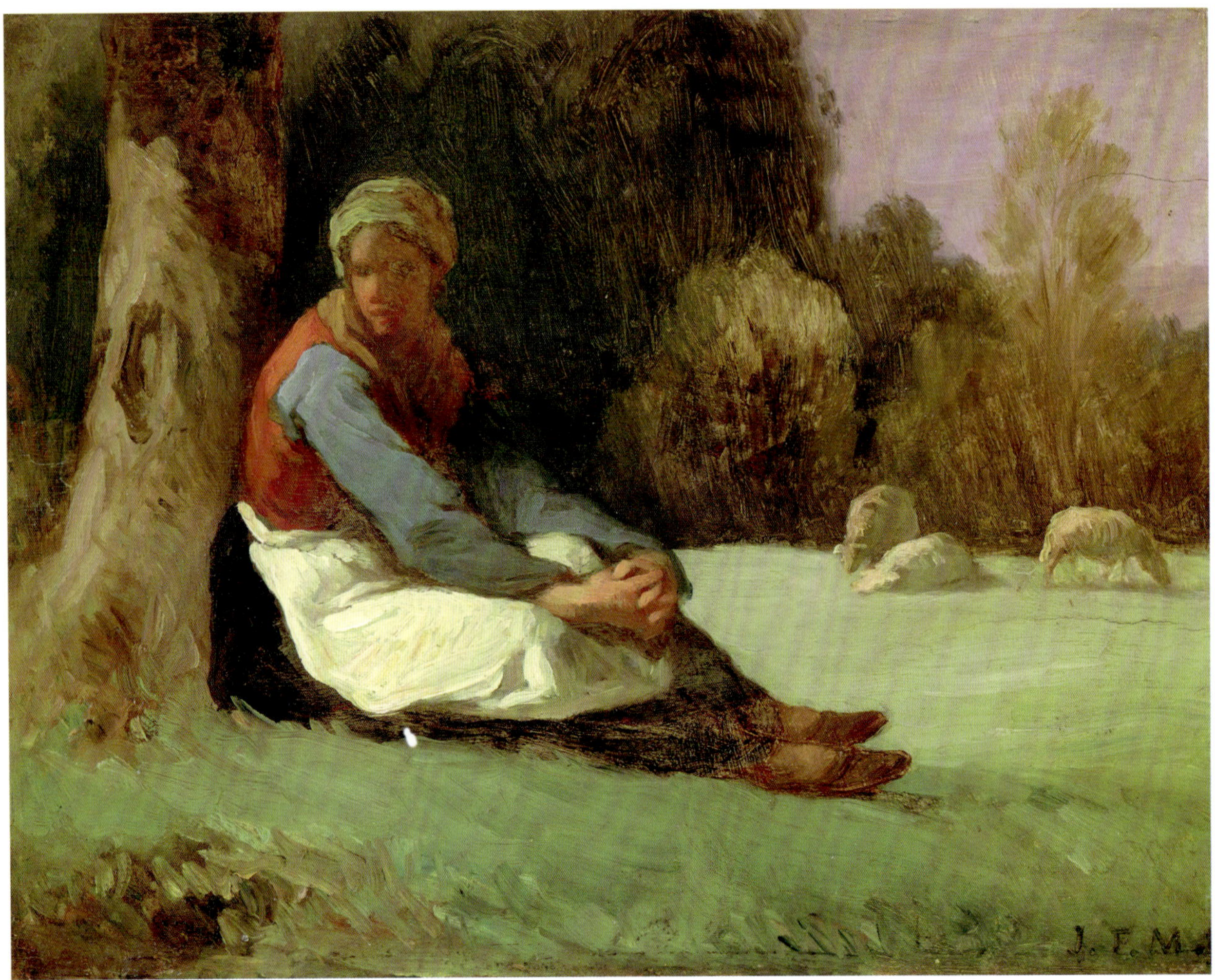

Seated Shepherdess

Bergère assise

Sitzende Schäferin

La pastora sentada

Pastora sentada

Zittende herderin

JEAN-FRANÇOIS MILLET (1814-1875)
n.d., Oil on wood/Huile sur bois, 18,6 × 24,3 cm,
National Museum Wales

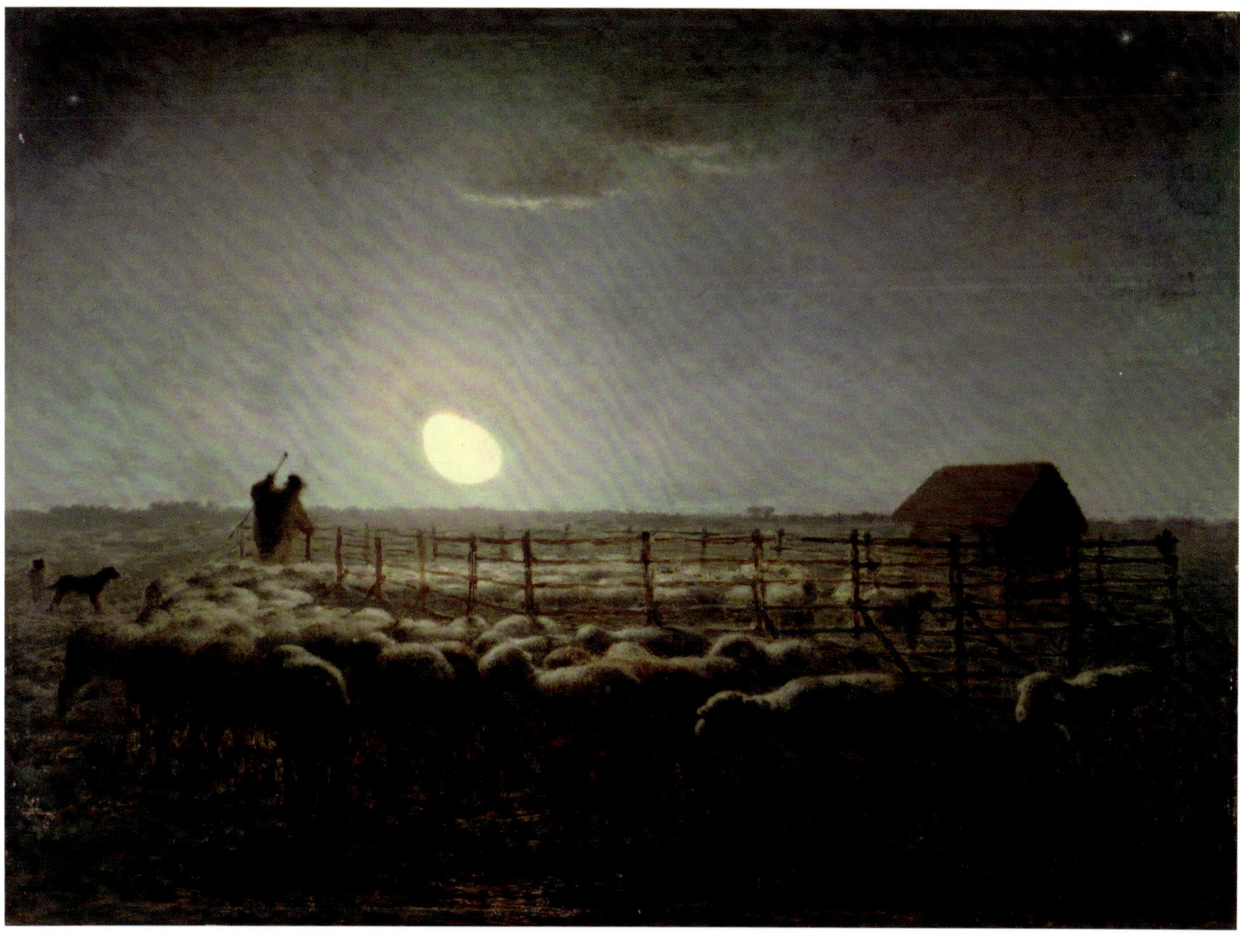

The Sheepfold

Whether in daylight or at night, Millet gave the representation of light the same priority as the motif. The strong contrasts give his figures a ghostly appearance.

Le Parc à moutons, clair de lune

De scènes diurnes en visions nocturnes, Millet accorde autant d'importance au sujet qu'au rendu des atmosphères. Ses puissants contrastes d'ombre et de lumière donnent à ses figures un aspect fantomatique.

JEAN-FRANÇOIS MILLET (1814-1875)

1856-60, Oil on panel/Huile sur panneau, 45,3 × 63,4 cm, Walters Art Museum, Baltimore

Schafpferch im Mondschein

Egal ob bei Tageslicht oder in der Nacht – Millet räumte der Darstellung des Lichts den gleichen Rang ein wie dem Motiv. Die starken Kontraste verleihen seinen Figuren eine geisterhafte Erscheinung.

Rebaño de ovejas a la luz de la luna

Tanto de día como de noche, Millet dio a la representación de la luz la misma prioridad que al motivo. Los fuertes contrastes dan a sus figuras una apariencia fantasmal.

Caneta de ovelhas ao luar

Seja à luz do dia ou à noite, Millet deu à representação da luz a mesma prioridade que o motivo. Os fortes contrastes dão às suas figuras uma aparência fantasmagórica.

De schaapskooi, maanlicht

Of het nu overdag of 's nachts is, voor Millet was de afbeelding van het licht even belangrijk als het onderwerp. De sterke contrasten geven zijn figuren iets spookachtigs.

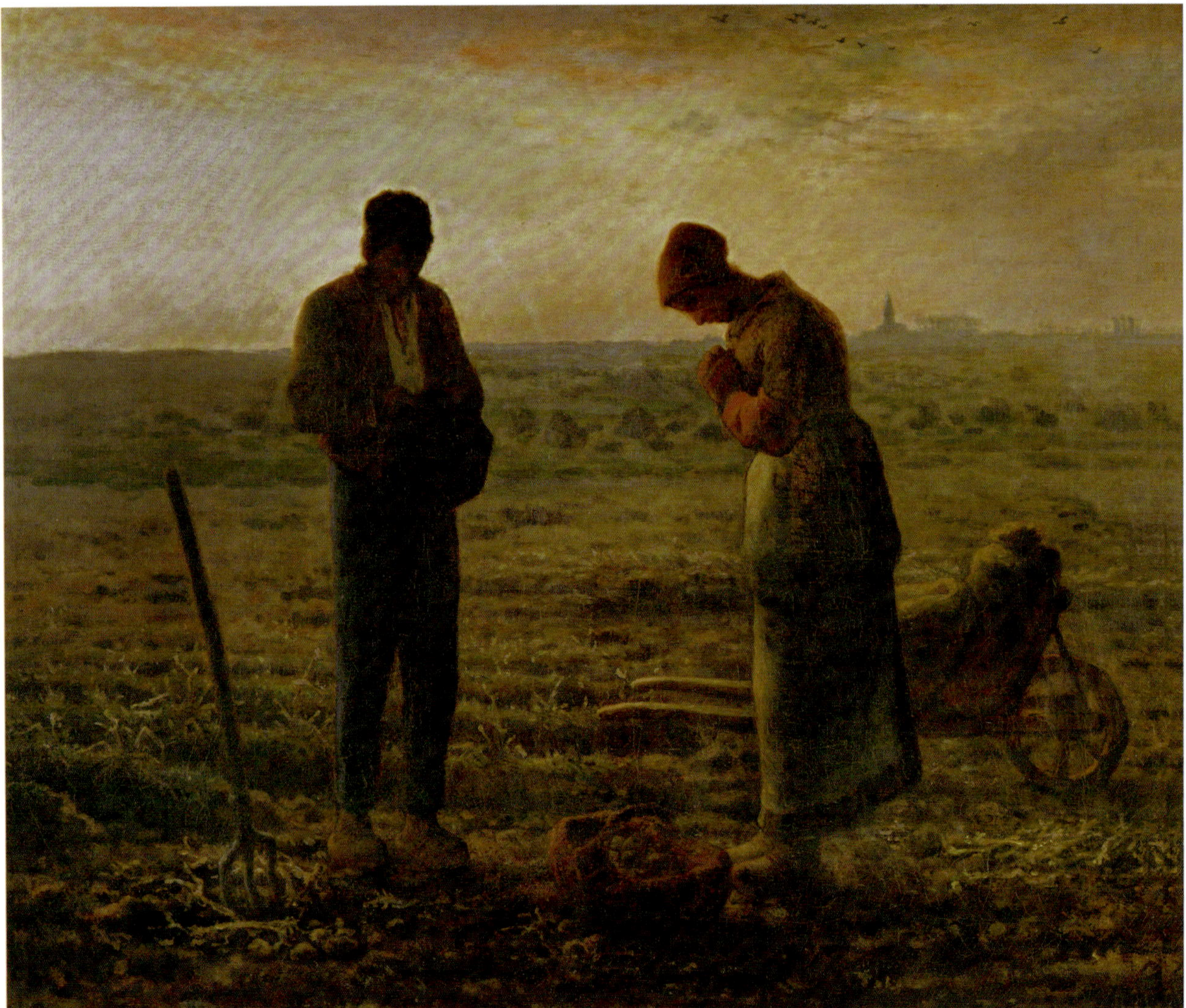

The Angelus

In the middle of a barren field, the tools of the potato harvest still at their feet, a woman and a man are reciting the Angelus prayer. The work is a silent homage to the everyday life of the farmers.

L'Angélus

Dans la nudité d'un champ, leurs outils à leurs pieds, un homme et une femme se sont arrêtés de ramasser les pommes de terre pour réciter l'angélus. Une évocation silencieuse du quotidien des paysans.

Das Angelusläuten

Inmitten eines kargen Feldes, die Werkzeuge der Kartoffelernte noch vor den Füßen, verrichten eine Frau und ein Mann das Angelusgebet. Das Werk ist eine stille Hommage an den Alltag der Bauern.

El Ángelus

En medio de un campo estéril, las herramientas de la cosecha a sus pies, una mujer y un hombre dejan de recoger patatas para realizan la oración del Ángelus. La obra es un homenaje silencioso a la vida cotidiana de los agricultores.

O toque do Angelus

No meio de um campo árido, as ferramentas da colheita da batata ainda diante dos pés, uma mulher e um homem fazem a oração do Angelus. O trabalho é uma homenagem silenciosa à vida cotidiana dos agricultores.

Het angelus

Midden op een kale akker, de werktuigen voor de aardappeloogst nog aan hun voeten, bidden een vrouw en een man het angelus. Het werk is a stille hommage aan het boerenbestaan.

JEAN-FRANÇOIS MILLET (1814-1875)

c. 1857-59, Oil on canvas/Huile sur toile, 55,5 × 66 cm, Musée d'Orsay, Paris

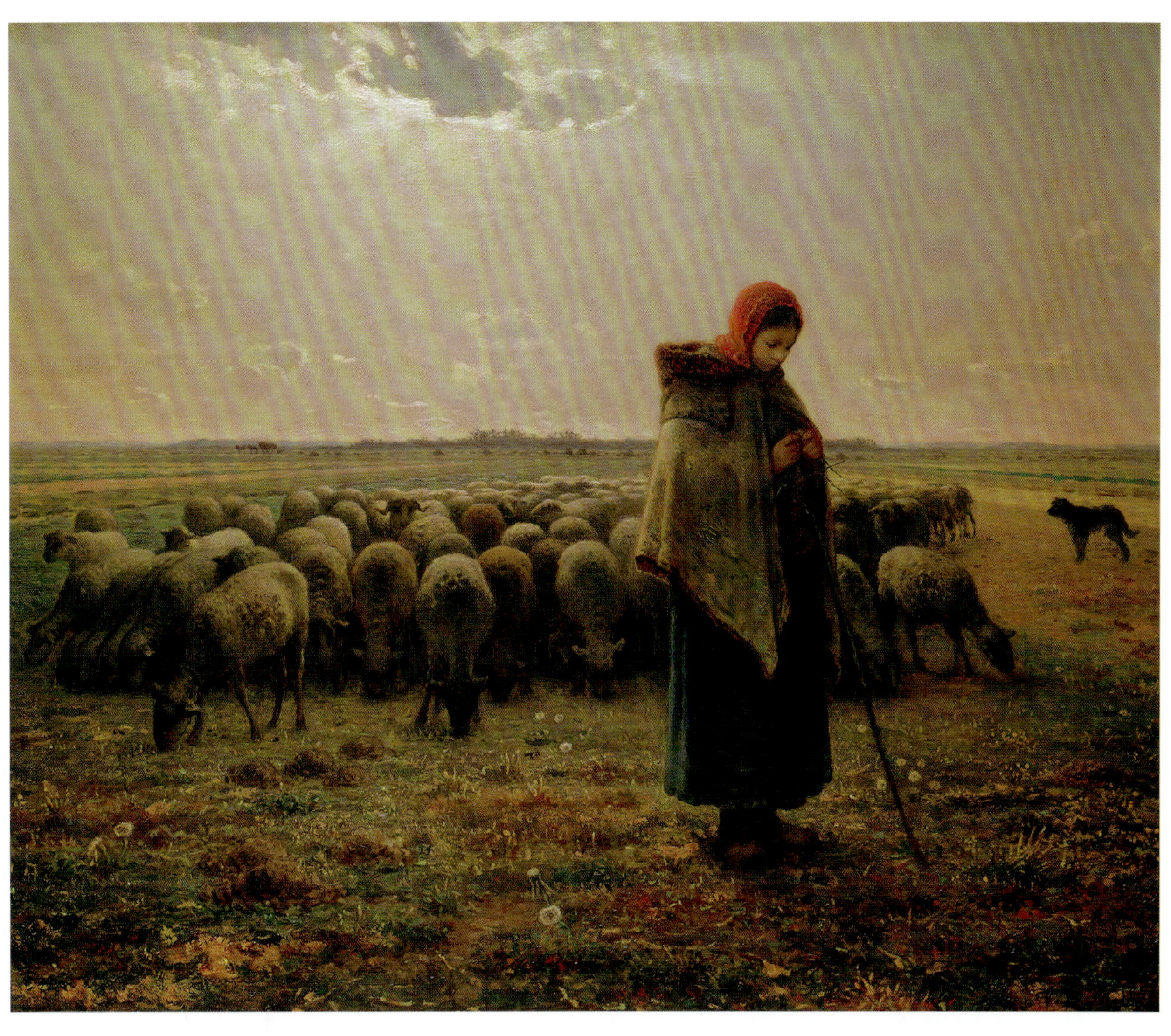

Shepherdess with her Flock

Bergère avec son troupeau

Hirtin mit ihrer Herde

La pastora con su rebaño

Pastora com o seu rebanho

Herderin met haar kudde

JEAN-FRANÇOIS MILLET (1814-1875)

c. 1863, Oil on canvas/Huile sur toile, 81 × 101 cm,
Musée d'Orsay, Paris

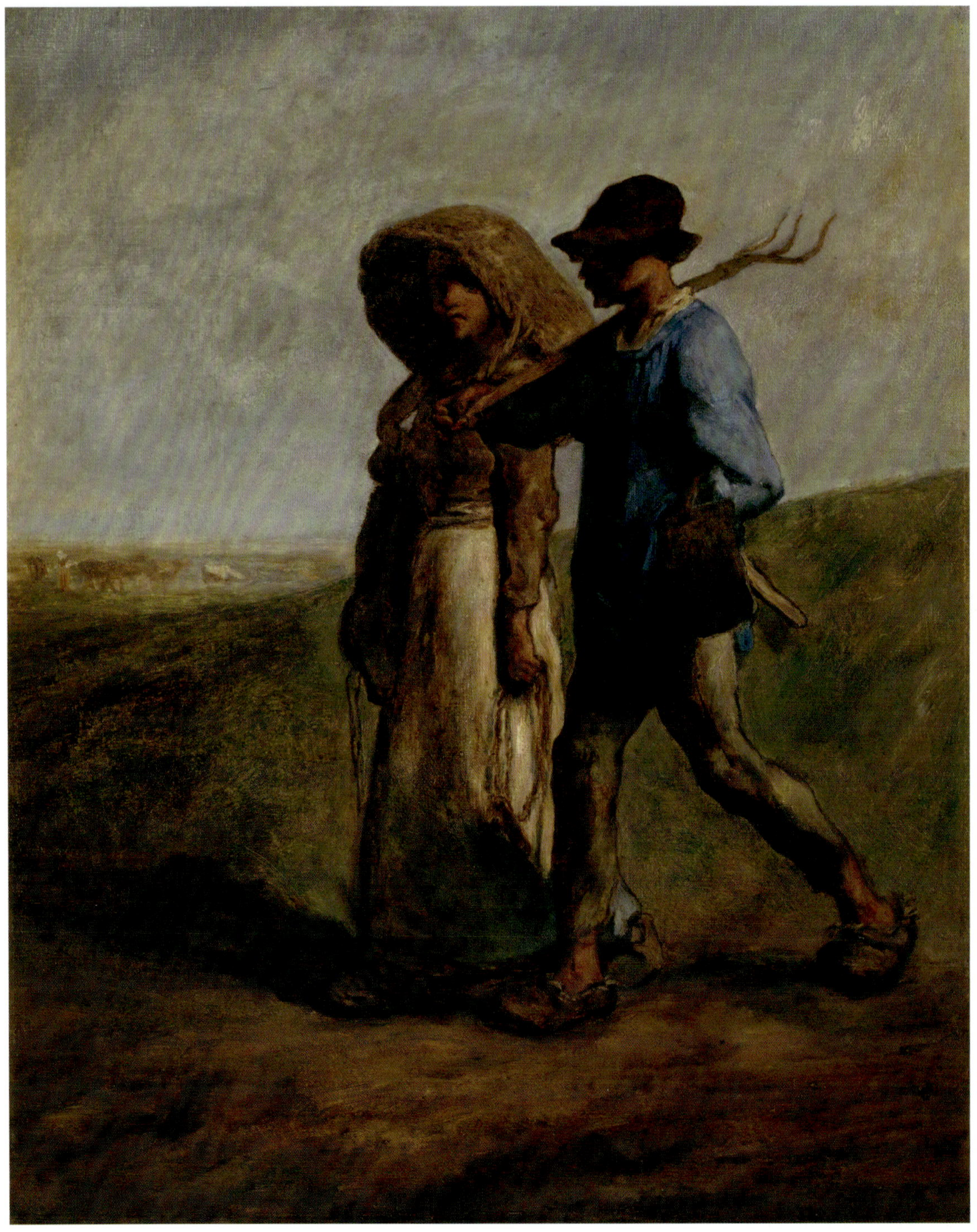

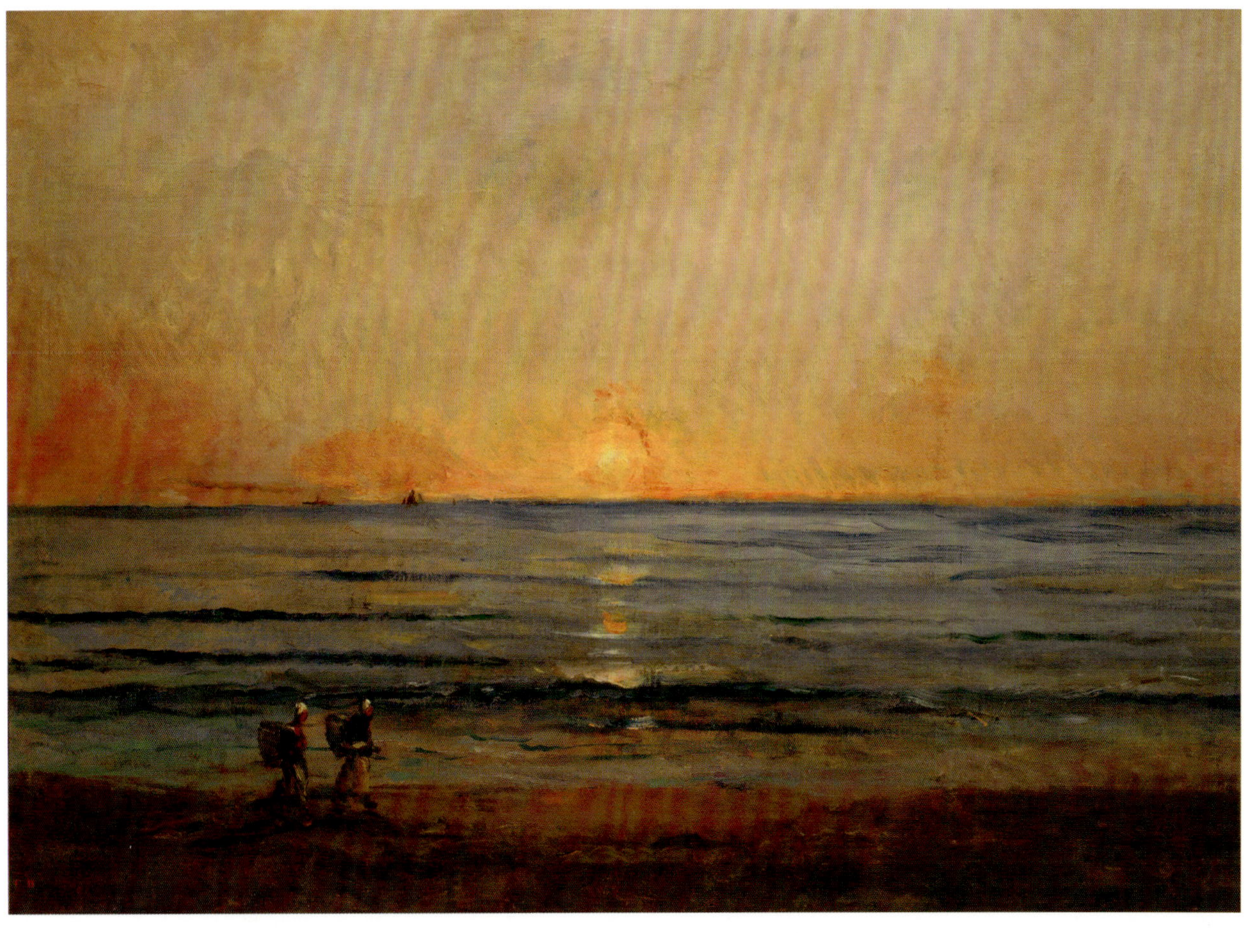

Sunset at Villerville

Coucher de soleil à Villerville

Sonnenuntergang bei Villerville

Atardecer en Villerville

Pôr-do-sol em Villerville

Zonsondergang in Villerville

CHARLES-FRANÇOIS DAUBIGNY (1817-1878)

1876, Oil on canvas/Huile sur toile, 89 × 130 cm,
De Mesdag collectie, Den Haag

Going to Work

Le Départ pour le travail

Der Weg zur Arbeit

En el camino al trabajo

A maneira de trabalhar

Op weg naar het werk

JEAN-FRANÇOIS MILLET (1814-1875)

c. 1850/51, Oil on canvas/Huile sur toile, 55,5 × 46 cm, Art Gallery and Museum, Glasgow

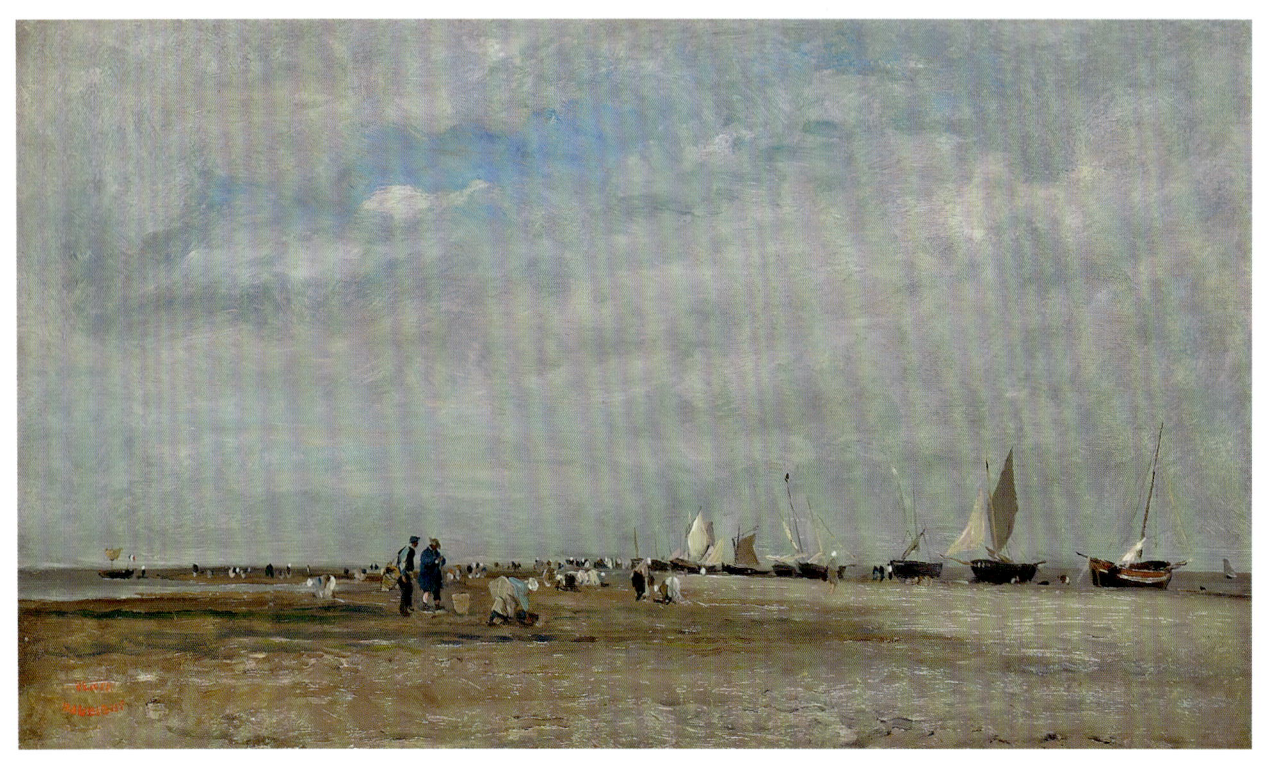

Les Ramasseurs de coquillages, Trouville

Les Ramasseurs de coquillages, Trouville

Muschelsammler bei Trouville

Coleccionista de conchas en Trouville

Colecionador de conchas em Trouville

Schelpenrapers bij Trouville

CHARLES-FRANÇOIS DAUBIGNY (1817-1878)

n.d., Oil on panel/Huile sur panneau, 31 × 52,5 cm, Private collection

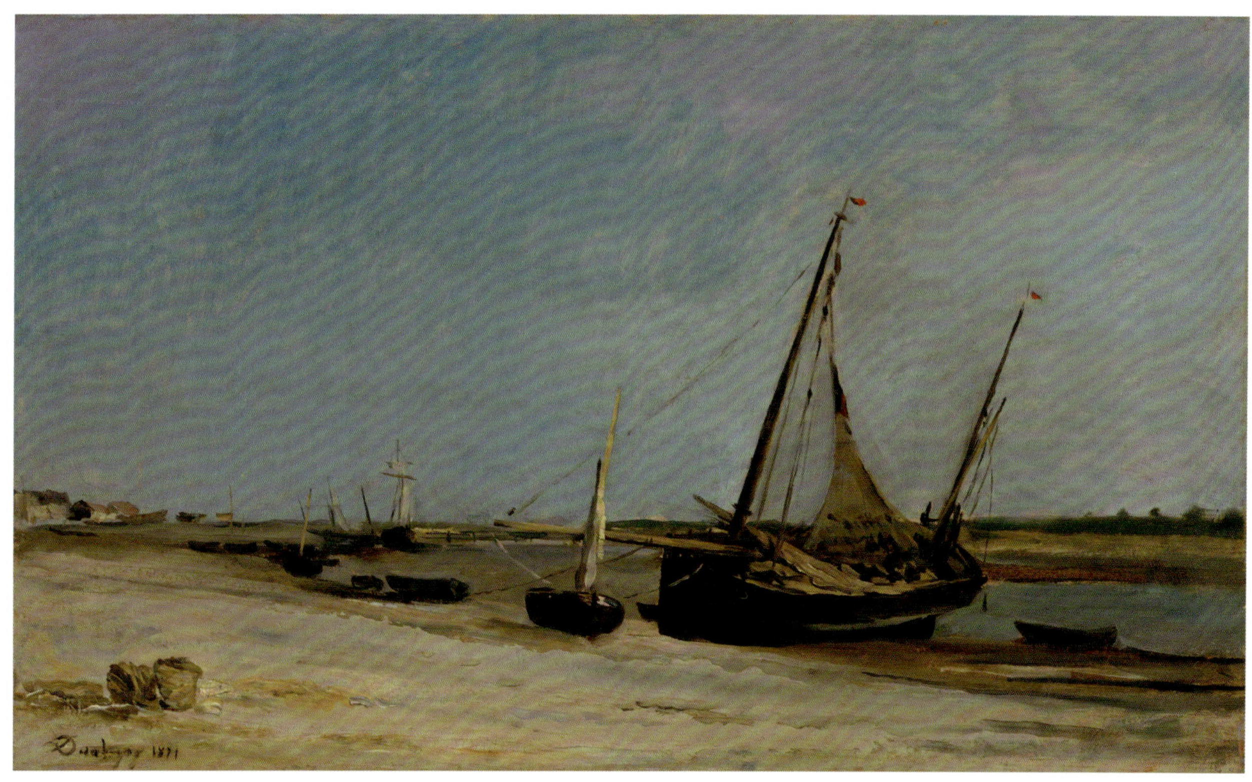

Boats on the Seacoast at Étaples

Bateaux sur le littoral à Étaples

Boote am Strand von Étaples

Barcos en la playa de Étaples

Barcos na praia de Étaples

Boten op het strand van Étaples

CHARLES-FRANÇOIS DAUBIGNY (1817-1878)

1871, Oil on wood/Huile sur bois, 34,3 × 58,1 cm, Metropolitan Museum of Art, New York

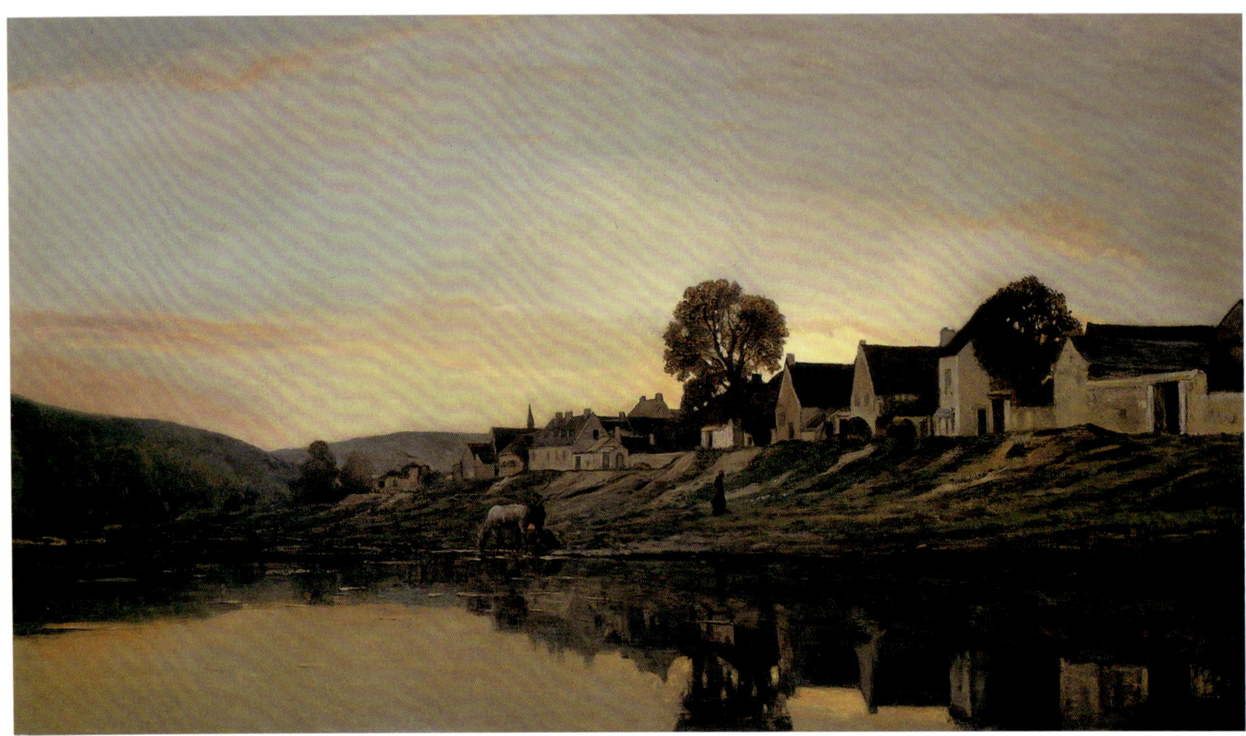

A Village near Bonnières

The landscape on the banks of the Seine is quiet and peaceful. More than ten years before the birth of Impressionism, the artist was concerned with the representation of light and mood.

Un village près de Bonnières

Calme et sérénité caractérisent ce paysage des bords de Seine. Plus de dix ans avant la naissance de l'impressionnisme, l'artiste se passionne pour les effets de lumière et les variations atmosphériques.

CHARLES-FRANÇOIS DAUBIGNY (1817-1878)

1861, Oil on canvas/Huile sur toile, 85 × 150 cm, Private collection

Dorf in der Nähe von Bonnières

Ruhig und friedlich liegt die Landschaft an den Ufern der Seine. Mehr als zehn Jahre vor der Geburt des Impressionismus befasst sich der Künstler mit der Darstellung des Lichts und der Stimmung.

Pueblo cerca de Bonnières

El paisaje a orillas del Sena es tranquilo y apacible. Más de diez años antes del nacimiento del Impresionismo, el artista se preocupó por la representación de la luz y el humor.

Vila perto de Bonnières

A paisagem nas margens do Sena é tranquila e pacífica. Mais de dez anos antes do nascimento do Impressionismo, o artista estava preocupado com a representação da luz e do humor.

Een dorp in de buurt van Bonnières

Het landschap aan de oevers van de Seine is rustig en vredig. Meer dan tien jaar voor de opkomst van het impressionisme hield de kunstenaar zich al bezig met de weergave van licht en sfeer.

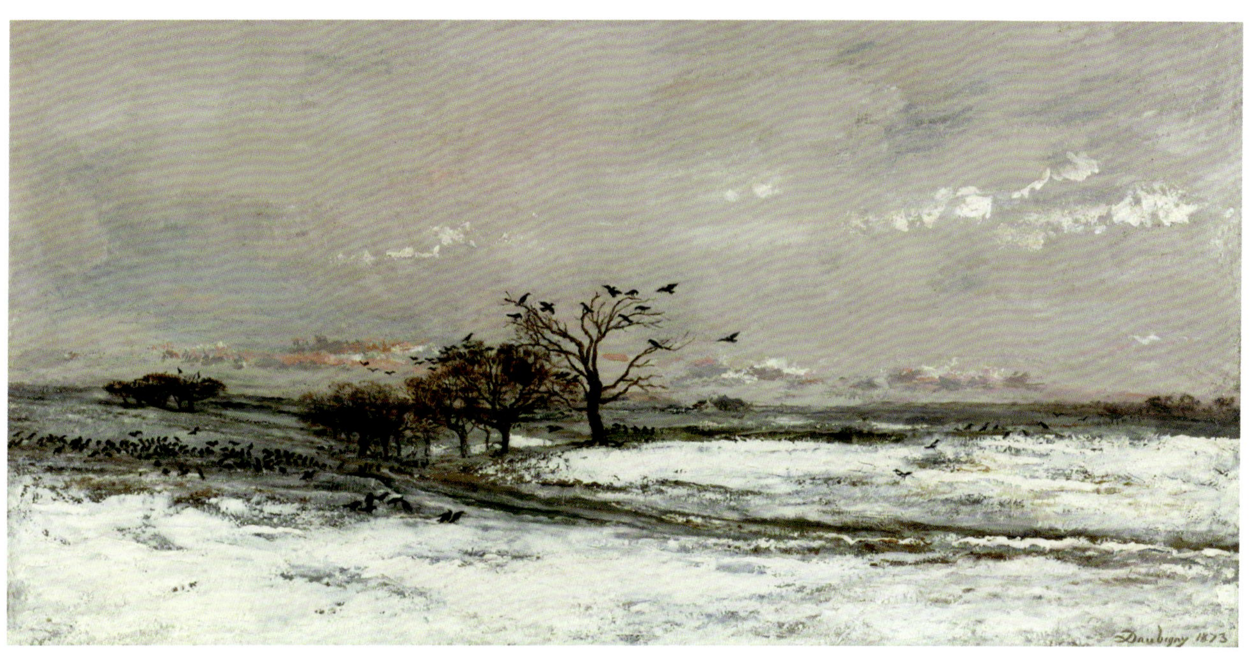

The Snow

La Neige

Schnee

La nieve

Nevar

De sneeuw

CHARLES-FRANÇOIS DAUBIGNY (1817-1878)
1873, Oil on canvas/Huile sur toile,
90 × 120 cm, Musée d'Orsay, Paris

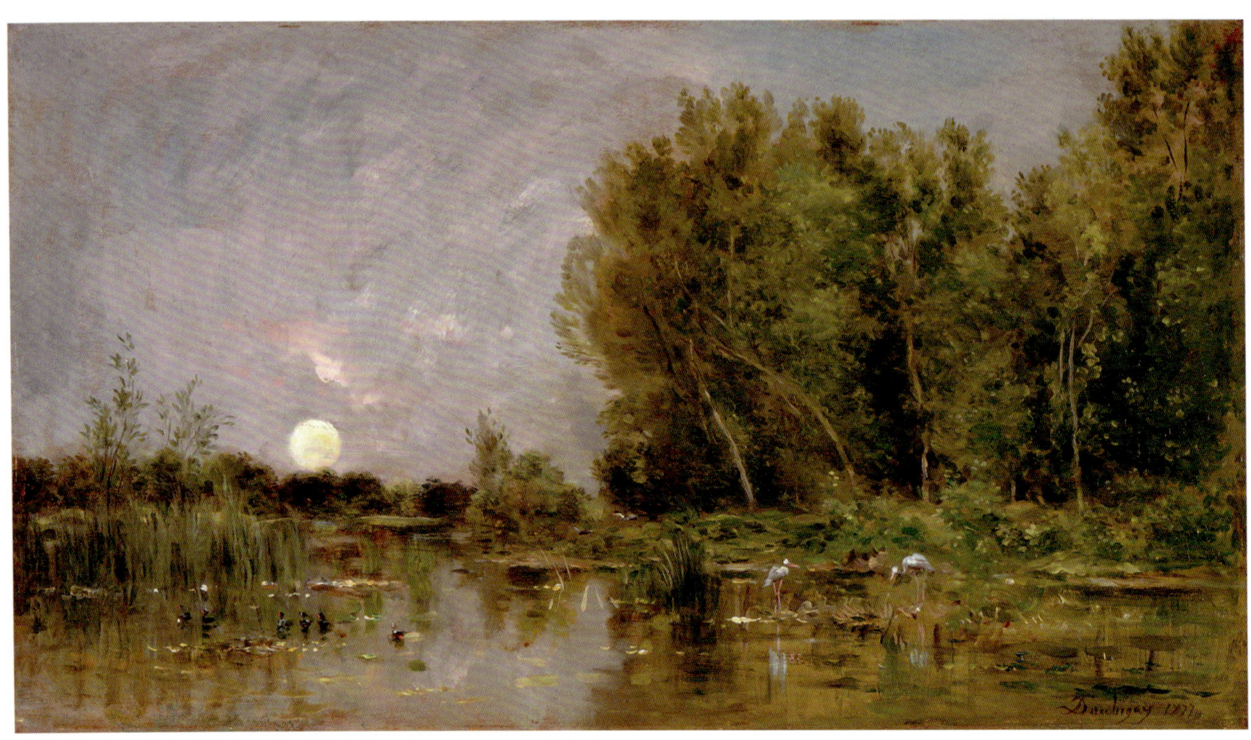

Moonrise

Le Lever de lune

Der Mondaufgang

La salida de la luna

O nascer da lua

De maansopgang

CHARLES-FRANÇOIS DAUBIGNY (1817-1878)
1877, Oil on panel/Huile sur panneau,
40,3 × 67,9 cm, Brooklyn Museum of Art, New York

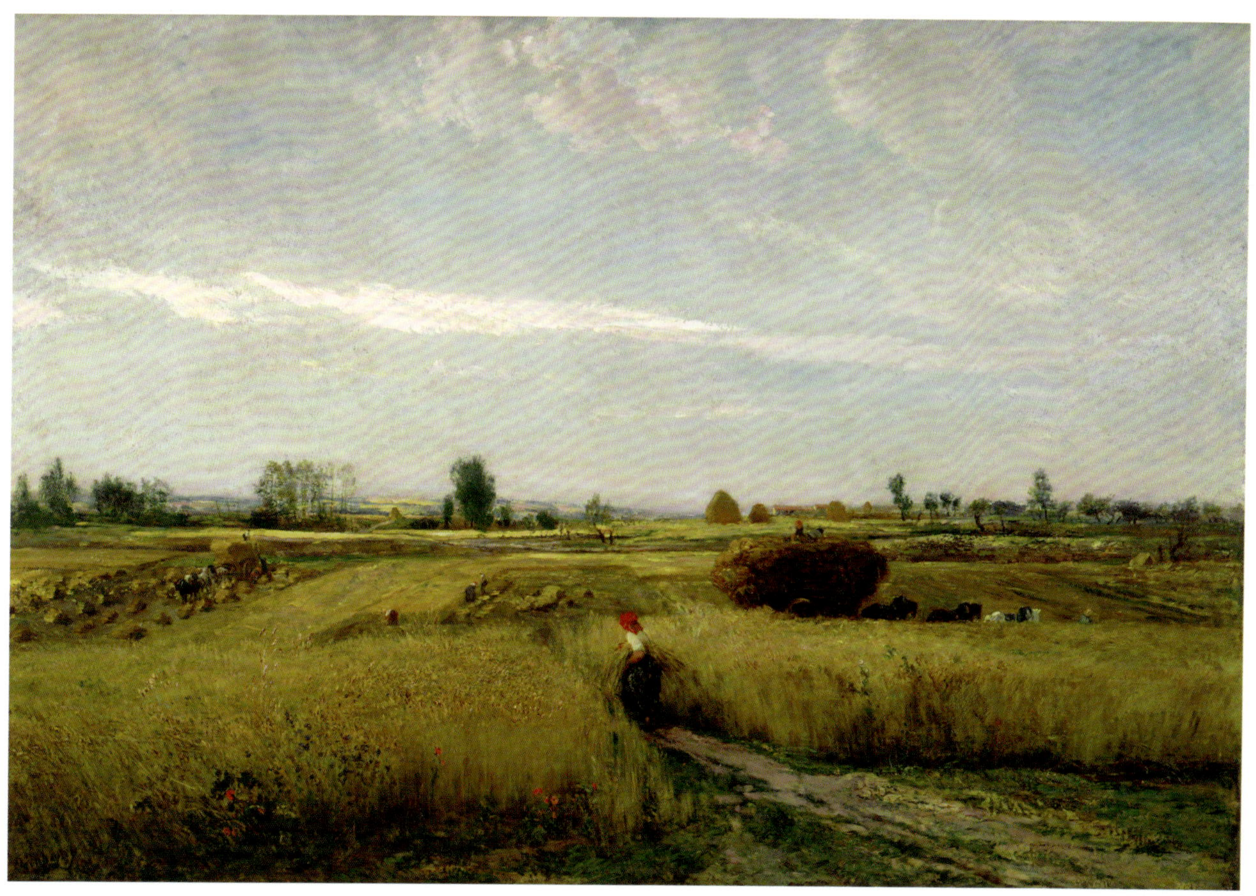

The Harvest

Moisson

Ernte

La cosecha

Colheita

De oogst

CHARLES-FRANÇOIS DAUBIGNY (1817-1878)
1851, Oil on canvas/Huile sur toile, 135 × 196 cm,
Musée d'Orsay, Paris

3

The Realism

Le réalisme

Der Realismus

El Realismo

O Realismo

Realisme

The Realism

Field work, industrial enterprises or simple people in their everyday activities - realism first manifested itself as a literary movement, before it was also reflected in painting during the Second Republic and the Second Empire. Shortly after the revolutionary year of 1848, it broke with the romanticism that prevailed in the first decades of the 19th century. Idealized representations decreased, but contemporary, social or political motifs were taking hold. Gustave Courbet's work *Burial at Ornans*, which could be seen at the Salon in 1850, became his manifesto. It caused a scandal during the presentation. Among other things, the painter was accused of having used a large format, which was reserved for historical paintings or religious motifs, for a banal, almost trivial scene.

In addition to Courbet, who created landscapes, hunting scenes, portraits and self-portraits, numerous other painters devoted themselves to realism. Through faces, gestures, postures or backgrounds they depicted, they bear witness to their epoch. Jules Breton devoted

Le réalisme

Le travail des champs, les ateliers industriels, les intérieurs de gens modestes dans leurs activités de tous les jours… Si le réalisme est d'abord un courant littéraire, il s'impose dans la peinture française entre le début de la IIe République et la fin du Second Empire. Au lendemain de la révolution de 1848, le réalisme rompt avec le romantisme des premières décennies du XIXe siècle. L'heure est aux sujets contemporains, sociaux, politiques, et l'idéalisation n'est pas de mise. Le tableau de Gustave Courbet intitulé *Un enterrement à Ornans*, présenté au Salon de 1850, est un véritable manifeste. Il fait d'ailleurs scandale à l'époque. On lui reproche, entre autres, d'avoir représenté une scène banale, voire triviale, dans un format monumental qui était jusqu'ici réservé à la peinture d'histoire ou religieuse.

Au-delà de Courbet – par ailleurs auteur de paysages, de scènes de chasse et de nombreux portraits ou autoportraits –, le réalisme réunit une quantité de peintres qui se sont attachés à rendre compte

Der Realismus

Feldarbeit, Industriebetriebe oder einfache Menschen bei ihren alltäglichen Beschäftigungen – der Realismus manifestiert sich zuerst als eine literarische Strömung, bevor er sich während der Zweiten Republik und dem Zweiten Kaiserreich in der Malerei niederschlägt. Kurz nach dem Revolutionsjahr 1848 bricht er mit der Romantik, die in den ersten Jahrzehnten des 19. Jahrhunderts vorherrscht. Idealisierte Darstellungen nehmen ab, dafür halten zeitgenössische, soziale oder politische Motive Einzug. Gustave Courbets Werk *Ein Begräbnis in Ornans*, das 1850 auf dem Salon gezeigt wird, wird zu seinem Manifest. Bei der Präsentation sorgt es für einen Skandal. Man wirft dem Maler unter anderem vor, ein großes Format, das Historiengemälden oder religiösen Motiven vorbehalten war, für eine banale, fast triviale Szene verwendet zu haben. Neben Courbet, der Landschaften, Jagdszenen, Porträts und Selbstbildnisse schuf, verschreiben sich zahlreiche weitere Maler dem Realismus. Durch ihre dargestellten Gesichter, Gesten, Körperhaltungen oder

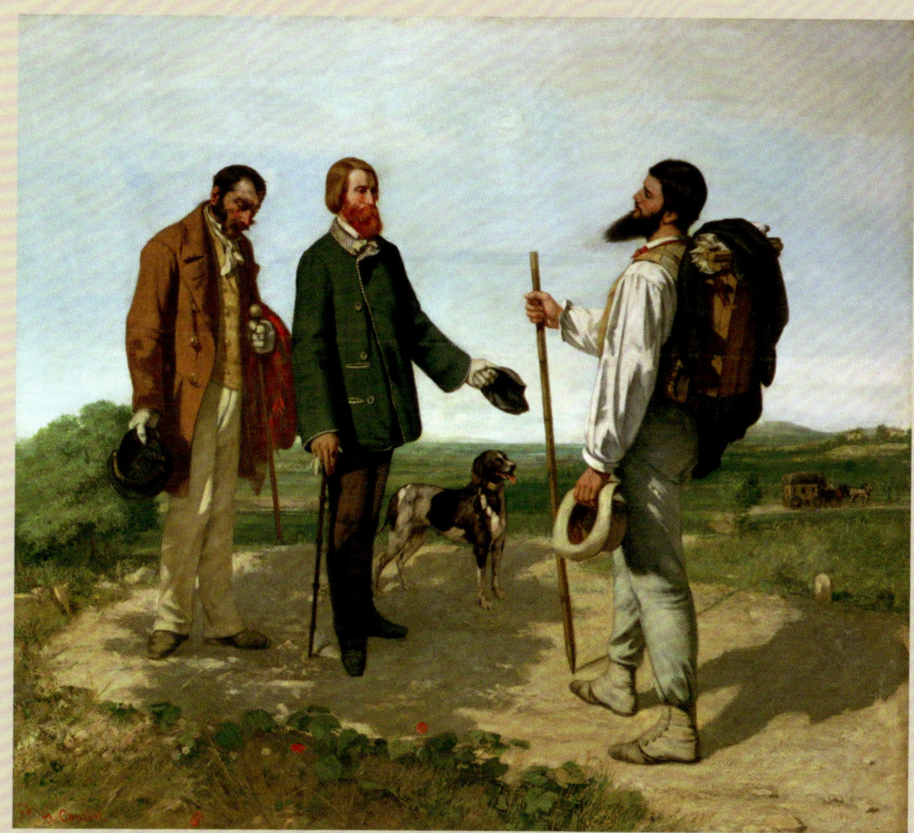

El Realismo

El trabajo de campo, las empresas industriales o las personas sencillas en sus actividades cotidianas - el realismo se manifiesta primero como un movimiento literario, antes de reflejarse también en la pintura durante la Segunda República y el Segundo Imperio. Poco después del año revolucionario de 1848, rompió con el romanticismo que reinaba en las primeras décadas del siglo XIX. Las representaciones idealizadas disminuyen, pero los motivos contemporáneos, sociales o políticos se están afianzando. La obra de Gustave Courbet *Un funeral en Ornans*, que puede verse en el Salón en 1850, se convierte en su manifiesto. Provoca un escándalo durante la presentación. Entre otras cosas, se acusa al pintor de haber utilizado un formato grande, reservado para pinturas históricas o motivos religiosos, para una escena banal, casi trivial.

Además de Courbet, que creó paisajes, escenas de caza, retratos y autorretratos, muchos otros pintores se dedicaron al realismo. A través de sus rostros, gestos, posturas o antecedentes, dan testimonio de su época.

O Realismo

Trabalho de campo, empresas industriais ou pessoas simples em suas atividades cotidianas - o realismo primeiro se manifesta como um movimento literário, antes que se reflita também na pintura durante a Segunda República e o Segundo Império. Pouco depois do ano revolucionário de 1848, ele rompeu com o romantismo que prevaleceu nas primeiras décadas do século XIX. As representações idealizadas diminuem, mas os motivos contemporâneos, sociais ou políticos estão se firmando. A obra de Gustave Courbet *Um Funeral em Ornans*, que pode ser vista no Salão em 1850, torna-se seu manifesto. Causa um escândalo durante a apresentação. Entre outras coisas, o pintor é acusado de ter usado um grande formato, que foi reservado para pinturas históricas ou motivos religiosos, para uma cena banal, quase trivial.

Além de Courbet, que criou paisagens, cenas de caça, retratos e auto-retratos, muitos outros pintores se dedicaram ao realismo. Através dos seus rostos, gestos, posturas ou fundos retratados, testemunham a sua

Realisme

Werk op het land, industriebedrijven of eenvoudige mensen bij hun dagelijkse doen en laten – het realisme manifesteerde zich eerst als een literaire stroming, voordat het tijdens de Tweede Franse Republiek en het Tweede Rijk ook in de schilderkunst zijn weerslag vond. Kort na het revolutiejaar 1848 brak het met de romantiek die in de eerste decennia van de 19e eeuw overheerste. Er kwamen minder geïdealiseerde voorstellingen, terwijl eigentijdse, maatschappelijke en politieke onderwerpen belangrijker werden. Gustave Courbets *Een begrafenis in Ornans*, dat te zien was op de Salon van 1850, werd het manifest van de stroming. Het veroorzaakte een schandaal bij de presentatie. De schilder werd er onder meer van beschuldigd dat hij een groot formaat gebruikte voor een banale, bijna triviale voorstelling, terwijl dat gereserveerd was voor historische en religieuze werken.

Naast Courbet, die landschappen, jachttaferelen, portretten en zelfportretten maakte, gaven tal van schilders zich over aan het realisme. De door

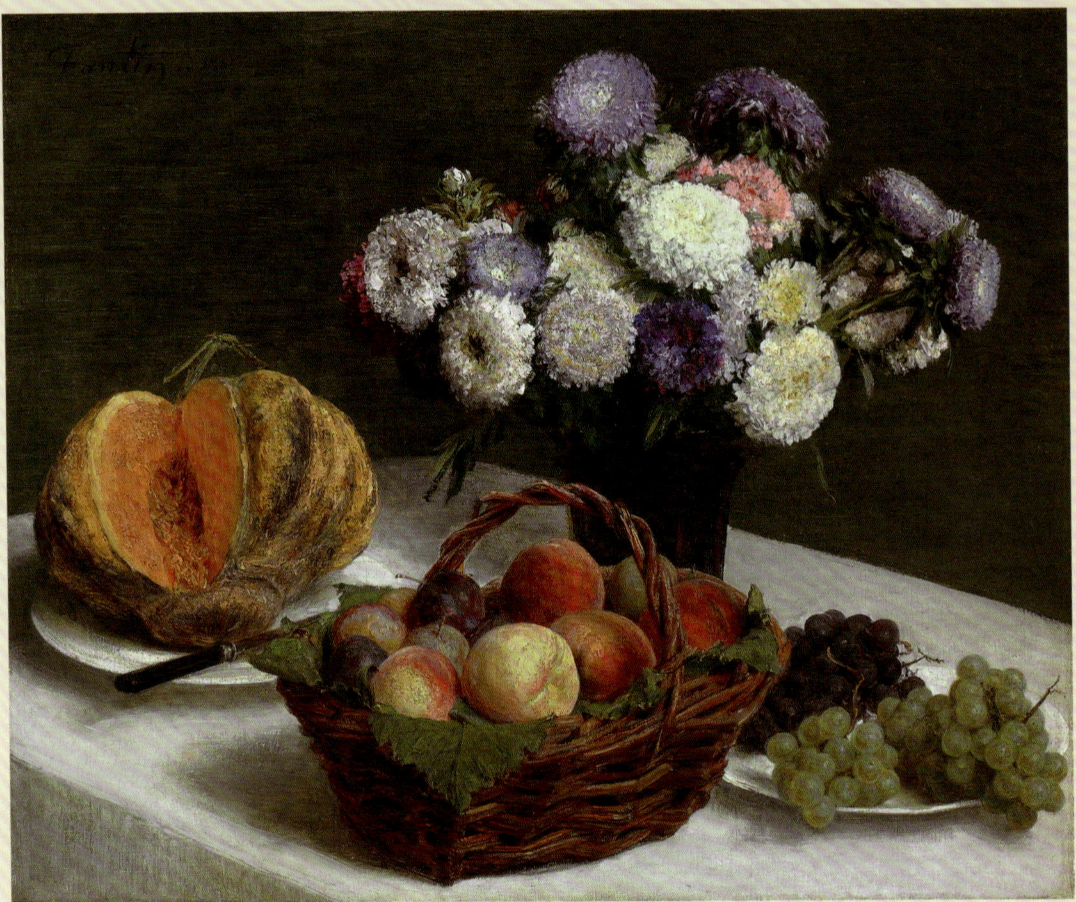

Flowers and fruits

Fleurs et fruits

Blumen und Früchte

Flores y frutas

Flores e frutos

Bloemen en vruchten

HENRI FANTIN-LATOUR (1836-1904)
1865, Oil on canvas/
Huile sur toile,
55,9 × 68,3 cm,
Private collection

himself to everyday rural life. Rosa Bonheur painted cows, lions and vultures with an extraordinary, almost photographic precision. Léon Lhermitte, Jules Bastien-Lepage and Théodule Ribot are distinguished by their portraits, genre paintings and still lifes. Henri Fantin-Latour, famous for his flower arrangements, fascinates today with his group portraits, in which he depicted his contemporaries (Verlaine, Rimbaud and the artists of the Batignolles school) very realistically. But his paintings are also testimonies to the loneliness and inability of people to communicate - themes that run like a common thread through his entire oeuvre, from *The Dubourg Family* to *The Reader*.

de leur époque, par la vérité des visages, des gestes, des postures, des décors. Jules Breton dépeint admirablement le monde rural. Rosa Bonheur peint des vaches, des lions ou des vautours avec une précision quasi photographique. Léon Lhermitte, Jules Bastien-Lepage, Théodule Ribot excellent dans les tableaux de figures, les scènes de genre et les natures mortes. Célèbre en son temps pour ses compositions florales, Henri Fantin-Latour fascine surtout par ses portraits collectifs. Il représente des personnages de son époque (Verlaine, Rimbaud, les artistes du groupe des Batignolles), avec beaucoup de vérité. Mais il est avant tout le peintre de la solitude et de l'incommunicabilité des êtres. Un sentiment qui traverse la quasi-totalité de ses scènes d'intérieurs, de l'austère *Famille Dubourg* à *La Lecture*.

Hintergründe legen sie Zeugnis von ihrer Epoche ab. Jules Breton widmete sich dem ländlichen Alltag. Rosa Bonheur malt mit einer außergewöhnlichen, fast schon fotografischen Präzession Kühe, Löwen und Geier. Léon Lhermitte, Jules Bastien-Lepage und Théodule Ribot zeichnen sich durch ihre Porträts, ihre Genrebilder und Stillleben aus. Der durch seine Blumenarrangements bekanntgewordene Henri Fantin-Latour fasziniert heute durch seine Gruppenporträts, auf denen er seine Zeitgenossen (Verlaine, Rimbaud und die Künstler der Schule von Batignolles) wahrheitsgetreu abbildet. Seine Gemälde sind aber auch Zeugnisse der Einsamkeit und der Kommunikationsunfähigkeit – Themen, die sich wie ein roter Faden durch sein gesamtes Werk ziehen, von *Die Familie Dubourg* bis hin zu *Die Lektüre*.

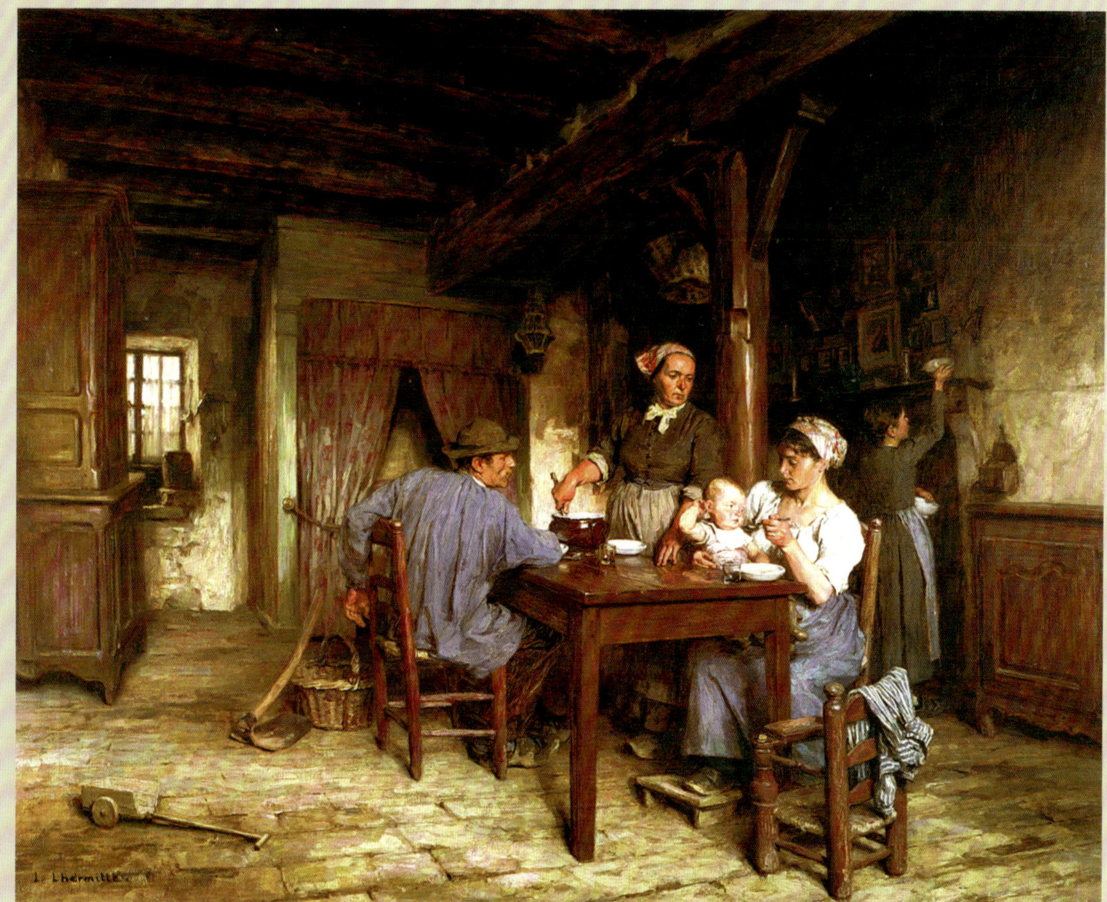

Jules Breton se dedicó a la vida rural cotidiana. Rosa Bonheur pinta vacas, leones y buitres con una precesión extraordinaria, casi fotográfica. Léon Lhermitte, Jules Bastien-Lepage y Théodule Ribot se distinguen por sus retratos, pinturas de género y bodegones. Henri Fantin-Latour, famoso por sus arreglos florales, fascina hoy con sus retratos de grupo, en los que retrata a sus contemporáneos (Verlaine, Rimbaud y los artistas de la escuela de Batignolles) de forma muy realista. Pero sus pinturas son también testimonios de la soledad y la incapacidad de la gente para comunicarse - temas que corren como un hilo rojo a través de toda su obra, desde *La familia Dubourg* hasta *La lectura*.

época. Jules Breton dedicou-se à vida rural quotidiana. Rosa Bonheur pinta vacas, leões e abutres com uma extraordinária, quase fotográfica precessão. Léon Lhermitte, Jules Bastien-Lepage e Théodule Ribot distinguem-se pelos seus retratos, pinturas de género e naturezas mortas. Henri Fantin-Latour, famoso por seus arranjos florais, fascina hoje com seus retratos de grupo, nos quais retrata seus contemporâneos (Verlaine, Rimbaud e os artistas da escola Batignolles) de forma muito realista. Mas as suas pinturas são também testemunhos da solidão e incapacidade de comunicação das pessoas - temas que percorrem como um fio vermelho toda a sua obra, desde *A Família Dubourg* à *Leitura*.

hen afgebeelde gezichten, gebaren, houdingen en achtergronden getuigen van hun tijd. Jules Breton legde zich toe op het dagelijks leven op het platteland. Rosa Bonheur schilderde met een buitengewone, bijna fotografische precisie koeien, leeuwen en gieren. Léon Lhermitte, Jules Bastien-Lepage en Théodule Ribot onderscheidden zich met hun portretten, genrestukken en stillevens. Henri Fantin-Latour, die beroemd was geworden door zijn bloemstukken, fascineert nog altijd met zijn groepsportretten, waarop hij zijn tijdgenoten (Verlaine, Rimbaud en de kunstenaars van de school van Batignolles) zeer realistisch afbeeldde. Maar zijn schilderijen getuigen ook van de eenzaamheid en het onvermogen van mensen om te communiceren – thema's die als een rode draad door zijn hele oeuvre lopen, van *De familie Dubourg* tot *Lezen*.

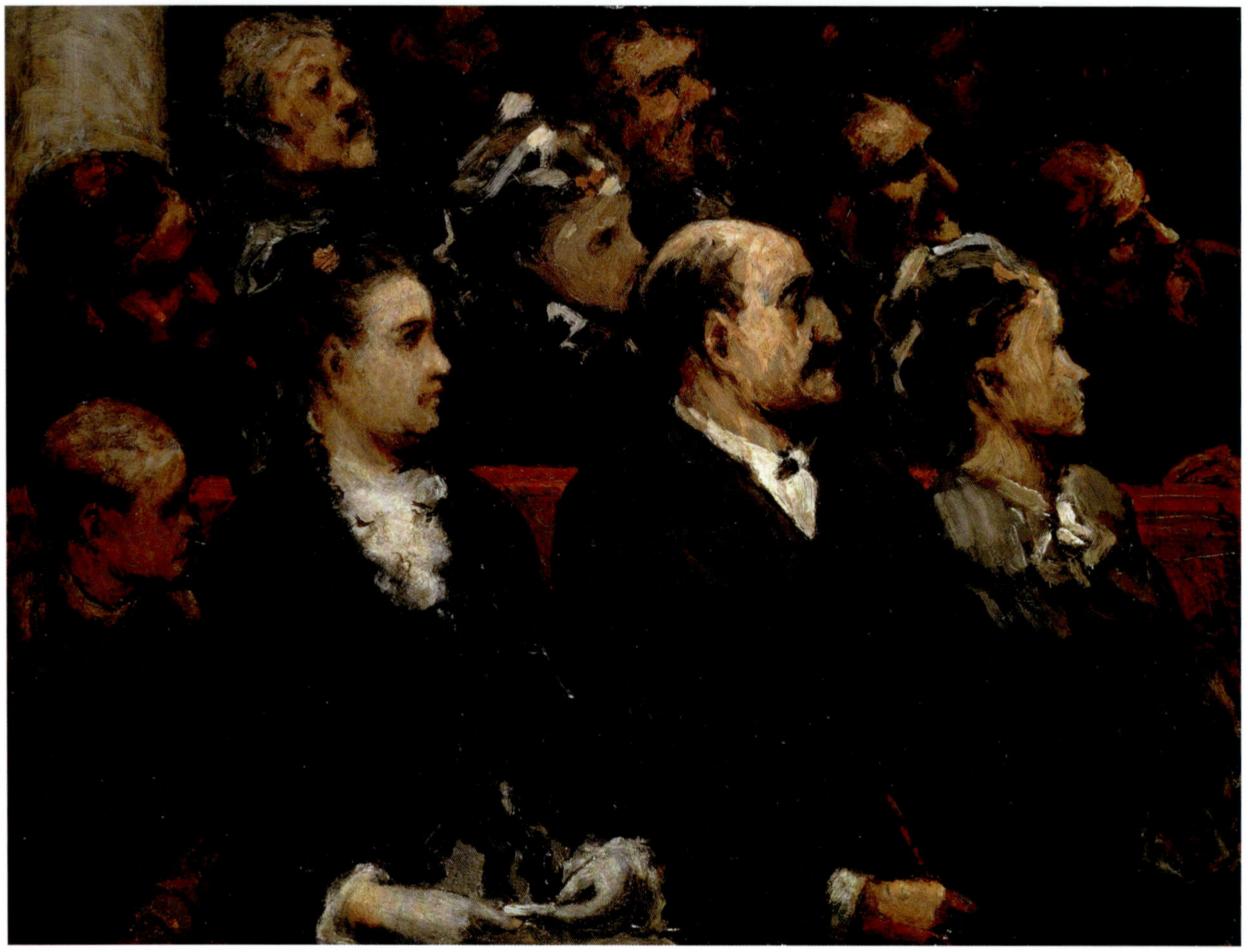

Attending the Theatre

Honoré Daumier's style cannot be clearly assigned to realism - his subjects, on the other hand, can. The painter, graphic artist and cartoonist reproduced the characters of his time with great precision.

Spectateurs de théâtre

Le style d'Honoré Daumier, peintre, graveur et caricaturiste, n'est pas à proprement parler réaliste. Mais ses sujets le sont. Il croque avec beaucoup de vérité les postures et les caractères de son temps.

Zuschauer im Theater

Honoré Daumiers Stil lässt sich nicht eindeutig dem Realismus zuordnen – seine Sujets hingegen schon. Mit großer Exaktheit gibt der Maler, Grafiker und Karikaturist die Charaktere seiner Zeit wieder.

Espectadores en el teatro

El estilo de Honoré Daumier, pintor, grabador y caricaturista, no es estrictamente realista. Pero sus súbditos sí. Reproduce con gran verdad las posturas y los personajes de su tiempo.

Espectadores no teatro

O estilo de Honoré Daumier não pode ser claramente atribuído ao realismo - os seus súbditos, por outro lado, podem. O pintor, artista gráfico e cartunista reproduz com grande precisão os personagens de seu tempo.

Toeschouwers in het theater

De stijl van Honoré Daumier laat zich niet eenduidig toewijzen aan het realisme, maar zijn onderwerpen wel. De schilder, graficus en karikaturist gaf de persoonlijkheden van zijn tijd zeer exact weer.

HONORÉ DAUMIER (1808-1879)

c. 1856, Oil on wood/Huile sur bois, 25,9 × 35 cm, National Gallery of Art, Washington

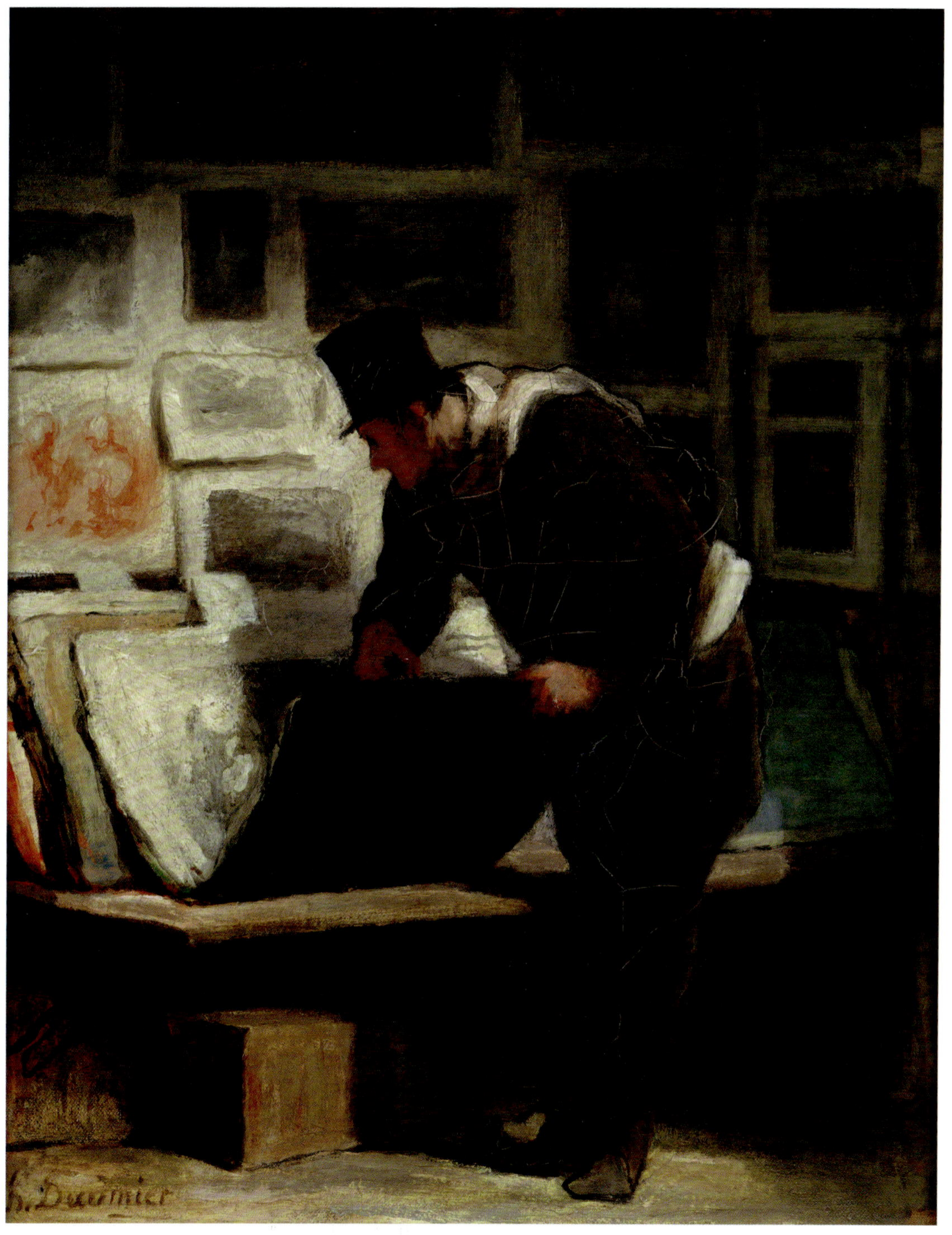

The Collecter
of Engravings

L'Amateur
d'estampes

Der
Grafikliebhaber

El amante gráfico

O amante
do gráfico

De liefhebber
van gravures

HONORÉ DAUMIER
(1808-1879)
c. 1860, Oil on
canvas/Huile sur
toile, 41 × 33,5 cm,
Petit Palais, Paris

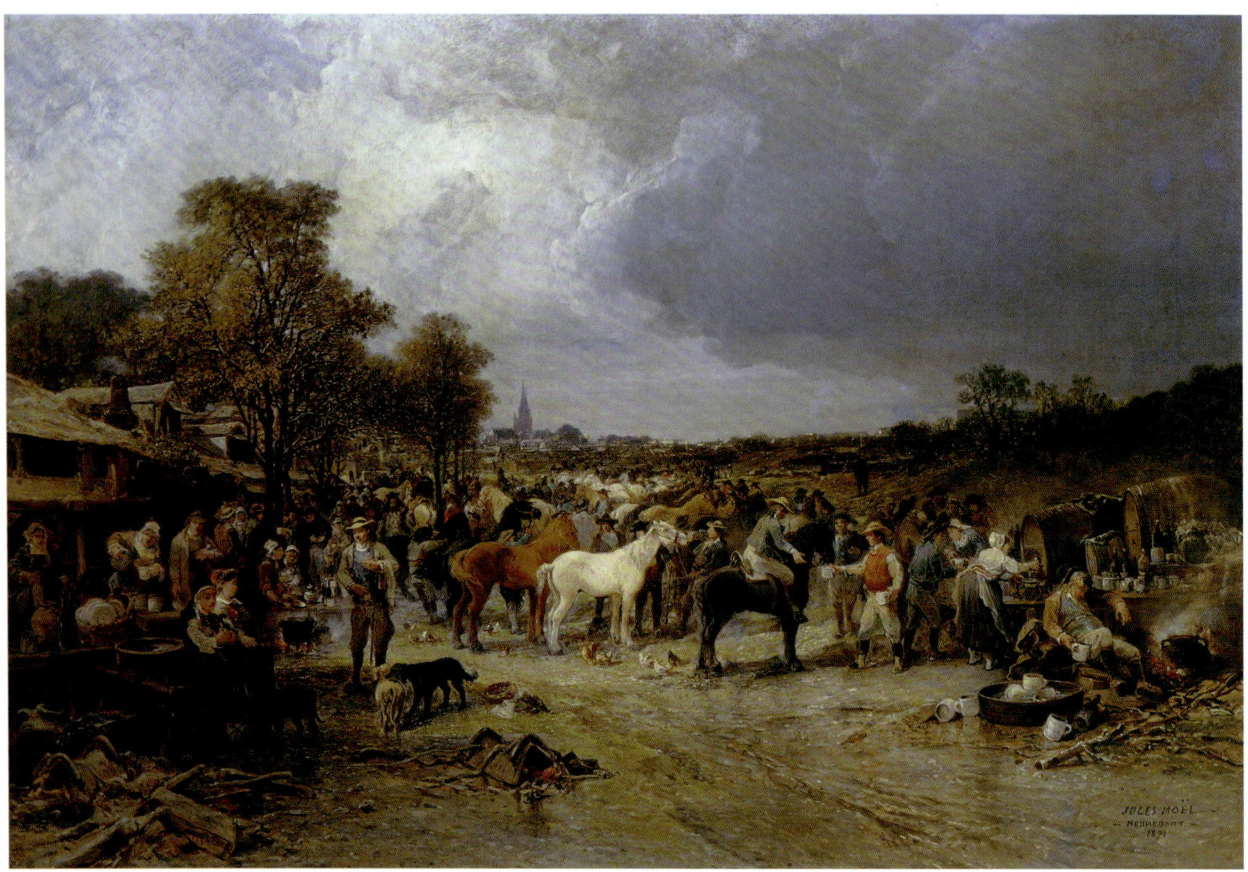

The Horse Market at Hennebont

La Foire aux chevaux à Hennebont

Der Pferdemarkt bei Hennebont

El mercado de caballos cerca de Hennebont

O mercado de cavalos perto de Hennebont

De paardenmarkt bij Hennebont

JULES NOËL (1810-1881)

1871, Oil on canvas/Huile sur toile,
74 × 110 cm, Private collection

Street Scene at Morlaix

Jules Noël not only painted landscapes and maritime subjects (Breton harbors, cliffs in Normandy), but also city views in which real architecture blends with fantastic street life.

Une rue à Morlaix en 1830

Paysagiste et peintre de marines (ports bretons, falaises normandes…), Jules Noël a également produit des vues de villes, où le réalisme de l'architecture se mêle au pittoresque de scènes très vivantes.

Eine Straßenszene in Morlaix

Jules Noël malte nicht nur Landschaften und maritime Sujets (bretonische Häfen, Klippen der Normandie), sondern auch Stadtansichten, in denen sich reale Architektur mit fantastischem Straßenleben mischt.

Una escena callejera en Morlaix

Jules Noël no sólo pintó paisajes y temas marítimos (puertos bretones, acantilados de Normandía), sino también vistas de la ciudad en las que la arquitectura real se mezcla con la fantástica vida de la calle.

Uma cena de rua em Morlaix

Jules Noël não só pintou paisagens e temas marítimos (portos bretões, penhascos da Normandia), mas também vistas da cidade em que a arquitetura real se mistura com a fantástica vida de rua.

Een straat in Morlaix

Jules Noël schilderde niet alleen landschappen en maritieme onderwerpen (Bretonse havens, Normandische kliffen), maar ook stadsgezichten, waarin hij echte architectuur combineerde met een verzonnen straatleven..

JULES NOËL (1810-1881)

1870, Oil on canvas/Huile sur toile, 121 × 91,2 cm, Musée des Beaux-Arts, Quimper

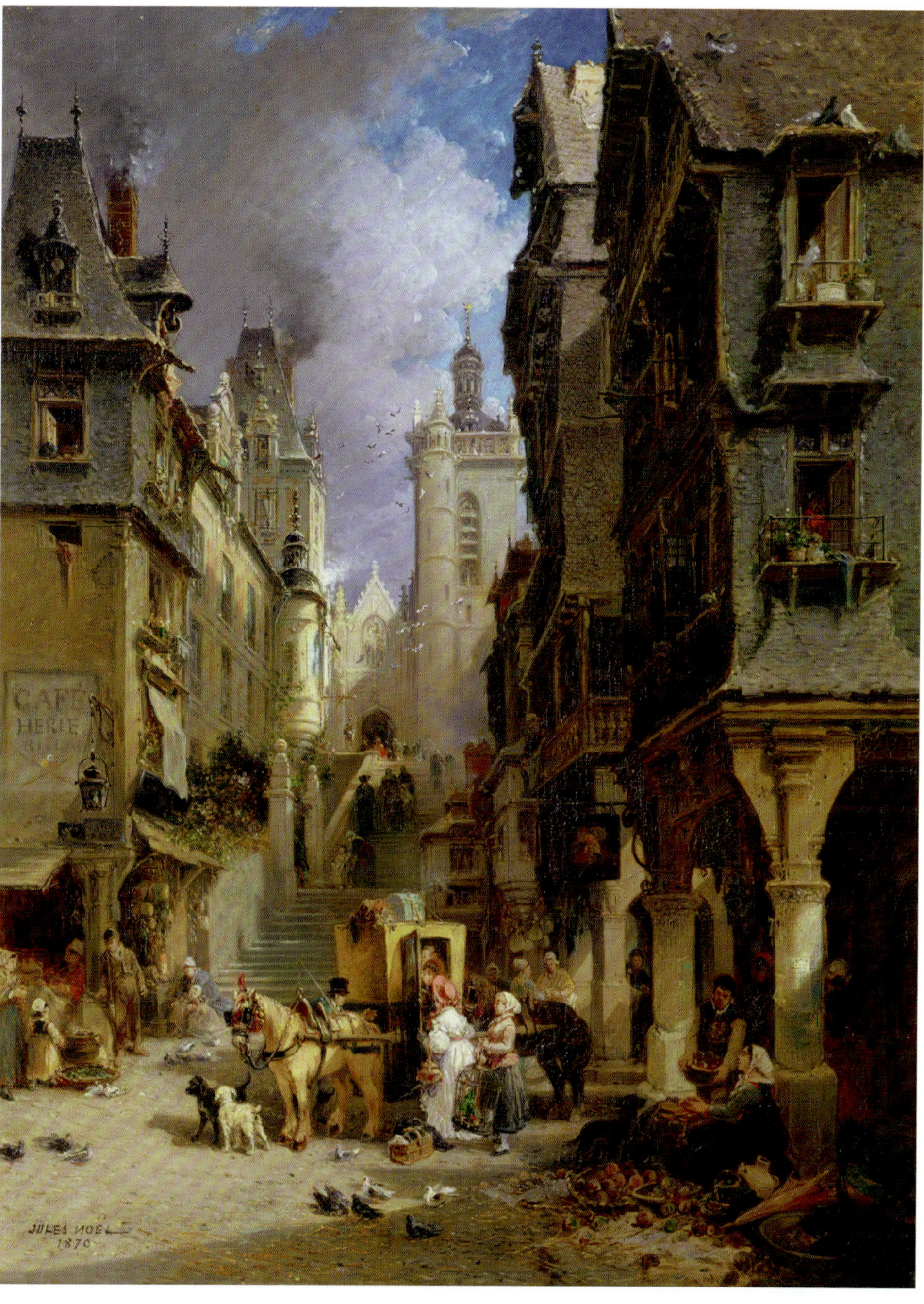

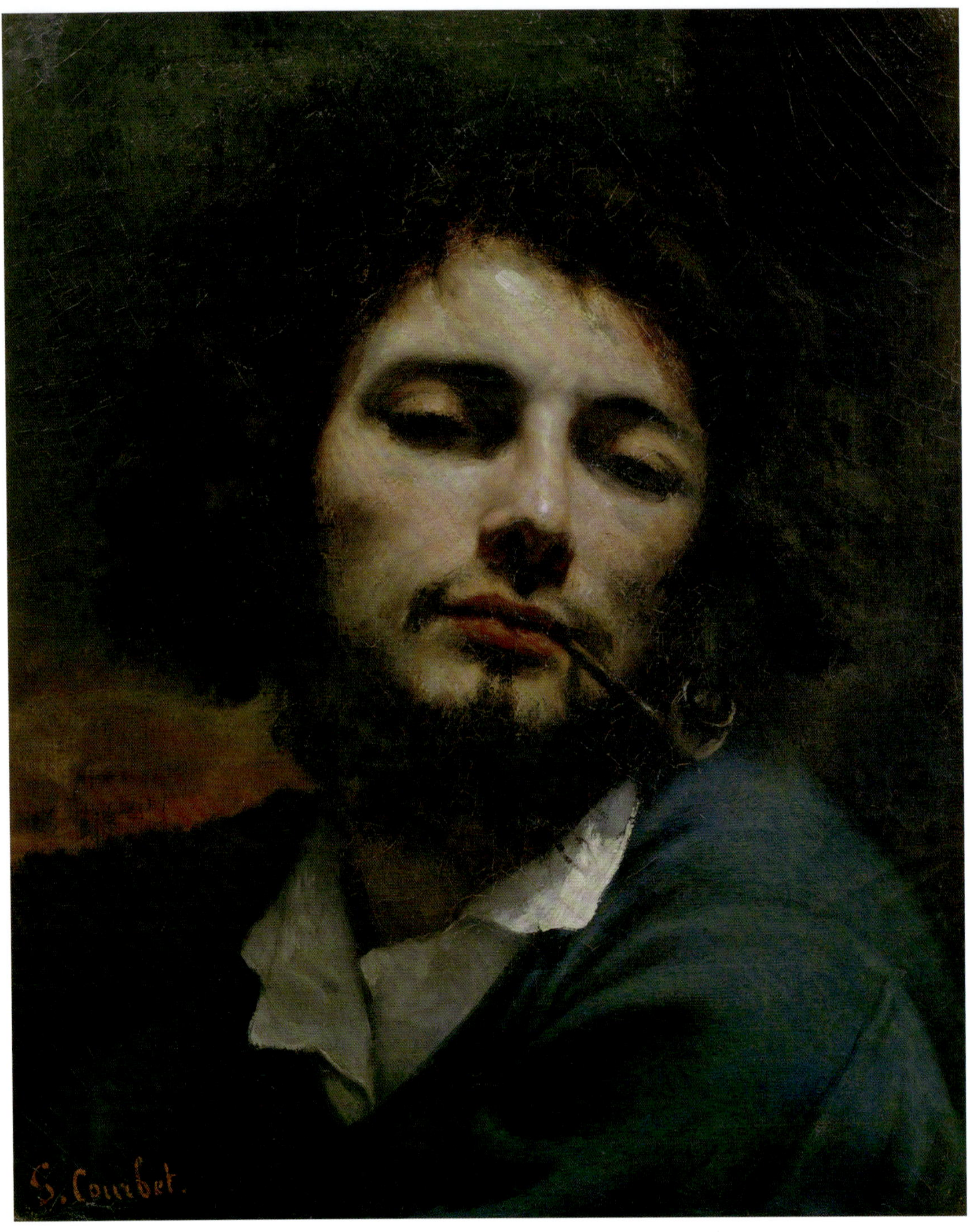

Self Portrait *or* **The Man with a Pipe**

Autoportrait *ou* **L'Homme à la pipe**

Selbstbildnis *oder* **Mann mit Pfeife**

Autorretrato *o* **hombre con pipa**

Auto-retrato *ou* **homem com cachimbo**

Zelfportret *of* **Man met pijp**

GUSTAVE COURBET (1819-1877)

c. 1848/49, Oil on canvas/ Huile sur toile, 45,8 × 37,8 cm, Musée Fabre, Montpellier

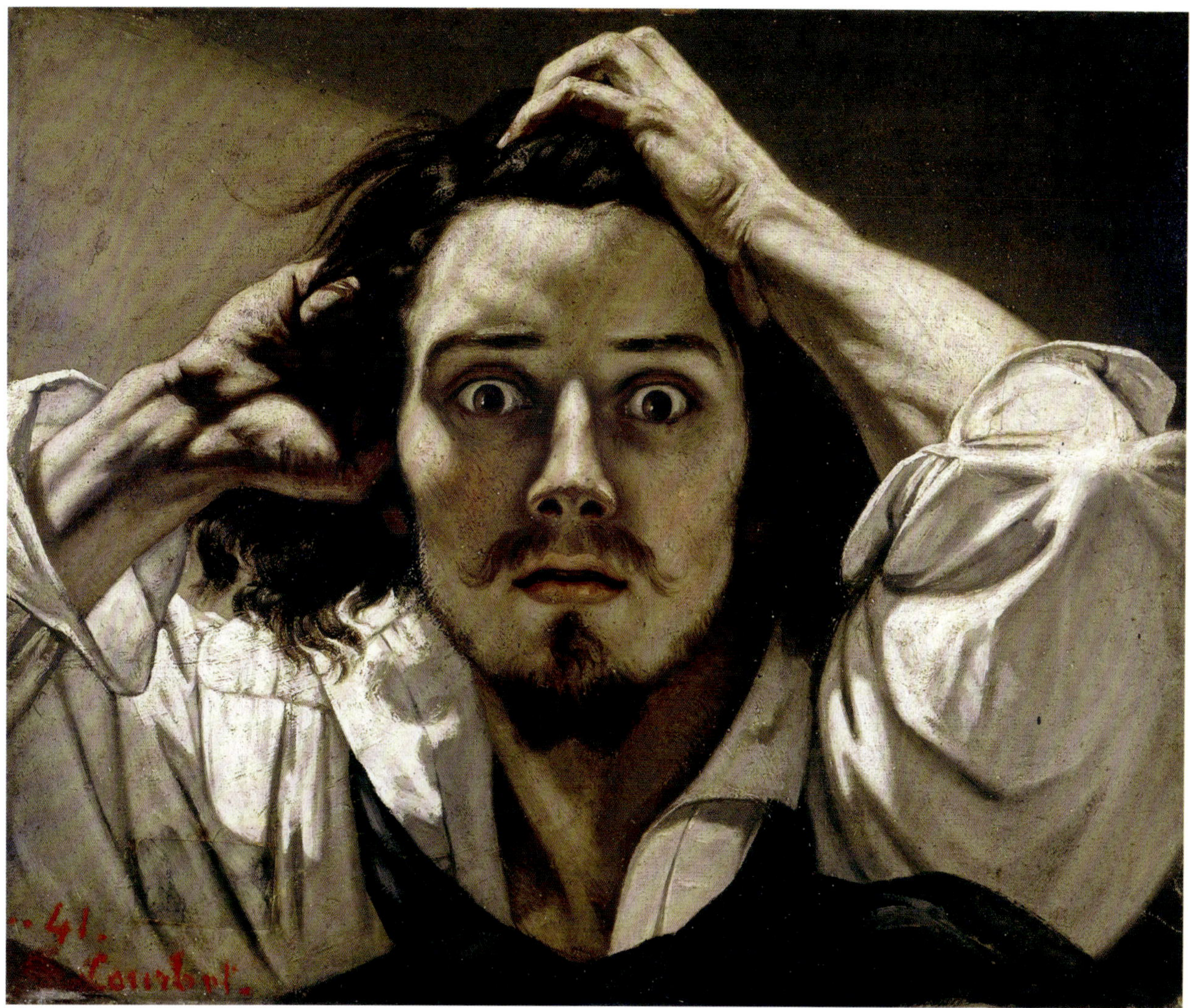

The Desperate Man (Self Portrait)

The expressive self-portrait of the young artist seems to literally emerge from the canvas. The wide open eyes and the large format intensify the feeling of closeness.

Le Désespéré (autoportrait)

Véritable tête d'expression, le visage de cet autoportrait de jeunesse, aux yeux écarquillés, semble surgir de la toile. L'effet de proximité avec le spectateur est renforcé par le cadrage en gros plan.

GUSTAVE COURBET (1819-1877)

1843-45, Oil on canvas/Huile sur toile, 45 × 54 cm, Private collection

Der Verzweifelte (Selbstbildnis)

Das ausdrucksstarke Selbstbildnis des jungen Künstlers scheint förmlich aus der Leinwand hervorzutreten. Die weit aufgerissenen Augen und das große Format verstärken das Gefühl der Nähe.

El Desesperado (autorretrato)

El autorretrato expresivo del joven artista parece emerger literalmente del lienzo. Los ojos bien abiertos y el gran formato intensifican la sensación de cercanía.

O Desesperado (auto-retrato)

O auto-retrato expressivo do jovem artista parece emergir literalmente da tela. Os olhos abertos e o grande formato intensificam a sensação de proximidade.

De wanhopige (zelfportret)

Het expressieve zelfportret van de jonge kunstenaar lijkt letterlijk uit het doek te komen. De wijd opengesperde ogen en het grote formaat versterken het gevoel van nabijheid.

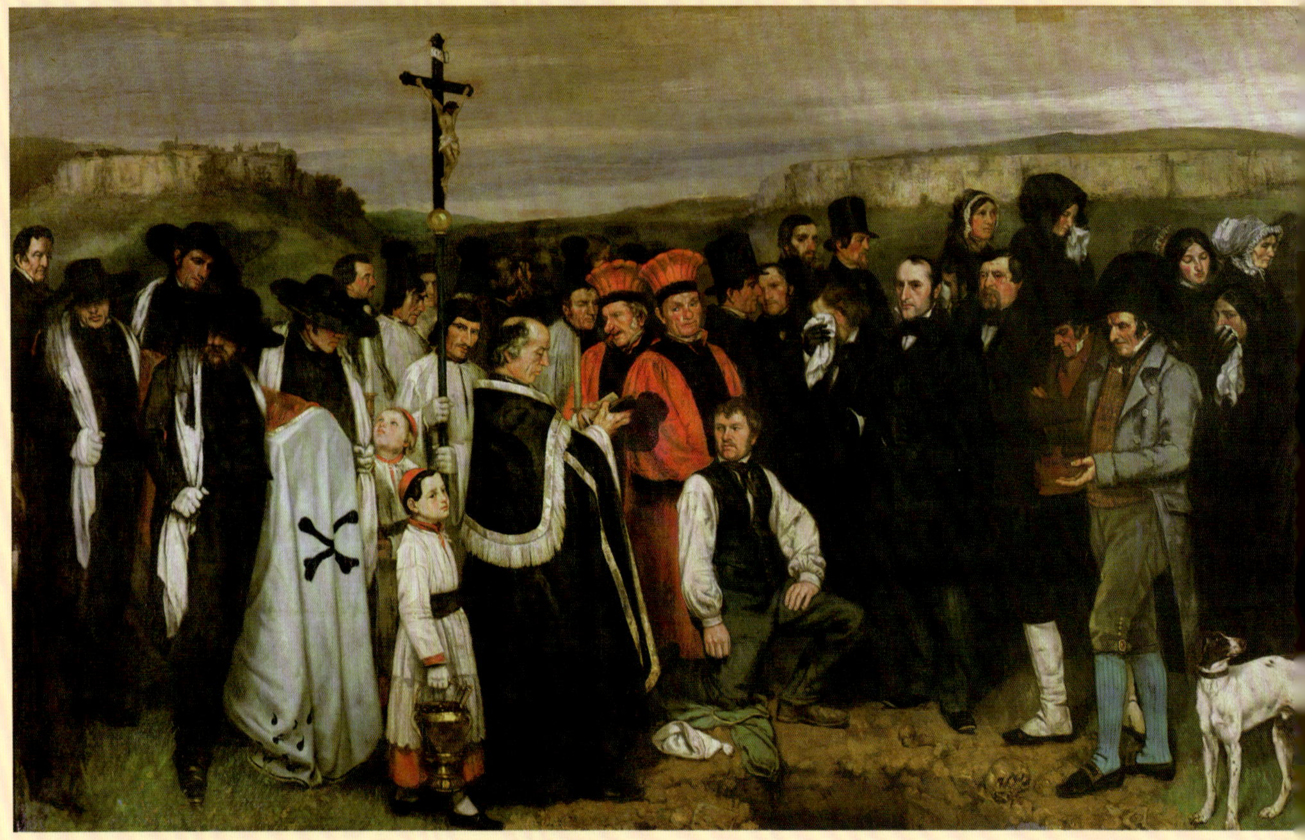

Gustave Courbet

Gustave Courbet (1819-1877) was a republican and a member of the Paris Commune in 1871 and became politically active. As a painter in 1850, he turned against academism by advocating a realistic form of art that provoked scandals. At the age of 20, Courbet, who came from a middle-class background, moved to Paris. There he copied the masters of the Louvre (Rembrandt, Rubens, Titian), was inspired by Géricault and Delacroix and exhibited his first works from 1848. In the course of his career he produced more than a thousand paintings. In addition to his masterpieces (*Burial at Ornans, The Studio of the Painter, The Origin of the World*), Courbet painted the landscapes of Franche-Comté and Normandy, hunting scenes, portraits (Hector Berlioz, Charles Baudelaire) and self-portraits. After the suppression of the Paris Commune, he was sentenced to six months in prison. When he was accused in 1873 of having participated in the destruction of the Colonne Vendôme, he fled to Switzerland, where he died, impoverished.

Gustave Courbet

Élu républicain et acteur de la Commune de Paris en 1871, Gustave Courbet (1819-1877) est un homme engagé. En tant qu'artiste, il s'affirme dès 1850 contre l'académisme, prônant un art de la vérité qui va provoquer le scandale. De milieu aisé, il arrive à Paris à 20 ans pour étudier le droit. Il copie les maîtres au Louvre (Rembrandt, Rubens, Titien…), admire Géricault et Delacroix, et expose à partir de 1848. Malgré l'incompréhension de la critique et du public, il connaîtra un vif succès et produira plus d'un millier d'œuvres. Outre les grands tableaux qui ont construit sa réputation *(Un enterrement à Ornans, L'Atelier du peintre, L'Origine du monde…)*, Courbet peint des paysages de sa Franche-Comté natale et de Normandie, des scènes de chasse, des portraits (Hector Berlioz, Charles Baudelaire…) et des autoportraits. Après la Commune de Paris, il est condamné à six mois de prison. Il s'exile en 1873 après avoir été accusé d'avoir participé à la destruction de la colonne Vendôme. Ruiné, il mourra en Suisse.

Gustave Courbet

Als Republikaner und Mitglied der Pariser Kommune 1871 engagierte sich Gustave Courbet (1819–1877) politisch. Als Maler wendet er sich 1850 gegen den Akademismus, indem er für eine realistische Kunst eintritt, die Skandale provoziert. Im Alter von 20 Jahren zieht der aus einem bürgerlichen Milieu stammende Courbet nach Paris. Dort kopiert er die Meister im Louvre (Rembrandt, Rubens, Tizian), lässt sich von Géricault und Delacroix inspirieren und stellt ab 1848 erste Werke aus. Im Laufe seiner Karriere wird er mehr als tausend Gemälde produzieren. Neben seinen Meisterwerken (*Ein Begräbnis in Ornans, Das Atelier des Künstlers, Der Ursprung der Welt*), malt Courbet die Landschaften der Franche-Comté und der Normandie, Jagdszenen, Porträts (Hector Berlioz, Charles Baudelaire) und Selbstbildnisse. Nach der Niederschlagung der Pariser Kommune wird er zu sechs Monaten Gefängnis verurteilt. Als er 1873 angeklagt wird, an der Zerstörung der Colonne Vendôme beteiligt gewesen zu sein, flieht er in die Schweiz, wo er verarmt stirbt.

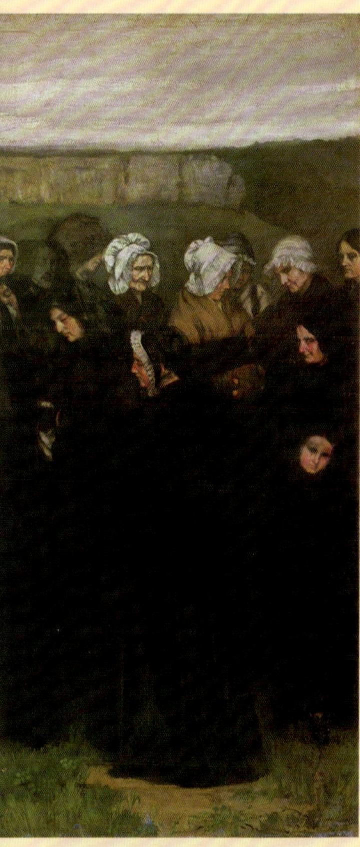

Burial at Ornans

Un enterrement à Ornans

Ein Begräbnis in Ornans

Un funeral en Ornans

Um funeral em Ornans

Een begrafenis in Ornans

GUSTAVE COURBET (1819-1877)

1849/50, Oil on canvas/Huile sur toile,
315 × 668 cm, Musée d'Orsay, Paris

Gustave Courbet

Gustave Courbet (1819-1877) fue republicano y miembro de la Comuna de París en 1871 y se volvió políticamente activo. Como pintor en 1850, se volvió contra el academicismo al abogar por un arte realista que provocaba escándalos. A los 20 años, Courbet, de origen burgués, se traslada a París. Allí copió a los maestros del Louvre (Rembrandt, Rubens, Tiziano), se inspiró en Géricault y Delacroix y expuso sus primeras obras de 1848. A lo largo de su carrera realizará más de mil pinturas. Además de sus obras maestras (*Entierro en Ornans, El taller delpintor , El origen del mundo*), Courbet pintó los paisajes de Franco Condado y Normandía, escenas de caza, retratos (Héctor Berlioz, Charles Baudelaire) y autorretratos. Tras la supresión de la Comuna de París, es condenado a seis meses de prisión. Cuando fue acusado en 1873 de haber participado en la destrucción de la Colonne Vendôme, huyó a Suiza, donde murió empobrecido.

Gustave Courbet

Gustave Courbet (1819-1877) foi republicano e membro da Comuna de Paris em 1871 e tornou-se politicamente activo. Como pintor, em 1850, ele se voltou contra o academismo, defendendo uma arte realista que provocou escândalos. Aos 20 anos, Courbet, que veio de uma classe média, mudou-se para Paris. Lá copiou os mestres do Louvre (Rembrandt, Rubens, Ticiano), foi inspirado por Géricault e Delacroix e expôs suas primeiras obras de 1848. Ao longo de sua carreira, ele vai produzir mais de mil pinturas. Além de suas obras-primas (*Um Funeral em Ornans, O Estúdio do Artista, A Origem do Mundo*), Courbet pintou as paisagens de Franche-Comté e Normandia, cenas de caça, retratos (Hector Berlioz, Charles Baudelaire) e auto-retratos. Após a supressão da Comuna de Paris, é condenado a seis meses de prisão. Quando foi acusado em 1873 de ter participado na destruição do Colonne Vendôme, fugiu para a Suíça, onde morreu empobrecido.

Gustave Courbet

Als republikein en lid van de Parijse Commune van 1871 was Gustave Courbet (1819-1877) politiek actief. Als schilder keerde hij zich in 1850 tegen het academisme door te pleiten voor een provocerende realistische kunst. Op 20-jarige leeftijd verhuisde de uit de middenklasse afkomstige Courbet naar Parijs. Daar kopieerde hij de meesters van het Louvre (Rembrandt, Rubens, Titiaan), liet hij zich inspireren door Géricault en Delacroix en exposeerde hij vanaf 1848 zijn eerste werken. In de loop van zijn carrière zou hij meer dan duizend schilderijen maken. Naast zijn meesterwerken (*Een begrafenis in Ornans, Het atelier van de schilder, De oorsprong van de wereld*) schilderde Courbet de landschappen van de Franche-Comté en Normandië, jachttaferelen, portretten (Hector Berlioz, Charles Baudelaire) en zelfportretten. Na het neerslaan van de Parijse Commune werd hij veroordeeld tot zes maanden gevangenisstraf. Toen hij in 1873 werd beschuldigd van deelname aan de vernieling van de Colonne Vendôme, vluchtte hij naar Zwitserland, waar hij verarmd stierf.

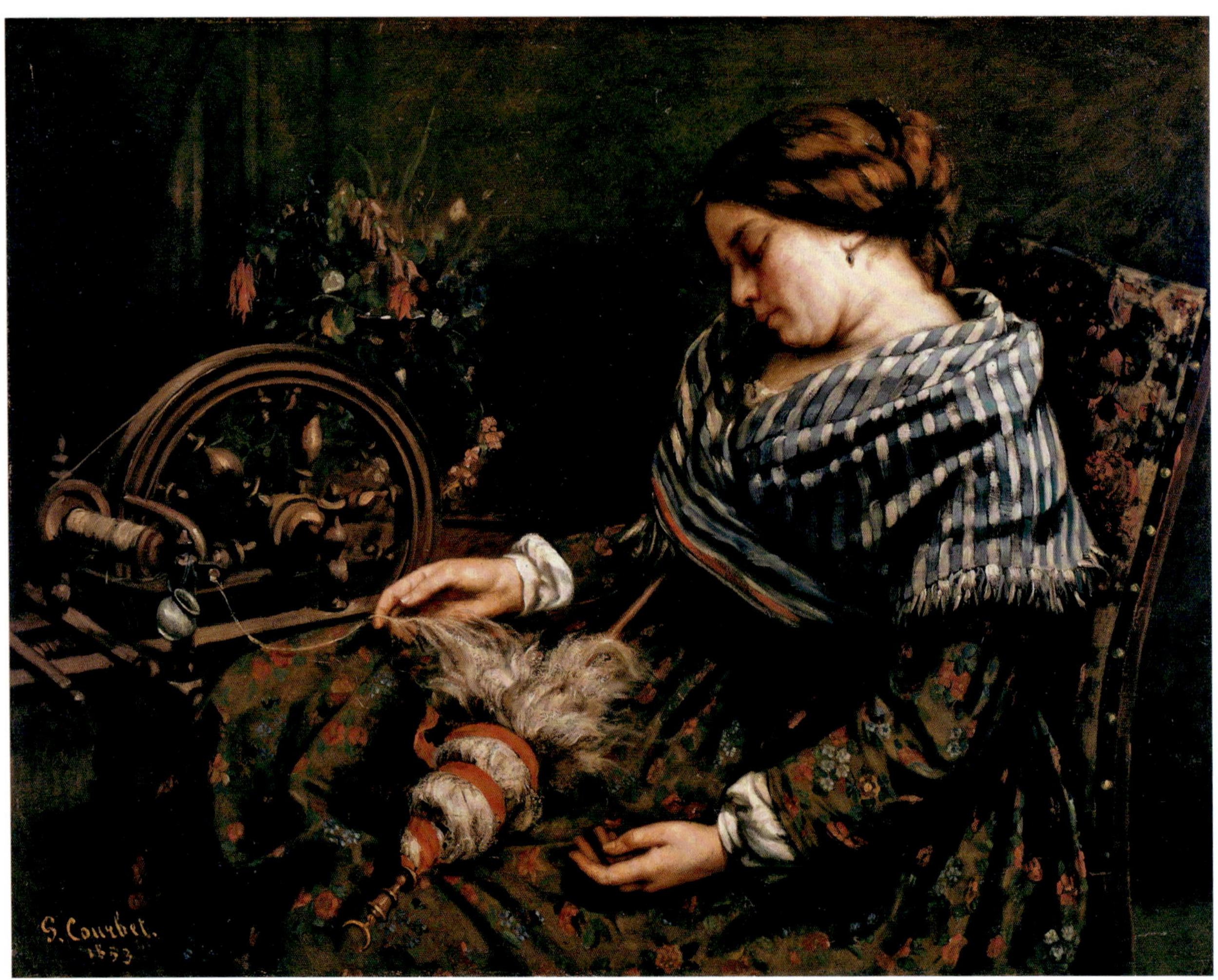

The Sleeping Spinner

La Fileuse endormie

Schlafende Spinnerin

La hilandera durmiente

Roda Adormecida

De slapende spinster

GUSTAVE COURBET (1819-1877)

1853, 91 × 116 cm, Musée Fabre, Montpellier

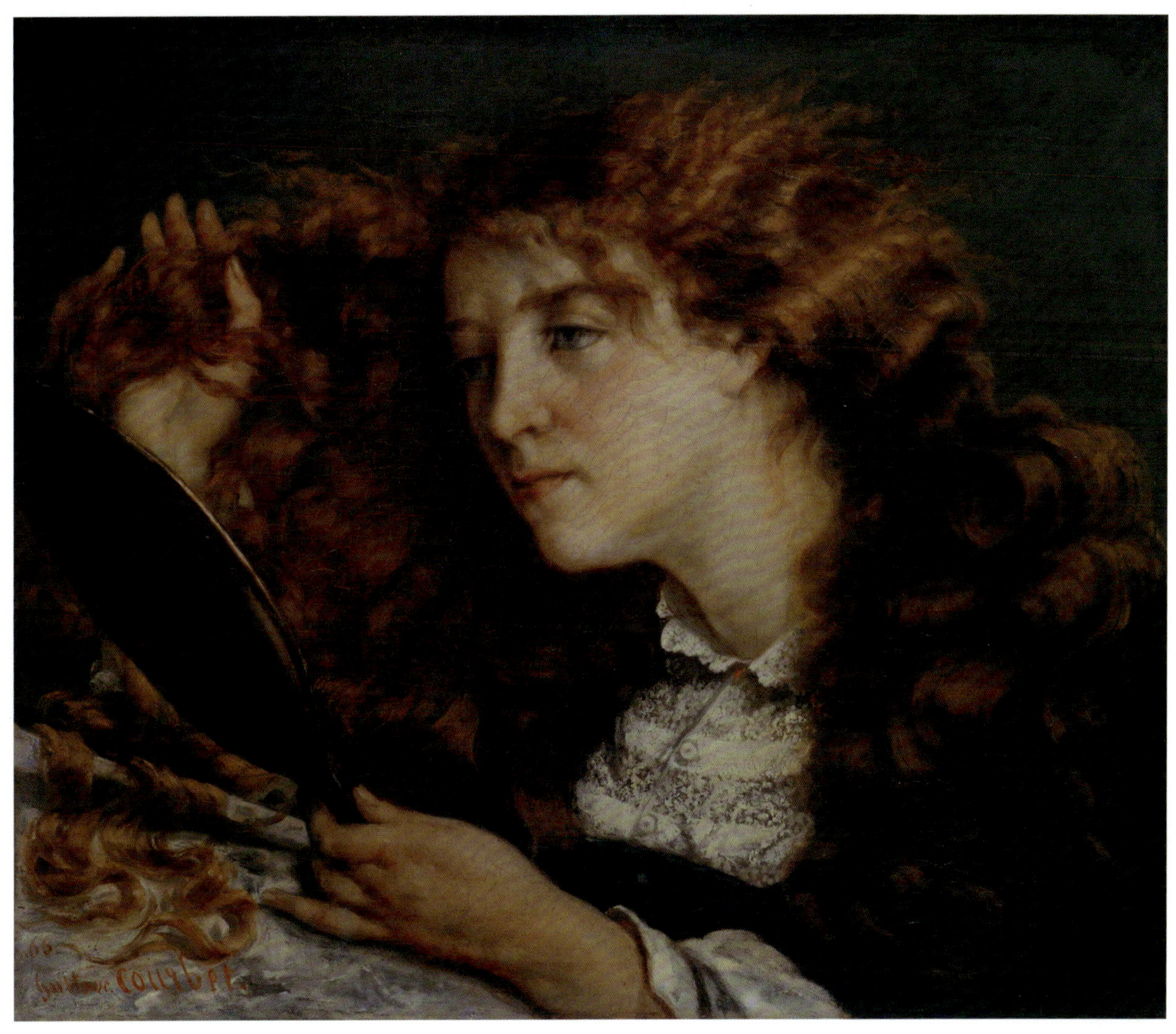

Jo, the beautiful Irishwoman

Jo, la belle Irlandaise

Jo, die schöne Irin

Jo, la bella irlandesa

Jo, a bela Irishwoman

Jo, de mooie Ierse

GUSTAVE COURBET (1819-1877)

1865/66, Oil on canvas/Huile sur toile,
55,9 × 66 cm,
Metropolitan Museum of Art, New York

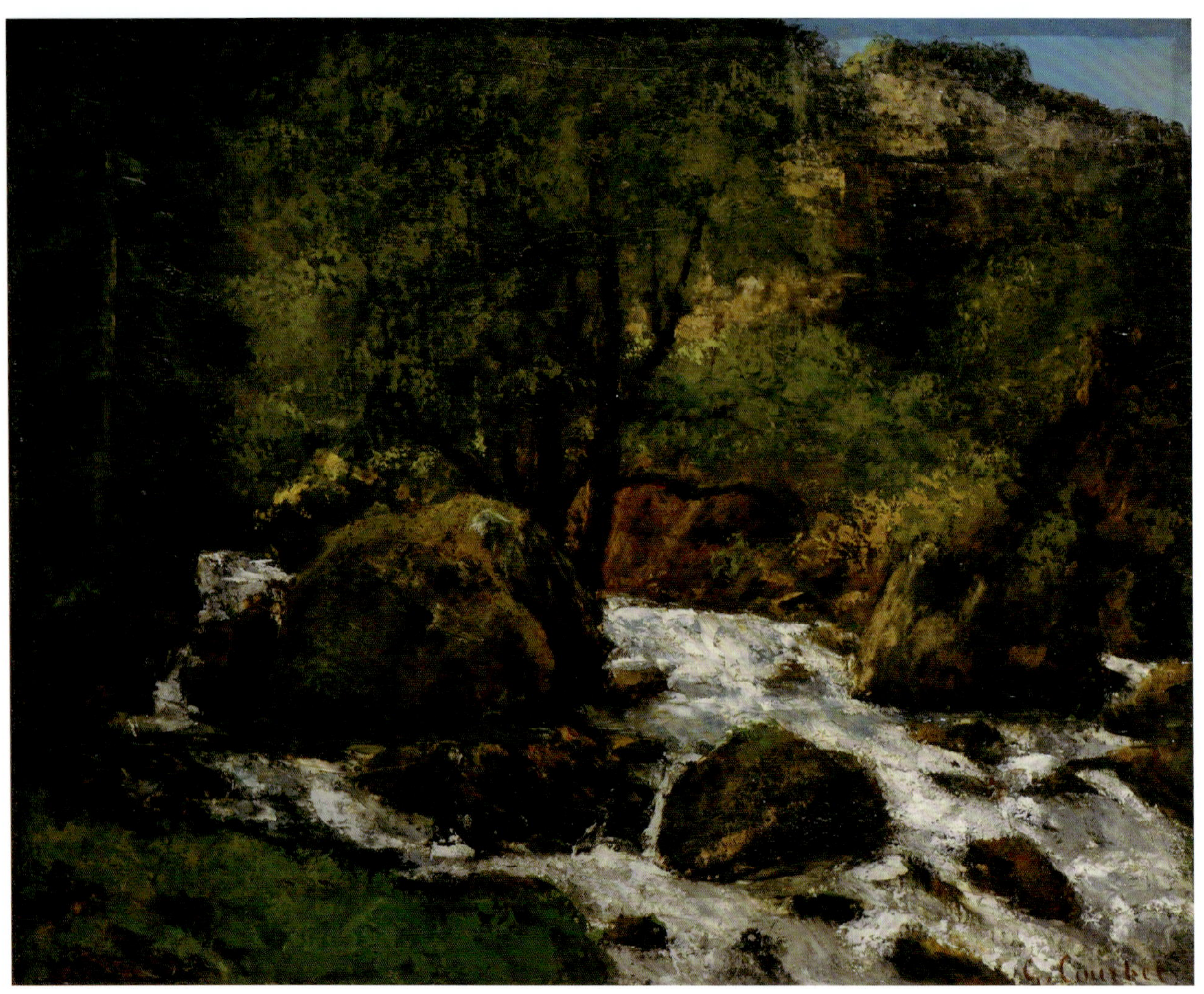

A Brook in the Forest

Un ruisseau dans la forêt, Jura

Ein Bach im Wald des Jura

Un arroyo en el bosque del Jura

Um riacho na floresta do Jura

Een beek in het bos van de Jura

GUSTAVE COURBET (1819-1877)
c. 1865, Oil on canvas/Huile sur toile,
59,9 × 74 cm, National Gallery, Oslo

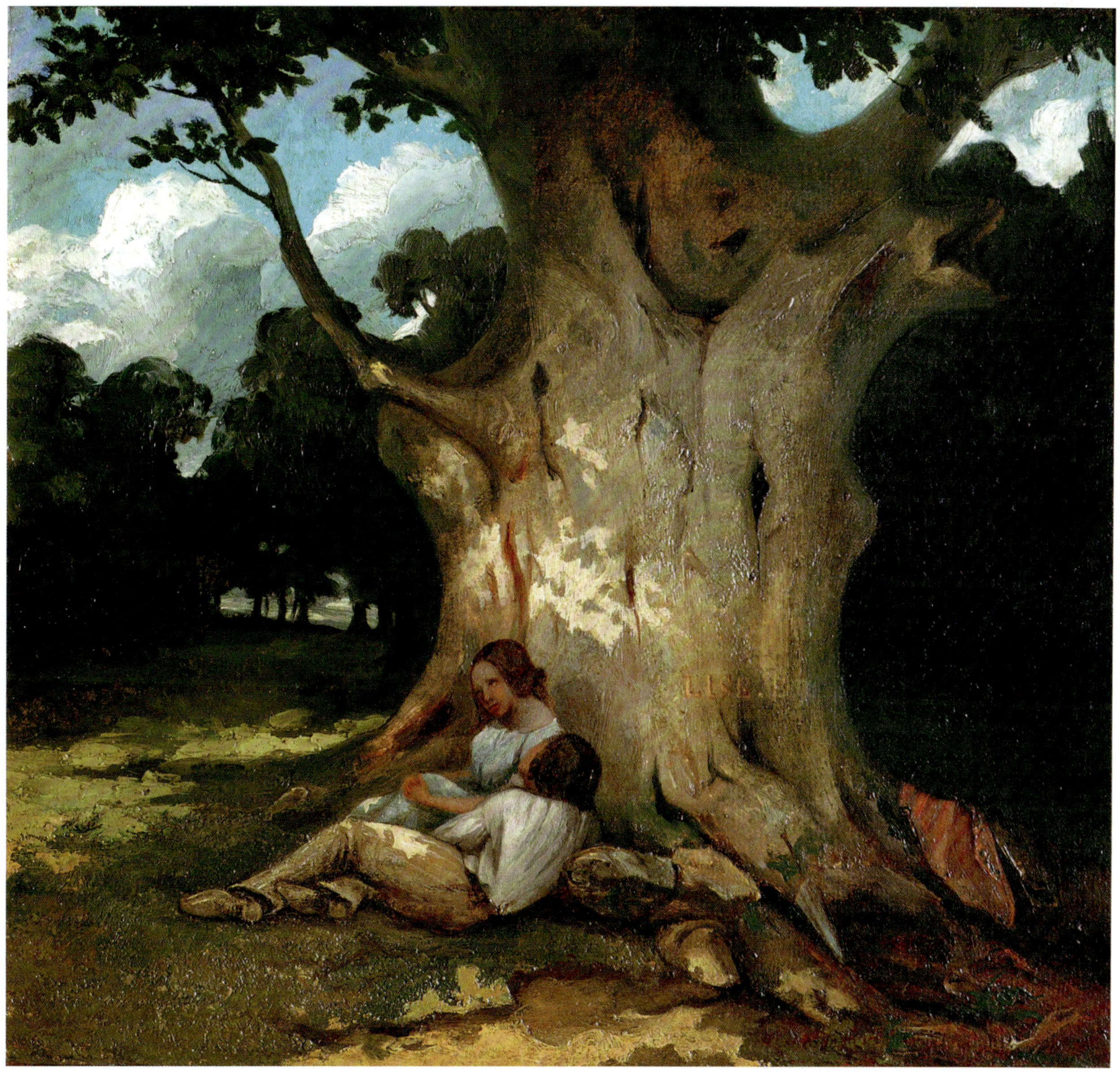

The Large Oak

Le Gros Chêne

GUSTAVE COURBET (1819-1877)
1843, Oil on canvas/Huile sur toile, 29,2 × 32,3 cm, Private collection

Die große Eiche

El gran roble

O Grande Carvalho

De grote eik

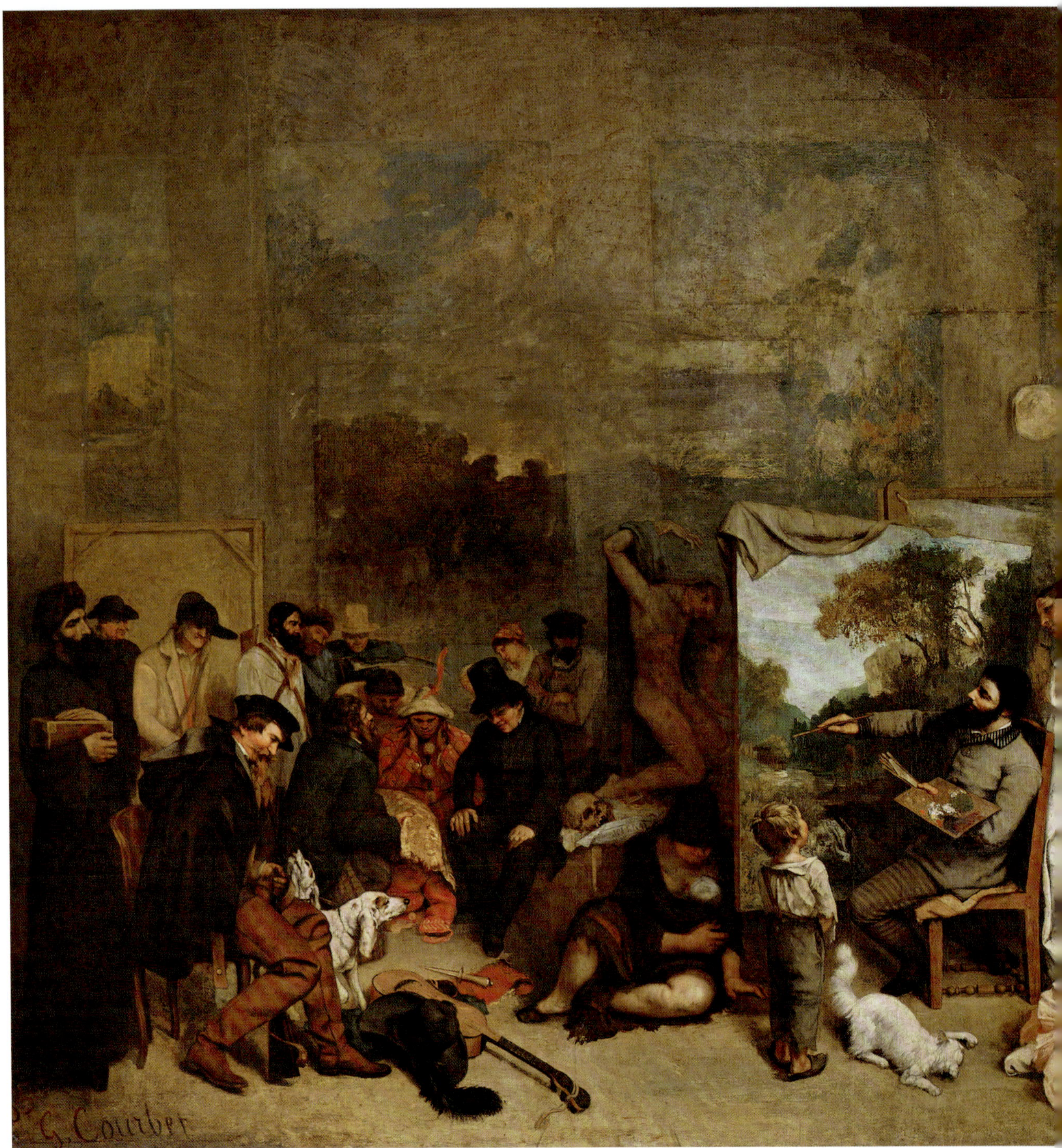
G. Courbet

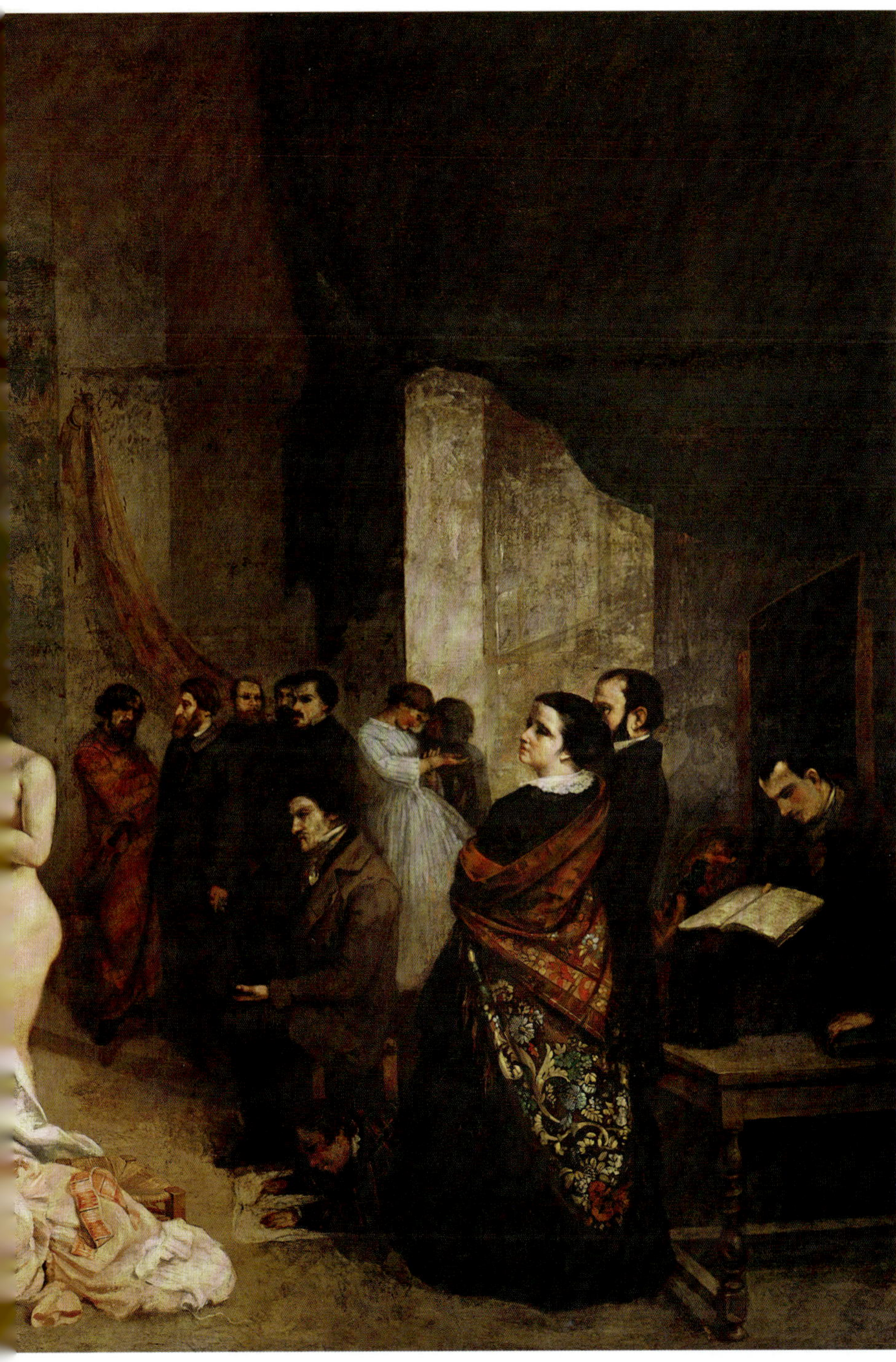

The Studio of the Painter

The painting, which was rejected by the Salon in 1855, goes far beyond classical depictions of an artist at work. The Republican Courbet created an uncompromising portrait of the society of his time.

L'Atelier du peintre

Refusé à l'Exposition universelle de 1855, ce tableau va bien au-delà du thème classique de l'artiste au travail. Républicain convaincu, Courbet dresse un portrait sans concession de la société de son temps.

Das Atelier des Künstlers

Das 1855 vom Salon abgelehnte Gemälde geht weit über klassische Darstellungen eines Künstlers bei der Arbeit hinaus. Der Republikaner Courbet schuf ein kompromissloses Porträt der Gesellschaft seiner Zeit.

El taller del artista

La pintura, que fue rechazada por el Salón en 1855, va mucho más allá de las representaciones clásicas de un artista trabajando. El republicano Courbet creó un retrato inflexible de la sociedad de su tiempo.

O estúdio do artista

A pintura, que foi rejeitada pelo Salão em 1855, vai muito além das representações clássicas de um artista em obra. O Republicano Courbet criou um retrato intransigente da sociedade do seu tempo.

Het atelier van de schilder

Dit schilderij, dat in 1855 door de Salon werd afgewezen, gaat veel verder dan de klassieke afbeelding van een schilder aan het werk. De republikeinse Courbet schilderde een compromisloos portret van de maatschappij van zijn tijd.

GUSTAVE COURBET (1819-1877)

1855, Oil on canvas/Huile sur toile, 361 × 598 cm, Musée d'Orsay, Paris

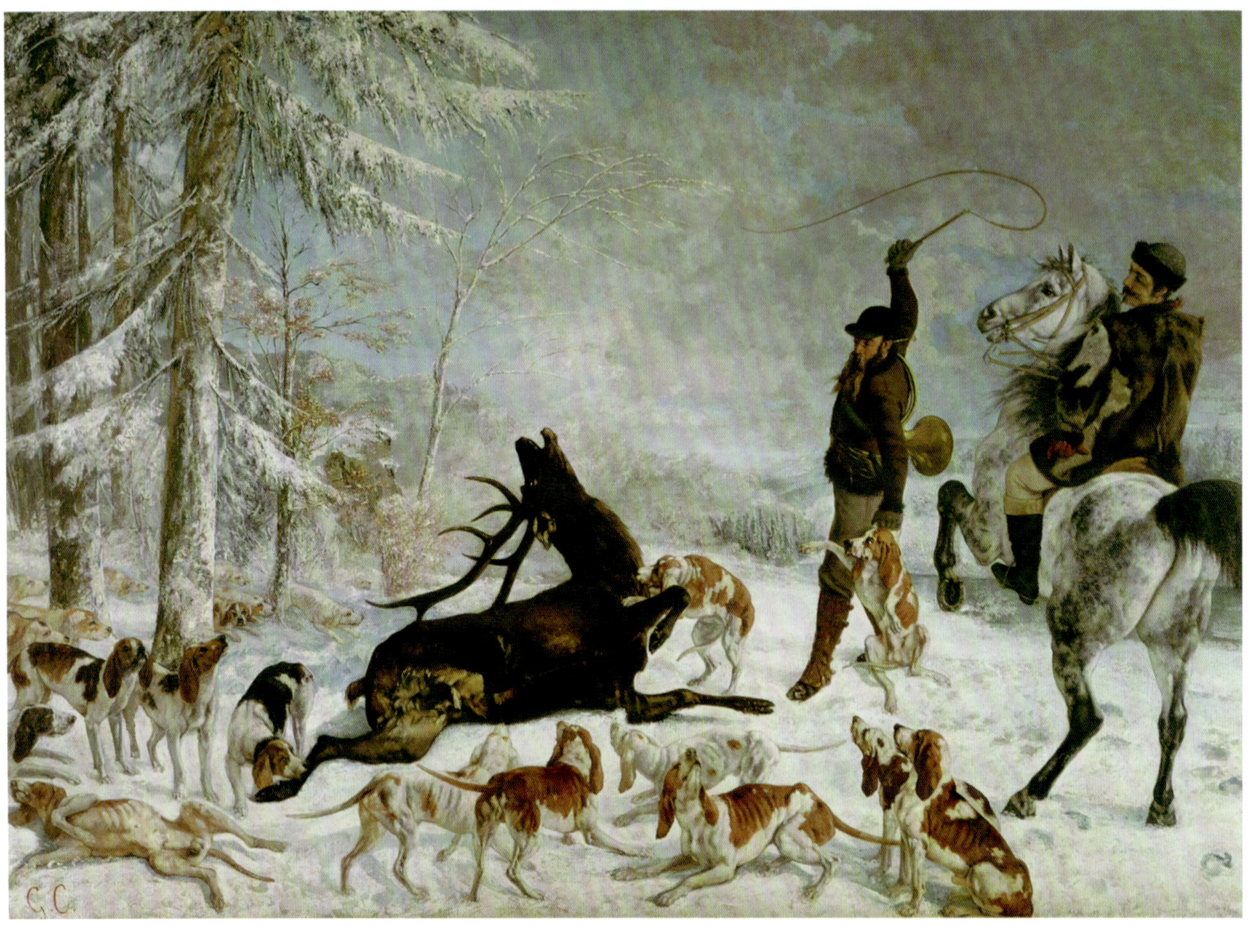

The Death of the Deer

L'Hallali du cerf

Hirschjagd im Winter

Caza de ciervo en invierno

Caça ao veado no inverno

Hertenjacht in de winter

GUSTAVE COURBET (1819-1877)
1867, Oil on canvas/Huile sur toile, 355 × 505 cm,
Musée des Beaux-Arts et d'Archéologie, Besançon

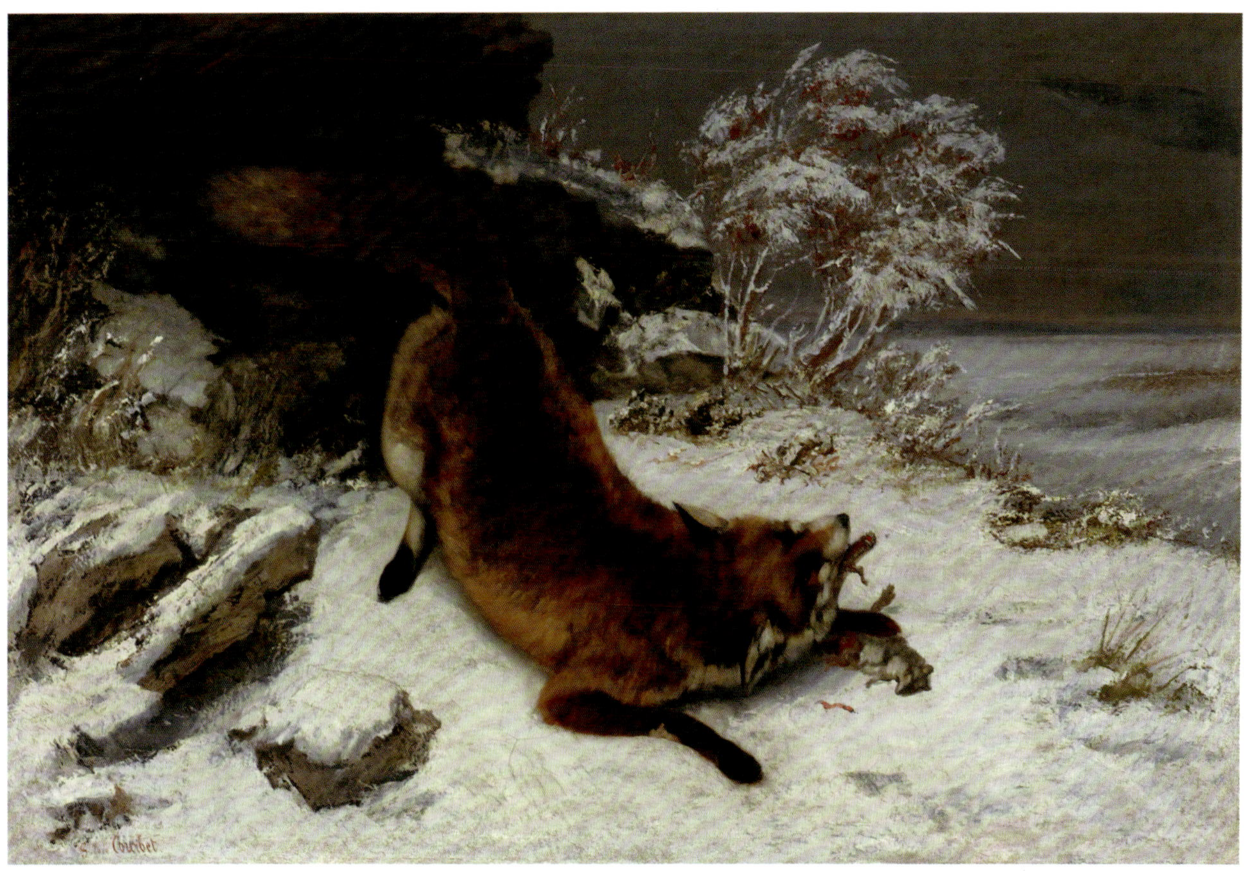

The Fox in the Snow

The hunting enthusiast Courbet painted more than 130 paintings, which often show surrealistic hunting scenes. Deer, roe deer or foxes seem to have been inserted into the landscape by the artist without a context.

Le Renard dans la neige

Passionné de chasse, Courbet a peint plus de cent trente tableaux sur le sujet. S'en dégage souvent une impression surréelle. Cerfs, chevreuils ou renards semblent avoir été « plaqués » sur le paysage.

Fuchs im Schnee

Der jagdbegeisterte Courbet malte mehr als 130 Gemälde, die oft surrealistische Jagdszenen zeigen. Hirsche, Rehe oder Füchse wirken, als wäre sie vom Künstler zusammenhanglos in die Landschaft eingefügt worden.

Zorro en la nieve

Apasionado por la caza, Courbet ha pintado más de ciento treinta cuadros sobre el tema. A menudo da una impresión surrealista. Ciervos, corzos o zorros parecen haber quedado «atrapados» en el paisaje.

Raposa na neve

O entusiasta da caça Courbet pintou mais de 130 pinturas, que muitas vezes mostram cenas de caça surrealistas. Veados, corços ou raposas parecem ter sido inseridos na paisagem pelo artista sem ligação.

Vos in de sneeuw

De jachtliefhebber Courbet maakte meer dan 130 schilderijen, waarop vaak surrealistische jachttaferelen te zien zijn. Herten, reeën of vossen lijken door de schilder zonder enige samenhang in het landschap te zijn ingevoegd.

GUSTAVE COURBET (1819-1877)

1860, Oil on canvas/Huile sur toile, 85,7 × 127,9 cm, Dallas Museum of Art, Dallas

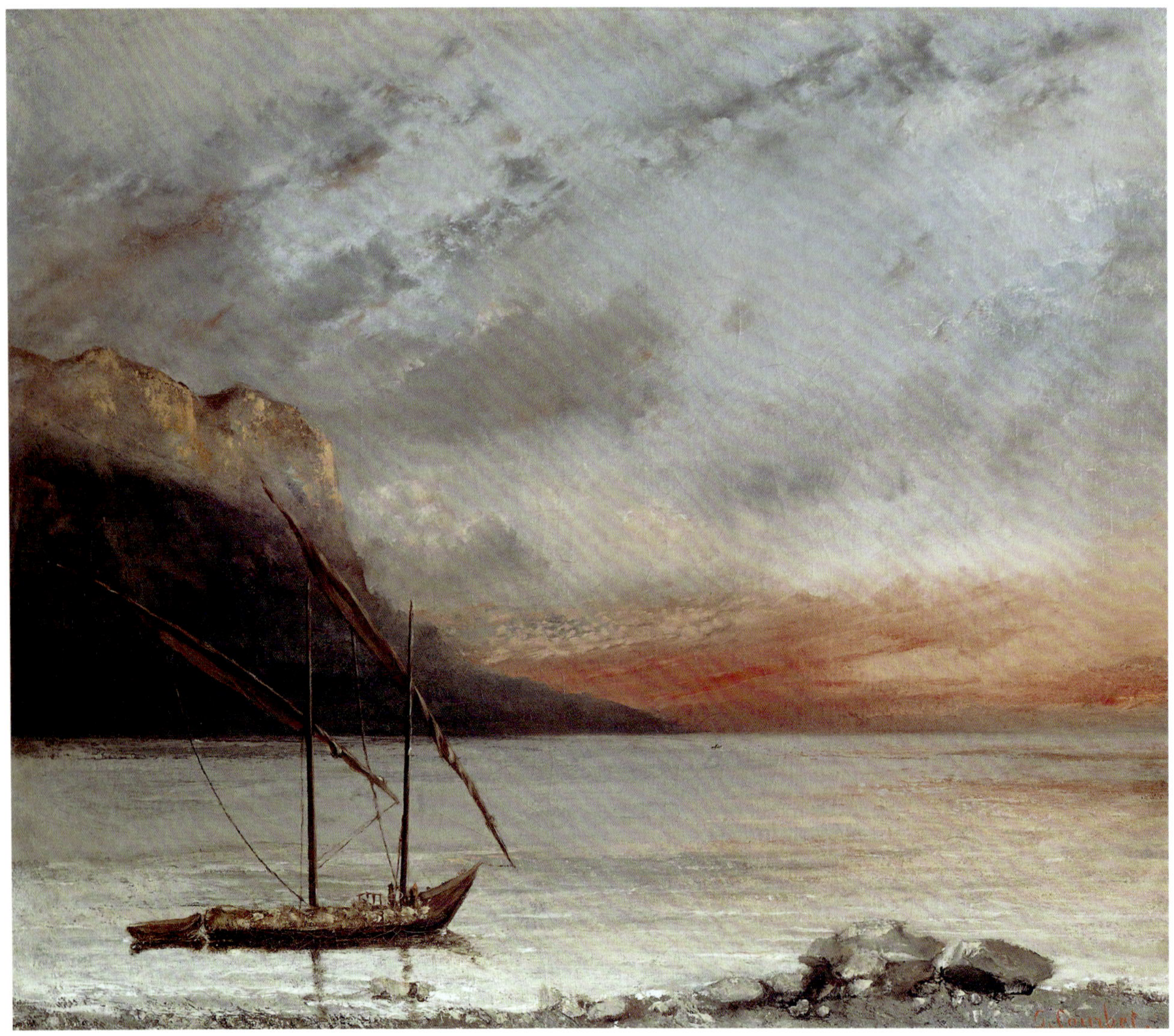

Sunset over Lake Geneva

Coucher de soleil sur le lac Léman

Sonnenuntergang über dem Genfersee

Atardecer sobre el Lago Lemán

Pôr-do-sol sobre o Lago Genebra

Zonsondergang boven het Meer van Genève

GUSTAVE COURBET (1819-1877)

1874, Oil on canvas/Huile sur toile, Musée Jenisch, Vevey

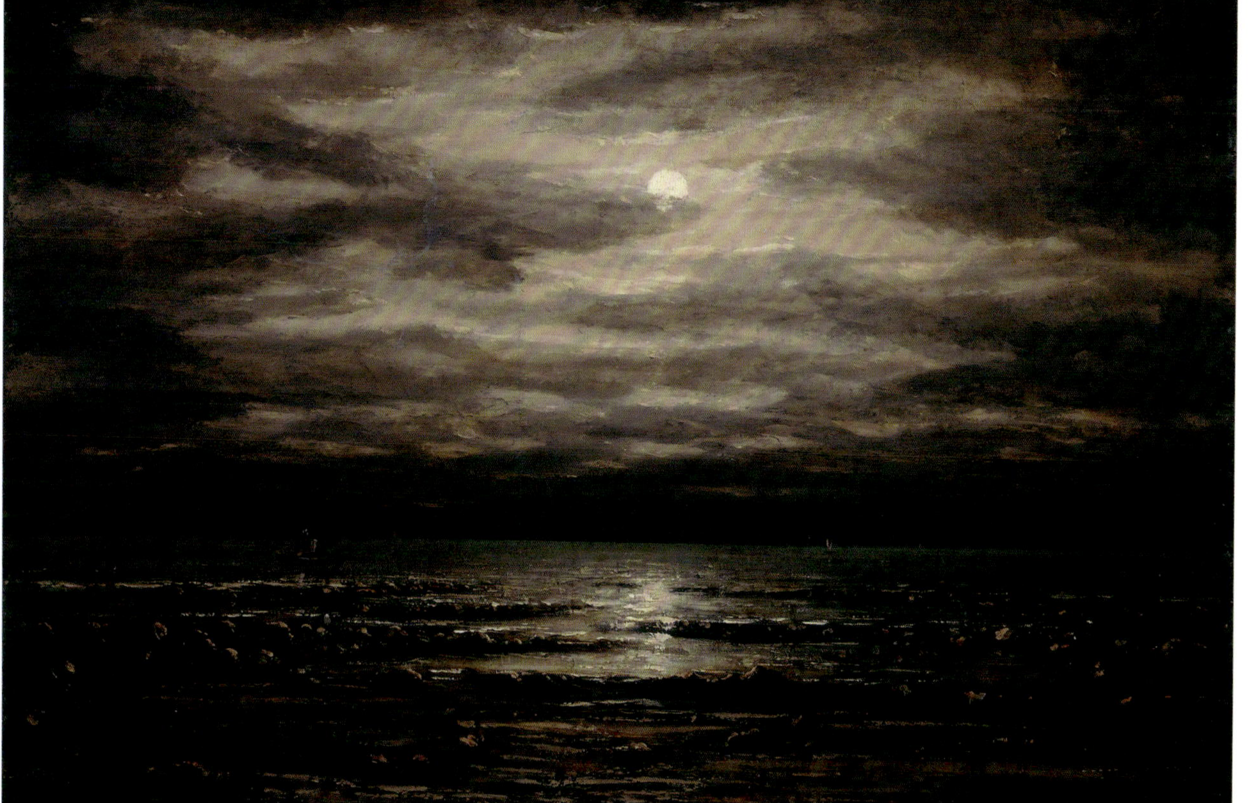

Lake Geneva at dusk near Bon-Pont

Le Lac Léman au crépuscule devant Bon-Port

Der Genfersee bei Bon-Pont in der Dämmerung

Lago Lemán al atardecer cerca de Bon-Pont

Lago Genebra ao anoitecer perto de Bon-Pont

Schemering boven het Meer van Genève in Bon-Port

GUSTAVE COURBET (1819-1877)

1876, Oil on canvas/Huile sur toile, 60 × 81 cm, Private collection

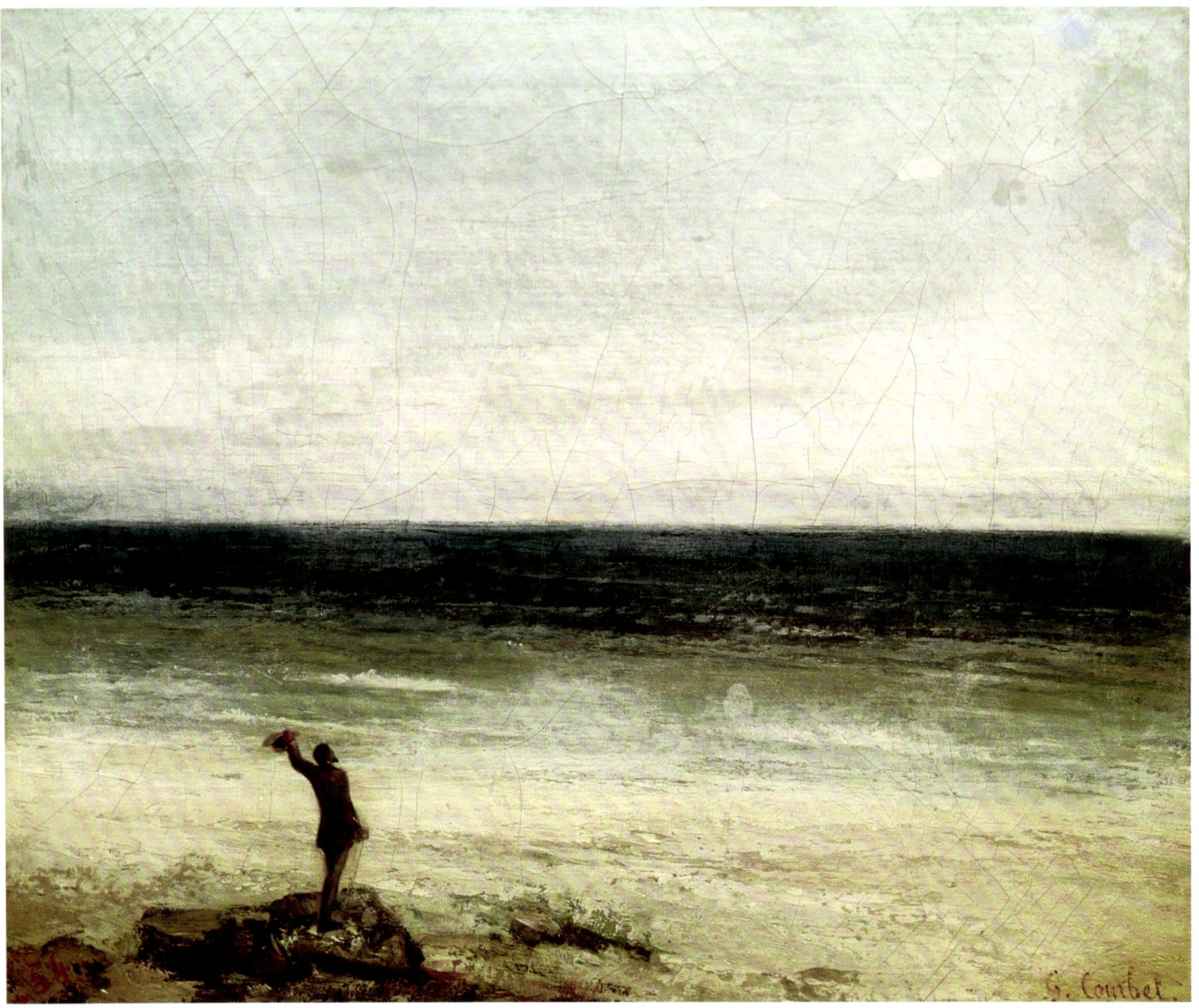

The Beach at Palavas

Le Bord de mer à Palavas

Die Küste bei Palavas

La costa de Palavas

A costa em Palavas

De kust bij Palavas

GUSTAVE COURBET (1819-1877)

1854, Oil on canvas/Huile sur toile, 37 × 46 cm,
Musée Fabre, Montpellier

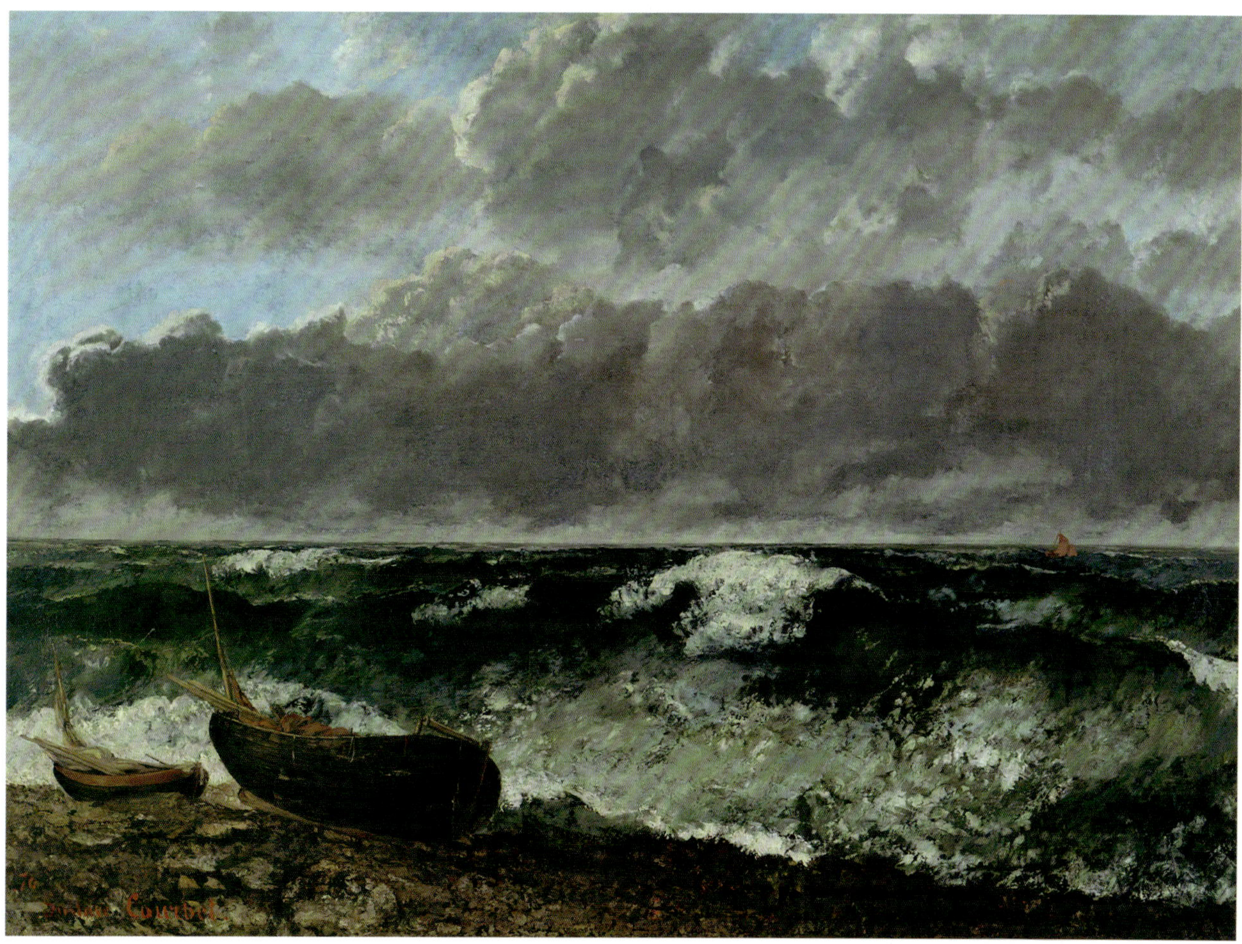

Stormy Sea *or* The Wave

Courbet worked out the power of the forces of nature by applying the paint thickly with a spatula. In the summer of 1869 he stayed in Étretat, where he studied the waves, the cliffs and the sky.

La Mer orageuse *ou* La Vague

D'une peinture épaisse, apposée au couteau, Courbet évoque la puissance de la mer. Durant l'été 1869, il est à Étretat où il multiplie les études de vagues, de falaises de craie et de ciels changeants.

Stürmische See *oder* Die Welle

Indem er mit einem Spachtel die Farbe dick aufträgt, arbeitet Courbet die Kraft der Naturgewalten heraus. Im Sommer 1869 hält er sich in Étretat auf, wo er die Wellen, die Klippen und den Himmel studiert.

Mar tormentoso *o* La Ola

Con una pintura espesa, aplicada con un cuchillo, Courbet evoca la fuerza del mar. En el verano de 1869, estuvo en Etretat donde multiplicó sus estudios de olas, acantilados de tiza y cielos cambiantes.

Mar Tempestuoso *ou* a Onda

Courbet calcula o poder das forças da natureza aplicando a tinta espalmadamente com uma espátula. No verão de 1869 ficou em Étretat, onde estudou as ondas, as falésias e o céu.

Stormachtige zee *of* De golf

Courbet werkte de kracht van de kracht van het natuurgeweld uit door de verf dik aan te brengen met een spatel. In de zomer van 1869 verbleef hij in Étretat, waar hij de golven, kliffen en luchten bestudeerde.

GUSTAVE COURBET (1819-1877)

1870, Oil on canvas/Huile sur toile, 117 × 160,5 cm, Musée d'Orsay, Paris

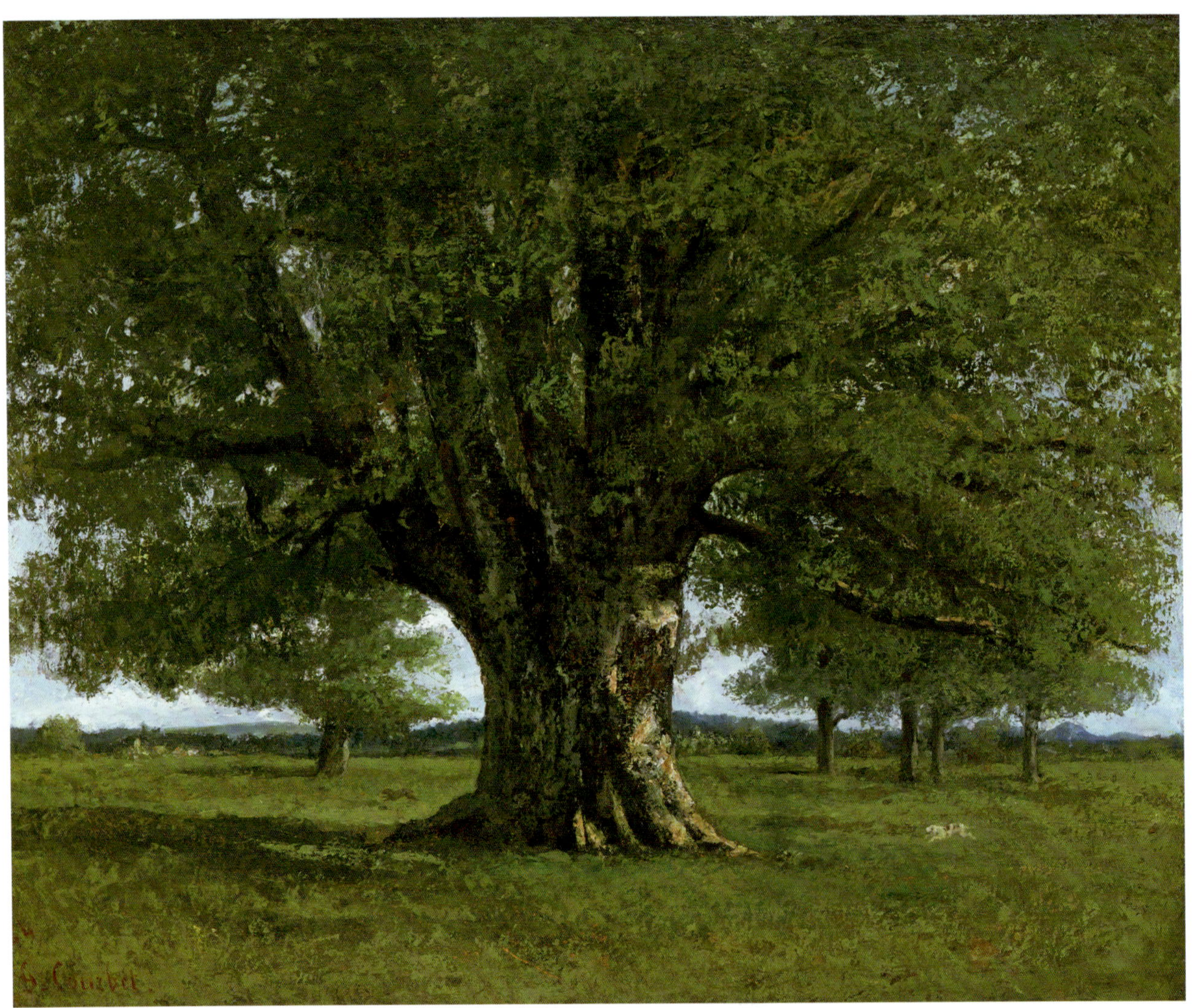

The Flagey Oak Tree

Le Chêne de Flagey

Die Eiche von Flagey

El roble de Flagey

O carvalho de Flagey

De eik van Flagey

GUSTAVE COURBET (1819-1877)
1864, Oil on canvas/Huile sur toile, 89 × 110 cm,
Musée-Maison natale Gustave Courbet, Ornans

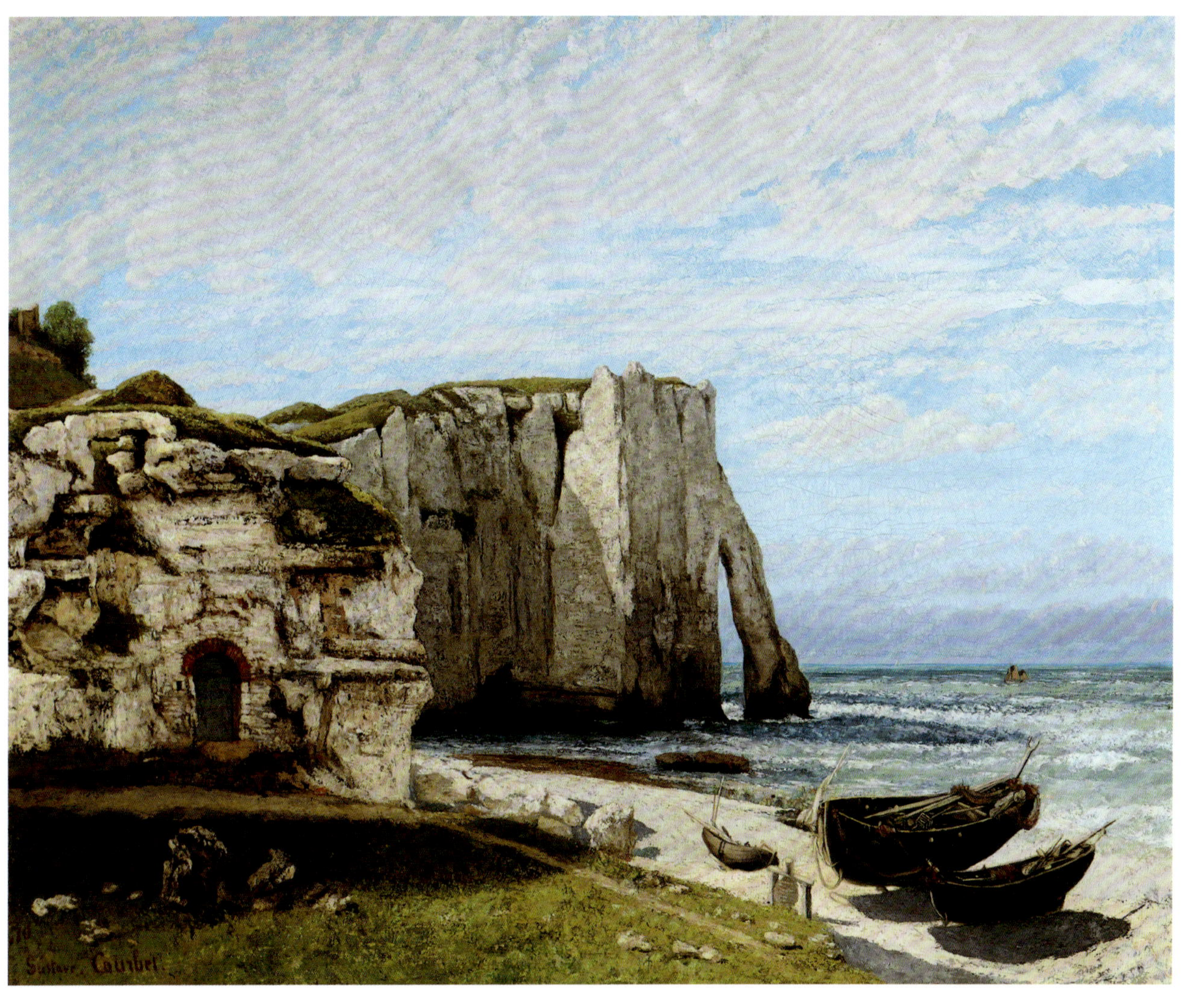

The Cliffs at Étretat after the Storm

Les Falaises d'Étretat après l'orage

Die Klippen von Étretat nach dem Sturm

Los acantilados de Étretat después de la tormenta

As falésias de Étretat após a tempestade

De kliffen van Étretat na de storm

GUSTAVE COURBET (1819-1877)

1870, Oil on canvas/Huile sur toile, 133 × 162 cm,
Musée d'Orsay, Paris

123

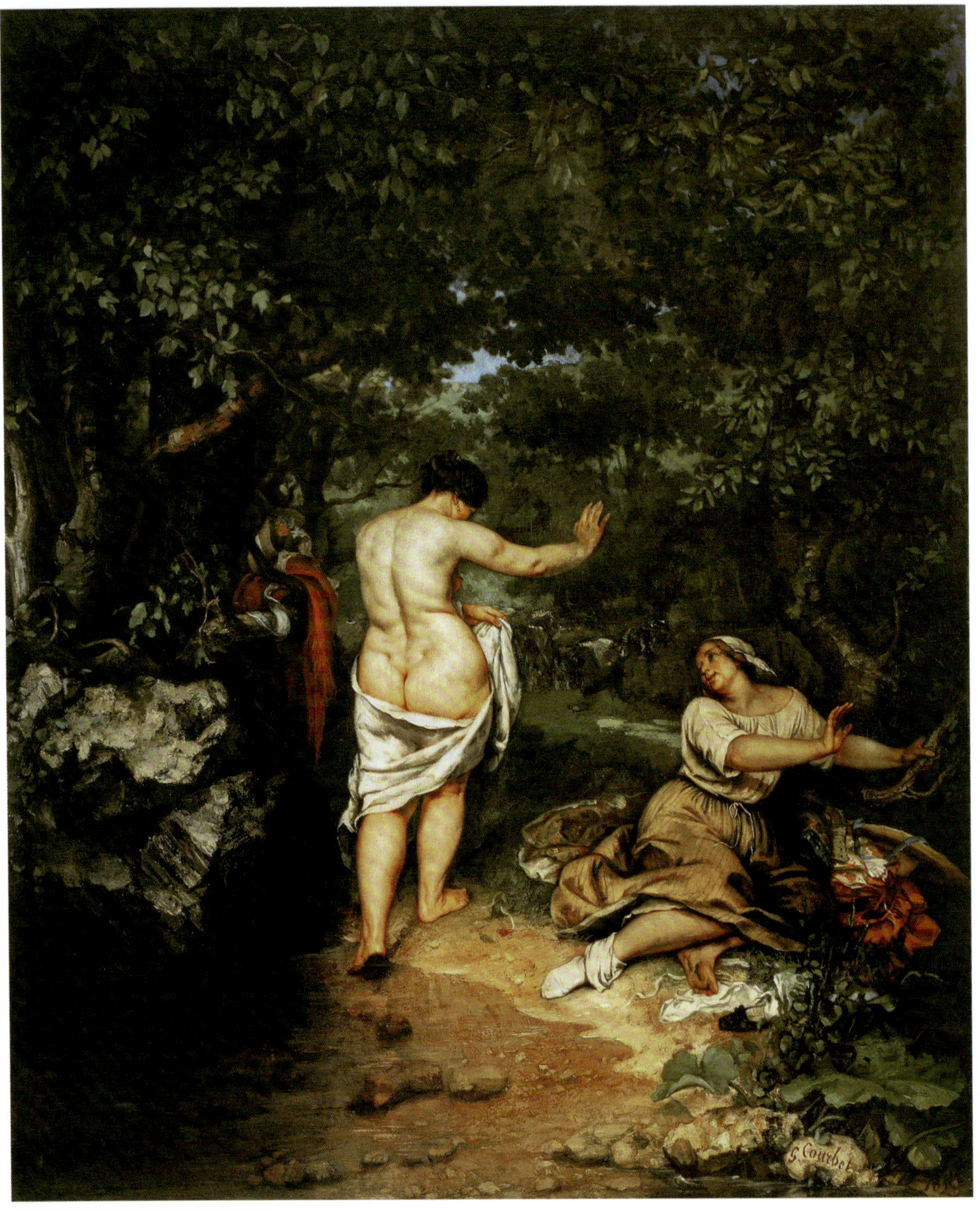

The Bathers

Les Baigneuses

Die Badenden

Los bañistas

Os banhistas

De baadsters

GUSTAVE COURBET
(1819-1877)
1853, Oil on canvas/
Huile sur toile,
227 × 193 cm, Musée
Fabre, Montpellier

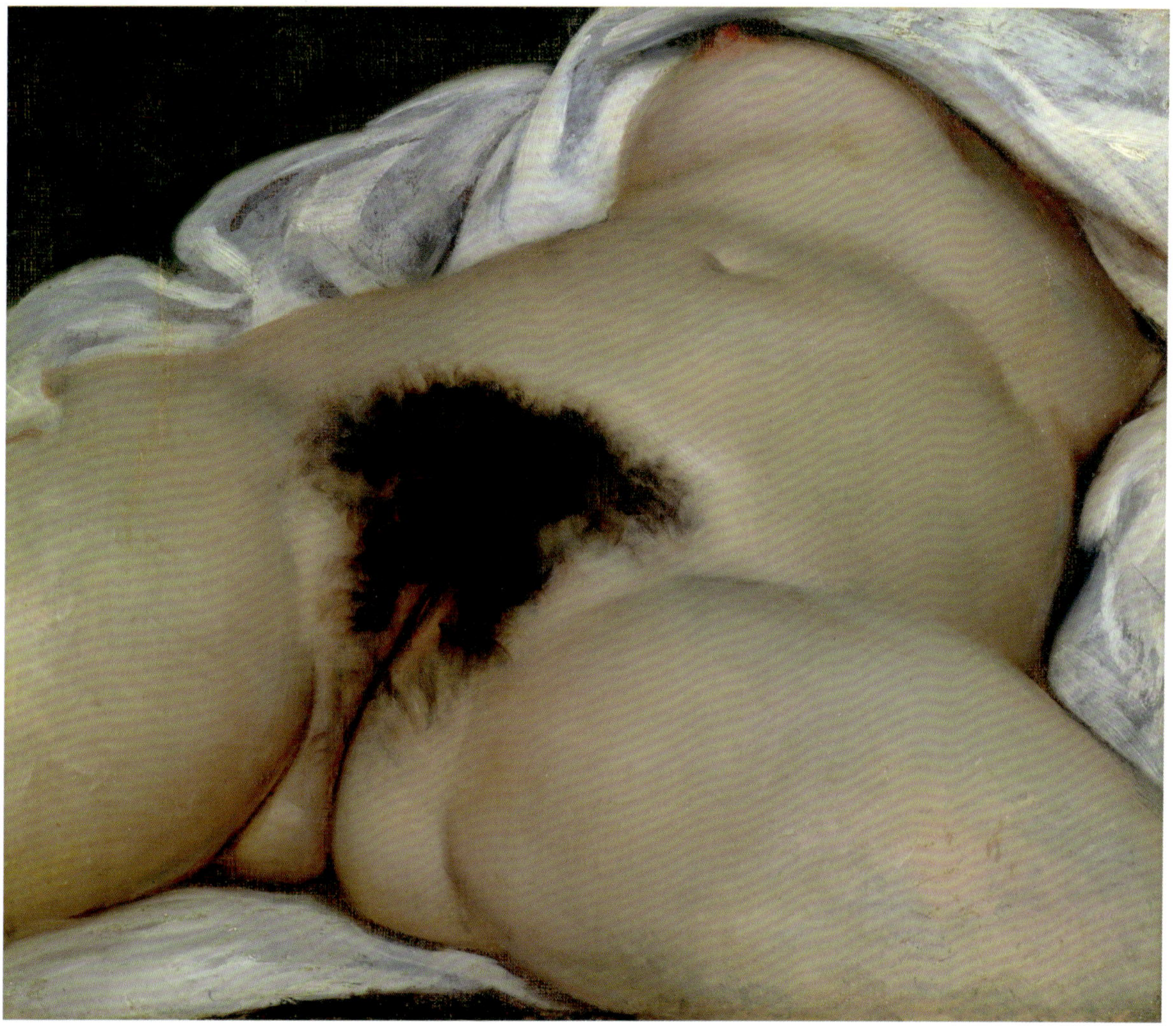

The Origin of the World

Some masterpieces retain their mystical effect to this day. The Origin of the World used to be in the possession of Jacques Lacan. The daring motif and the realistic representation are still fascinating.

L'Origine du monde

Certaines œuvres iconiques ont su garder leur mystère. *L'Origine du monde*, qui a appartenu à Jacques Lacan, continue de fasciner par son audace, sa frontalité, et l'extrême réalisme du traitement du sujet.

Der Ursprung der Welt

Einige Meisterwerke bewahren ihre mystische Wirkung bis heute. Der Ursprung der Welt befand sich zuletzt im Besitz von Jacques Lacan. Immer noch fasziniert das gewagte Motiv und die realistische Darstellung.

El origen del mundo

Algunas obras maestras conservan su efecto místico hasta el día de hoy. El origen del mundo estuvo por última vez en manos de Jacques Lacan. El motivo atrevido y la representación realista siguen siendo fascinantes.

A origem do mundo

Algumas obras-primas mantêm o seu efeito místico até hoje. A origem do mundo foi a última na posse de Jacques Lacan. O motivo ousado e a representação realista ainda são fascinantes.

De oorsprong van de wereld

Sommige meesterwerken behouden tot op heden hun mystieke werking. De oorsprong van de wereld was het laatst in het bezit van Jacques Lacan. Het gedurfde onderwerp en de realistische weergave boeien nog altijd.

GUSTAVE COURBET (1819-1877)

1866, Oil on canvas/Huile sur toile, 46 × 55 cm, Musée d'Orsay, Paris

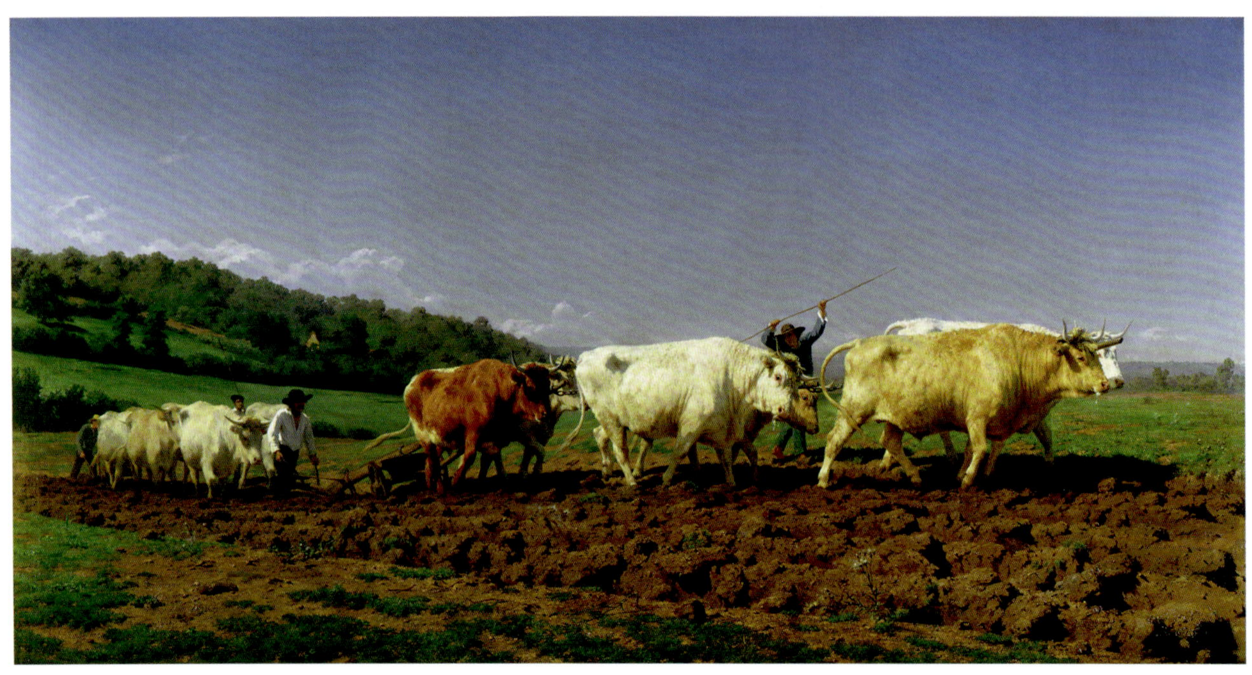

Ploughing in Nievernais

Labourage nivernais *ou* Le Sombrage

Ackerbau in der Nièvre

El arado en Nivernais *o* Le Sombrage

Agricultura em Nièvre

Werk op het land in Nièvre

ROSA BONHEUR (1822-1899)

1849, Oil on canvas/Huile sur toile, 134 × 260 cm, Musée d'Orsay, Paris

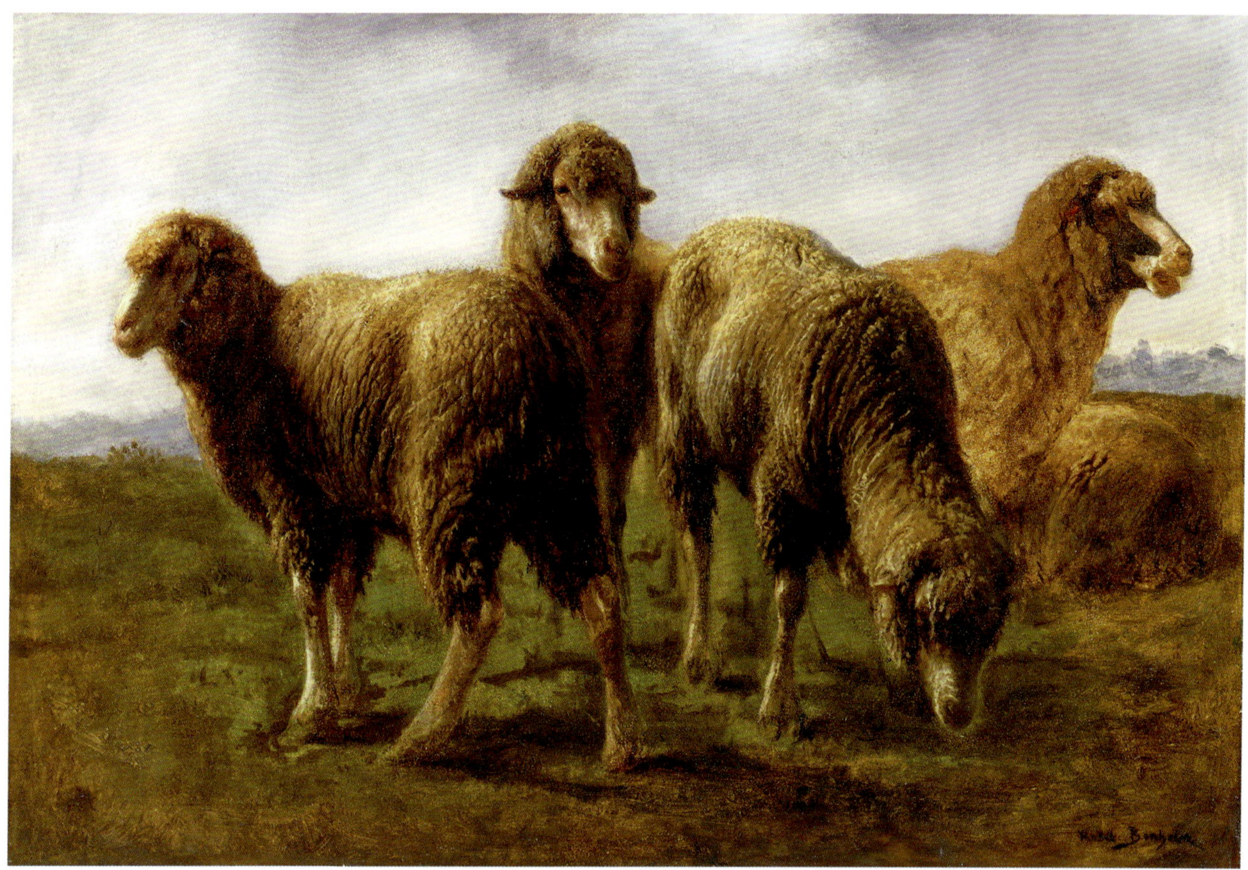

Sheep Grazing in a Meadow

After her death, Rosa Bonheur, who had been highly
regarded during her lifetime, fell into oblivion - animal
painting was no longer fashionable. In her works she
depicted cows, sheep and horses with almost photographic
precision.

Moutons paissant dans un pré

Célèbre de son vivant, Rosa Bonheur est tombée dans l'oubli
à sa mort, la peinture animalière étant passée de mode.
Vaches, moutons, chevaux… sont représentés avec
une précision quasi photographique.

ROSA BONHEUR (1822-1899)

Oil on canvas/Huile sur toile, 36,8 × 53,4 cm, Private collection

Schafe auf einer Weide

Nach ihrem Tod geriet die zu Lebzeiten beachtete Rosa
Bonheur in Vergessenheit – die Tiermalerei war nicht mehr
in Mode. In ihren Werken bildete sie Kühe, Schafe und
Pferde mit fast fotografischer Präzession ab.

Ovejas pastando en el prado

Famosa durante su vida, Rosa Bonheur cayó en el olvido
cuando murió, ya que la pintura animal había quedado
obsoleta. Vacas, ovejas, caballos… están representados con
una precisión casi fotográfica.

Ovelhas num pasto

Após sua morte, Rosa Bonheur, que havia sido notada
durante sua vida, caiu no esquecimento - a pintura animal
não estava mais na moda. Em suas obras ela retratava vacas,
ovelhas e cavalos com precessão quase fotográfica.

Grazende schapen in een wei

Na haar dood raakte de tijdens haar leven wel opgemerkte
Rosa Bonheur in de vergetelheid. Schilderijen van dieren
waren niet meer in de mode. In haar werk beeldde ze koeien,
schapen en paarden met bijna fotografische precisie af.

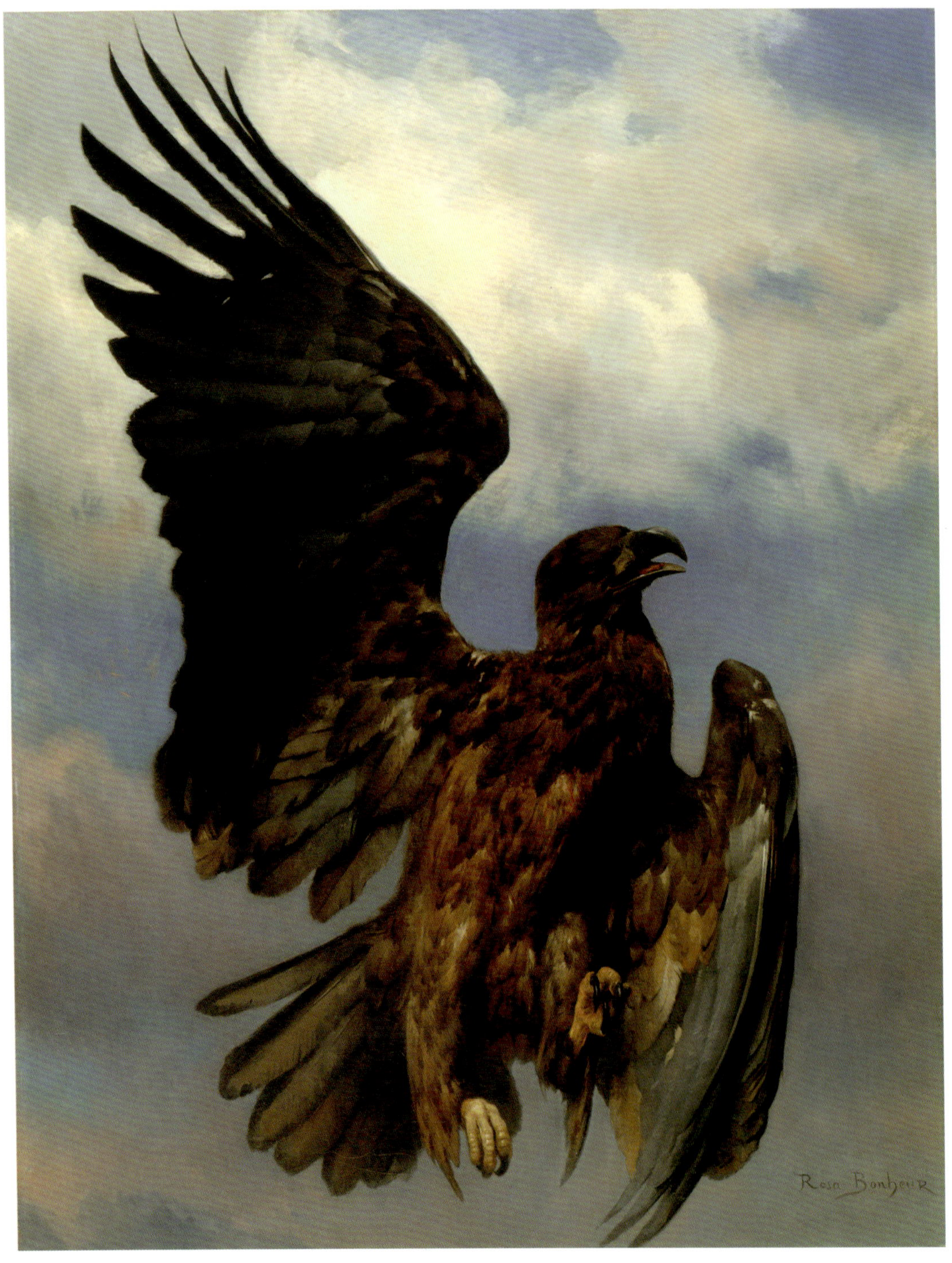

The Wounded Eagle

L'Aigle blessé

Der verwundete Adler

El águila herida

A águia ferida

De gewonde adelaar

ROSA BONHEUR
(1822-1899)
c. 1870, Oil on canvas/
Huile sur toile,
147,6 × 114,6 cm,
Los Angeles County
Museum of Art,
Los Angeles

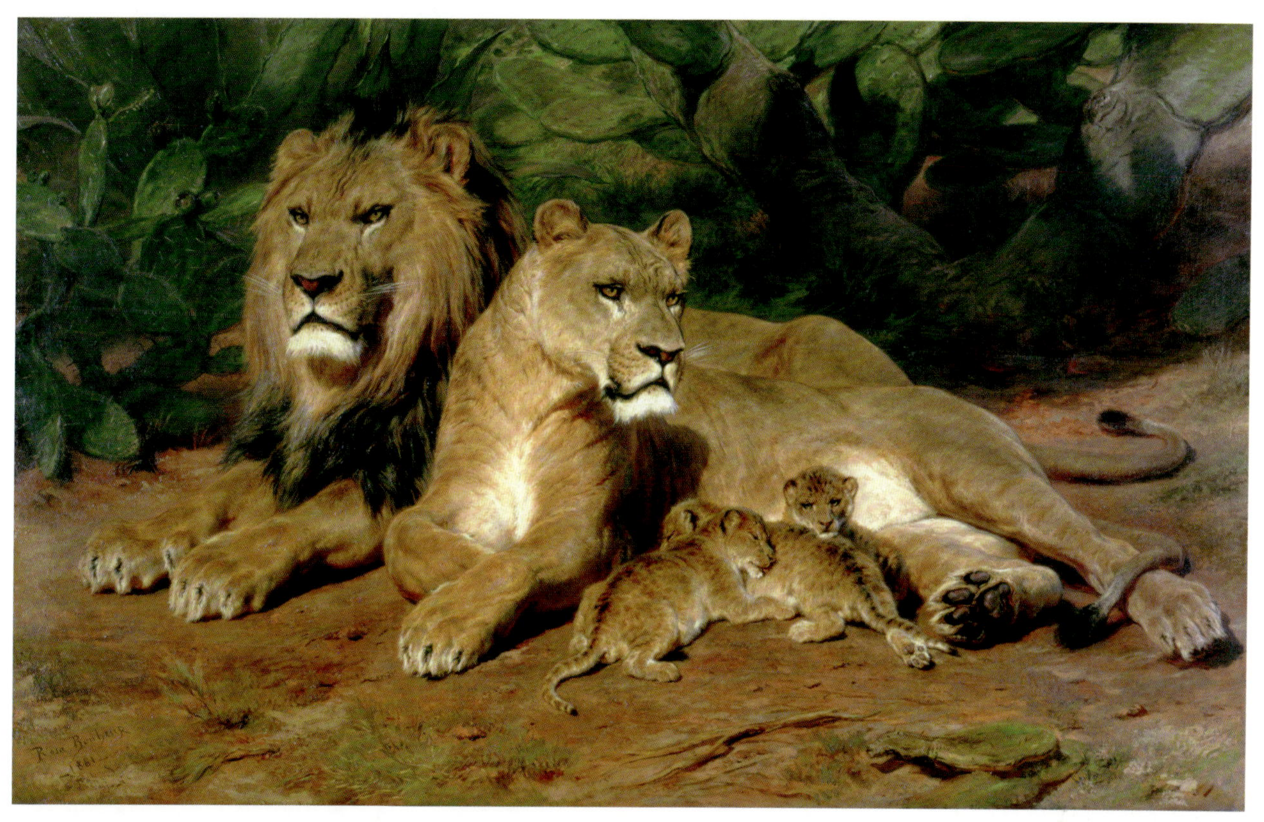

The Lions at Home

Les Lions à la maison

Eine Löwenfamilie

Una familia de leones

Uma família de leões

Een leeuwenfamilie

ROSA BONHEUR (1822-1899)

1881, Oil on canvas/Huile sur toile,
162,3 × 262,3 cm, Hull Museums,
Kingston upon Hull

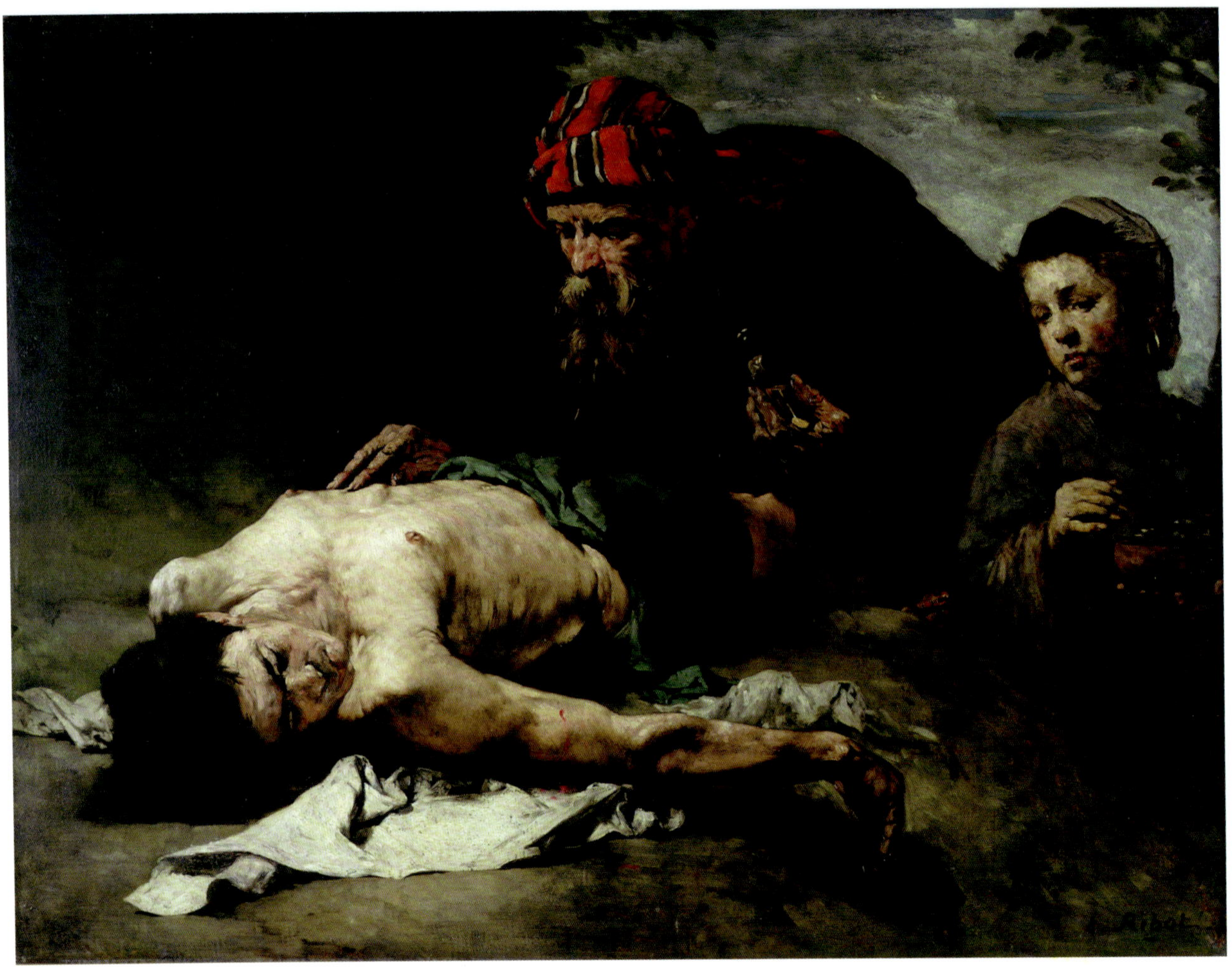

The Good Samaritan

Le Bon Samaritain

Der barmherzige Samariter

El buen samaritano

O Bom Samaritano

De barmhartige Samaritaan

THÉODULE RIBOT (1823-1891)

before 1870, Oil on canvas/
Huile sur toile, 98 × 131 cm,
Musée des Beaux-Arts, Pau

The Three Cooks

Théodule Ribot made a name for himself at the 1861 Salon with his paintings of restaurant kitchens and backyards. In addition to his genre paintings, he also devoted himself to historical and religious motifs..

Les Trois Cuisiniers

Ses toiles d'intérieurs de cuisine et de basse-cour ont permis à Théodule Ribot de se faire connaître au Salon de 1861. Maître de la scène de genre, il a aussi peint des tableaux historiques et religieux.

Die drei Köche

Mit seinen Gemälden von Restaurantküchen und Hinterhöfen machte sich Théodule Ribot auf dem Salon 1861 einen Namen. Neben seinen Genrebildern widmete er sich aber auch historischen und religiösen Motiven.

Los tres chefs

Théodule Ribot se hizo un nombre en el Salón de 1861 con sus pinturas de cocinas de restaurantes y patios traseros. Además de sus pinturas de género, también se dedicó a los motivos históricos y religiosos.

Os três chefs

éodule Ribot ganhou fama no Salão de 1861 com suas pinturas de cozinhas de restaurantes e quintais. Além de suas pinturas de gênero, ele também se dedicou a motivos históricos e religiosos.

De drie koks

Théodule Ribot maakte met zijn schilderijen van restaurantkeukens en binnenplaatsen naam op de Salon van 1861. Naast genrestukken schilderde hij ook historische en religieuze onderwerpen.

THÉODULE RIBOT (1823-1891)

1860-69, Oil on canvas/Huile sur toile,
45,7 × 38,7 cm, Private collection

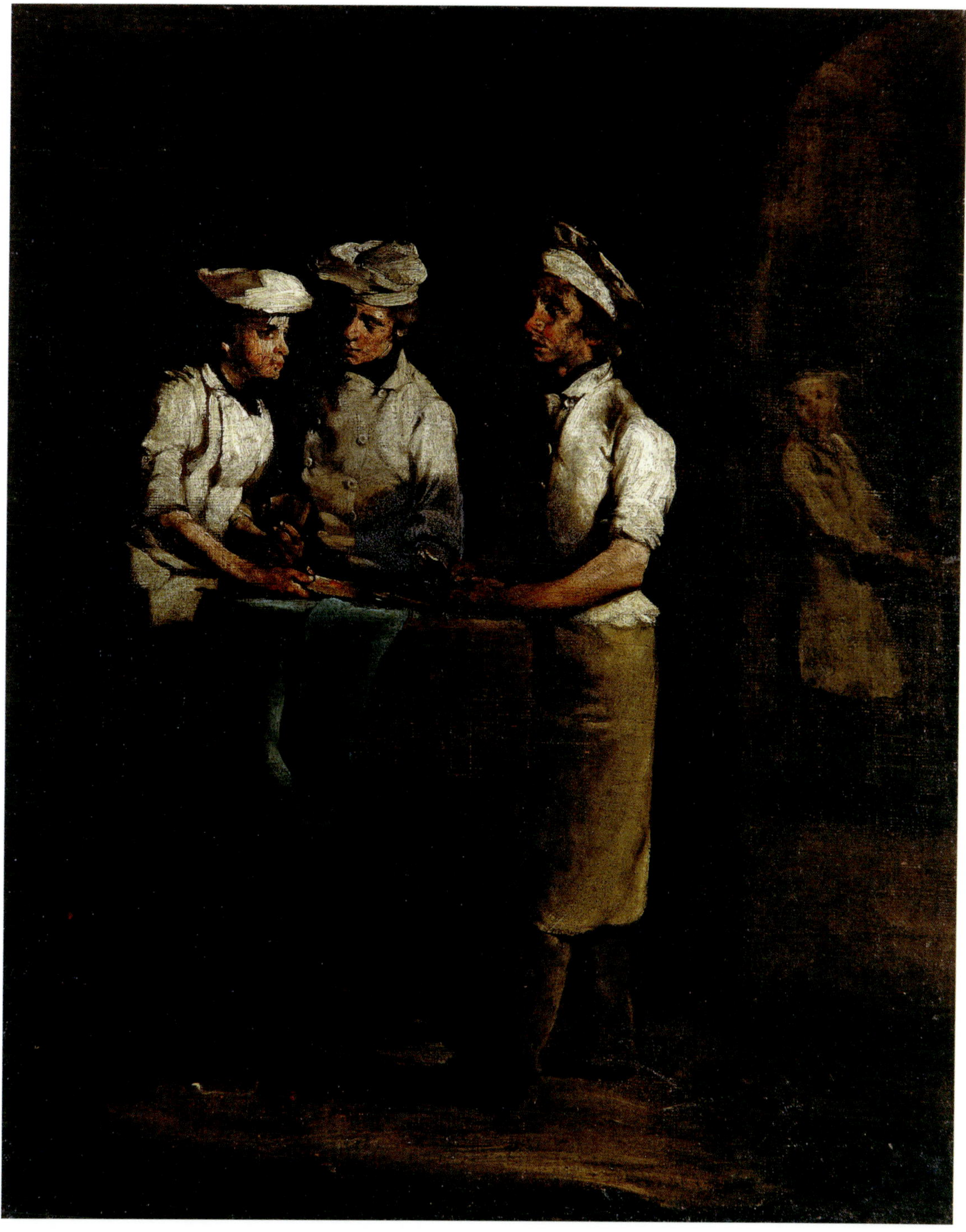

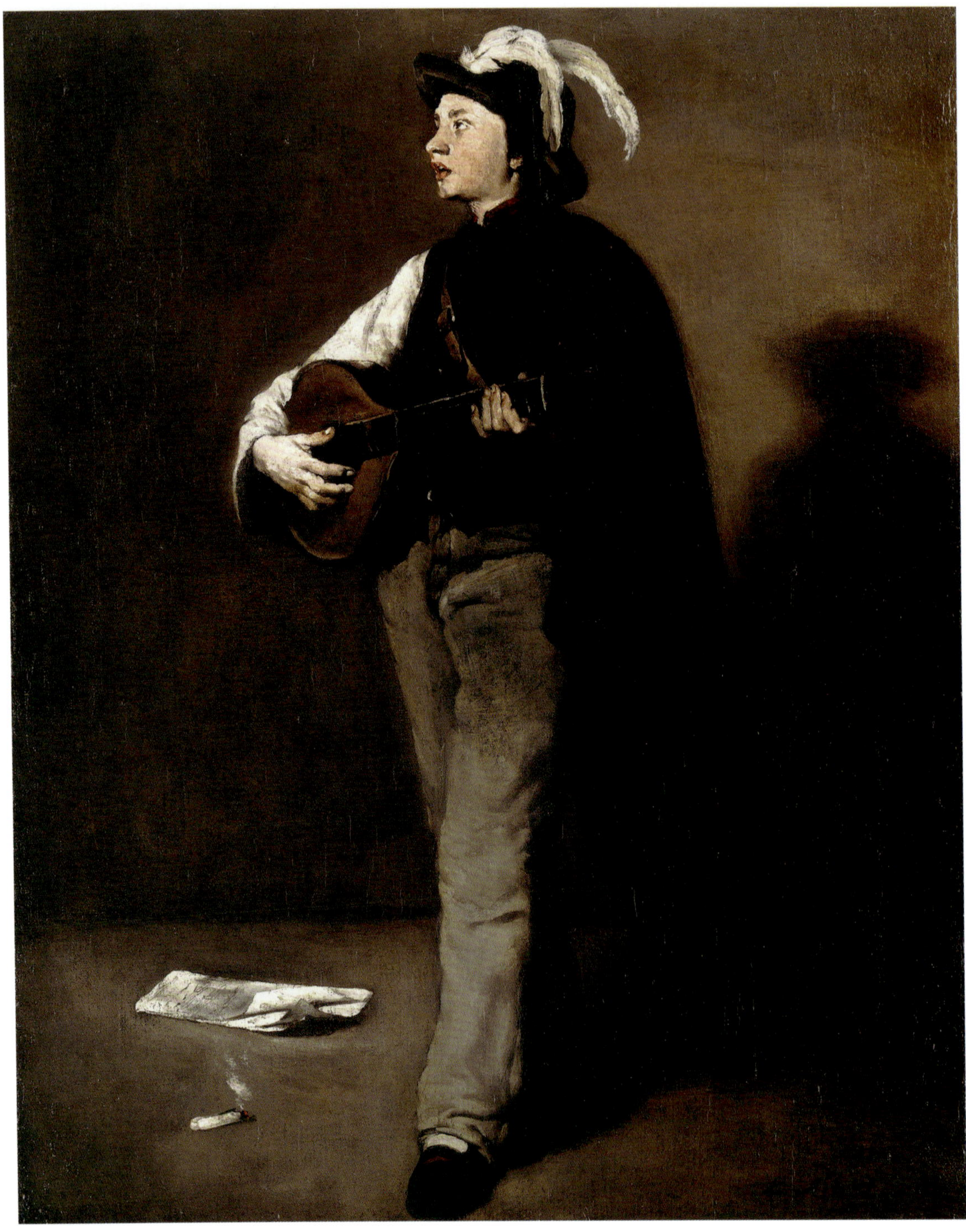

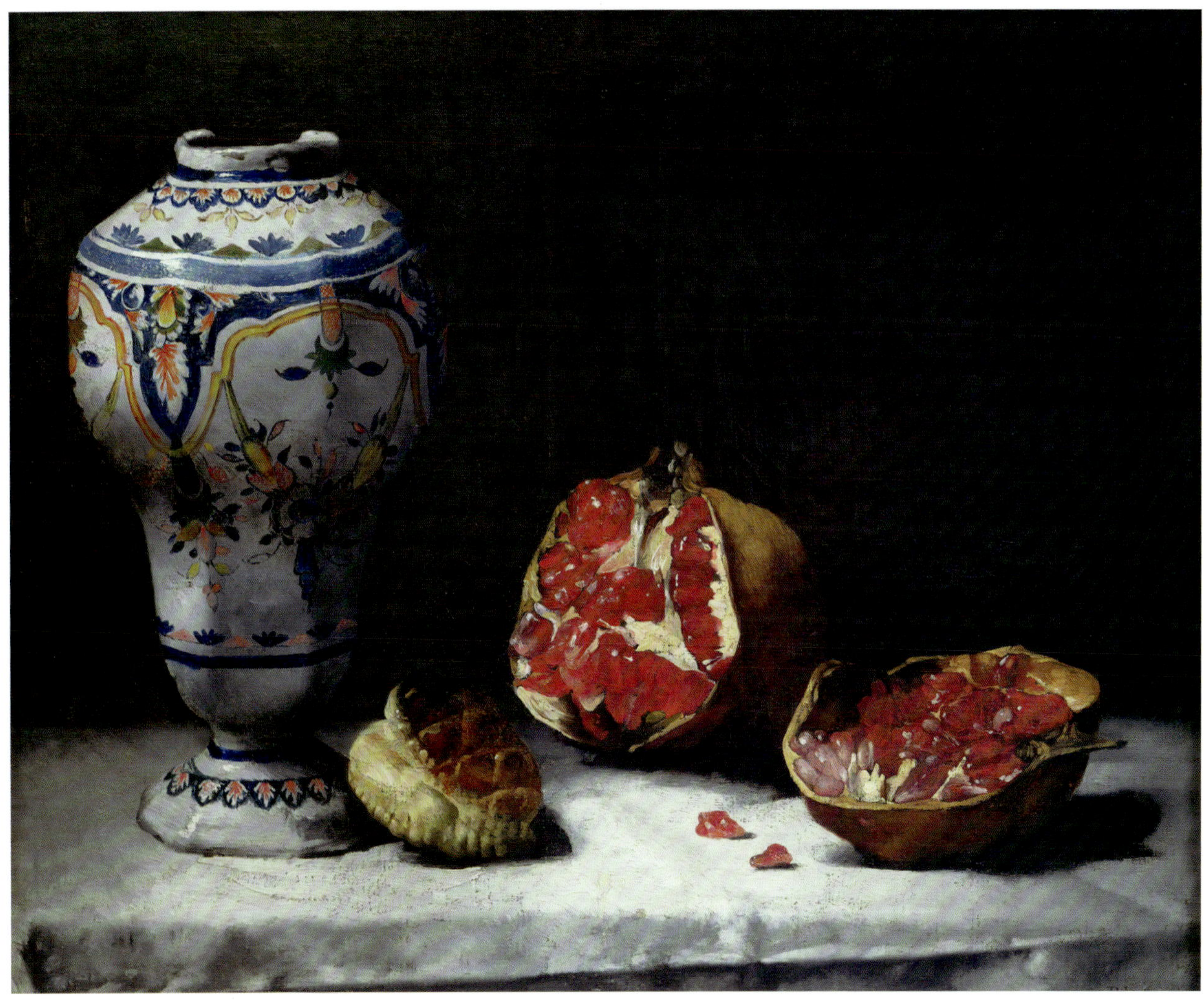

The Mandolin Player

Le Joueur de mandoline

Der Mandolinenspieler

El mandolinero

O Jogador de Bandolim

De mandolinespeler

THÉODULE RIBOT (1823-1891)

1862, Oil on canvas/Huile sur toile,
73 × 59,7 cm, Private collection

Still Life with a Pomegranate

Nature morte à la grenade

Stillleben mit Granatapfel

Naturaleza muerta con granada

Natureza morta com romã

Stilleven met granaatappel

THÉODULE RIBOT (1823-1891)

Oil on canvas/Huile sur toile,
Musée des Beaux-Arts, Arras

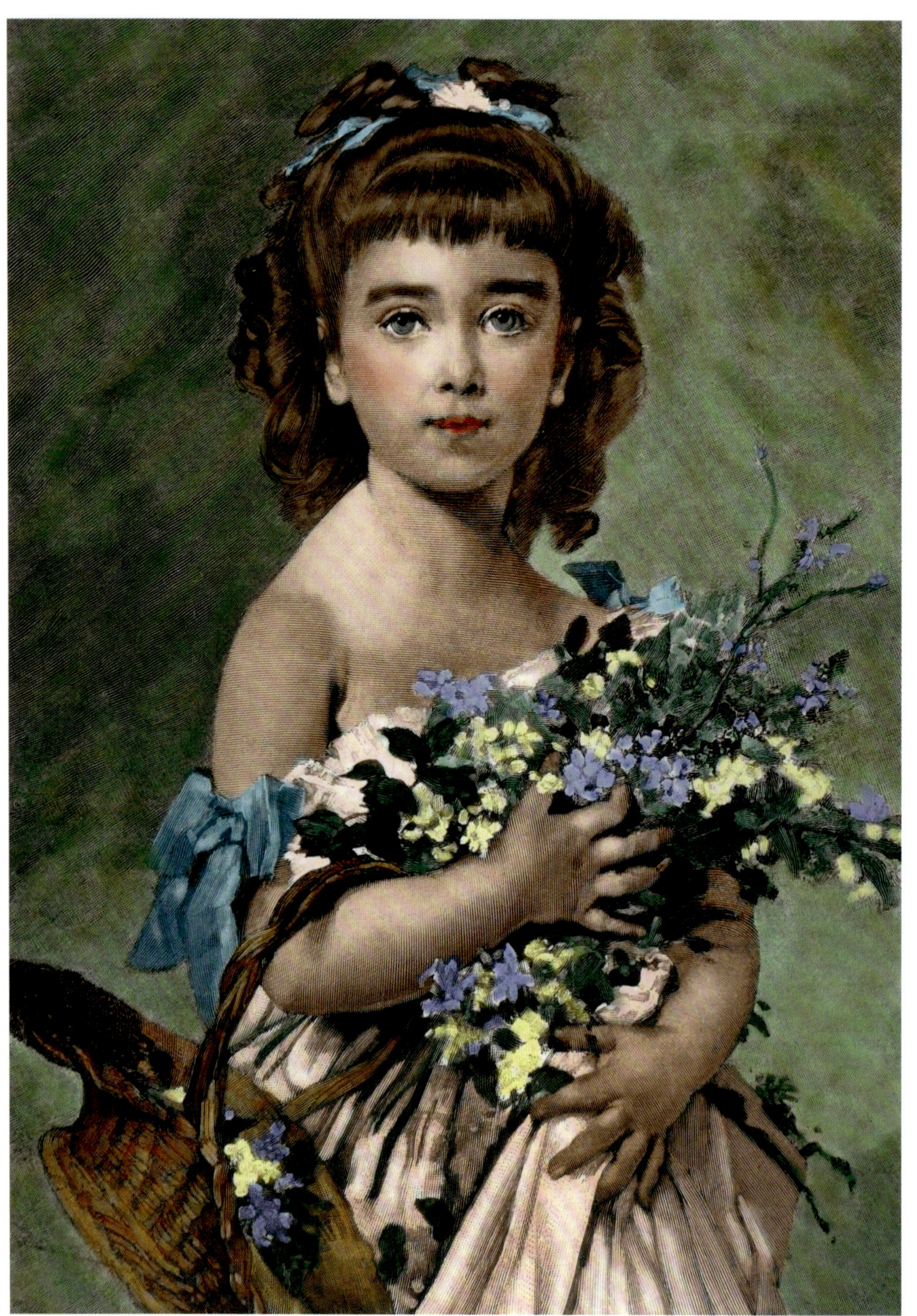

Young Girl with Flower Basket
Charles Chaplin, now forgotten, was known in his day for his genre paintings and portraits. He also painted decorations for the Opéra Garnier and the Élysée Palace in Paris.

Jeune Fille au panier de fleurs
Aujourd'hui tombé dans l'oubli, Charles Chaplin est en son temps apprécié pour ses scènes de genre et ses portraits. Il a aussi peint des décors pour l'Opéra Garnier et le palais de l'Élysée, à Paris.

Junges Mädchen mit Blumenkorb
Der heute in Vergessenheit geratene Charles Chaplin war zu seiner Zeit für seine Genrebilder und Porträts bekannt. Darüber hinaus malte er Dekore für die Opéra Garnier und den Élysée-Palast in Paris.

Chica joven con cesta de flores
Charles Chaplin, ahora olvidado, era conocido en su época por sus pinturas y retratos de género. También pintó decoraciones para la Ópera Garnier y el Palacio del Elíseo en París.

Menina jovem com cesta de flores
Charles Chaplin, agora esquecido, era conhecido em seu tempo por suas pinturas de gênero e retratos. Também pintou decorações para a Opéra Garnier e para o Palácio do Eliseu em Paris.

Jong meisje met bloemenmandje
De nu vergeten Charles Chaplin stond in zijn tijd bekend om zijn genrestukken en portretten. Daarnaast schilderde hij decors voor de Opéra Garnier en het Elysée-paleis in Parijs.

CHARLES JOSHUA CHAPLIN (1825-1891)
1882, Engraving/Gravure, Private collection

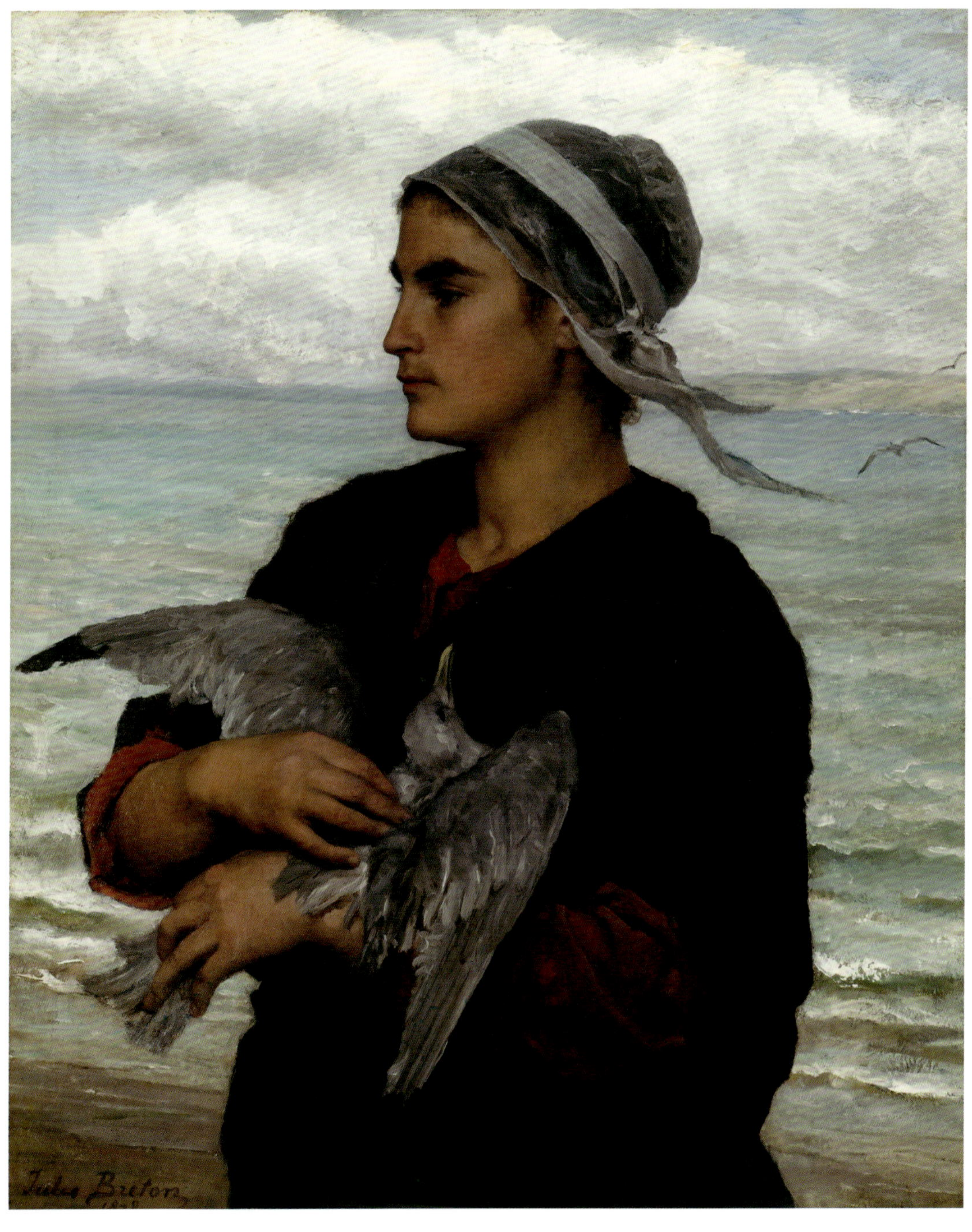

The Wounded
Sea Gull

La Mouette blessée

Die verwundete
Möwe

La gaviota herida

A gaivota ferida

De gewonde
meeuw

JULES BRETON
(1827-1906)

1878, Oil on canvas/
Huile sur toile,
92,7 × 77,2 cm,
Saint-Louis Art
Museum, Saint-Louis

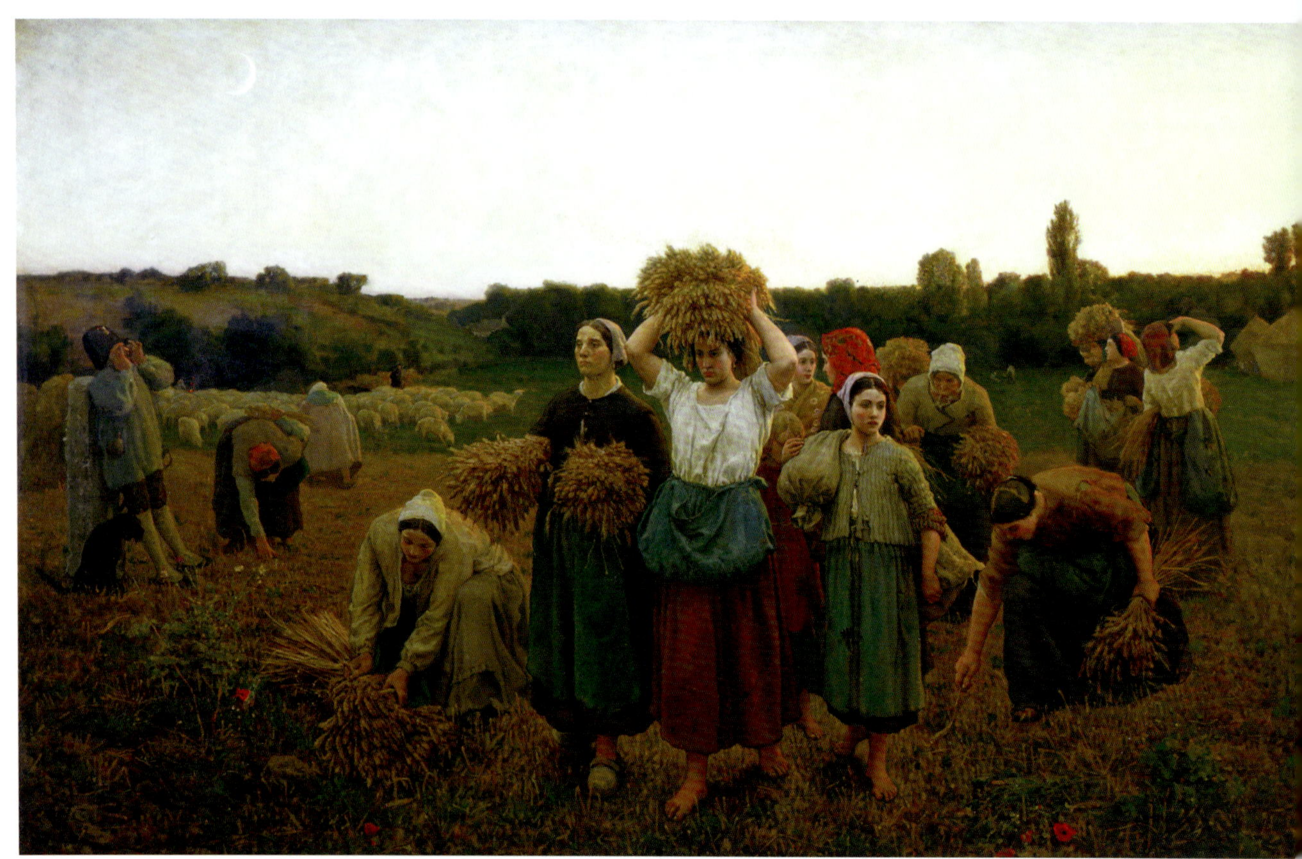

Calling in the Gleaners

Le Rappel des glaneuses

Die Rückkehr der Ährenleserinnen

La retirada de las espigadoras

O Retorno dos Leitores Orelhas

De terugkeer van de arenleessters

JULES BRETON (1827-1906)
1859, Oil on canvas/Huile sur toile,
90,5 × 176 cm, Musée d'Orsay, Paris

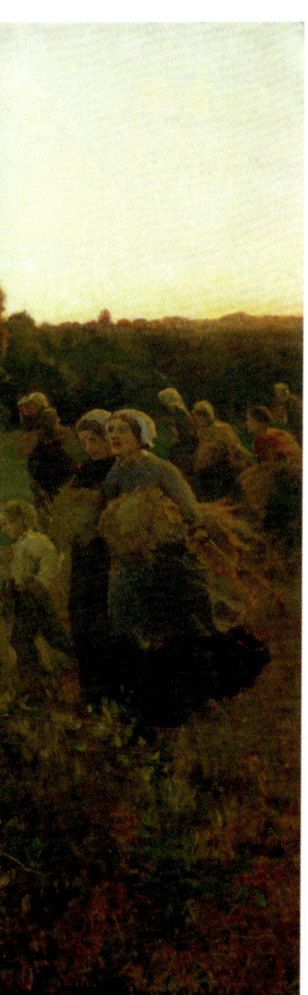

The Gleaner

Jules Breton quickly made his way as a painter of rural life. The large-format painting lends his gleaner an almost sculptural presence, which is reinforced by the slight worm's-eye view.

La Glaneuse

Jules Breton se qualifiait lui-même de peintre paysan. Occupant la quasi-totalité de la toile, la glaneuse impose une présence sculpturale, impression renforcée par le point de vue en légère contre-plongée.

Die Ährenleserin

Jules Breton schlug schnell seinen Weg als Maler des Landlebens ein. Das großformatige Gemälde verleiht seiner Ährenleserin eine fast skulpturale Präsenz, die durch die leichte Froschperspektive verstärkt wird.

Las espigadoras

Jules Breton se llamaba a sí mismo pintor campesino. Ocupando casi todo el lienzo, el espigador impone una presencia escultórica, una impresión reforzada por el ángulo de visión ligeramente bajo.

O leitor de orelha

Jules Breton rapidamente fez o seu caminho como pintor da vida rural. A pintura em grande formato confere ao seu leitor de orelha uma presença quase escultórica, que é reforçada pela ligeira vista aérea do verme.

De arenleesster

Jules Breton koos er al snel voor het plattelandsleven te schilderen. Door het grote formaat lijkt zijn arenleesster een bijna sculpturale aanwezigheid, een effect dat nog wordt versterkt door het lichte kikkerperspectief.

JULES BRETON (1827-1906)

1877, Oil on canvas/Huile sur toile, 230 × 124 cm, Musée des Beaux-Arts, Arras

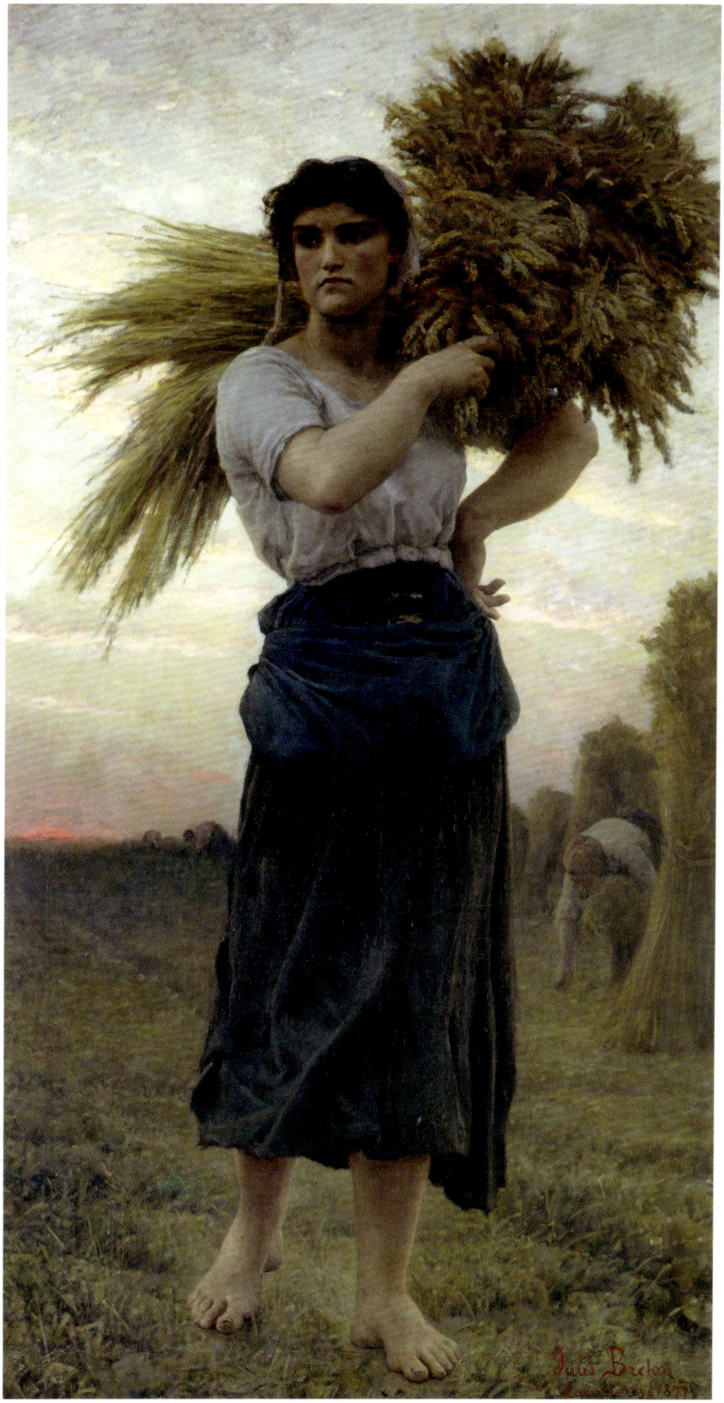

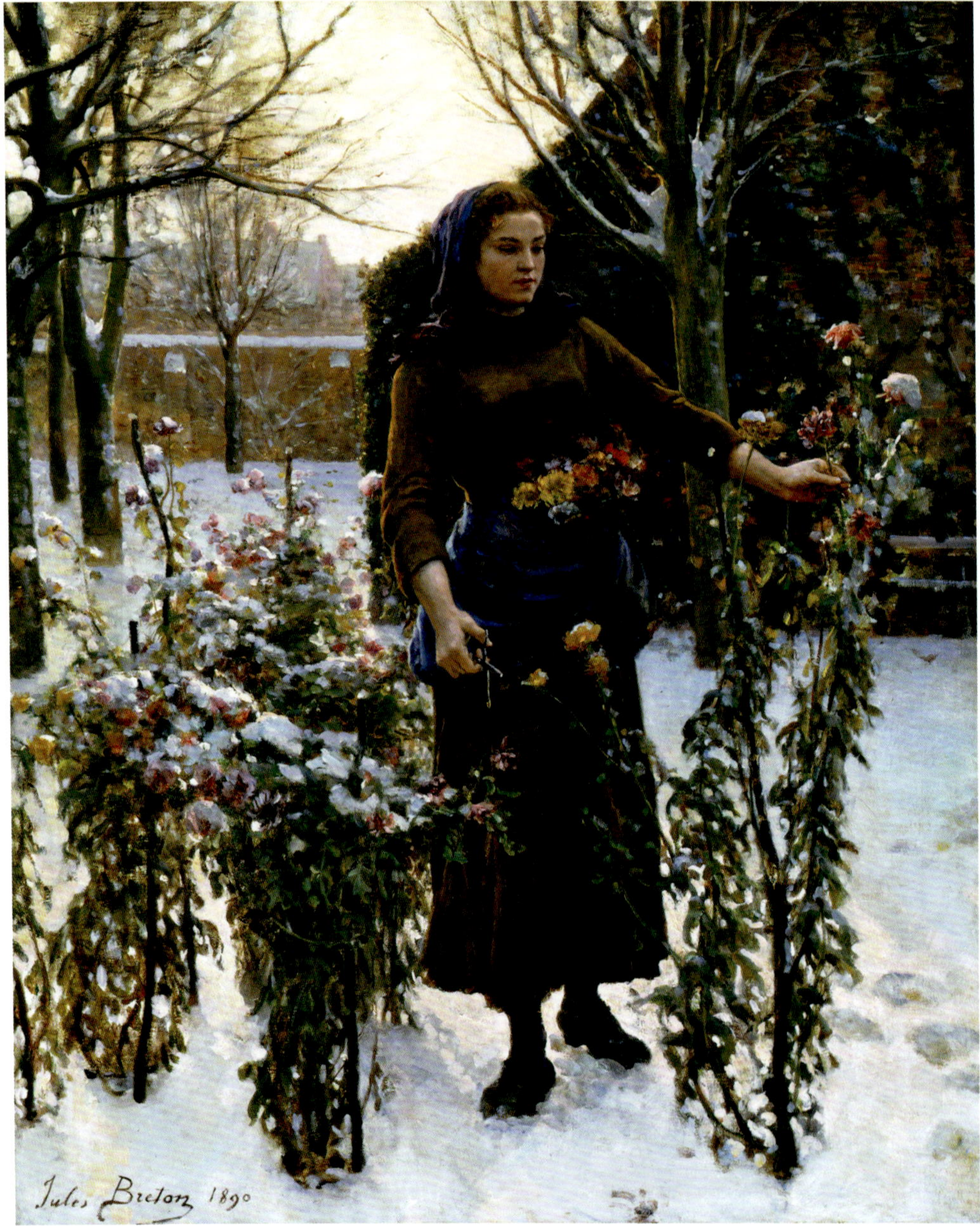

Last Flowers

Dernières fleurs

Die letzten Blumen

Las últimas flores

As últimas flores

De laatste bloemen

JULES BRETON (1827-1906)
1890, Oil on canvas/Huile sur
toile, 101,6 × 81,3 cm, Cincinnati
Art Museum, Cincinnati

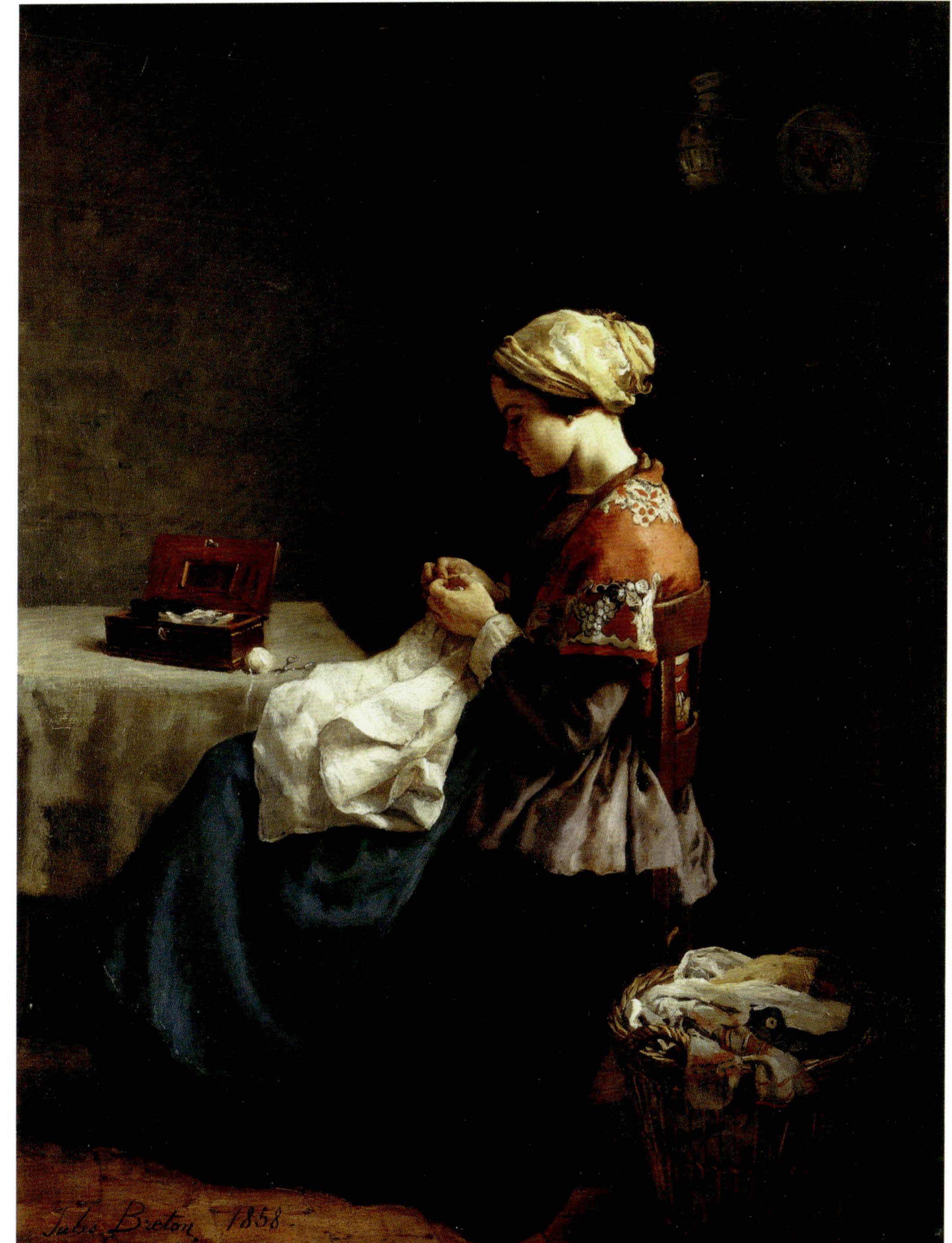

The Little Seamstress

La Petite Couturière

Die kleine Näherin

La pequeña costurera

A pequena costureira

Het naaistertje

JULES BRETON
(1827-1906)

1858, Oil on canvas/
Huile sur toile,
55,5 × 43 cm, Private
collection

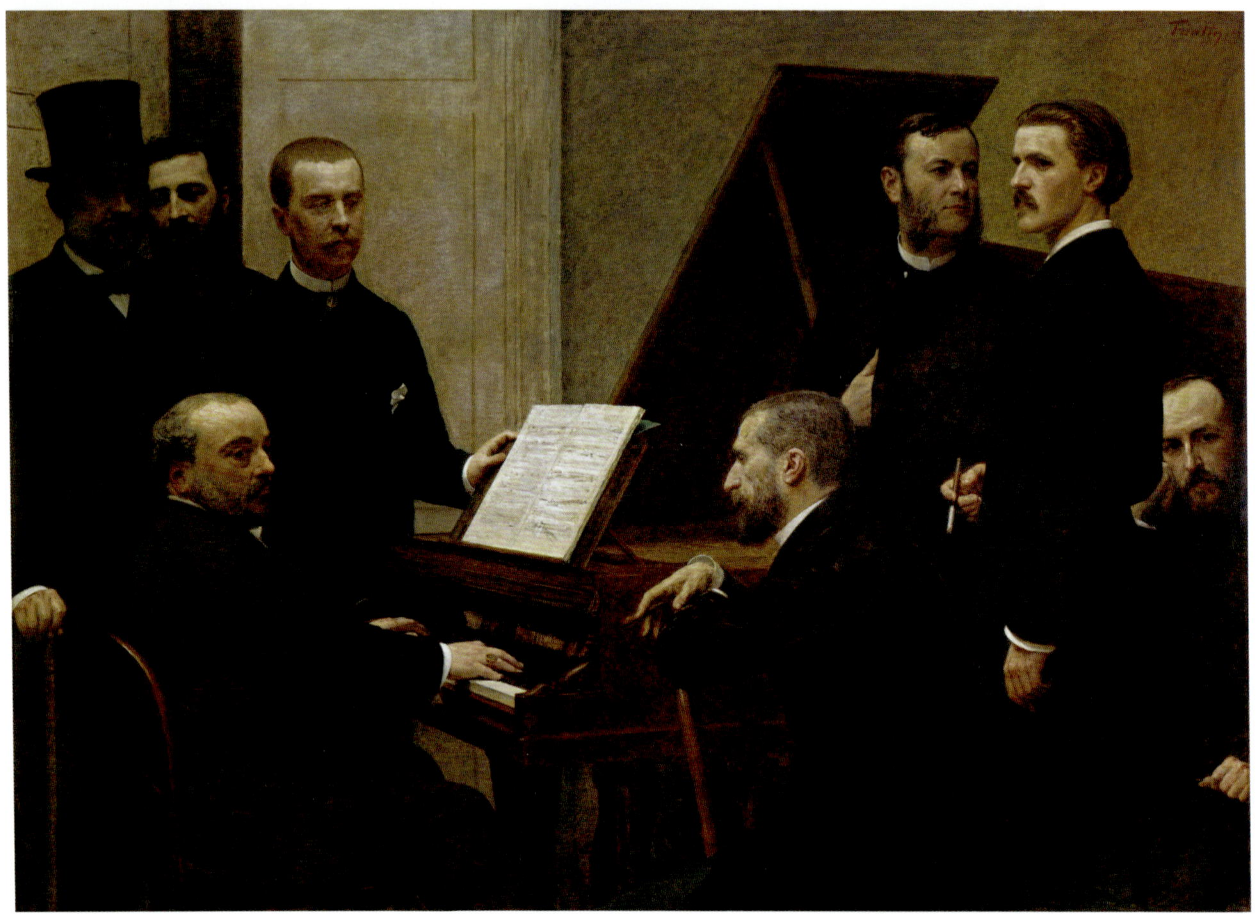

Around the Piano

Autour du piano

Um das Klavier

Alrededor del piano

Para tocar piano

Rond het klavier

HENRI FANTIN-LATOUR (1836-1904)
1885, Oil on canvas/Huile sur toile,
160 × 220 cm,
Musée d'Orsay, Paris

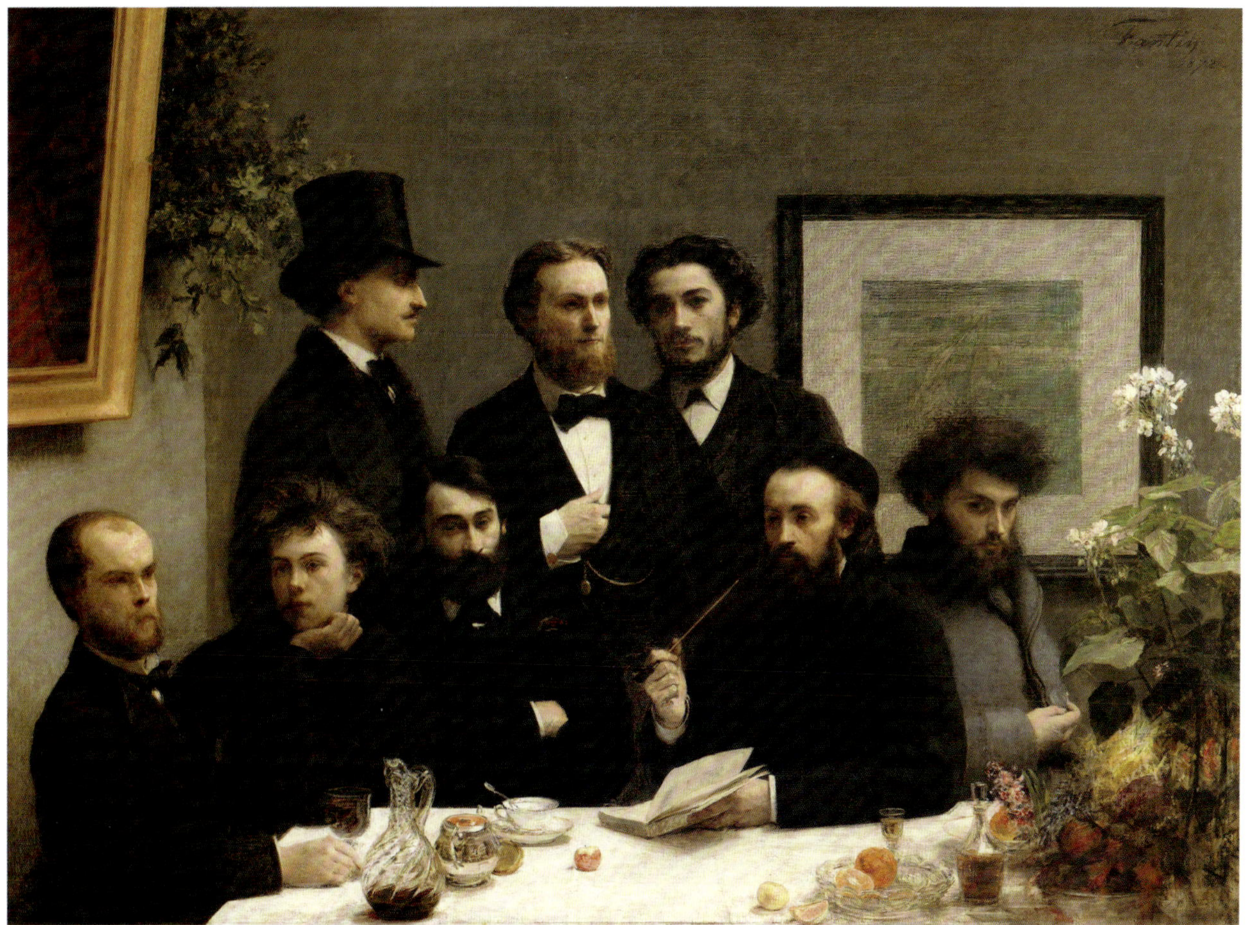

A Corner of the Table
Fantin-Latour's group portraits stand out due to the lack of interaction between the people. Here he united the poets of the Parnassian group. The Duo Rimbaud-Verlaine is on the left in the picture.

Un coin de table
Les portraits de groupe de Fantin-Latour fascinent par le fait qu'il n'y a aucune interaction entre les personnages. Il réunit ici des poètes parnassiens, dont le couple Rimbaud-Verlaine, à gauche.

Französische Dichter an einem Tisch
Fantin-Latours Gruppenporträts fallen durch den Mangel an Interaktion zwischen den Personen auf. Hier vereinigte er die Dichter der Gruppe Parnassiens. Links im Bild befindet sich das Duo Rimbaud-Verlaine.

Poetas franceses en una mesa
Los retratos de grupo de Fantin-Latour destacan por la falta de interacción entre las personas. Aquí reunió a los poetas del grupo parnasiano. El dúo Rimbaud-Verlaine está a la izquierda en la foto.

Poetas franceses à mesa
Os retratos de grupo de Fantin-Latour destacam-se pela falta de interação entre as pessoas. Aqui ele uniu os poetas do grupo Parnassian. O Duo Rimbaud-Verlaine está à esquerda na foto.

Een hoek van de tafel
De groepsportretten van Fantin-Latour vallen op door het gebrek aan interactie tussen de mensen. Hier verenigde hij de dichters van de Parnassiens. Het duo Rimbaud-Verlaine bevindt zich links op het doek.

HENRI FANTIN-LATOUR (1836-1904)
1872, Oil on canvas/Huile sur toile, 160 × 225 cm, Musée d'Orsay, Paris

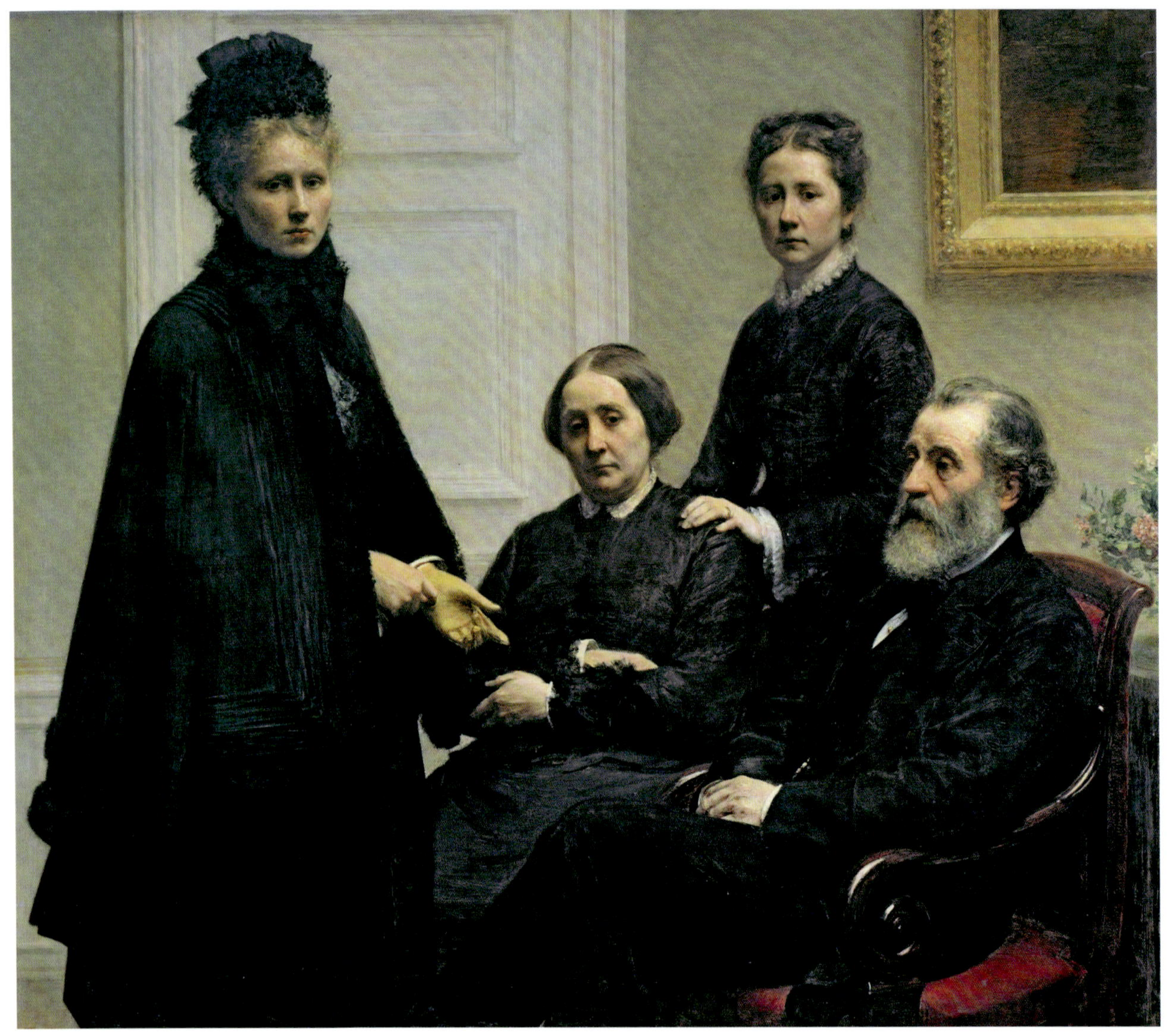

The Dubourg Family

La Famille Dubourg

Die Familie Dubourg

La familia Dubourg

A Família Dubourg

De familie Dubourg

HENRI FANTIN-LATOUR (1836-1904)

1878, Oil on canvas/Huile sur toile, 146,5 × 170,5 cm, Musée d'Orsay, Paris

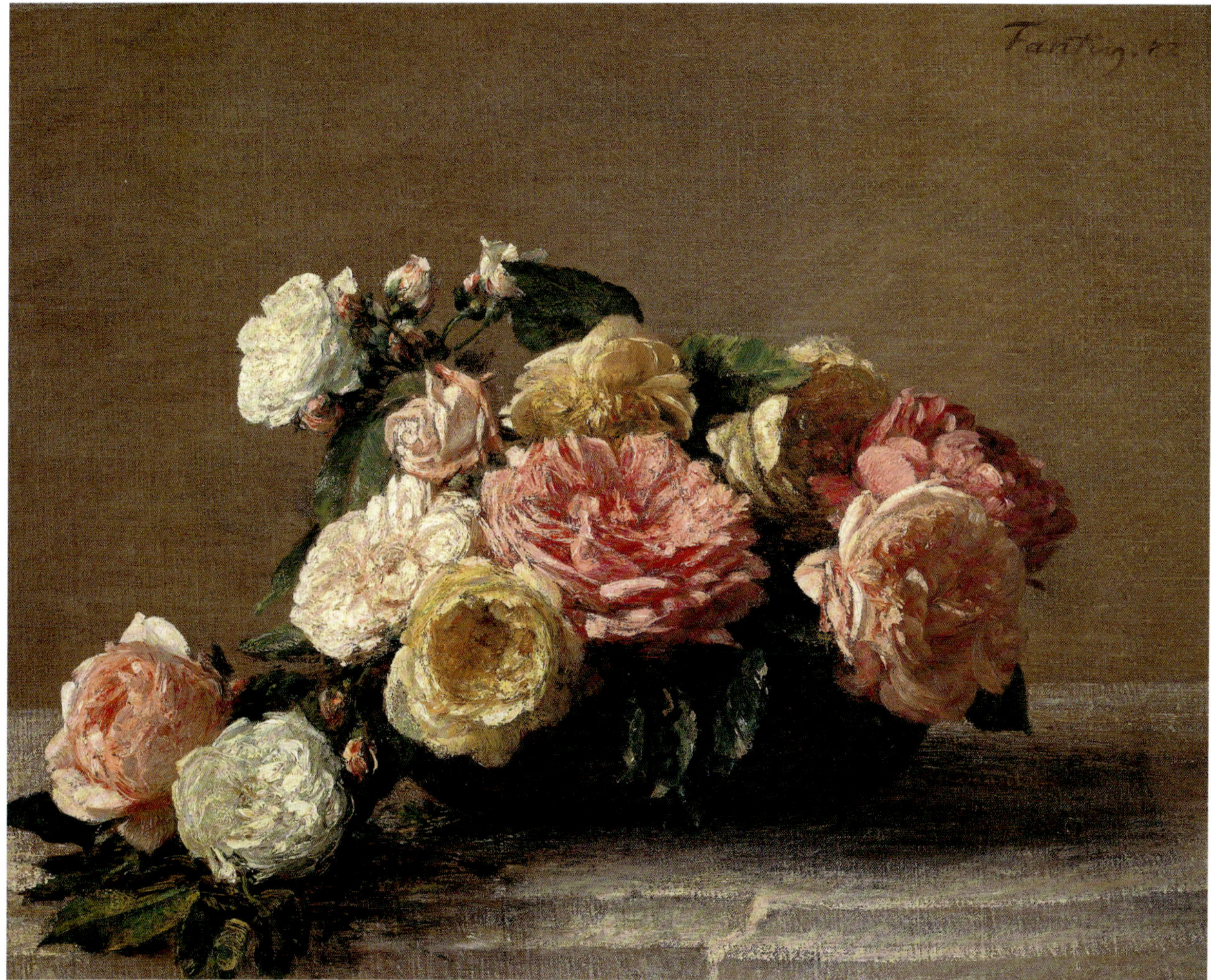

Roses in a Dish

Still lifes, especially bouquets of flowers, were the basis for the artist's commercial success, which he had mainly with English buyers. In this genre he was able to develop his talent for color design.

Roses dans une coupe

Les natures mortes, et les bouquets de fleurs en particulier, ont fait le succès commercial de l'artiste, notamment auprès d'une clientèle anglaise. Un genre où s'épanouissent ses talents de coloriste.

HENRI FANTIN-LATOUR (1836-1904)
1882, Oil on canvas/Huile sur toile, 36,5 × 46 cm, Musée d'Orsay, Paris

Rosen in einer Schale

Stillleben, insbesondere Blumenbouquets, begründeten den kommerziellen Erfolg des Künstlers, den er vor allem bei englischen Käufern hatte. In dem Genre konnte er sein Talent für die Farbgestaltung entfalten.

Rosas en un cuenco

Las naturalezas muertas, especialmente los ramos de flores, fueron la base del éxito comercial del artista, que tuvo principalmente con compradores ingleses. En este género pudo desarrollar su talento para el diseño de color.

Rosas numa tigela

As naturezas mortas, especialmente bouquets de flores, foram a base para o sucesso comercial do artista, que ele tinha principalmente com compradores ingleses. Neste género, conseguiu desenvolver o seu talento para o design de cores.

Rozen in een kom

Stillevens, vooral van boeketten, vormden de basis voor het commerciële succes van de kunstenaar, die vooral Engelse kopers had. In dit genre kon hij zijn talent voor kleurgebruik ontwikkelen.

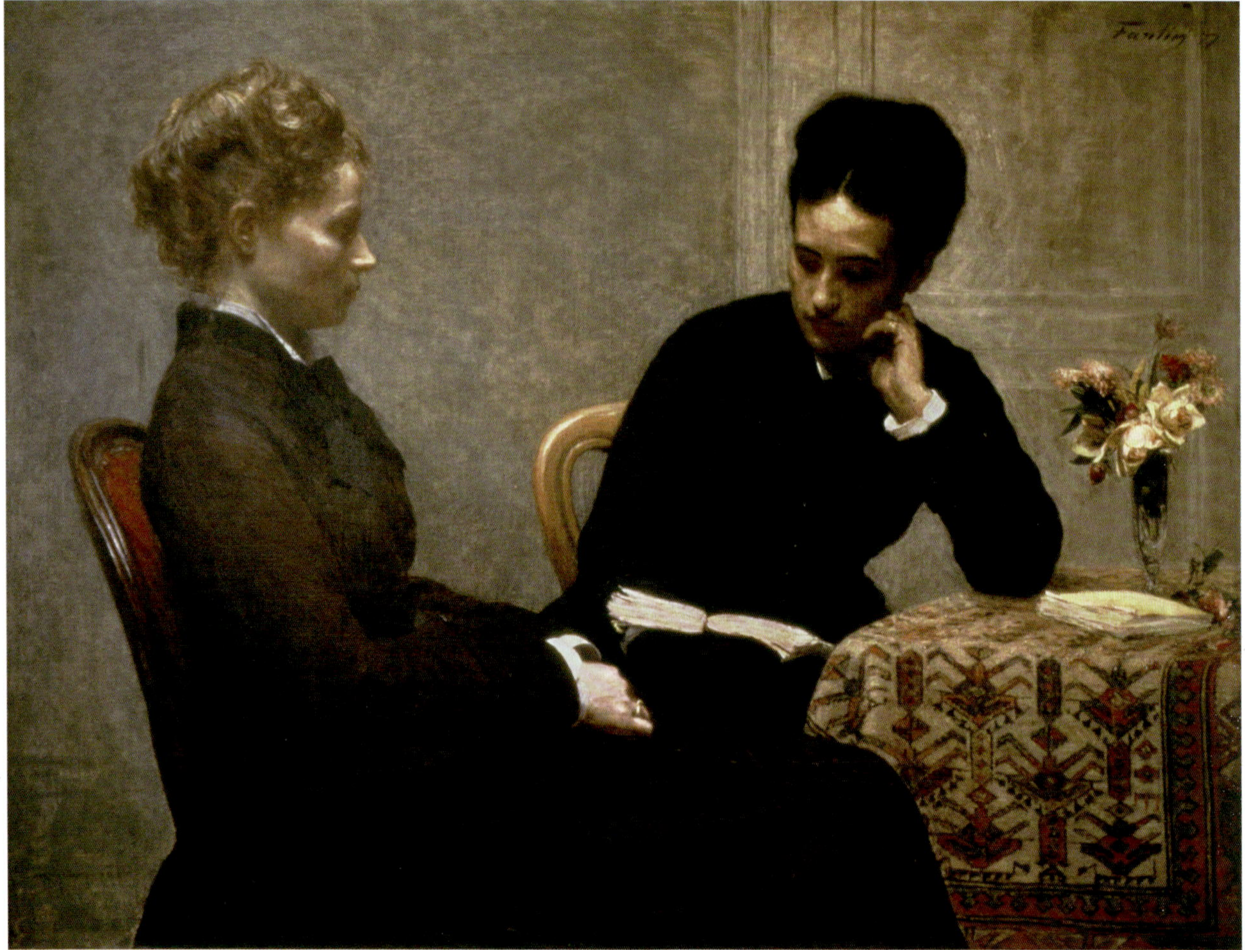

Reading

Fantin-Latour's interiors are characterised by mysterious
austerity. While one woman is reading, the other does not
seem to follow it and is deeply absorbed in her thoughts.

La Lecture

Une certaine austérité caractérise les mystérieuses scènes
d'intérieur de Fantin-Latour. Ici, une femme est en train
de lire, et la seconde, censée l'écouter, semble plutôt perdue
dans ses pensées.

Die Lektüre

Fantin-Latours Interieurs zeichnen sich durch eine
mysteriöse Strenge aus. Während eine Frau ließt, scheint
die zweite der Lektüre nicht zu folgen und ist tief in ihre
Gedanken versunken.

La lectura

Los interiores de Fantin-Latour se caracterizan por una
misteriosa austeridad. Mientras una mujer lee, la otra no
parece seguir la lectura y está profundamente absorta en sus
pensamientos.

A leitura

Os interiores de Fantin-Latour são caracterizados por uma
austeridade misteriosa. Enquanto uma mulher está lendo,
a outra não parece seguir a leitura e está profundamente
absorvida em seus pensamentos.

Lezen

De interieurs van Fantin-Latour worden gekenmerkt door
een mysterieuze strengheid. Terwijl de ene vrouw aan het
lezen is, lijkt de andere vrouw daarmee te zijn gestopt en in
gedachten verzonken te zijn.

HENRI FANTIN-LATOUR (1836-1904)

1877, Oil on canvas/Huile sur toile, 97 × 130,5 cm, Musée des Beaux-Arts, Lyon

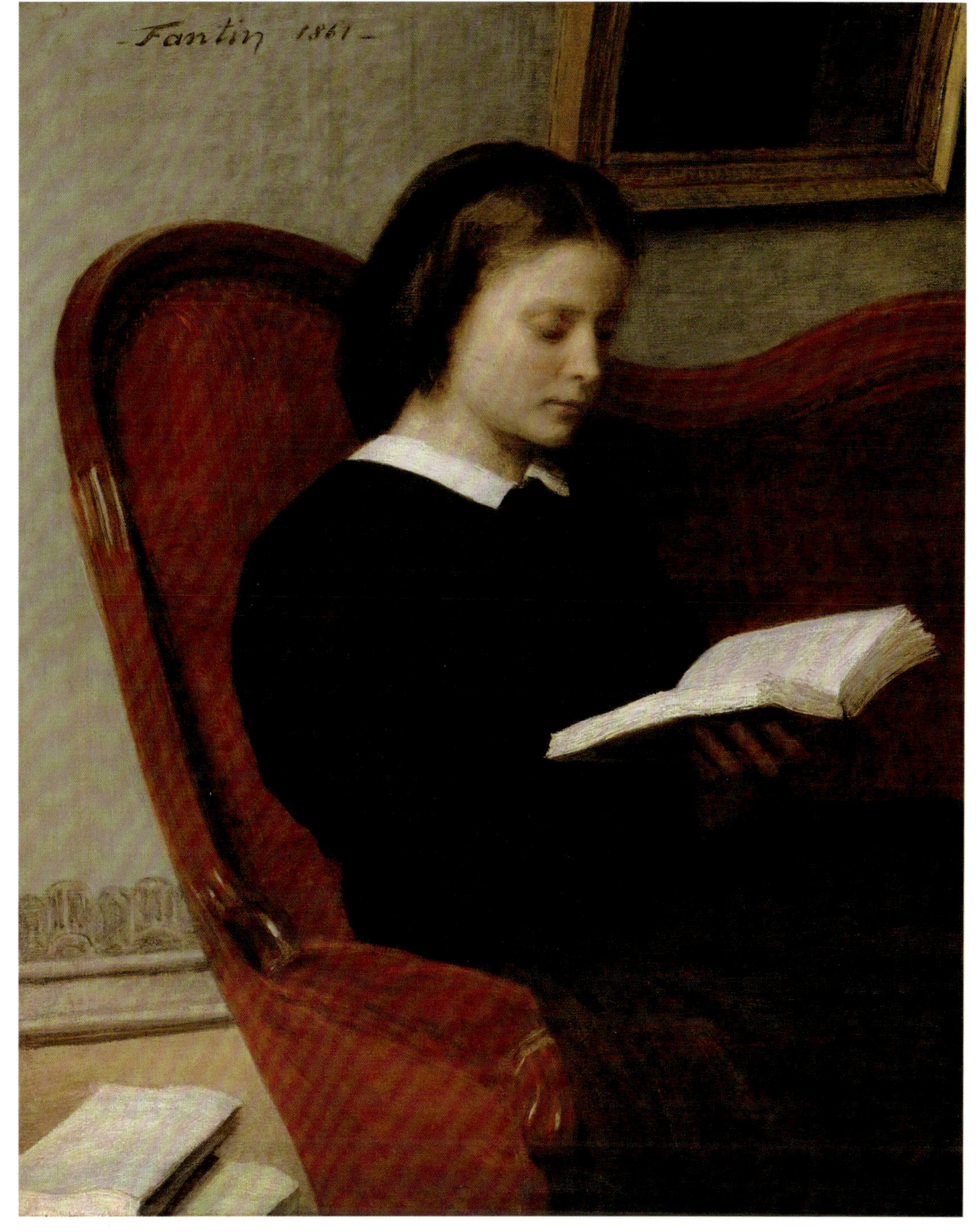

The Reader

La Liseuse

Die Lesende

La lectora

O leitor

Lezende vrouw

HENRI FANTIN-LATOUR
(1836-1904)

1861, Oil on canvas/
Huile sur toile,
100 × 83 cm,
Musée d'Orsay, Paris

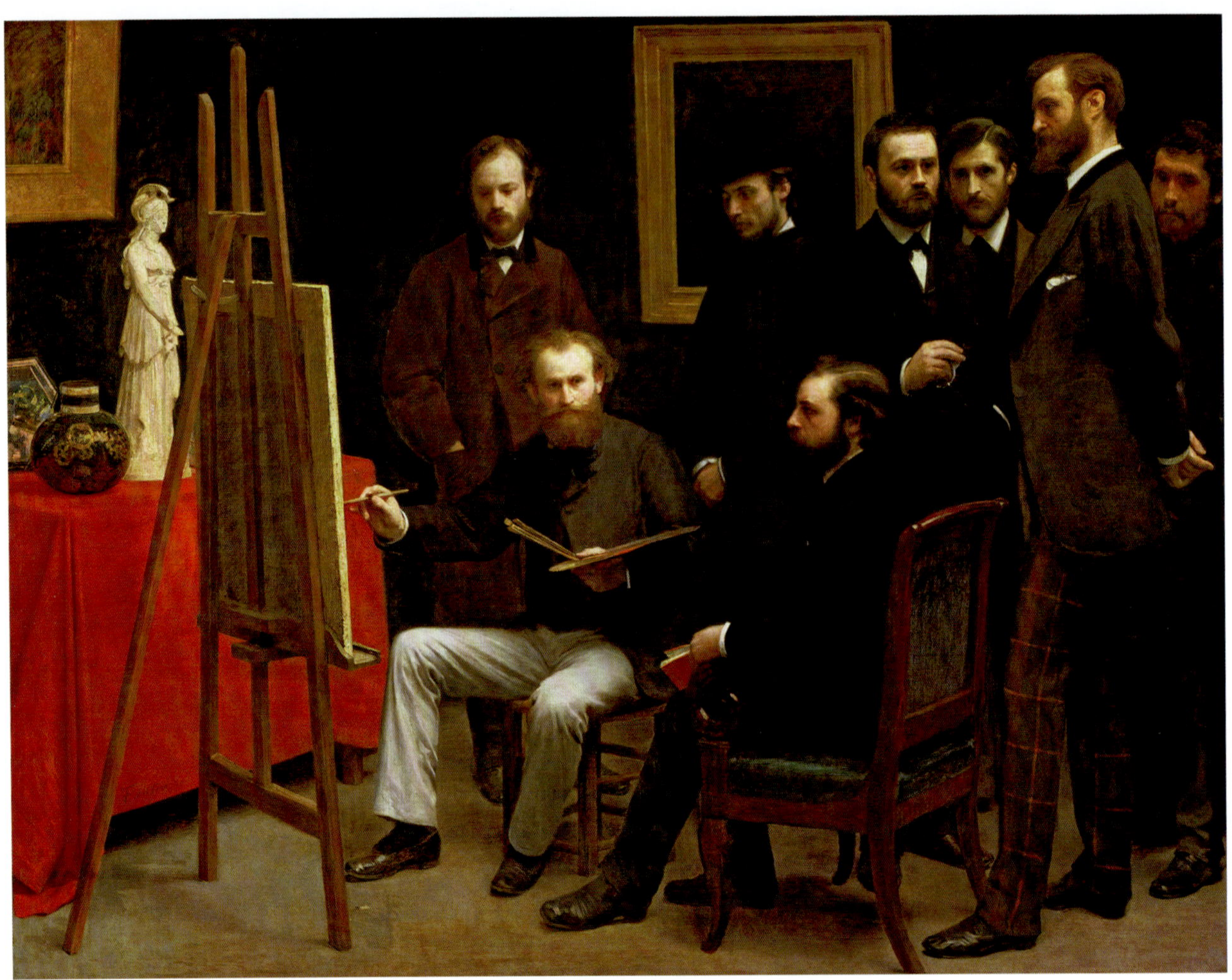

Studio at Batignolles

Un atelier aux Batignolles

Ein Atelier in Batignolles

Un estudio en Batignolles

Um estúdio em Batignolles

Een atelier in Batignolles

HENRI FANTIN-LATOUR (1836-1904)
1870, Oil on canvas/Huile sur toile,
204 × 273,5 cm, Musée d'Orsay, Paris

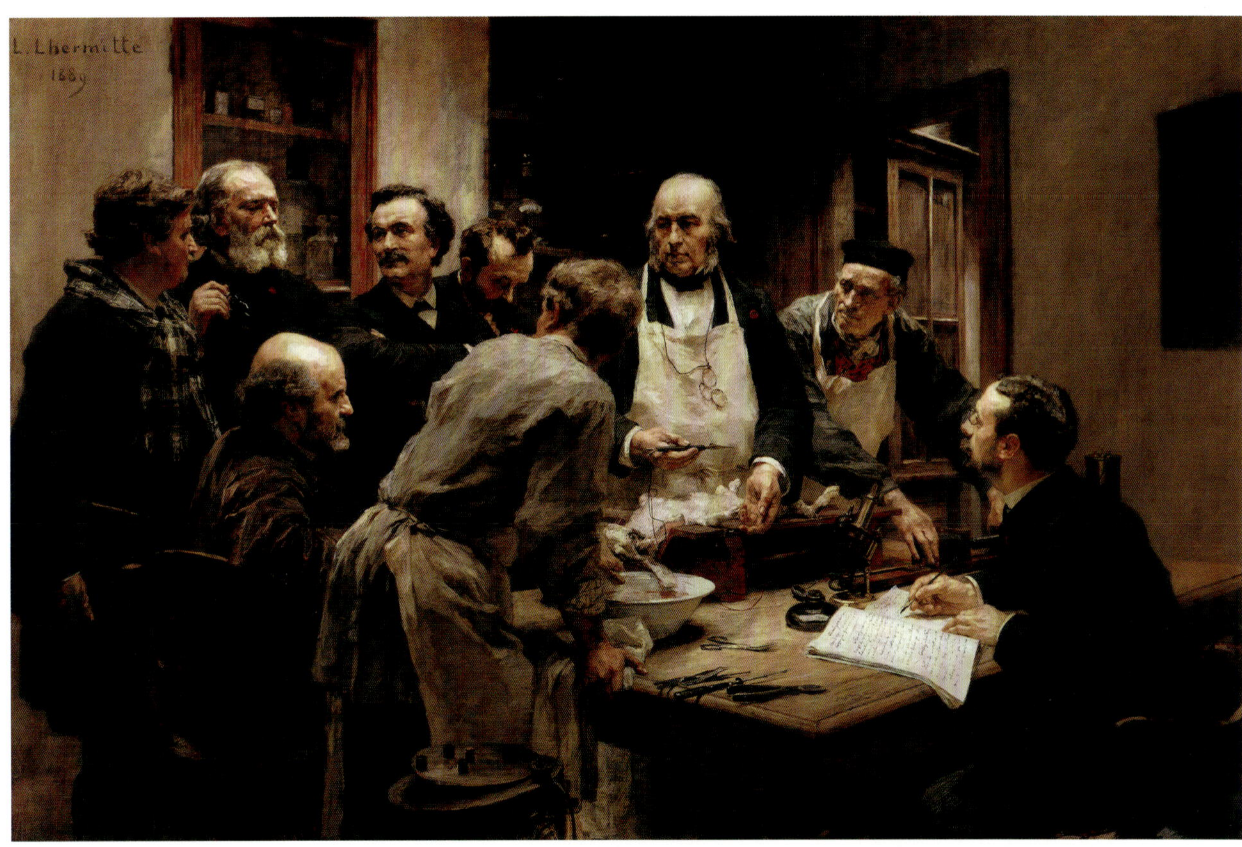

The Lesson of Claude Bernard *or*
Session at the Vivisection Laboratory

In 1886, the Sorbonne commissioned two paintings from Léon Augustin Lhermitte, including this one showing the physician Claude Bernard in his laboratory at the Collège de France during a vivisection.

La Leçon de Claude Bernard *ou*
Séance au laboratoire de vivisection

En 1886, l'artiste reçoit la commande de deux tableaux pour la Sorbonne, dont celui-ci qui montre le médecin Claude Bernard dans son laboratoire du Collège de France, en pleine séance de vivisection.

Claude Bernard und seine Schüler *oder*
Unterricht im Labor der Vivisektion

1886 gab die Sorbonne zwei Gemälde bei Léon Augustin Lhermitte in Auftrag, darunter dieses Werk, das den Arzt Claude Bernard in seinem Labor im Collège de France bei einer Vivisektion zeigt.

Claude Bernard y sus alumnos *o*
clases en el laboratorio de vivisección

En 1886, la Sorbona encargó a Léon Augustin Lhermitte dos cuadros, entre los cuales éste muestra al médico Claude Bernard en su laboratorio del Collège de France durante una vivisección.

Claude Bernard e seus alunos *ou*
aulas no laboratório de vivissecção

Em 1886, a Sorbonne encomendou dois quadros a Léon Augustin Lhermitte, incluindo este que mostrava o médico Claude Bernard no seu laboratório no Collège de France durante uma vivissecção.

De les van Claude Bernard *of*
Les in het vivisectielaboratorium

In 1886 bestelde de Sorbonne twee schilderijen bij Léon Augustin Lhermitte, waaronder dit schilderij dat de arts Claude Bernard tijdens een vivisectie in zijn laboratorium aan het Collège de France toont.

LÉON AUGUSTIN LHERMITTE (1844-1925)
1889, Oil on canvas/Huile sur toile, 180 × 282 cm, Académie de médecine, Paris

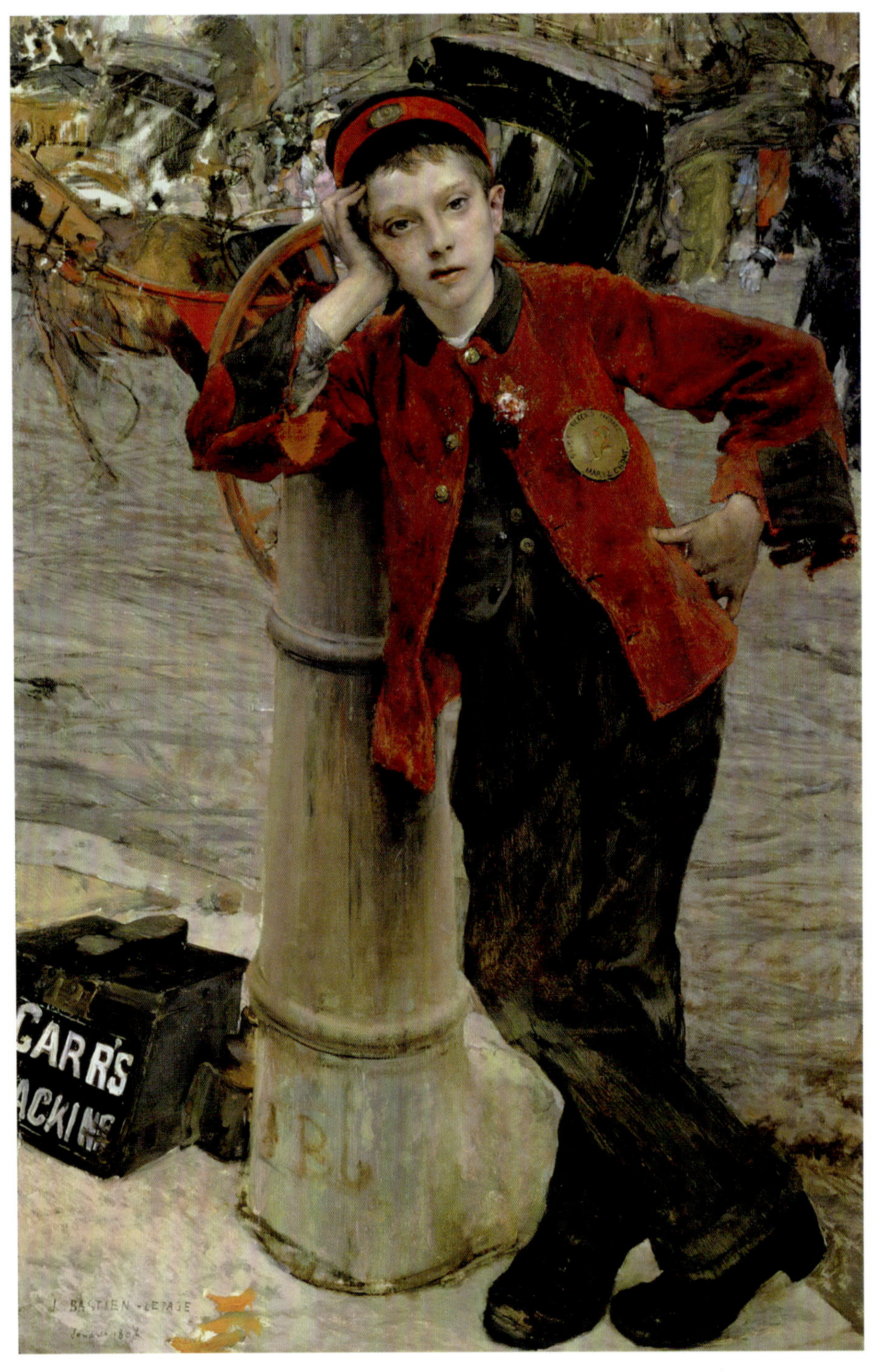

London Bootblack

Petit Cireur de bottes à Londres

Der kleine Schuhputzer

Pequeño lustrabotas en Londres

O menino engraxador de sapatos

De jonge schoenenpoetser

JULES BASTIEN-LEPAGE (1848-1884)

1882, Oil on canvas/Huile sur toile,
132 × 89 cm, Musée des Arts Décoratifs, Paris

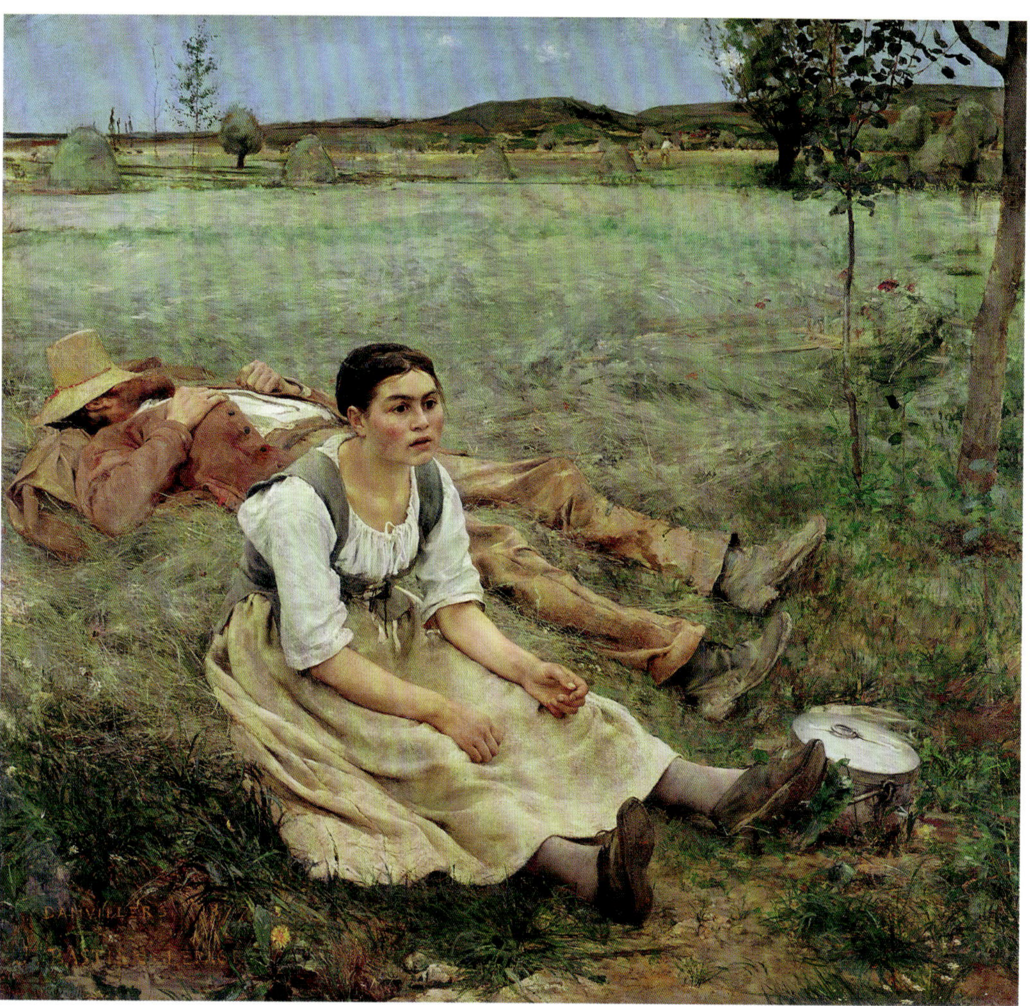

Hay Makers

The painting, which appears very modern due to the shortened distance to the motif and the high horizon, was praised by Zola at the Salon 1878. The woman's empty gaze testifies to the exhaustion caused by her work.

Les Foins

Moderne par son cadrage en plan rapproché et sa ligne d'horizon haute, ce tableau fit l'admiration de Zola au Salon de 1878. L'émouvant portrait d'une jeune femme fatiguée par le labeur, au regard perdu.

Heuernte

Das durch den verkürzten Abstand zum Motiv und den hohen Horizont sehr modern wirkende Gemälde wurde auf dem Salon 1878 von Zola gelobt. Der leere Blick der Frau zeugt von der Erschöpfung durch die Arbeit.

Cosecha de heno

La pintura, que parece muy moderna debido a la distancia acortada al motivo y al alto horizonte, fue elogiada por Zola en el Salón de 1878. La mirada vacía de la mujer atestigua el agotamiento causado por su trabajo.

Colheita de feno

A pintura, que parece muito moderna devido à curta distância ao motivo e ao horizonte alto, foi elogiada por Zola no Salão de 1878. O olhar vazio da mulher testemunha a exaustão causada pelo seu trabalho.

Hooien

Het schilderij, dat door de verkorte afstand tot het onderwerp en de hoge horizon zeer modern oogt, werd door Zola op de Salon van 1878 geprezen. De lege blik van de vrouw getuigt van de uitputting door haar werk.

JULES BASTIEN-LEPAGE (1848-1884)

1877, Oil on canvas/Huile sur toile, 160 × 195 cm, Musée d'Orsay, Paris

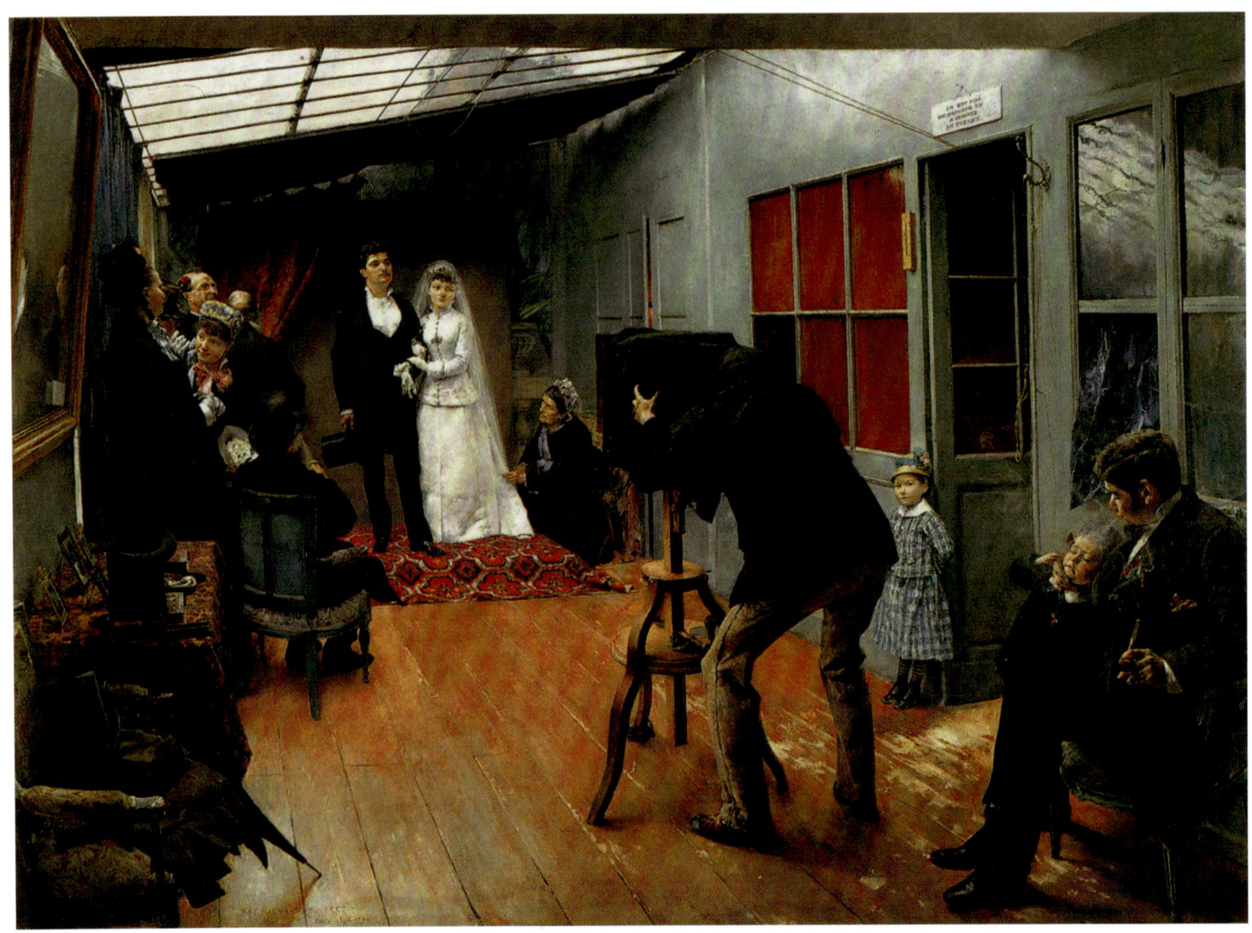

Wedding at the Photographer's

La Noce chez le photographe

Hochzeitspaar beim Fotografen

Pareja de novios en casa del fotógrafo

Casamento de casal com o fotógrafo

Huwelijkspaar bij de fotograaf

JEAN DAGNAN-BOUVERET (1852-1929)
1879, Oil on canvas mounted on cardboard/
Huile sur toile marouflée sur carton,
85 × 122 cm, Musée des Beaux-Arts, Lyon

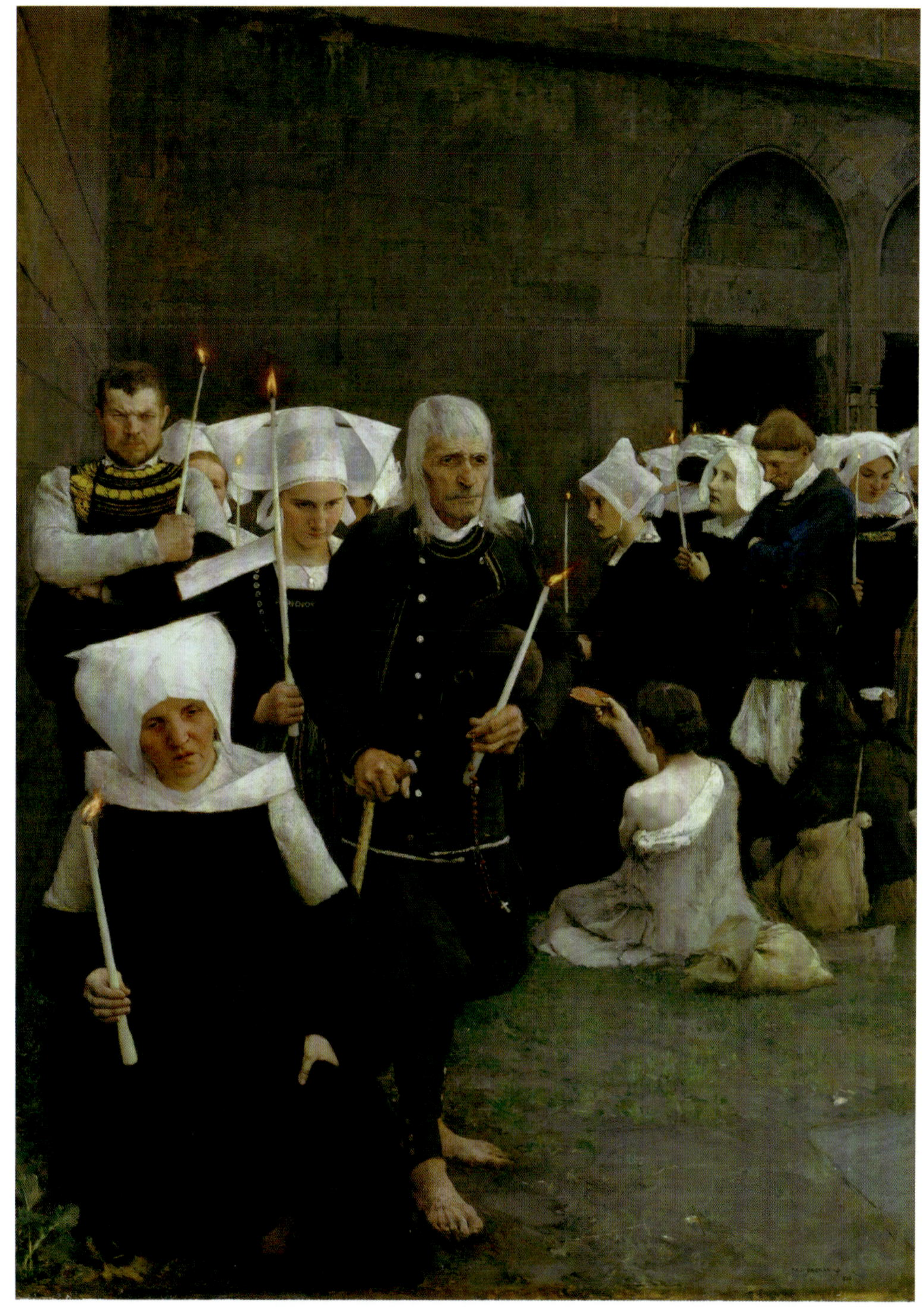

The Pardon in Brittany

Le Pardon en Bretagne

Pardon in der Bretagne

Perdón en Bretaña

Perdão na Bretanha

Het pardon in Bretagne

JEAN DAGNAN-BOUVERET
(1852-1929)

1886, Oil on canvas/
Huile sur toile, 114,6 × 84,8 cm,
Metropolitan Museum of Art,
New York

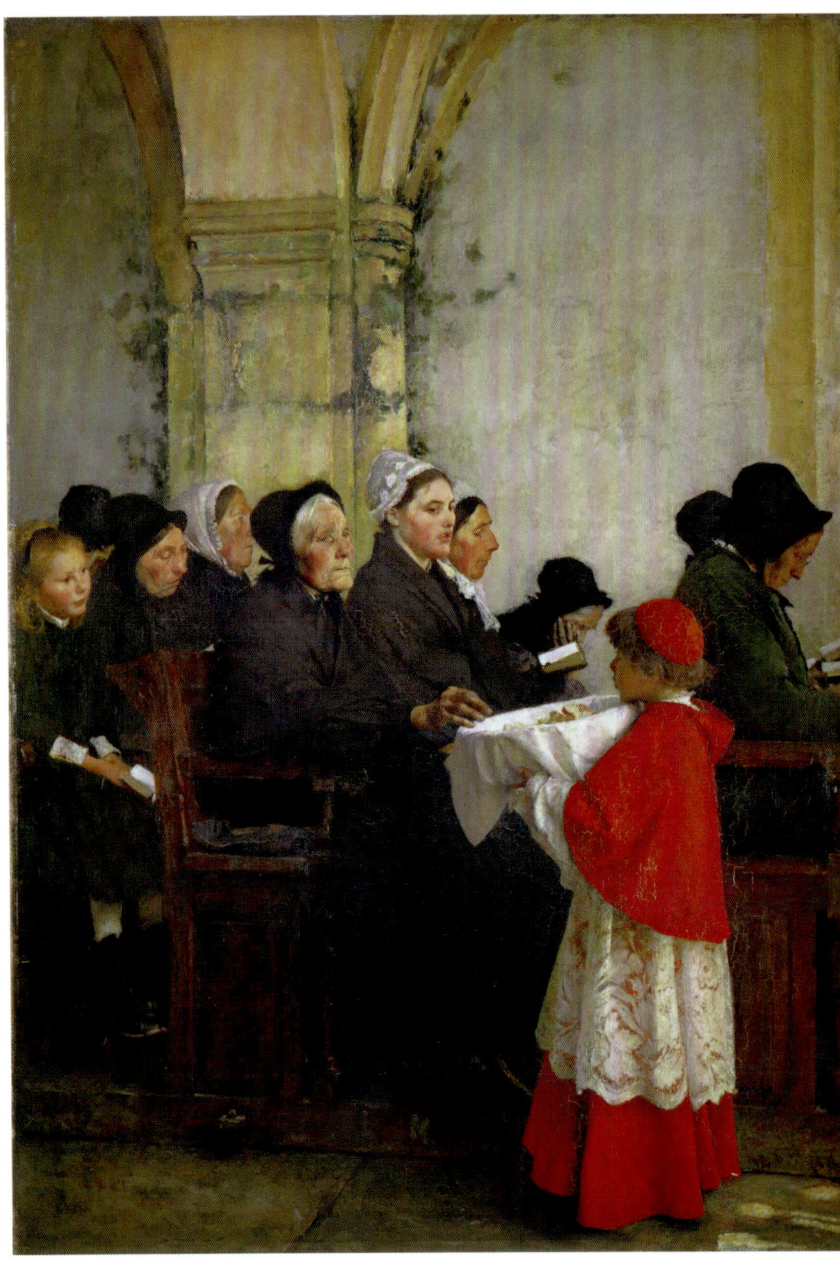

The Ex Voto

Royer, who was born in Nancy, traveled widely. His stay in Brittany in 1896 was most influential, and four years later he was awarded the silver medal for this work at the World Exhibition.

L'Ex-Voto

Né à Nancy, Henri Royer a beaucoup voyagé, et a été fortement marqué par son séjour en Bretagne en 1896. Quatre ans plus tard, il obtiendra pour ce tableau la médaille d'argent à l'Exposition universelle.

Ex voto

Der in Nancy geborene Royer reiste viel. Am prägendsten war sein Aufenthalt in der Bretagne im Jahr 1896. Vier Jahre später wurde ihm für dieses Werk die Silbermedaille auf der Weltausstellung verliehen.

Ex voto

Royer, nacido en Nancy, viajaba mucho. Su estancia en Bretaña en 1896 fue muy influyente, y cuatro años más tarde fue galardonado con la medalla de plata por esta obra en la Exposición Universal.

Ex voto

A Nancy, nascida em Royer, viajou muito. Sua estadia na Bretanha em 1896 foi mais influente, e quatro anos depois, ele foi agraciado com a medalha de prata para este trabalho na Exposição Mundial.

Ex voto

De in Nancy geboren Royer reisde veel. Zijn verblijf in Bretagne in 1896 zou hem het sterkst beïnvloeden. Vier jaar later kreeg hij voor dit werk de zilveren medaille op de Wereldtentoonstelling.

HENRI ROYER (1869-1938)
1898, Oil on canvas/Huile sur toile,
219,5 × 181 cm, Musée des Beaux-Arts, Quimper

Le Pain bénit

Le Pain bénit

Geweihtes Brot

Pan bendecido

Pão melado

Gewijd brood

JEAN DAGNAN-BOUVERET (1852-1929)
1885, Oil on canvas/Huile sur toile,
121 × 84,5 cm, Musée d'Orsay, Paris

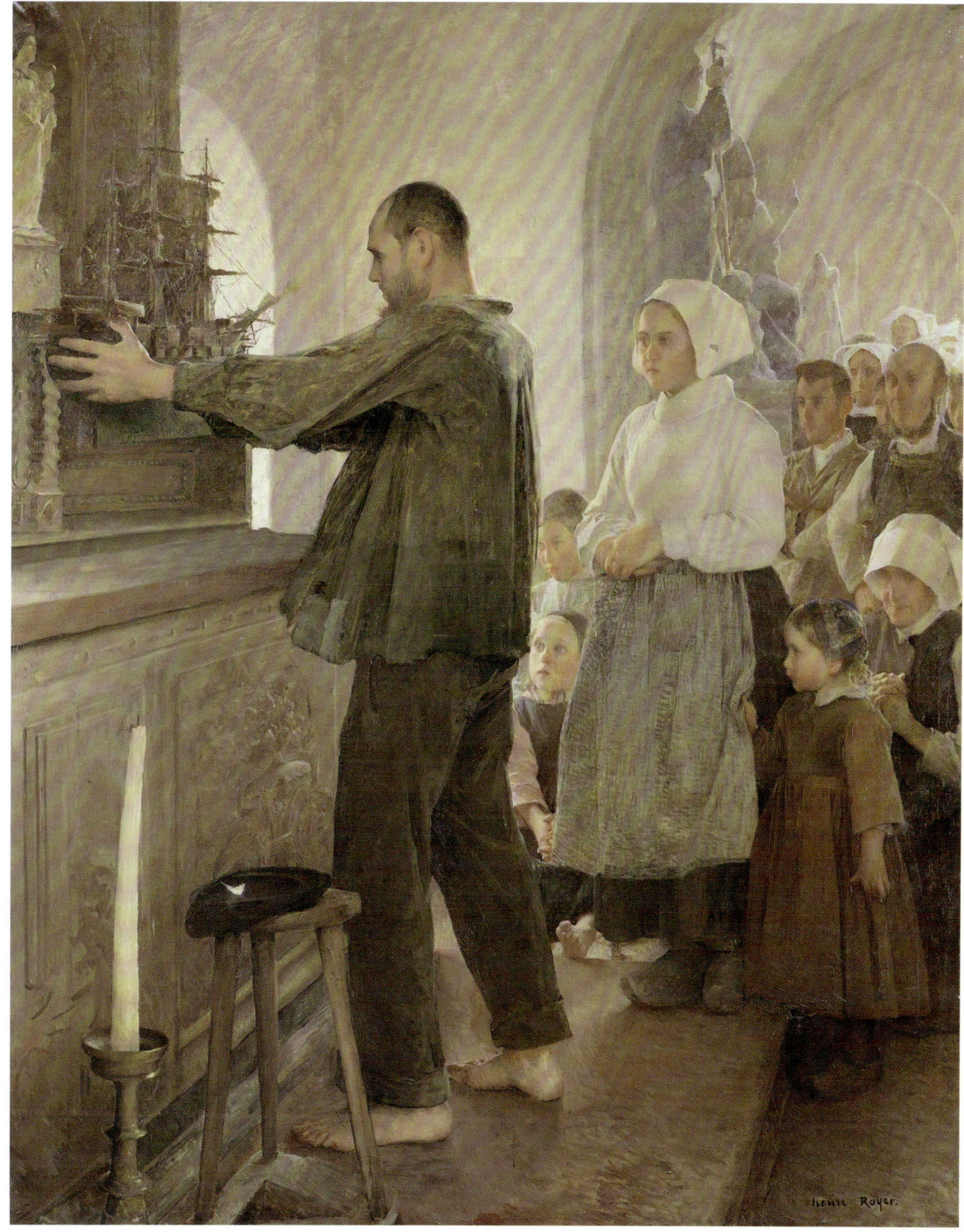

4

The Forerunners of Impressionism

Les précurseurs de l'impressionnisme

Die Vorläufer des Impressionismus

Los Precursores des Impresionismo

O Provisório do Impressionismo

De Voorlopers van het Impressionsme

The Forerunners of Impressionism

In 1874 the first exhibition of the Impressionists took place. The principles of their painting, however, go back further. Towards the middle of the 19th century, Romanticism, Naturalism and Realism emerged as parallel currents. Eugène Delacroix, Jean-Baptiste Camille Corot, the painters of the Barbizon School and Gustave Courbet all contributed to the emergence of Impressionism. Eugène Boudin, following the example of the Dutch painter Johan Barthold Jongkind, studied the theories of light and sky at the beginning of the 1850s. The sky and the sea become his favourite motifs. "If I have ever become a painter, I owe it to Eugène Boudin," Claude Monet said about the Normandy painter.

In the course of the 1860s, Édouard Manet established himself in Parisian painting circles. With his work *Olympia*, shown at the 1863 Salon, Manet, who was simultaneously interested in historical and contemporary themes, shaped his reputation as a representative of "new painting". Between 1869 and 1875

Les précurseurs de l'impressionnisme

Si l'année 1874 est celle de la première exposition des impressionnistes, les grands principes de leur peinture sont posés bien plus tôt. Le milieu du XIXᵉ siècle est une période complexe où cohabitent le romantisme, le naturalisme et le réalisme. Eugène Delacroix, Jean-Baptiste Camille Corot, les peintres de l'école de Barbizon, Gustave Courbet, vont jouer leur rôle dans la genèse de l'impressionnisme. Eugène Boudin également. À l'instar du Néerlandais Johan Barthold Jongkind, le peintre normand se passionne dès le début des années 1850 pour les effets atmosphériques, les variations de la lumière, en faisant du ciel et de la mer ses sujets de prédilection. « Si je suis devenu peintre, c'est à Eugène Boudin que je le dois », dira Claude Monet au crépuscule de sa vie.

Au cours des années 1860, une autre personnalité va devenir incontournable, Édouard Manet. Partagé entre son intérêt pour la peinture du passé et sa volonté d'être un témoin de son époque, il apparaît, dès le Salon de 1863 avec *Olympia*, comme l'homme de la « nouvelle

Die Vorläufer des Impressionismus

Im Jahr 1874 findet die erste Ausstellung der Impressionisten statt. Die Grundsätze ihrer Malerei reichen aber weiter zurück. Gegen Mitte des 19. Jahrhunderts bilden sich die Romantik, der Naturalismus und der Realismus als parallel existierende Strömungen heraus. Eugène Delacroix, Jean-Baptiste Camille Corot, die Maler der Schule von Barbizon und Gustave Courbet tragen alle zur Entstehung des Impressionismus bei. So wie Eugène Boudin, der dem Beispiel des niederländischen Malers Johan Barthold Jongkind folgt, und sich zu Beginn der 1850er-Jahre mit dem Studium des Lichts und des Himmels auseinandersetzt. Dieser und das Meer werden seine bevorzugten Motive. „Sollte ich jemals Maler geworden sein, verdanke ich dies Eugène Boudin", wird Claude Monet über den Maler aus der Normandie sagen.

Im Laufe der 1860er-Jahre etabliert sich Édouard Manet in den Pariser Malerkreisen. Der gleichzeitig an historischen und zeitgenössischen Themen

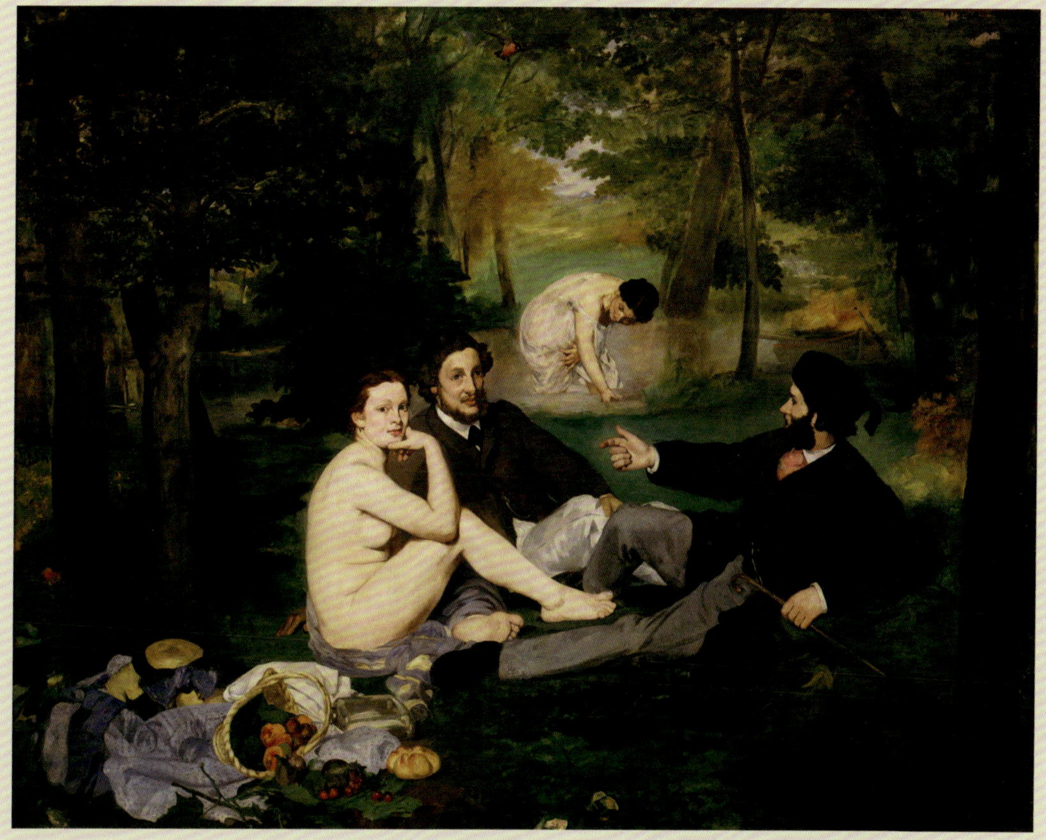

Los Precursores del Impresionismo

En 1874 tuvo lugar la primera exposición de los impresionistas. Los principios de su pintura, sin embargo, van más atrás. Hacia mediados del siglo XIX, el Romanticismo, el Naturalismo y el Realismo surgieron como corrientes paralelas. Eugène Delacroix, Jean-Baptiste Camille Corot, los pintores de la Escuela Barbizon y Gustave Courbet contribuyeron a la aparición del impresionismo. Eugène Boudin, siguiendo el ejemplo del pintor holandés Johan Barthold Jongkind, estudió el estudio de la luz y el cielo a principios de la década de 1850. El cielo y el mar se convierten en sus motivos favoritos. "Si alguna vez me he convertido en pintor, se lo debo a Eugène Boudin", dirá Claude Monet sobre el pintor normando.

A lo largo de la década de 1860, Édouard Manet se estableció en los círculos de la pintura parisina. Con su obra *Olympia*, expuesta en el Salón de 1863, Manet, interesado a la vez en temas históricos y contemporáneos, forjó su reputación como representante de la "nueva pintura". Entre 1869 y 1875

O Provisório do Impressionismo

Em 1874 realizou-se a primeira exposição dos Impressionistas. Os princípios da sua pintura, no entanto, remontam mais atrás. Em meados do século XIX, o Romantismo, o Naturalismo e o Realismo surgiram como correntes paralelas. Eugène Delacroix, Jean-Baptiste Camille Corot, os pintores da Escola Barbizon e Gustave Courbet contribuíram para a emergência do Impressionismo. Eugène Boudin, seguindo o exemplo do pintor holandês Johan Barthold Jongkind, estudou o estudo da luz e do céu no início dos anos 1850. O céu e o mar tornam-se os seus motivos favoritos. "Se alguma vez me tornei pintor, devo isso a Eugène Boudin", dirá Claude Monet sobre o pintor da Normandia.

No decorrer da década de 1860, Édouard Manet estabeleceu-se nos círculos de pintura parisienses. Com seu trabalho *Olympia*, exibido no Salão 1863, Manet, que se interessou simultaneamente por temas históricos e contemporâneos, moldou sua reputação como representante da "nova pintura". Entre 1869 e

De Voorlopers van het Impressionisme

In 1874 vond de eerste tentoonstelling van de impressionisten plaats. De principes van hun schilderkunst gingen echter verder terug in de tijd. Halverwege de 19e eeuw kwamen de romantiek, het naturalisme en realisme als naast elkaar bestaande stromingen op. Eugène Delacroix, Jean-Baptiste Camille Corot, de schilders van de school van Barbizon en Gustave Courbet droegen allemaal bij aan het ontstaan van het impressionisme. Eugène Boudin bestudeerde omstreeks 1850, naar het voorbeeld van de Nederlandse schilder Johan Barthold Jongkind, het licht en de luchten. De lucht en de zee werden zijn favoriete onderwerpen. 'Dat ik ooit schilder ben geworden, heb ik aan Eugène Boudin te danken,' zei Claude Monet over deze schilder uit Normandië. In de loop van de jaren 1860 vestigde Édouard Manet zich in de Parijse schilderskringen. Met zijn werk *Olympia*, dat op de Salon van 1863 te zien was, gaf Manet, die tegelijkertijd geïnteresseerd was in historische en eigentijdse thema's, vorm aan zijn

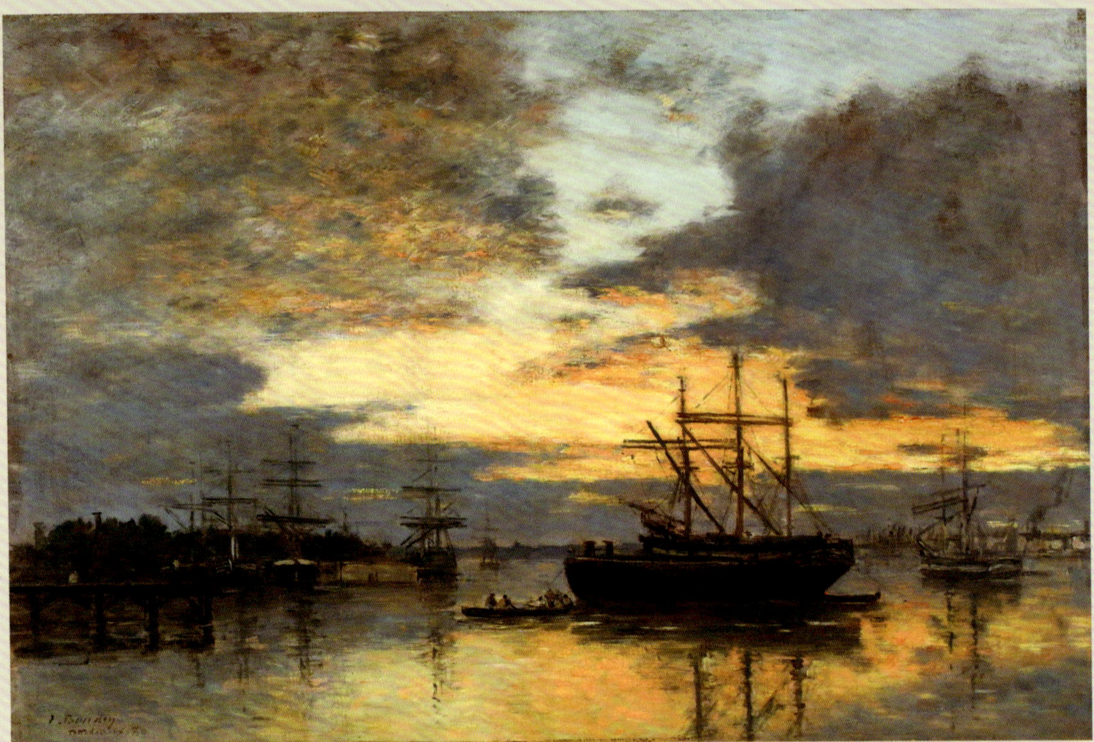

he gathered around him a group of young artists who would become known as the School of Batignolles. They were immortalized by Henri Fantin-Latour in 1870. Regular visitors to Café Guerbois, the group's meeting place, included Claude Monet, Auguste Renoir, Alfred Sisley, Edgar Degas, Camille Pissarro and Frédéric Bazille, who in the course of his short life - he died at the age of 28 - created portraits and nudes between classicism and modernism. His strokes are prudent and precise, yet his hunger for light and bright colors is palpable in his plein-air paintings. He would no longer experience the first exhibition of the Impressionists in 1874. During the second in 1876, Manet ensured that he was posthumously present - among other things through a portrait that Auguste Renoir created of him.

peinture ». Entre 1869 et 1875, il fédère autour de lui de jeunes artistes qui vont constituer, de manière informelle, le groupe des Batignolles (immortalisé par Henri Fantin-Latour en 1870). Parmi les habitués du café Guerbois où ils se réunissent, figurent Claude Monet, Auguste Renoir, Alfred Sisley, Edgar Degas, Camille Pissarro ou encore Frédéric Bazille. Au cours de sa brève carrière (il meurt à 28 ans), ce dernier produit des portraits, des scènes de groupes, des nus masculins, entre classicisme et modernité. Sa touche est sage et appliquée, mais il a le goût du plein air, de la lumière, de la couleur claire. La première exposition impressionniste aura lieu quatre ans après le décès de Bazille. Manet veillera à ce qu'il soit présent, à titre posthume, à la deuxième exposition en 1876, par le biais d'un portrait qu'Auguste Renoir avait fait de lui.

interessierte Manet prägt mit seinem Werk *Olympia*, das 1863 auf dem Salon gezeigt wird, seinen Ruf als Vertreter der „neuen Malerei". Zwischen 1869 und 1875 sammelt er eine Gruppe junger Künstler um sich, die als Schule von Batignolles bekannt werden sollte. Sie werden von Henri Fantin-Latour 1870 verewigt. Zu den regelmäßigen Besuchern des Café Guerbois, dem Treffpunkt der Gruppe, gehören Claude Monet, Auguste Renoir, Alfred Sisley, Edgar Degas, Camille Pissarro und Frédéric Bazille, der im Laufe seines kurzen Lebens – er starb mit 28 Jahren – Porträts und Akte zwischen Klassizismus und Moderne schuf. Seine Striche setzt er besonnen und präzise, dennoch ist in seinen Pleinairgemälden sein Hunger nach Licht und hellen Farben spürbar. Die erste Ausstellung der Impressionisten, wird er nicht mehr erleben. Bei der zweiten im Jahr 1876 sorgt Manet dafür, dass er posthum präsent ist – unter anderem durch ein Porträt, das Auguste Renoir von ihm schuf.

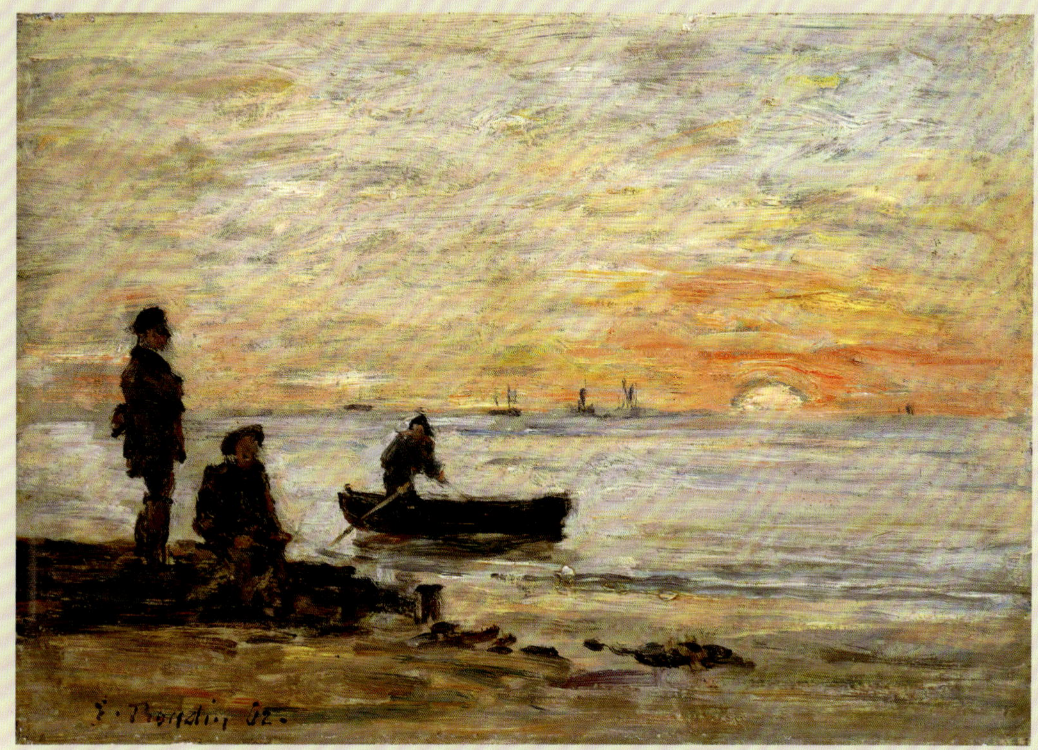

reunió a su alrededor a un grupo de jóvenes artistas que serían conocidos como la Escuela de Batignolles. Son inmortalizados por Henri Fantin-Latour en 1870. El Café Guerbois, lugar de encuentro del grupo, es visitado regularmente por Claude Monet, Auguste Renoir, Alfred Sisley, Edgar Degas, Camille Pissarro y Frédéric Bazille, que a lo largo de su corta vida -cuando murió a la edad de 28 años- creó retratos y desnudos entre clasicismo y modernismo. Sus trazos son prudentes y precisos, pero su sed de luz y colores brillantes es palpable en sus pinturas al aire libre. Ya no vivirá la primera exposición de los impresionistas en 1874. Durante la segunda, en 1876, Manet se aseguró de que estuviera presente a título póstumo, entre otras cosas a través de un retrato que Augusto Renoir creó de él.

1875 ele se reuniu em torno dele um grupo de jovens artistas que se tornaria conhecido como a Escola de Batignolles. São imortalizados por Henri Fantin-Latour em 1870. Visitantes regulares do Café Guerbois, ponto de encontro do grupo, incluem Claude Monet, Auguste Renoir, Alfred Sisley, Edgar Degas, Camille Pissarro e Frédéric Bazille, que ao longo da sua curta vida - quando morreu aos 28 anos - criaram retratos e nus entre o classicismo e o modernismo. Seus traços são prudentes e precisos, mas sua fome por luz e cores brilhantes é palpável em suas pinturas plein-air. Ele não vai mais experimentar a primeira exposição dos Impressionistas em 1874. Durante a segunda, em 1876, Manet assegurou que ele estava postumamente presente - entre outras coisas através de um retrato que Augusto Renoir criou dele.

reputatie als vertegenwoordiger van de 'nieuwe schilderkunst'. Tussen 1869 en 1875 verzamelde hij een groep jonge kunstenaars om zich heen die bekend zouden worden als de school van Batignolles. Ze werden in 1870 vereeuwigd door Henri Fantin-Latour. Tot de vaste bezoekers van Café Guerbois, de ontmoetingsplaats van de groep, behoorden Claude Monet, Auguste Renoir, Alfred Sisley, Edgar Degas, Camille Pissarro en Frédéric Bazille. Die laatste schilderde in de loop van zijn korte leven – hij stierf op 28-jarige leeftijd – portretten en naakten in een stijl die het midden hield tussen classicisme en modernisme. Zijn penseelvoering was bedachtzaam en precies, maar zijn honger naar licht en felle kleuren is duidelijk zichtbaar in zijn plein-airschilderijen. De eerste tentoonstelling van de impressionisten in 1874 zou hij niet meer meemaken. Tijdens de tweede tentoonstelling in 1876 zorgde Manet ervoor dat hij postuum aanwezig was – onder meer door een portret dat Auguste Renoir van hem maakte.

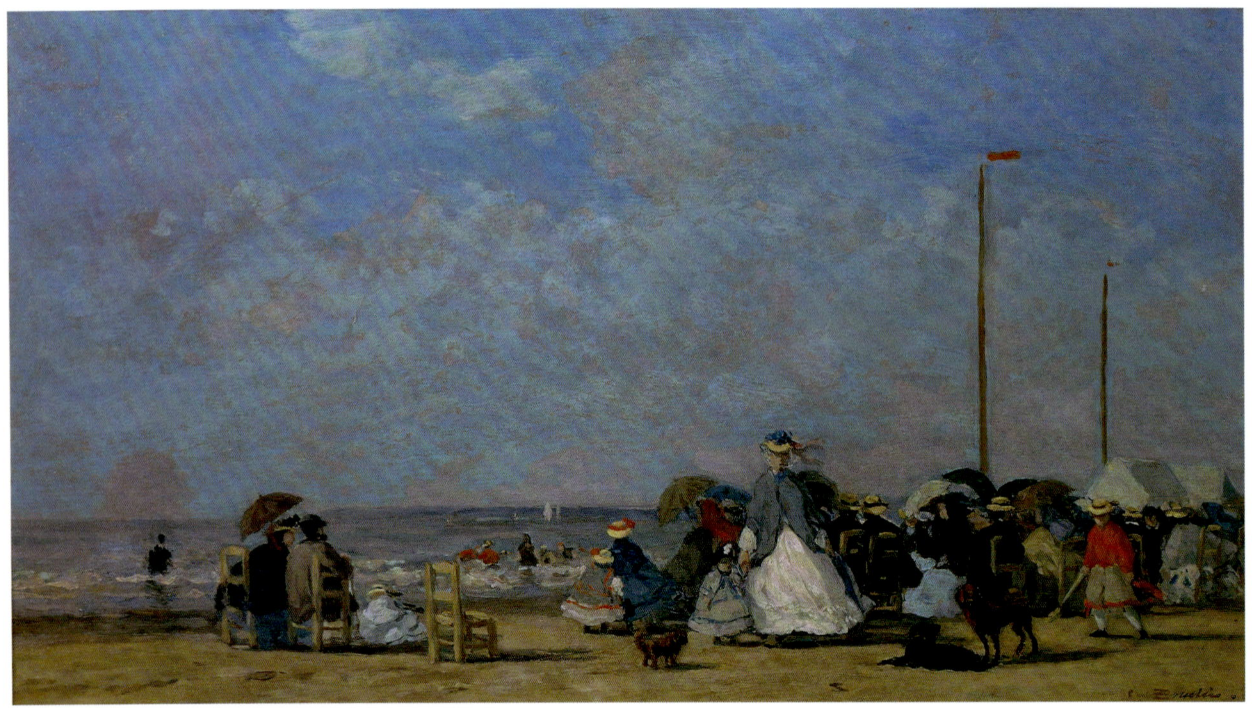

On Trouville Beach

Sur la plage de Trouville

EUGÈNE BOUDIN (1824-1898)

n.d., Oil on panel/Huile sur panneau, Mahmoud Khalil Museum, Cairo

Am Strand von Trouville

En la playa de Trouville

Na praia de Trouville

Op het strand van Trouville

The Jetty at High Tide, Trouville
Boudin's true motif extends over the colorful sails of the boats: the sky, which occupies three quarters of the composition. With innumerable shades of grey, he depicts the light and the movement of the clouds.

La Jetée à marée haute
Au-delà des voiles colorées des bateaux, le vrai sujet chez Boudin est le ciel, qui occupe ici les trois quarts de la composition. Il en traduit la lumière, et la course des nuages aux mille nuances de gris.

Die Mole bei Flut
Über den bunten Segeln der Boote erstreckt sich Boudins wahres Motiv: Der Himmel, der dreiviertel der Komposition einnimmt. Mit unzähligen Grauabstufungen bildet er das Licht und den Zug der Wolken ab.

El muelle en marea alta
Más allá de las coloridas velas de los barcos, el verdadero tema de Boudin es el cielo, que aquí ocupa tres cuartas partes de la composición. Traduce la luz de la misma, y el curso de las nubes con mil matices de gris.

A toupeira na maré alta
O verdadeiro motivo de Boudin estende-se sobre as velas coloridas dos barcos: o céu, que ocupa três quartos da composição. Com inúmeras tonalidades de cinza, retrata a luz e o trem das nuvens.

Het havenhoofd bij hoogwater
Boudins echte onderwerp strekt zich uit boven de kleurige zeilen van de boten: de lucht, die drie kwart van de compositie beslaat. Met ontelbare grijstinten verbeeldde hij het licht en de voorbijdrijvende wolken.

EUGÈNE BOUDIN (1824-1898)

n. d., Oil on panel/Huile sur panneau, 27 × 217 cm, Association Peindre en Normandie, Caen

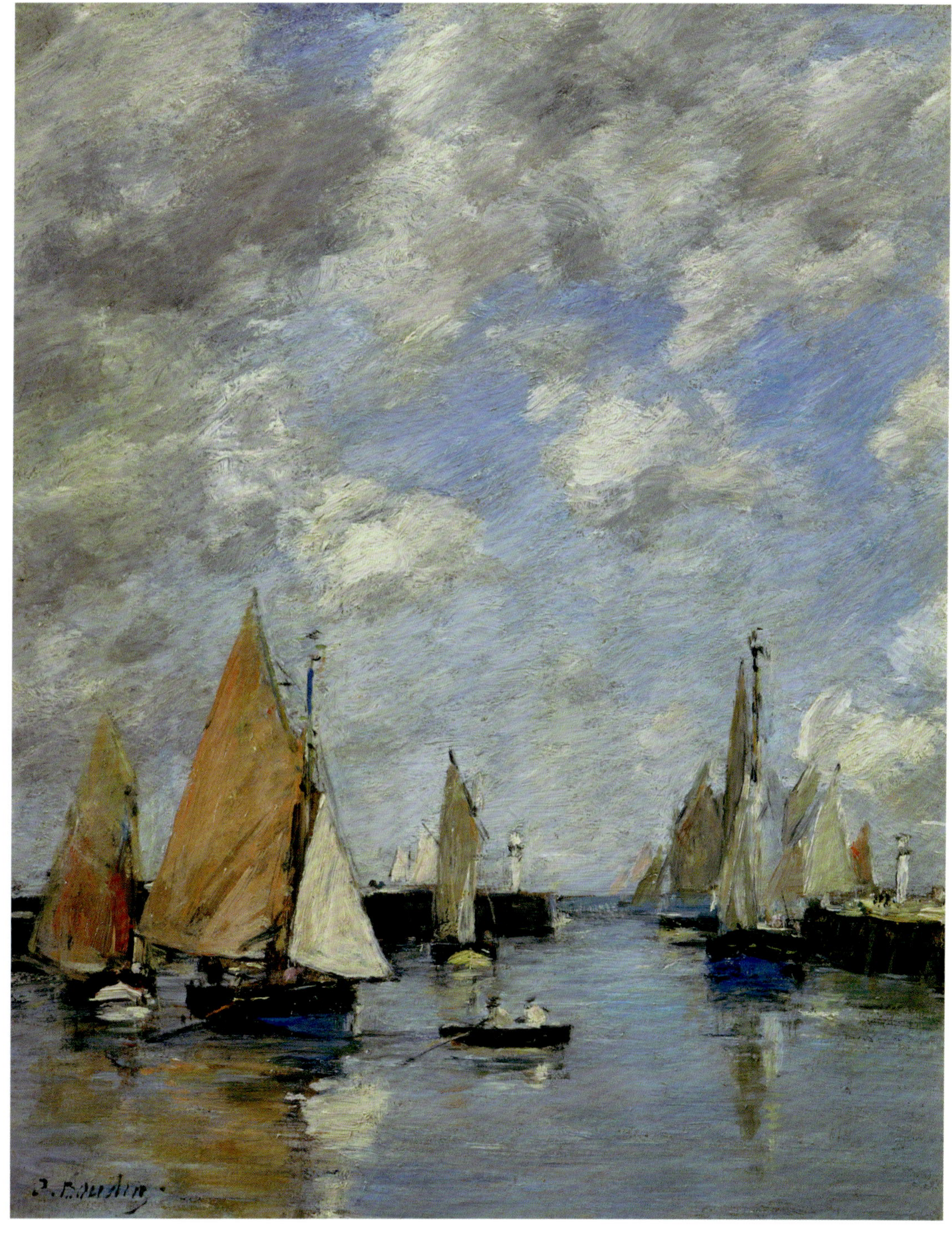

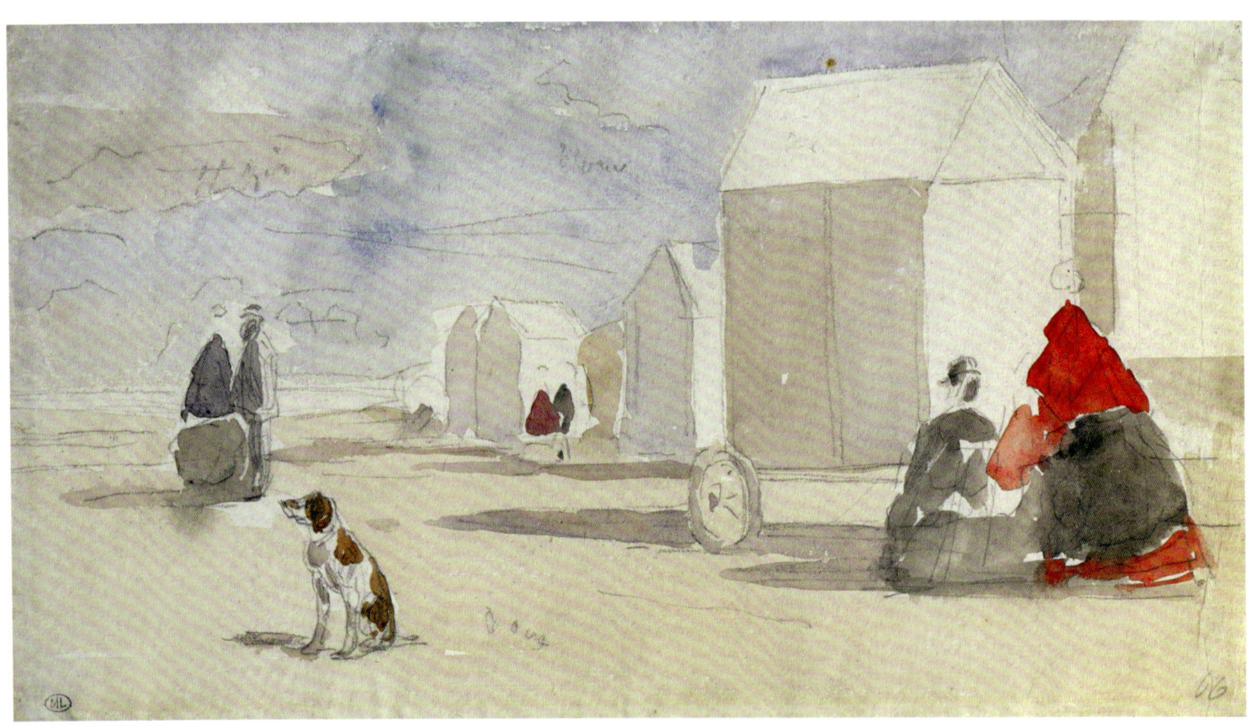

By the Bathing Machines

The beach life of Normandy was one of the artist's favourite
motifs. The sparse strokes and colorful expanse of the
watercolor are enough to bring to mind the bathing pleasure
of a summer afternoon.

Près des cabines

Les scènes de plages normandes comptent parmi
les thèmes de prédilection de l'artiste. Quelques traits
et masses colorées à l'aquarelle suffisent à évoquer
les plaisirs balnéaires d'un après-midi d'été.

Bei den Umkleidekabinen

Das Strandleben der Normandie zählte zu den
Lieblingsmotiven des Künstlers. Die spärlichen Striche
und farbigen Volumina des Aquarells reichen aus, um das
Badevergnügen eines Sommernachmittags vor Augen zu rufen.

En los vestuarios

La vida playera de Normandía fue uno de los motivos
favoritos del artista. Las escasas pinceladas y los coloridos
volúmenes de la acuarela son suficientes para recordar el
placer de bañarse en una tarde de verano.

Nos camarins

A vida na praia da Normandia era um dos motivos
preferidos do artista. Os traços esparsos e os volumes
coloridos da aquarela são suficientes para trazer à mente o
prazer de banho de uma tarde de verão.

Bij de kleedhokjes

Het strandleven van Normandië was een geliefd onderwerp
van de kunstenaar. De spaarzame penseelstreken en kleurige
vlakken van de aquarel zijn genoeg om het zwemplezier van
een zomermiddag op te roepen.

EUGÈNE BOUDIN (1824-1898)

1866, Watercolour on paper/Aquarelle sur papier, 14,8 × 27 cm, Musée d'Orsay, Paris

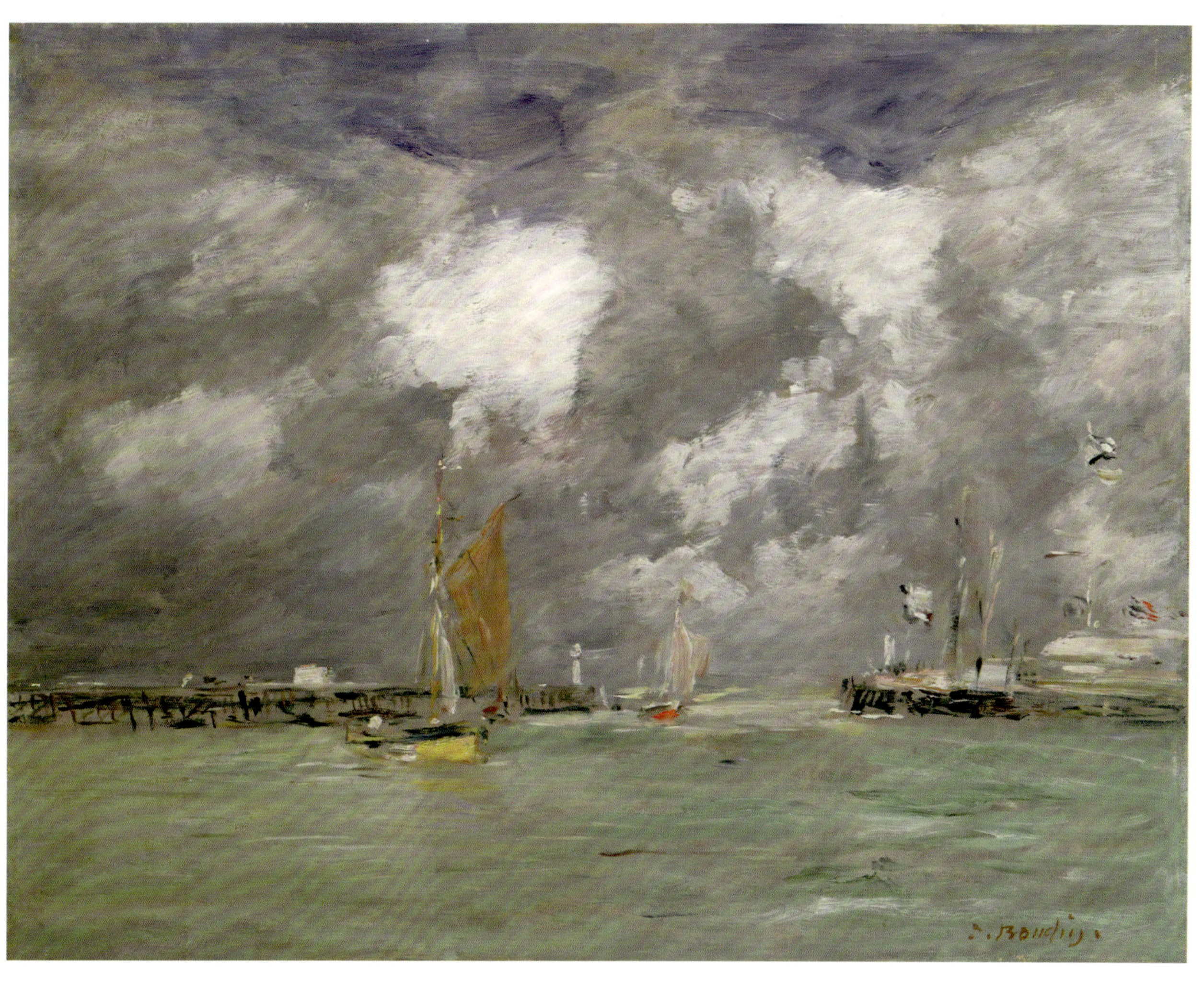

High Tide at Trouville

Marée haute à Trouville

Flut bei Trouville

Marea alta en Trouville

Inundação em Trouville

Vloed bij Trouville

EUGÈNE BOUDIN (1824-1898)
c. 1892-96, Oil on panel/Huile sur panneau,
31 × 39 cm, Private collection

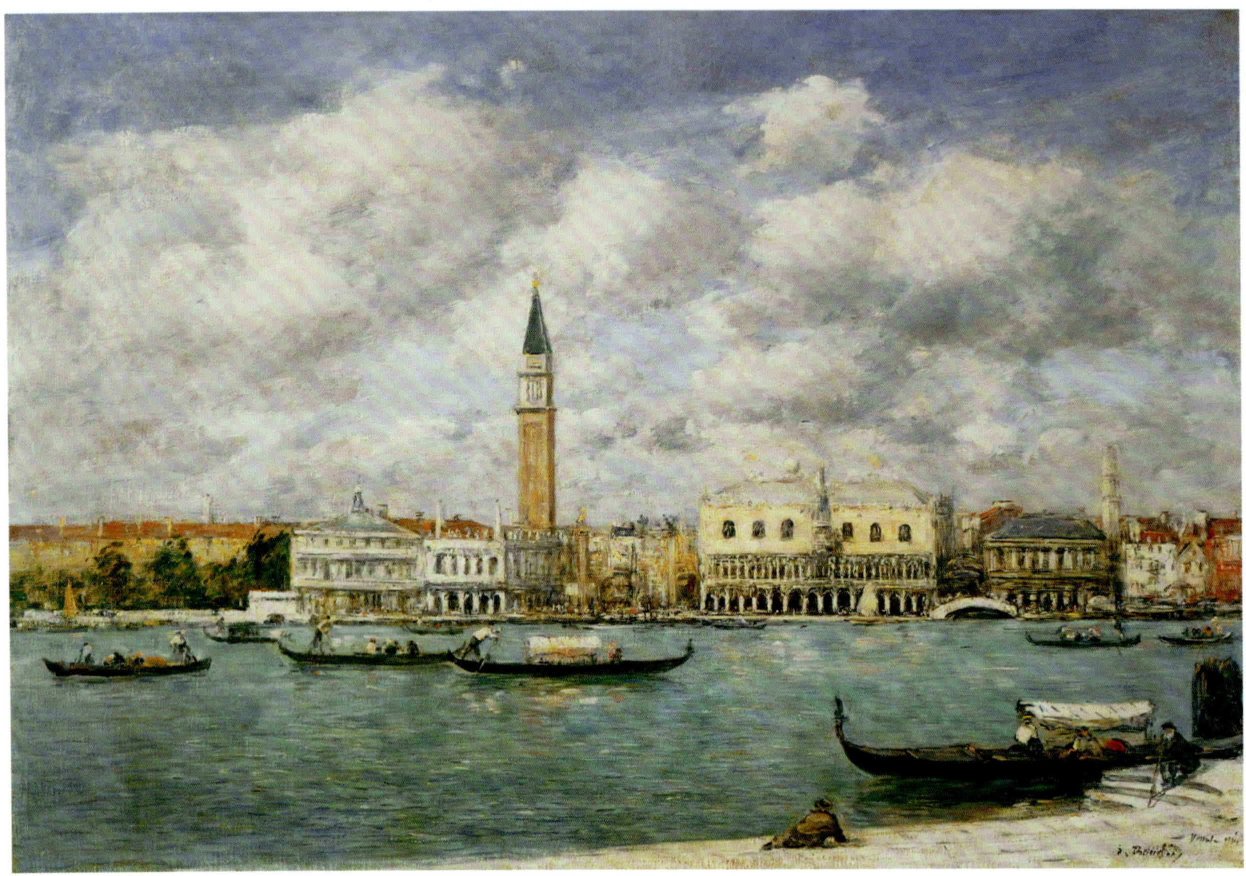

**Venice, Campanile, St Mark's, View of
the Canal from San Giorgio**

His trip to Venice in 1895 inspired Boudin to create some of
his best works, combining the precision of his brushstrokes
with the subtle shades of blue and grey.

**Venise, le Campanile, vue du canal
San Marco prise de San Giorgio**

Son voyage à Venise, en 1895, a inspiré à Boudin quelques-
unes de ses œuvres les plus raffinées, où la précision
du dessin se mêle à la délicatesse de la couleur, toute
en nuances de gris et de bleus.

EUGÈNE BOUDIN (1824-1898)

1895, Oil on canvas/Huile sur toile, 50 × 75 cm, Private collection

**Venedig, der Campanile, Blick auf den Canale
San Marco von San Giorgio Maggiore**

Seine Venedigreise im Jahr 1895 inspirierte Boudin zu
einigen seiner besten Werke, in denen sich die Genauigkeit
seiner Pinselführung mit den feinen Farbabstufungen der
Blau- und Grautöne verbindet.

**Venecia, el Campanile, vista del Canal San
Marco de San Giorgio Maggiore**

Su viaje a Venecia en 1895 inspiró a Boudin a crear algunas
de sus mejores obras, combinando la precisión de sus
pinceladas con los sutiles tonos de azul y gris.

**Veneza, a Campanile, vista do Canale San
Marco de San Giorgio Maggiore**

Sua viagem a Veneza em 1895 inspirou Boudin a criar alguns
de seus melhores trabalhos, combinando a precisão de suas
pinceladas com os tons sutis de azul e cinza.

**Venetië, de Campanile, uitzicht op het
Canale San Marco vanaf San Giorgio**

Zijn reis naar Venetië in 1895 inspireerde Boudin tot enkele
van zijn beste werken, waarbij hij de precisie van zijn
penseelvoering combineerde met het subtiele kleurverloop
van blauw- en grijstinten.

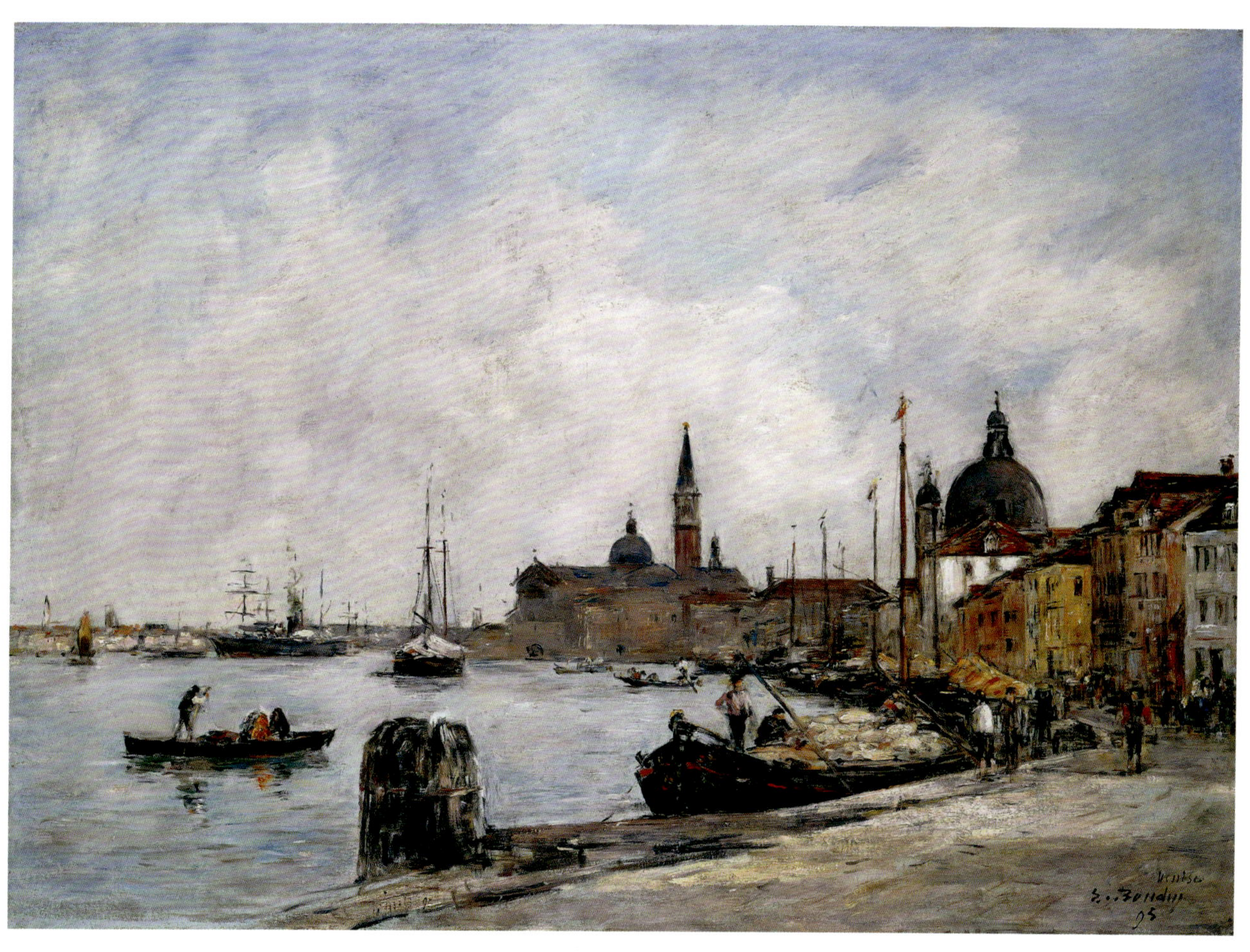

The Quay on Giudecca, Venice

Le Quai de la Giudecca, Venise

Der Kai von Giudecca, Venedig

El muelle de Giudecca, Venecia

O cais de Giudecca, Veneza

De kade van Giudecca, Venetië

EUGÈNE BOUDIN (1824-1898)

1895, Oil on canvas/Huile sur toile,
47 × 65,5 cm, Private collection

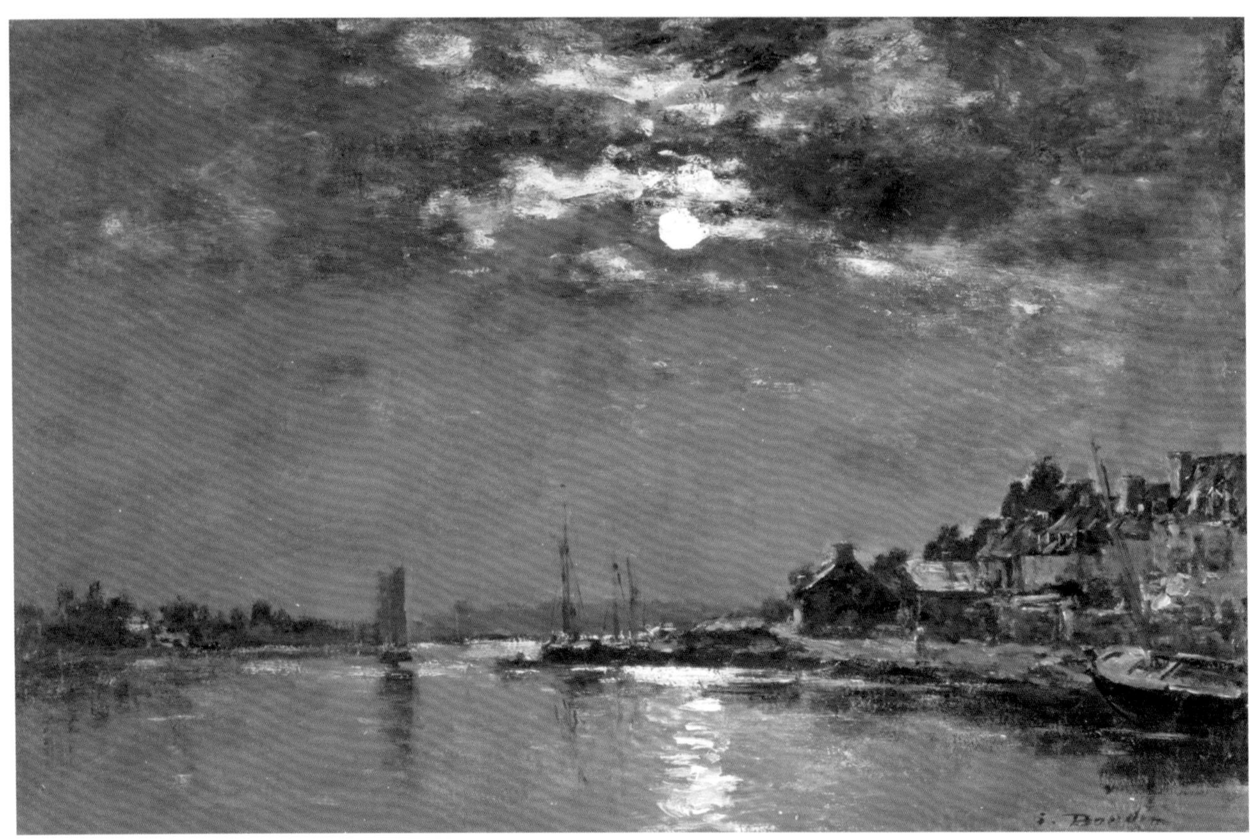

Moonlight Village Scene, Le Faou, Brittany

Le Village du Faou au clair de lune

Das Dorf Faou im Mondschein

El pueblo de Faou a la luz de la luna

A aldeia de Faou ao luar

Het dorp Faou bij maanlicht

EUGÈNE BOUDIN (1824-1898)

1860-65, Oil on canvas/Huile sur toile,
30,5 × 46,5 cm, Southampton City Art Gallery, Southampton

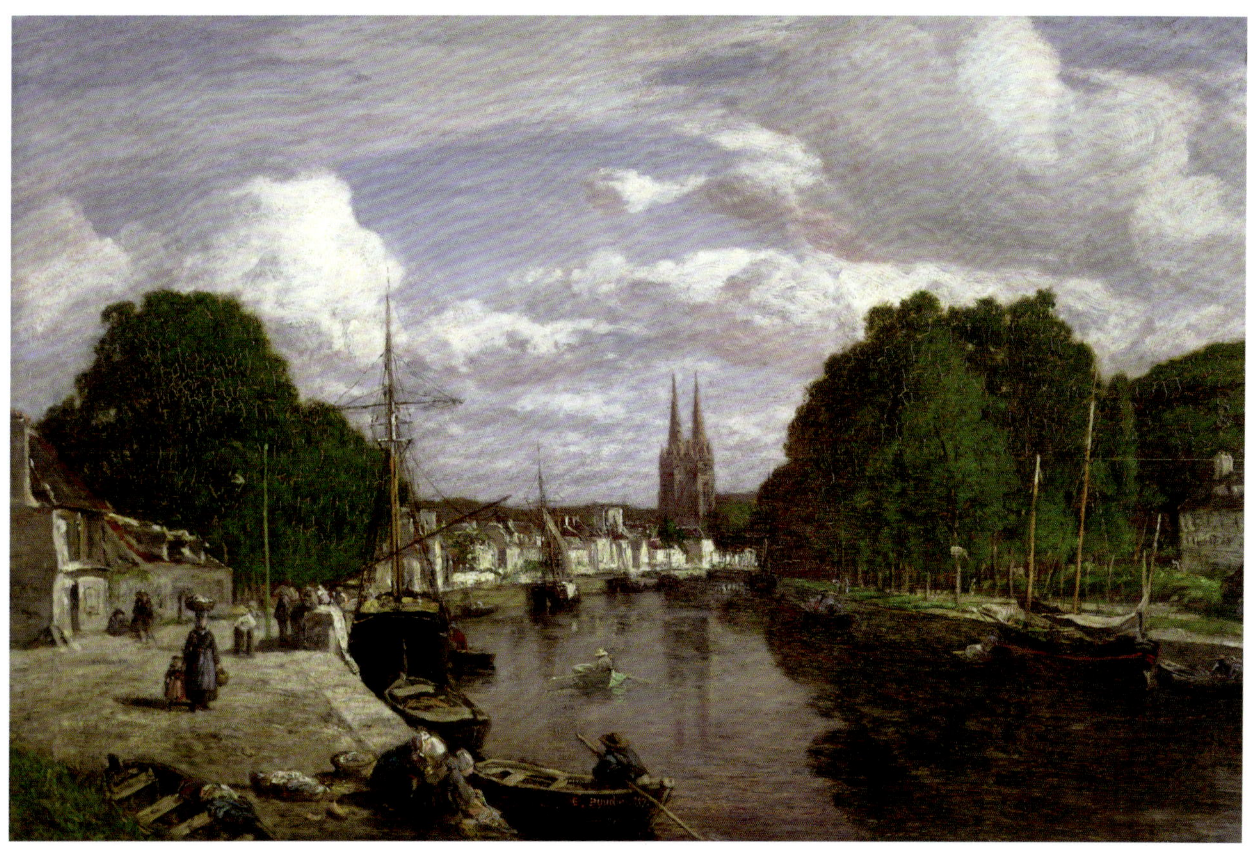

The Port at Quimper

Boudin traveled aroung Brittany in 1885. He was to return 27 times by 1897. He painted the view of Quimper from the harbor, on the banks of the Odet. In the background you can see the towers of the cathedral.

Le port de Quimper

Boudin découvre la Bretagne en 1885. Il s'y rendra vingt-sept fois jusqu'en 1897. Pour cette vue de Quimper, avec les flèches de la cathédrale au fond, il se place du côté du port, au bord de l'Odet.

EUGÈNE BOUDIN (1824-1898)

1857, Oil on wood/Huile sur bois, 27 × 35 cm, Musée des Beaux-Arts, Quimper

Der Hafen von Quimper

Boudin bereist 1885 die Bretagne. Bis 1897 sollte er 27 Mal wiederkommen. Die Ansicht von Quimper malt er vom Hafen aus, an den Ufern des Odet. Im Hintergrund sind die Türme der Kathedrale zu sehen.

El puerto de Quimper

Boudin viaja a Bretaña en 1885. Hasta 1897 regresaría unas 27 veces. Pinta la vista de Quimper desde el puerto, a orillas del Odet. En el fondo se pueden ver las torres de la catedral.

O porto de Quimper

Boudin viaja pela Bretanha em 1885. Ele devia voltar 27 vezes até 1897. Ele pinta a vista do Quimper do porto, nas margens do Odet. Ao fundo pode ver as torres da catedral.

De haven van Quimper

Boudin reisde in 1885 door Bretagne. Hij zou er tot 1897 27 keer terugkomen. Hij schilderde het zicht op Quimper vanuit de haven, aan de oevers van de Odet. Op de achtergrond zijn de torens van de kathedraal te zien.

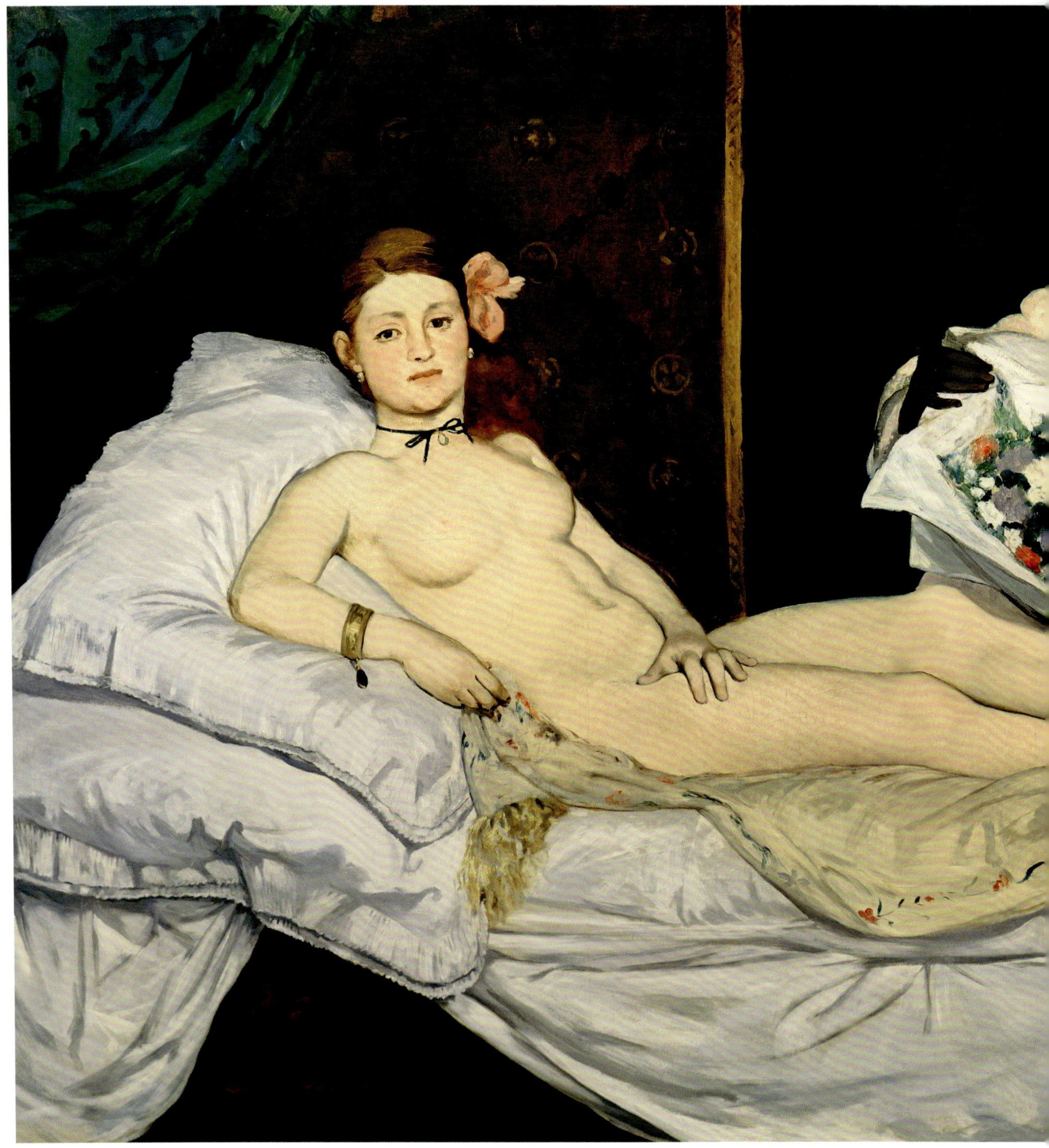

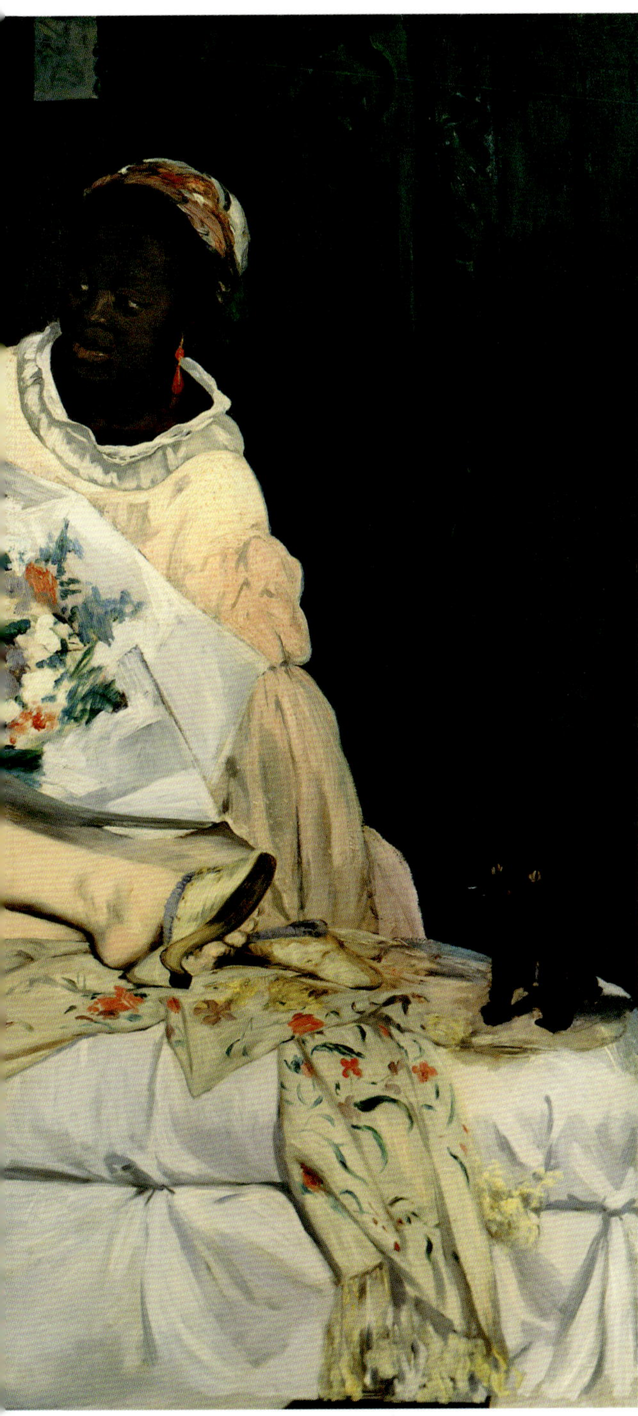

Olympia

The painting caused a scandal at the Salon in 1865.
Based on Titian's *Venus of Urbino*, Manet painted
the non-idealized nude of a prostitute looking
directly at the viewer.

Olympia

Dans cette toile qui fit scandale au Salon de 1865,
Manet ose un nu féminin non idéalisé. Malgré la référence à
la *Vénus d'Urbin* de Titien, il peint une prostituée
bien réelle, qui regarde le spectateur.

Olympia

Das Gemälde sorgte auf dem Salon 1865 für einen Skandal.
Angelehnt an Tizians *Venus von Urbino* malt Manet
den nicht idealisierten Akt einer Prostituierten, die den
Betrachter direkt anblickt.

Olympia

La pintura causó un escándalo en el Salón en 1865.
Basada en la *Venus de Urbino* de Tiziano, Manet pinta
el desnudo no idealizado de una prostituta mirando
directamente al espectador.

Olympia

A pintura causou um escândalo no Salão em 1865.
Baseado na *Vénus de Urbino* de Ticiano, Manet pinta
o ato não idealizado de uma prostituta olhando
diretamente para o espectador.

Olympia

Het schilderij veroorzaakte een schandaal op de
Salon van 1865. Gebaseerd op Titiaans *Venus van Urbino*
schilderde Manet het niet-geïdealiseerde naakt van een
prostituee die de kijker aankijkt.

ÉDOUARD MANET (1832-1883)

1863, Oil on canvas/Huile sur toile, 130 × 190 cm,
Musée d'Orsay, Paris

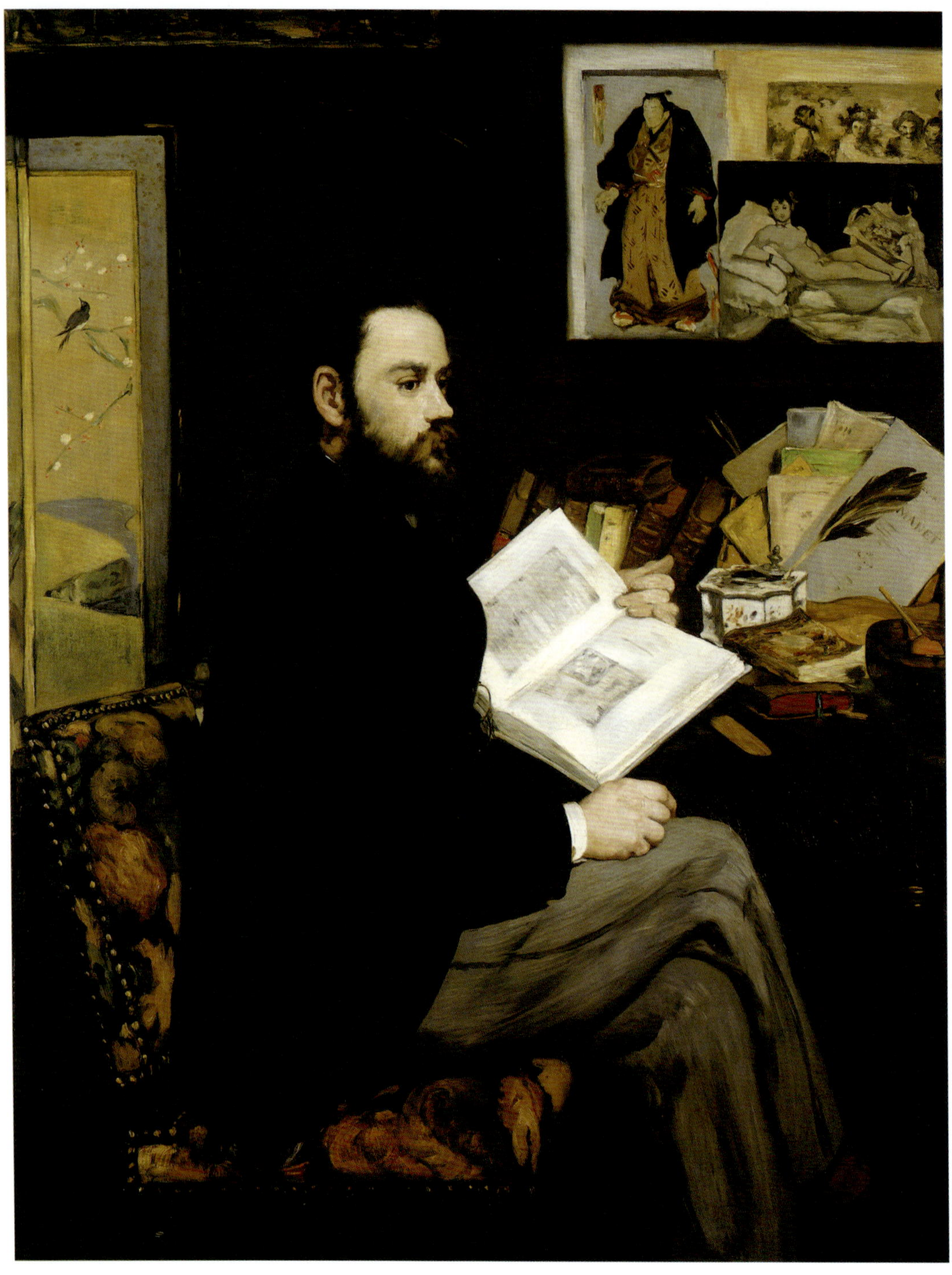

Émile Zola
(1840-1902)

ÉDOUARD MANET
(1832-1883)
1868, Oil on canvas/
Huile sur toile,
146,5 × 114 cm,
Musée d'Orsay, Paris

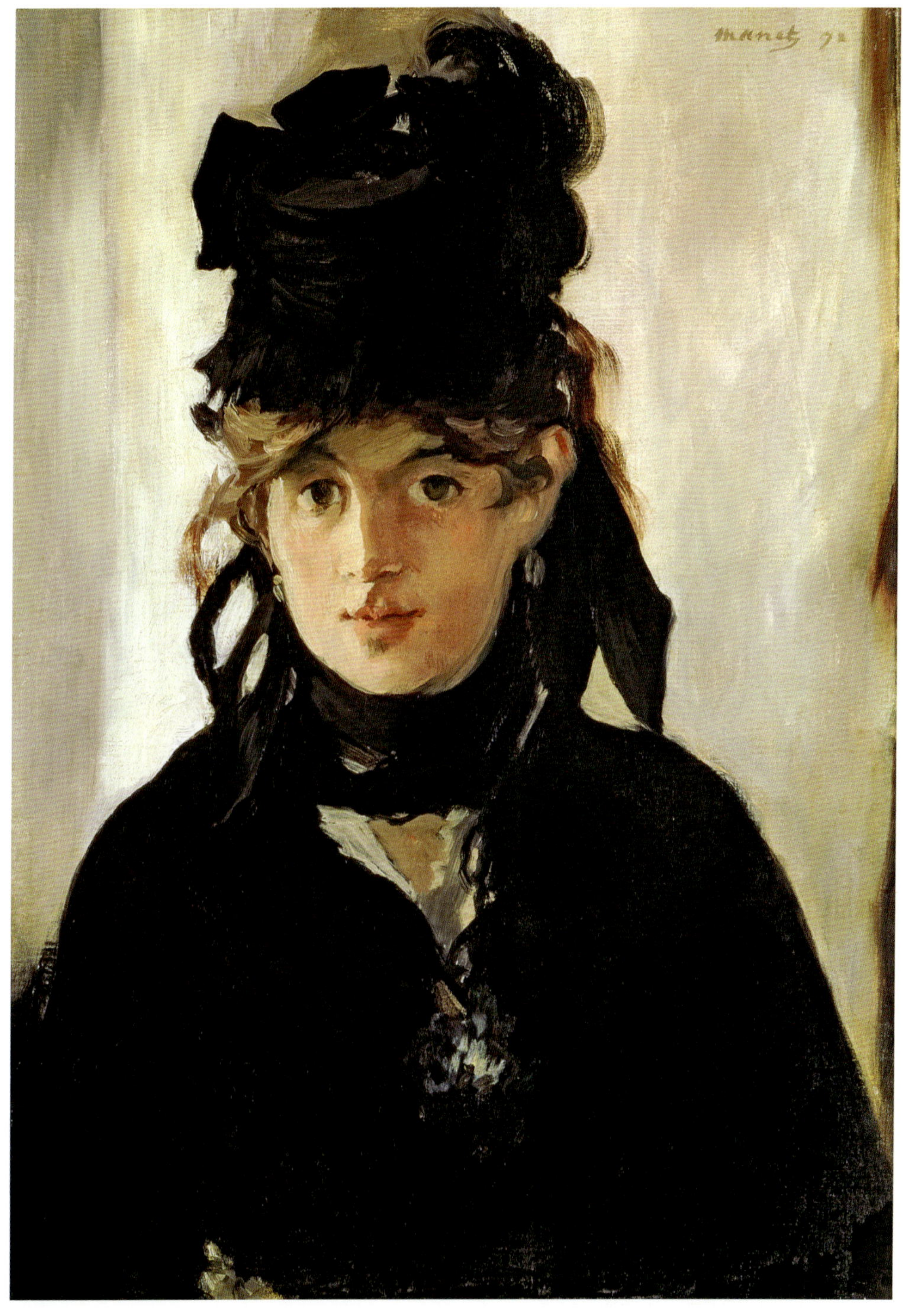

Berthe Morisot with a Bouquet of Violets

Twelve paintings testify to the friendship between Manet and Berthe Morisot, and she married his brother. The predominant black tones of the portrait underline the pale complexion of the face.

Berthe Morisot au bouquet de violettes

Douze tableaux attestent de l'amitié qui unit Édouard Manet et Berthe Morisot. Elle épousera le frère de l'artiste. Dans ce portrait, la pâleur du visage est accentuée par la prédominance du noir.

Berthe Morisot mit Veilchenstrauß

Zwölf Gemälde zeugen von der Freundschaft zwischen Manet und Berthe Morisot. Sie wird seinen Bruder heiraten. Die vorherrschenden Schwarztöne des Porträts unterstreichen den blassen Teint des Gesichts.

Berthe Morisot con ramo de violetas

Doce cuadros dan testimonio de la amistad entre Manet y Berthe Morisot, la cual se va a casar con su hermano. Los tonos negros predominantes del retrato subrayan la tez pálida de la cara.

Berthe Morisot com bouquet de violetas

Doze pinturas testemunham a amizade entre Manet e Berthe Morisot. Ela vai casar com o irmão dele. Os tons pretos predominantes do retrato sublinham a tez pálida do rosto.

Berthe Morisot met boeket viooltjes

Twaalf schilderijen getuigen van de vriendschap tussen Manet en Berthe Morisot. Ze zou met zijn broer trouwen. De overheersende zwarttinten van het portret accentueren de bleke teint van het gezicht.

ÉDOUARD MANET (1832-1883)

1872, Oil on canvas/Huile sur toile, 55 × 3940 cm, Musée d'Orsay, Paris

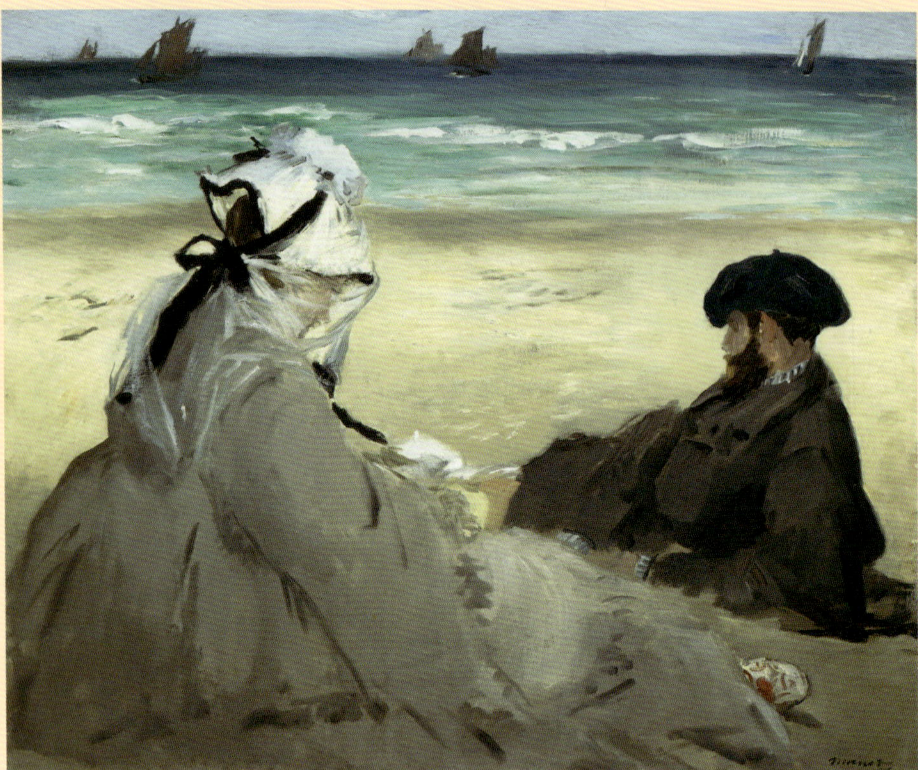

Édouard Manet

Édouard Manet (1832-1883) did much to free painting
from the constraints of academism. The bourgeois
painter was trained from 1850 in the studio of
Thomas Couture. His first works were genre
paintings influenced by Spanish painters. In 1863,
his infamous painting *Luncheon on the Grass*, with
its real nudes, made him the star of the Salon des
Refusés. In 1865 he celebrated a success at the Salon
with *Olympia*, which is based on Titian's *Venus of
Urbino*. He skilfully mixed allusions to the past
and art history with contemporary influences,
which earned him his reputation as a "painter of
modern life". He also had a decisive influence on the
Impressionists. Manet was older than Bazille, Cézanne,
Monet or Renoir, but also devoted to plein air painting
and some impressionist themes such as rowing, horse
racing or cafés. But he was much more interested in
people and scenes of everyday life. In the course of his
career he created over 400 paintings.

Édouard Manet

Né dans un milieu bourgeois, Édouard Manet
(1832-1883) a largement contribué à libérer la peinture
des carcans de l'académisme. Il débute en 1850 dans
l'atelier de Thomas Couture. Ses premières œuvres
sont des scènes de genre marquées par la peinture
espagnole. « Star » du Salon des Refusés en 1863 avec
son sulfureux *Déjeuner sur l'herbe*, au nu trop réel, puis
du Salon de 1865 avec *Olympia* – très librement inspiré
de la *Vénus d'Urbin* de Titien –, il mêle habilement
les références au passé et les clins d'œil à l'histoire
de l'art à la réalité de son temps. Il est considéré
comme « le peintre de la vie moderne ». Plus âgé que
Bazille, Cézanne, Monet ou Renoir, il a joué auprès
des impressionnistes un rôle décisif. S'il s'adonne à
la peinture en plein air et traite de certains sujets qui
leur seront chers, comme les canotiers, les courses
de chevaux, les scènes de cafés, Manet sera toujours
davantage intéressé par les personnages, les portraits,
la vie quotidienne, que par le paysage pur. Il a peint plus
de quatre cents toiles.

Édouard Manet

Édouard Manet (1832–1883) trug viel dazu bei, um
die Malerei aus den Zwängen des Akademismus zu
befreien. Ausgebildet wurde der bourgeoise Maler
ab 1850 im Atelier von Thomas Couture. Seine ersten
Werke werden Genrebilder, die von spanischen Malern
beeinflusst sind. 1863 macht ihn sein anrüchiges
Gemälde *Das Frühstück im Grünen* durch die realen
Aktdarstellungen zum Star des Salons des Refusés. 1865
feiert er mit *Olympia*, das an Tizians *Venus von Urbino*
angelehnt ist, einen Erfolg auf dem Salon. Gekonnt
mischt er Anspielungen auf die Vergangenheit und
die Kunstgeschichte mit zeitgenössischen Einflüssen,
was ihm seinen Ruf als „Maler des modernen Lebens
einbringt". Auch die Impressionisten beeinflusst er
entscheidend. Manet ist älter als Bazille, Cézanne,
Monet oder Renoir, widmet sich aber ebenfalls der
Pleinairmalerei und einigen impressionistischen
Themen, wie Ruderern, Pferderennen oder Cafés. Viel
mehr interessieren ihn jedoch Menschen und Szenen
des alltäglichen Lebens. Im Laufe seiner Karriere wird
er über 400 Gemälde schaffen.

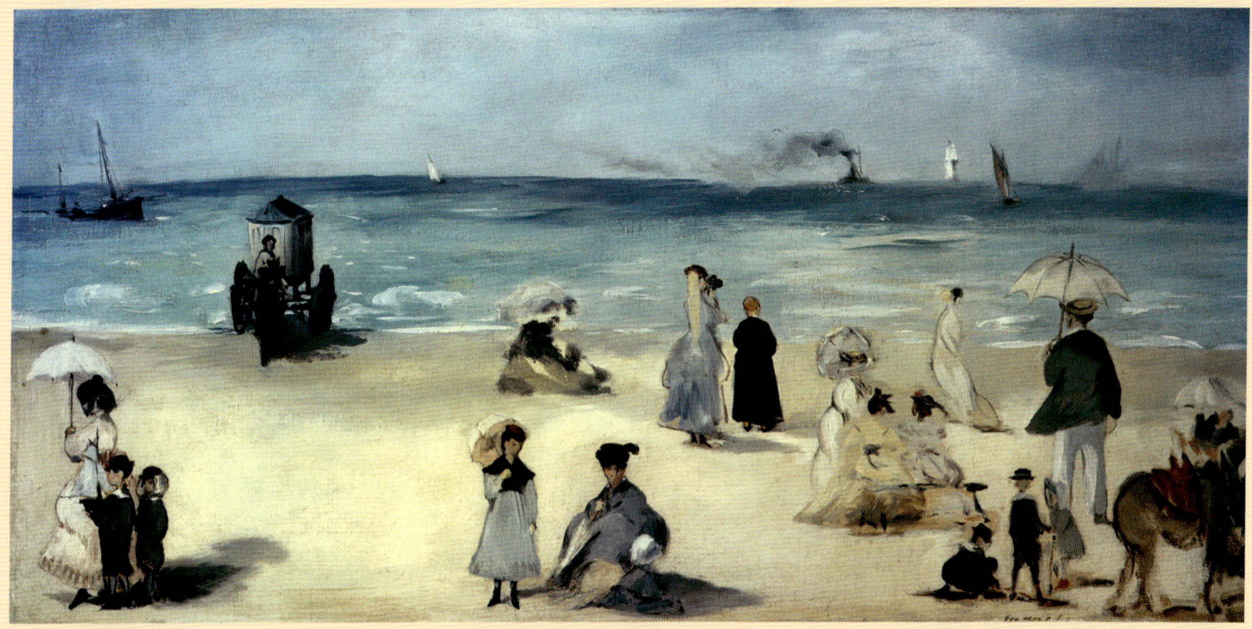

On the Beach, Boulogne-sur-Mer

Sur la plage à Boulogne

Am Strand vom Boulogne-sur-Mer

En la playa de Boulogne-sur-Mer

Na praia de Boulogne-sur-Mer

Op het strand van Boulogne-sur-Mer

ÉDOUARD MANET (1832-1883)
1868, Oil on canvas/Huile sur toile, 32,4 × 66,04 cm, Virginia Museum of Fine Arts, Richmond

Édouard Manet

Édouard Manet (1832-1883) hizo mucho para liberar a la pintura de las limitaciones del academicismo. El pintor burgués se formó a partir de 1850 en el taller de Thomas Couture. Sus primeras obras se convirtieron en pinturas de género influenciadas por pintores españoles. En 1863, su infame pintura *Desayunosobre la hierba*, con sus desnudos reales, lo convirtió en la estrella del Salón de los Rechazados. En 1865 celebró un éxito en el Salón con *Olympia*, que se basa en *La Venus de Urbino* de Tiziano. Mezcla hábilmente alusiones al pasado y a la historia del arte con influencias contemporáneas, lo que le valió la fama de "pintor de la vida moderna". También tuvo una influencia decisiva en los impresionistas. Manet es más viejo que Bazille, Cézanne, Monet o Renoir, pero también se dedica a la pintura al aire libre y a algunos temas impresionistas como el remo, las carreras de caballos o los cafés. Pero está mucho más interesado en las personas y en las escenas de la vida cotidiana. A lo largo de su carrera creará más de 400 cuadros.

Édouard Manet

Édouard Manet (1832-1883) fez muito para libertar a pintura das restrições do academismo. O pintor burguês foi treinado desde 1850 no estúdio de Thomas Couture. Suas primeiras obras tornaram-se pinturas de gênero influenciadas por pintores espanhóis. Em 1863, sua infame pintura *O piquenique no bosque*, com seus verdadeiros nus, fez dele a estrela do Salon des Refusés. Em 1865 ele comemorou um sucesso no Salão com Olympia, que é baseado na *Venus de Urbino* de Ticiano. Ele habilmente mistura alusões ao passado e à história da arte com influências contemporâneas, o que lhe valeu sua reputação de "pintor da vida moderna". Ele também teve uma influência decisiva nos impressionistas. Manet é mais velho do que Bazille, Cézanne, Monet ou Renoir, mas também dedicado à pintura aérea plein e alguns temas impressionistas, como remo, corridas de cavalos ou cafés. Mas ele está muito mais interessado em pessoas e cenas da vida cotidiana. Ao longo de sua carreira, ele vai criar mais de 400 pinturas.

Édouard Manet

Édouard Manet (1832-1883) deed veel om de schilderkunst te bevrijden van de beperkingen van het academisme. De uit de burgerij afkomstige schilder kreeg zijn opleiding vanaf 1850 in het atelier van Thomas Couture. Zijn eerste werken waren genrestukken, beïnvloed door Spaanse schilders. In 1863 werd hij met zijn beruchte schilderij *Le Déjeuner sur l'herbe*, met zijn realistische naakten, de ster van de Salon des Refusés. In 1865 had hij op de Salon succes met *Olympia*, dat gebaseerd was op Titiaans *Venus van Urbino*. Vakkundig combineerde hij toespelingen op het verleden en de kunstgeschiedenis met eigentijdse invloeden, wat hem zijn reputatie als 'schilder van het moderne leven' opleverde. Hij had ook een beslissende invloed op de impressionisten. Manet was ouder dan Bazille, Cézanne, Monet en Renoir, maar hield zich eveneens bezig met de plein-airschilderkunst en enkele impressionistische thema's, zoals roeiers, paardenraces en cafés. Maar hij was nog veel meer geïnteresseerd in mensen en alledaagse taferelen. In de loop van zijn carrière zou hij meer dan 400 schilderijen maken.

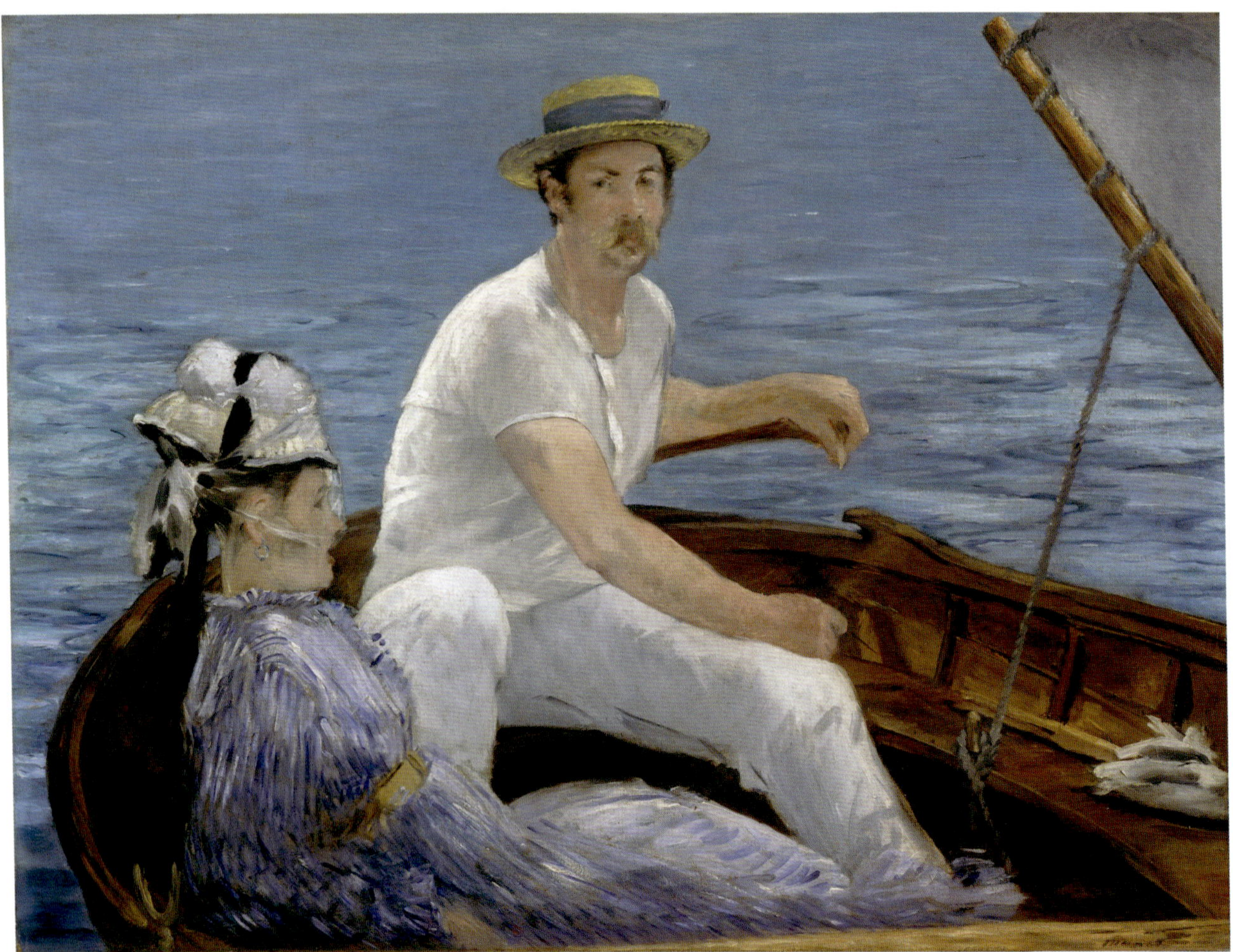

Boating

En Bateau

Im Boot

En el barco

No barco

In de boot

ÉDOUARD MANET (1832-1883)

1874, Oil on canvas/Huile sur toile, 97,2 × 130,2 cm, Metropolitan Museum of Art, New York

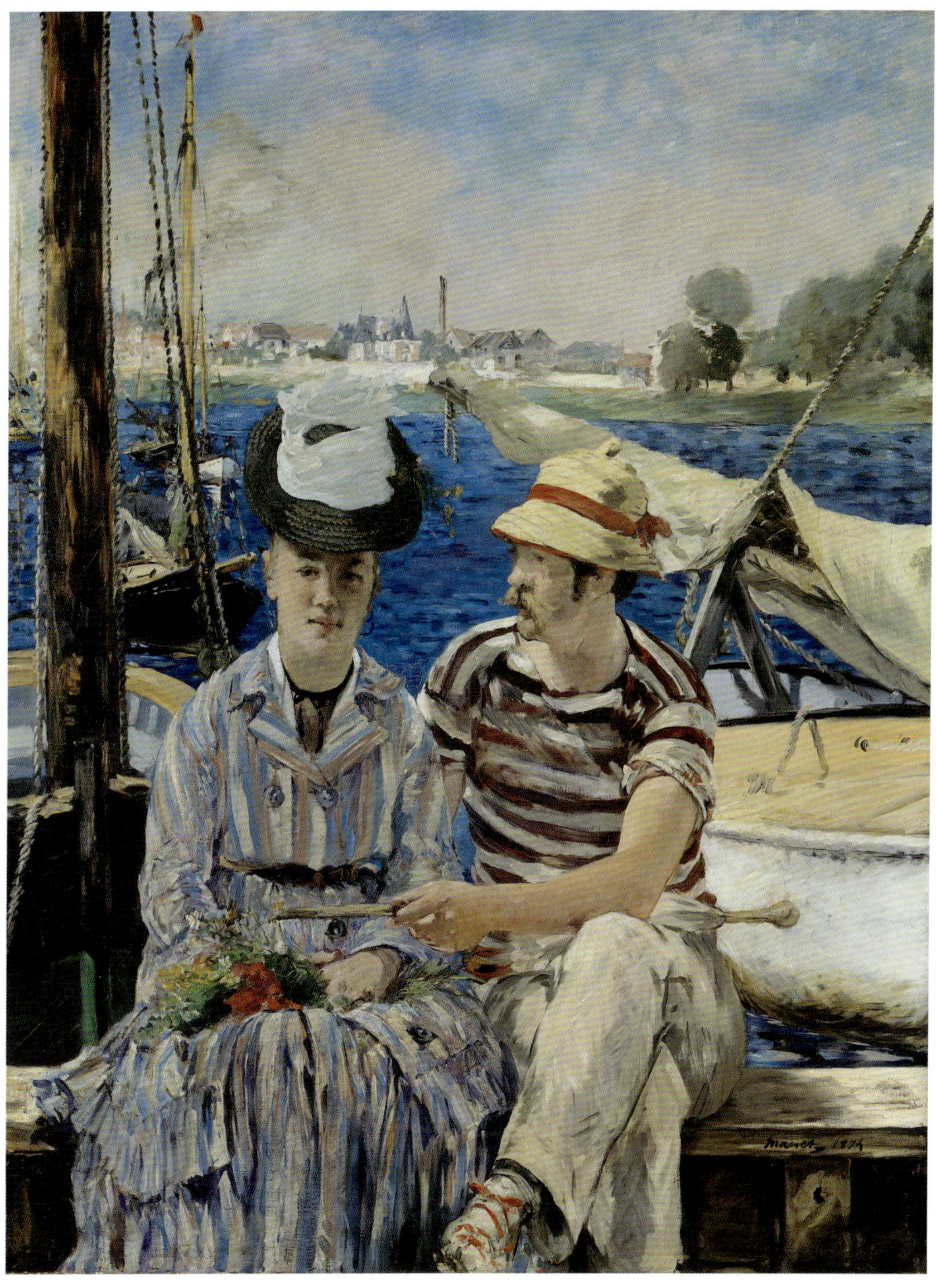

Argenteuil

ÉDOUARD MANET
(1832-1883)

1874, Oil on canvas/
Huile sur toile, 149 × 115 cm,
Musée des Beaux-Arts,
Tournai

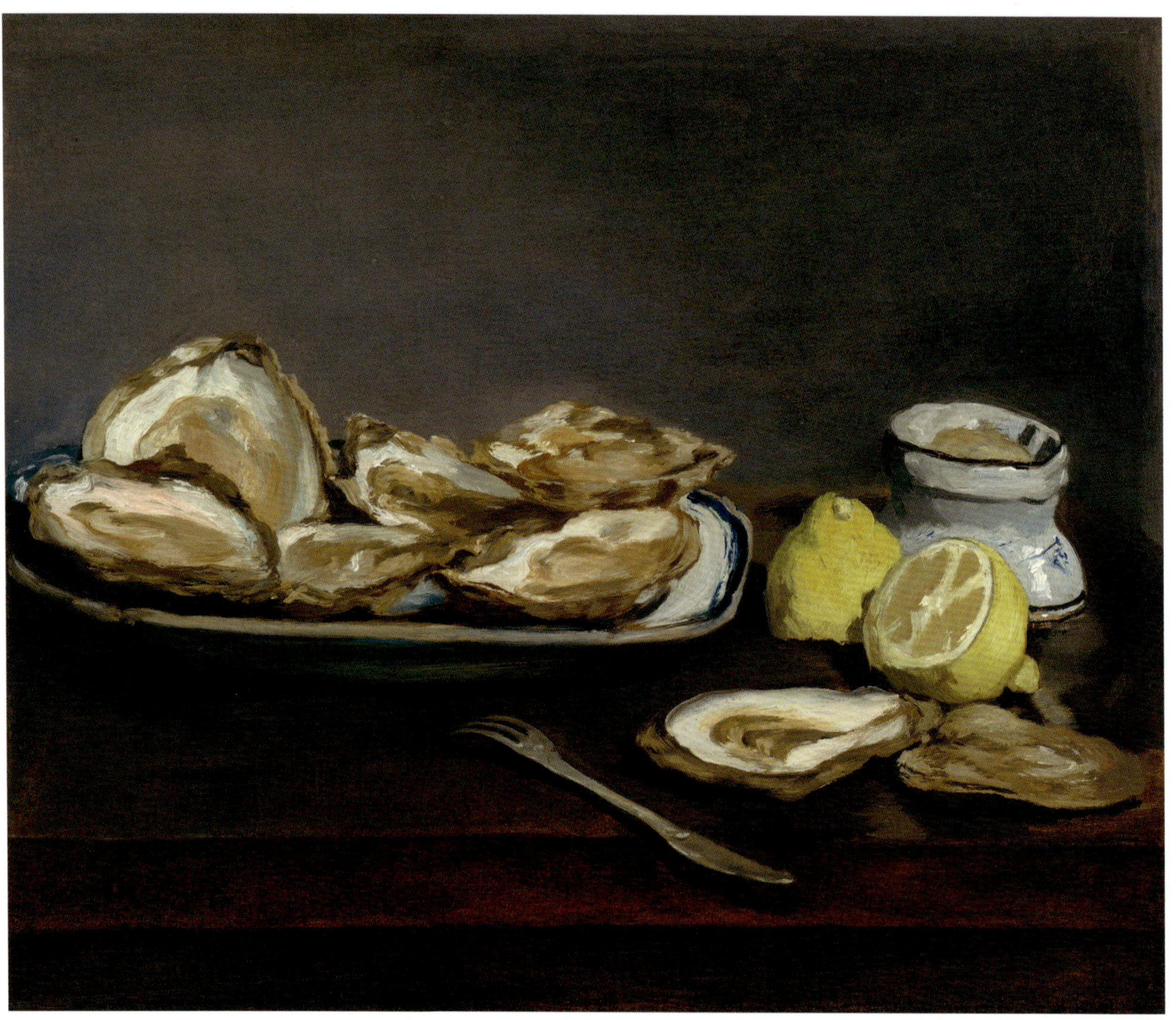

Still life with oysters and lemons

Nature morte avec huîtres et citrons

Stillleben mit Austern und Zitronen

Bodegón con ostras y limones

Natureza morta com ostras e limões

Stilleven met oesters en citroen

ÉDOUARD MANET (1832-1883)

1862, Oil on canvas/Huile sur toile, 39,2 × 46,8 cm,
National Gallery of Art, Washington

Pinks and Clematis in a Crystal Vase

Manet applied himself with devotion to the still life. Throughout his life he always painted new motifs. His works were unanimously praised, even by his most vehement critics.

Œillets et clématite dans un vase de cristal

Le peintre attachait une grande importance aux natures mortes. Il en peindra tout au long de sa carrière, et ces œuvres firent l'unanimité, y compris chez les critiques les plus virulents à son égard.

Nelken und Klematis

Manet widmet sich mit Hingabe dem Stillleben. Zeit seines Lebens malt er immer wieder neue Motive. Seine Werke werden einstimmig gelobt, selbst von seinen heftigsten Kritikern.

Claveles y clemátides

Manet se dedica con devoción a la naturaleza muerta. A lo largo de su vida pintó siempre nuevos motivos. Sus obras son elogiadas unánimemente, incluso por sus críticos más vehementes.

Cravos e Clematis

Manet dedica-se com devoção à natureza morta. Ao longo da sua vida ele sempre pintou novos motivos. As suas obras são unanimemente elogiadas, mesmo pelos seus críticos mais veementes.

Anjers en clematissen in een kristallen vaas

Manet stortte zich met toewijding op stillevens. Hij schilderde ze zijn hele leven, steeds met nieuwe onderwerpen. Zijn werken worden unaniem geprezen, zelfs door zijn grootste critici.

ÉDOUARD MANET (1832-1883)

c. 1882, Oil on canvas/Huile sur toile, 56 × 35,5 cm, Musée d'Orsay, Paris

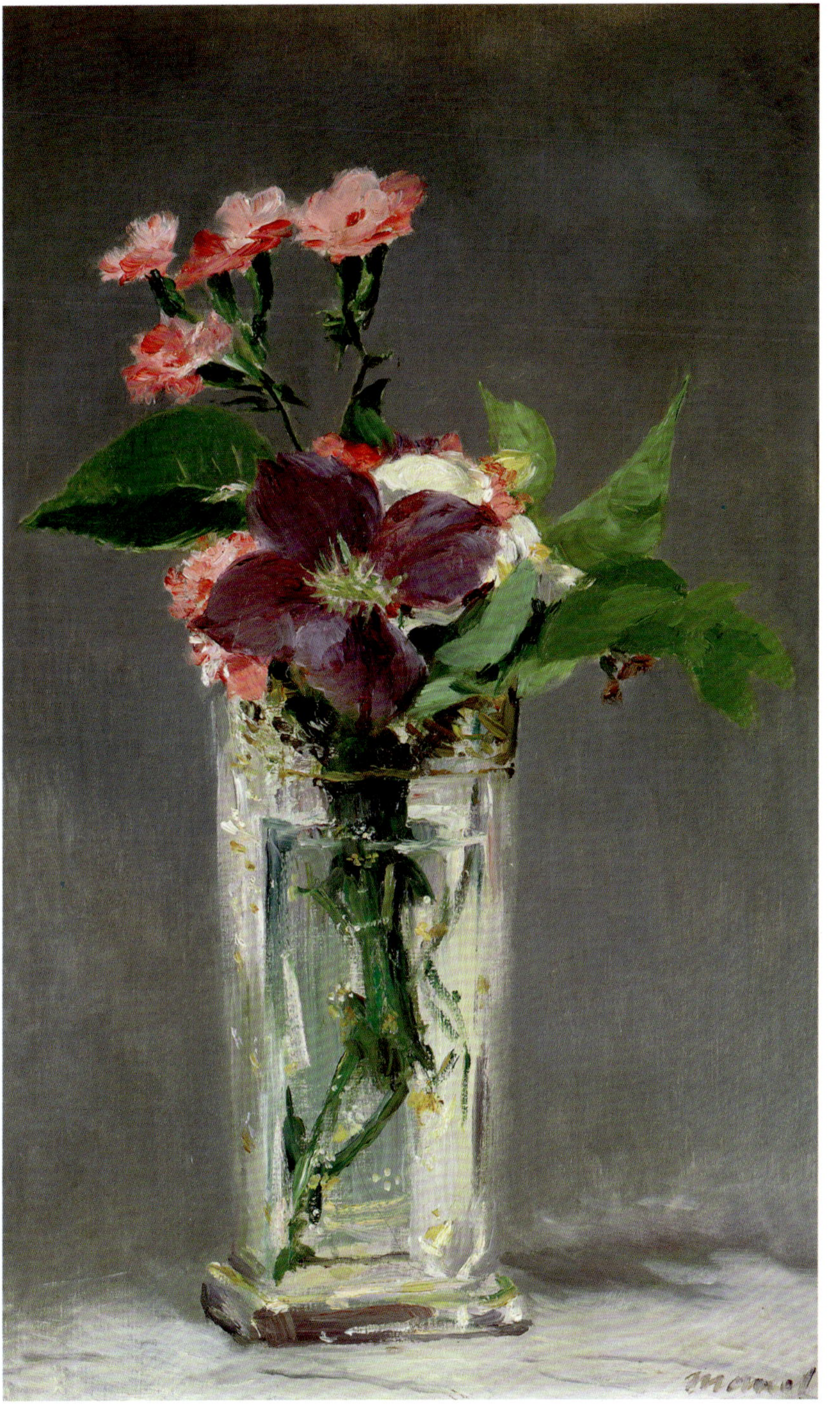

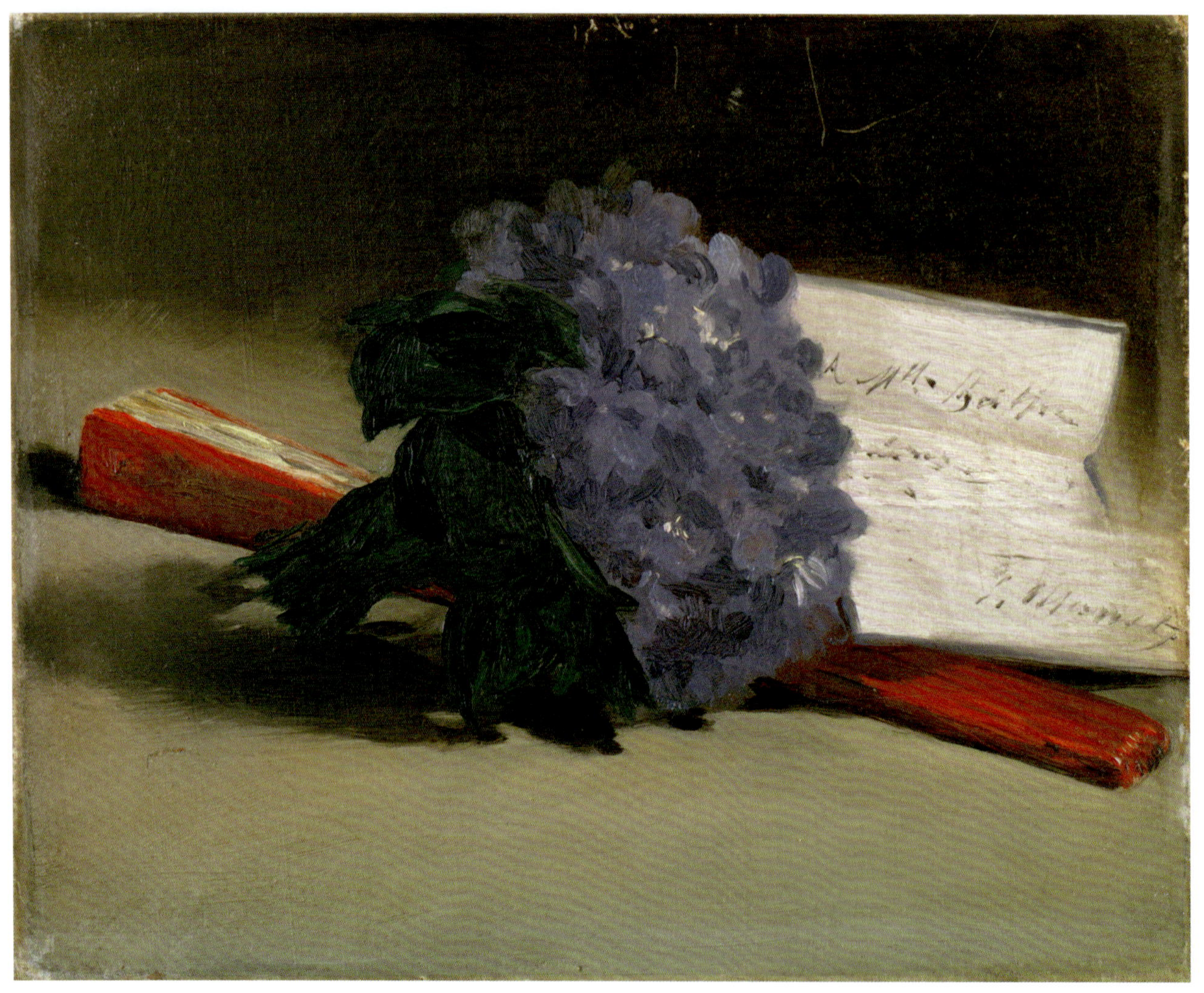

Bouquet of Violets

Bouquet de violettes

Veilchenstrauß

Ramo de violetas

Bouquet de violetas

Bosje viooltjes

ÉDOUARD MANET (1832-1883)

1872, Oil on canvas/Huile sur toile, 22 × 27 cm, Private collection

Horsewoman

The design is part of an unfinished
series on the four seasons that Antonin
Proust, the then Minister of the Arts,
commissioned from Manet. Two years
after the assignment, Manet died.

Cavalière

Cette esquisse appartient à une série
laissée inachevée sur le thème
des quatre saisons, commandée à Manet
par son ami Antonin Proust, alors
ministre des Beaux-Arts, deux ans
avant la mort de l'artiste.

Die Reiterin

Der Entwurf gehört zu einer
unvollendeten Serie über die vier
Jahreszeiten, die Antonin Proust, der
damalige Minister für die Künste, bei
Manet in Auftrag gab. Zwei Jahre nach
der Erteilung stirbt Manet.

La jinete

El diseño forma parte de una serie
inacabada sobre las cuatro estaciones
que Antonin Proust, el entonces
Ministro de las Artes, encargó a Manet.
Dos años después de la concesión,
Manet muere.

O Cavaleiro

O design faz parte de uma série
inacabada sobre as quatro estações que
Antonin Proust, o então Ministro das
Artes, encomendou a Manet. Dois anos
depois da concessão, Manet morre.

Paardrijdster

Het ontwerp maakt deel uit van een
onvoltooide serie over de vier seizoenen
die Antonin Proust, de toenmalige
minister van Kunst, Manet in opdracht
gaf. Twee jaar na het verstrekken van de
opdracht stierf Manet.

ÉDOUARD MANET (1832-1883)

c. 1882, Oil on canvas/Huile sur toile,
73 × 52 cm, Museo
Thyssen-Bornemisza, Madrid

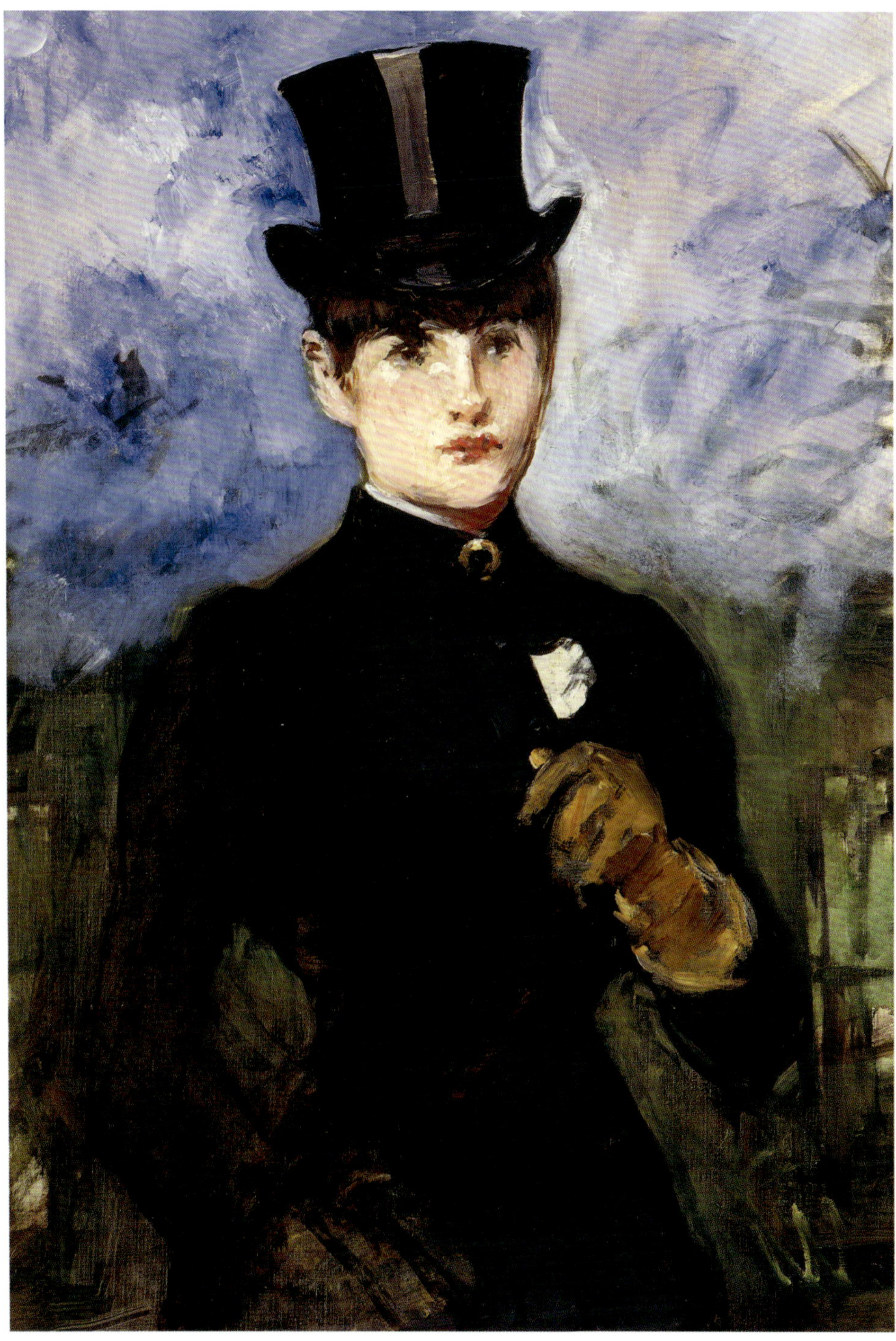

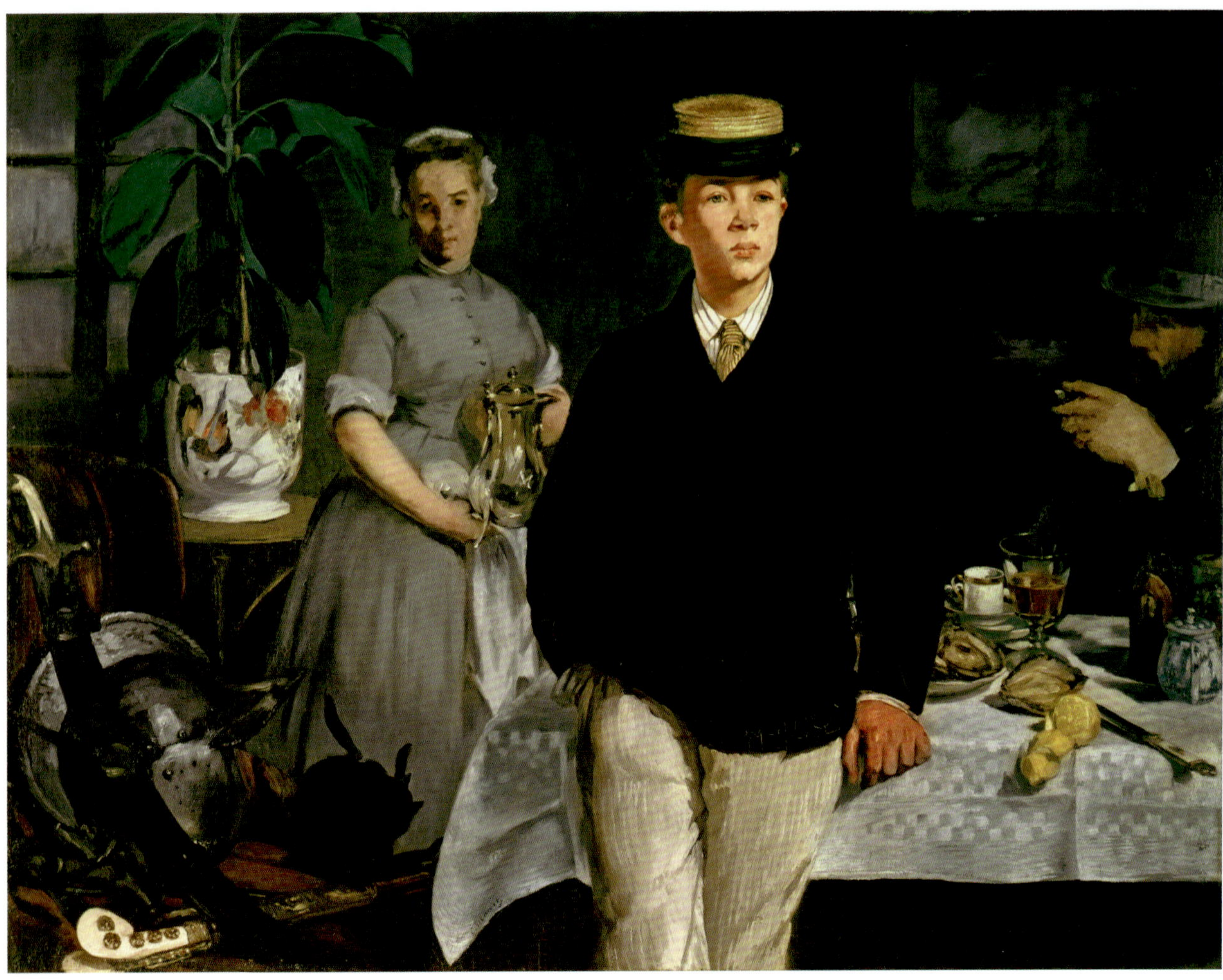

Luncheon in the Studio

Le Déjeuner dans l'atelier

Frühstück im Atelier

Desayuno en el estudio

Café da manhã no estúdio

De lunch in in de studio

ÉDOUARD MANET (1832-1883)

1868, Oil on canvas/Huile sur toile, 118 × 154 cm, Neue Pinakothek, München

Nana

Manet painted the figure two years
before the publication of Zola's novel
Nana. The portrait shows a prostitute
standing in her boudoir dressed
only in her lingerie and putting
on make-up.

Nana

Dans ce portrait en pied peint
deux ans avant la publication du
Nana de Zola, le peintre montre
une prostituée dans son intérieur,
simplement vêtue de ses dessous, en
train de se poudrer le visage.

Nana

Manet malt die Ganzfigur zwei Jahre
vor der Veröffentlichung von Zolas
Roman Nana. Das Porträt zeigt
eine Prostituierte, die nur mit ihren
Dessous bekleidet in ihrem Boudoir
steht und sich schminkt.

Nana

Manet pinta toda la figura dos años
antes de la publicación de la novela
Nana de Zola. El retrato muestra a
una prostituta de pie en su tocador
vestida sólo con su ropa interior
y maquillada.

Nana

Manet pinta toda a figura dois anos
antes da publicação do romance de
Zola, Nana. O retrato mostra uma
prostituta de pé em seu boudoir
vestida apenas com sua lingerie
e maquiagem.

Nana

Manet schilderde de figuur ten
voeten uit twee jaar voor de
publicatie van Zola's roman Nana.
Het portret toont een prostituee in
haar boudoir, die slechts gekleed in
lingerie haar make-up aanbrengt.

ÉDOUARD MANET (1832-1883)

1877, Oil on canvas/Huile sur toile,
150 × 116 cm, Hamburger Kunsthalle

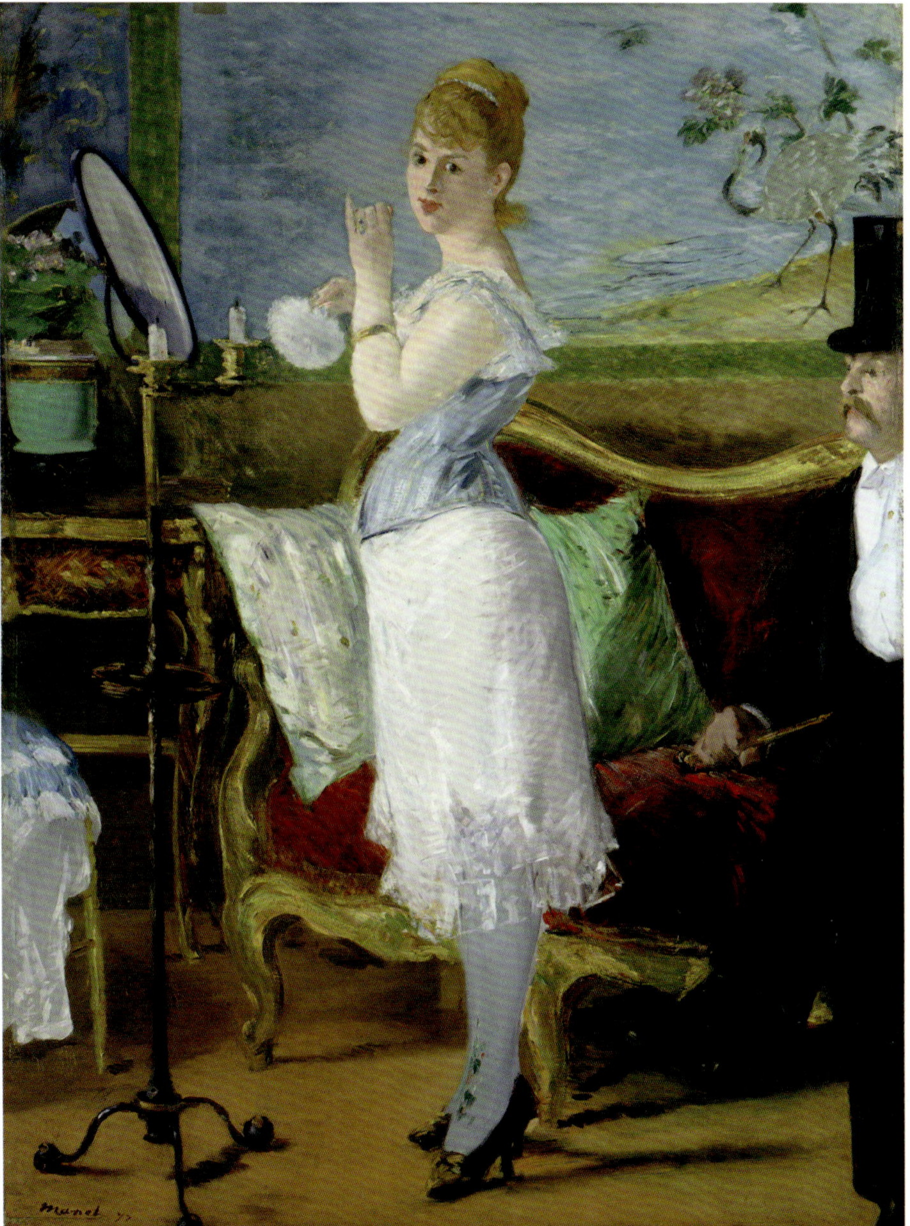

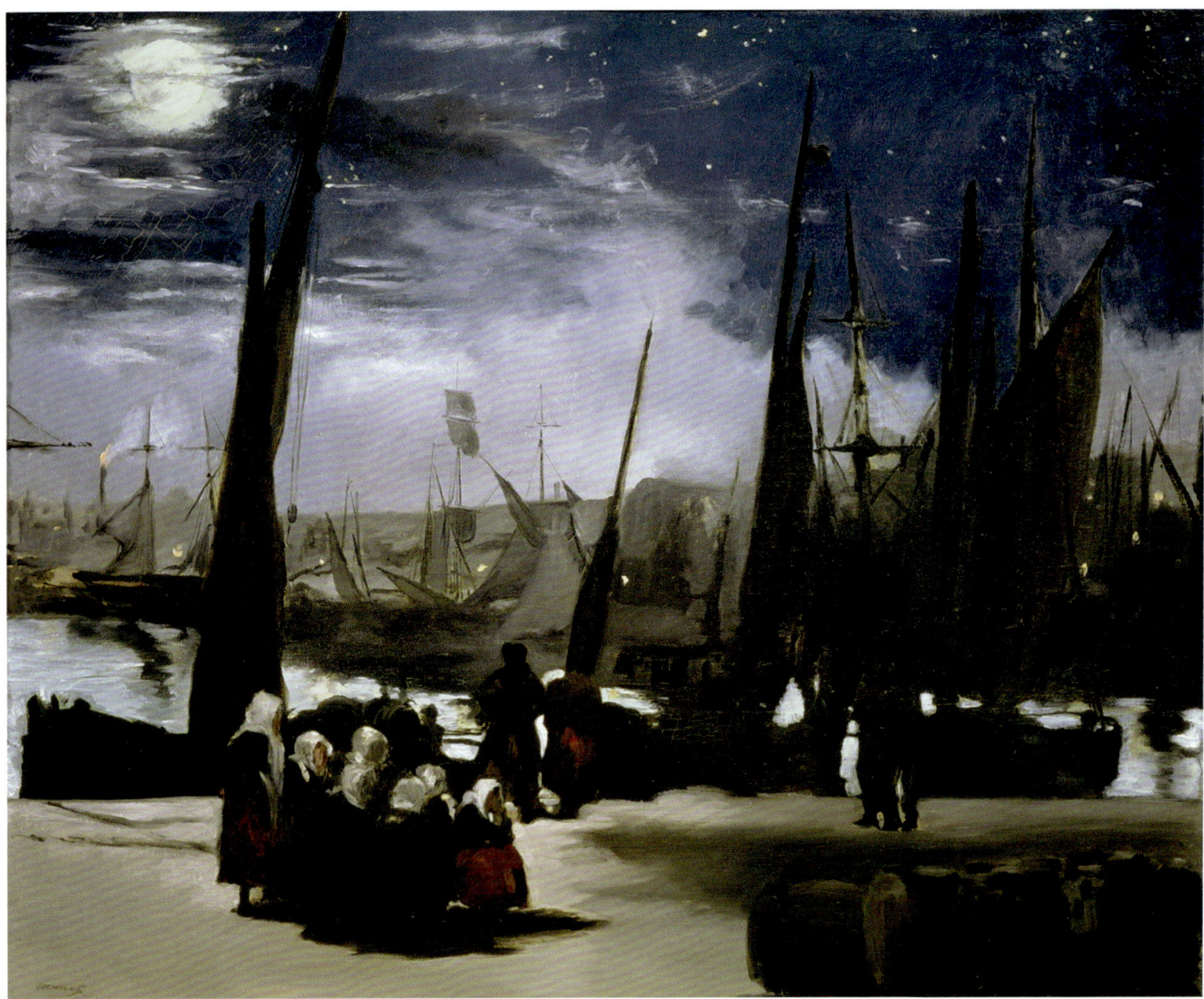

Moonlight on Boulogne Harbour

Clair de lune sur le port de Boulogne

Mondlicht über dem Hafen von Boulogne

La luz de la luna sobre el puerto de Boulogne

O luar sobre o porto de Boulogne

Maanlicht boven de haven van Boulogne

ÉDOUARD MANET (1832-1883)

1868, Oil on canvas/Huile sur toile,
82 × 101 cm, Musée d'Orsay, Paris

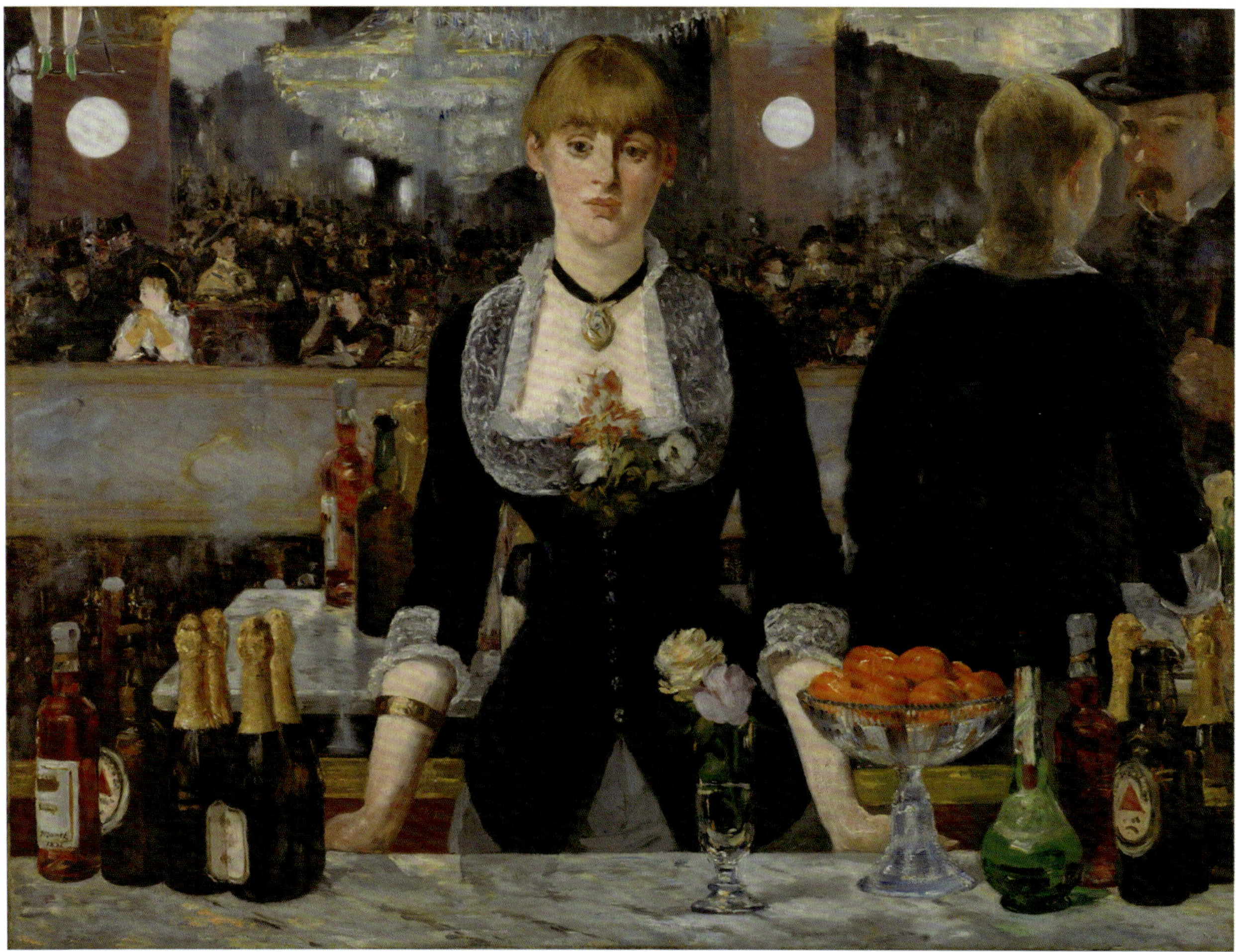

A Bar at the Folies Bergère

Opposite the waitress with the absent-minded gaze is a man who is only visible as a mirror image. At the centre of the complex composition is the loneliness of the woman in the midst of the crowd.

Un bar aux Folies Bergère

Les yeux dans le vague, la serveuse fait face à un homme qui, étrangement, n'apparaît que dans le reflet du miroir. Au sein d'une composition complexe, Manet peint la solitude d'une femme parmi la foule.

Bar in den Folies Bergère

Gegenüber der Bedienung mit dem geistesabwesenden Blick befindet sich ein Mann, der nur als Spiegelbild sichtbar ist. Im Zentrum der komplexen Komposition steht die Einsamkeit der Frau inmitten der Menschenmenge.

Bar en el Folies Bergère

Frente a la camarera con la mirada distraída hay un hombre que sólo es visible como un espejo. En el centro de la compleja composición está la soledad de la mujer en medio de la multitud.

Bar no Folies Bergère

Em frente à garçonete com o olhar distraído está um homem que só é visível como uma imagem de espelho. No centro da composição complexa está a solidão da mulher no meio da multidão.

Bar in de Folies Bergère

Tegenover de serveerster met de afwezige blik staat een man die alleen zichtbaar is als spiegelbeeld. Centraal in de complexe compositie staat de eenzaamheid van de vrouw midden in een mensenmenigte.

ÉDOUARD MANET (1832-1883)

1881/82, Oil on canvas/Huile sur toile, 96 × 130 cm, The Courtauld Gallery, London

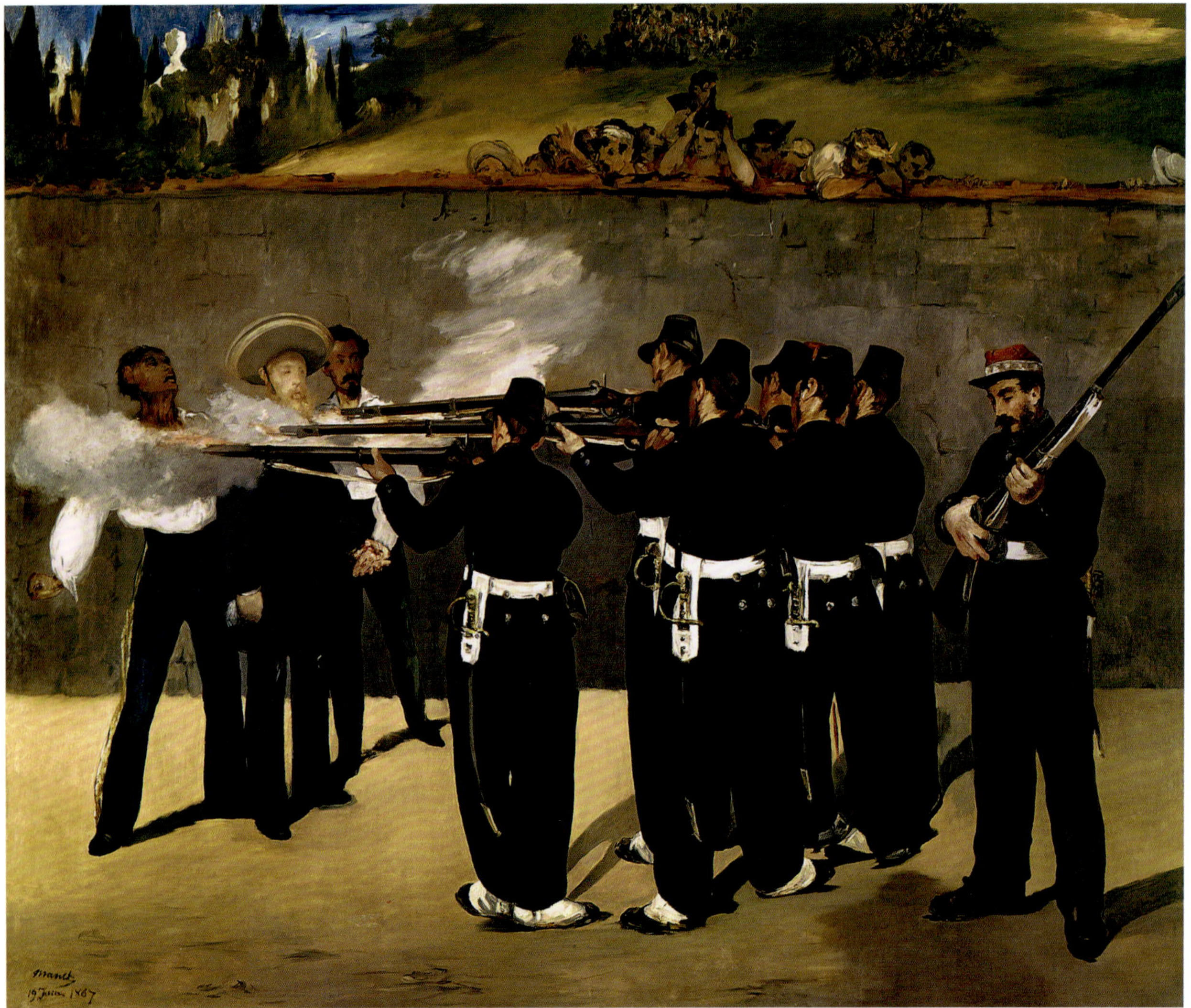

The Execution of the Emperor Maximilian

The background to the painting was the execution of
Maximilian I, Emperor of Mexico, and two of his generals
on 19 June 1867. Manet's composition was inspired by
Goya's *The Third of May 1808*.

L'Exécution de Maximilien

L'exécution de l'empereur Maximilien du Mexique et de
deux de ses généraux, le 19 juin 1867 a inspiré cinq œuvres
à Manet. La composition du tableau est empruntée
au *Tres de Mayo* de Francisco de Goya.

Die Erschießung des Kaisers Maximilian

Hintergrund des Gemäldes war die Hinrichtung von
Maximilian I., Kaiser von Mexiko, und zwei seiner Generäle
am 19. Juni 1867. Bei der Komposition lehnte sich Manet an
Goyas Erschießung der Aufständischen an.

La ejecución del emperador Maximiliano

El trasfondo del cuadro fue la ejecución de Maximiliano I,
emperador de México, y dos de sus generales el 19 de junio
de 1867, y la composición de Manet se inspiró en el disparo
de Goya a los insurgentes.

A Execução do Imperador Maximiliano

O pano de fundo da pintura foi a execução de Maximiliano
I, Imperador do México, e dois de seus generais em 19 de
junho de 1867. A composição de Manet foi inspirada pela
filmagem dos rebeldes por Goya.

De executie van keizer Maximiliaan

De achtergrond van het schilderij was de executie van
Maximiliaan I, keizer van Mexico, en twee van diens
generaals op 19 juni 1867. Manets compositie was
geïnspireerd op Goya's Executie van de opstandelingen.

ÉDOUARD MANET (1832-1883)

1868/69, Oil on canvas/Huile sur toile, 252 × 305 cm, Stadtische Kunsthalle, Mannheim

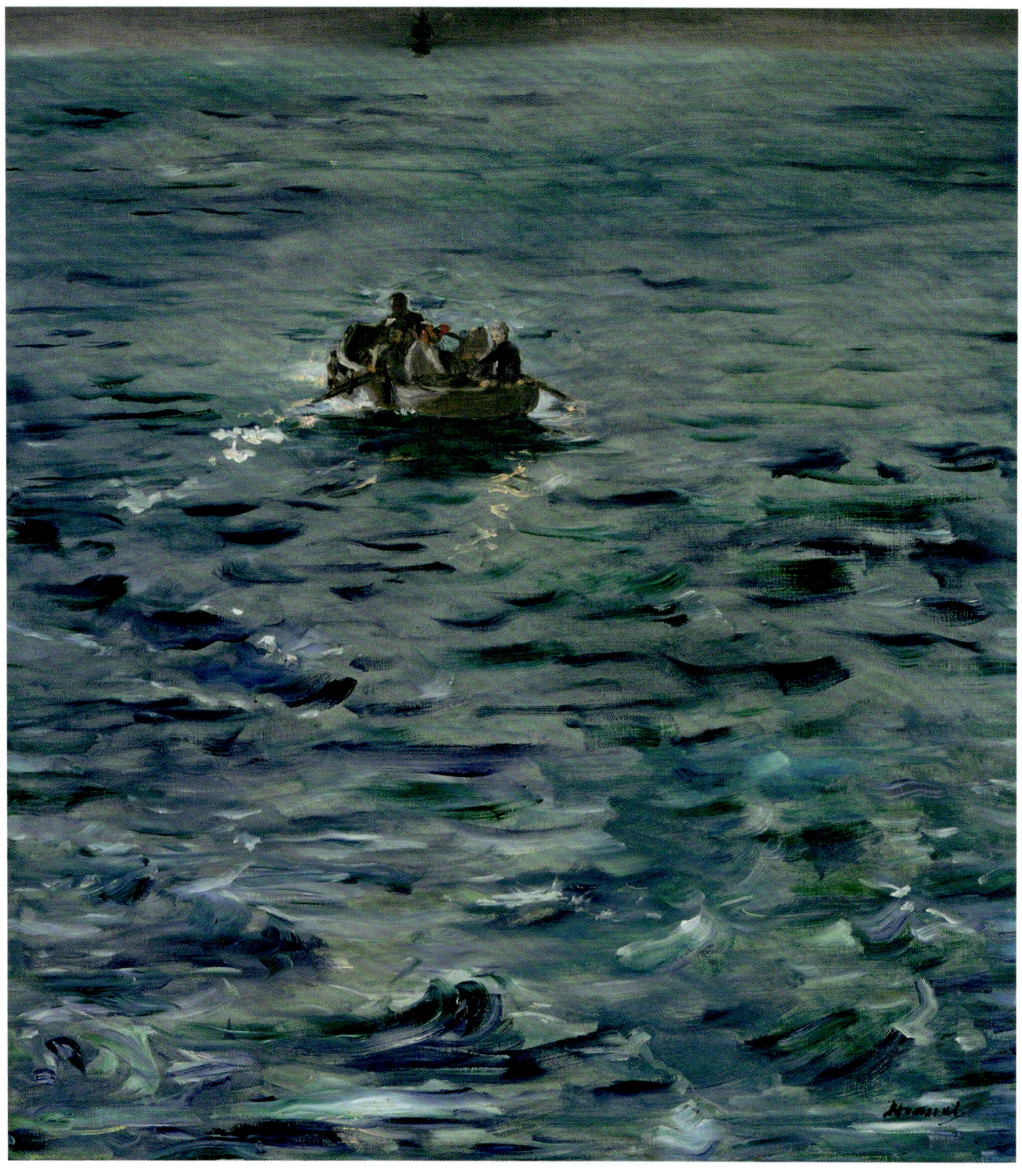

The Escape of Henri de Rochefort (1831-1915)

L'Évasion de Henri de Rochefort (1831-1915)

Die Flucht Henri de Rocheforts (1831-1915)

La fuga de Henri de Rochefort (1831-1915)

Henri Rocheforts (1831-1915) Fuga

De vlucht van Henri Rochefort (1831-1915)

ÉDOUARD MANET (1832-1883)

c. 1881, Oil on canvas/Huile sur toile, 80 × 73 cm, Musée d'Orsay, Paris

183

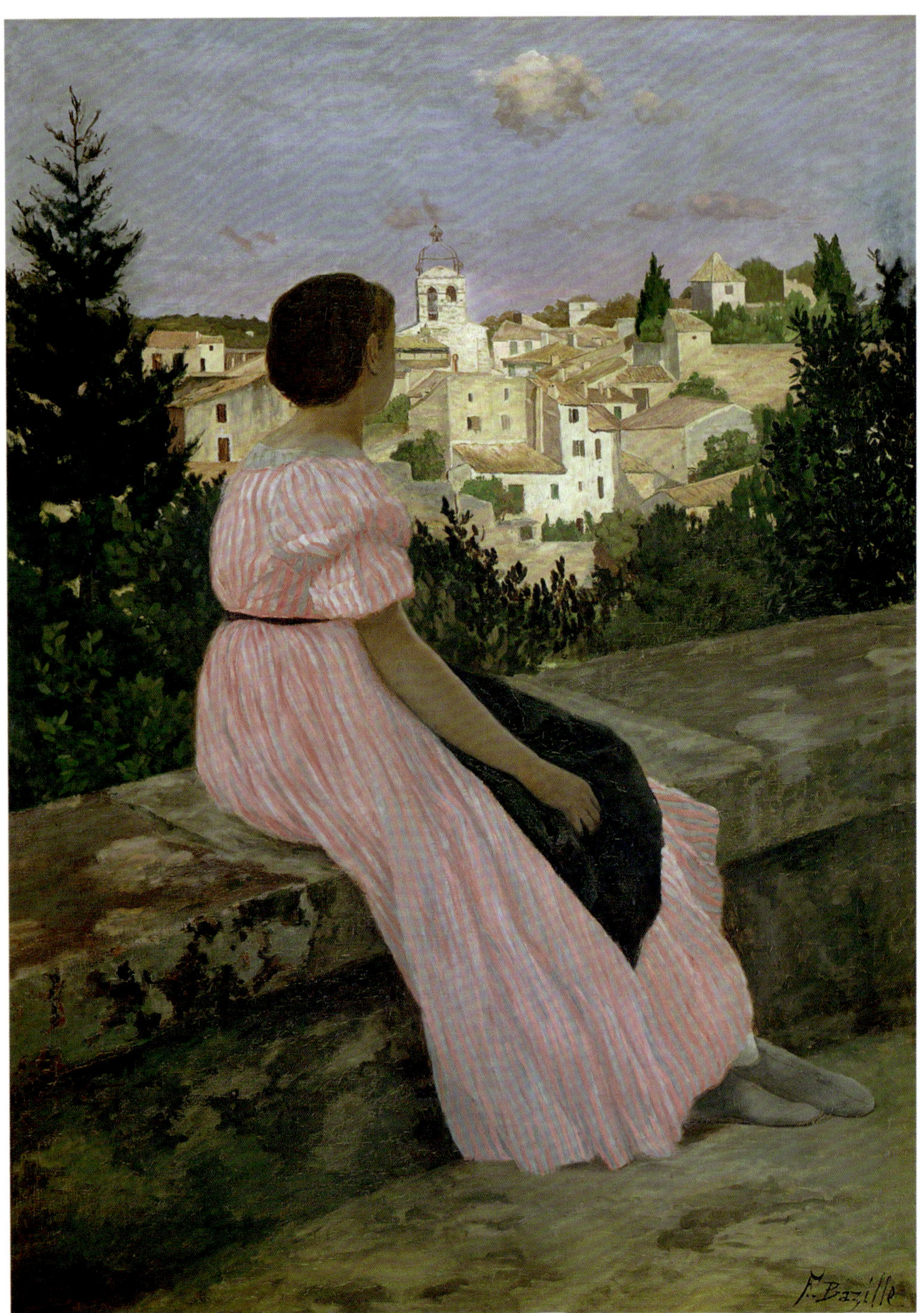

The Pink Dress

The painting, created in the summer of 1864, testifies to Frédéric Bacillle's penchant for depicting people in the open air. The model sitting on the wall is one of his cousins, Thérèse des Hours.

La Robe rose

Peint pendant l'été 1864, *La Robe rose* témoigne du goût de Frédéric Bazille pour la représentation de figures en plein air. Assise sur le muret, il s'agit ici de l'une de ses cousines, Thérèse des Hours.

Das rosa Kleid

Das im Sommer 1864 entstandene Gemälde zeugt von Frédéric Bazilles Faible für die Darstellung von Personen unter freiem Himmel. Das auf der Mauer sitzende Modell ist eine seiner Cousinen, Thérèse des Hours.

El vestido rosa

La pintura, creada en el verano de 1864, da testimonio de la afición de Frédéric Bacillle por representar a la gente al aire libre. La modelo sentada en la pared es una de sus primas, Thérèse des Hours.

O vestido rosa

A pintura, criada no verão de 1864, testemunha a propensão de Frédéric Bacillle para representar as pessoas ao ar livre. O modelo sentado na parede é uma das suas primas, Thérèse des Hours.

De roze jurk

Het in de zomer van 1864 gemaakte schilderij toont Frédéric Bazillles neiging om mensen in de buitenlucht af te beelden. Het model op het muurtje is een van zijn nichten, Thérèse des Hours.

JEAN-FRÉDÉRIC BAZILLE (1841-1870)

1864, Oil on canvas/Huile sur toile, 147 × 110 cm, Musée d'Orsay, Paris

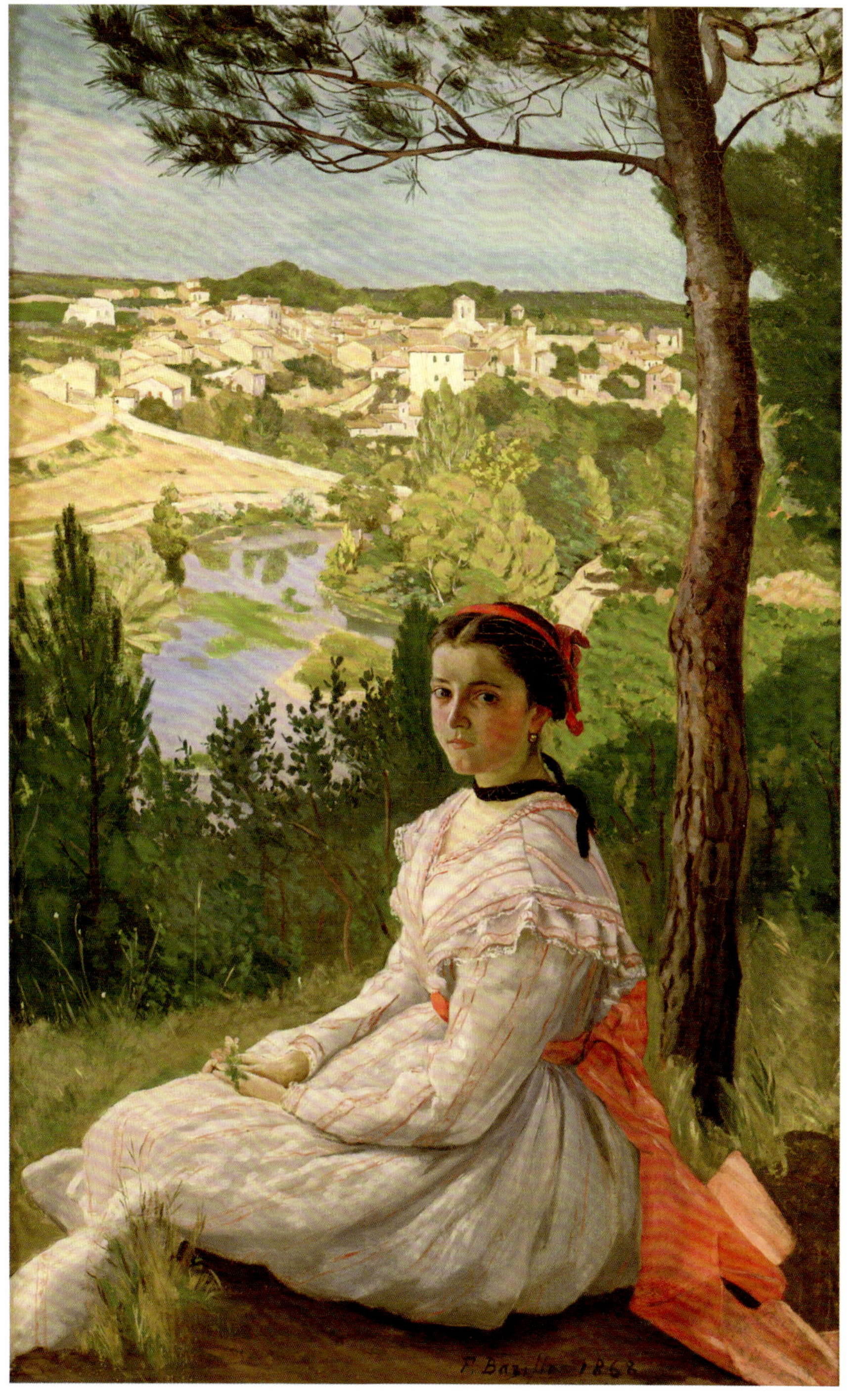

View of the Village

Vue du village

Dorfansicht

Vista al pueblo

Vista da aldeia

Gezicht op het dorp

JEAN-FRÉDÉRIC BAZILLE (1841-1870)
1868, Oil on canvas/Huile sur toile,
130 × 89 cm, Musée Fabre, Montpellier

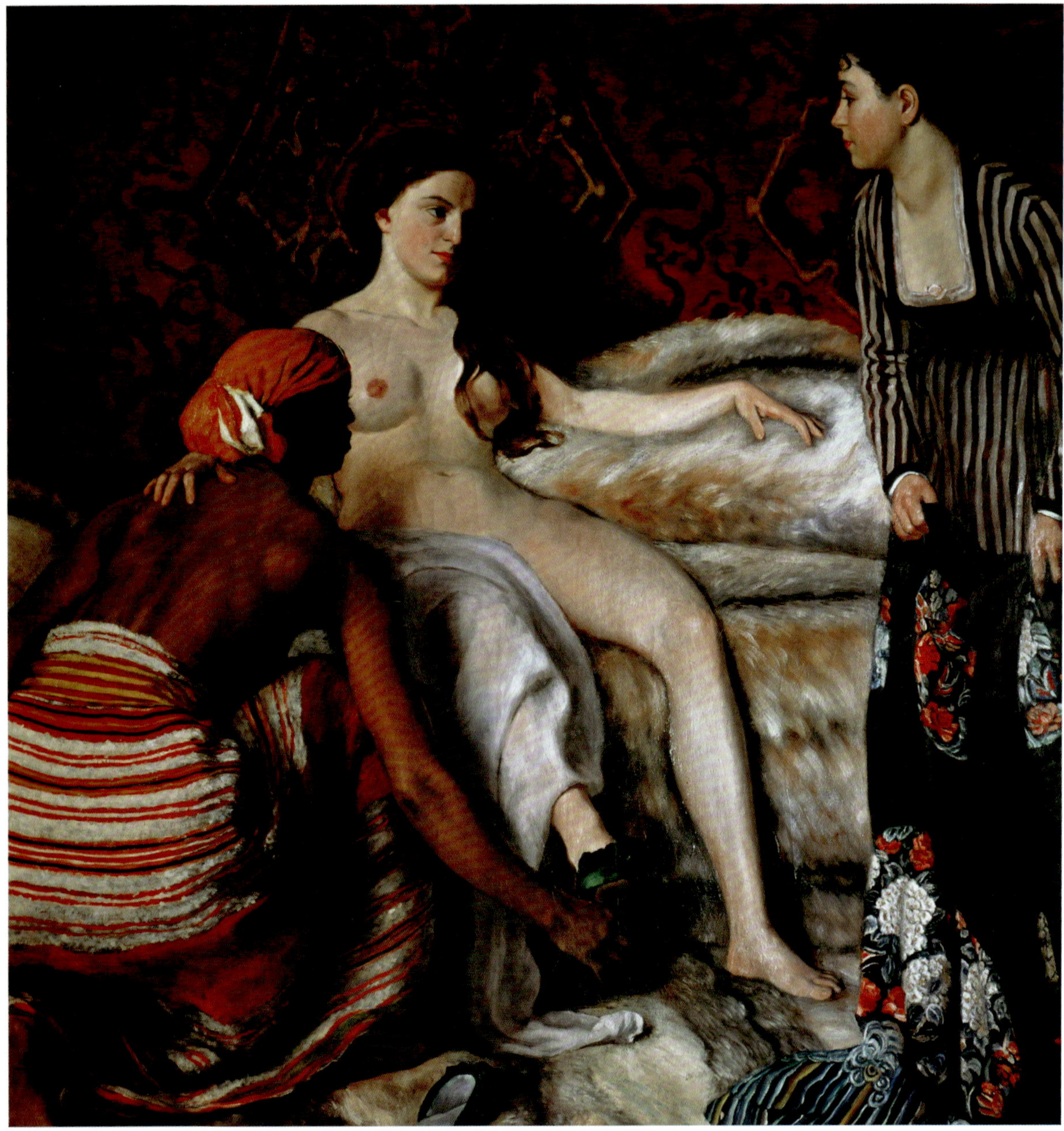

The Toilette

La Toilette

Die Toilette

La Toilette

A casa de banho

Het toilet

JEAN-FRÉDÉRIC BAZILLE (1841-1870)

1869/70, Oil on canvas/Huile sur toile, 153 × 148,5 cm, Musée Fabre, Montpellier

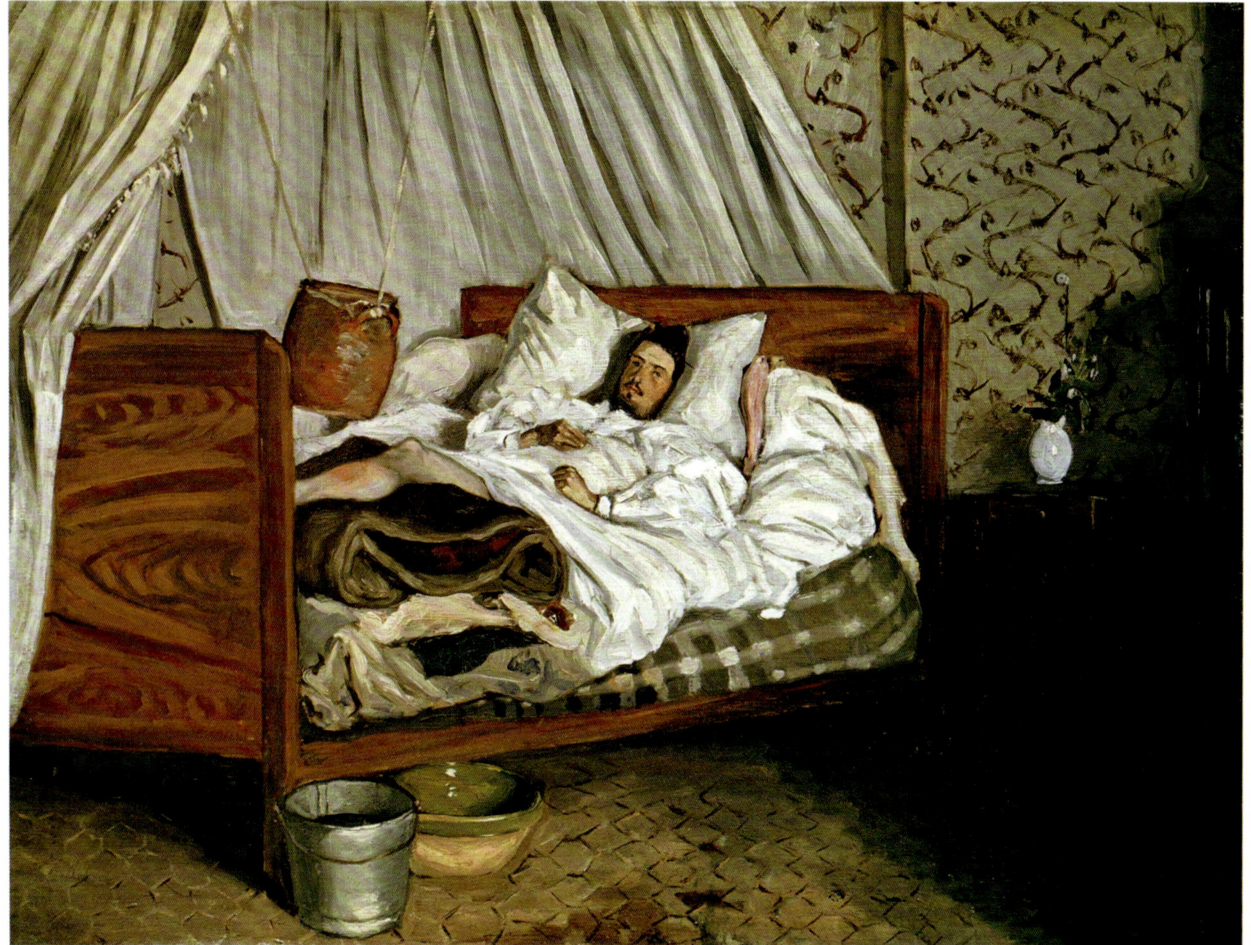

The Improvised Field Hospital

On several occasions Frédéric Bazille painted his artist
friends from the future group of Impressionists. Here it was
Monet - with whom he will share his studio - who had to
stay in bed because of a leg injury.

L'Ambulance improvisée

Frédéric Bazille a peint à plusieurs reprises ses amis du
futur groupe impressionniste. Monet, avec qui il partagera
un temps son atelier, est alité pour soigner une blessure à la
jambe après un accident.

JEAN-FRÉDÉRIC BAZILLE (1841-1870)
1865, Oil on canvas/Huile sur toile, 48 × 65 cm, Musée d'Orsay, Paris

Improvisiertes Krankenbett

Frédéric Bazille malte bei mehreren Gelegenheiten seine
Malerfreunde der zukünftigen Impressionisten. Hier war
es Monet – mit dem er sein Atelier teilen wird – der wegen
einer Beinverletzung das Bett hüten musste.

Cama de hospital improvisada

Frédéric Bazille pintó en varias ocasiones a sus amigos
pintores del grupo de los futuros impresionistas. Aquí fue
Monet -con quien compartirá su estudio- quien tuvo que
quedarse en cama debido a una lesión en la pierna.

Cama de hospital improvisada

Frédéric Bazille pintou em várias ocasiões de seus pintores
amigos dos futuros impressionistas. Aqui foi Monet - com
quem ele vai compartilhar seu estúdio - que teve que ficar
na cama por causa de uma lesão na perna.

Geïmproviseerd ziekenhuisbed

Frédéric Bazille schilderde zijn vrienden, de toekomstige
impressionisten, bij verschillende gelegenheden. Hier was
het Monet, met wie hij zijn atelier zou delen, die vanwege
een beenblessure in bed moest blijven.

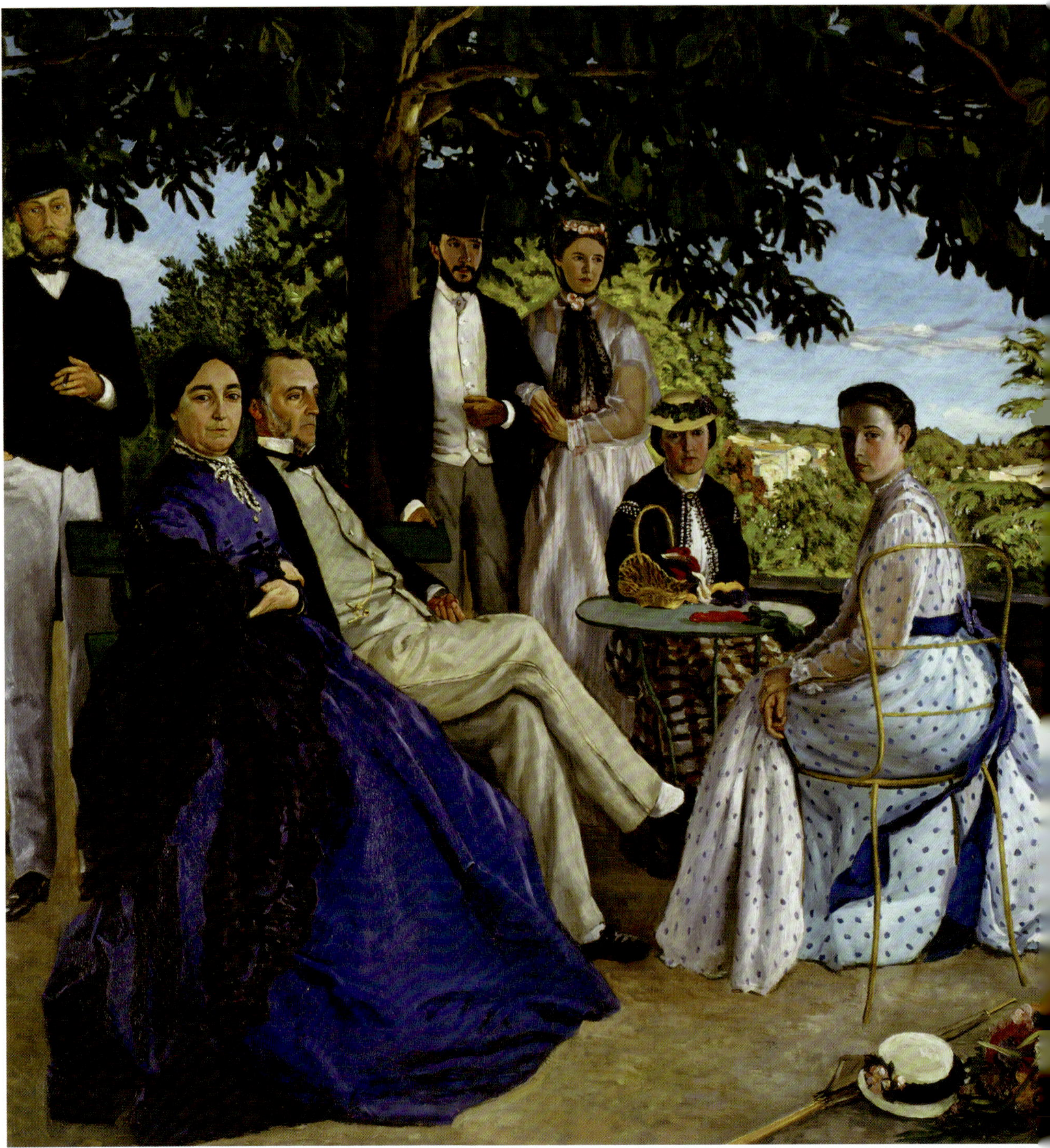

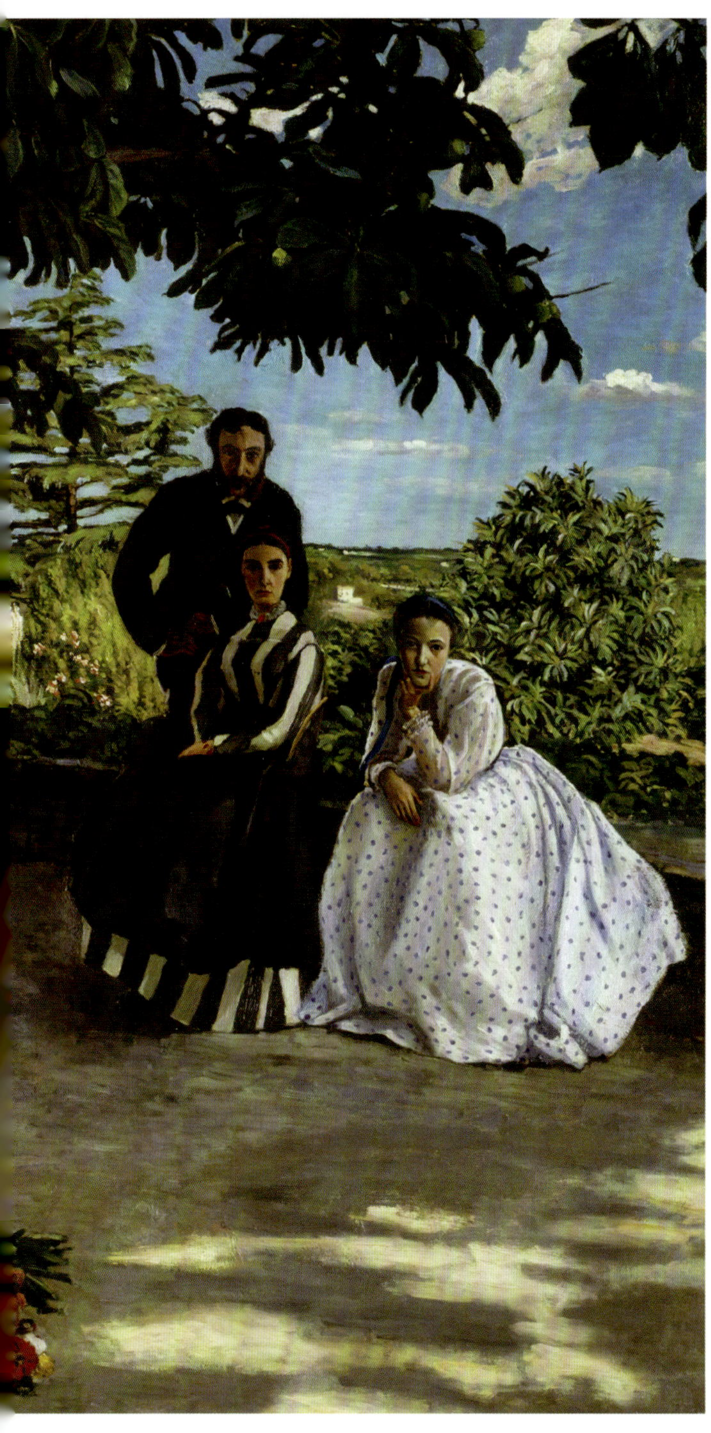

Family Reunion

The group portrait was made on the terrace of the Mérics family estate near Montpellier. All of those present return the gaze of the beholder, including the painter who depicted himself on the far left.

Réunion de famille

Sur la terrasse de la propriété familiale de Méric, près de Montpellier, Bazille réalise un ambitieux portrait de groupe. Tous les modèles regardent le spectateur, et le peintre figure à l'extrême gauche.

Das Familientreffen

Das Gruppenporträt entstand auf der Terrasse des Familienanwesens der Mérics in der Nähe von Montpellier. Alle Anwesenden erwidern den Blick des Betrachters, inklusive des Malers, der sich ganz links abbildete.

La reunión familiar

El retrato de grupo fue tomado en la terraza de la finca de la familia Mérics, cerca de Montpellier. Todos los presentes devuelven la mirada al espectador, incluido el pintor que se representaba a sí mismo en el extremo izquierdo.

A reunião de família

O retrato do grupo foi tirado no terraço da propriedade da família Mérics, perto de Montpellier. Todos os presentes retornam o olhar do espectador, incluindo o pintor que se descreveu no extremo esquerdo.

De familiebijeenkomst

Het groepsportret is geschilderd op het terras van het landgoed van de familie Méric bij Montpellier. Alle aanwezigen beantwoorden de blik van de toeschouwer, inclusief de schilder, die zichzelf uiterst links afbeeldde.

JEAN-FRÉDÉRIC BAZILLE (1841-1870)

1867, Oil on canvas/Huile sur toile, 152 × 230 cm, Musée d'Orsay, Paris

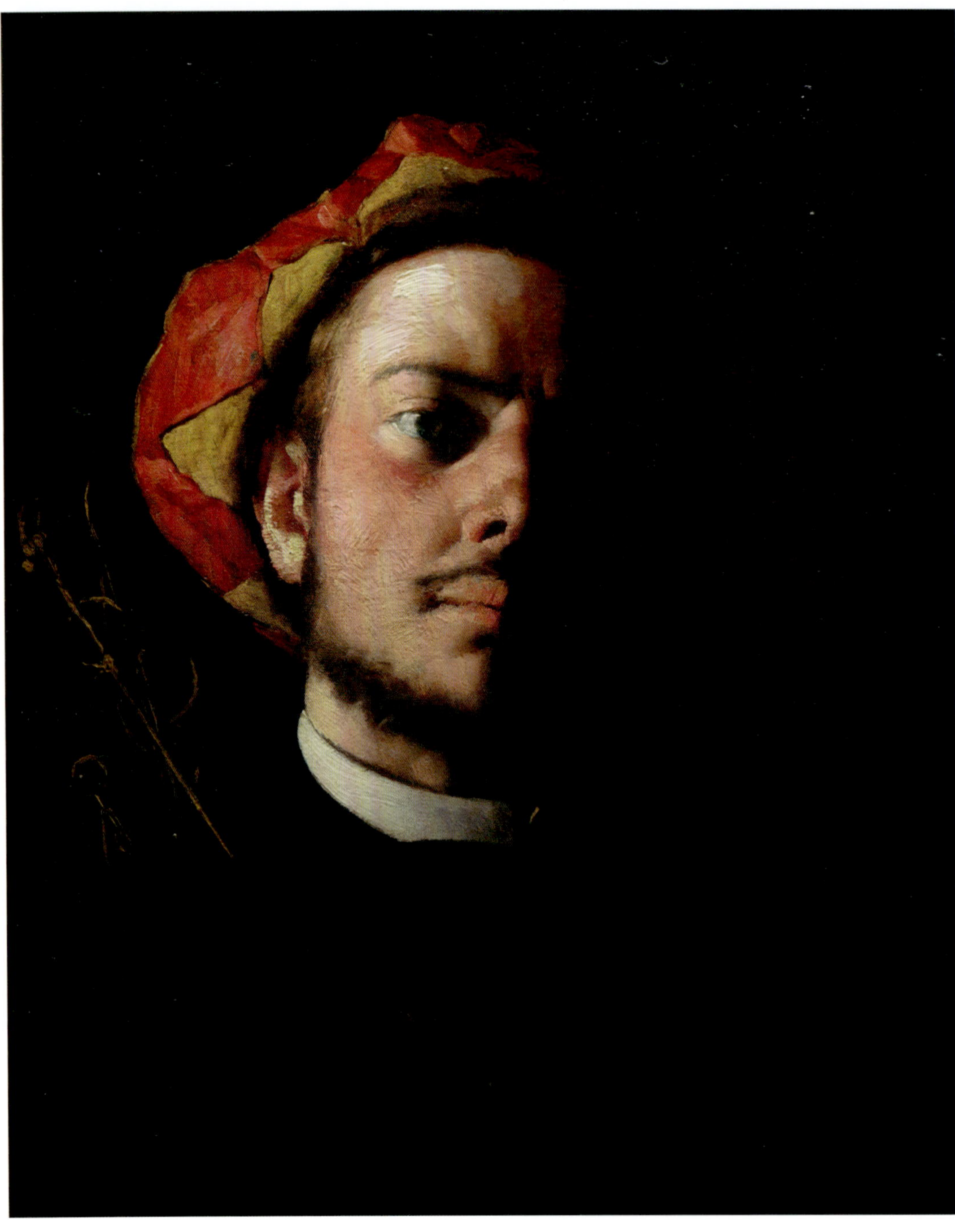

Portrait of Paul
Verlaine as a
Troubadour

Portrait de Paul
Verlaine en
troubadour

Paul Verlaine als
Troubadour

Paul Verlaine
como trovador

Paul Verlaine
como Trovador

Paul Verlaine als
troubadour

**JEAN-FRÉDÉRIC
BAZILLE (1841-1870)**
1868, Oil on canvas/
Huile sur toile,
45,8 × 38,1 cm,
Dallas Museum
of Art, Dallas

Portrait of Pierre-Auguste Renoir

In depicting Renoir, then at the beginning of his career, Bazille did not resort to the traditional attributes of an artist's portrait, such as a brush or easel, but painted him in a casual pose.

Pierre-Auguste Renoir

Aux traditionnels portraits posés d'artistes représentés le pinceau à la main ou assis devant leur chevalet, Bazille oppose une vision des plus décontractées de son camarade Renoir, alors à ses débuts.

Pierre-Auguste Renoir

Bei der Darstellung Renoirs, damals am Anfang seine Karriere, greift Bazille nicht auf die traditionellen Attribute eines Künstlerporträts, wie Pinsel oder Staffelei, zurück, sondern malt ihn in einer lockeren Pose.

Pierre-Auguste Renoir

A los tradicionales retratos de artistas representados con pinceles en la mano o sentados frente a su caballete, Bazille contrasta con la visión más relajada de su camarada Renoir, entonces en sus inicios.

Pierre-Auguste Renoir

Ao representar Renoir, então no início de sua carreira, Bazille não recorre aos atributos tradicionais do retrato de um artista, como um pincel ou cavalete, mas pinta-o em uma pose solta.

Pierre-Auguste Renoir

Bij het portret van Renoir, destijds nog aan het begin van zijn carrière, maakte Bazille geen gebruik van de traditionele attributen van een kunstenaarsportret, zoals een penseel of ezel, maar schilderde hij hem in een losse pose.

JEAN-FRÉDÉRIC BAZILLE (1841-1870)

1867, Oil on canvas/Huile sur toile, 61,2 × 50 cm, Musée d'Orsay, Paris

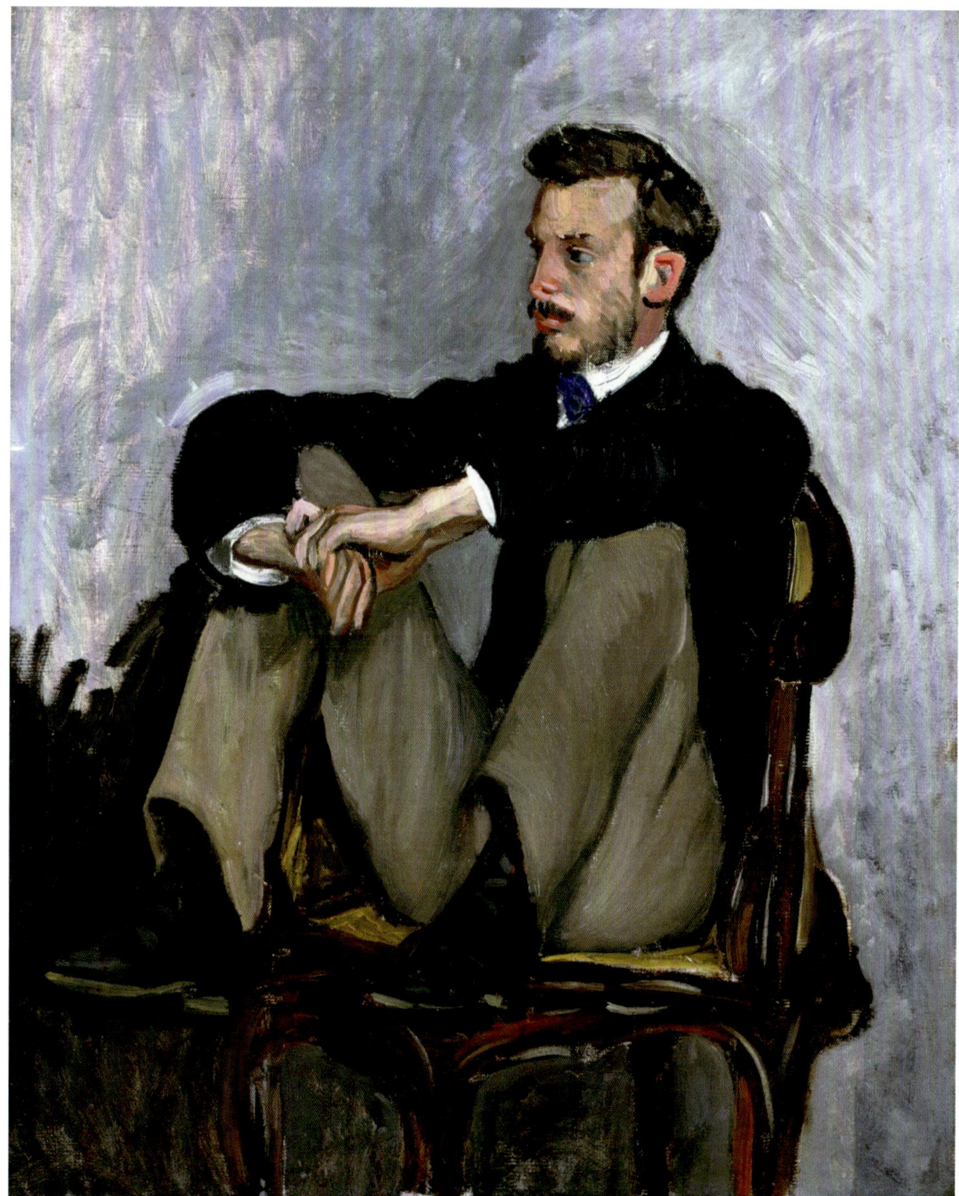

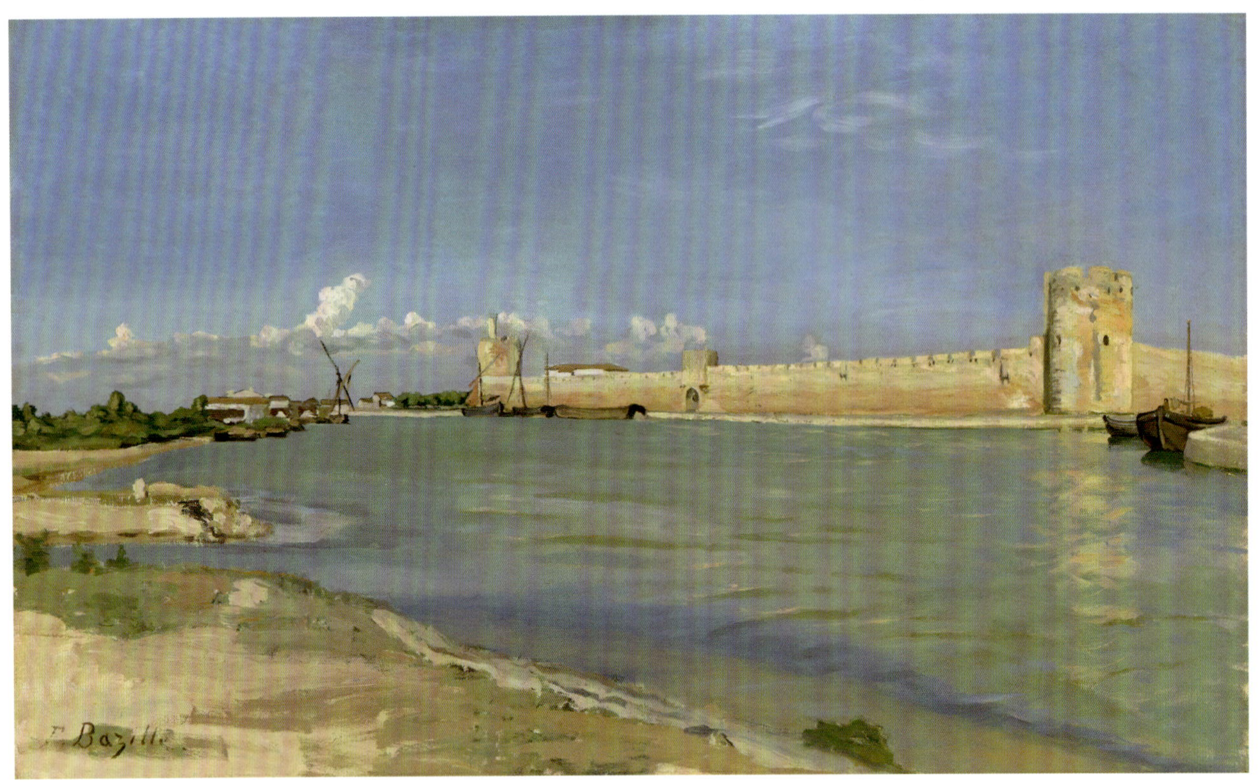

The Ramparts at Aigues-Mortes

Les Remparts d'Aigues-Mortes

JEAN-FRÉDÉRIC BAZILLE (1841-1870)

1867, Oil on canvas/Huile sur toile, 60 × 100 cm, National Gallery of Art, Washington

Die Festungsmauern von Aigues-Mortes

Las murallas de Aigues-Mortes

As muralhas da fortaleza de Aigues-Mortes

De vestingmuren van Aigues-Mortes

Summer Scene *or* The Bathers
Bazille broke new ground with his motif - men bathing had never been presented before. The bathers are depicted in an idyllic, light-flooded clearing on the banks of the Lez.

Scène d'été *ou* Les Baigneurs
Le thème de la baignade masculine n'avait encore jamais été traité à l'époque. Les hommes, en costume de bain, évoluent dans le cadre bucolique d'une clairière baignée de soleil, en bordure du Lez.

Sommerszene *oder* Die Badenden
Mit seinem Motiv betritt Bazille Neuland – Männer beim Bad wurden vorher noch nie behandelt. Die Badenden stellt er auf einer idyllischen, lichtdurchfluteten Lichtung dar, an den Ufern des Lez.

Escena de verano *o* Los bañistas
Bazille abre nuevos caminos con su motivo: los hombres en el baño es un tema que nunca antes se había tratado en la pintura. Los bañistas están representados en un idílico y luminoso claro a orillas del Lez.

Cena de Verão *ou* Os banhistas
Bazille abre novos caminhos com o seu motivo - os homens na casa de banho nunca foram tratados antes. Os banhistas são representados numa clareira idílica e cheia de luz nas margens do Lez.

Zomers tafereel *of* De zwemmers
Bazille betrad nieuwe wegen met zijn onderwerp: badende mannen waren nog nooit eerder geschilderd. De zwemmers zijn afgebeeld op een idyllische, zonovergoten open plek aan de oevers van de Lez.

JEAN-FRÉDÉRIC BAZILLE (1841-1870)

1869, Oil on canvas/Huile sur toile, 160 × 160,7 cm, Fogg Art Museum, Harvard

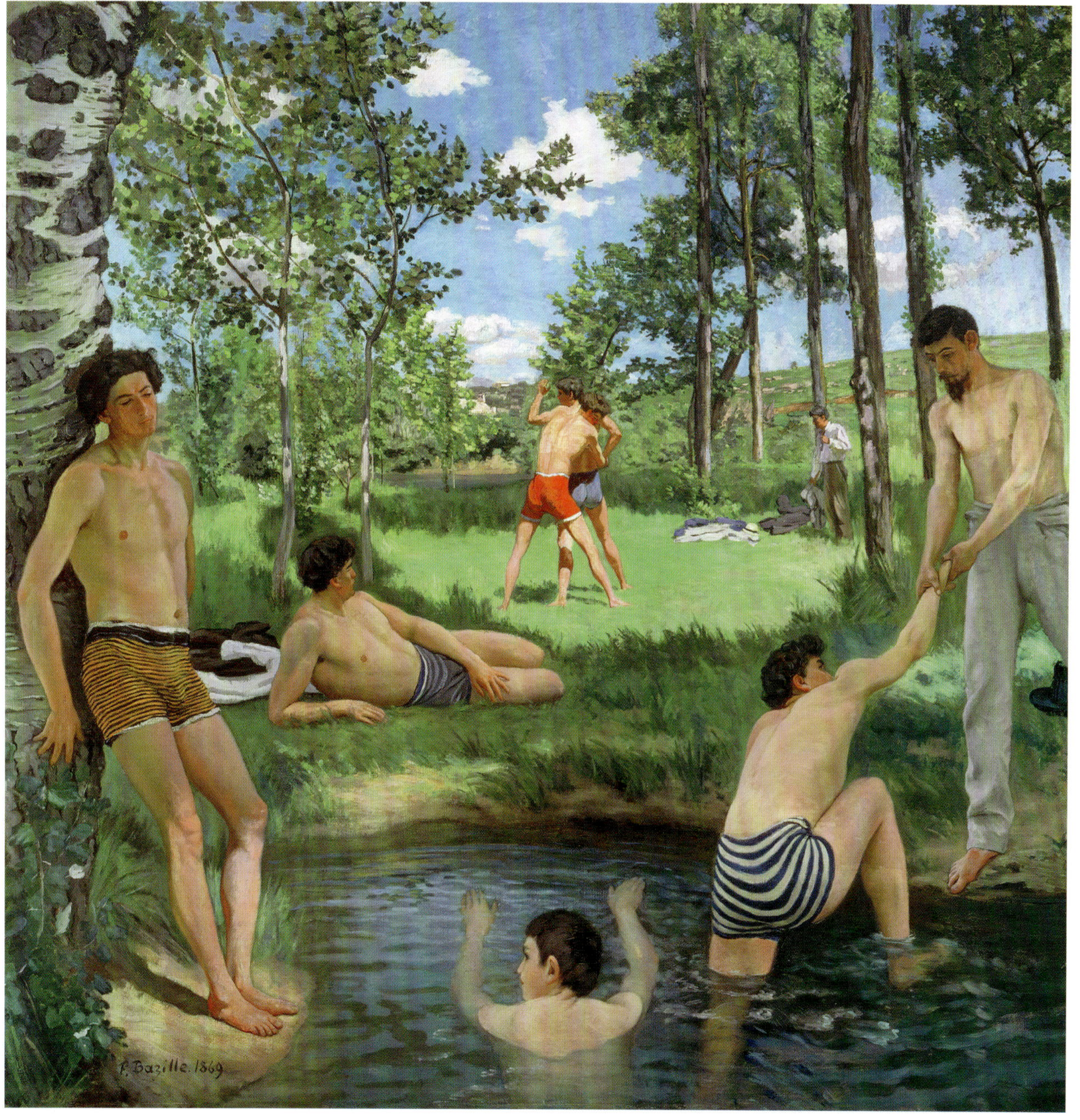

Impressionism

L'impressionnisme

Der Impressionismus

Impressionismo

Impressionismo

Impressionisme

Impressionism

Impressionism exhibitions are among the biggest crowd-pullers today - in stark contrast to the early years of the style. In 1874, Paul Cézanne, Claude Monet, Alfred Sisley, Eugène Boudin, Edgar Degas, Auguste Renoir, Camille Pissarro and Berthe Morisot, who regarded official art as rigid in its principles, decided to exhibit their works outside the Salon, independent of the jury and the awarding of medals. The group's first exhibition, entitled "Société anonyme coopérative des artistes peintres, sculpteurs et graveurs", took place in spring in the studio of the photographer Nadar in Paris. Claude Monet showed his work *Impression, Sunrise.* The art critic Louis Leroy then used the term "impressionists" for the first time in the magazine *Le Charivari.* Six more exhibitions followed until 1886, in which Gustave Caillebotte, Mary Cassatt, Paul Gauguin, Georges Seurat and Paul Signac took part over the years.

L'impressionnisme

L'impressionnisme est aujourd'hui, incontestablement, le mouvement qui attire le plus de monde dans les expositions. Il n'en a pas toujours été ainsi, loin de là. Considérant l'art officiel sclérosé, Paul Cézanne, Claude Monet, Alfred Sisley, Eugène Boudin, Edgar Degas, Auguste Renoir, Camille Pissarro, Berthe Morisot… décident en 1874 de présenter leurs œuvres hors du Salon, sans se soucier de jury et de médailles. La première « Exposition de la Société anonyme des artistes, peintres, sculpteurs, graveurs » ouvre au printemps dans l'atelier du photographe Nadar, boulevard des Capucines, à Paris. Claude Monet présente alors son tableau *Impression, soleil levant.* Le terme « impressionnisme » apparaît pour la première fois à cette occasion, sous la plume railleuse du critique Louis Leroy, dans les pages du journal *Le Charivari.* Sept expositions de groupe suivront jusqu'en 1886, auxquelles participeront également, selon les années, Gustave Caillebotte, Mary Cassatt, Paul Gauguin, Georges Seurat, Paul Signac…

Der Impressionismus

Impressionismusausstellungen zählen heute zu den großen Publikumsmagneten – ganz im Gegensatz zu den Anfangsjahren des Stils. 1874 beschließen Paul Cézanne, Claude Monet, Alfred Sisley, Eugène Boudin, Edgar Degas, Auguste Renoir, Camille Pissarro und Berthe Morisot, die die offizielle Kunst als in ihren Prinzipien erstarrt betrachten, ihre Werke außerhalb des Salons auszustellen – unabhängig von der Jury und der Vergabe von Medaillen. Die erste Ausstellung der Gruppe mit dem Namen „Société anonyme coopérative des artistes peintres, sculpteurs et graveurs" findet im Frühling im Pariser Atelier des Fotografen Nadar statt. Claude Monet zeigt sein Werk *Impression, Sonnenaufgang.* Der Kunstkritiker Louis Leroy verwendet daraufhin in der Zeitschrift *Le Charivari* zum ersten Mal abwertend den Begriff „Impressionisten". Bis 1886 sollten sechs weitere Ausstellungen der Gruppe folgen, an denen im Laufe der Jahre Gustave Caillebotte, Mary Cassatt, Paul Gauguin, Georges Seurat und Paul Signac teilnehmen werden.

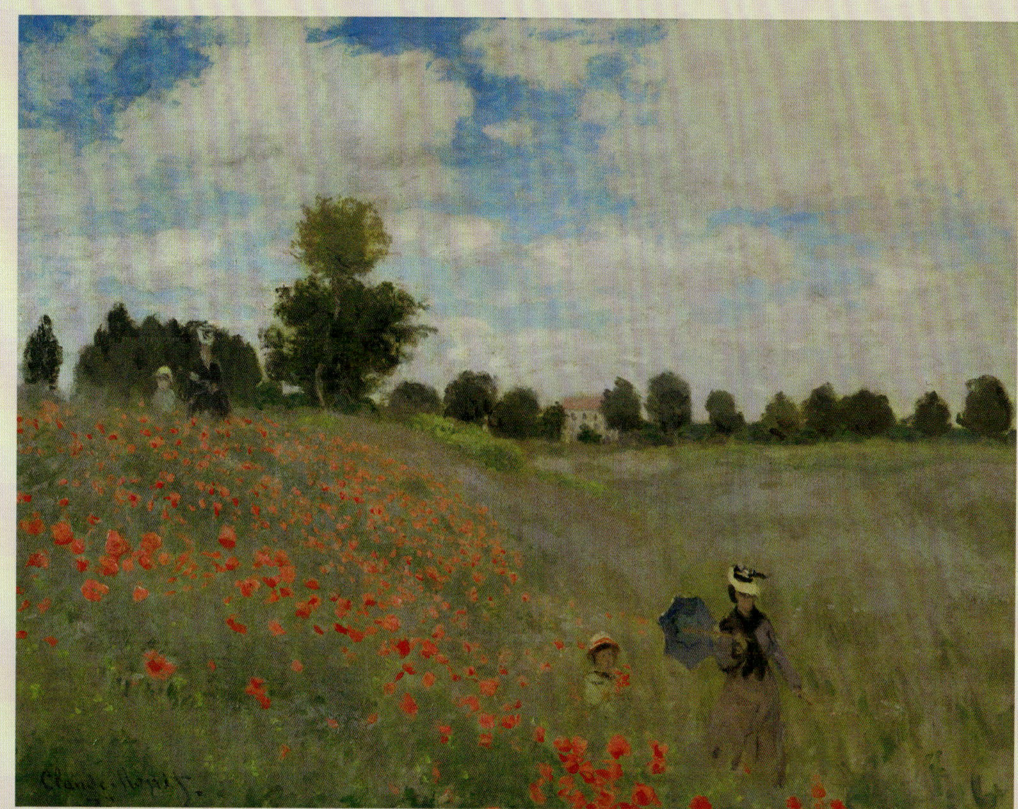

Poppy Field

Les Coquelicots

Mohnfeld

Campo de amapolas

Campo de papoila

Papaverveld

CLAUDE MONET (1840-1926)
1873, Oil on canvas/Huile sur toile,
50 × 65 cm, Musée d'Orsay, Paris

Impresionismo

Las exposiciones de impresionismo se encuentran entre las que más atraen a las multitudes en la actualidad, en marcado contraste con los primeros años del estilo. En 1874, Paul Cézanne, Claude Monet, Alfred Sisley, Eugène Boudin, Edgar Degas, Auguste Renoir, Camille Pissarro y Berthe Morisot, que consideraban el arte oficial rígido en sus principios, decidieron exponer sus obras fuera del Salón, independientemente del jurado y de la entrega de medallas. La primera exposición del grupo, titulada *"Société anonyme coopérative des artistes peintres, sculpteurs et graveurs"*, tendrá lugar esta primavera en el estudio del fotógrafo Nadar en París. Claude Monet muestra su obra *Impresión. Sol naciente*. El crítico de arte Louis Leroy utilizó por primera vez el término "impresionistas" en la revista *Le Charivari*. Seis exposiciones más siguieron hasta 1886, en las que Gustave Caillebotte, Mary Cassatt, Paul Gauguin, Georges Seurat y Paul Signac participaron a lo largo de los años.

Impressionismo

as exposições de impressionismo estão entre as maiores do mundo de hoje - em grande contraste com os primeiros anos do estilo. Em 1874, Paul Cézanne, Claude Monet, Alfred Sisley, Eugène Boudin, Edgar Degas, Auguste Renoir, Camille Pissarro e Berthe Morisot, que consideravam a arte oficial rígida nos seus princípios, decidiram expor as suas obras fora do salão, independentemente do júri e da atribuição de medalhas. A primeira exposição do grupo, intitulada "Société anonyme coopérative des artistes peintres, sculpteurs et graveurs", terá lugar esta Primavera no estúdio do fotógrafo Nadar em Paris. Claude Monet mostra o seu trabalho *Impression, Sunrise.* O crítico de arte Louis Leroy utilizou pela primeira vez o termo "impressionistas" na revista *Le Charivari*. Seguiram-se mais seis exposições até 1886, nas quais Gustave Caillebotte, Mary Cassatt, Paul Gauguin, Georges Seurat e Paul Signac participariam ao longo dos anos.

Impressionisme

Impressionistische tentoonstellingen behoren tegenwoordig tot de grootste publiekstrekkers. Hoe anders was dat in de beginjaren van de stijl! In 1874 besloten Paul Cézanne, Claude Monet, Alfred Sisley, Eugène Boudin, Edgar Degas, Auguste Renoir, Camille Pissarro en Berthe Morisot, die de officiële kunst door al haar principes als te rigide beschouwden, hun werken buiten de Salon te exposeren, onafhankelijk van een jury en zonder medailles. De eerste tentoonstelling van de groep, getiteld 'Société anonyme coopérative des artistes peintres, sculpteurs et graveurs', zou dat voorjaar plaatsvinden in het atelier van fotograaf Nadar in Parijs. Claude Monet exposeerde zijn werk *Impressie, zonsopgang*. De kunstcriticus Louis Leroy gebruikte naar aanleiding daarvan voor het eerst de term 'impressionisten' in het tijdschrift *Le Charivari*. Tot 1886 volgden nog zes tentoonstellingen, waaraan in de loop der jaren Gustave Caillebotte, Mary Cassatt, Paul Gauguin, Georges Seurat en Paul Signac deelnamen.

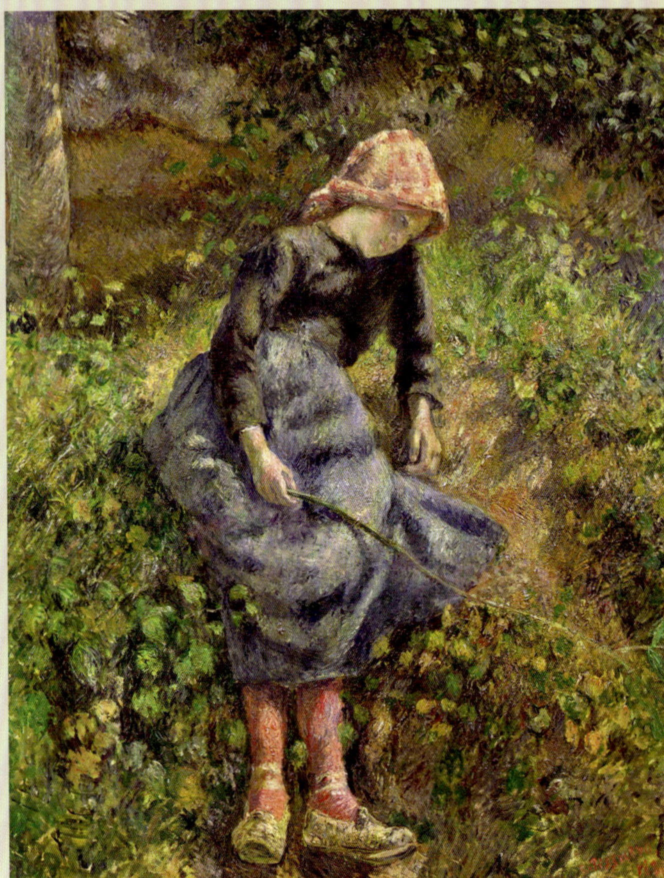

The Shepherdess

La Bergère

Die Schäferin

La pastora

A pastora

De herderin

CAMILLE PISSARRO (1830-1903)
1881, Oil on canvas/Huile sur toile,
81 × 64,8 cm, Musée d'Orsay, Paris

The criticism of the Impressionists was great. The group was accused of painting motifs without depth in a sketchy style that had nothing to do with a finished painting. They were supported by the writer Émile Zola and the art dealer Paul Durand-Ruel. The members of the group followed different paths, but had the same goal - the renewal of painting. They all worked with natural light and a fragmented brushstroke. Monet, Renoir, Pissarro and Guillaumin were dedicated to landscape, everyday life and leisure. Berthe Morisot preferred portraits and intimate motifs. Edgar Degas was fascinated by the world of opera, dancers and horse racing, while Gustave Caillebotte dealt with Haussmann's modern Paris in photograph-like image details.

À leurs débuts, les peintres impressionnistes sont vivement critiqués, pour leurs sujets jugés anecdotiques, sans profondeur, et leur style plus proche de l'esquisse que du tableau achevé. Ils sont néanmoins soutenus par l'écrivain Émile Zola, et défendus avec ardeur par le grand marchand de tableaux Paul Durand-Ruel. Réunis par un même idéal – renouveler la peinture – et des principes communs – la lumière naturelle, la touche fragmentée… –, les artistes suivent chacun leur propre chemin. Monet, Renoir, Pissarro, Guillaumin se passionnent pour le paysage, le quotidien et les loisirs, Berthe Morisot privilégie les portraits et les scènes intimes. Edgar Degas se montre fasciné par l'opéra, les danseuses et les courses de chevaux, Gustave Caillebotte par la modernité du Paris haussmannien, au travers de cadrages très photographiques.

Die Kritik gegenüber den Impressionisten ist groß. Der Gruppe wird vorgeworfen Motive ohne Tiefe in einem skizzenhaften Stil zu malen, der nichts mit einem fertigen Gemälde zu tun hat. Unterstützung erhalten sie von dem Schriftsteller Emil Zola und von dem Kunsthändler Paul Durand-Ruel. Die Mitglieder der Gruppe verfolgen unterschiedliche Pfade, haben aber dasselbe Ideal – die Erneuerung der Malerei. Sie arbeiten alle mit natürlichem Licht und einer fragmentierten Pinselführung. Monet, Renoir, Pissarro und Guillaumin widmen sich der Landschaft, dem Alltagsleben und dem Freizeitvergnügen. Berthe Morisot zieht Porträts und intime Motive vor. Edgar Degas ist fasziniert von der Welt der Oper, den Tänzerinnen und den Pferderennen, während sich Gustave Caillebotte in fotografisch wirkenden Bildausschnitten mit dem modernen Paris Haussmanns auseinandersetzt.

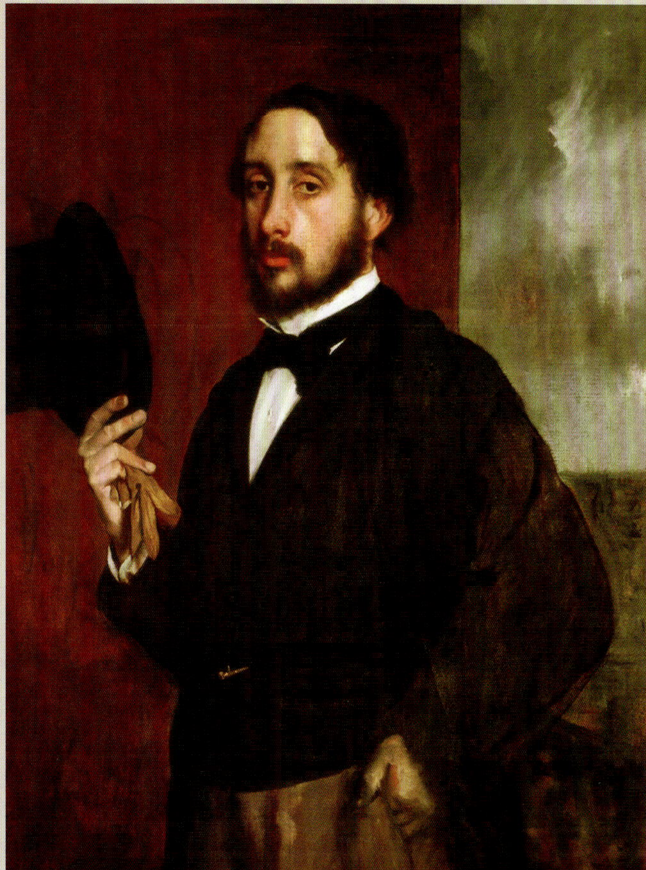

EDGAR DEGAS (1834-1917)
c. 1863, Oil on canvas/Huile sur toile, 92,1 × 69 cm,
Museu Calouste Gulbenkian, Lisboa

La crítica de los impresionistas es grande. Se acusa al grupo de pintar motivos sin profundidad en un estilo esquemático que no tiene nada que ver con una pintura terminada. Están apoyados por el escritor Émile Zola y el marchante de arte Paul Durand-Ruel. Los miembros del grupo siguen caminos diferentes, pero tienen el mismo ideal: la renovación de la pintura. Todos ellos trabajan con luz natural y una pincelada fragmentada. Monet, Renoir, Pissarro y Guillaumin se dedican al paisaje, a la vida cotidiana y al ocio. Berthe Morisot prefiere retratos y motivos íntimos. Edgar Degas está fascinado por el mundo de la ópera, los bailarines y las carreras de caballos, mientras que Gustave Caillebotte se ocupa de los modernos Haussmanns de París en los detalles de imagen fotográfica.

A crítica aos impressionistas é grande. O grupo é acusado de pintar motivos sem profundidade num estilo esquemático que nada tem a ver com uma pintura acabada. Eles são apoiados pelo escritor Émile Zola e pelo comerciante de arte Paul Durand-Ruel. Os membros do grupo seguem caminhos diferentes, mas têm o mesmo ideal - a renovação da pintura. Todos eles trabalham com luz natural e uma pincelada fragmentada. Monet, Renoir, Pissarro e Guillaumin são dedicados à paisagem, vida cotidiana e lazer. Berthe Morisot prefere retratos e motivos íntimos. Edgar Degas é fascinado pelo mundo da ópera, dança e corridas de cavalos, enquanto Gustave Caillebotte lida com os modernos Paris Haussmanns em detalhes fotográficos.

De kritiek op de impressionisten was groot. De groep werd ervan beschuldigd onderwerpen zonder diepte in een schetsmatige stijl te schilderen die niets met een afgewerkt schilderij te maken had. Ze werden gesteund door de schrijver Émile Zola en de kunsthandelaar Paul Durand-Ruel. De groepsleden volgden verschillende wegen, maar hadden hetzelfde ideaal: vernieuwing van de schilderkunst. Ze werkten allemaal met natuurlijk licht en een gefragmenteerde penseelvoering. Monet, Renoir, Pissarro en Guillaumin hielden zich bezig met landschappen, het dagelijks leven en de vrije tijd. Berthe Morisot verkoos portretten en intieme onderwerpen. Edgar Degas was gefascineerd door de wereld van opera, danseressen en paardenraces, terwijl Gustave Caillebotte het moderne Parijs van Haussmann in fotografisch aandoende beelduitsneden vastlegde.

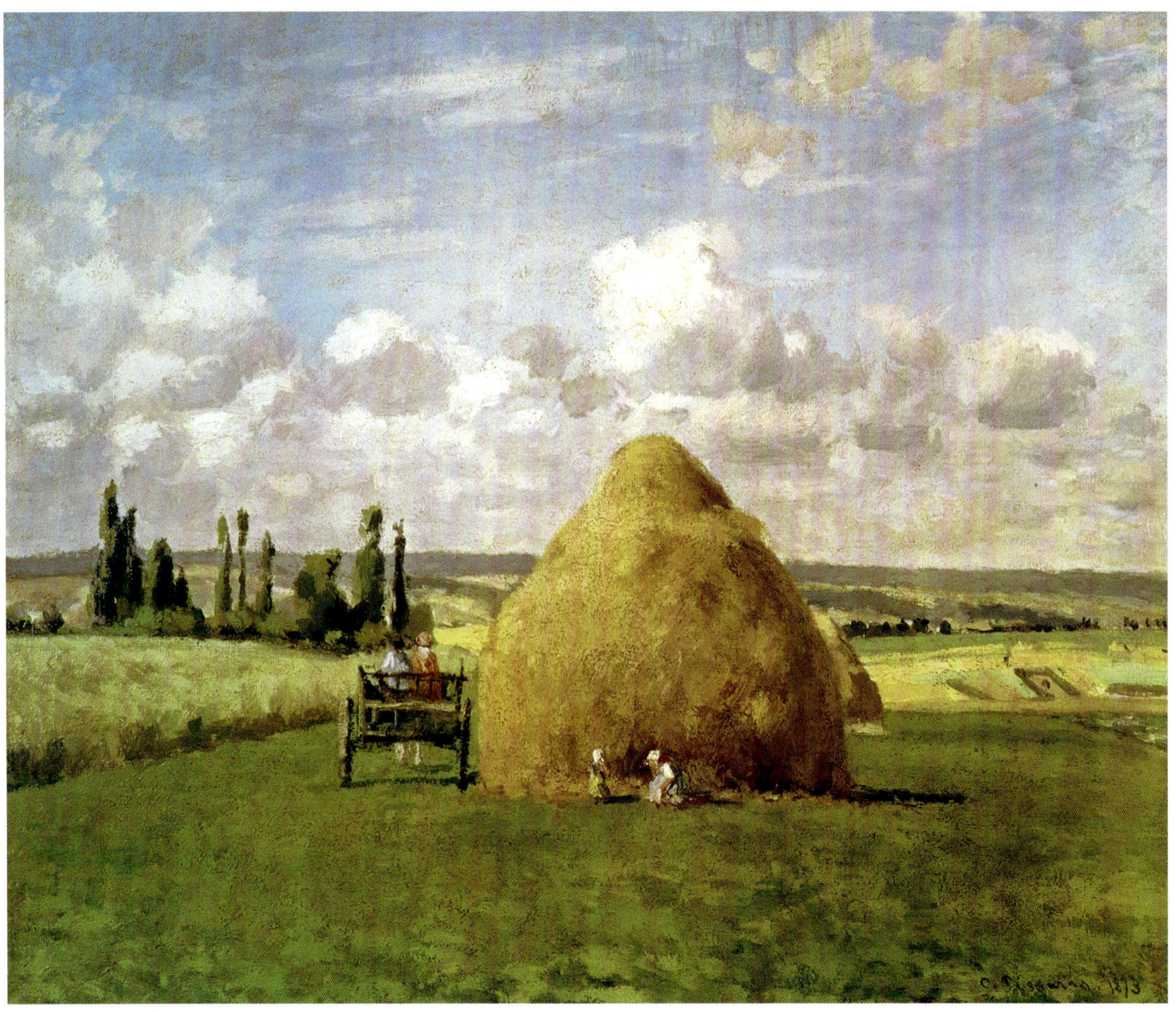

The Haystack, Pontoise

Meule de foin, Pontoise

Heuschober bei Pontoise

Graneros de heno cerca de Pontoise

Palheiros de feno perto de Pontoise

Hooiberg bij Pontoise

CAMILLE PISSARRO (1830-1903)
1873, Oil on canvas/Huile sur toile, 45 x 54 cm,
Private collection

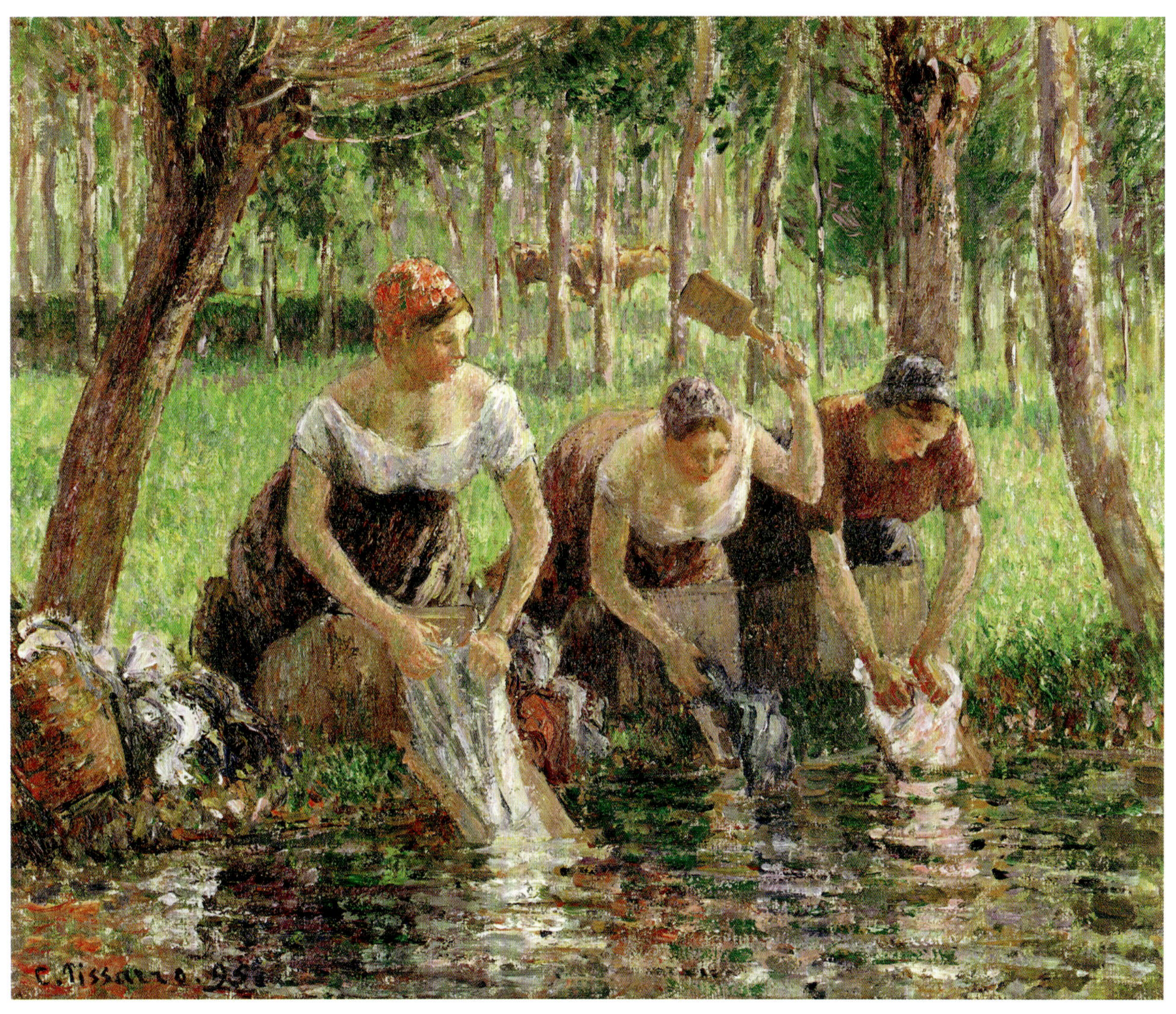

The Washerwomen, Éragny

Les Lavandières, Éragny

Wäscherinnen, Éragny

Las lavanderas, Éragny

Lavandarias, Éragny

De wasvrouwen, Éragny

CAMILLE PISSARRO (1830-1903)
1895, Oil on canvas/Huile sur toile,
38 × 46 cm, Private collection

199

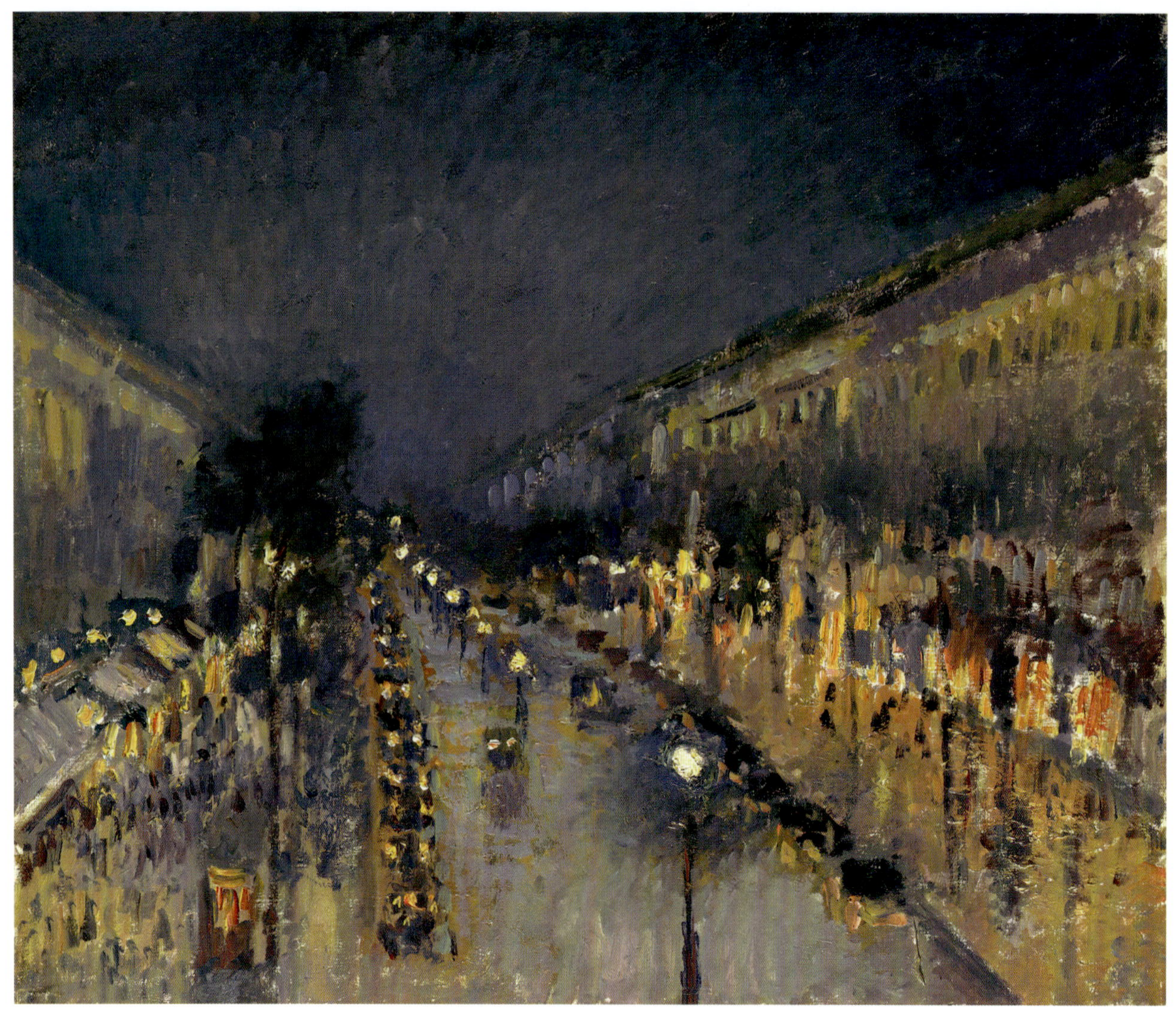

The Boulevard Montmartre at Night

Boulevard Montmartre, effet de nuit

Der Boulevard Montmartre bei Nacht

Boulevard Montmartre de noche

Boulevard Montmartre à noite

De Boulevard Montmartre bij nacht

CAMILLE PISSARRO (1830-1903)
1897, Oil on canvas/Huile sur toile,
53,3 × 64,8 cm, The National Gallery, London

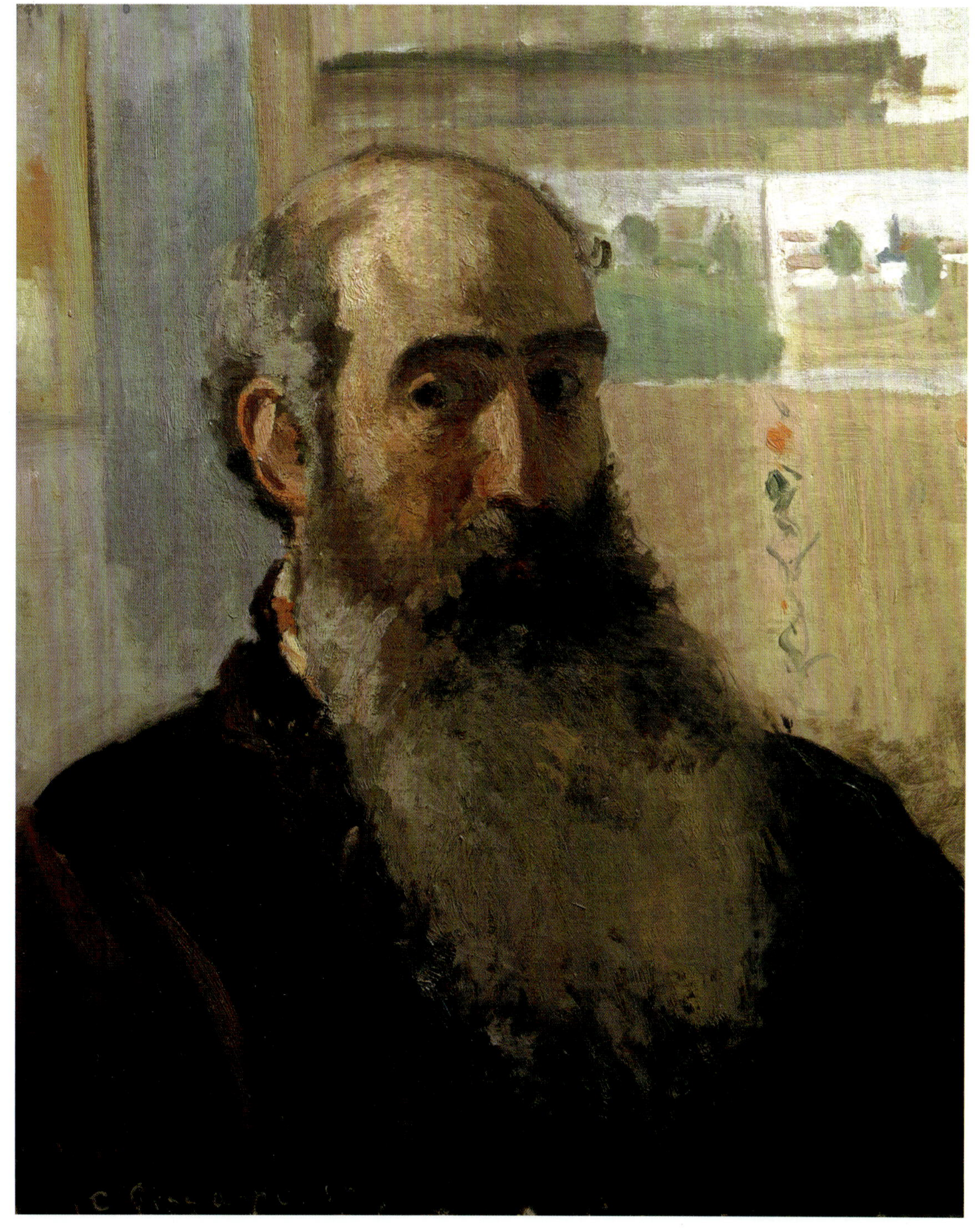

Self Portrait

Autoportrait

Selbstbildnis

Autorretrato

Auto-retrato

Zelfportret

CAMILLE PISSARRO
(1830-1903)
1873, Oil
on canvas/
Huile sur toile,
55,5 × 46 cm,
Musée d'Orsay,
Paris

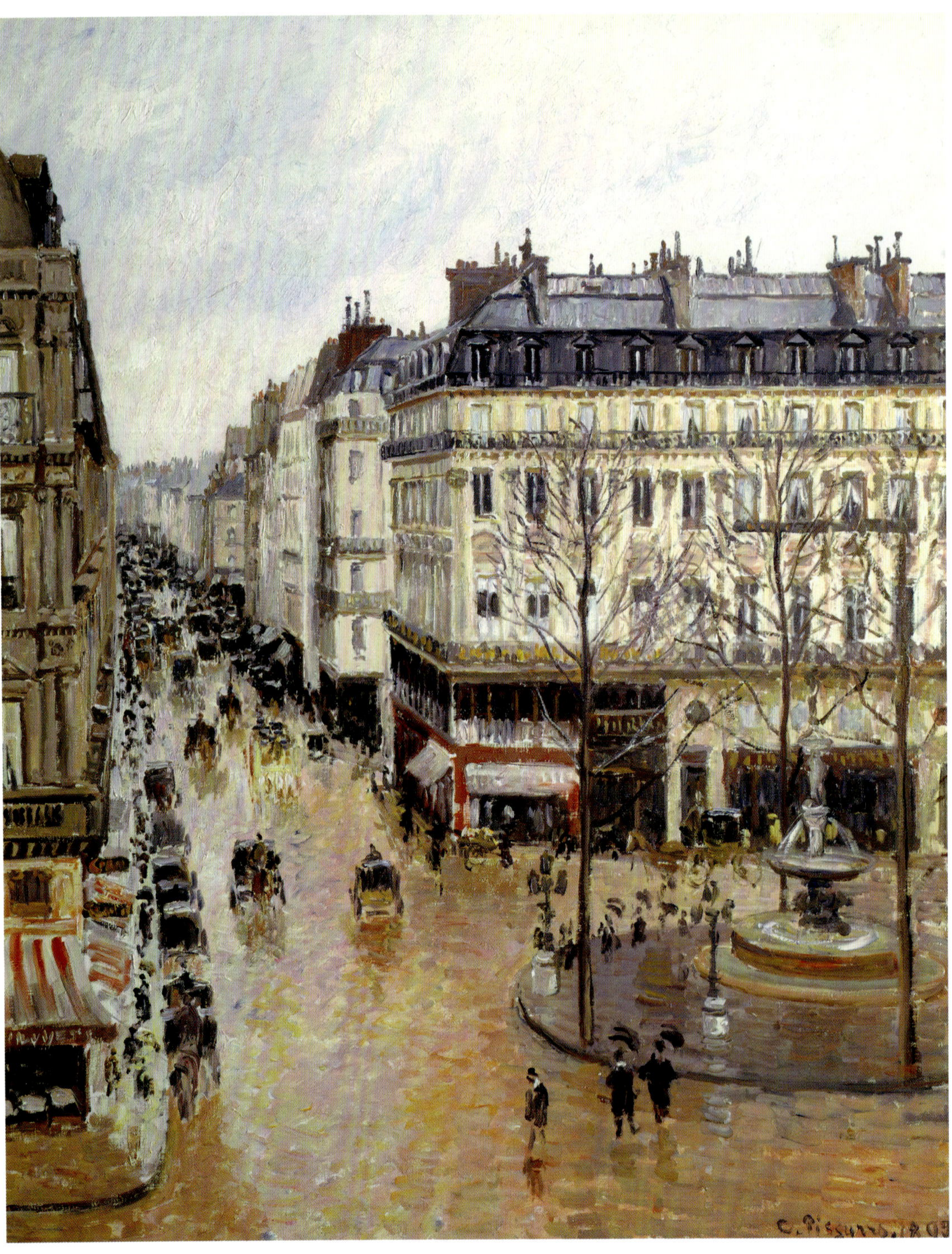

Rue Saint-Honoré, Afternoon, Rain Effect

Rue Saint-Honoré dans l'après-midi, effet de pluie

Rue Saint-Honoré am Nachmittag bei Regen

Rue Saint-Honoré por la tarde bajo la lluvia

Rue Saint-Honoré à tarde na chuva

Rue Saint-Honoré in de namiddag in de regen

CAMILLE PISSARRO (1830-1903)
1897, Oil on canvas/Huile sur toile, 81 × 65 cm, Museo Thyssen-Bornemisza, Madrid

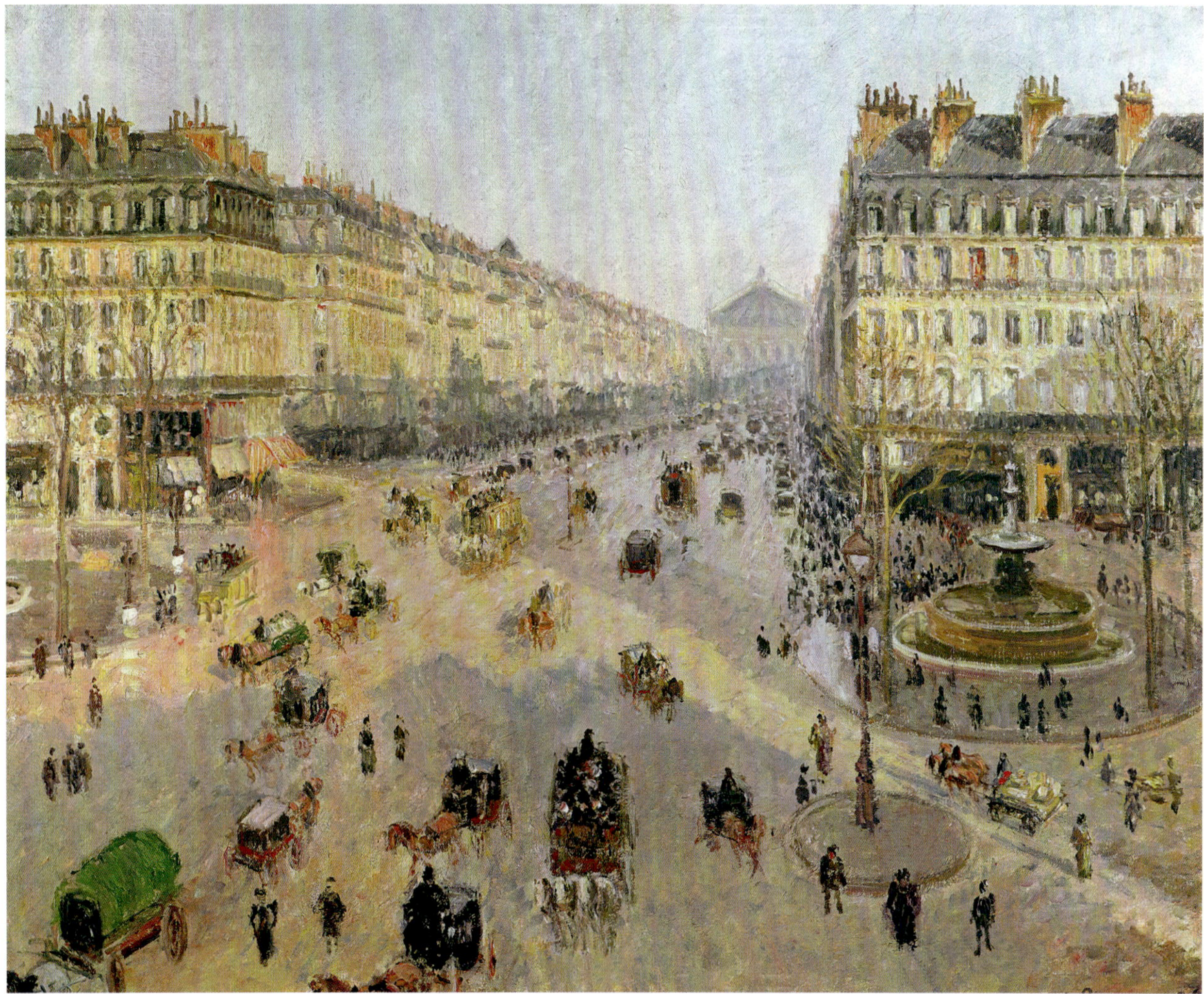

The Avenue de l'Opéra, Sunlight, Winter Morning

From 1897 to 1899, Pissarro resided at the Hôtel du Louvre. His room offered a wide view over the square in front of the Comédie-Française and the Avenue de l'Opéra, where pedestrians and cabs mingle.

Avenue de l'Opéra, soleil, matinée d'hiver

Entre 1897 et 1899, Pissarro loge au Grand Hôtel du Louvre. Il bénéficie depuis sa chambre d'une vue plongeante sur la place de la Comédie-Française et le boulevard de l'Opéra, où passent piétons et fiacres.

Die Avenue de l'Opéra bei Sonne an einem Wintermorgen

Von 1897 bis 1899 residiert Pissarro im Hôtel du Louvre. Sein Zimmer bietet einen weiten Blick über den Platz vor der Comédie-Française und die Avenue de l'Opéra, auf der sich Fußgänger und Droschken tummeln.

Avenue de l'Opéra al sol en una mañana de invierno

De 1897 a 1899, Pissarro residió en el Hôtel du Louvre. Su habitación ofrece una amplia vista sobre la plaza frente a la Comédie-Française y la Avenue de l'Opéra, donde los peatones y los taxis se divierten.

Avenue de l'Opéra ao sol numa manhã de inverno

De 1897 a 1899, Pissarro residiu no Hôtel du Louvre. Seu quarto oferece uma ampla vista sobre a praça em frente à Comédie-Française e à Avenida da Ópera, onde pedestres e táxis cavortam.

Avenue de l'Opéra op een winterochtend in de zon

Van 1897 tot 1899 verbleef Pissarro in het Hôtel du Louvre. Zijn kamer bood een weids uitzicht over het plein voor de Comédie-Française en de Avenue de l'Opéra, waar het krioelt van de voetgangers en huurrijtuigen.

CAMILLE PISSARRO (1830-1903)
1898, Oil on canvas/Huile sur toile, 73 × 92 cm, Musée des Beaux-Arts, Reims

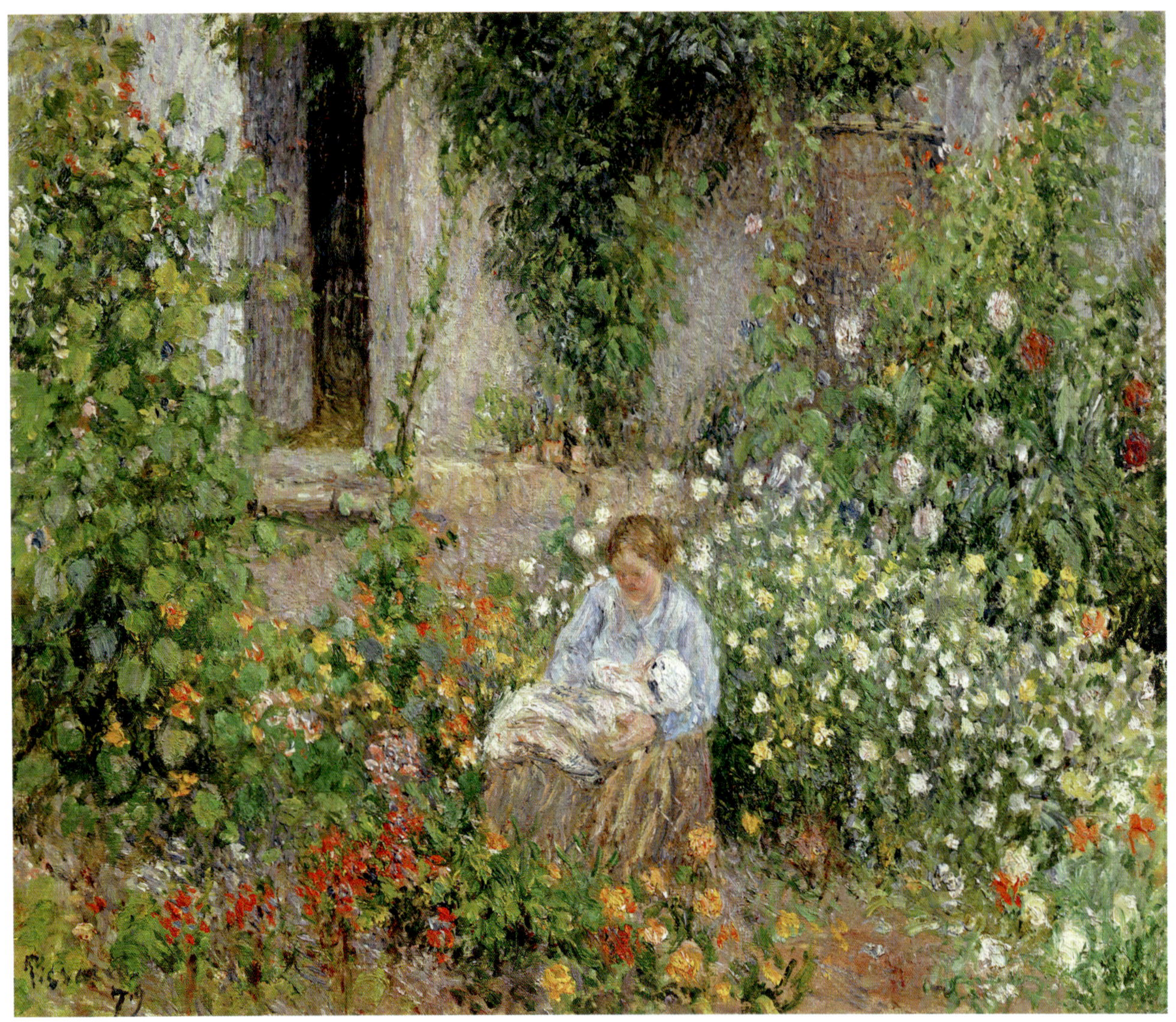

Mother and Child in the Flowers

Mère et enfant dans les fleurs

Mutter mit Kind zwischen Blumen

Madre con su hijo entre flores

Mãe com filho entre flores

Moeder met kind tussen de bloemen

CAMILLE PISSARRO (1830-1903)

1879, Oil on canvas/Huile sur toile, 38 × 46 cm, Private collection

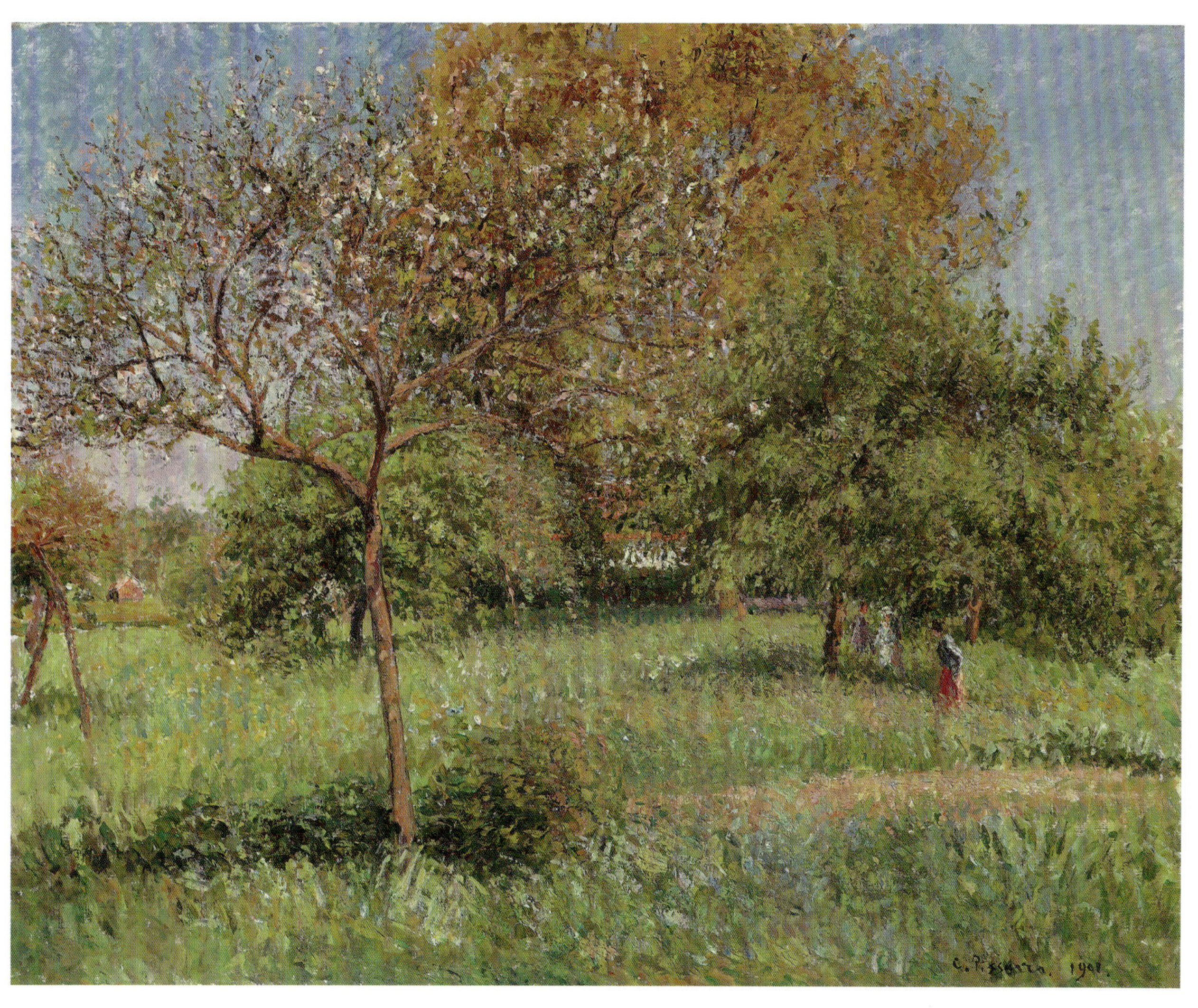

The Great Walnut Tree, Morning, Éragny

Le Grand Noyer, Matin, Éragny

Der große Walnussbaum am Morgen, Éragny

El gran nogal por la mañana, Éragny

A grande nogueira de manhã, Éragny

De grote walnotenboom in de ochtend, Éragny

CAMILLE PISSARRO (1830-1903)

1901, Oil on canvas/Huile sur toile, 73 × 92 cm, Private collection

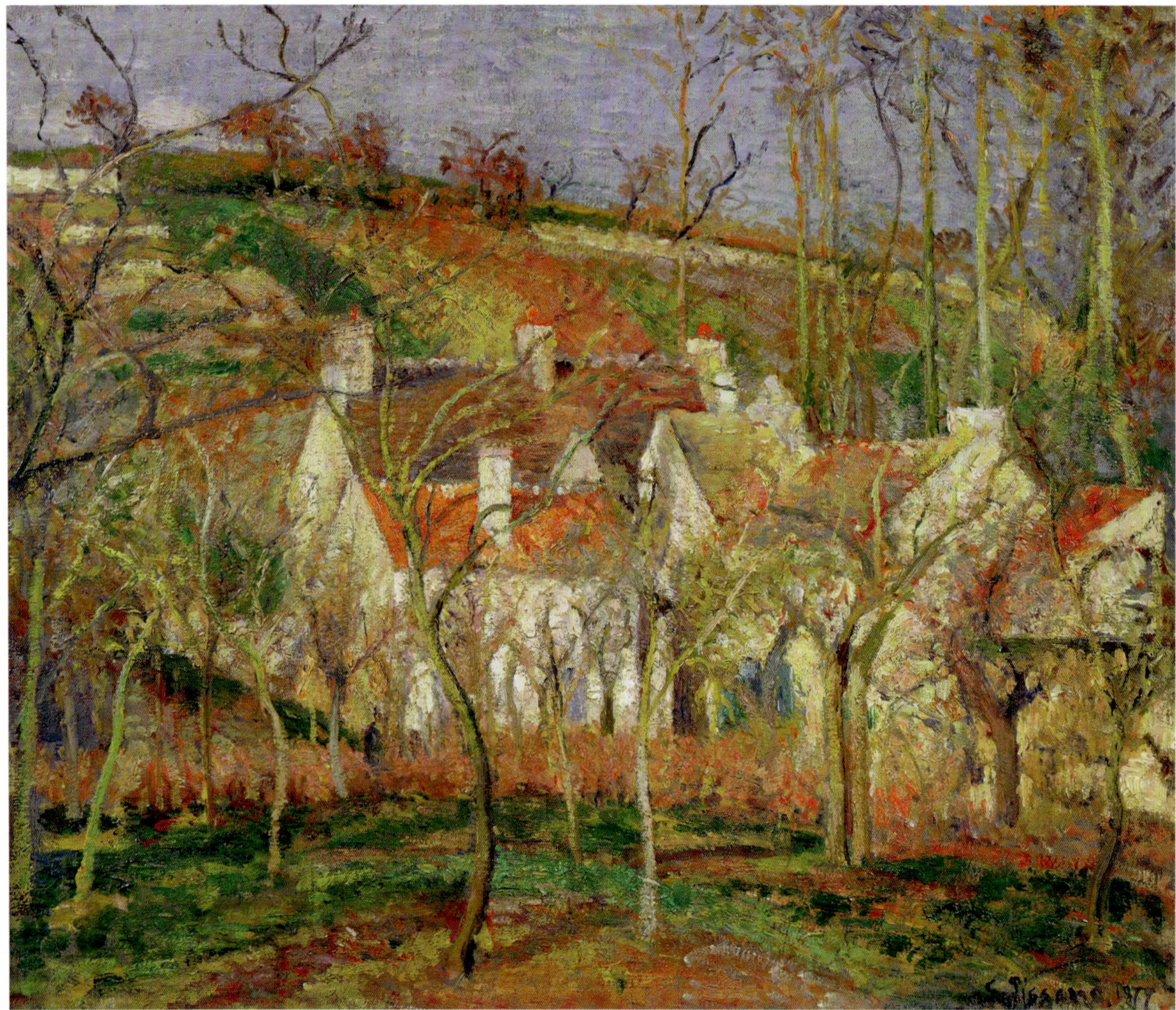

The Red Roofs, Corner of a Village, Winter

Pissarro painted the village of Pontoise several times. This is the most famous work. At the foot of the Saint-Denis hillside, between the trunks of bare trees, the outlines of the houses subtly shine through.

Les Toits rouges

Pissarro a peint de nombreux tableaux à Pontoise. *Les Toits rouges* est sans doute le plus connu. Les maisons apparaissent subtilement, au pied de la côte Saint-Denis, entre les troncs des arbres dénudés.

Rote Dächer, Dorfausschnitt, winterliche Stimmung

Pissarro malte das Dorf Pontoise mehrere Male. Dieses ist das bekannteste Werk. Am Fuße des Hanges Saint-Denis scheinen zwischen den Stämmen kahler Bäume subtil die Umrisse der Häuser hindurch.

Techos rojos, rincón del pueblo, atmósfera invernal

Pissarro pintó el pueblo de Pontoise varias veces. Esta es la obra más famosa. Al pie de la ladera de Saint-Denis, entre los troncos de los árboles desnudos, los contornos de las casas brillan sutilmente.

Telhados vermelhos, recortes de aldeia, atmosfera invernal

Pissarro pintou várias vezes a aldeia de Pontoise. Este é o trabalho mais famoso. No sopé da encosta de Saint-Denis, entre troncos de árvores nuas, os contornos das casas brilham sutilmente.

Rode daken, hoek van een dorp, winter

Pissarro schilderde het dorp Pontoise meerdere malen. Dit is het bekendste werk. Aan de voet van de helling van Saint-Denis, tussen de stammen van kale bomen, schijnen subtiel de contouren van huizen door.

CAMILLE PISSARRO (1830-1903)

1877, Oil on canvas/Huile sur toile, 54,5 × 65,5 cm, Musée d'Orsay, Paris

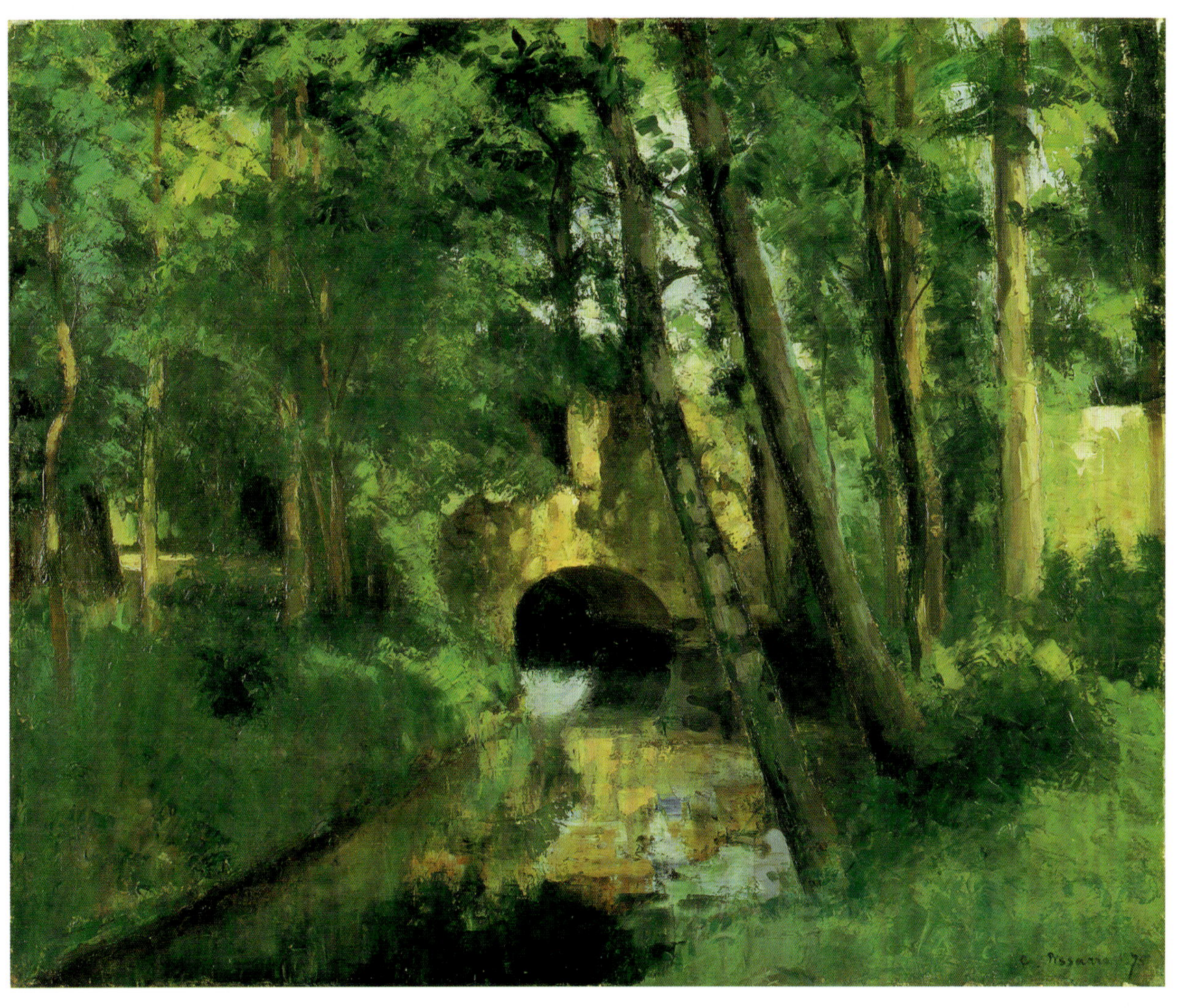

The Little Bridge, Pontoise

Le Petit Pont, Pontoise

Die kleine Brücke, Pontoise

Pequeño puente, Pontoise

A pequena ponte, Pontoise

Het bruggetje, Pontoise

CAMILLE PISSARRO (1830-1903)

1875, Oil on canvas/Huile sur toile,
65 × 81 cm, Kunsthalle Mannheim

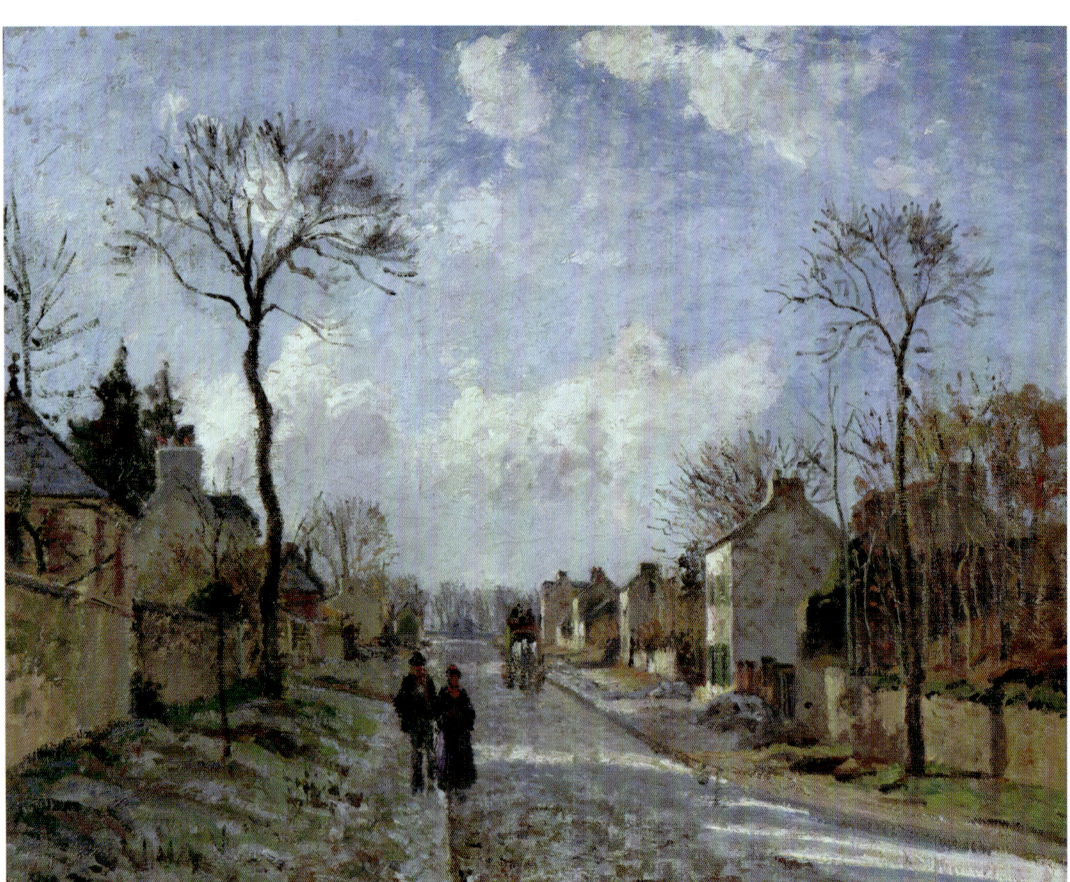

Woman wearing a Green Headscarf

The young woman sitting in front of a table turns her head slightly towards the viewer. The painting belongs to the late work of the artist. It stands out due to the relationships between the colors and the dotted background.

Femme au fichu vert

Assise devant une table, de profil, la jeune femme tourne légèrement la tête vers le spectateur. Œuvre tardive du peintre, ce portrait surprend par ses rapports de couleurs vives et son fond moucheté.

Frau mit grünem Kopftuch

Die vor einem Tisch sitzende junge Frau wendet ihren Kopf leicht dem Betrachter zu. Das Gemälde zählt zum Spätwerk des Künstlers. Es sticht durch die Beziehungen der Farben und den getupften Hintergrund hervor.

Mujer con pañuelo verde

La joven sentada frente a una mesa gira ligeramente la cabeza hacia el espectador. La pintura pertenece a la obra tardía del artista. Destaca por la relación entre los colores y el fondo manchado.

Mulher com lenço verde

A jovem sentada em frente a uma mesa vira a cabeça ligeiramente para o espectador. A pintura pertence ao trabalho tardio do artista. Destaca-se pelas relações entre as cores e o fundo manchado.

Vrouw met groene hoofddoek

De jonge vrouw die voor een tafel zit, draait haar hoofd een beetje naar de kijker toe. Het schilderij behoort tot het late werk van de schilder. Het boeit door de relatie tussen de kleuren en de gestippelde achtergrond.

CAMILLE PISSARRO (1830-1903)
1893, Oil on canvas/Huile sur toile, 65,5 × 54,5 cm, Musée d'Orsay, Paris

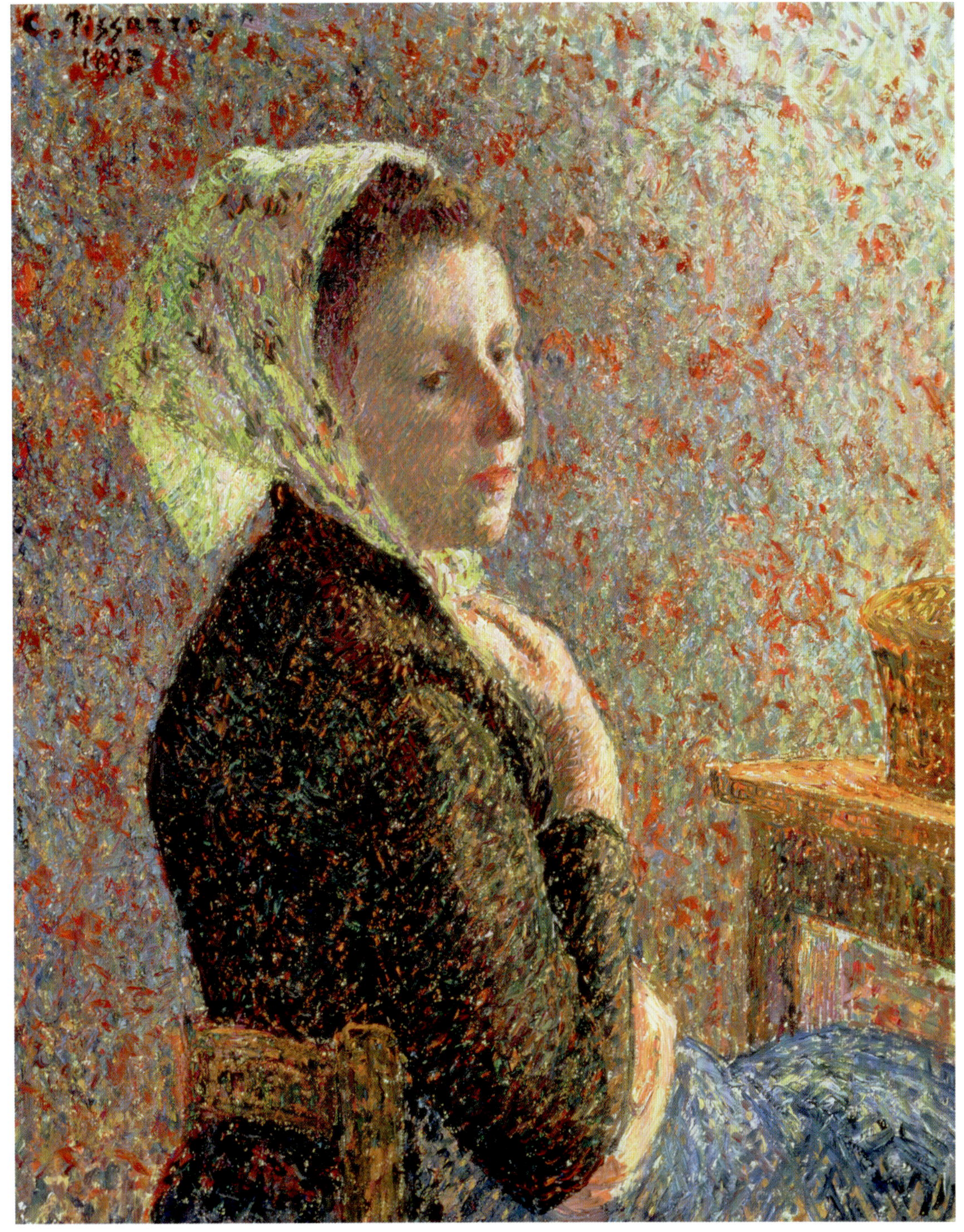

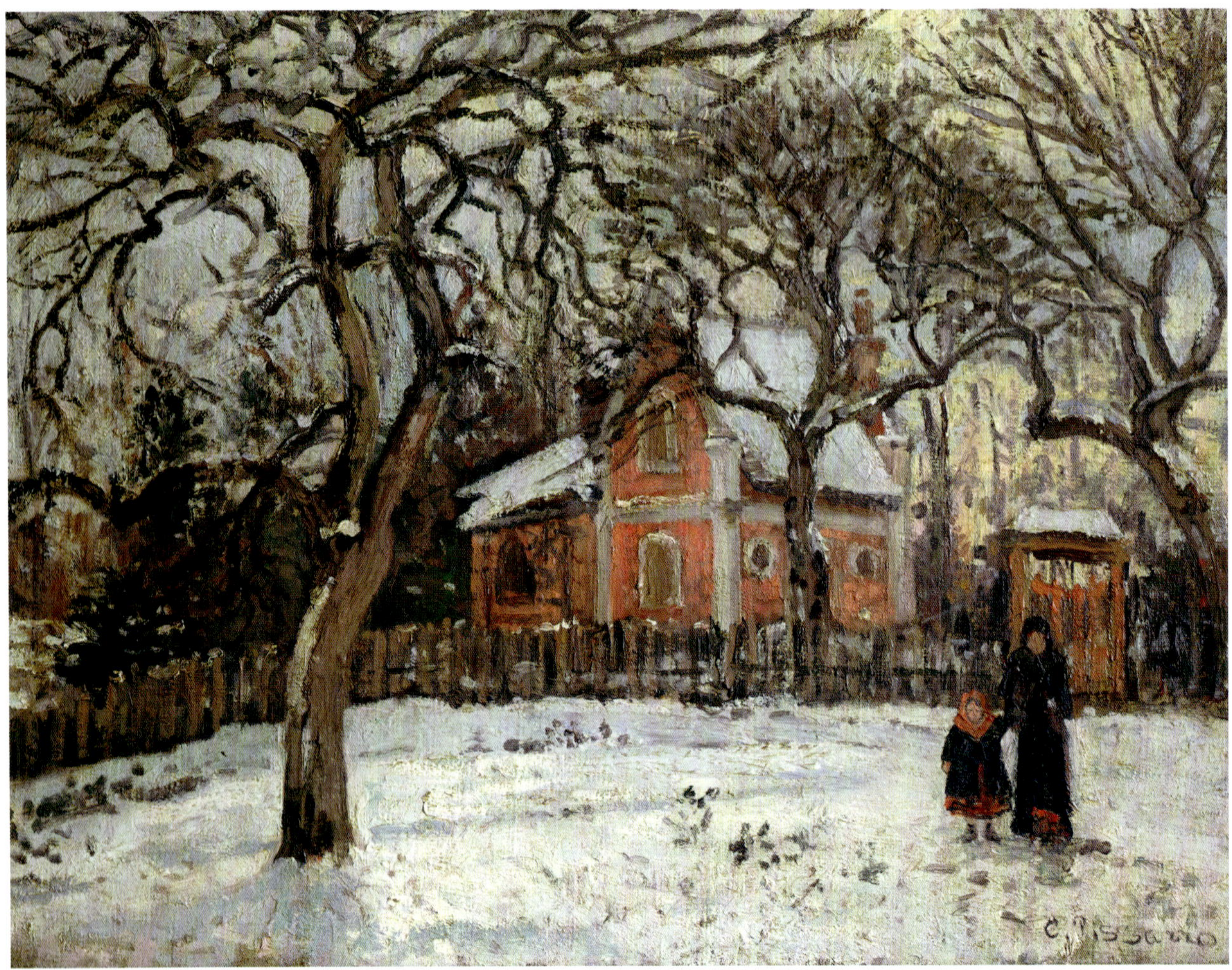

Chestnut Trees at Louveciennes

Châtaignier à Louveciennes

Kastanienbäume in Louveciennes

Castaños en Louveciennes

Castanheiros em Louveciennes

Kastanjebomen in Louveciennes

CAMILLE PISSARRO (1830-1903)

1879, Oil on canvas/Huile sur toile, 41 × 54 cm, Musée d'Orsay, Paris

In a Café *or* The Absinthe

Through her deep melancholy the woman dominates the painting, which makes the man next to her fade into the background. The picture was modelled by the actress Ellen Andrée and the painter Marcellin Desboutin.

Dans un café *dit aussi* L'Absinthe

D'une infinie mélancolie, la figure féminine est si présente qu'elle en ferait presque oublier l'homme assis à côté d'elle. Les modèles sont l'actrice Ellen Andrée et le peintre Marcellin Desboutin.

In einem Café *oder* Der Absinth

Durch ihre tiefe Melancholie beherrscht die Frau das Gemälde, was den Mann neben ihr in den Hintergrund treten lässt. Für das Bild standen die Schauspielerin Ellen Andrée und der Maler Marcellin Desboutin Modell.

El ajenjo *también llamado* Los bebedores de absenta

Con una melancolía infinita, la figura femenina está tan presente que casi te hace olvidar al hombre sentado a su lado. Las modelos son la actriz Ellen Andrée y el pintor Marcelino Desboutin.

Num Café *ou* no Absinto

Através de sua profunda melancolia a mulher domina a pintura, o que faz com que o homem ao lado de seu passo para o fundo. O quadro foi modelado pela atriz Ellen Andrée e pelo pintor Marcellin Desboutin.

De absintdrinkster *of* In een café

Door haar diepe melancholie overheerst de vrouw het schilderij, waardoor de man naast haar op de achtergrond raakt. Voor dit werk zaten de actrice Ellen Andrée en de schilder Marcellin Desboutin model.

EDGAR DEGAS (1834-1917)

c. 1875/76, Oil on canvas/Huile sur toile, 92 × 68,5 cm, Musée d'Orsay, Paris

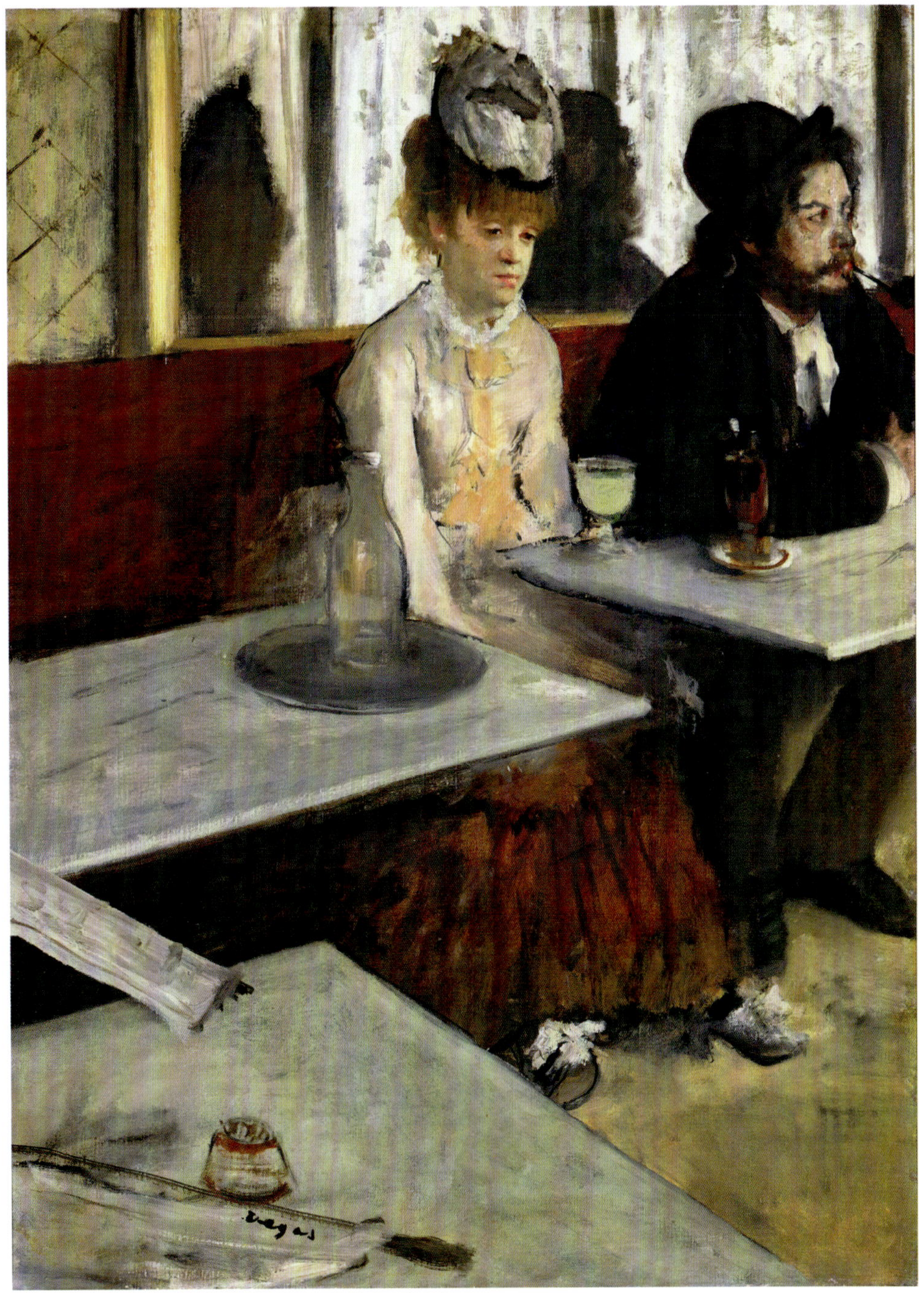

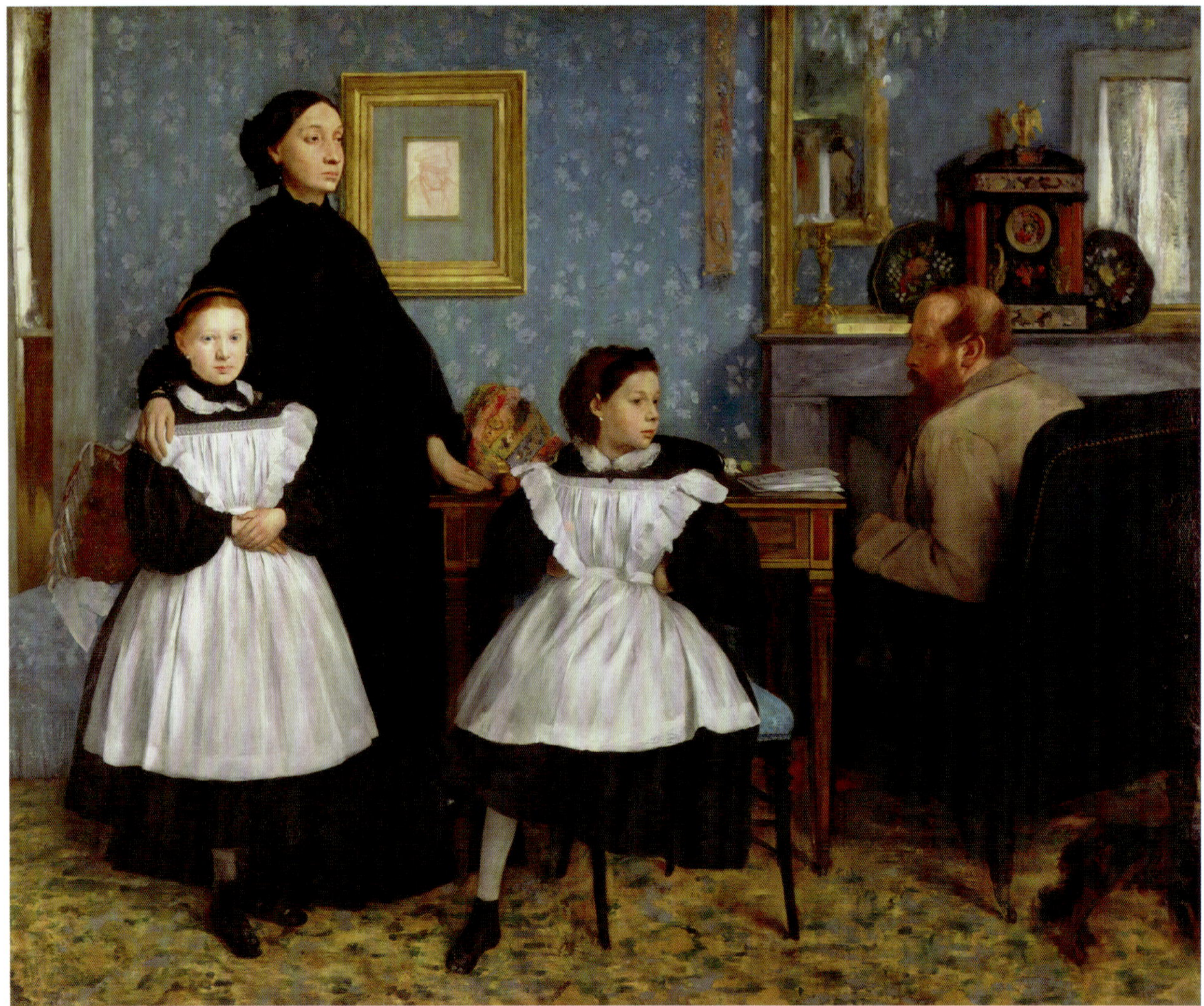

The Bellelli family

In the portrait Degas immortalized his paternal aunt, her husband, Baron Bellelli, and her two daughters. The mother, dressed in black, was mourning for her father at that time.

La Famille Bellelli

Dans cette œuvre de jeunesse, la tante paternelle de Degas et son époux le baron Bellelli prennent la pose, accompagnés de leurs deux filles. La mère, vêtue de noir, porte le deuil de son propre père.

Die Familie Bellelli

In dem Porträt verewigte Degas seine Tante väterlicherseits, ihren Ehemann, den Baron Bellelli, und ihre beiden Töchter. Die in schwarz gekleidete Mutter trauerte zu dem Zeitpunkt um ihren Vater.

La familia Bellelli

En el retrato, Degas inmortalizó a su tía por parte de su padre, su marido, el barón Bellelli, y sus dos hijas. La madre, vestida de negro, lloraba a su padre en ese momento.

A família Bellelli

No retrato Degas imortalizou sua tia do lado do pai, seu marido, Barão Bellelli, e suas duas filhas. A mãe, vestida de preto, chorou o pai naquela altura.

De familie Bellelli

Op het portret vereeuwigde Degas zijn tante van vaders kant, haar echtgenoot, baron Bellelli, en haar twee dochters. De moeder, gekleed in het zwart, rouwde destijds om haar vader.

EDGAR DEGAS (1834-1917)
1858-67, Oil on canvas/Huile sur toile, 200 × 250 cm, Musée d'Orsay, Paris

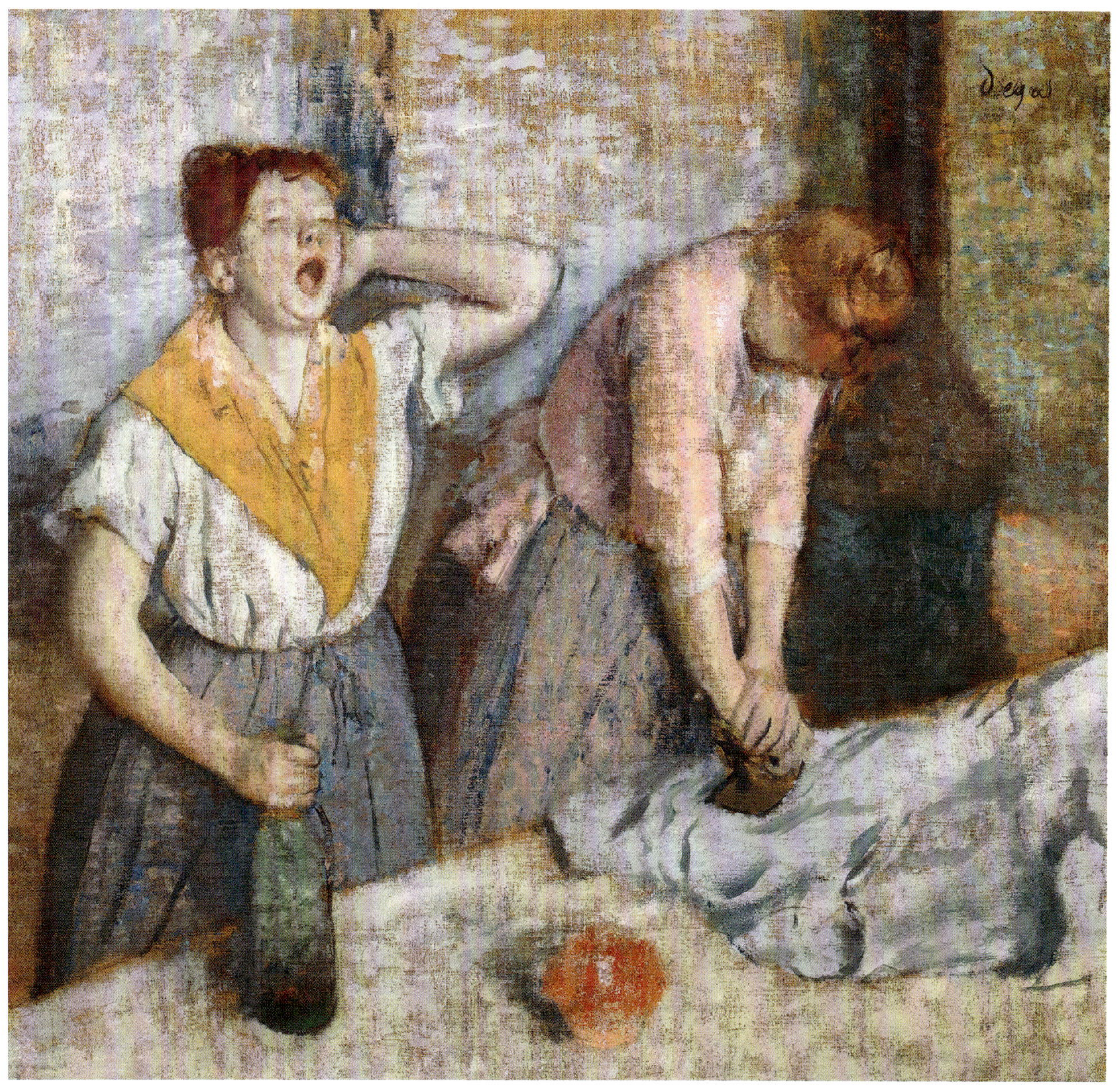

The Laundresses   Die Büglerinnen   As engomadoras

Repasseuses   Las planchadoras   De strijksters

EDGAR DEGAS (1834-1917)

c. 1884-86, Oil on canvas/Huile sur toile, 76 × 81,4 cm, Musée d'Orsay, Paris

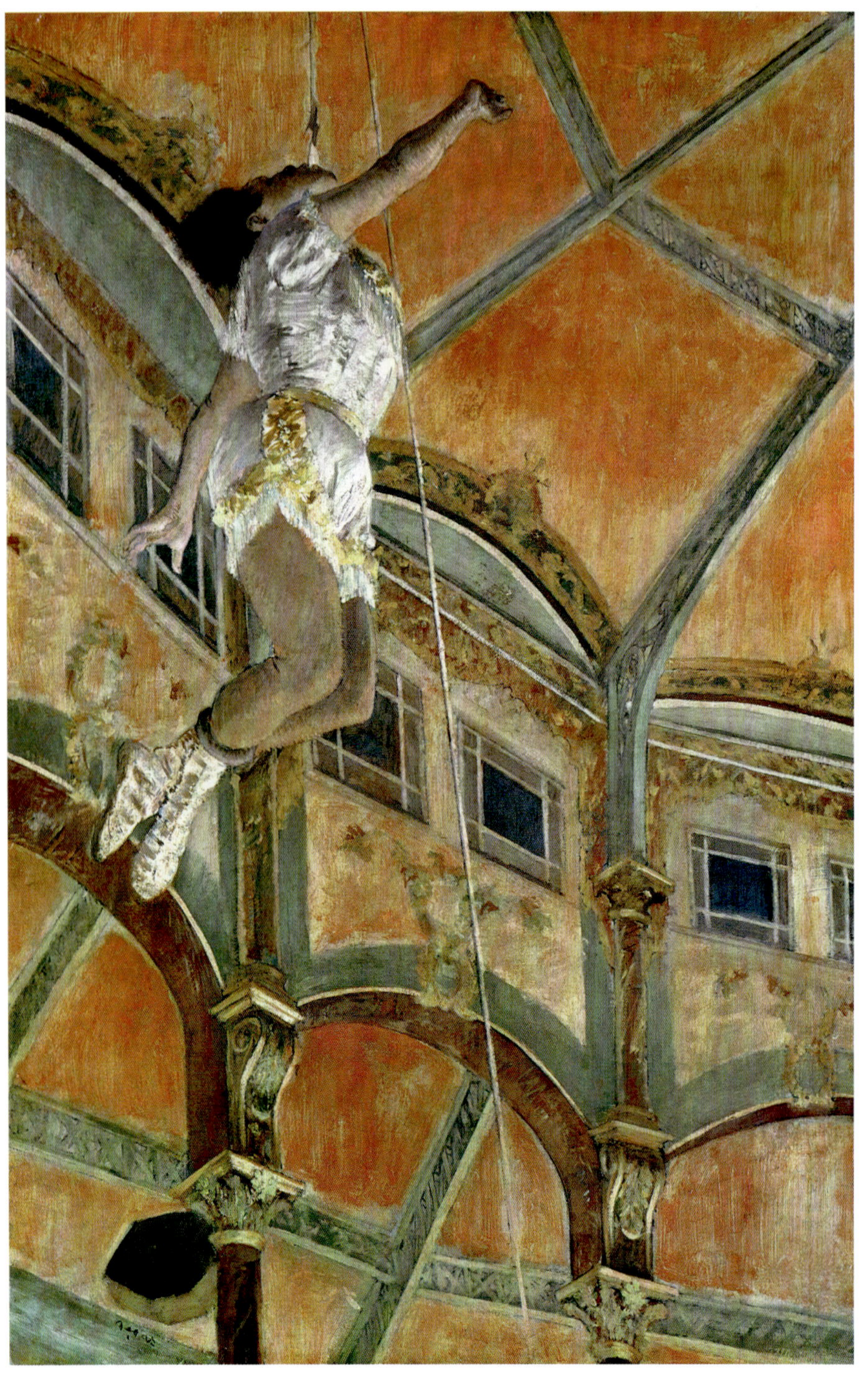

Miss La La at the Cirque Fernando

Miss Lala au cirque Fernando

Miss Lala im Zirkus Fernando

La Srta. Lala en el Circo Fernando

Miss Lala no Circo Fernando

Miss Lala van Circus Fernando

EDGAR DEGAS (1834-1917)

1879, Oil on canvas/Huile sur toile,
117,2 × 77,5 cm, The National Gallery, London

The Opera Orchestra

L'Orchestre de l'Opéra

Das Orchester der Oper

La orquesta de la ópera

A Orquestra da Ópera

Het orkest van de Opera

EDGAR DEGAS (1834-1917)

c. 1870, Oil on canvas/Huile sur toile,
56,6 × 46 cm, Musée d'Orsay, Paris

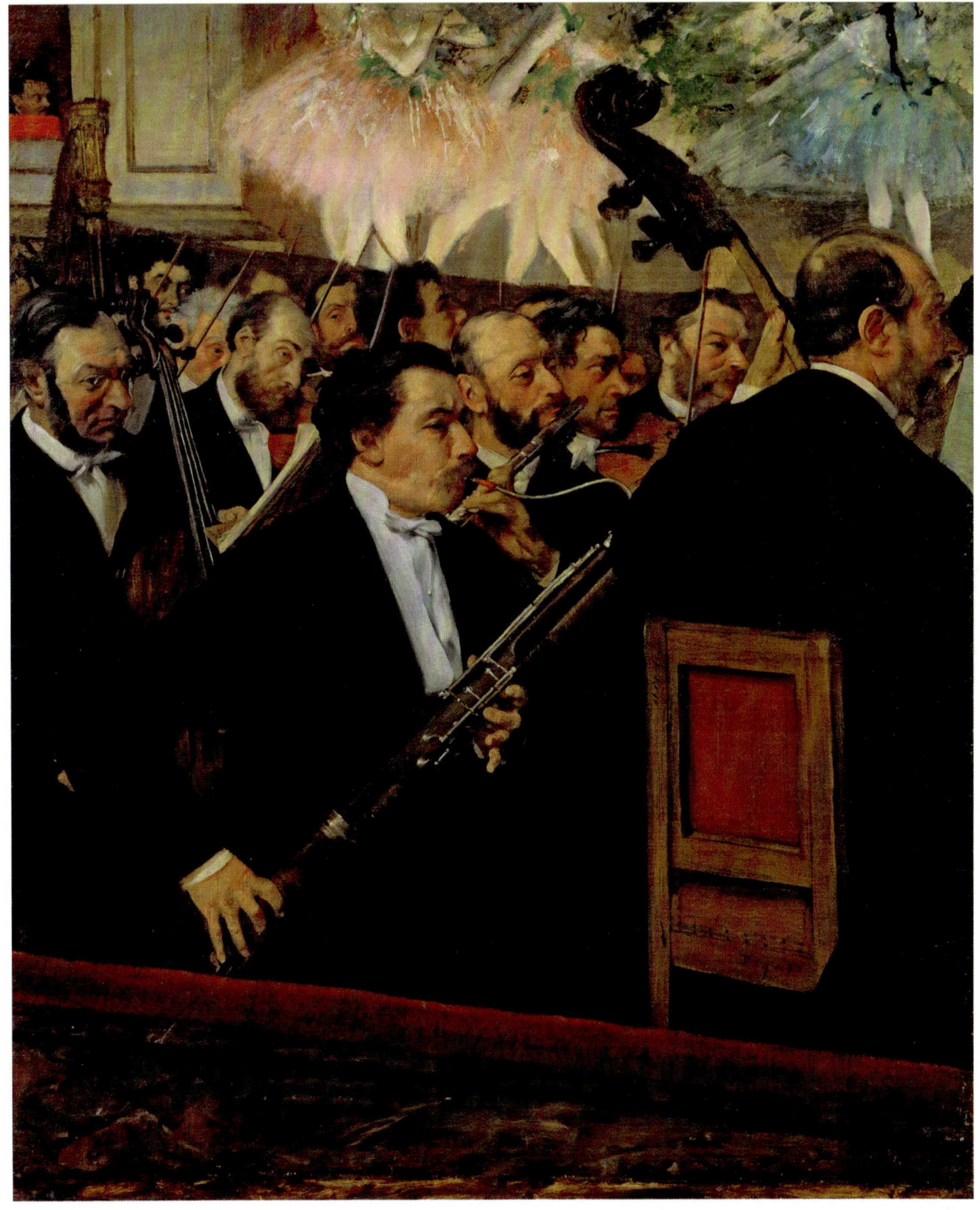

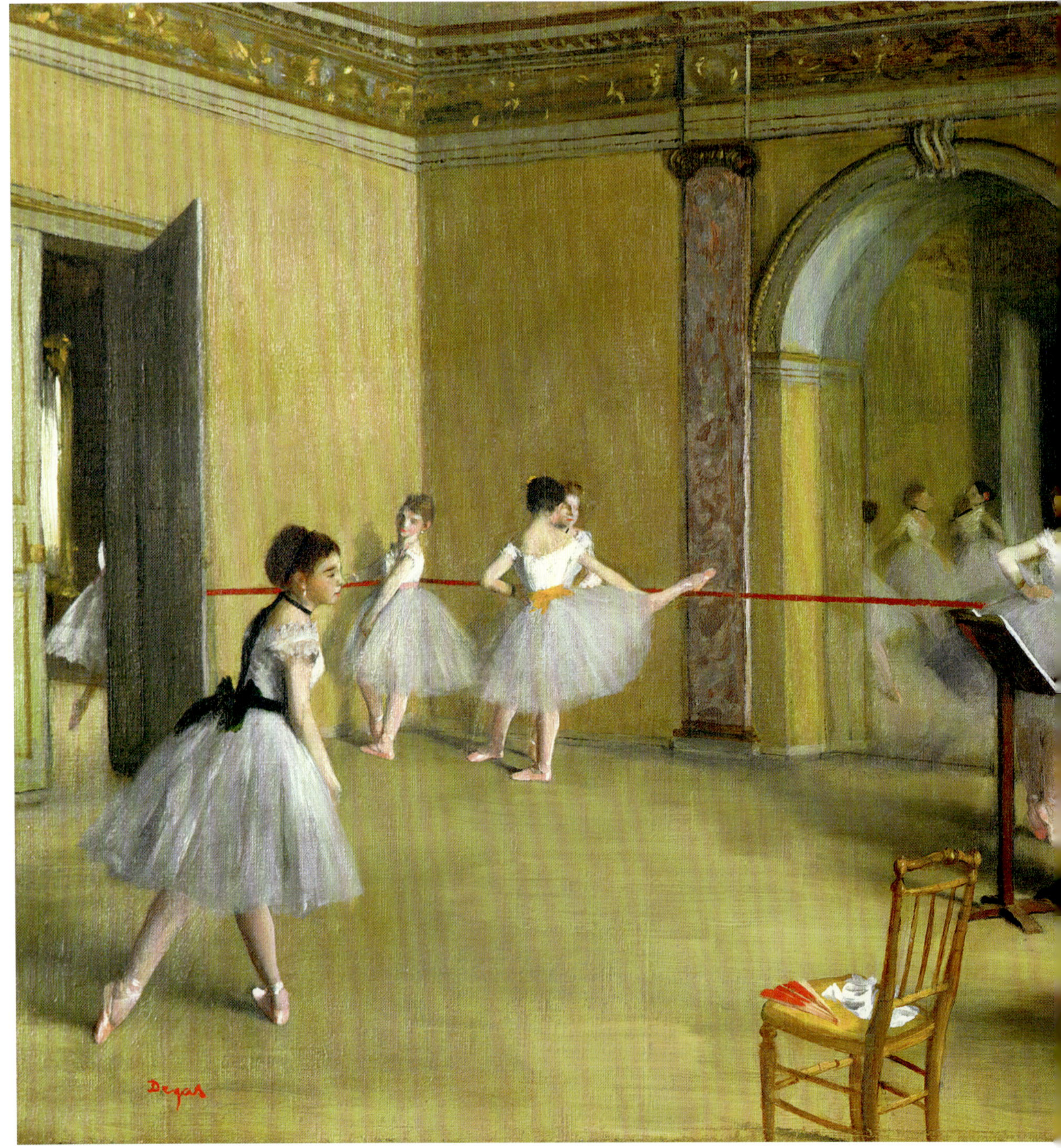

Degas

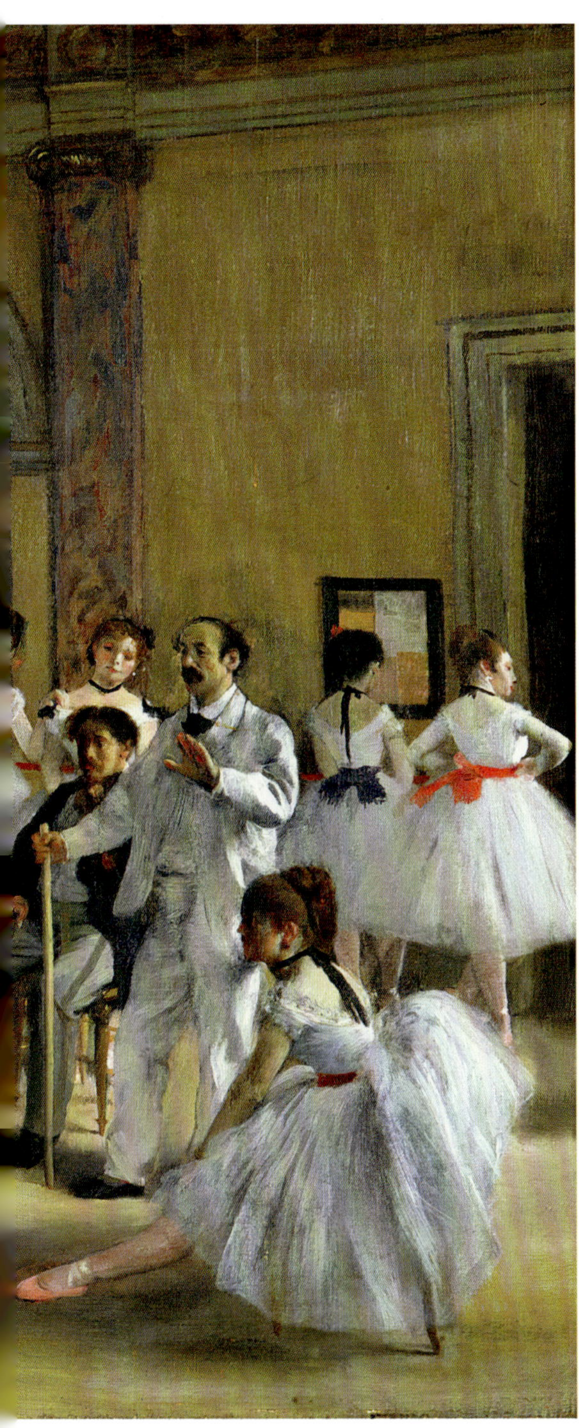

The Dance Foyer at the Opera on the Rue Le Peletier

The events at the Paris Opera were among Degas favourite motifs. He created numerous paintings and pastels. We can see the dancers at rehearsal under the guidance of the choreographer Louis Mérante.

Le Foyer de la danse à l'Opéra de la rue Le Peletier

L'Opéra de Paris n'a aucun secret pour Degas, qui a produit une multitude de peintures et de pastels sur le sujet. Les danseuses sont ici en répétition, sous la direction du maître de ballet Louis Mérante.

Ballettsaal der Oper in der Rue Le Peletier

Die Vorgänge in der Pariser Oper zählten zu Degas Lieblingsmotiven. Er schuf zahlreiche Gemälde und Pastelle. Unter der Anleitung des Choreografen Louis Mérante sehen wir die Tänzerinnen bei der Probe.

Sala de ballet de la ópera de la Rue Le Peletier

Los eventos de la Ópera de París fueron uno de los motivos favoritos de Degas. Creó numerosas pinturas y pasteles. Bajo la dirección del coreógrafo Louis Mérante vemos a los bailarines en el ensayo.

Salão de Ballet da Ópera na Rue Le Peletier

Os eventos da Ópera de Paris estavam entre os motivos favoritos da Degas. Ele criou inúmeras pinturas e pastéis. Sob a orientação do coreógrafo Louis Mérante, vemos os dançarinos no ensaio.

Balletzaal van de Opera aan de Rue Le Peletier

Het reilen en zeilen in de Parijse Opera was een geliefd onderwerp van Degas. Hij maakte er talrijke schilderijen en pastels van. We zien danseressen tijdens een repetitie onder leiding van de choreograaf Louis Mérante.

EDGAR DEGAS (1834-1917)

1872, Oil on canvas/Huile sur toile, 32,7 × 46,3 cm, Musée d'Orsay, Paris

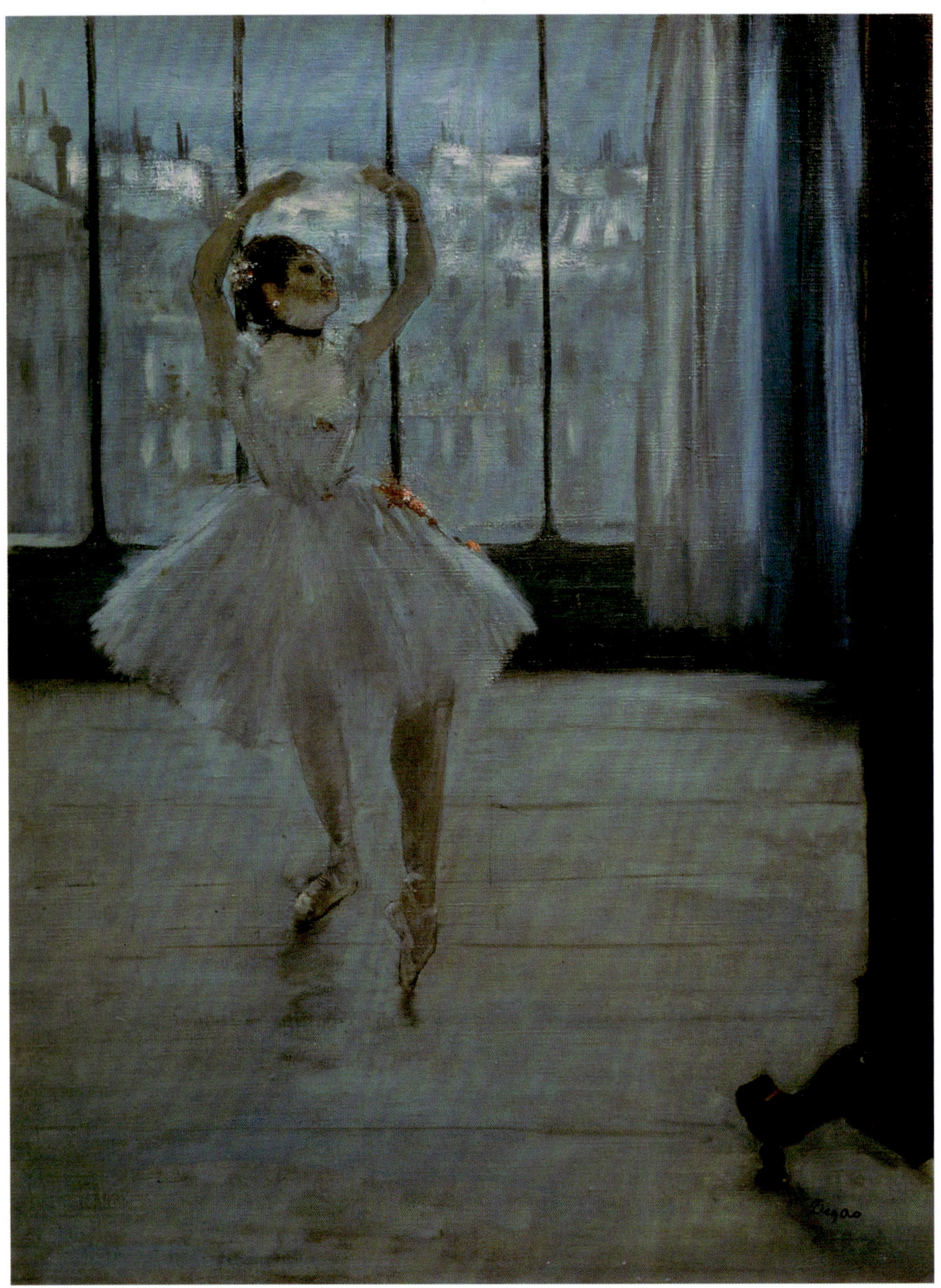

Dancer in Front of
the Window

Danseuse devant
la fenêtre

Tänzerin vor
einem Fenster

Bailarina delante
de una ventana

Dançarina em frente
a uma janela

Danseres voor een raam

EDGAR DEGAS (1834-1917)
c. 1873-76, Oil on canvas/
Huile sur toile, 65 × 50 cm,
Pushkin Museum, Moscow

The Dancing Class

La Classe de danse

Tanzunterricht

La clase de danza

Aulas de dança

De dansles

EDGAR DEGAS (1834-1917)
c. 1873-76, Oil on canvas/
Huile sur toile,
85,5 × 75 cm,
Musée d'Orsay, Paris

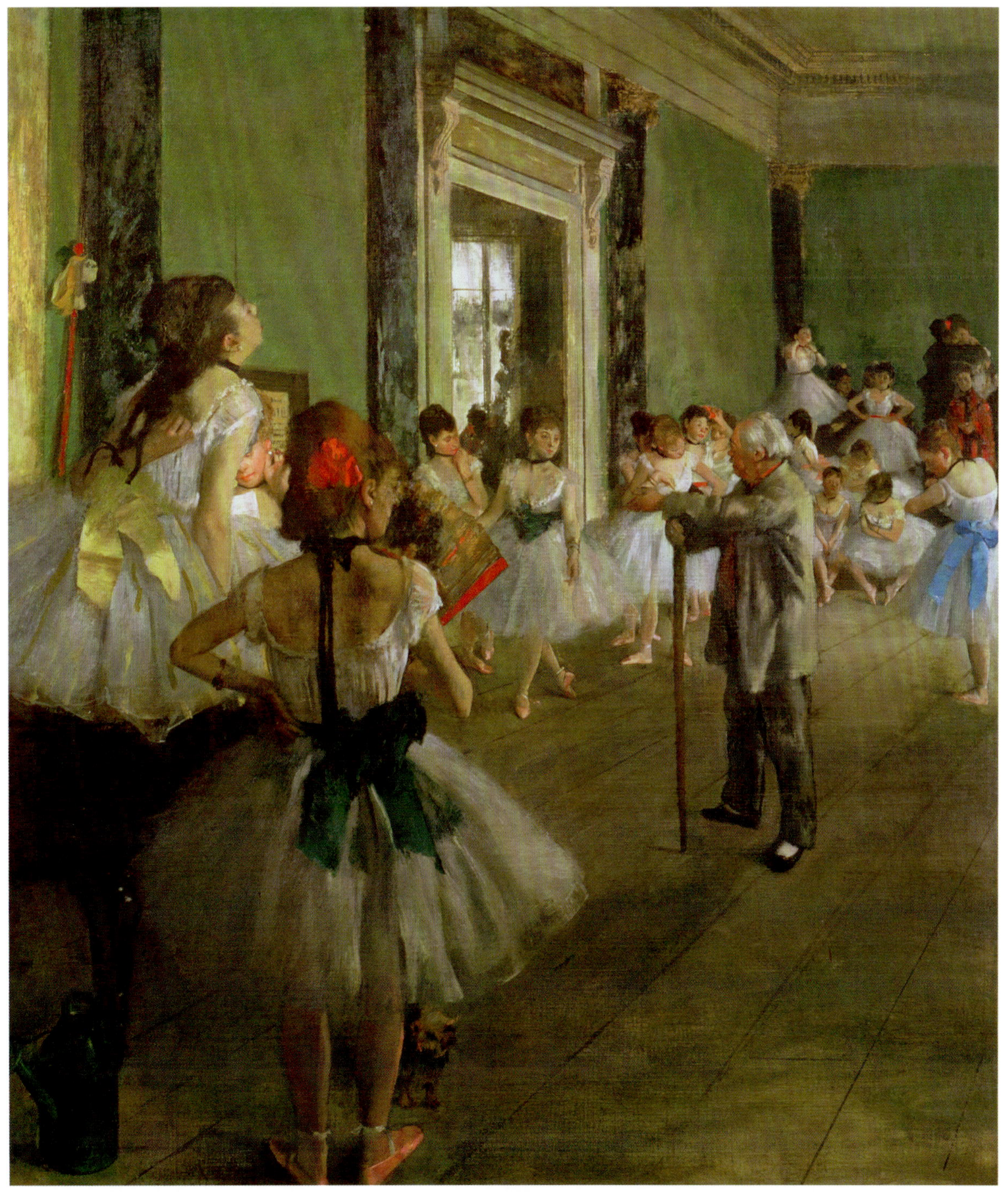

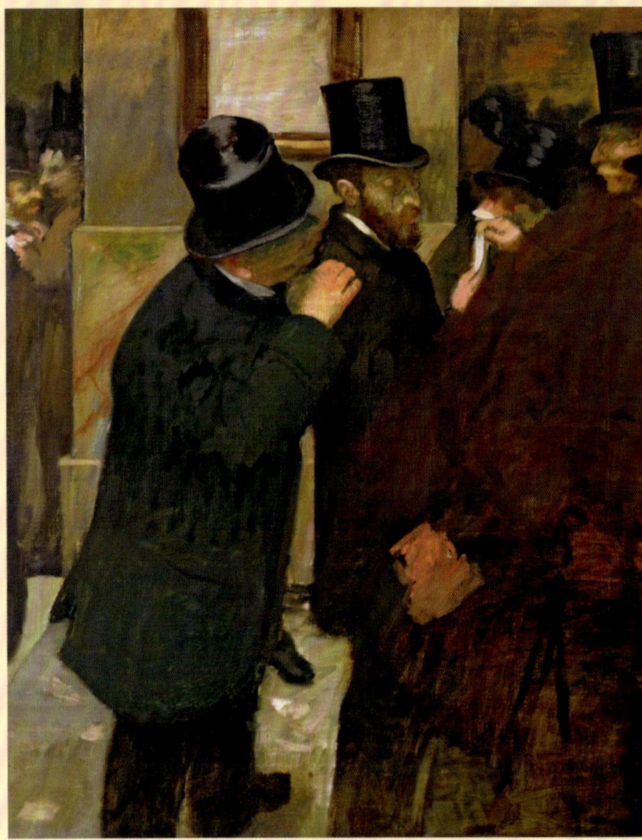

Edgar Degas

Like Gustave Caillebotte, Edgar Degas (1834-1917) was one of the Impressionists, but was distinguished from them by his well-structured compositions, metropolitan motifs, precise depiction of forms and his talent as a pastel painter. He admired Jean-Auguste-Dominique Ingres for his mature brushstrokes and Eugène Delacroix for his lively poses and sense of color. At the beginning of his career Degas was still occupied with historical painting before he quickly developed into an outstanding portraitist. He then devoted himself to the presentation of modern life and movement - with sketches of horse races, but also with his depictions of dancers, whose movements he studied during lessons and rehearsals at the Paris Opera. The actors on stage, the musicians in the orchestra pit and the spectators in their boxes are also among his motifs. He also created outstanding genre paintings and sensual nudes of women at their body care.

Edgar Degas

À l'instar de Gustave Caillebotte, Edgar Degas (1834-1917) est une figure un peu à part dans le cercle des impressionnistes. Par l'audace de ses compositions, ses sujets puisés dans la vie moderne, mais aussi par ses talents de dessinateur et de pastelliste. Il est un fervent admirateur de Jean-Auguste-Dominique Ingres pour la perfection du trait, et d'Eugène Delacroix pour l'énergie et le sens de la couleur. Degas s'essaie à ses débuts à la peinture d'histoire et se révèle rapidement un fin portraitiste. Il devient par la suite un peintre de la vie moderne, et du mouvement. Celui des chevaux, qu'il croque sur les champs de courses, mais surtout celui des danseuses, dont il observe le moindre mouvement à l'Opéra de Paris, notamment pendant les classes et les répétitions. Il se passionne tout autant pour les artistes qui évoluent sur la scène, que pour les musiciens de la fosse d'orchestre ou les spectateurs assis dans leur loge. On doit également à Edgar Degas de saisissantes scènes de genre, et de délicieux nus féminins à la toilette.

Edgar Degas

Wie Gustave Caillebotte wird Edgar Degas (1834–1917) zu den Impressionisten gezählt, hebt sich von diesen aber durch durchstrukturierte Kompositionen, Großstadtmotive, die präzise Darstellung der Formen und sein Talent als Pastellmaler ab. Er bewundert Jean-Auguste-Dominique Ingres für seine ausgereifte Pinselführung und Eugène Delacroix für seine lebendigen Posen und das Gespür für Farben. Zu Beginn seiner Karriere befasst sich Degas noch mit der Historienmalerei, bevor er sich schnell zu einem herausragenden Porträtisten entwickelt. Anschließend widmet er sich der Darstellung des modernen Lebens und der Bewegung – mit Skizzen von Pferderennen, aber auch mit seinen Darstellungen von Tänzerinnen, deren Bewegungen er während des Unterrichts und der Proben in der Pariser Oper studiert. Ebenso zählen die Schauspieler auf der Bühne, die Musiker im Orchestergraben und die Zuschauer in ihren Logen zu seinen Motiven. Außerdem realisiert er herausragende Genrebilder und sinnliche Akte von Frauen bei der Körperpflege.

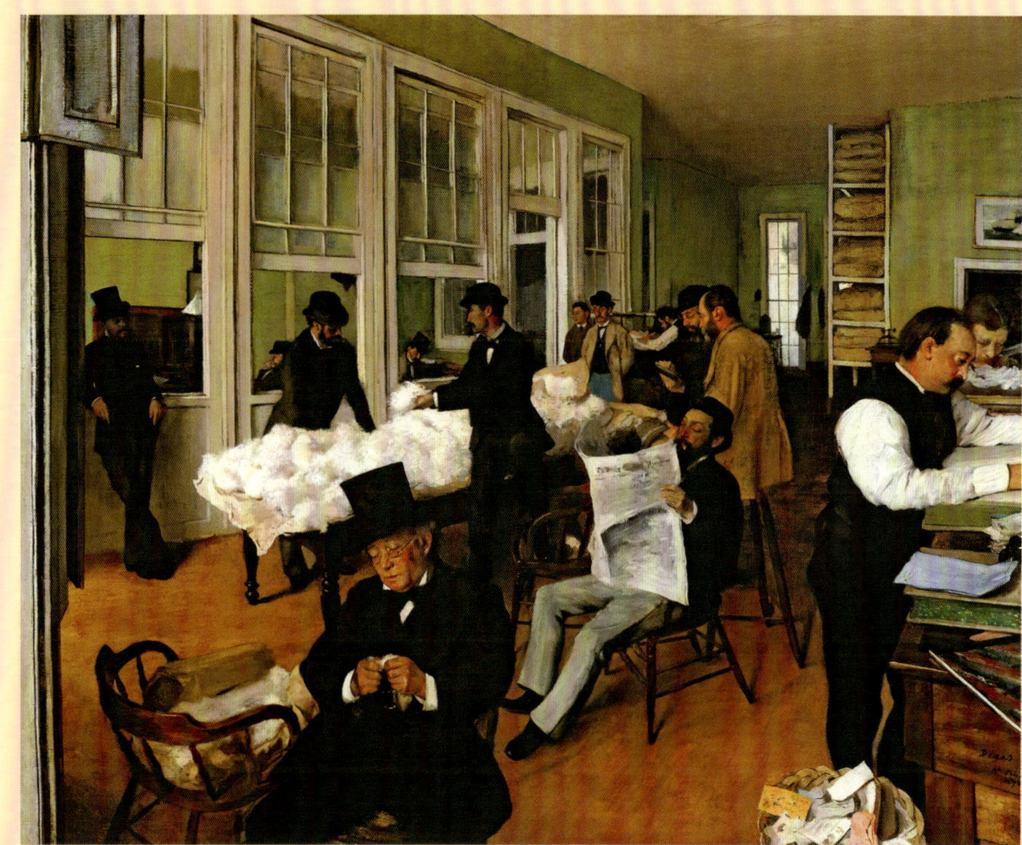

Edgar Degas

Como Gustave Caillebotte, Edgar Degas (1834-1917)
fue uno de los impresionistas, pero se distinguió de
ellos por sus composiciones bien estructuradas, sus
motivos metropolitanos, su precisa representación de
las formas y su talento como pintor de pastel. Admira
a Jean-Auguste-Dominique Ingres por sus pinceladas
maduras y a Eugène Delacroix por sus poses vivas y
su sentido del color. Al principio de su carrera, Degas
todavía estaba ocupado con la pintura de historia
antes de convertirse rápidamente en un retratista
sobresaliente. Luego se dedicó a la representación de la
vida moderna y el movimiento, con bocetos de carreras
de caballos, pero también con sus representaciones
de bailarines, cuyos movimientos estudió durante las
clases y los ensayos en la Ópera de París. Los actores
en el escenario, los músicos en el foso de la orquesta y
los espectadores en sus cajas también están entre sus
motivos. También crea pinturas de género y desnudos
sensuales de mujeres en el cuidado del cuerpo.

Edgar Degas

Como Gustave Caillebotte, Edgar Degas (1834-
1917) foi um dos impressionistas, mas distinguiu-se
por suas composições bem estruturadas, motivos
metropolitanos, representação precisa de formas
e seu talento como pintor pastel. Ele admira Jean-
Auguste-Dominique Ingres pelas suas pinceladas
maduras e Eugène Delacroix pelas suas poses vivas e
sentido de cor. No início de sua carreira Degas ainda
estava ocupado com pintura de história antes que
ele rapidamente se transformou em um retratista
excepcional. Em seguida, dedicou-se à representação
da vida e do movimento modernos - com esboços
de corridas de cavalos, mas também com suas
representações de dançarinos, cujos movimentos
estudou durante as aulas e ensaios da Ópera de Paris.
Os atores no palco, os músicos no fosso da orquestra
e os espectadores em suas caixas também estão entre
seus motivos. Ele também cria excelentes pinturas de
gênero e nus sensuais de mulheres no cuidado do corpo.

Edgar Degas

Net als Gustave Caillebotte wordt Edgar Degas
(1834-1917) gerekend tot de impressionisten, maar hij
onderscheidde zich van hen door zijn goed opgebouwde
composities, grootstedelijke onderwerpen, precieze
weergave van vormen en zijn talent als pastelschilder.
Hij bewonderde Jean-Augustuse-Dominique Ingres
om zijn uitgerijpte penseelvoering en Eugène Delacroix
om zijn levendige poses en gevoel voor kleur. Aan het
begin van zijn carrière hield Degas zich nog bezig met de
historieschilderkunst, voordat hij al snel zou uitgroeien
tot een uitstekende portretschilder. Vervolgens wijdde
hij zich aan de weergave van het moderne leven en
van bewegingen — met schetsen van paardenraces,
maar ook met zijn afbeeldingen van danseressen, wier
bewegingen hij tijdens de lessen en repetities in de Parijse
Opera bestudeerde. De toneelspelers op het podium,
de muzikanten in de orkestbak en de toeschouwers in
hun loges behoren ook tot zijn onderwerpen. Verder
schilderde hij uitstekende genrestukken en sensuele
naakten van vrouwen tijdens de lichaamsverzorging.

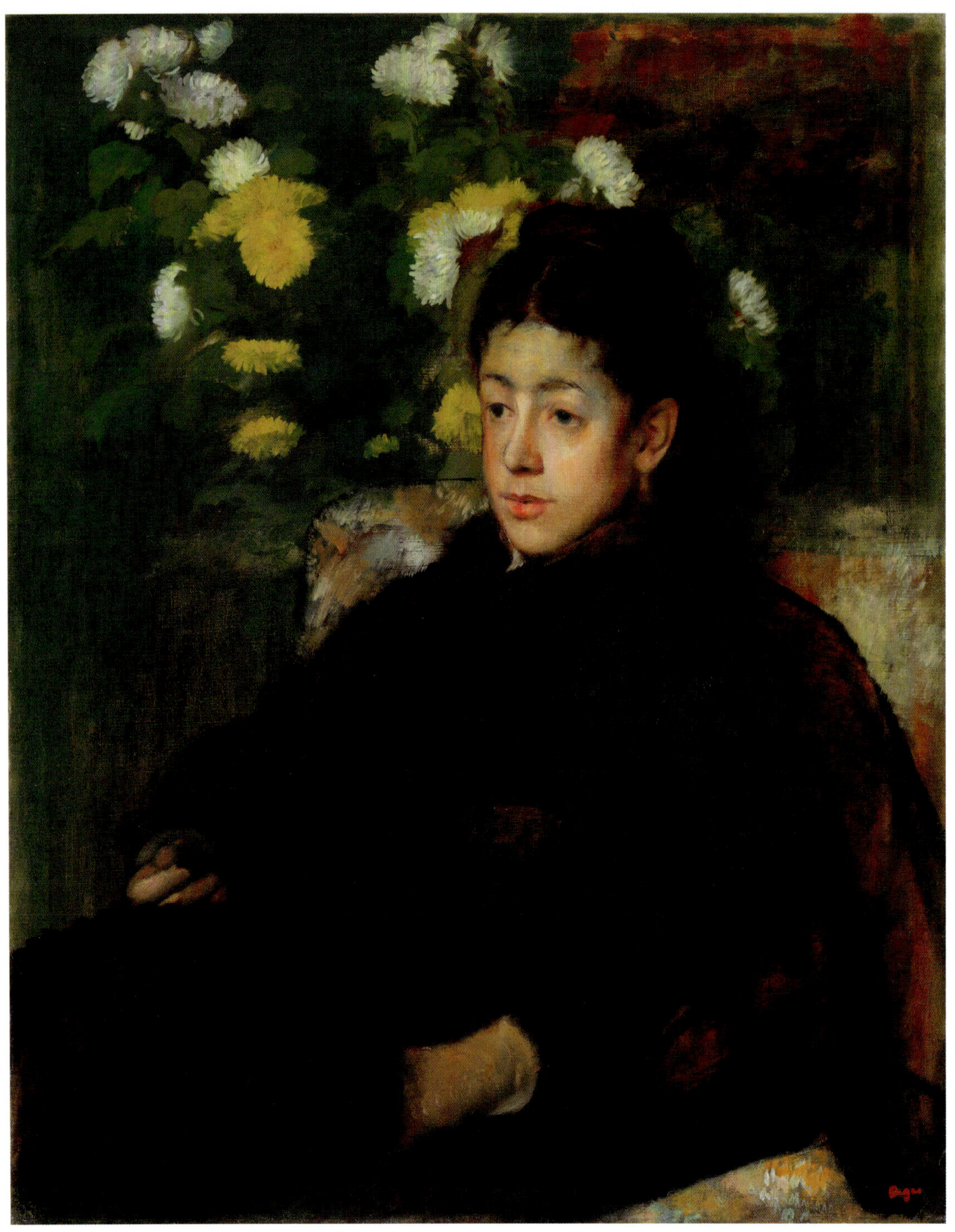

Mademoiselle
Malo

**EDGAR DEGAS
(1834-1917)**
c. 1877,
Oil on canvas/
Huile sur toile,
81,1 × 65,1 cm,
National Gallery
of Art, Washington

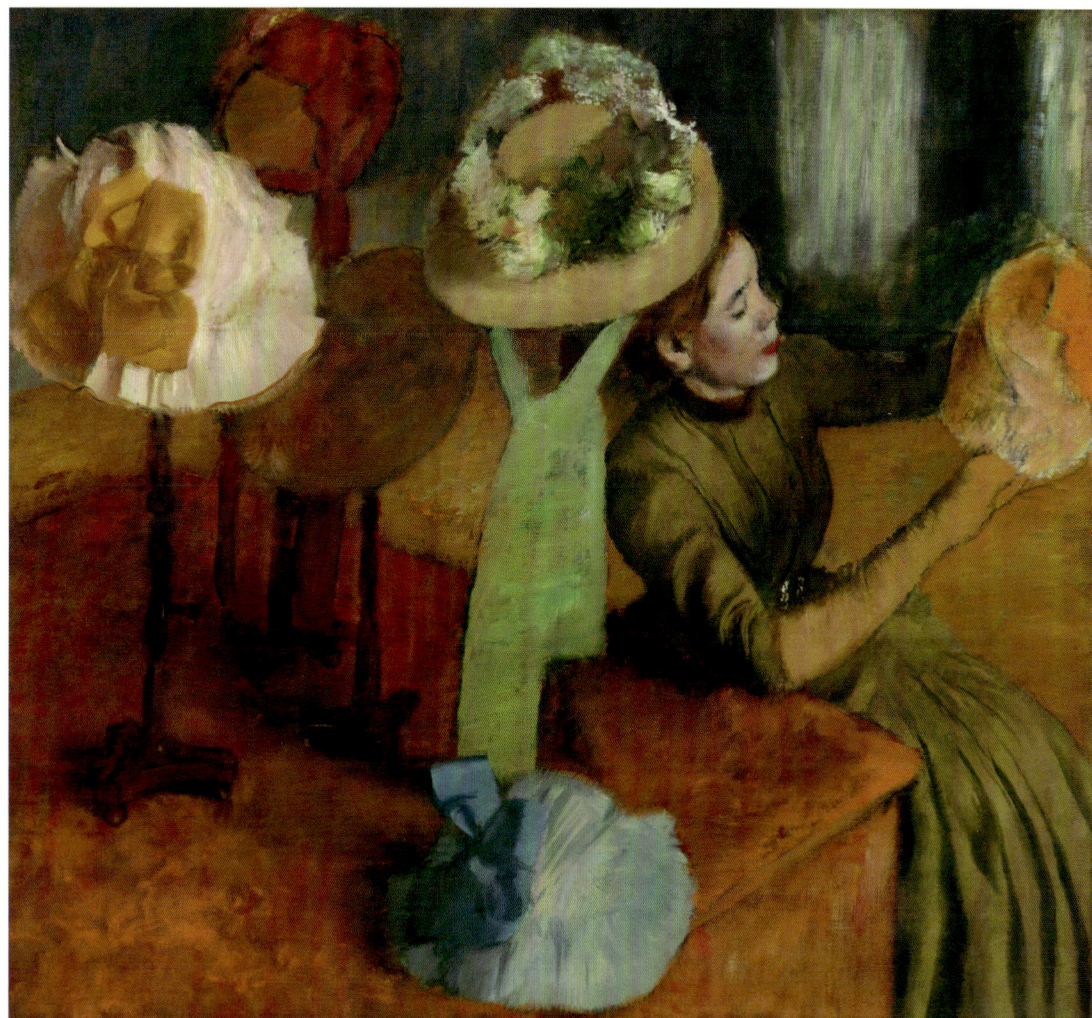

The Millinery Shop

Degas was inspired by all aspects of modern life - including fashion. The hats occupy most of the canvas and create a symphony of colors dominated by ochre and green.

La Chapellerie

Degas s'est intéressé à tous les aspects de la vie moderne. La mode en fait partie. Les chapeaux occupent l'essentiel de la toile et donnent lieu à une symphonie de couleurs dominée par l'ocre et le vert.

Die Hutmacherin

Degas ließ sich von allen Aspekten des modernen Lebens inspirieren – auch von der Mode. Die Hüte nehmen den Großteil der Leinwand ein und ergeben eine Farbsymphonie, die von Ocker und Grün beherrscht wird.

La sombrerera

Degas se inspiró en todos los aspectos de la vida moderna, incluida la moda. Los sombreros ocupan la mayor parte del lienzo y crean una sinfonía de colores dominados por el ocre y el verde.

O chapeleiro

Degas foi inspirado por todos os aspectos da vida moderna - incluindo moda. Os chapéus ocupam a maior parte da tela e criam uma sinfonia de cores dominadas pelo ocre e pelo verde.

De hoedenmaakster

Degas werd geïnspireerd door alle aspecten van het moderne leven, inclusief mode. De hoeden beslaan het grootste deel van het doek en vormen een kleurensymfonie die gedomineerd wordt door oker en groen.

EDGAR DEGAS (1834-1917)

1879-86, Oil on canvas/Huile sur toile, 100 × 110,7 cm, The Art Institute of Chicago

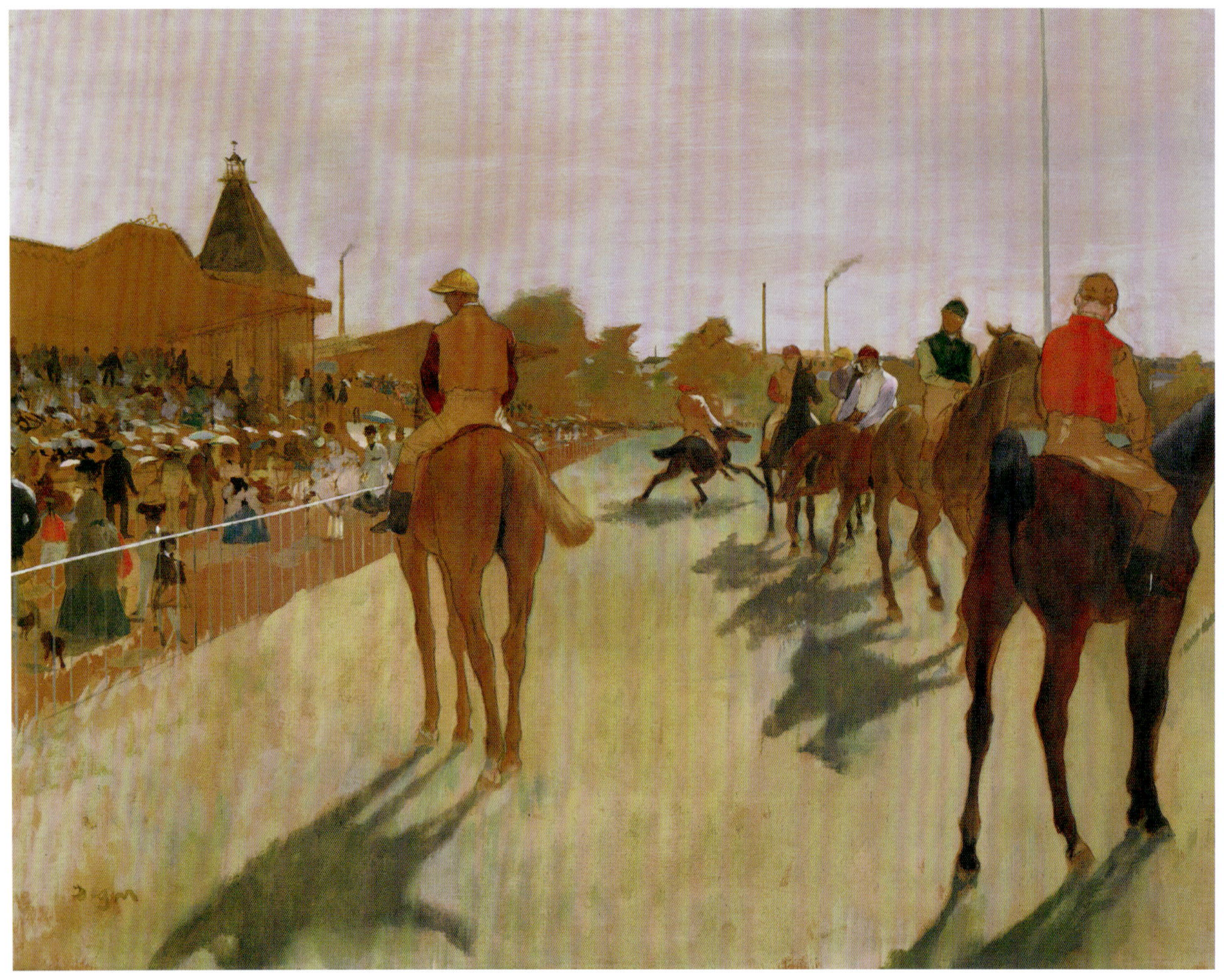

The Parade *or* Racehorses in front of the Stands

Le Défilé *ou* Chevaux de course devant les tribunes

Die Parade *oder* Rennpferde vor den Tribünen

El desfile *o* los caballos de carrera delante de las tribunas

O desfile *ou* cavalos de corrida em frente às arquibancadas

Het defilé *of* Renpaarden voor de tribunes

EDGAR DEGAS (1834-1917)

c. 1866-68, Oil on paper mounted on canvas/Huile sur papier marouflé sur toile, 46 × 61 cm, Musée d'Orsay, Paris

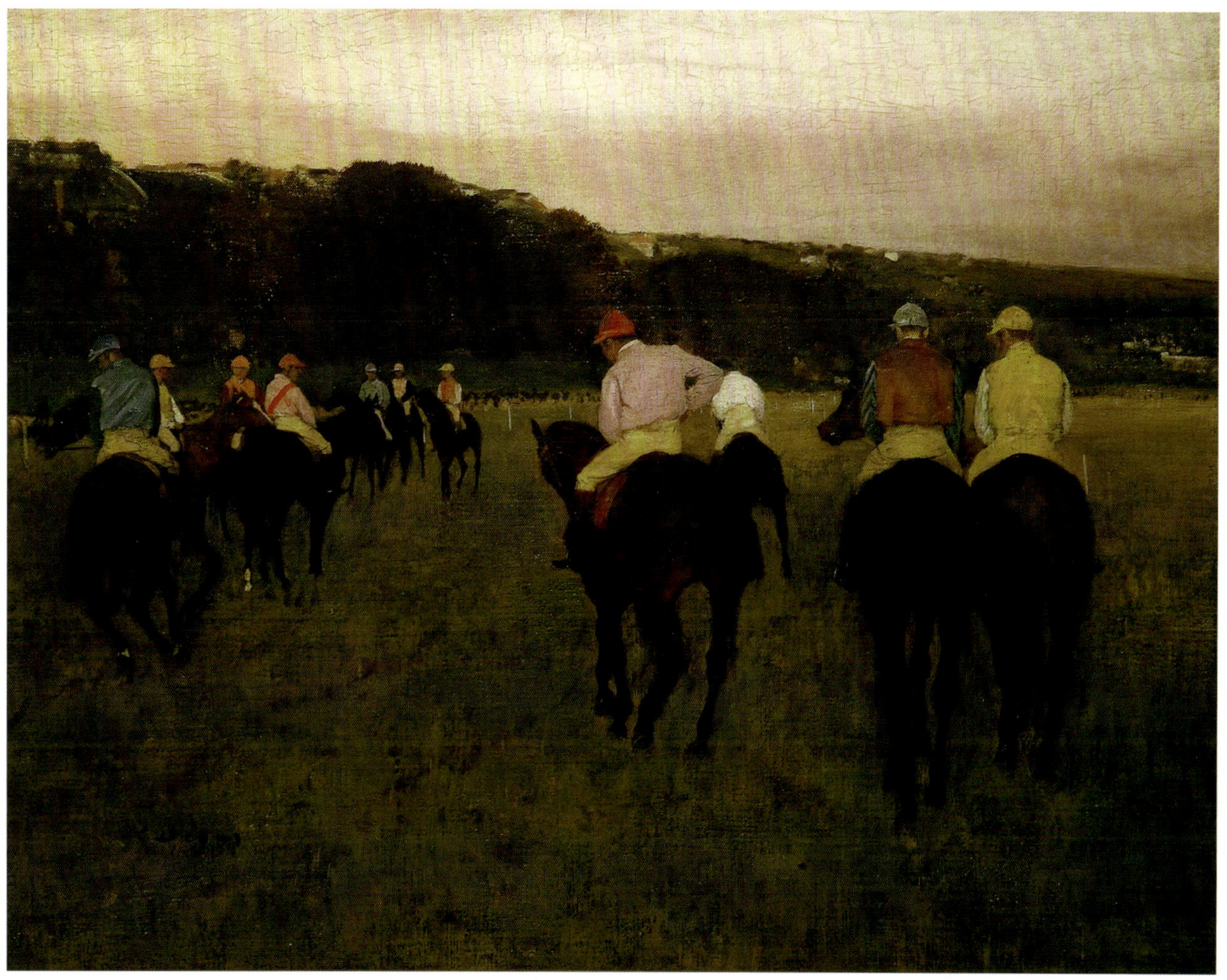

Racehorses at Longchamp

Horse racing was a popular entertainment in the 19th century. Degas also regularly visited the racecourses in Longchamp or Vésinet in order to capture horses and jockeys standing or moving.

Chevaux de course à Longchamp

Au XIXe siècle, les courses hippiques sont un sport très populaire. Degas a beaucoup fréquenté les hippodromes de Longchamp et du Vésinet, et excelle à figurer chevaux et jockeys, immobiles ou en mouvement.

Pferderennen in Longchamp

Pferderennen sind im 19. Jahrhundert eine beliebte Unterhaltung. Auch Degas besucht regelmäßig die Rennbahnen in Longchamp oder Vésinet, um Pferde und Jockeys stehend oder in der Bewegung festzuhalten.

Carreras de caballos en Longchamp

Las carreras de caballos son un entretenimiento popular en el siglo XIX. Degas también visita regularmente los hipódromos de Longchamp o Vésinet para reproducir a los caballos y jinetes de pie o en movimiento.

Corridas de cavalos em Longchamp

As corridas de cavalos são um entretenimento popular no século XIX. Degas também visita regularmente os hipódromos de Longchamp ou Vésinet para manter os cavalos e jóqueis em pé ou em movimento.

Paardenrennen in Longchamp

Paardenrennen waren een populaire vorm van vermaak in de 19e eeuw. Ook Degas bezocht regelmatig de renbanen van Longchamp of Vésinet om paarden en jockeys staand of in beweging vast te leggen.

EDGAR DEGAS (1834-1917)

1871, Oil on canvas/Huile sur toile, 30 × 40 cm, Museum of Fine Arts, Boston

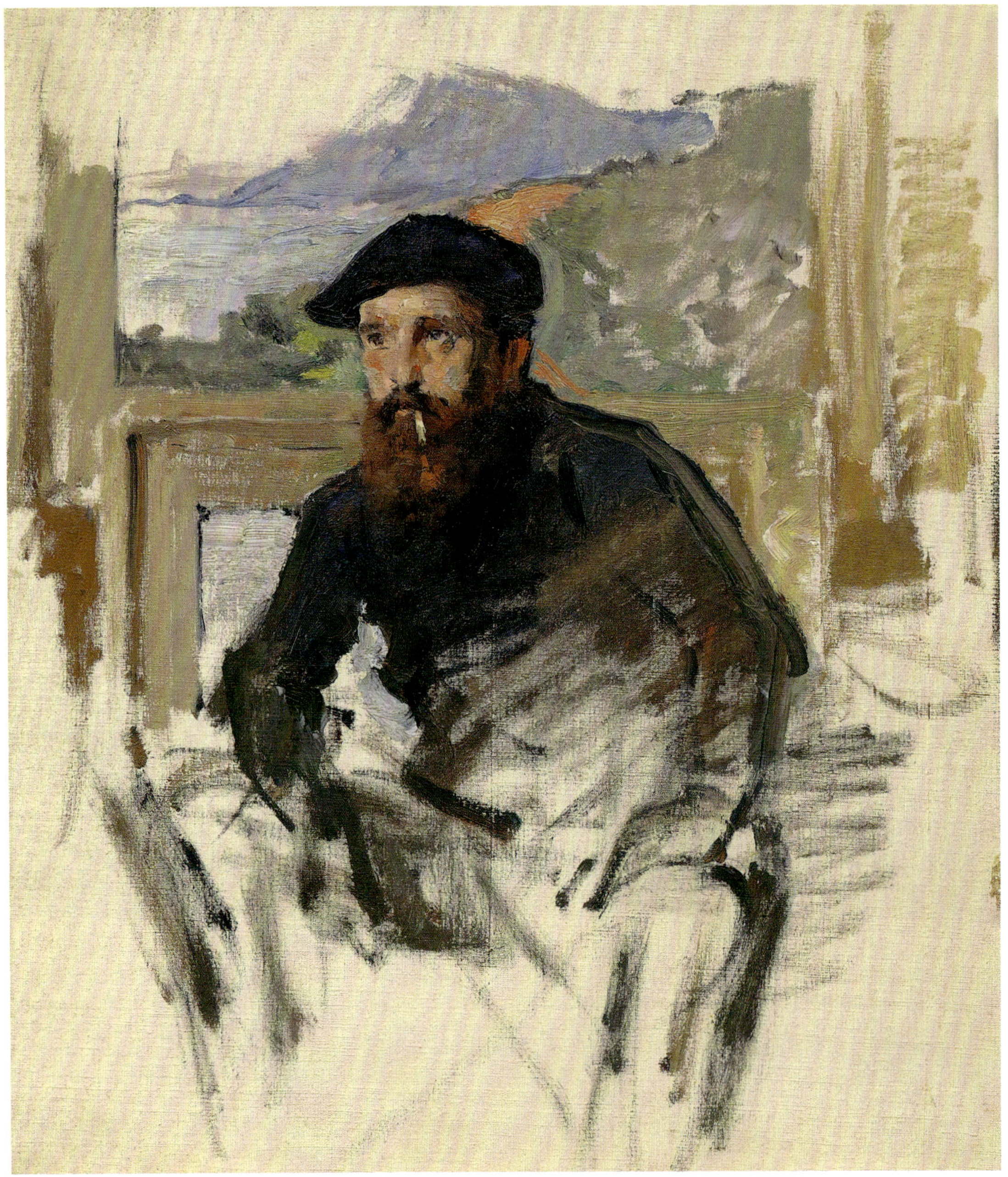

Self Portrait in
his Atelier

Autoportrait
dans son atelier

Selbstbildnis
im Atelier

Autorretrato
en el estudio

Auto-retrato
no estúdio

Zelfportret in
het atelier

CLAUDE MONET
(1840-1926)
c. 1884, Oil on
canvas/Huile sur
toile, 85 × 54 cm,
Musée Marmottan
Monet, Paris

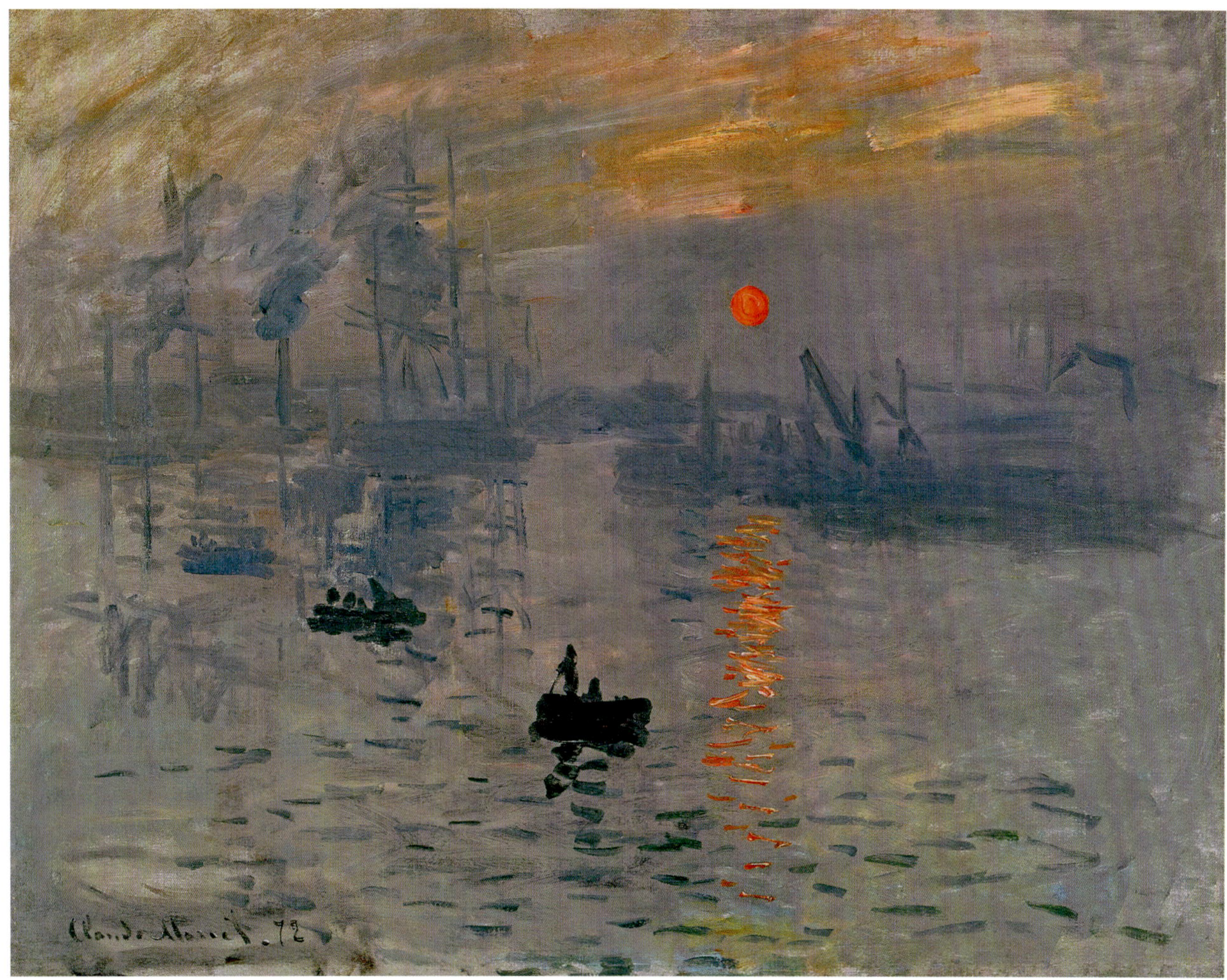

Impression, Sunrise

One morning in 1872, from his hotel room, Claude
Monet painted the foggy sunrise over the industrial port
of Le Havre. The painting was to become the eponym of
Impressionism.

Impression, soleil levant

Un matin de 1872, Claude Monet peint, depuis sa chambre
d'hôtel, cette vue du port industriel du Havre au soleil
levant. Toute en effets de brumes et de fumées, elle donnera
son nom à l'impressionnisme.

Impression, Sonnenaufgang

Eines Morgens im Jahr 1872 malt Claude Monet von seinem
Hotelzimmer aus den in Nebel gehüllten Sonnenaufgang
über dem Industriehafen von Le Havre. Das Gemälde sollte
der Namensgeber des Impressionismus werden.

Impresión, sol naciente

Una mañana de 1872, desde su habitación de hotel, Claude
Monet pintó el nublado amanecer sobre el puerto industrial
de Le Havre. La pintura se convertiría en el epónimo del
Impresionismo.

Impressão, Nascer do Sol

Numa manhã de 1872, de seu quarto de hotel, Claude
Monet pintou o nebuloso nascer do sol sobre o porto
industrial de Le Havre. A pintura se tornaria o epônimo do
Impressionismo.

Inmpressie, zonsopgang

Op een ochtend in 1872 schilderde Claude Monet
vanuit zijn hotelkamer de mistige zonsopgang over de
industriehaven van Le Havre. Het schilderij zou het
impressionisme zijn de naam geven.

CLAUDE MONET (1840-1926)
1872, Oil on canvas/Huile sur toile, 48 × 63 cm, Musée Marmottan Monet, Paris

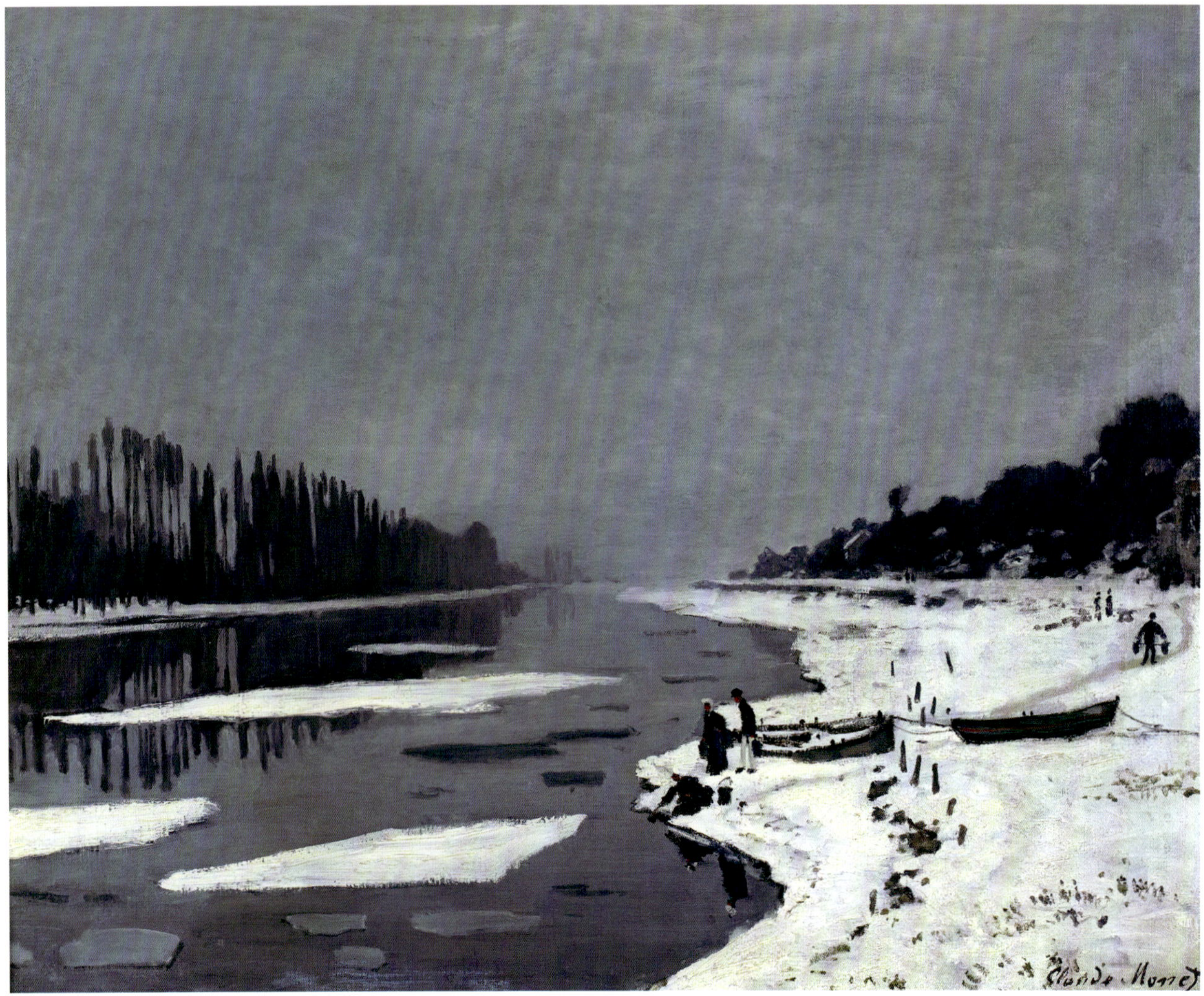

Ice Floes on the Seine at Bougival

When Monet created this painting, he had not yet turned to Impressionism. The calm, precise composition is based on the interplay of colors, which are almost monochrome.

Glaçons sur la Seine à Bougival

À cette époque, Monet n'est pas encore l'impressionniste que l'on connaît. D'une beauté silencieuse, ce paysage au dessin précis est construit par la couleur, en larges aplats presque monochromes.

Treibeis auf der Seine bei Bougival

Als Monet das Gemälde schuf, hatte er sich noch nicht dem Impressionismus zugewandt. Die ruhige, präzise Komposition basiert auf dem Wechselspiel der Farben, die fast monochrom ausgeführt sind.

Témpanos de hielo en el Sena cerca de Bougival

Cuando Monet creó el cuadro, aún no había recurrido al Impresionismo. La composición tranquila y precisa se basa en el juego de colores, que son casi monocromos.

Gelo flutuante no Sena perto de Bougival

Quando Monet criou a pintura, ainda não se tinha voltado para o Impressionismo. A composição calma e precisa baseia-se na interacção das cores, que são quase monocromáticas.

Drijvend ijs op de Seine bij Bougival

Toen Monet het schilderij maakte, had hij zich nog niet tot het impressionisme gekeerd. De rustige, precieze compositie is gebaseerd op het samenspel van bijna monochrome kleuren.

CLAUDE MONET (1840-1926)

c. 1867/68, Oil on canvas/Huile sur toile, 65 × 81 cm, Musée du Louvre, Paris

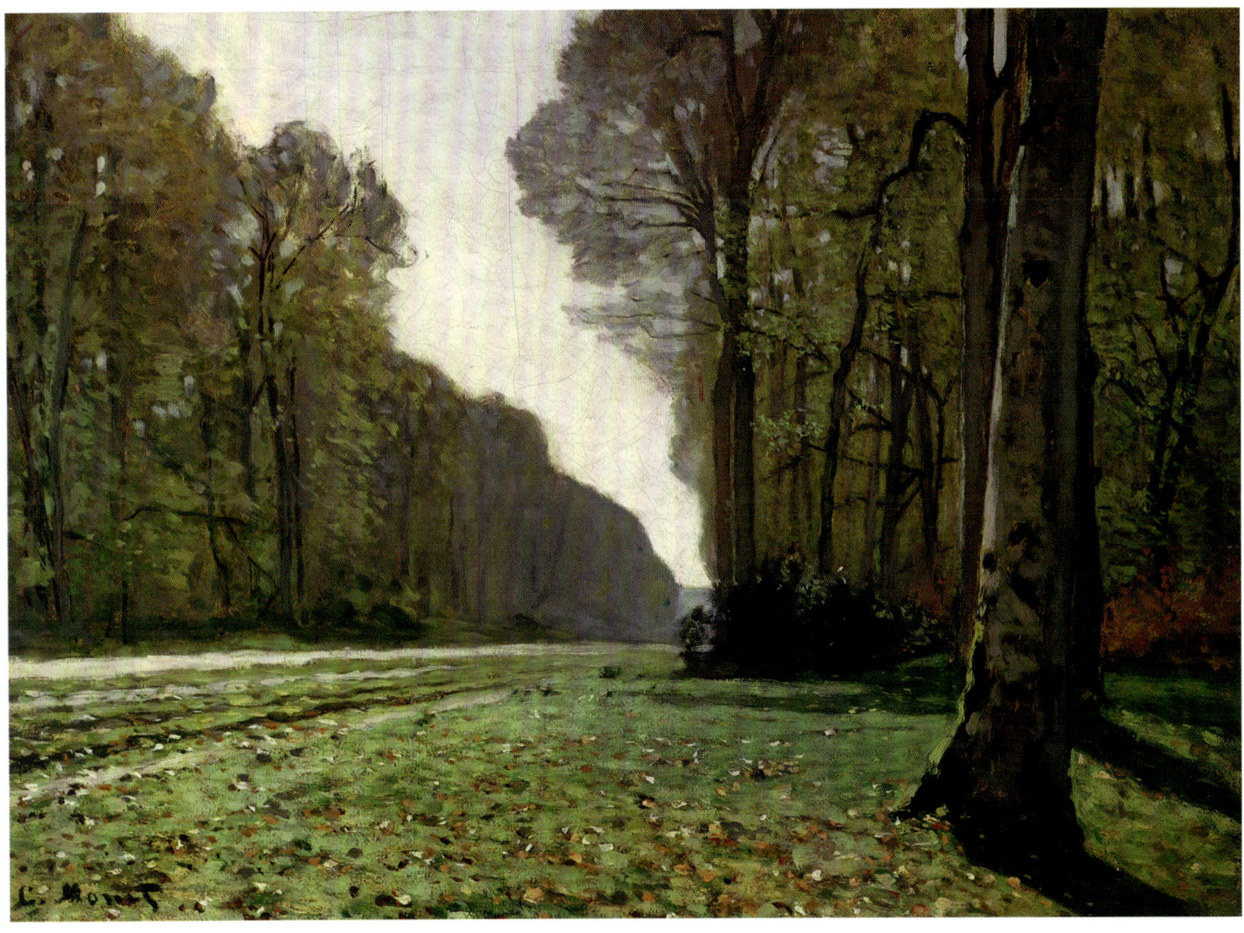

The Road to Bas-Bréau, Fontainebleu

Le Pavé de Chailly *dit autrefois* Route du Bas-Bréau

Die Straße nach Bas-Bréau

El camino a Bas-Bréau

A estrada para Bas-Bréau

De weg naar Bas-Bréau

CLAUDE MONET (1840-1926)

c. 1865, Oil on canvas/Huile sur toile, 43,5 × 59,3 cm, Musée d'Orsay, Paris

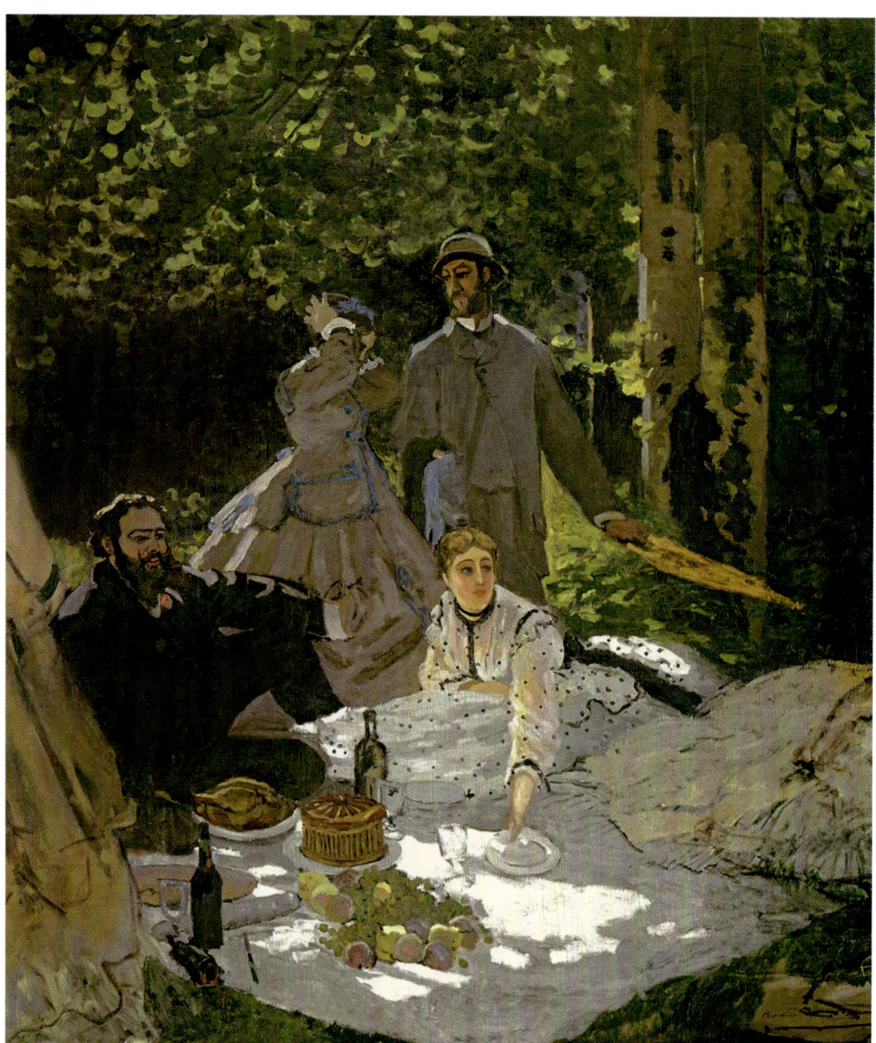

Luncheon on the Grass

In response to Manet's work of the same name, Monet painted his breakfast in 1863 in the countryside. Of the monumental painting in the format of four by six metres, only two fragments have survived, including the one depicted.

Le Déjeuner sur l'herbe

En réponse à celui de Manet, peint en 1863, Monet réalise son propre *Déjeuner sur l'herbe*. Il ne reste aujourd'hui que deux fragments (dont celui-ci) d'une œuvre monumentale de quatre mètres sur six.

Das Frühstück im Grünen

Als Antwort auf Manets gleichnamiges Werk malt Monet 1863 sein Frühstück im Grünen. Von dem monumentalen Gemälde im Format von vier mal sechs Metern sind nur zwei Fragmente erhalten geblieben, darunter das abgebildete.

Desayuno sobre la hierba

En respuesta a la obra de Manet del mismo nombre, Monet pintó su Desayuno sobre la hierba en 1863. De la pintura monumental en formato de cuatro por seis metros, sólo se conservan dos fragmentos, entre ellos el representado.

O piquenique no bosque

Em resposta ao trabalho de Manet com o mesmo nome, Monet pintou seu café da manhã em 1863 no campo. Da pintura monumental em formato de quatro por seis metros, apenas dois fragmentos sobreviveram, incluindo o retratado.

Das Frühstück im Grünen

Als reactie op het gelijknamige werk van Manet schilderde Monet in 1863 zijn lunch in het groen. Van het monumentale schilderij met een formaat van 4 x 6 meter zijn slechts twee fragmenten bewaard gebleven, waaronder het afgebeelde.

CLAUDE MONET (1840-1926)

1865/66, Oil on canvas/Huile sur toile, 248 × 217 cm, Musée d'Orsay, Paris

Women in the
Garden

Femmes au jardin

Frauen im Garten

Mujeres en
el jardín

Mulheres no jardim

Vrouwen in de tuin

CLAUDE MONET
(1840-1926)
1866, Oil on canvas/
Huile sur toile,
255 × 205 cm, Musée
d'Orsay, Paris

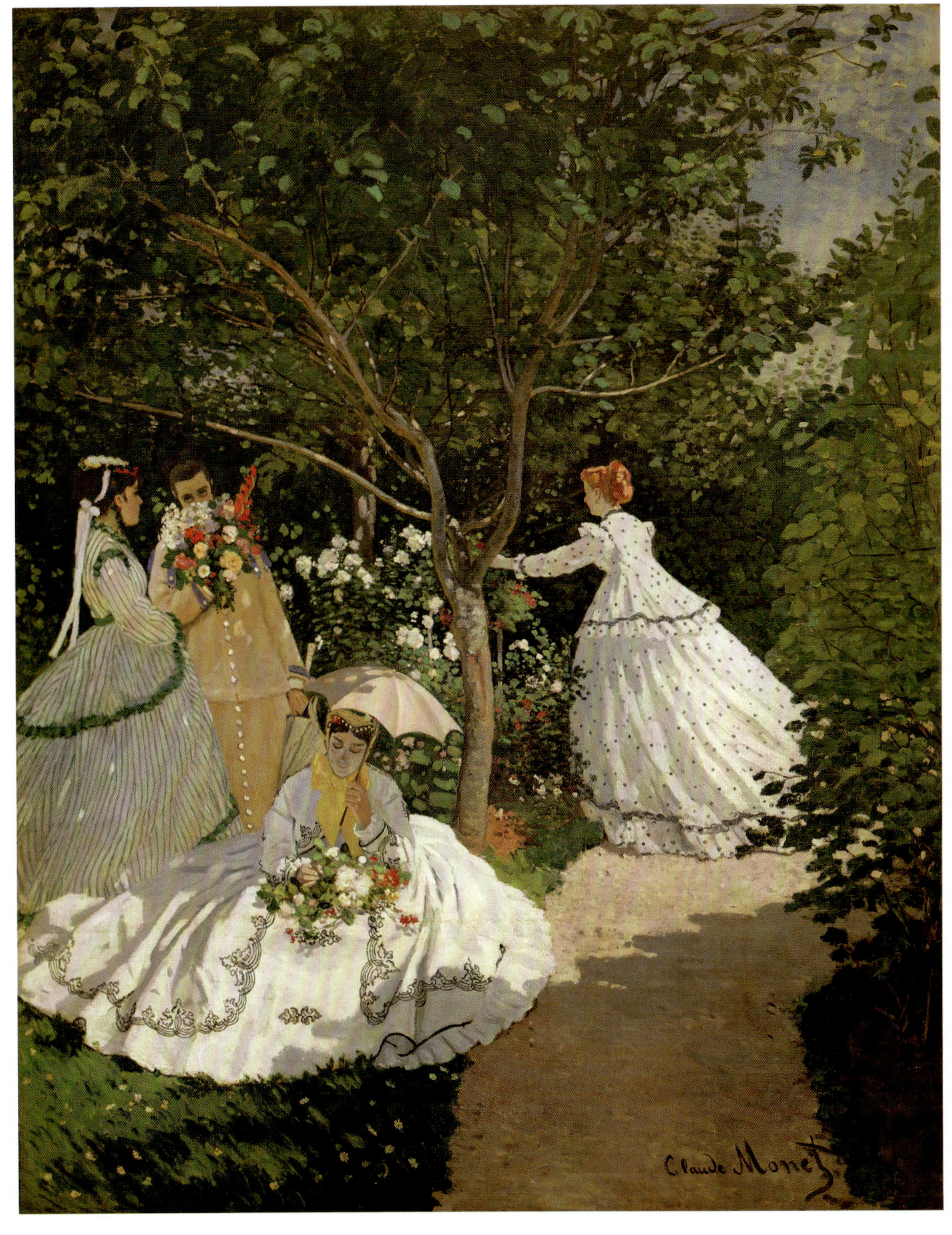

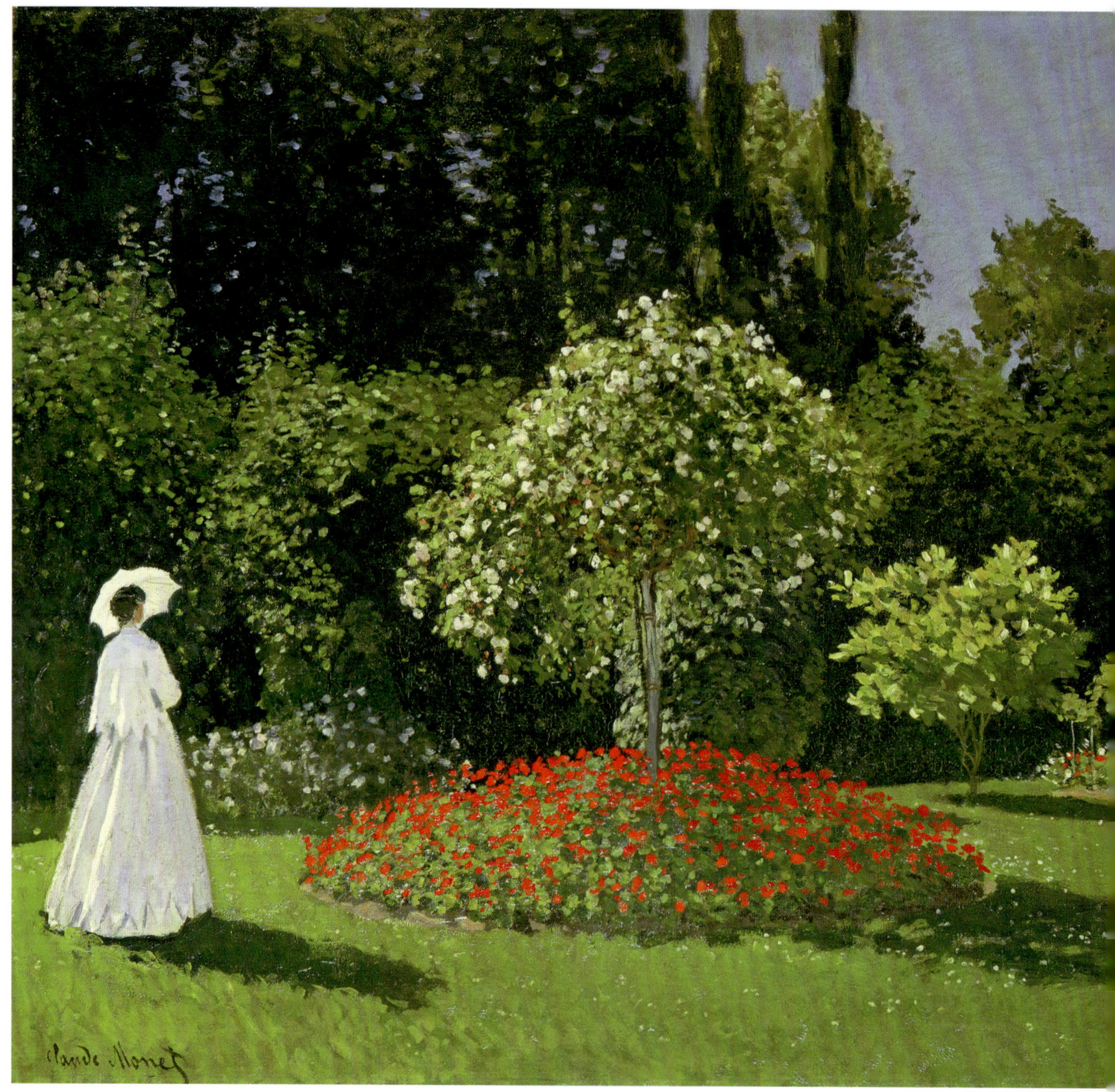

Jeanne-Marguerite Lecadre in the Garden

Dame en blanc au jardin (Jeanne-Marguerite Lecadre)

Jeanne-Marguerite Lecadre im Garten

Jeanne-Marguerite Lecadre en el jardín

Jeanne-Marguerite Lecadre no jardim

Jeanne-Marguerite Lecadre in de tuin

CLAUDE MONET (1840-1926)

1866, Oil on canvas/Huile sur toile, 82 × 101 cm, State Hermitage Museum, St. Petersburg

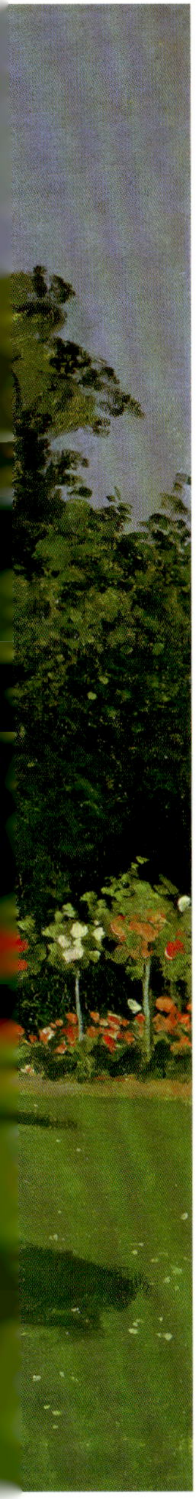

Woman with
a Parasol

Femme à
l'ombrelle
tournée vers
la gauche

Frau mit
Sonnenschirm

Mujer con
sombrilla

Mulher com
guarda-sol

Vrouw met
parasol gedraaid
naar links

**CLAUDE MONET
(1840-1926)**
1886, Oil on canvas/
Huile sur toile,
131 × 88 cm, Musée
d'Orsay, Paris

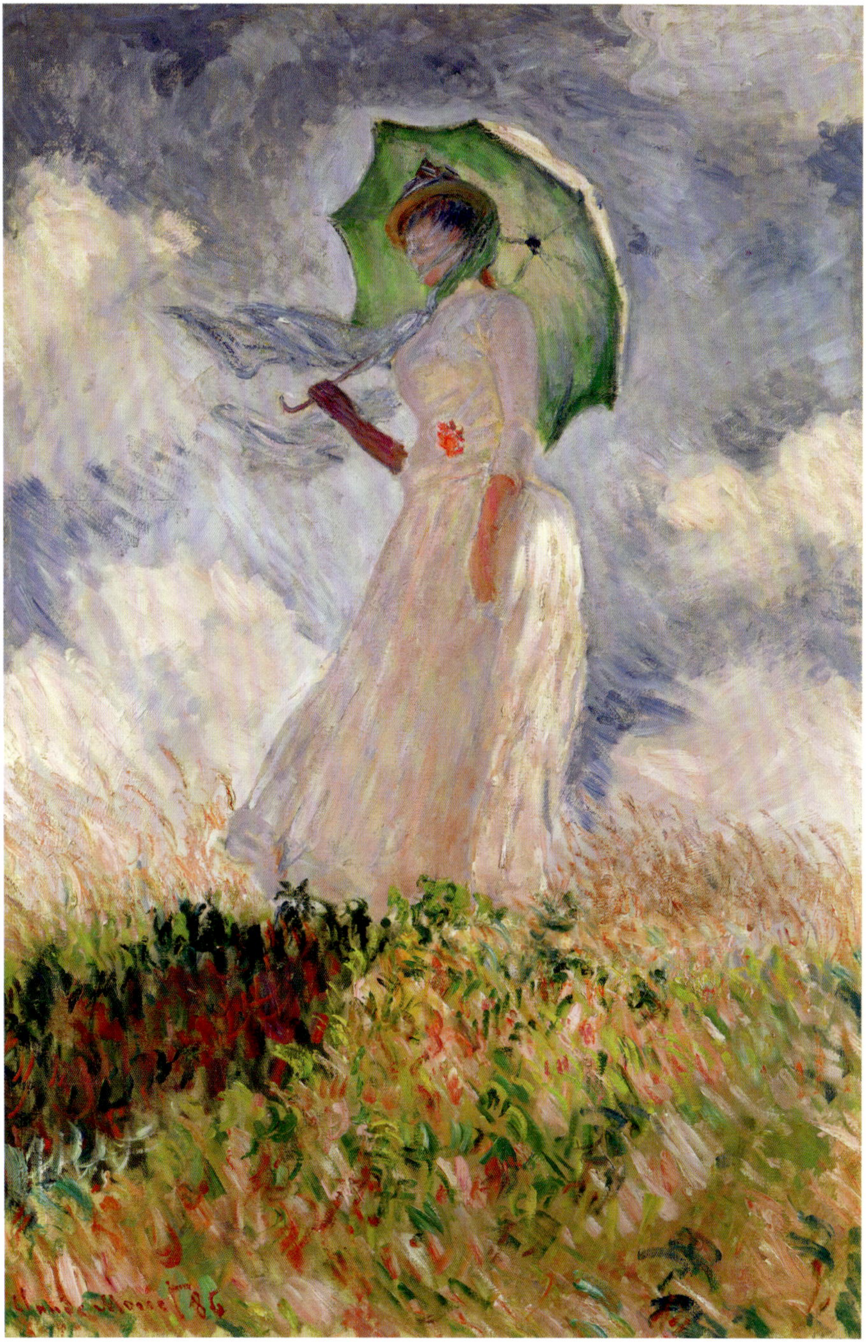

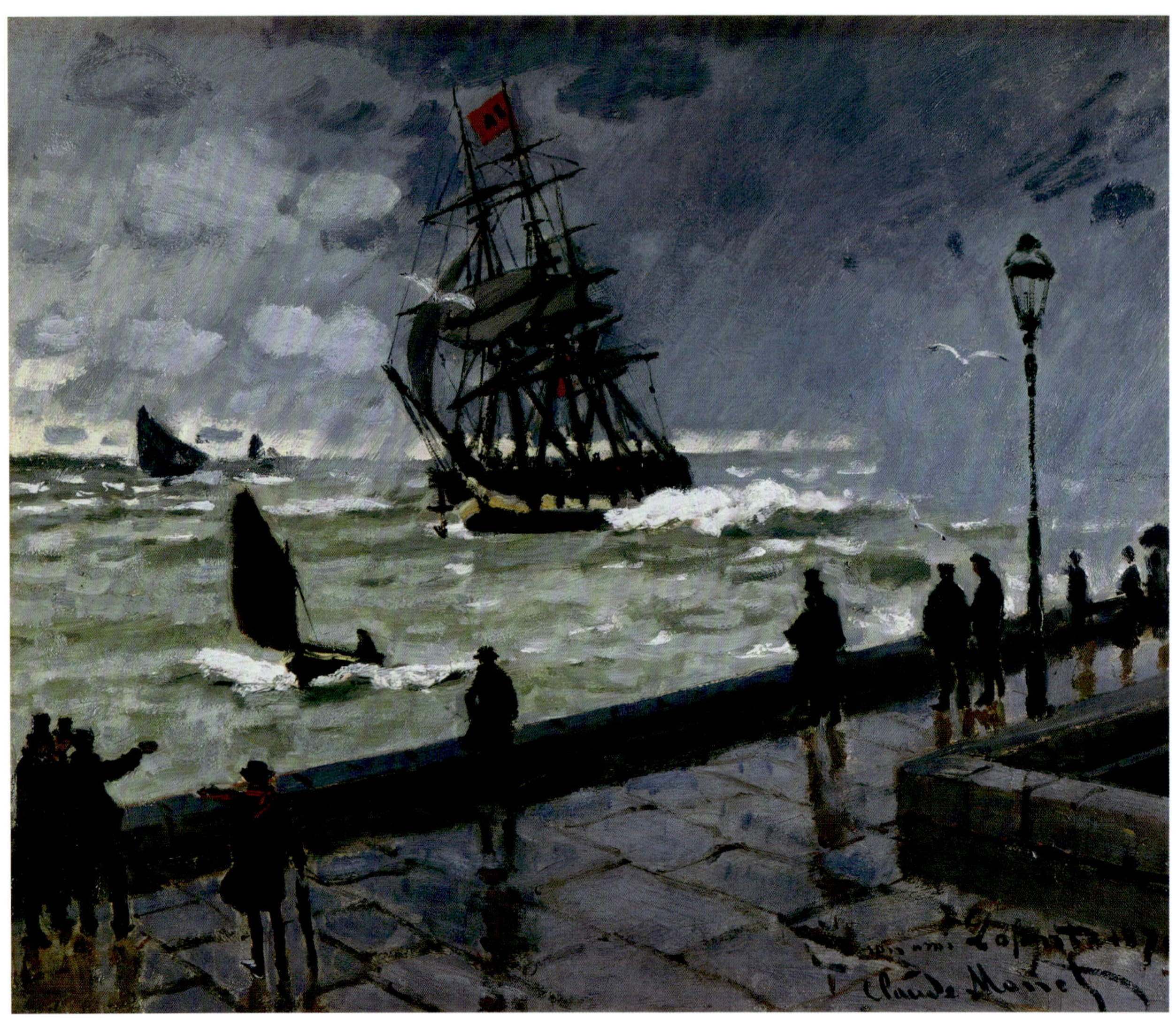

The Jetty of Le Havre, Bad Weather

La Jetée du Havre par mauvais temps

Die Mole von Le Havre bei schlechtem Wetter

El muelle de Le Havre con mal tiempo

O cais de Le Havre com mau tempo

Het havenhoofd van Le Havre bij slecht weer

CLAUDE MONET (1840-1926)

1867, Oil on canvas/Huile sur toile, 50 × 61 cm,
Private collection

The Hôtel des Roches Noires at Trouville

During the summer of 1870, Monet and his wife Camille stayed in Trouville. The painting impresses with the contrast between the severity of the facades in the shade and the movement of the flags in the sun.

Hôtel des roches noires. Trouville

Durant l'été 1870, Monet et son épouse Camille séjournent à Trouville. Cette vue opère un contraste entre la rigueur des façades, à l'ombre, et le mouvement des drapeaux qui flottent dans le soleil.

Hôtel des roches noires. Trouville

Während des Sommers 1870 halten sich Monet und seine Ehefrau Camille in Trouville auf. Das Gemälde wirkt durch den Kontrast zwischen der Strenge der Fassaden im Schatten und der Bewegung der Flaggen in der Sonne.

Hôtel des roches noires. Trouville

Durante el verano de 1870, Monet y su esposa Camille se quedaron en Trouville. La pintura trabaja a través del contraste entre la severidad de las fachadas a la sombra y el movimiento de las banderas al sol.

Hôtel des roches noires. Trouville

Durante o verão de 1870, Monet e sua esposa Camille ficaram em Trouville. A pintura trabalha através do contraste entre a severidade das fachadas à sombra e o movimento das bandeiras ao sol.

Hôtel des Roches Noires, Trouville

In de zomer van 1870 verbleven Monet en zijn vrouw Camille in Trouville. Het schilderij is effectief door het contrast tussen de strengheid van de gevels in de schaduw en de beweging van de vlaggen in de zon.

CLAUDE MONET (1840-1926)

1870, Oil on canvas/Huile sur toile, 81 × 58,5 cm, Musée d'Orsay, Paris

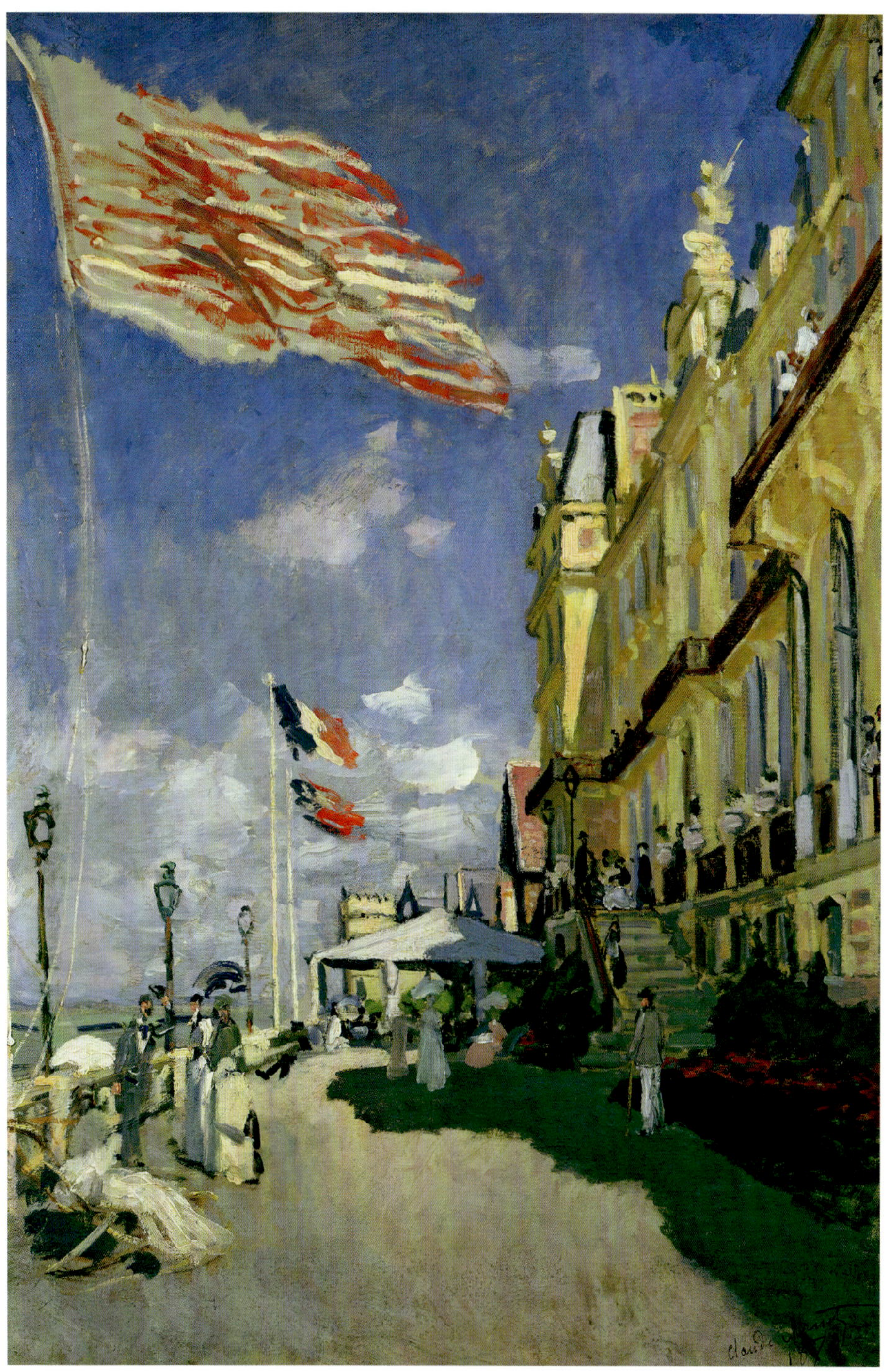

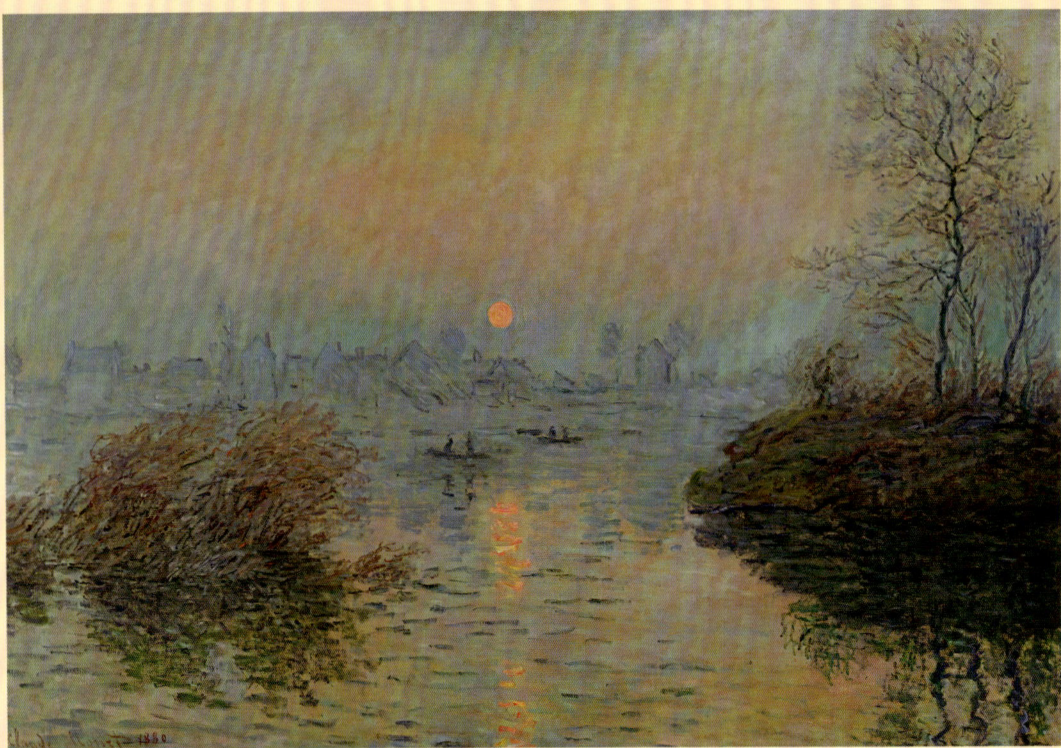

Claude Monet

The most famous Impressionist painter dedicated
most of his career to the landscape. After his arrival
in Paris in 1859, he attended the free painting school
Académie Suisse. At the beginning of his career, he was
inspired by the atmospheric studies of Eugène Boudin
and the diffuse, colored visions of William Turner,
whose paintings he studied at the National Gallery in
London in 1870. His obsession was the reproduction of
light, which he captured with short and vivid strokes.
Haystacks, *Poplars* or *Rouen Cathedral* - Claude Monet
(1840-1926) painted series depicting the same motif
at different times of the day or year. His travels took
him to Brittany, the Netherlands, Southern France,
London, Venice and Norway. He developed his skills
to the full in Normandy, where he settled in Giverny in
1883. His *Water Lilies* paintings, which since 1927 are
being shown in a permanent exhibition at the Musée de
l'Orangerie in Paris, were installed there a few months
after the artist's death.

Claude Monet

Arrivé à Paris en 1859 où il se forme à l'Académie suisse,
le plus célèbre des peintres impressionnistes a voué
l'essentiel de sa vie et de sa carrière au paysage. Il est
influencé, à ses débuts, par les études atmosphériques
d'Eugène Boudin et les visions brumeuses de William
Turner, dont il découvre les toiles à la National
Gallery de Londres en 1870. Quel que soit le sujet, son
obsession est le rendu de la lumière, au travers d'une
touche vibrante et fragmentée. *Meules, Peupliers* ou
Cathédrales, Claude Monet (1840-1926) va souvent
procéder selon le principe de la série, pour capter, aux
différentes heures et saisons, les variations d'un même
paysage. Monet a beaucoup voyagé, en Bretagne, dans le
Midi, aux Pays-Bas, à Londres, à Venise, en Norvège…
Mais c'est en Normandie, et plus précisément dans sa
propriété de Giverny, où il s'installe en 1883, que va
s'épanouir pleinement sa peinture. Jusqu'à l'élaboration
du cycle décoratif des *Nymphéas*, installé à l'Orangerie,
à Paris, et inauguré en 1927, quelques mois après
le décès de l'artiste.

Claude Monet

Der berühmteste Maler der Impressionisten widmete
den Großteil seiner Karriere der Landschaft. Nach
seiner Ankunft in Paris im Jahr 1859 besucht er die
freie Malschule Académie Suisse. Zu Beginn seiner
Karriere lässt er sich von den atmosphärischen Studien
Eugène Boudins und William Turners diffusen, farbigen
Visionen inspirieren, dessen Gemälde er 1870 in der
Londoner National Gallery studiert. Seine Obsession
wird die Wiedergabe des Lichts, das er mit kurzen
und lebhaften Strichen einfängt. *Getreideschober*,
Pappeln oder die *Kathedrale von Rouen* – Claude
Monet (1840–1926) malt Serien, um dasselbe Motiv
zu unterschiedlichen Tages- oder Jahreszeiten
darzustellen. Seine Reisen führen ihn in die Bretagne,
die Niederlande, nach Südfrankreich, London, Venedig
und Norwegen. Zur vollen Entfaltung bringt er sein
Können in der Normandie, wo er sich 1883 in Giverny
niederlässt. Dort entstehen seine *Seerosenbilder*, die ab
1927 in einer permanenten Ausstellung im Musée de
l'Orangerie in Paris gezeigt werden, einige Monate nach
dem Tod des Künstlers.

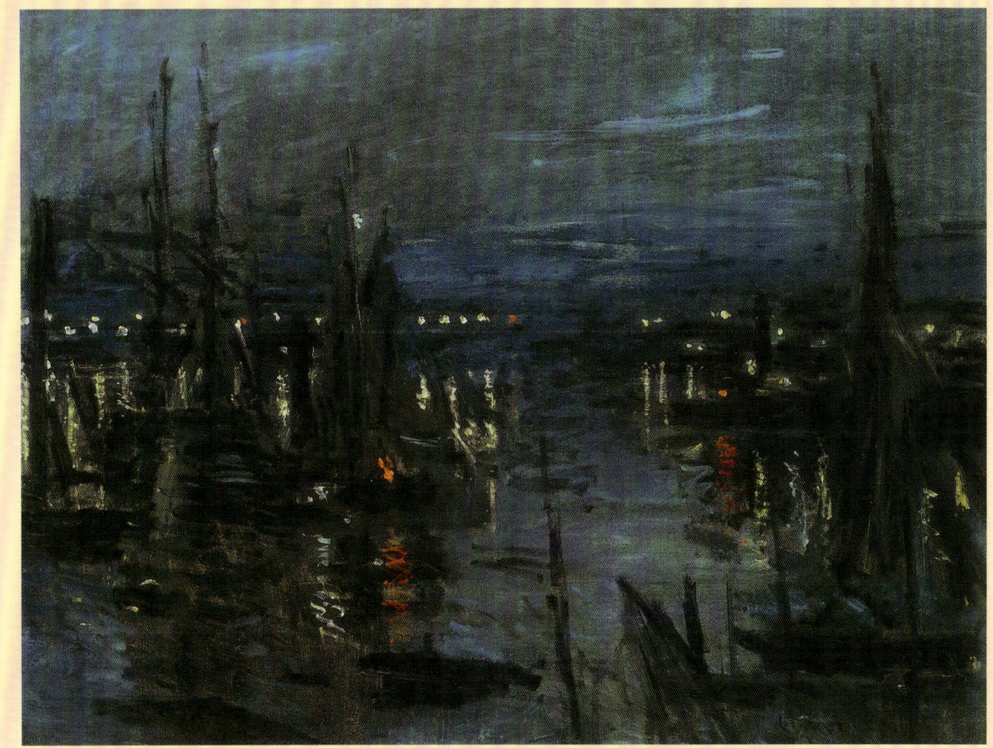

Claude Monet

El pintor impresionista más famoso dedicó la mayor parte de su carrera al paisaje. Después de su llegada a París en 1859, asistió a la escuela de pintura gratuita *Académie Suisse.* Al principio de su carrera se inspiró en los estudios atmosféricos de Eugène Boudin y William Turner, cuyas pinturas, de visiones difusas y coloreadas, estudió en la *National Gallery* de Londres en 1870. Su obsesión se convierte en la reproducción de la luz, que capta con trazos cortos y vivos *Almiares, Álamos* o *La Catedral de Rouen* - Claude Monet (1840-1926) pinta series para representar el mismo motivo en diferentes momentos del día o del año. Sus viajes lo llevan a Bretaña, los Países Bajos, el sur de Francia, Londres, Venecia y Noruega. Desarrolló sus habilidades al máximo en Normandía, donde se instaló en Giverny en 1883. Sus pinturas de los *Nenúfares*, que fueron expuestas en una exposición permanente en el Museo de la Orangerie de París a partir de 1927, fueron creadas allí pocos meses después de la muerte del artista.

Claude Monet

O mais famoso pintor impressionista dedicou a maior parte da sua carreira à paisagem. Após a sua chegada a Paris em 1859, frequentou a escola de pintura gratuita Académie Suisse. No início da sua carreira, inspirou-se nos estudos atmosféricos de Eugène Boudin e William Turner, cujas pinturas estudou na National Gallery de Londres em 1870, de visões difusas e coloridas. Sua obsessão torna-se a reprodução da luz, que ele capta com traços curtos e vívidos. *Ricos de grãos, choupos* ou *a catedral de Rouen* - Claude Monet (1840-1926) pinta a série para retratar o mesmo motivo em diferentes momentos do dia ou do ano. Suas viagens o levam à Bretanha, Holanda, sul da França, Londres, Veneza e Noruega. Ele desenvolveu suas habilidades ao máximo na Normandia, onde se estabeleceu em Giverny em 1883. Suas pinturas de lírios de água, que foram expostas em uma exposição permanente no Musée de l'Orangerie de Paris em 1927, foram criadas ali alguns meses após a morte do artista.

Claude Monet

De beroemdste impressionistische schilder hield zich het grootste deel van zijn carrière bezig met het landschap. Na aankomst in Parijs in 1859 ging hij naar de vrije schilderschool Académie Suisse. Aan het begin van zijn loopbaan liet hij zich inspireren door de atmosferische studies van Eugène Boudin en de diffuse, kleurige visioenen van William Turner, wiens schilderijen hij in 1870 in de Londense National Gallery bestudeerde. Hij raakte geobsedeerd door de weergave van het licht, dat hij met korte en levendige penseelstreken vastlegde. *Hooibergen, Populieren* en de *Kathedraal van Rouen* – Claude Monet (1840-1926) schilderde series om hetzelfde onderwerp op verschillende tijdstippen van de dag of momenten van het jaar weer te geven. Zijn reizen voerden hem naar Bretagne, Nederland, Zuid-Frankrijk, Londen, Venetië en Noorwegen. Hij ontwikkelde zijn vaardigheden ten volle in Normandië, waar hij in 1883 in Giverny ging wonen. Zijn schilderijen van waterlelies, die vanaf 1927, enkele maanden na zijn dood, in een permanente tentoonstelling in het Musée de l'Orangerie in Parijs te zien zijn, maakte hij daar.

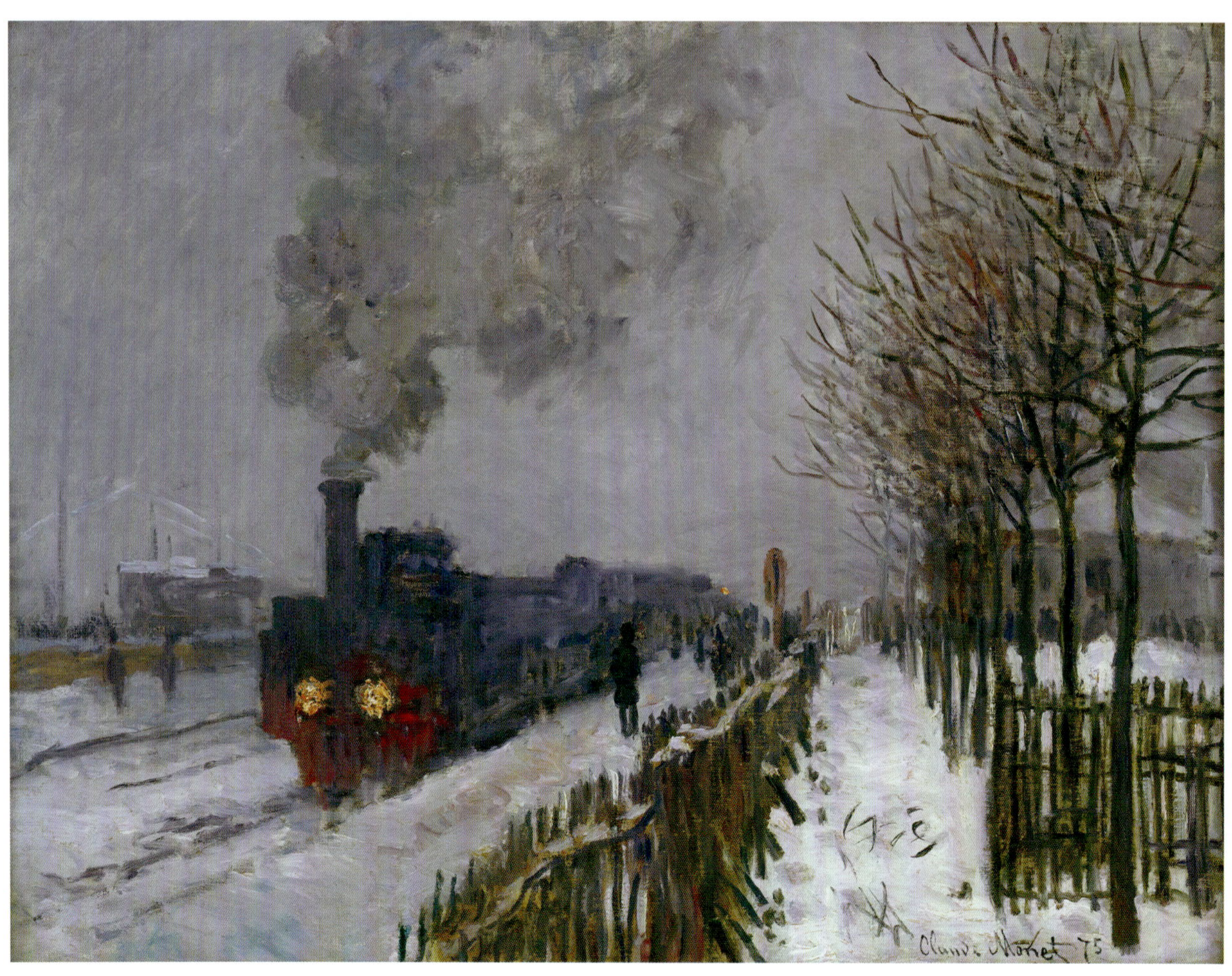

Train in the Snow *or* The Locomotive

Le Train dans la neige *ou* La Locomotive

Der Zug im Schnee *oder* Die Lokomotive

El tren en la nieve *o* la locomotora

O comboio na neve *ou* a locomotiva

De trein in de sneeuw *of* De locomotief

CLAUDE MONET (1840-1926)

1875, Oil on canvas/Huile sur toile, 59 × 78 cm,
Musée Marmottan Monet, Paris

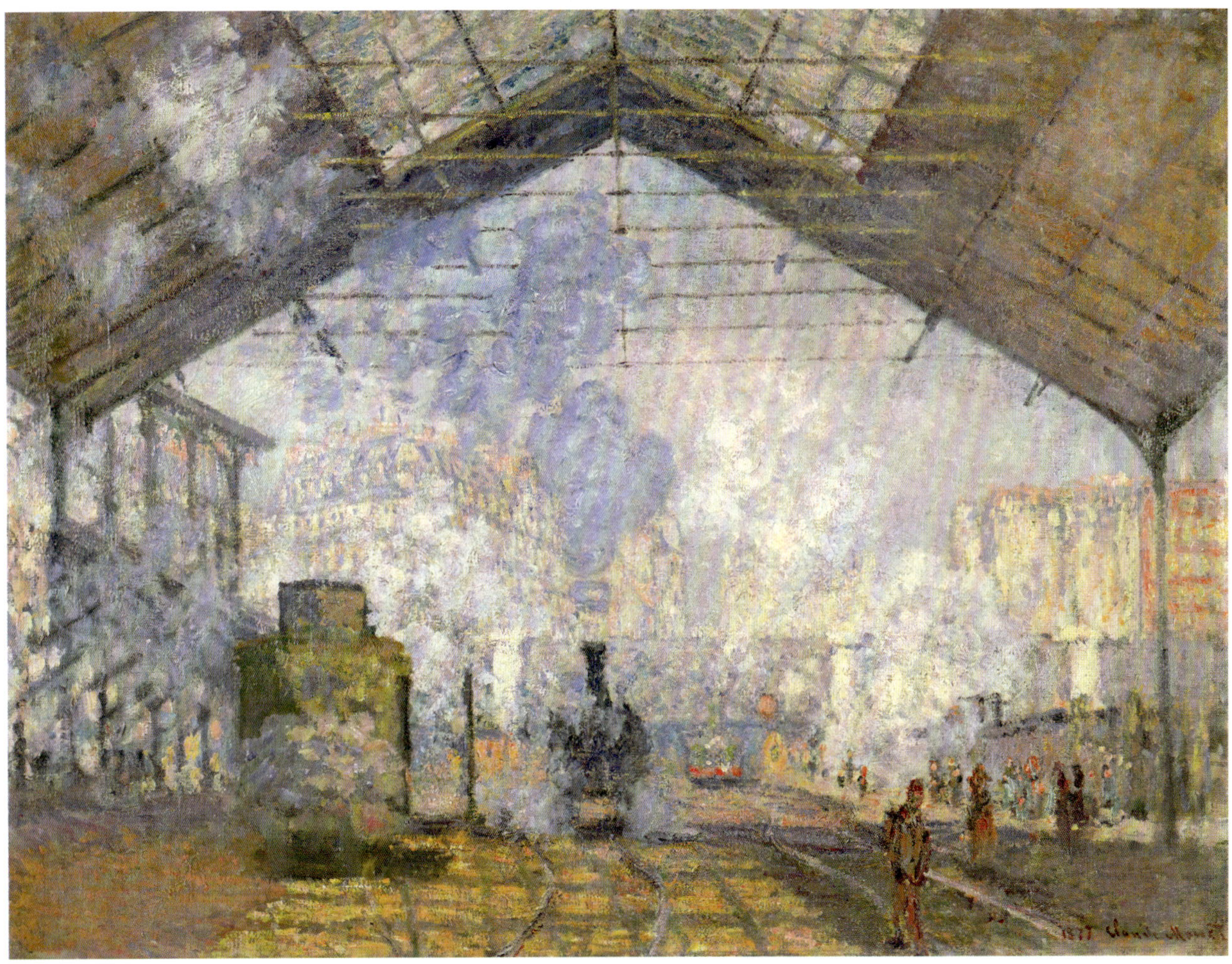

The Gare Saint-Lazare

Monet painted several variations of the motif. He used
the stations and locomotives - a symbol of progress - as a
pretext to depict the effects of steam under the huge glass
roof.

La Gare Saint-Lazare

L'artiste a réalisé douze variations sur ce thème. Emblèmes
de la modernité, les gares et les locomotives lui offrent avant
tout un prétexte pour représenter les effets de fumée sous
l'immense verrière.

Der Bahnhof Saint-Lazare

Von dem Motiv malte Monet mehrere Variationen. Er
nutzt die Bahnhöfe und Lokomotiven – ein Symbol des
Fortschritts – als Vorwand, um die Effekte des Dampfes
unter dem riesigen Glasdach darzustellen.

La estación de Saint-Lazare

Monet pintó varias variaciones del motivo. Utiliza las
estaciones y las locomotoras -un símbolo de progreso-
como pretexto para representar los efectos del vapor bajo el
enorme techo de cristal.

A estação ferroviária de Saint-Lazare

Monet pintou várias variações do motivo. Ele usa as
estações e locomotivas - um símbolo de progresso - como
pretexto para descrever os efeitos do vapor sob o enorme
telhado de vidro.

Het Gare Saint-Lazare

Monet schilderde verschillende doeken met dit onderwerp.
Hij gebruikte de stations en locomotieven – symbolen van
de vooruitgang – als voorwendsel om de effecten van stoom
onder het enorme glazen dak weer te geven.

CLAUDE MONET (1840-1926)

1877, Oil on canvas/Huile sur toile, 75 × 104 cm, Musée d'Orsay, Paris

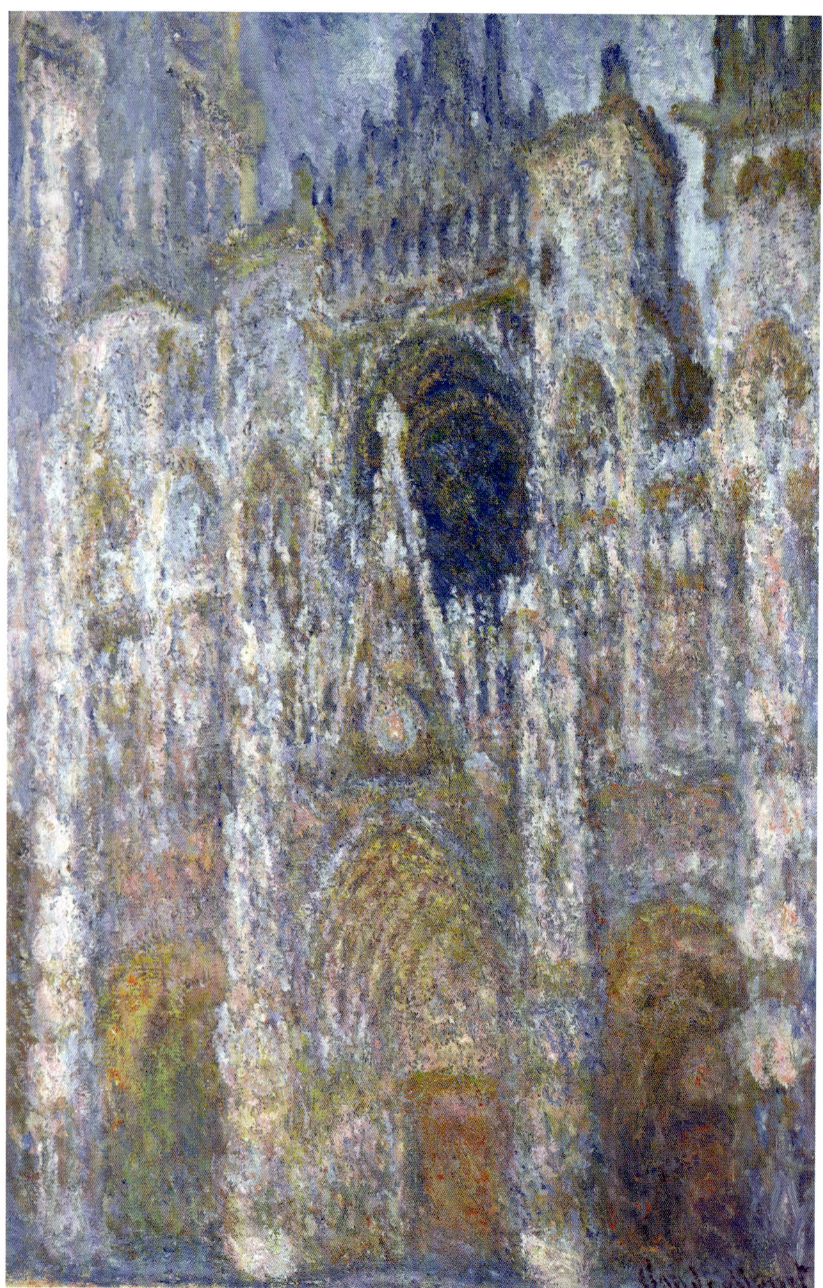

Rouen Cathedral, Blue Harmony, Morning Sunlight

Monet often approached his motifs through series in order to capture different light situations and moods - as in his Hayricks, Poplars, The Parliament of London and the Cathedral of Rouen.

La Cathédrale de Rouen. Le Portail, soleil matinal. Harmonie bleue

S'attachant à peindre un même sujet en plusieurs saisons ou heures de la journée, Monet procède souvent par séries. Ainsi des Meules, des Peupliers, du Parlement de Londres ou de la Cathédrale de Rouen.

Kathedrale von Rouen. Das Portal bei Morgensonne. Harmonie in Blau

An seine Motive nähert sich Monet oft durch Serien an, um verschiedene Lichtsituationen und Stimmungen festzuhalten – wie bei seinen Getreideschobern, Pappeln, dem Parlament von London und der Kathedrale von Rouen.

Catedral de Rouen. El portal con el sol de la mañana. Armonía en azul

Centrándose en pintar el mismo tema en varias estaciones u horas del día, Monet a menudo procede en serie. Así lo en las series de Almiares, los Álamos, el Parlamento de Londres o la Catedral de Rouen.

Catedral de Rouen. O portal ao sol da manhã. Harmonia em Azul

Monet aborda frequentemente os seus motivos através de séries para captar diferentes situações de luz e humores - como nas suas pás de cereais, choupos, o parlamento de Londres e a catedral de Rouen.

Kathedraal van Rouen. Het portaal bij ochtendzon. Harmonie in blauw

Monet benaderde zijn onderwerpen vaak seriematig om verschillende lichtsituaties en stemmingen vast te leggen – zoals in zijn Hooibergen, Populieren, Parlementsgebouwen in Londen en Kathedraal van Rouen.

CLAUDE MONET (1840-1926)

1893, Oil on canvas/Huile sur toile, 92,2 × 63 cm, Musée d'Orsay, Paris

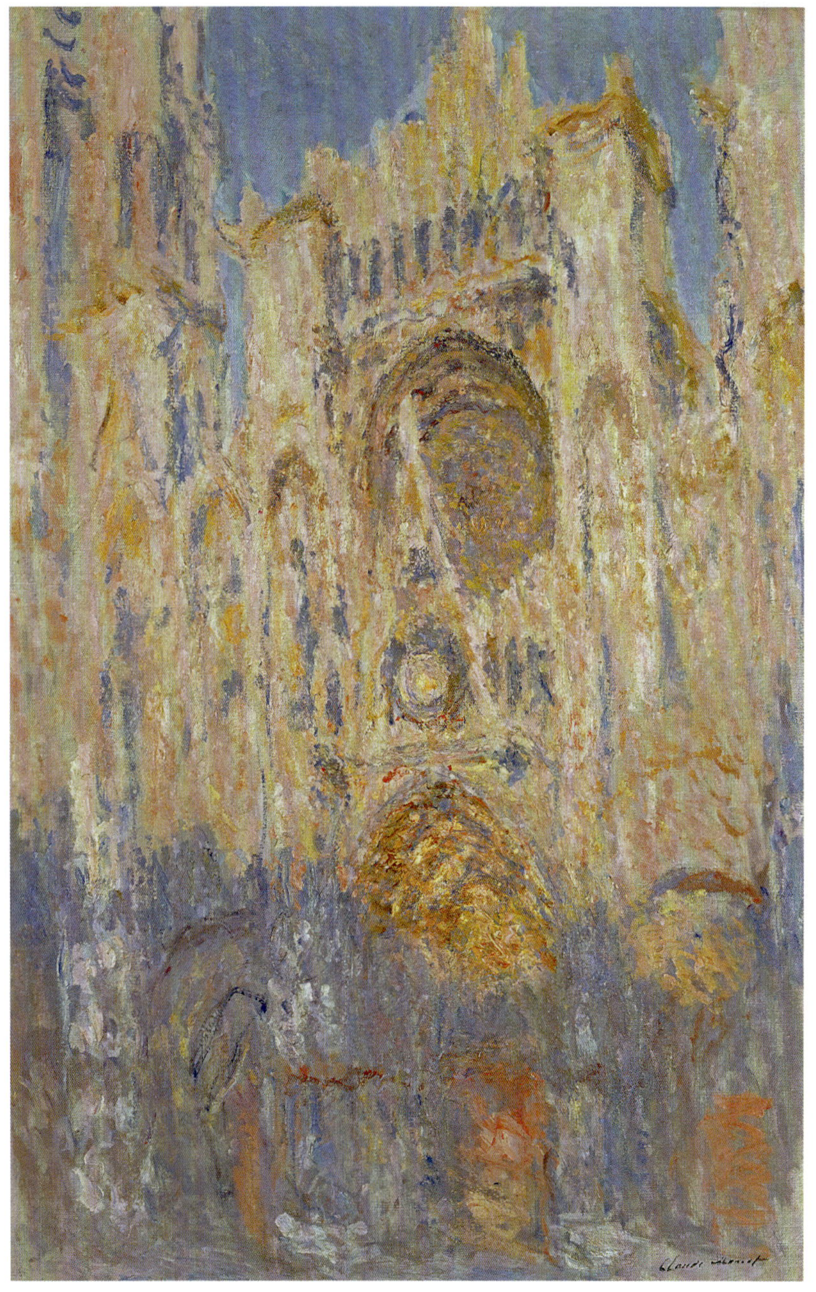

Rouen Cathedral, Effects
of Sunlight, Sunset

La Cathédrale de Rouen, effet
de soleil, fin de journée

Kathedrale von Rouen. Das Portal
im Sonnenlicht. Sonnenuntergang

Catedral de Rouen. El portal a
la luz del sol. Puesta de sol

Catedral de Rouen. O portal
à luz do sol. Pôr-do-sol

Kathedraal van Rouen.
Het portaal in het zonlicht.
Eind van de dag

CLAUDE MONET (1840-1926)
1892, Oil on canvas/
Huile sur toile, 100 × 65 cm,
Musée Marmottan Monet, Paris

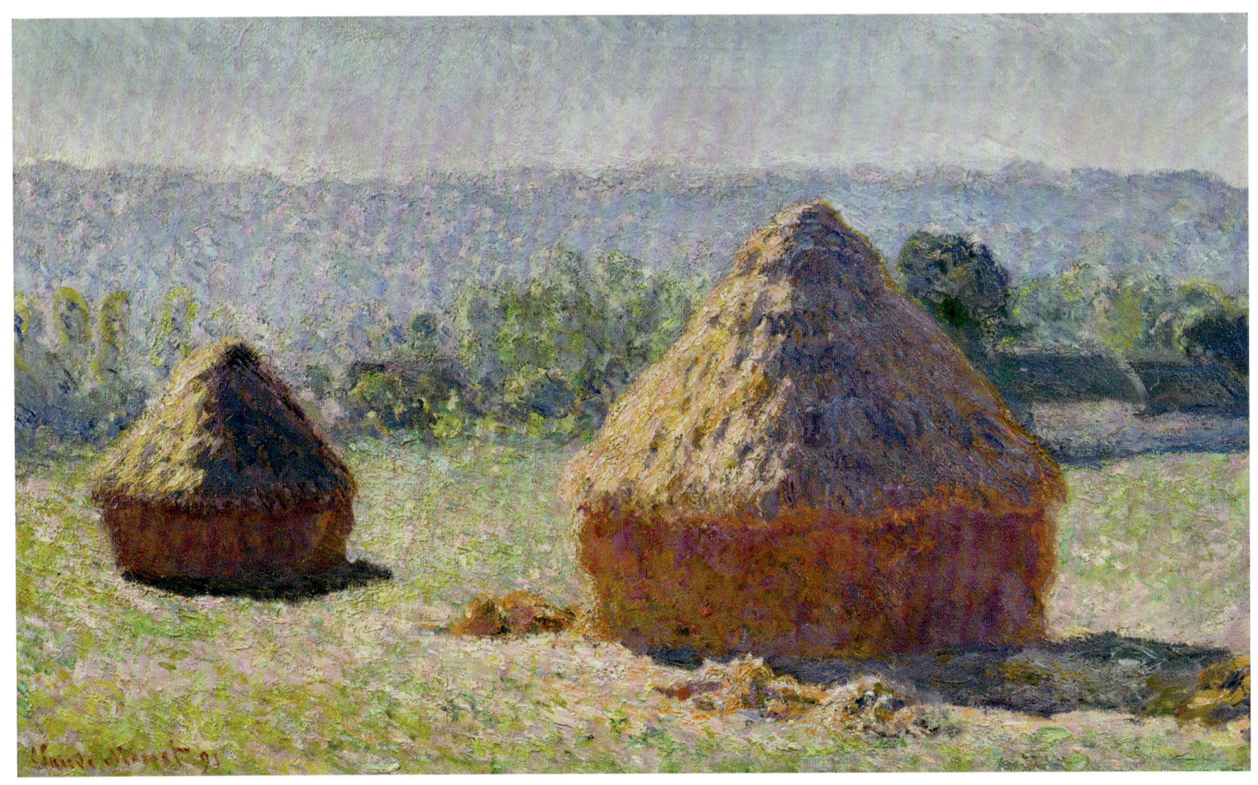

Haystacks at the End of the Summer

Meules, fin de l'été

Getreideschober im Spätsommer

Almiares al final del verano

Galpão de grãos no final do verão

Hooibergen in de nazomer

CLAUDE MONET (1840-1926)
1891, Oil on canvas/Huile sur toile, 60,5 × 100,8 cm,
Musée d'Orsay, Paris

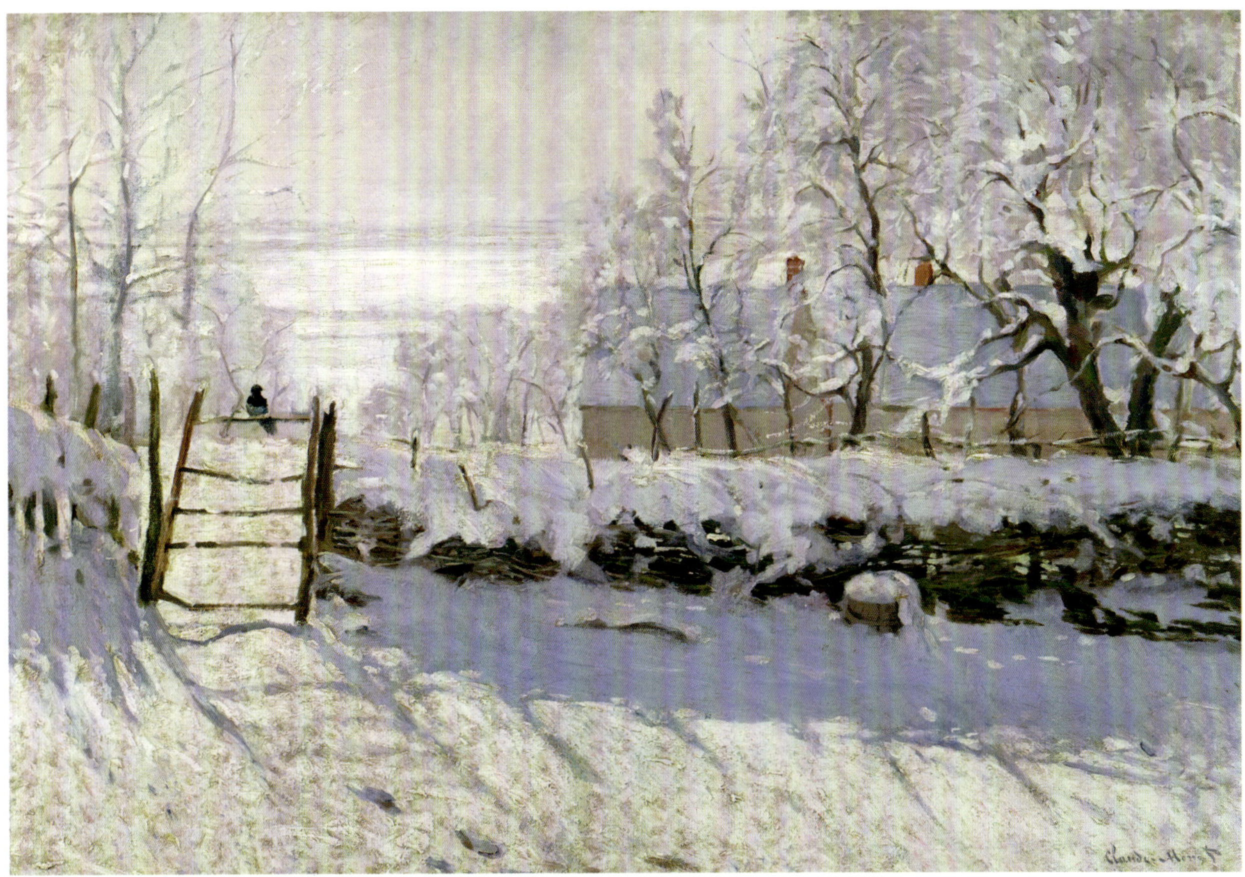

The Magpie

Only the black spot of the magpie on the gate enlivens
the symphony of white and bluish grey tones. With this
tiny detail, Monet gives the snow-covered landscape
its full effect.

La Pie

Que serait ce paysage de neige sans l'infime détail qui lui
donne vie ? L'extraordinaire symphonie de blancs et de gris
bleutés vibre grâce à une pointe de noir, celle de la pie
posée sur la barrière.

Die Elster

Erst der schwarze Fleck der Elster auf dem Tor belebt die
Symphonie aus Weiß und bläulichen Grautönen. Durch
das winzige Detail verleiht Monet der schneebedeckten
Landschaft ihre volle Wirkung.

La Urraca

¿Qué sería de este paisaje nevado sin el pequeño detalle
que le da vida? La extraordinaria sinfonía de blancos
y grises azulados vibra gracias a un toque de negro,
el de la urraca en la valla.

A Magia

Apenas o ponto negro da pega no portão anima a sinfonia
dos tons branco e cinza azulado. Com seus pequenos
detalhes, Monet dá à paisagem coberta de neve seu
efeito total.

De ekster

Alleen de zwarte vlek van de ekster op het hek verlevendigt
de symfonie van witte en blauwgrijze tinten. Met dit
kleine detail geeft Monet het besneeuwde landschap
zijn volle effect.

CLAUDE MONET (1840-1926)

1868/69, Oil on canvas/Huile sur toile, 89 × 130 cm, Musée d'Orsay, Paris

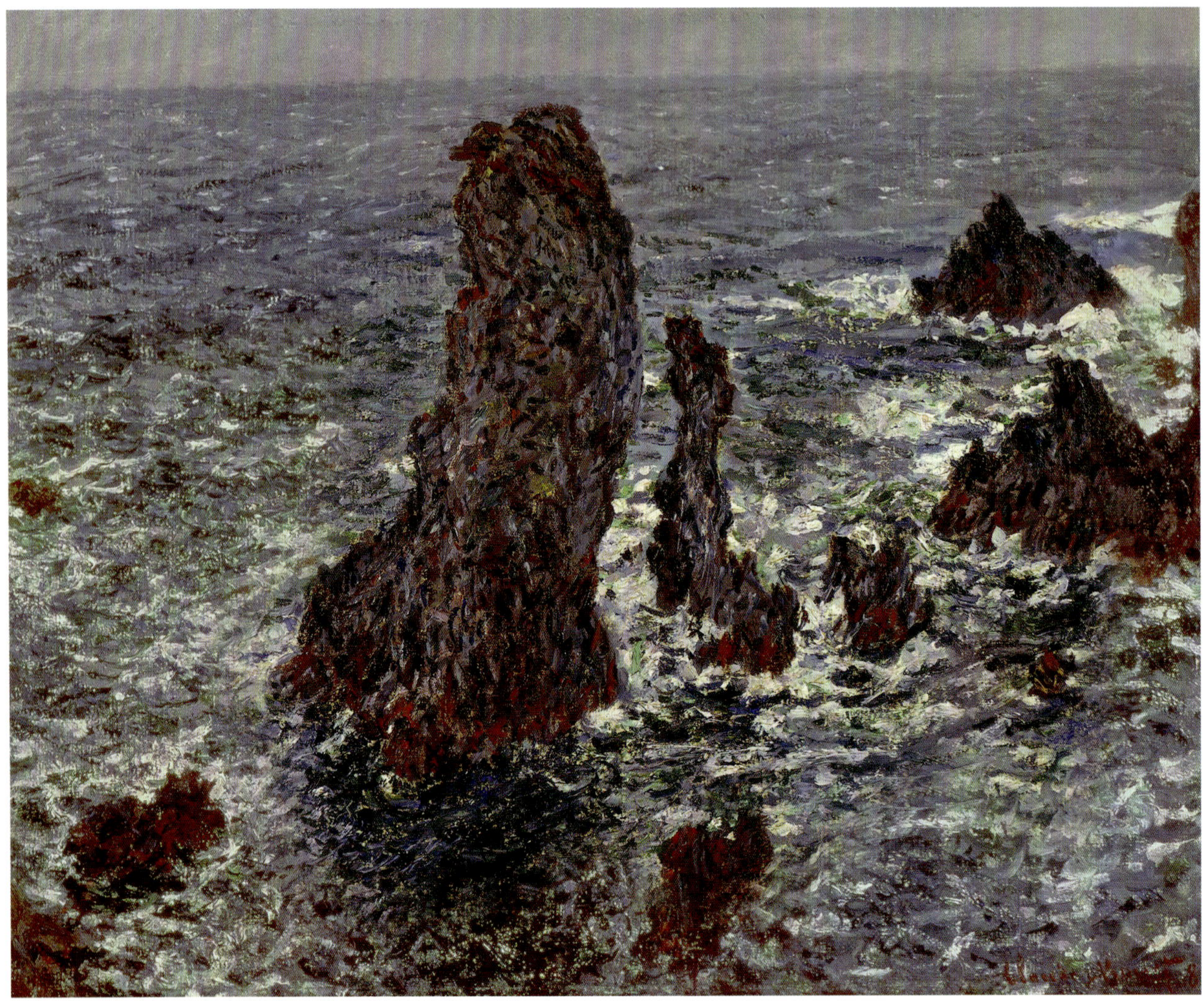

The Rocks at Belle-Ile

Between September and November 1886, the painter stayed on the Breton island of Belle-Île. There he painted five paintings that testify to his enthusiasm for the landscape and the untamed sea.

Les Aiguilles de Port-Coton, mer sauvage

Le peintre séjourne à Belle-Île, en Bretagne, entre septembre et novembre 1886. Il en rapportera cinq toiles, qui témoignent de son émerveillement devant le paysage et la beauté d'une mer indomptable.

Die Aiguilles de Port-Coton

Zwischen September und November 1886 hält sich der Maler auf der bretonischen Insel Belle-Île auf. Dort entstehen fünf Gemälde, die von seiner Begeisterung für die Landschaft und das ungezähmte Meer zeugen.

Las Agujas de Port-Coton

Entre septiembre y noviembre de 1886, el pintor permaneció en la isla bretona de Belle-Île. Allí pintó cinco cuadros que atestiguan su entusiasmo por el paisaje y el mar indómito.

Os Aiguilles de Port-Coton

Entre setembro e novembro de 1886, o pintor ficou na ilha bretã de Belle-Île. Lá ele pintou cinco pinturas que testemunham o seu entusiasmo pela paisagem e pelo mar selvagem.

De Aiguilles de Port-Coton

Tussen september en november 1886 verbleef de schilder op het Bretonse eiland Belle-Île. Daar maakte hij vijf schilderijen die getuigen van zijn enthousiasme voor het landschap en de ongetemde zee.

CLAUDE MONET (1840-1926)

1886, Oil on canvas/Huile sur toile, 66 × 81 cm, Pushkin Museum, Moscow

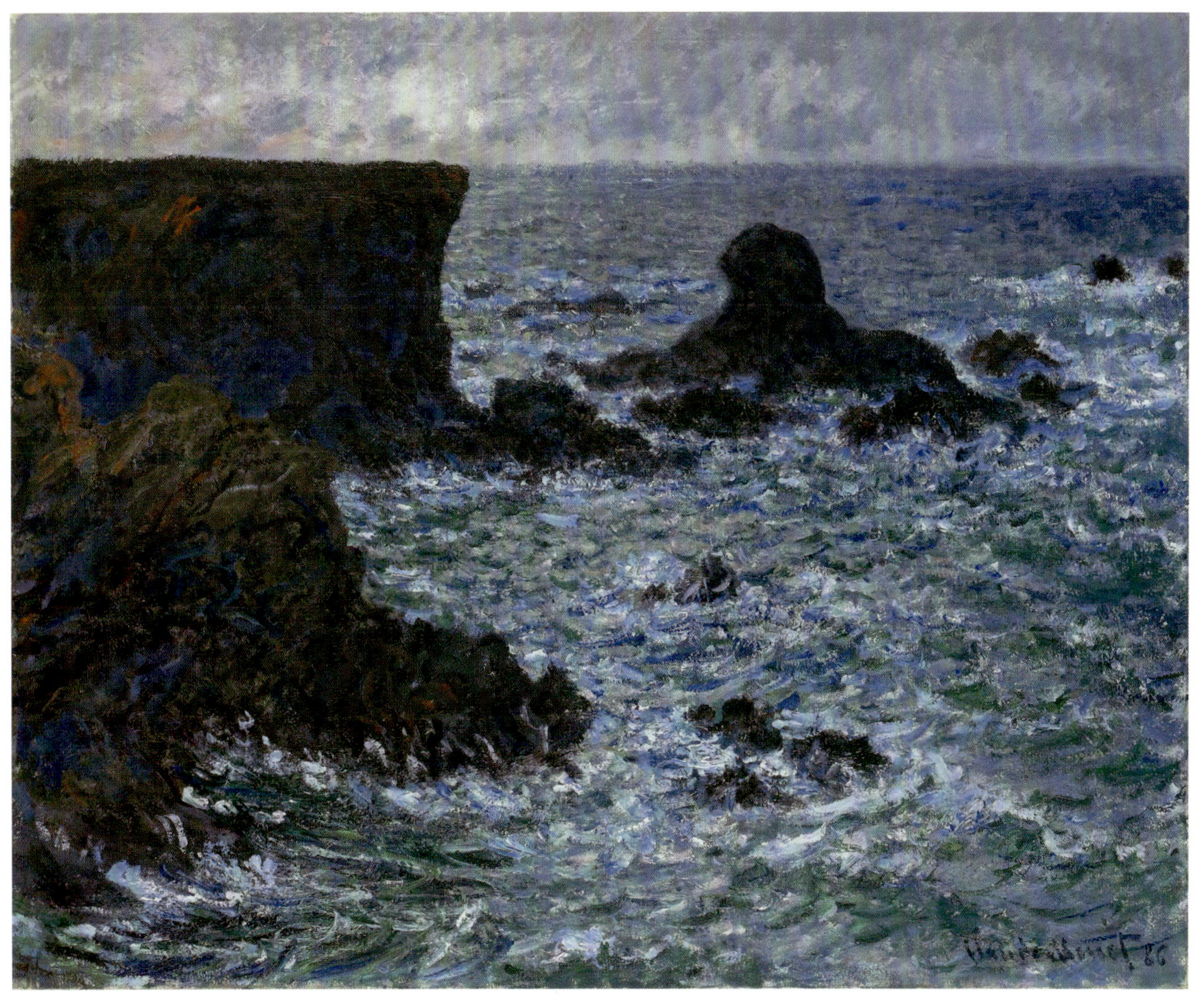

Le Rocher du Lion, Belle-Île-en-mer

CLAUDE MONET (1840-1926)

1886, Oil on canvas/Huile sur toile, 65,4 × 81,2 cm,
Fitzwilliam Museum, Cambridge

245

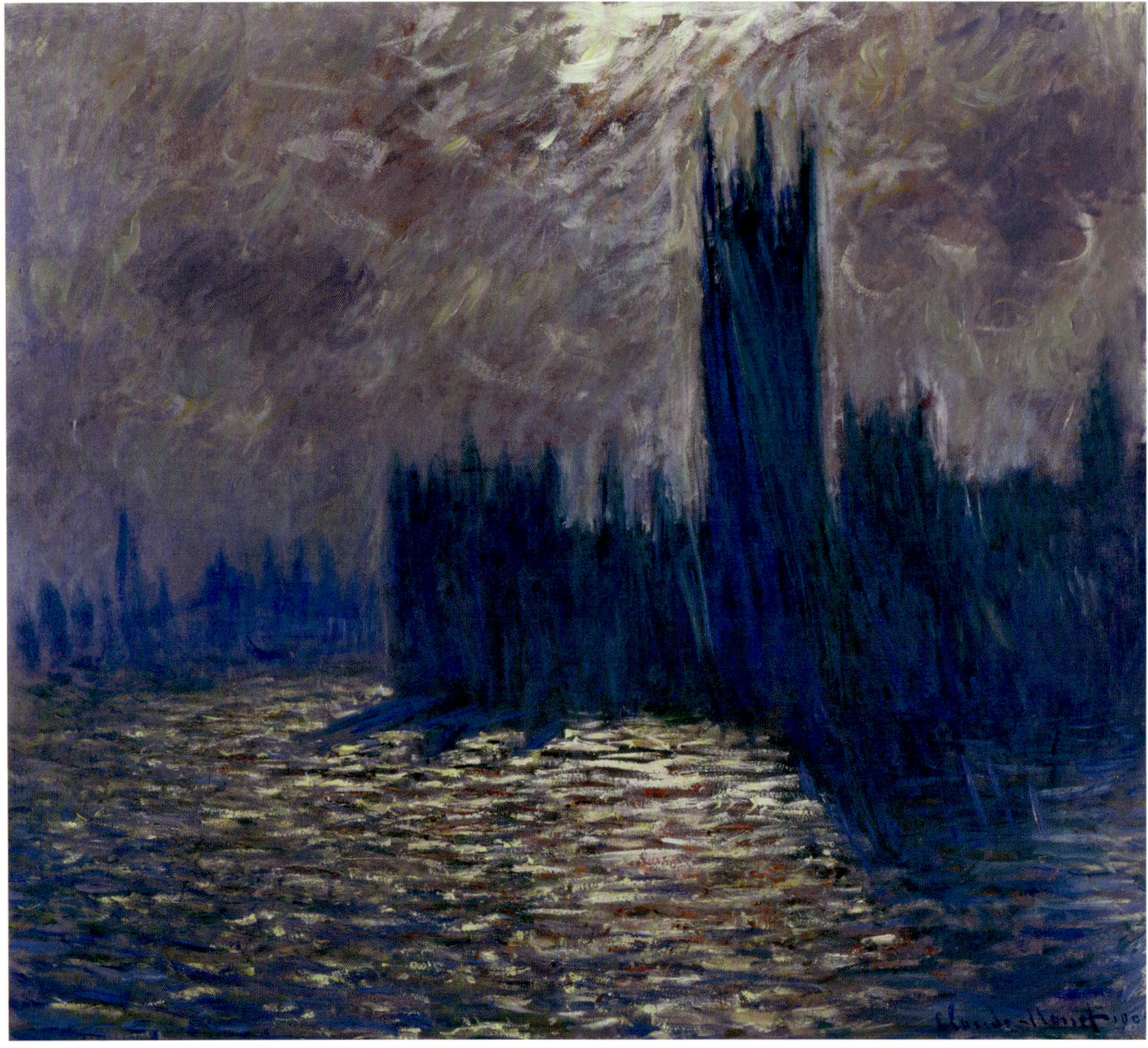

Parliament, Reflections on the Thames

Londres. Le Parlement. Reflets sur la Tamise

Das Parlament, Spiegelungen auf der Themse

El Parlamento, reflejos sobre el Támesis

O Parlamento, reflexões sobre o Tamisa

Parlementsgebouwen, weerspiegelingen op de Theems

CLAUDE MONET (1840-1926)

1905, Oil on canvas/Huile sur toile, 81 × 92 cm, Musée Marmottan Monet, Paris

The London Parliament series comprises 19 paintings created between 1900 and 1904. In turn Monet painted it at sunset, in the fog, in the rain or in a storm.

L'ensemble de la série consacrée au Parlement de Londres compte dix-neuf tableaux, produits entre 1900 et 1904. Il le peint tour à tour au soleil couchant, dans le brouillard, sous la pluie ou l'orage.

Die Serie des Parlaments von London umfasst 19 Gemälde, die zwischen 1900 und 1904 entstanden sind. Nach und nach malt Monet es im Sonnenuntergang, im Nebel, im Regen oder bei Sturm.

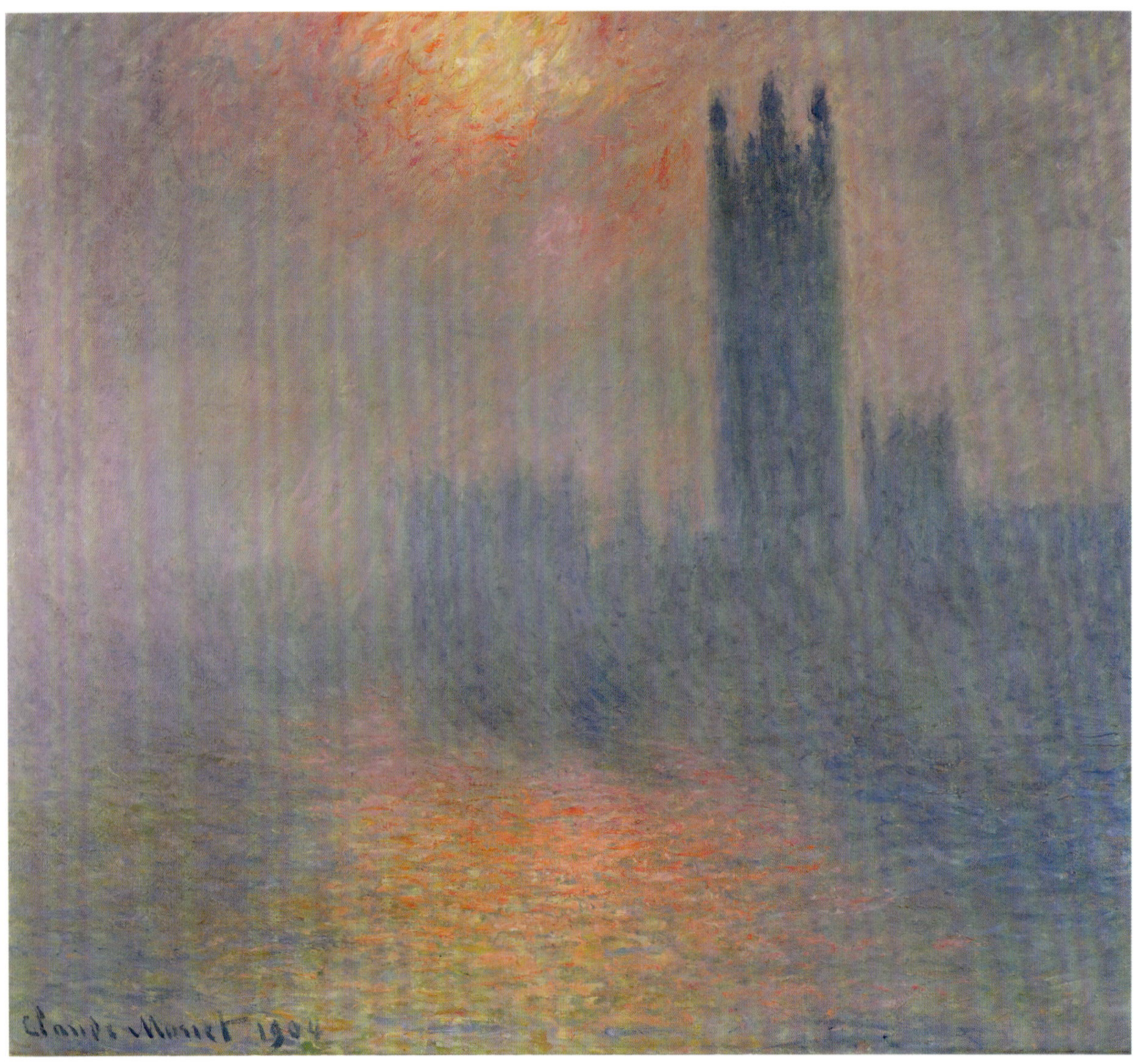

London, The Houses of Parliament.
The Sun Shining through the Fog

Londres, le Parlement. Trouée
de soleil dans le brouillard

London, das Parlament, die Sonne
bricht durch den Nebel

Londres, el parlamento, el sol se
abre paso entre la niebla

Londres, o parlamento,
o sol rompe o nevoeiro

Londen, parlementsgebouwen,
de zon breekt door de mist

CLAUDE MONET (1840-1926)

1904, Oil on canvas/Huile sur toile, 81 × 92 cm, Musée d'Orsay,

La serie del Parlamento de Londres comprende 19 cuadros creados entre 1900 y 1904. Poco a poco Monet lo pinta en la puesta de sol, en la niebla, en la lluvia o en una tormenta.

A série do Parlamento de Londres compreende 19 pinturas criadas entre 1900 e 1904. Pouco a pouco, Monet pinta-o no pôr-do-sol, no nevoeiro, na chuva ou numa tempestade.

De serie met Londense parlementsgebouwen bestaat uit 19 schilderijen, die tussen 1900 en 1904 zijn gemaakt. Keer op keer schilderde Monet ze bij zonsondergang, in de mist, in de regen of bij storm.

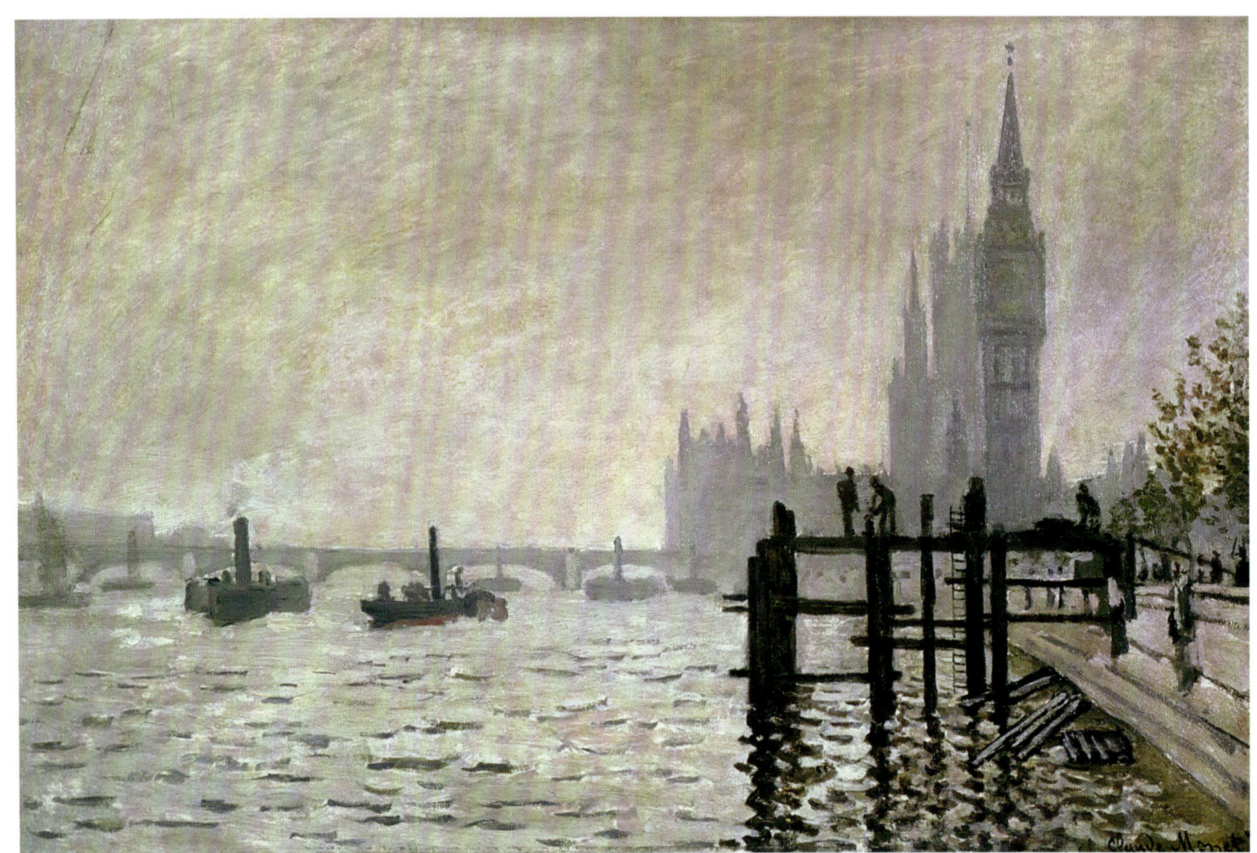

The Thames below Westminster

La Tamise à Westminster

Die Themse bei Westminster

El Támesis cerca de Westminster

O Tamisa perto de Westminster

De Theems bij Westminster

CLAUDE MONET (1840-1926)

1871, Oil on canvas/Huile sur toile, 47 × 73 cm, The National Gallery, London

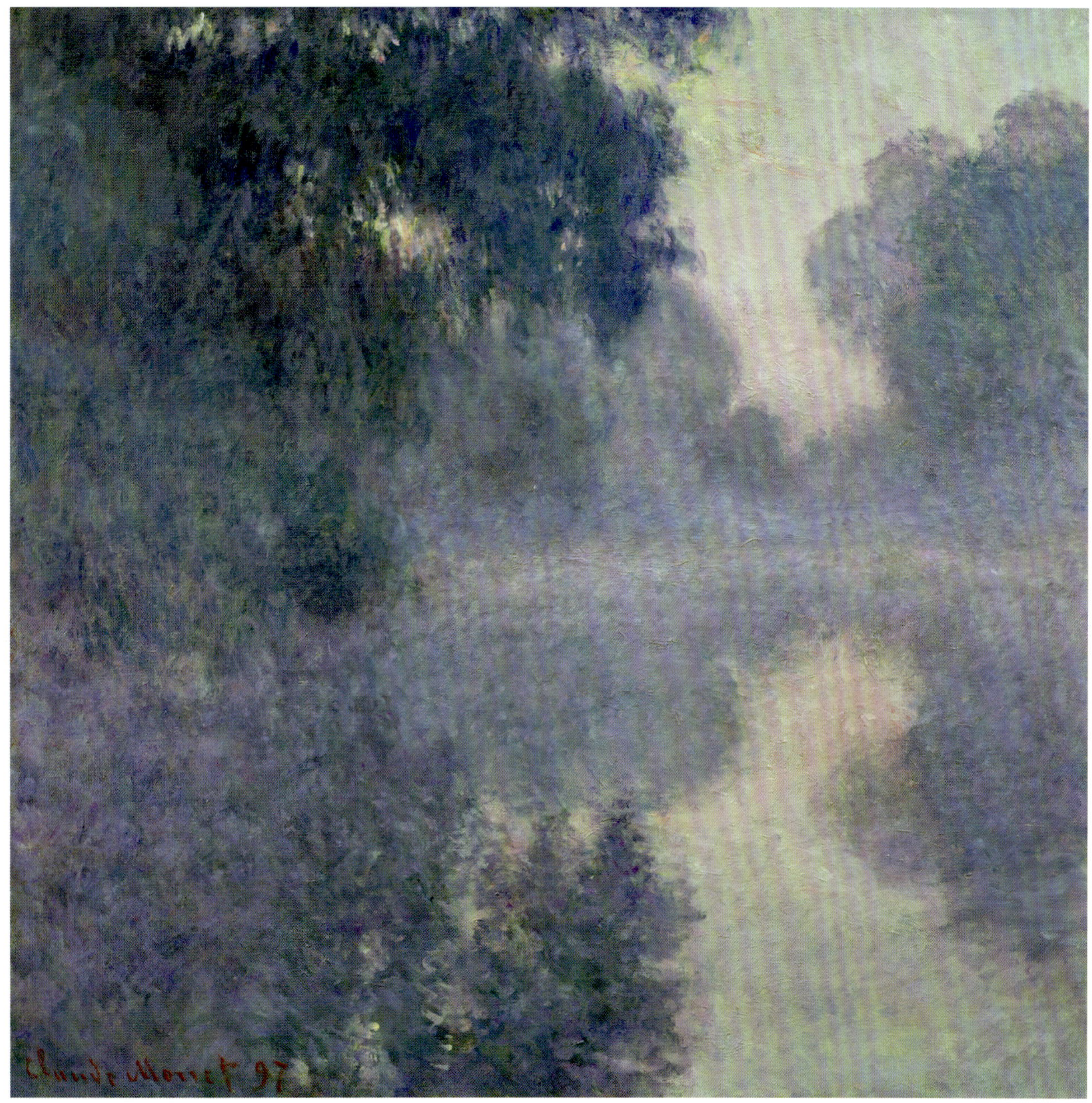

Branch of the Seine near Giverny

Bras de Seine près de Giverny

Arm der Seine bei Giverny

Brazo del Sena en Giverny

Braço do Sena em Giverny

Arm van de Seine bij Giverny

CLAUDE MONET (1840-1926)

1897, Oil on canvas/Huile sur toile, 91 × 93 cm, Musée Marmottan Monet, Paris

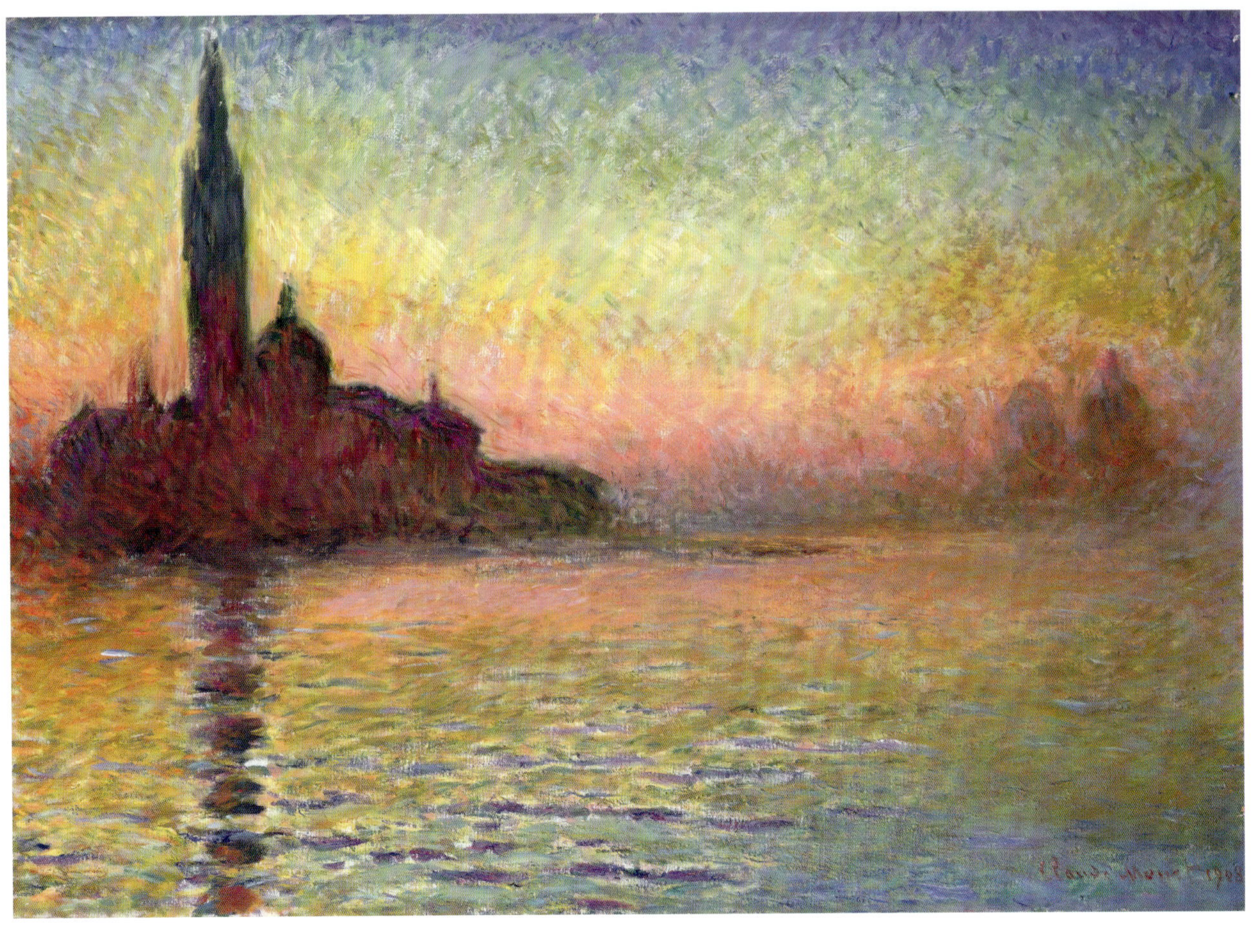

San Giorgio Maggiore by Twilight

Saint-Georges-Majeur au crépuscule

San Giorgio Maggiore in der Dämmerung

San Giorgio Maggiore al atardecer

San Giorgio Maggiore ao anoitecer

San Giorgio Maggiore in de avondschemering

CLAUDE MONET (1840-1926)

1908-12, Oil on canvas/Huile sur toile, 65,2 × 92,4 cm,
National Museum Wales, Cardiff

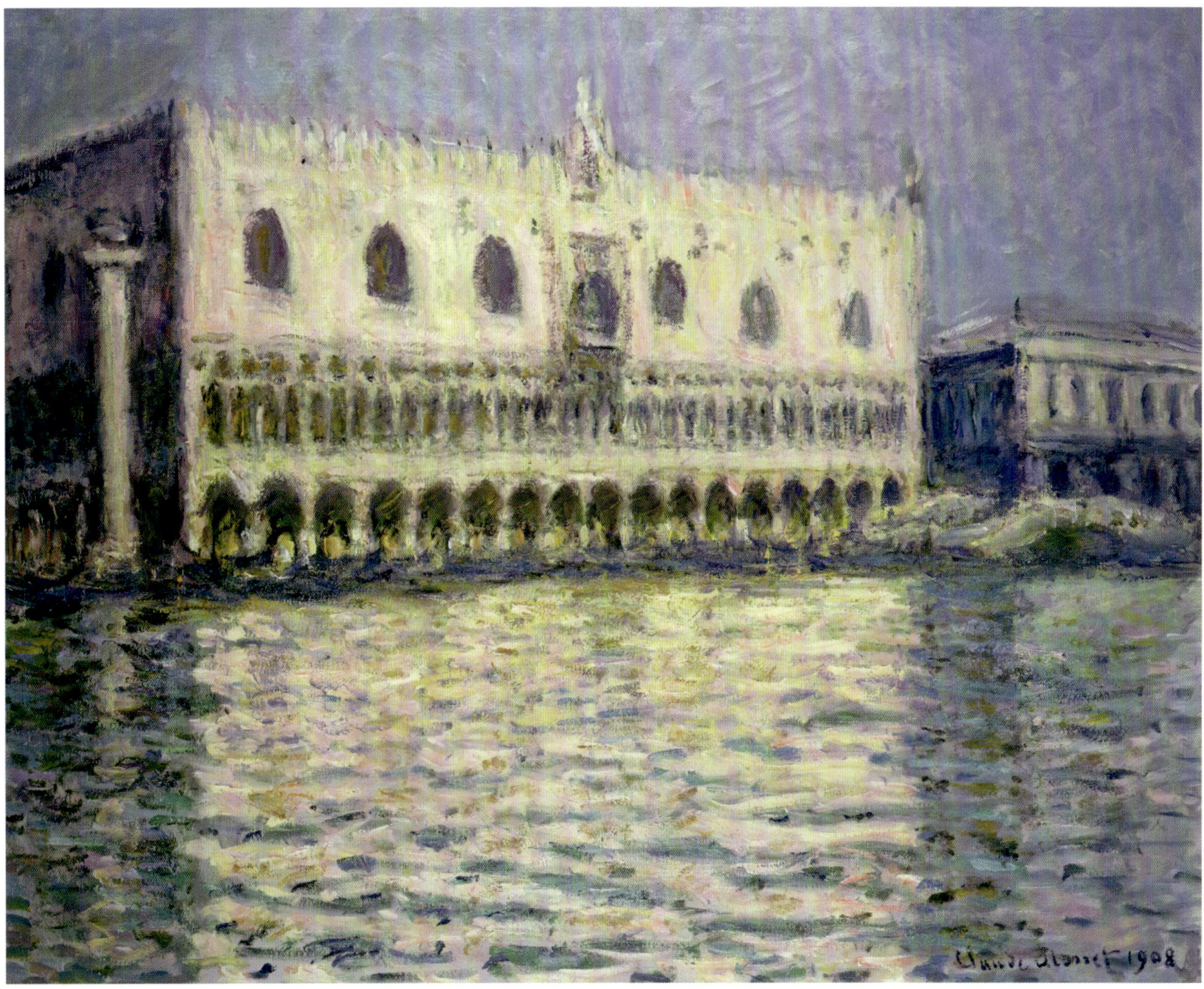

The Ducal Palace, Venice

Monet visited Venice only once in the autumn of 1908, but nevertheless he produced 37 paintings, many of which were completed in his studio. For the artist who loved light and water, the city offered the ideal motif.

Le Palais ducal, Venise

Si Monet n'a séjourné qu'une fois à Venise, à l'automne 1908, il prit le temps de concevoir trente-sept toiles, souvent terminées en atelier. Une ville idéale pour cet amoureux de l'eau et de la lumière.

Der Dogenpalast in Venedig

Monet besuchte Venedig nur einmal im Herbst 1908. Trotzdem entstehen 37 Gemälde, von denen viele im Atelier vollendet werden. Für den Künstler, der das Licht und das Wasser liebt, bietet die Stadt das ideale Motiv.

El Palacio Ducal en Venecia

Monet visitó Venecia sólo una vez en el otoño de 1908, pero sin embargo produjo 37 pinturas, muchas de las cuales fueron terminadas en su estudio. Para el artista que ama la luz y el agua, la ciudad ofrece el motivo ideal.

O Palácio do Doge em Veneza

Monet visitou Veneza apenas uma vez no outono de 1908, mas ainda assim ele produziu 37 pinturas, muitas das quais foram concluídas em seu estúdio. Para o artista que adora luz e água, a cidade oferece o motivo ideal.

Het Dogepaleis in Venetië

Monet bezocht Venetië slechts één keer, in de herfst van 1908, maar hij maakte er desalniettemin 37 schilderijen, waarvan hij een groot deel in zijn atelier voltooide. Voor de schilder die van licht en water hield, bood de stad het ideale onderwerp.

CLAUDE MONET (1840-1926)
1908, Oil on canvas/Huile sur toile, 81,3 × 99,1 cm, Brooklyn Museum of Art, New York

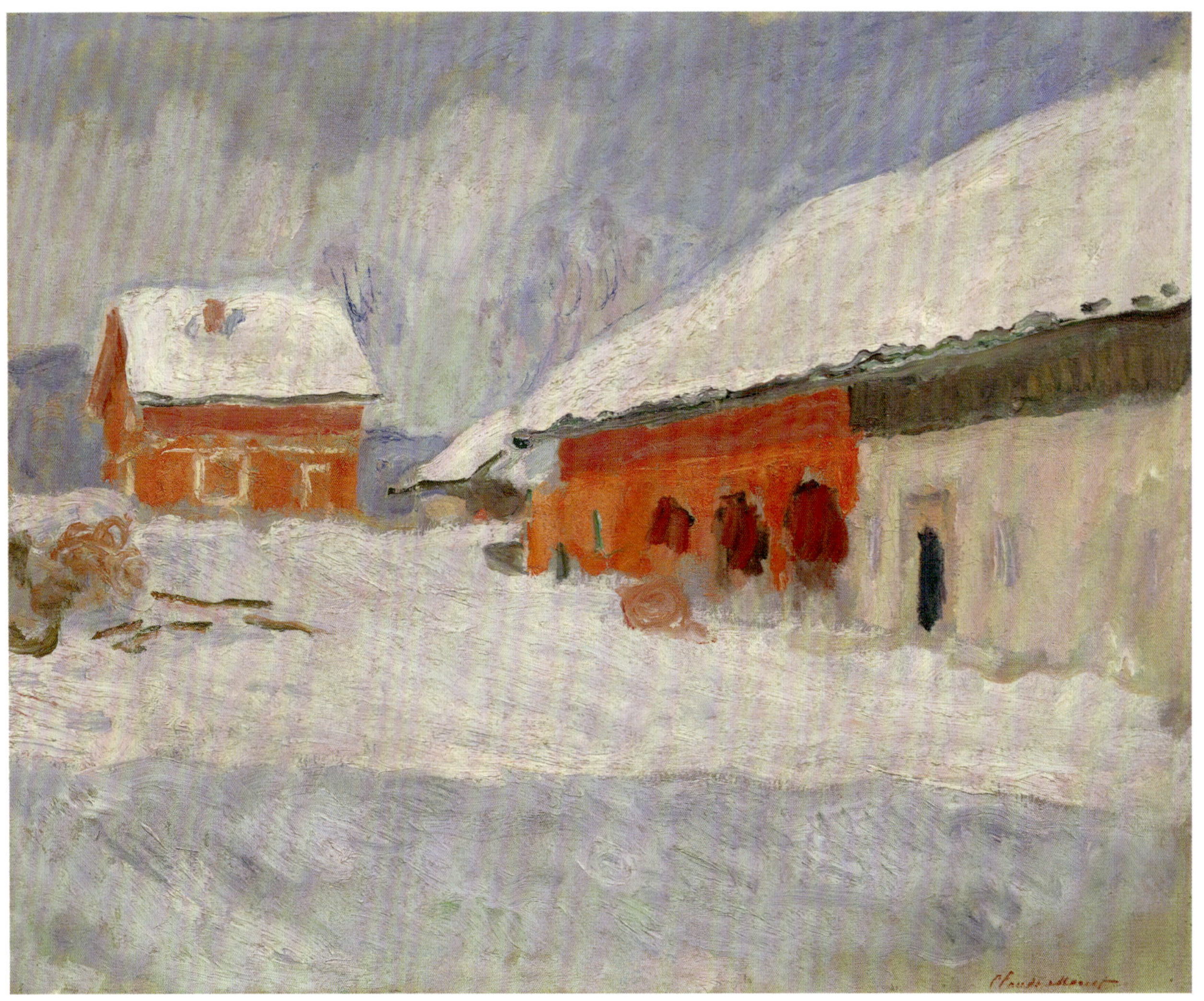

Norway, Red Houses at Bjørnegård

Norvège, maisons rouges à Bjørnegård

Norwegen, rote Häuser bei Bjørnegård

Noruega, casas rojas cerca de Bjørnegård

Noruega, casas vermelhas perto de Bjørnegård

Noorwegen, rode huizen bij Bjørnegård

CLAUDE MONET (1840-1926)

1895, Oil on canvas/Huile sur toile, 65 × 81 cm, Musée Marmottan Monet, Paris

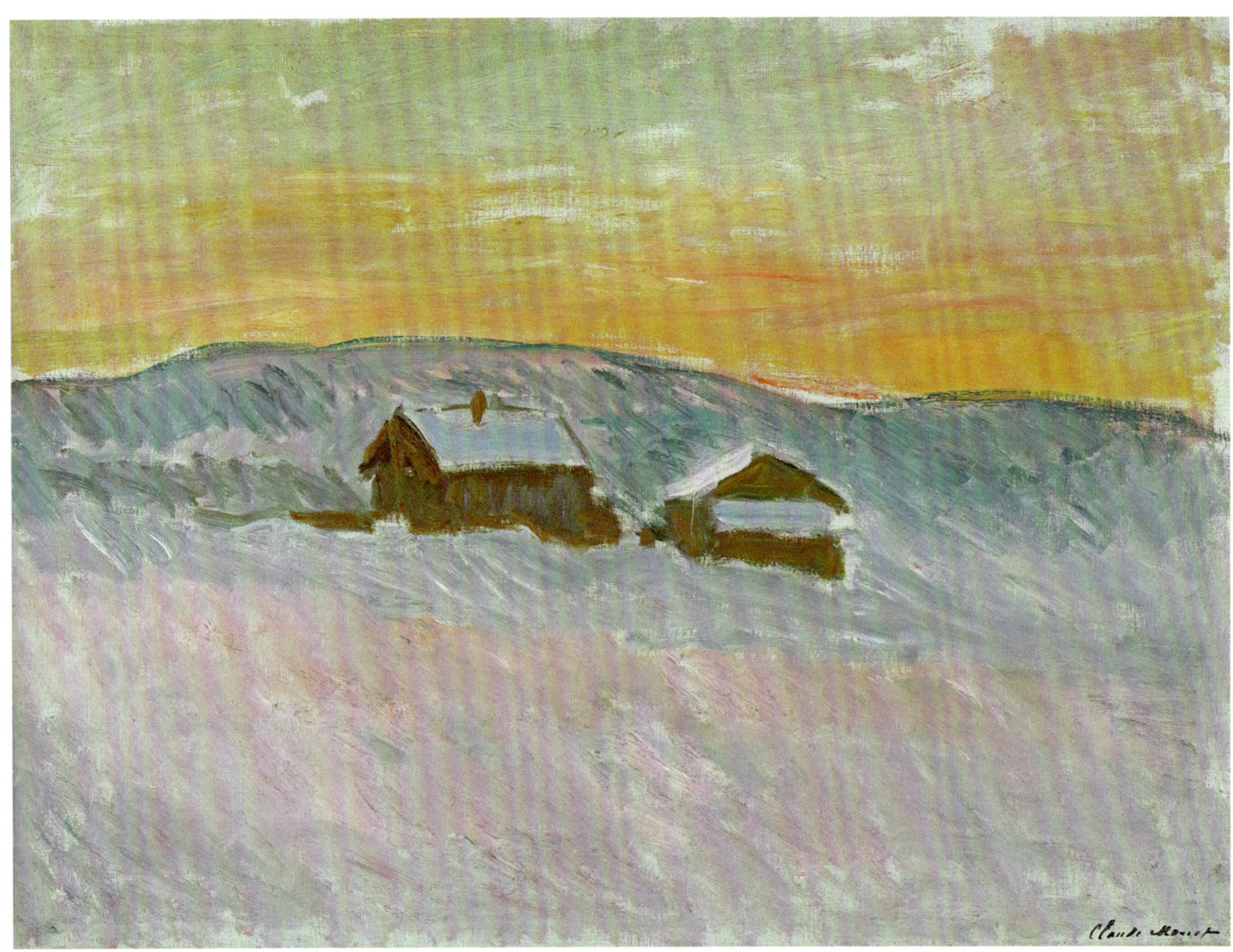

Norwegian Landscape, Blue Houses

1895 Monet traveled in Norway. He himself described the works created there as successful. They show unique views of the fjords and villages with traditional wooden houses.

Paysage de Norvège, les maisons bleues

En 1895, Monet s'offre une escapade en Norvège. Très appréciés de leur auteur, les tableaux qui en résultent offrent de superbes visions des fjords et des maisons traditionnelles en bois des villages.

Norwegische Landschaft, blaue Häuser

1895 bereist Monet Norwegen. Die dort entstandenen Werke, bezeichnet er selber als gelungen. Sie zeigen einmalige Ansichten der Fjorde und der Dörfer aus traditionellen Holzhäusern.

Paisaje noruego, casas azules

En 1895, Monet hizo un viaje a Noruega. Muy apreciadas por su autor, las pinturas resultantes ofrecen magníficas visiones de los fiordos y las casas de madera tradicionales de los pueblos.

Paisagem norueguesa, casas azuis

1895 Monet viaja pela Noruega. Ele próprio descreve as obras ali criadas como bem sucedidas. Mostram vistas únicas dos fiordes e aldeias a partir de casas de madeira tradicionais.

Noors landschap, blauwe huizen

In 1895 reisde Monet door Noorwegen. Zelf noemde hij de werken die hij daar maakte geslaagd. Ze tonen unieke gezichten op fjorden en dorpen met traditionele houten huizen.

CLAUDE MONET (1840-1926)

1895, Oil on canvas/Huile sur toile, 61 × 84 cm, Musée Marmottan Monet, Paris

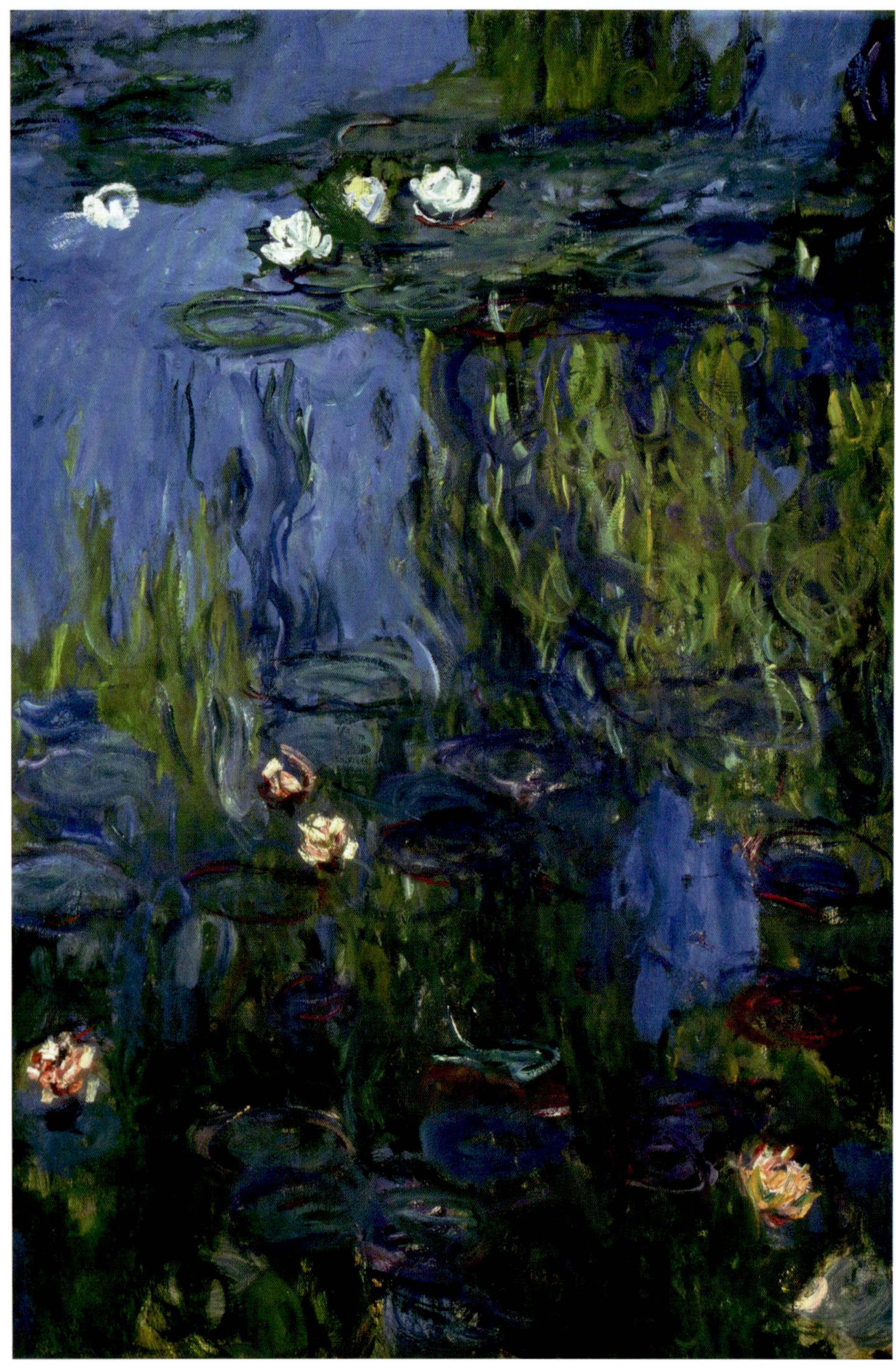

Water Lilies

Nymphéas

Seerosen

Nenúfares

Lírios de água

Waterlelies

CLAUDE MONET (1840-1926)
1914-17, Oil on canvas/Huile sur toile,
169 × 123,2 cm, Private collection

The Agapanthus

1883 Monet moved to Giverny. Ten years later he had a water garden laid out on his property. The banks of the pond are lined with decorative lilies whose mirror images unite with the water lilies on the water.

Agapanthes

Installé à Giverny depuis 1883, Monet fait aménager dix ans plus tard un jardin d'eau dans sa propriété. Les bords du bassin sont plantés d'agapanthes, dont les reflets se mêlent aux feuilles des nymphéas.

Schmucklilien

1883 zieht Monet nach Giverny. Zehn Jahre später lässt er auf seinem Grundstück einen Wassergarten anlegen. Die Ufer des Teichs säumen Schmucklilien, deren Spiegelbilder sich auf dem Wasser mit den Seerosen vereinen.

Agapantos

Instalado en Giverny desde 1883, Monet hizo construir un jardín acuático en su propiedad diez años después. Los bordes de la cuenca están plantados con agapantos, cuyos reflejos se mezclan con las hojas de los nenúfares.

lírios decorativos

1883 Monet muda-se para Giverny. Dez anos mais tarde, ele tinha um jardim de água na sua propriedade. As margens do tanque estão forradas de lírios decorativos cujas imagens espelhadas se unem aos lírios de água sobre a água.

Agapanthus

In 1883 verhuisde Monet naar Giverny. Tien jaar later liet hij een watertuin aanleggen op zijn erf. Langs de oevers van de vijver groeien agapanthussen. Het spiegelbeeld daarvan verenigt zich met de waterlelies op het water.

CLAUDE MONET (1840-1926)

1914-17, Oil on canvas/Huile sur toile, Musée Marmottan Monet, Paris

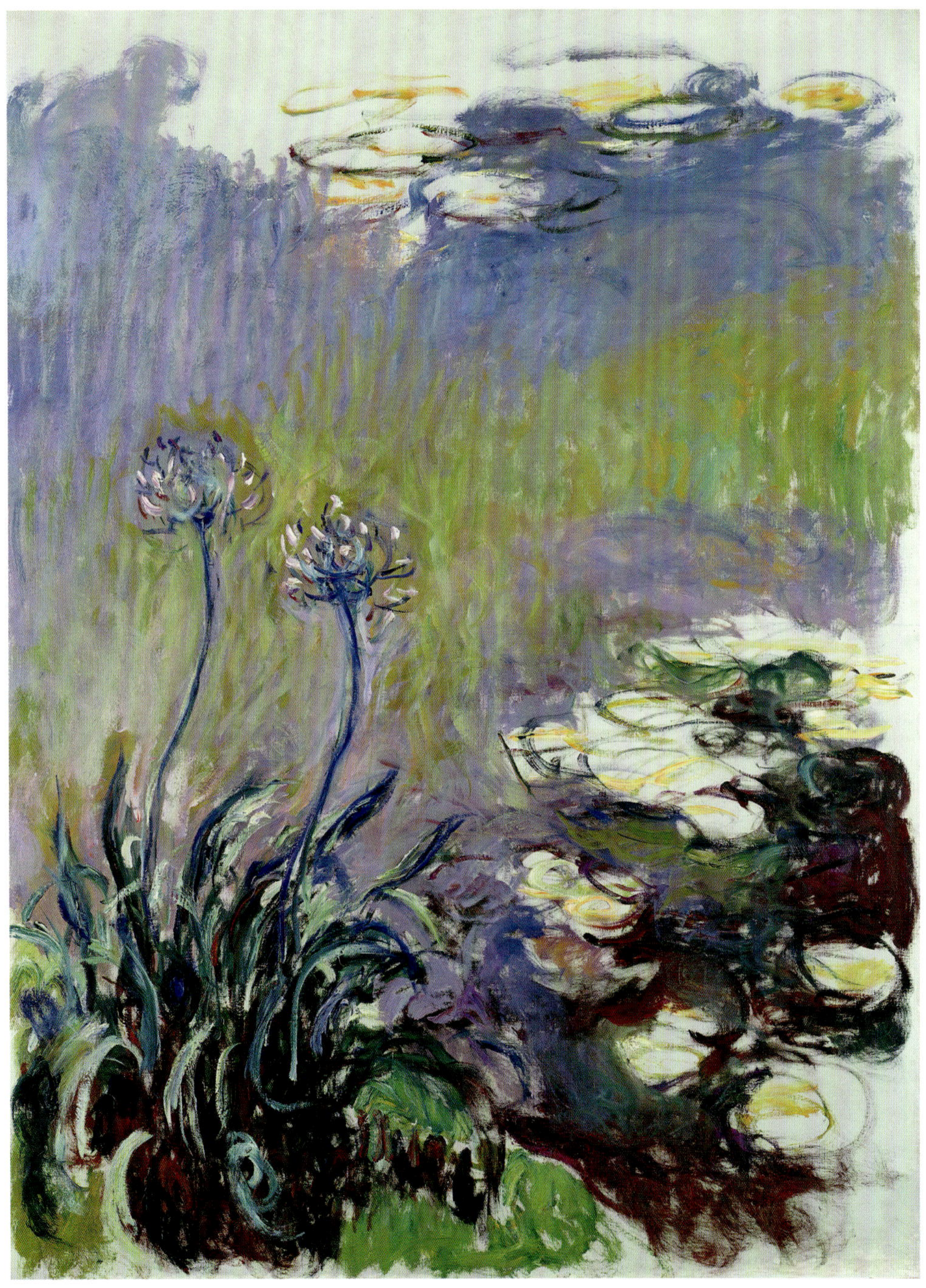

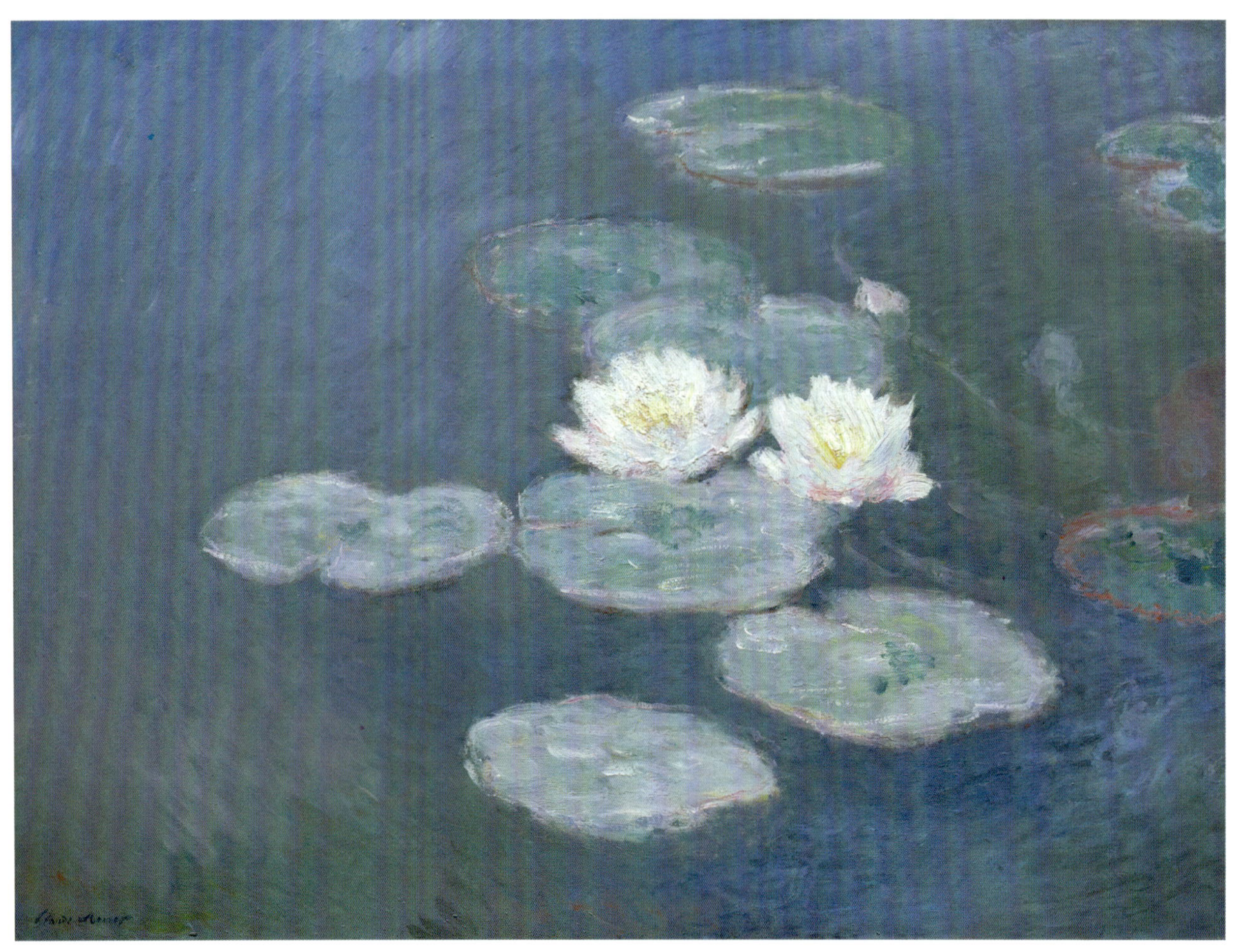

Water Lilies, Evening

Nymphéas, effet du soir

Seerosen, Abend

Lirios de agua, por la noche

Lírios de água, noite

Waterlelies, avond

CLAUDE MONET (1840-1926)
1897, Oil on canvas/Huile sur toile, 73 × 100 cm,
Musée Marmottan Monet, Paris

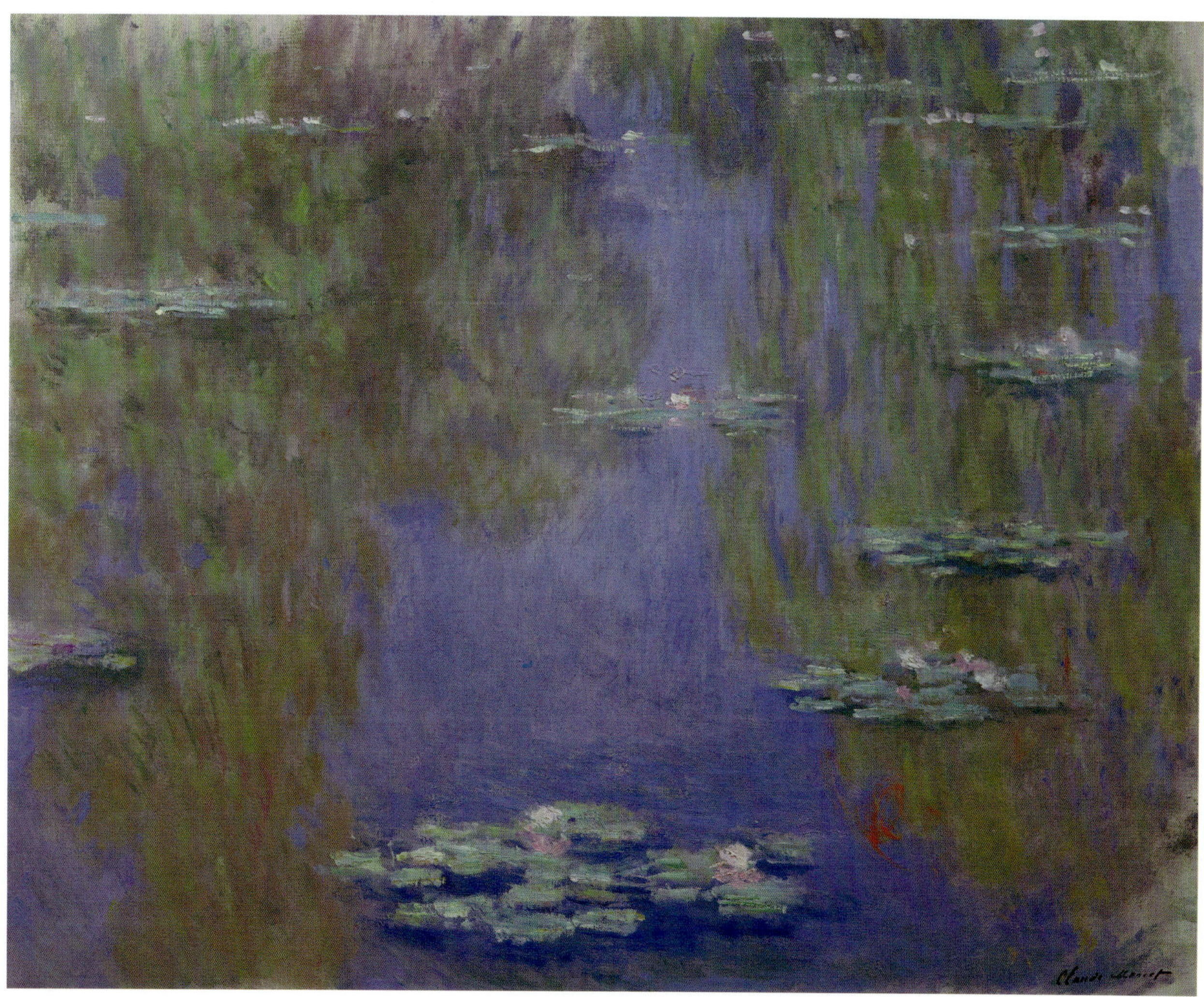

Water Lilies

Nymphéas

Seerosen

Lirios de agua

Lírios de água

Waterlelies

CLAUDE MONET (1840-1926)

1903, Oil on canvas/Huile sur toile,

73 × 92 cm, Musée Marmottan Monet, Paris

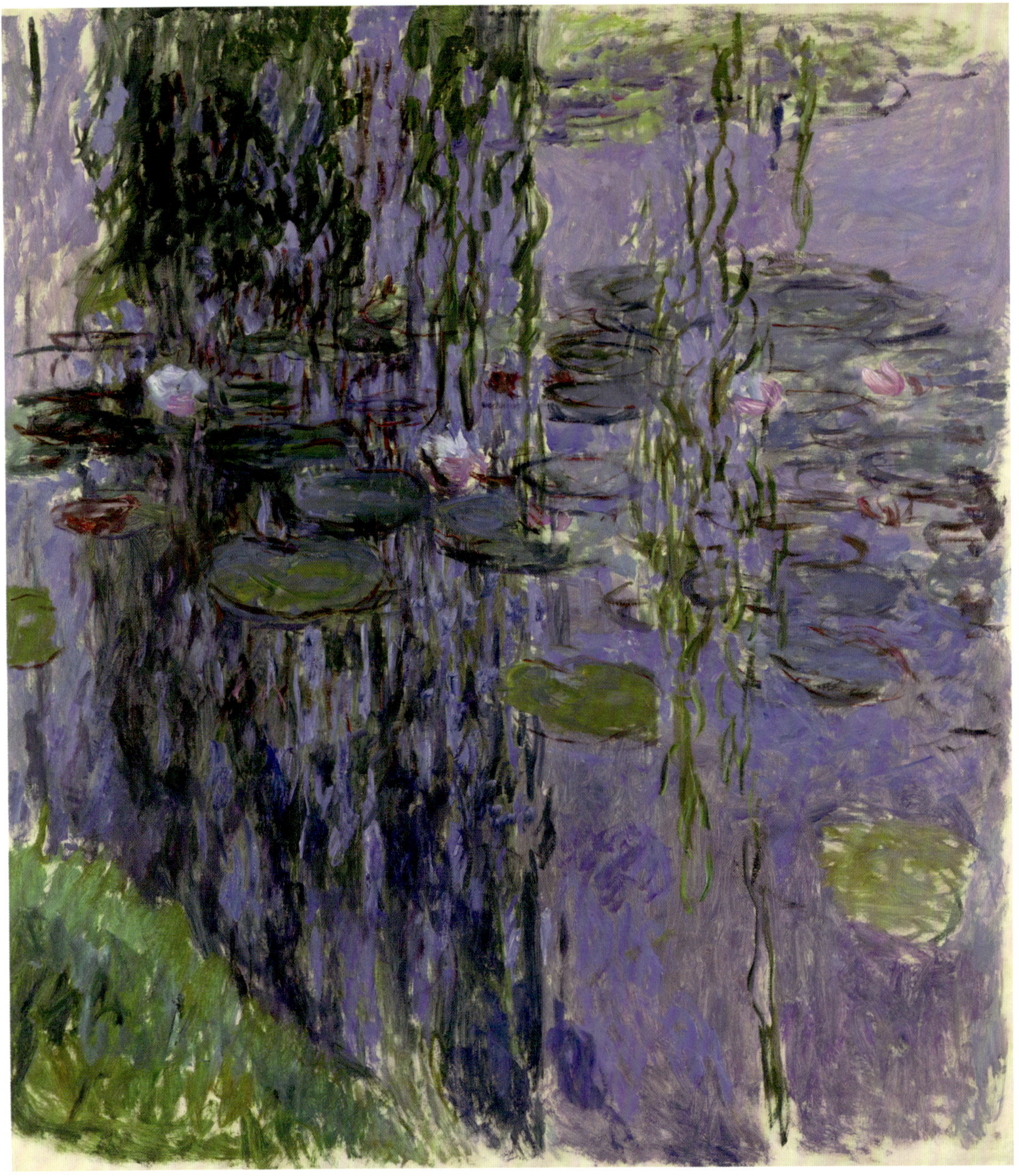

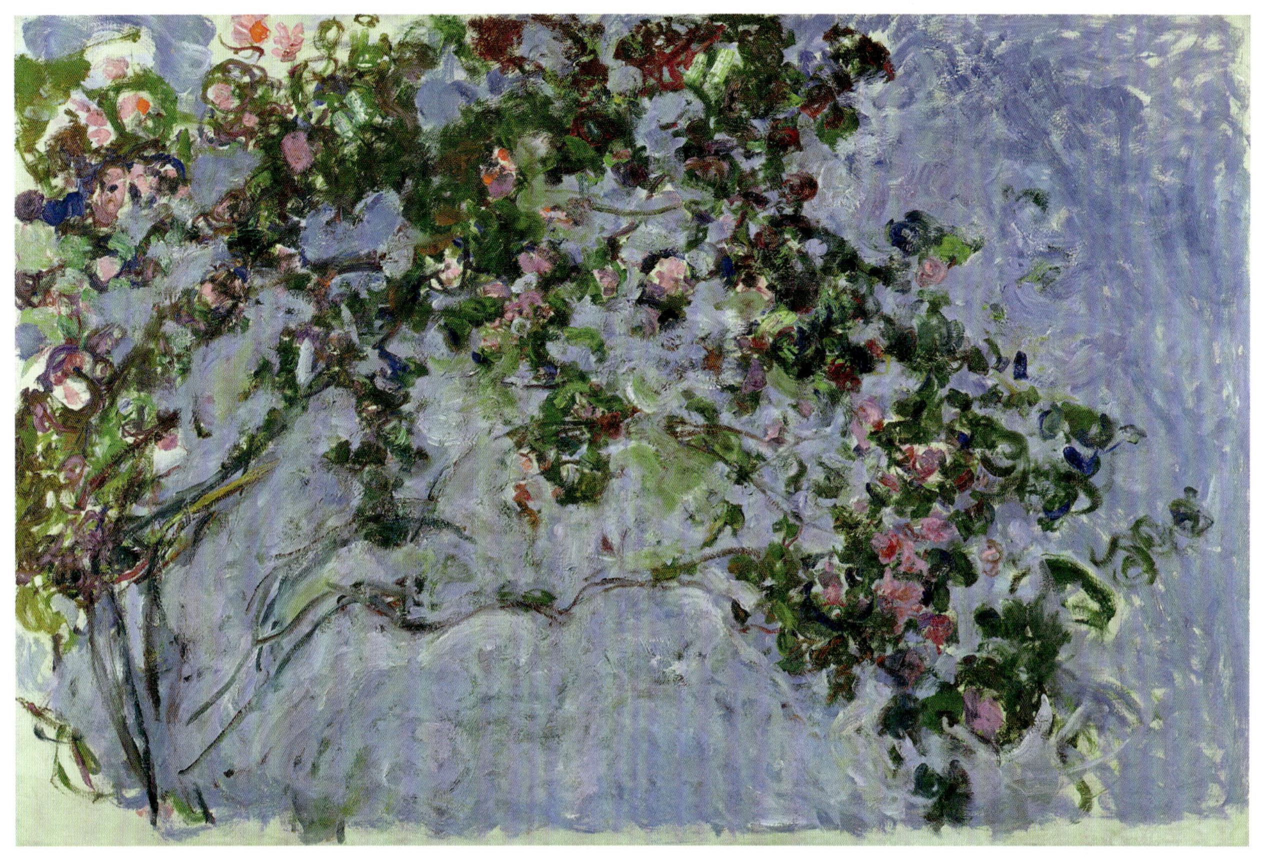

The Roses   Die Rosen   As Rosas

Les Roses   Las rosas   De rozen

CLAUDE MONET (1840-1926)

1925/26, Oil on canvas/Huile sur toile, 130 × 200 cm, Musée Marmottan Monet, Paris

Nympheas (Water Lilies)

Monet painted his first water lily pictures in 1893. More than 250 paintings with the motif are listed in the catalog of works. One of his most famous works is the Panorama, which he created for the Musée de l'Orangerie.

Nymphéas

Monet peint ses premiers *Nymphéas* en 1893. Le catalogue raisonné de l'artiste fait état de plus deux cent cinquante œuvres sur ce sujet qui l'obsèdera jusqu'au grand cycle décoratif de l'Orangerie, à Paris.

Seerosen

Seine ersten Seerosenbilder malt Monet 1893. Im Werksverzeichnis sind mehr als 250 Arbeiten mit dem Motiv aufgelistet. Zu den bekanntesten Werken gehört das Panorama, das er für das Musée de l'Orangerie schuf.

Nenúfares

Monet pintó sus primeros nenúfares en 1893. El catálogo del artista incluye más de doscientas cincuenta obras sobre este tema, que le obsesionarán hasta el gran ciclo decorativo que creó para el Museo de l'Orangerie.

Lírios de água

Monet pintou seus primeiros quadros de lírios de água em 1893. Mais de 250 obras com o motivo estão listadas no catálogo de obras. Uma de suas obras mais famosas é o Panorama, que ele criou para o Musée de l'Orangerie.

Waterlelies

Monet schilderde zijn eerste waterlelies in 1893. Meer dan 250 werken met dit ondewerp zijn opgenomen in zijn oeuvrecatalogus. Een van zijn bekendste is het panorama dat hij maakte voor het Musée de l'Orangerie.

CLAUDE MONET (1840-1926)

1916-19, Oil on canvas/Huile sur toile, 150 × 197 cm, Musée Marmottan Monet, Paris

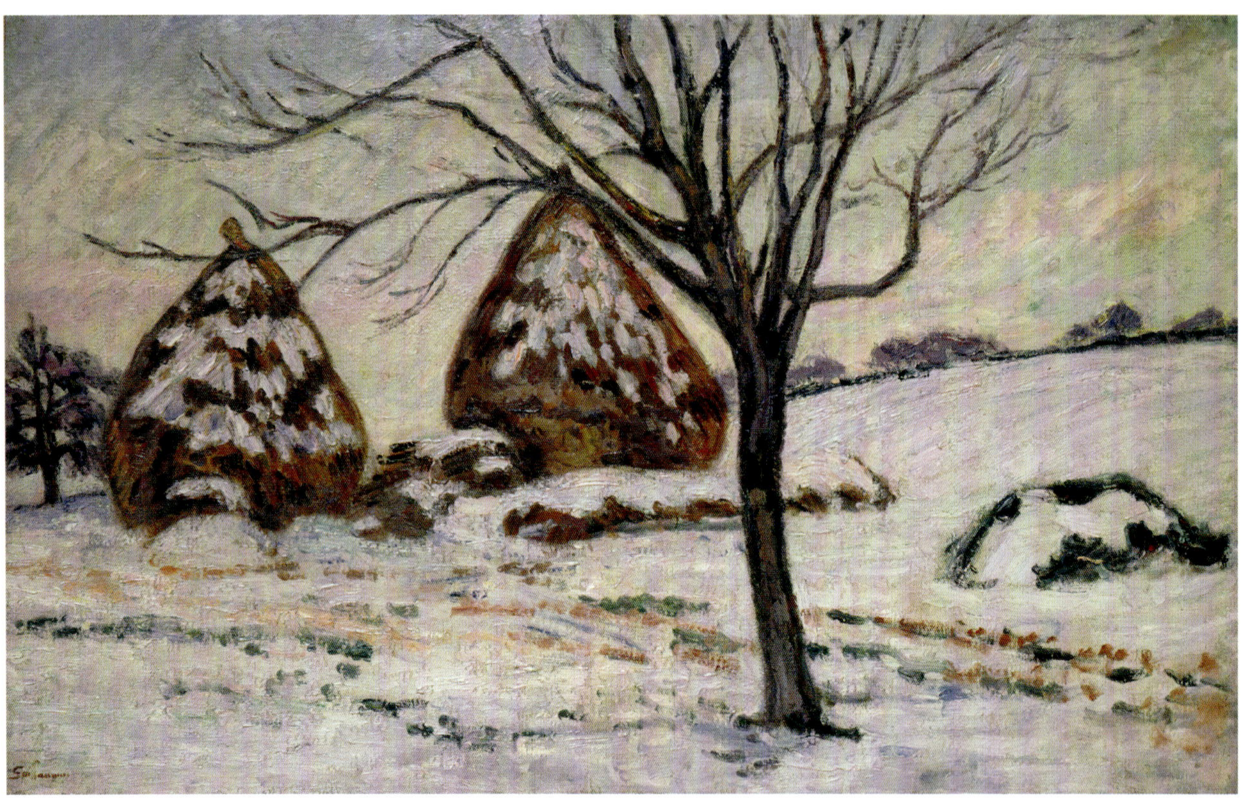

Haystacks in winter at Palaiseau

Armand Guillaumin is one of the rather unknown Impressionists, but he was an outstanding artist with a lively palette of colors. He painted the surroundings of Paris and the landscapes in the Département Creuse.

Les Meules en hiver à Palaiseau

Figure discrète du mouvement impressionniste, Armand Guillaumin n'en demeure pas moins un excellent artiste, à la palette vive. Il a peint les environs de Paris, mais surtout les paysages de la Creuse.

ARMAND GUILLAUMIN (1841-1927)

1898, Oil on canvas/Huile sur toile, 35,3 × 51,7 cm, Private collection

Palaiseau, Heuschober im Schnee

Armand Guillaumin zählt zu den eher unbekannten Impressionisten, war jedoch ein herausragender Künstler mit einer lebhaften Farbpalette. Er malte die Umgebung von Paris und die Landschaften im Département Creuse.

Palaiseau, granero en la nieve

Armand Guillaumin es uno de los impresionistas más desconocidos, pero fue un artista excepcional con una paleta de colores muy viva. Pinta los alrededores de París y los paisajes del departamento de Creuse.

Palaiseau, celeiro na neve

Armand Guillaumin é um dos impressionistas bastante desconhecidos, mas era um artista excepcional com uma paleta de cores vivas. Ele pintou os arredores de Paris e as paisagens no Département Creuse.

Palaiseau, hooibergen in de sneeuw

Armand Guillaumin is een tamelijk onbekende impressionist, maar hij was een voortreffelijk schilder met een levendig kleurenpalet. Hij schilderde de omgeving van Parijs en de landschappen in het departement Creuse.

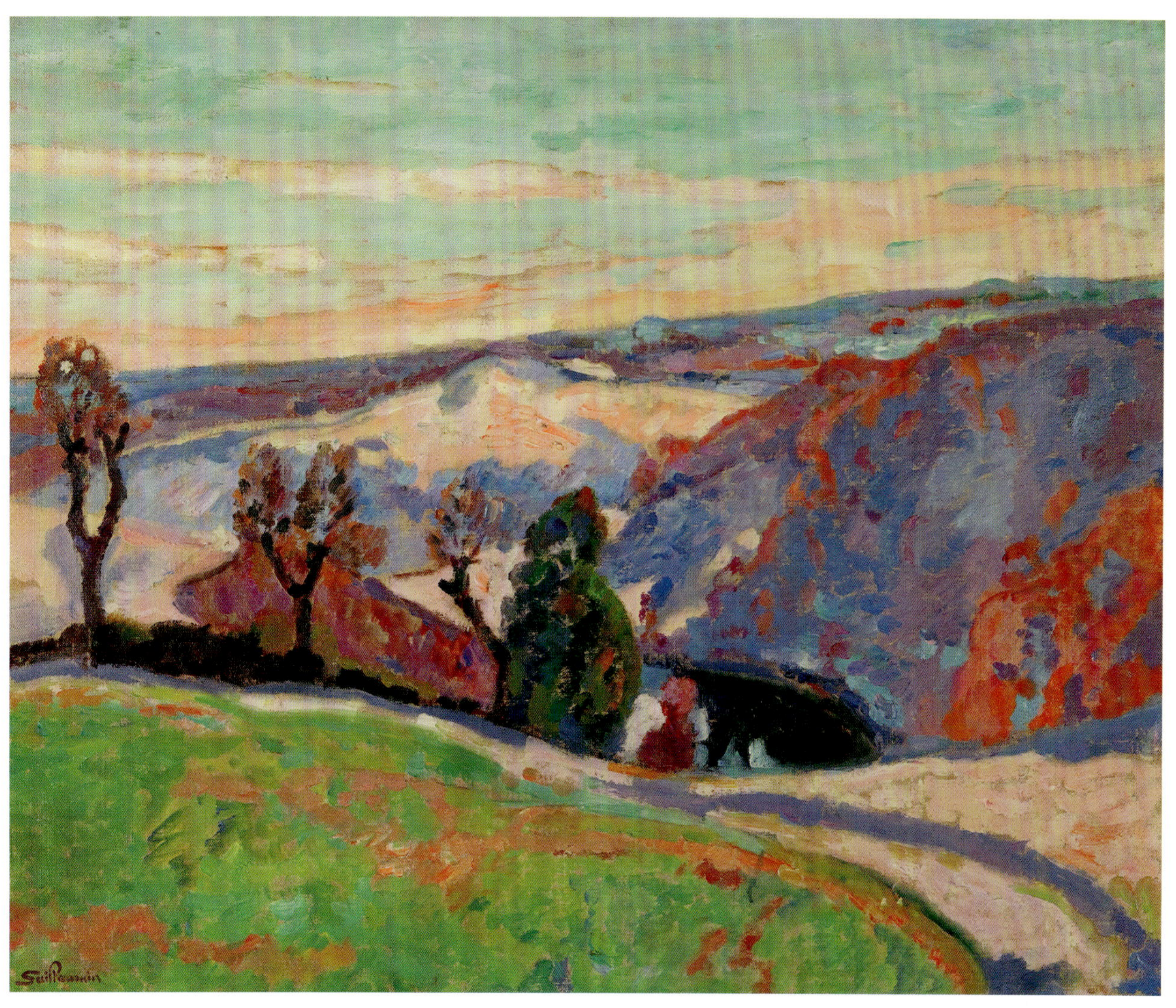

Puy Barriou and the Valley of the Creuse

Puy Barriou et la vallée de la Creuse

Der Puy Barriou und das Tal der Creuse

El Puy Barriou y el Valle de Creuse

O Puy Barriou e o Creuse Valley

De Puy Barriou en het dal van de Creuse

ARMAND GUILLAUMIN (1841-1927)

c. 1915, Oil on canvas/Huile sur toile, 60 × 73 cm,
Musée Marmottan Monet, Paris

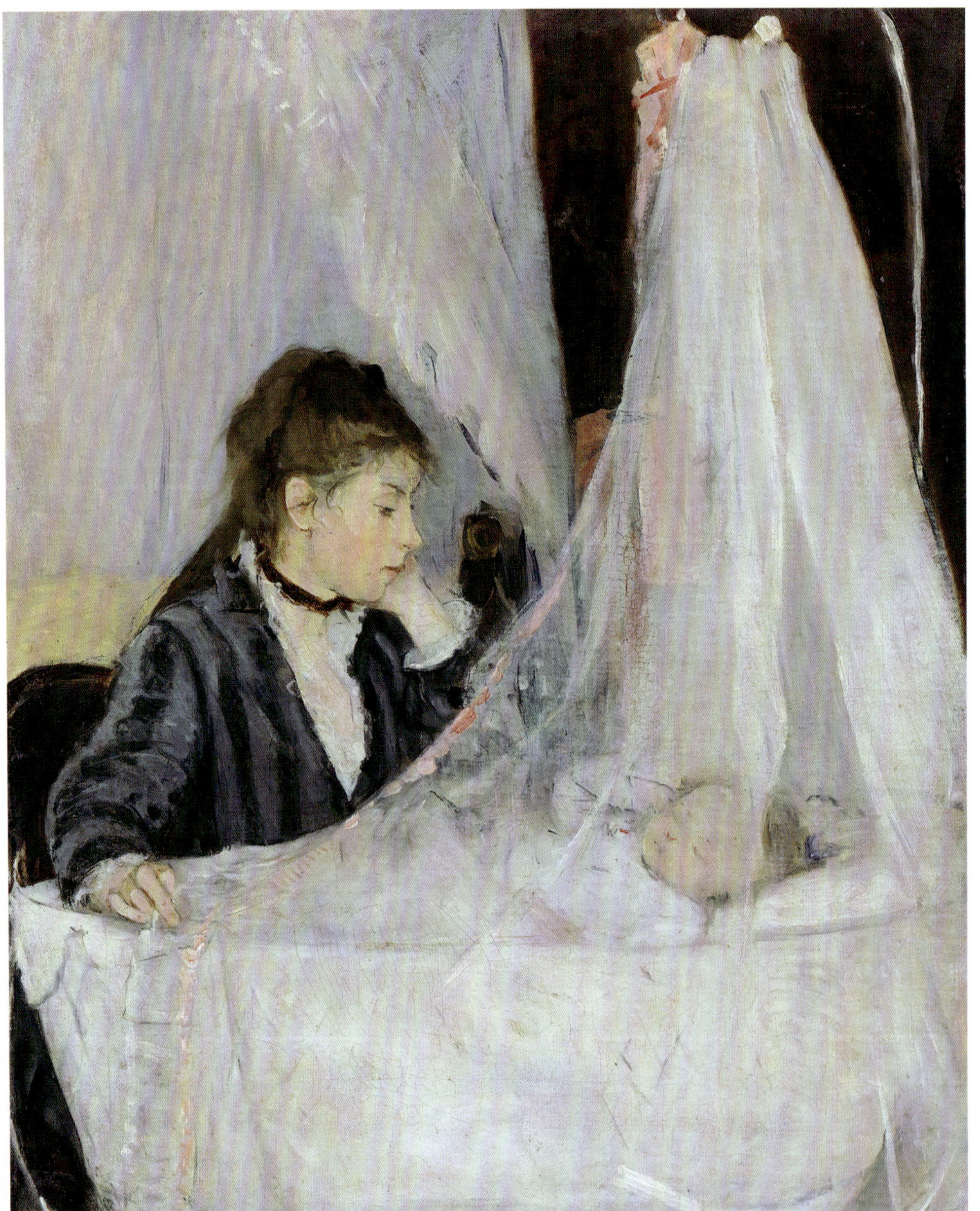

The Cradle
The artist's sister looks tenderly at her sleeping daughter. The painting is one of Morisot's most famous works. It was the prelude to a long series on motherhood.

Le Berceau
De profil, la sœur de l'artiste regarde avec tendresse sa petite fille endormie. Ce tableau, l'un des plus célèbres de Berthe Morisot, est le premier d'une longue série d'œuvres autour de la maternité.

Die Wiege
Zärtlich betrachtet die Schwester der Künstlerin ihre schlafende Tochter. Das Gemälde gehört zu den bekanntesten Werken Morisots. Es wurde der Auftakt zu einer langen Serie über Mutterschaft.

La cuna
La hermana del artista mira tiernamente a su hija dormida. El cuadro es una de las obras más famosas de Morisot. Fue el preludio de una larga serie sobre la maternidad.

O berço
A irmã do artista olha ternamente para a sua filha adormecida. A pintura é uma das obras mais famosas de Morisot. Foi o prelúdio de uma longa série sobre maternidade.

De wieg
De zus van de schilderes kijkt vertederd naar haar slapende dochter. Het is een van Morisots bekendste werken. Het was de opmaat tot een lange serie schilderijen over het moederschap.

BERTHE MORISOT (1841-1895)
1872, Oil on canvas/Huile sur toile, 56 × 46 cm, Musée d'Orsay, Paris

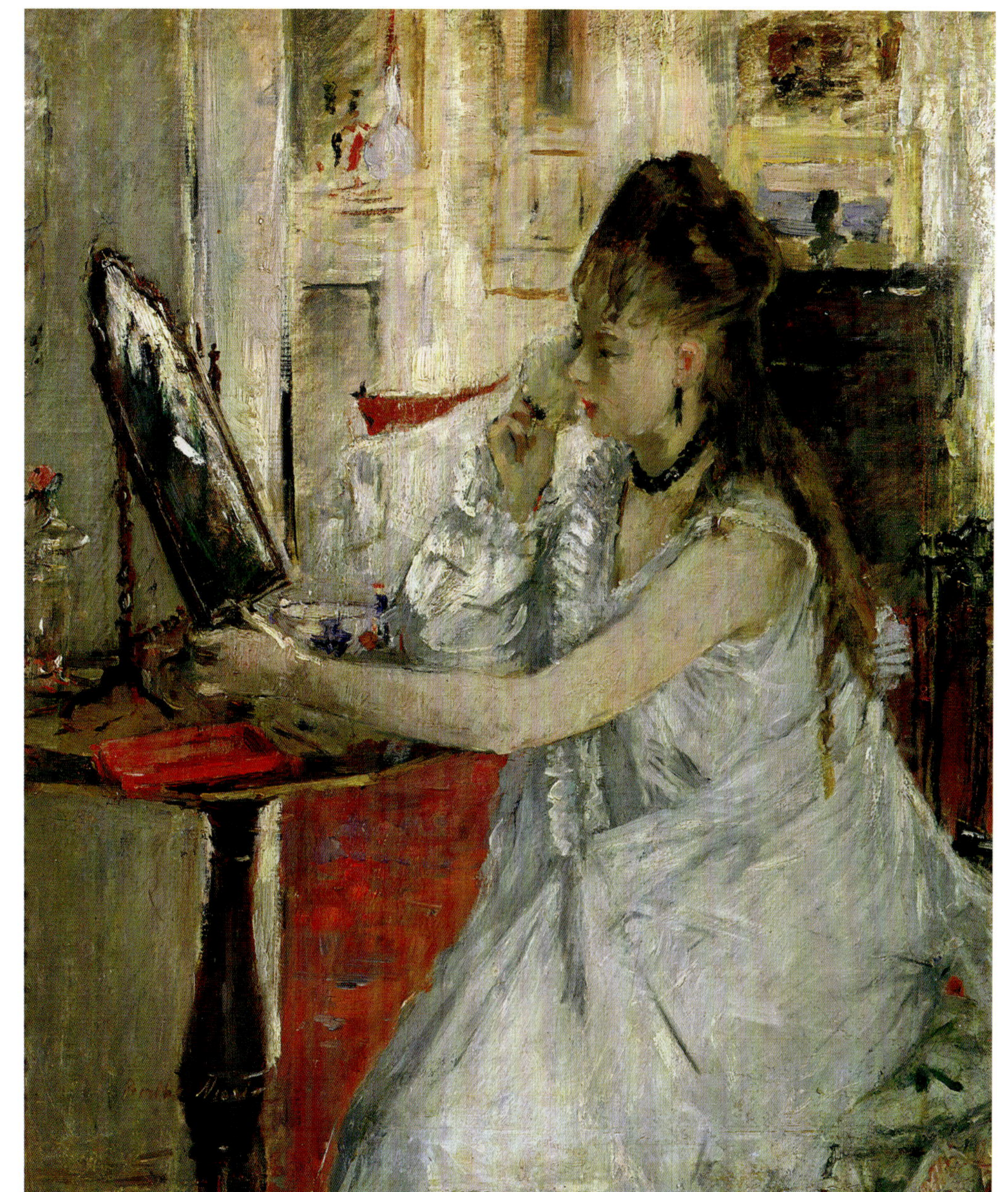

Young Woman
Powdering her Face

Jeune femme se poudrant

Junge Frau, sich pudernd

Mujer joven, empolvándose

Jovem mulher,
empoeirando-se

Jonge vrouw die haar
gezicht poedert

BERTHE MORISOT (1841-1895)

1877, Oil on canvas/
Huile sur toile, 46 × 39 cm,
Musée Marmottan Monet, Paris

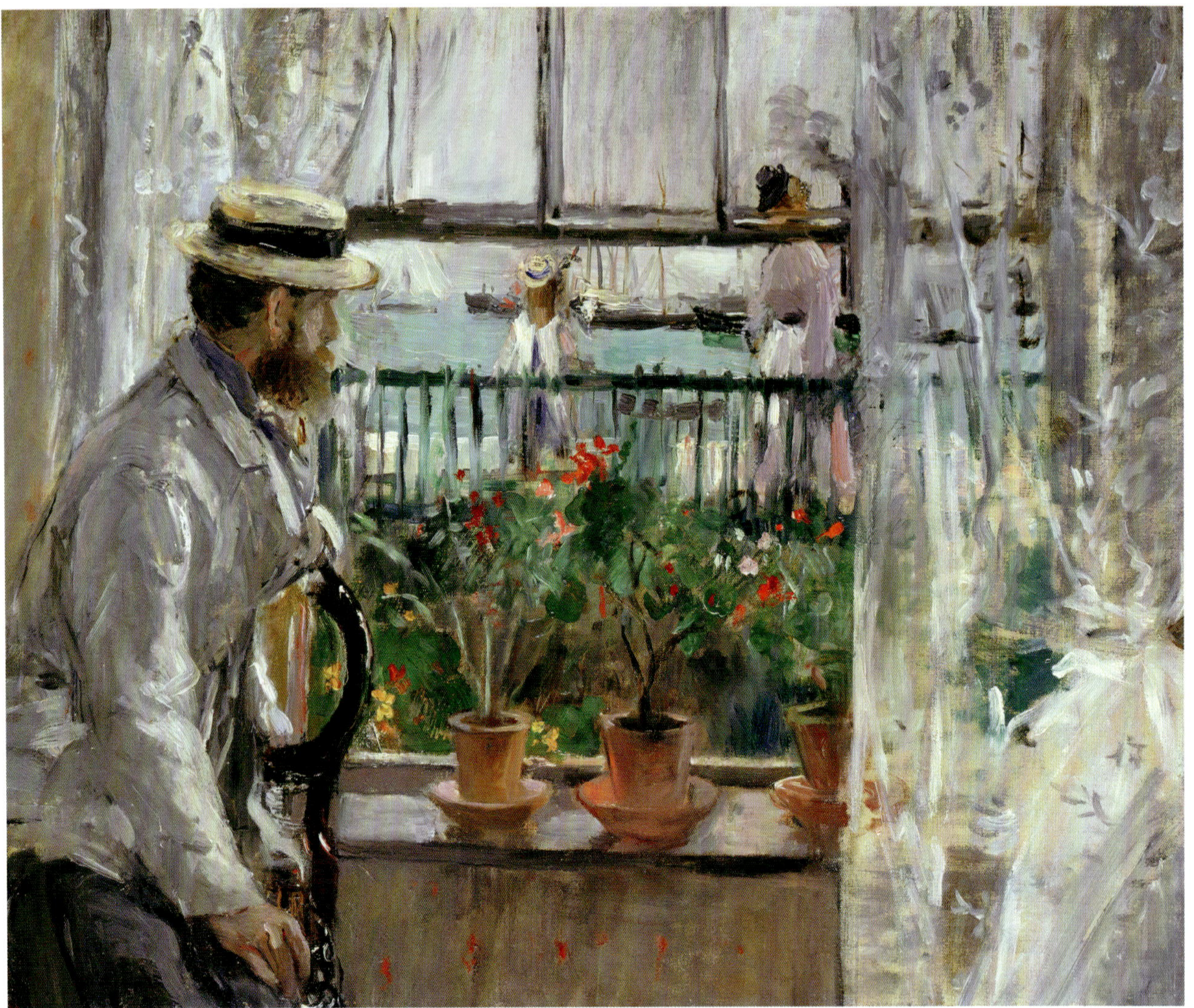

Eugène Manet on the Isle of Wight

Morisot depicted her husband Eugène Manet, Édouard's brother, in a complex composition structured by successive levels: Interior, garden, people, sea and the sailing boats on the horizon.

Eugène Manet à l'île de Wight

Berthe Morisot peint son époux Eugène Manet, frère d'Édouard. Complexe, la composition est structurée en plans successifs, l'intérieur, le jardin, les personnages, la mer et les voiliers à l'horizon.

Eugène Manet auf der Isle of Wight

Morisot bildet ihren Ehemann Eugène Manet, den Bruder von Édouard, in einer komplexen Komposition ab, die durch aufeinanderfolgende Ebenen strukturiert ist: Innenraum, Garten, Personen, Meer und die Segelboote am Horizont.

Eugène Manet en la Isla de Wight

Morisot representa a su marido Eugène Manet, hermano de Édouard, en una compleja composición estructurada por niveles sucesivos: interior, jardín, gente, mar y los veleros en el horizonte.

Eugène Manet na Ilha de Wight

Morisot retrata seu marido Eugène Manet, irmão de Édouard, em uma complexa composição estruturada por níveis sucessivos: Interior, jardim, pessoas, mar e barcos à vela no horizonte.

Eugène Manet op het Isle of Wight

Morisot schilderde hier haar man Eugène Manet, de broer van Édouard, in een complexe compositie, die is opgebouwd uit opeenvolgende niveaus: interieur, tuin, mensen, zee en de zeilboten aan de horizon.

BERTHE MORISOT (1841-1895)

1875, Oil on canvas/Huile sur toile, 38 × 46 cm, Musée Marmottan Monet, Paris

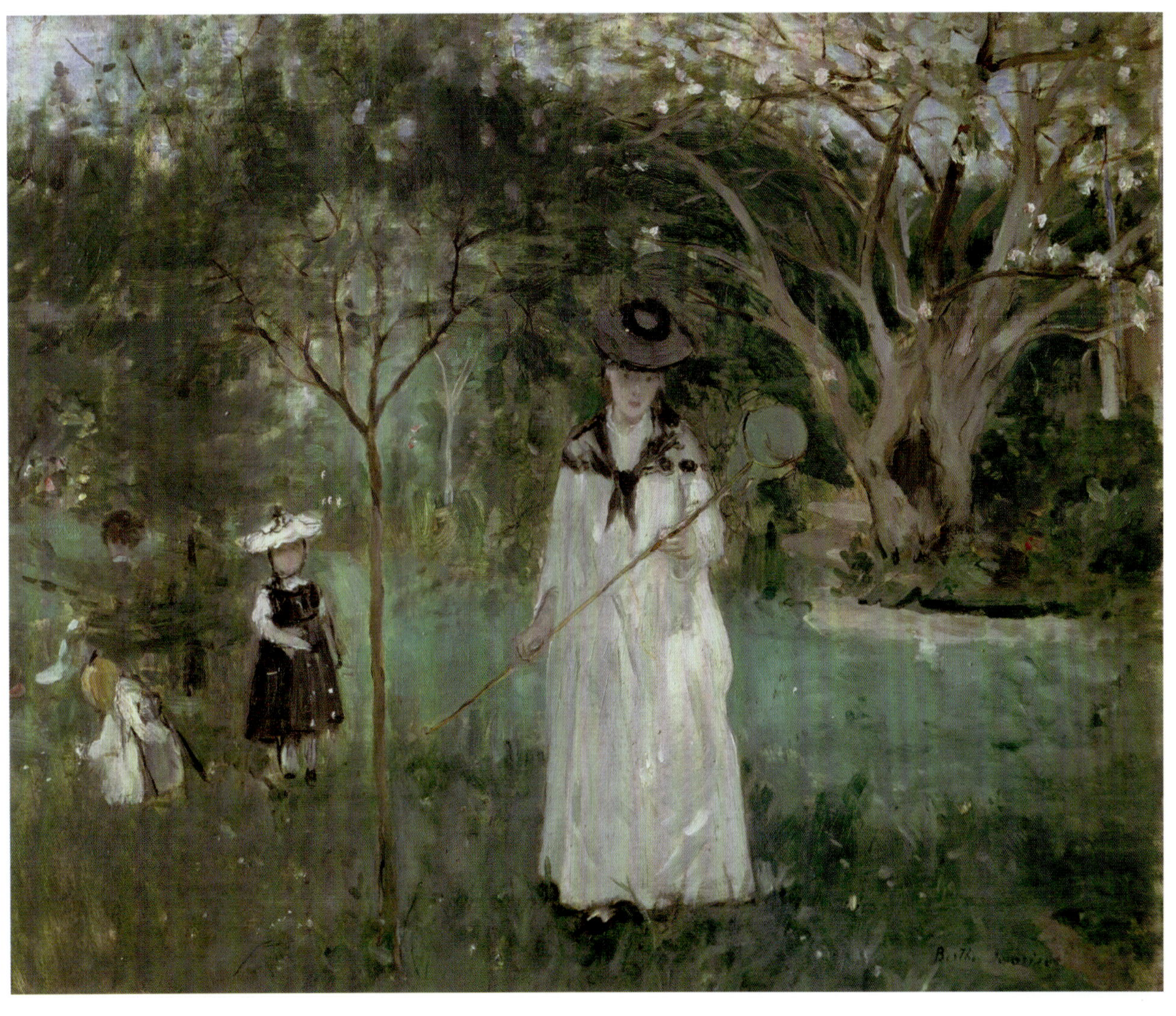

The Butterfly Hunt

La Chasse aux papillons

Die Schmetterlingsjagd

La caza de mariposas

A caça às borboletas

De vlinderjacht

BERTHE MORISOT (1841-1895)

1874, Oil on canvas/Huile sur toile, 46 × 56 cm,
Musée d'Orsay, Paris

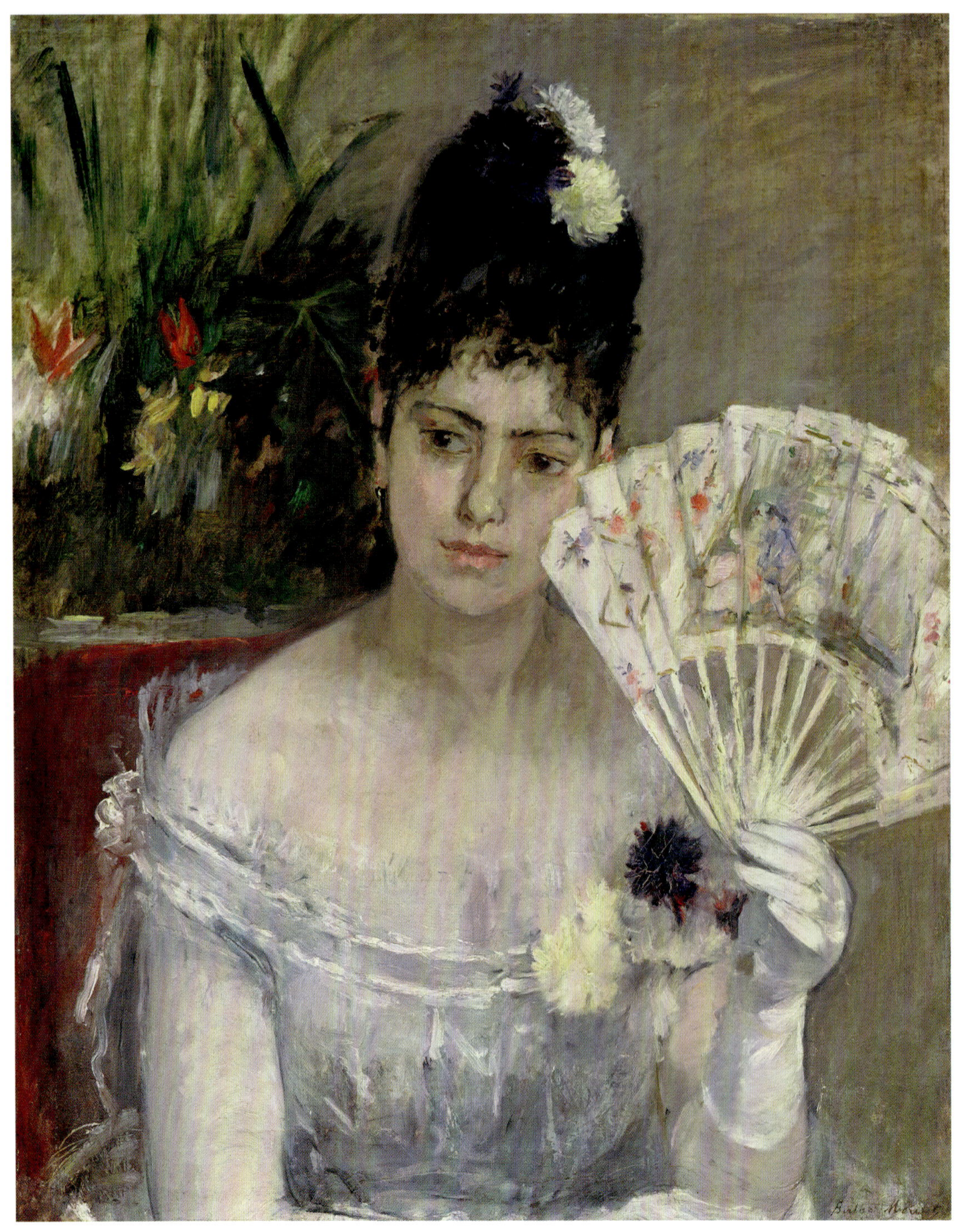

At the Ball

Au bal

Auf dem Ball

En el baile

No baile

Op het bal

**BERTHE MORISOT
(1841-1895)**
1875, Oil on
canvas/Huile sur
toile, 62 × 52 cm,
Musée Marmottan
Monet, Paris

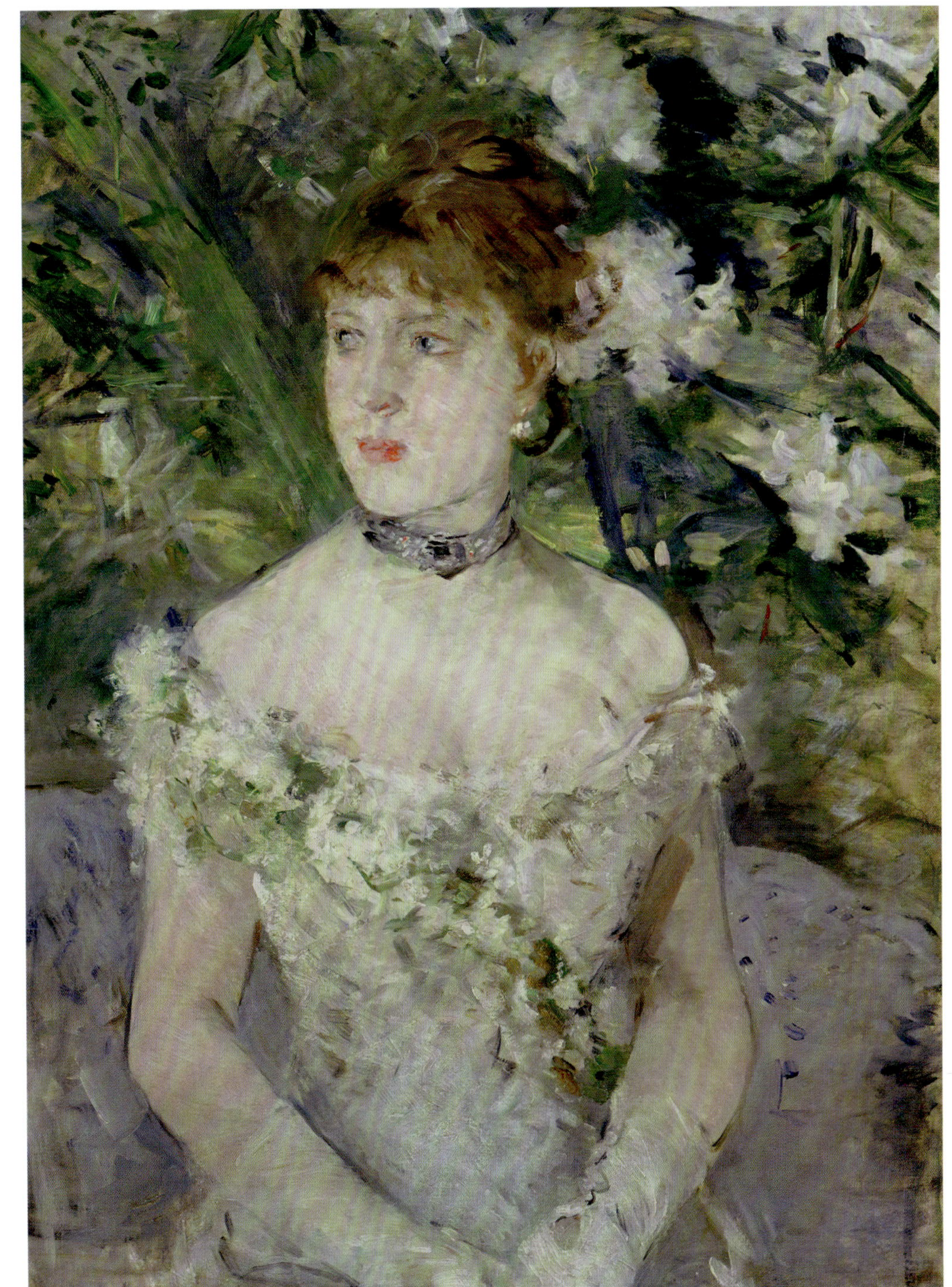

Young Girl in a Ball Gown

**Jeune Femme
en toilette de bal**

Junge Frau im Ballkleid

**Mujer joven con
vestido de baile**

**Jovem mulher com um
vestido de baile**

Jonge vrouw in een baljurk

BERTHE MORISOT (1841-1895)
1879, Oil on canvas/Huile sur toile,
71 × 54 cm, Musée d'Orsay, Paris

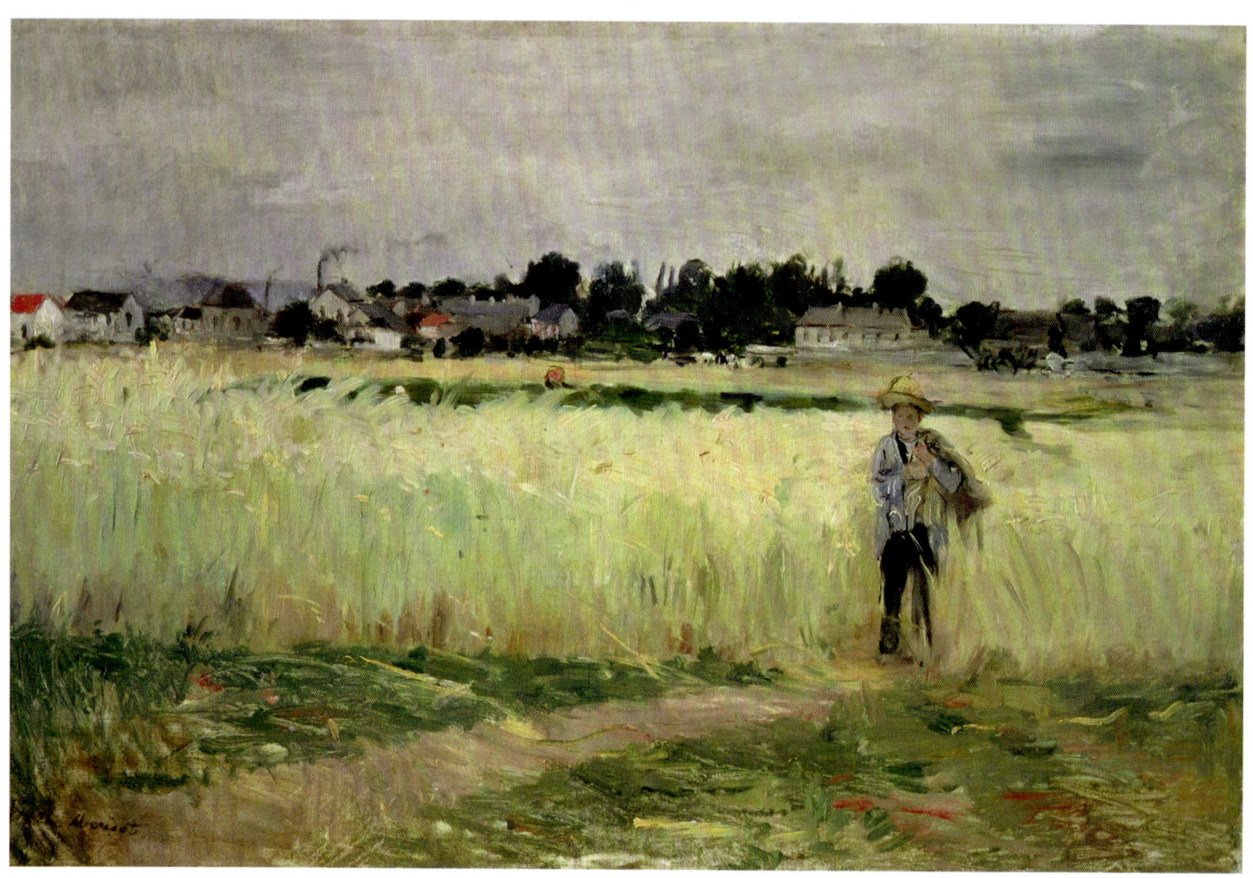

In the Wheatfield at Gennevilliers

Starting from an ordinary landscape, Morisot demonstrates her finely tuned palette of colors, with which she immerses the wheat field in golden shades. A solitary figure enlivens the homage to nature.

Dans les blés

À partir d'un simple paysage rural, Berthe Morisot parvient à envoûter par la délicatesse de sa palette, et les tonalités dorées du champ de blé. Une figure solitaire vient animer cet hymne à la nature.

Im Weizenfeld bei Gennevilliers

Ausgehend von einer gewöhnlichen Landschaft, stellt Morisot ihre fein abgestimmte Farbpalette unter Beweis, mit der sie das Weizenfeld in goldene Schattierungen taucht. Eine Figur belebt die Hommage an die Natur.

En el campo de trigo cerca de Gennevilliers

Partiendo de un paisaje ordinario, Morisot muestra su paleta de colores delicadamente afinada, con la que sumerge el campo de trigo en tonalidades doradas. Una figura anima el homenaje a la naturaleza.

No campo de trigo perto de Gennevilliers

Partindo de uma paisagem comum, Morisot demonstra sua paleta de cores finamente afinadas, com as quais imerge o campo de trigo em tons dourados. Uma figura anima a homenagem à natureza.

In het tarweveld nabij Gennevilliers

Uitgaand van een gewoon landschap toont Morisot hier haar fijn afgestemde kleurenpalet, waarmee ze het tarweveld in gouden schaduwen dompelt. Een figuur verlevendigt dit eerbetoon aan de natuur.

BERTHE MORISOT (1841-1895)

1875, Oil on canvas/Huile sur toile, 46,5 × 69 cm, Musée d'Orsay, Paris

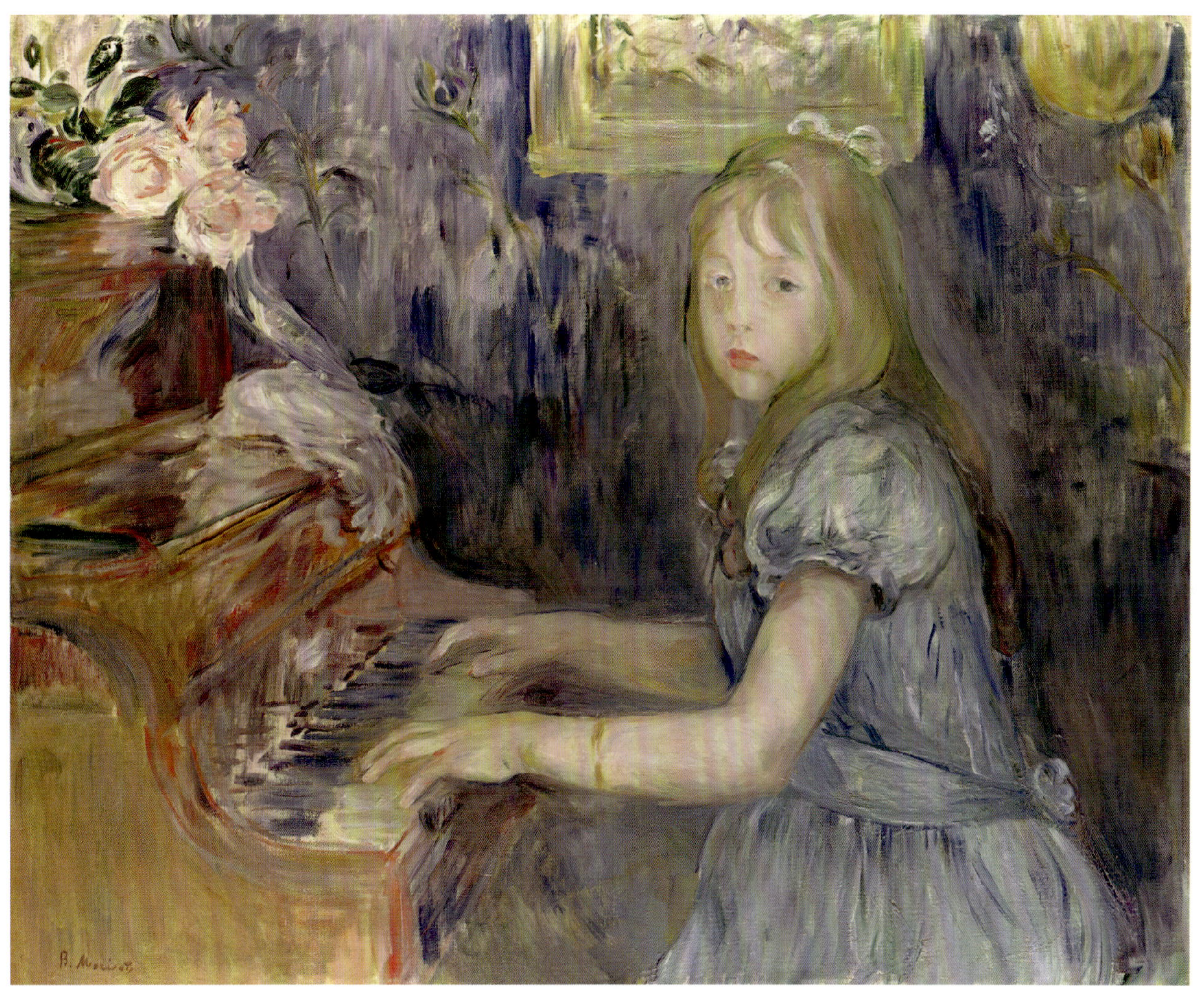

Lucie Léon at the Piano

Lucie Léon au piano

Lucie Léon am Klavier

Lucie Léon al piano

Lucie Léon ao piano

Lucie Léon aan de piano

BERTHE MORISOT (1841-1895)

1892, Oil on canvas/Huile sur toile, 65 × 80 cm, Private collection

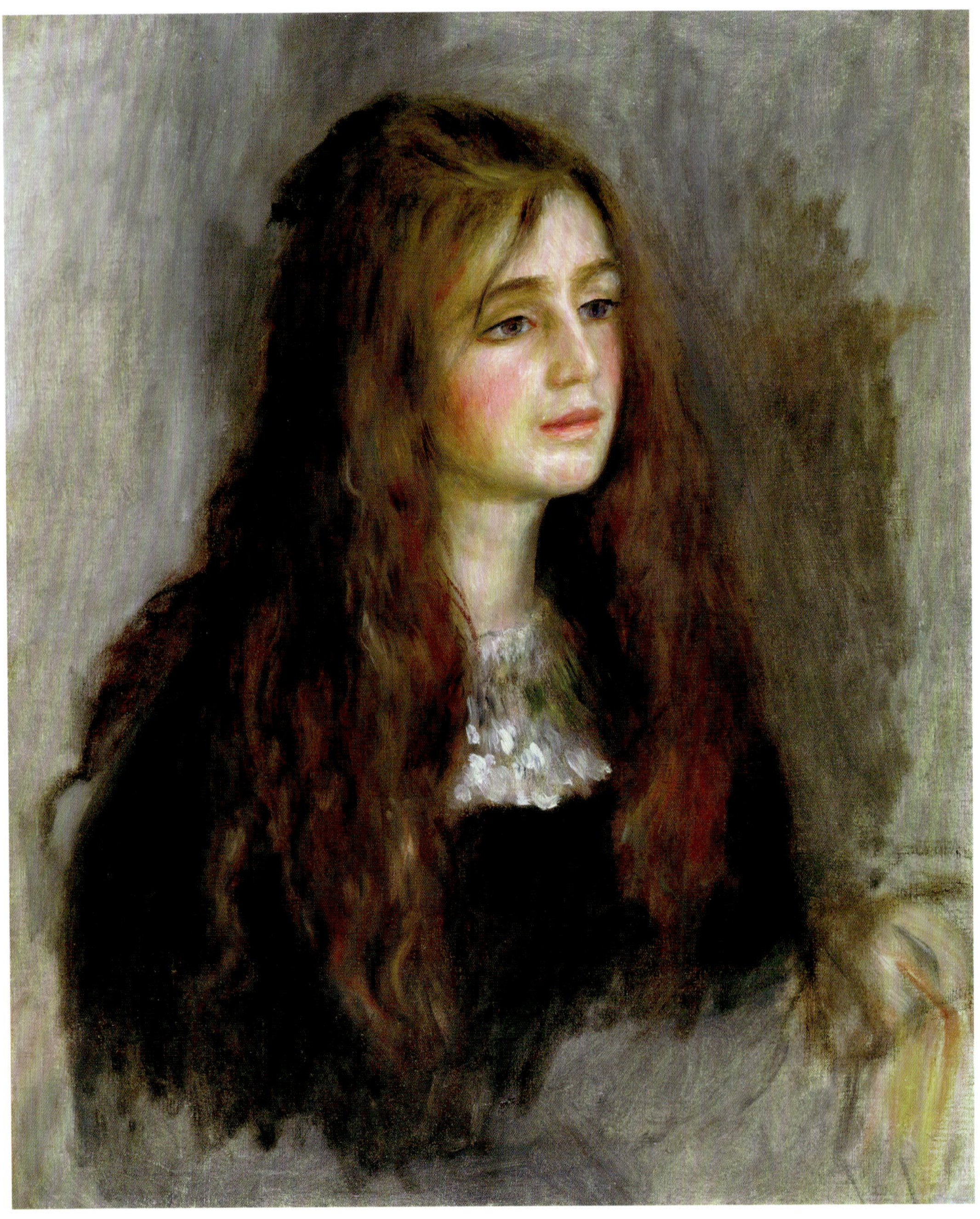

Julie Manet

AUGUSTE RENOIR
(1841-1919)
1894, Oil on canvas/
Huile sur toile,
55 × 46 cm, Musée
Marmottan Monet, Paris

270

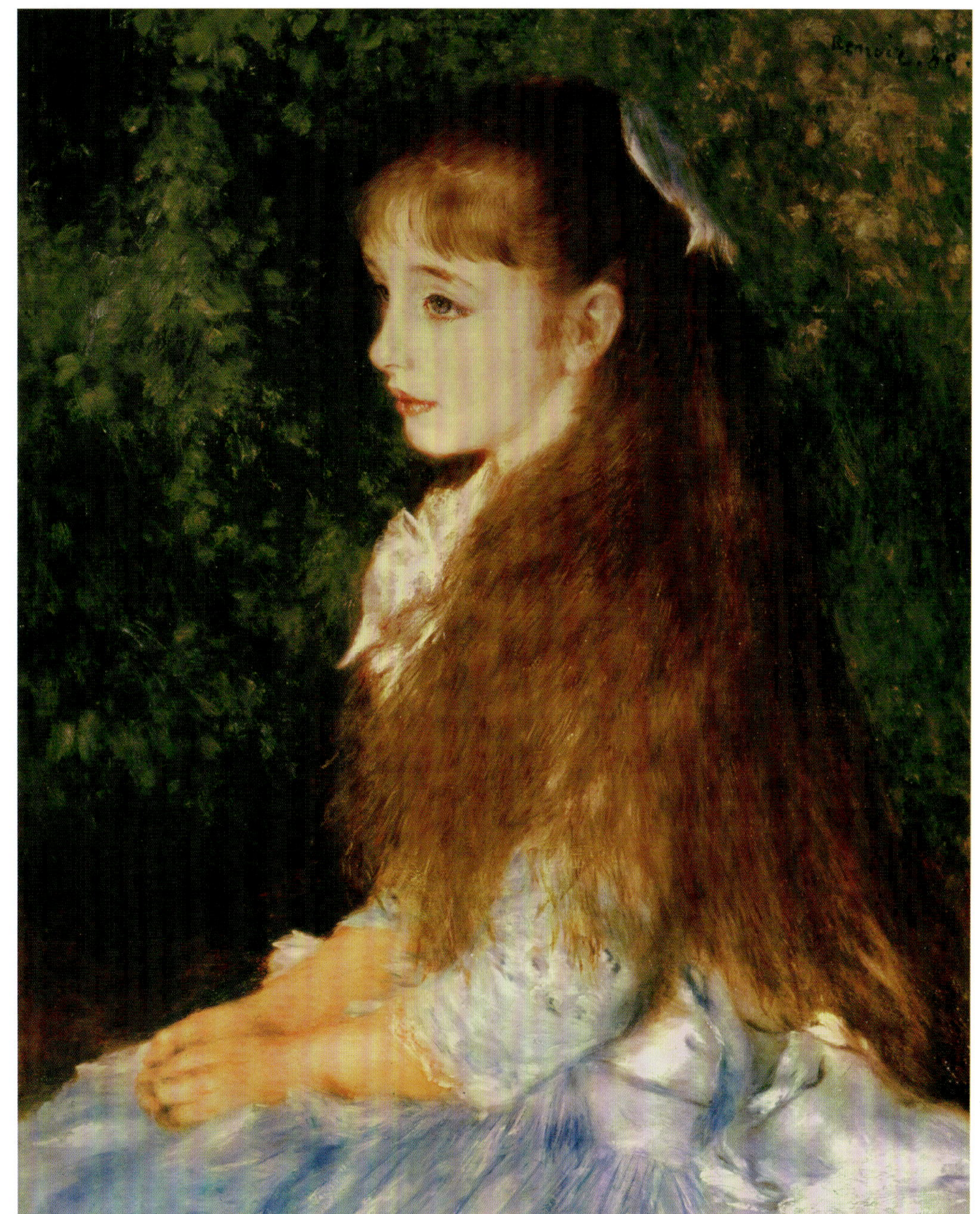

Irène Cahen d'Anvers

AUGUSTE RENOIR
(1841-1919)
1880, Oil on canvas/
Huile sur toile,
65 × 54 cm, Foundation
E.G. Bührle, Zürich

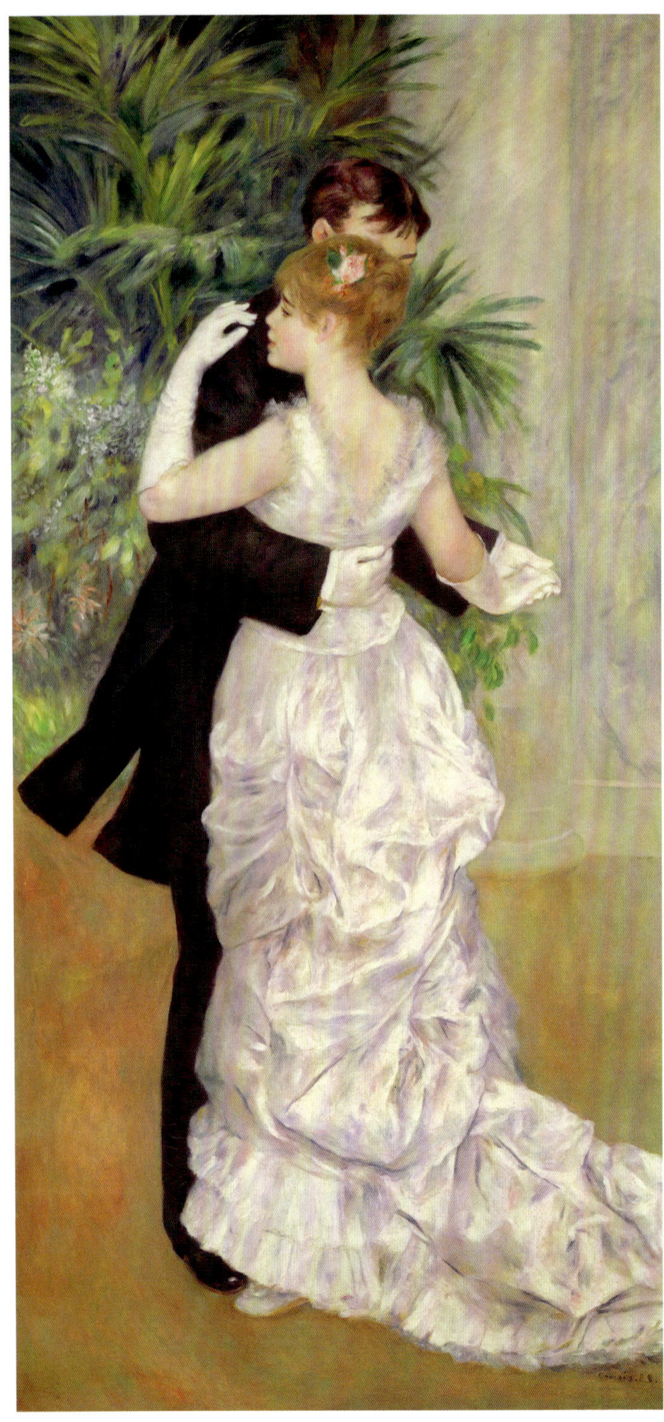

Dance in the City

Danse à la ville

Tanz in der Stadt

Baile en la ciudad

Dança na cidade

Dans in de stad

AUGUSTE RENOIR (1841-1919)

1883, Oil on canvas/Huile sur toile,
180 × 90 cm, Musée d'Orsay, Paris

A Dance in the Country

Both paintings belong to a series. They represent
two kinds of dancing entertainment. One in the
upmarket surroundings of a salon, the other in a
more relaxed atmosphere in the country.

Danse à la campagne

Ces deux tableaux ont été pensés comme des
pendants. S'y opposent deux manières de s'adonner
aux plaisirs de la danse, dans le cadre feutré d'un
salon, ou, de façon plus décontractée, à la campagne.

Tanz auf dem Land

Beide Gemälde gehören zu einer Serie. Sie stellen
zwei Arten des Tanzvergnügens dar. Das eine in der
gehobenen Umgebung eines Salons, das andere in
einer lockereren Atmosphäre auf dem Land.

Baile en el campo

Ambas pinturas pertenecen a una serie. Representan
dos tipos de espectáculos de danza. Una en el
exclusivo entorno de un salón de belleza, la otra en
un ambiente más relajado en el campo.

Dança no país

Ambos os quadros pertencem a uma série. Eles
representam dois tipos de entretenimento de dança.
Um no ambiente sofisticado de um salão de beleza, o
outro em uma atmosfera mais relaxada no país.

Dans op het platteland

Beide schilderijen maken deel uit van een serie. Ze
vertegenwoordigen twee soorten dansvermaak. Het
een in de chique omgeving van een salon, het ander
in een ontspannener sfeer op het platteland.

1883, Oil on canvas/Huile sur toile,
180 × 90 cm, Musée d'Orsay, Paris

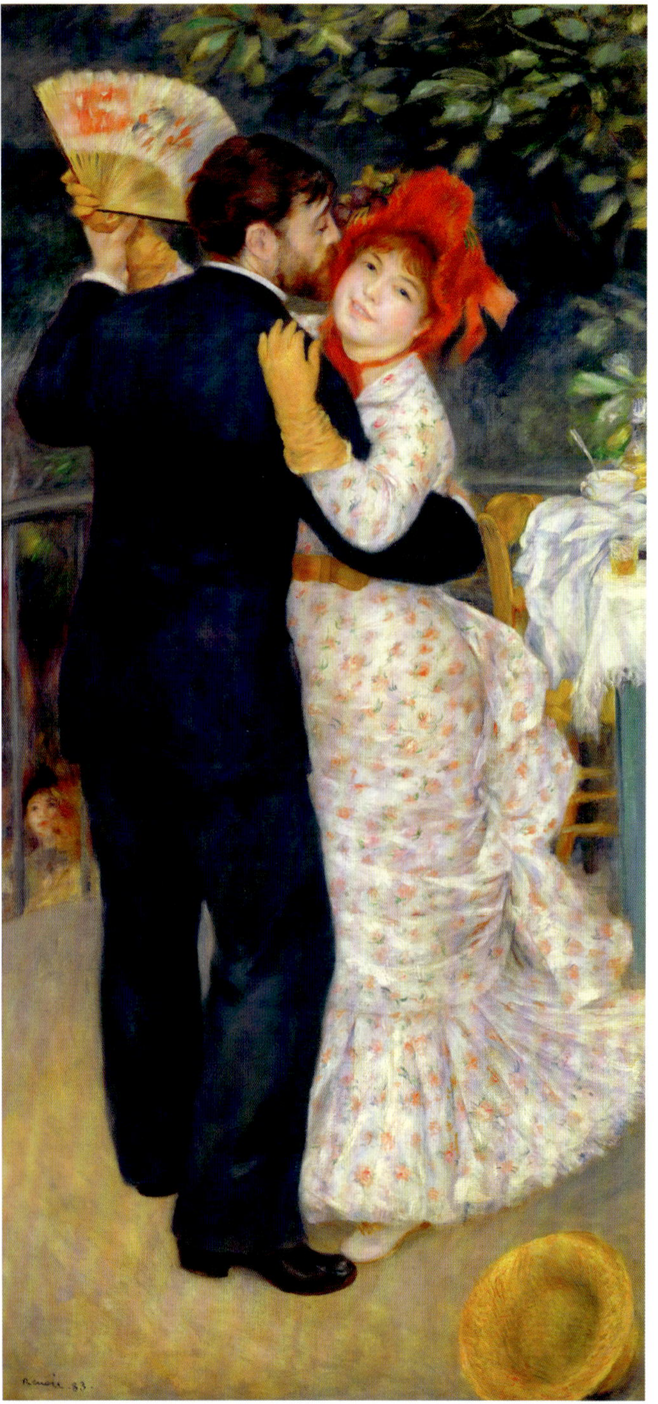

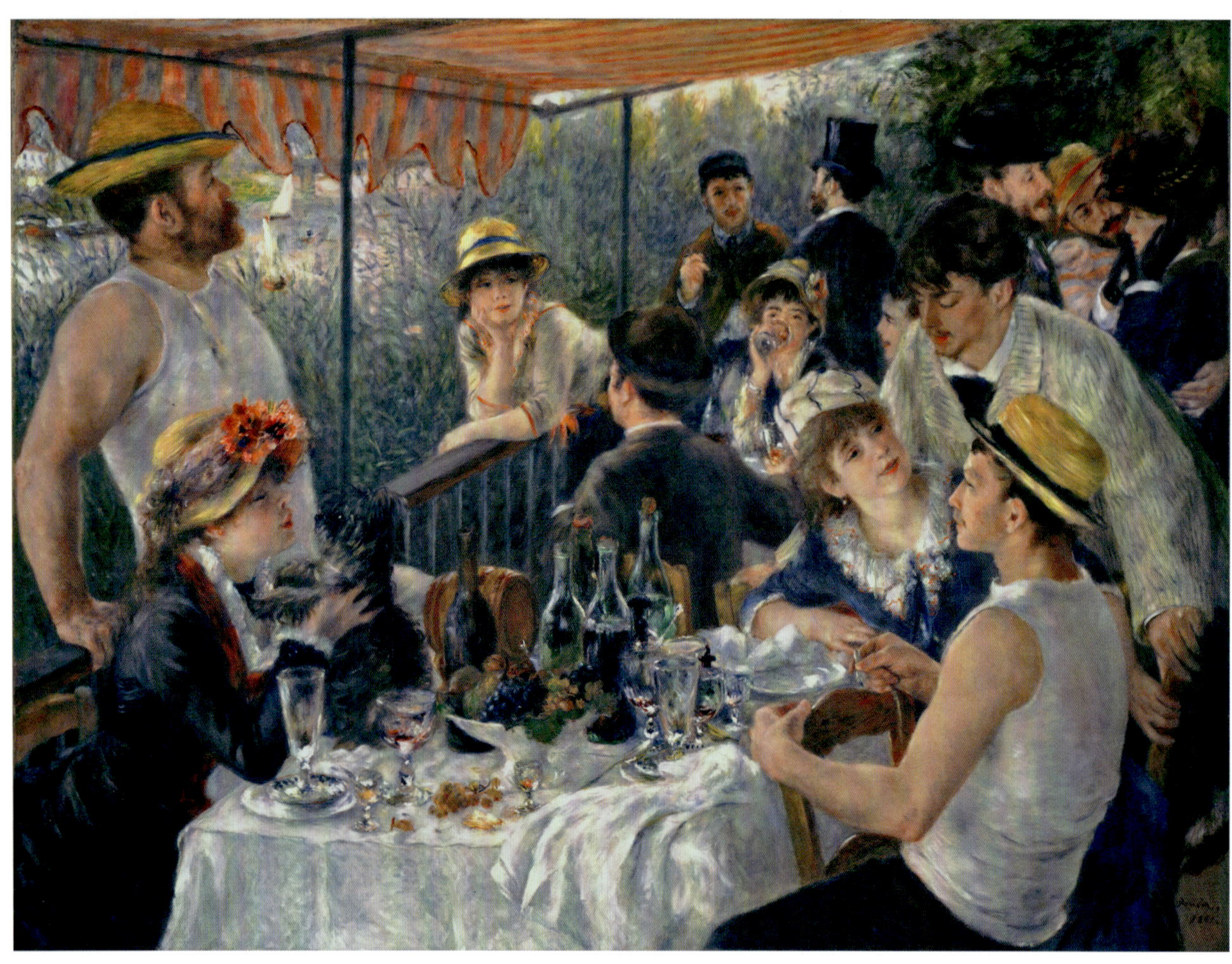

Luncheon of the Boating Party

Le Déjeuner des canotiers

Das Frühstück der Ruderer

El almuerzo de los remeros

Café da manhã dos remadores

De lunch van de roeiers

AUGUSTE RENOIR (1841-1919)

1880-1881, Oil on canvas/Huile sur toile,
130 × 173 cm, Private collection

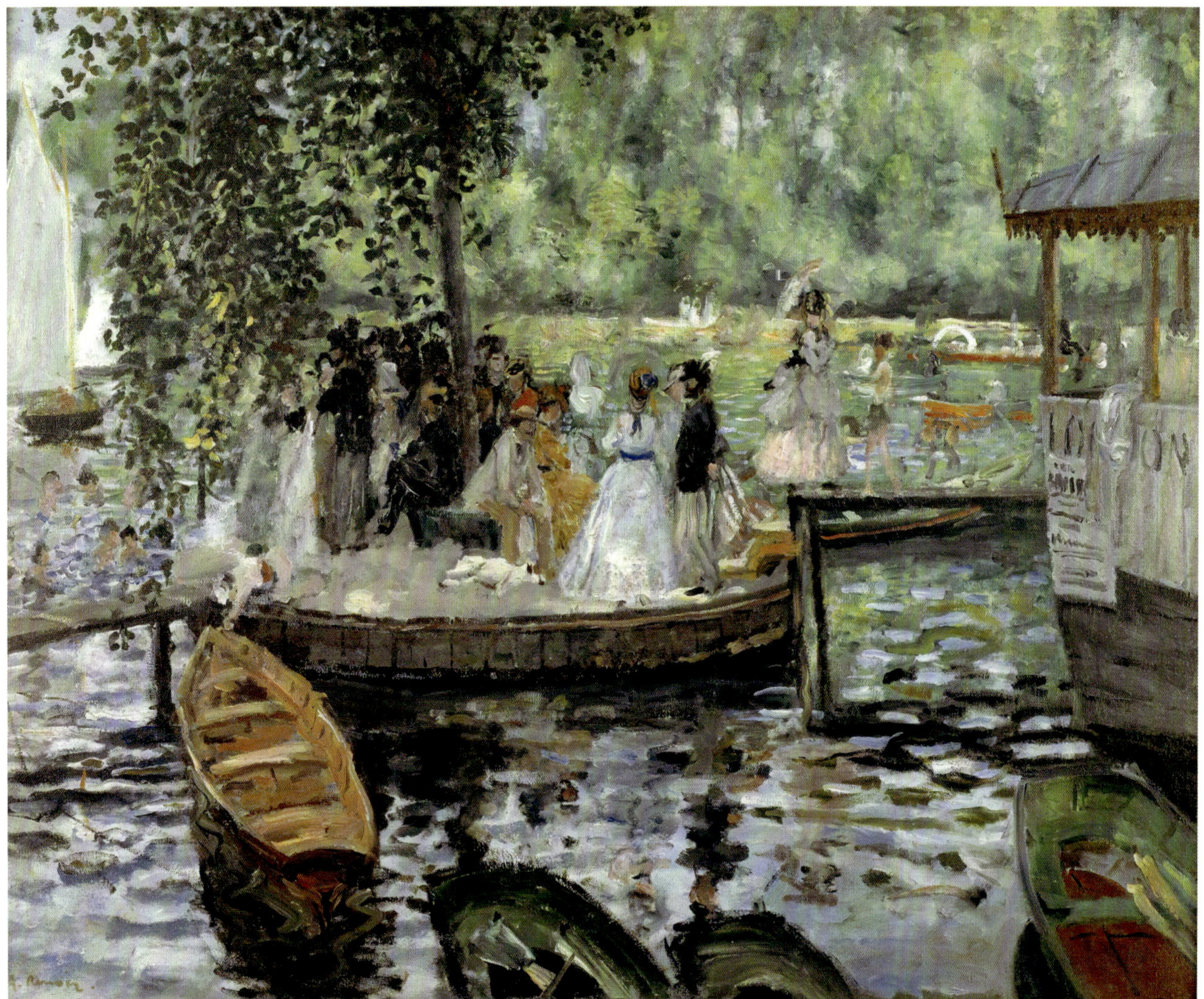

La Grenouillère

Five years before the birth of Impressionism (1874), this painting had all its characteristics. Renoir pays homage to plein air painting and outdoor pleasure with a light and short stroke.

La Grenouillère

Cinq ans avant la naissance de l'impressionnisme (première exposition en 1874), cette toile en a déjà toutes les caractéristiques. Elle célèbre les joies du plein air, dans une touche claire et fragmentée.

La Grenouillère

Das Gemälde weißt bereits fünf Jahre vor der Geburt des Impressionismus (1874) alle seine Charakteristika auf. Mit hellem und kurzem Strich huldigt Renoir der Pleinairmalerei und dem Vergnügen im Freien.

La Grenouillère

Cinco años antes del nacimiento del Impresionismo (1874), la pintura tenía todas sus características. Renoir rinde homenaje a la pintura al aire libre y al placer de la vida al aire libre con un trazo ligero y corto.

La Grenouillère

Cinco anos antes do nascimento do Impressionismo (1874), a pintura tinha todas as suas características. Renoir presta homenagem a plein pintura a ar puro e prazer ao ar livre com um leve e curto curso.

La Grenouillère

Vijf jaar voor het ontstaan van het impressionisme (1874) bezat dit schilderij al alle kenmerken daarvan. Renoir bracht met lichte en korte penseelstreken hulde aan het plein-airschilderen en de genoegens van het buitenleven.

AUGUSTE RENOIR (1841-1919)

1869, Oil on canvas/Huile sur toile, 66 × 81 cm, Nationalmuseum, Stockholm

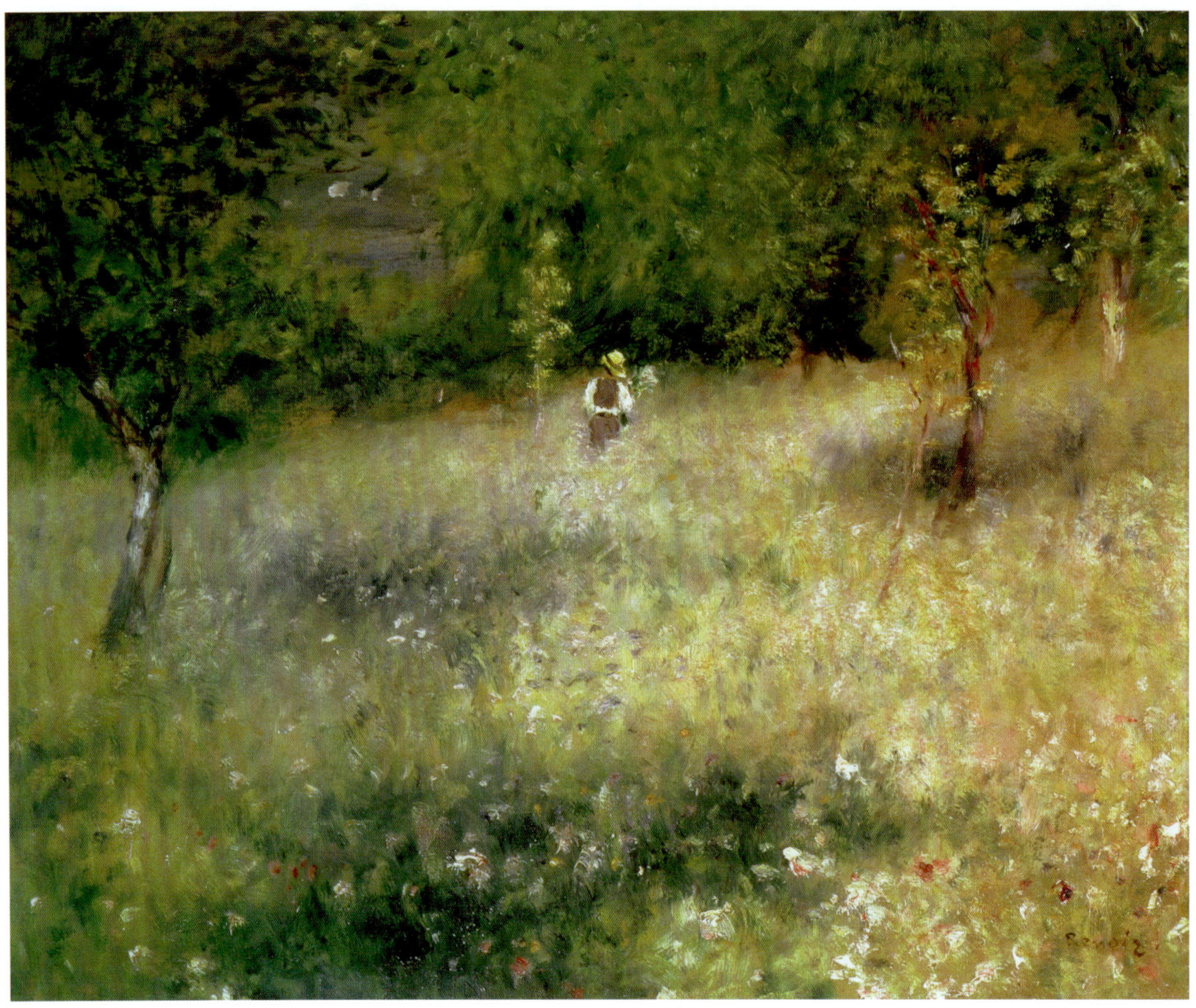

Spring at Chatou

Printemps à Chatou

Frühling in Chatou

Primavera en Chatou

Primavera em Chatou

Voorjaar in Chatou

AUGUSTE RENOIR (1841-1919)

c. 1872-75, Oil on canvas/Huile sur toile,

59 × 74 cm, Private collection

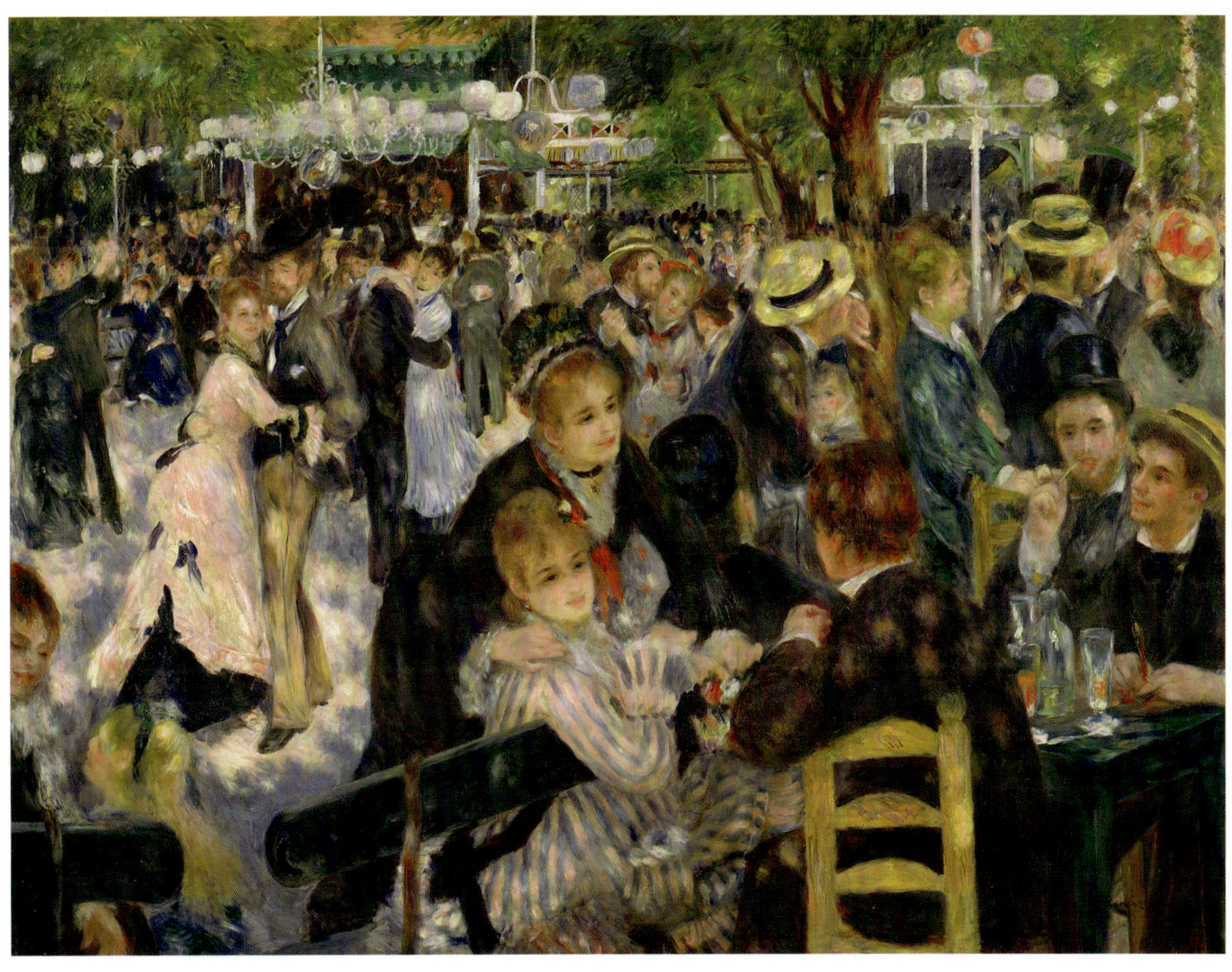

Ball at the Moulin de la Galette

The picture, painted with a lively and bright line, is one of the most famous by Auguste Renoir. It skilfully recreates the atmosphere of the festivals at Butte Montmartre in the last decades of the 19th century.

Bal du Moulin de la Galette

Peinte d'une touche vive et lumineuse, la plus célèbre des toiles d'Auguste Renoir traduit parfaitement l'ambiance festive et populaire de la butte Montmartre dans les dernières décennies du XIXe siècle.

Der Tanz im Moulin de la Galette

Das mit lebhaftem und hellen Strich gemalte Bild ist eines der bekanntesten von Auguste Renoir. Es gibt gekonnt die Atmosphäre der Feste an der Butte Montmartre in den letzten Jahrzehnten des 19. Jahrhunderts wieder.

El baile en el Moulin de la Galette

El cuadro, pintado con una línea viva y brillante, es uno de los más famosos de Auguste Renoir. Recrea hábilmente el ambiente de las fiestas de Butte Montmartre de las últimas décadas del siglo XIX.

A dança no Moulin de la Galette

O quadro, pintado com uma linha viva e brilhante, é um dos mais famosos de Auguste Renoir. Ele habilmente recria a atmosfera dos festivais em Butte Montmartre nas últimas décadas do século 19.

Het bal van de Moulin de la Galette

PHet met levendige en heldere streken geschilderde doek is een van de bekendste van Auguste Renoir. Het geeft kundig de sfeer van de feesten op de heuvel van Montmartre in de laatste decennia van de 19e eeuw weer.

AUGUSTE RENOIR (1841-1919)
1876, Oil on canvas/Huile sur toile, 131 × 175 cm, Musée d'Orsay, Paris

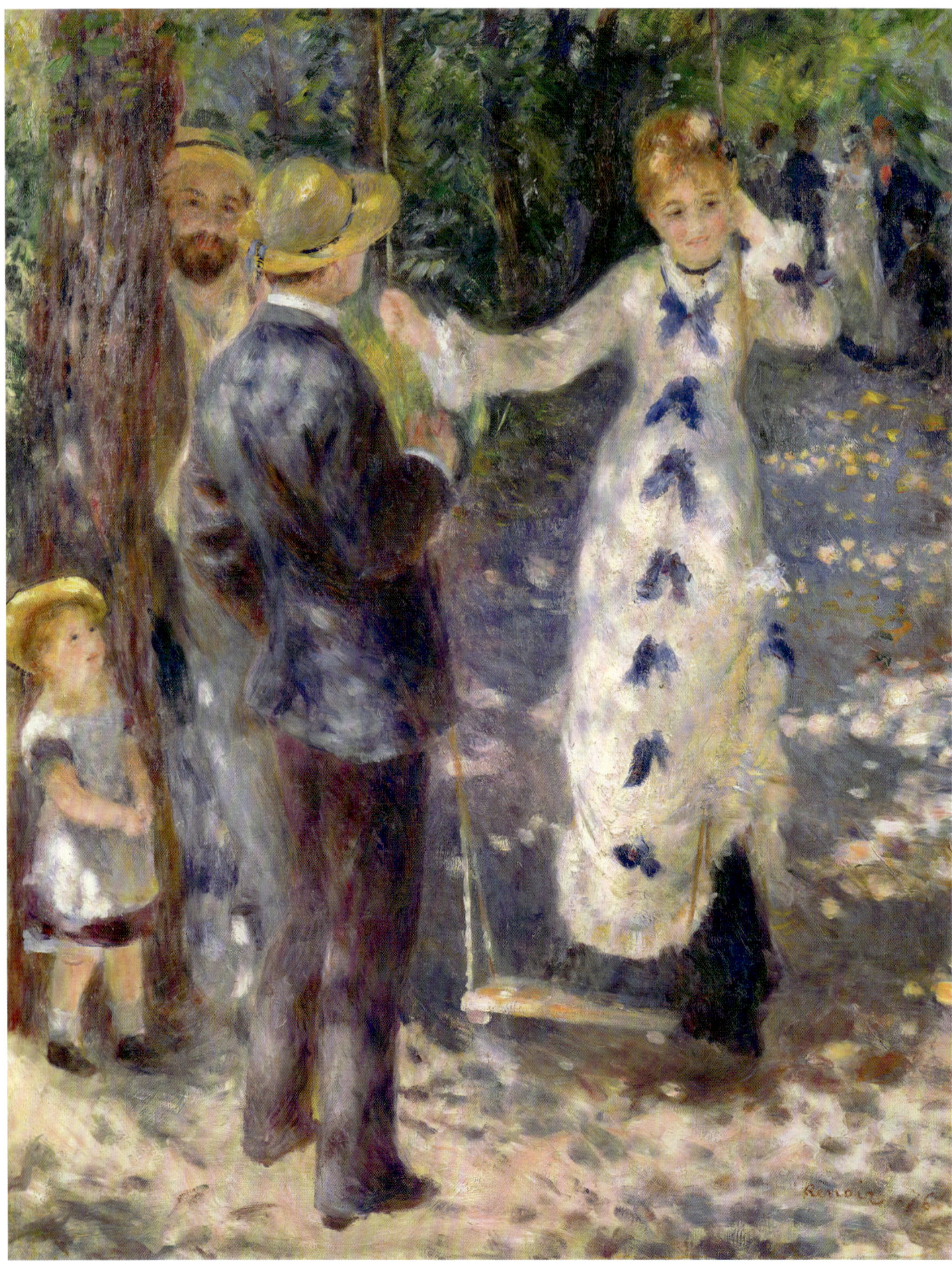

The Swing

La Balançoire

Die Schaukel

El columpio

O balanço

De schommel

AUGUSTE RENOIR (1841-1919)
1876, Oil on canvas/ Huile sur toile, 92 × 73 cm, Musée d'Orsay, Paris

Study. Torso, Effect of Sunlight

The torso and the background in
different shades of blue and green
are in perfect harmony. The rays
of sunlight refracted by the canopy
of leaves play around the woman's
body as fine spots of color.

Étude. Torse, effet de soleil

Le personnage en buste et le décor
en camaïeu de bleu-vert sont en
parfaite osmose. Les éclats de
soleil, qui traversent le feuillage
des arbres, éclairent la peau de la
jeune femme par touches délicates.

Studie. Torso, Sonnenlicht

Der Torso und der in
unterschiedlichen Blau- und
Grüntönen gehaltene Hintergrund
stehen in perfekter Harmonie. Die
durch das Blätterdach gebrochenen
Sonnenstrahlen umspielen als feine
Farbtupfer den Körper der Frau.

Estudio. Torso, luz solar

El torso y el fondo en diferentes
tonos de azul y verde están en
perfecta armonía. Los rayos de sol
refractados por el dosel de las hojas
juegan alrededor del cuerpo de la
mujer como finas manchas de color.

Estudar. Torso, luz do sol

O tronco e o fundo em diferentes
tonalidades de azul e verde estão
em perfeita harmonia. Os raios
de sol refratados pela copa das
folhas brincam à volta do corpo da
mulher como finas manchas de cor.

Studie. Torso, zonlicht

De torso en de achtergrond in
verschillende tinten blauw en
groen zijn perfect met elkaar in
harmonie. De door het bladerdak
gebroken zonnestralen spelen
als fijne verfstippen rond het
lichaam van de vrouw.

AUGUSTE RENOIR (1841-1919)

c. 1876, Oil on canvas/Huile sur toile,
81 × 65 cm, Musée d'Orsay, Paris

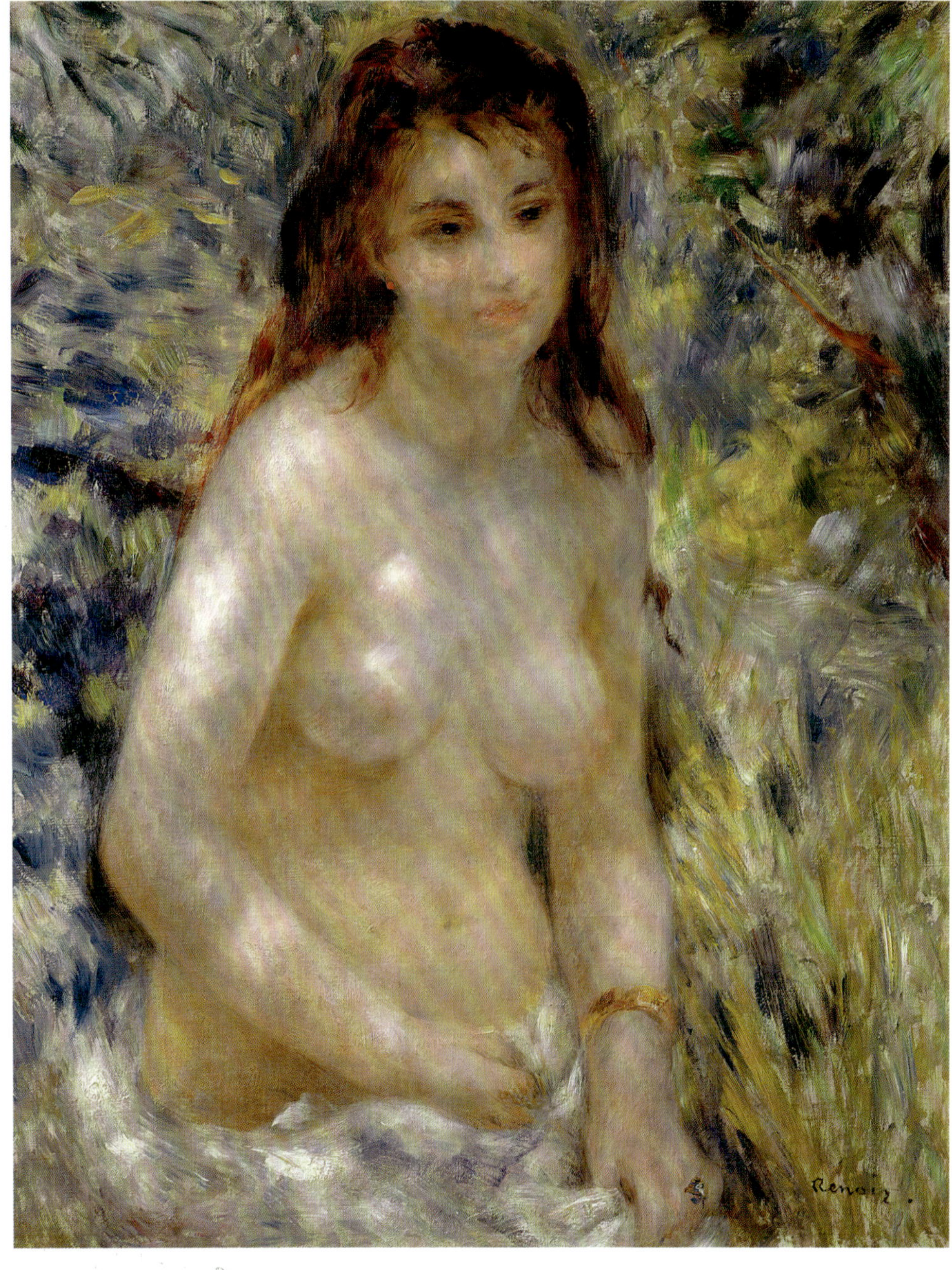

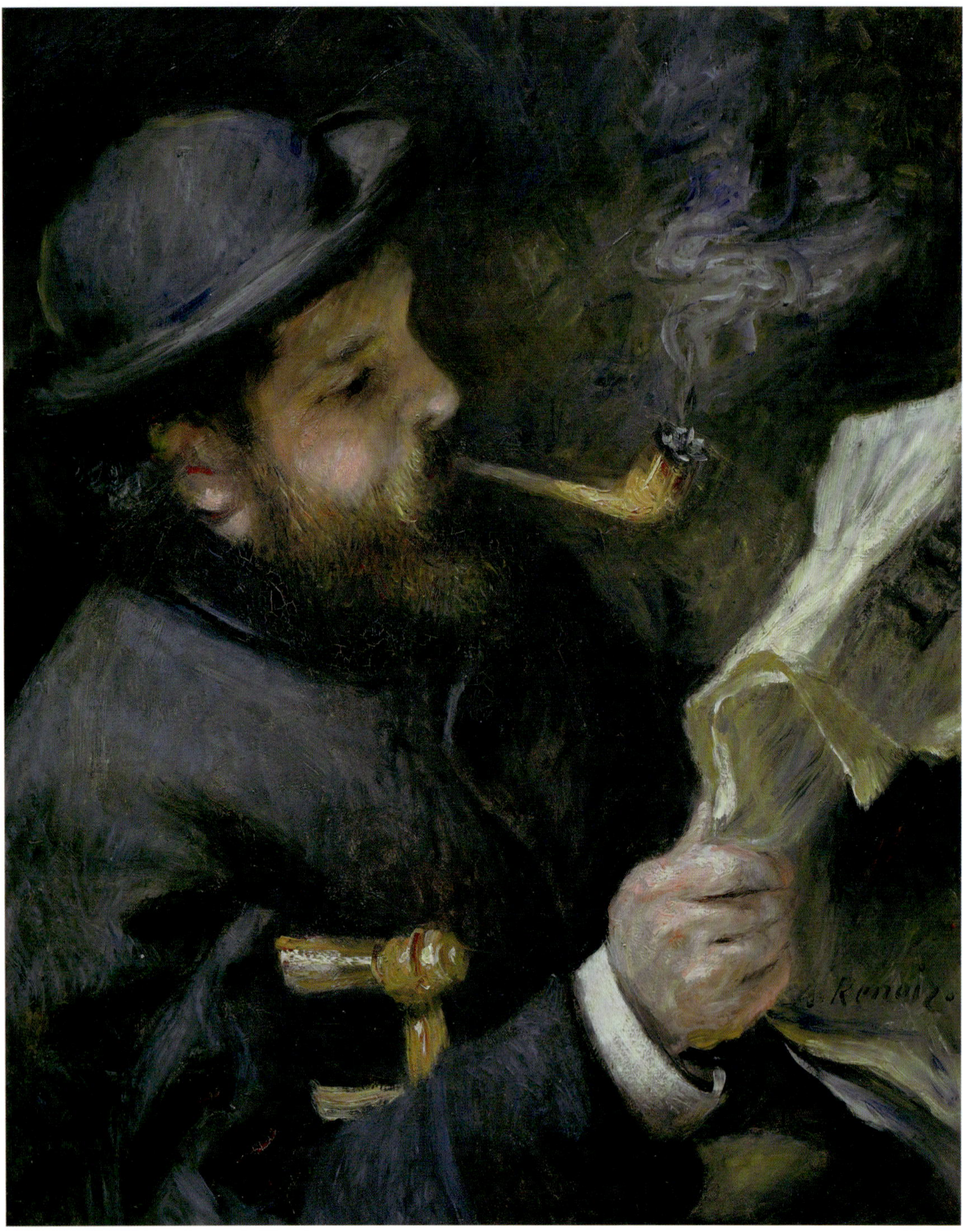

Claude Monet
Reading a
Newspaper

Claude
Monet lisant

Claude Monet
lesend

Claude Monet
leyendo

Claude Monet
lendo

Claude Monet
lezend

**AUGUSTE
RENOIR
(1841-1919)**
c. 1873,
Oil on canvas/
Huile sur toile,
61,7 × 50 cm,
Musée
Marmottan
Monet, Paris

Marie-Thérèse Durand-Ruel Sewing

In 1882 Paul Durand-Ruel, the Impressionist art dealer, asked his friend Renoir to paint portraits of his children. He painted several images, including that of Marie-Thérèse with a red hat.

Marie-Thérèse Durand-Ruel cousant

En 1882, Paul Durand-Ruel, le marchand des impressionnistes, demande à son ami Renoir de peindre ses enfants. L'artiste réalisera plusieurs portraits, dont celui-ci de Marie-Thérèse au chapeau rouge.

Marie-Thérèse Durand-Ruel nähend

1882 bittet Paul Durand-Ruel, der Kunsthändler der Impressionisten, seinen Freund Renoir, Porträts seine Kinder zu malen. Es entstehen mehrere Gemälde, darunter das von Marie-Thérèse mit einem roten Hut.

Marie-Thérèse Durand-Ruel cosiendo

En 1882, Paul Durand-Ruel, el marchante de arte impresionista, pidió a su amigo Renoir que pintara retratos de sus hijos. Pintó varios cuadros, entre ellos el de Marie-Thérèse con un sombrero rojo.

Costura Marie-Thérèse Durand-Ruel

Em 1882, Paul Durand-Ruel, o comerciante de arte impressionista, pediu a seu amigo Renoir para pintar retratos de seus filhos. Ele pintou vários quadros, incluindo o de Marie-Thérèse com um chapéu vermelho.

Marie-Thérèse Durand-Ruel naaiend

In 1882 vroeg Paul Durand-Ruel, de kunsthandelaar van de impressionisten, zijn vriend Renoir om portretten van zijn kinderen te schilderen. Renoir maakte verschillende schilderijen, waaronder dat van Marie-Thérèse met een rode hoed.

AUGUSTE RENOIR (1841-1919)

1882, Oil on canvas/Huile sur toile, 64,9 × 54 cm, The Clark, Williamstown

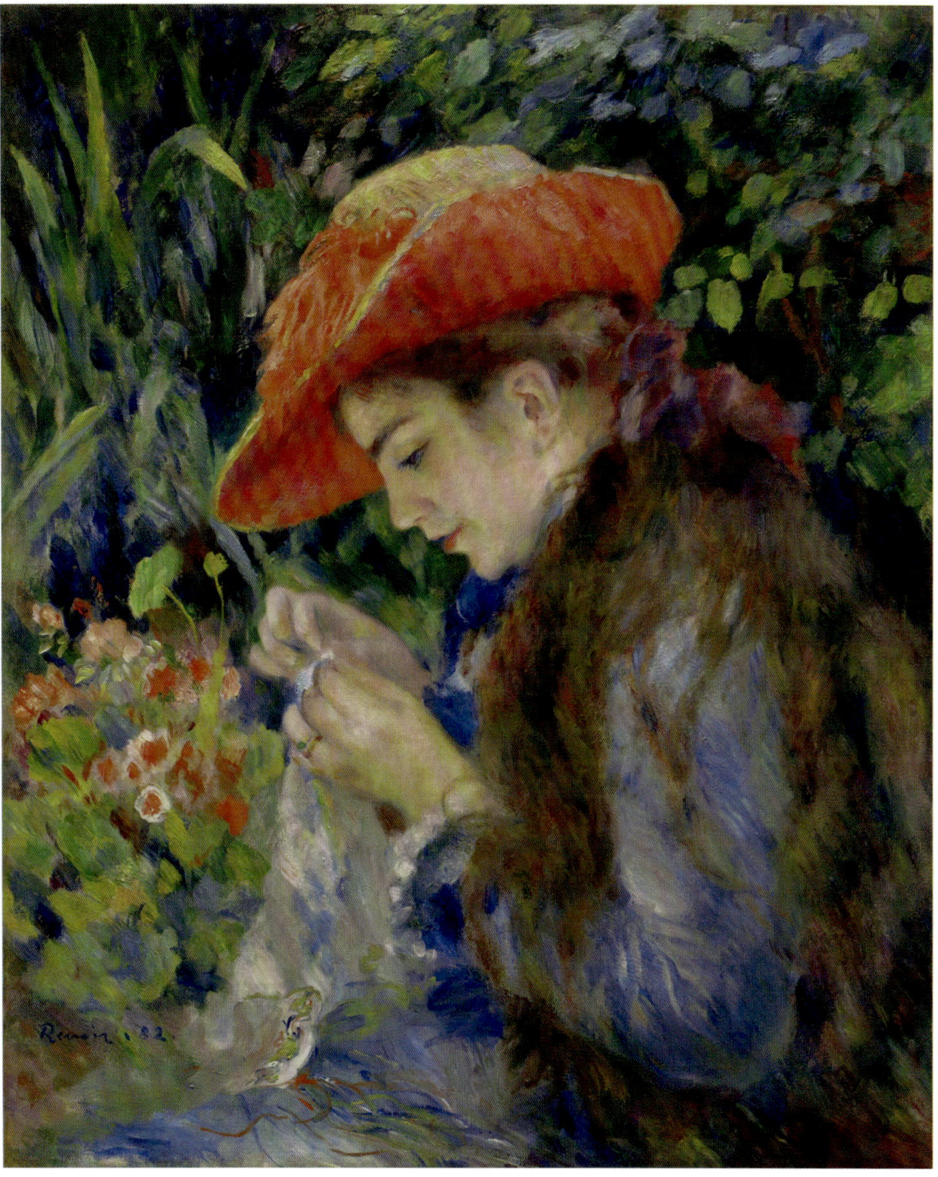

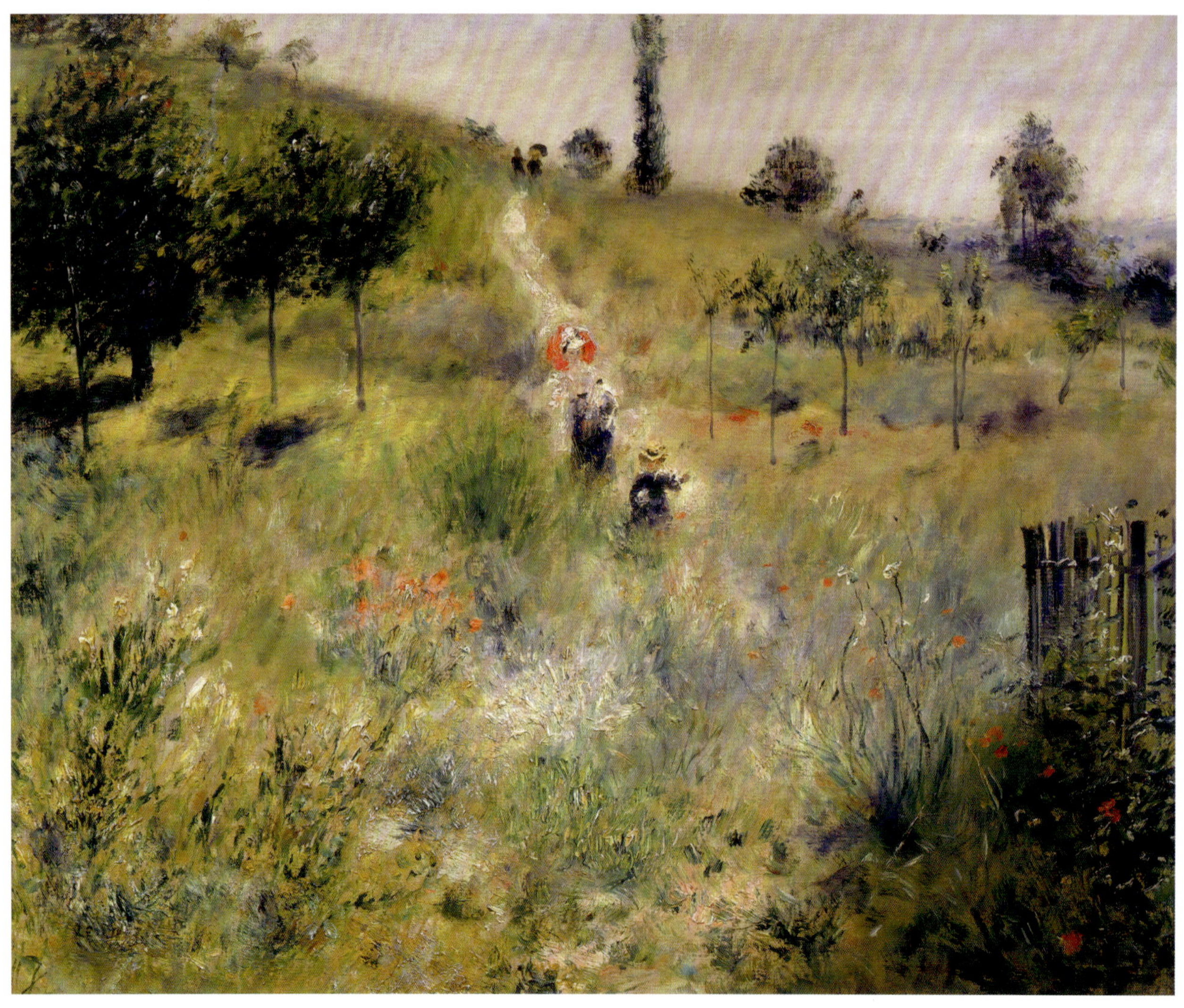

The Path through the Long Grass

Chemin montant dans les hautes herbes

Ansteigender Weg durch hohes Gras

Sendero cuesta arriba a través de la hierba alta

Caminho de subida através da relva alta

Oplopend pad door hoog gras

AUGUSTE RENOIR (1841-1919)
c. 1875, Oil on canvas/Huile sur toile, 60 × 74 cm,
Musée d'Orsay, Paris

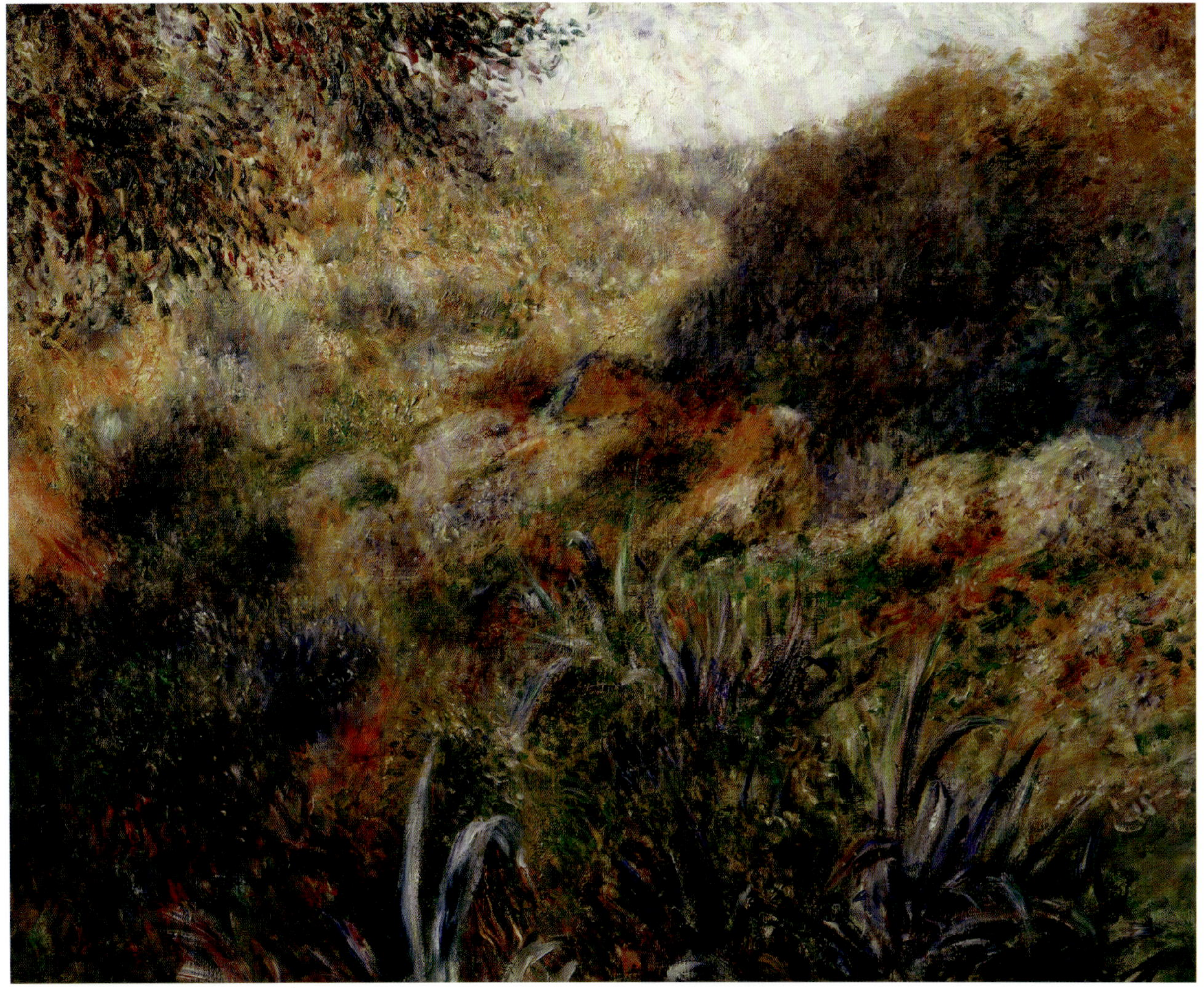

Algerian Landscape

Renoir traveled twice to Algeria. The country inspired him to make portraits of women, but also to create a series of landscapes. He succeeded in realistically capturing the colors and the bright light.

Paysage algérien

L'Algérie, où il a séjourné deux fois, a inspiré à Renoir des figures féminines, mais surtout un bel ensemble de paysages où il parvient à traduire la vérité des couleurs sous l'éclat d'une lumière écrasante.

Algerische Landschaft

Renoir hält sich zweimal in Algerien auf. Das Land inspiriert ihn zu Frauenporträts, aber auch zu einer Reihe an Landschaften. Ihm gelingt es, die Farben und das grelle Licht naturgetreu einzufangen.

Paisaje argelino

Argelia, país en el que estuvo dos veces, inspiró a Renoir a crear figuras femeninas, pero sobre todo un bello conjunto de paisajes donde consigue traducir la verdad de los colores bajo el resplandor de una luz aplastante.

Paisagem argelina

Renoir está na Argélia duas vezes. O país o inspirou a fazer retratos de mulheres, mas também a criar uma série de paisagens. Ele consegue capturar as cores e a luz brilhante verdadeira para a natureza.

Algerijns landschap

Renoir verbleef twee keer in Algerije. Het land inspireerde hem tot het schilderen van vrouwenportretten, maar ook tot een serie landschappen. Hij slaagde erin de kleuren en het felle licht natuurgetrouw vast te leggen.

AUGUSTE RENOIR (1841-1919)

1881, Oil on canvas/Huile sur toile, 65 × 81,5 cm, Musée d'Orsay, Paris

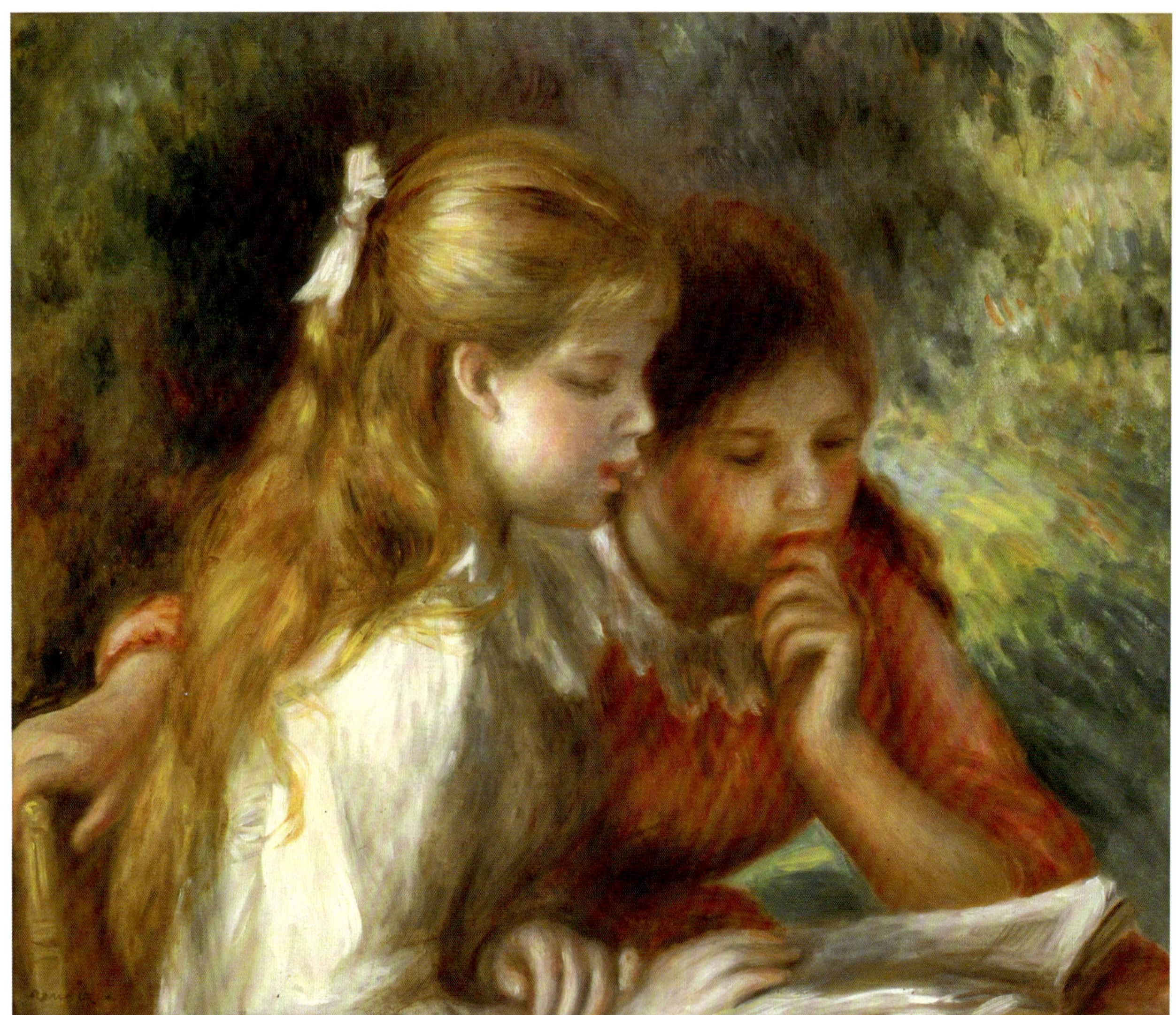

The Reading

La Lecture

Die Lektüre

La lectura

A leitura

Het lezen

AUGUSTE RENOIR (1841-1919)

1892, Oil on canvas/Huile sur toile, 55 × 65,5 cm,
Musée du Louvre, Paris

Two Young Girls
at the Piano

Jeunes Filles au piano

Junge Mädchen
am Klavier

Niñas jóvenes al piano

Meninas jovens
ao piano

Jonge meisjes
aan de piano

AUGUSTE RENOIR
(1841-1919)

1892, Oil on canvas/
Huile sur toile, 116 × 90 cm,
Musée d'Orsay, Paris

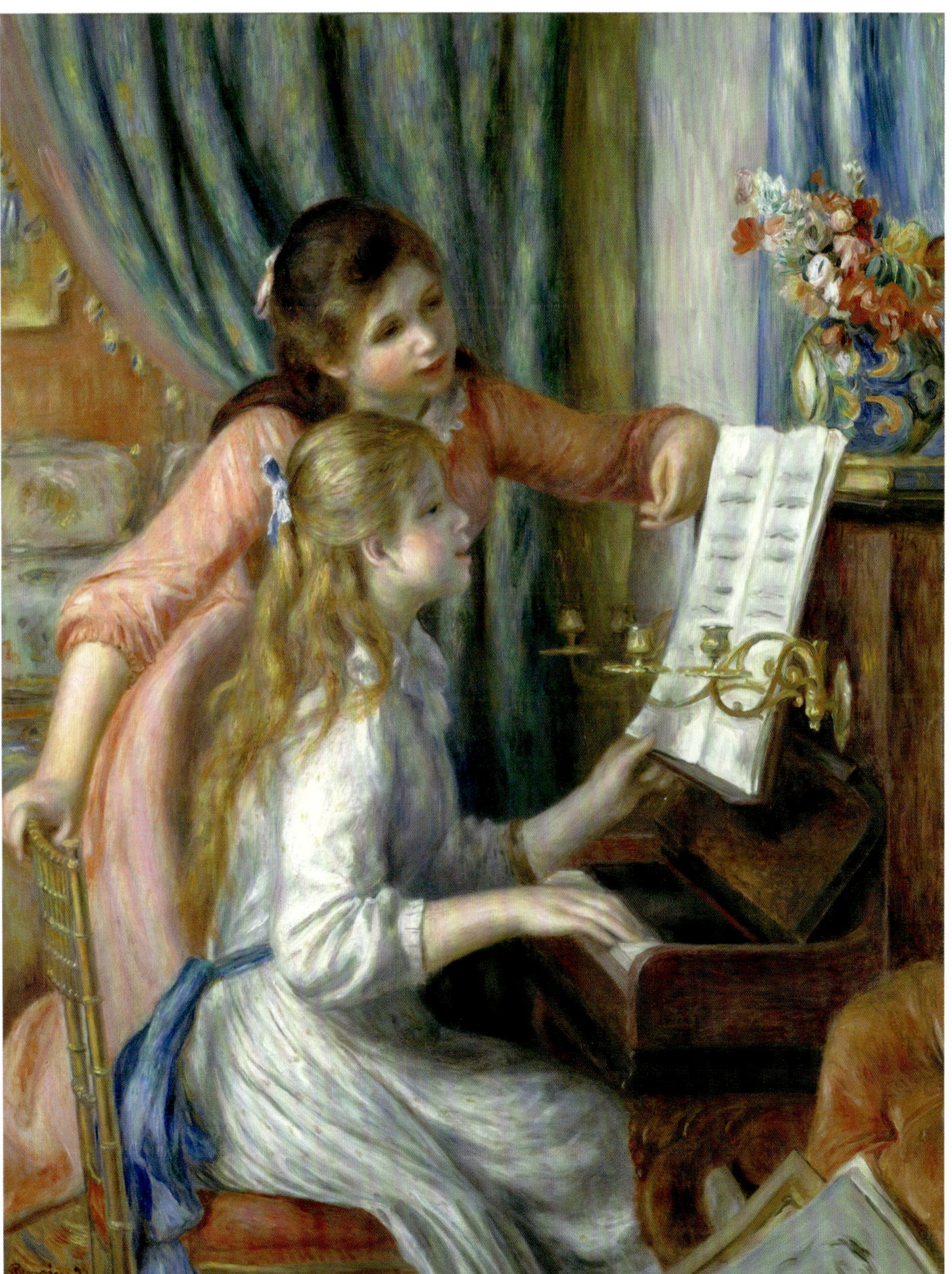

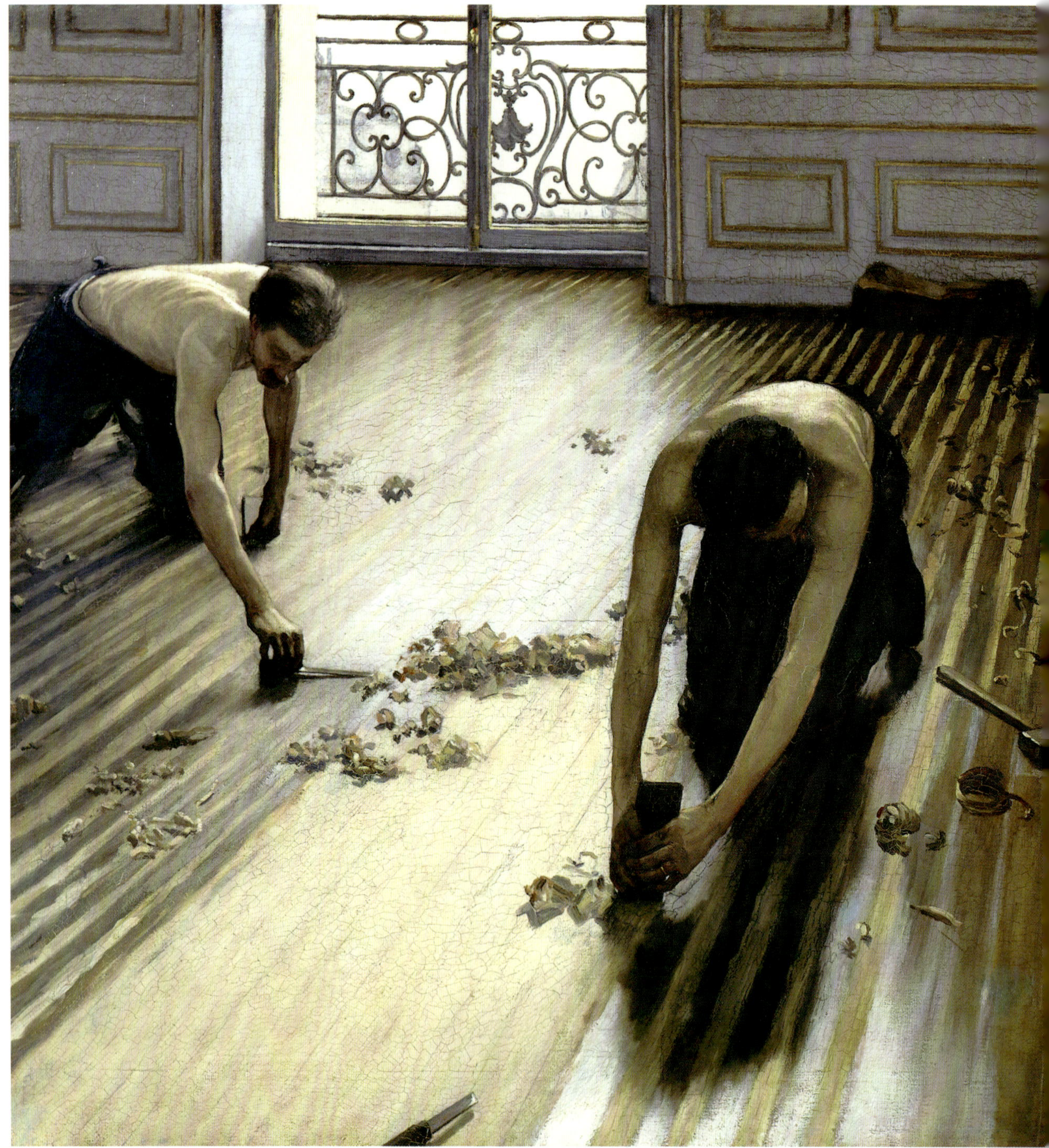

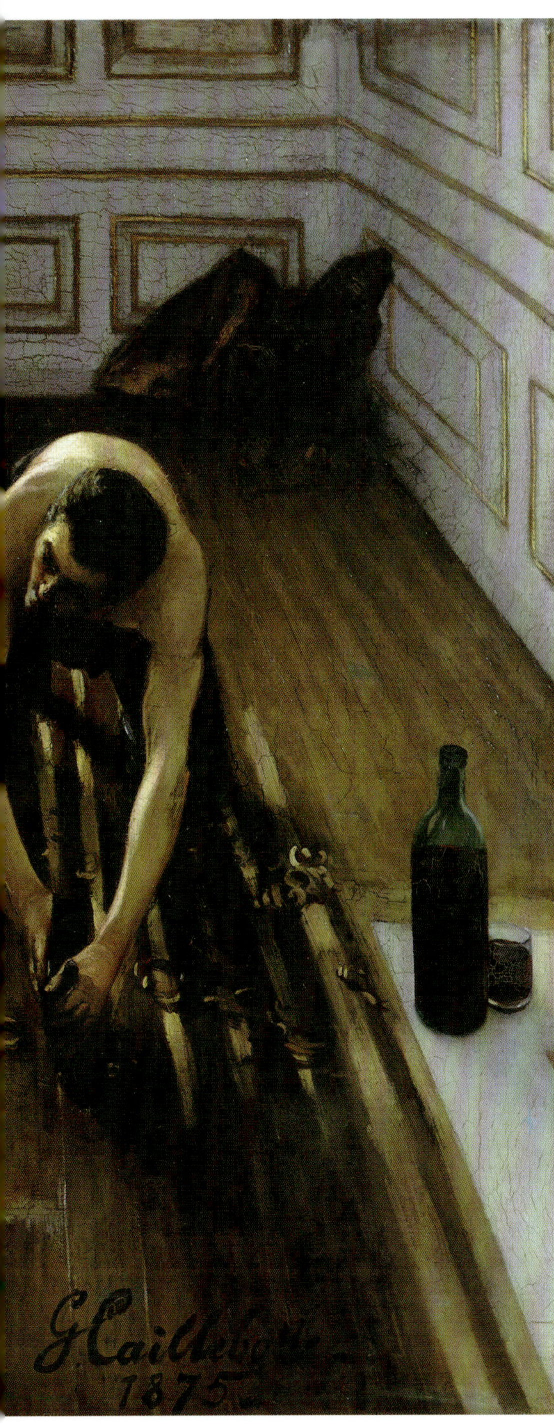

The Parquet Planers

The presentation impresses with its relentless realism. The novel motif of the technically perfect painting, however, was strongly criticized by the jury at the 1875 Salon and described as vulgar.

Les Raboteurs de parquet

La technique est parfaite, et le rendu irréprochable. Mais le sujet de cette œuvre très réaliste, inédit dans la peinture, sera qualifié de vulgaire lors de la présentation du tableau au Salon de 1874.

Die Parkettschleifer

Die Darstellung beeindruckt durch ihren schonungslosen Realismus. Das neuartige Motiv des technisch perfekten Gemäldes wird allerdings von der Jury auf dem Salon 1875 heftig kritisiert und als vulgär bezeichnet.

Los acuchilladores de parquét

La representación impresiona por su implacable realismo. Sin embargo, el motivo novedoso de la pintura técnicamente perfecta fue fuertemente criticado por el jurado en el Salón de 1875 y descrito como vulgar.

As lixadeiras de parquet

O desempenho impressiona pelo seu realismo implacável. O motivo do romance da pintura tecnicamente perfeita, no entanto, foi fortemente criticado pelo júri no Salão de Salão de 1875 e descrito como vulgar.

De parketschavers

De voorstelling maakt indruk door zijn zuivere realisme. Het nieuwe onderwerp van het technisch perfecte schilderij werd door de jury van de Salon van 1875 echter hevig bekritiseerd en als vulgair omschreven.

GUSTAVE CAILLEBOTTE (1848-1894)

1875, Oil on canvas/Huile sur toile, 102 × 146,5 cm, Musée d'Orsay, Paris

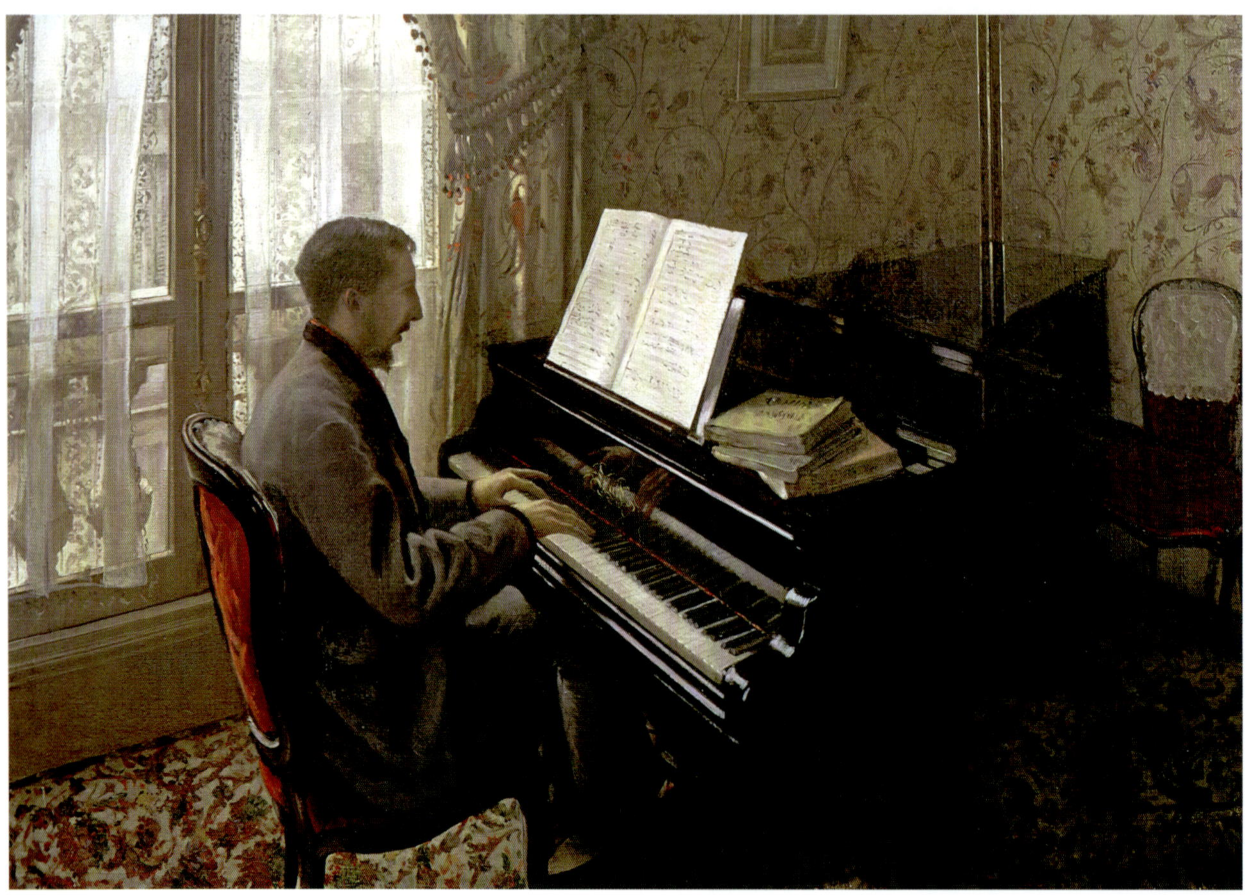

Young Man Playing the Piano

Caillebotte painted his brother Martial against a carefully executed background. He worked out the smallest details - from the wallpaper, the curtains and the carpet, to the reflection of the fingers.

Jeune Homme au piano

Dans un décor aux détails soignés – papier peint, rideaux, moquette… –, Gustave Caillebotte a peint son frère Martial. Le reflet de ses doigts dans le noir laqué du piano est particulièrement réussi.

Junger Mann am Klavier

Caillebotte malt seinen Bruder Martial vor einem sorgfältig ausgeführten Hintergrund. Er arbeitet die kleinsten Details heraus – von der Tapete über die Vorhänge und den Teppich bis hin zu der Spiegelung der Finger.

Joven al piano

Caillebotte pinta a su hermano Marcial sobre un fondo cuidadosamente ejecutado. Trabaja con los detalles más pequeños, desde el papel pintado, las cortinas y la alfombra, hasta el reflejo de los dedos.

Jovem ao piano

Caillebotte pinta o seu irmão Martial contra um fundo cuidadosamente executado. Ele trabalha os menores detalhes - desde o papel de parede até as cortinas e o tapete, passando pelo reflexo dos dedos.

Jongeman aan de piano

Caillebotte schilderde zijn broer Martial tegen een zorgvuldig uitgevoerde achtergrond. Hij werkte de kleinste details uit: van behang tot de gordijnen en van het tapijt tot de reflectie van de vingers.

GUSTAVE CAILLEBOTTE (1848-1894)

1876, Oil on canvas/Huile sur toile, 81,3 × 116,8 cm, Bridgestone Museum, Tokyo

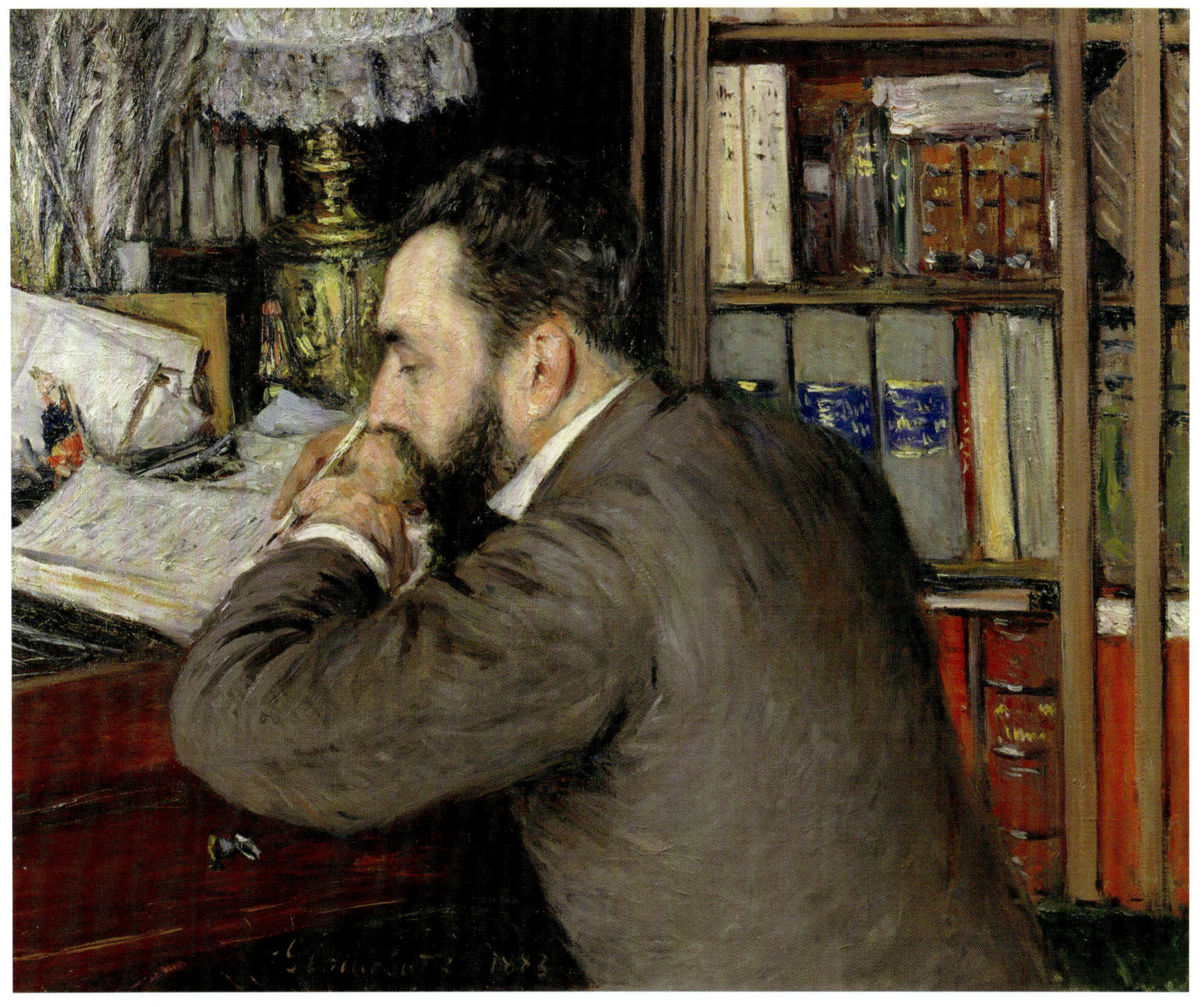

Henri Cordier

GUSTAVE CAILLEBOTTE (1848-1894)

1883, Oil on canvas/Huile sur toile, 65 × 82 cm,

Musée d'Orsay, Paris

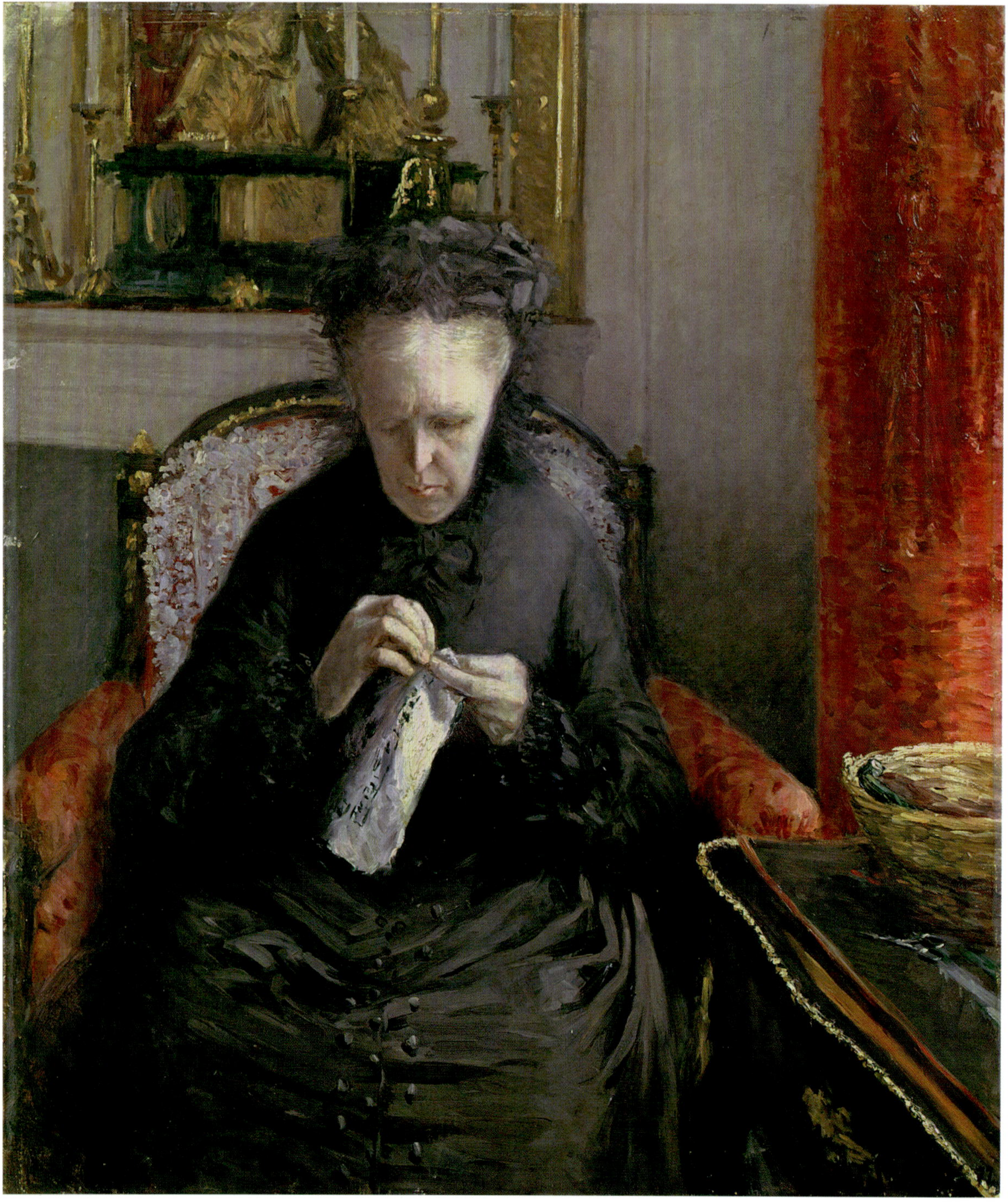

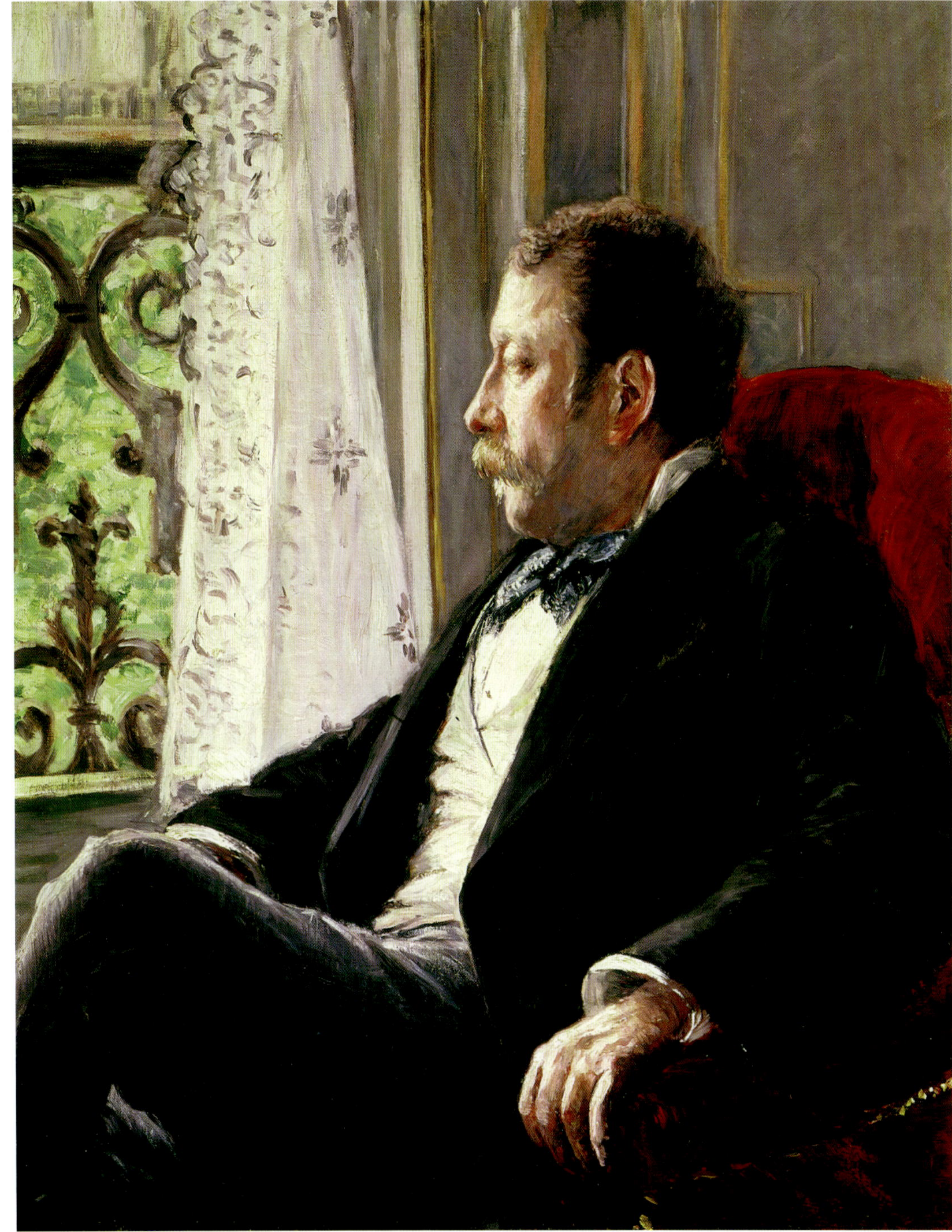

Madame Martial
Caillebotte

**GUSTAVE
CAILLEBOTTE
(1848-1894)**
1877, Oil on canvas/
Huile sur toile,
83 × 72 cm,
Private collection

Portrait of a Man

Portrait d'un
homme

Porträt eines
Mannes

Retrato de un
hombre

Retrato de
um homem

Portret van
een man

**GUSTAVE
CAILLEBOTTE
(1848-1894)**
1880, Oil on canvas/
Huile sur toile,
82 × 65 cm,
Private collection

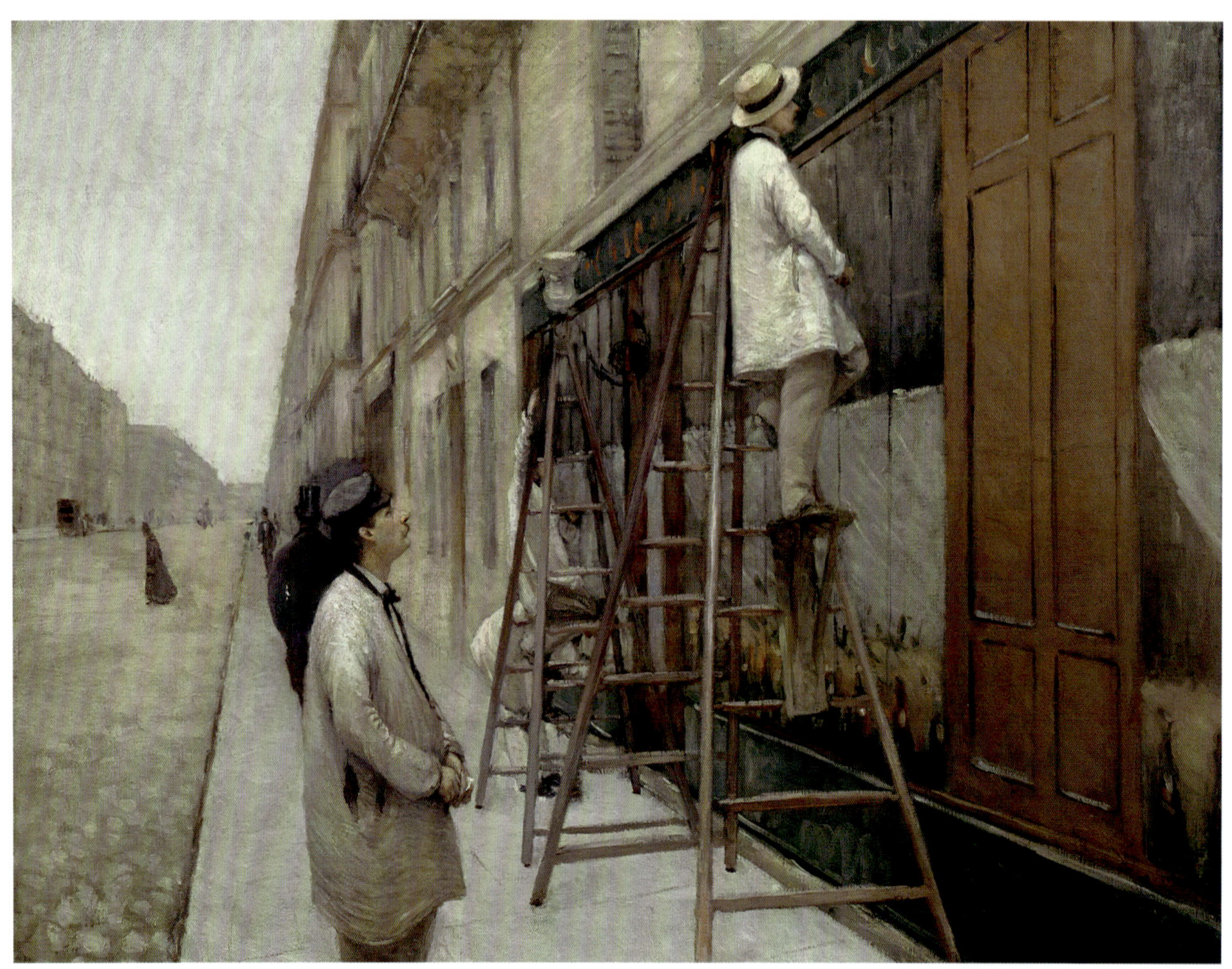

The Painters

Les Peintres

Die Anstreicher

Los pintores

Os pintores

De schilders

GUSTAVE CAILLEBOTTE (1848-1894)

1877, Oil on canvas/Huile sur toile, 60 × 73 cm,
Private collection

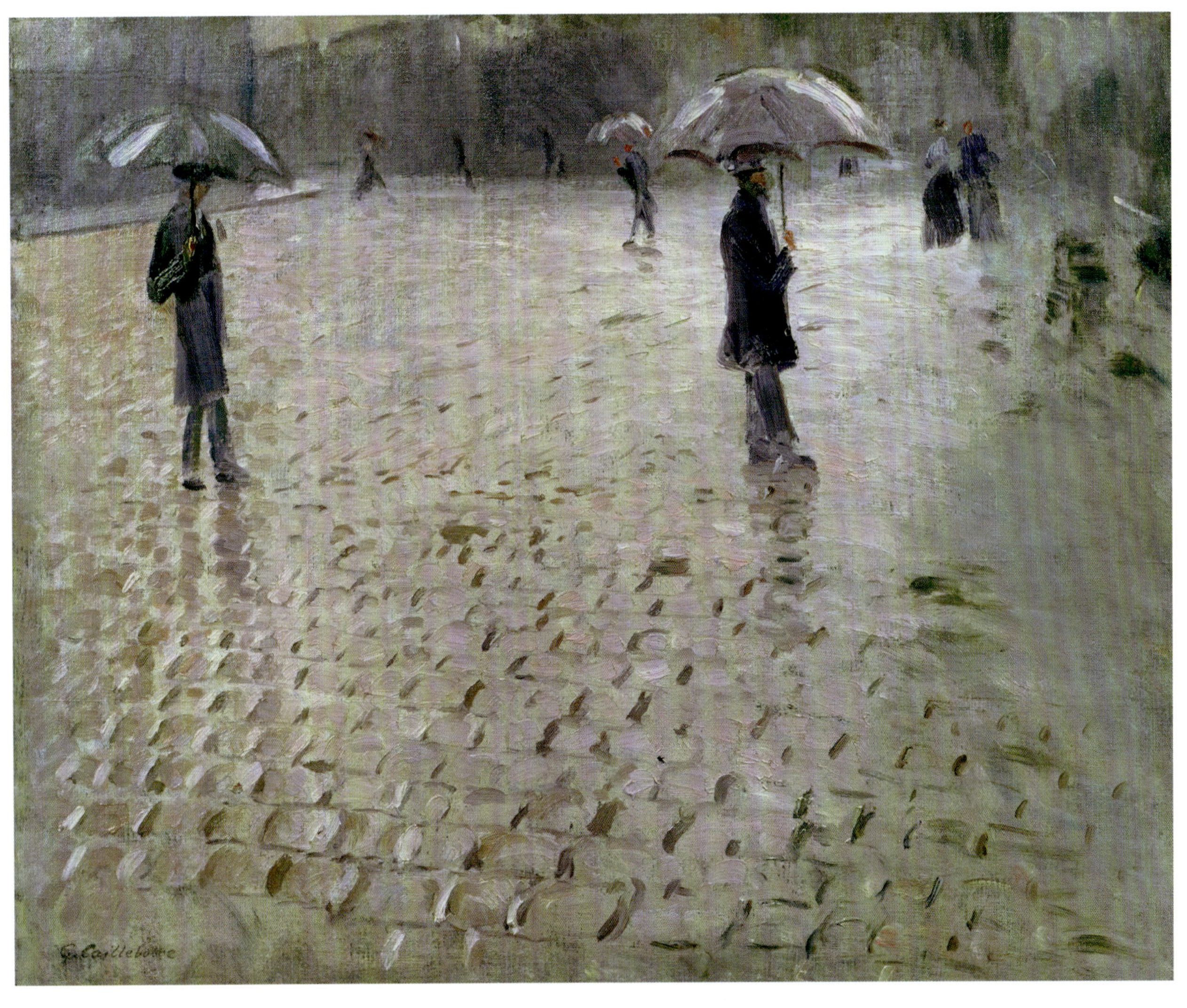

Study for a Paris Street, Rainy Day

Étude pour une rue de Paris, temps de pluie

Studie einer Pariser Straße, Regenwetter

Estudio de una calle parisina, tiempo lluvioso

Estudo de uma rua parisiense, tempo chuvoso

Studie van een Parijse straat, regenachtige dag

GUSTAVE CAILLEBOTTE (1848-1894)

1877, Oil on canvas/Huile sur toile, 54 × 65 cm,
Private collection

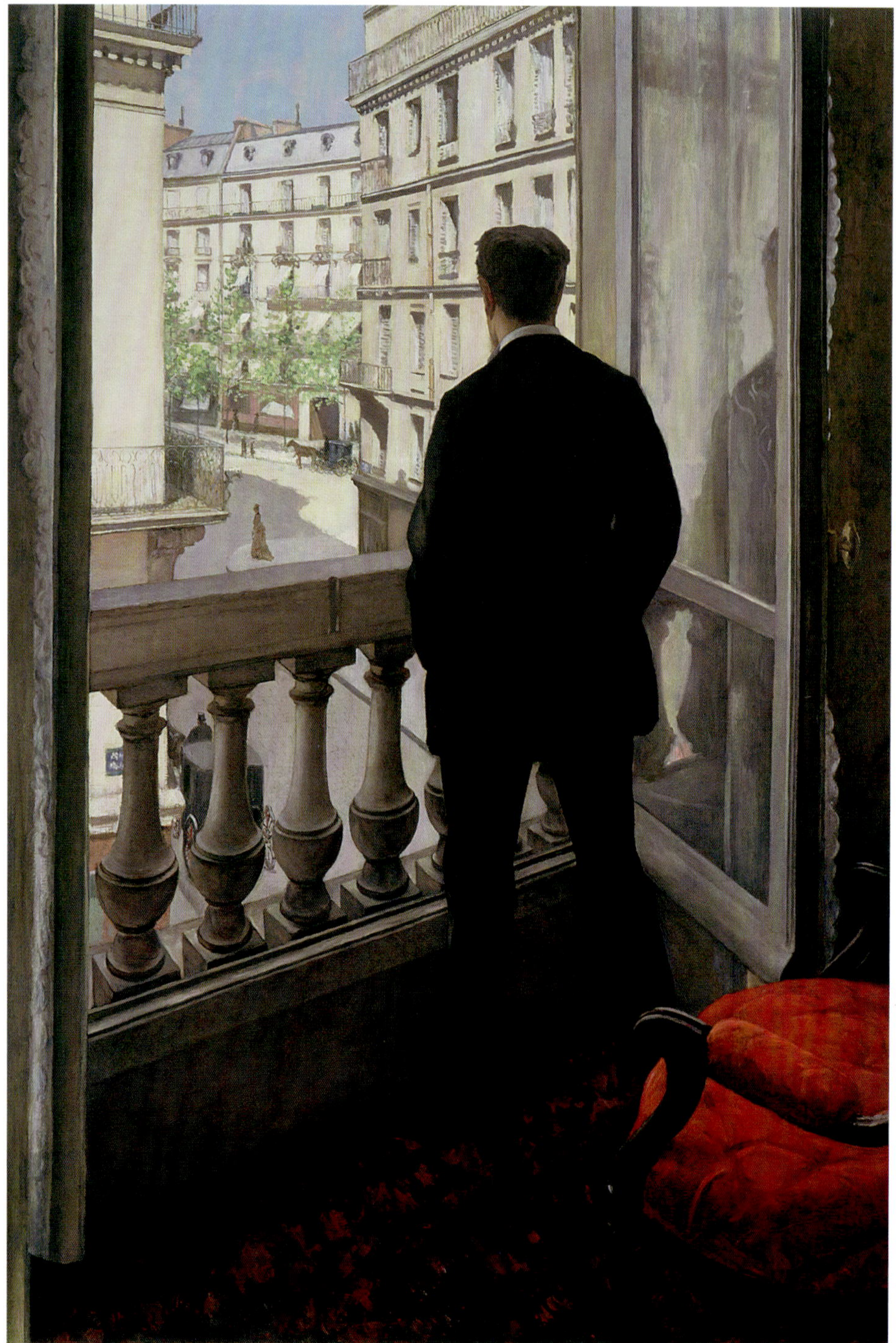

Man at the Window

Five years lie between the two paintings
with the same motif. Both show a person
standing at the window looking outwards
- a snapshot between daydream and
loneliness.

Jeune Homme à la fenêtre

À cinq ans d'intervalle, Caillebotte peint
ces deux tableaux, sur le même thème.
Les personnages, homme et femme, sont
debout à la fenêtre et regardent dehors.
Deux visions entre rêverie et solitude.

Der Blick aus dem Fenster

Fünf Jahre liegen zwischen den zwei
Gemälden mit demselben Motiv. Beide
zeigen eine stehende Person am Fenster
mit nach Außen gerichtetem Blick – eine
Momentaufnahme zwischen Tagtraum
und Einsamkeit.

Joven en la ventana

Cinco años se encuentran entre las
dos pinturas con el mismo motivo.
Ambos muestran a una persona de pie
en la ventana con vista al exterior, una
instantánea entre la fantasía y la soledad.

A vista da janela

Cinco anos entre as duas pinturas com
o mesmo motivo. Ambos mostram uma
pessoa em pé na janela com uma vista para
o exterior - um instantâneo entre sonho
acordado e solidão.

Jongeman bij het raam

Er ligt vijf jaar tussen de twee schilderijen
met hetzelfde onderwerp. Beide tonen
een staande, naar buiten kijkende persoon
voor het raam - een momentopname
tussen dagdroom en eenzaamheid.

GUSTAVE CAILLEBOTTE (1848-1894)
1875, Oil on canvas/Huile sur toile,
117 × 82 cm, Private collection

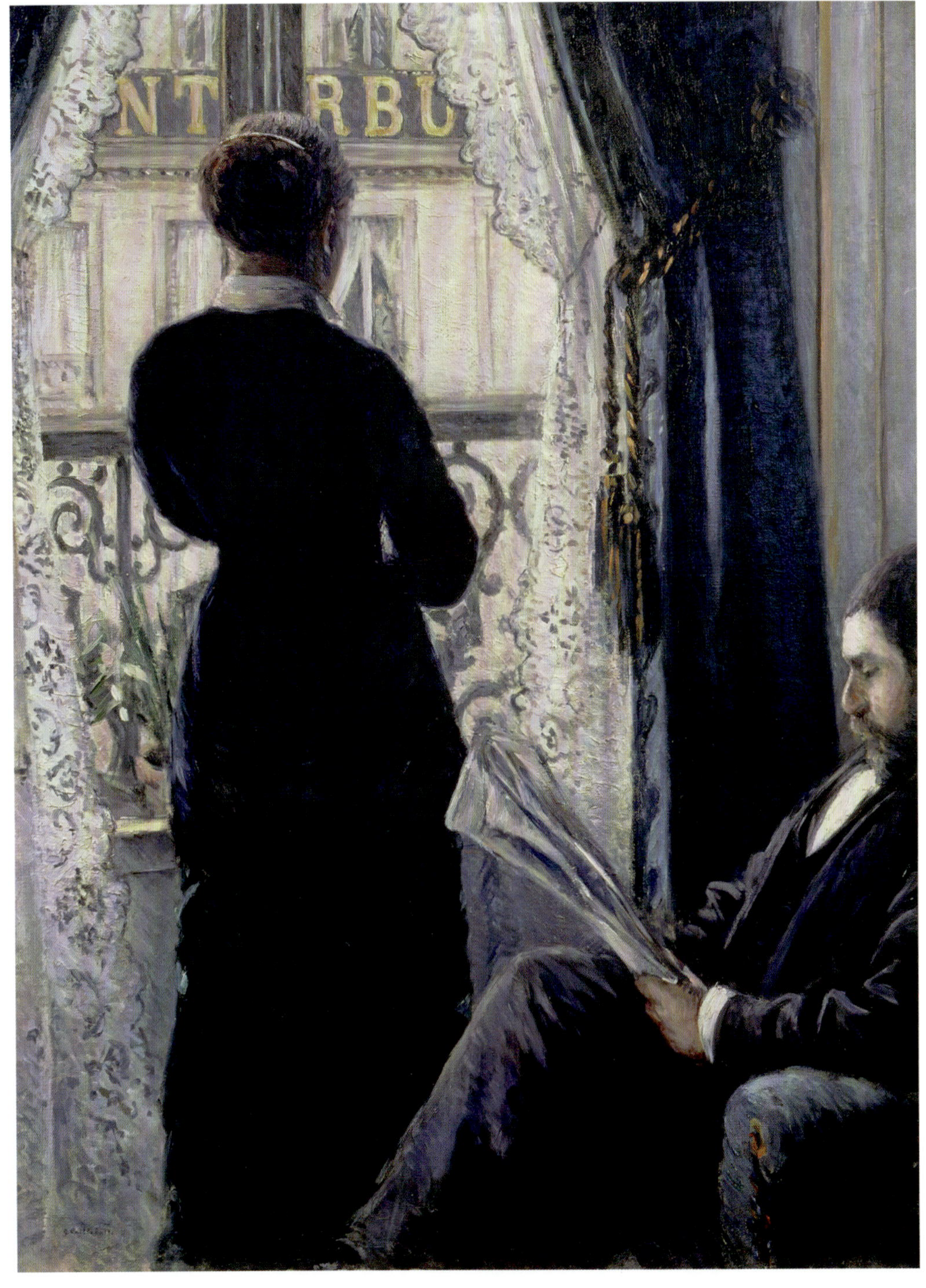

Interior, Woman at
the Window

Intérieur, femme à la fenêtre

Innenansicht, Frau am Fenster

Vista interior, mujer
en la ventana

Vista interior, mulher
na janela

Interieur, vrouw
voor het raam

GUSTAVE CAILLEBOTTE
(1848-1894)
1880, Oil on canvas/Huile sur toile,
116 × 89 cm, Private collection

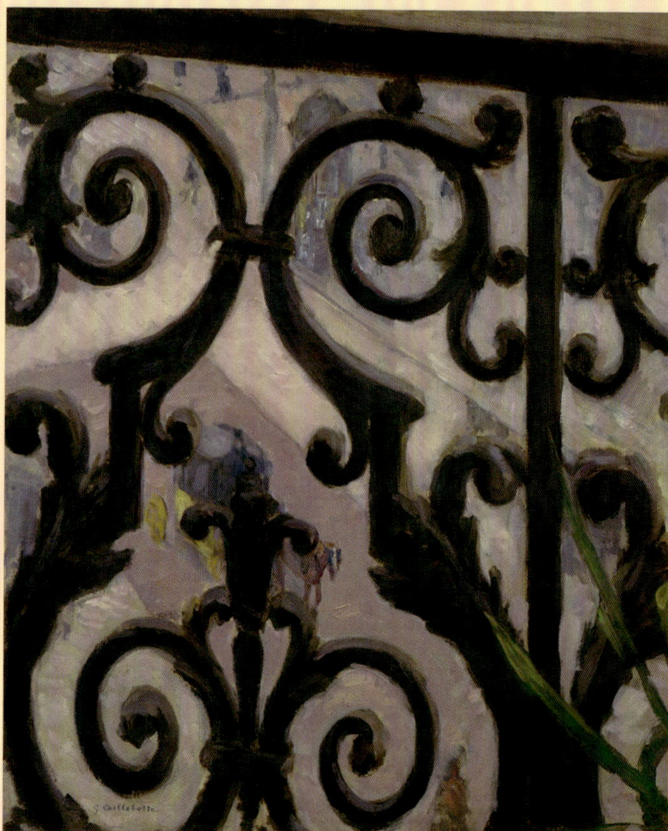

View from a Balcony

Vue d'un balcon

Blick vom Balkon

Vista desde el balcón

Vista da varanda

Uitzicht vanaf een balkon

GUSTAVE CAILLEBOTTE (1848-1894)

1880, Oil on canvas/Huile sur toile, 65,6 × 54,9 cm,

Van Gogh Museum, Amsterdam

Gustave Caillebotte

In 1872 Gustave Caillebotte (1848-1894) met Monet, who lived in Argenteuil at that time. After the death of his father, he used his inherited fortune to support his Impressionist friends by buying their paintings. In 1875 his work *The Parquet Planers* was rejected by the Salon. As a reaction he took part in five exhibitions of the Impressionists between 1876 and 1882. His feeling for the detail of the picture, the shortened representation of the perspective and the views from a bird's or frog's perspective make him one of the most progressive painters in the group. In addition to the typical motifs from nature, he depicted the transformation of the city - the buildings, the boulevards and the bridges of the Paris of Haussmann. He found his subjects in the open air, but painted them in the quiet of his studio. In contrast to the short strokes of Monet, Renoir or Pissarro, Caillebotte preferred a calm brushstroke. At the age of only 45 the artist, who also worked as a boat builder, gardener, art collector and patron, died.

Gustave Caillebotte

Gustave Caillebotte (1848-1894) rencontre Monet en 1872, qui habite alors Argenteuil. À la mort de son père en 1874, il hérite d'une somme importante qui lui permettra de soutenir ses amis impressionnistes, en leur achetant des œuvres. En 1875, ses *Raboteurs de parquet* sont refusés au Salon. Il exposera ensuite avec les impressionnistes, participant à cinq de leurs expositions, entre 1876 et 1882. Caillebotte est sans doute le plus moderne d'entre eux, par son sens du cadrage, ses effets de perspectives tronquées, ses vues en plongée et en contre-plongée. Au-delà des sujets habituels de ses camarades, principalement axés sur la nature, l'artiste peint la ville en mutation, les immeubles, les boulevards et les ponts du Paris haussmannien. Il puise ses sujets à l'extérieur, mais peint dans la tranquillité de son atelier. À la touche fractionnée de Monet, Renoir ou Pissarro, il préfère une peinture plus lisse. Il meurt prématurément à l'âge de 45 ans. Peintre, Caillebotte fut aussi architecte naval, horticulteur, collectionneur et mécène.

Gustave Caillebotte

1872 lernt Gustave Caillebotte (1848–1894) Monet kennen, der zu dieser Zeit in Argenteuil wohnt. Nach dem Tod seines Vaters unterstützt er mit dem geerbten Vermögen die befreundeten Impressionisten, indem er ihre Gemälde kauft. 1875 wird sein Werk *Die Parkettschleifer* vom Salon abgelehnt. Als Reaktion nimmt er zwischen 1876 und 1882 an fünf Ausstellungen der Impressionisten teil. Sein Gefühl für den Bildausschnitt, die verkürzte Darstellung der Perspektive und die Ansichten aus der Vogel- und Froschperspektive machen ihn zu einem der fortschrittlichsten Maler der Gruppe. Neben den typischen Motiven aus der Natur bildet er die Transformation der Stadt ab – die Gebäude, die Boulevards und die Brücken des Paris Haussmanns. Seine Sujets findet er unter freiem Himmel, malt sie aber in der Ruhe seines Ateliers. Im Gegensatz zu den kurzen Strichen Monets, Renoirs oder Pissarros bevorzugt Caillebotte eine ruhige Pinselführung. Im Alter von nur 45 Jahren stirbt der Künstler, der auch als Bootsbauer, Gärtner, Kunstsammler und Mäzen tätig war.

GUSTAVE CAILLEBOTTE (1848-1894)
1880, Oil on canvas/Huile sur toile,
65 × 54 cm, Private collection

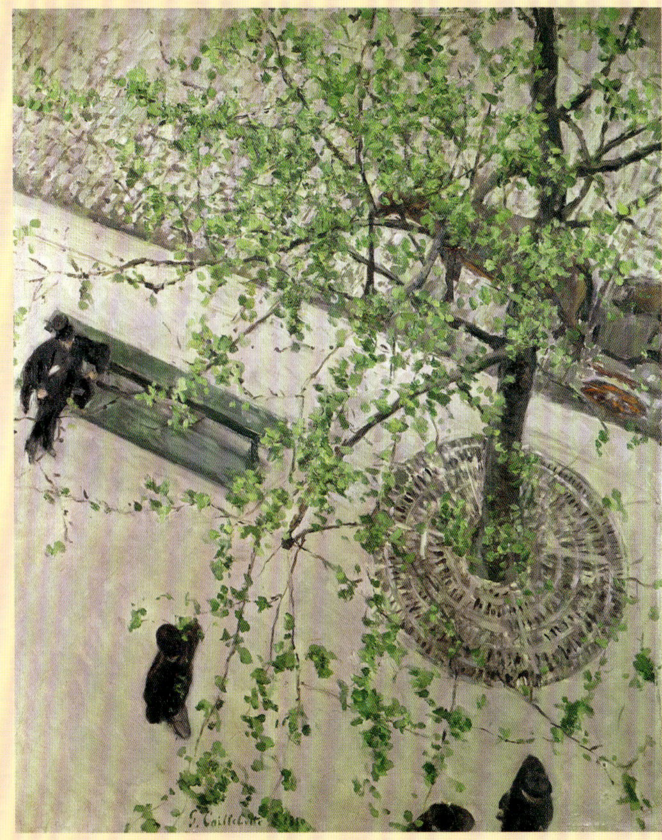

Gustave Caillebotte

1872 Gustave Caillebotte (1848-1894) conoce a Monet, que vive en Argenteuil en ese momento. Después de la muerte de su padre, utilizó su fortuna heredada para apoyar a sus amigos impresionistas comprando sus pinturas. En 1875 su obra *Los acuchilladores de parqué* fue rechazada por el Salón. Como reacción participó en cinco exposiciones de los impresionistas entre 1876 y 1882. Su sensibilidad por el detalle del cuadro, la representación acortada de la perspectiva y las vistas desde la perspectiva del pájaro y la rana lo convierten en uno de los pintores más progresistas del grupo. Además de los motivos típicos de la naturaleza, representa la transformación de la ciudad: los edificios, los bulevares y los puentes de la Haussmann de París. Encuentra a sus súbditos al aire libre, pero los pinta en la tranquilidad de su estudio. En contraste con los trazos cortos de Monet, Renoir o Pissarro, Caillebotte prefiere una pincelada tranquila. El artista, que también trabajó como constructor de barcos, jardinero, coleccionista de arte y mecenas, muere con tan solo 45 años.

Gustave Caillebotte

1872 Gustave Caillebotte (1848-1894) encontra Monet, que vive em Argenteuil na época. Após a morte de seu pai, ele usou sua fortuna herdada para sustentar seus amigos impressionistas comprando suas pinturas. Em 1875, seu trabalho *Die Parkettschleifer* foi rejeitado pelo Salão. Como reacção, participou em cinco exposições dos Impressionistas entre 1876 e 1882. O seu sentimento pelo detalhe do quadro, a representação abreviada da perspectiva e os pontos de vista da perspectiva do pássaro e da rã fazem dele um dos pintores mais progressistas do grupo. Além dos motivos típicos da natureza, retrata a transformação da cidade - os edifícios, as avenidas e as pontes da Paris Haussmann. Ele encontra os seus súbditos ao ar livre, mas pinta-os no silêncio do seu estúdio. Em contraste com as pinceladas curtas de Monet, Renoir ou Pissarro, Caillebotte prefere uma pincelada calma. Com apenas 45 anos de idade morre o artista, que também trabalhou como construtor de barcos, jardineiro, colecionador de arte e patrono.

Gustave Caillebotte

In 1872 leerde Gustave Caillebotte (1848-1894) Monet kennen, die in die tijd in Argenteuil woonde. Na de dood van zijn vader gebruikte Caillebotte zijn geërfde vermogen om zijn impressionistische vrienden te steunen door hun schilderijen te kopen. In 1875 werd zijn werk *De parketschavers* afgewezen door de Salon. Als reactie hierop nam hij tussen 1876 en 1882 deel aan vijf impressionistententoonstellingen. Zijn gevoel voor de juiste beelduitsnede, verkort perspectief en aanzichten vanuit vogel- en kikkerperspectief maken hem tot een van de meest vooruitstrevende schilders van de groep. Naast de typische onderwerpen uit de natuur schilderde hij de transformatie van de stad – de gebouwen, boulevards en bruggen van het Parijs van Haussmann. Hij vond zijn onderwerpen in de open lucht, maar schilderde ze in de rust van zijn atelier. In tegenstelling tot de korte penseelstreken van Monet, Renoir en Pissarro verkoos Caillebotte een rustige penseelvoering. Op 45-jarige leeftijd overleed de schilder, die ook actief was als botenbouwer, tuinier, kunstverzamelaar en mecenas.

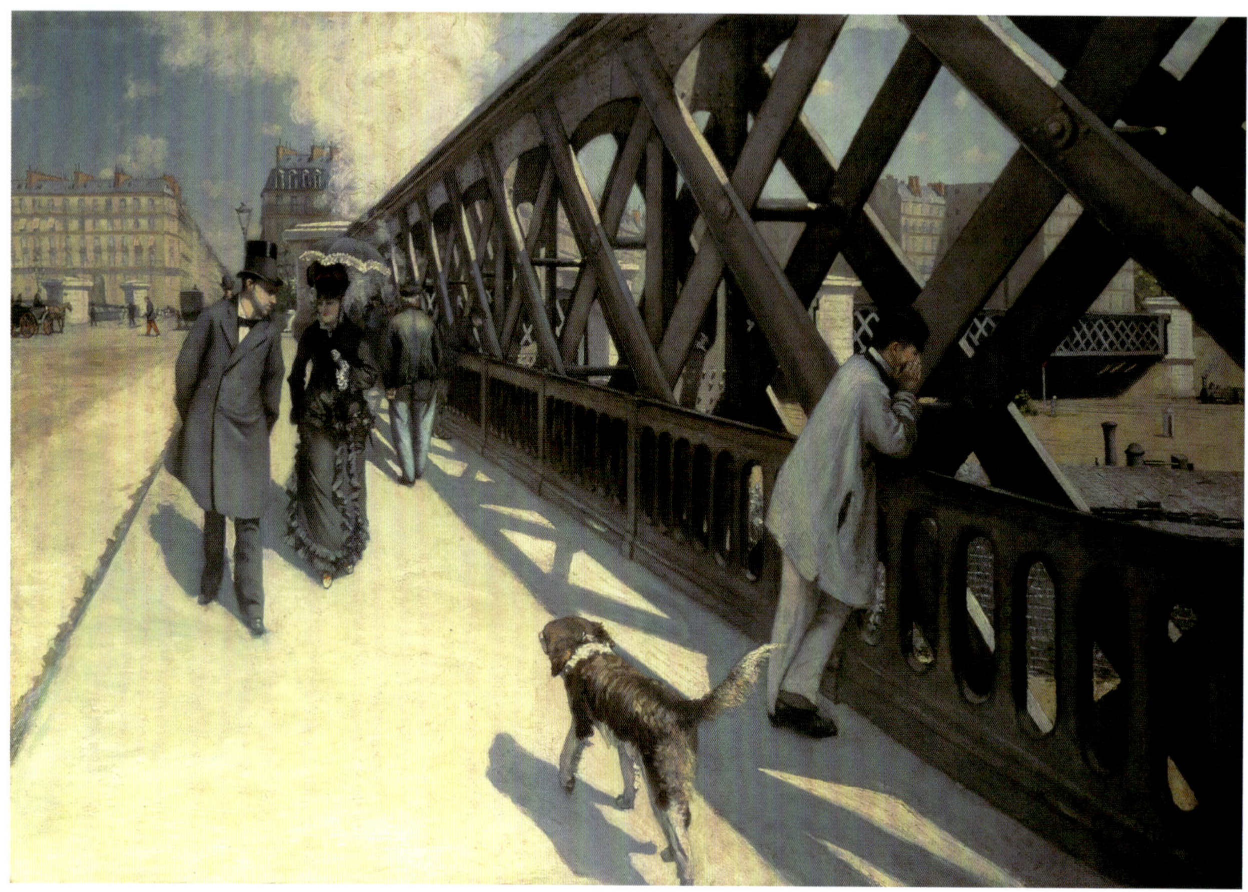

Le Pont de l'Europe

Le Pont de l'Europe

Der Pont de l'Europe

El Puente de Europa

O Ponto da Europa

De Pont de l'Europe

GUSTAVE CAILLEBOTTE (1848-1894)

1876, Oil on canvas/Huile sur toile, 125 × 180 cm,
Petit Palais, Genève

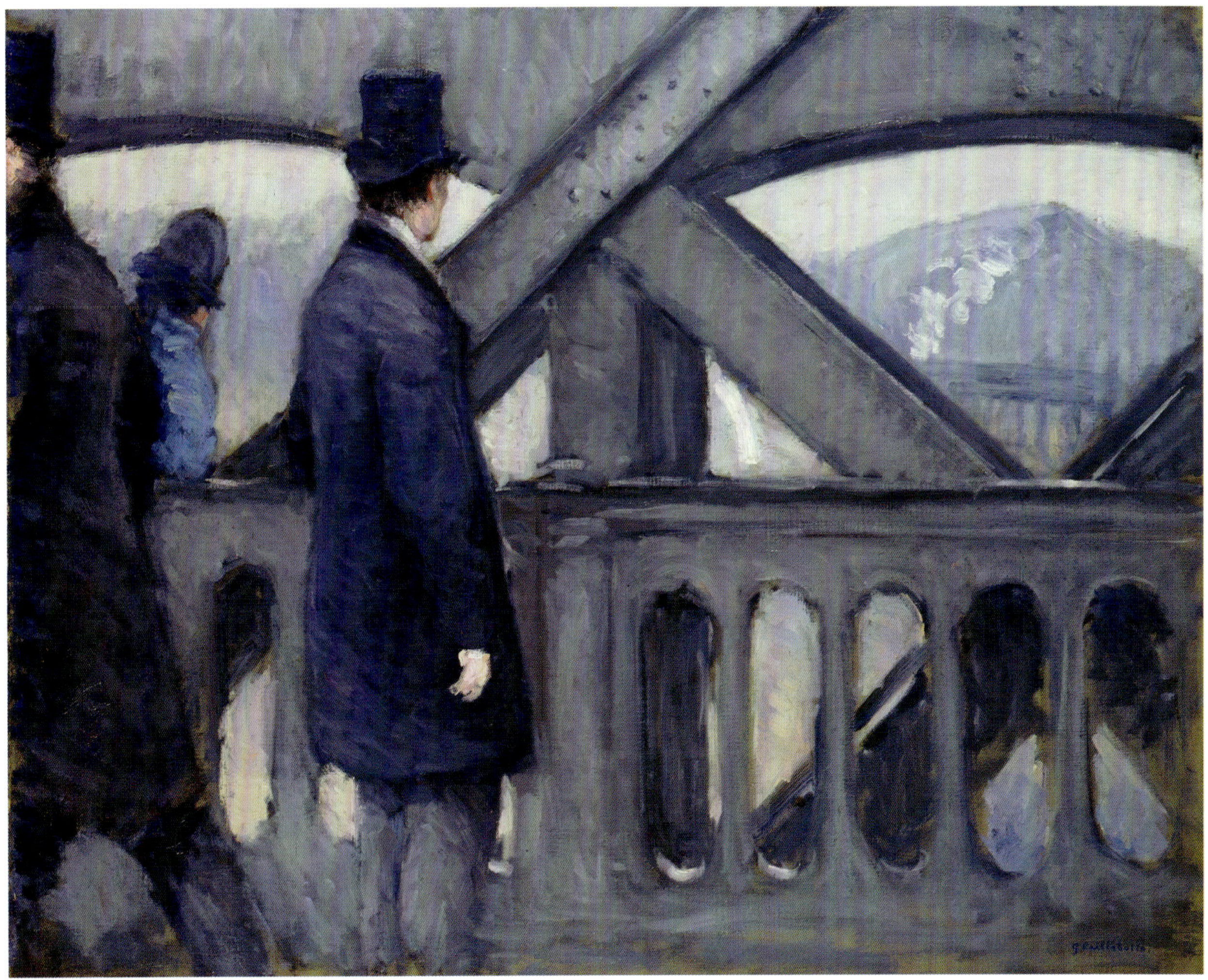

Le Pont de l'Europe

The painter created several paintings of the Pont de l'Europe in Paris, a masterpiece of modernism. In this view, the metallic structure of the bridge occupies the majority of the image section.

Le Pont de l'Europe

Le peintre a réalisé plusieurs tableaux autour de cet ouvrage moderne qu'est le pont de l'Europe, à Paris. Dans ce cadrage en plan rapproché, la structure métallique occupe l'essentiel de l'espace.

Der Pont de l'Europe

Der Maler schuf mehrere Gemälde der Pont de l'Europe in Paris, einem Meisterwerk der Moderne. Bei dieser Ansicht nimmt die metallische Struktur der Brücke den Großteil des Bildausschnitts ein.

El Puente de Europa

El pintor realizó varias pinturas del Pont de l'Europe en París, una obra maestra del modernismo. En esta vista, la estructura metálica del puente ocupa la mayor parte de la sección de la imagen.

O Ponto da Europa

O pintor criou várias pinturas da Pont de l'Europe em Paris, uma obra-prima do modernismo. Nesta vista, a estrutura metálica da ponte ocupa a maior parte da secção de imagem.

De Pont de l'Europe

De schilder maakte verschillende schilderijen van de Pont de l'Europe in Parijs, een meesterwerk van moderniteit. Bij deze aanblik beslaat de metalen brugconstructie het grootste deel van het beeldvlak.

GUSTAVE CAILLEBOTTE (1848-1894)

c. 1876/77, Oil on canvas/Huile sur toile, 64,8 × 81 cm, Private collection

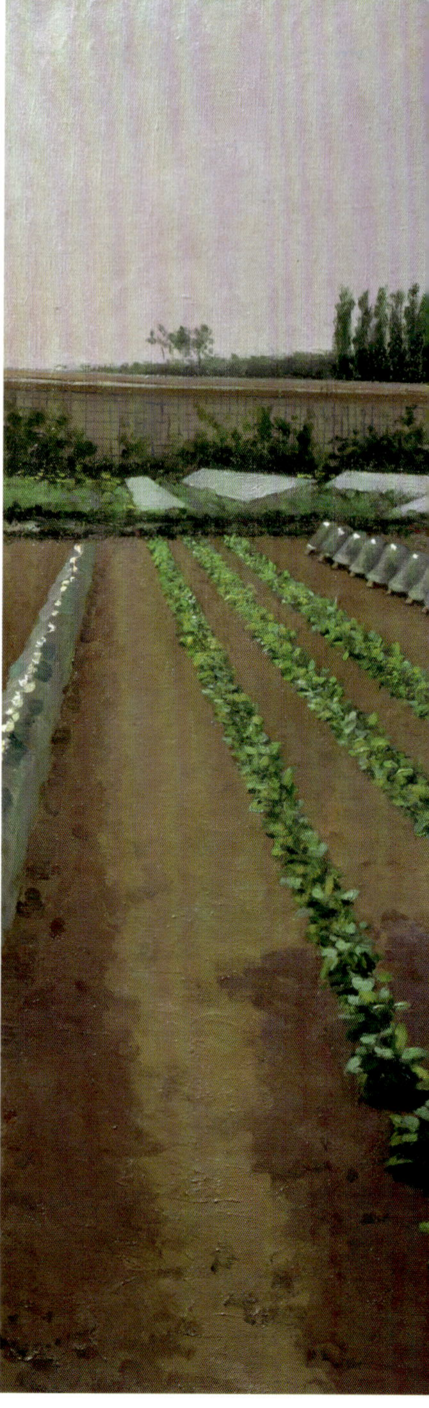

The Gardeners

The painting stands out in Caillebotte's work. Never before - apart from *The Parquet Planers* - has he gone so far in the direction of realism. The impressionistic brushwork gives way to a precise representation.

Les Jardiniers

Ce tableau est étonnant. Jamais, mis à part dans ses *Raboteurs de parquet*, Caillebotte n'avait poussé aussi loin son souci de réalisme. La touche impressionniste a laissé place à la précision du dessin.

Die Gärtner

Das Gemälde hebt sich von Caillebottes Werk ab. Nie zuvor – abgesehen von den *Parkettschleifern* – begab er sich soweit in Richtung Realismus. Die impressionistische Pinselführung weicht einer präzisen Darstellung.

Los jardineros

Esta obra de Caillebotte es increíble. Nunca antes -aparte de *Los acuchilladores de parqué*- ha ido tan lejos en la dirección del realismo. La pincelada impresionista da paso a una representación precisa.

Os jardineiros

A pintura destaca-se do trabalho de Caillebotte. Nunca antes - além *das lixadeiras de parquet* - ele foi tão longe na direção do realismo. A escova impressionista dá lugar a uma representação precisa.

De tuinmannen

Dit schilderij van Caillebotte valt uit de toon. Nooit eerder - afgezien van *De parketschuurschavers* - bewoog hij zich zo ver richting realisme. De impressionistische penseelvoering maakte plaats voor een precieze weergave.

GUSTAVE CAILLEBOTTE (1848-1894)

1877, Oil on canvas/Huile sur toile, 90 × 117 cm, Private collection

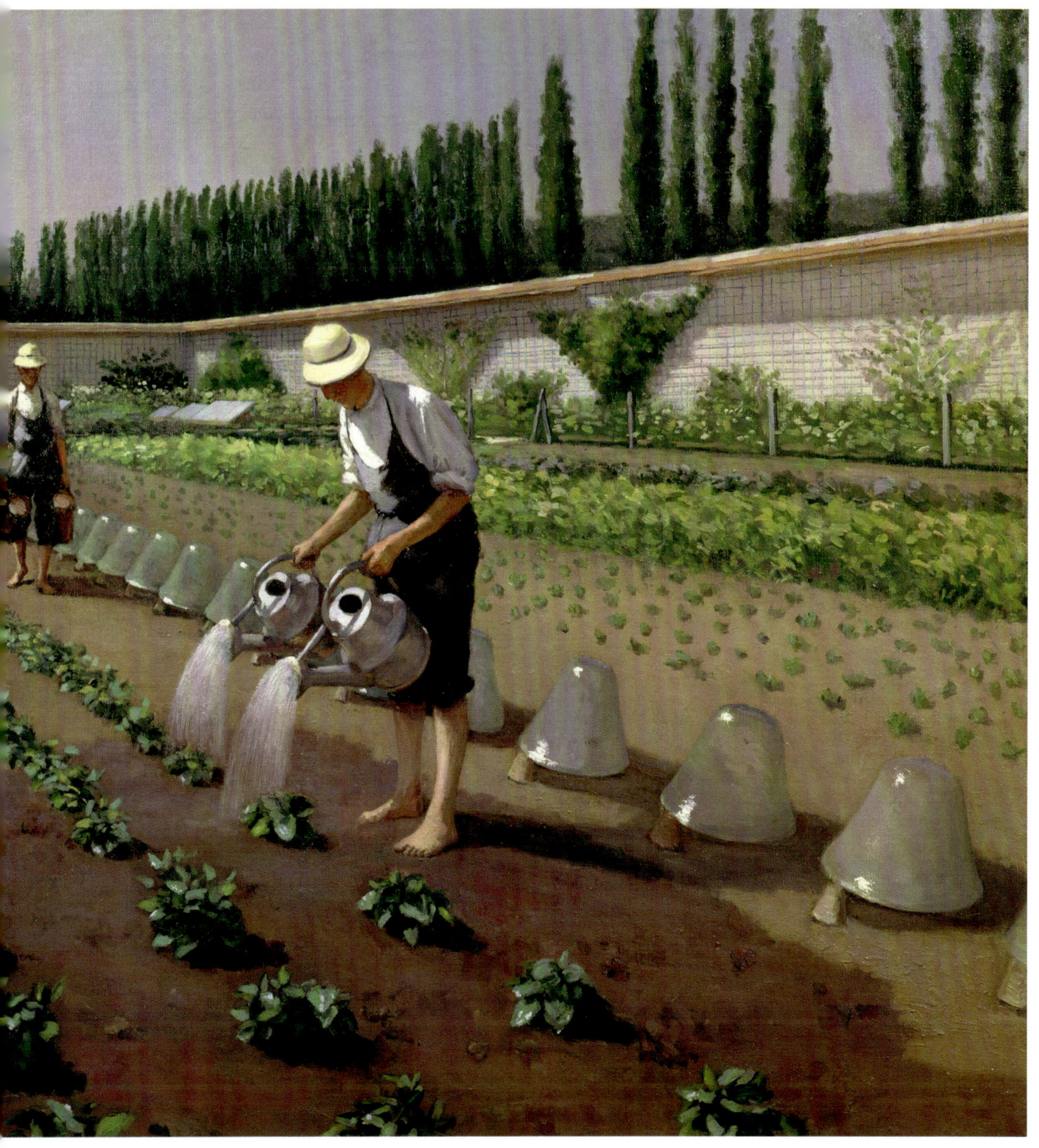

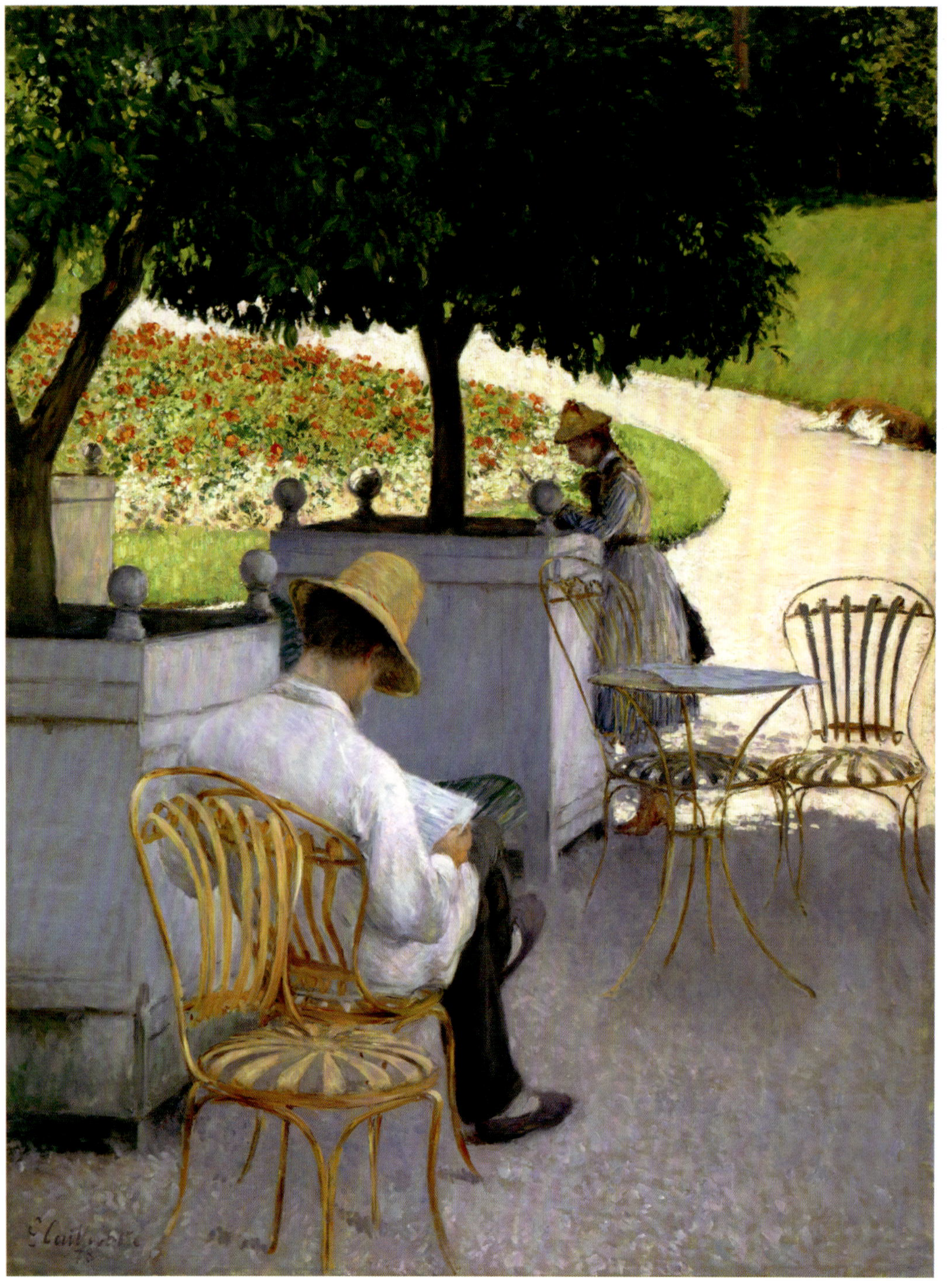

The Orange Trees or
The Artist's Brother
in His Garden

Les Orangers

Die Orangenbäume

Los naranjos

As Árvores Laranja

De sinaasappelbomen

GUSTAVE CAILLEBOTTE
(1848-1894)

1878, Oil on canvas/Huile sur
toile, 155 × 117 cm, Museum
of Fine Arts, Houston

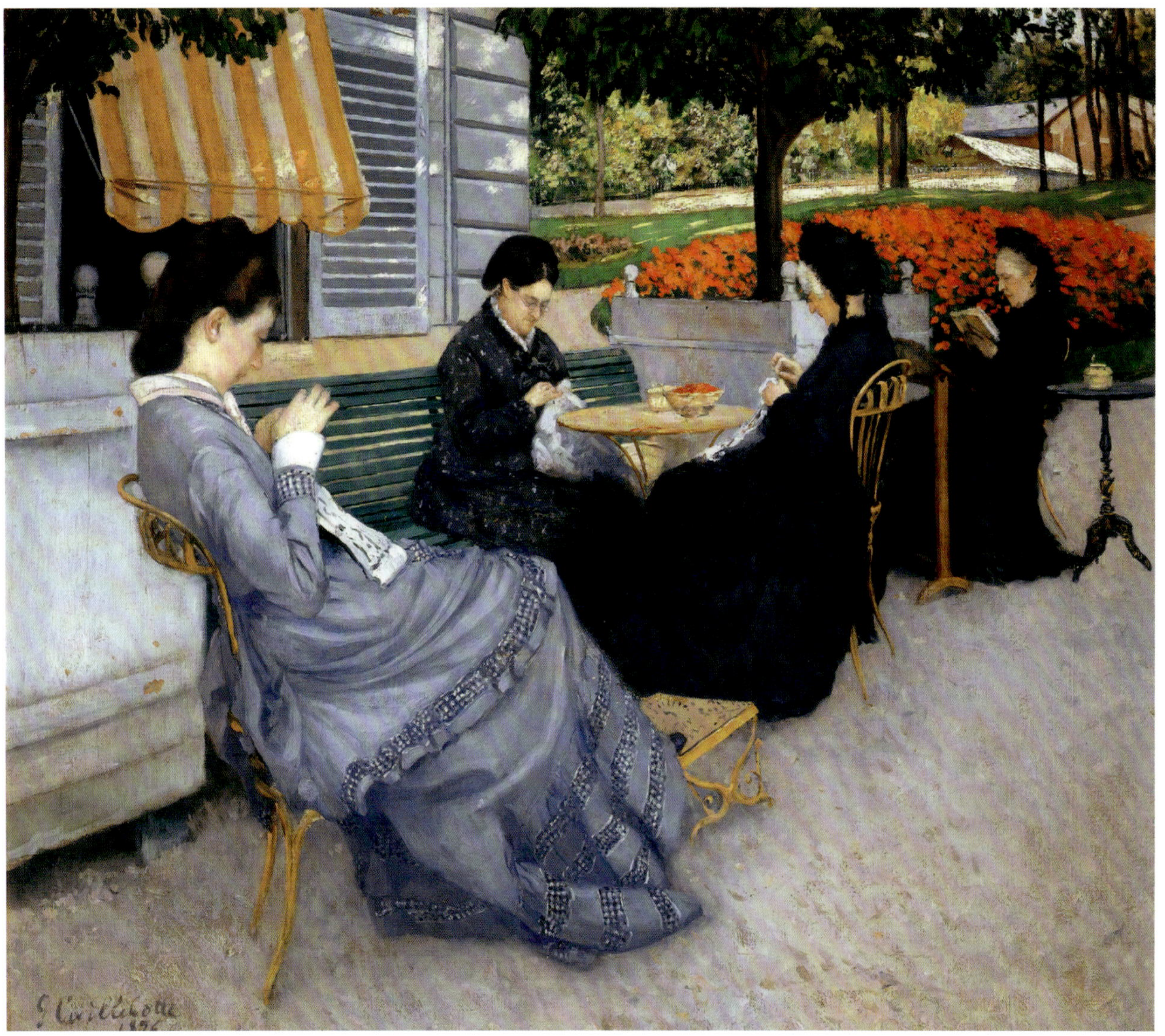

Ladies Sewing

The painting was made on the Caillebotte family's country estate in Yerres, southeast of Paris. On the terrace in front of the house the women occupy themselves with sewing and reading.

Femmes cousant

C'est à Yerres, au sud-est de Paris, dans la propriété familiale des Caillebotte, que l'artiste peint cette scène. Les femmes s'adonnent à la couture et à la lecture sur la terrasse, devant la maison.

Porträts auf dem Land oder Frauen beim Nähen

Das Gemälde entsteht auf dem Landsitz der Familie Caillebotte in Yerres südöstlich von Paris. Auf der Terrasse vor dem Haus widmen sich die Frauen dem Nähen und der Lektüre.

Mujeres cosiendo

El cuadro fue pintado en la finca de la familia Caillebotte en Yerres, al sureste de París. En la terraza, frente a la casa, las mujeres se dedican a la costura y a la lectura.

Retratos no país ou mulheres costurando

A pintura foi pintada na propriedade rural da família Caillebotte em Yerres, sudeste de Paris. No terraço em frente à casa, as mulheres se dedicam à costura e à leitura.

Naaiende vrouwen

Het schilderij is gemaakt op het landgoed van de familie Caillebotte in Yerres, ten zuidoosten van Parijs. Op het terras voor het huis zitten de vrouwen te naaien en te lezen.

GUSTAVE CAILLEBOTTE (1848-1894)

1878, Oil on canvas/Huile sur toile, Musée d'art et d'histoire Baron Gérard, Bayeux

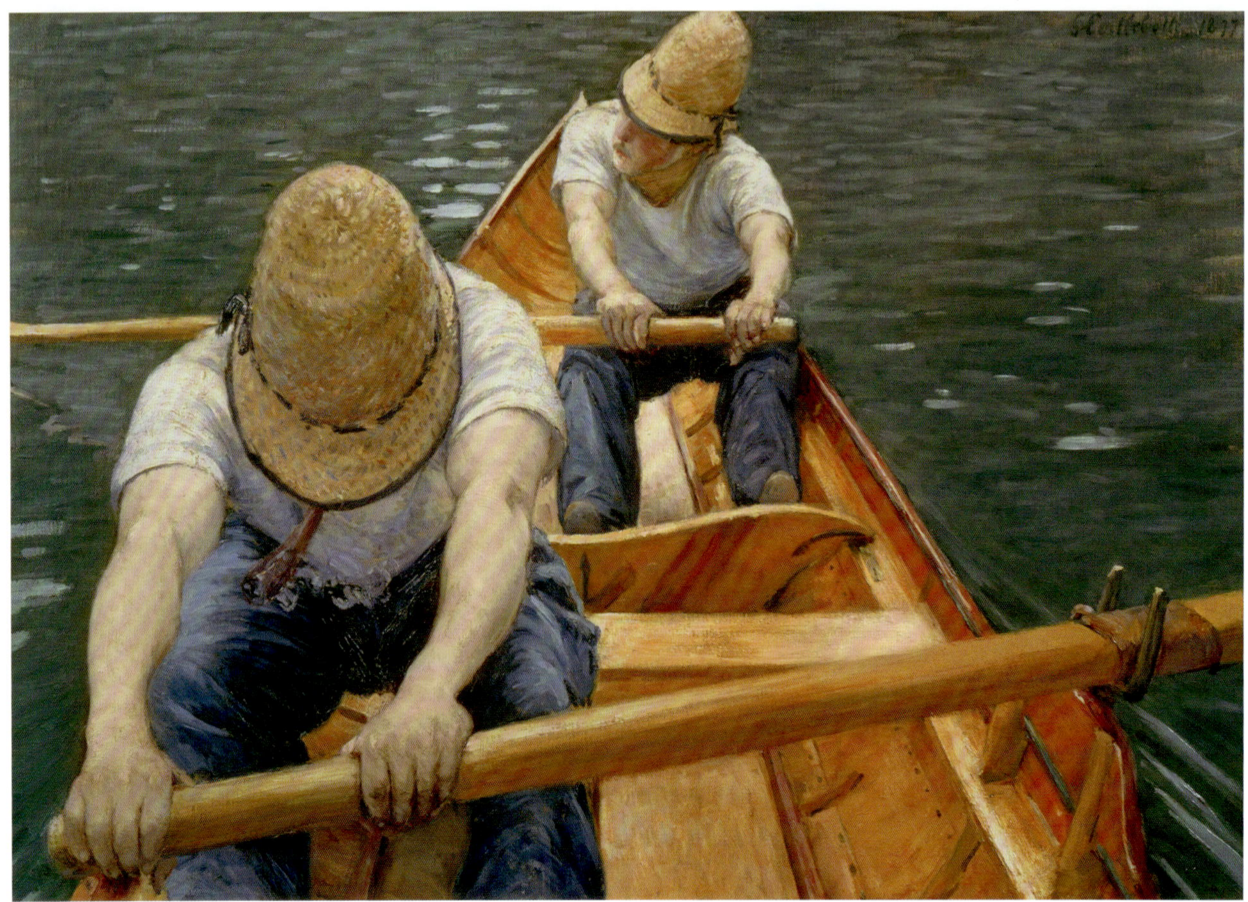

Boaters Rowing on the Yerres

The photograph-like image detail and the slight aeriel view bear witness to Caillebotte's modern approaches, which concentrate on the body posture of the rowers and conceal their faces under the straw hats.

Canotiers ramant sur l'Yerre

Le cadrage photographique et la vue en plongée témoignent de la modernité de l'artiste, qui s'est focalisé sur le geste des rameurs. Au point de dissimuler le visage d'un personnage sous son chapeau.

Ruderer auf der Yerres

Der fotografisch wirkende Bildausschnitt und die leichte Draufsicht zeugen von den modernen Ansätzen Caillebottes, der sich auf die Körperhaltung der Ruderer konzentriert und die Gesichter unter den Strohhüten verbirgt.

Remeros en el Yerres

El detalle de la imagen fotográfica y la ligera vista superior son testigos de los modernos enfoques de Caillebotte, que se concentran en la postura corporal de los remeros y ocultan los rostros bajo los sombreros de paja.

Oarsmen on the Yerres

O detalhe fotográfico da imagem e a ligeira vista de cima testemunham as abordagens modernas de Caillebotte, que se concentram na postura corporal dos remadores e escondem os rostos sob os chapéus de palha.

Roeiers op de Yerres

De fotografisch aandoende beelduitsnede en het lichte bovenaanzicht getuigen van Caillebottes moderne benadering, die zich concentreert op de lichaamshouding van de roeiers en de gezichten onder de strohoeden verbergt.

GUSTAVE CAILLEBOTTE (1848-1894)

1877, Oil on canvas/Huile sur toile, 81 × 116 cm, Private collection

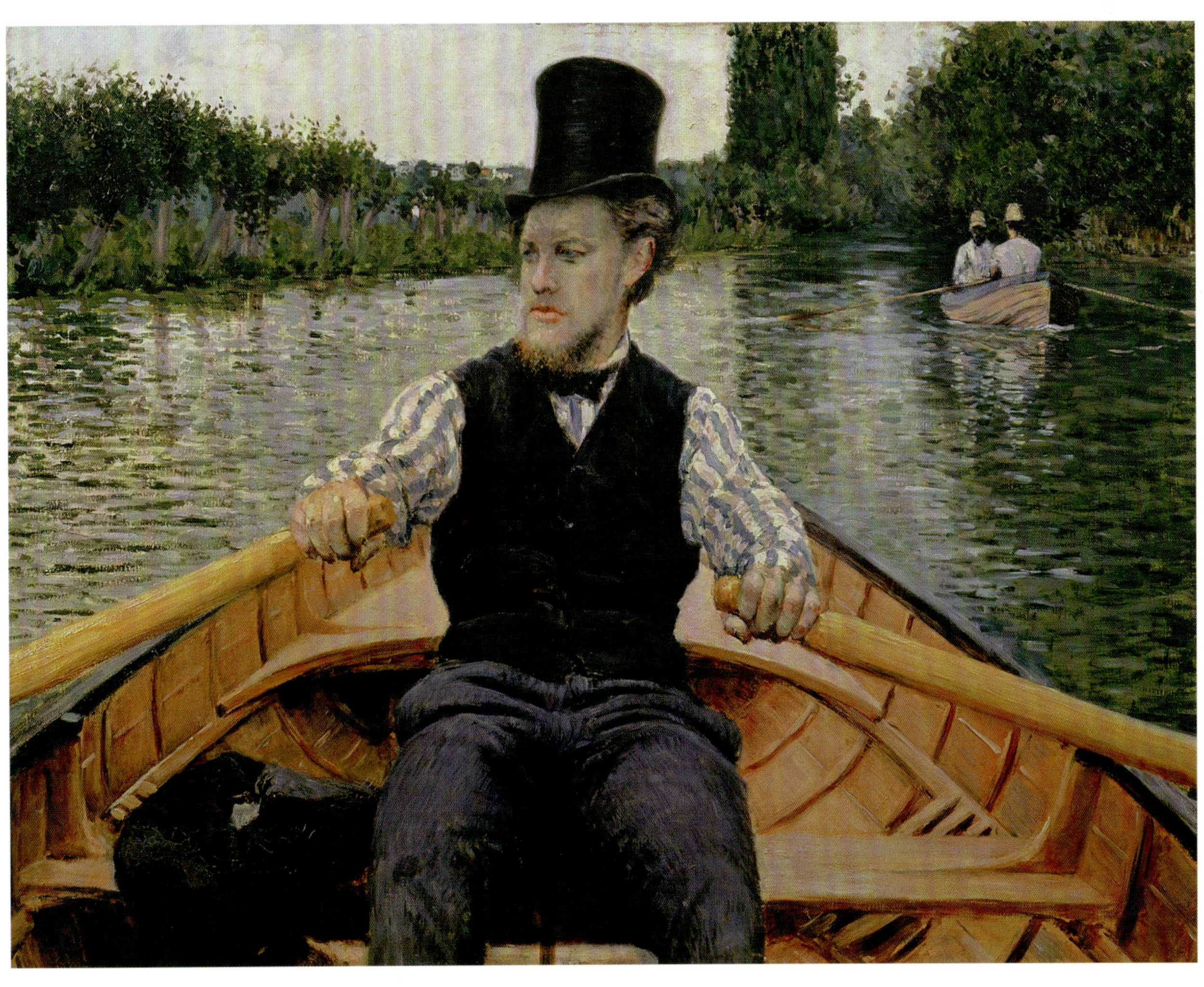

The Boat Party *or* Rower in a Top Hat

La Partie de bateau *ou* Le Canotier au chapeau haut-de-forme

Die Bootfahrt *oder* Der Ruderer mit dem Zylinder

Navegación *o* Remero con chistera

Boating *ou* O remador com o cilindro

De boottocht *of* De roeier met de hoge hoed

GUSTAVE CAILLEBOTTE (1848-1894)

1878, Oil on canvas/Huile sur toile, 90 × 117 cm, Private collection

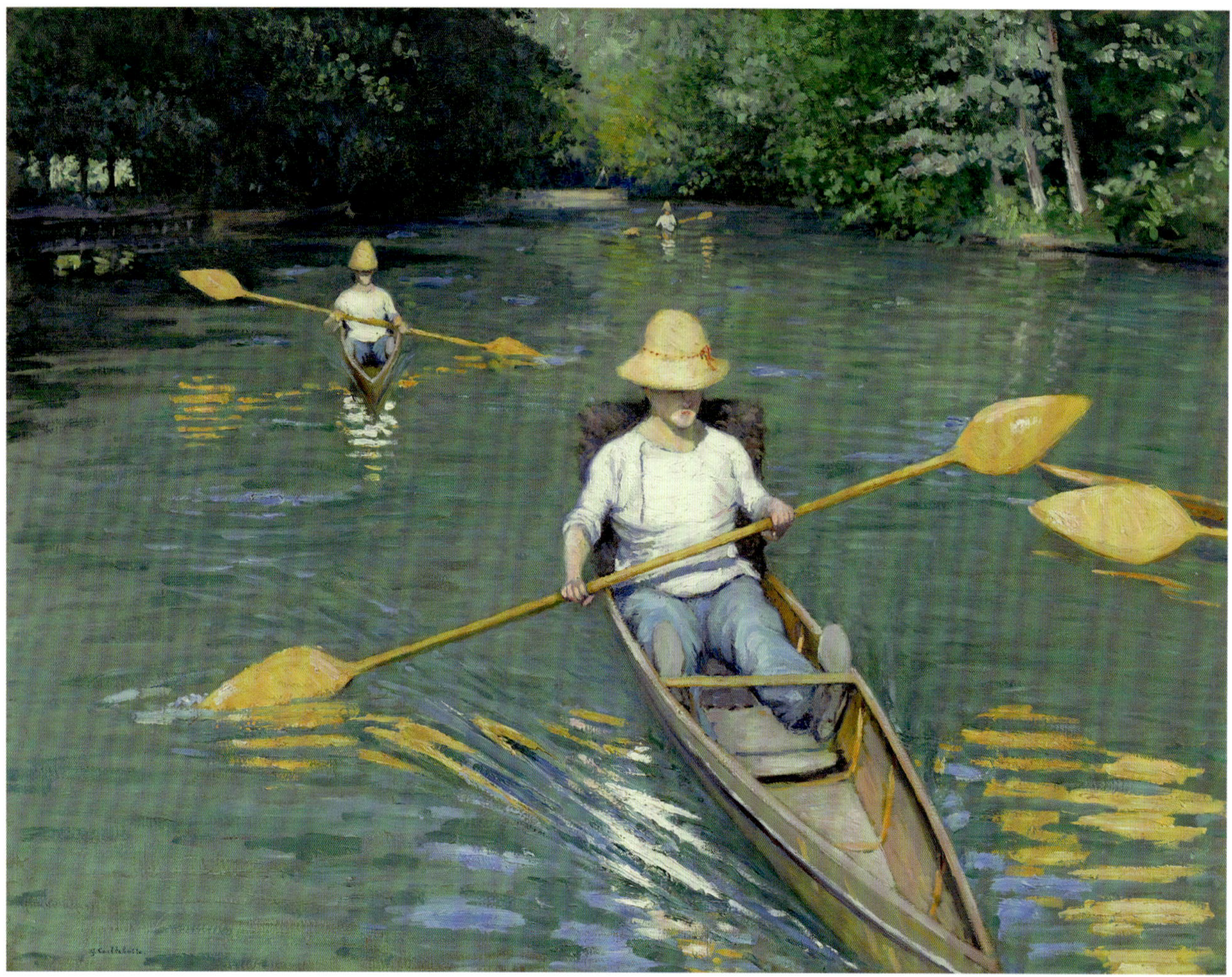

Skiffs

Avirons

Kanus auf der Yerres

Canoas en el Yerres

Canoas sobre os Yerres

Kano's op de Yerre

GUSTAVE CAILLEBOTTE (1848-1894)

1877, Oil on canvas/Huile sur toile, 88,9 × 116,2 cm,
National Gallery of Art, Washington

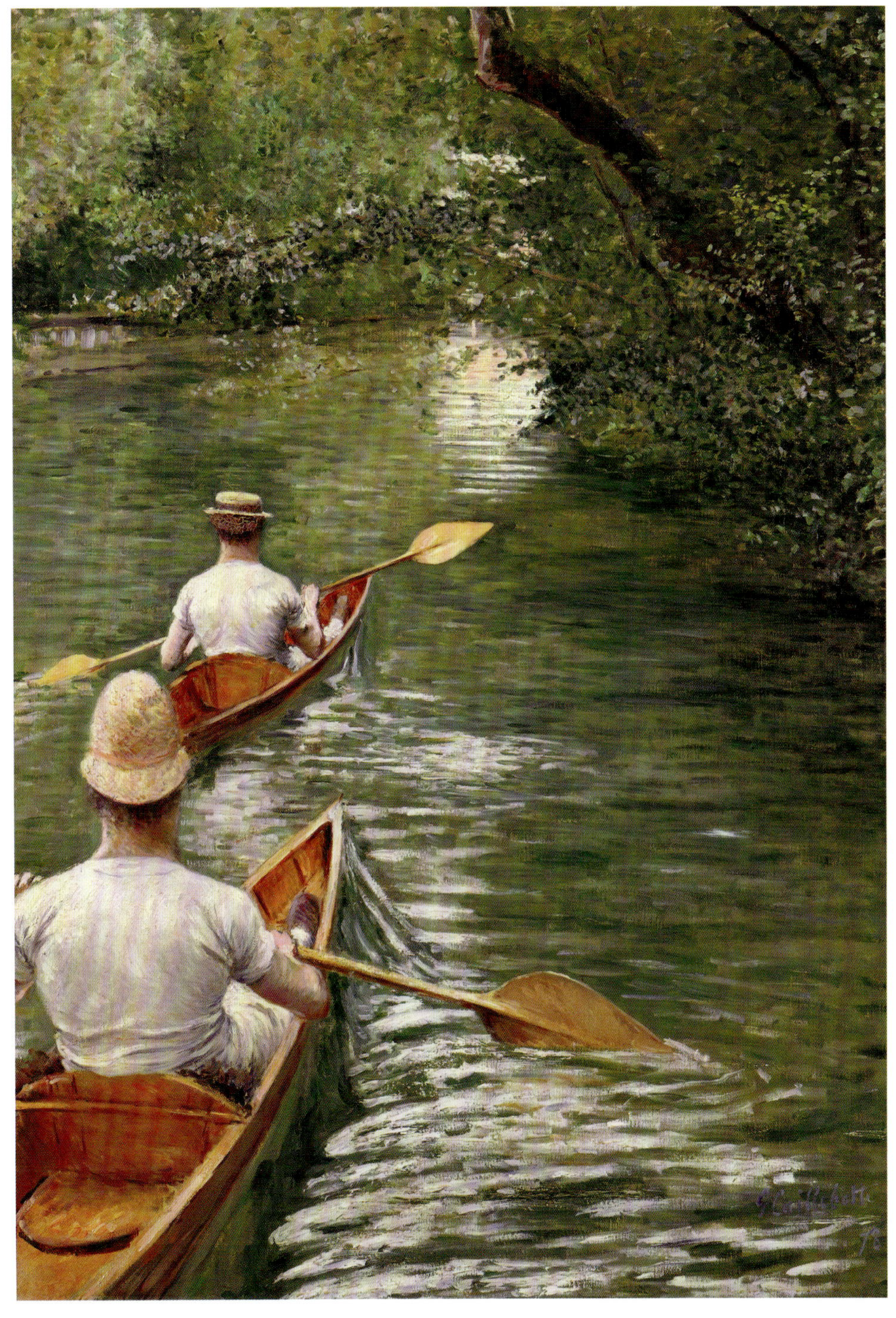

The Canoes

Les Canoës

Die Kanus

Las canoas

As canoas

De kano's

GUSTAVE CAILLEBOTTE (1848-1894)
1878, Oil on canvas/
Huile sur toile, 155 × 108,5 cm,
Musée des Beaux-Arts, Rennes

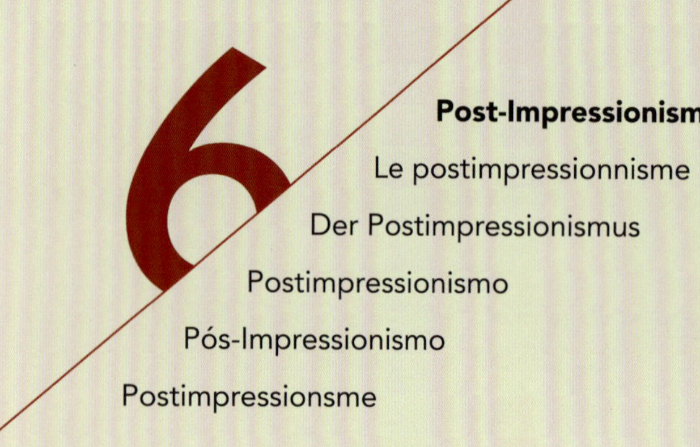

Post-Impressionism

Le postimpressionnisme

Der Postimpressionismus

Postimpressionismo

Pós-Impressionismo

Postimpressionsme

Post-Impressionism

The term Post-Impressionism refers to several styles that emerged from the mid-1880s onwards under the influence of the Impressionists, whose last group exhibition took place in 1886. While Paul Gauguin and the painters of the School of Pont-Aven developed Synthetism, Georges Seurat - the most important figure of Post-Impressionism - as well as Paul Signac, Henri Edmond Cross and Maximilien Luce increasingly devoted themselves to Pointillism.

Paul Cézanne questioned the rules of perspective and carried out innovative studies on the deconstruction of form. The simplification into geometric forms and the abandonment of traditional representation produced balanced compositions of colored bodies and volumes. They lend landscapes, still lifes, figures and portraits a novel visual effect. The development of Cézanne's style is remarkable - from his landscapes from the 1870s, which still bear witness to Impressionism, to the views of Mont Sainte-Victoire bordering on abstraction from 1904-1906.

Le postimpressionnisme

Derrière le terme de postimpressionnisme se cachent plusieurs tendances. Elles s'épanouissent à partir du milieu des années 1880 dans le sillage des impressionnistes, dont la dernière exposition collective a lieu en 1886. Si, Paul Gauguin et ses camarades de l'école de Pont-Aven s'orientent vers le synthétisme, Georges Seurat, chef de file du néo-impressionnisme, s'adonne au pointillisme, tout comme Paul Signac, Henri Edmond Cross ou Maximilien Luce.

De son côté, Paul Cézanne remet en cause les lois de la perspective, et développe des recherches innovantes autour de la déconstruction de la forme. La simplification et la géométrisation, l'abandon du dessin traditionnel au profit de compositions construites par des masses et des volumes colorés, métamorphosent paysages, natures mortes, figures et portraits. L'évolution de la peinture de Cézanne est saisissante, de ses paysages des années 1870, marquées par l'impressionnisme, à ses ultimes vues de la montagne Sainte-Victoire des années 1904-1906, aux frontières de l'abstraction.

Der Postimpressionismus

Unter der Bezeichnung Postimpressionismus werden mehrere Stile zusammengefasst, die ab der Mitte der 1880er-Jahre unter dem Einfluss der Impressionisten entstanden, deren letzte Gruppenausstellung 1886 stattfand. Während Paul Gauguin und die Maler der Schule von Pont-Aven den Synthetismus entwickeln, widmen sich Georges Seurat – die wichtigste Figur des Postimpressionismus – sowie Paul Signac, Henri Edmond Cross oder Maximilien Luce verstärkt dem Pointillismus.

Paul Cézanne hinterfragt die Regeln der Perspektive und führt innovative Studien zur Dekonstruktion der Form durch. Die Vereinfachung in geometrische Formen und die Abkehr von der traditionellen Darstellung bringt ausgewogene Kompositionen aus farbigen Körpern und Volumen hervor. Sie verleihen Landschaften, Stillleben, Figuren und Porträts eine neuartige Bildwirkung. Die Entwicklung von Cézannes Stil ist bemerkenswert – angefangen bei seinen Landschaften aus den 1870er-Jahren, die noch vom

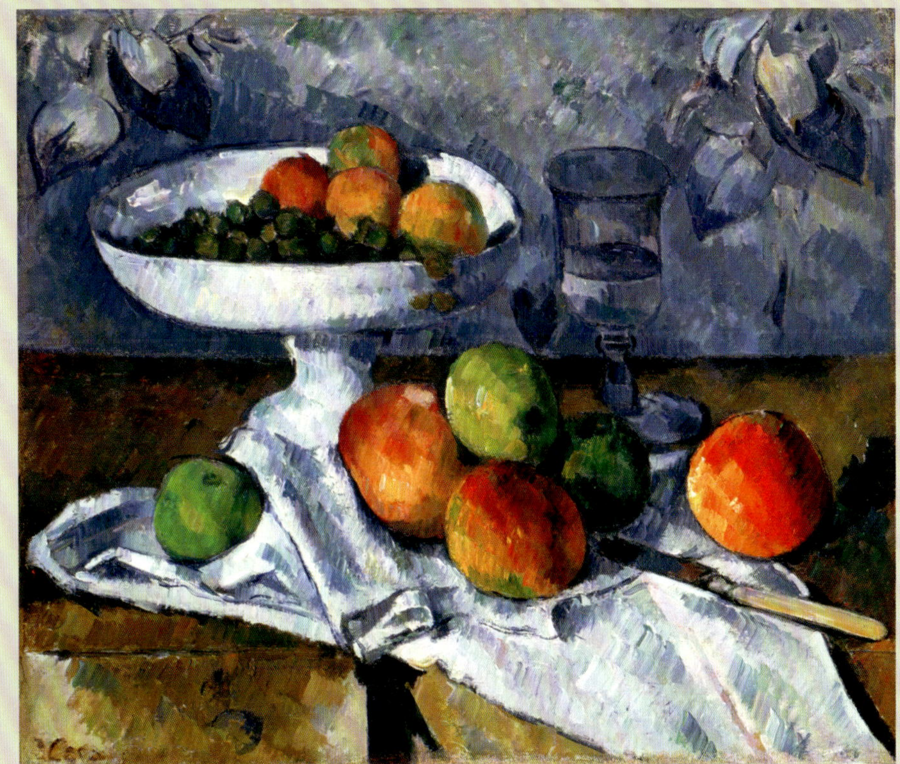

Postimpresionismo

El término Post-Impresionismo se refiere a varios estilos que surgieron a partir de mediados de la década de 1880 bajo la influencia de los impresionistas, cuya última exposición colectiva tuvo lugar en 1886. Mientras Paul Gauguin y los pintores de la Escuela de Pont-Aven desarrollaban el sintetismo, Georges Seurat -la figura más importante del postimpresionismo-, así como Paul Signac, Henri Edmond Cross y Maximilien Luce se dedicaban cada vez más al puntillismo.

Paul Cézanne cuestiona las reglas de la perspectiva y realiza estudios innovadores sobre la deconstrucción de la forma. La simplificación en formas geométricas y el abandono de la representación tradicional produce composiciones equilibradas de cuerpos y volúmenes coloreados. Confieren a los paisajes, bodegones, figuras y retratos un novedoso efecto visual. El desarrollo del estilo de Cézanne es notable, desde sus paisajes de la década de 1870, que todavía dan testimonio del impresionismo, hasta las vistas del Monte Sainte-Victoire en los límites de la abstracción de 1904-1906.

Pós-Impressionismo

O termo Pós-Impressionismo refere-se a vários estilos que surgiram a partir de meados dos anos 1880 sob a influência dos Impressionistas, cuja última exposição colectiva teve lugar em 1886. Enquanto Paul Gauguin e os pintores da Escola de Pont-Aven desenvolveram o Sintético, Georges Seurat - a figura mais importante do Pós-Impressionismo - assim como Paul Signac, Henri Edmond Cross e Maximilien Luce se dedicaram cada vez mais ao Pontifício.

Paul Cézanne questiona as regras da perspectiva e realiza estudos inovadores sobre a desconstrução da forma. A simplificação em formas geométricas e o abandono da representação tradicional produzem composições equilibradas de corpos e volumes coloridos. Eles emprestam paisagens, naturezas mortas, figuras e retratos a um novo efeito visual. O desenvolvimento do estilo de Cézanne é notável - desde as suas paisagens da década de 1870, que ainda testemunham o impressionismo, até às vistas do Monte Sainte-Victoire nos limites da abstracção de 1904-1906.

Postimpressionisme

De term postimpressionisme verwijst naar verschillende stijlen die vanaf halverwege de jaren 1880 opkwamen onder invloed van de impressionisten, wier laatste groepstentoonstelling in 1886 plaatsvond. Terwijl Paul Gauguin en de schilders van de school van Pont-Aven het synthetisme ontwikkelden, legden Georges Seurat (de belangrijkste persoonlijkheid van het postimpressionisme), Paul Signac, Henri Edmond Cross en Maximilien Luce zich steeds meer toe op het pointillisme.

Paul Cézanne vroeg naar het waarom van de perspectiefregels en bracht vernieuwende studies naar de deconstructie van de vorm ten uitvoer. De vereenvoudiging door geometrische vormen en het loslaten van de traditionele manier van weergeven leverden evenwichtige composities van kleurige lichamen en volumes op. Ze verleenden landschappen, stillevens, figuren en portretten een nieuwe visuele werking. De ontwikkeling van Cézannes stijl is opmerkelijk – van landschappen uit de jaren 1870

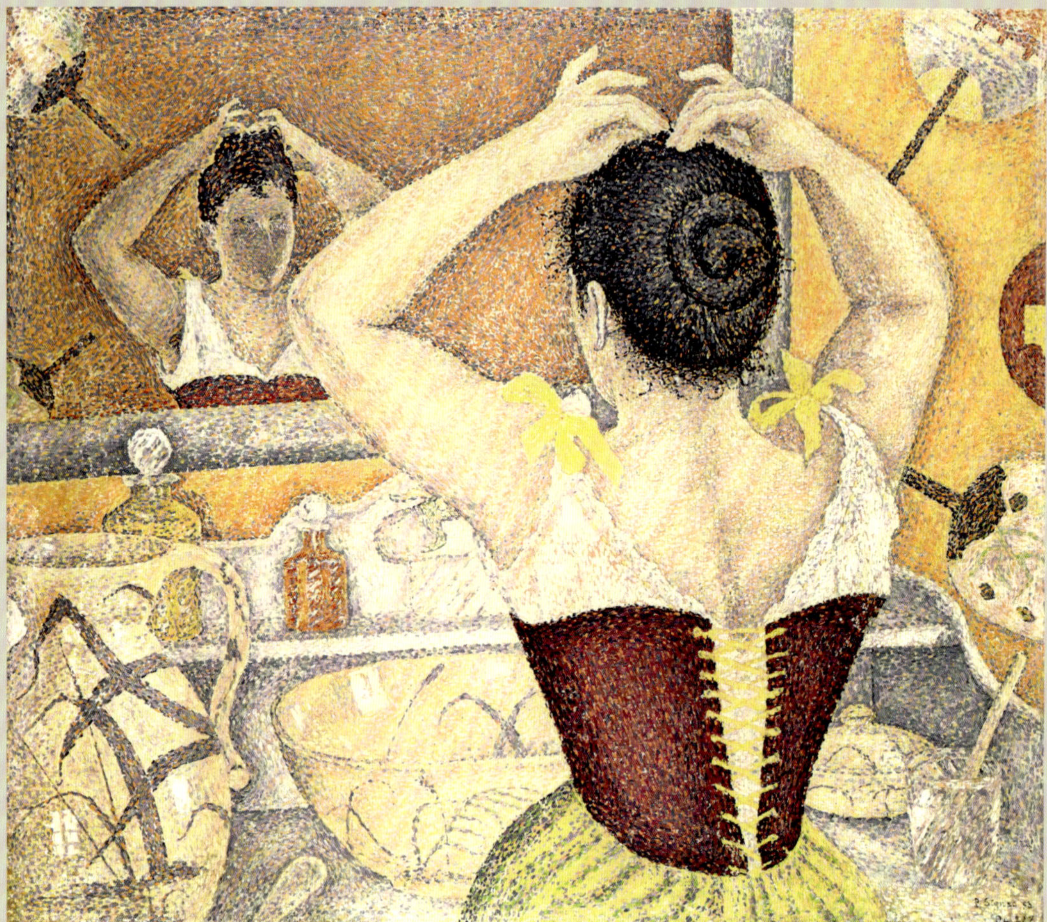

The last decades of the 19th century were also the time of Henri de Toulouse-Lautrec. The painter, illustrator and graphic artist, who drew inspiration from every current, is an indispensable part of Montmartre's artistic life. He captured the atmosphere of an epoch with a lively stroke, sometimes in sketchy paintings. Comedians, singers, circus artists, prostitutes - Toulouse-Lautrec is the painter of women, of nightly pleasure, joys and melancholy. He presents his models with dignity and respect - in intimate, lonely and bored moments, during body care, in the box of a theatre or waiting for customers in the lounge of a brothel.

Enfin, difficile d'évoquer les dernières décennies du XIXᵉ siècle sans parler d'Henri de Toulouse-Lautrec. Peintre, dessinateur, illustrateur et affichiste, ce personnage haut en couleur, en marge de tout courant ou mouvement, est indissociable de la vie montmartroise. D'une touche vive, au travers de tableaux qui s'apparentent parfois à des esquisses, il capte le parfum d'une époque. Comédiennes, chanteuses, artistes de cirque ou prostituées, Toulouse-Lautrec est le peintre des femmes, du spectacle et de la nuit. Du plaisir, et de la mélancolie. Avec dignité et respect, il saisit ses modèles dans des moments intimes, de solitude ou d'ennui, à leur toilette, dans la loge d'un théâtre, en train d'attendre le client dans le salon d'une maison close.

Impressionismus zeugen, bis hin zu den Ansichten des Mont Sainte-Victoire an den Grenzen der Abstraktion aus den Jahren 1904–1906.
Die letzten Jahrzehnte des 19. Jahrhunderts waren auch die Zeit von Henri de Toulouse-Lautrec. Der aus jeder Strömung schöpfende Maler, Illustrator und Grafiker ist aus dem Künstlerleben Montmartres kaum wegzudenken. Mit lebhaftem Strich, in manchmal skizzenhaften Gemälden fängt er die Atmosphäre einer Epoche ein. Komikerinnen, Sängerinnen, Zirkuskünstlerinnen, Prostituierte – Toulouse-Lautrec ist der Maler der Frauen, des nächtlichen Vergnügens, der Freuden und der Melancholie. Mit Würde und Respekt stellt er seine Modelle dar – in intimen, einsamen und gelangweilten Augenblicken, bei der Körperpflege, in der Loge eines Theaters oder beim Warten auf Kunden im Salon eines Bordells.

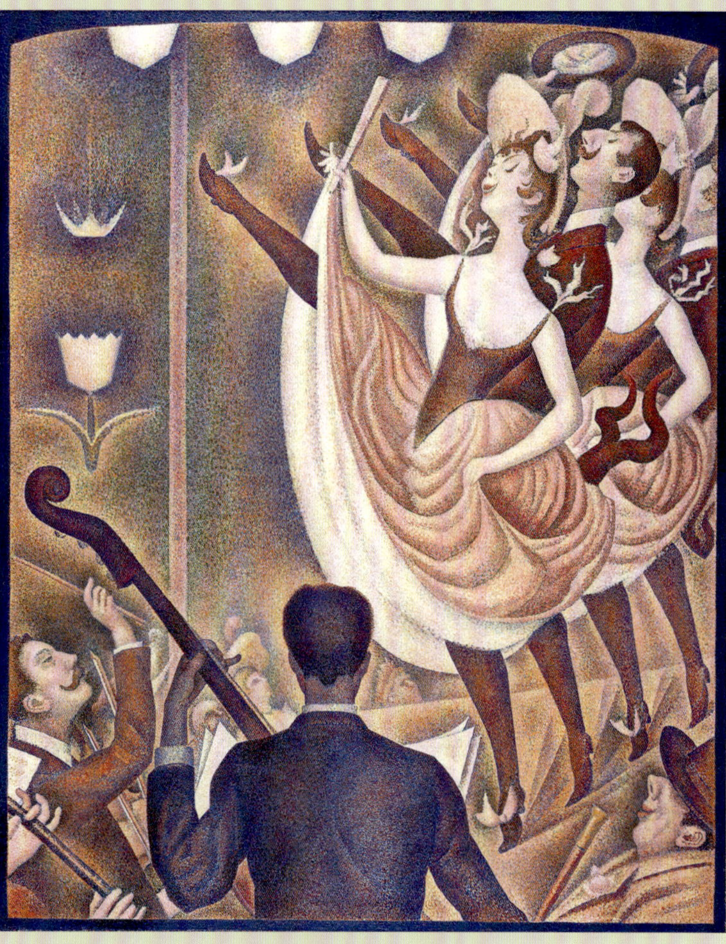

Las últimas décadas del siglo XIX fueron también la época de Henri de Toulouse-Lautrec. El pintor, ilustrador y grafista, que se nutre de todas las corrientes, es una parte indispensable de la vida artística de Montmartre. Captura la atmósfera de una época con un trazo vivo, a veces en cuadros incompletos. Comediantes, cantantes, artistas de circo, prostitutas - Toulouse-Lautrec es el pintor de las mujeres, del placer nocturno, de las alegrías y de la melancolía. Presenta a sus modelos con dignidad y respeto - en momentos íntimos, solitarios y aburridos, en el cuidado del cuerpo, en el palco de un teatro o esperando a los clientes en el salón de un burdel.

As últimas décadas do século XIX foram também a época de Henri de Toulouse-Lautrec. O pintor, ilustrador e artista gráfico, que tira de cada corrente, é uma parte indispensável da vida artística de Montmartres. Ele capta a atmosfera de uma época com uma pincelada viva, às vezes em pinturas esquemáticas. Comediantes, cantores, artistas de circo, prostitutas - Toulouse-Lautrec é a pintora das mulheres, do prazer noturno, das alegrias e da melancolia. Apresenta os seus modelos com dignidade e respeito - em momentos íntimos, solitários e aborrecidos, no body care, na caixa de um teatro ou à espera de clientes no salão de um bordel.

die nog getuigen van het impressionisme tot de aan abstractie grenzende blikken op de Mont Sainte-Victoire van 1904-1906.
De laatste decennia van de 19e eeuw waren ook de tijd van Henri de Toulouse-Lautrec. De uit alle stromingen puttende schilder, illustrator en graficus is bijna niet weg te denken uit het kunstenaarsleven van Montmartre. Hij legde de sfeer van een tijdperk in soms schetsmatige schilderijen met levendige penseelstreken vast. Comédiennes, zangeressen, circusartiestes, prostituees – Toulouse-Lautrec was de schilder van vrouwen, van nachtelijk plezier, van vreugde en melancholie. Hij gaf zijn modellen met waardigheid en respect weer – tijdens intieme, eenzame en langdradige momenten, bij de lichaamsverzorging, in de loge van een theater of wachtend op klanten in de salon van een bordeel.

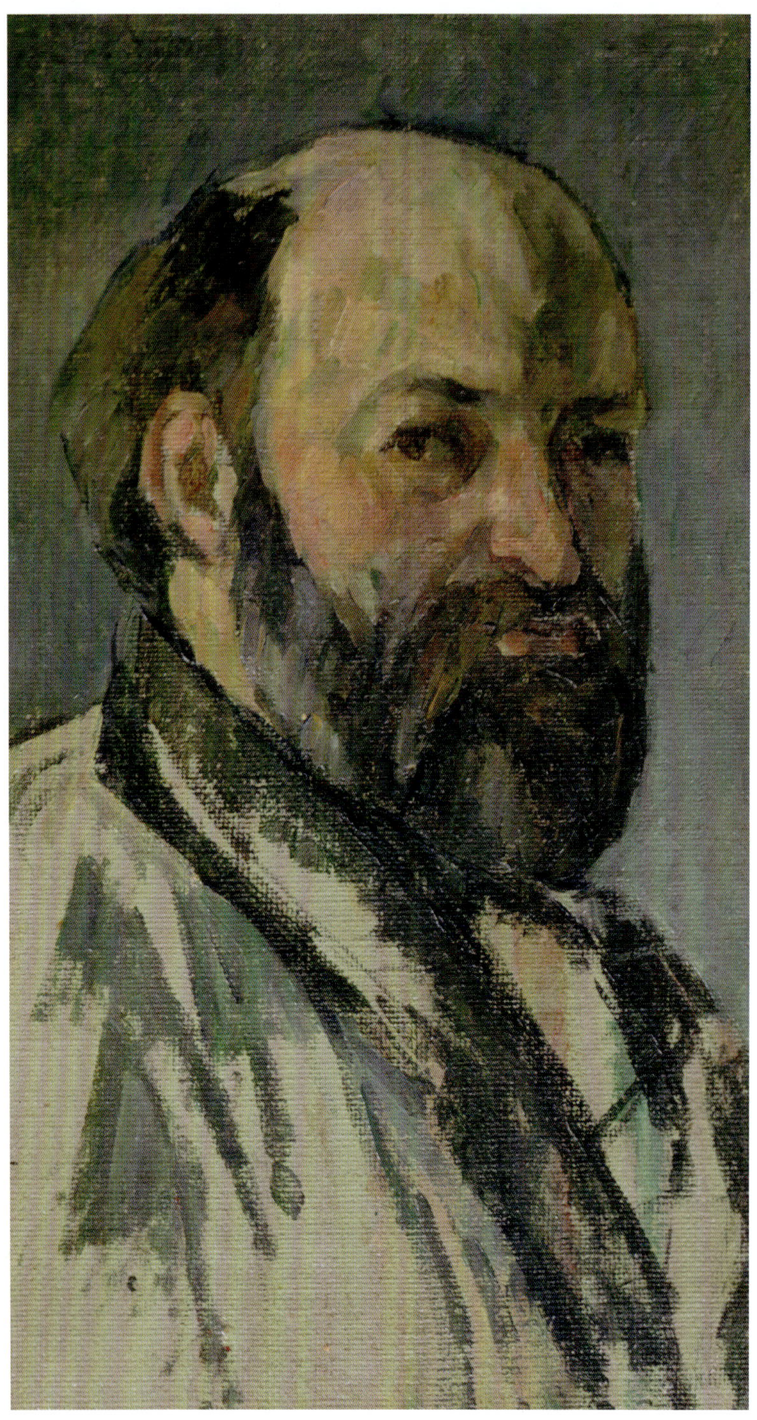

Self Portrait

Autoportrait

Selbstbildnis

Autorretrato

Auto-retrato

Zelfportret

PAUL CÉZANNE (1839-1906)
c. 1877, Oil on canvas/
Huile sur toile, 25,5 × 14,3 cm,
Musée d'Orsay, Paris

Madame Cézanne sewing

Madame Cézanne cousant

Madame Cézanne, nähend

Madame Cézanne cosiendo

Madame Cézanne, costura

Madame Cézanne naaiend

PAUL CÉZANNE (1839-1906)
1877, Oil on canvas/
Huile sur toile, 59,5 x 49,5 cm,
Nationalmuseum, Stockholm

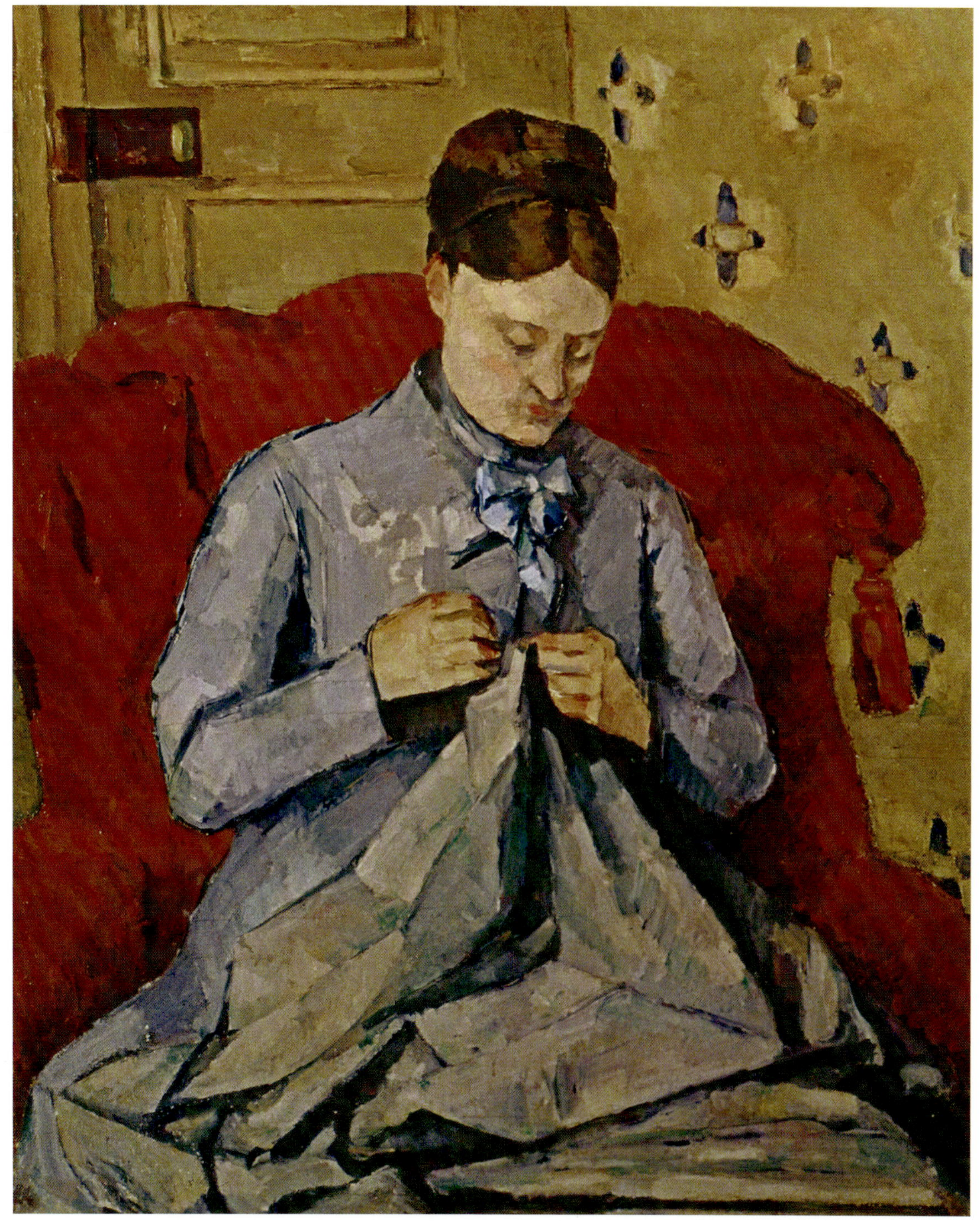

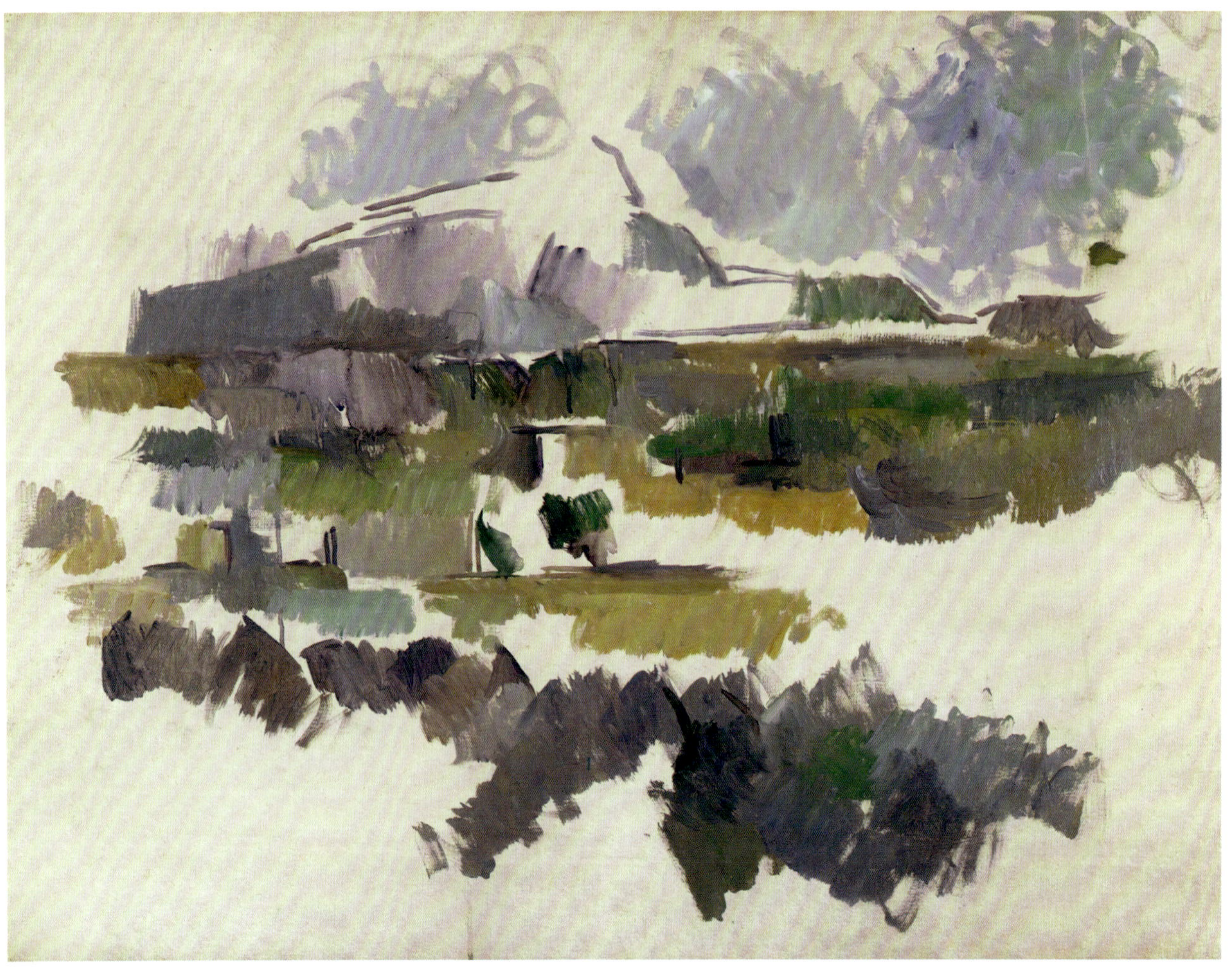

Montagne Sainte-Victoire

Cézanne painted the Montagne Sainte-Victoire mountain
range near Aix-en-Provence countless times. More than
80 paintings, watercolors and sketches were created,
some of them bordering on abstraction.

La Montagne Sainte-Victoire

Sujet quasi obsessionnel de Cézanne, la montagne Sainte-
Victoire, près d'Aix-en-Provence, donnera lieu à plus de
quatre-vingts peintures, aquarelles et esquisses, parfois
aux frontières de l'abstraction.

PAUL CÉZANNE (1839-1906)

1904/05, Oil on canvas/Huile sur toile, 54 × 73 cm, Fondation Beyeler, Basel

Montagne Sainte-Victoire

Cézanne malt das Gebirge Montagne Sainte-Victoire in der
Nähe von Aix-en-Provence unzählige Male. Es entstehen
mehr als 80 Gemälde, Aquarelle und Skizzen, manche
davon an der Grenze zum Abstrakten.

Montaña Sainte-Victoire

Cézanne pinta la cadena montañosa de la Montaña
Sainte-Victoire cerca de Aix-en-Provence en innumerables
ocasiones. Se crean más de 80 pinturas, acuarelas y bocetos,
algunos de ellos en el borde de lo abstracto.

Montagne Sainte-Victoire

Cézanne pinta a cordilheira Montagne Sainte-Victoire perto
de Aix-en-Provence inúmeras vezes. Mais de 80 pinturas,
aquarelas e esboços são criados, alguns deles na fronteira
do abstrato.

Montagne Sainte-Victoire

Cézanne schilderde de Montagne Sainte-Victoire in de
buurt van Aix-en-Provence talloze malen. Hij maakte
er meer dan 80 schilderijen, aquarellen en schetsen van,
waarvan sommige grenzen aan het abstracte.

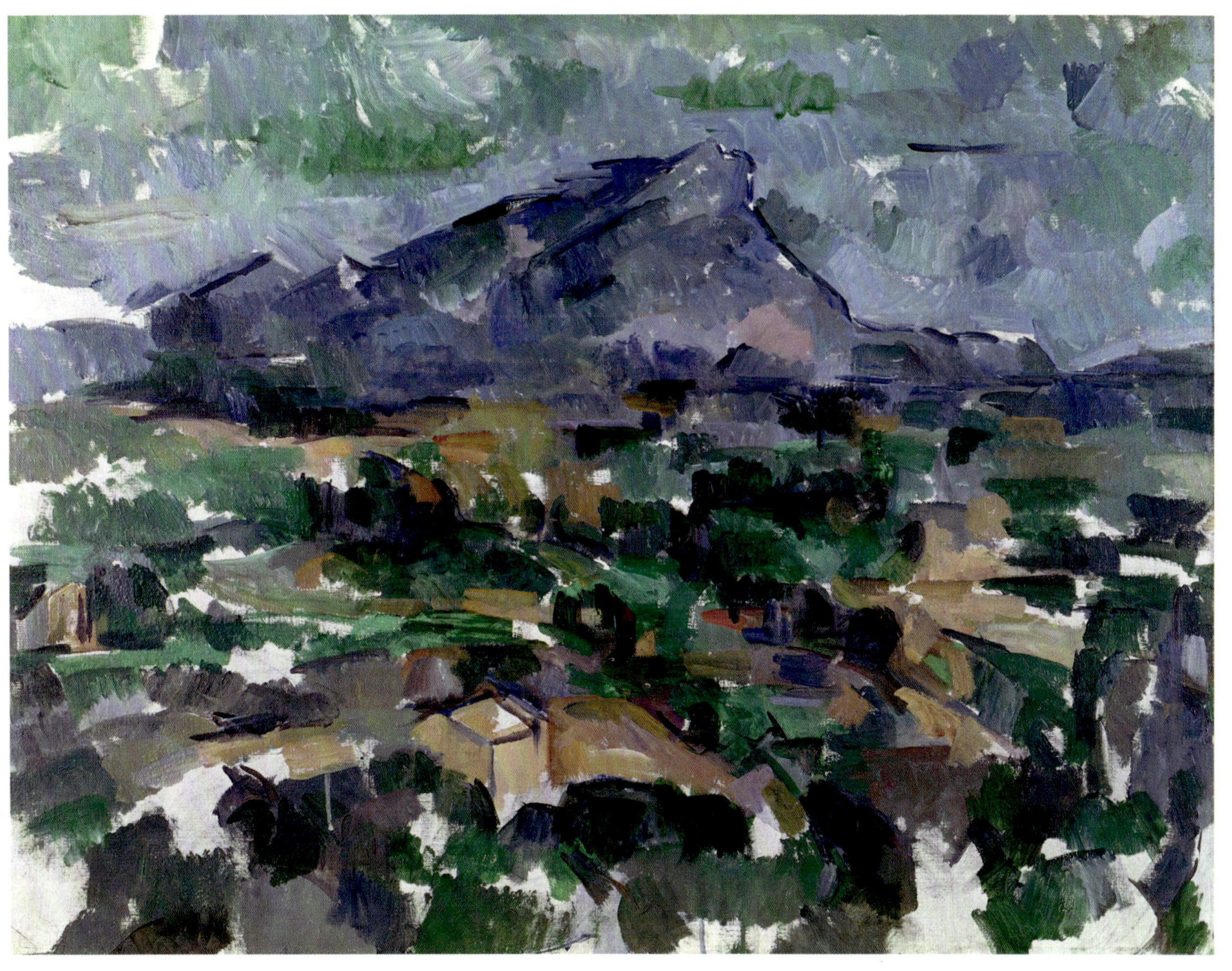

Montagne Sainte-Victoire

La Montagne Sainte-Victoire

Mont Sainte-Victoire

Montaña Sainte-Victoire

Mont Sainte-Victoire

Montagne Sainte-Victoire

PAUL CÉZANNE (1839-1906)

1904-06, Oil on canvas/
Huile sur toile,
63,5 × 83 cm, Kunsthaus Zürich

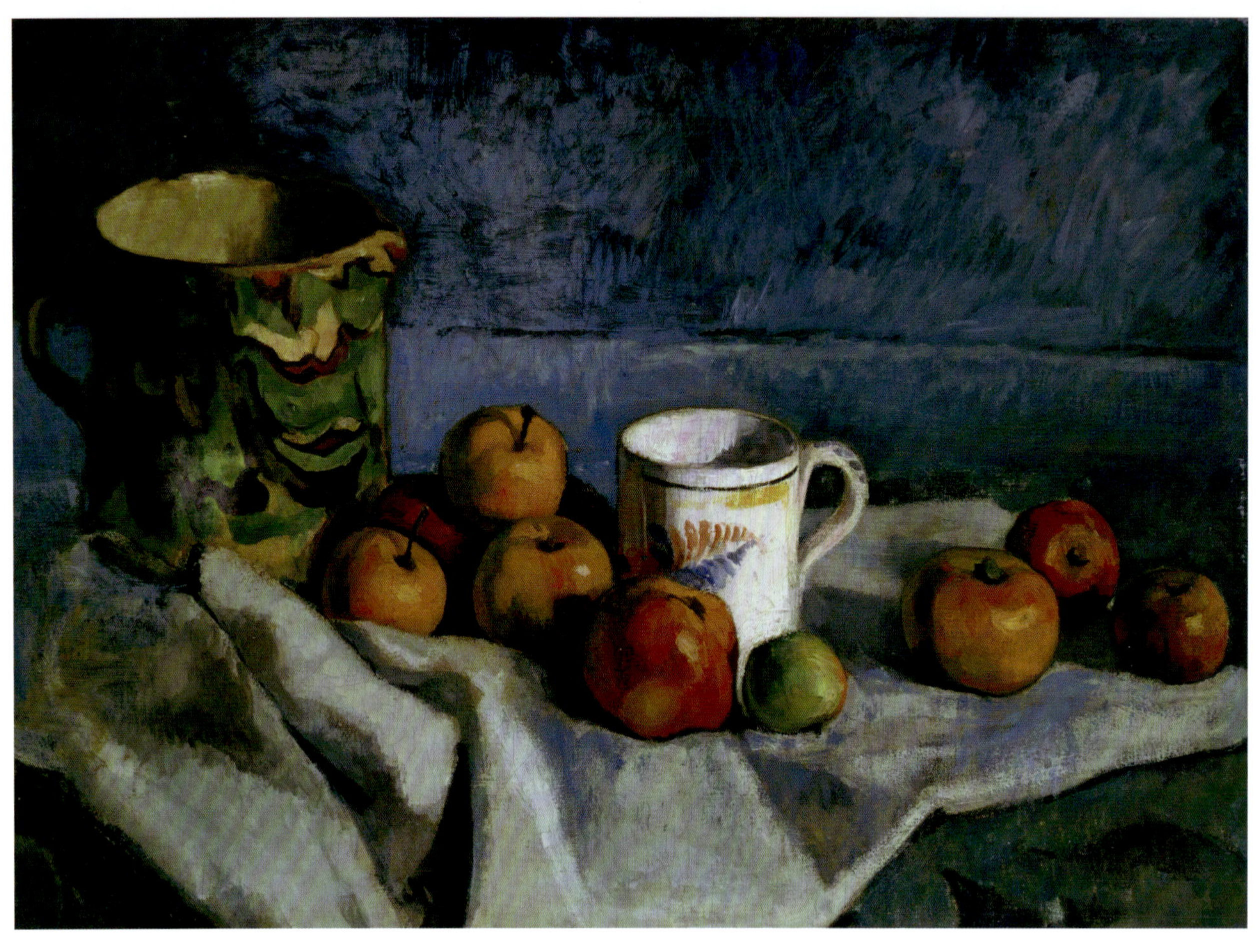

Still Life with Apples, Cup and Pitcher

Nature morte aux pommes, tasse et pichet

Stillleben mit Äpfeln, Tasse und Krug

Bodegón con manzanas, taza y jarra

Natureza morta com maçãs, chávena e jarro

Stilleven met appels, beker en kan

PAUL CÉZANNE (1839-1906)

n.d., Oil on canvas/Huile sur toile, Private collection

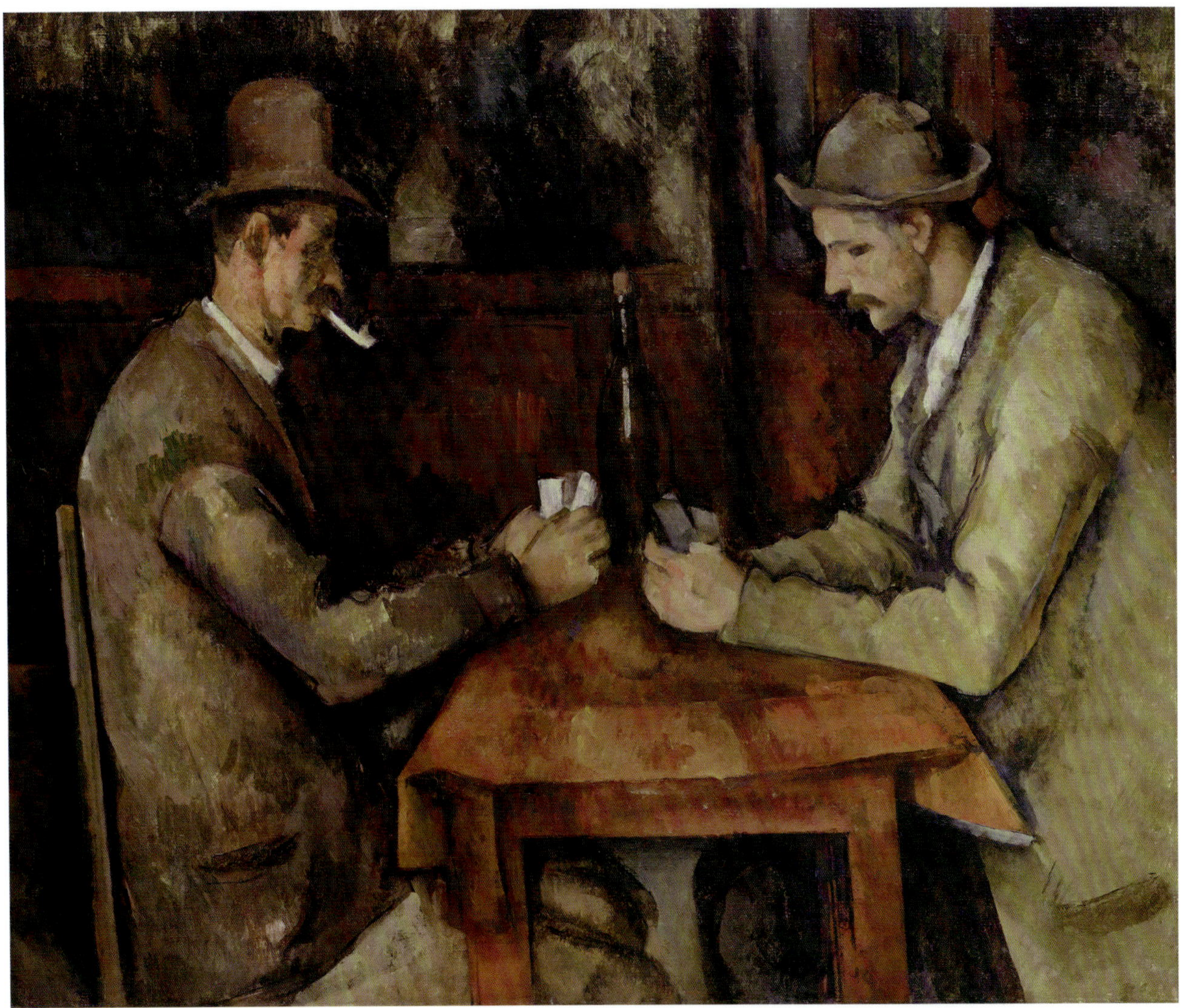

The Card Players

Cézanne has reinterpreted the Caravaggio theme. The symmetrical composition of two men sitting opposite each other is divided by the bottle in the middle.

Les Joueurs de cartes

Le thème caravagesque des joueurs de cartes est ici réinterprété par Paul Cézanne, qui confronte deux hommes au sein d'une composition symétrique, partagée en son milieu par le motif de la bouteille.

Die Kartenspieler

Das an Caravaggio angelehnte Sujet wird von Cézanne neu interpretiert. Die symmetrische Komposition aus zwei sich gegenüber sitzenden Männern wird durch die Flasche in der Mitte geteilt.

Los jugadores de cartas

Cézanne reinterpreta el tema de Caravaggio. La composición simétrica de dos hombres sentados uno frente al otro está dividida por la botella en el centro.

Os jogadores de cartas

Cézanne reinterpreta o tema Caravaggio. A composição simétrica de dois homens sentados em frente um do outro é dividida pela garrafa no meio.

De kaartspelers

Cézanne herinterpreteerde het Caravaggio-achtige onderwerp. De symmetrische compositie van twee tegenover elkaar zittende mannen wordt door de fles in tweeën gedeeld.

PAUL CÉZANNE (1839-1906)

1890-95, Oil on canvas/Huile sur toile, 47,5 × 57 cm, Musée d'Orsay, Paris

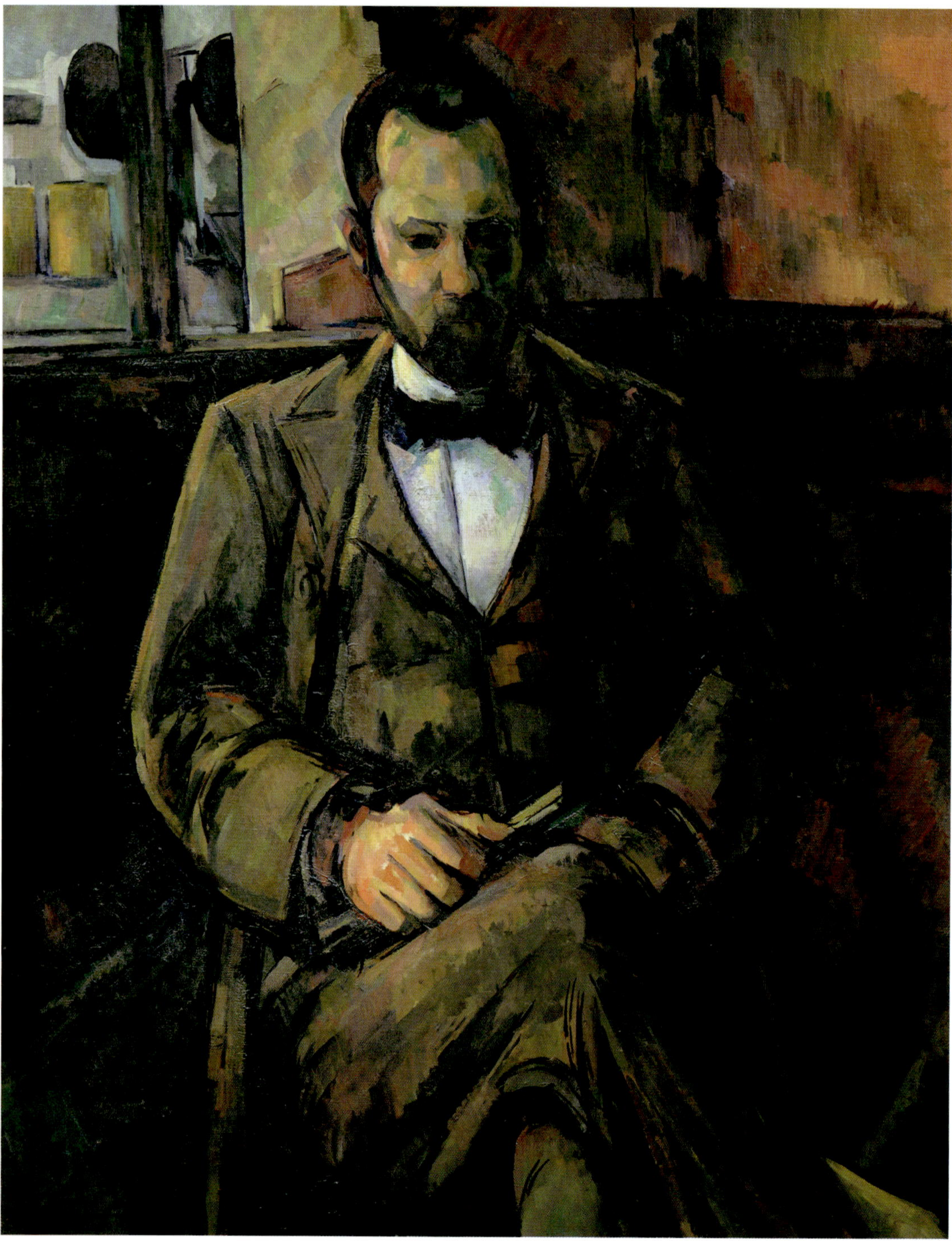

Ambroise Vollard

PAUL CÉZANNE
(1839-1906)
1899, Oil on canvas/
Huile sur toile,
100,3 × 81,3 cm,
Petit Palais, Paris

Woman with a Coffee Pot

Cézanne's portraits are rarely psychological studies. He concentrated on the formal elements. Already far removed from Impressionism, he simplified his figures and turned to geometric forms.

La Femme à la cafetière

Les portraits de Cézanne sont rarement des études psychologiques. Ses préoccupations sont d'abord formelles. Déjà loin de l'impressionnisme, il simplifie ses figures, première étape vers la géométrisation.

Frau mit Kaffeekanne

Cézannes Porträts sind selten psychologische Studien. Er konzentriert sich auf die formellen Elemente. Bereits weit vom Impressionismus entfernt, vereinfacht er seine Figuren und wendet sich geometrischen Formen zu.

Mujer con cafetera

Los retratos de Cézanne rara vez son estudios psicológicos. Se concentra en los elementos formales. Ya muy alejado del Impresionismo, simplificó sus figuras y recurrió a las formas geométricas.

Mulher com cafeteira

Os retratos de Cézanne raramente são estudos psicológicos. Ele concentra-se nos elementos formais. Já longe do Impressionismo, ele simplificou suas figuras e se voltou para formas geométricas.

Vrouw met koffiekan

Cézannes portretten zijn zelden psychologische studies. Hij concentreerde zich op vormelementen. Hij vereenvoudigde zijn figuren, al ver verwijderd van het impressionisme, en hield zich bezig met geometrische vormen.

PAUL CÉZANNE (1839–1906)

c. 1890–95, Oil on canvas/Huile sur toile, 130 × 97 cm, Musée d'Orsay, Paris

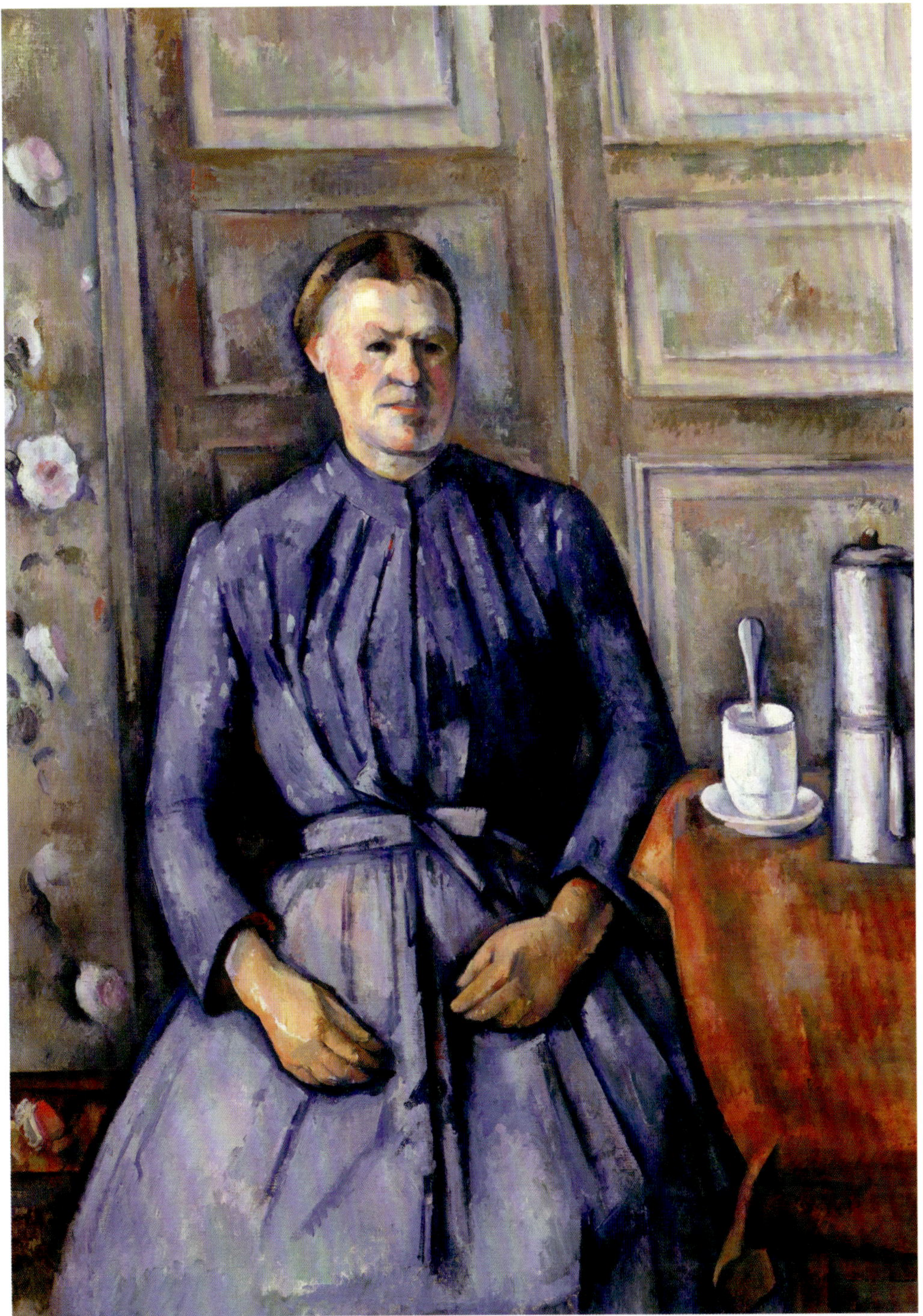

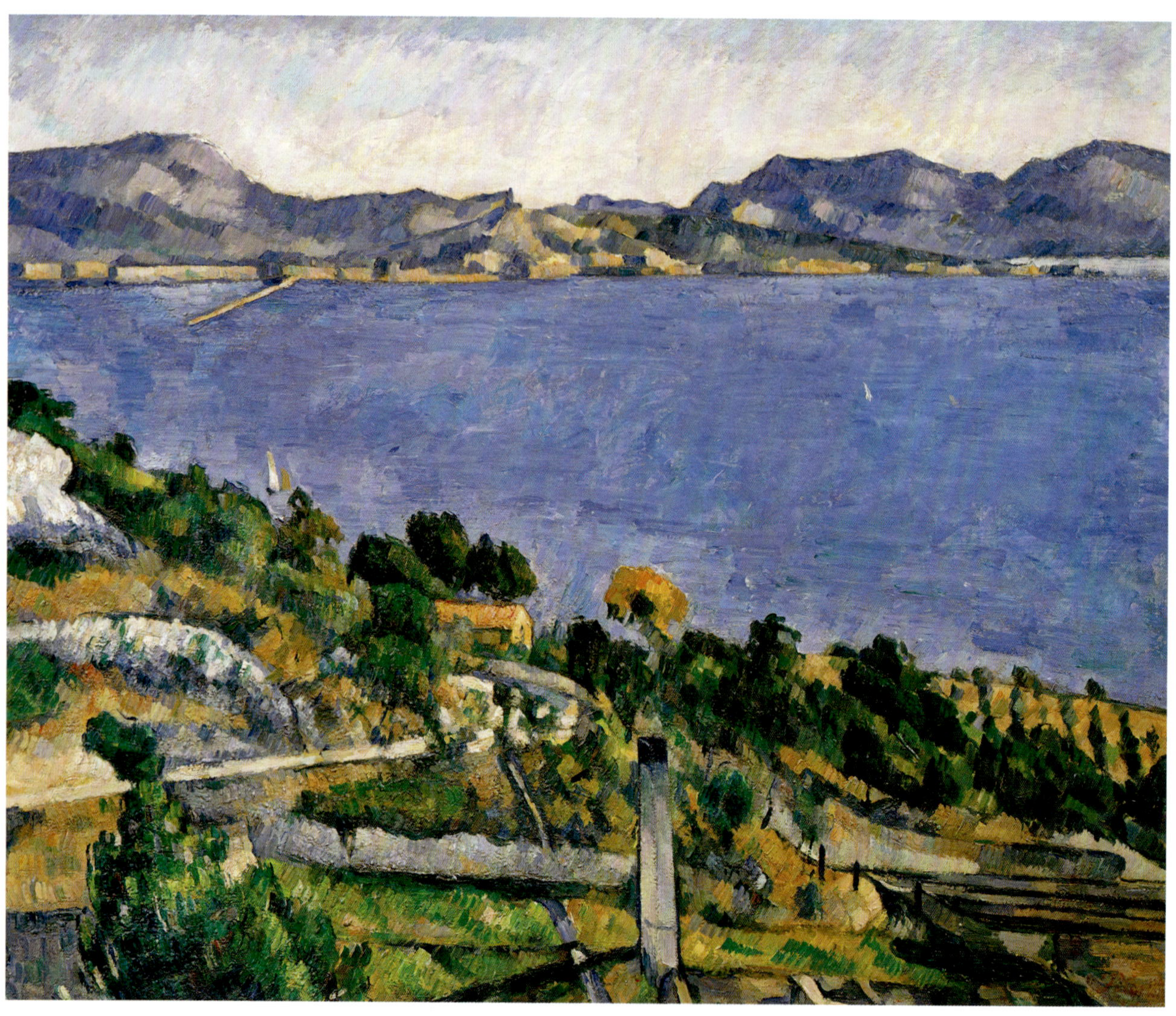

The Bay of Marseille seen from L'Estaque *or* L'Estaque

Le Golfe de Marseille vu de l'Estaque, *dit aussi* L'Estaque

Die Bucht von Marseille, von L'Estaque aus gesehen *oder* L'Estaque

La bahía de Marsella, vista desde l'Estaque, *también llamado* L'Estaque

A baía de Marselha, vista de L'Estaque *ou* L'Estaque

De baai van Marseille gezien vanaf l'Estaque *of* L'Estaque

PAUL CÉZANNE (1839-1906)

c. 1878/79, Oil on canvas/Huile sur toile, 58 × 72 cm, Musée d'Orsay, Paris

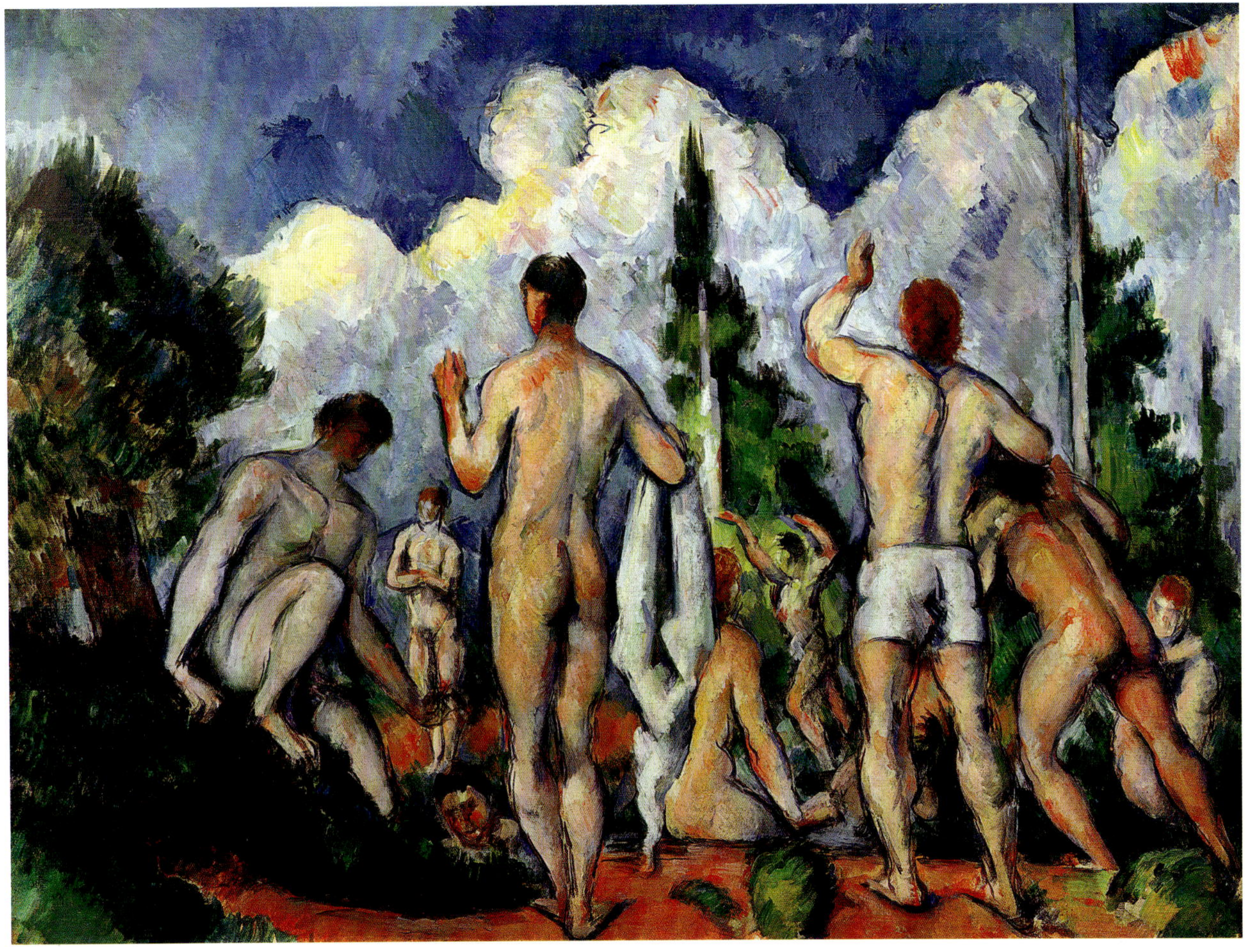

The Bathers

In his bathing series, the artist tried to create a perfect harmony between landscape and figure. The bodies, like the trees and the clouds are only structural elements in the painting.

Baigneurs

Parvenir à une fusion parfaite du paysage et de la figure, telle est l'ambition du peintre dans ses multiples scènes de baigneurs. Les corps, comme les arbres et les nuages, sont des éléments de structure.

Badende

In seiner Badenden-Serie versuchte der Künstler, eine perfekte Harmonie aus Landschaft und Figur zu schaffen. Die Körper, die Bäume und die Wolken sind nur noch strukturelle Einheiten, die das Gemälde gliedern.

Bañistas

En su serie de baño, el artista trató de crear una perfecta armonía entre el paisaje y la figura. Los cuerpos, los árboles y las nubes son sólo unidades estructurales que estructuran la pintura.

Banhistas

Em sua série de banhos, o artista tentou criar uma perfeita harmonia entre paisagem e figura. Os corpos, as árvores e as nuvens são apenas unidades estruturais que estruturam a pintura.

De baders

In zijn serie van badenden probeerde de schilder een perfecte harmonie tussen landschap en figuur te creëren. De lichamen, bomen en wolken zijn nog slechts structurele eenheden die het schilderij indelen.

PAUL CÉZANNE (1839-1906)

c. 1890, Oil on canvas/Huile sur toile, 60 × 82 cm, Musée d'Orsay, Paris

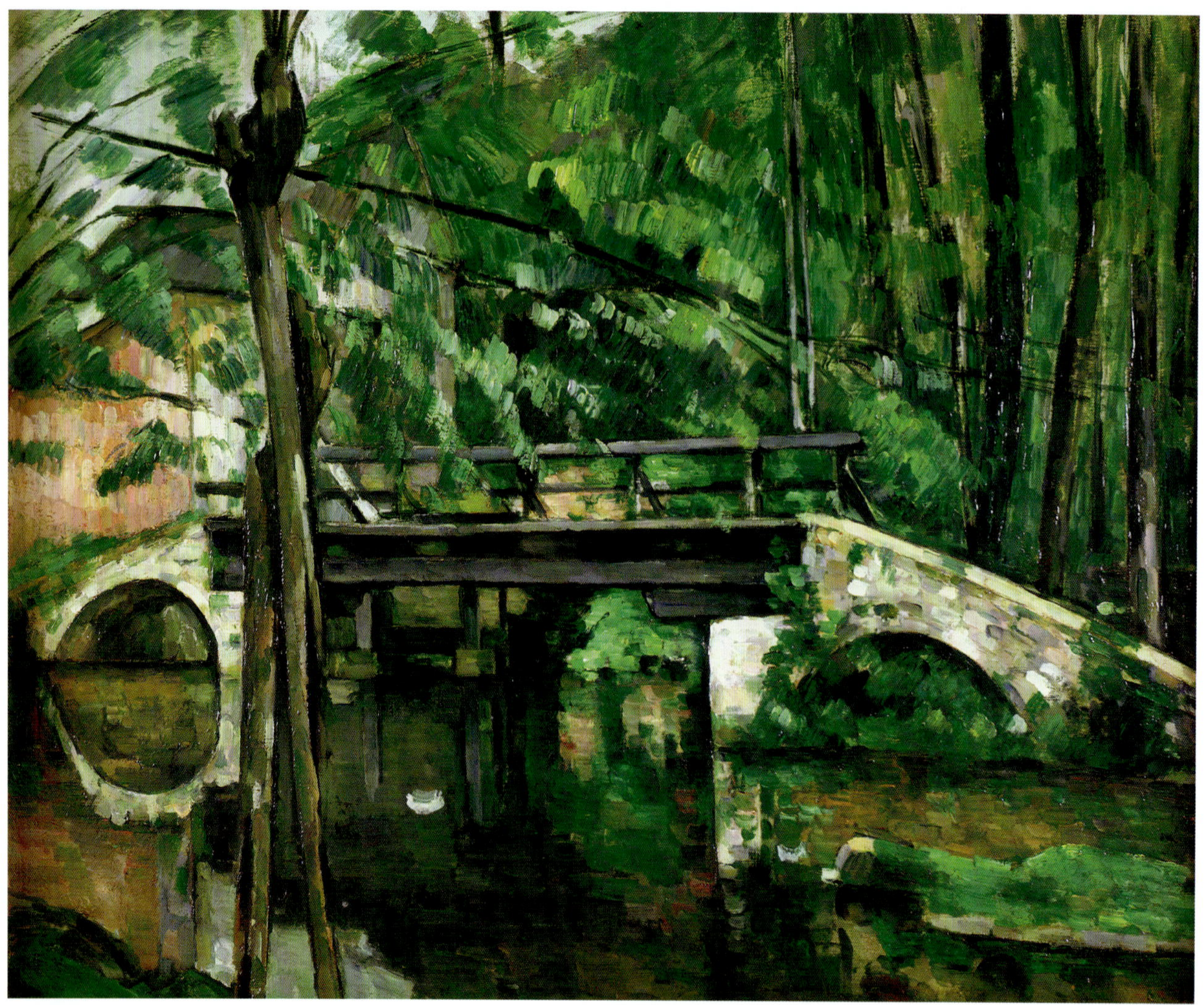

Maincy Bridge

Pont de Maincy

Brücke von Maincy

Puente de Maincy

Ponte de Maincy

Brug van Maincy

PAUL CÉZANNE (1839-1906)

c. 1879, Oil on canvas/Huile sur toile,
58,5 × 72,5 cm, Musée d'Orsay, Paris

The Big Trees

Grands Arbres

Die hohen Bäume

Grandes árboles

As árvores altas

De hoge bomen

PAUL CÉZANNE
(1839-1906)
c. 1902-04, Oil on canvas/Huile sur toile, 81 × 65 cm, National Galleries of Scotland, Edinburgh

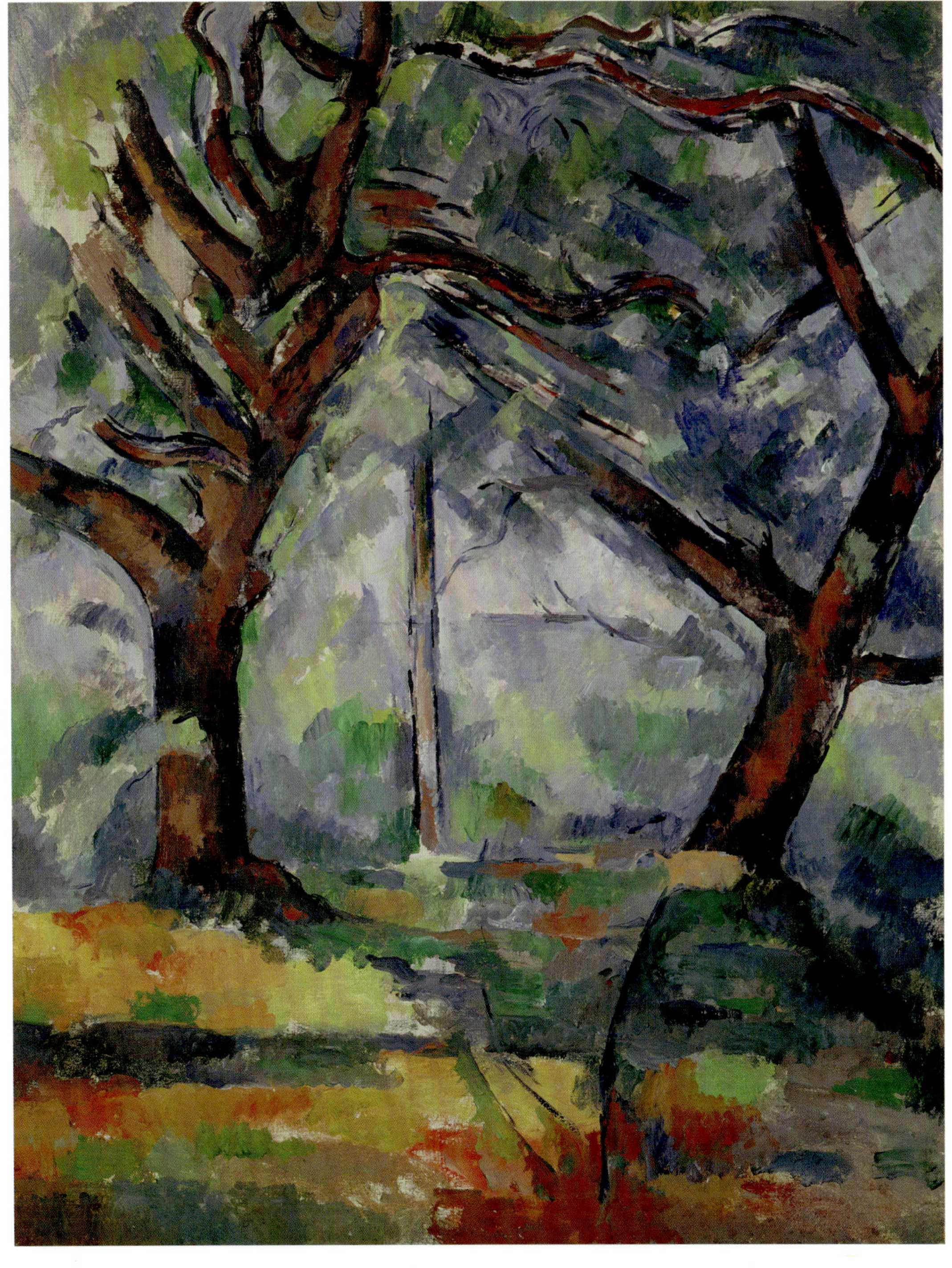

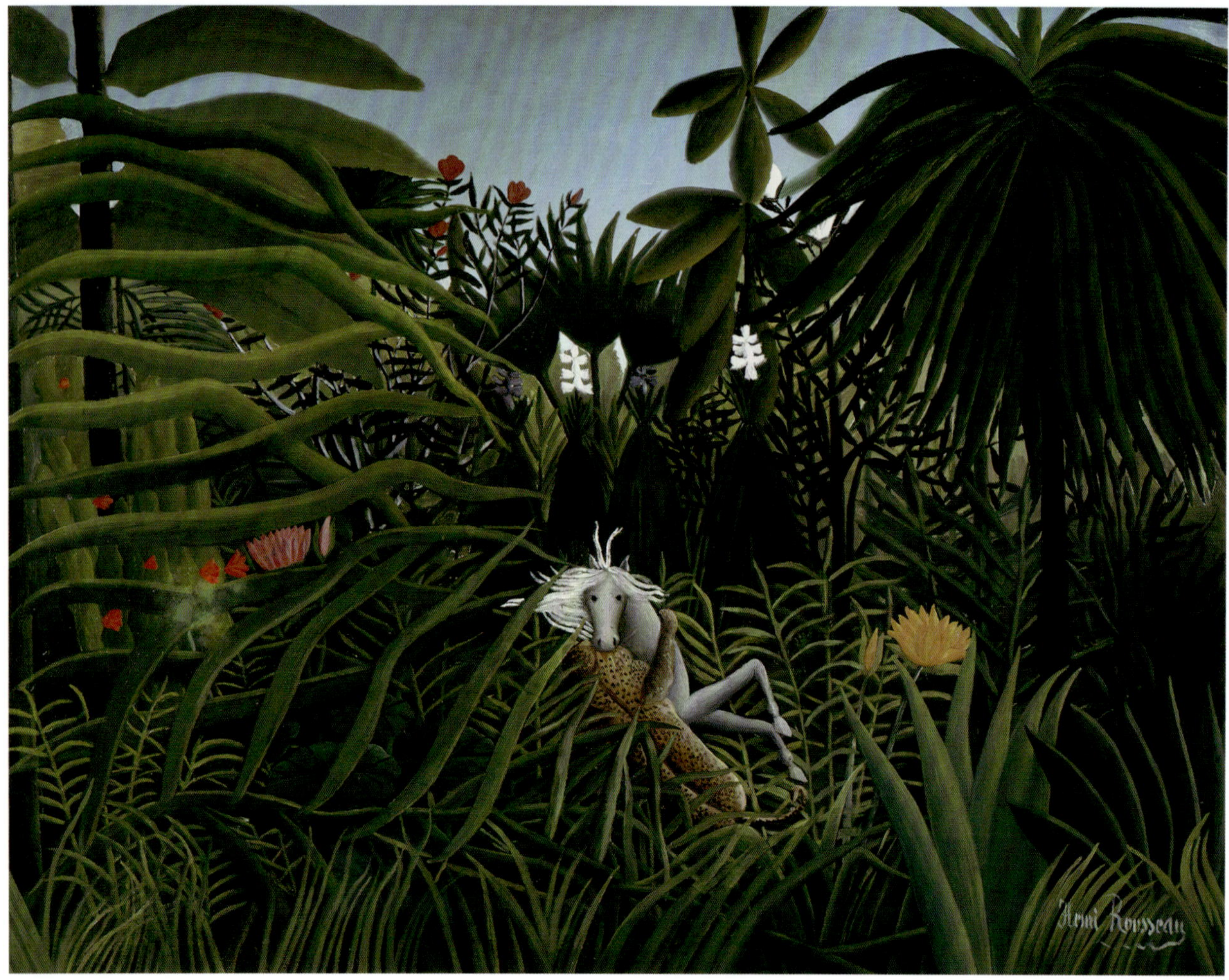

Jaguar attacking a Horse

Cheval attaqué par un jaguar

Pferd, von einem Jaguar angefallen

Caballo, atacado por un jaguar

Cavalo, atacado por um jaguar

Paard, aangevallen door een jaguar

HENRI ROUSSEAU (1844-1910)

1910, Oil on canvas/Huile sur toile,
89 × 116 cm,
Pushkin Museum, Moscow

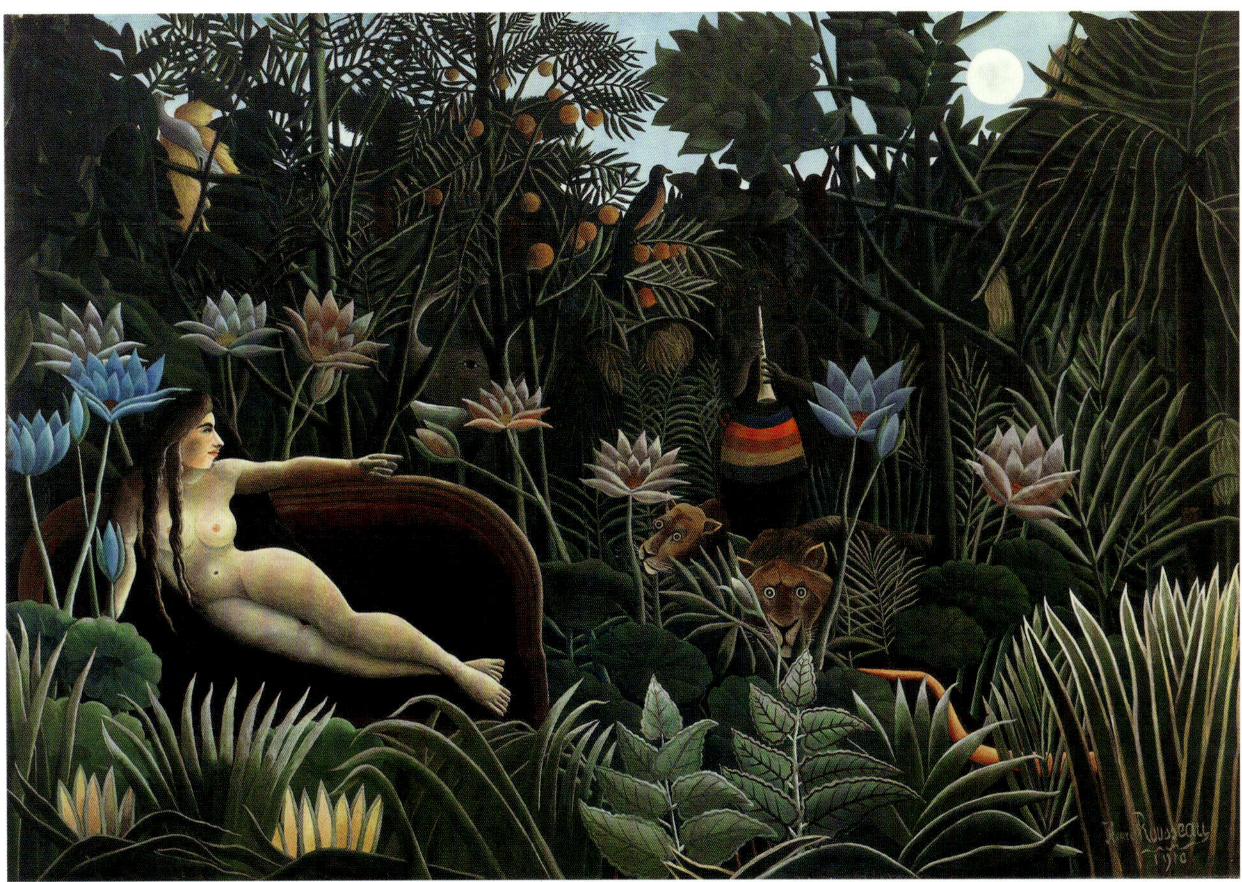

The Dream

Rousseau's lush jungle displays made him famous. Yet he never left France once. He found his inspirations in the Imagerie Populaire or in the plants of the Jardin des Plantes.

Le Rêve

Ses jungles luxuriantes ont fait la réputation du Douanier Rousseau. Il n'a jamais quitté la France, et puise son inspiration exotique dans l'imagerie populaire ou devant les fauves du Jardin des plantes.

Der Traum

Seine üppigen Urwalddarstellungen machten Rousseau bekannt. Trotzdem verließ er Frankreich kein einziges Mal. Seine Inspirationen fand er in der Imagerie Populaire oder in den Anlagen des Jardin des Plantes.

El sueño

Las exuberantes exhibiciones en la selva de Rousseau lo hicieron famoso. Sin embargo, no salió de Francia ni una sola vez. Se inspiró en la Imagerie Populaire o en las plantas del Jardin des Plantes.

O Sonho

As exibições exuberantes da selva de Rousseau tornaram-no famoso. No entanto, nunca deixou a França uma única vez. Ele encontrou suas inspirações na Imagerie Populaire ou nas plantas do Jardin des Plantes.

De droom

Rousseau werd beroemd om zijn weelderige oerwoudvoorstellingen. Toch is hij nooit buiten Frankrijk geweest. Hij haalde zijn inspiratie uit prentenboeken of uit de tuinen van de Jardin des Plantes.

HENRI ROUSSEAU (1844-1910)
1910, Oil on canvas/Huile sur toile, 298,5 × 204,5 cm, Museum of Modern Art, New York

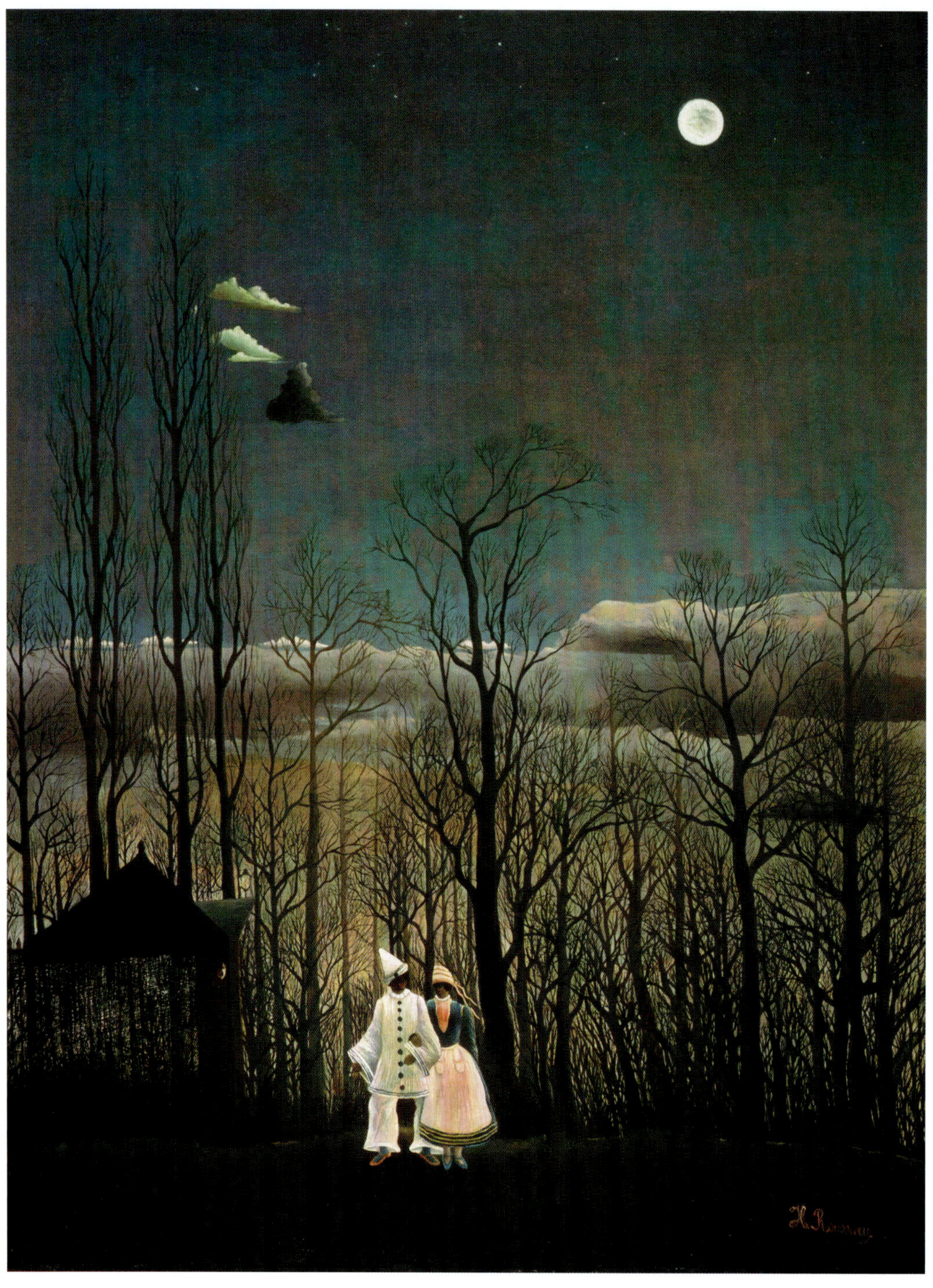

Carnival Evening

Une soirée au carnaval

Eine Karnevalsnacht

Una noche de carnaval

Uma noite de carnaval

Een carnavalsnacht

HENRI ROUSSEAU (1844-1910)

1886, Oil on canvas/Huile sur toile, 117,4 × 89,61 cm, Philadelphia Museum of Art, Pennsylvania

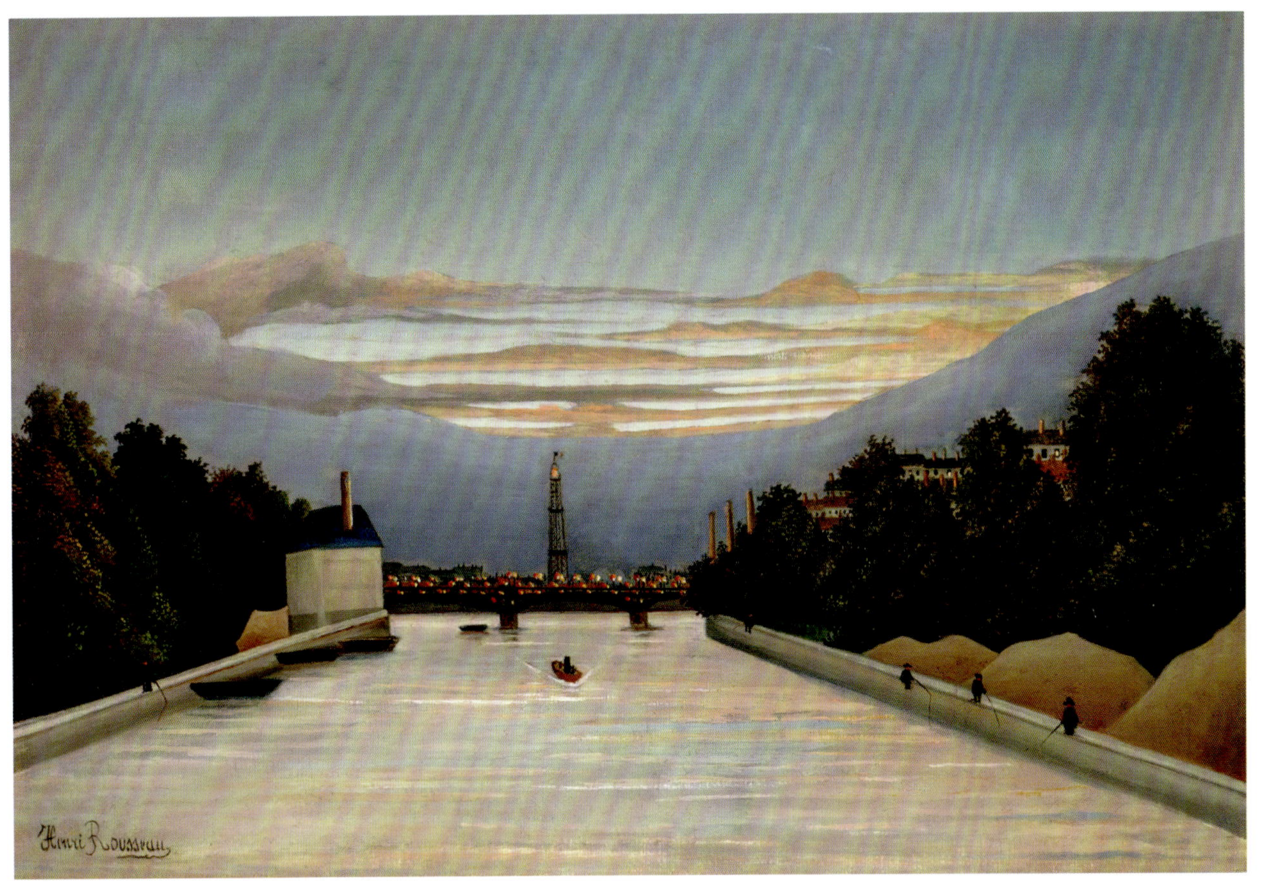

The Eiffel Tower

La Tour Eiffel

Der Eiffelturm

La Torre Eiffel

A Torre Eiffel

De Eiffeltoren

HENRI ROUSSEAU (1844-1910)

c. 1898, Oil on canvas/Huile sur
toile, 52,4 × 77,2 cm, Museum
of Fine Arts, Houston

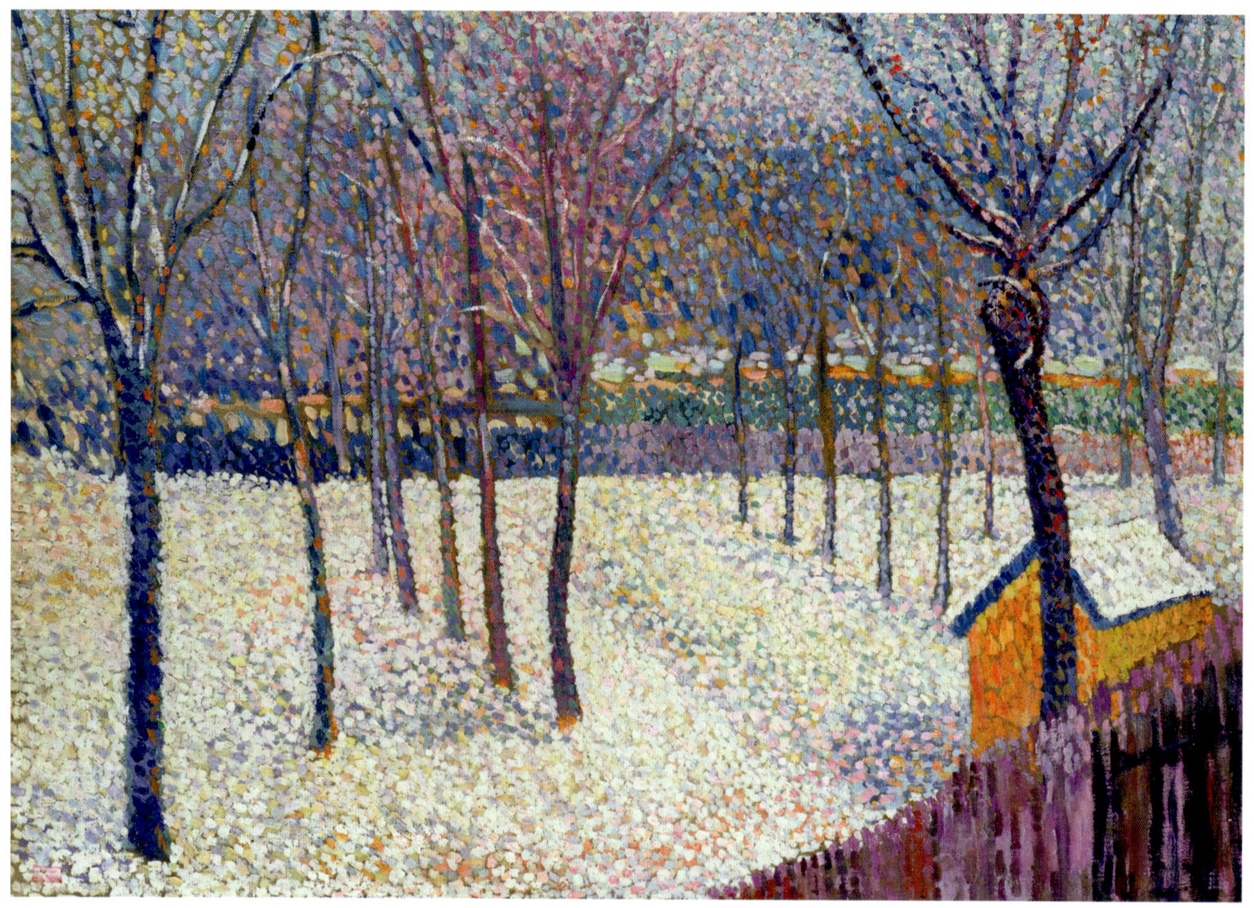

The Orchard under the Snow

Verger sous la neige

Obstgarten unter einer Schneedecke

Huerto bajo un manto de nieve

Pomar sob uma manta de neve

Boomgaard onder een deken van sneeuw

HIPPOLYTE PETITJEAN (1854-1929)

n. d., Oil on canvas/Huile sur toile, 49 × 69 cm, Private collection

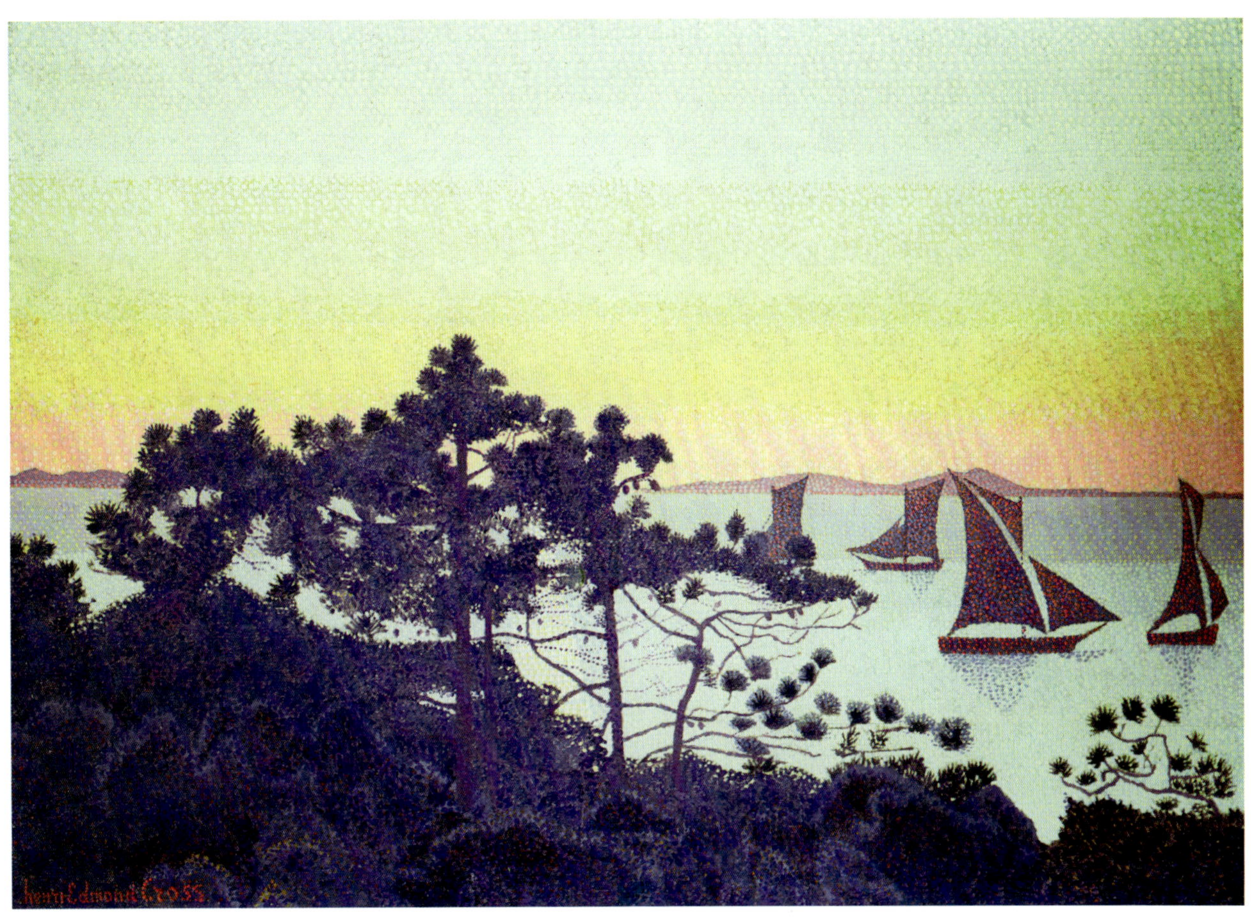

The Pointe de la Galère

La Pointe de la Galère

Der Pointe de la Galère

La punta de la Galera

A Pointe de la Galère

De Pointe de la Galère

HENRI-EDMOND CROSS (1856-1910)

1891/92, Oil on canvas/Huile sur toile, 63 × 91 cm, Private collection

HENRI-EDMOND CROSS (1856-1910)
1896, Oil on canvas/
Huile sur toile,
54 × 65,4 cm,
Metropolitan Museum
of Art, New York

The Îles d'Or

In this masterpiece of pointillism, the sky, the sea and the sand merge with harmoniously graded shades - as if they were dissolved by light. This makes the poetic motif seem almost abstract.

Les Îles d'Or

Dans ce chef-d'œuvre du pointillisme, le ciel, la mer et le sable se fondent en dégradés harmonieux de tons, comme dissous dans la lumière. Ce tableau éminemment poétique en devient presque abstrait.

Die goldenen Inseln

In dem Meisterwerk des Pointillismus verschmelzen der Himmel, das Meer und der Sand durch harmonisch abgestufte Farbtöne – als würden sie durch das Licht aufgelöst. Dadurch wirkt das poetische Motiv fast abstrakt.

Las islas doradas

En esta obra maestra del puntillismo, el cielo, el mar y la arena se funden con matices armoniosamente escalonados, como si fueran disueltos por la luz. Esto hace que el motivo poético parezca casi abstracto.

As ilhas douradas

Nesta obra-prima do pontilhismo, o céu, o mar e a areia fundem-se com tons harmoniosamente graduados - como se fossem dissolvidos pela luz. Isso faz com que o motivo poético pareça quase abstrato.

De gouden eilanden

In dit meesterwerk van het pointillisme versmelten hemel, zee en zand met elkaar door harmonieus verlopende tinten - alsof ze door het licht worden opgelost. Hierdoor komt het poëtische onderwerp bijna abstract over.

HENRI-EDMOND CROSS (1856-1910)
c. 1891/92, Oil on canvas/Huile sur toile, 59 × 54 cm, Musée d'Orsay, Paris

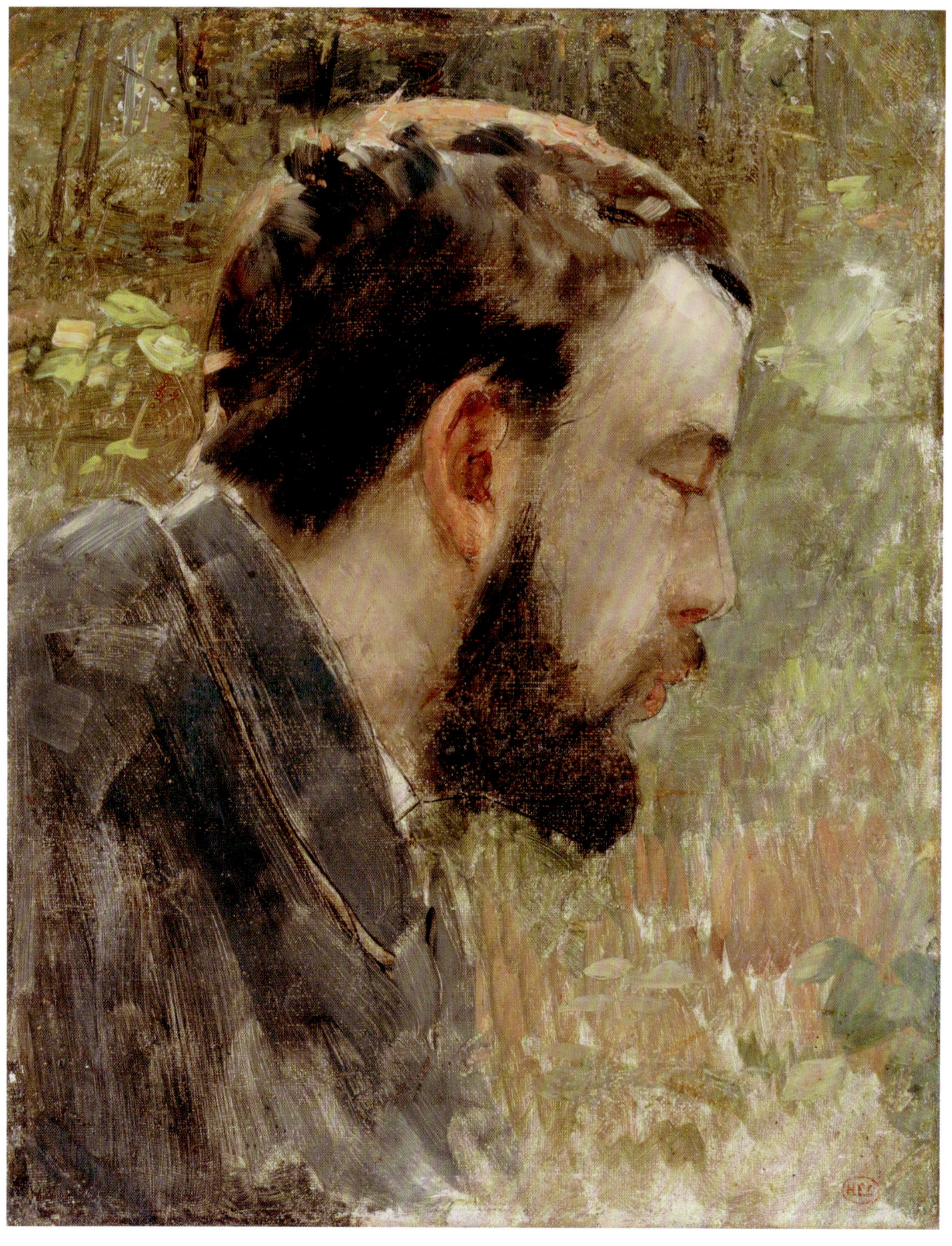

Portrait of Seurat

Portrait de Seurat

Bildnis Seurats

Retrato de Seurat

Retrato dos Seurats

Portret van Seurat

HENRI-EDMOND CROSS (1856-1910)
n.d., Oil on canvas/
Huile sur toile,
41,6 × 33,6 cm,
Private collection

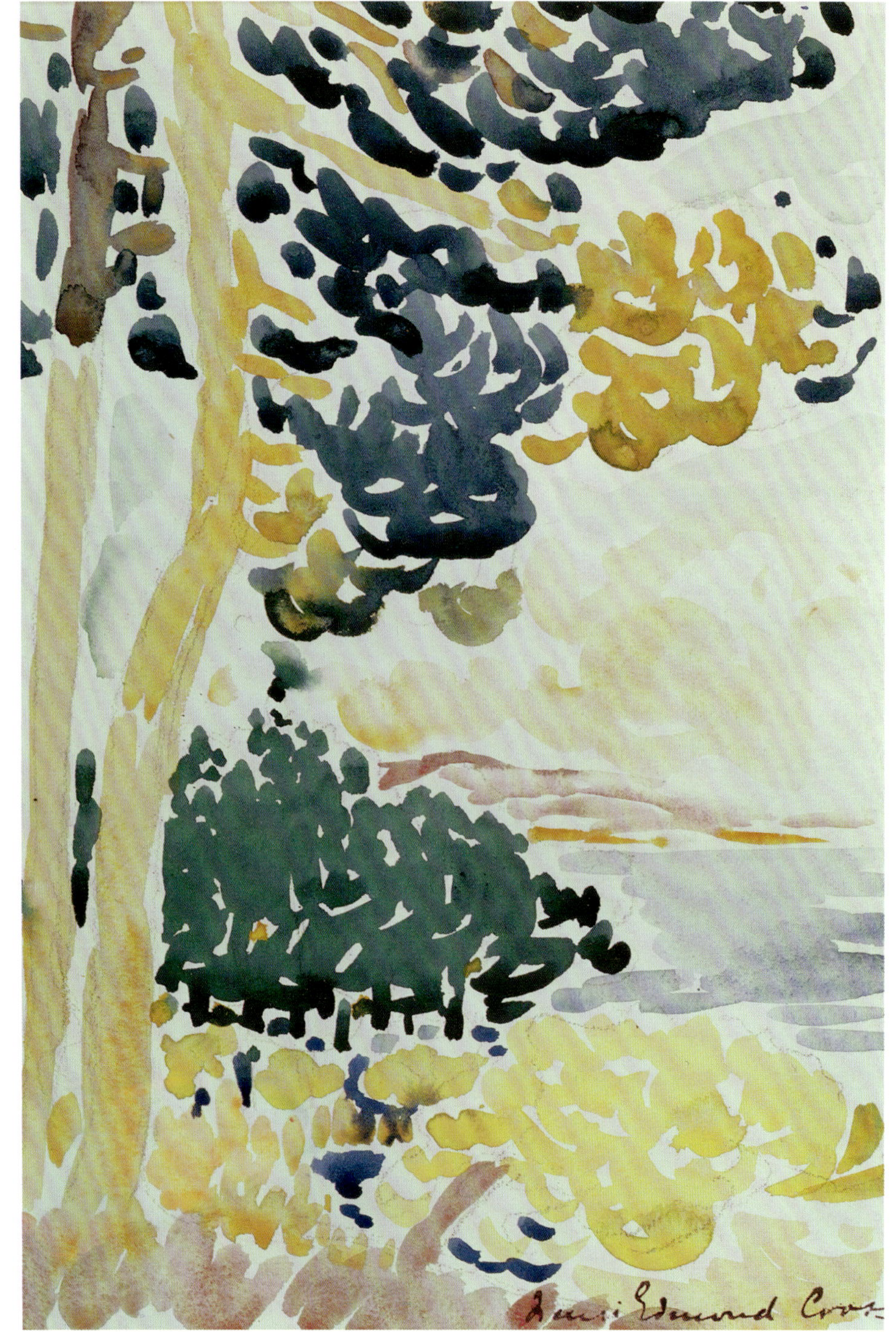

Pardigon

HENRI-EDMOND CROSS (1856-1910)

1908, Watercolour/Aquarelle, 24 × 16 cm, Musée
des Beaux-Arts et d'Archéologie, Besançon

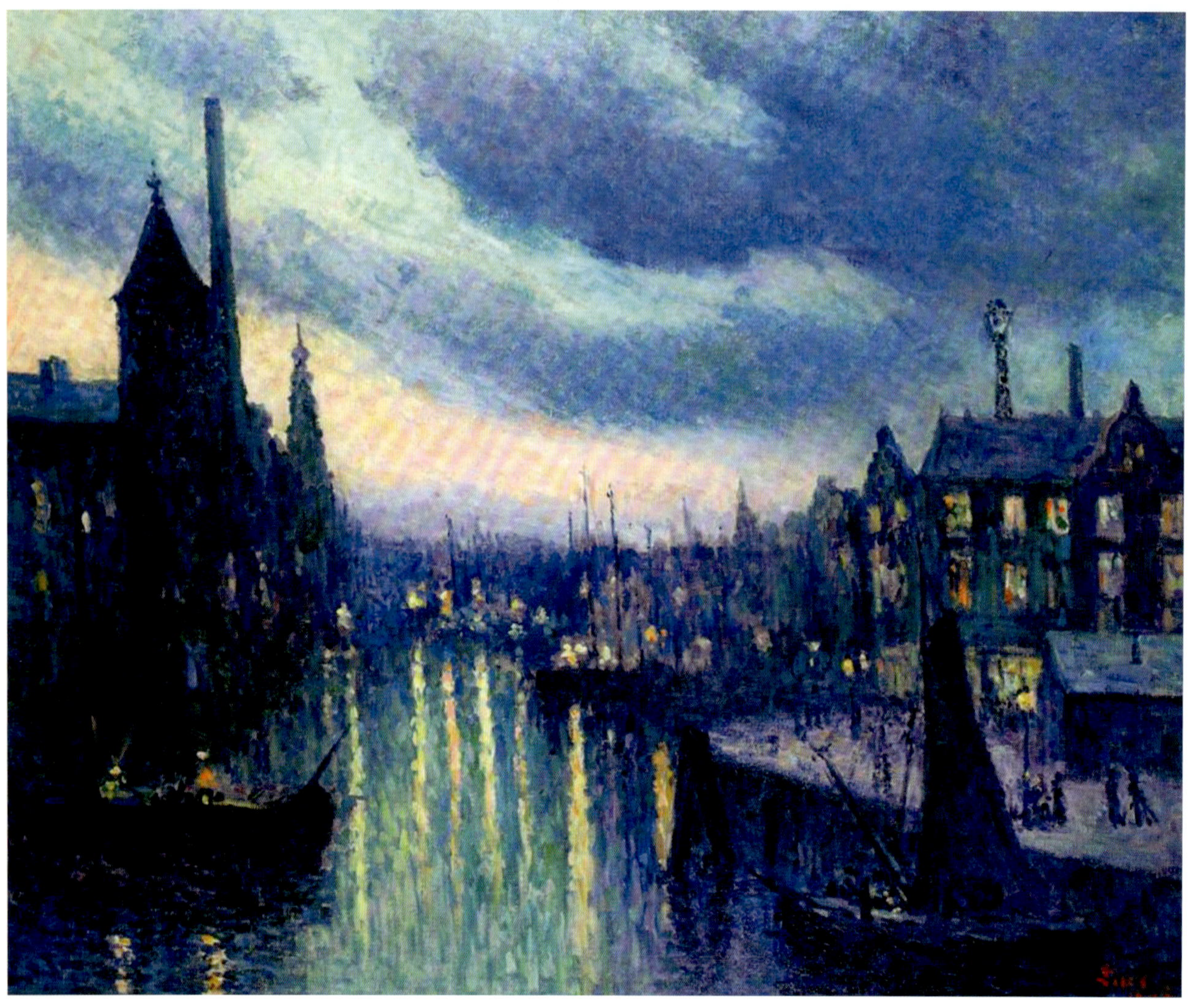

The Port of Rotterdam at Night

Le Port de Rotterdam la nuit

Der Hafen von Rotterdam bei Nacht

El puerto de Rotterdam de noche

O porto de Roterdão à noite

De haven van Rotterdam bij nacht

MAXIMILIEN LUCE (1858-1941)

1908, Oil on canvas/Huile sur toile, 65 × 81 cm, Private collection

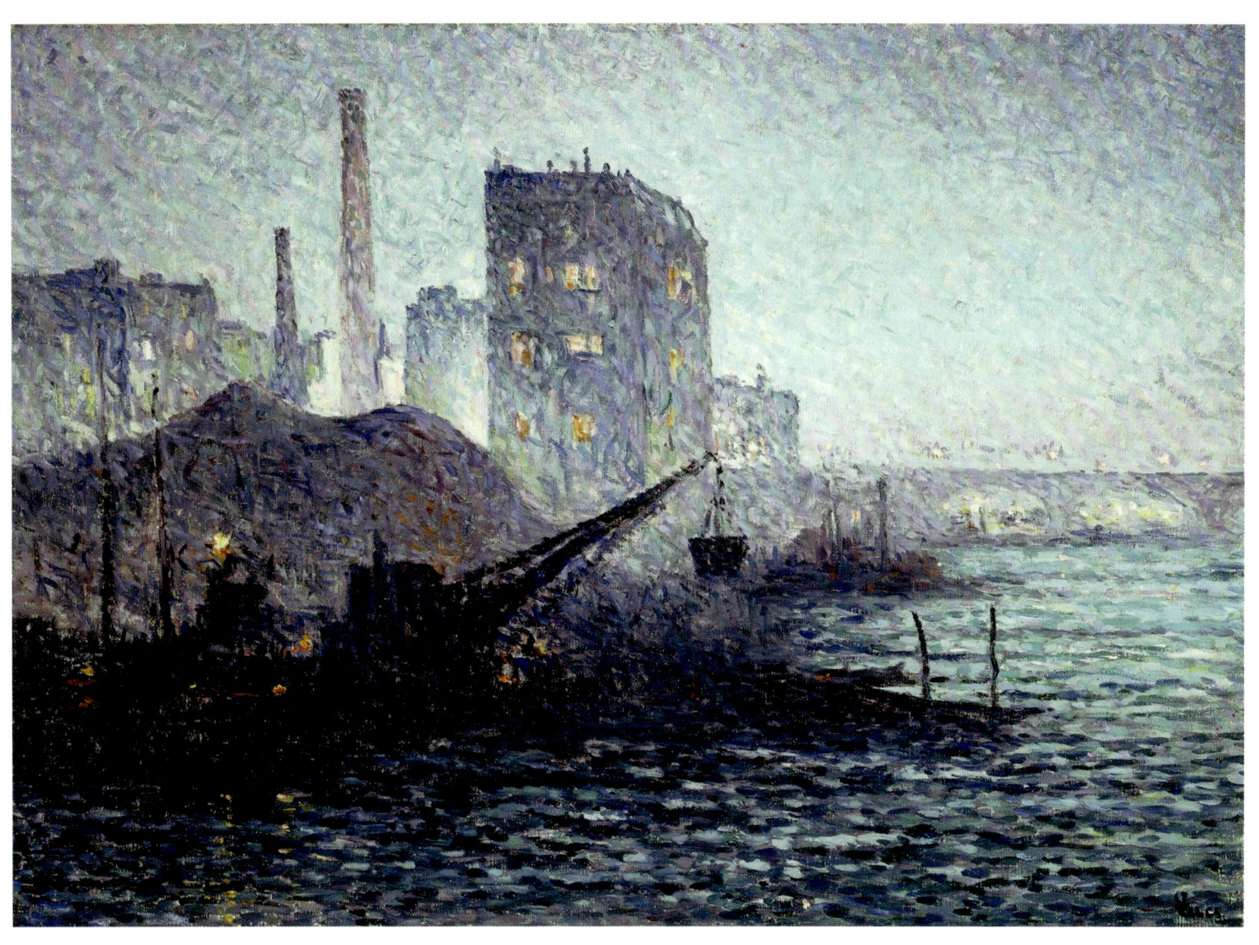

The Thames in London

La Tamise à Londres

Die Themse in London

El Támesis en Londres

O Tamisa em Londres

De Theems in Londen

MAXIMILIEN LUCE (1858-1941)

c. 1893, Oil on canvas/Huile sur toile, 46 × 65 cm, Private collection

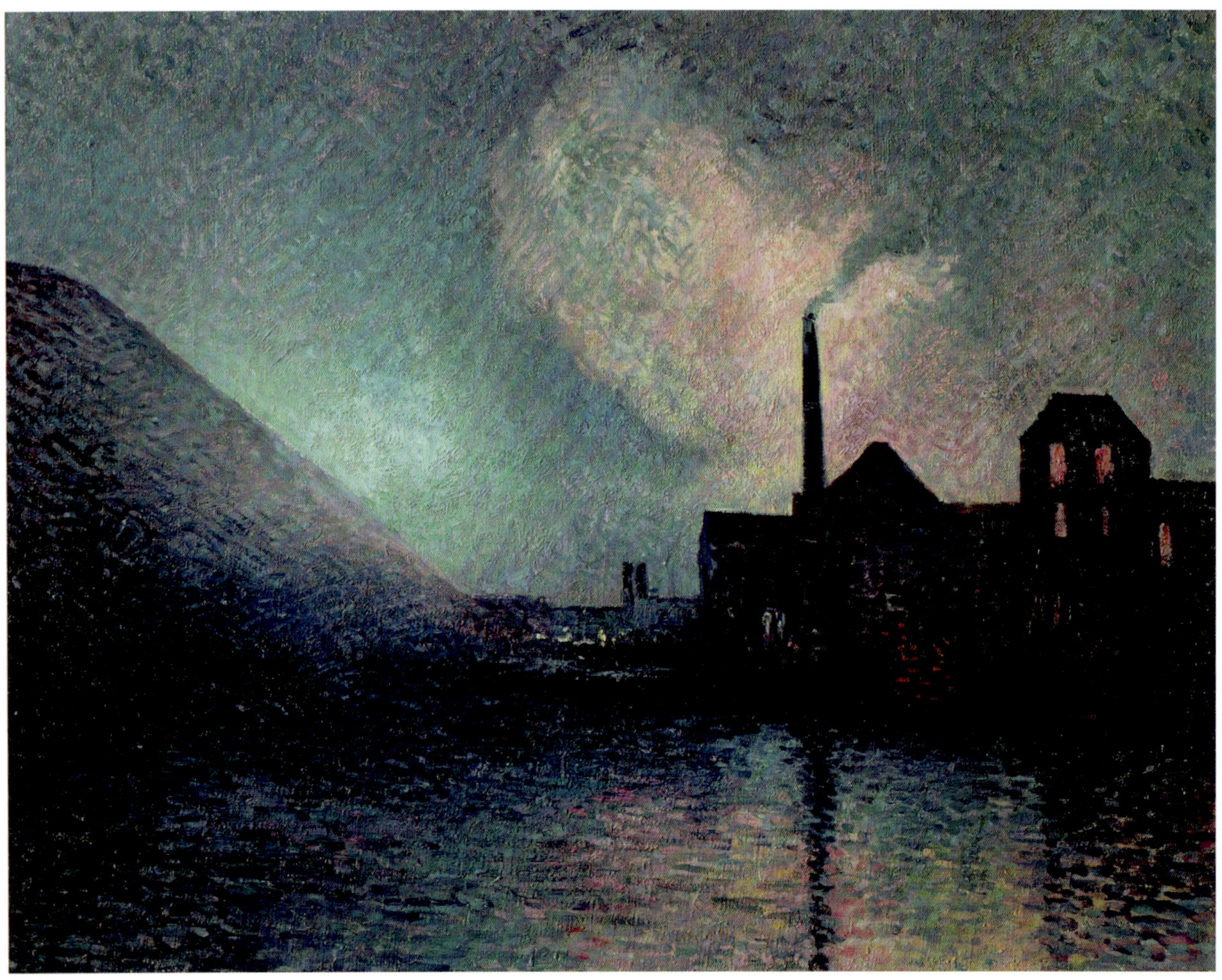

Couillet by Night

The politically committed Maximilien Luce dealt with
working conditions. Inspired by Georges Seurat, he painted
contemporary motifs such as factories and buildings in the
Divisionist style.

Couillet la nuit

Politiquement engagé et sensible à la condition des
ouvriers, Maximilien Luce s'intéresse à des sujets
modernes, comme les usines ou les chantiers. Dans une
veine divisionniste, proche de Georges Seurat.

MAXIMILIEN LUCE (1858-1941)

1895, Oil on canvas/Huile sur toile, 50 × 65 cm, Private collection

Couillet bei Nacht

Der politisch engagierte Maximilien Luce setzte sich mit
Arbeitsbedingungen auseinander. Inspiriert durch Georges
Seurat, malt er zeitgenössische Motive wie Fabriken und
Bauarbeiten im Stil des Divisionismus.

Couillet de noche

El políticamente comprometido Maximilien Luce se ocupó
de las condiciones de trabajo. Inspirado en Georges Seurat,
pinta motivos contemporáneos como fábricas y edificios de
estilo divisionista.

Couillet à noite

A Maximilien Luce, politicamente empenhada, tratava das
condições de trabalho. Inspirado por Georges Seurat, ele
pinta motivos contemporâneos como fábricas e edifícios
no estilo divisionista.

Couillet bij nacht

De politiek geëngageerde Maximilien Luce hield zich bezig
met arbeidsomstandigheden. Geïnspireerd door Georges
Seurat schilderde hij eigentijdse onderwerpen zoals
fabrieken en gebouwen in divisionistische stijl.

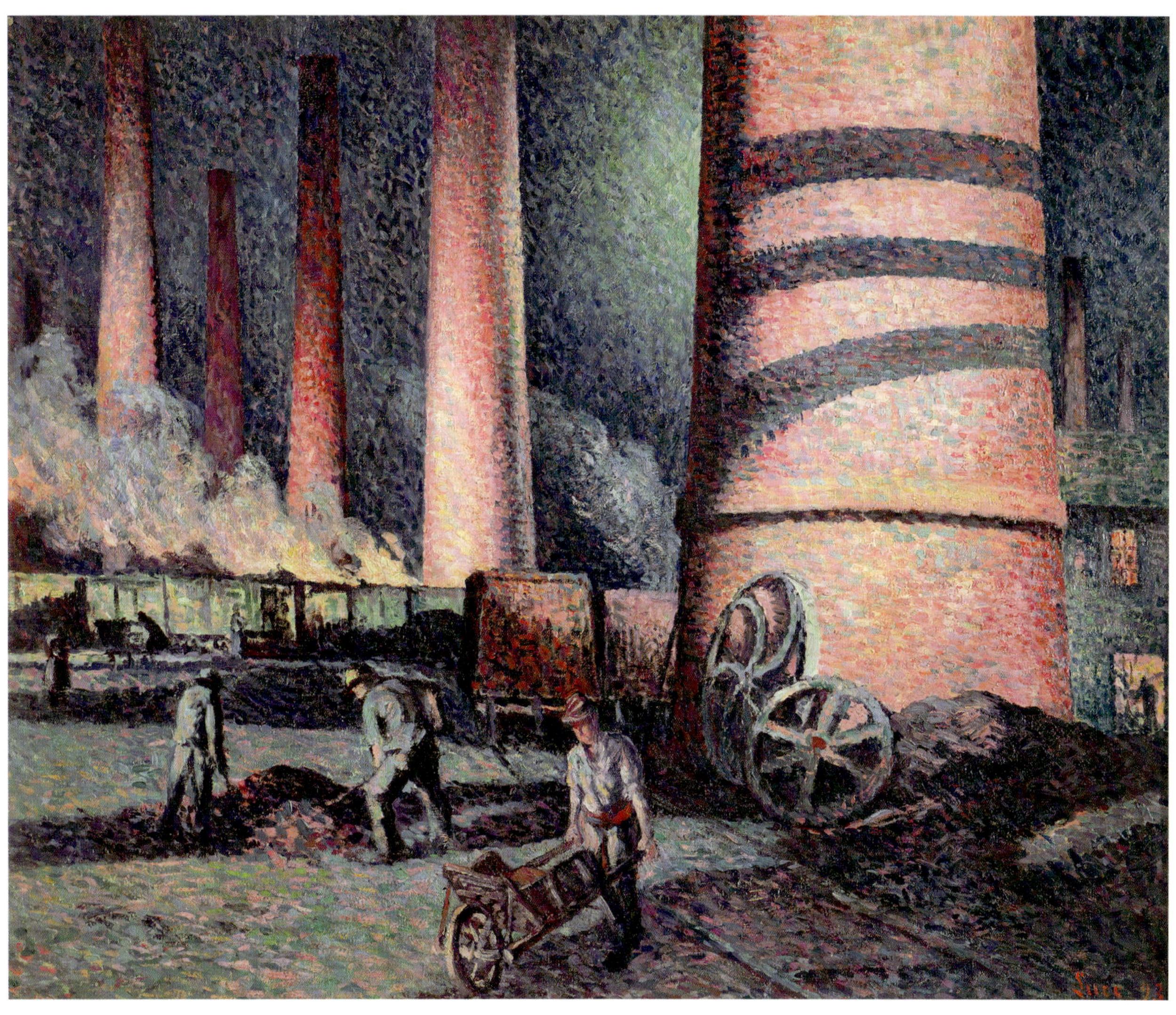

Factory Chimneys

Cheminées d'usine

Fabrikschornsteine

Chimeneas industriales

Chaminés de fábrica

Fabrieksschoorstenen

MAXIMILIEN LUCE (1858-1941)
1896, Oil on canvas/Huile sur toile, 60 × 73 cm,
Petit Palais, Genève

337

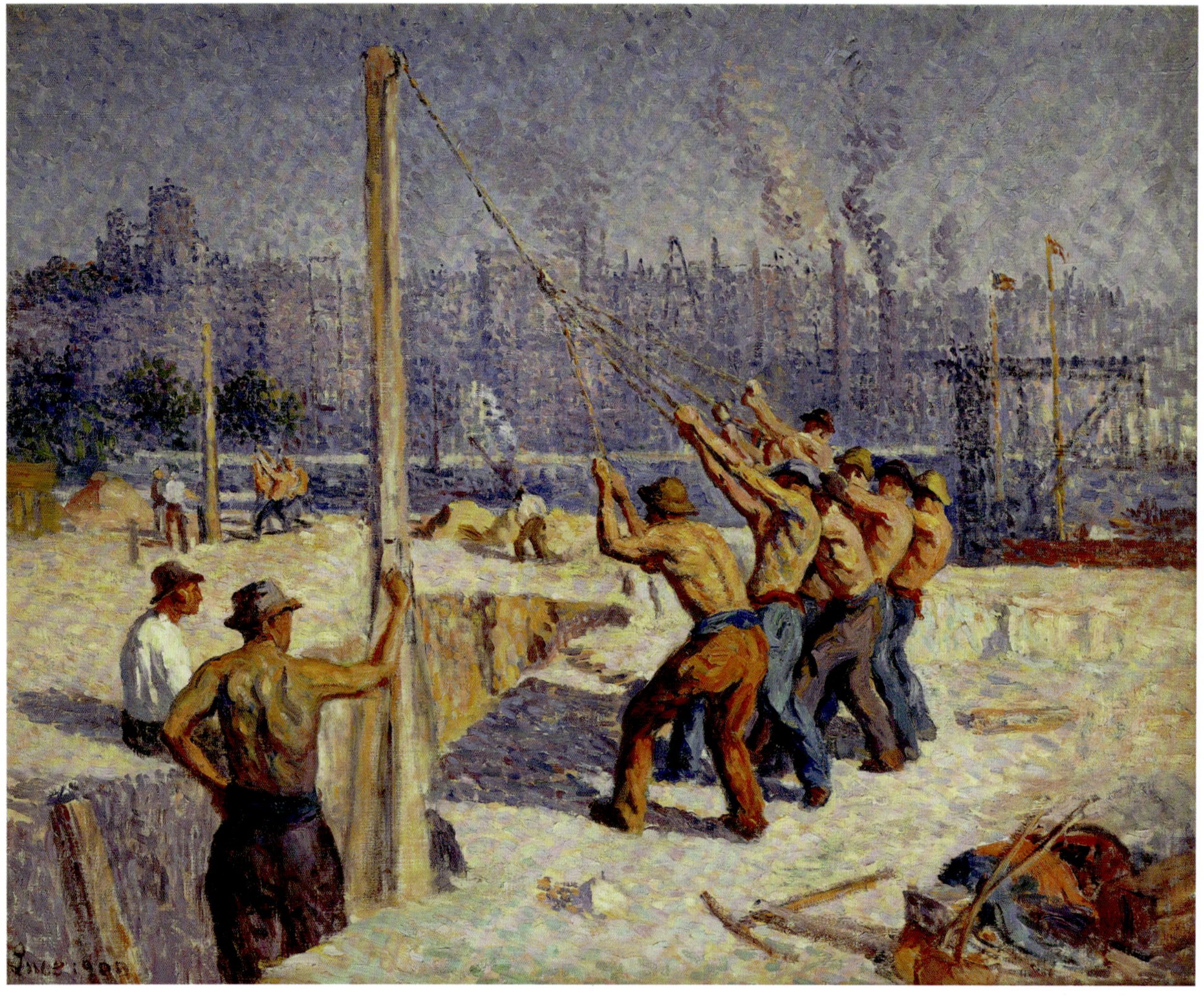

The Pile Drivers

Les Batteurs de pieux

Die Pfahlrammer

Los batedores de postes

O empilhador de estacas

Het heiblok

MAXIMILIEN LUCE (1858-1941)

1902/03, Oil on canvas/Huile sur toile,
154 × 196 cm, Musée d'Orsay, Paris

The Building Sites of Paris, Boulevard de la Madeleine

Les Chantiers de Paris, boulevard de la Madeleine

Die Baustellen von Paris, Boulevard de la Madeleine

Las obras de construcción de París,
Boulevard de la Madeleine

Os estaleiros de construção de Paris,
Boulevard de la Madeleine

De bouwplaatsen van Parijs, Boulevard de la Madeleine

MAXIMILIEN LUCE (1858-1941)

n. d., Oil on canvas/Huile sur toile, 65 × 54 cm, Private collection

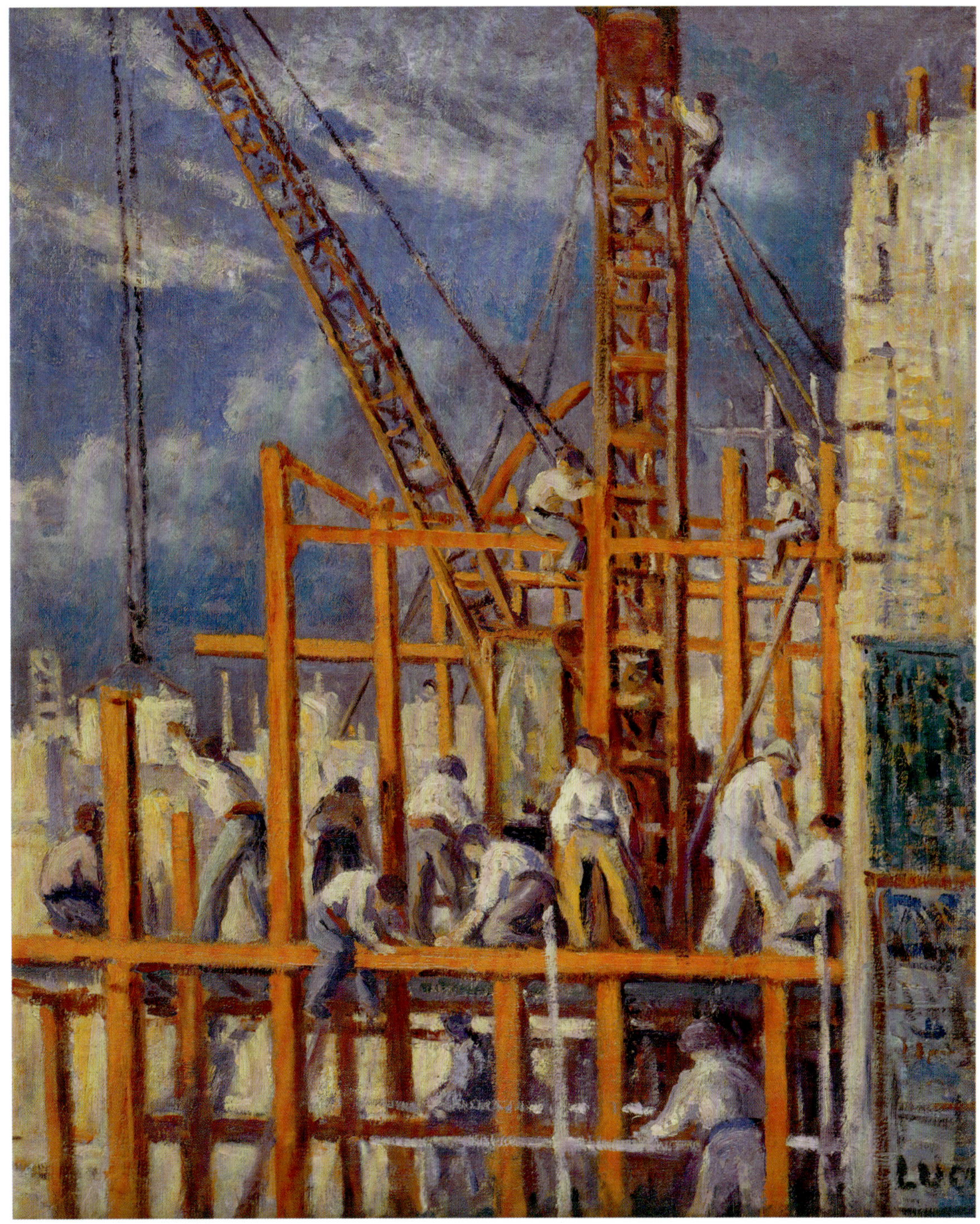

Luc

A Sunday on La Grande Jatte

The depiction of an afternoon on the banks of the Seine was a technical masterpiece. The Neo-Impressionist Manifesto is the result of two years of preparation based on sketches and studies.

Un dimanche après-midi à l'île de la Grande Jatte

Véritable manifeste du néo-impressionnisme, cette image d'un après-midi oisif en bord de Seine est une prouesse technique. De dessins préparatoires en études peintes, elle résulte de deux ans de travail.

Ein Sonntagnachmittag auf der Insel La Grande Jatte

Die Darstellung eines Nachmittags an den Ufern der Seine war eine technische Meisterleistung. Das Manifest des Neoimpressionismus ist das Resultat einer zweijährigen Vorbereitung anhand von Skizzen und Studien.

Una tarde de domingo en la isla de La Grande Jatte

La representación de Una tarde a orillas del Sena fue una obra maestra de la técnica. El manifiesto Neo-Impresionista es el resultado de dos años de preparación basada en bocetos y estudios.

Uma tarde de domingo na ilha de La Grande Jatte

A representação de uma tarde nas margens do Sena foi uma obra-prima técnica. O Manifesto Neo-Impressionista é o resultado de dois anos de preparação baseada em esboços e estudos.

Een zondagmiddag op het eiland La Grande Jatte

De weergave van een middag aan de oever van de Seine was een technisch meesterwerk. Dit manifest van het neo-impressionisme is het resultaat van twee jaar voorbereiding aan de hand van schetsen en studies.

GEORGES SEURAT (1859-1891)

1886, Oil on canvas/Huile sur toile, 207,5 × 308,1 cm, The Art Institute of Chicago

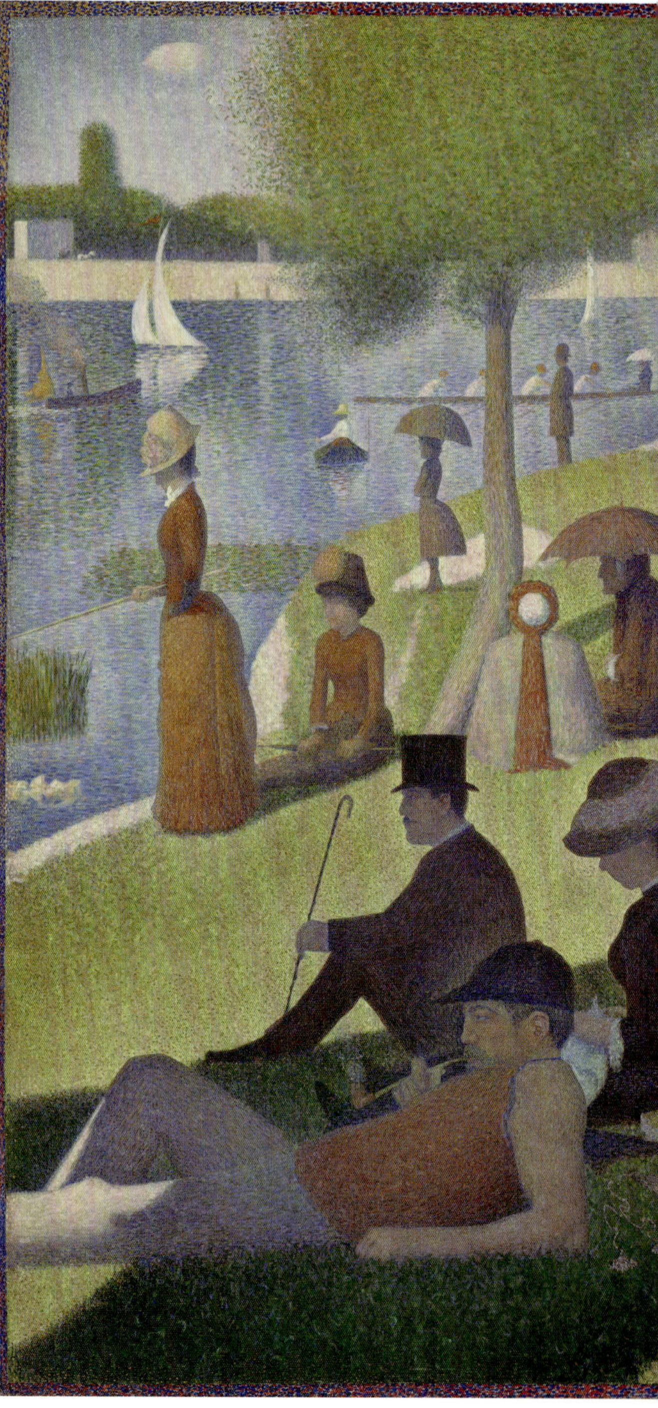

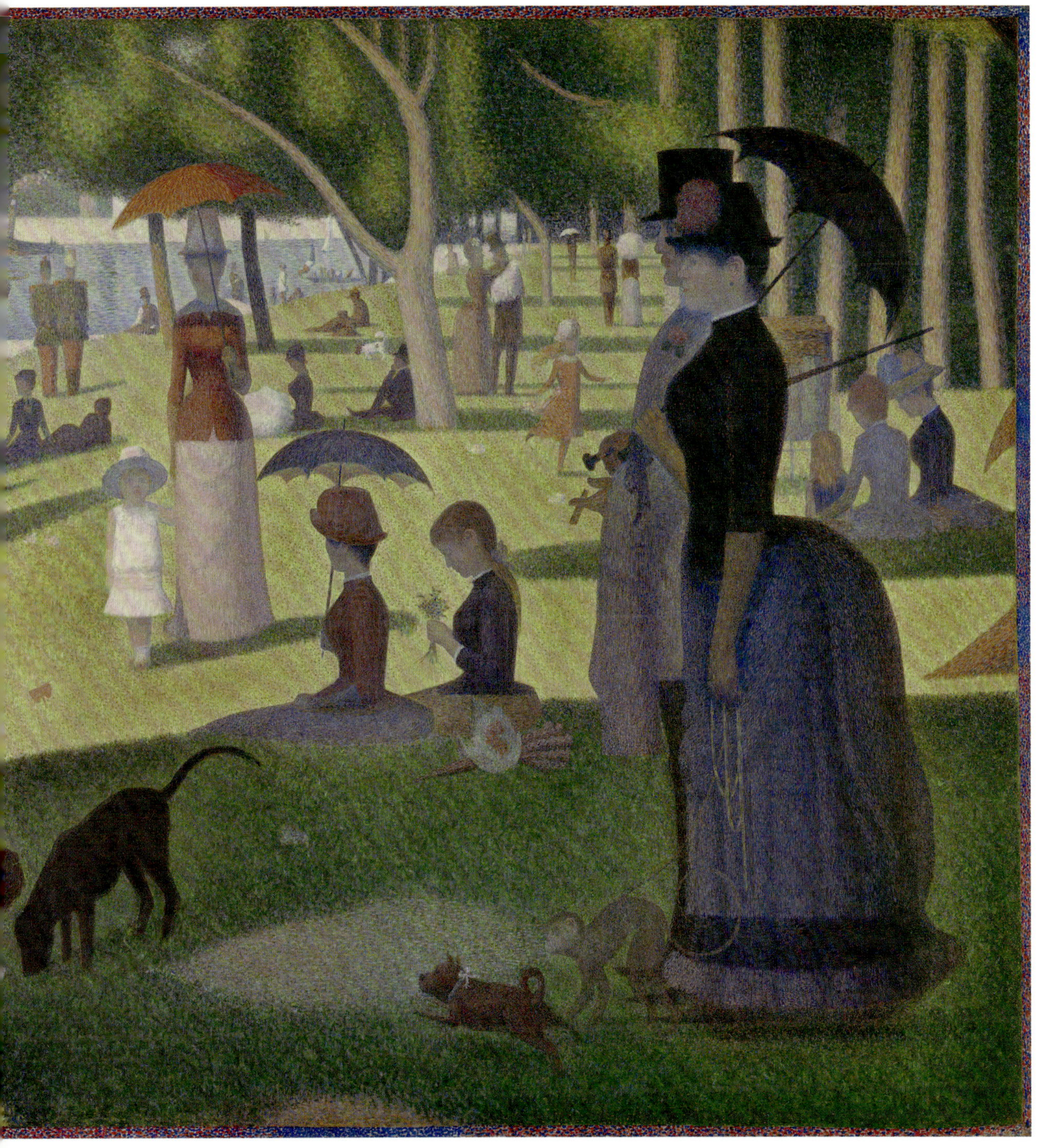

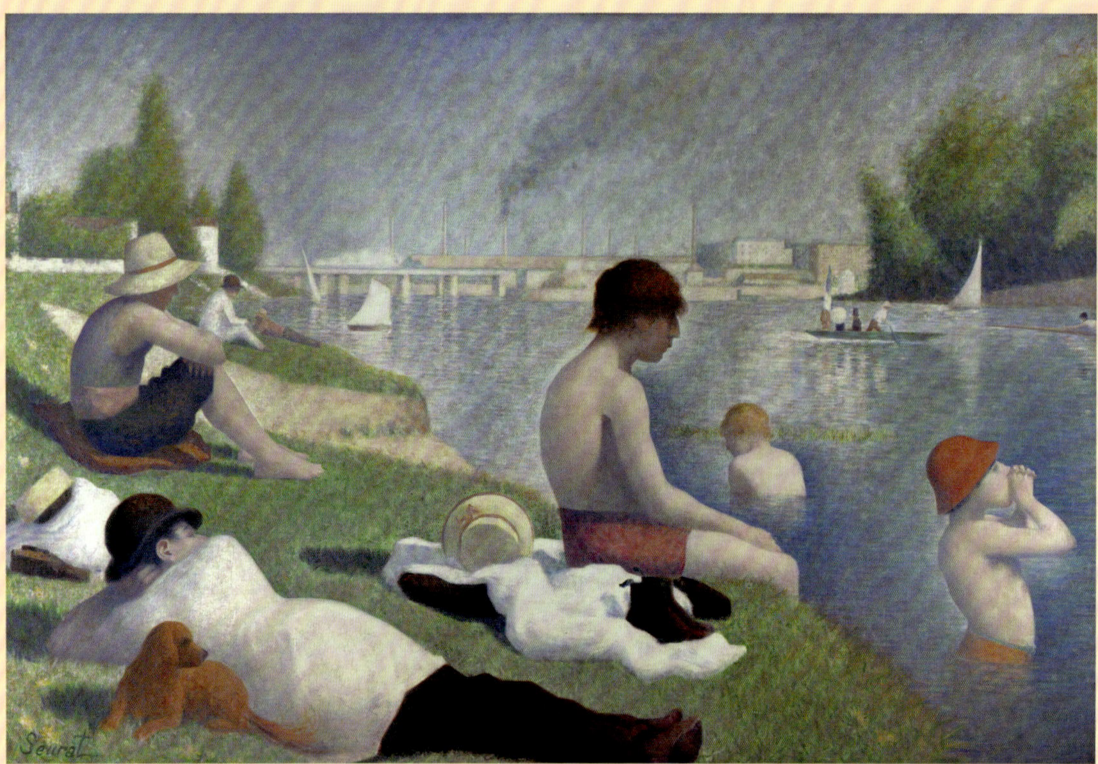

Bathers at
Asnières

Une baignade
à Asnières

Die Badenden,
Asnières

Los bañistas,
Asnières

Os banhistas,
Asnières

Baders bij
Asnières

**GEORGES
SEURAT
(1859-1891)**
1884, Oil on
canvas/
Huile sur toile,
201 × 300 cm,
The National
Gallery, London

Pointillism

Pointillism produced meticulously executed works
composed of thousands of dots of color. If they are
viewed from a greater distance, the dots applied in pure
colors mix to form color transitions. Georges Seurat's
A Sunday on La Grande Jatte, which enjoys the
reputation of a manifesto, provided the model for
this lengthy and time-consuming technique, which
many painters were to try their hand at. Above all Paul
Signac, who made Pointillism the basis of his paintings
and watercolors, but also Charles Angrand, Hippolyte
Petitjean, Maximilien Luce, Henri Martin, Henri
Le Sidaner and Henri Edmond Cross - who created
masterpieces such as *The Iles d'Or*. Henri Matisse also
devoted himself to style before turning to Fauvism. His
work *Luxury, Serenity and Pleasure*, created in 1904
while with Paul Signac in Saint-Tropez, deserves special
mention. For a time, the Cubists and Futurists used
Pointillism as a starting point for their new approaches.

Le pointillisme

Au sein du néo-impressionnisme, le pointillisme a
donné naissance à des œuvres d'une extrême minutie.
Le principe consiste à juxtaposer des milliers de points
de couleurs pures sur la toile. L'œil du spectateur, en
observant le tableau de loin, opère lui-même le
mélange des couleurs. *Un dimanche après-midi à l'île
de la Grande Jatte* de Georges Seurat est le modèle
absolu du genre, et a valeur de manifeste. Nombre de
peintres se sont essayés à cette technique longue et
contraignante. Paul Signac bien sûr, qui en fit l'essentiel
de son style (toiles et aquarelles), mais aussi Charles
Angrand, Hippolyte Petitjean, Henri-Edmond Cross
– avec quelques grands chefs-d'œuvre comme *Les Îles
d'or* –, Maximilien Luce, Henri Martin ou Henri
Le Sidaner. Jusqu'à Henri Matisse, qui, avant de devenir
le peintre fauve que l'on connaît, s'est essayé lui aussi au
pointillisme, notamment dans *Luxe, calme et volupté*,
réalisé auprès de Paul Signac, en 1904, à Saint-Tropez.
Les cubistes et les futuristes s'y intéresseront un temps,
comme point de départ de recherches nouvelles.

Der Pointillismus

Der Pointillismus brachte minutiös ausgeführte Werke
hervor, die sich aus Tausenden von Farbpunkten
zusammensetzen. Werden sie aus einem größeren
Abstand betrachtet, mischen sich die in puren Farben
aufgetragenen Punkte zu Farbübergängen.
Georges Seurats *Ein Sonntagnachmittag auf der
Insel La Grande Jatte*, das den Ruf eines Manifests
genießt, lieferte die Vorlage für diese langwierige
und zeitaufwendige Technik, an der sich zahlreiche
Maler versuchen sollten. Allen voran Paul Signac,
der den Pointillismus zur Grundlage seiner Gemälde
und Aquarelle machte, aber auch Charles Angrand,
Hippolyte Petitjean, Maximilien Luce, Henri Martin,
Henri Le Sidaner und Henri Edmond Cross – der
Meisterwerke wie *Die goldenen Inseln* schuf. Auch
Henri Matisse widmete sich dem Stil, bevor er sich
dem Fauvismus zuwandte. Hervorzuheben ist sein
Werk *Luxus, Stille und Begierde*, das 1904 im Umfeld
von Paul Signac in Saint-Tropez entstand. Den Kubisten
und Futuristen diente der Pointillismus eine Zeit lang
als Ausgangspunkt für ihre neuartigen Ansätze.

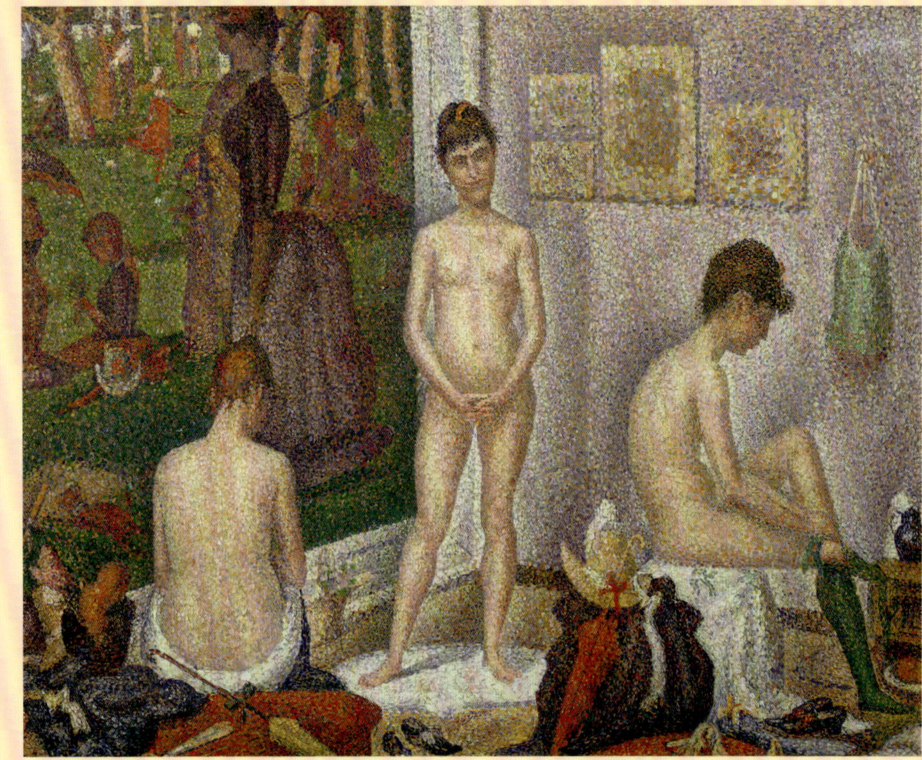

Puntillismo

El puntillismo produjo obras meticulosamente
ejecutadas compuestas de miles de puntos de color.
Si se observan a mayor distancia, los puntos aplicados
en colores puros se mezclan para formar transiciones
de color. La obra de Georges Seurats *Una tarde de
domingo en la isla de La Grande Jatte*, que goza de la
reputación de un manifiesto, proporcionó el modelo
para esta técnica larga y lenta, que muchos pintores
iban a probar. Sobre todo Paul Signac, que hizo del
puntillismo la base de sus pinturas y acuarelas, pero
también Charles Angrand, Hippolyte Petitjean,
Maximilien Luce, Henri Martin, Henri Le Sidaner y
Henri Edmond Cross, que crearon obras maestras como
Las islas doradas. Henri Matisse también se dedicó al
estilo antes de recurrir al fauvismo. Mención especial
merece su obra *Lujo, calma y voluptuosidad*, creada en
1904 en los alrededores de Paul Signac en Saint-Tropez.
Durante un tiempo, los cubistas y futuristas utilizaron
el puntillismo como punto de partida para sus nuevos
enfoques.

Pontilhismo

O pontilhismo produziu obras meticulosamente
executadas compostas por milhares de pontos de cor.
Se forem vistos de uma distância maior, os pontos
aplicados em cores puras misturam-se para formar
transições de cor. Georges Seurats *A tarde de domingo
na ilha de La Grande Jatte*, que goza da reputação de
um manifesto, forneceu o modelo para esta técnica
demorada e demorada, que muitos pintores estavam a
tentar a sua mão. Acima de tudo, Paul Signac, que fez
do pontilhismo a base das suas pinturas e aquarelas,
mas também Charles Angrand, Hippolyte Petitjean,
Maximilien Luce, Henri Martin, Henri Le Sidaner e
Henri Edmond Cross - que criou obras-primas como
As Ilhas Douradas. Henri Matisse também se dedicou
ao estilo antes de se voltar para o fauvismo. Sua obra
Luxo, Silêncio e Desejo, criada em 1904 nos arredores
de Paul Signac em Saint-Tropez, merece menção
especial. Durante algum tempo, os cubistas e futuristas
usaram o pontilhismo como ponto de partida para as
suas novas abordagens.

Pointillisme

Het pointillisme bracht minutieus uitgevoerde werken
voort die zijn opgebouwd uit duizenden verfstippen.
Als ze van een grotere afstand worden bekeken,
vermengen de in zuivere kleuren aangebrachte stippen
zich tot kleurovergangen. Georges Seurats werk
Een zondagmiddag op het eiland La Grande Jatte,
dat de reputatie van een manifest geniet, vormde
het voorbeeld voor deze tijdrovende techniek,
die veel schilders zouden uitproberen. Als eerste
Paul Signac, die van het pointillisme de basis voor
zijn schilderijen en aquarellen maakte, maar ook
Charles Angrand, Hippolyte Petitjean, Maximilien Luce,
Henri Martin, Henri Le Sidaner, Henri Le Sidaner
en Henri Edmond Cross – die meesterwerken als
De gouden eilanden maakte. Henri Matisse werkte ook
in deze stijl voordat hij zich tot het fauvisme zou keren.
Zijn schilderij *Luxe, calm et volupté*, gemaakt in 1904
in de omgeving van Paul Signac in Saint-Tropez,
verdient bijzondere vermelding. Het pointillisme
diende de kubisten en futuristen enige tijd als
uitgangspunt voor hun nieuwe aanpak.

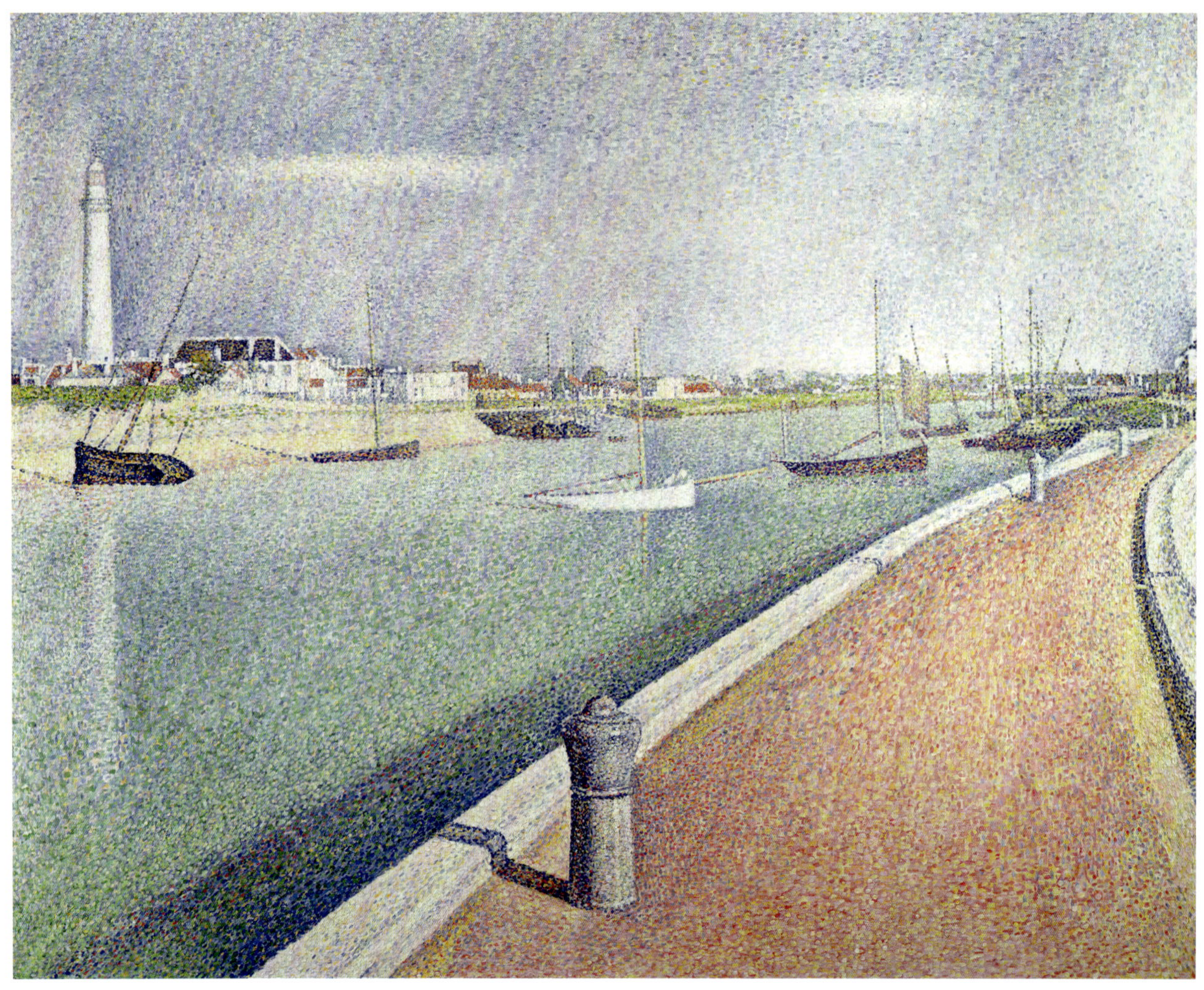

The Channel of Gravelines, Petit-Fort-Philippe

Le Canal de Gravelines, Petit-Fort-Philippe

Der Kanal von Gravelines, Petit-Fort-Philippe

El Canal de Gravelines, Petit-Fort-Philippe

O Canal de Gravelines, Petit-Fort-Philippe

Het kanaal van Gravelines, Petit-Fort-Philippe

GEORGES SEURAT (1859-1891)

1890, Oil on canvas/Huile sur toile, 73 × 92,7 cm, Indianapolis Museum of Art, Newfields

Man leaning on a Parapet

The dynamic silhouette of a tree and a man standing contrast with a strictly composed background of vertical and horizontal lines that cannot be identified more closely.

Homme se penchant sur un parapet

Sur un fond construit par de larges plans et des lignes verticales et horizontales, se détachent la silhouette dansante d'un arbre et celle d'un homme debout devant un paysage, impossible à identifier.

Mann an der Brüstung

Vor einem streng komponierten Hintergrund aus vertikalen und horizontalen Linien, der nicht näher identifiziert werden kann, hebt sich die dynamische Silhouette eines Baumes und eines stehenden Mannes ab.

Hombre en la balaustrada

La silueta dinámica de un árbol y un hombre de pie se destaca sobre un fondo estrictamente compuesto de líneas verticales y horizontales que no pueden ser identificadas más de cerca.

Homem na balaustrada

A silhueta dinâmica de uma árvore e de um homem em pé destaca-se sobre um fundo estritamente composto por linhas verticais e horizontais que não podem ser identificadas mais de perto.

Man leunend op een balustrade

Het dynamische silhouet van een boom en een staande man steekt af tegen een streng gecomponeerde achtergrond van verticale en horizontale lijnen die niet nader te identificeren is.

GEORGES SEURAT (1859-1891)

c. 1881, Oil on canvas/Huile sur toile, 62 x 83 cm, Private collection

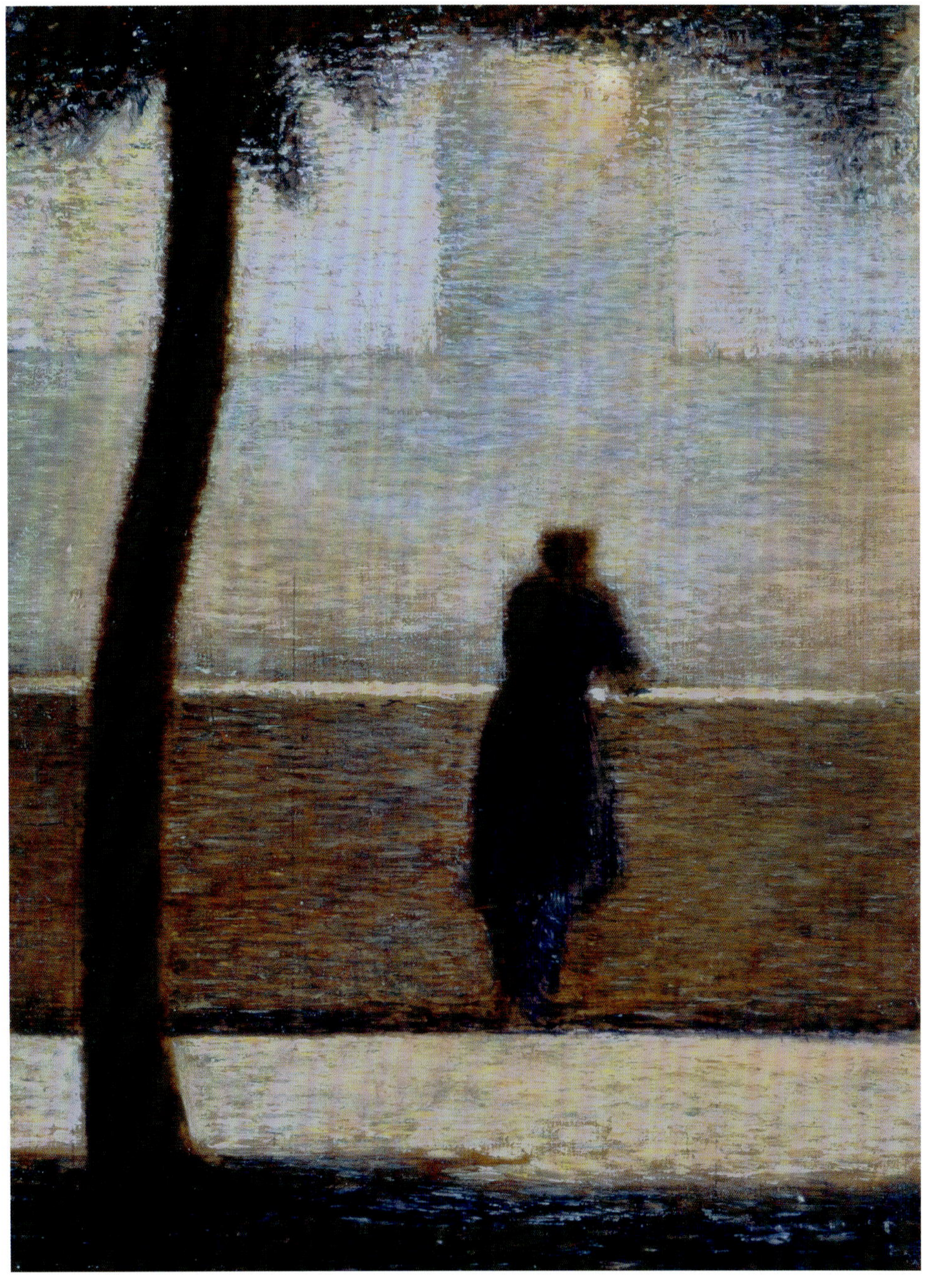

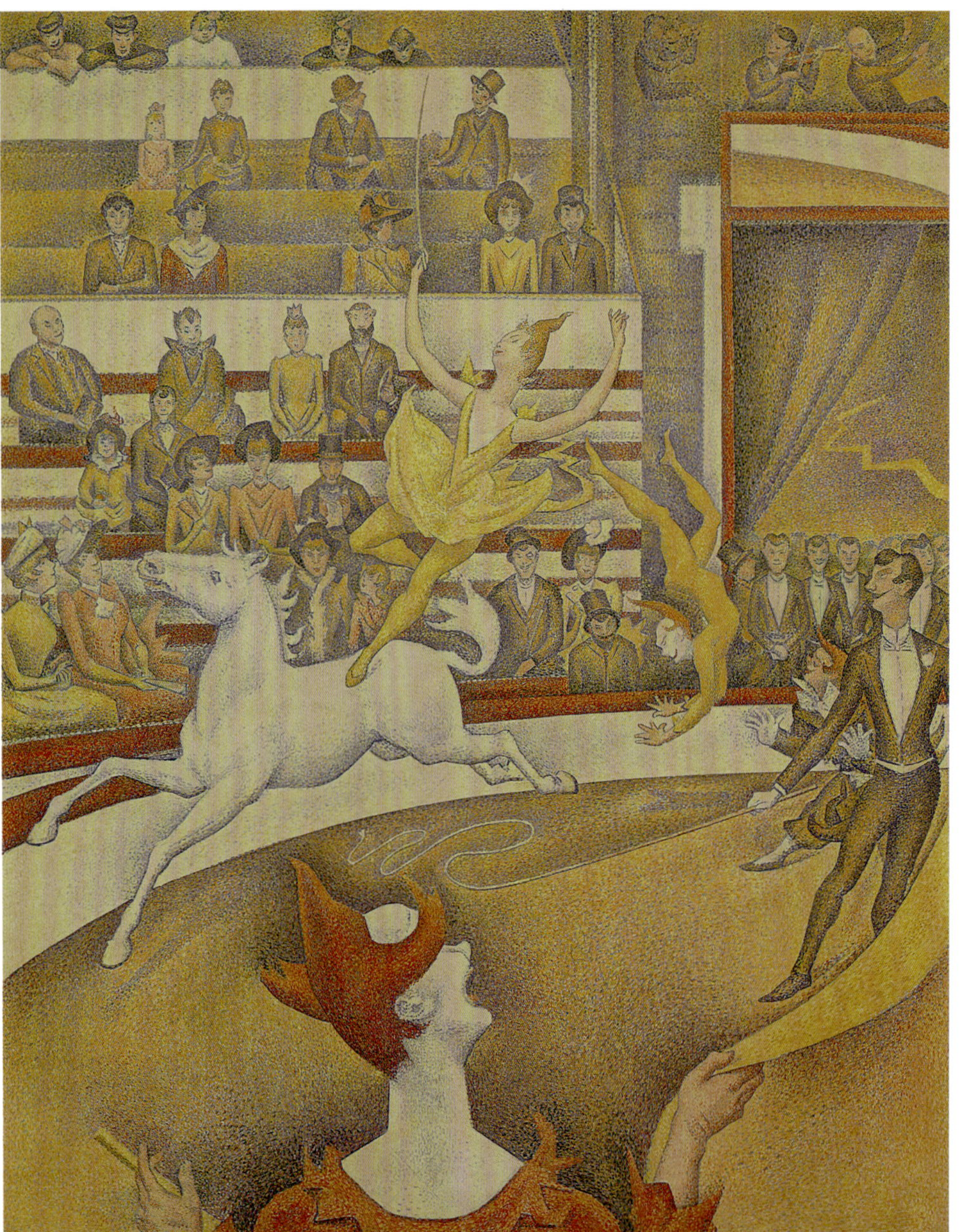

The Circus

The arena of the Circus Fernando shines in a symphony of yellow and orange tones. Seurat plays with the interaction between the movements in the ring and the severity of the horizontal spectator stands.

Le Cirque

L'écuyère du cirque Fernando évolue dans une symphonie de tons jaune orangé. Seurat joue sur l'opposition entre le mouvement tourbillonnant de la piste et la rigueur des lignes horizontales des gradins.

Der Zirkus

Die Manege des Zirkus Fernando erstrahlt in einer Symphonie aus Gelb- und Orangetönen. Seurat spielt mit der Wechselwirkung zwischen den Bewegungen in der Manege und der Strenge der horizontalen Zuschauerränge.

El Circo

La amazona del circo Fernando evoluciona en una sinfonía de tonos anaranjados y amarillos. Seurat juega con la oposición entre el movimiento giratorio de la pista y el rigor de las líneas horizontales de las gradas.

O Circo

O anel circense do circo Fernando brilha numa sinfonia de tons amarelos e alaranjados. Seurat brinca com a interação entre os movimentos no anel e a gravidade da posição do espectador horizontal.

Het circus

De piste van het Circus Fernando straalt als een symfonie van gele en oranje tinten. Seurat speelde met de wisselwerking tussen de bewegingen in de piste en de strenge horizontale lijnen van de tribunes.

GEORGES SEURAT (1859-1891)

1890/91, Oil on canvas/Huile sur toile, 186 × 152 cm, Musée d'Orsay, Paris

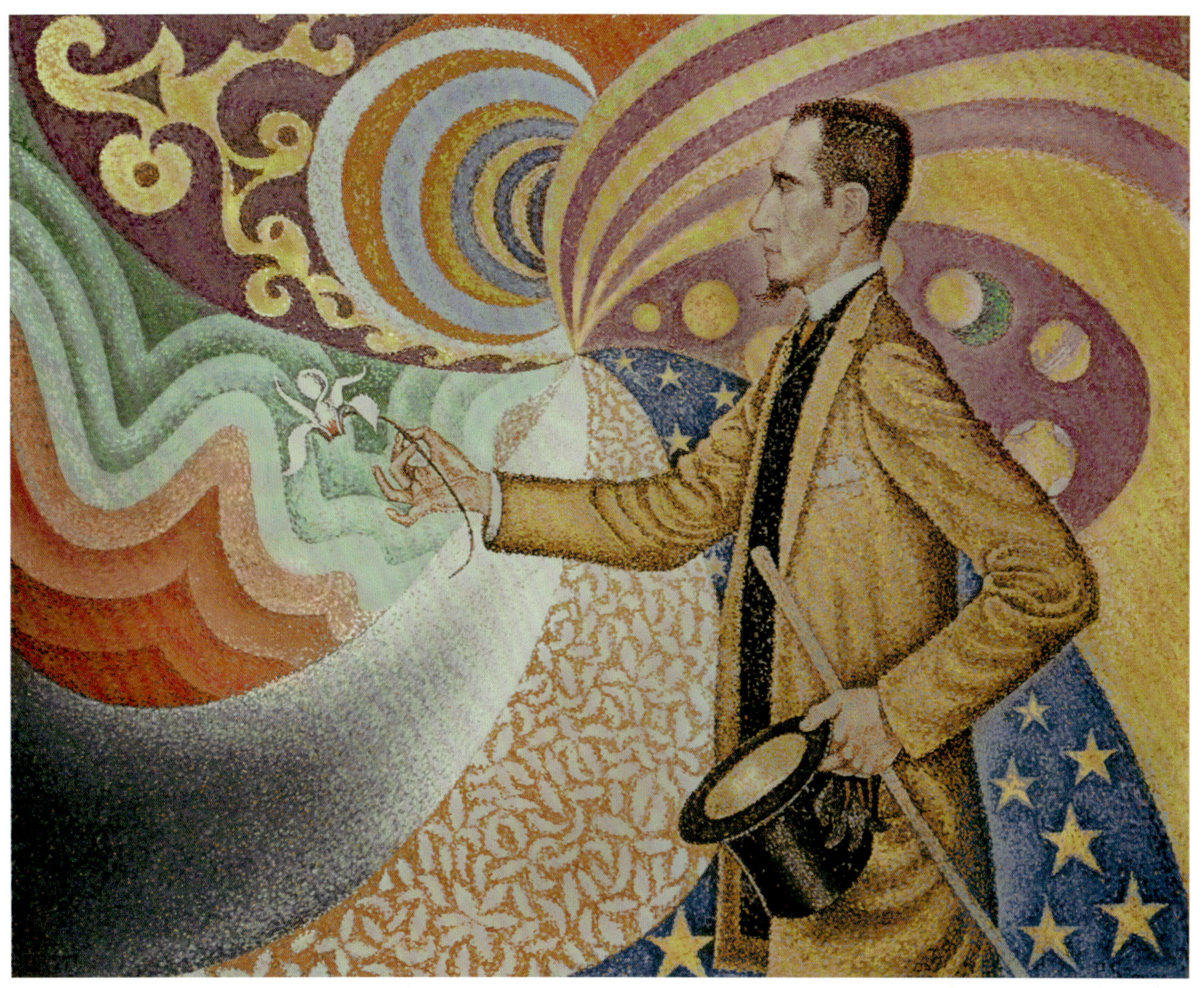

Opus 217

PAUL SIGNAC (1863-1935)

1890, Oil on canvas/Huile sur toile, 73,5 × 92,5 cm,

Museum of Modern Art, New York

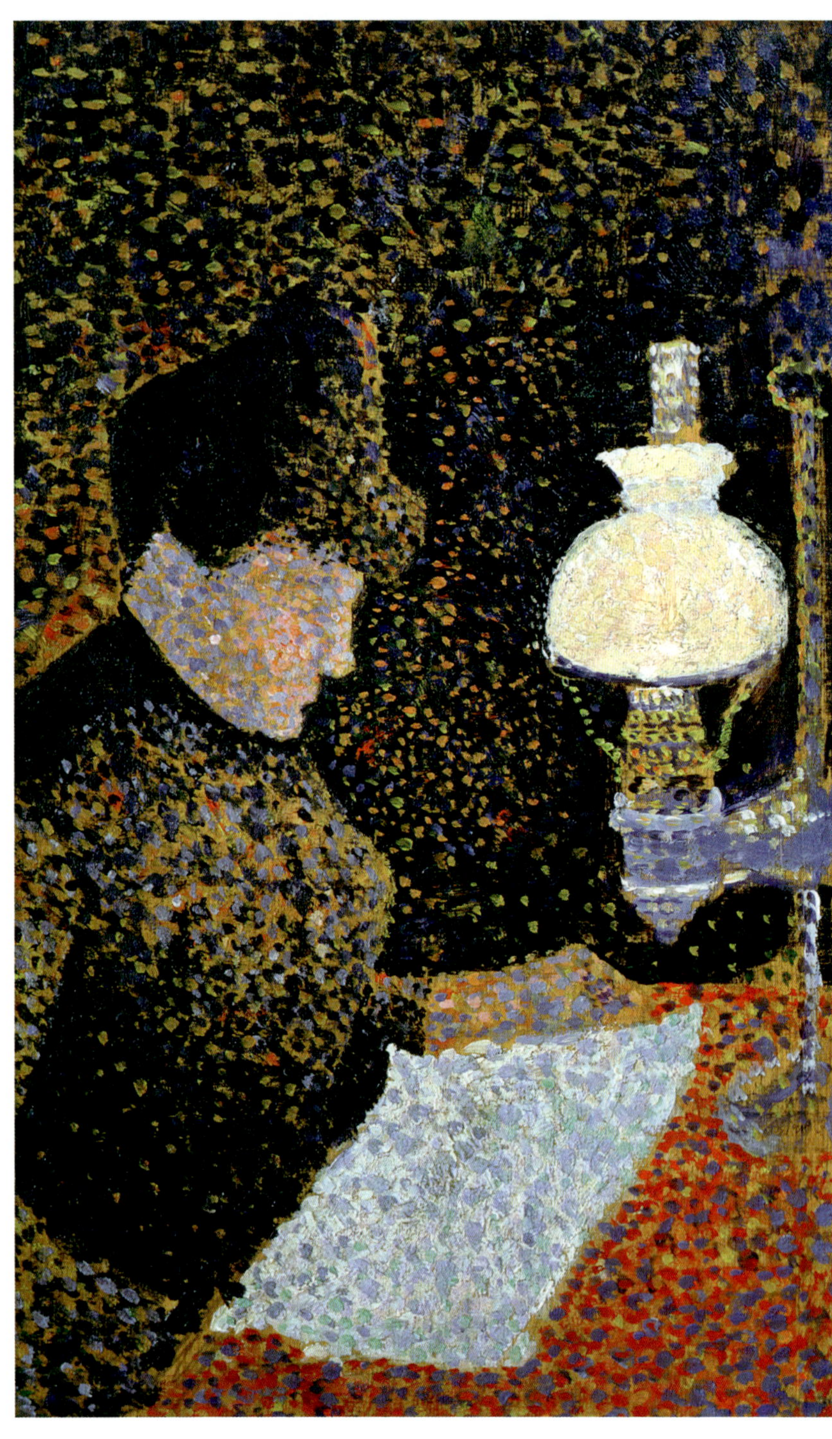

Woman by a Lamp

Femme sous la lampe

Frau unter der Lampe

La mujer bajo la lámpara

Mulher debaixo da lâmpada

Vrouw bij een lamp

PAUL SIGNAC (1863-1935)

1890, Oil on wood/Huile sur bois,
26,1 × 16,6 cm, Musée d'Orsay, Paris

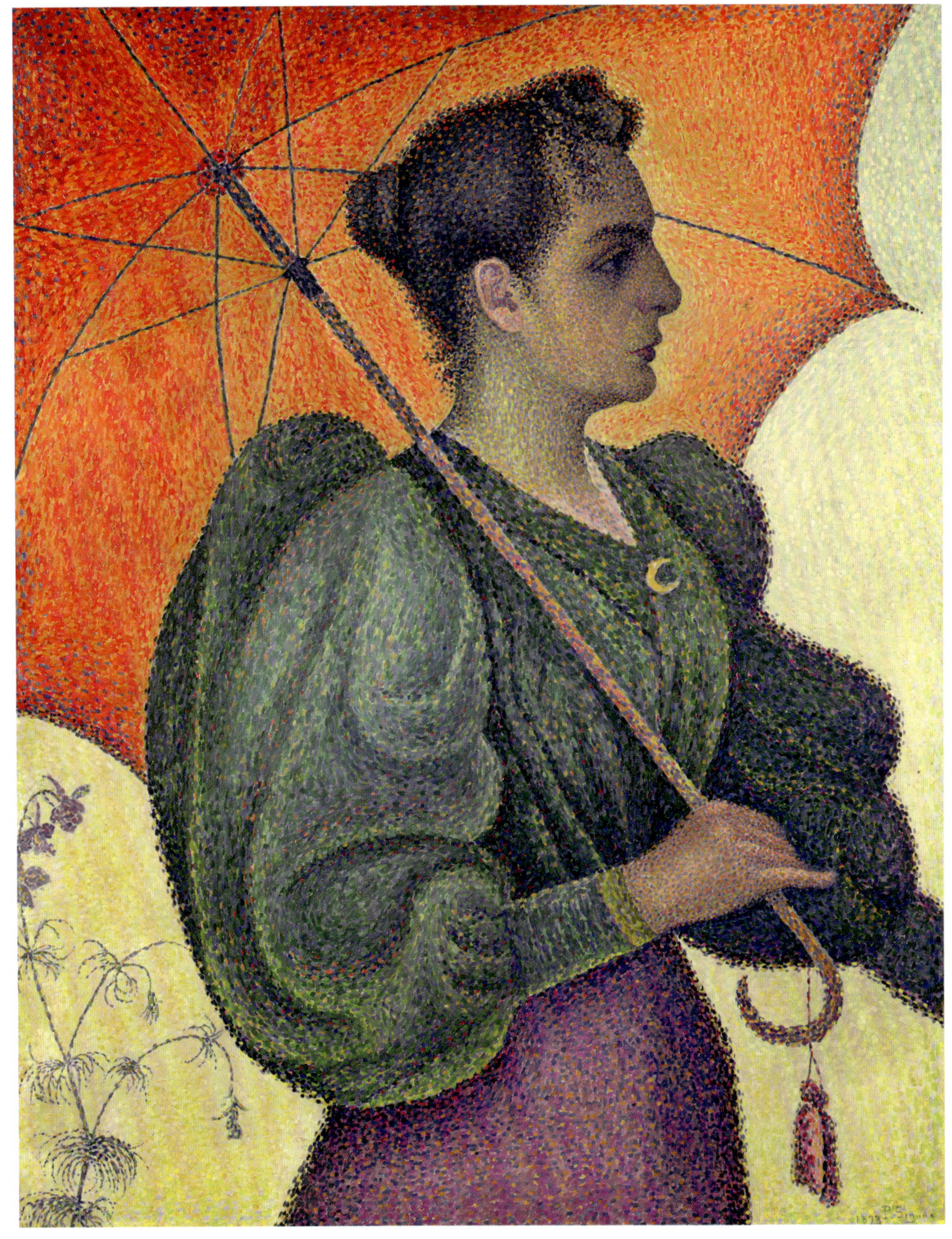

Woman with a
Parasol (Opus 243)

Femme à l'ombrelle
(Opus 243, Effigie)

Frau mit
Sonnenschirm
(Opus 243, Bildnis)

Mujer con
sombrilla (Opus
243, retrato)

Mulher com
guarda-sol (Opus
243, retrato)

Vrouw met parasol
(Opus 243, portret)

PAUL SIGNAC
(1863-1935)
1893, Oil on canvas/
Huile sur toile,
81 × 65 cm, Musée
d'Orsay, Paris

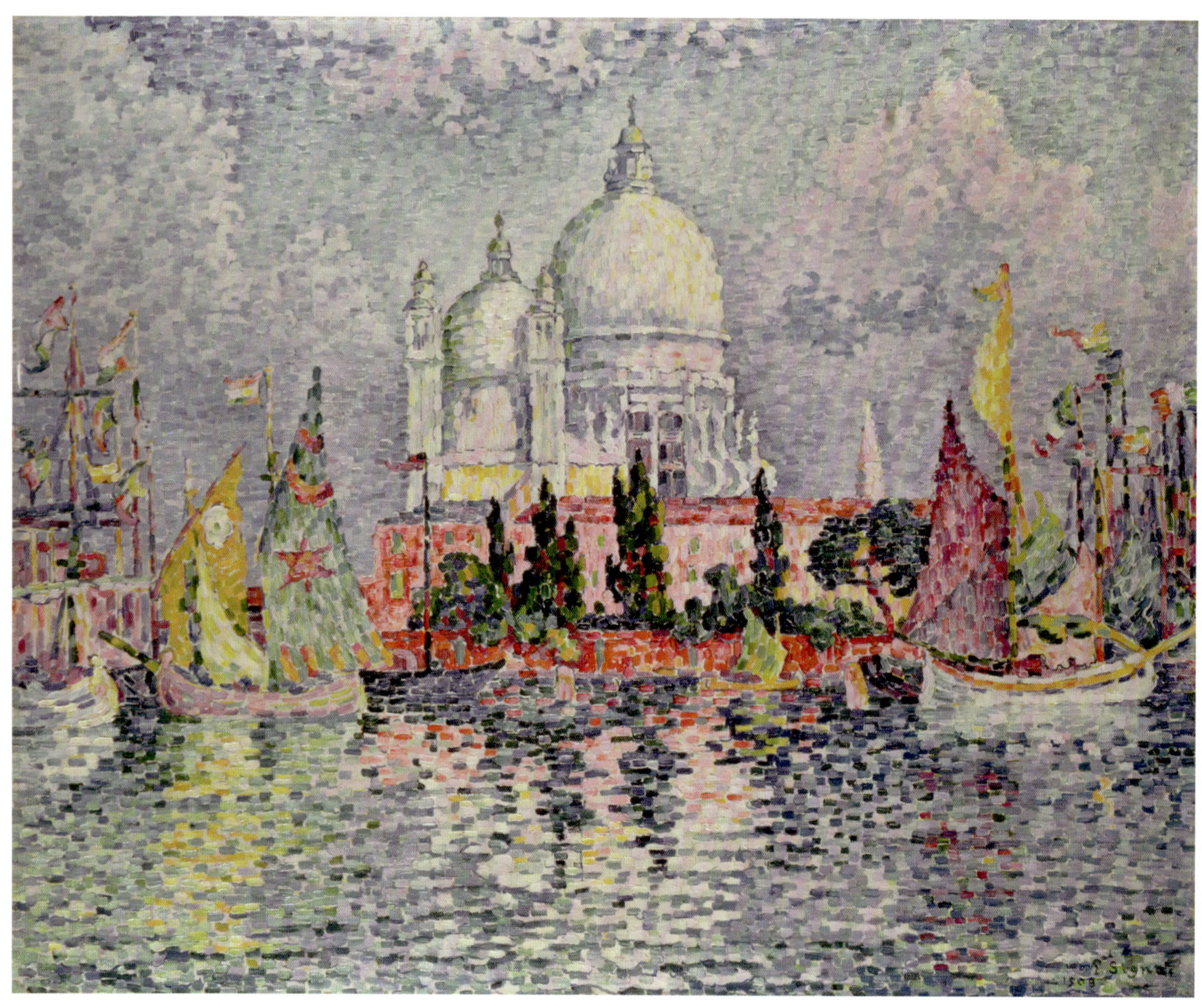

Santa Maria della Salute

PAUL SIGNAC (1863-1935)

1908, Oil on canvas/Huile sur toile, 73 × 91,5 cm, Private collection

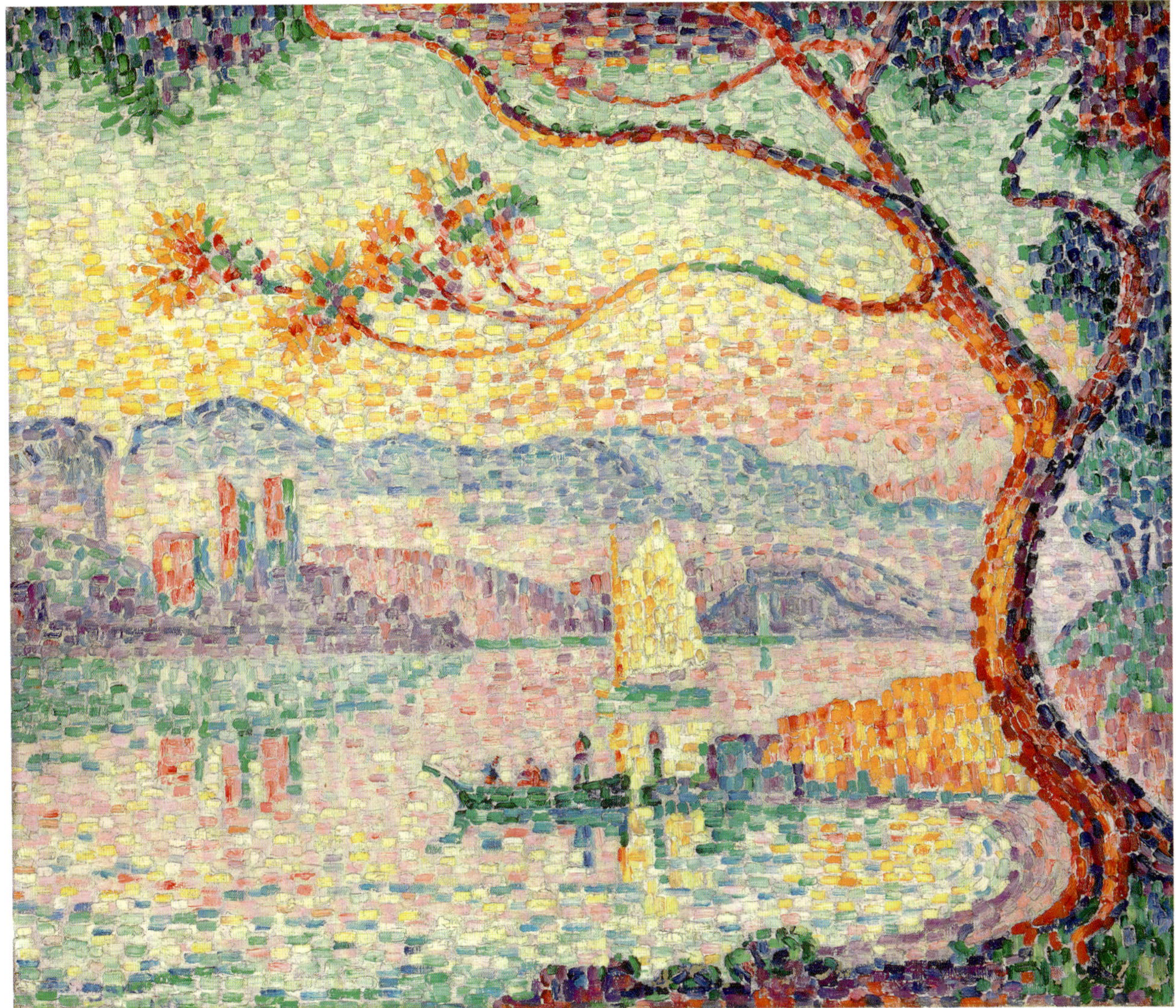

The Port of Antibes

In this painting, based on Japanese arabesques, Signac juxtaposes luminous colours in a bold mixture. He painted his motif in pure blue, red, green and violet tones.

Le Port d'Antibes

Dans cette toile aux arabesques japonisantes, Signac ose les tons vifs, et les rapports de couleurs les plus audacieux, juxtaposant sans mélange des touches de bleu et de rouge, de vert et de violet.

Der Hafen von Antibes

Bei dem an japanische Arabesken angelehnten Gemälde setzt Signac leuchtende Farben in einer kühnen Mischung nebeneinander. Sein Motiv malt er in reinen Blau-, Rot-, Grün- und Violetttönen.

El puerto de Antibes

En este cuadro, basado en arabescos japoneses, Signac yuxtapone colores luminosos en una mezcla atrevida. Pinta su motivo en tonos puros de azul, rojo, verde y violeta.

O porto de Antibes

Nesta pintura, baseada em arabescos japoneses, Signac justapõe cores luminosas numa mistura arrojada. Pinta o seu motivo em tons de azul puro, vermelho, verde e violeta.

De haven van Antibes

In dit op Japanse arabesken geïnspireerde schilderij zette Signac lichte kleuren in een gedurfde mix naast elkaar. Hij schilderde zijn onderwerp met zuivere blauw-, rood-, groen- en paarstinten.

PAUL SIGNAC (1863-1935)

1917, Oil on canvas/Huile sur toile, 54 × 64,8 cm, Private collection

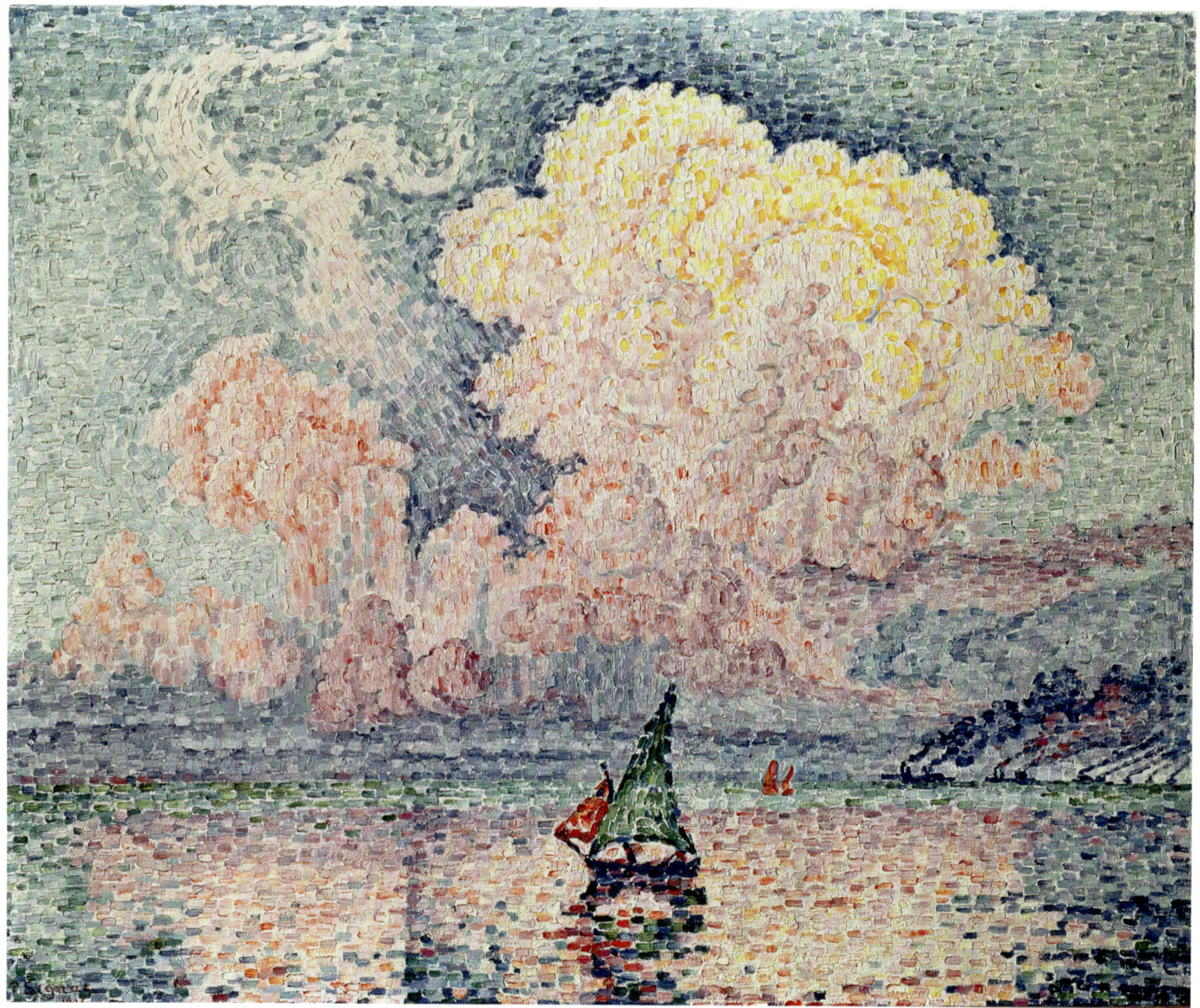

Antibes, the Pink Cloud

Antibes, le nuage rose

Antibes, die rosa Wolke

Antibes, la nube rosa

Antibes, a nuvem rosa

Antibes, de roze wolk

PAUL SIGNAC (1863-1935)

1916, Oil on canvas/Huile sur toile, 73 × 92 cm, Private collection

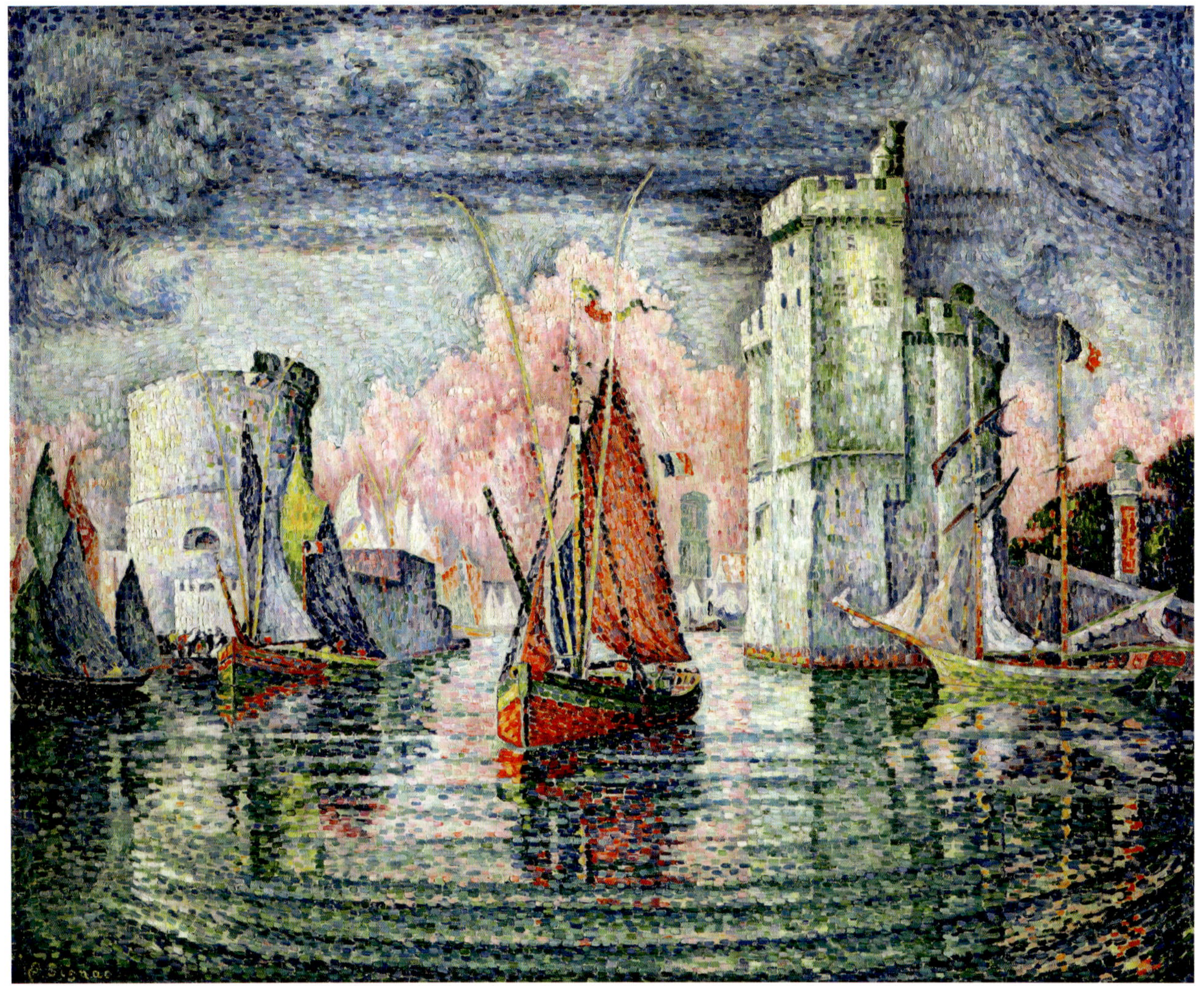

The Port at La Rochelle

Venice, Saint-Tropez, Marseille or La Rochelle - Signac was a lover of ports and dedicated about ten paintings to them. Despite the abstraction of the colors, the port of La Rochelle is clearly recognizable.

Entrée du port de La Rochelle

Venise, Saint-Tropez, Marseille ou La Rochelle, les ports inspirent Signac, qui leur consacrera plusieurs dizaines œuvres. Malgré l'irréalité des couleurs, le site est ici immédiatement reconnaissable.

Der Hafen von La Rochelle

Venedig, Saint-Tropez, Marseille oder La Rochelle – Signac ist ein Liebhaber der Häfen und widmet ihnen um die zehn Gemälde. Trotz der Abstrahierung der Farben ist der Hafen von La Rochelle eindeutig zu erkennen.

El puerto de La Rochelle

Venecia, Saint-Tropez, Marsella o La Rochelle - Signac es un amante de los puertos y les dedica una decena de cuadros. A pesar de la abstracción de los colores, el puerto de La Rochelle es claramente visible.

O porto de La Rochelle

Veneza, Saint-Tropez, Marselha ou La Rochelle - Signac é um amante dos portos e dedica cerca de dez pinturas a eles. Apesar da abstracção das cores, o porto de La Rochelle é claramente visível.

De haven van La Rochelle

Venetië, Saint-Tropez, Marseille of La Rochelle - Signac hield van havens en wijdde er een tiental schilderijen aan. Ondanks de abstractie van de kleuren is de haven van La Rochelle duidelijk herkenbaar.

PAUL SIGNAC (1863-1935)
1921, Oil on canvas/Huile sur toile, 130,5 × 162 cm, Musée d'Orsay, Paris

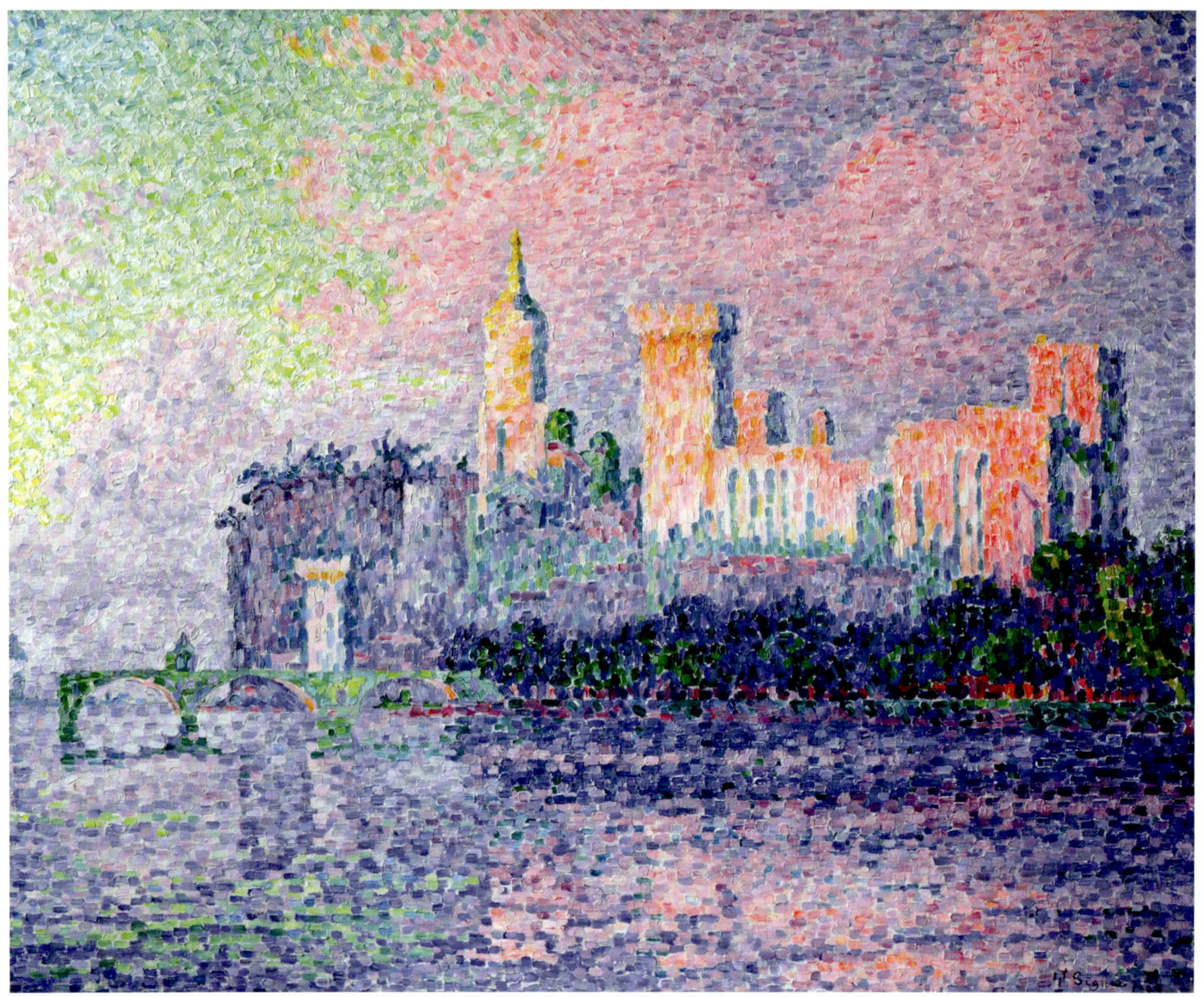

The Palais des Papes, Avignon

Le Palais des Papes, Avignon

Der Papstpalast, Avignon

El Palacio de los Papas, Aviñón

O Palácio dos Papas, Avignon

Het Pausenpaleis, Avignon

PAUL SIGNAC (1863-1935)

1909, Oil on canvas/Huile sur toile, 73,3 × 91,9 cm, Musée d'Orsay, Paris

The Pont des Arts,
Inondation

Pont des arts, inondation

Der Pont des Arts,
Überschwemmung

El Puente de las Artes,
inundaciones

A Pont des Arts,
Inundação

De Pont des Arts,
overstroming

PAUL SIGNAC (1863-1935)
1930, Oil on canvas/
Huile sur toile, 35 × 27 cm,
Private collection

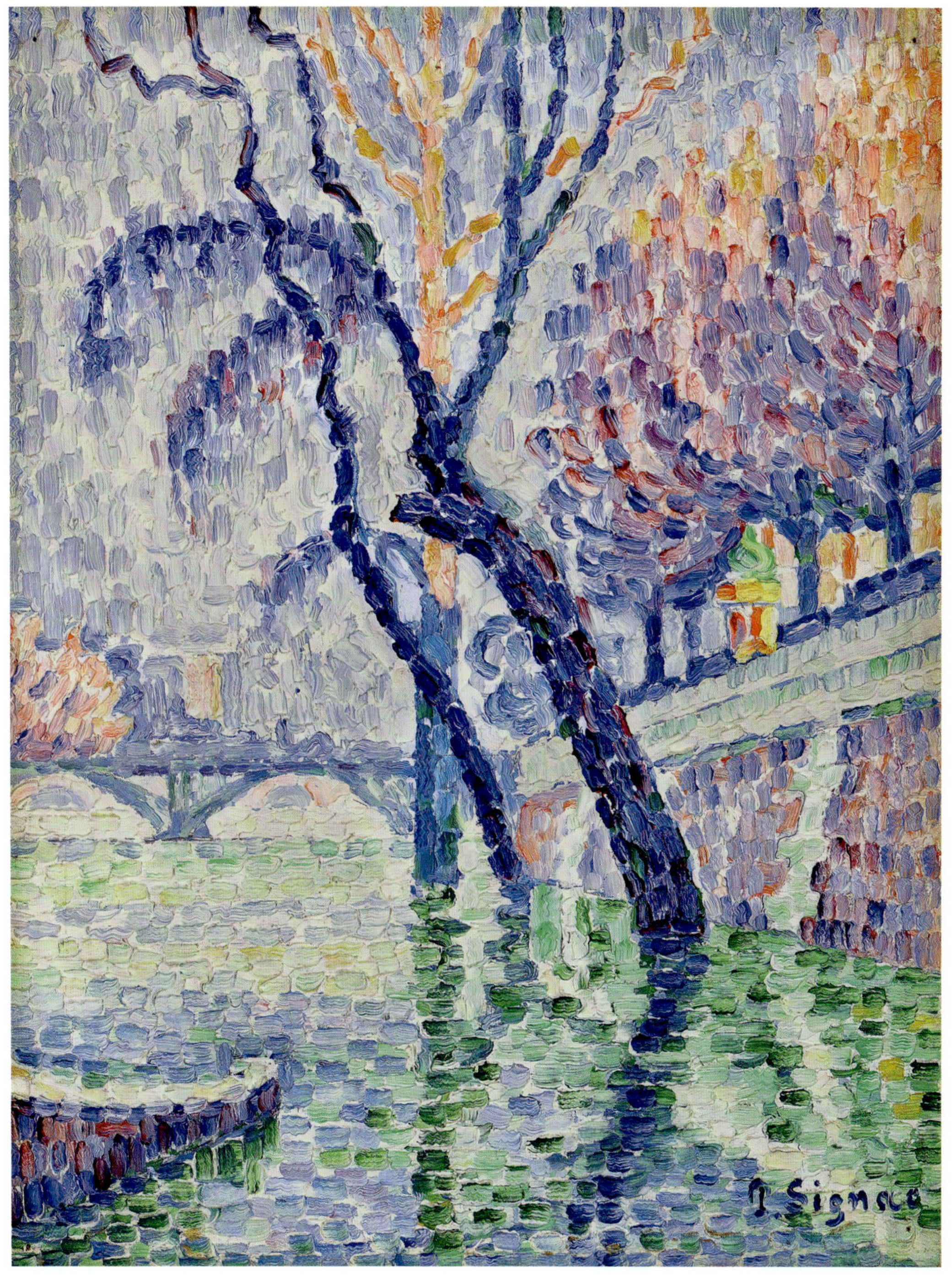

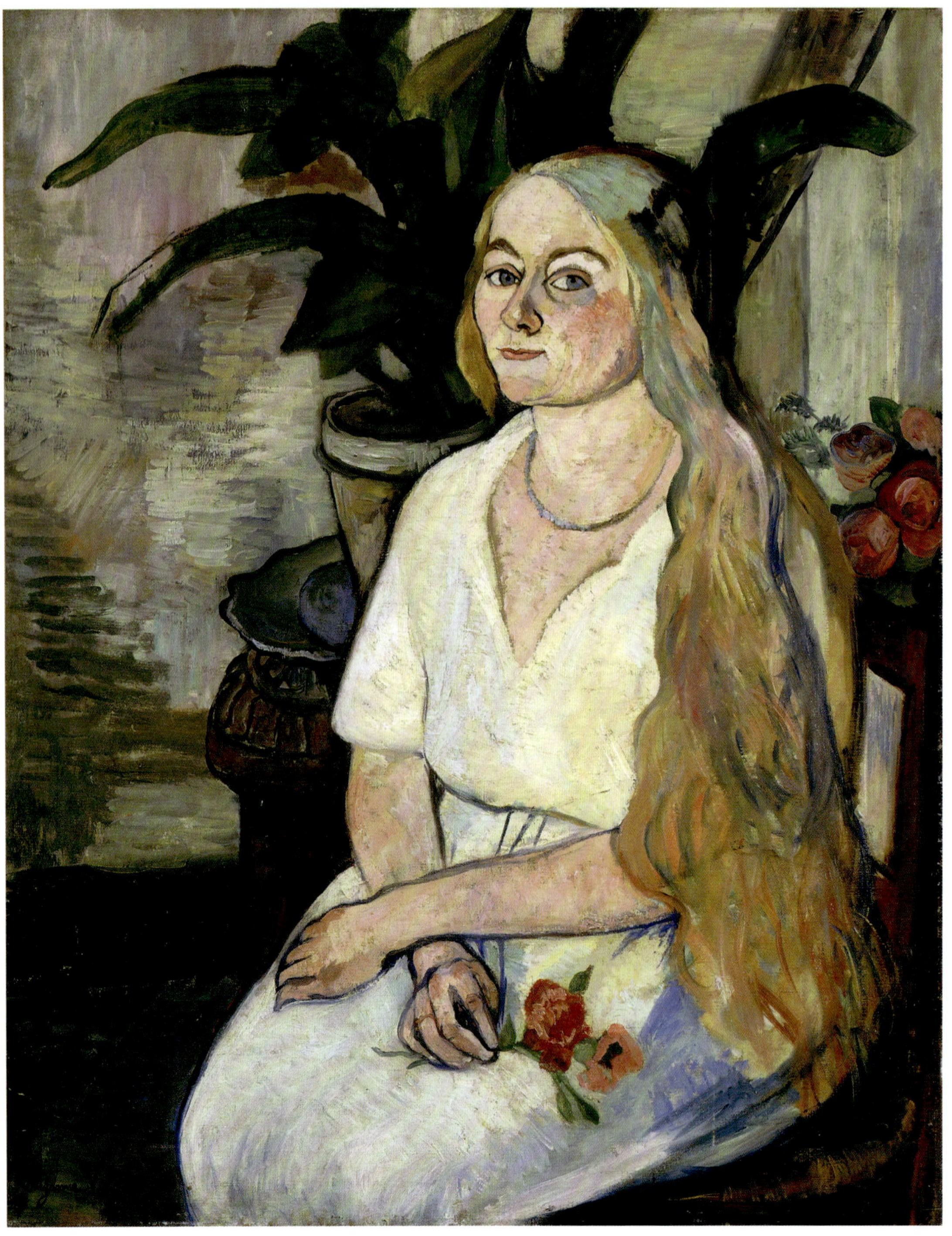

Germaine Utter

**SUZANNE
VALADON**
(1865-1938)
1922, Oil on canvas/
Huile sur toile,
82 × 64,8 cm,
Private collection

Study of a Cat

Suzanne Valadon was not only the mother of the painter Maurice Utrillo and as a model popular with Renoir or Toulouse-Lautrec. Encouraged by Degas, she developed into a recognized artist.

Étude de chat

Mère du peintre de Montmartre Maurice Utrillo, Suzanne Valadon fut un modèle apprécié d'Auguste Renoir ou d'Henri de Toulouse-Lautrec, mais aussi une artiste à part entière, encouragée par Edgar Degas.

Studie einer Katze

Suzanne Valadon war nicht nur die Mutter des Malers Maurice Utrillo und als Modell beliebt bei Renoir oder Toulouse-Lautrec. Ermuntert durch Degas, entwickelt sie sich selbst zu einer anerkannten Künstlerin.

Estudio de un gato

Suzanne Valadon no sólo fue la madre del pintor Maurice Utrillo y como modelo popular entre Renoir o Toulouse-Lautrec. Animada por Degas, se convierte en una artista reconocida.

Estudo de um gato

Suzanne Valadon não foi apenas a mãe do pintor Maurice Utrillo e como modelo popular com Renoir ou Toulouse-Lautrec. Encorajada por Degas, ela se desenvolve como uma artista reconhecida.

Studie van een kat

Suzanne Valadon was niet alleen de moeder van de schilder Maurice Utrillo en als model geliefd bij Renoir en Toulouse-Lautrec. Aangemoedigd door Degas groeide ze uit tot een erkend kunstenares.

SUZANNE VALADON (1865-1938)

1918, Oil on canvas/Huile sur toile, 52 × 40 cm, Private collection

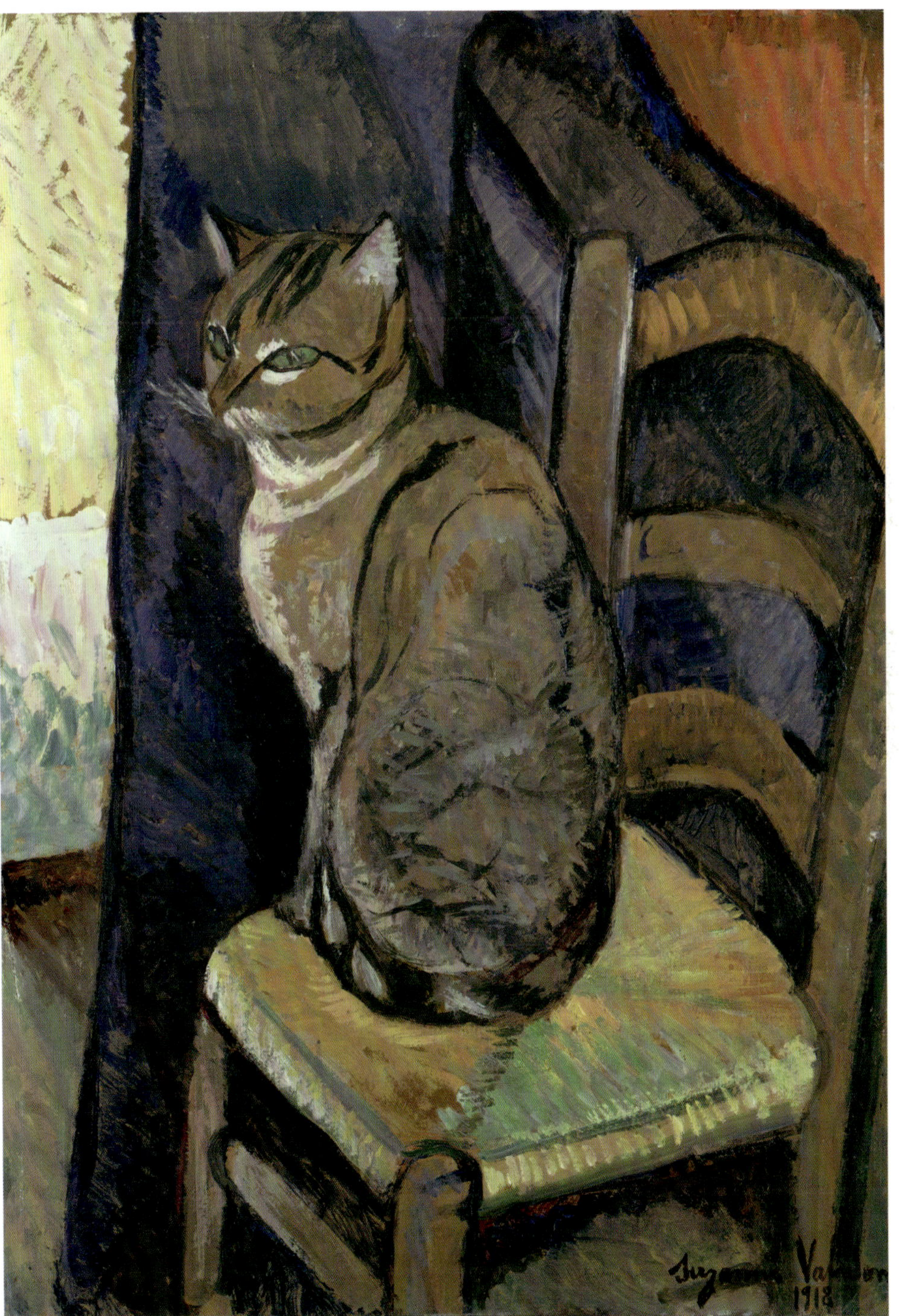

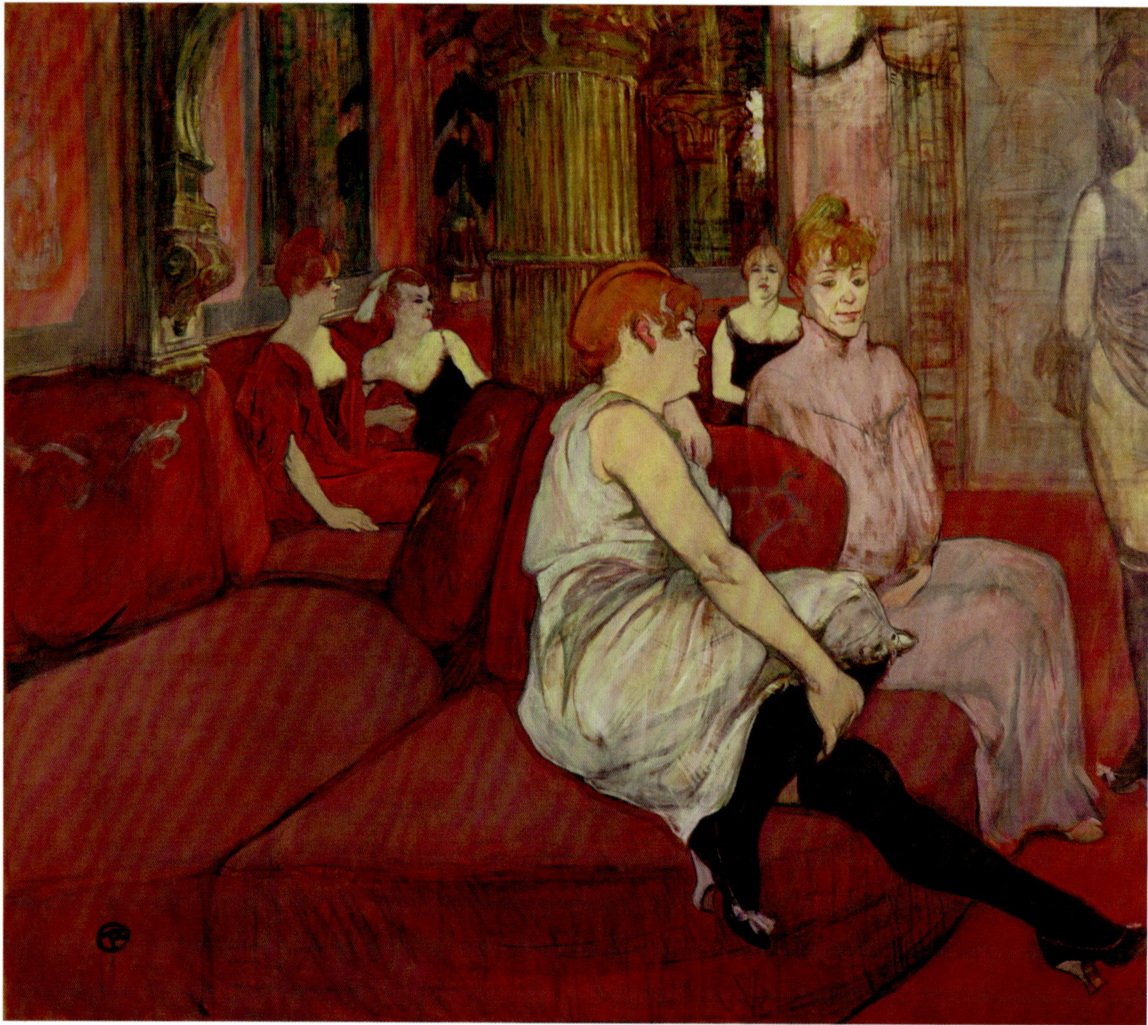

In the salon in the Rue des Moulins

Toulouse-Lautrec regularly found his subjects in brothels. The painting in pink and purple tones emphasizes the faces of the prostitutes, who oscillate between expectation, boredom, and melancholy.

Au salon de la rue des Moulins

Le thème des maisons closes passionne Lautrec. Cette toile, dominée par le rose et le pourpre, met l'accent sur les postures et les visages individualisés des prostituées, entre attente, ennui et mélancolie.

Der Salon in der Rue des Moulins

Toulouse-Lautrec fand seine Sujets regelmäßig in Bordellen. Das in Rosa- und Purpurtönen gehaltene Gemälde betont die Gesichter der Prostituierten, die zwischen Erwartung, Langeweile und Melancholie schwanken.

El salón de la Rue des Moulins

Toulouse-Lautrec encontró a sus súbditos regularmente en burdeles. La pintura en tonos rosados y morados enfatiza los rostros de las prostitutas, que oscilan entre la expectación, el aburrimiento y la melancolía.

O salão na Rue des Moulins

Toulouse-Lautrec encontrava os seus súbditos regularmente em bordéis. A pintura em tons rosa e roxo enfatiza os rostos das prostitutas, que oscilam entre expectativa, tédio e melancolia.

In de salon aan de Rue des Moulins

Toulouse-Lautrec vond zijn onderwerpen regelmatig in bordelen. Het schilderij in roze en paarse tinten benadrukt de gezichten van de prostituees, die schommelen tussen verwachting, verveling en melancholie.

HENRI DE TOULOUSE-LAUTREC (1864-1901)

1894, Oil on cardboard/Huile sur carton, 115,5 × 132 cm, Musée Toulouse-Lautrec, Albi

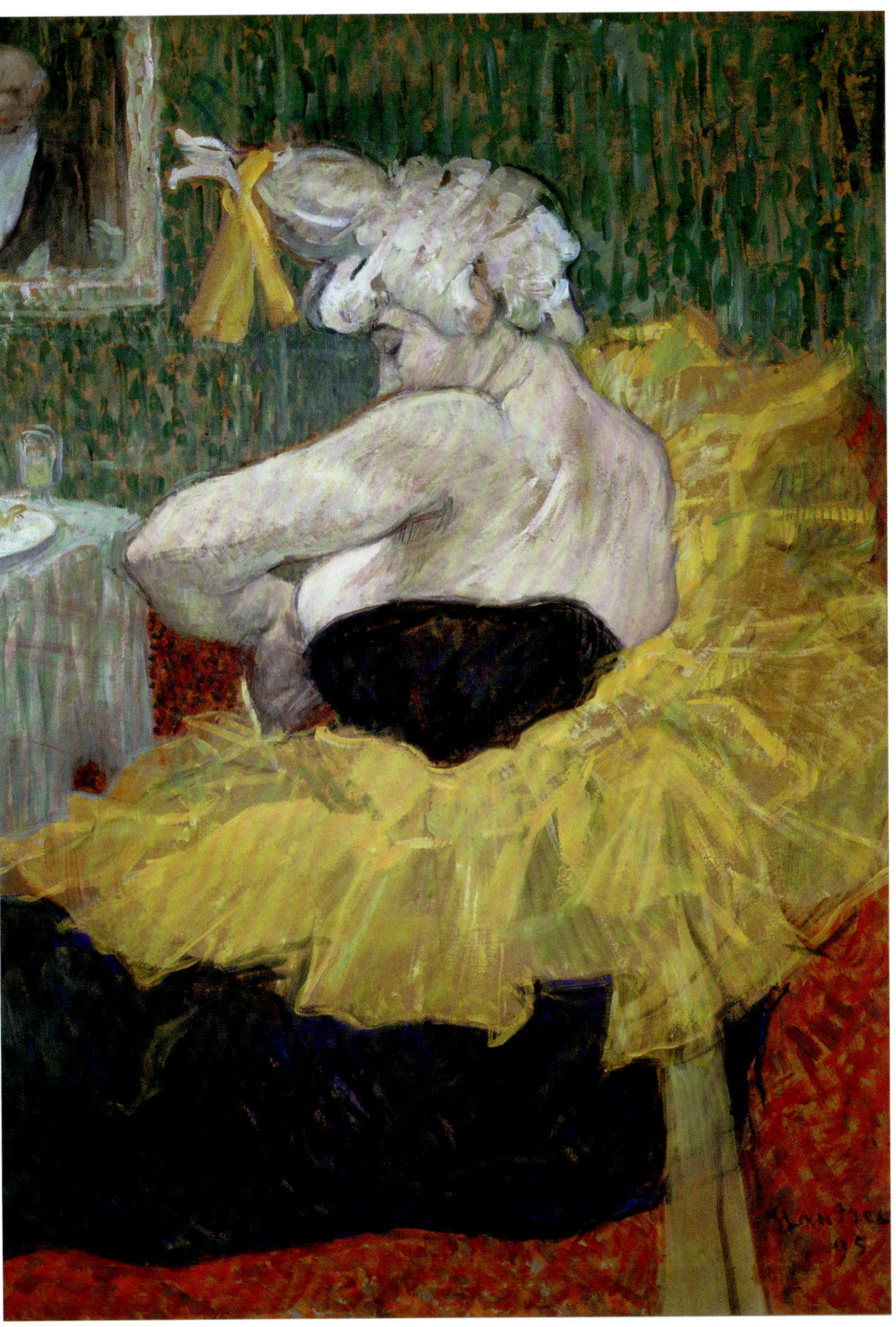

The Clown Cha-U-Kao

La Clownesse Cha-U-Kao

Die Clownesse Cha-U-Kao

La Clownesse Cha-U-Kao

O Palhaço Cha-U-Kao

De vrouwelijke clown Cha-U-Kao

HENRI DE TOULOUSE-LAUTREC
(1864-1901)

1895, Oil on cardboard/Huile sur carton,
64 × 49 cm, Musée d'Orsay, Paris

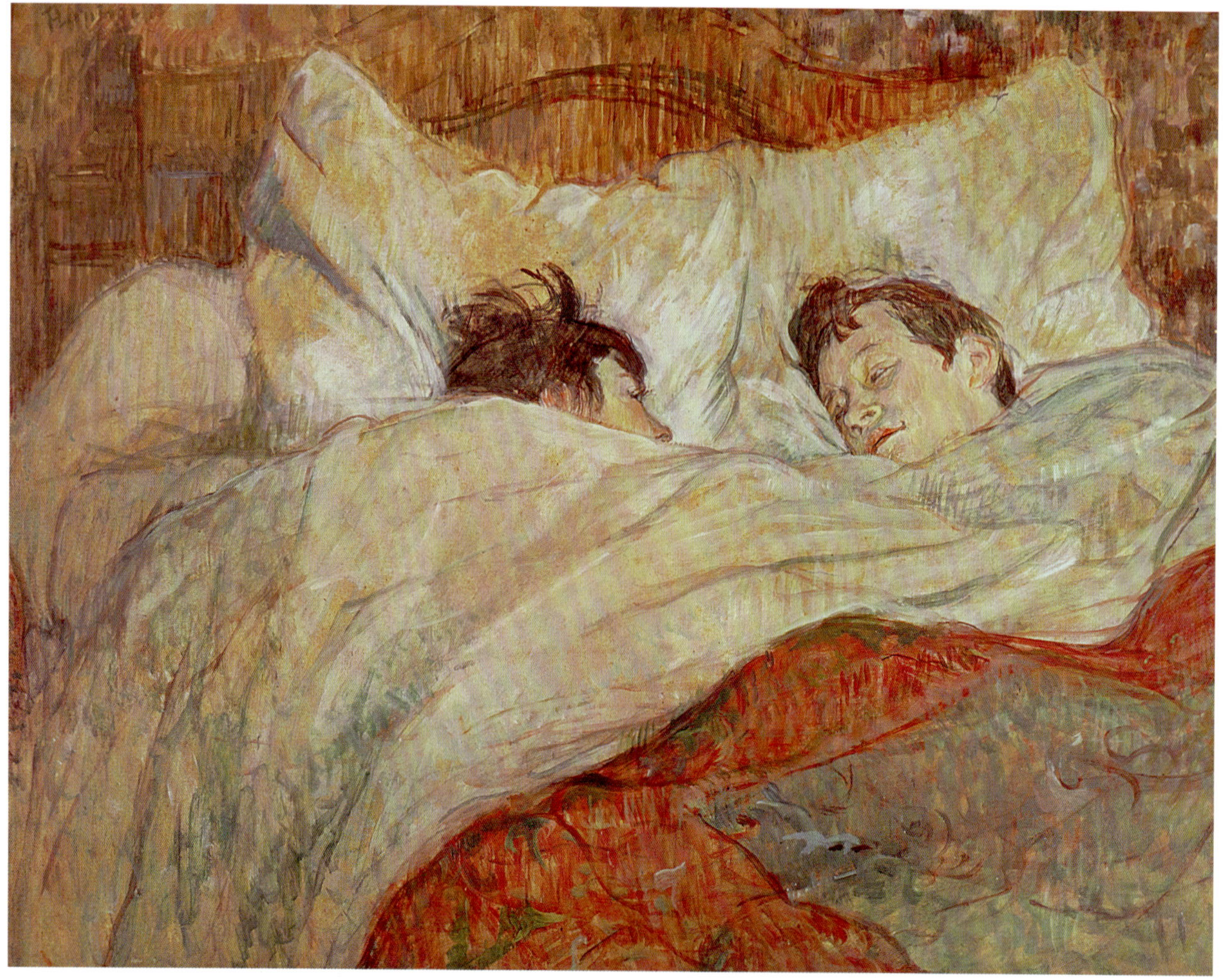

The Bed

The painting belongs to a series of four works dedicated to intimate moments between prostitutes. Away from any voyeurism, the painter depicted them in a tender and sensitive moment.

Le Lit

Ce tableau fait partie d'une série de quatre œuvres consacrées à des moments d'intimité partagés entre des prostituées. Le peintre fait preuve de tendresse et de délicatesse, loin de tout voyeurisme.

Das Bett

Das Gemälde gehört zu einer Serie von vier Werken, die sich intimen Momenten zwischen Prostituierten widmen. Abseits jeglichen Voyeurismus stellt der Maler sie in einem zärtlichen und feinfühligen Augenblick dar.

La cama

El cuadro pertenece a una serie de cuatro obras dedicadas a momentos íntimos entre prostitutas. Lejos de cualquier voyeurismo, el pintor la representa en un momento tierno y sensible.

A cama

A pintura pertence a uma série de quatro obras dedicadas a momentos íntimos entre prostitutas. Longe de qualquer voyeurismo, o pintor retrata-a num momento delicado e sensível.

Het bed

Dit schilderij maakt deel uit van een serie van vier werken die gewijd zijn aan intieme momenten tussen prostituees. Weg van elk voyeurisme geeft de schilder hen op een teder en gevoelig moment weer.

HENRI DE TOULOUSE-LAUTREC (1864-1901)

c. 1892, Oil on cardboard mounted on parquet flooring/Huile sur carton marouflé sur bois parqueté, 53,5 × 70 cm, Musée d'Orsay, Paris

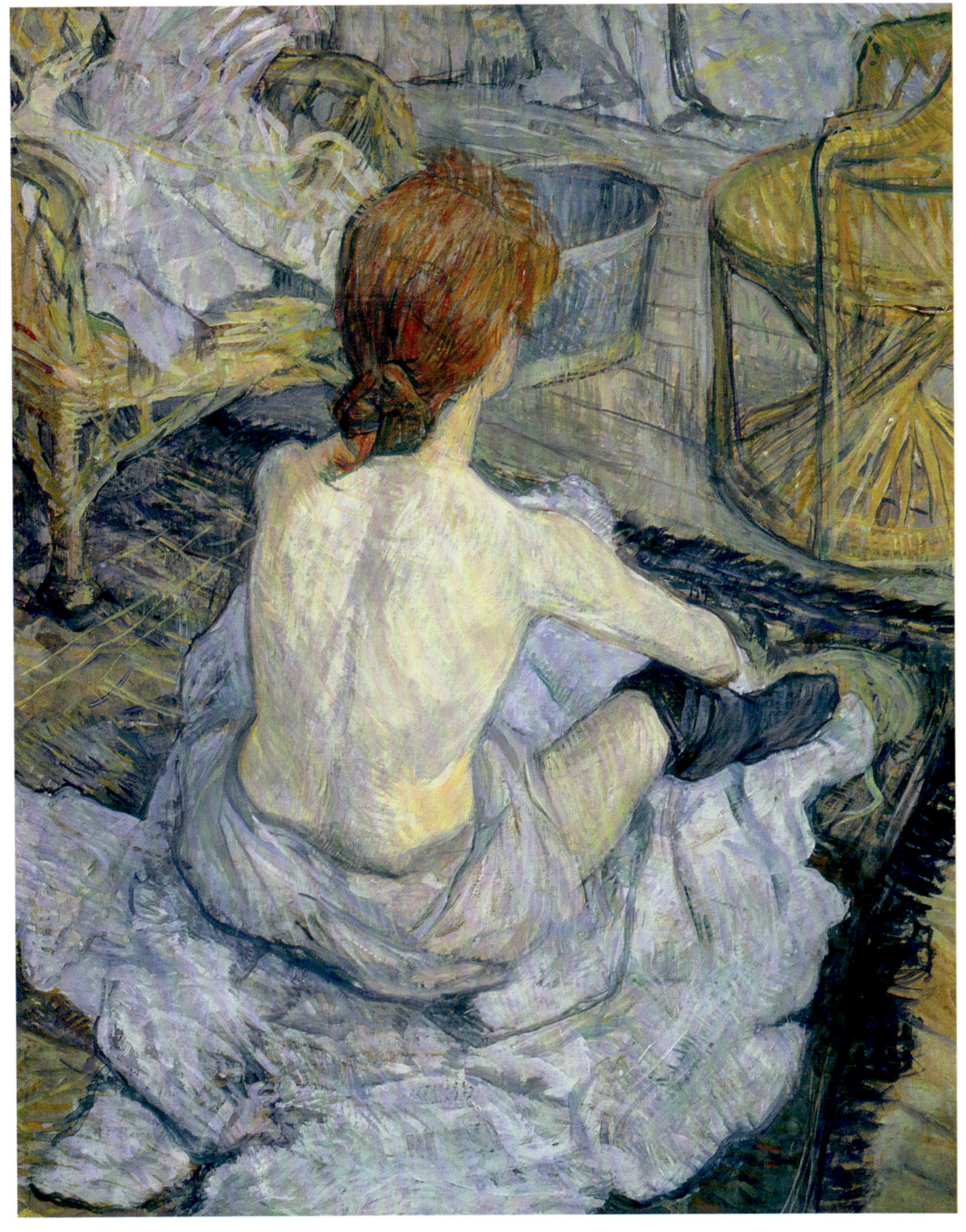

Rousse *or* Toilet

Rousse *ou* La toilette

Die Rothaarige *oder*
Bei der Toilette

La pelirroja *o*
En el baño

A ruiva *ou* Na
casa de banho

De roodharige
of La toilette

**HENRI DE
TOULOUSE-LAUTREC
(1864-1901)**

1889, Oil on cardboard/
Huile sur carton,
67 × 54 cm,
Musée d'Orsay, Paris

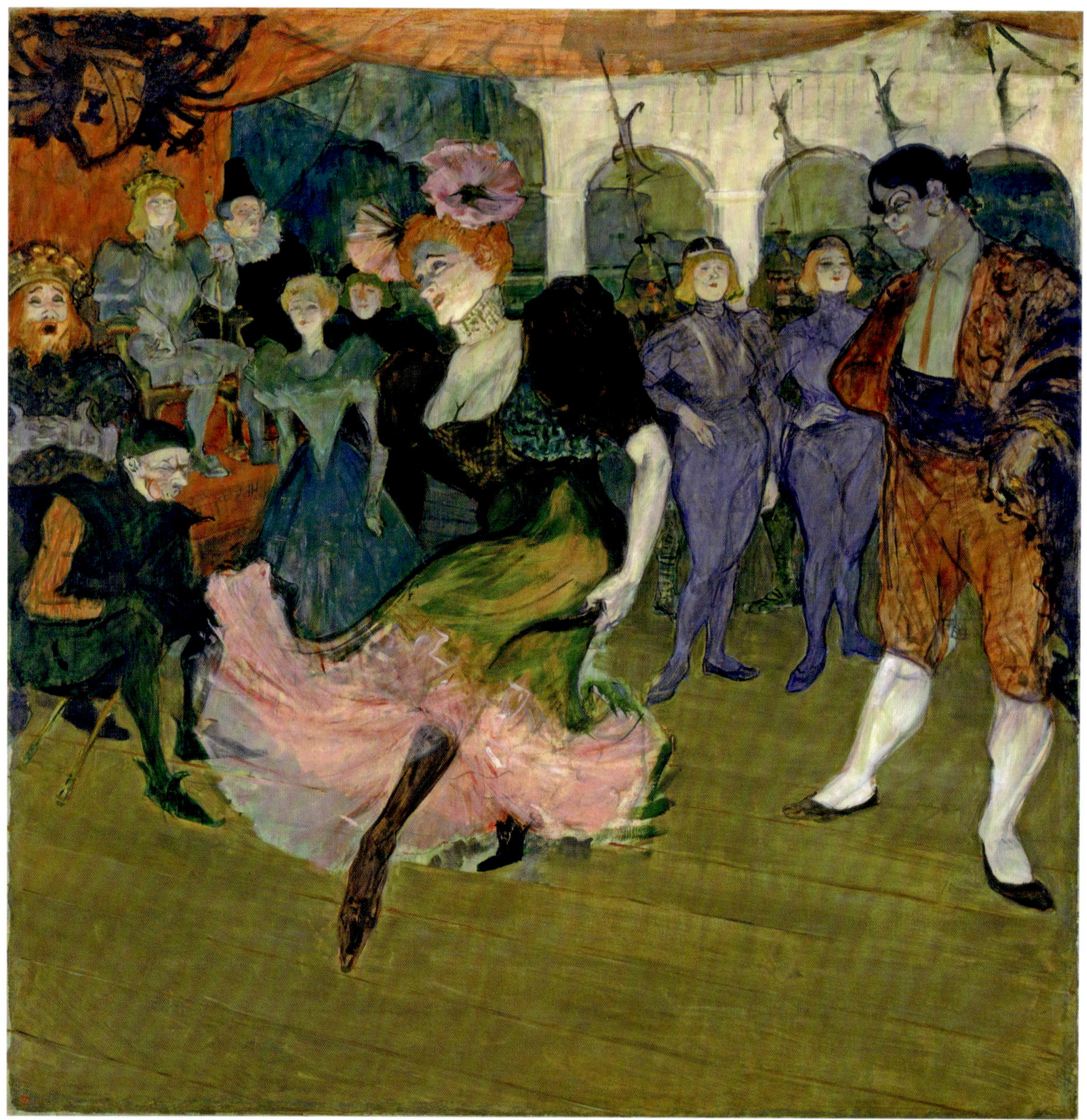

Marcelle Lender Dancing the Bolero in "Chilpéric"

Marcelle Lender dansant le pas du Boléro dans « Chilpéric »

Marcelle Lender tanzt den Bolero im „Chilpéric"

Marcelle Lender baila el bolero en el Chilpéric

Marcelle Lender dança o bolero no Chilpéric

Marcelle Lender danst de bolero in 'Chilpéric'

HENRI DE TOULOUSE-LAUTREC (1864-1901)

1895, Oil on canvas/Huile sur toile, 145 × 149 cm, National Gallery of Art, Washington

Jane Avril dancing

Jane Avril dansant

Die tanzende Jane Avril

Jane Avril bailando

A dançarina Jane Avril

Dansende Jane Avril

HENRI DE TOULOUSE-LAUTREC (1864-1901)
c. 1892, Oil on cardboard/Huile sur carton,
85,5 × 45 cm, Musée d'Orsay, Paris

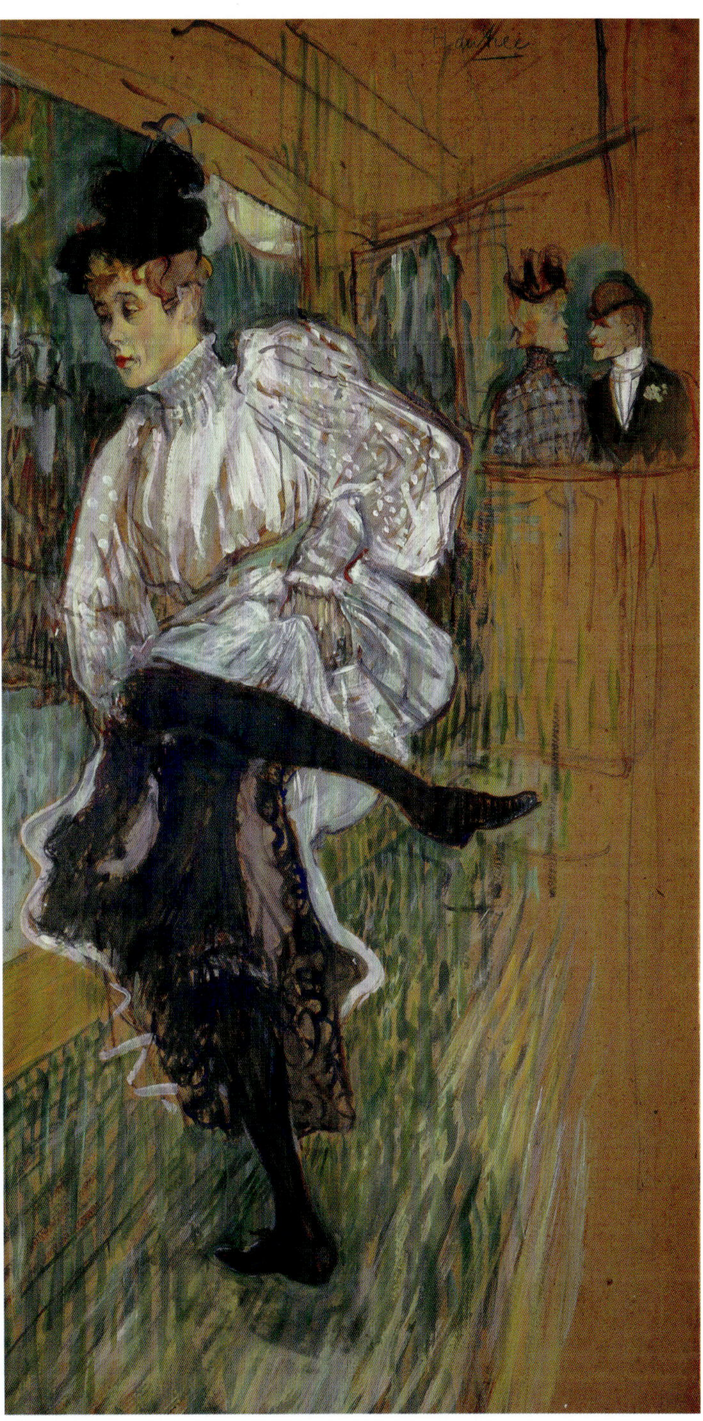

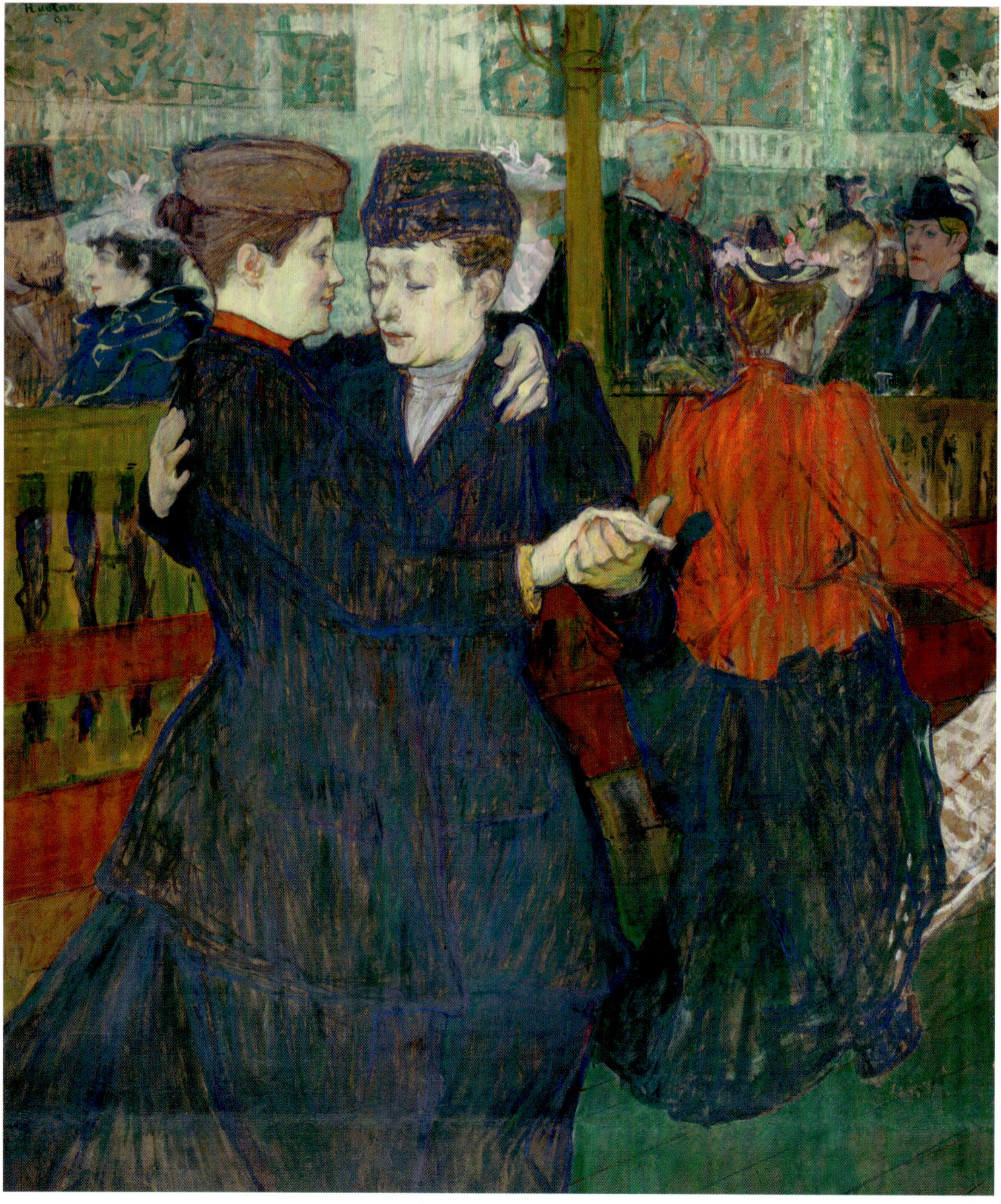

At the Moulin Rouge, Two Women walzing

Au Moulin-Rouge, deux femmes dansant

Im Moulin Rouge, zwei tanzende Frauen

En el Moulin Rouge, dos bailarinas

No Moulin Rouge, duas mulheres dançarinas

In de Moulin Rouge, twee dansende vrouwen

HENRI DE TOULOUSE-LAUTREC (1864-1901)
1892, Oil on cardboard/Huile sur carton,
93 × 80 cm, Národní Galerie, Praha

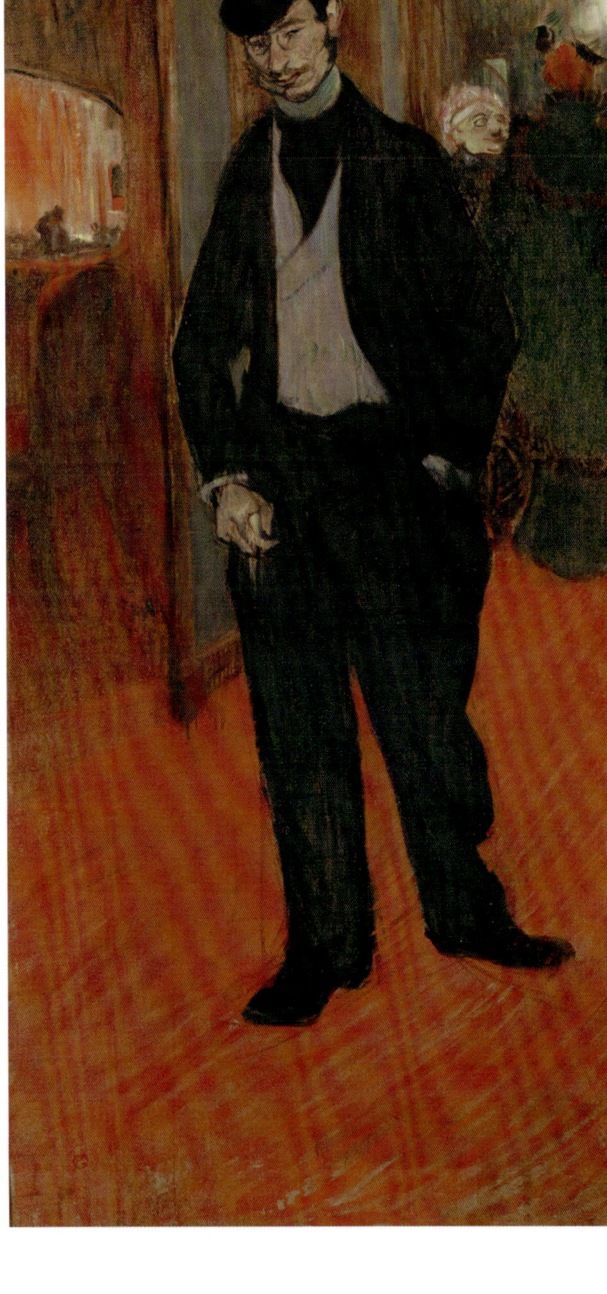

Doctor Gabriel Tapié de Céleyran

Le Docteur Gabriel Tapié de Céleyran

Der Arzt Gabriel Tapié de Céleyran

El Doctor Gabriel Tapié de Céleyran

O Doutor Gabriel Tapié de Céleyran

Dokter Gabriel Tapié de Céleyran

HENRI DE TOULOUSE-LAUTREC (1864-1901)
1894, Oil on canvas/Huile sur toile,
110 × 56 cm, Musée Toulouse-Lautrec, Albi

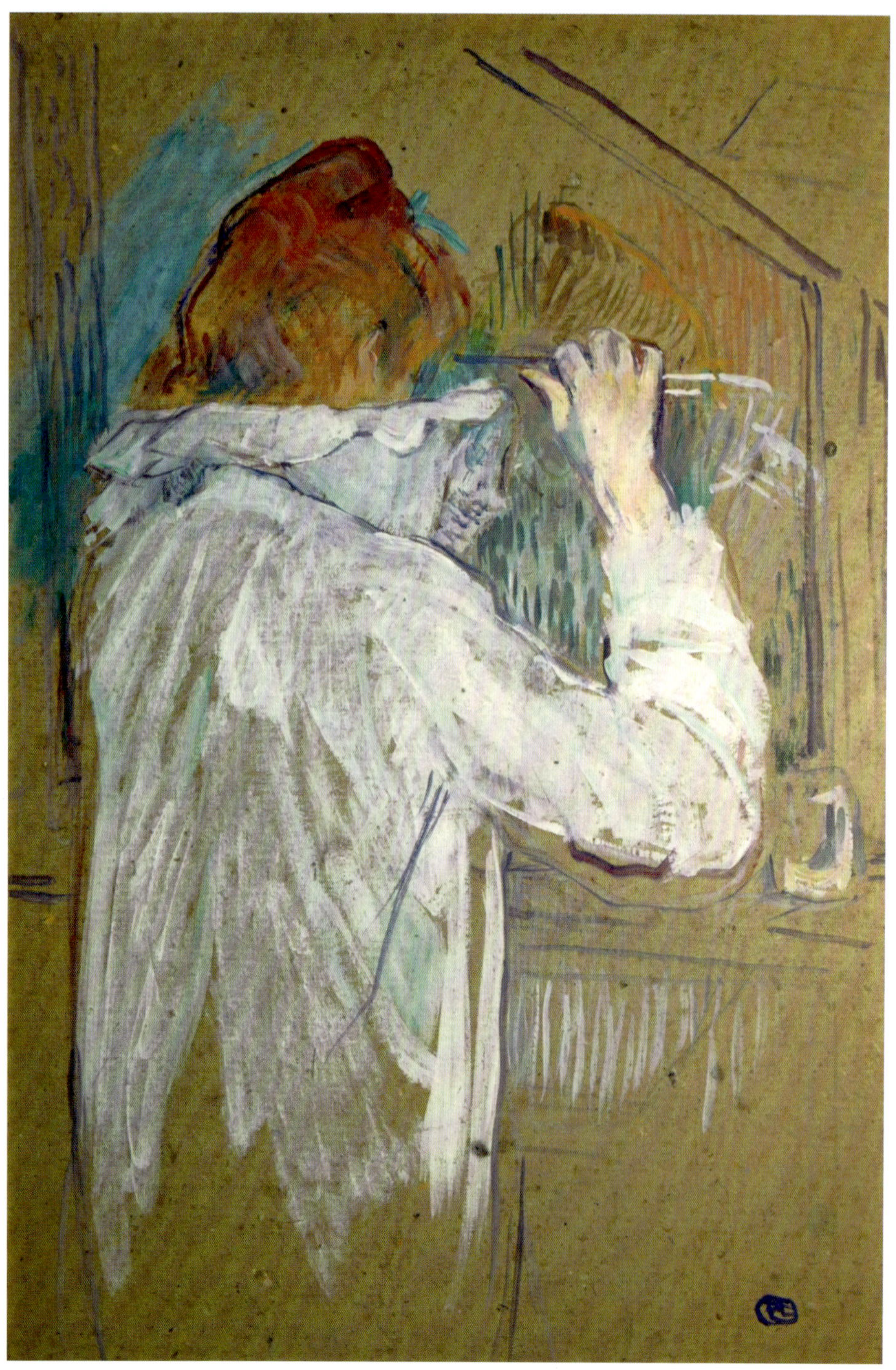

Woman curling her Hair

Femme se frisant

Frau beim Kämmen

Mujer peinándose

Pentear mulher

Vrouw die haar haren kamt

HENRI DE TOULOUSE-LAUTREC (1864-1901)

c. 1876-1900, Oil on cardboard/Huile sur carton,
56 × 39 cm, Musée des Augustins, Toulouse

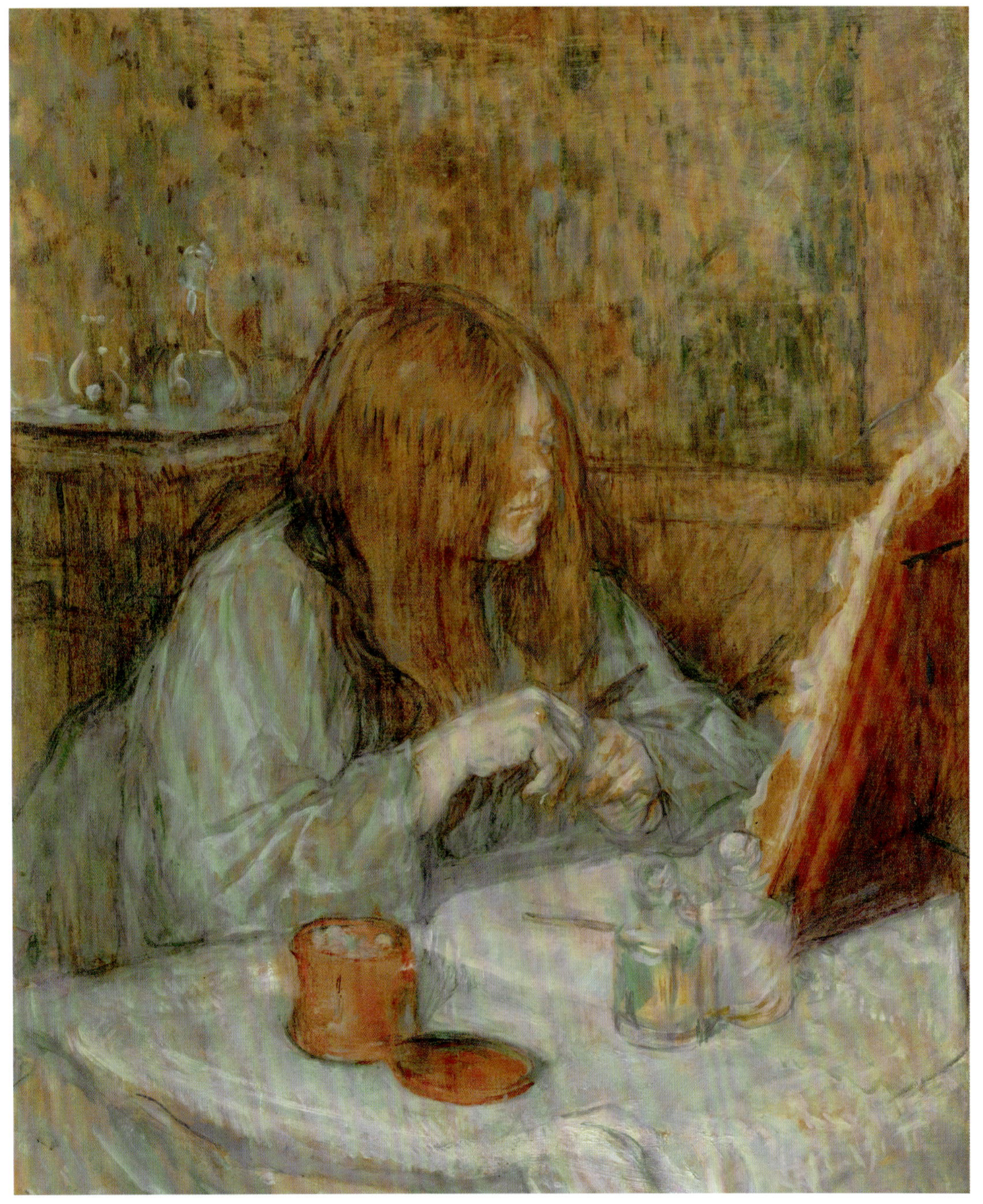

Madame Poupoule
at her toilette

Madame Poupoule
à sa toilette

Madame Poupoule
bei der Toilette

Madame Poupoule
aseándose

Madame Poupoule
alla toilette

Madame Poupoule
bij het toilet

**HENRI DE
TOULOUSE-LAUTREC
(1864-1901)**
1898, Oil on
cardboard/
Huile sur carton,
60,8 × 49,6 cm, Musée
Toulouse-Lautrec, Albi

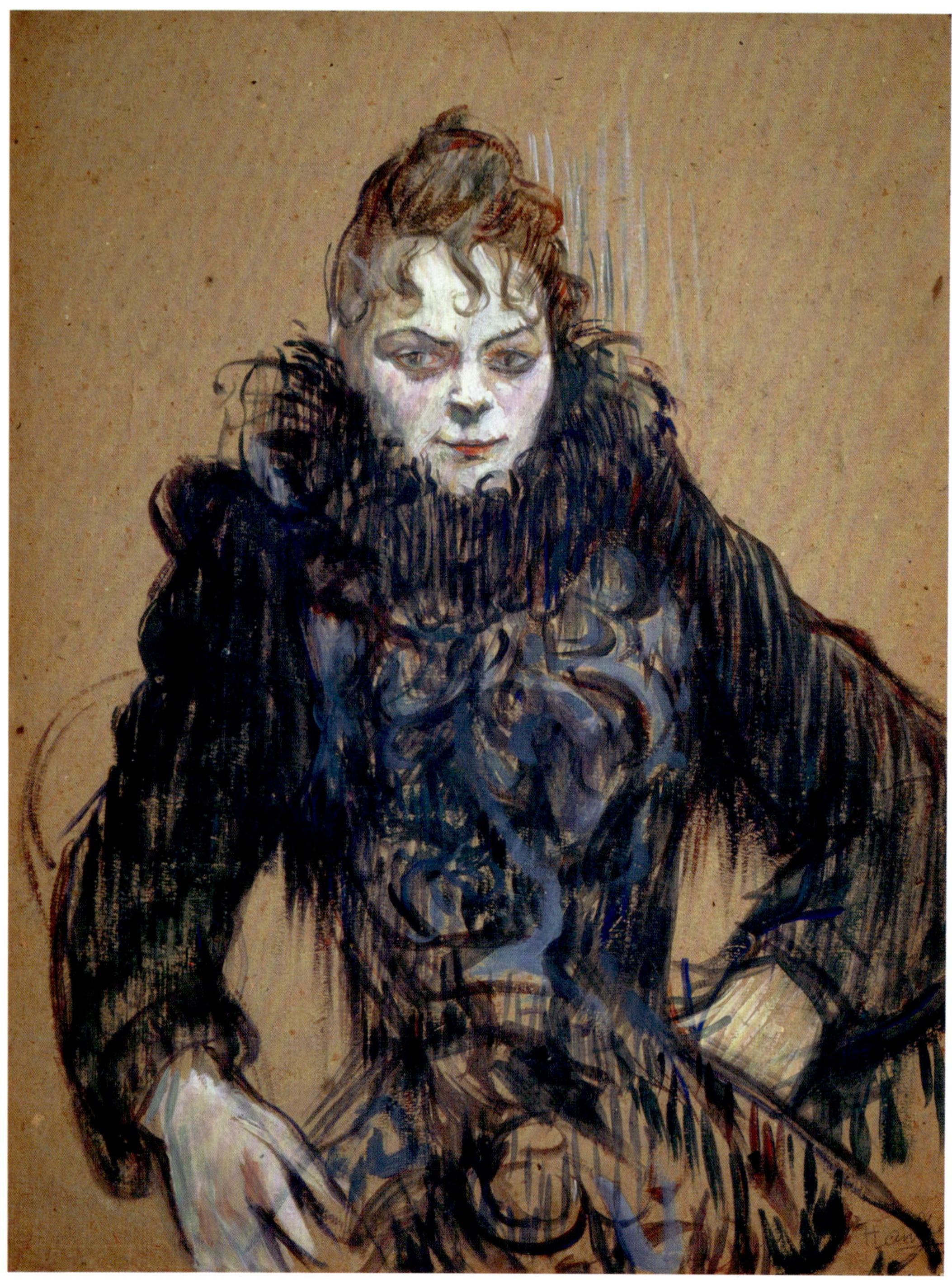

Portrait of A Woman
in the Black Boa

Femme au boa noir

*Die Frau mit der
schwarzen Boa*

Mujer con boa negra

*A mulher com a
jibóia negra*

*De vrouw met
de zwarte boa*

**HENRI DE TOULOUSE-
LAUTREC (1864-1901)**
1892, Oil on cardboard/
Huile sur carton, 50 × 40
cm, Musée d'Orsay, Paris

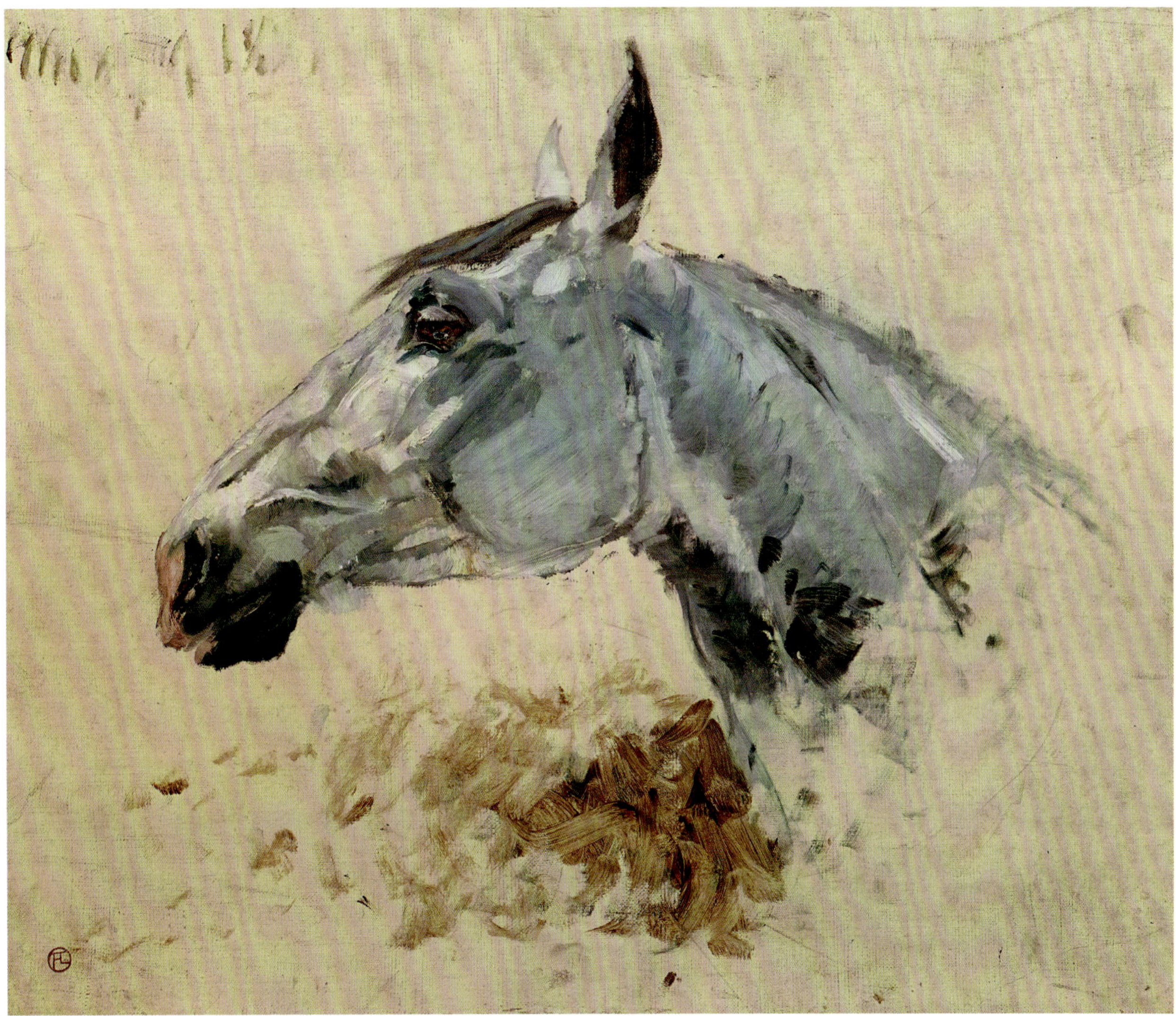

White Horse "Gazelle"

Like in a portrait Toulouse-Lautrec painted the grey horse «Gazelle» in profile. The study illustrates his deep affection for the horses found in many of his compositions.

Cheval blanc Gazelle

De profil, la tête de Gazelle est traitée exactement comme un portrait. Par cette belle esquisse, Lautrec témoigne de son affection profonde pour les chevaux, qui animent nombre de ses compositions.

Weißes Pferd, „Gazelle"

Wie bei einem Porträt malte Toulouse-Lautrec den Schimmel „Gazelle" im Profil. Die Studie verdeutlicht seine tiefe Zuneigung zu den Pferden, die in zahlreichen seiner Kompositionen zu finden sind.

Caballo blanco, Gacela

Como en un retrato, Toulouse-Lautrec pintó de perfil el caballo Gazela. El estudio ilustra su profundo afecto por los caballos que aparecen en muchas de sus composiciones.

Cavalo branco, Gazela

Como num retrato Toulouse-Lautrec pintou o cavalo cinzento «Gazelle» em perfil. O estudo ilustra sua profunda afeição pelos cavalos encontrados em muitas de suas composições.

Wit paard, 'Gazelle'

Als bij een portret schilderde Toulouse-Lautrec het paard 'Gazelle' en profil. De studie illustreert zijn diepe genegenheid voor paarden, die in veel van zijn composities te zien zijn.

HENRI DE TOULOUSE-LAUTREC (1864-1901)

1881, Oil on canvas/Huile sur toile, 49,6 × 56,1 cm, Musée Toulouse-Lautrec, Albi

Paul Gauguin and the Nabis

Paul Gauguin et les Nabis

Paul Gauguin und die Nabis

Paul Gauguin y los Nabis

Paul Gauguin e o Nabis

Paul Gauguin en de Nabis

Paul Gauguin and the Nabis

paul Gauguin's first works can be attributed to the Impressionist environment. Very quickly, however, the artist moved on and developed his own style - between Brittany and French Polynesia, where he lived from 1891. In 1871 Gauguin still worked as a stockbroker. Three years later, he met Camille Pissarro. Until 1886 he took part in five group exhibitions of the Impressionists. In the same year he spent his first year in Pont-Aven, where he made the acquaintance of Émile Bernard. The artist traveled throughout Martinique from June to October 1887. There he created 17 paintings. After his return, he set off again for Brittany to develop his style under the influence of Bernard. In 1888 he painted his first paintings in the style of Synthetism - among them his symbolic work *Vision of the Sermon*. They are characterised by a departure from the traditional perspective, a simplification of form and uniform color areas surrounded by a dark line. In the summer of the same year, Paul Sérusier painted a small open-air picture in the Bois d'Amour wood under Gauguin's gaze. During the creation the master is supposed to

Paul Gauguin et les Nabis

Les premières œuvres de Paul Gauguin s'inscrivent dans la mouvance de l'impressionnisme. Mais très vite, l'artiste va s'en détacher pour développer son propre style, entre la Bretagne et la Polynésie française, où il s'installera définitivement en 1891. Rien ne prédisposait l'artiste à la peinture. En 1871, il est agent de change. Trois ans plus tard, il fait la connaissance de Camille Pissarro. Il participera à cinq expositions du groupe impressionniste, jusqu'en 1886. Cette année-là, Gauguin séjourne pour la première fois à Pont-Aven, où il rencontre Émile Bernard. De juin à octobre 1887, il est à la Martinique, où il peint dix-sept toiles, avant de revenir à Paris, puis de repartir pour la Bretagne. Son style évolue sous l'influence d'Émile Bernard. En 1888, il peint ses premières œuvres synthétistes (abolition de la perspective traditionnelle, simplification des formes, couleurs en aplat cernées par une ligne sombre), dont l'emblématique *Vision après le sermon*. Cette même année, pendant l'été, Paul Sérusier peint un petit tableau sous l'œil de Gauguin, directement sur le motif, dans le cadre verdoyant du bois d'Amour.

Paul Gauguin und die Nabis

Die ersten Werke Paul Gauguins sind dem Umfeld des Impressionismus zuzuordnen. Sehr schnell entfernt sich der Künstler jedoch davon und entwickelt seinen eigenen Stil – zwischen der Bretagne und französisch Polynesien, wo er ab 1891 lebt. Im Jahr 1871 arbeitet Gauguin noch als Börsenmakler. Drei Jahre später lernt er Camille Pissarro kennen. Bis 1886 wird er an fünf Gruppenausstellungen der Impressionisten teilnehmen. Im selben Jahr hält er sich zum ersten Mal in Pont-Aven auf, wo er die Bekanntschaft von Émile Bernard macht. Von Juni bis Oktober 1887 bereist der Künstler Martinique. Dort entstehen 17 Gemälde. Nach seiner Rückkehr bricht er wieder in die Bretagne auf, um seinen Stil unter dem Einfluss Bernards weiterzuentwickeln. 1888 malt er seine ersten Gemälde im Stil des Synthetismus – darunter sein symbolträchtiges Werk *Die Vision der Predigt*. Sie sind geprägt durch die Abkehr von der traditionellen Perspektive, der Vereinfachung der Form und gleichmäßigen Farbflächen, die von einer dunklen Linie umschlossen werden. Im Sommer desselben Jahres malt Paul Sérusier unter den Blicken Gauguins ein kleines Bild

PIERRE BONNARD (1867-1947)

1908/09, Oil on canvas/Huile sur toile, 124 × 109 cm, Musée d'Art moderne, Bruxelles

Paul Gauguin y los Nabis

Las primeras obras de Paul Gauguin se pueden atribuir al ambiente impresionista. Muy rápidamente, sin embargo, el artista se mudó y desarrolló su propio estilo, entre Bretaña y la Polinesia Francesa, donde vivió a partir de 1891. En 1871 Gauguin todavía trabajaba como corredor de bolsa. Tres años después, conoció a Camille Pissarro. Hasta 1886 participará en cinco exposiciones colectivas de los impresionistas. Ese mismo año pasó su primer año en Pont-Aven, donde conoció a Émile Bernard. El artista viajó a Martinica de junio a octubre de 1887. Allí creó 17 pinturas. Después de su regreso, partió de nuevo hacia Bretaña para desarrollar su estilo bajo la influencia de Bernard. En 1888 pintó sus primeras pinturas al estilo del sintetismo, entre ellas su obra simbólica *La Visión tras el Sermón*. Se caracterizan por un alejamiento de la perspectiva tradicional, una simplificación de las formas y unas zonas de color uniforme rodeadas de una línea oscura. En el verano del mismo año, Paul Sérusier pinta un pequeño cuadro al aire libre en el bosque del Bois d'Amour bajo la mirada de Gauguin. Durante la

Paul Gauguin e o Nabis

os primeiros trabalhos de Paul Gauguin podem ser atribuídos ao ambiente impressionista. Muito rapidamente, porém, o artista se afastou e desenvolveu seu próprio estilo - entre a Bretanha e a Polinésia Francesa, onde viveu desde 1891. Em 1871, Gauguin ainda trabalhava como corretor da bolsa. Três anos depois, conheceu a Camille Pissarro. Até 1886 participará em cinco exposições colectivas dos Impressionistas. No mesmo ano, passou seu primeiro ano em Pont-Aven, onde conheceu Émile Bernard. O artista viajou pela Martinica de junho a outubro de 1887. Lá ele criou 17 quadros. Após seu retorno, ele partiu novamente para a Bretanha para desenvolver seu estilo sob a influência de Bernard. Em 1888 ele pintou suas primeiras pinturas no estilo do Sintético - entre elas sua obra simbólica *A Visão do Sermão*. Caracterizam-se por um afastamento da perspectiva tradicional, uma simplificação da forma e áreas de cor uniformes rodeadas por uma linha escura. No verão do mesmo ano, Paul Sérusier pinta um pequeno quadro ao ar livre na madeira de Bois d'Amour sob o olhar de

Paul Gauguin en de Nabis

Paul Gauguins eerste werken zijn nog impressionistisch te noemen. Al snel nam de kunstenaar echter afstand van het impressionisme en ontwikkelde hij zijn eigen stijl – tussen Bretagne en Frans-Polynesië, waar hij vanaf 1891 woonde. In 1871 werkte Gauguin nog als effectenmakelaar. Drie jaar later ontmoette hij Camille Pissarro. Tot 1886 nam hij deel aan vijf groepstentoonstellingen van de impressionisten. In datzelfde jaar verbleef hij voor het eerst in Pont-Aven, waar hij kennismaakte met Émile Bernard. De kunstenaar reisde tussen juni en oktober 1887 over Martinique. Daar maakte hij 17 schilderijen. Na terugkeer vertrok hij weer naar Bretagne, om onder invloed van Bernard zijn eigen stijl verder te ontwikkelen. In 1888 maakte hij zijn eerste schilderijen in de stijl van het synthetisme, waaronder het symbolische *Het visioen na de preek*. Ze worden gekenmerkt door het opgeven van het traditionele perspectief, vereenvoudigde vormen en gelijkmatige kleurvlakken die met een donkere contourlijn zijn omsloten. In de zomer van datzelfde jaar maakte Paul

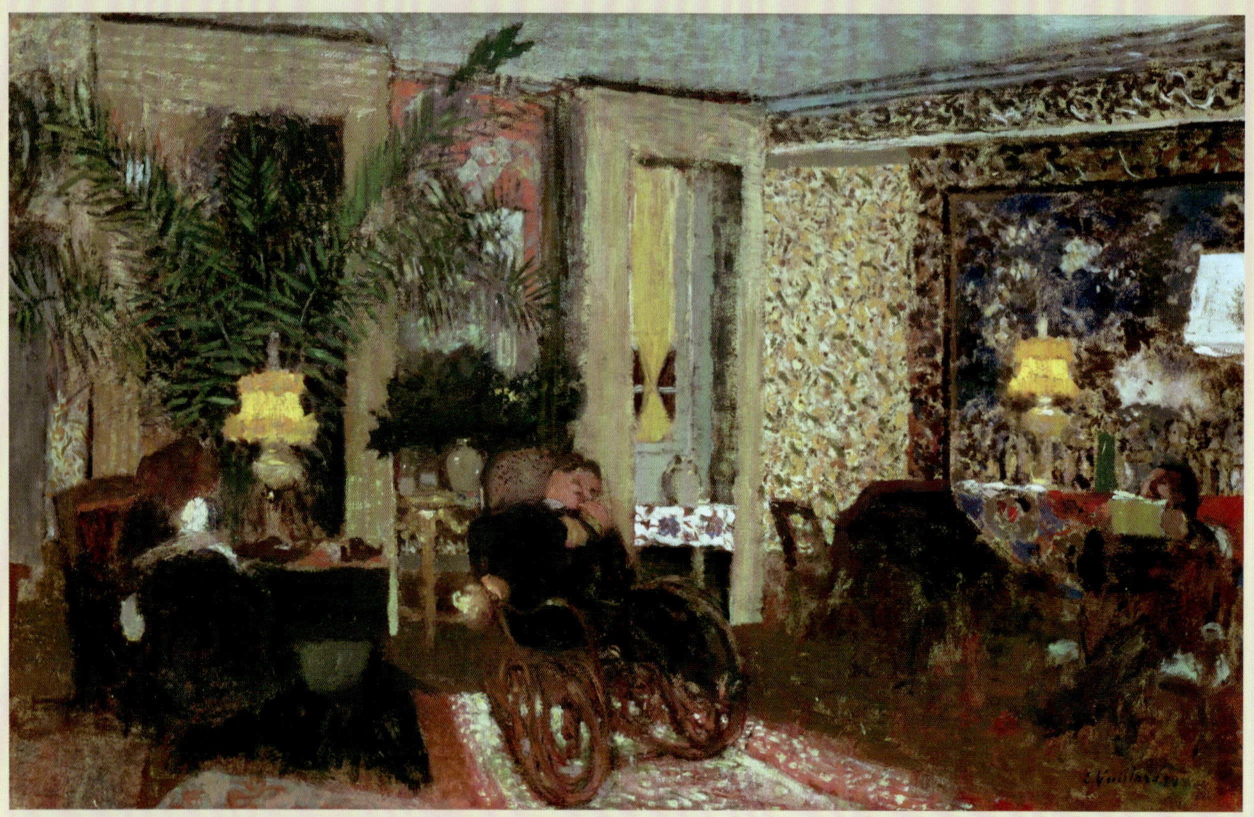

Interior with Three Lamps, Rue Saint-Florentin

Le Salon aux trois lampes, rue Saint-Florentin

Der Salon mit den drei Lampen, Rue Saint-Florentin

El salón con las tres lámparas, Rue Saint-Florentin

O salão com as três lâmpadas, Rue Saint-Florentin

De salon met drie lampen, Rue Saint-Florentin

ÉDOUARD VUILLARD (1868-1940)
1899, Tempera on paper glued on canvas/Peinture à la colle sur papier marouflé sur toile, 59,7 × 96 cm, Musée d'Orsay, Paris

have said to his disciple: "How do you see these trees? They're yellow. Then take yellow. This shadow? Rather blue. Then paint it in pure ultramarine blue. These leaves are red? Then take vermilion." Today it is known as *The Talisman*.

The syntheticism of the Pont-Aven school was to be continued during the 1890s in the work of the Nabis group of artists. In addition to Paul Sérusier, the members included Maurice Denis, Pierre Bonnard, Édouard Vuillard, Ker-Xavier Roussel, Jan Verkade, Paul Ranson, Georges Lacombe and Félix Vallotton. Influenced by Japanese woodblock prints, their works move between decorative art and symbolism.

« Comment voyez-vous ces arbres ? Ils sont jaunes. Eh bien, mettez du jaune ; cette ombre, plutôt bleue, peignez-la avec de l'outremer pur ; ces feuilles rouges ? Mettez du vermillon », aurait dit le maître à son jeune ami, en train de produire l'œuvre que l'on connaît aujourd'hui sous le titre de *Talisman*.

Le synthétisme cher à l'école de Pont-Aven trouvera un prolongement dans les recherches des Nabis, tout au long des années 1890. Autour de Paul Sérusier, ce groupe réunit Maurice Denis, Pierre Bonnard, Édouard Vuillard, Ker-Xavier Roussel, Jan Verkade, Paul Ranson, Georges Lacombe, Félix Vallotton... Marquées par l'esthétique des estampes japonaises, leurs œuvres oscillent, selon les artistes, entre compositions décoratives et symbolisme.

unter freiem Himmel in dem Wäldchen Bois d'Amour. Während der Entstehung soll der Meister zu seinem Schüler gesagt haben: „Wie sehen Sie diese Bäume? Sie sind gelb. Dann nehmen Sie Gelb. Diesen Schatten? Eher blau. Dann malen Sie ihn in reinem Ultramarinblau. Diese Blätter sind rot? Dann nehmen Sie Zinnoberrot." Heute ist es unter dem Titel *Der Talisman* bekannt.

Der Synthetismus der Schule von Pont-Aven sollte während der 1890er-Jahre seine Fortsetzung im Schaffen der Künstlergruppe der Nabis finden. Neben Paul Sérusier gehörten ihr Maurice Denis, Pierre Bonnard, Édouard Vuillard, Ker-Xavier Roussel, Jan Verkade, Paul Ranson, Georges Lacombe und Félix Vallotton an. Beeinflusst durch japanische Farbholzschnitte bewegen sich ihre Werke zwischen dekorativer Kunst und dem Symbolismus.

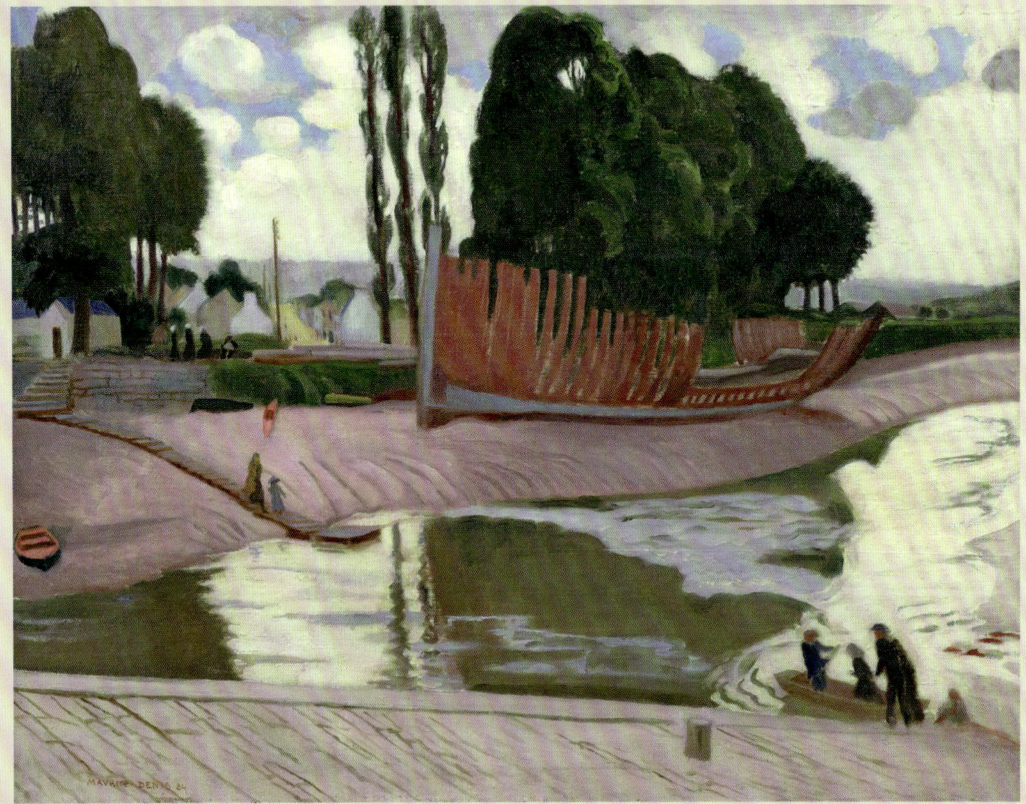

creación se supone que el maestro le dijo a su discípulo: "¿Cómo ves estos árboles? Son amarillos. Entonces toma el amarillo. ¿Esta sombra? Bastante azul. Luego píntalo en azul ultramarino puro. ¿Estas hojas son rojas? Entonces toma bermellón." Hoy en día se le conoce como *El Talismán*.

El sintetismo de la escuela de Pont-Aven continuaría durante la década de 1890 en el trabajo del grupo de artistas Nabis. Además de Paul Sérusier, sus miembros incluían a Maurice Denis, Pierre Bonnard, Édouard Vuillard, Ker-Xavier Roussel, Jan Verkade, Paul Ranson, Georges Lacombe y Félix Vallotton. Influenciada por los grabados japoneses en madera, sus obras se mueven entre el arte decorativo y el simbolismo.

Gauguin. Durante a criação, o mestre deve ter dito a seu discípulo: "Como você vê estas árvores? São amarelos. Então leva amarelo. Esta sombra? Bastante azul. Depois pinta-o em azul ultramarino puro. Estas folhas são vermelhas? Então toma vermelhão." Hoje é conhecido como *O Talismã*.

O sintetismo da escola Pont-Aven deveria ser continuado durante a década de 1890 no trabalho do grupo de artistas Nabis. Para além de Paul Sérusier, os seus membros incluíam Maurice Denis, Pierre Bonnard, Édouard Vuillard, Ker-Xavier Roussel, Jan Verkade, Paul Ranson, Georges Lacombe e Félix Vallotton. Influenciada pelas gravuras japonesas em blocos de madeira, suas obras se movem entre a arte decorativa e o simbolismo.

Sérusier onder het toeziend oog van Gauguin een klein schilderij in de buitenlucht in het Bois d'Amour. Tijdens het schilderen zou de meester tegen zijn leerling hebben gezegd: 'Hoe zie je deze bomen? Ze zijn geel. Gebruik dan geel. Deze schaduw? Tamelijk blauw. Schilder hem dan in zuiver ultramarijnblauw. Zijn deze bladeren rood? Gebruik dan vermiljoen.' Tegenwoordig is het werk bekend als *De talisman*.

Het synthetisme van de school van Pont-Aven werd in de jaren 1890 voortgezet in het werk van de Nabis. Naast Paul Sérusier behoorden Maurice Denis, Pierre Bonnard, Édouard Vuillard, Ker-Xavier Roussel, Jan Verkade, Paul Ranson, Georges Lacombe en Félix Vallotton tot deze kunstenaarsgroep. Onder invloed van Japanse houtsneden schommelden hun werken tussen decoratieve kunst en het symbolisme.

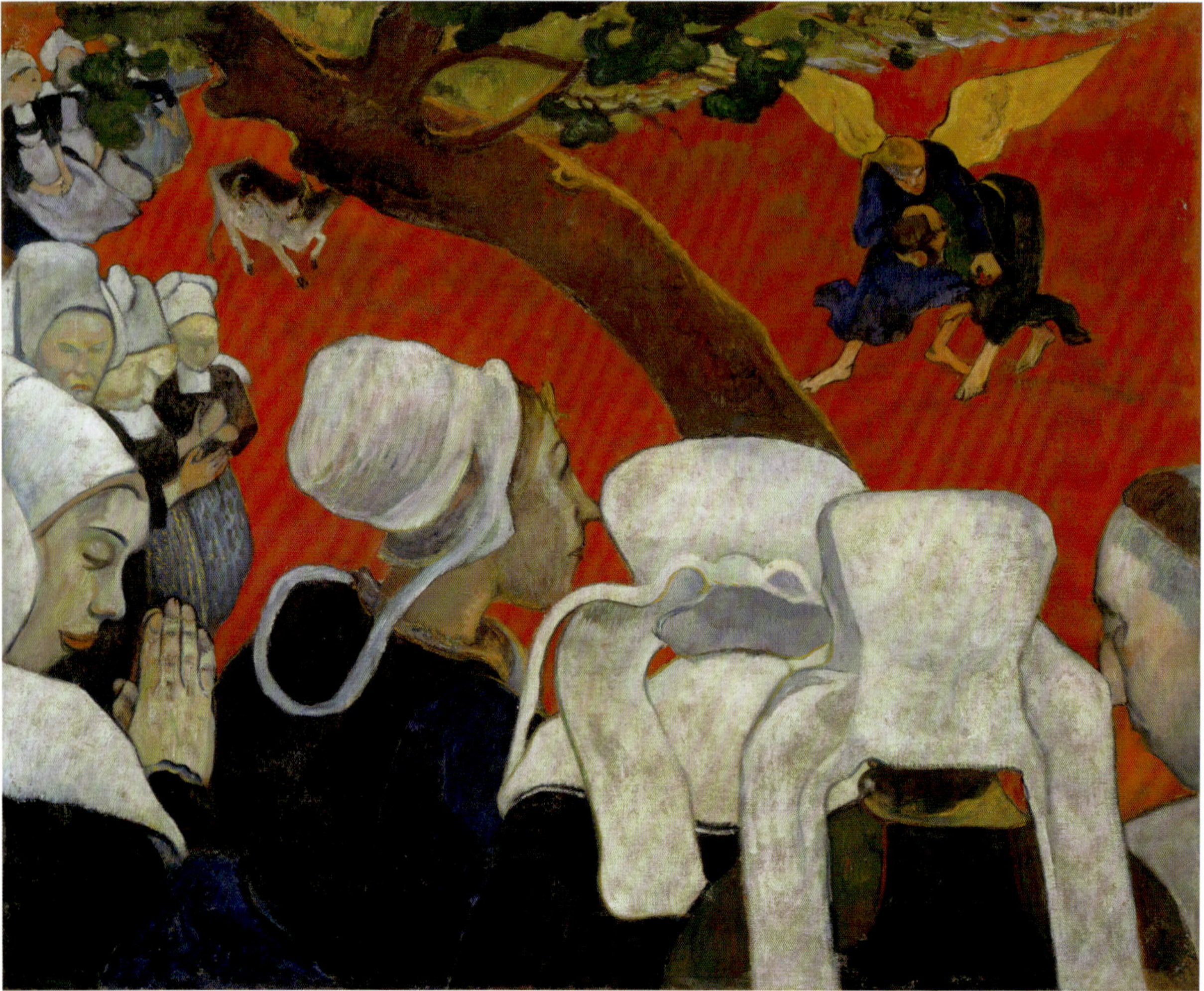

Vision of the Sermon *or* Jacob Wrestling with the Angel
The painting is one of Gauguin's first works in the style of Synthetism and Cloisonism. He used areas of color and delimited his figures with a closed line. Perspective also takes a back seat.

La Vision après le sermon *ou*
La Lutte de Jacob avec l'ange
Il s'agit d'une des toutes premières œuvres synthétistes et cloisonnistes de Gauguin. En Bretagne, il traite la couleur en aplats, et cerne ses figures d'un trait continu, en abolissant la perspective.

Die Vision nach der Predigt *oder*
Der Kampf Jakobs mit dem Engel
Das Bild ist eines der ersten Werke Gauguins im Stil des Synthetismus und Cloisonismus. Er nutzt Farbflächen und grenzt seine Figuren durch eine geschlossene Linie ab. Auch die Perspektive tritt in den Hintergrund.

La visión después del sermón *o*
La lucha de Jacob con el ángel
La pintura es una de las primeras obras de Gauguin en el estilo del Sintetismo y el Cloisonismo. Utiliza áreas de color y delimita sus figuras con una línea cerrada. La perspectiva también ocupa un segundo plano.

A visão após o sermão *ou* A luta de Jacó com o anjo
A pintura é uma das primeiras obras de Gauguin no estilo do Sintético e do Cloisonismo. Ele usa áreas de cor e delimita suas figuras com uma linha fechada. A perspectiva também fica em segundo plano.

Het visioen na de preek *of* Jakobs gevecht met de engel
Het gaat hier om een van Gauguins eerste werken in de stijl van het synthetisme en cloisonnisme. Hij gebruikte kleurvlakken en trok zijn figuren om met gesloten lijnen. Ook het perspectief was van ondergeschikt belang.

PAUL GAUGUIN (1848-1903)

1888, Oil on canvas/Huile sur toile, 72,2 × 91 cm, National Galleries of Scotland, Edinburgh

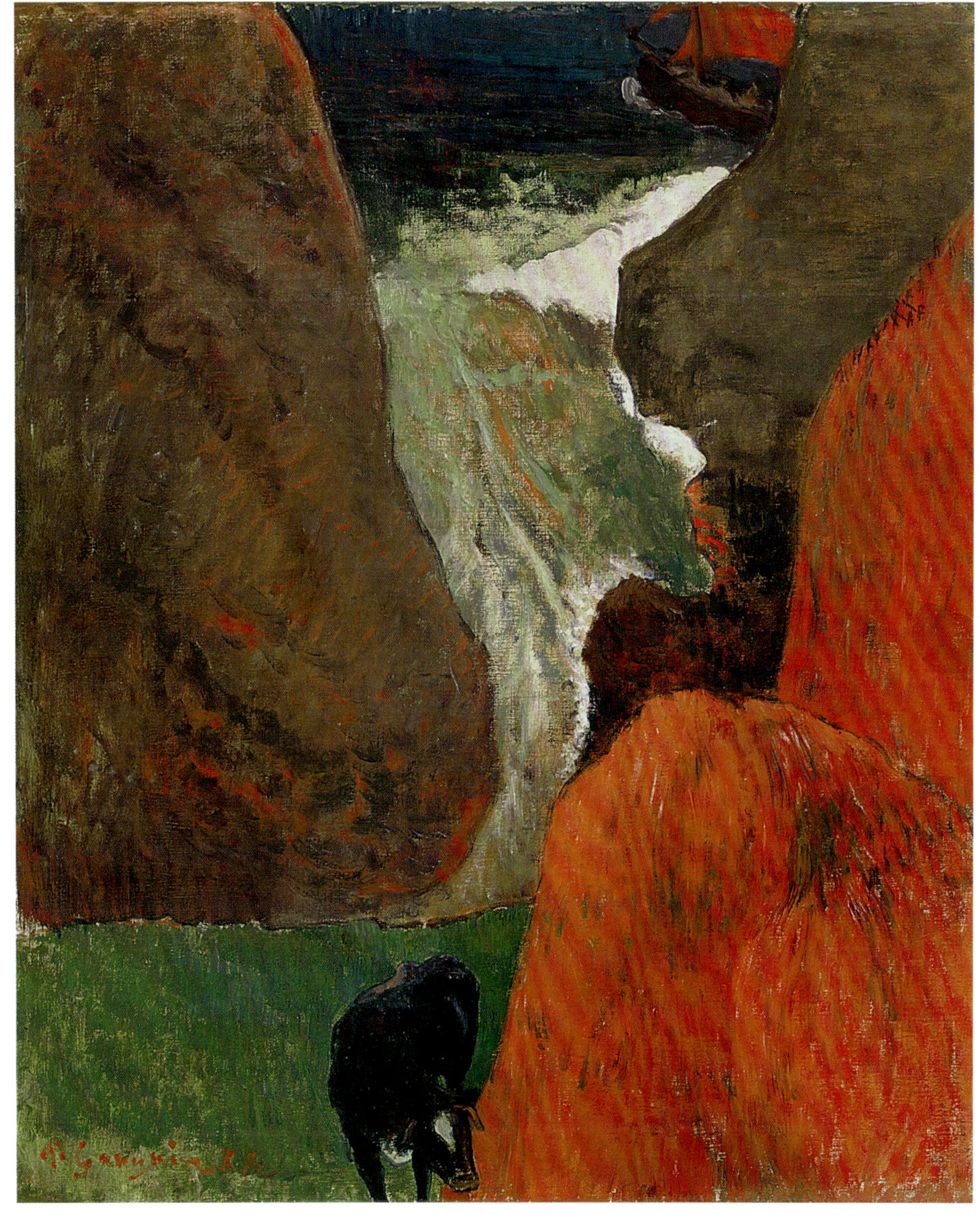

Seascape
with Cow

Marine avec
vache

Seestück mit Kuh

Marina con vaca

Pedaço de mar
com vaca

Zeestuk met koe

PAUL GAUGUIN
(1848-1903)
1888, Oil on canvas/
Huile sur toile,
72,5 × 61 cm, Musée
d'Orsay, Paris

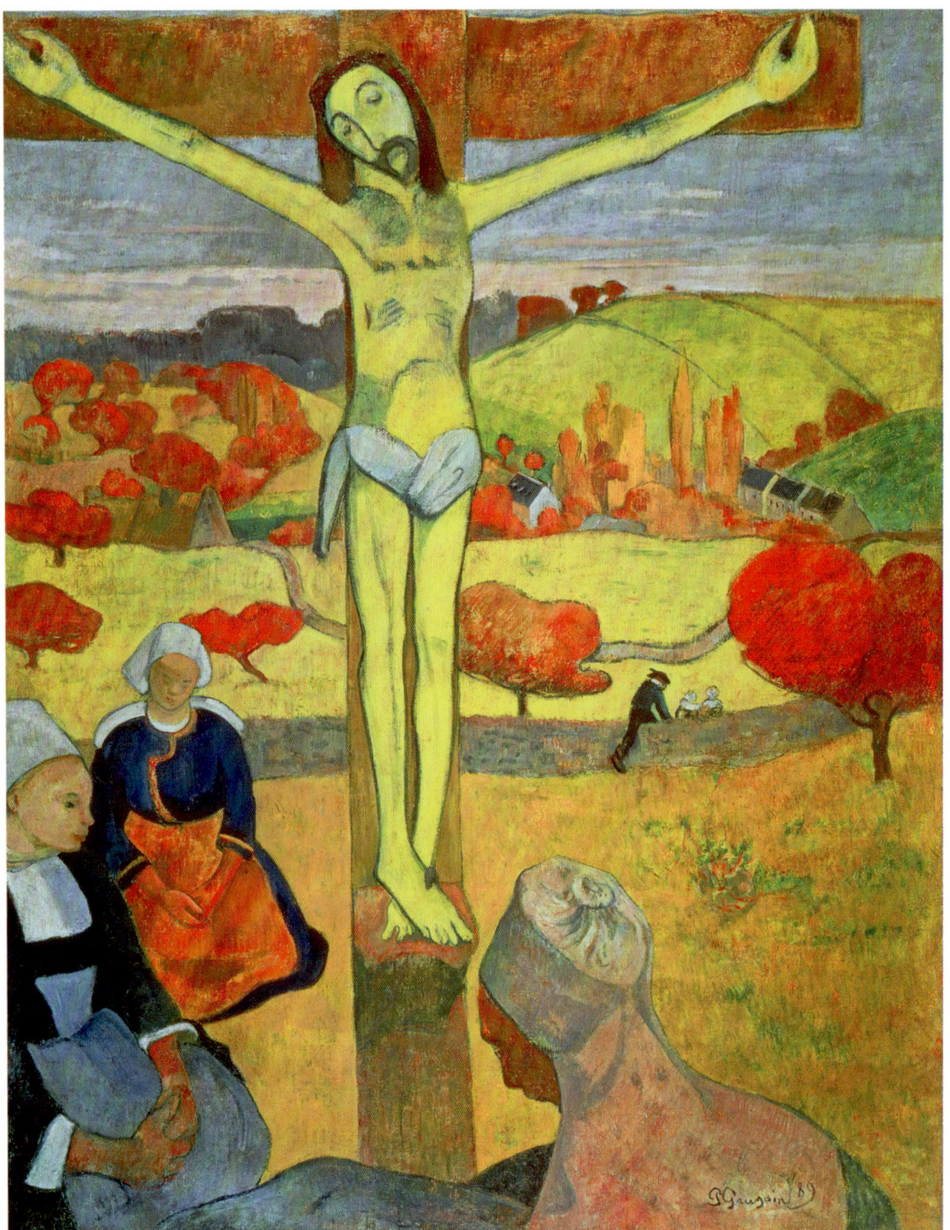

The Yellow Christ

When Gauguin returned to Pont-Aven in 1889, he visited the Trémalo chapel near the Bois d'Amour. Its multicolored crucifix inspired him to create two works: this one and the *Self Portrait with a yellow Christ.*

Le Christ jaune

Lorsqu'il revient à Pont-Aven en 1889, Gauguin visite la chapelle de Trémalo, à proximité du bois d'Amour. Le crucifix polychrome qu'elle abrite lui inspire cette œuvre, et *l'Autoportrait au Christ jaune.*

Der gelbe Christus

Als Gauguin 1889 nach Pont-Aven zurückkehrt, besucht er die Kapelle von Trémalo in der Nähe des Bois d'Amour. Ihr mehrfarbiges Kruzifix inspiriert ihn zu zwei Werken: diesem und dem *Selbstbildnis mit gelbem Christus.*

El Cristo Amarillo

Cuando Gauguin regresó a Pont-Aven en 1889, visitó la capilla de Trémalo, cerca del Bois d'Amour. Su crucifijo multicolor le inspiró a crear dos obras: ésta y el *Autorretrato con Cristo amarillo.*

O Cristo Amarelo

Quando Gauguin regressou a Pont-Aven em 1889, visitou a capela de Trémalo, perto do Bois d'Amour. O seu crucifixo multicolorido inspirou-o a criar duas obras: esta e o *Auto-retrato com um Cristo amarelo.*

De gele Christus

Toen Gauguin in 1889 terugkeerde naar Pont-Aven, bezocht hij de kapel van Trémalo bij het Bois d'Amour. Het veelkleurige kruisbeeld daar inspireerde hem tot twee werken: dit werk en *Zelfportret met De gele Christus.*

PAUL GAUGUIN (1848-1903)

1889, Oil on canvas/Huile sur toile, 91,1 × 73,4 cm, Albright Knox Art Gallery, New York

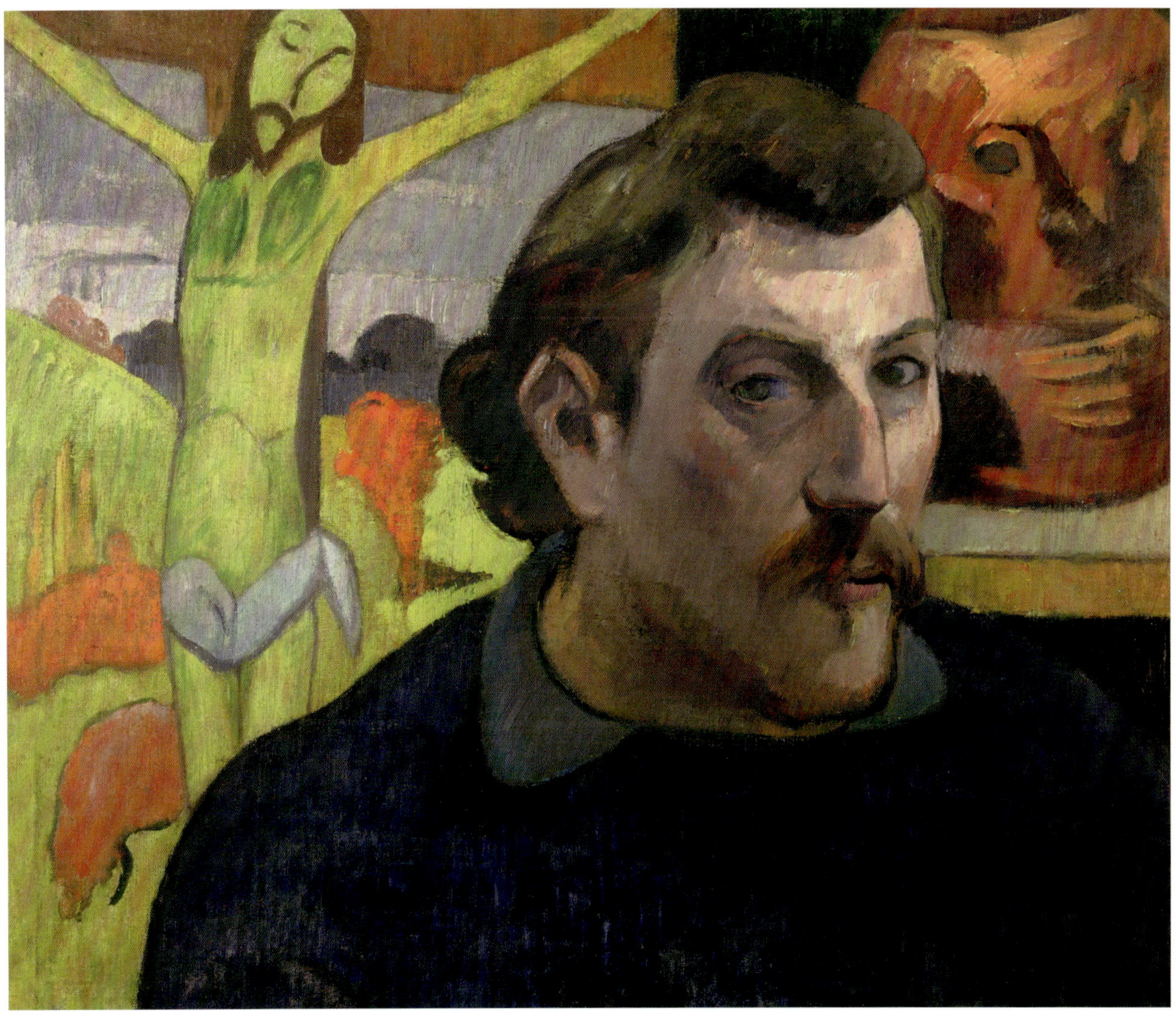

Self Portrait with Yellow Christ

Autoportrait au Christ jaune

Selbstbildnis mit gelbem Christus

Autorretrato con Cristo amarillo

Auto-retrato com Cristo Amarelo

Zelfportret met De gele Christus

PAUL GAUGUIN (1848-1903)

1890/91, Oil on canvas/Huile sur toile, 30 × 46 cm, Musée d'Orsay, Paris

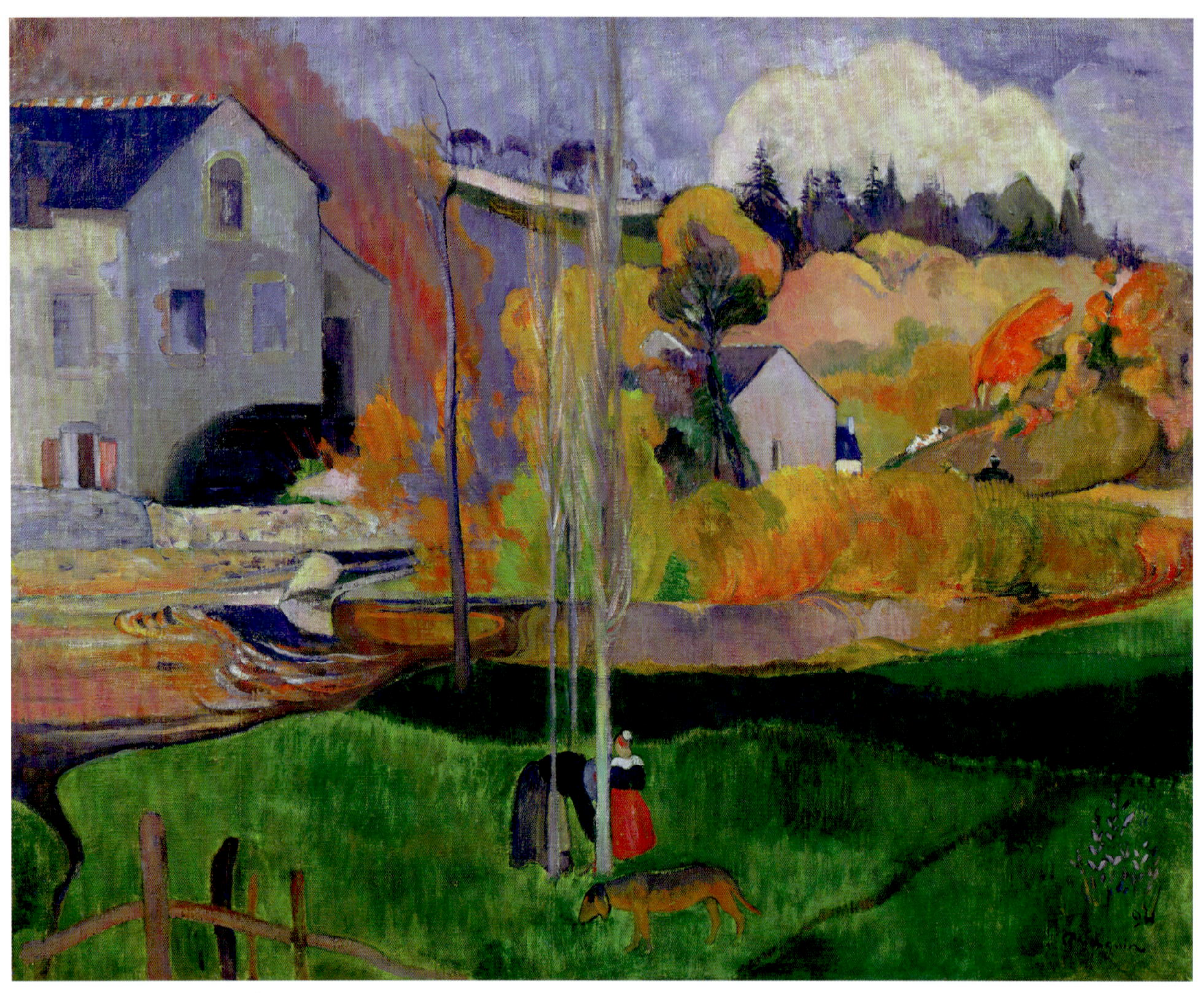

Landscape in Brittany. The David Mill

Paysage de Bretagne. Le Moulin de David

PAUL GAUGUIN (1848-1903)
1894, Oil on canvas/Huile sur toile, 73 × 92,2 cm, Musée d'Orsay, Paris

Bretonische Landschaft. Die Moulin de David

Paisaje bretón. El Moulin de David

Paisagem bretã. O Moulin de David

Bretons landschap. De Moulin de David

La Belle Angèle

Inspired by the very popular Japanese woodcuts, Gauguin painted in Pont-Aven the portrait of the hotel owner Marie-Angélique Satre, who is said to have titled it «How terrible!»

La Belle Angèle

Inspiré par les estampes japonaises alors très en vogue à Paris, ce portrait à l'effigie de Marie-Angélique Satre, aubergiste à Pont-Aven, déplut au modèle qui eut ces mots : « Quelle horreur ! »

La Belle Angèle

Inspiriert durch die sehr populären japanischen Holzschnitte, malt Gauguin in Pont-Aven das Porträt der Hotelbesitzerin Marie-Angélique Satre, die es mit den Worten „Wie schrecklich!" betitelt haben soll.

La Belle Angèle

Inspirado en los famosos grabados en madera japoneses, Gauguin pinta en Pont-Aven el retrato de la dueña del hotel, Marie-Angélique Satre, que se dice que lo tituló «¡Qué horror!»

La Belle Angèle

Inspirado pelos muito populares xilogravuras japonesas, Gauguin pinta em Pont-Aven o retrato da proprietária do hotel Marie-Angélique Satre, que se diz ter intitulado «Que terrível»!

La Belle Angèle

Geïnspireerd door de zeer populaire Japanse houtsneden schilderde Gauguin in Pont-Aven het portret van herbergierster Marie-Angélique Satre, die bij het zien ervan 'Wat verschrikkelijk!' zou hebben geroepen.

PAUL GAUGUIN (1848-1903)

1889, Oil on canvas/Huile sur toile, 92 × 73 cm, Musée d'Orsay, Paris

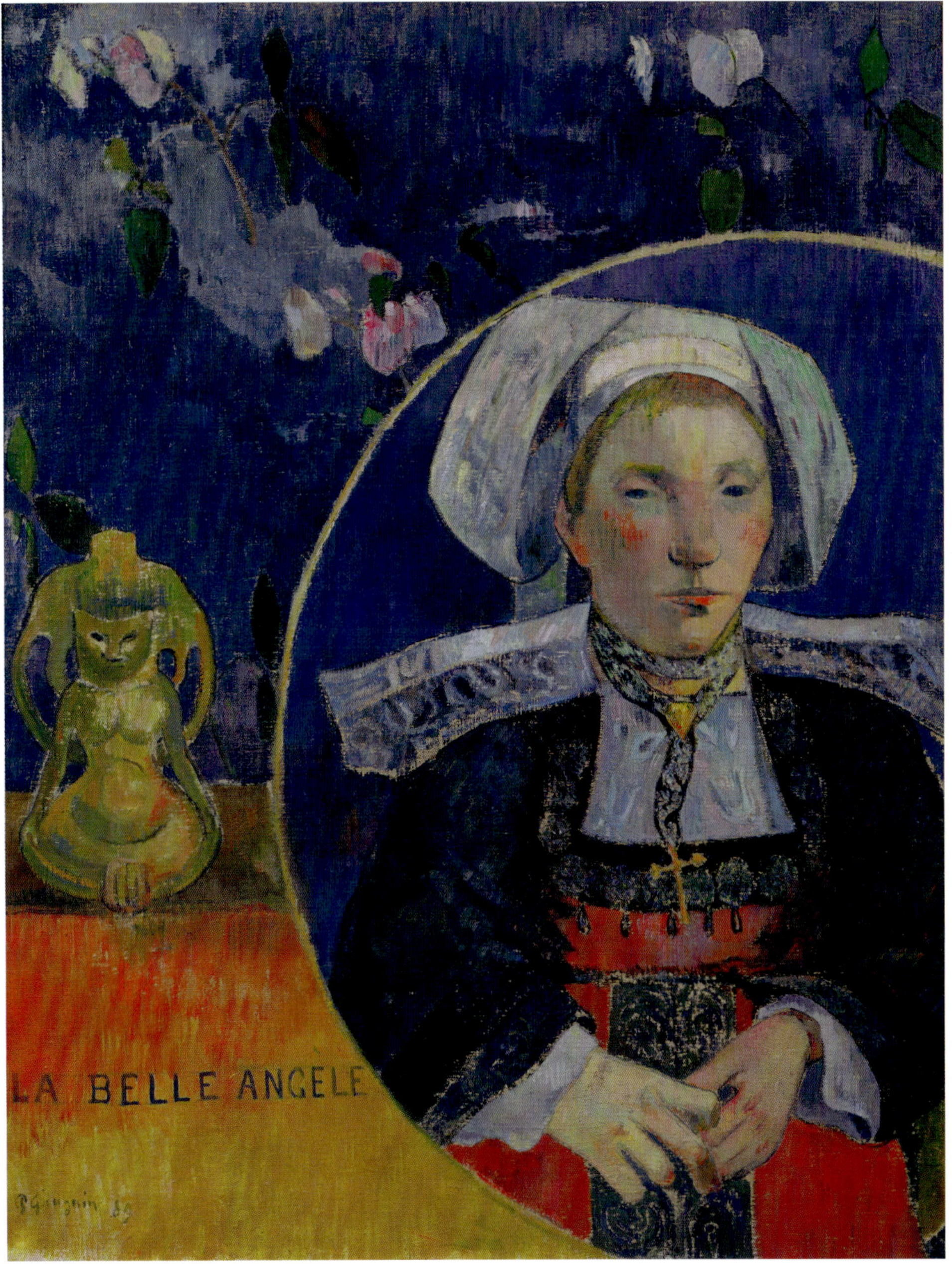

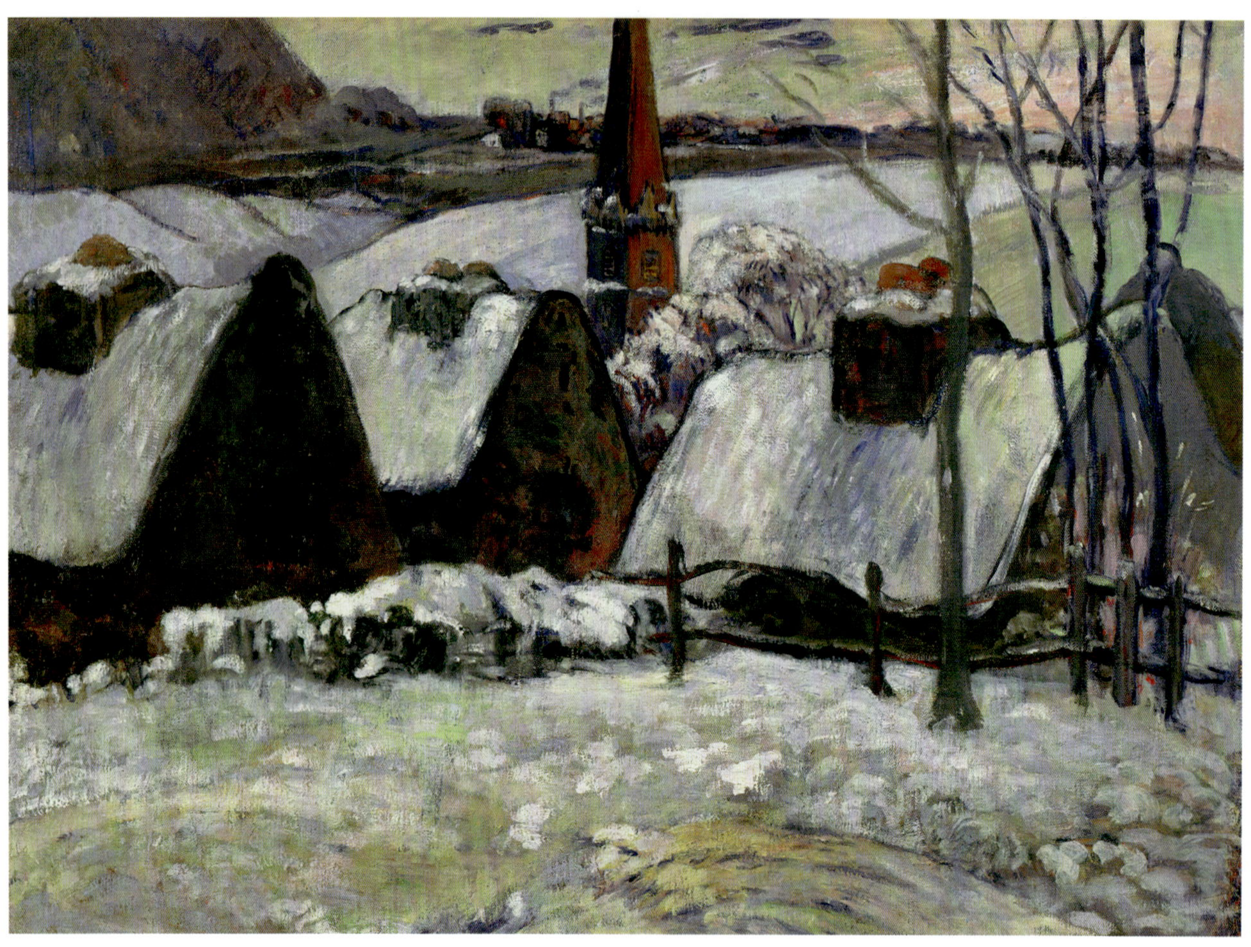

Breton Village under Snow

Village breton sous la neige

Bretonisches Dorf im Schnee

Pueblo bretón en la nieve

Aldeia bretã na neve

Bretons dorp in de sneeuw

PAUL GAUGUIN (1848-1903)

1894, Oil on canvas/Huile sur toile, 62 × 87 cm, Musée d'Orsay, Paris

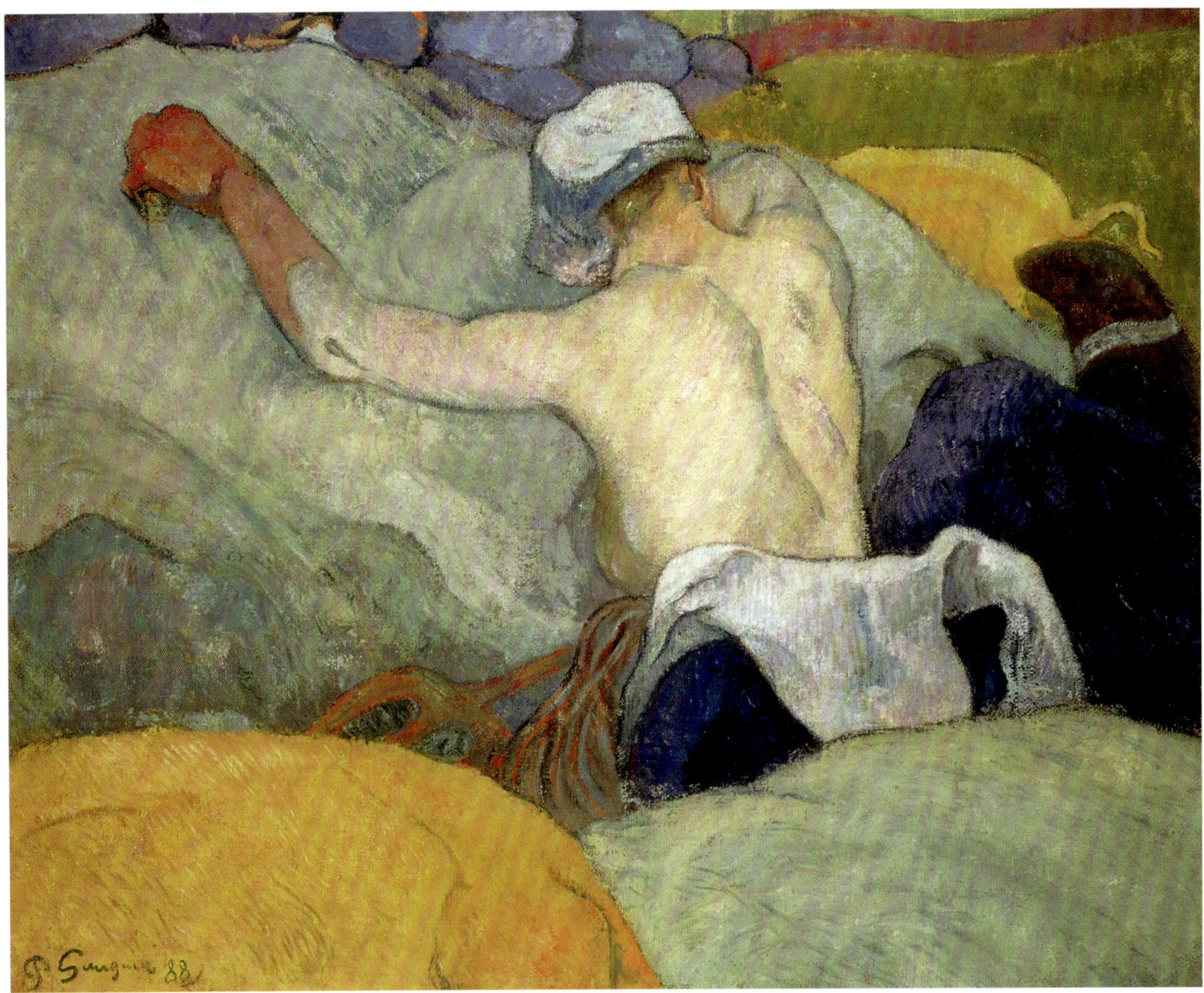

The Woman with the Pigs

Gauguin painted the back view of a woman exhausted by the heat with a naked upper body in the middle of an abstract background. The pigs surrounding them are only partially indicated.

La Femme aux cochons, en pleine chaleur

La vision est étrange et la composition audacieuse. Une femme au buste dénudé, de dos, accablée par la chaleur, dans un décor presque abstrait, est entourée de cochons dont on ne voit que des fragments.

PAUL GAUGUIN (1848-1903)

1888, Oil on canvas/Huile sur toile, 73 × 92 cm, Private collection

Die Frau mit den Schweinen

Gauguin malt die Rückenansicht einer durch die Hitze erschöpften Frau mit nacktem Oberkörper inmitten eines abstrakten Hintergrundes. Die sie umgebenden Schweine sind nur in Teilen angedeutet.

La mujer de los cerdos o En el calor

La visión es extraña y la composición atrevida. Una mujer con el pecho desnudo, de espaldas, abrumada por el calor, en un entorno casi abstracto, está rodeada de cerdos de los que sólo se pueden ver fragmentos.

A mulher com os porcos

Gauguin pinta a vista traseira de uma mulher exausta pelo calor com o tronco nu no meio de um fundo abstrato. Os porcos que os rodeiam são apenas parcialmente indicados.

Vrouw met varkens

Gauguin schilderde de op de rug geziene, door de hitte uitgeputte vrouw met ontbloot bovenlichaam midden voor een abstracte achtergrond. De varkens om haar heen zijn slechts ten dele aangeduid.

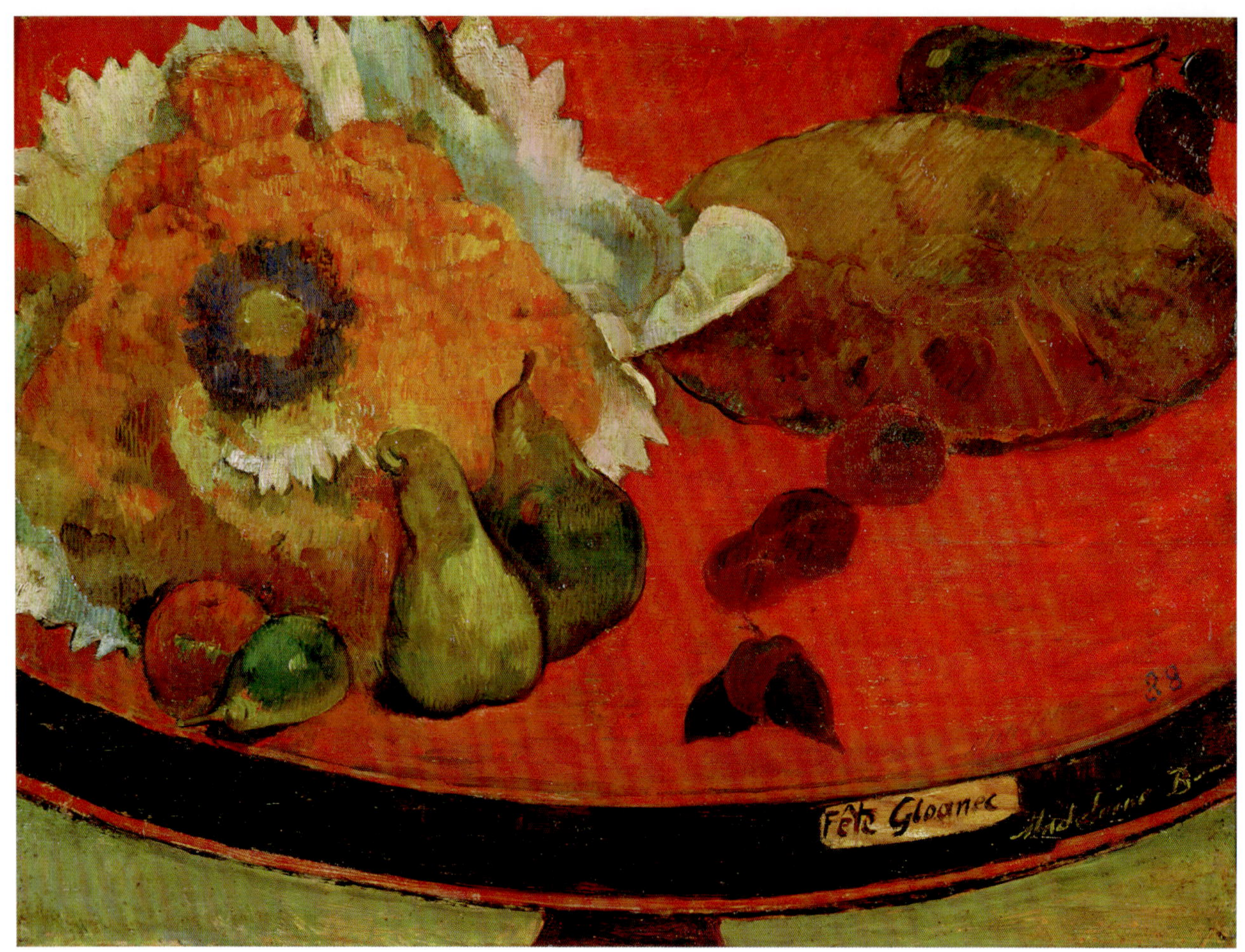

Fête Gloanec

PAUL GAUGUIN (1848-1903)

1888, Oil on wood/Huile sur bois, 36,5 × 52 cm, Musée des Beaux-Arts, Orléans

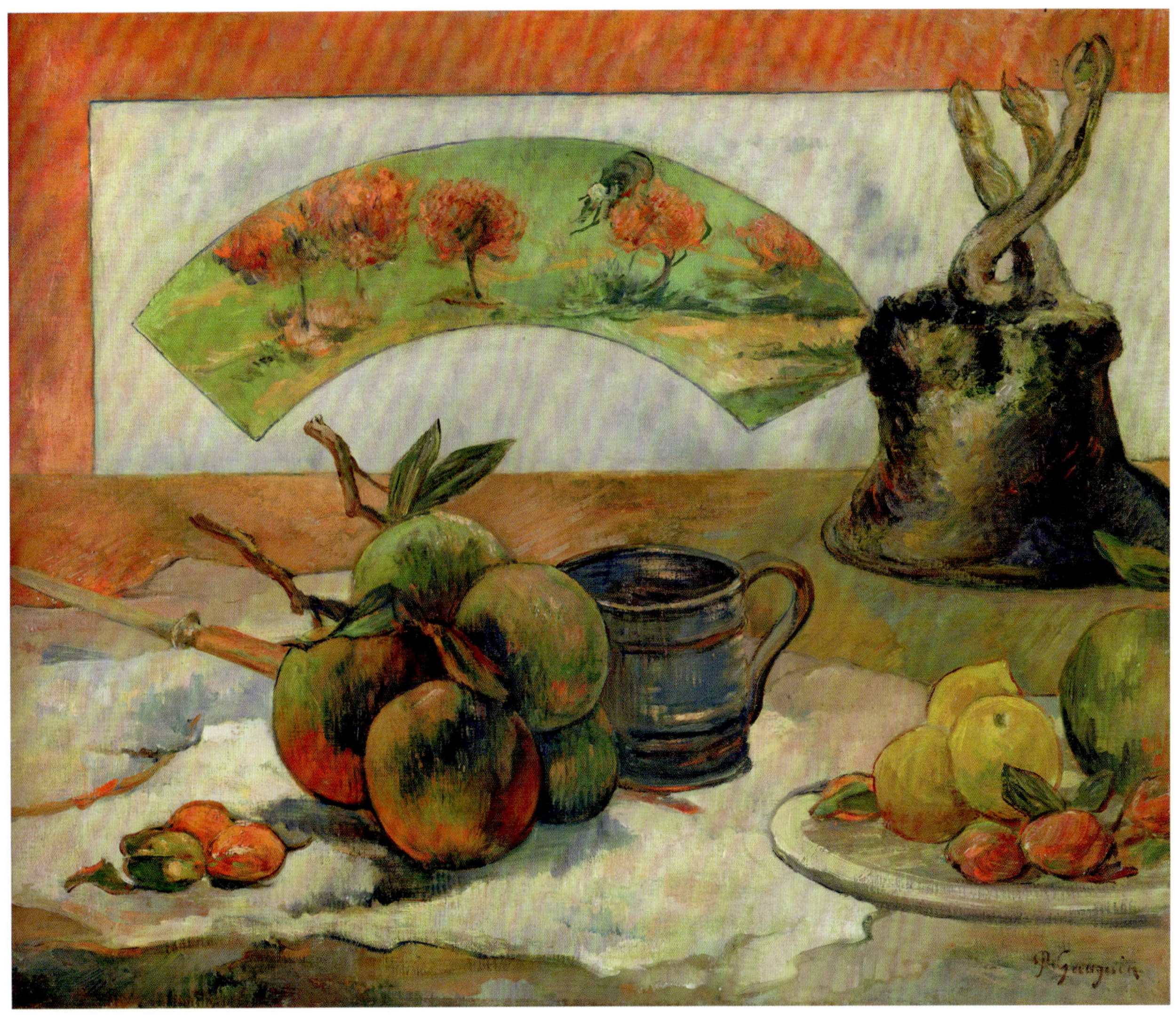

Still Life with a Fan

Nature morte à l'éventail

Stillleben mit Fächer

Bodegón con ventilador

Natureza morta com ventilador

Stilleven met waaier

PAUL GAUGUIN (1848-1903)

c. 1889, Oil on canvas/Huile sur toile, 50,5 × 61,5 cm, Musée d'Orsay, Paris

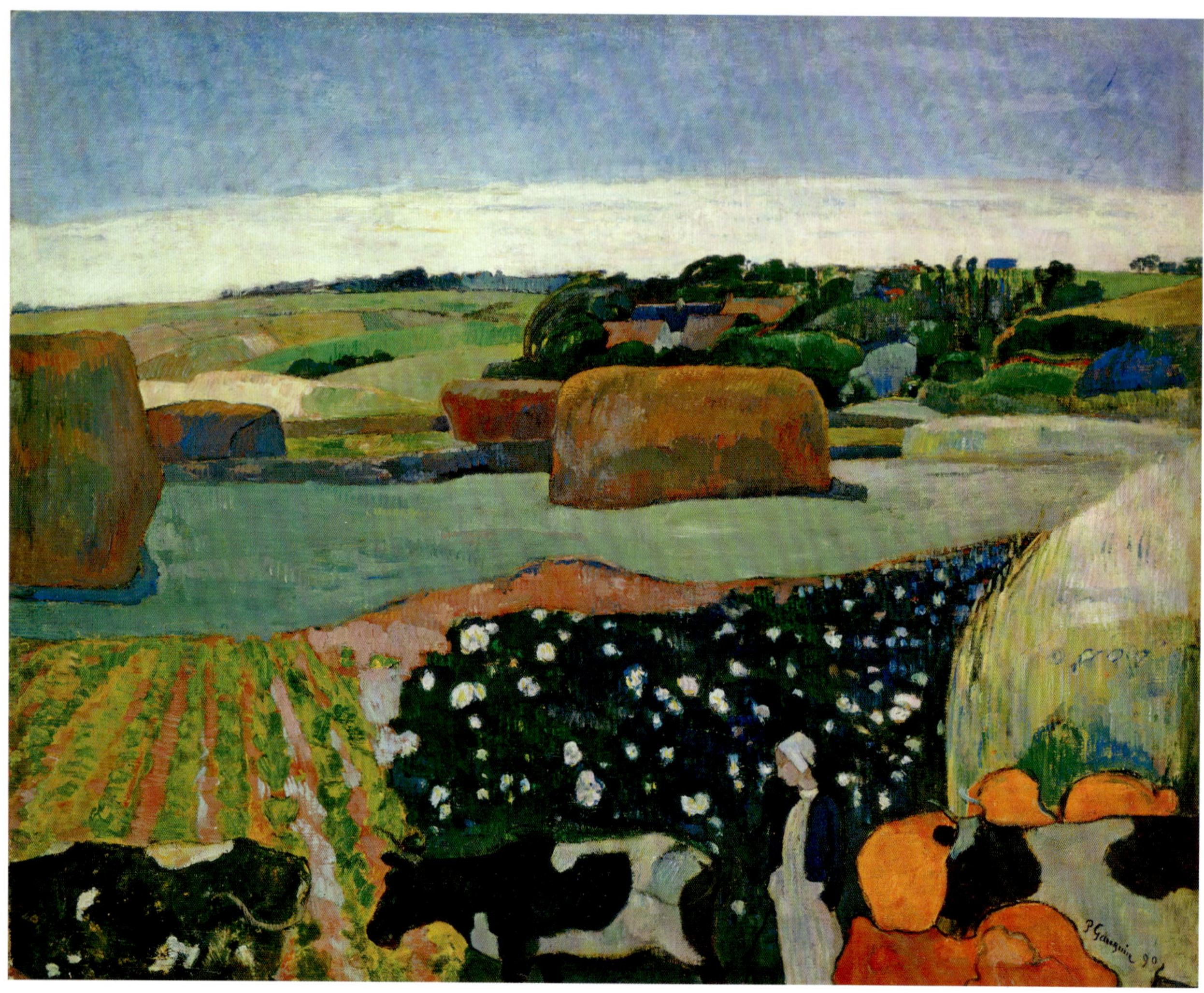

Haystacks in Brittany

Meules de foin en Bretagne

Heuhaufen in der Bretagne

Pajares en Bretaña

Palheiros na Bretanha

Hooibergen in Bretagne

PAUL GAUGUIN (1848-1903)

1890, Oil on canvas/Huile sur toile,
74,3 × 93,6 cm, National Gallery of Art, Washington

Still life with Profile of Laval

Nature morte au profil de Laval

Stillleben mit dem Profil von Charles Laval

Bodegón con el perfil de Charles Laval

Natureza morta com o perfil de Charles Laval

Stilleven met het profiel van Charles Laval

PAUL GAUGUIN (1848-1903)

1886, Oil on canvas/Huile sur toile, 46 × 38 cm,
Indianapolis Museum of Art, Newfields

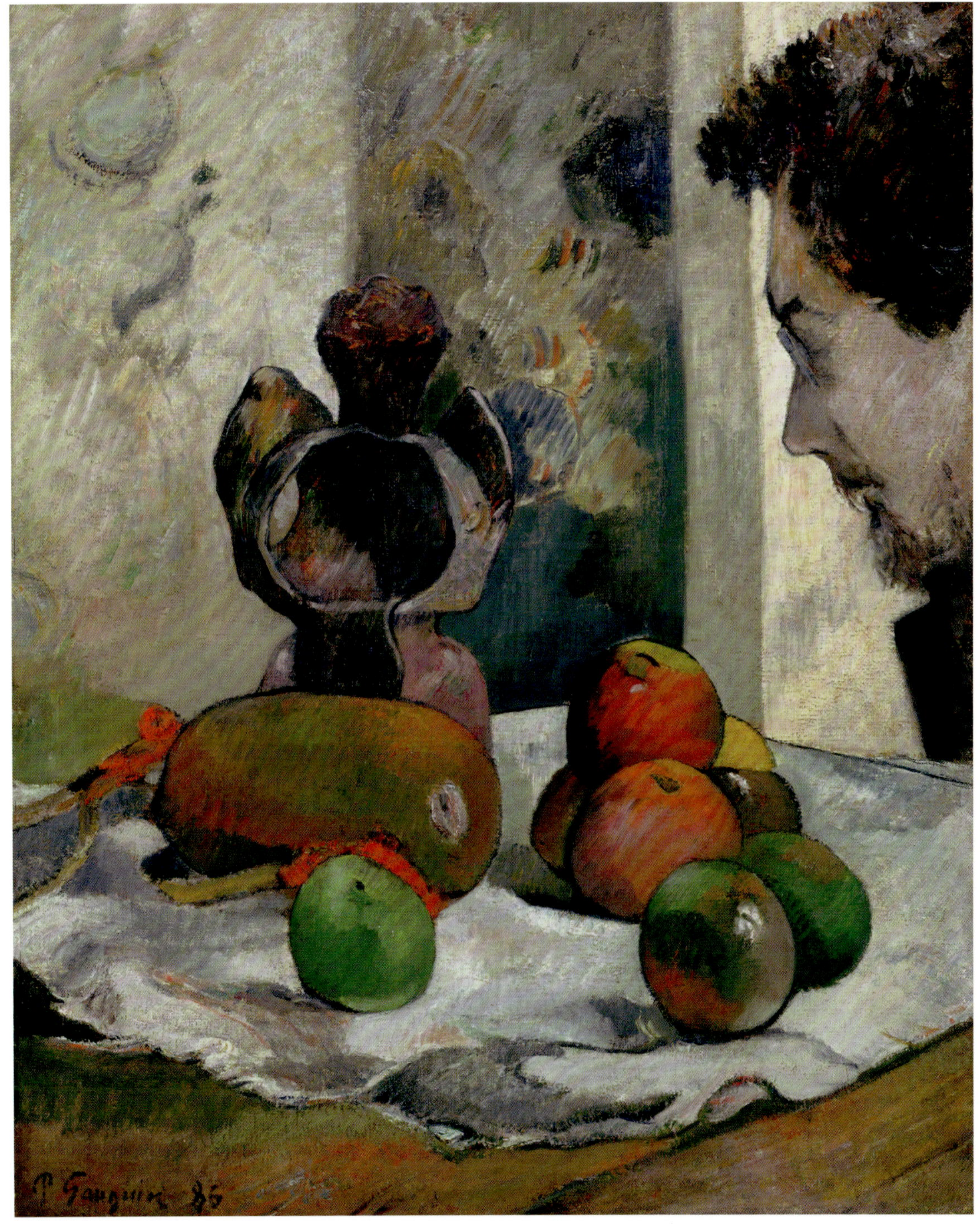

P Gauguin 85

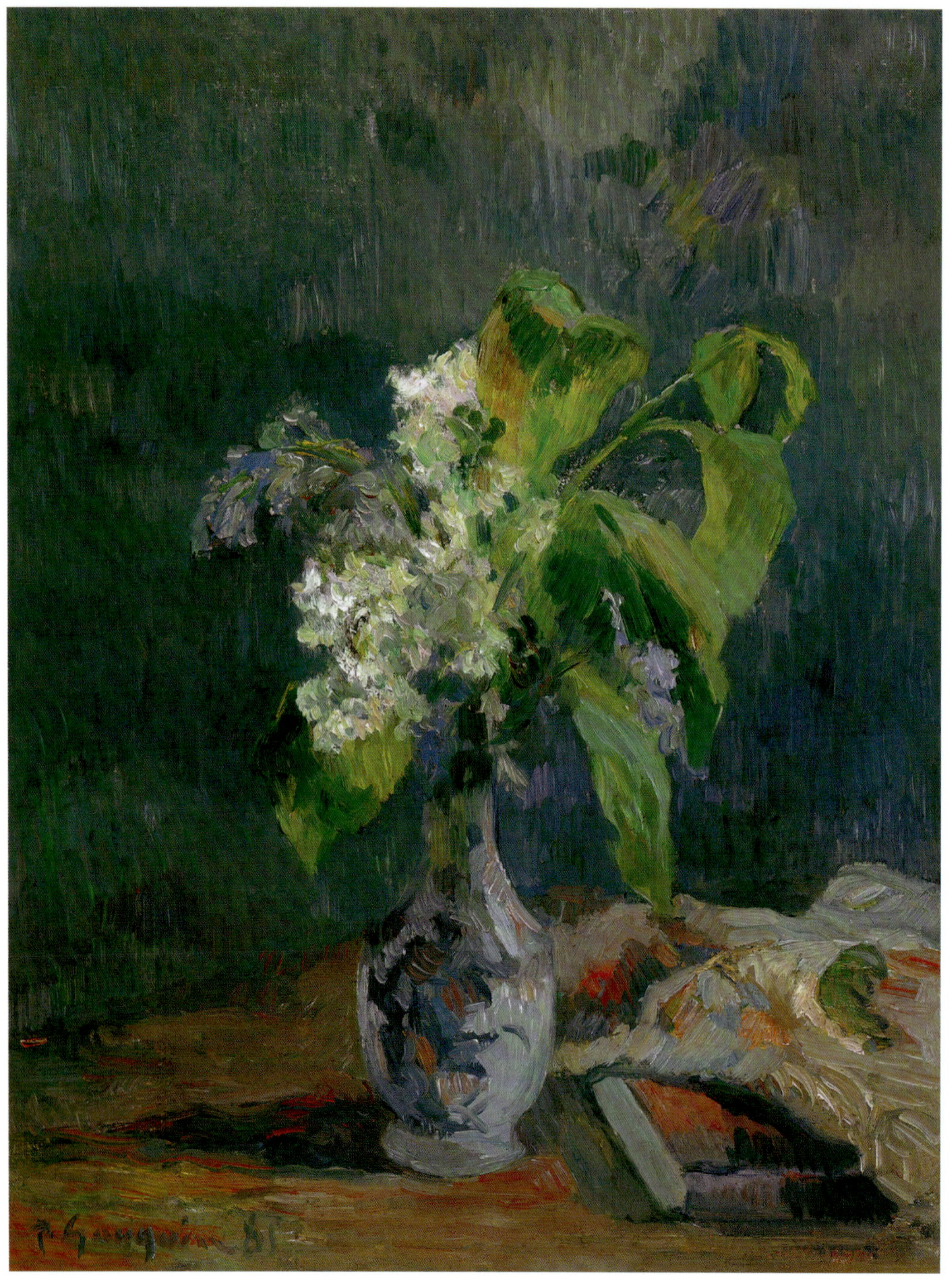

Lilacs

Lilas

Flieder

Lilas

Lilás

Seringen

PAUL GAUGUIN
(1848-1903)
1885, Oil on canvas/
Huile sur toile, 34,9 x 27 cm,
Museo Thyssen-Bornemisza,
Madrid

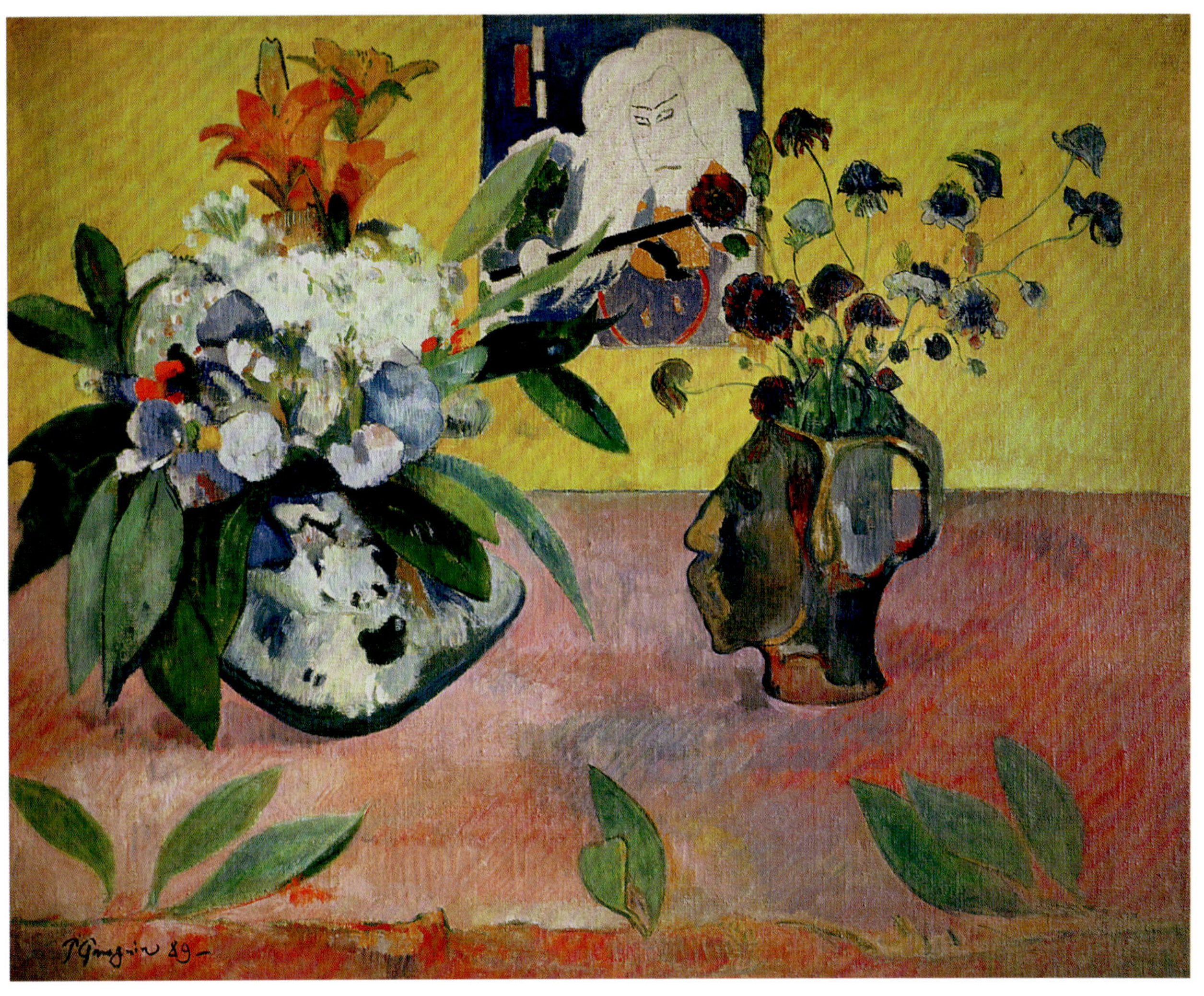

Still Life with Japanese Woodcut

Nature morte à l'estampe japonaise

Stillleben mit japanischem Holzschnitt

Bodegón con xilografía japonesa

Natureza morta com Woodcut Japonês

Stilleven met hoofdvormige vaas en Japanse houtsnede

PAUL GAUGUIN (1848-1903)

1889, Oil on canvas/Huile sur toile, 72 × 94 cm,
Muze honarhā-ye mohasser Tehran

387

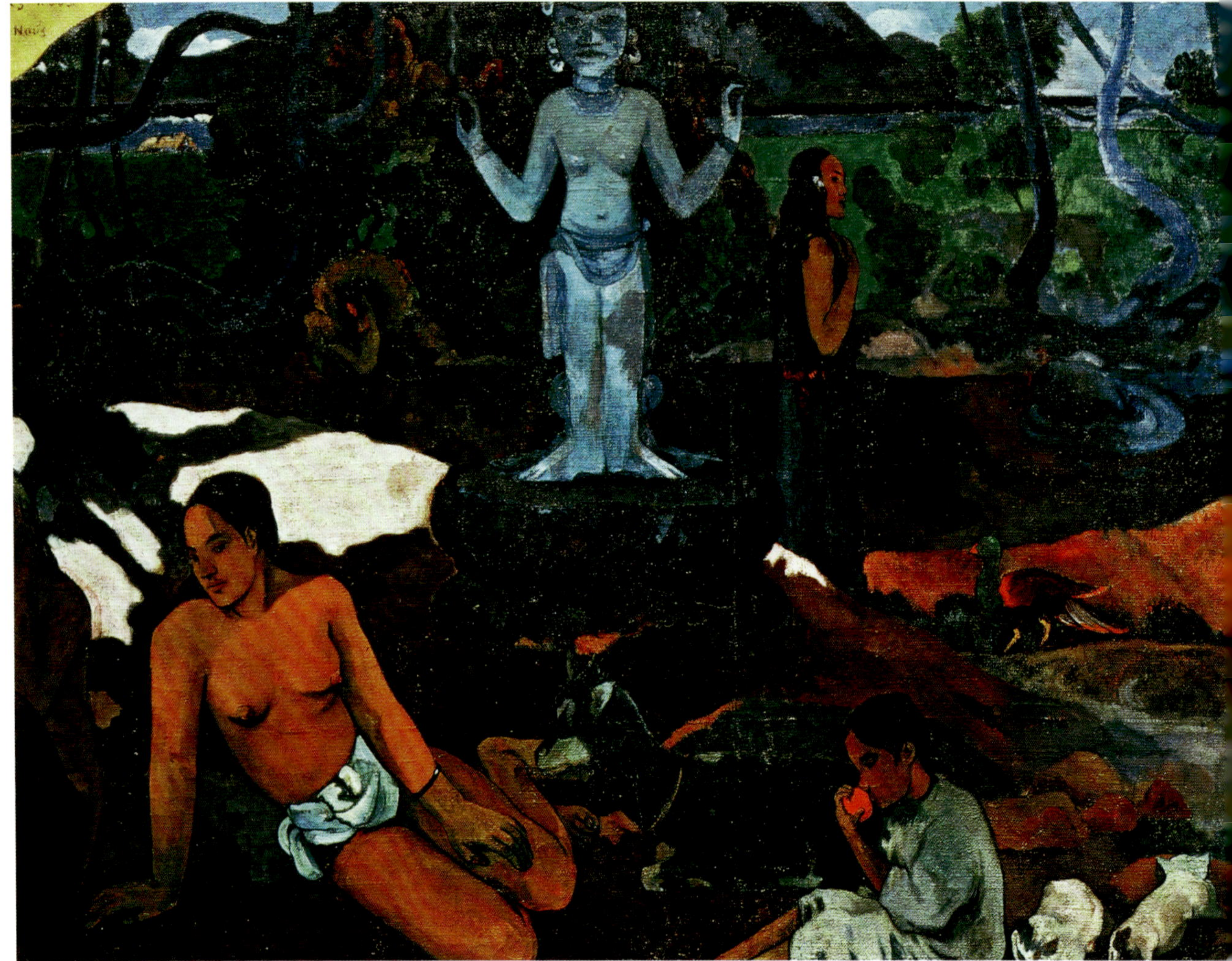

**Where Do we Come From? What Are We?
Where Are We Going?**

Penniless and shaken by the death of his daughter Aline,
Gauguin thought of suicide. He painted his will - a symbolic
representation between lost paradise, simple life and
metaphysical allusions.

**D'où venons-nous ? Que sommes-nous ?
Où allons-nous ?**

Ruiné et brisé par le décès de sa fille chérie Aline, Gauguin
pense au suicide. Ce tableau a des allures de testament.
Une vision symboliste entre paradis perdu, vie primitive
et questions métaphysiques.

Woher kommen wir? Wer sind wir? Wohin gehen wir?

Mittellos und durch den Tod seiner Tochter Aline
erschüttert, denkt Gauguin an Selbstmord. Er malt sein
Testament – eine symbolische Darstellung zwischen
verlorenem Paradies, einfachem Leben und metaphysischen
Anspielungen.

PAUL GAUGUIN (1848-1903)
1897/98, Oil on canvas/Huile sur toile, 139,1 × 374,6 cm, Museum of Fine Arts, Boston

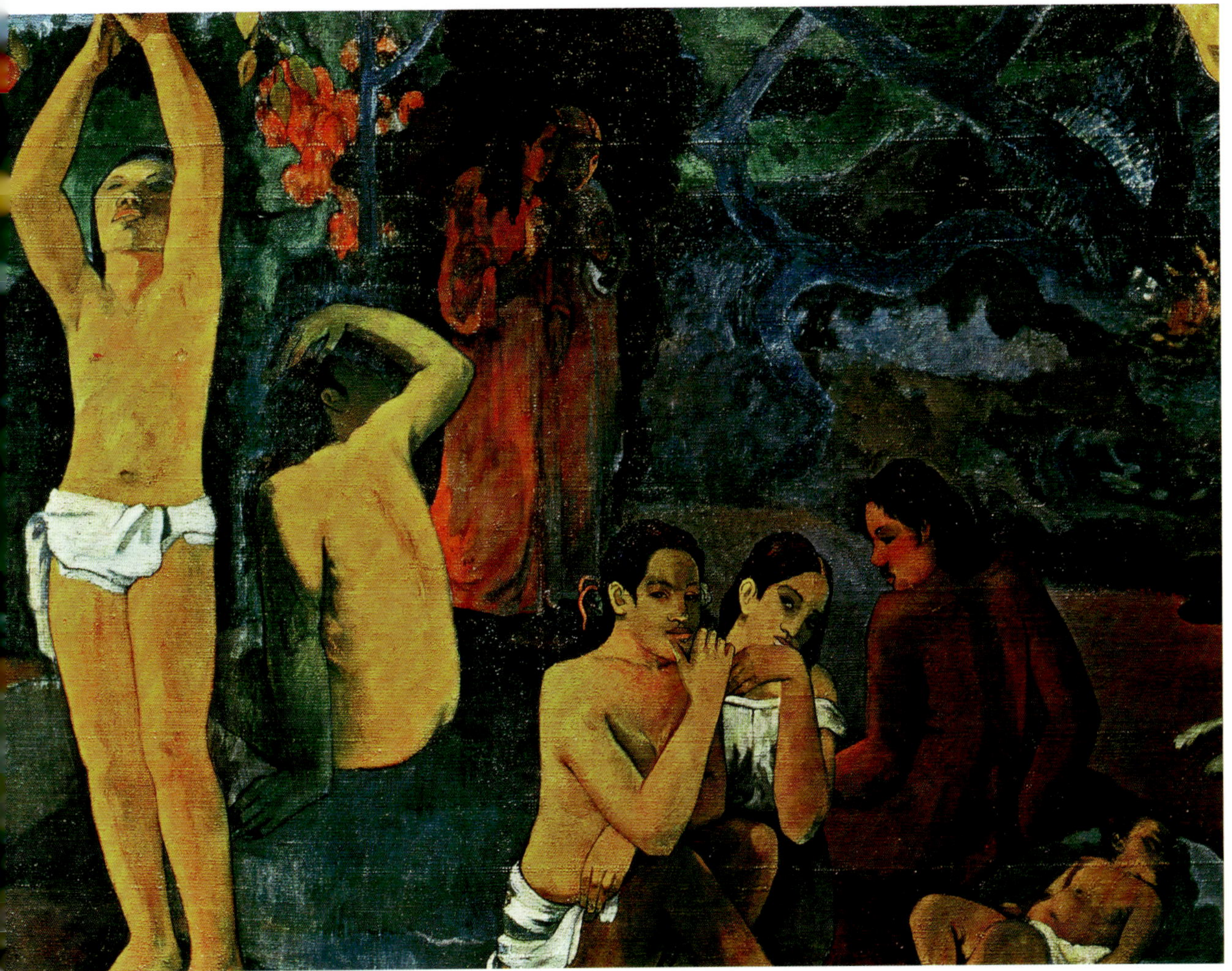

¿De dónde venimos? ¿Quiénes somos?
¿Adónde vamos, hombre?

Sin dinero y conmocionado por la muerte de su hija Aline,
Gauguin piensa en el suicidio. Pinta su voluntad, una
representación simbólica entre el paraíso perdido, la vida
sencilla y las alusiones metafísicas.

De onde somos? Quem somos nós? Onde vamos, meu?

Sem dinheiro e abalado pela morte de sua filha Aline,
Gauguin pensa em suicídio. Ele pinta a sua vontade - uma
representação simbólica entre o paraíso perdido, a vida
simples e as alusões metafísicas.

Waar komen wij vandaan? Wie zijn wij?
Waar gaan wij naartoe?

Gauguin was geschokt door de dood van zijn dochter Aline
en overwoog zelfmoord. Hij schilderde zijn testament:
een symbolische voorstelling tussen verloren paradijs,
eenvoudig leven en metafysische verwijzingen.

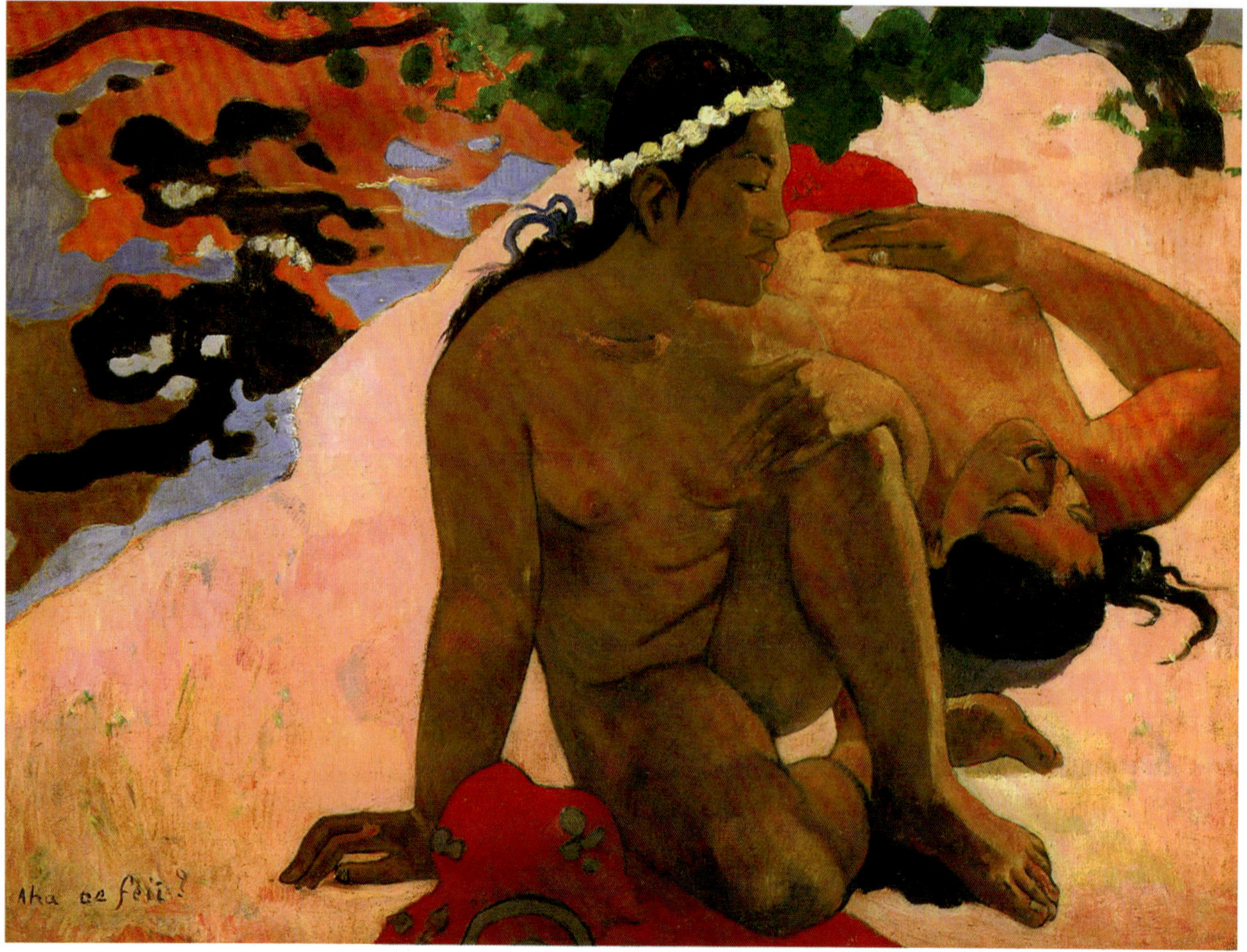

Aha oe feii? (What? Are you jealous?)

The two Tahitian women on the shore appear sculptural
and sensual – the first seated and contemplative, the second
sunbathing. They are surrounded by a stylized landscape
dominated by a pink surface.

Aha oe Feii? (Eh quoi ! Tu es jalouse ?)

Sculpturales et sensuelles, deux vahinés sont au bord de
l'eau, l'une assise, pensive, le visage de profil, la seconde
allongée au soleil, au cœur d'un paysage stylisé dominé
par un aplat rose lumineux.

PAUL GAUGUIN (1848-1903)

1892, Oil on canvas/Huile sur toile, 66 × 89 cm, Pushkin Museum, Moscow

Aha oe Feii? (Wie? Bist du eifersüchtig?)

Skulptural und sinnlich erscheinen die beiden Tahitianerinnen
am Ufer – die erste sitzend und nachdenklich, die zweite beim
Sonnen. Sie umgibt eine stilisierte Landschaft, die durch eine
rosa Fläche beherrscht wird.

Aha oe feii? (¿Cómo? ¿Estás celoso?)

Las dos mujeres tahitianas aparecen esculturales y sensuales
en la orilla - la primera sentada y contemplativa, la segunda
tomando el sol. Rodea un paisaje estilizado dominado por
una superficie de color rosa.

Aha oe feii? (Como? Estás com ciúmes?)

As duas mulheres taitianas aparecem escultóricas e sensuais
na costa - a primeira sentada e contemplativa, a segunda a
apanhar sol. Envolve uma paisagem estilizada dominada por
uma superfície rosa.

Aha oe feii? (Wat? Ben je jaloers?)

De twee Tahitiaanse vrouwen zien er sculpturaal en
sensueel uit op het strand - de eerste zittend en peinzend,
de tweede zonnebadend. Zij omringt een gestileerd
landschap dat beheerst wordt door een roze vlak.

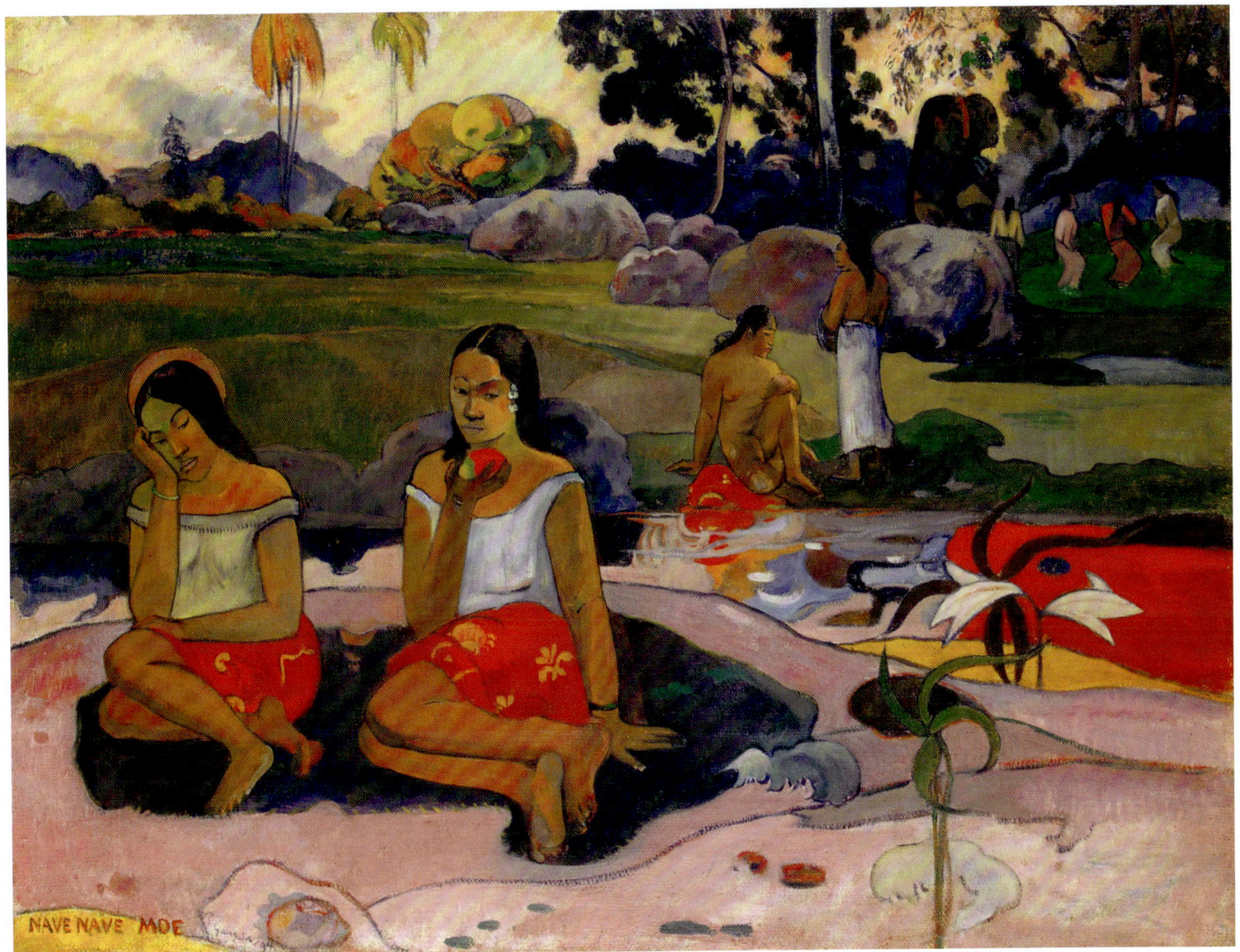

Nave Nave Moe (Sweet Dreams)

Nave Nave Moe (Douces Rêveries)

Nave Nave Moe (Süße Träume)

Nave Nave Moe (Sweet Dreams)

Nave Nave Nave Moe (Sonhos Doces)

Nave Nave Moe (Zoete dromen)

PAUL GAUGUIN (1848-1903)

1894, Oil on canvas/Huile sur toile, 74 × 100 cm, State Hermitage Museum, St. Petersburg

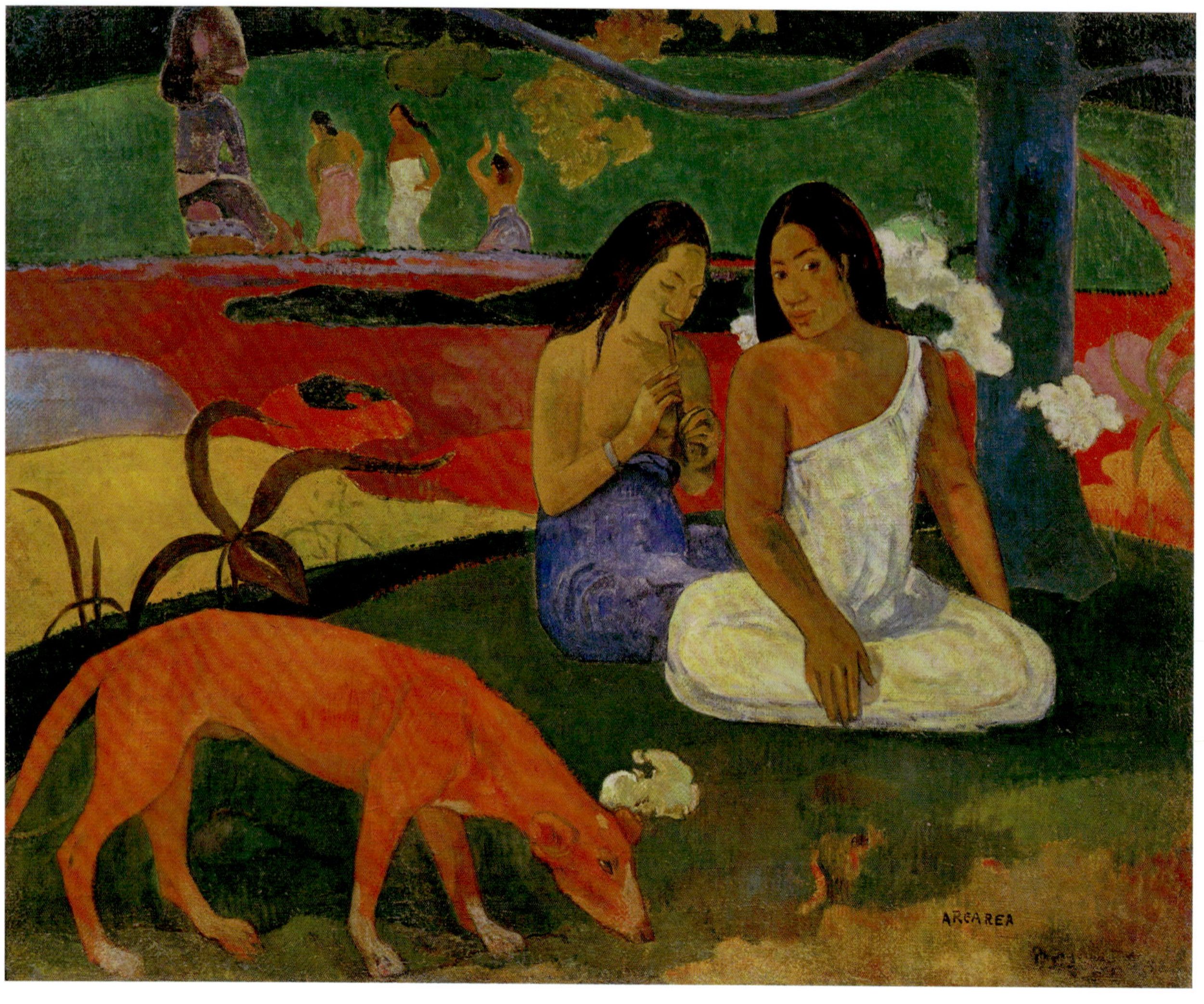

Arearea, Jokes (The Red Dog)

Arearea (Joyeusetés)

Arearea, Zeitvertreib (Der rote Hund)

Arearea, Pasatiempo (El perro rojo)

Arearea, Passatempo (O Cão Vermelho)

Arearea (De rode hond)

PAUL GAUGUIN (1848–1903)

1892, Oil on canvas/Huile sur toile, 74,5 × 93,5 cm, Musée d'Orsay, Paris

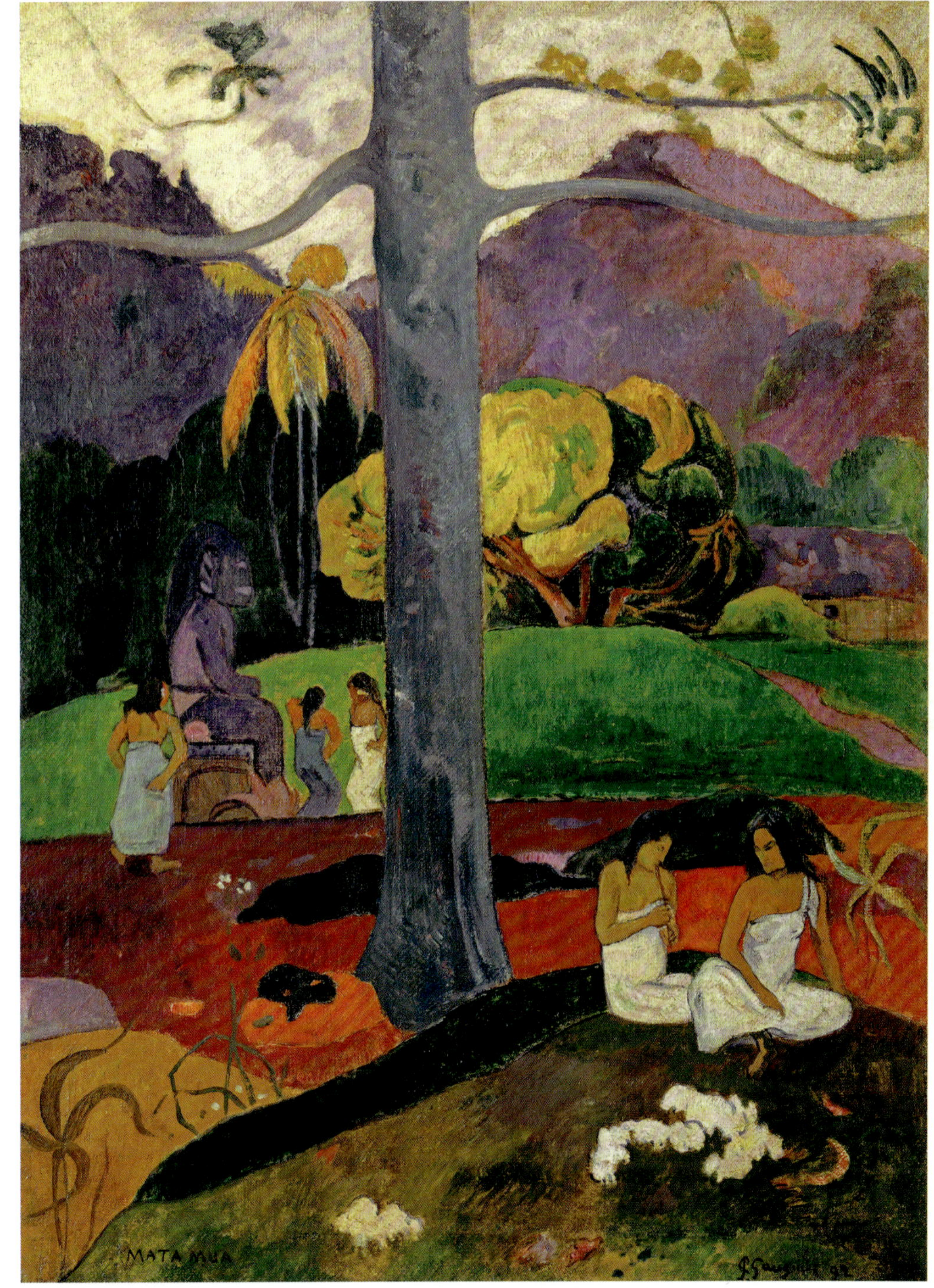

In Olden Times, Mata Mua

Autrefois, Mata Mua

Früher, Mata Mua

En el pasado, Mata Mua

No passado, Mata Mua

Vroeger, Mata Mua

PAUL GAUGUIN (1848-1903)

1892, Oil on canvas/
Huile sur toile, 91 × 69 cm,
Museo Thyssen-Bornemisza,
Madrid

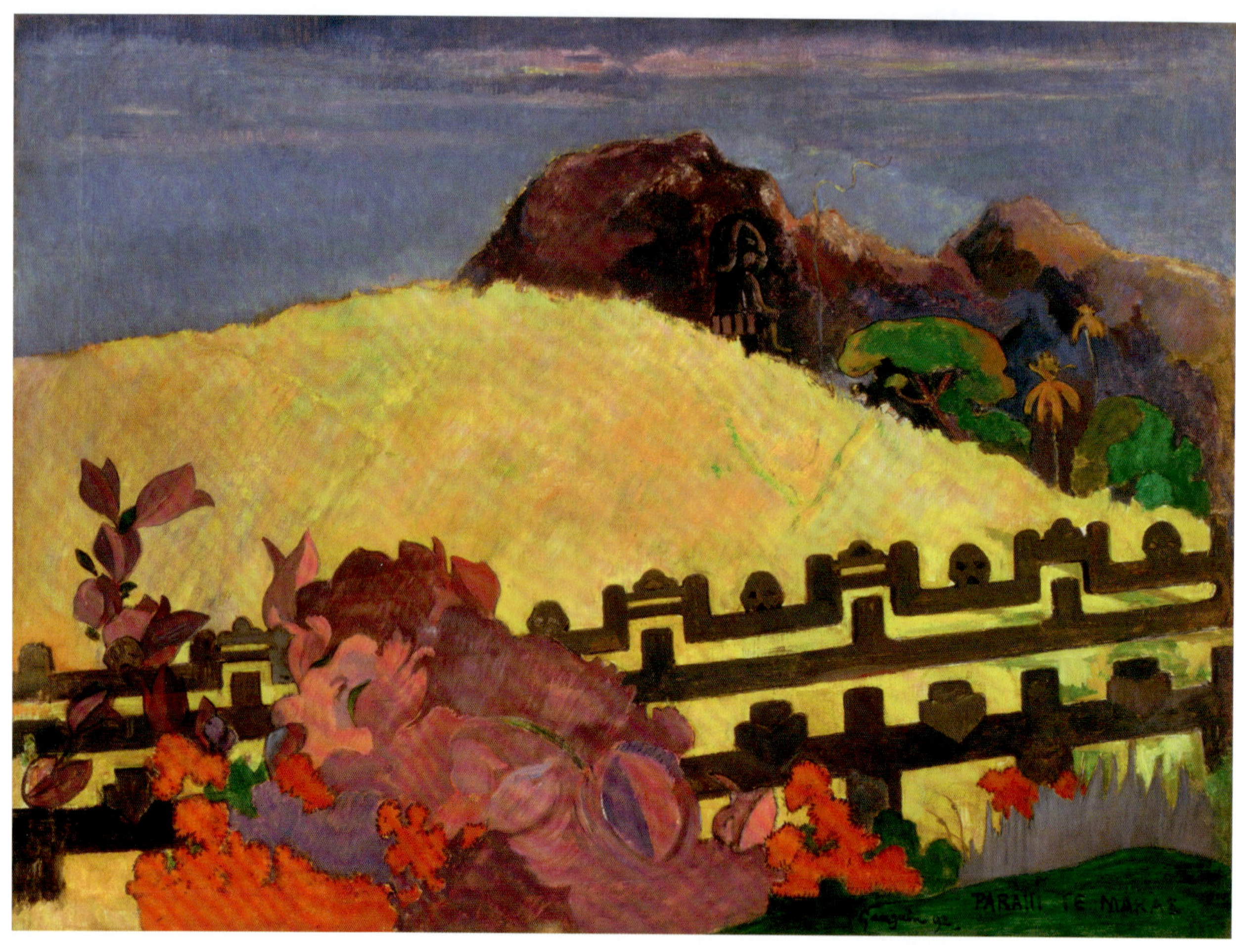

The Sacred Mountain (Parahi Te Marae)

Der heilige Berg (Parahi Te Marae)

A montanha sagrada (Parahi Te Marae)

La Montagne sacrée (Parahi Te Marae)

La montaña sagrada (Parahi Te Marae)

De heilige berg (Parahi Te Marae)

PAUL GAUGUIN (1848-1903)

1892, Oil on canvas/Huile sur toile, 66 × 89,9 cm, Philadelphia Museum of Art, Philadelphia

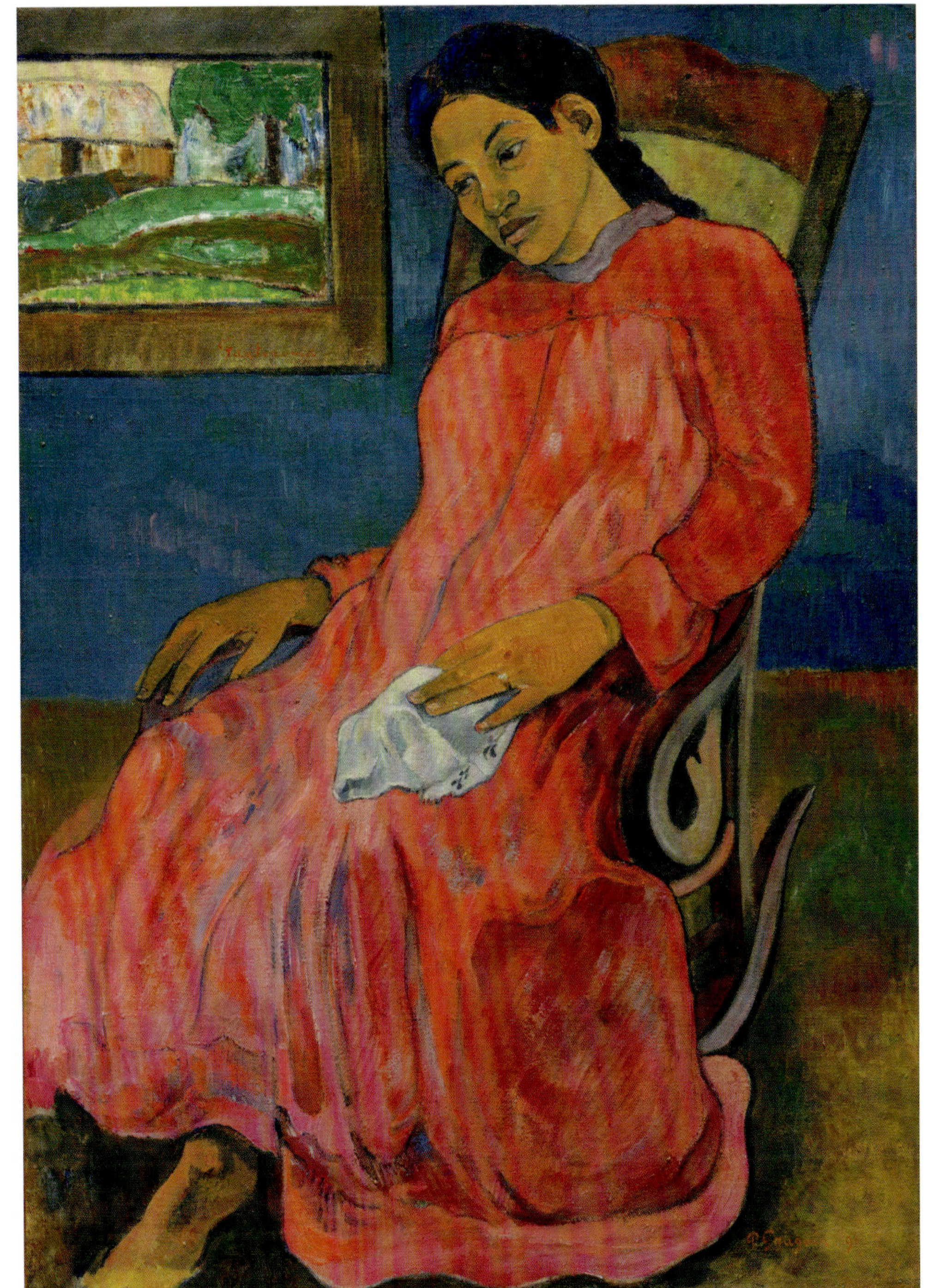

Faaturuma (Melancholic)

Faaturuma (Rêverie)

Faaturuma (Träumerei)

Faaturuma (Soñando)

Faaturuma (Sonhando)

Faaturuma (Melancholiek)

PAUL GAUGUIN (1848-1903)
1891, Oil on canvas/Huile sur toile,
93,9 × 68,2 cm, Nelson-Atkins
Museum of Art, Kansas City

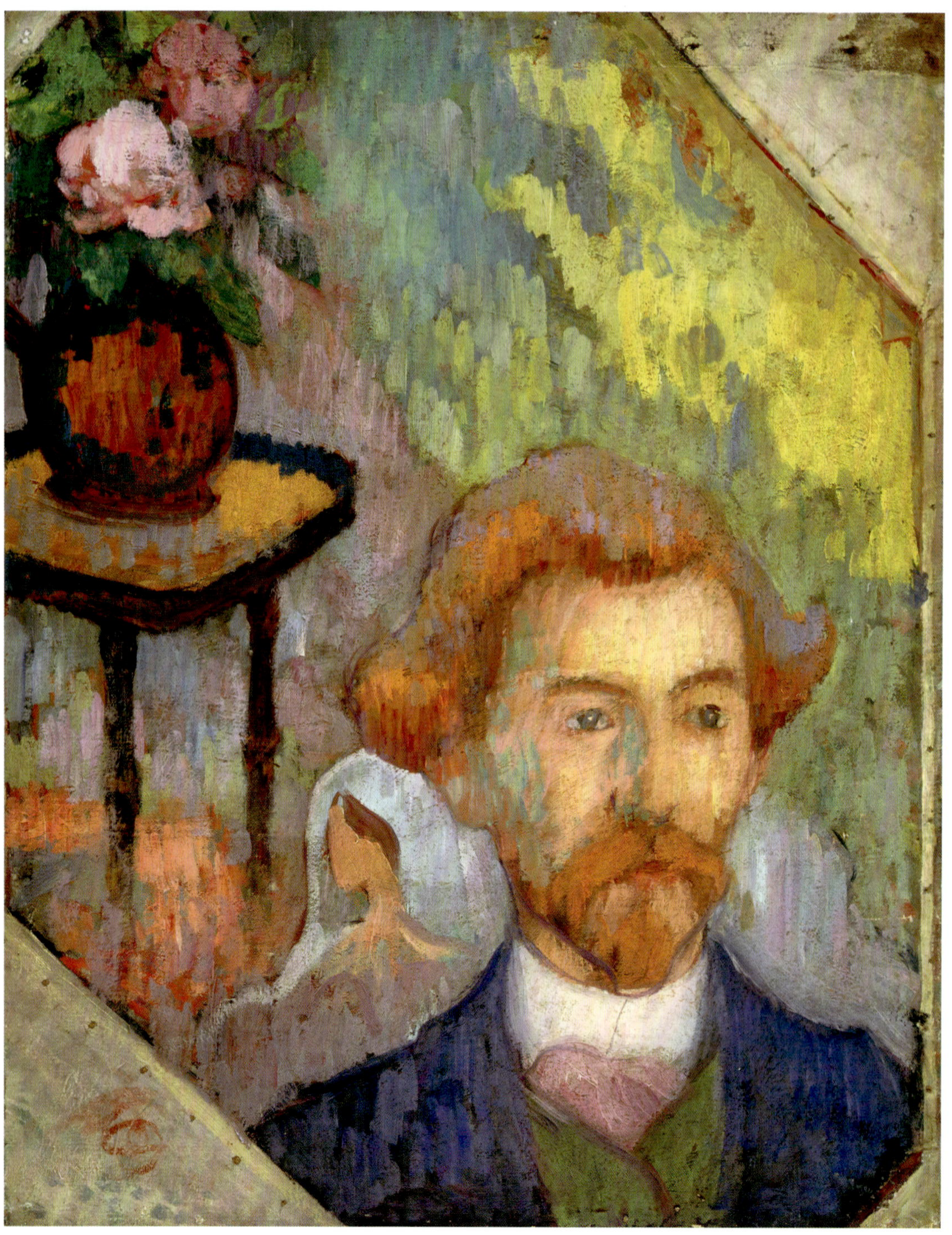

Émile Bernard

ÉMILE SCHUFFENECKER
(1851-1934)
1889, Oil on canvas/Huile sur toile, 58,4 × 46 cm, Museum of Fine Arts, Houston

Les Falaises au bord de la mer

As a member of the Pont-Aven School, Moret moved in the field of tension between Synthetism and Impressionism. The painter who was supported by Paul Durand-Ruel created more than 600 paintings.

Les Falaises au bord de la mer

Figure de l'école de Pont-Aven, Henry Moret oscille entre la tentation du synthétisme et la persistance d'un impressionnisme hérité de Monet. Soutenu par Paul Durand-Ruel, il a peint plus de six cents toiles.

Die Klippen am Meer

Als Mitglied der Schule von Pont-Aven bewegt sich Moret im Spannungsfeld zwischen Synthetismus und Impressionismus. Der von Paul Durand-Ruel unterstützte Maler schafft mehr als 600 Gemälde.

Los acantilados junto al mar

Figura de la escuela de Pont-Aven, Moret oscila entre la tentación de sintetizar y la persistencia de un impresionismo heredado de Monet. Apoyado por Paul Durand-Ruel, ha pintado más de seiscientos lienzos.

As falésias à beira-mar

Como membro da Pont-Aven School, Moret move-se no campo da tensão entre o Synthetismo e o Impressionismo. O pintor apoiado por Paul Durand-Ruel cria mais de 600 pinturas.

De kliffen bij de zee

Als lid van de school van Pont-Aven bewoog Moret zich in het spanningsveld tussen synthetisme en impressionisme. De door Paul Durand-Ruel gesteunde schilder maakte meer dan 600 schilderijen.

HENRY MORET (1856-1913)

1895, Oil on canvas/Huile sur toile, 73 × 60 cm, Private collection

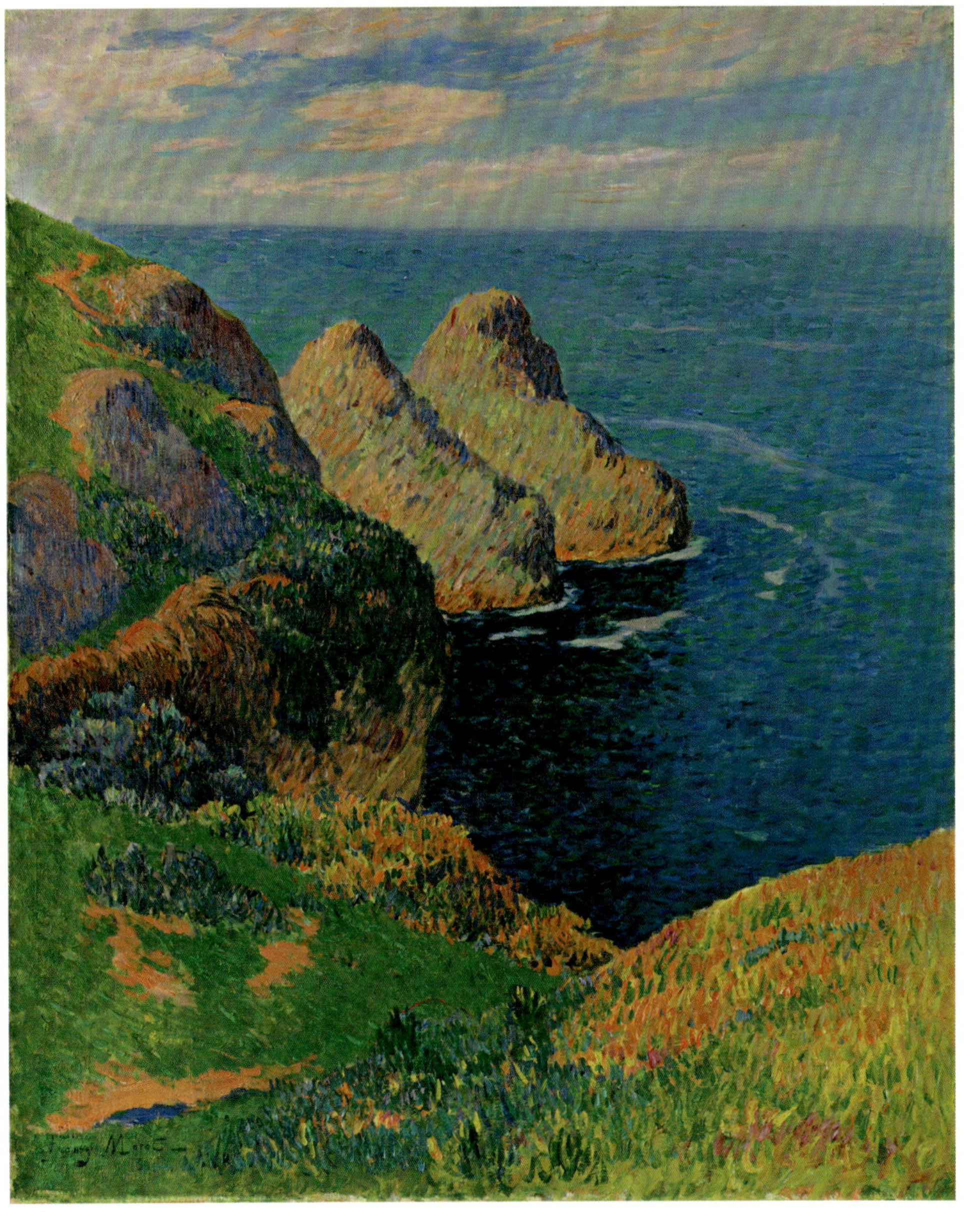

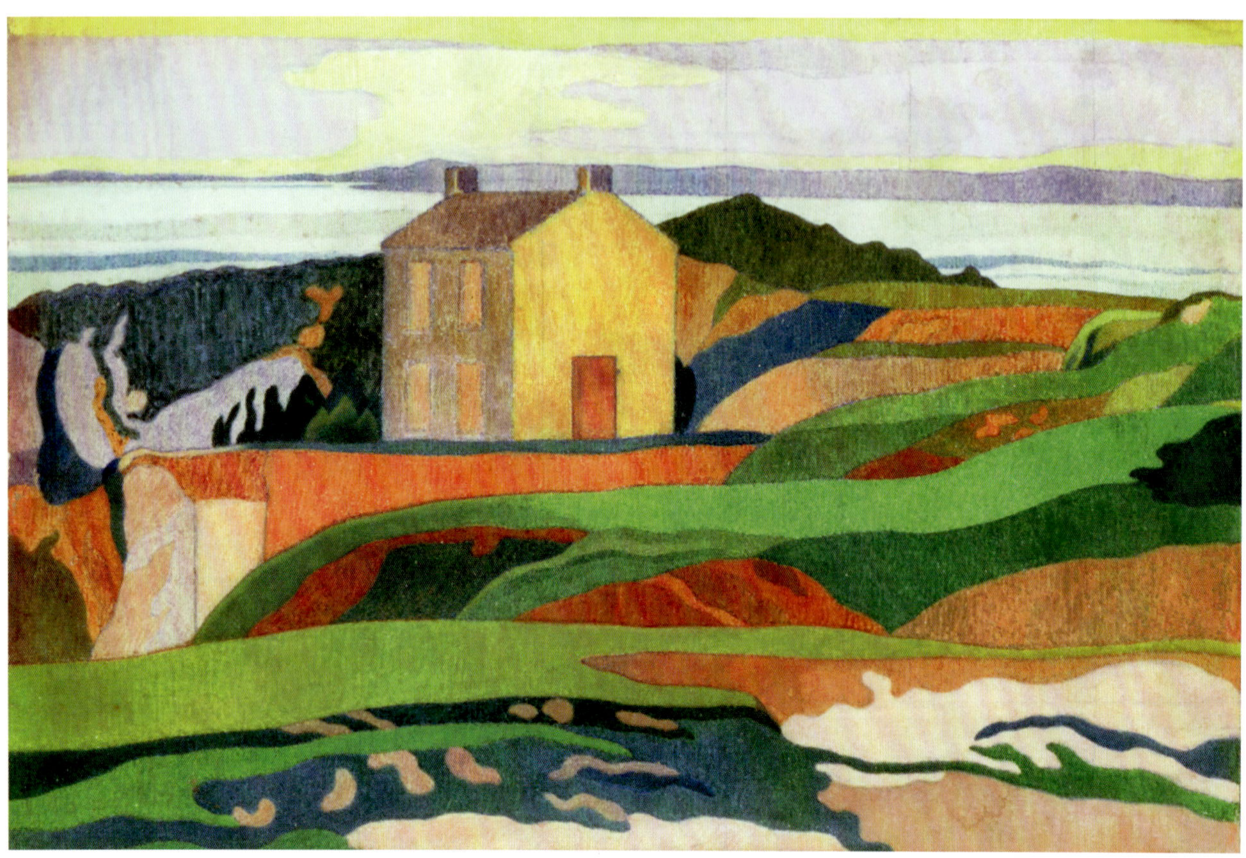

The Hangman's House

La Maison du Pen-Du, paysage parabolique

Das Haus des Gehängten

La Maison du Pen-Du, paisaje parabólico

A Casa do Enforcado

Het huis van de beul

CHARLES FILIGER (1863-1928)

c. 1890, Gouache on cardboard/Gouache sur carton, 25 × 37,5 cm, Private collection

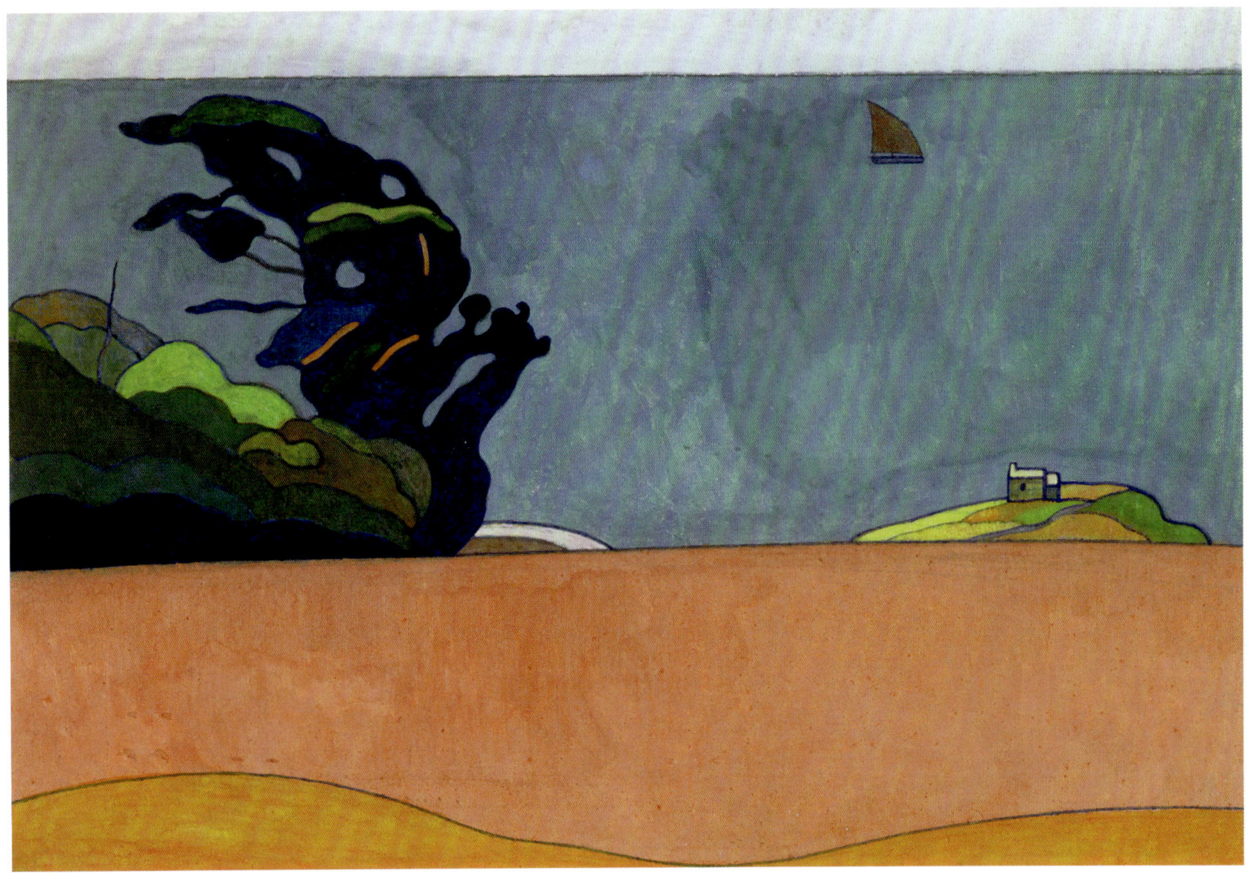

Pouldu Landscape

The influence of Japanese woodcuts is reflected in the composition of colored surfaces and fine lines. Filiger spent most of his life impoverished and withdrawn in Brittany.

Paysage du Pouldu

L'esprit des estampes japonaises habite cette composition épurée, construite par des aplats de couleurs et quelques lignes fines. Filiger passa l'essentiel de sa vie en Bretagne, reclus dans la misère.

Landschaft bei Pouldu

Der Einfluss japanischer Holzschnitte spiegelt sich in der Komposition aus Farbflächen und feinen Linien wider. Filiger verbrachte den Großteil seines Lebens verarmt und zurückgezogen in der Bretagne.

Paisaje cerca de Pouldu

La influencia de la xilografía japonesa se refleja en la composición de las superficies coloreadas y las líneas finas. Filiger pasó la mayor parte de su vida empobrecido y retirado en Bretaña.

Paisagem perto de Pouldu

A influência das xilogravuras japonesas reflecte-se na composição das superfícies coloridas e das linhas finas. Filiger passou a maior parte da sua vida empobrecido e retirado na Bretanha.

Landschap bij Pouldu

De invloed van Japanse houtsneden wordt weerspiegeld in de compositie van kleurvlakken en fijne lijnen. Filiger bracht het grootste deel van zijn leven verarmd en teruggetrokken door in Bretagne.

CHARLES FILIGER (1863-1928)

c. 1892, Gouache on paper/Gouache sur papier, 26 × 38,5 cm, Musée des Beaux-Arts, Quimper

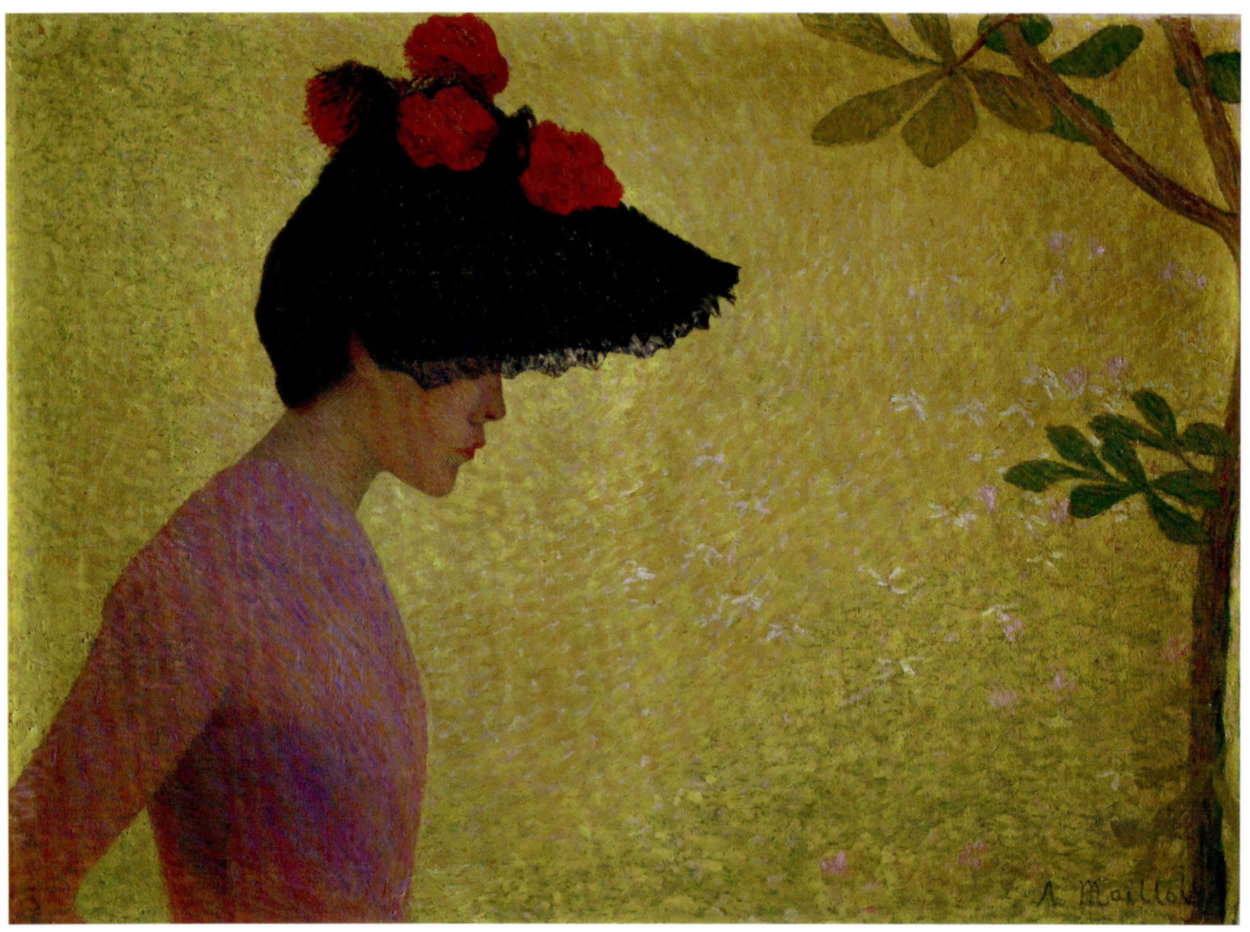

Woman in Profile

Maillol, known as a sculptor, also created some paintings, especially portraits of women. The delicate profile with Japanese influences stands out against a background of a stylized tree.

Profil de femme

Plus connu comme sculpteur, Maillol a également peint, principalement des figures féminines. Ce portrait japonisant, tout en délicatesse, se détache d'un fond dont le seul décor est un arbre stylisé.

Frau im Profil

Der als Bildhauer bekannte Maillol, schuf auch einige Gemälde, insbesondere Frauenporträts. Das zarte Profil mit japanischen Einflüssen hebt sich von einem Hintergrund mit einem stilisierten Baum ab.

Mujer de perfil

Maillol, conocido como escultor, también realizó algunas pinturas, especialmente retratos de mujeres. El delicado perfil con influencias japonesas destaca sobre el fondo de un árbol estilizado.

Mulher em perfil

Maillol, conhecido como escultor, também criou algumas pinturas, especialmente retratos de mulheres. O perfil delicado com influências japonesas destaca-se no fundo de uma árvore estilizada.

Vrouw en profil

De als beeldhouwer bekende Maillol maakte ook enkele schilderijen, vooral vrouwenportretten. Het delicate profiel met Japanse invloeden komt los van de achtergrond met een gestileerde boom.

ARISTIDE MAILLOL (1861-1944)

c. 1896, Oil on canvas/Huile sur toile, 73,5 × 103 cm, Musée Hyacinthe Rigaud, Perpignan

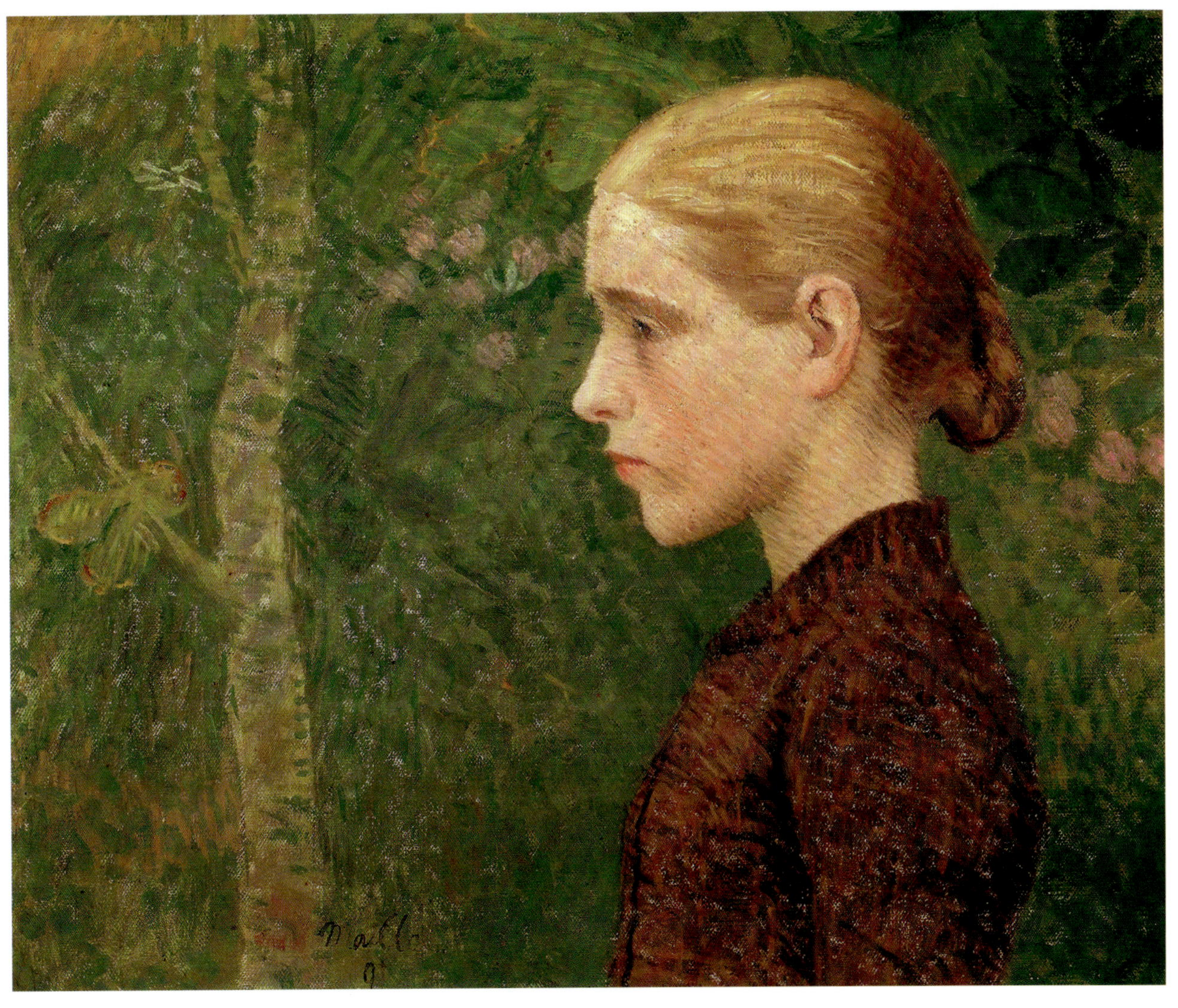

Bust of a young Peasant

Buste de jeune paysanne

Brustbild einer jungen Bäuerin

Retrato de una joven granjera

Retrato de meio comprimento da mulher de um jovem agricultor

Buste van een jonge boerin

ARISTIDE MAILLOL (1861-1944)

1891, Oil on canvas/Huile sur toile, 46 × 55,8 cm, Musée des Beaux-Arts, Reims

Landscape at Pont-Aven

Maufra met Gauguin in 1890 in Pont-Aven. Shortly thereafter he resided at Mary Henry's inn in Pouldu. In 1893 he moved into a studio in the Bateau-Lavoir in Paris. Brittany remained his greatest inspiration.

Vue du port de Pont-Aven

Maufra rencontre Gauguin à Pont-Aven en 1890, puis fréquente l'auberge de Mary Henry au Pouldu. S'il s'installe au Bateau-Lavoir, à Paris, en 1893, la Bretagne restera sa principale source d'inspiration.

Blick auf den Hafen von Pont-Aven

Maufra lernt Gauguin 1890 in Pont-Aven kennen. Kurz danach residiert er im Gasthaus von Mary Henry in Pouldu. 1893 bezieht er ein Atelier im Bateau-Lavoir in Paris. Die Bretagne blieb seine größte Inspiration.

Vista del puerto de Pont-Aven

Maufra conoció a Gauguin en 1890 en Pont-Aven. Poco después reside en la posada de Mary Henry en Pouldu. En 1893 se traslada a un estudio en el Bateau-Lavoir de París. La Bretaña sigue siendo su mayor inspiración.

Vista do porto de Pont-Aven

Maufra conheceu Gauguin em 1890 em Pont-Aven. Pouco depois, ele reside na pousada de Mary Henry em Pouldu. 1893 muda-se para um estúdio no Bateau-Lavoir em Paris. A Bretanha continuou a ser a sua maior inspiração.

Gezicht op de haven van Pont-Aven

Maufra leerde Gauguin in 1890 in Pont-Aven kennen. Kort daarna verbleef hij in de herberg van Mary Henry in Pouldu. In 1893 betrok hij en atelier in Le Bateau-Lavoir in Parijs. Bretagne bleef zijn grootste inspiratiebron.

MAXIME MAUFRA (1861-1918)
c. 1894, Oil on canvas/Huile sur toile, 150 × 300,5 cm, Musée des Beaux-Arts, Quimper

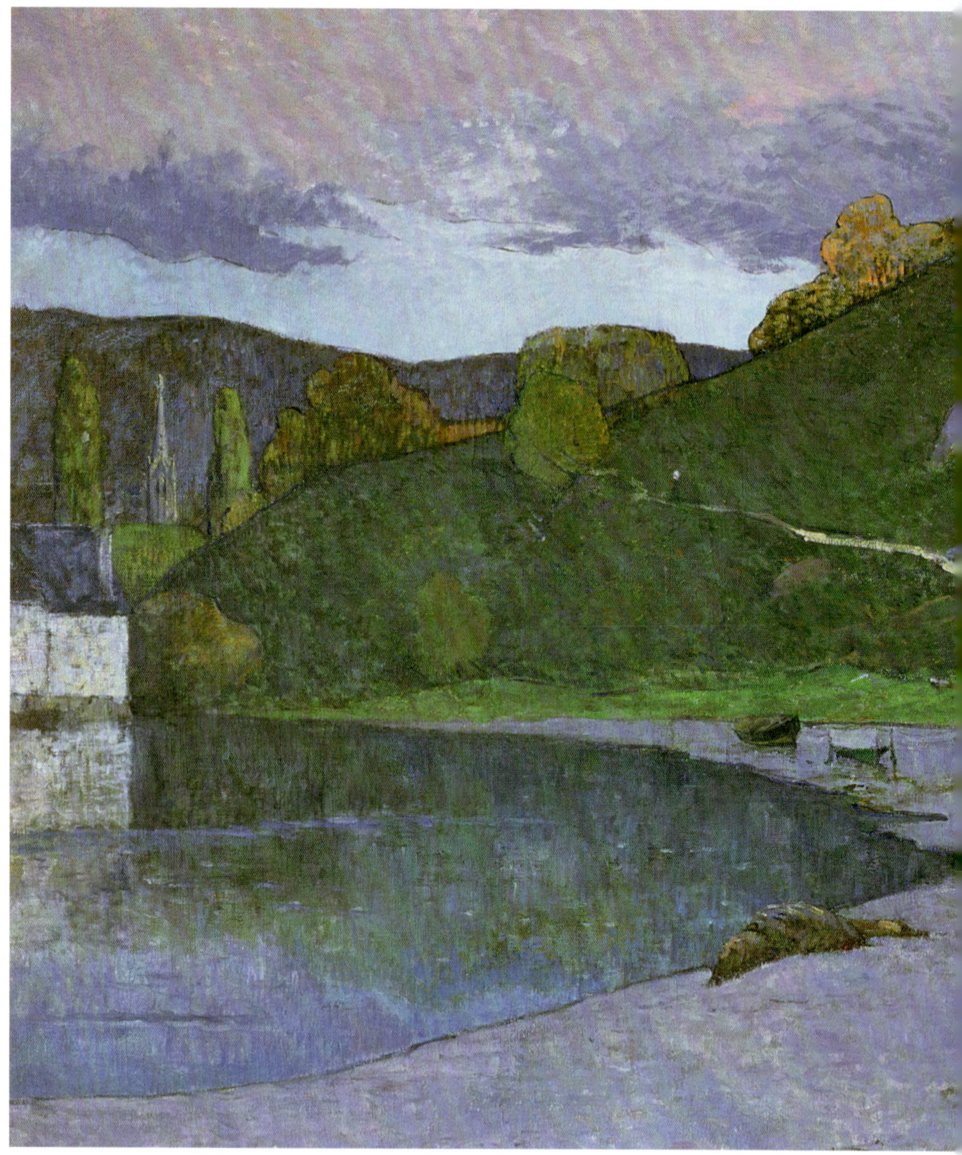

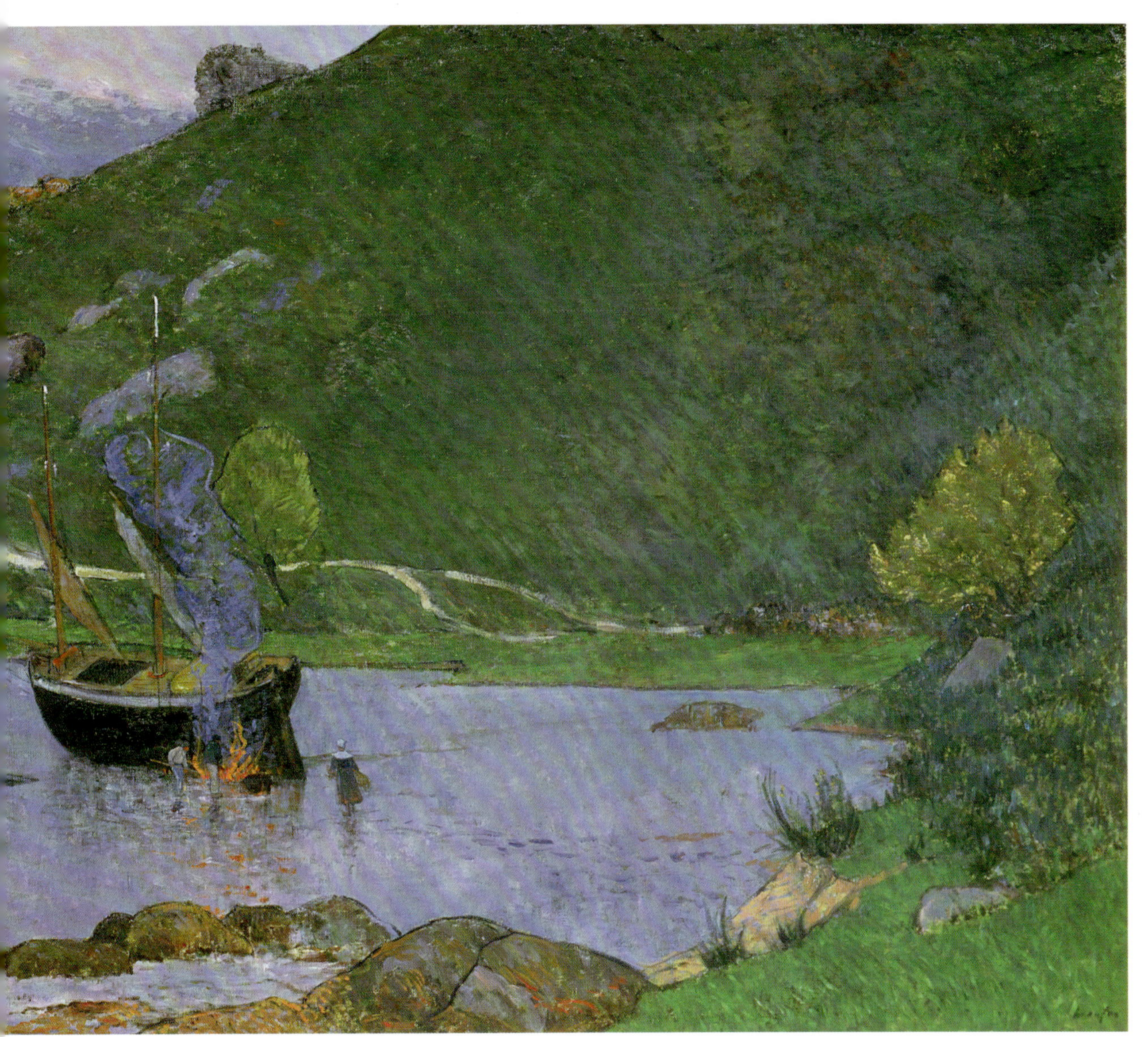

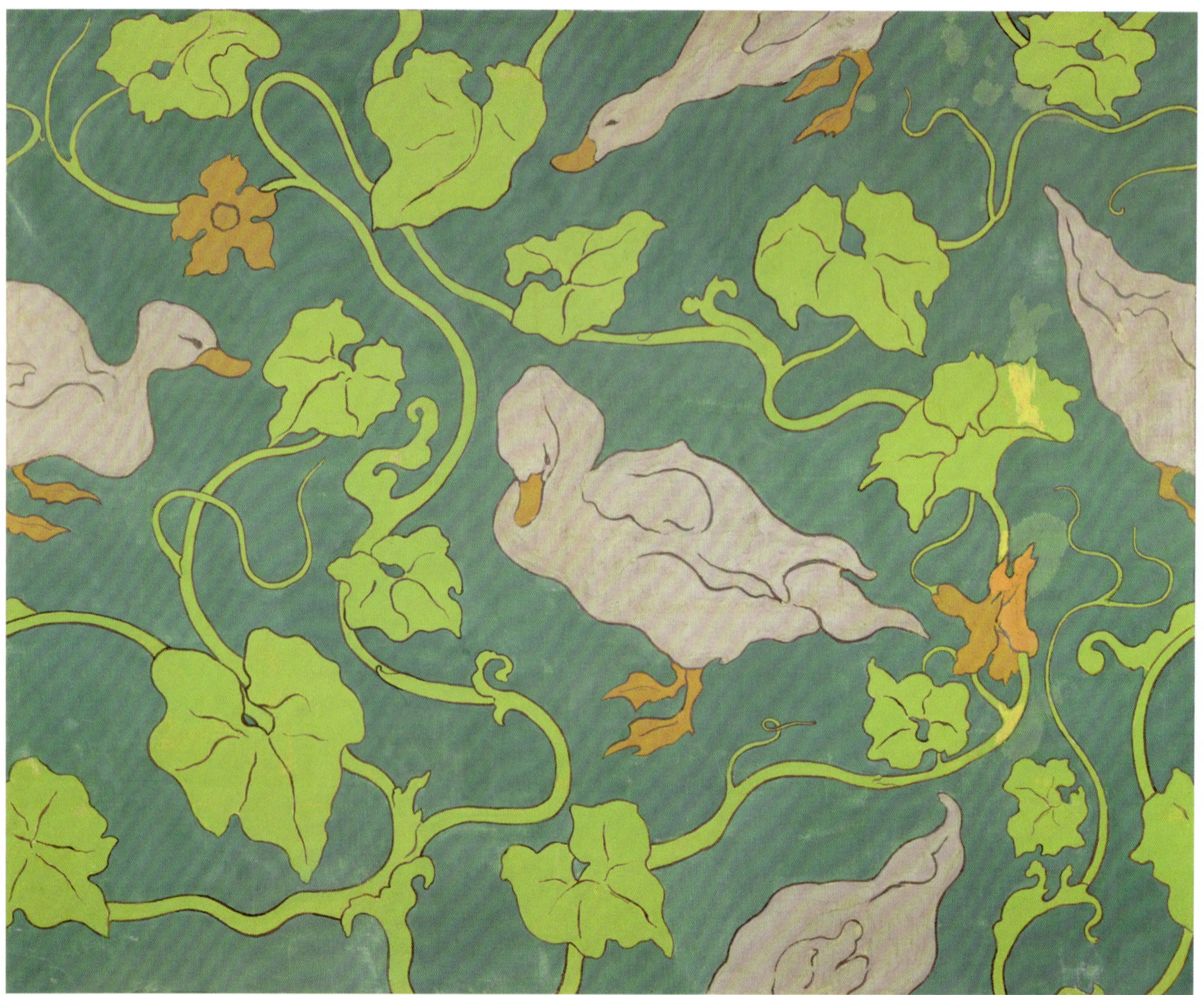

The Ducks

Les Canards

Die Enten

Los patos

Os patos

De eenden

PAUL RANSON (1861-1909)

c. 1884/85, Wallpaper design/Projet de papier peint, 65 × 81 cm, Musée des Beaux-Arts, Quimper

404

A Woman in Red

Une femme en rouge

Eine Frau in Rot

Una mujer de rojo

Uma mulher de vermelho

Een vrouw in het rood

PAUL RANSON (1861-1909)

1893, 150 x 100 cm,
Collection Ranson, Paris

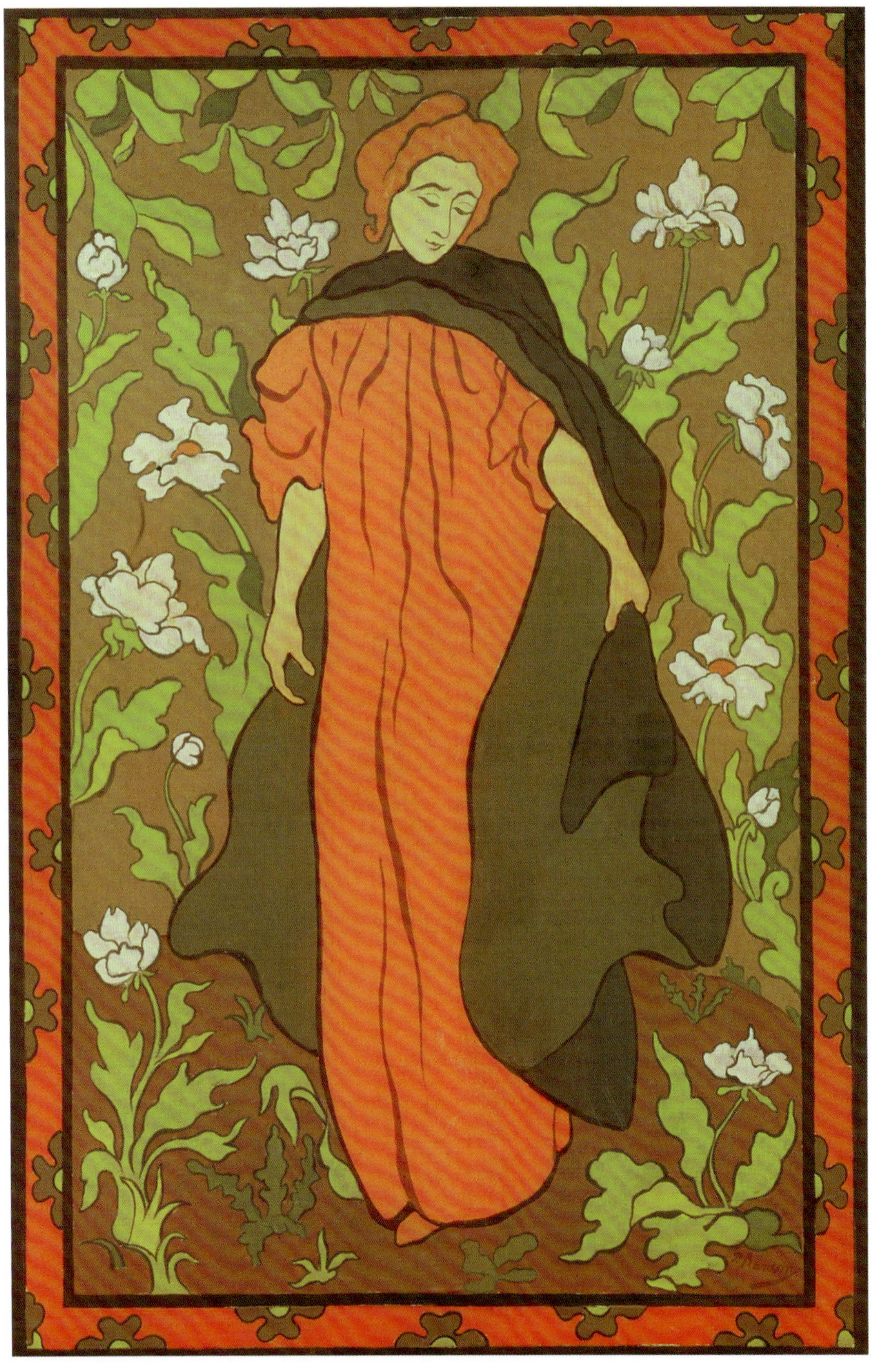

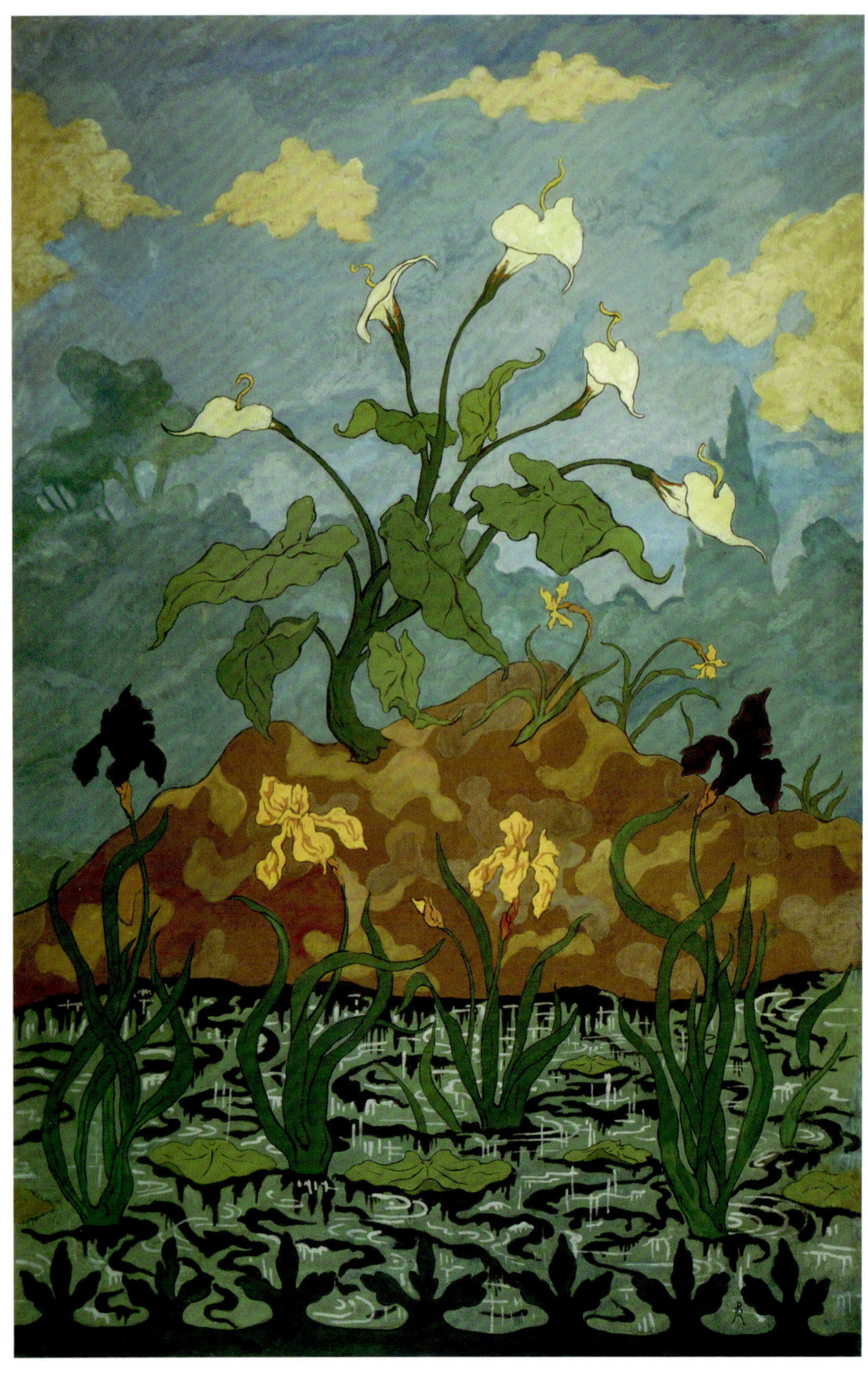

Lilies, Purple and Yellow Irises

Arums et iris violets et jaunes

Aronstab, lila und gelbe Lilien

Arum, lirios morados y amarillos

Arum, lírios roxos e amarelos

Aronskelk, paarse en gele lelies

PAUL RANSON (1861-1909)

1899, Oil on canvas/Huile sur toile,
245,2 × 163,9 cm, Private collection

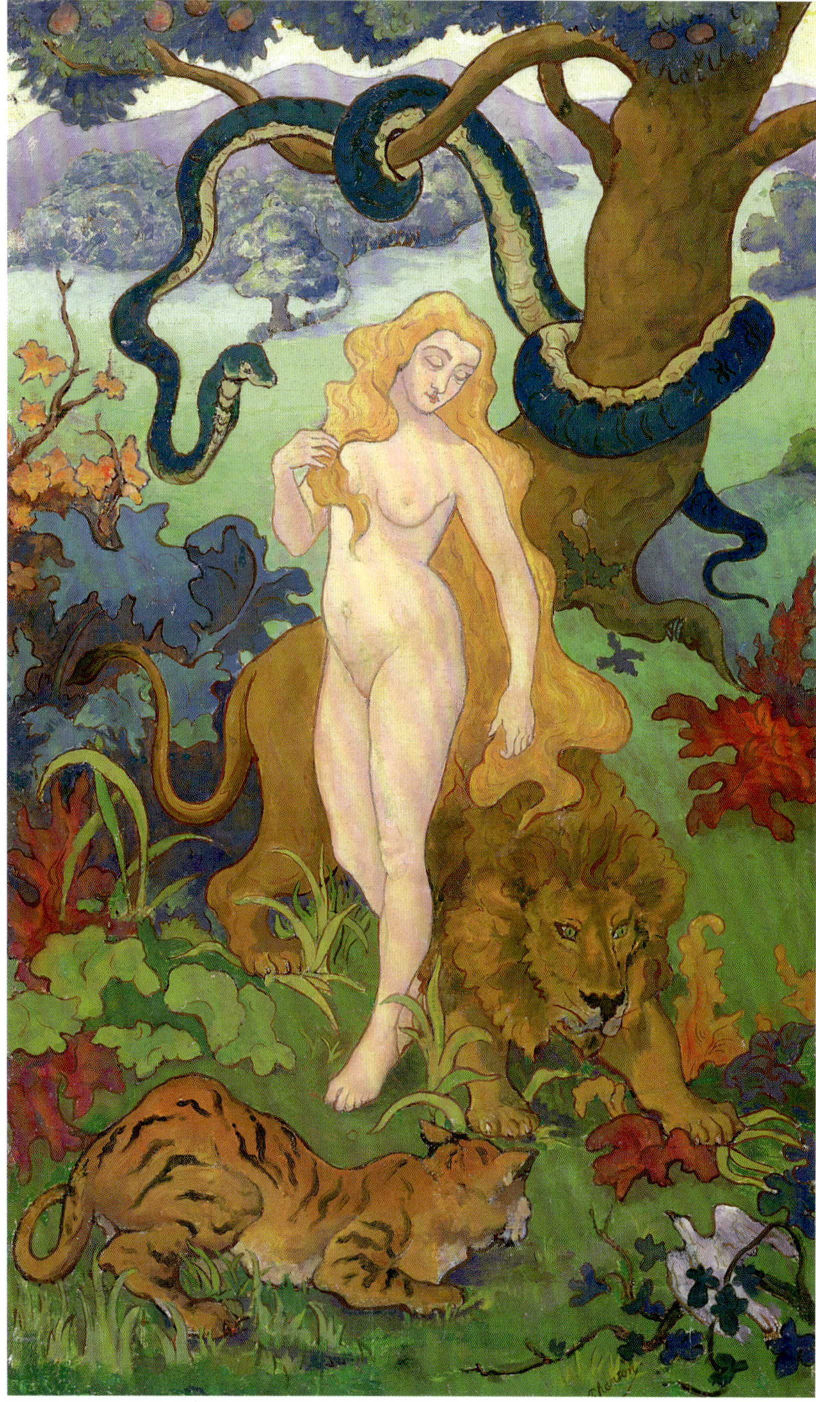

Eve

Ève

Eva

Eva

Eva

Eva

PAUL RANSON (1861-1909)

c. 1895, Oil on canvas/Huile sur toile,
85 × 51 cm, Musée des Beaux-Arts, Rennes

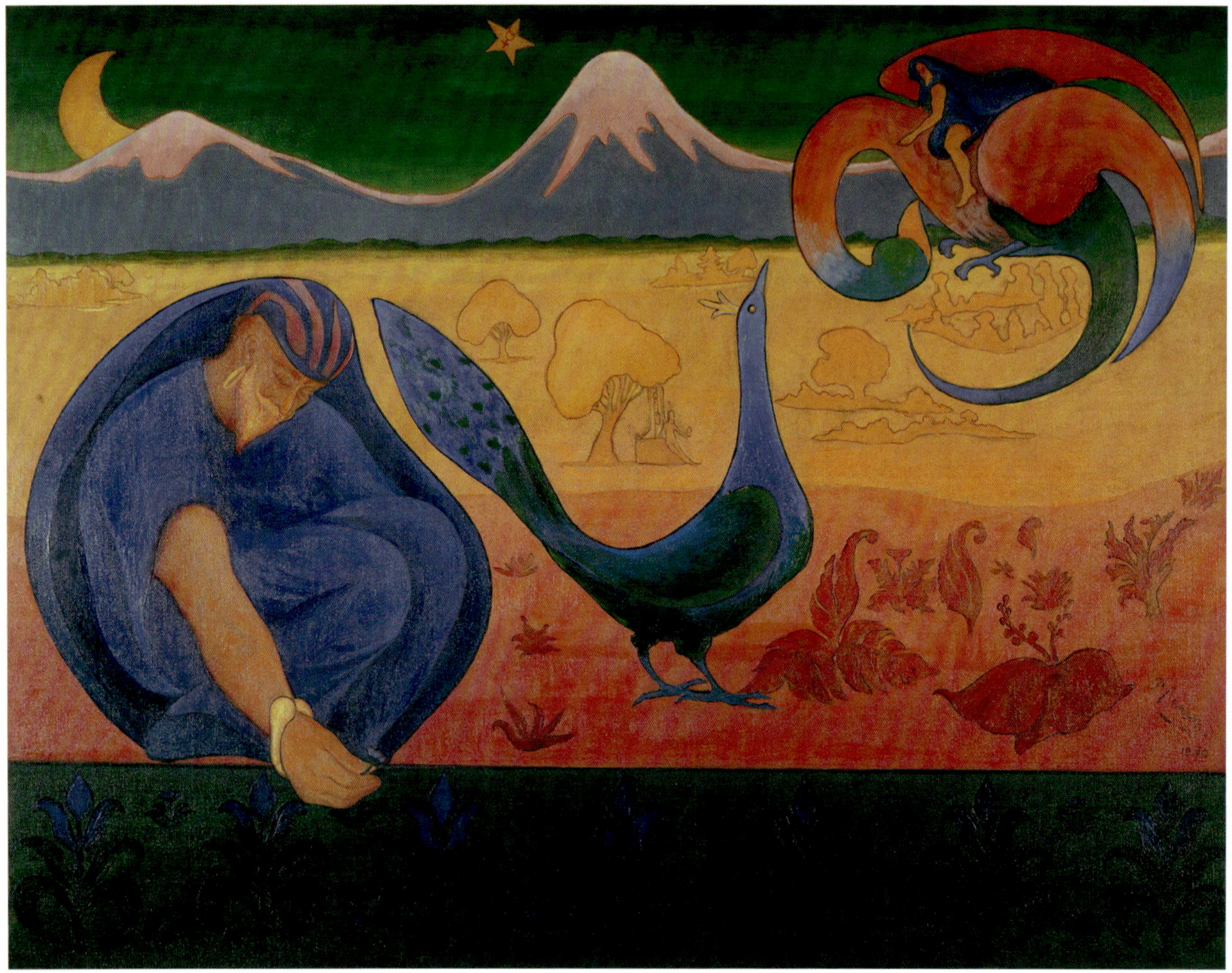

Nabi Landscape

Le Paysage nabique

Nabi-Landschaft

Paisaje de Nabi

Paisagem Nabi

Paesaggio nabi

PAUL RANSON (1861-1909)

1890, Oil on canvas/Huile sur toile, 90 × 114 cm, Private collection

Lustral

The title alludes to the holy water for the purification of souls. The artist from the Nabis group depicts a naked woman at her toilet between floral motifs in shades of blue and green.

Lustral

Allusion au Moyen Âge, le titre évoque l'eau lustrale qui purifie les âmes. L'artiste nabi peint une femme nue à sa toilette, entourée de motifs floraux, dans un sublime camaïeu de bleus et de verts.

Lustral

Der Titel spielt auf das heilige Wasser zur Seelenreinigung an. Der Künstler aus der Gruppe der Nabis stellt eine nackte Frau bei der Toilette zwischen floralen Motiven dar, die in Blau- und Grüntönen gehalten sind.

Lustral

El título alude al agua bendita para la purificación de las almas. El artista del grupo Nabis representa a una mujer desnuda en el baño entre motivos florales en tonos azules y verdes.

Lustral

O título alude à água benta para a purificação das almas. O artista do grupo Nabis retrata uma mulher nua na sanita entre motivos florais em tons de azul e verde.

Lustral

De titel verwijst naar het heilige water voor de zuivering van de zielen. De schilder, lid van de Nabis, schilderde een naakte vrouw bij haar toilet tussen bloemmotieven in blauw- en groentinten.

PAUL RANSON (1861–1909)

1891, Tempera on canvas/Tempera sur toile, 35,5 × 24 cm, Musée d'Orsay, Paris

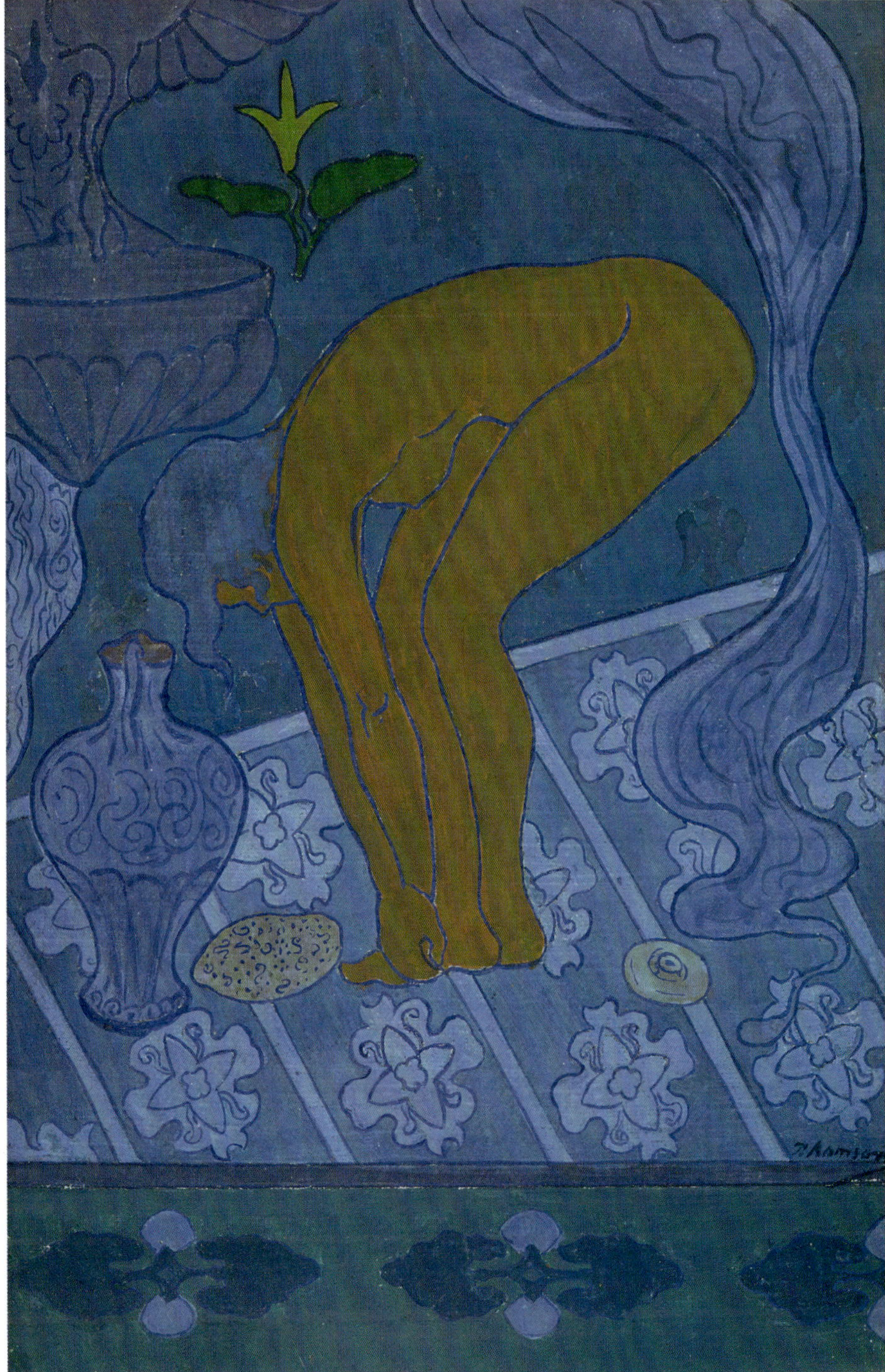

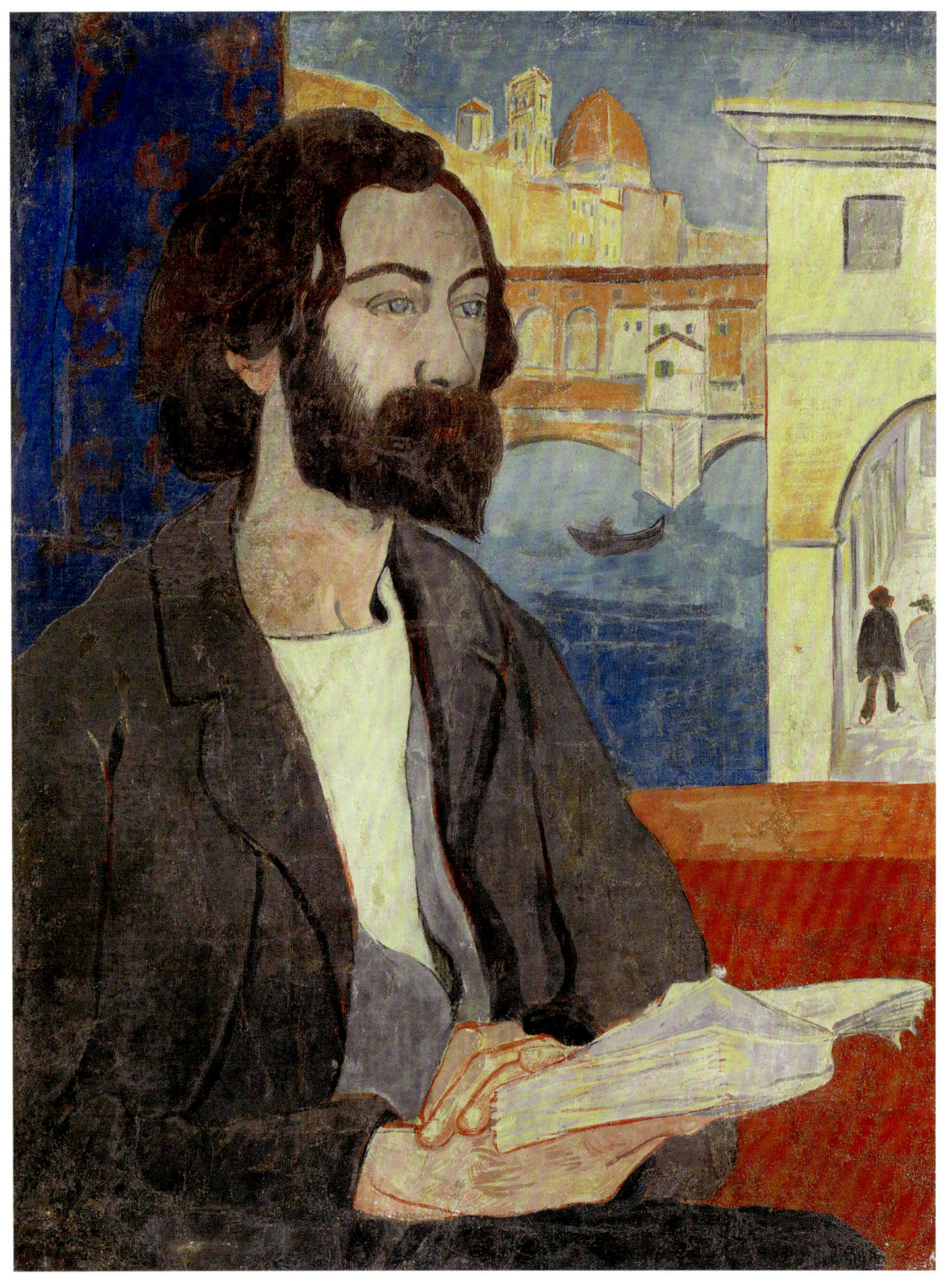

Portrait of Émile
Bernard in Florence

Portrait d'Émile
Bernard à Florence

Porträt des Émile
Bernard in Florenz

Retrato de Émile
Bernard en Florencia

Retrato de Émile
Bernard em Florença

Portret van Émile
Bernard in Florence

PAUL SÉRUSIER
(1864-1927)

1893, Tempera on canvas/
Tempera sur toile,
73,3 × 56,1 cm,
Private collection

The Talisman *or* The Swallow-hole in the Bois d'Amour

The work, written in 1888 in Pont-Aven, became a manifesto of Syntheticism. During a lesson, Gauguin encouraged his student Sérusier to give free rein to his feelings by looking at the landscape.

Le Talisman, l'Aven au bois d'Amour

Cette œuvre est considérée comme le manifeste du synthétisme, né à Pont-Aven en 1888. Au cours d'une « leçon » de peinture devenue célèbre, Gauguin encourage Sérusier à peindre sa sensation face au paysage.

Der Talisman

Das 1888 in Pont-Aven entstandene Werk wurde zum Manifest des Synthetismus. Im Verlauf einer Unterrichtsstunde ermutigt Gauguin seinen Schüler Sérusier, seinen Gefühlen beim Anblick der Landschaft freien Lauf zu lassen.

El Talismán

La obra, creada en 1888 en Pont-Aven, se convirtió en un manifiesto de sintetismo. Durante una clase, Gauguin anima a su alumno Sérusier a dar rienda suelta a sus sentimientos mirando el paisaje.

O Talismã

A obra, escrita em 1888 em Pont-Aven, tornou-se um manifesto de sintetismo. Durante uma aula, Gauguin encoraja o seu aluno Sérusier a dar rédea solta aos seus sentimentos ao olhar para a paisagem.

De talisman

Het in 1888 in Pont-Aven geschilderde werk werd het manifest van het synthetisme. Tijdens een les had Gauguin zijn leerling Sérusier aangemoedigd om bij het bekijken van het landschap zijn gevoelens de vrije loop te laten.

PAUL SÉRUSIER (1864-1927)

1888, Oil on wood/Huile sur bois, 27 × 21 cm, Musée d'Orsay, Paris

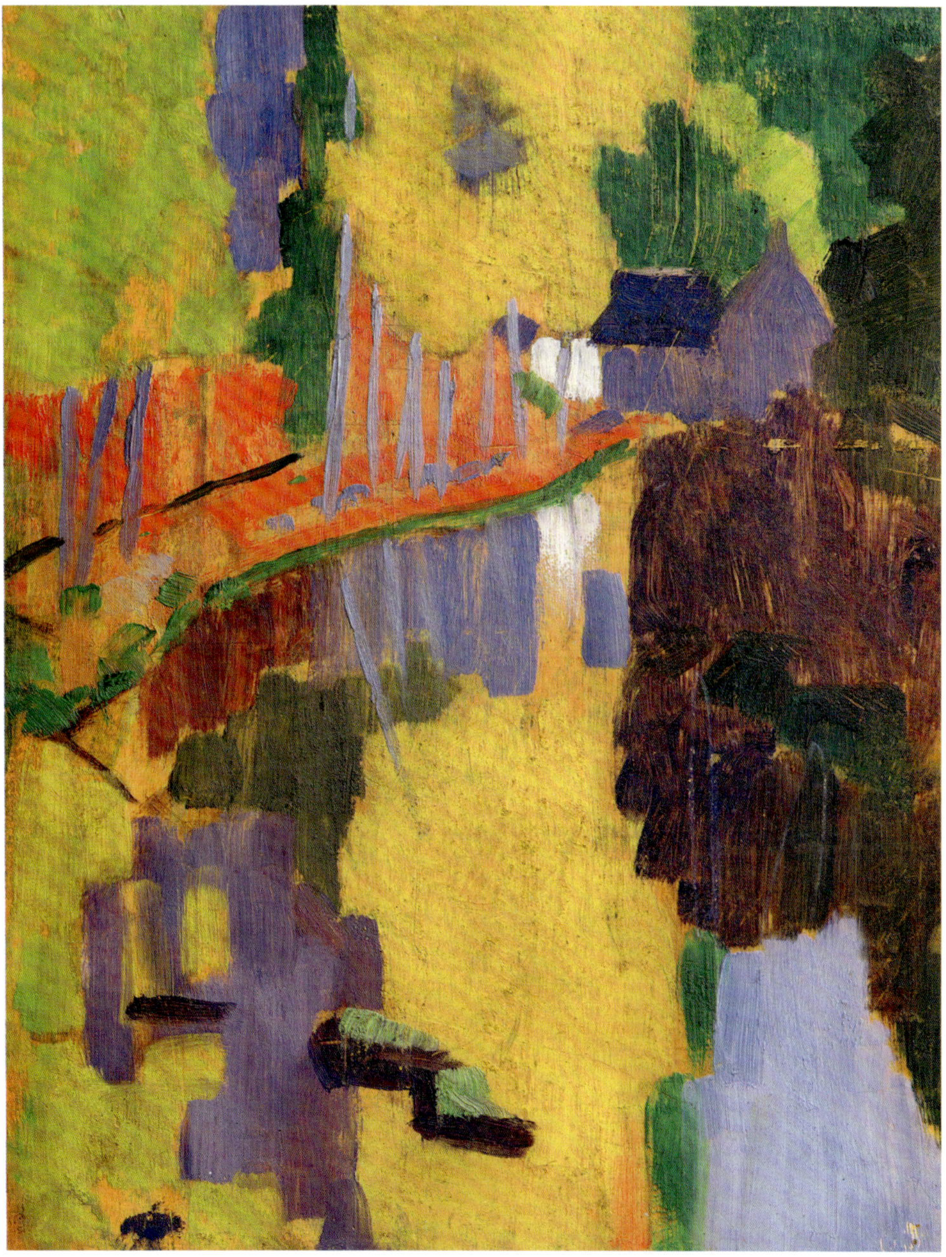

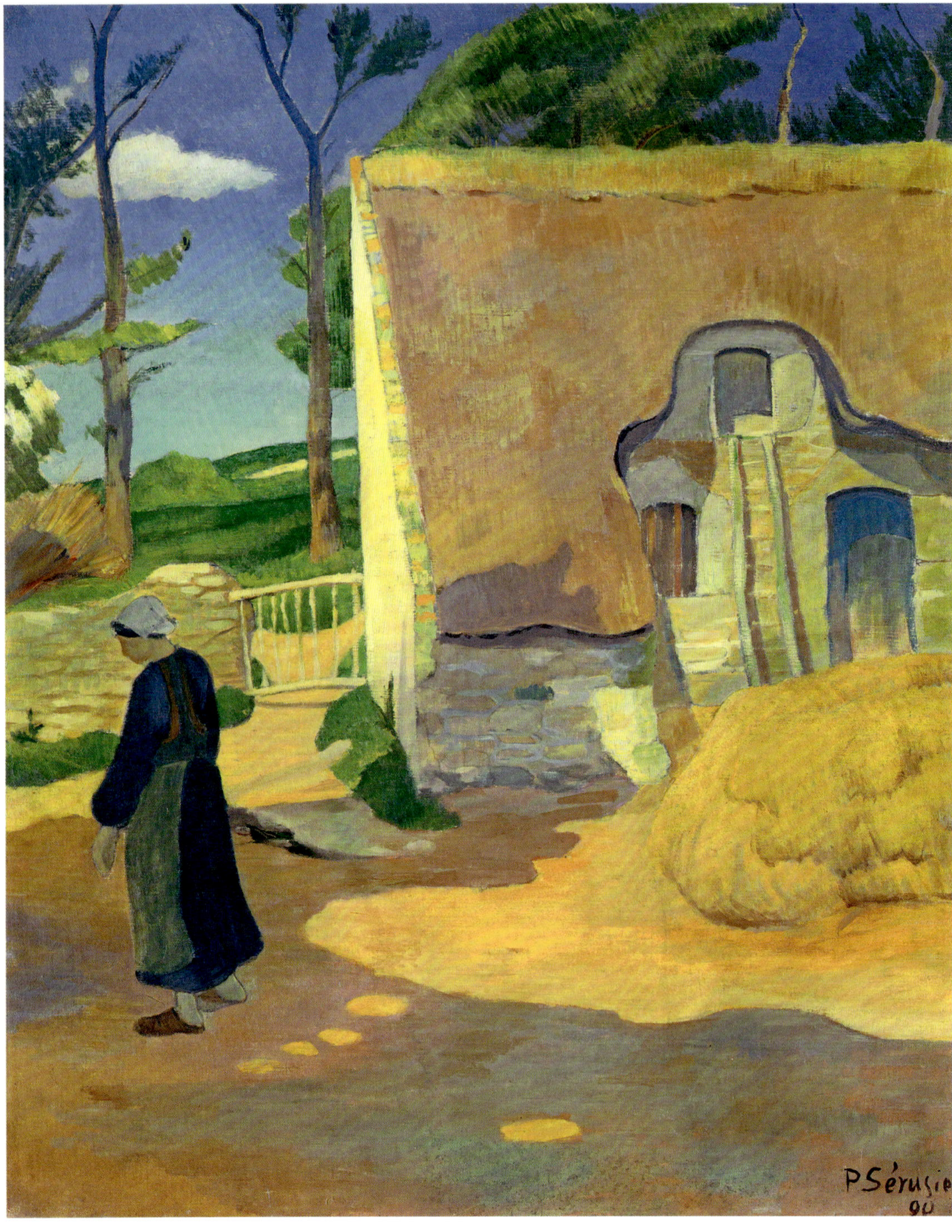

Farmhouse
at Le Pouldu

Ferme au
Pouldu

Bauernhaus
in Le Pouldu

Masía en
Le Pouldu

Quinta em
Le Pouldu

Boerderij in
Le Pouldu

PAUL SÉRUSIER
(1864-1927)
1890, Oil on
canvas/
Huile sur toile,
72 × 60 cm,
National
Gallery of Art,
Washington

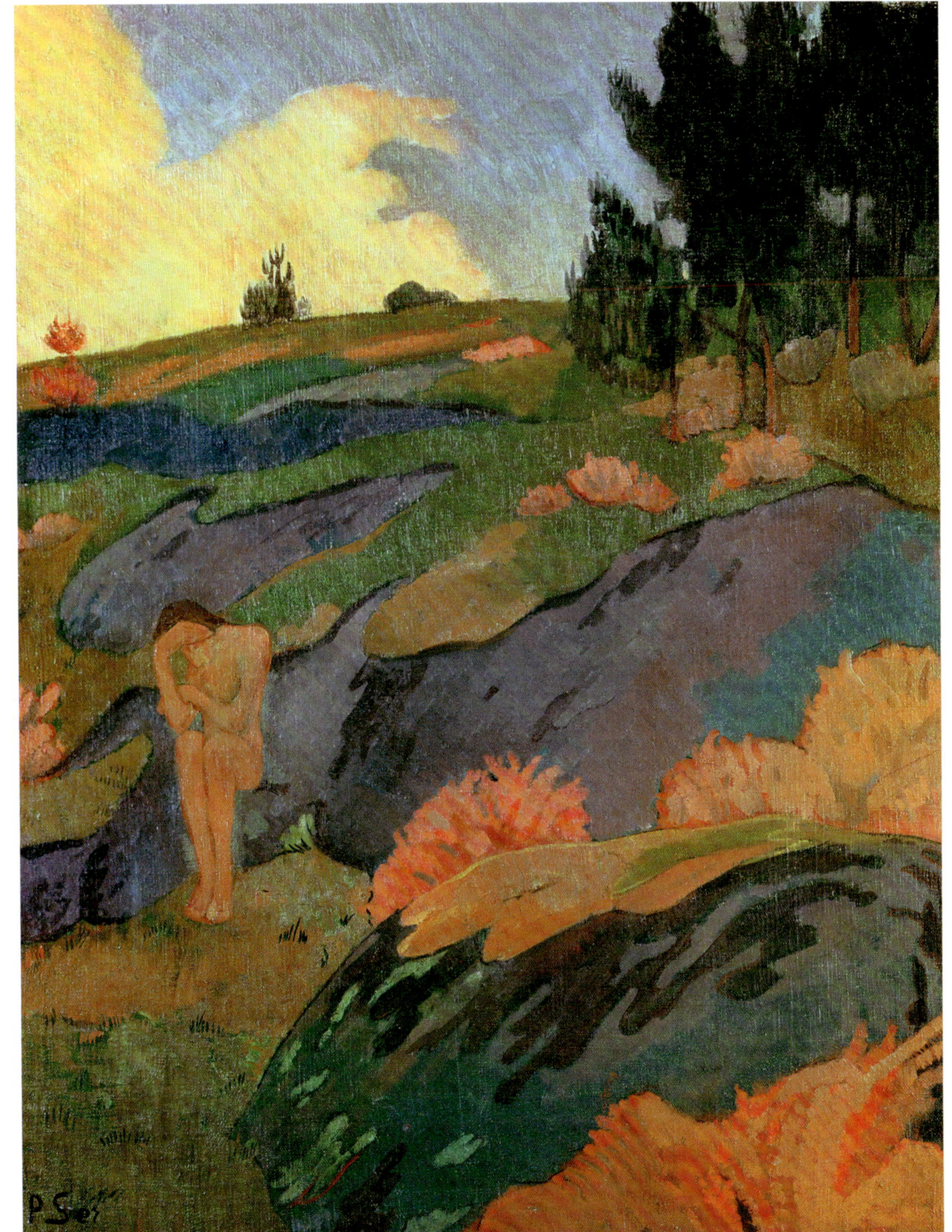

Breton Eve *or*
melancholy

Ève bretonne *ou*
Mélancolie

Bretonische Eva
oder Melancholie

La víspera bretona
o la melancolía

Bretão Eva *ou*
melancolia

Bretonse Eva *of*
Melancholie

PAUL SÉRUSIER
(1864-1927)
1890, Oil on canvas/Huile
sur toile, 72,6 × 58,3 cm,
Musée d'Orsay, Paris

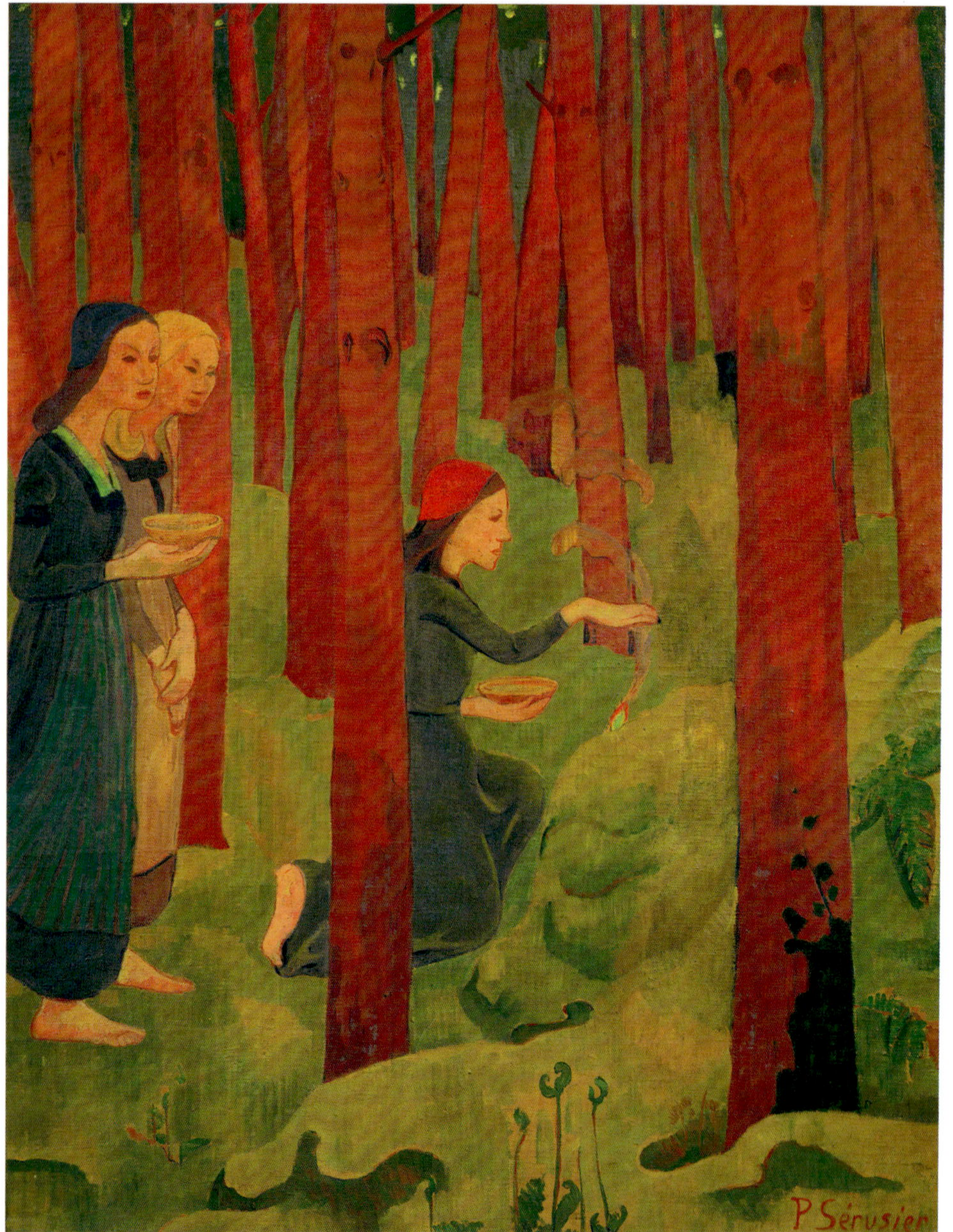

The Incantation *or* **The Holy Wood**

Sérusier was enthusiastic about Breton rituals, cults and legends. The sacred forest was often taken up as a theme by the Nabis. The artist staged a mysterious festival between the dense reddish trees.

L'Incantation *ou* **Le Bois sacré**

Rites, cultes et légendes bretonnes passionnent Sérusier, et le thème du bois sacré est très prisé des Nabis. L'artiste met en scène une étrange célébration, parmi les arbres rouges d'une forêt dense.

Die Beschwörung *oder* **Der heilige Hain**

Sérusier begeistert sich für bretonische Rituale, Kulte und Legenden. Der heilige Wald wird oft von den Nabis als Thema aufgegriffen. Der Künstler inszeniert ein mysteriöses Fest zwischen den dichten rötlichen Bäumen.

El conjuro *o* **El bosque sagrado**

Serusier es un apasionado de los rituales, cultos y leyendas bretonas, y el tema del bosque sagrado es muy popular entre los Nabis. El artista escenifica una extraña celebración entre los árboles rojos de un denso bosque.

A Convocação *ou* **o Bosque Sagrado**

Sérusier é entusiasta dos rituais, cultos e lendas bretões. A floresta sagrada é muitas vezes abordada como tema pela Nabis. O artista encena um misterioso festival entre as densas árvores avermelhadas.

De bezwering *of* **Het heilige bos**

Sérusier hield van Bretonse rituelen, culten en legenden. Het heilige bos wordt door de Nabis vaak als thema gebruikt. De schilder ensceneerde een mysterieus feest tussen de dichte, roodachtige bomen.

PAUL SÉRUSIER (1864-1927)

1891, Oil on canvas/Huile sur toile, 91,5 × 72 cm, Musée des Beaux-Arts, Quimper

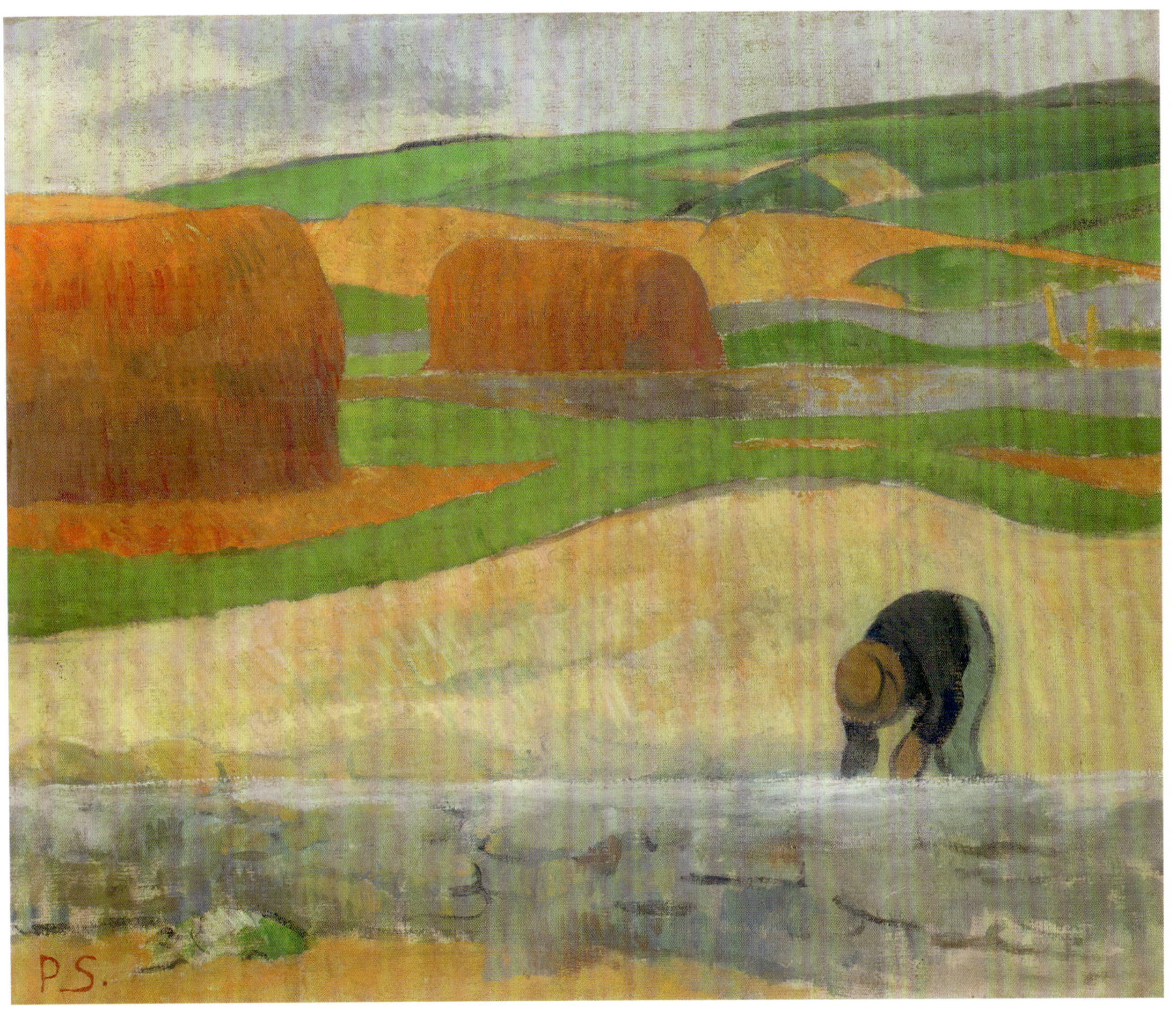

Seaweed Gatherer

Le Ramasseur de goémons

Der Tangsammler

Recolector de algas

O Coletor Tang

De zeewierverzamelaar

PAUL SÉRUSIER (1864-1927)

c. 1889, Oil on canvas/Huile sur toile, 46 × 55 cm, Indianapolis Museum of Art, Newfields

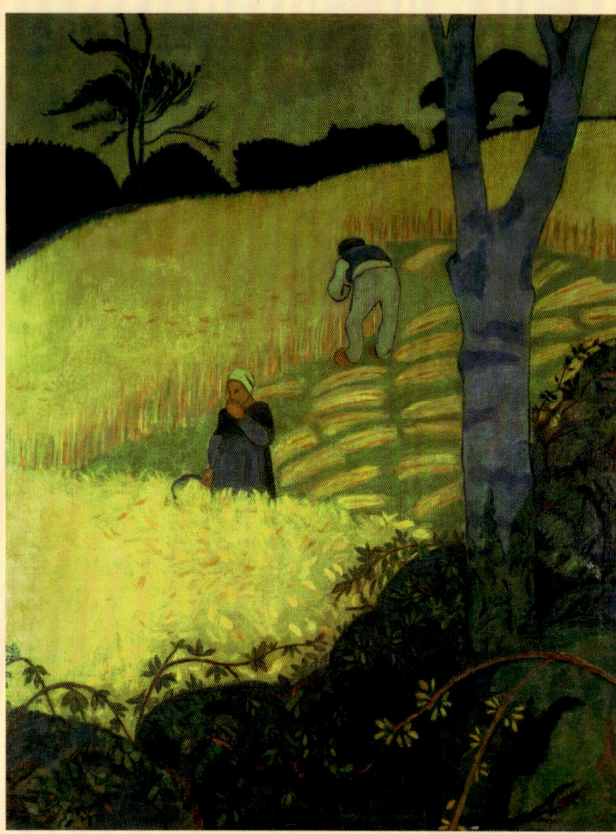

Harvest Scene

Scène de récolte

Ernte-Szene

Escena de cosecha

Cena de colheita

Oogstscène

PAUL SÉRUSIER (1864-1927)

n. d., Oil on canvas/Huile sur toile,
Private collection

The School of Pont-Aven

The School of Pont-Aven brought together artists
from various backgrounds, all of whom lived in the
environment of Paul Gauguin in the village of the same
name in Finistère, Brittany. Their "master" visited Pont-
Aven five times between 1886 and 1894. He boasted
of "being able to dare to do anything" and developed
Cloisonism with Émile Bernard in 1888. His followers
included Paul Sérusier, Charles Filiger, Émile Jourdan as
well as the Dane Mogens Ballin, the Dutchman Meijer
de Haan and the Irishman Roderic O'Connor. On the
one hand they stayed in Pont-Aven because of Gauguin,
on the other hand because Brittany is a suitable region
with picturesque charm. The numerous legends and
folk tales provided the inspiration for their paintings.
Not everyone painted them in the style of syntheticism.
In the region, however, they found a climate of creative
exchange that encouraged inspiration and new
approaches. Many of the artists surpassed themselves
and painted according to Gauguin's principles - "free
and crazy".

L'école de Pont-Aven

L'histoire de l'art a réuni sous le qualificatif d'école de Pont-
Aven les artistes, d'horizons très divers, qui à un moment
ou un autre, ont gravité autour de Paul Gauguin dans ce
village breton du Finistère. Le maître y séjourne à cinq
reprises, entre 1886 et 1894. Avec Émile Bernard, il met au
point en 1888 le principe du cloisonnisme. Gauguin prône
le « droit de tout oser ». Paul Sérusier, Charles Filiger,
Émile Jourdan..., mais aussi le Danois Mogens Ballin, le
Hollandais Meijer de Haan, l'Irlandais Roderic O'Connor,
séjourneront à Pont-Aven. La présence de tous ces peintres
dans le village s'explique en partie, bien sûr, par la présence
de Gauguin, mais aussi, simplement, parce que la Bretagne
est une région bon marché au charme pittoresque, une
terre de légendes et de croyances propice à nourrir la
peinture. Les artistes n'ont pas tous produit des œuvres
synthétistes. Mais ils ont trouvé là un climat d'échange
stimulant, un bouillonnement créatif, une inspiration et
des idées nouvelles qui leur ont permis de se dépasser,
et de travailler, selon les propres mots de Gauguin,
« librement et follement ».

Die Schule von Pont-Aven

Unter der Schule von Pont-Aven werden Künstler
verschiedener Ansätze zusammengefasst, die sich aber
alle im Umfeld Paul Gauguins in dem gleichnamigen
Dorf im bretonischen Finistère aufhielten. Ihr Meister
weilte zwischen 1886 und 1894 fünfmal in Pont-Aven.
Er rühmt sich „alles wagen zu können" und entwickelt
1888 mit Émile Bernard den Cloisonismus. Zu seinen
Anhängern zählen Paul Sérusier, Charles Filiger,
Émile Jourdan sowie der Däne Mogens Ballin, der
Niederländer Meijer de Haan und der Ire Roderic
O'Connor. Zum einen halten sie sich wegen Gauguin
in Pont-Avens auf, zum anderen, weil die Bretagne
eine günstige Region mit pittoreskem Charme ist.
Die zahlreichen Legenden und Volkssagen liefern die
Inspiration für ihre Malerei. Nicht alle malen sie im Stil
des Synthetismus. Vor Ort finden sie aber ein Klima
des kreativen Austausches vor, das Inspiration und
neue Ansätze begünstigt. Viele der Künstler wachsen
dadurch über sich selbst hinaus und malen nach den
Grundsätzen Gauguins – „frei und verrückt".

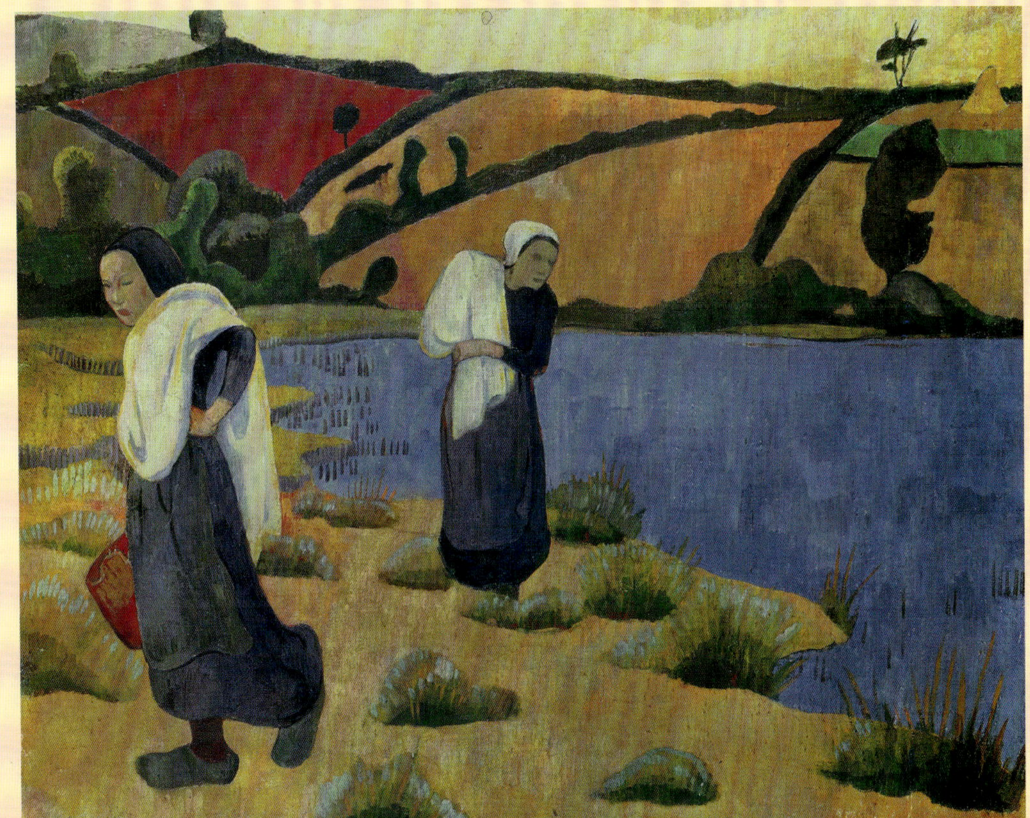

La escuela de Pont-Aven

La Escuela de Pont-Aven reúne a artistas de diversos orígenes, todos los cuales vivían en los alrededores de Paul Gauguin en el pueblo bretón de Finistère. Su maestro visitó Pont-Aven cinco veces entre 1886 y 1894. Se jacta de "ser capaz de atreverse a todo" y desarrolló el cloisonismo con Émile Bernard en 1888. Entre sus seguidores se encuentran Paul Sérusier, Charles Filiger, Émile Jourdan, así como el danés Mogens Ballin, el holandés Meijer de Haan y el irlandés Roderic O'Connor. Por un lado, se alojan en Pont-Aven debido a Gauguin y, por otro, porque Bretaña es una región idónea con un encanto pintoresco. Las numerosas leyendas y cuentos populares proporcionan la inspiración para sus pinturas. No todo el mundo las pinta al estilo del sintetismo. En el lugar, sin embargo, encuentran un clima de intercambio creativo que fomenta la inspiración y los nuevos enfoques. Muchos de los artistas crecen más allá de sí mismos y pintan según los principios de Gauguin: "libres y locos".

A escola de Pont-Aven

A Escola de Pont-Aven reúne artistas de diversas origens, todos eles residentes nos arredores de Paul Gauguin, na aldeia de mesmo nome em Finistère, Bretanha. Seu mestre visitou Pont-Aven cinco vezes entre 1886 e 1894. Orgulha-se de "ser capaz de ousar qualquer coisa" e desenvolveu o cloisonismo com Émile Bernard em 1888. Os seus seguidores incluem Paul Sérusier, Charles Filiger, Émile Jourdan, bem como o dinamarquês Mogens Ballin, o holandês Meijer de Haan e o irlandês Roderic O'Connor. Por um lado, eles ficam em Pont-Aven por causa de Gauguin, por outro lado, porque a Bretanha é uma região adequada com charme pitoresco. As numerosas lendas e contos populares fornecem a inspiração para suas pinturas. Nem toda a gente os pinta ao estilo do sintético. No local, no entanto, eles encontram um clima de intercâmbio criativo que incentiva a inspiração e novas abordagens. Muitos dos artistas crescem além de si mesmos e pintam de acordo com os princípios de Gauguin - "livres e loucos".

De school van Pont-Aven

Onder de school van Pont-Aven worden kunstenaars met uiteenlopende achtergronden geschaard, die allemaal in de buurt van Paul Gauguin in het gelijknamige dorp in Finistère (Bretagne) verbleven. Hun meester bezocht Pont-Aven tussen 1886 en 1894 vijf keer. Hij ging er prat op dat hij 'alles durfde' en ontwikkelde in 1888 samen met Émile Bernard het cloisonnisme. Zijn volgelingen waren Paul Sérusier, Charles Filiger, Émile Jourdan en de Deen Mogens Ballin, de Nederlander Meijer de Haan en de Ier Roderic O'Connor. Zij verbleven enerzijds in Pont-Aven vanwege Gauguin, anderzijds omdat Bretagne een geschikt gebied was met een schilderachtige charme. De vele legenden en volksverhalen leverden de inspiratie voor hun schilderijen. Niet iedereen schilderde in de stijl van het synthetisme. Ter plaatse troffen ze echter een klimaat van creatieve uitwisseling aan dat inspireerde en nieuwe benaderingen stimuleerde. Veel kunstenaars oversteen zichzelf en schilderden volgens de principes van Gauguin: 'vrij en gek'.

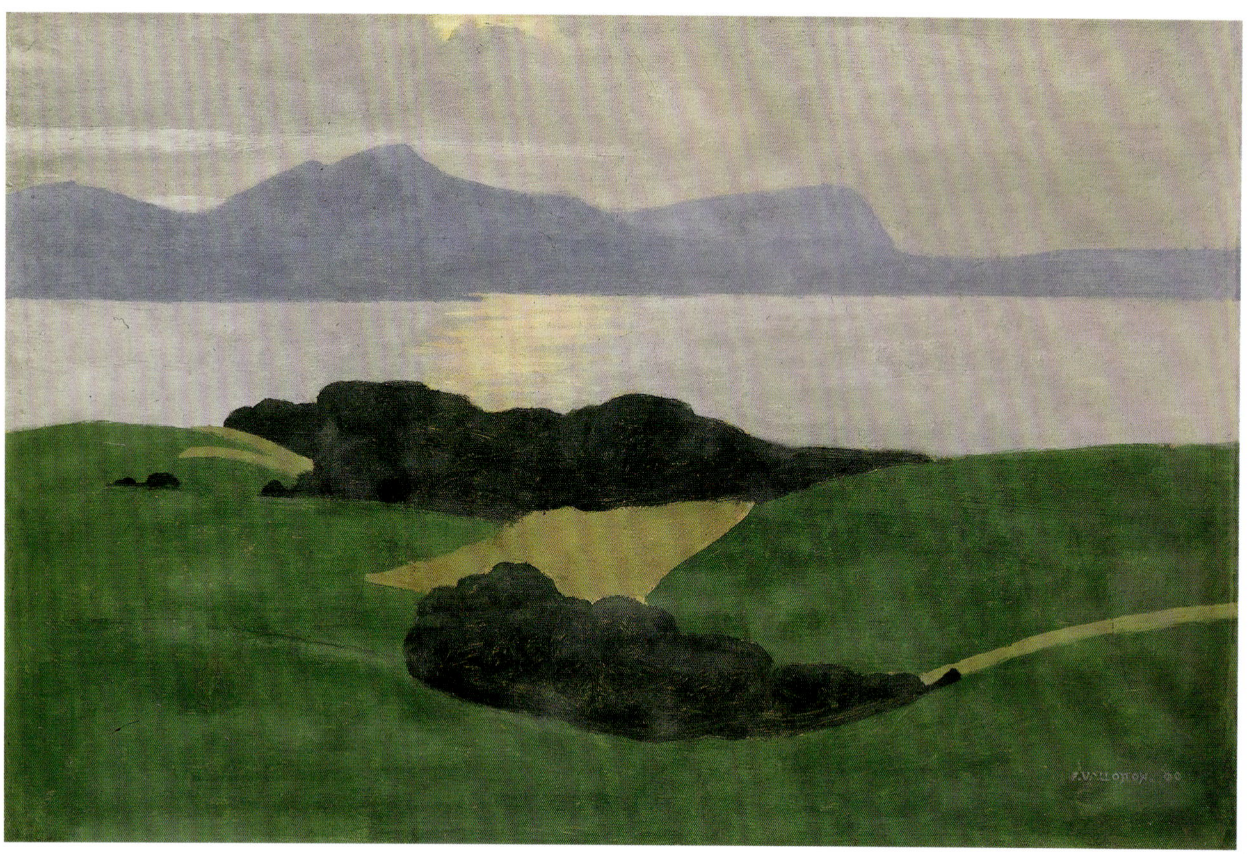

The Salève and the Lake

Le Salève et le lac

**Der Mont Salève
und der See**

Mont Salève y el lago

Mont Salève e o lago

Mont Salève en het meer

**FÉLIX VALLOTTON
(1865-1925)**

1900, Oil on canvas/
Huile sur toile,
31,5 × 47,5 cm,
Private collection

Nude Seated in a Red Armchair

Born in Switzerland, Vallotton was naturalised in France in 1900. Under the nickname «Nabi from abroad» the painter, wood engraver and graphic artist created interiors, portraits, nudes and landscapes.

Femme nue assise dans un fauteuil rouge

Né en Suisse, Vallotton est naturalisé Français en 1900. Surnommé le « Nabi étranger », le peintre, graveur et illustrateur partage son temps entre scènes d'intérieurs, portraits, nus et paysages épurés.

Akt in einem roten Lehnstuhl

Der in der Schweiz geborene Vallotton wird 1900 in Frankreich eingebürgert. Unter dem Spitznamen „Nabi aus dem Ausland" schafft der Maler, Holzstecher und Grafiker Interieurs, Porträts, Akte und Landschaften.

Desnudo en un sillón rojo

Nacido en Suiza, Vallotton se naturalizó en Francia en 1900. Bajo el apodo «Nabi el extranjero» el pintor, grabador de madera y artista gráfico crea interiores, retratos, desnudos y paisajes.

Nua numa poltrona vermelha

Nascido na Suíça, Vallotton foi naturalizado na França em 1900. Sob o apelido de «Nabi from abroad» o pintor, gravador de madeira e artista gráfico cria interiores, retratos, nus e paisagens.

Naakte vrouw zittend op een rode stoel

De in Zwitserland geboren Vallotton werd in 1900 Frans staatsburger. Onder de bijnaam 'buitenlandse Nabi' maakte de schilder, houtgraveur en graficus interieurs, portretten, naakten en landschappen.

FÉLIX VALLOTTON (1865-1925)

1897, Oil on cardboard/Huile sur carton, 28 × 28 cm, Musée de Grenoble, Grenoble

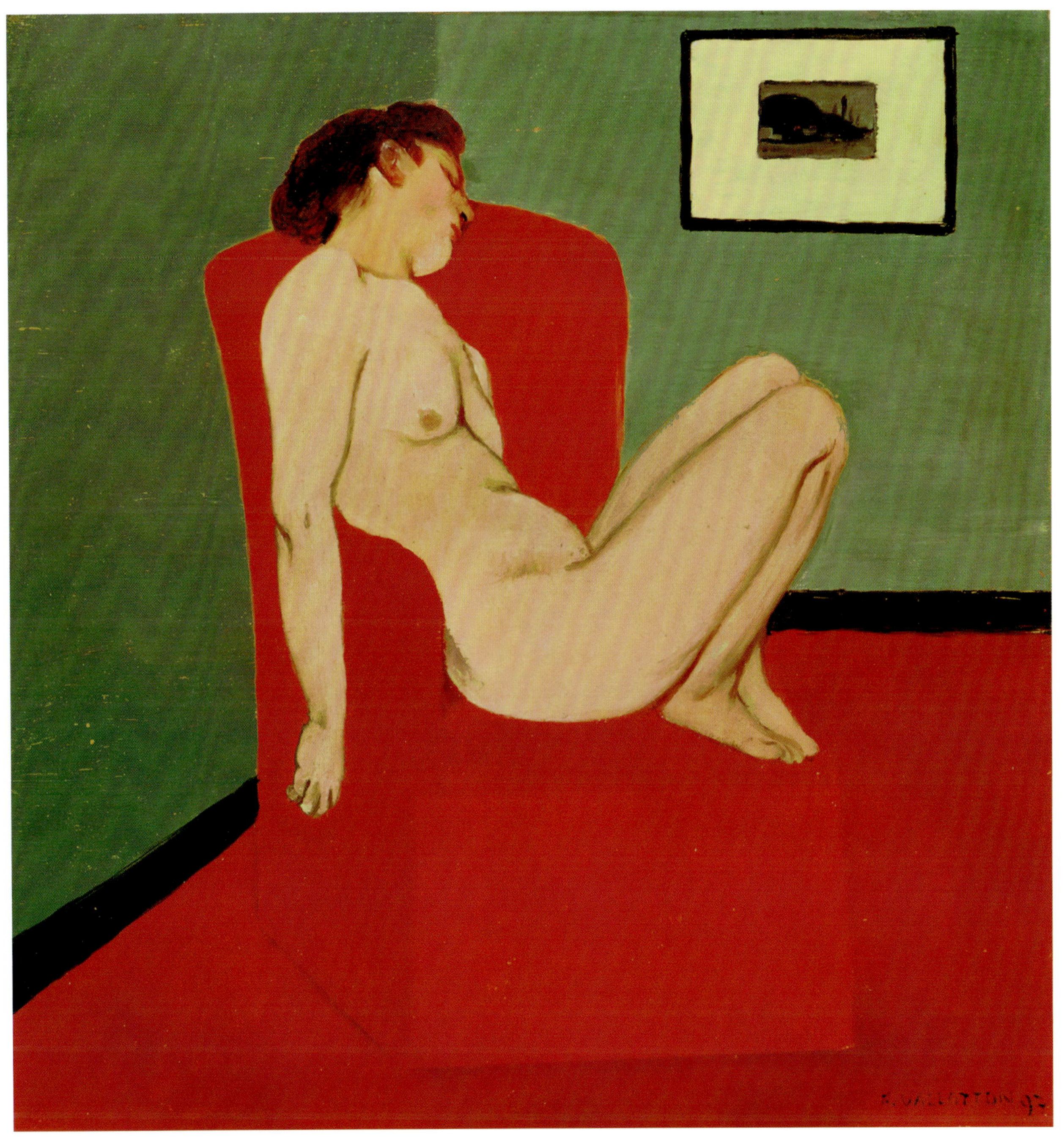

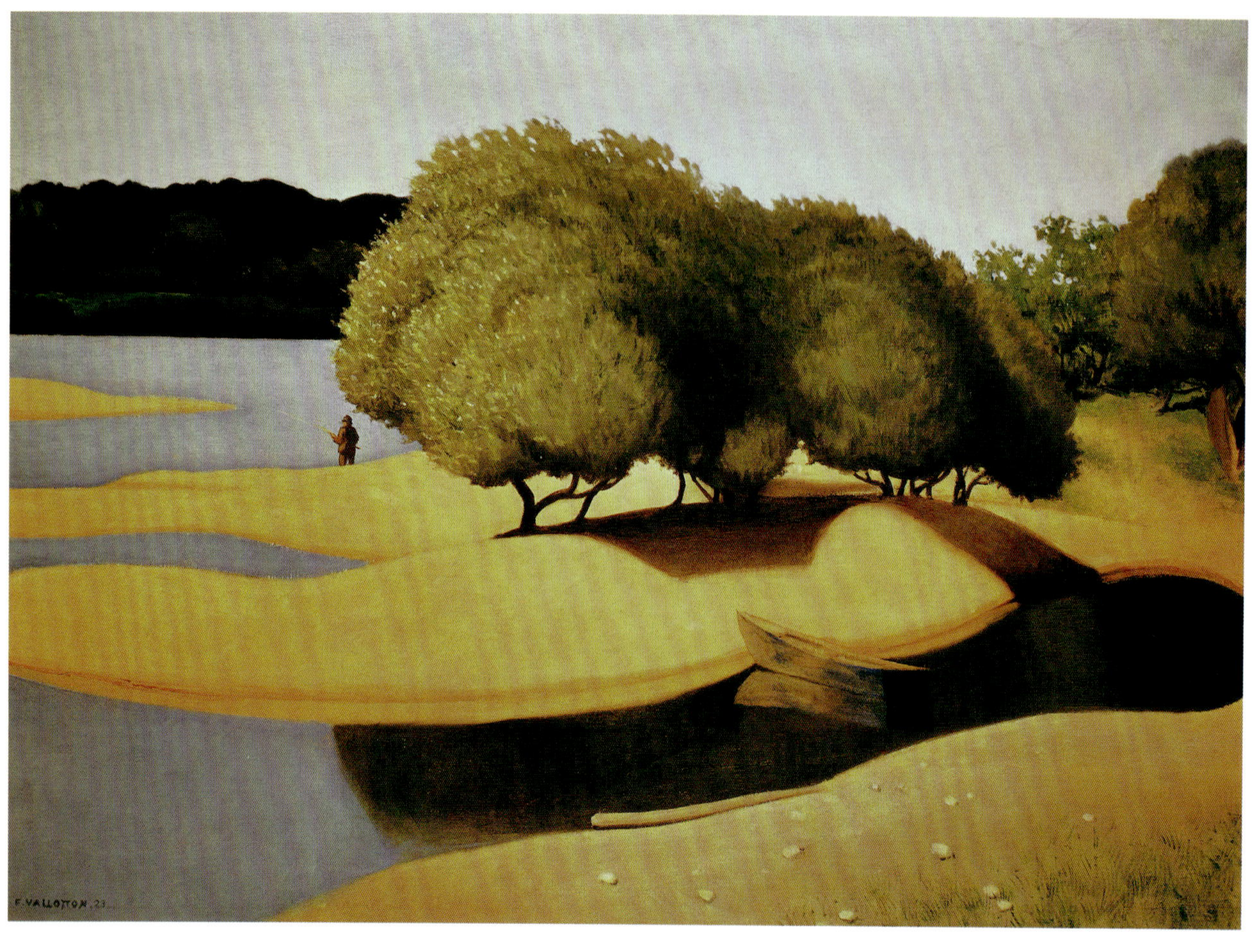

Sandbanks on the Loire

Bancs de sable au bord de Loire

Sandbänke an der Loire

Bancos de arena en el Loira

Bancos de areia no Loire

Zandbanken aan de Loire

FÉLIX VALLOTTON (1865-1925)

1923, Oil on canvas/Huile sur toile, 73 × 100 cm, Kunsthaus Zürich

420

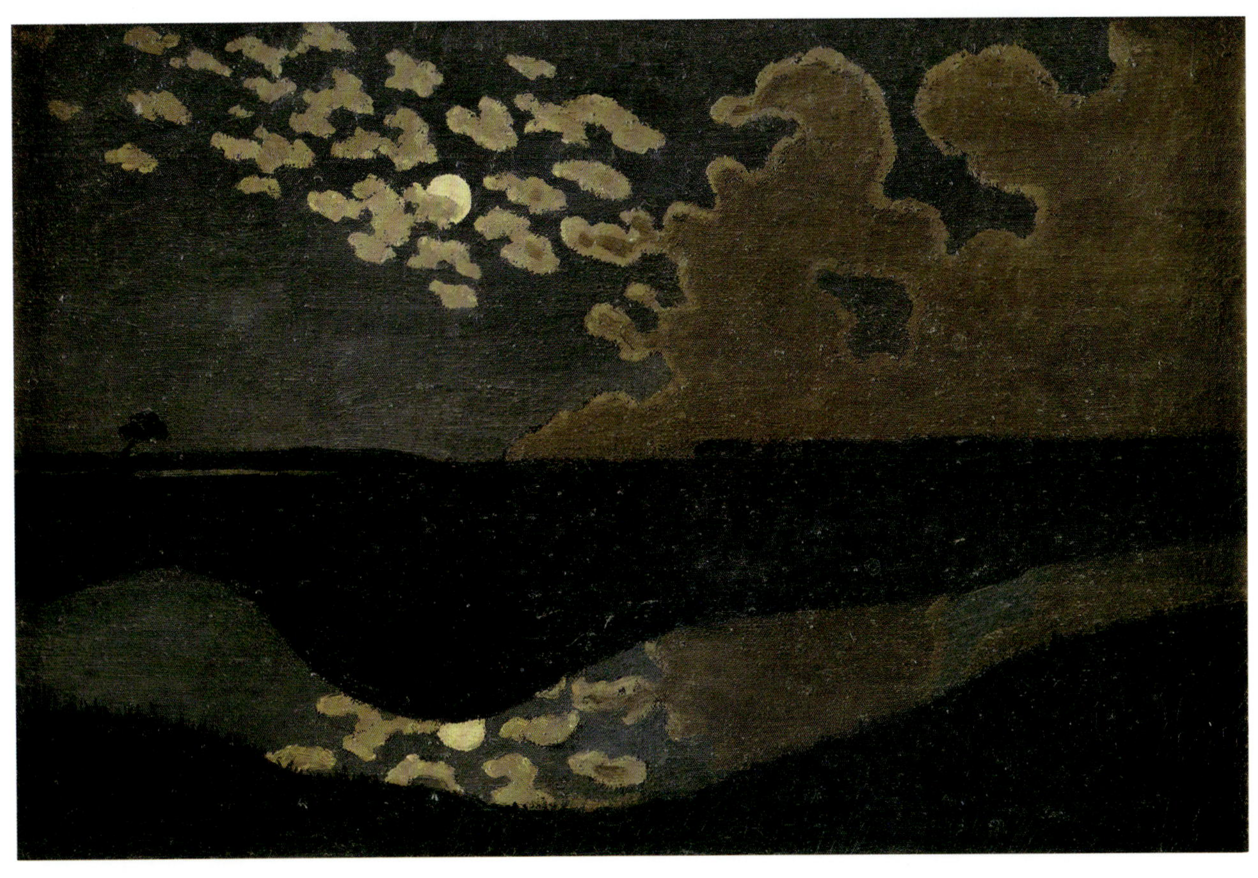

Moonlight

Clair de lune

Mondschein

Luz de luna

Luar

Maanlicht

FÉLIX VALLOTTON (1865-1925)

c. 1895, Oil on canvas/Huile sur toile, 27 × 41 cm, Musée d'Orsay, Paris

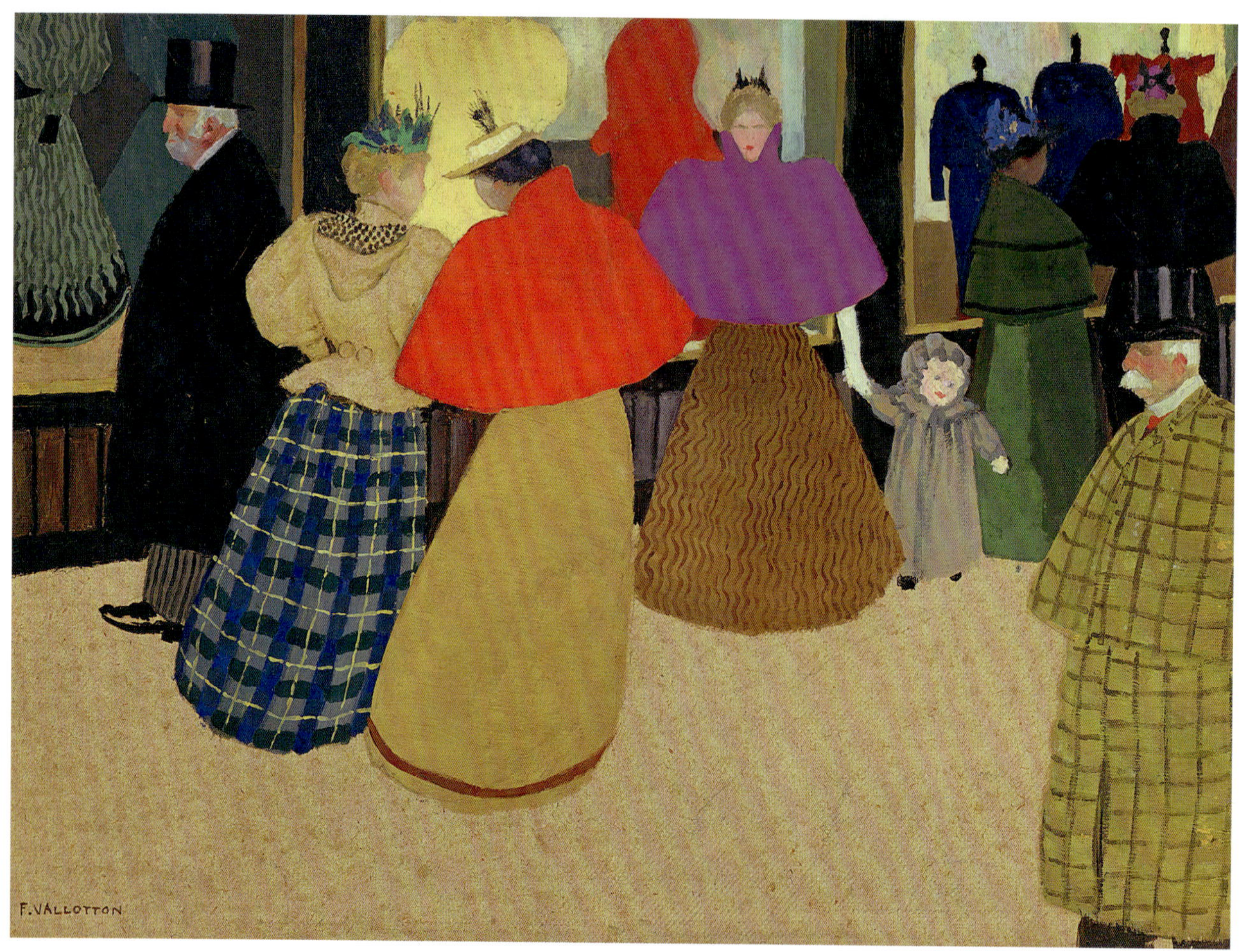

Les Passants *or* Street Scene

Les Passants *ou* Scène de rue

Die Passanten *oder* Straßenszene

Los transeúntes *o* La escena de la calle

Os transeuntes *ou* a cena da rua

De voorbijgangers *of* Straatbeeld

FÉLIX VALLOTTON (1865-1925)

1897, Tempera on cardboard/Détrempe, 33 × 46 cm, Private collection

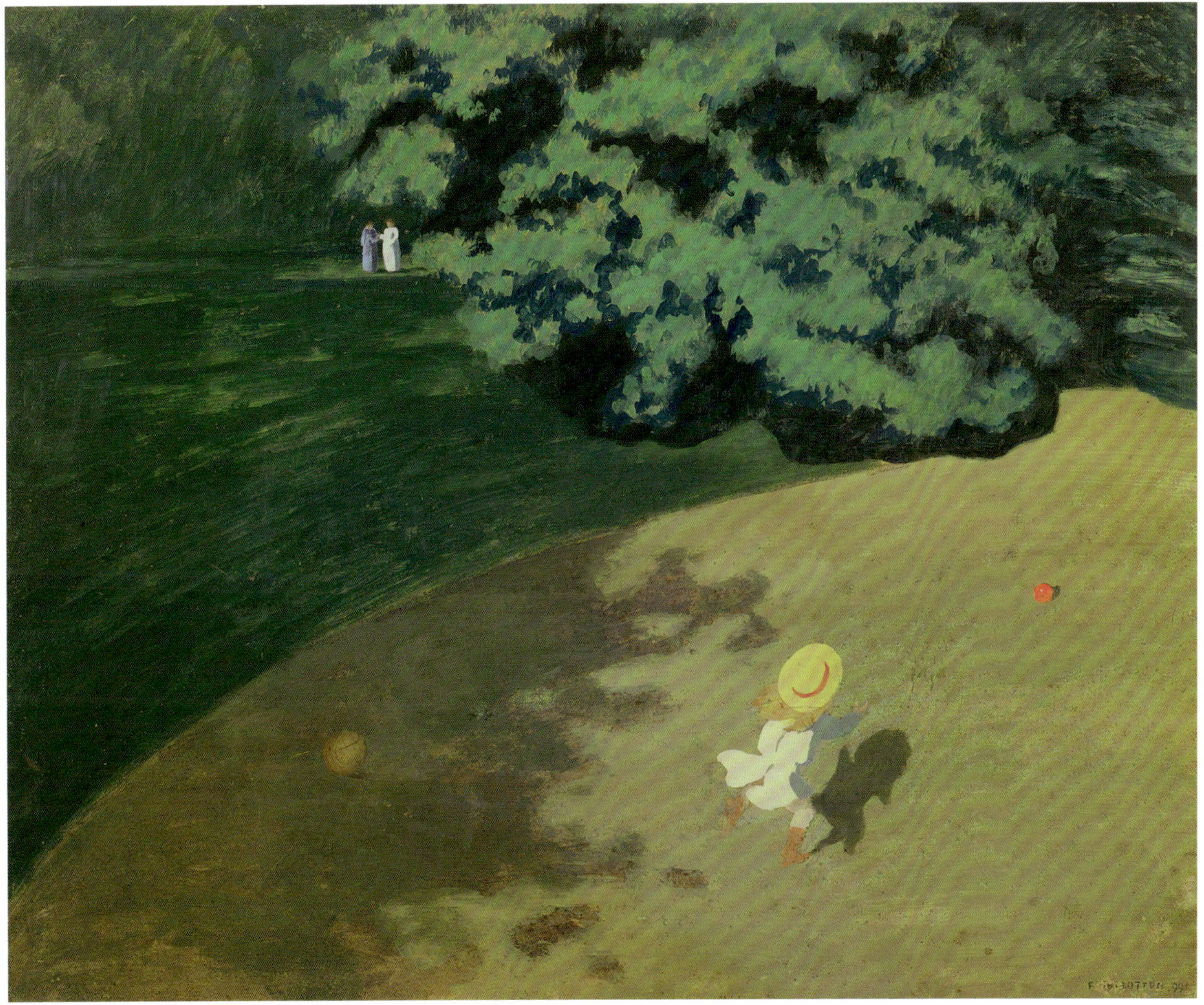

The Ball

The motif and coloring of the painting are close to those of Vuillard and Bonnard. The spatial effect results from the ratio between the child and the two people in the background.

Le Ballon

Par son thème – le jardin – et ses couleurs, cette œuvre rapproche Vallotton de Vuillard et Bonnard. L'effet de perspective est donné par le rapport d'échelle entre l'enfant et les deux figures du fond.

Der Ball

Durch das Motiv und die Farbgebung steht das Gemälde den Werken von Vuillard und Bonnard nahe. Die räumliche Wirkung ergibt sich aus dem Größenverhältnis zwischen dem Kind und den zwei Personen im Hintergrund.

La pelota

El motivo y el colorido de la pintura son similares a los de Vuillard y Bonnard. El efecto espacial resulta de la relación de tamaño entre el niño y las dos personas en el fondo.

A bola

O motivo e a coloração da pintura estão próximos aos de Vuillard e Bonnard. O efeito espacial resulta da relação de tamanho entre a criança e as duas pessoas no fundo.

De bal

Door het onderwerp en kleurgebruik staat het schilderij dicht bij het werk van Vuillard en Bonnard. De ruimtewerking ontstaat door de verhouding in grootte tussen het kind en de twee personen op de achtergrond.

FÉLIX VALLOTTON (1865-1925)

1899, Oil on cardboard glued on wood/Huile sur carton collé sur bois, 48 × 61 cm, Musée d'Orsay, Paris

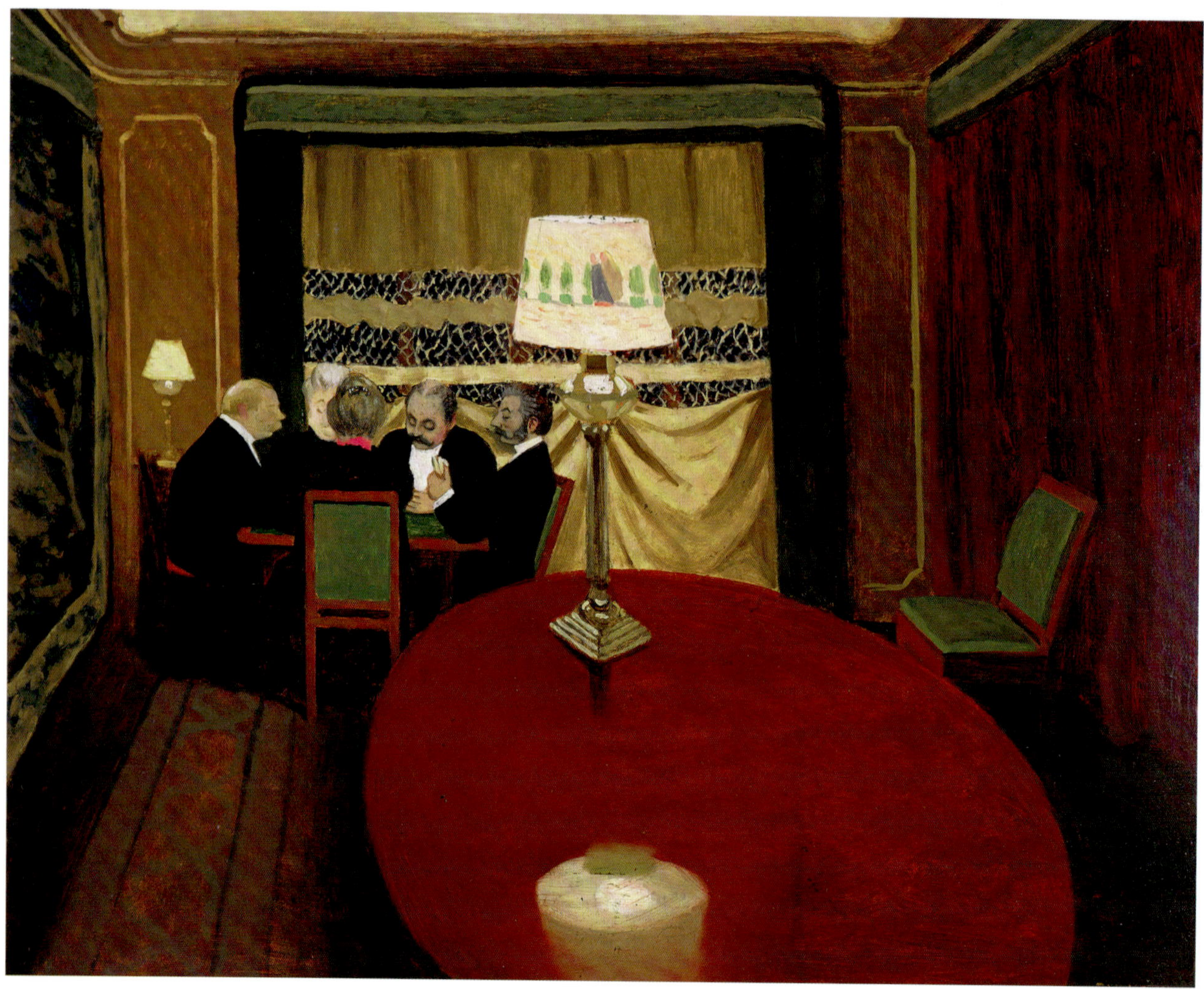

A Round of Poker

Le Poker

Das Pokerspiel

El juego de póquer

O Jogo de Poker

Het pokerspel

FÉLIX VALLOTTON (1865-1925)

1902, Oil on canvas/Huile sur toile, 52,5 × 67,4 cm, Musée d'Orsay, Paris

Landscape with Trees

In the light of the last rays of the sun, the stylized trees appear like dancing shadows against a background of a color gradient from orange to blue. The influence of Japanese art is unmistakable.

Paysage avec des arbres

À l'heure des derniers feux du soleil couchant, les arbres stylisés se détachent d'un fond en dégradé (de l'orange au bleu), comme des ombres qui dansent. L'influence du japonisme est manifeste.

Fünf Bäume

Im Licht der letzten Sonnenstrahlen wirken die stilisierten Bäume wie tanzende Schatten vor einem Hintergrund aus einem Farbverlauf von Orange nach Blau. Der Einfluss japanischer Kunst ist unverkennbar.

Cinco árboles

A la luz de los últimos rayos del sol, los árboles estilizados aparecen como sombras danzantes sobre un fondo degradado que va del naranja al azul. La influencia del arte japonés es inconfundible.

Cinco árvores

À luz dos últimos raios de sol, as árvores estilizadas aparecem como sombras dançantes sobre um fundo de gradiente de cor de laranja a azul. A influência da arte japonesa é inconfundível.

Vijf bomen

In het licht van de laatste zonnestralen verschijnen de gestileerde bomen als dansende schaduwen tegen een achtergrond met een kleurverloop van oranje naar blauw. De invloed van de Japanse kunst is onmiskenbaar.

FÉLIX VALLOTTON (1865-1925)

1911, Oil on canvas/
Huile sur toile, 100 × 73 cm,
Musée des Beaux-Arts, Quimper

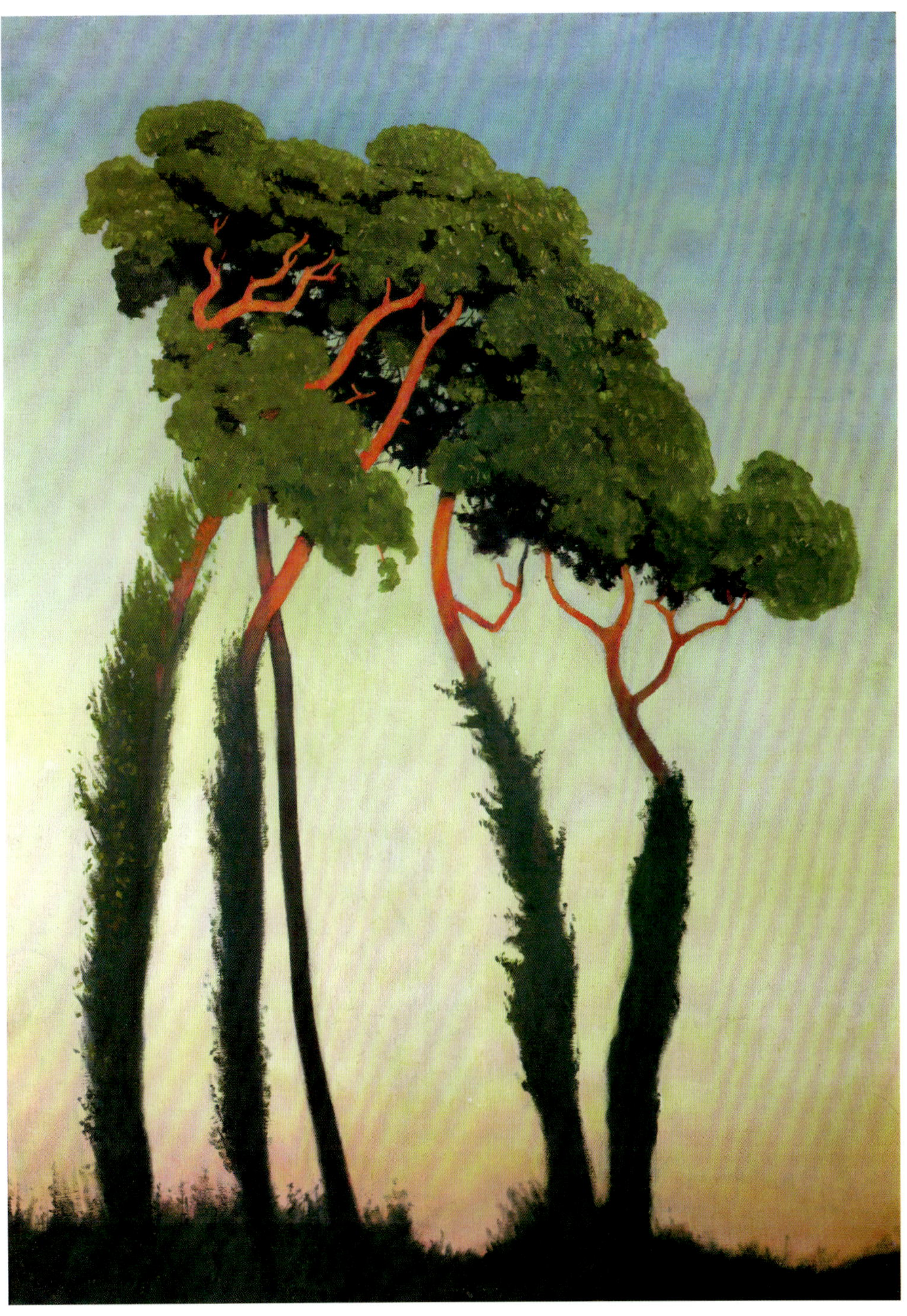

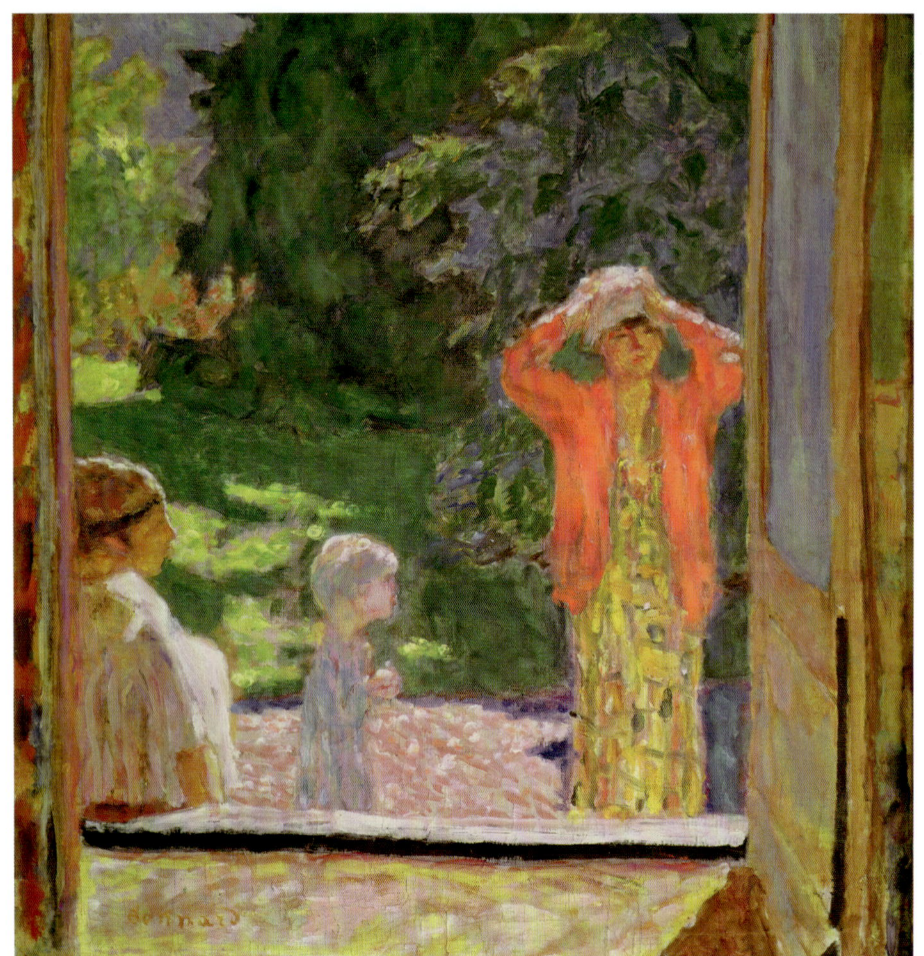

In Front of the Window at Le Grand Lemps

Devant la fenêtre au Grand Lemps

Vor dem Fenster bei Le Grand Lemps

Frente a la ventana de Le Grand Lemps

Em frente à janela de Le Grand Lemps

Voor het raam bij Le Grand Lemps

PIERRE BONNARD (1867-1947)

1923, Oil on canvas/Huile sur toile,
65 × 64,5 cm, Musée des Beaux-Arts,
Besançon

The Studio with Mimosa

In 1936, the artist began in Le Cannet a hymn to color and light, which he revised in 1949. From the studio in the villa «Le Bosquet» Bonnard had a free view of the lush garden.

L'Atelier au mimosa

Peint au Cannet en 1936, cet hymne à la couleur et à la lumière sera repris par l'artiste en 1946. Depuis l'atelier de sa villa Le Bosquet, Bonnard bénéficie d'une vue imprenable sur son jardin luxuriant.

Atelier mit Mimosen

1936 beginnt der Künstler in Le Cannet eine Hymne an die Farbe und das Licht, die er 1949 überarbeitet. Von dem Atelier in der Villa „Le Bosquet" aus bot sich Bonnard ein freier Blick auf den üppigen Garten.

Atelier con mimosas

En 1936, el artista comenzó en Le Cannet un himno al color y a la luz, que revisó en 1949. Desde el estudio de la villa «Le Bosquet» Bonnard tenía una vista libre del exuberante jardín.

Atelier com mimosas

Em 1936, o artista começou em Le Cannet um hino à cor e à luz, que ele revisou em 1949. Do estúdio na villa «Le Bosquet» Bonnard tinha uma vista livre do exuberante jardim.

Het atelier met mimosa

In 1936 begon de schilder in Le Cannet met een lofzang op kleur en licht, die hij in 1949 overschilderde. Vanuit zijn atelier in de villa 'Le Bosquet' had Bonnard een vrij uitzicht op de weelderige tuin.

PIERRE BONNARD (1867-1947)

1939-46, Oil on canvas/Huile sur toile, 127,5 × 127,5 cm, Centre Pompidou, Paris

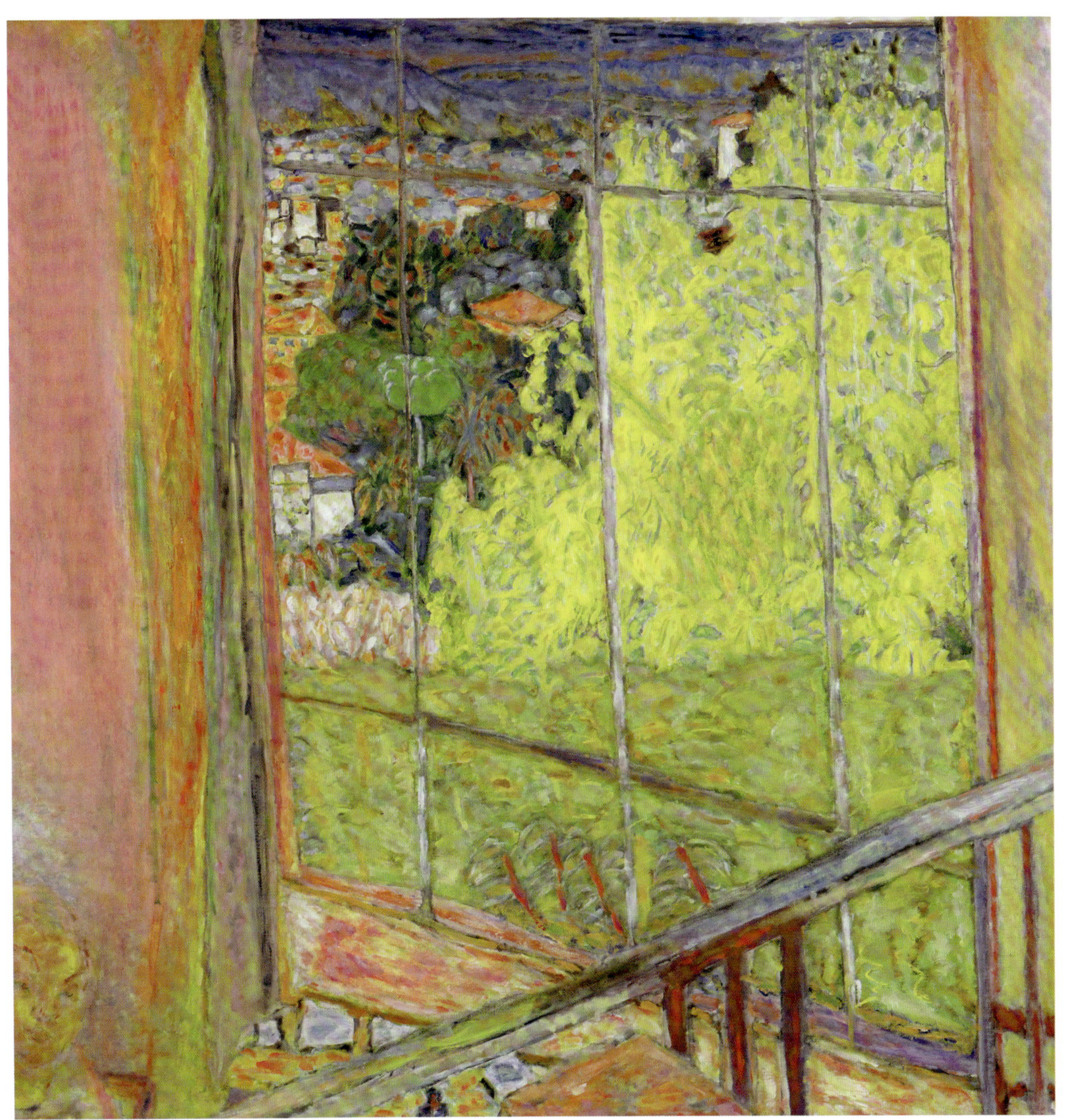

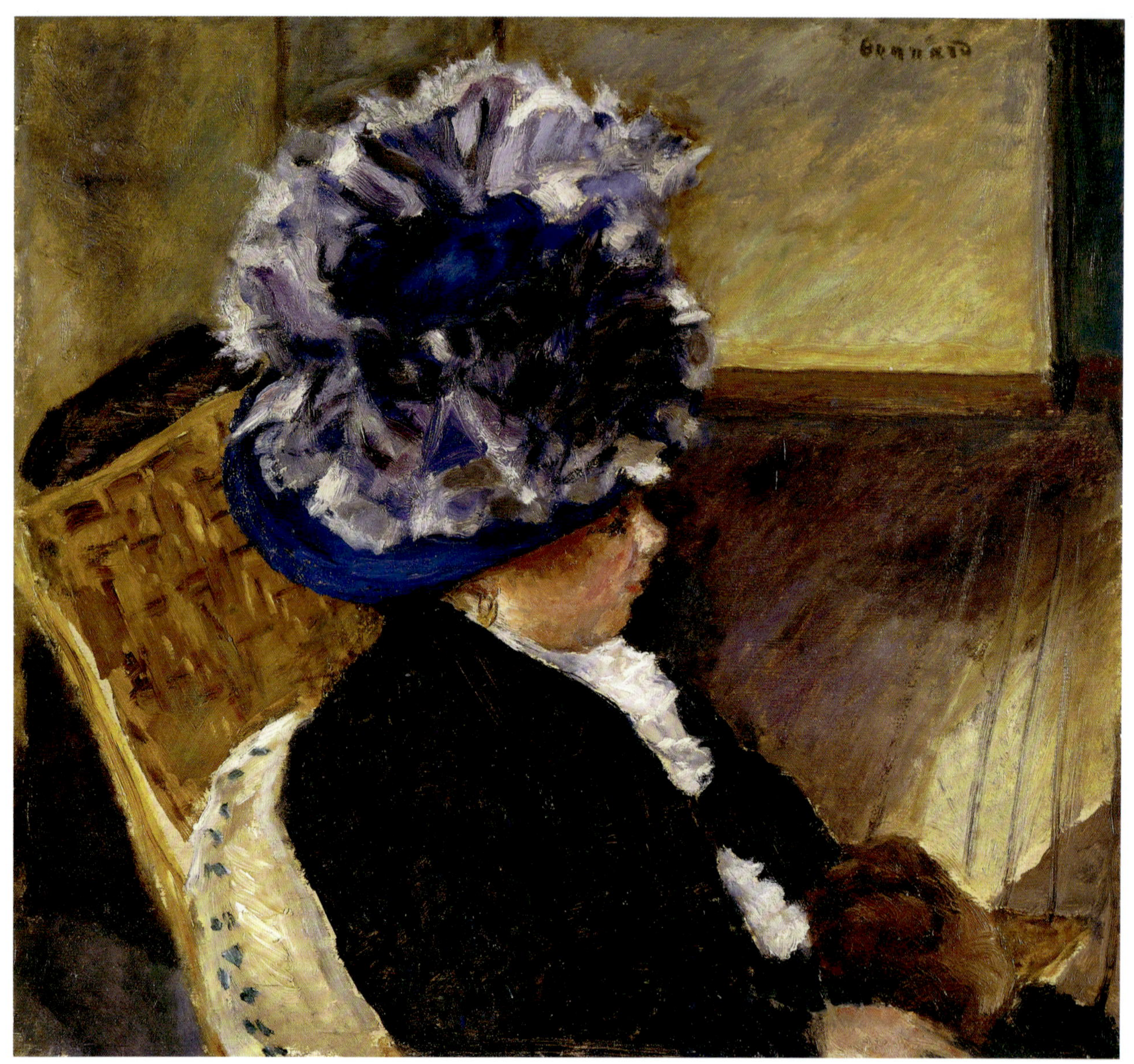

Young Woman in a Blue Hat

Jeune Femme au chapeau bleu

Junge Frau mit blauem Hut

Mujer joven con sombrero azul

Jovem mulher com chapéu azul

Jonge vrouw met blauwe hoed

PIERRE BONNARD (1867-1947)

1908, Oil on canvas/Huile sur toile, 55,2 × 60,3 cm, Private collection

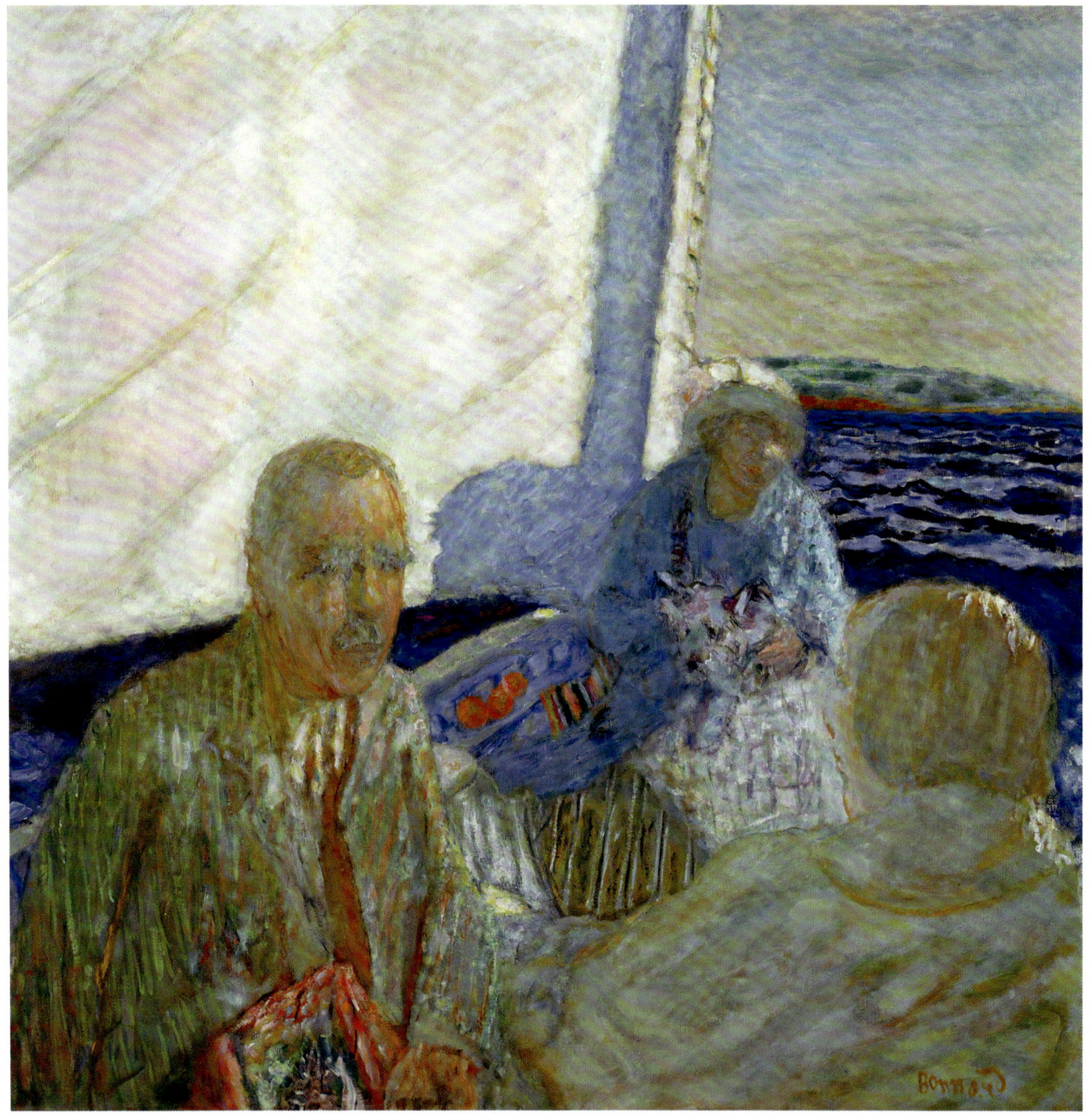

At Sea

En mer

Segelpartie auf dem Meer

En el mar

Velejar no mar

Op zee

PIERRE BONNARD (1867-1947)

1924, Oil on canvas/Huile sur toile, 98 × 103 cm, Private collection

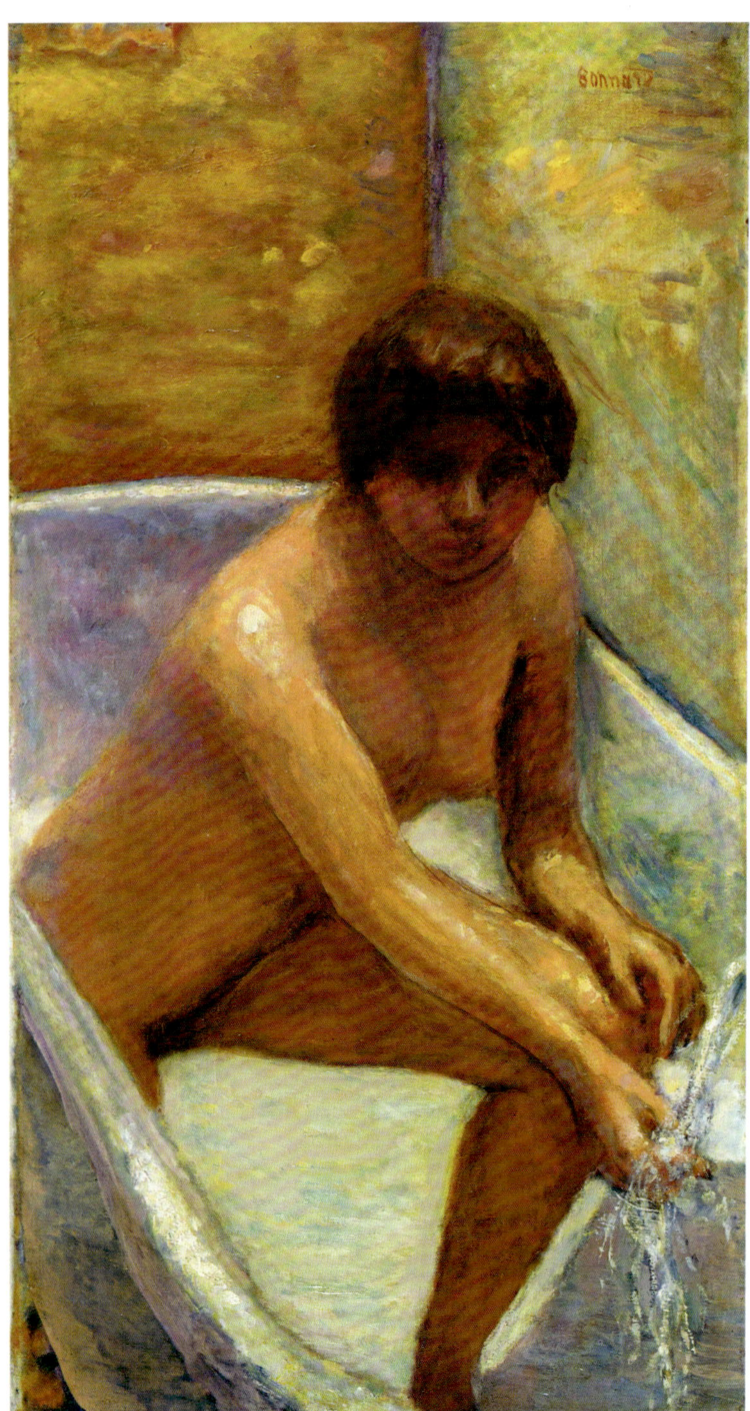

The Spring *or* Nude in a Bath

La Source *ou* Nu dans le bain

Die Quelle *oder* Akt in der Badewanne

La fuente *o* Desnudo en la bañera

A fonte *ou* ato na banheira

De bron *of* Naakt in het bad

PIERRE BONNARD (1867-1947)
1917, Oil on canvas/Huile sur toile, 85 × 50 cm,
Private collection

Nude at the Fireplace
His wife Marthe was Bonnard's only model, whom he immortalized in his numerous nudes. The painting shows her naked rear view. The mirror opens a second level with the glimpse of her face.

Nu devant la cheminée
Pierre Bonnard a fait de son épouse Marthe le seul et unique modèle de ses nombreux nus féminins. Elle est ici saisie avec pudeur, debout, de dos, son visage n'étant visible que par le reflet du miroir.

Rückenakt vor dem Kamin
Seine Ehefrau Marthe war Bonnards einziges Modell, das er in seinen zahlreichen Akten verewigte. Das Gemälde zeigt ihre nackte Rückenansicht. Der Spiegel eröffnet eine zweite Ebene mit dem Antlitz ihres Gesichtes.

Desnudo de espaldas delante de la chimenea
Su esposa Marthe fue la única modelo de Bonnard, la cual inmortalizó en sus numerosos archivos. La pintura muestra su desnudo de espaldas y su rostro solo es visible por el reflejo del espejo.

Agir de costas em frente à lareira
Sua esposa Marthe era o único modelo de Bonnard, que ele imortalizou em seus numerosos arquivos. O quadro mostra a vista traseira nua. O espelho abre um segundo nível com o rosto do rosto dela.

Naakt op de rug gezien bij de haard
Zijn vrouw Marthe was het enige model dat Bonnard in zijn talrijke naakten vereeuwigde. Het schilderij toont haar naakt op de rug gezien. De spiegel opent een tweede niveau met het gelaat van haar gezicht.

PIERRE BONNARD (1867-1947)
1919, Oil on canvas/Huile sur toile, 77,5 × 59,5 cm,
Musée de l'Annonciade, Saint-Tropez

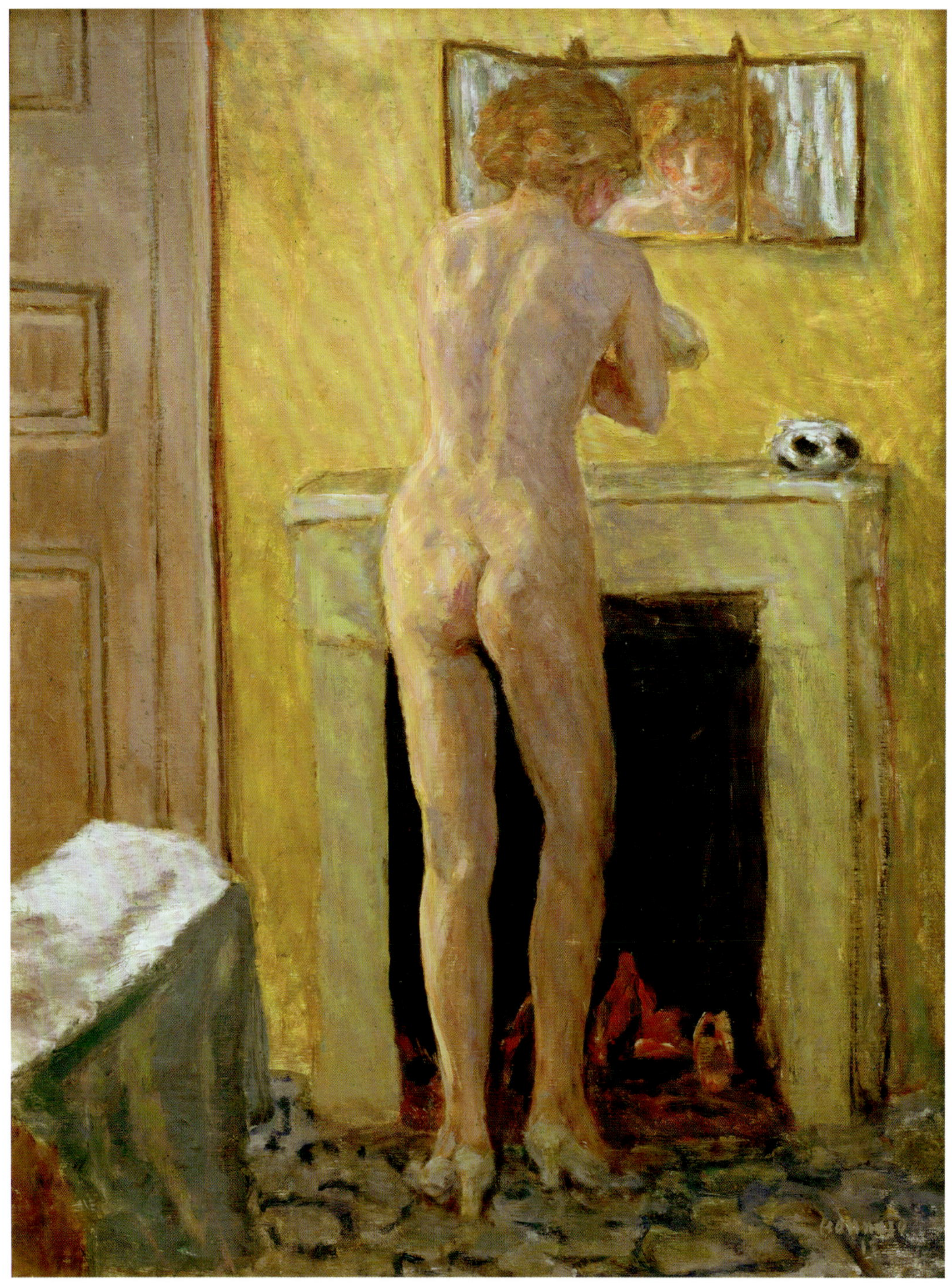

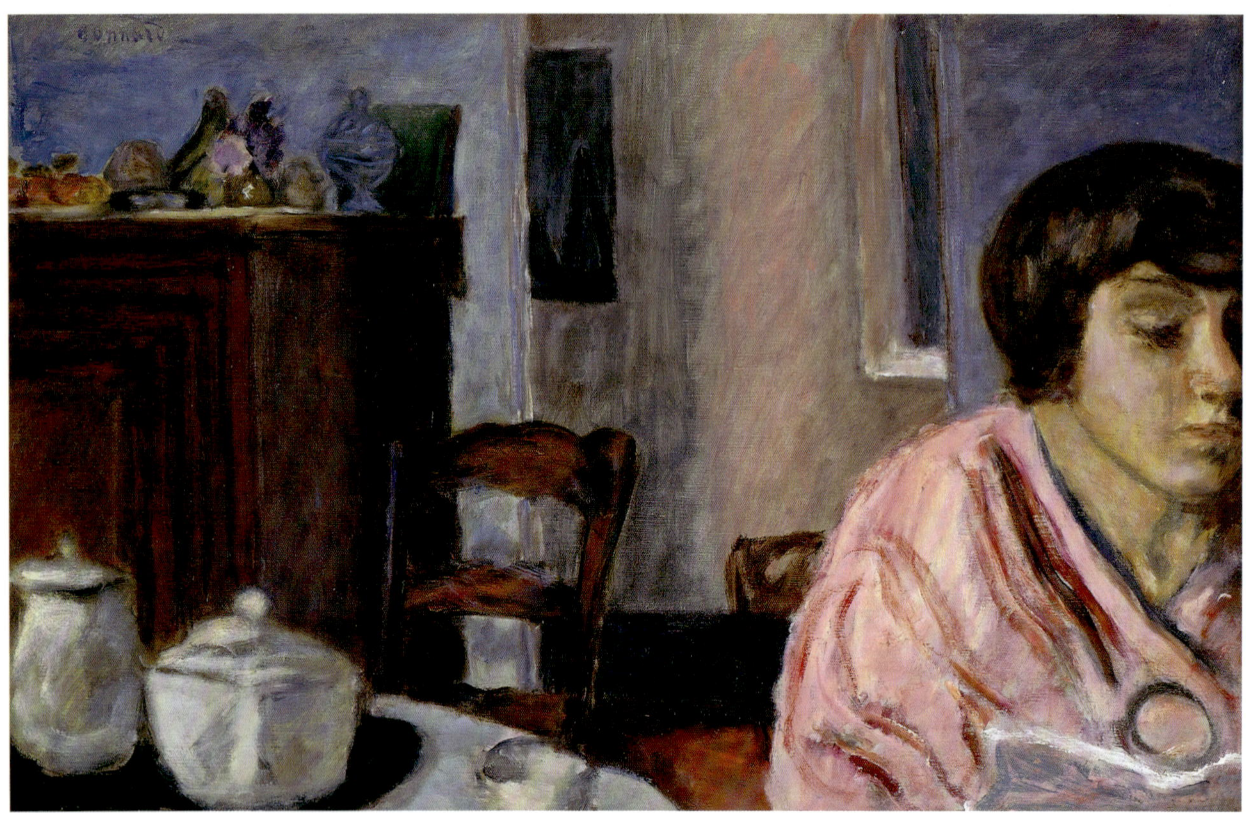

Interior with Figure

Intérieur avec figure

Interieur mit Gestalt

Interior con figura

Interior com forma

Interieur met figuur

PIERRE BONNARD (1867-1947)

1914/15, Oil on canvas/Huile sur toile, 42,2 × 66,4 cm, Private collection

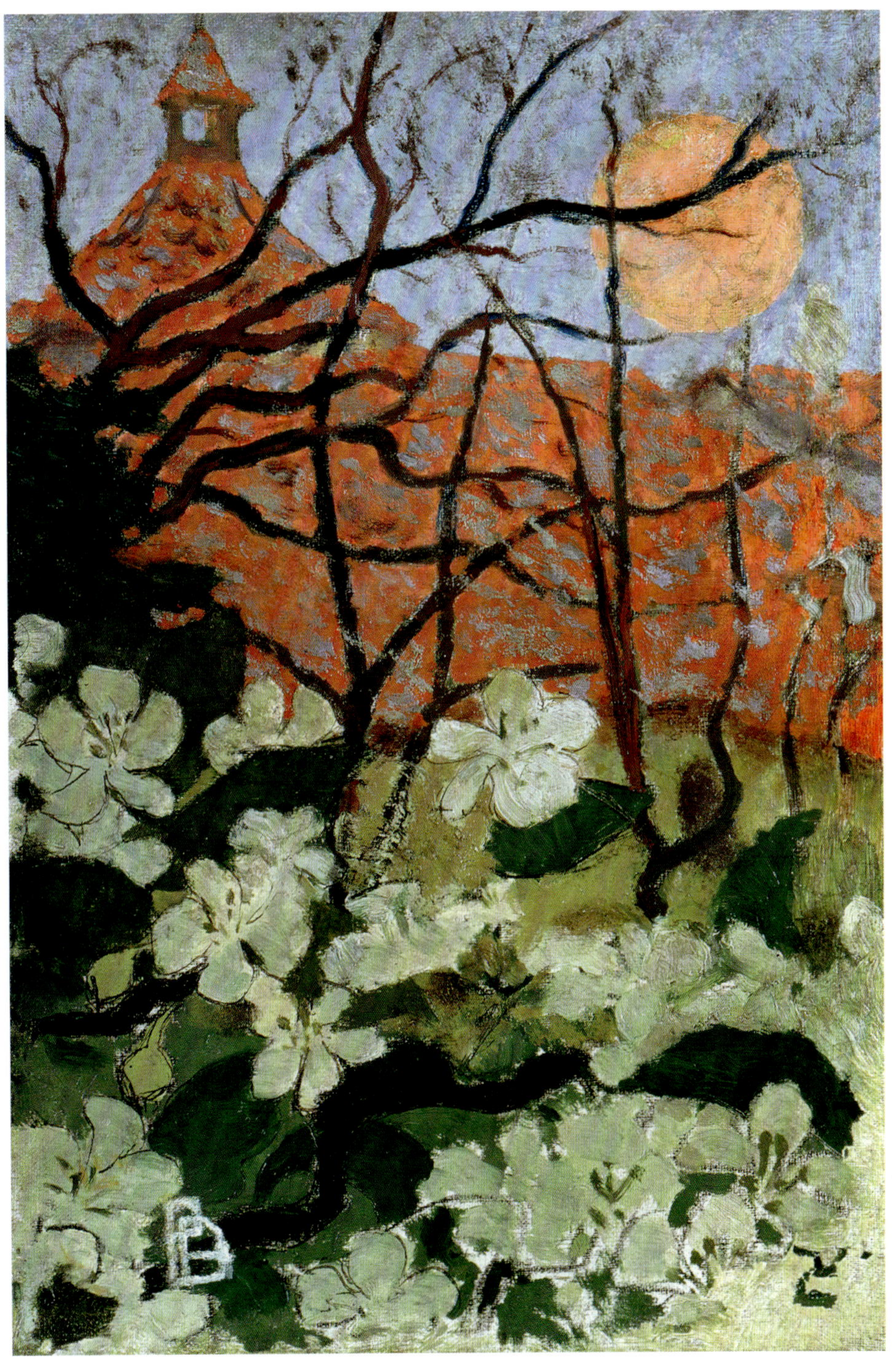

Le Grand-Lemps

PIERRE BONNARD (1867-1947)

c. 1892, Oil on canvas/Huile sur toile,
35 × 24 cm, Private collection

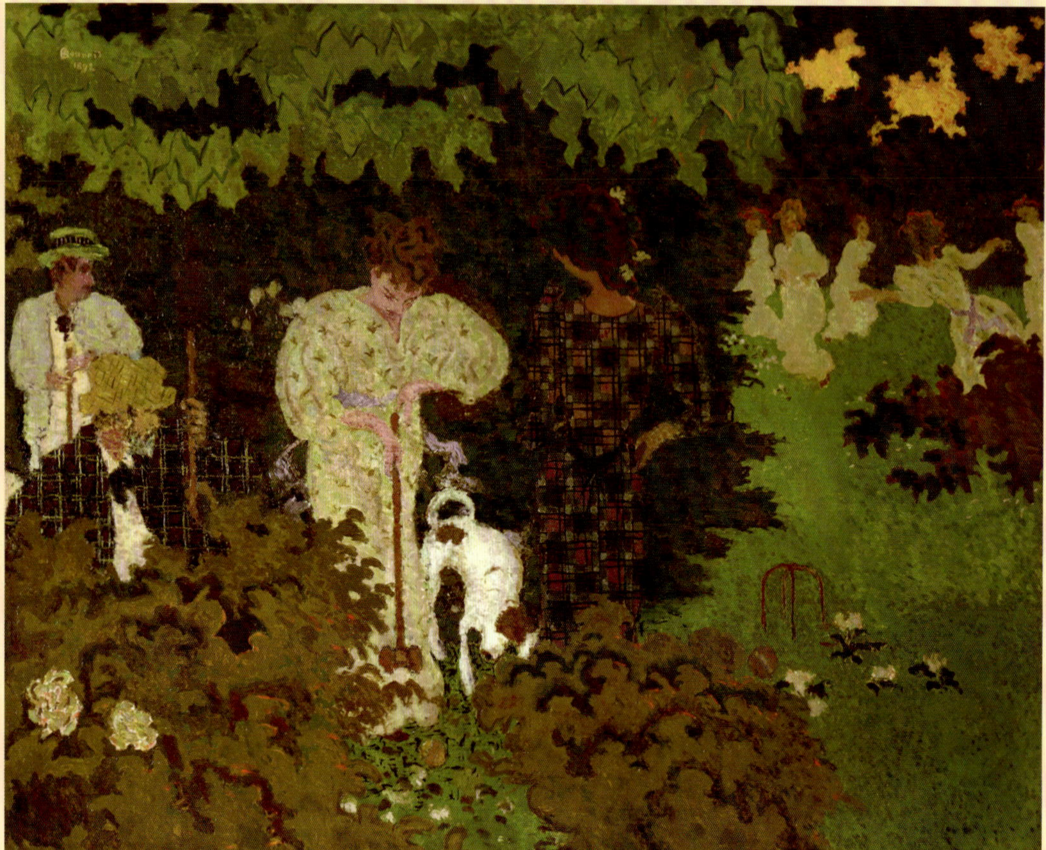

Pierre Bonnard

Pierre Bonnard (1867-1947) developed his own style -
apart from the prominent currents that prevailed
in the first half of the 20th century. Alongside
Édouard Vuillard, Maurice Denis, Paul Ranson and
Félix Vallotton, he was a member of the Nabis
artist group at the beginning of his career. Later he
turned to intimate scenes, portraits, nudes, still lifes
and landscapes. His subjects were classical - their
representation very contemporary. Bonnard created
complex compositions by constructing them as pictures
within pictures. Through frames and reflections, he
multiplied the levels depicted. His colors are the central
element in the reproduction of light, the rural views
and gardens that he painted from Normandy to the
Mediterranean coast. He subtly developed his style
further - without large breaks - towards a palette of light
shades. The only exception are his self-portraits, whose
mysterious severity contrasts with the rest of his work.

Pierre Bonnard

C'est à l'écart des grands courants et mouvements de
la première moitié du XXe siècle que Pierre Bonnard
(1867-1947) a trouvé sa voie. Assimilé au début
de sa carrière au groupe des Nabis, aux côtés
d'Édouard Vuillard, Maurice Denis, Paul Ranson ou
Félix Vallotton, Bonnard va continuer ses recherches
entre scènes intimistes, portraits, nus féminins, natures
mortes et paysages. Ses sujets sont donc classiques,
mais leur traitement très moderne. Bonnard construit
des compositions complexes, usant du principe du
tableau dans le tableau, en multipliant et démultipliant
les plans par des effets de cadrages et de miroirs. Côté
couleur, il est le peintre de la lumière, de la campagne
et des jardins normands aux rivages de la Méditerranée.
L'évolution de Bonnard est subtile, continue, sans
ruptures radicales. Année après année, il poursuit son
cheminement vers une peinture à la palette toujours
plus claire. À l'exception d'énigmatiques autoportraits,
dont l'austérité tranche avec le reste de son œuvre.

Pierre Bonnard

Pierre Bonnard (1867–1947) entwickelte seinen eigenen
Stil – abseits der prominenten Strömungen, die in der
ersten Hälfte des 20. Jahrhunderts vorherrschten. Neben
Édouard Vuillard, Maurice Denis, Paul Ranson oder
Félix Vallotton gehörte er zu Beginn seiner Karriere
der Künstlergruppe der Nabis an. Später wandte er
sich intimen Szenen, Porträts, Akten, Stillleben und
Landschaften zu. Seine Sujets sind klassisch – ihre
Darstellung sehr zeitgenössisch. Bonnard schuf komplexe
Kompositionen, indem er sie als Bild im Bild aufbaut.
Durch Rahmen und Spiegelungen vervielfältigt er die
dargestellten Ebenen. Seine Farben sind das zentrale
Element in der Wiedergabe des Lichts, der ländlichen
Ansichten und der Gärten, die er von der Normandie
bis an die Küste des Mittelmeeres malt. Seinen Stil
entwickelt er subtil weiter – ohne große Brüche – hin zu
einer Palette aus hellen Farbtönen. Die einzige Ausnahme
bilden seine Selbstbildnisse, deren geheimnisumwobene
Strenge mit dem Rest seines Werks kontrastiert.

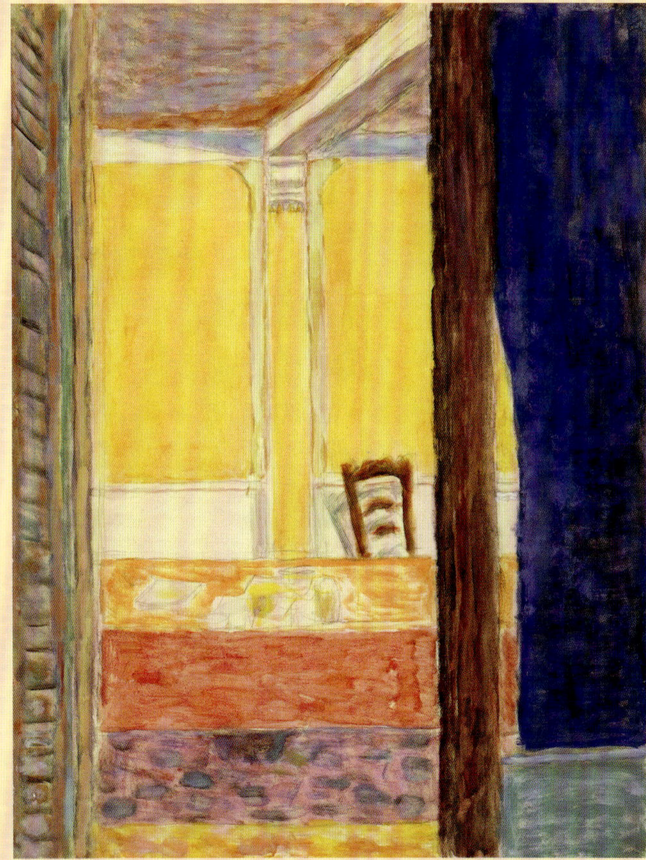

Pierre Bonnard

Pierre Bonnard (1867-1947) desarrolló su propio estilo - aparte de las corrientes prominentes que prevalecieron en la primera mitad del siglo XX. Junto a Édouard Vuillard, Maurice Denis, Paul Ranson y Félix Vallotton, fue miembro del grupo de artistas Nabis al principio de su carrera. Más tarde se dedicó a escenas íntimas, retratos, desnudos, bodegones y paisajes. Sus temas son clásicos - su representación muy contemporánea. Bonnard creó composiciones complejas construyéndolas como un cuadro dentro de otro. A través de marcos y reflexiones, multiplica los niveles representados. Sus colores son el elemento central en la reproducción de la luz, las vistas rurales y los jardines que pinta desde Normandía hasta la costa mediterránea. Desarrolla sutilmente su estilo - sin grandes interrupciones - hacia una paleta de tonos claros. La única excepción son sus autorretratos, cuya misteriosa severidad contrasta con el resto de su obra.

Pierre Bonnard

Pierre Bonnard (1867-1947) desenvolveu o seu próprio estilo - para além das correntes proeminentes que prevaleceram na primeira metade do século XX. Ao lado de Édouard Vuillard, Maurice Denis, Paul Ranson e Félix Vallotton, foi membro do grupo de artistas Nabis no início da sua carreira. Mais tarde virou-se para cenas íntimas, retratos, nus, naturezas mortas e paisagens. Os seus temas são clássicos - a sua representação é muito contemporânea. Bonnard criou composições complexas construindo-as como imagem dentro da imagem. Através de frames e reflexões, ele multiplica os níveis retratados. As suas cores são o elemento central na reprodução da luz, das vistas rurais e dos jardins que pinta desde a Normandia até à costa mediterrânica. Ele desenvolve sutilmente seu estilo ainda mais - sem grandes rupturas - em direção a uma paleta de tons claros. A única exceção são seus autoretratos, cuja misteriosa gravidade contrasta com o resto de seu trabalho.

Pierre Bonnard

Pierre Bonnard (1867-1947) ontwikkelde een heel eigen stijl – ver weg van de prominente stromingen die in de eerste helft van de 20e eeuw overheersten. Naast Édouard Vuillard, Maurice Denis, Paul Ranson en Félix Vallotton was hij aan het begin van zijn carrière lid van de Nabis. Later richtte hij zich op intieme taferelen, portretten, naakten, stillevens en landschappen. Zijn onderwerpen zijn klassiek, de weergave ervan zeer eigentijds. Bonnard schilderde complexe composities door ze als schilderij in een schilderij op te bouwen. Met kaders en weerspiegelingen vermenigvuldigde hij de afgebeelde niveaus. Zijn kleuren vormen het centrale element in de weergave van licht, landelijke vergezichten en tuinen, die hij schilderde van Normandië tot aan de Middellandse Zeekust. Hij ontwikkelde zijn stijl subtiel verder – zonder grote breuken – tot een palet van lichte tinten. De enige uitzondering vormen zijn zelfportretten, waarvan de mysterieuze strengheid contrasteert met de rest van zijn werk.

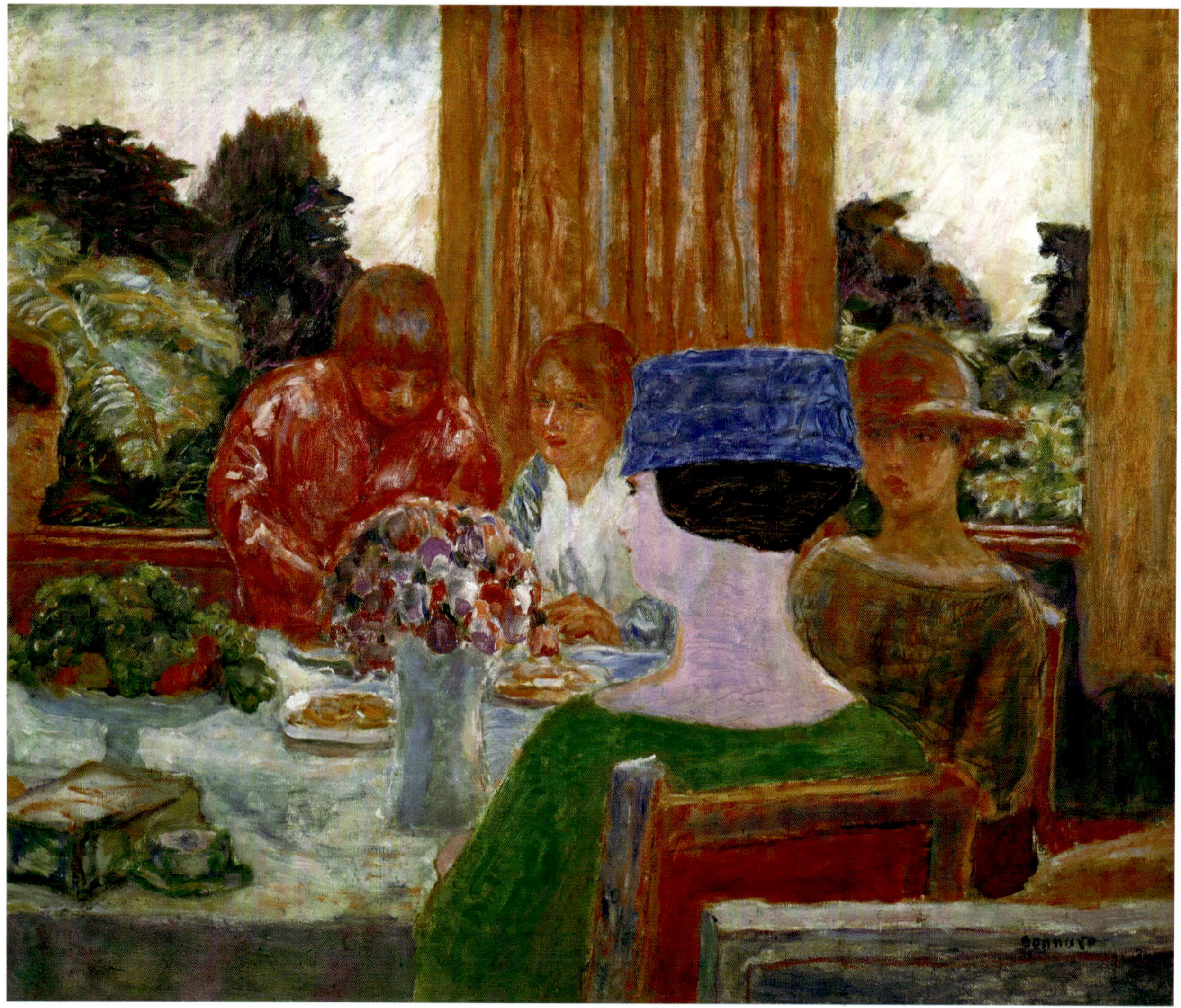

Teatime

The composition is divided into three levels: the woman in green with a blue hat in a side profile, the ladies sitting opposite her at the table and the landscape behind the large windows.

L'Heure du thé

Ce tableau est construit en trois plans : la femme en vert de dos et de trois quarts, coiffée d'un chapeau bleu, les femmes lui faisant face autour de la table, et le paysage derrière les larges fenêtres.

PIERRE BONNARD (1867-1947)

1917, Oil on canvas/Huile sur toile, 67,5 × 80 cm, Villa Flora, Winterthur

Die Teestunde

Die Komposition ist in drei Ebenen gegliedert: der Frau in Grün mit blauem Hut im verlorenen Profil, den ihr gegenübersitzenden Damen am Tisch und der Landschaft hinter den großen Fenstern.

La hora del té

La composición se divide en tres niveles: la mujer de verde con un sombrero azul en un perfil perdido, las señoras sentadas frente a ella en la mesa y el paisaje detrás de los grandes ventanales.

A hora do chá

A composição é dividida em três níveis: a mulher em verde com um chapéu azul num perfil perdido, as senhoras sentadas em frente à mesa e a paisagem atrás das grandes janelas.

Theetijd

De compositie is verdeeld in drie vlakken: de vrouw in het groen met een blauwe hoed, de dames tegenover haar aan de tafel en het landschap achter de grote ramen.

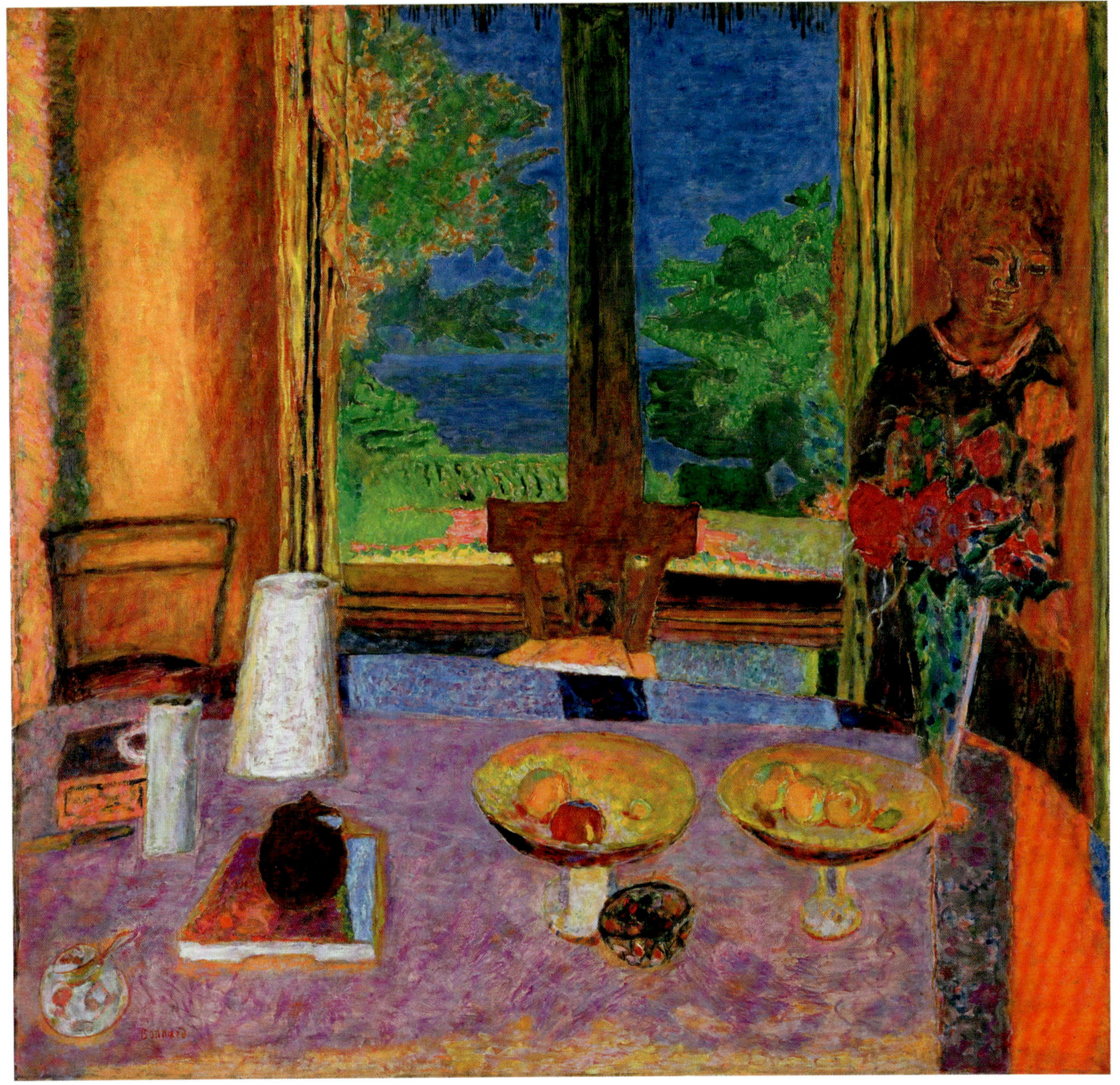

Dining Room on the Garden

Salle à manger donnant sur le jardin

Esszimmer mit Blick auf den Garten

Comedor con vista al jardín

Sala de jantar com vista para o jardim

Eetkamer met uitzicht op de tuin

PIERRE BONNARD (1867-1947)

1934/35, Oil on canvas/Huile sur toile, 126,8 × 135,3 cm, Solomon R. Guggenheim Museum, New York

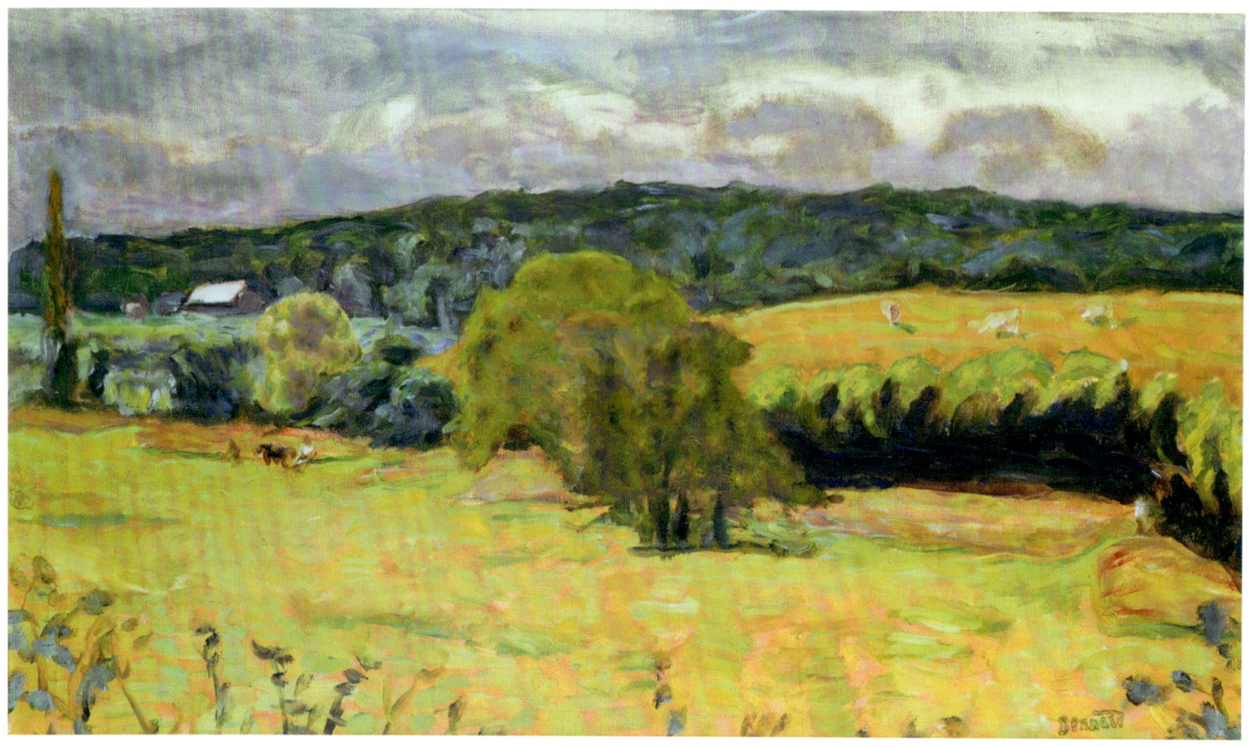

Dauphiné Landscape

Paysage du Dauphiné

PIERRE BONNARD (1867-1947)
1915, Oil on canvas/Oil on canvas, 31 × 53,5 cm, Private collection

Landschaft der Dauphiné

Paisaje de Dauphiné

Terra do Dauphiné

Landschap in de Dauphiné

The Terrace at Vernon

After his time with the Nabis, Bonnard found a new inspiration in the beauty of Normandy. Sometimes he enlivened his compositions with characters. They are structured by the colors without contour lines.

La Terrasse à Vernon

Après sa période nabie, Bonnard trouve dans la beauté sereine des paysages normands un souffle nouveau. La couleur structure ses compositions, animées ou non de figures, sans aucune ligne de contour.

Die Terrasse in Vernon

Nach seiner Zeit bei den Nabis findet Bonnard in der Schönheit der Normandie eine neue Inspiration. Manchmal belebt er seine Kompositionen durch Personen. Sie werden ohne Konturlinien durch die Farben strukturiert.

La terraza en Vernon

Después de su paso por los Nabis, Bonnard encontró una nueva inspiración en la belleza de Normandía. A veces anima sus composiciones con personajes. Están estructurados por los colores sin líneas de contorno.

O terraço em Vernon

Depois do seu tempo com a Nabis, Bonnard encontrou uma nova inspiração na beleza da Normandia. Às vezes ele anima suas composições com personagens. Eles são estruturados pelas cores sem linhas de contorno.

Het terras in Vernon

Na zijn tijd bij de Nabis vond Bonnard nieuwe inspiratie in de schoonheid van Normandië. Soms verlevendigde hij zijn composities met personen. Ze zijn opgebouwd uit kleuren zonder contourlijnen.

PIERRE BONNARD (1867-1947)
1923, Oil on canvas/Huile sur toile, 120 × 105 cm, Private collection

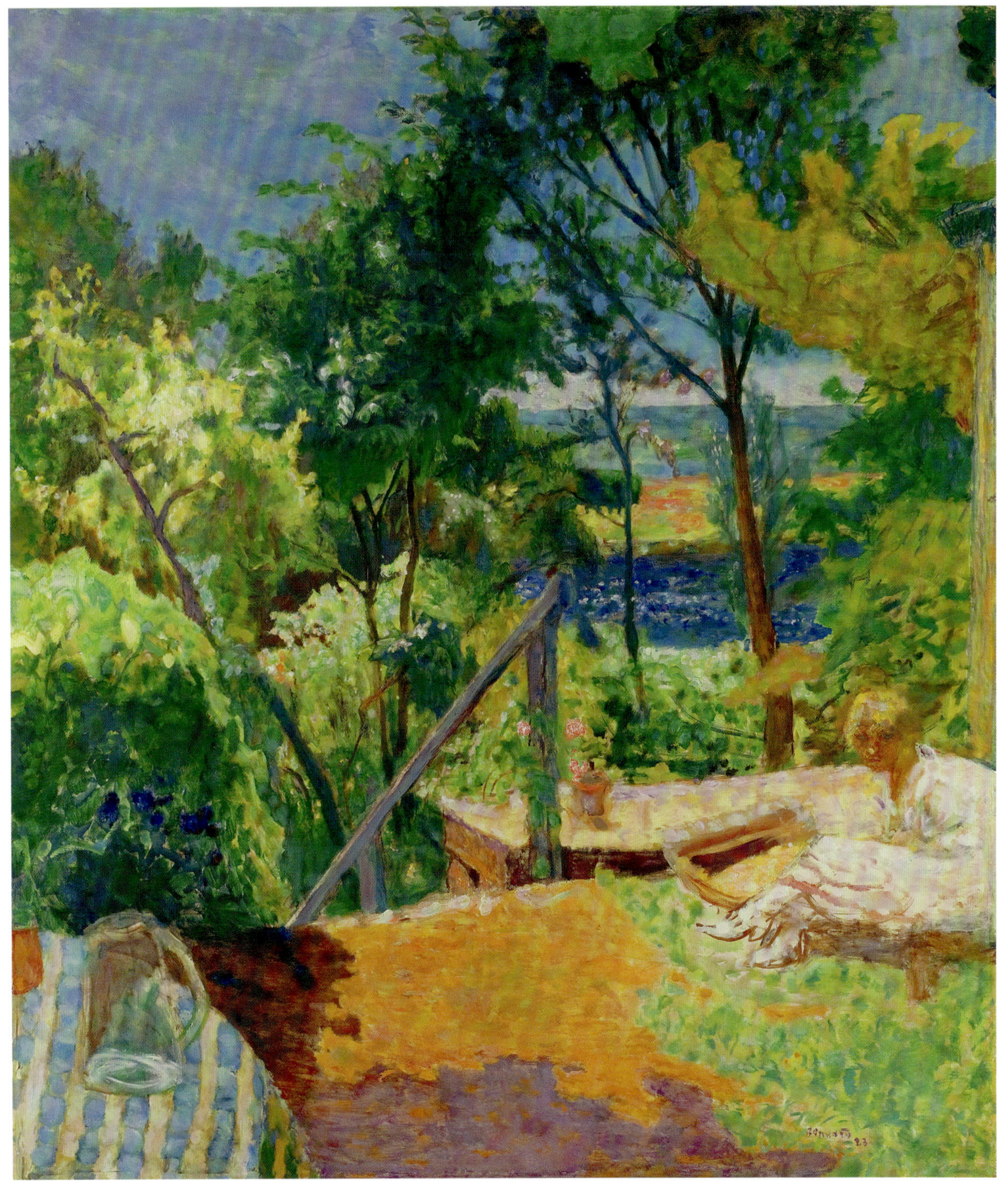

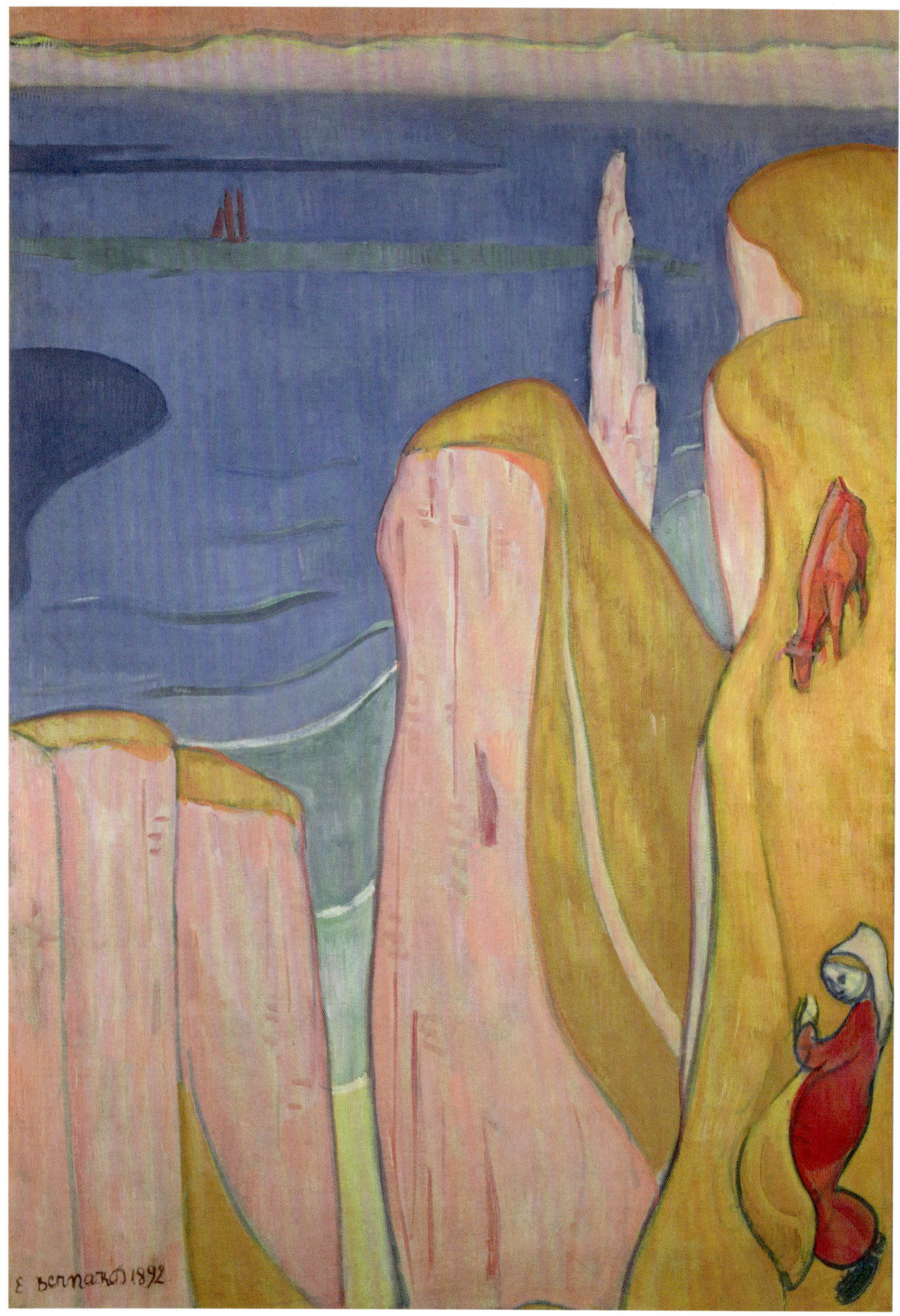

The Cliffs of Yport

Les Falaises d'Yport

Steilküste bei Yport

Costa escarpada cerca de Yport

Costa íngreme perto de Yport

Steile kust bij Yport

ÉMILE BERNARD (1868-1941)

1892, Oil on canvas/Huile sur toile,
91,7 × 65,8 cm, Private collection

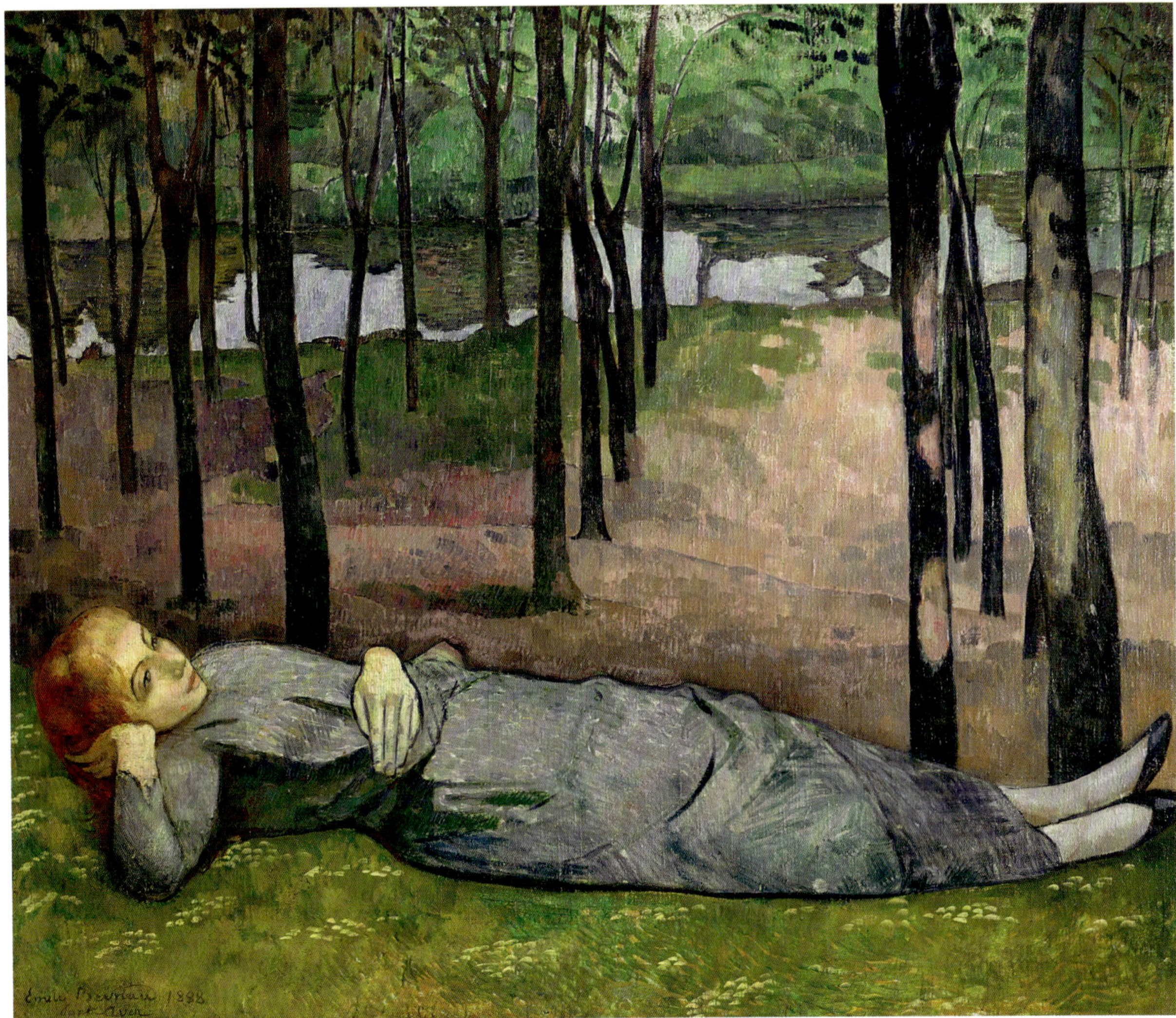

Madeleine in the Bois d'Amour

At the age of 20 Émile Bernard painted this surreal work. It is characterized by the representation of his sister Madeleine, who he placed in an unnatural position in front of the landscape.

Madeleine au bois d'Amour

Une atmosphère d'irréalité règne sur ce tableau, peint en atelier à l'âge de 20 ans. La figure allongée de Madeleine, la sœur d'Émile Bernard, semble artificiellement « plaquée » sur le paysage.

ÉMILE BERNARD (1868-1941)

1888, Oil on canvas/Huile sur toile, 138 × 163 cm, Musée d'Orsay, Paris

Madeleine im Bois d'Amour

Im Alter von 20 Jahren malt Émile Bernard das surreal wirkende Gemälde. Es ist geprägt durch die Darstellung seiner Schwester Madeleine, die er in einer unnatürlichen Position vor der Landschaft platziert.

Madeleine en el Bois d'Amour

A la edad de 20 años Émile Bernard crea una pintura surrealista. Se caracteriza por la representación de su hermana Madeleine, la cual coloca en una posición antinatural frente al paisaje.

Madeleine no Bois d'Amour

Aos 20 anos, Émile Bernard pinta a pintura surrealista. Caracteriza-se pela representação da sua irmã Madeleine, que ele coloca numa posição antinatural em frente à paisagem.

Madeleine in het Bois d'Amour

Op 20-jarige leeftijd schilderde Émile Bernard dit surrealistisch aandoende schilderij. Het wordt getekend door de afbeelding van zijn zus Madeleine, die hij in een onnatuurlijke houding voor het landschap plaatste.

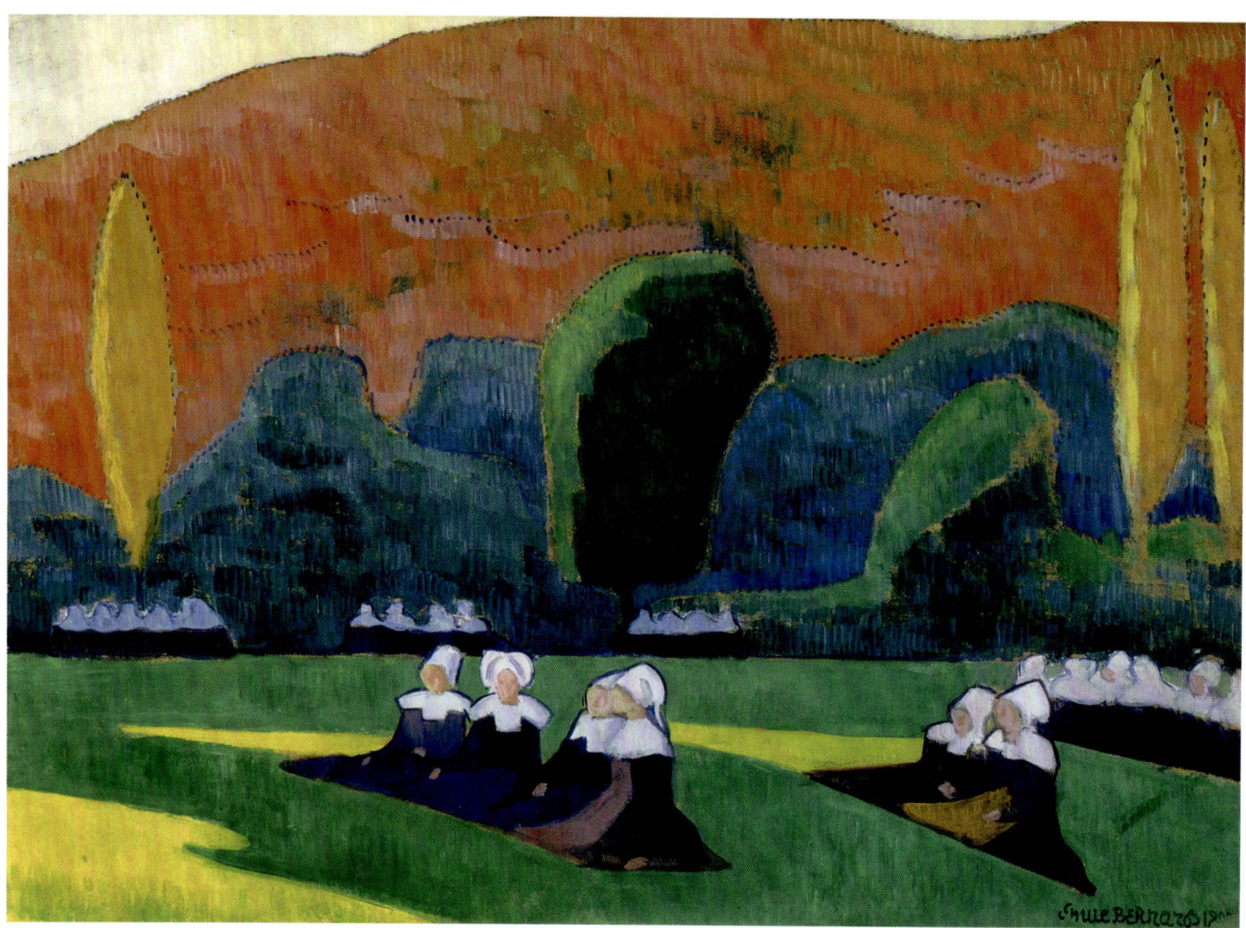

Breton Women Attending a Pardon

Femmes bretonnes assistant à un pardon

Bretonische Frauen bei einem Pardon

Mujeres bretonas que asisten a un indulto

Mulheres bretãs com perdão

Bretonse vrouwen bij een gratieverzoek

ÉMILE BERNARD (1868-1941)

1892, Oil on cardboard/Huile sur carton, 82,2 × 116,2 cm, Dallas Museum of Art, Dallas

The Apple Harvest

The painting in extreme portrait format, reminiscent of a Japanese kakemono, renounces any rules of perspective. The effect of depth is created solely by the overlapping of the figures.

Le Gaulage des pommes

Dans un format vertical allongé qui rappelle les kakemonos japonais, ce tableau abolit toute perspective traditionnelle. La profondeur n'est suggérée que par les effets de superposition des figures.

Die Apfelernte

Das Gemälde im extremen Hochformat, das an ein japanisches Kakemono erinnert, verzichtet auf jegliche Regeln der Perspektive. Die Tiefenwirkung wird allein durch die Überschneidung der Figuren erzeugt.

La cosecha de manzanas

La pintura en formato de retrato extremo, que recuerda a un kakemono japonés, renuncia a cualquier regla de perspectiva. El efecto de profundidad se crea únicamente por la superposición de las figuras.

A colheita da maçã

A pintura em formato de retrato extremo, reminiscente de um kakemono japonês, renuncia a qualquer regra de perspectiva. O efeito de profundidade é criado apenas pela sobreposição das figuras.

De appeloogst

Het extreem langwerpige schilderij, dat qua formaat doet denken aan een Japanse kakemono, negeert alle perspectiefregels. De dieptewerking ontstaat puur door de overlapping van de figuren.

ÉMILE BERNARD (1868-1941)

1890, Oil on canvas/Huile sur toile, 105 × 45 cm, Musée des Beaux-Arts, Nantes

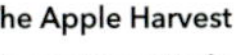

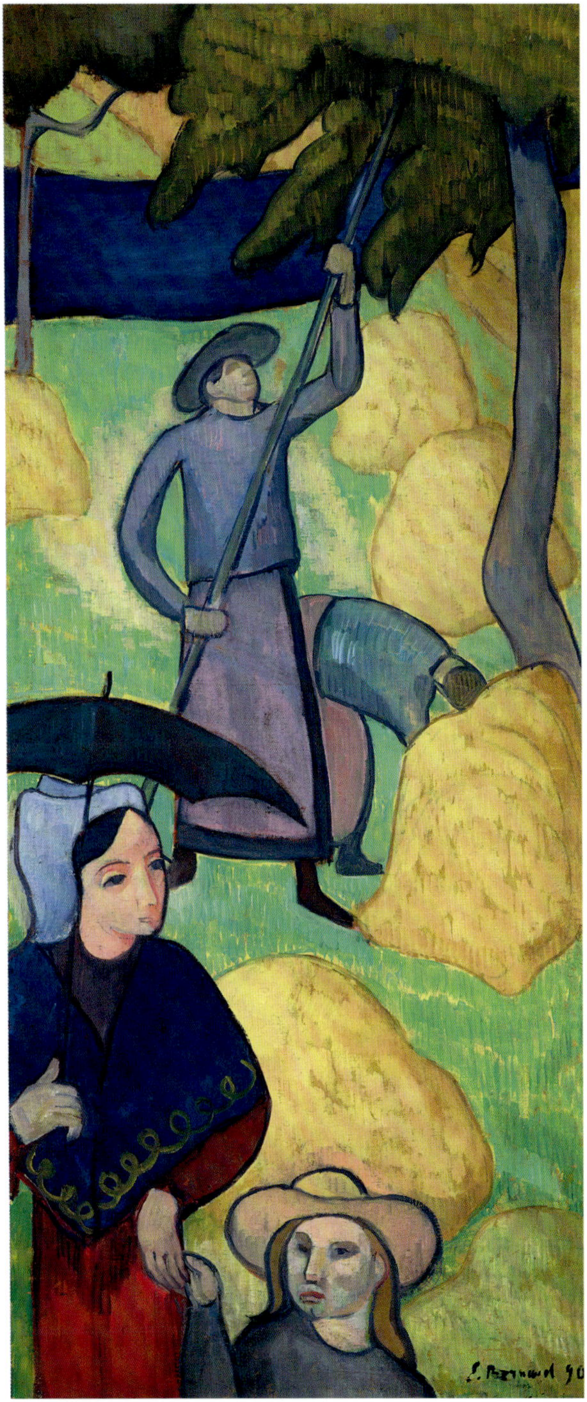

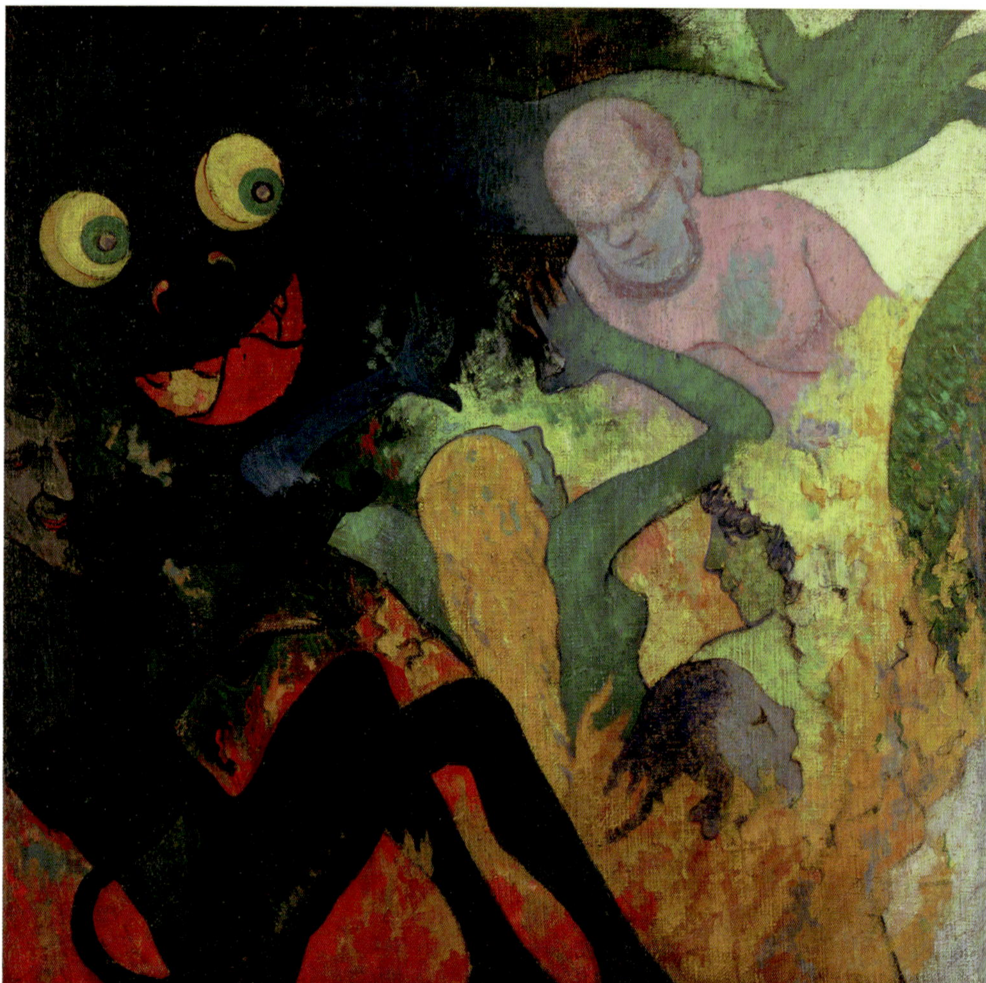

Les Paradis artificiels

Seguin has driven Syntheticism into the fantastic. With his works he referred to Baudelaire but also to Verlaine, who is depicted on the right like a ghost under the influence of drugs.

Les Paradis artificiels

Seguin fait basculer le synthétisme dans le fantastique. Il rend hommage à Baudelaire, mais aussi à Verlaine, représenté à droite du tableau comme un fantôme halluciné sous l'emprise de drogues.

Paradies

Seguin treibt den Synthetismus in das Fantastische. Mit seinen Werken bezieht er sich auf Baudelaire aber auch auf Verlaine, der rechts im Bild wie ein Geist unter dem Einfluss von Drogen dargestellt ist.

Paraíso artificial

Seguin convierte la síntesis en fantasía. Rinde homenaje a Baudelaire, pero también a Verlaine, representada a la derecha del cuadro como un fantasma alucinado bajo la influencia de las drogas.

Paraíso

Seguin leva o sintético para o fantástico. Com suas obras, ele se refere a Baudelaire, mas também a Verlaine, que é retratado à direita como um fantasma sob a influência de drogas.

Kunstmatig paradijs

Seguin dreef het synthetisme door tot het fantastische. Met zijn werken verwees hij naar Baudelaire, maar ook naar Verlaine, die rechts is afgebeeld als een geest onder invloed van drugs.

ARMAND SEGUIN (1869-1903)

c. 1895, Oil on canvas/Huile sur toile, 53 × 55 cm, Private collection

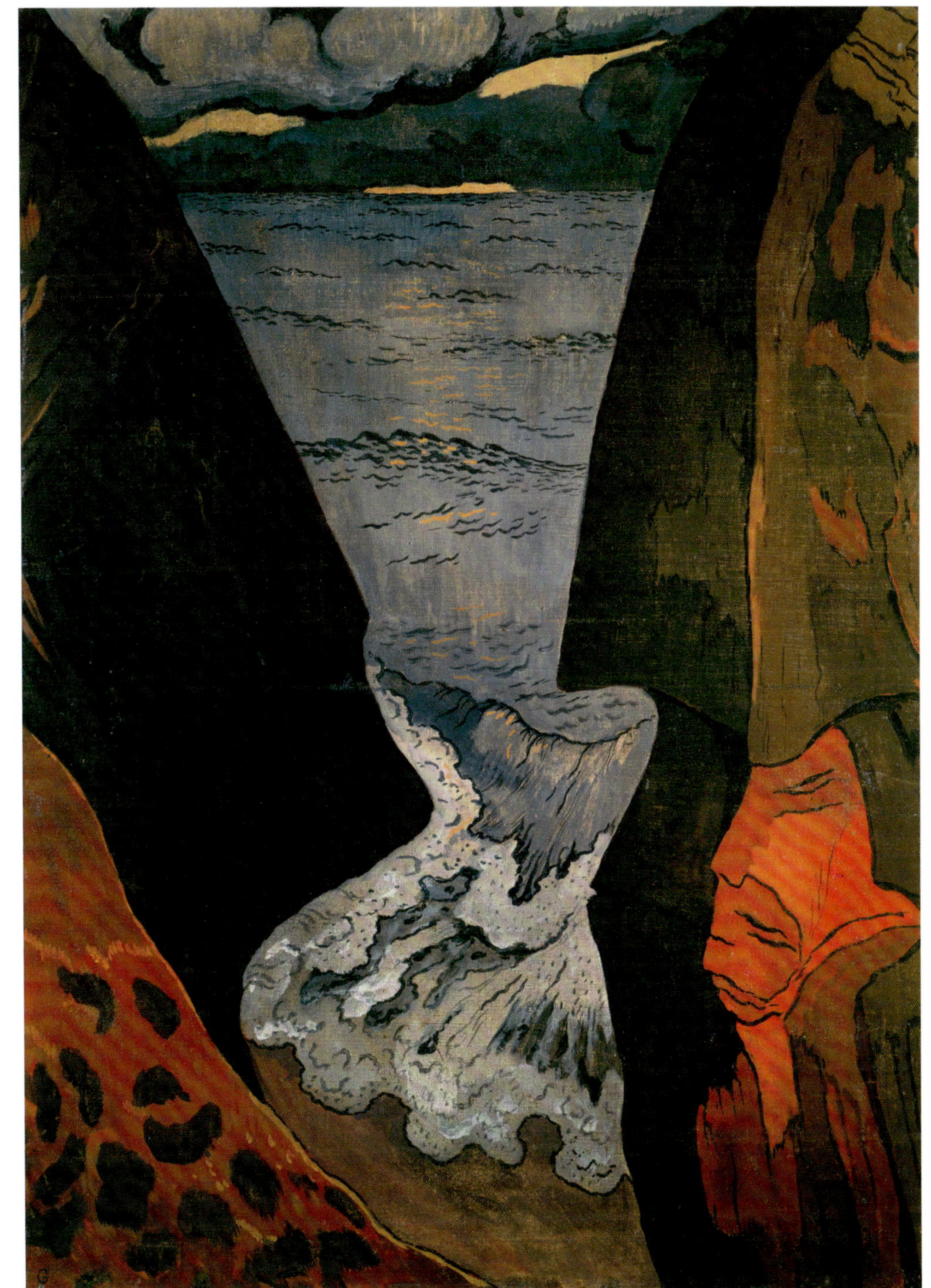

Cliffs near Camaret

Vorhor, vague grise
dit aussi Falaises à Camaret

Felsküste bei Camaret

Costa rocosa cerca de Camaret

Costa rochosa perto de Camaret

Rotskust bij Camaret

GEORGES LACOMBE (1868-1916)

c. 1892, Painting with egg on canvas/
Peinture à l'œuf sur toile,
82,5 x 61 cm, Musée des
beaux-arts de Brest

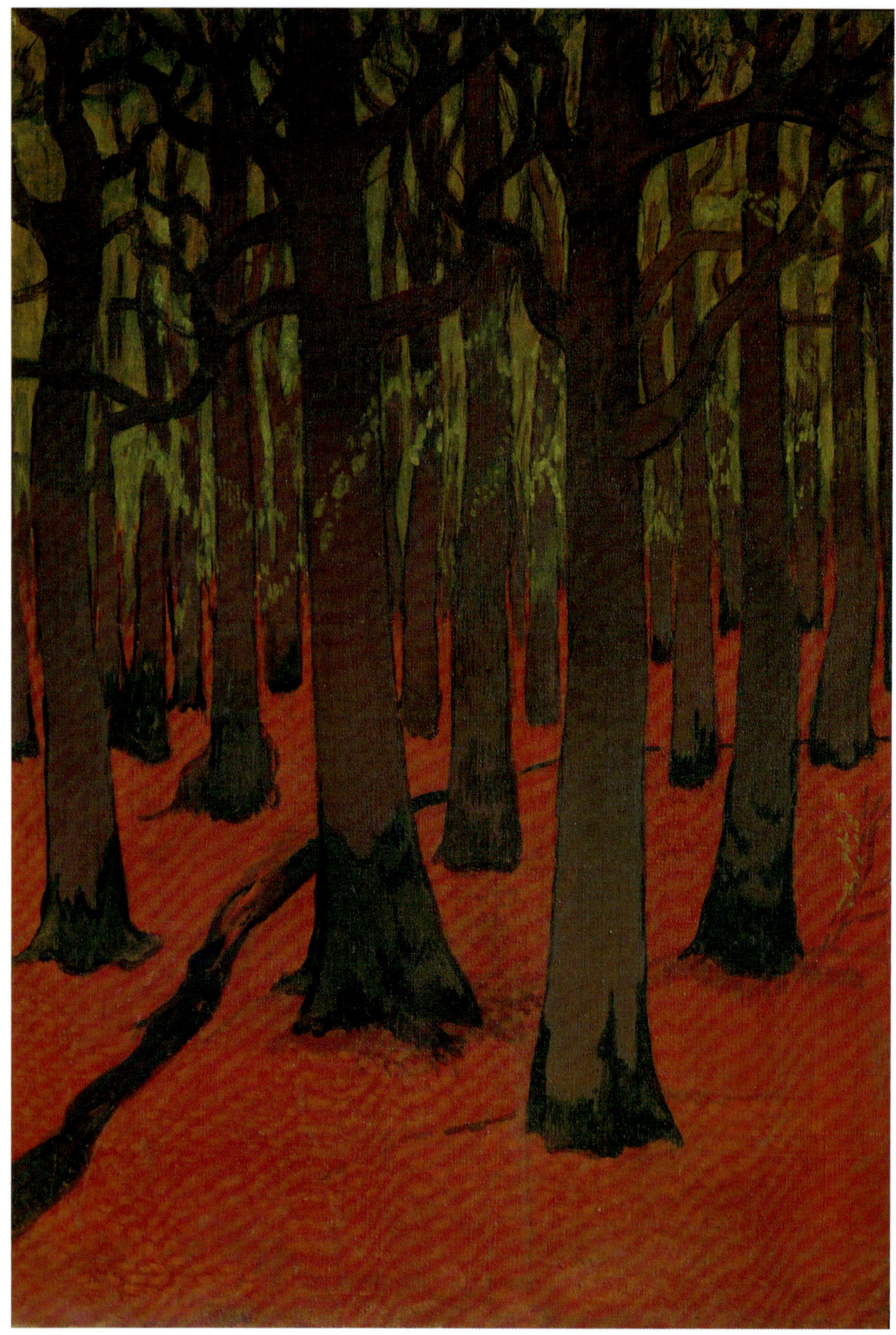

The Forest with Red Earth

La Forêt au sol rouge

Wald mit roter Erde

Bosque con tierra roja

Floresta com terra vermelha

Bos met rode aarde

GEORGES LACOMBE (1868-1916)
1891, Oil on canvas/Huile sur toile,
71,3 × 50,5 cm, Musée des
Beaux-Arts, Quimper

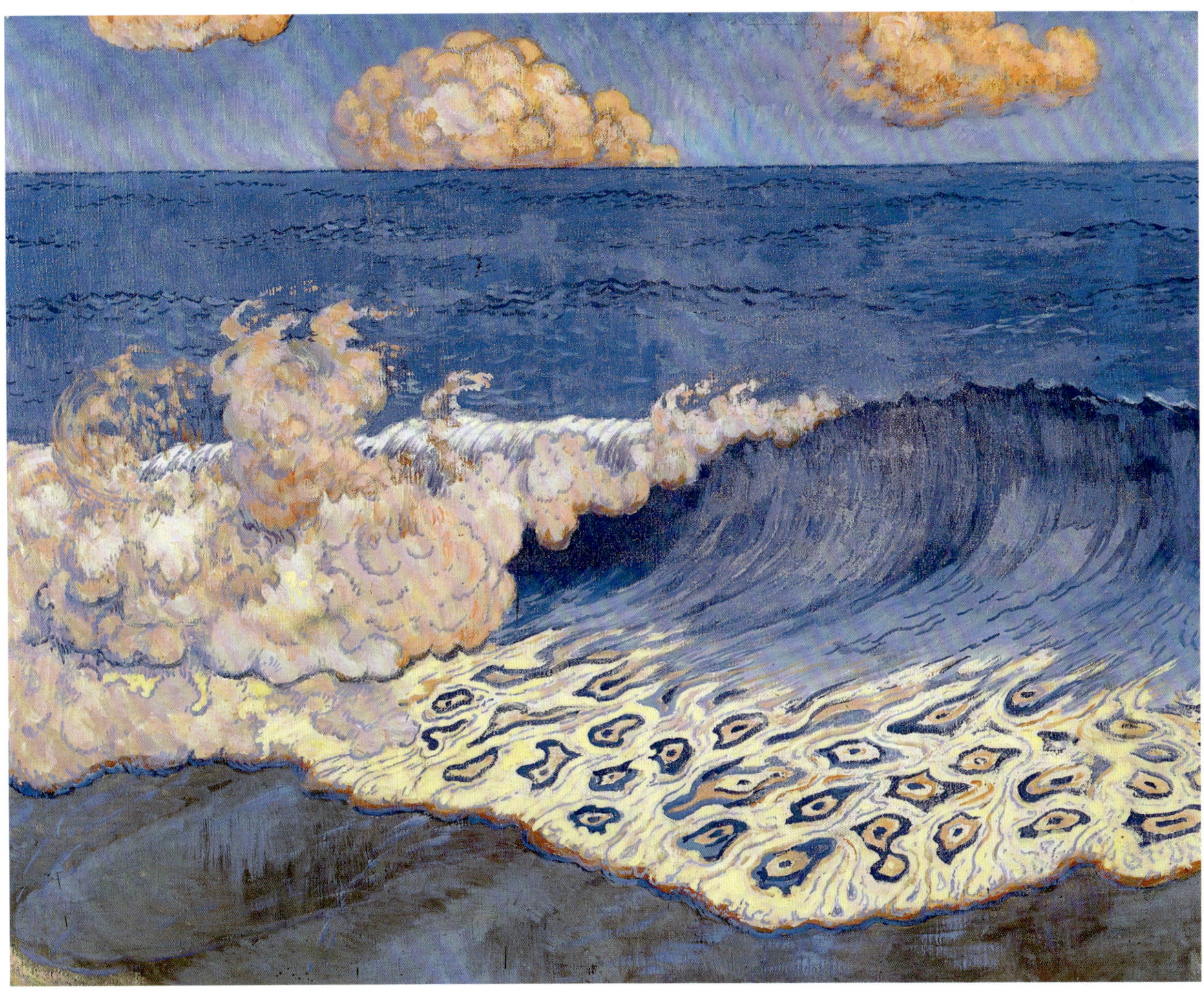

Blue Seascape, Wave Effect

With its high horizon, bright colors and decorative elements that make up the foam, Lacombe referred to Japanese woodcuts. His work is reminiscent of the waves of Hokusai or Hiroshige.

Marine bleue, effet de vague

Horizon haut, couleurs claires, effets décoratifs pour figurer l'écume : peut-on faire œuvre plus inspirée par les estampes japonaises ? Difficile de ne pas penser aux vagues d'Hokusai ou d'Hiroshige.

Blaues Seestück, Wellen

Mit dem hohen Horizont, den hellen Farben und den dekorativen Elementen, die den Schaum bilden, nimmt Lacombe Bezug auf japanische Holzschnitte. Sein Werk erinnert an die Wellen von Hokusai oder Hiroshige.

Pieza de mar azul, olas

Con su alto horizonte, los colores vivos y los elementos decorativos que componen la espuma, Lacombe se refiere a la xilografía japonesa. Su obra recuerda a las olas de Hokusai o Hiroshige.

Blue sea piece, ondas

Com o seu horizonte alto, cores vivas e elementos decorativos que compõem a espuma, Lacombe refere-se às xilogravuras japonesas. Seu trabalho lembra as ondas de Hokusai ou Hiroshige.

Blauw zeestuk, golven

Met zijn hoge horizon, heldere kleuren en decoratieve elementen die het schuim vormen, verwijst Lacombe naar Japanse houtsneden. Zijn werk herinnert aan de golven van Hokusai en Hiroshige.

GEORGES LACOMBE (1868-1916)

c. 1893, Tempera on canvas/Tempera sur toile, 43 × 64,2 cm, Musée des Beaux-Arts, Rennes

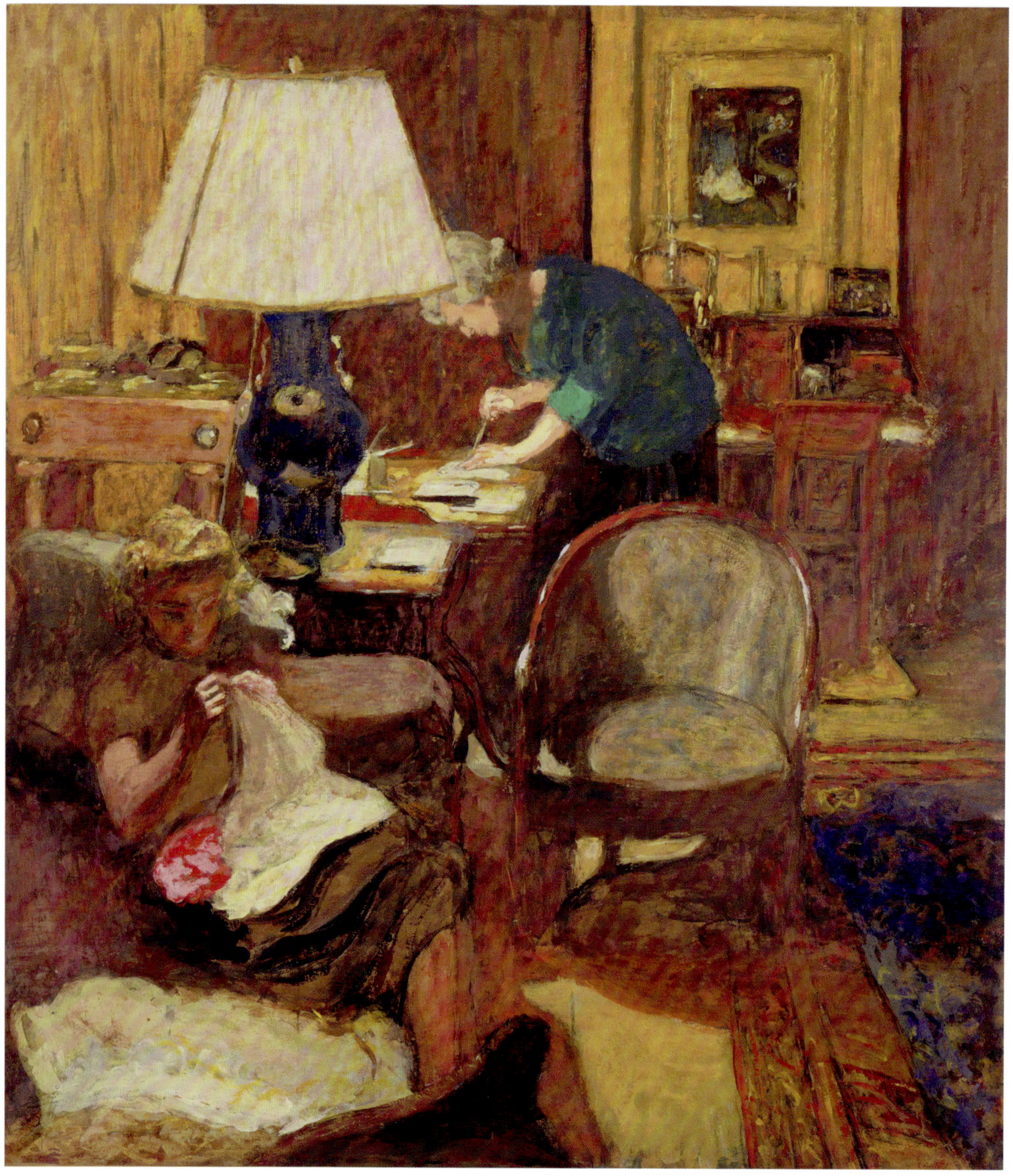

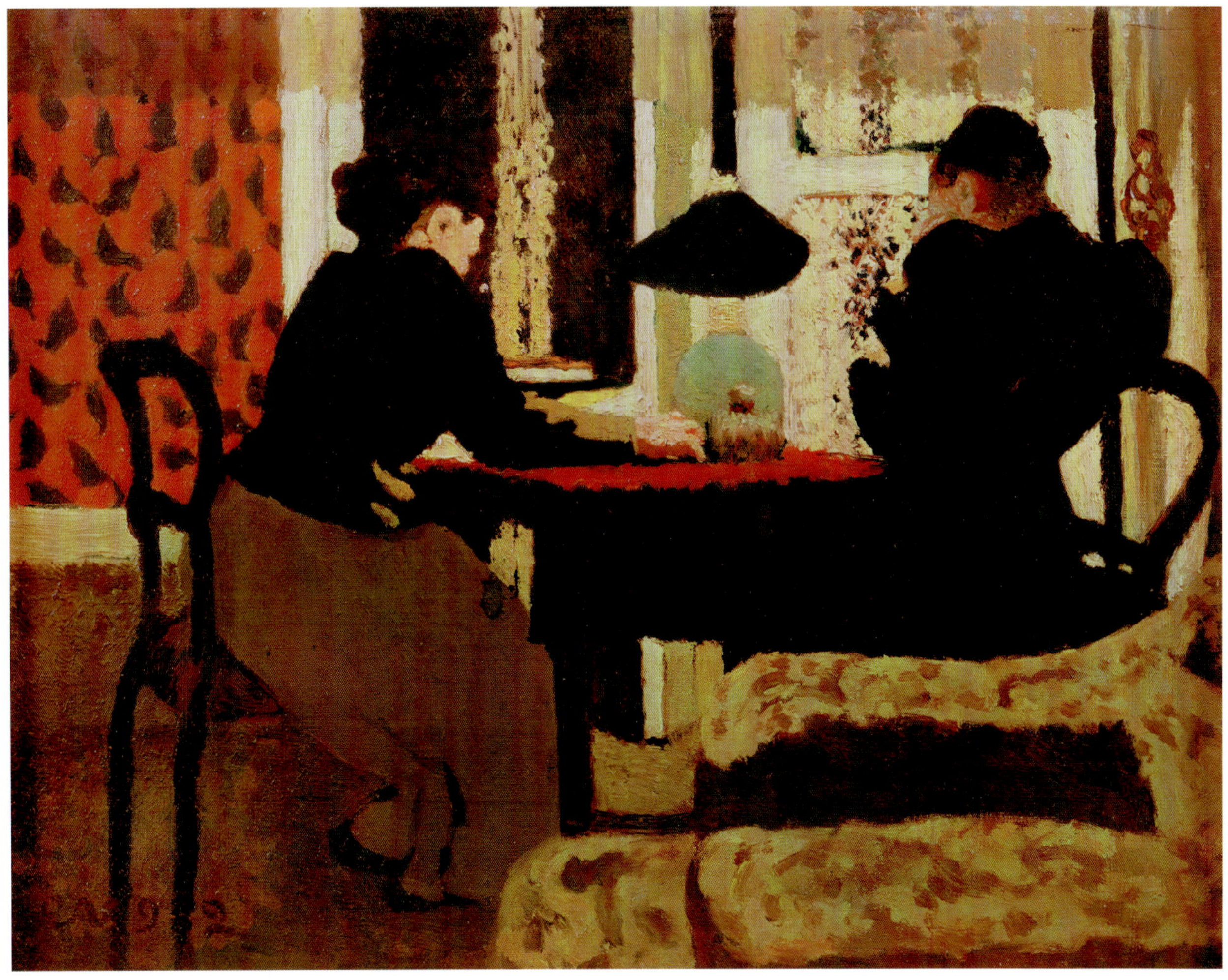

The Book Maker

Le Fabricant de livres

Der Buchbinder

La encuadernadora

O Encadernador de livros

De boekbinder

ÉDOUARD VUILLARD
(1868-1940)

n. d., Oil on panel/
Huile sur panneau,
123 × 110 cm, Private collection

Women by Lamplight

Deux femmes sous la lampe

Zwei Frauen im Lampenlicht

Dos mujeres a la luz de la lámpara

Duas mulheres no lampião

Twee vrouwen bij lamplicht

ÉDOUARD VUILLARD (1868-1940)

1892, Oil on canvas mounted on wood/
Huile sur toile marouflée sur bois, 33 × 41,5 cm,
Musée de l'Annonciade, Saint-Tropez

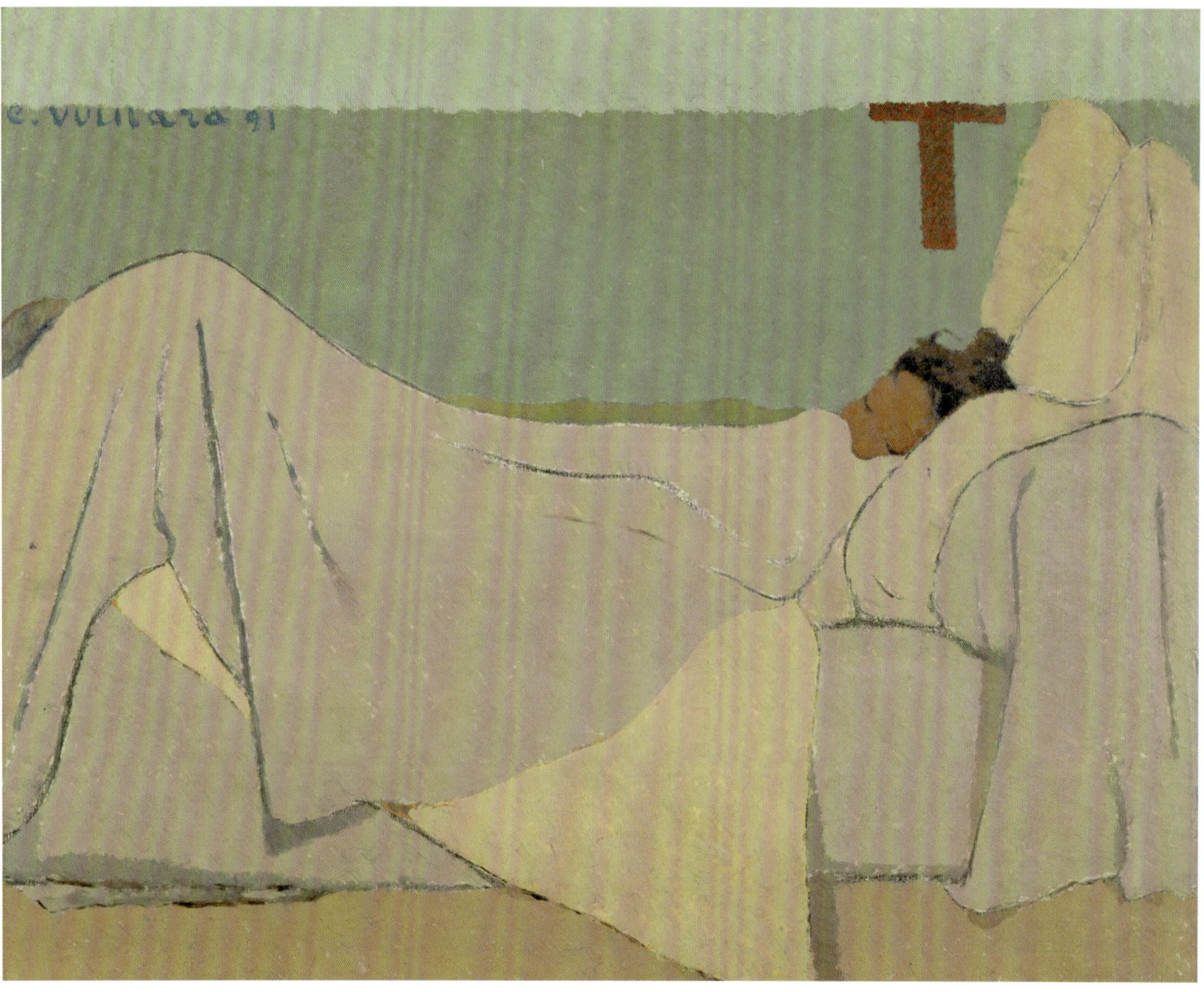

In Bed

The background is composed of three simple stripes of color. The bed and the person consist solely of composite color surfaces, to which Vuillard lends plasticity through horizontal and oblique lines.

Au lit

Sur un fond structuré par trois bandes de couleurs, le lit et le personnage ne sont figurés que par un jeu d'aplats juxtaposés, et quelques lignes droites et obliques qui suffisent à les faire exister.

Im Bett

Der Hintergrund setzt sich aus drei einfachen Farbstreifen zusammen. Das Bett und die Person bestehen allein aus zusammengesetzten Farbflächen, denen Vuillard durch horizontale und schräge Linien Plastizität verleiht.

En la cama

El fondo se compone de tres simples franjas de color. La cama y la persona están formadas únicamente por superficies de color compuestas, a las que Vuillard confiere plasticidad a través de líneas horizontales y oblicuas.

Na cama

O fundo é composto por três faixas coloridas simples. A cama e a pessoa consistem unicamente em superfícies de cor compostas, às quais Vuillard empresta plasticidade através de linhas horizontais e oblíquas.

In bed

De achtergrond is opgebouwd uit drie eenvoudige kleurstroken. Het bed en de persoon bestaan uitsluitend uit naast elkaar geplaatste kleurvlakken, waaraan Vuillard door horizontale en schuine lijnen plasticiteit verleende.

ÉDOUARD VUILLARD (1868-1940)

1891, Oil on canvas/Huile sur toile, 74 × 92,5 cm, Musée d'Orsay, Paris

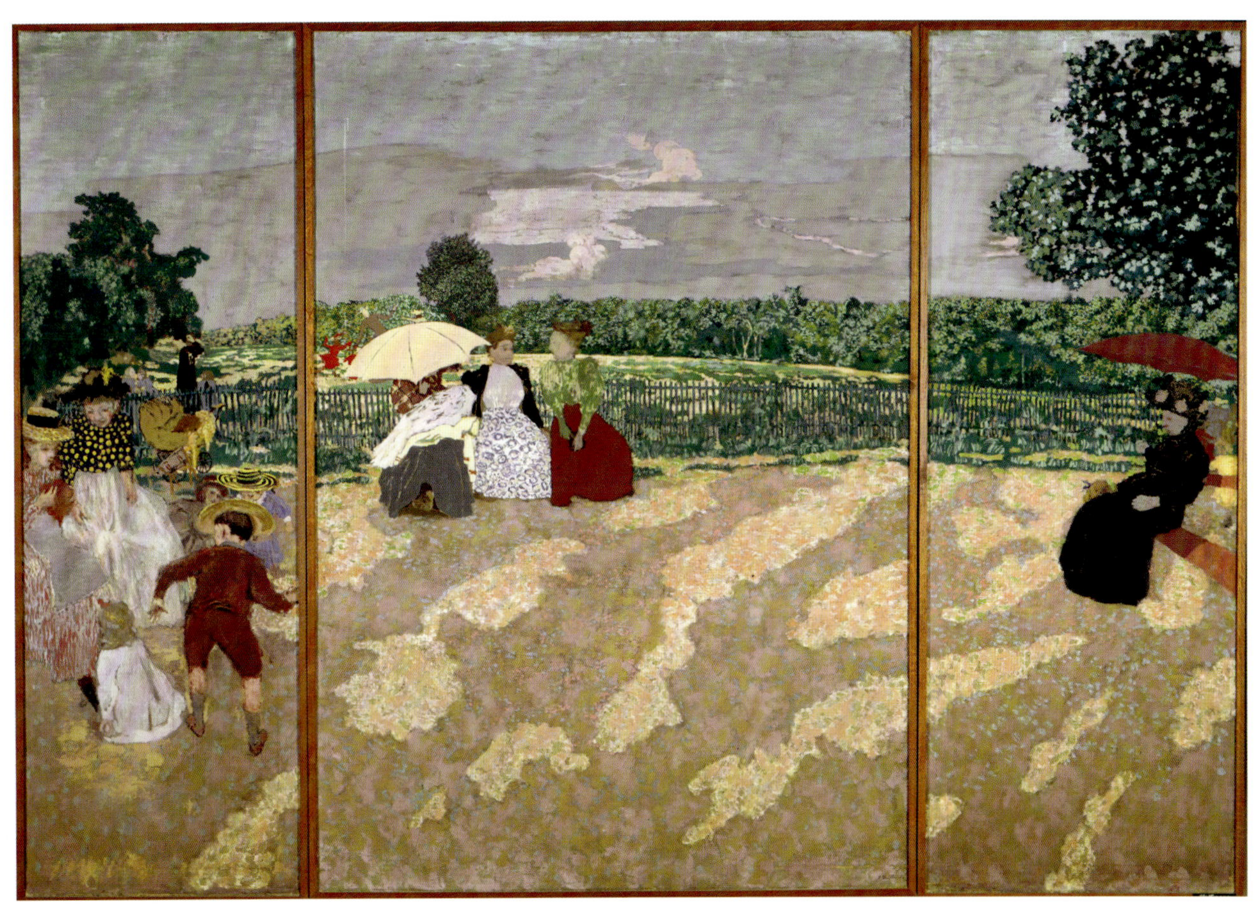

Public Gardens: The Conversation, Nannies, The Red Parasol

Jardins publics : La Conversation, Les Nourrices, L'Ombrelle rouge

Öffentliche Gärten: Die Unterhaltung, Die Ammen, Der rote Sonnenschirm

Jardines Públicos: el entretenimiento, las enfermeras, la sombrilla roja

Jardins Públicos: O Entretenimento, Os Enfermeiros, O Parasol Vermelho

Publieke tuin: de conversatie, de voedsters, de rode parasol

ÉDOUARD VUILLARD (1868-1940)

1894, Tempera on canvas/ Détrempe sur toile, 213,5 × 154 cm, Musée d'Orsay, Paris

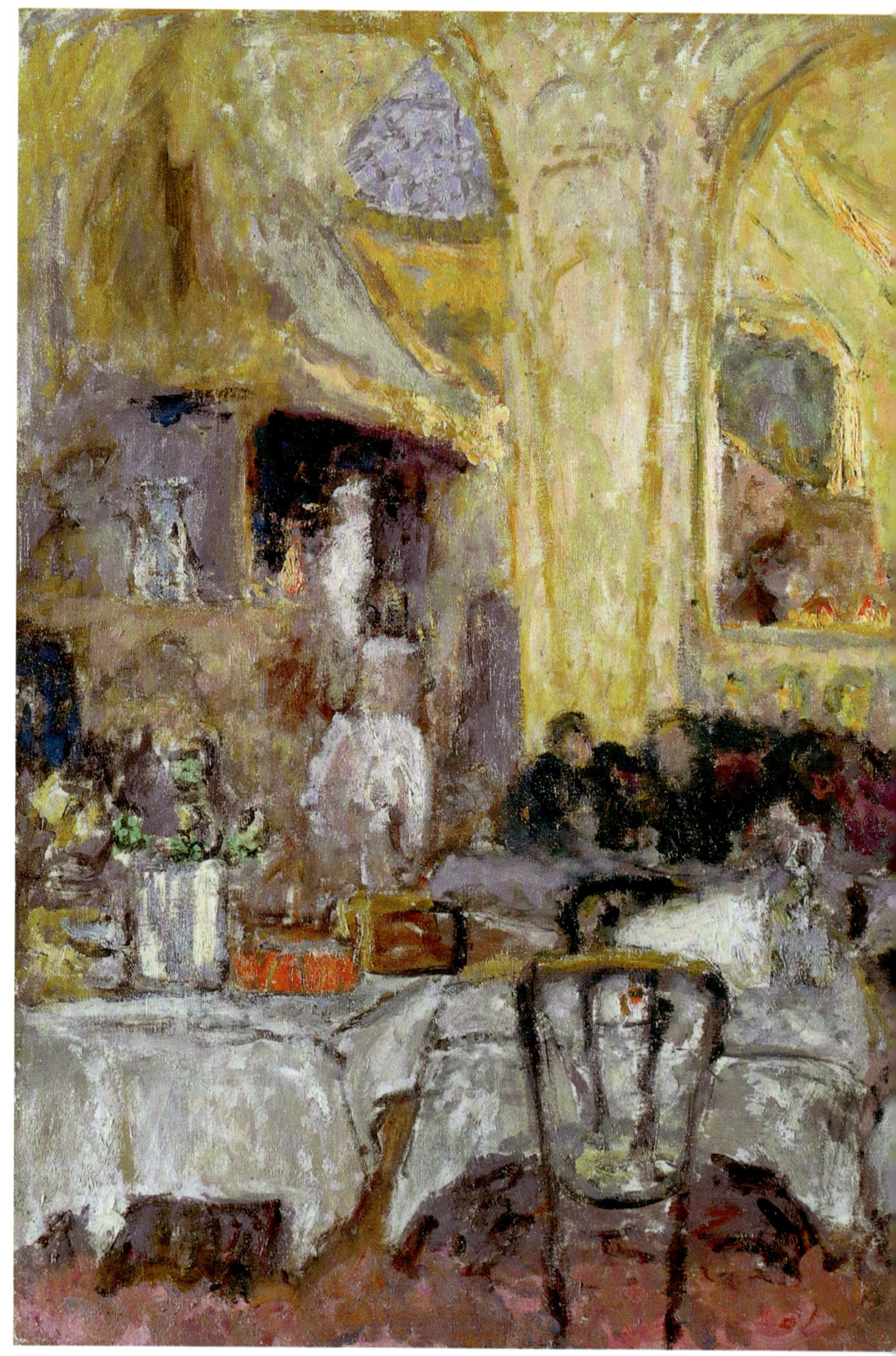

Café Wepler

Le Café Wepler

Das Café Wepler

El Café Wepler

O Café Wepler

Café Wepler

ÉDOUARD VUILLARD (1868-1940)
c. 1908-10, Oil on canvas/Huile sur toile, 91,8 × 132,7 cm,
Cleveland Museum of Art, Cleveland

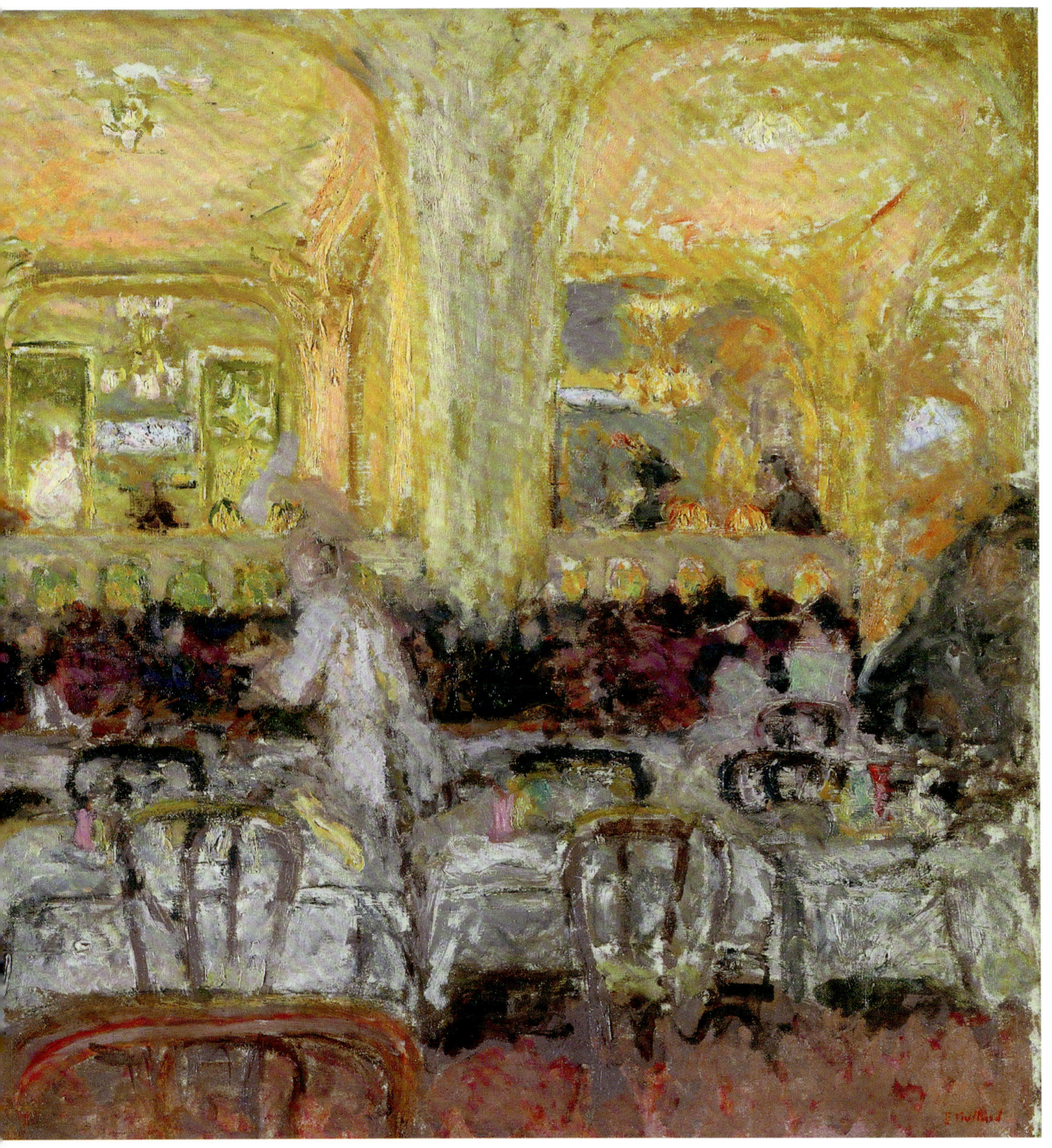

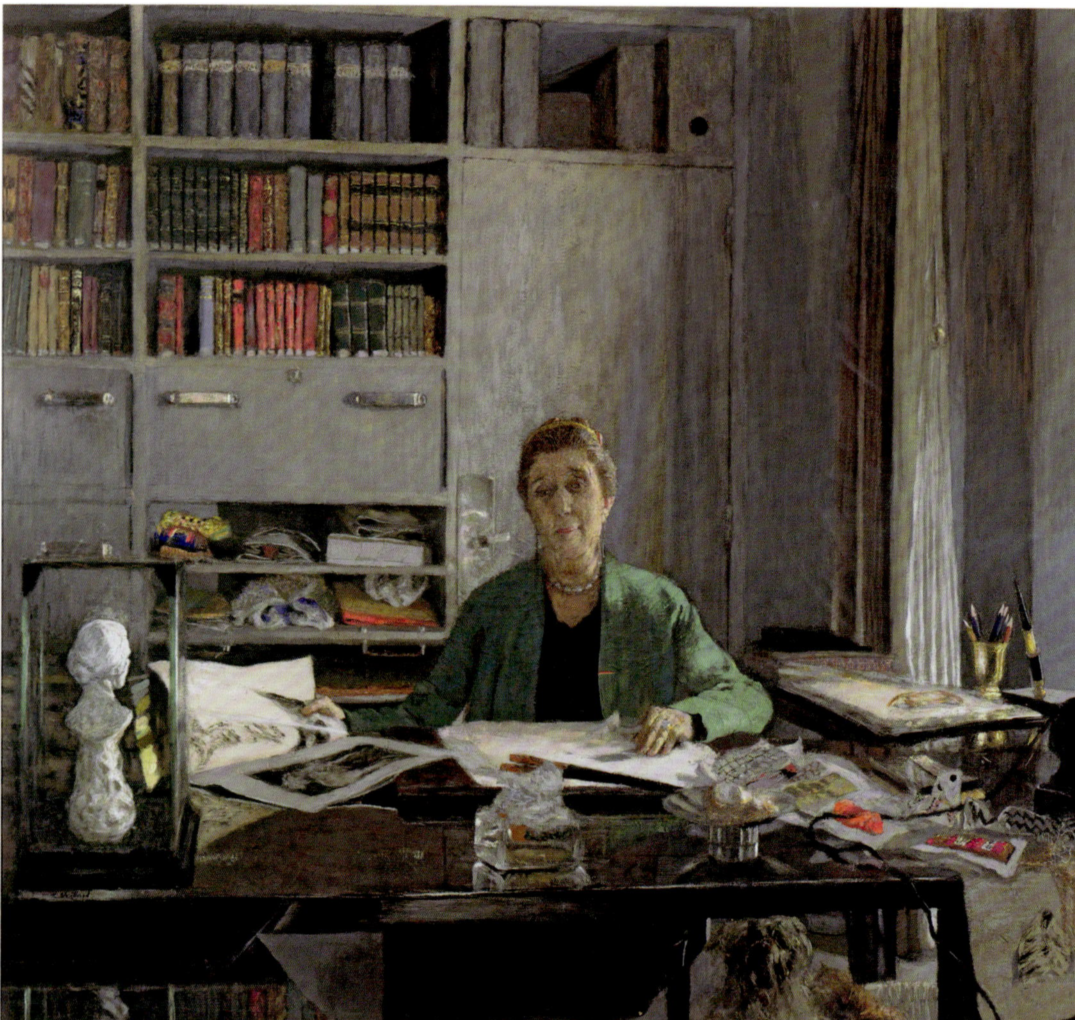

Jeanne Lanvin

The painting, commissioned by the famous fashion designer Jeanne Lanvin, is in the tradition of Vuillard's other interiors, in which the people and the furnishings merge into a unit.

Jeanne Lanvin

Commandé par la grande couturière française Jeanne Lanvin, ce portrait au dessin précis tranche avec les scènes d'intérieurs habituelles d'Édouard Vuillard, où figure et décor se mêlent et se fondent.

Jeanne Lanvin

Das von der berühmten Modeschöpferin Jeanne Lanvin in Auftrag gegebene Gemälde steht in der Tradition von Vuillards anderen Interieurs, auf denen die Personen und die Einrichtung zu einer Einheit verschmelzen.

Jeanne Lanvin

La pintura, encargada por la famosa diseñadora de moda Jeanne Lanvin, contrasta con las escenas interiores de Vuillard, en las que las personas y el mobiliario se funden en una unidad.

Jeanne Lanvin

A pintura, encomendada pela famosa estilista Jeanne Lanvin, está na tradição dos outros interiores de Vuillard, nos quais as pessoas e os móveis se fundem em uma unidade.

Jeanne Lanvin

Het schilderij dat hij maakte in opdracht van de beroemde modeontwerpster Jeanne Lanvin, past in de traditie van Vuillards andere interieurs, waarop personen en inrichting versmelten tot een geheel.

ÉDOUARD VUILLARD (1868-1940)

1933, Tempera on canvas/Peinture à la colle sur toile, 124,5 × 136,5 cm, Musée d'Orsay, Paris

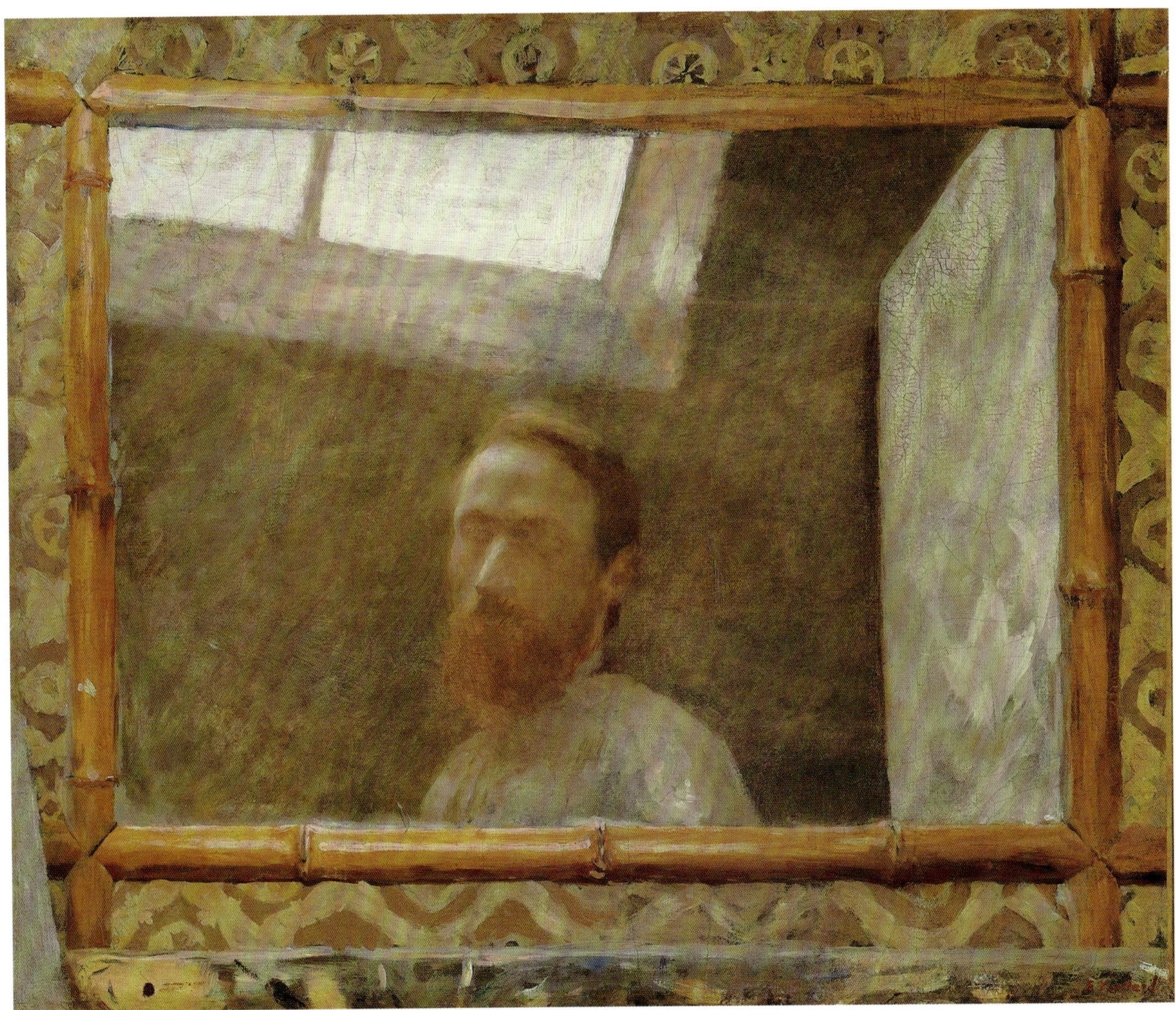

Self Portrait with a Bamboo Mirror

Like his friend Pierre Bonnard, Vuillard depicted himself in front of a mirror. He used it to create a picture within a picture. The muted colors lend his work a melancholic mood.

Autoportrait au miroir de bambou

À l'instar de son ami Pierre Bonnard, Vuillard se représente face à son miroir, et crée ainsi un effet de tableau dans le tableau. Les tonalités sourdes de la toile renforcent le sentiment de mélancolie.

Selbstbildnis im Bambusspiegel

Wie sein Freund Pierre Bonnard bildet sich Vuillard vor einem Spiegel ab. Er kreiert damit ein Bild im Bild. Die gedämpften Farbtöne verleihen seinem Werk eine melancholische Stimmung.

Autorretrato en un espejo de bambú

Como su amigo Pierre Bonnard, Vuillard se representa a sí mismo frente a su espejo, creando así un efecto pictórico en el cuadro. Las tonalidades apagadas de la tela refuerzan la sensación de melancolía.

Auto-retrato num espelho de bambu

Como seu amigo Pierre Bonnard, Vuillard se apresenta em frente a um espelho. Ele usa-o para criar uma imagem dentro de uma imagem. As cores suaves emprestam ao seu trabalho um humor melancólico.

Zelfportret in een bamboespiegel

Net als zijn vriend Pierre Bonnard schilderde Vuillard zichzelf voor een spiegel. Hij maakte daarbij een schilderij in een schilderij. De gedempte kleuren geven dit werk een melancholieke sfeer.

ÉDOUARD VUILLARD (1868-1940)

c. 1890, Oil on canvas/Huile sur toile, 44,5 × 53,3 cm, Private collection

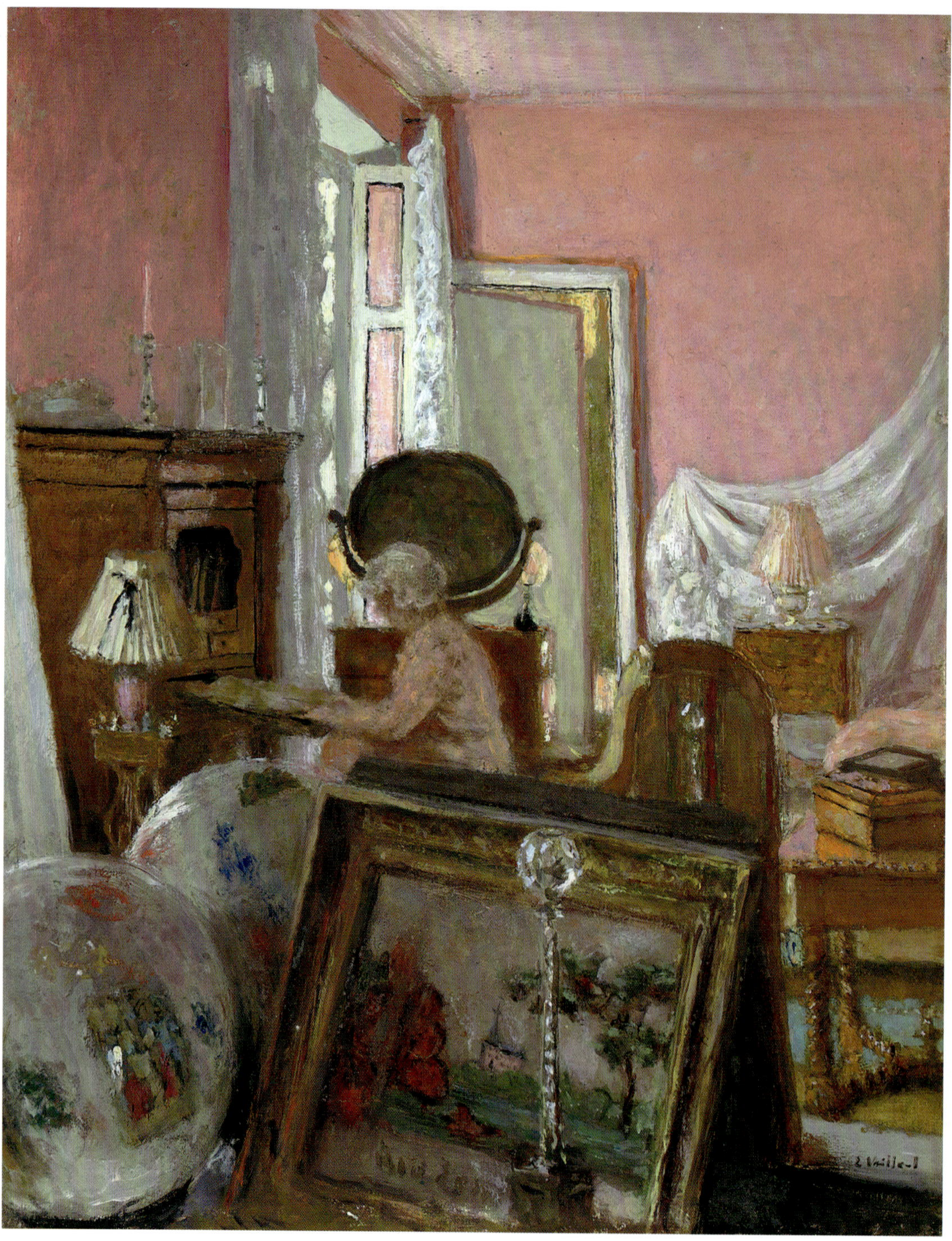

Madame Hessel
in her Room at
the Château
des Clayes

Madame Hessel
dans sa chambre
au château
des Clayes

Madame Hessel
in ihrem Zimmer
im Château
des Clayes

Madame Hessel
en su habitación
del Château
des Clayes

Madame Hessel
no seu quarto
no Château
des Clayes

Madame Hessel
in haar kamer
in het Château
des Clayes

**ÉDOUARD
VUILLARD
(1868-1940)**

c. 1930-35,
Oil on panel/
Huile sur panneau,
41,1 × 32,8 cm,
Private collection

Calvary *or* The Road to Calvary

The effect of the picture is characterized by the sloping diagonal, which is composed of the women's bodies. The artist painted them as stylized black forms with white highlights.

Montée au calvaire, *ou* Le calvaire

La composition attire immédiatement le regard par la puissante diagonale ascendante formée par le mouvement des femmes, dont la présence est réduite à des masses noires stylisées, soulignées de blanc.

Der Kalvarienberg *oder* Der Aufstieg zum Kalvarienberg

Die Wirkung des Bildes ist geprägt durch die abfallende Diagonale, die sich aus den Frauenkörpern zusammensetzt. Der Künstler malte sie als stilisierte schwarze Formen mit weißen Akzenten.

El Calvario *o* El ascenso al Calvario

El efecto de la imagen se caracteriza por la diagonal inclinada, que se compone de los cuerpos de las mujeres. El artista las pintó como estilizadas formas negras con acentos blancos.

O Calvário *ou* a ascensão ao Calvário

O efeito da figura é caracterizado pela diagonal inclinada, que é composta pelos corpos das mulheres. O artista pintou-as como formas negras estilizadas com sotaques brancos.

De Calvarieberg *of* De weg naar de Calvarieberg

Het effect van het schilderij wordt bepaald door de schuine diagonaal van de vrouwenlichamen. De kunstenaar schilderde ze als gestileerde zwarte vormen met witte accenten.

MAURICE DENIS (1870–1943)

1889, Oil on canvas/Huile sur toile, 41 × 33 cm, Musée d'Orsay, Paris

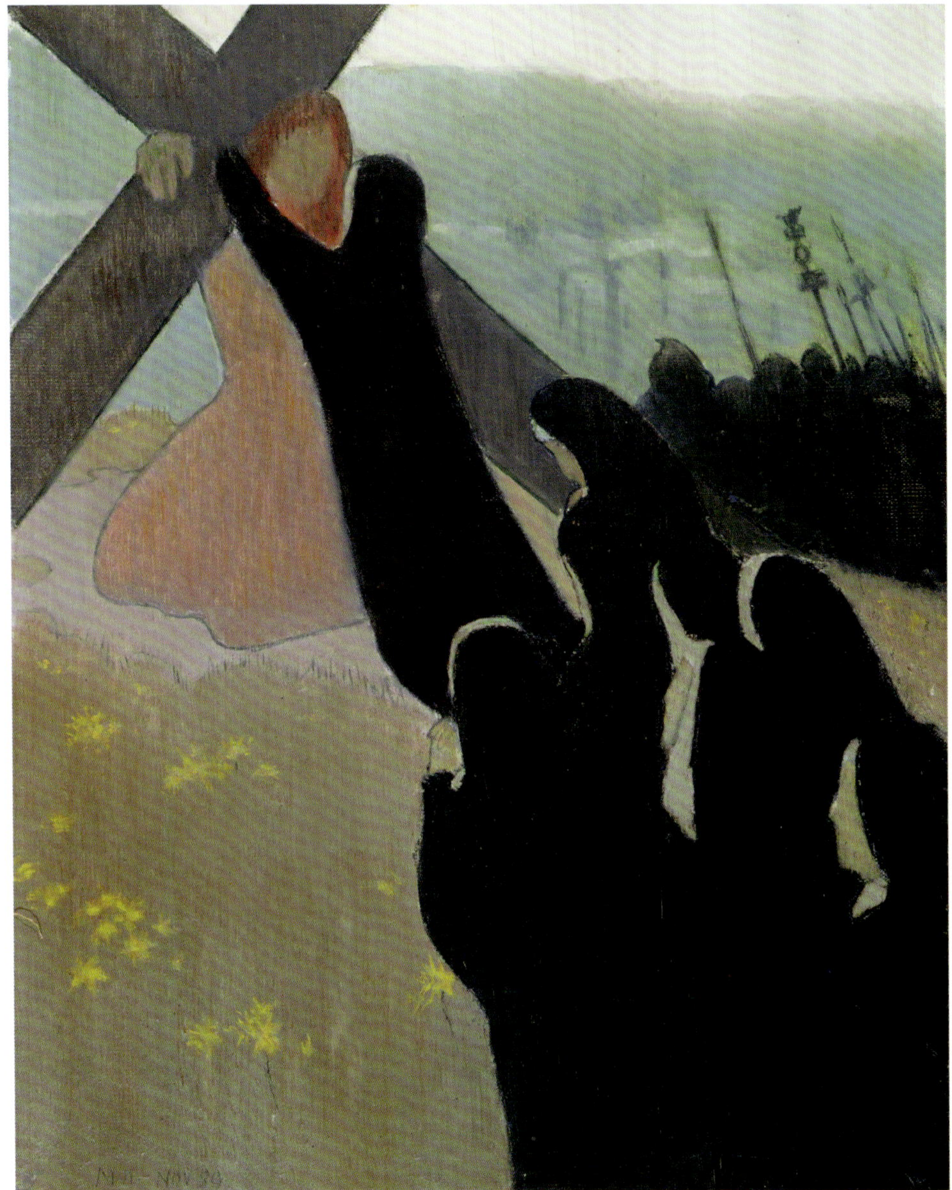

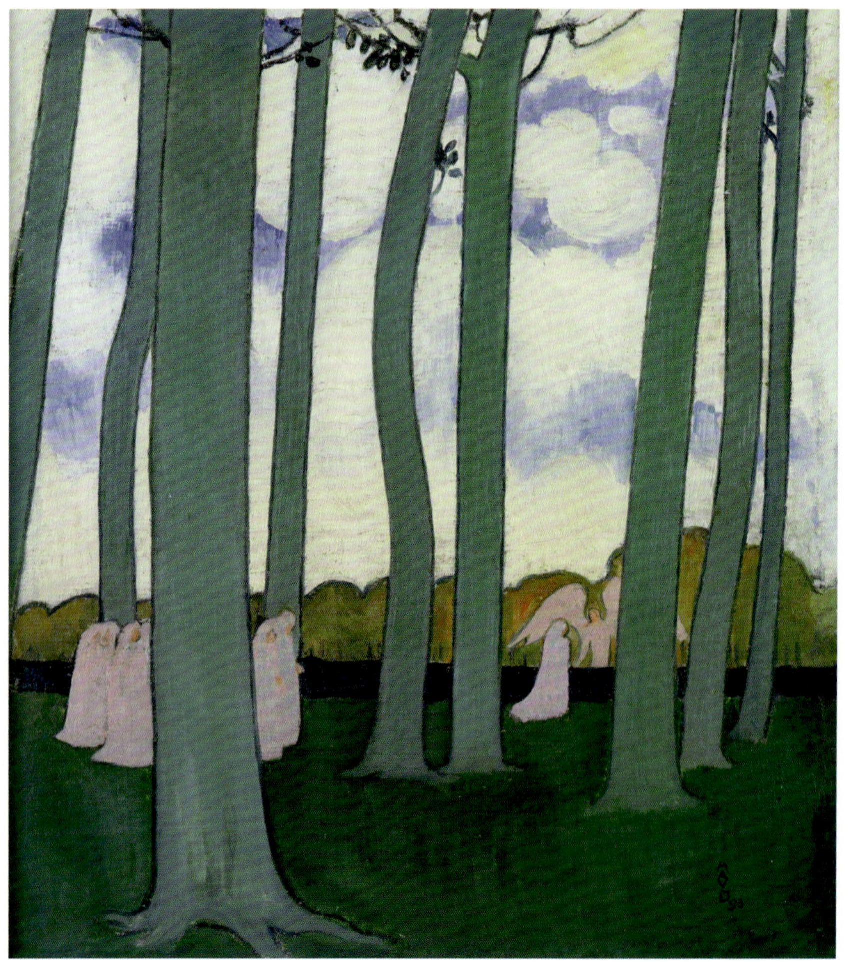

Landscape with Green Trees *or*
The Beeches in Kerduel

Denis was one of the Symbolists among the Nabis. The mystical view was created in the same year as his work *The Muses*. It shows a procession from which a girl moves away to approach an angel.

Les Hêtres de Kerduel *ou* La Procession sous les arbres

Denis est le plus symboliste des Nabis. Réalisé la même année que *Les Muses*, ce tableau offre la vision onirique d'une jeune fille qui s'éloigne d'une mystérieuse procession pour rejoindre un ange.

Landschaft mit grünen Bäumen *oder*
Die Buchen von Kerduel

Denis zählte zu den Symbolisten unter den Nabis. Die mystische Ansicht entstand im selben Jahr wie sein Werk *Die Musen*. Sie zeigt eine Prozession, von der sich ein Mädchen entfernt, um auf einen Engel zuzugehen.

Paisaje con árboles verdes *o* Las hayas de Kerduel

Denis era uno de los simbolistas entre los Nabis. La visión mística fue creada en el mismo año que su obra *Las musas*. Muestra una procesión desde la que una niña se aleja para acercarse a un ángel.

Paisagem com árvores verdes *ou* As faias de Kerduel

Denis era um dos simbolistas entre os Nabis. A visão mística foi criada no mesmo ano da sua obra *As Musas*. Mostra uma procissão da qual uma rapariga se afasta para se aproximar de um anjo.

Landschap met groene bomen *of* Beuken in Kerduel

Denis behoorde tot de symbolisten onder de Nabis. Deze mystieke aanblik maakte hij in hetzelfde jaar als *De muzen*. Het werk toont een optocht waaruit een meisje zich verwijdert om naar een engel te lopen.

MAURICE DENIS (1870-1943)

1893, Oil on canvas/Huile sur toile,
46,3 × 42,8 cm, Musée d'Orsay, Paris

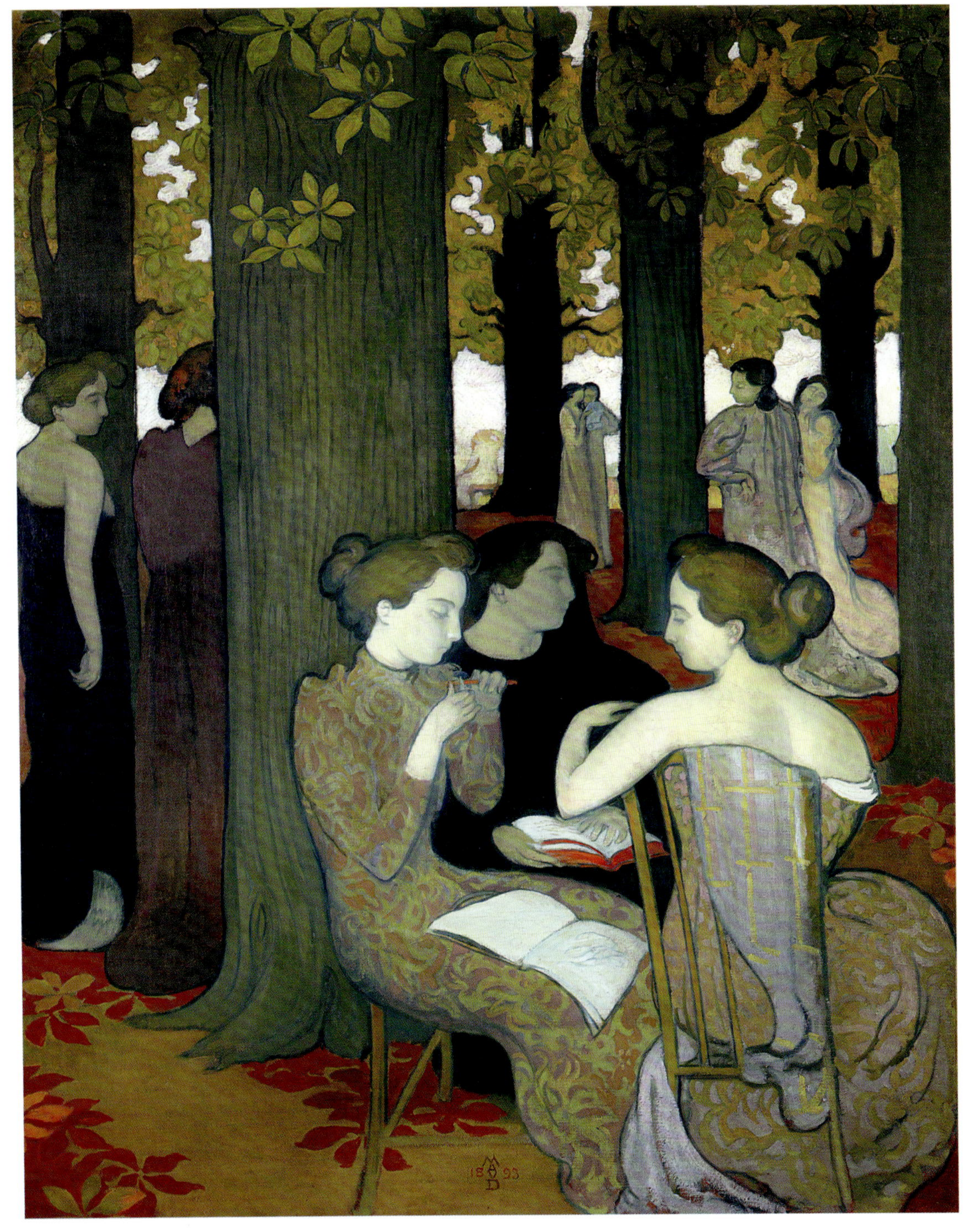

MAURICE DENIS
(1870-1943)
1893, Oil on
canvas/
Huile sur toile,
171,5 × 137,5 cm,
Musée d'Orsay,
Paris

The Muses

Les Muses

Die Musen

Las musas

As Musas

De muzen

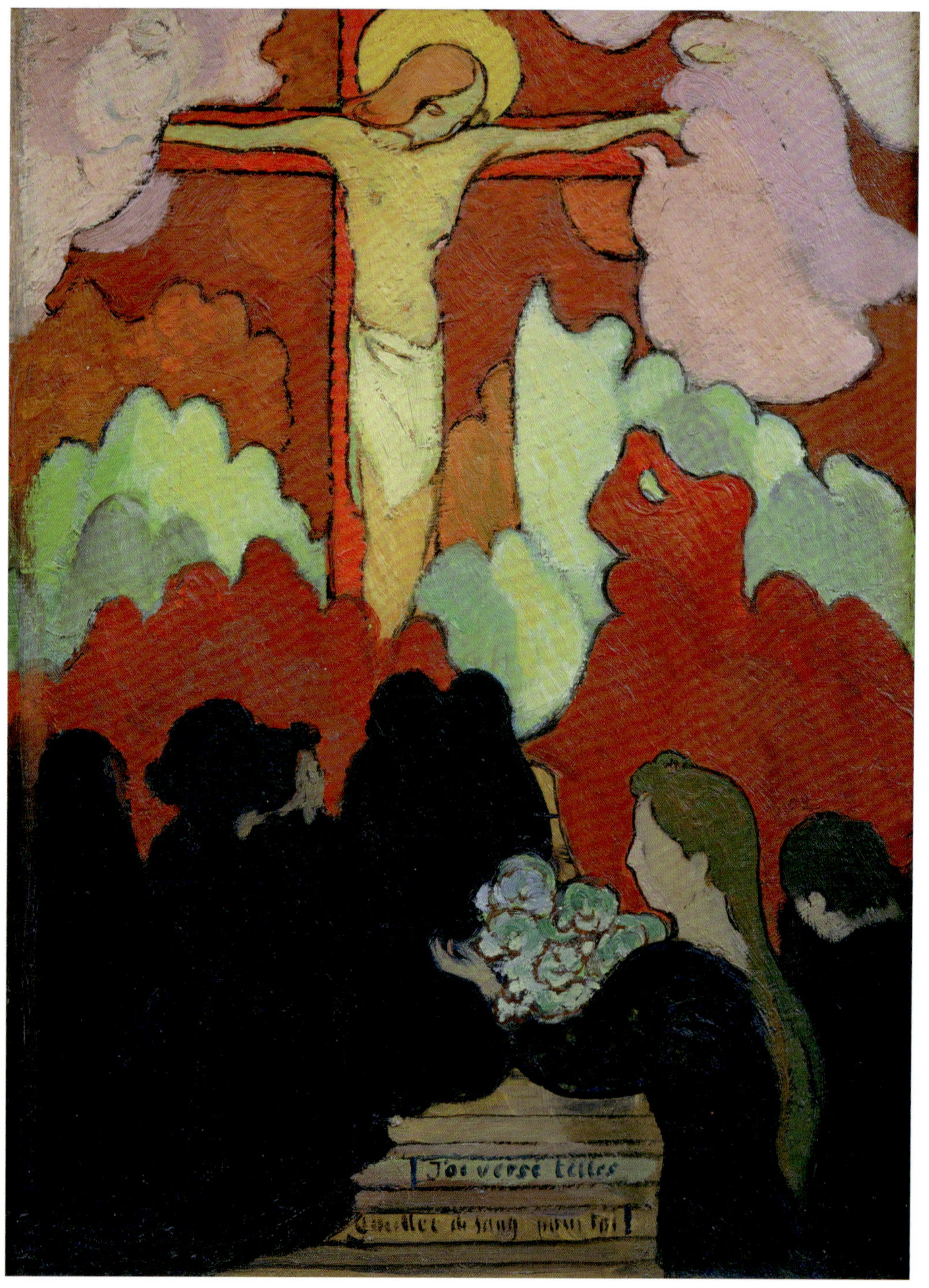

The Offertory at Calvary

L'Offrande au calvaire

Opferszene vor
einem Kruzifix

Escena de la víctima
frente a un crucifijo

Cena da vítima em
frente a um crucifixo

Offer voor een kruisbeeld

MAURICE DENIS (1870-1943)
c. 1890, Oil on canvas/
Huile sur toile, 32 × 23,5 cm,
Musée d'Orsay, Paris

Evening Memory I

Souvenir de soir I

Erinnerungen an
einen Abend I

Recuerdos de una noche I

Memórias de uma noite I

Herinneringen
aan een avond I

MAURICE DENIS
(1870-1943)
1890, Oil on canvas/
Huile sur toile, 55,7 × 46,4 cm,
Museum of Fine Arts, Houston

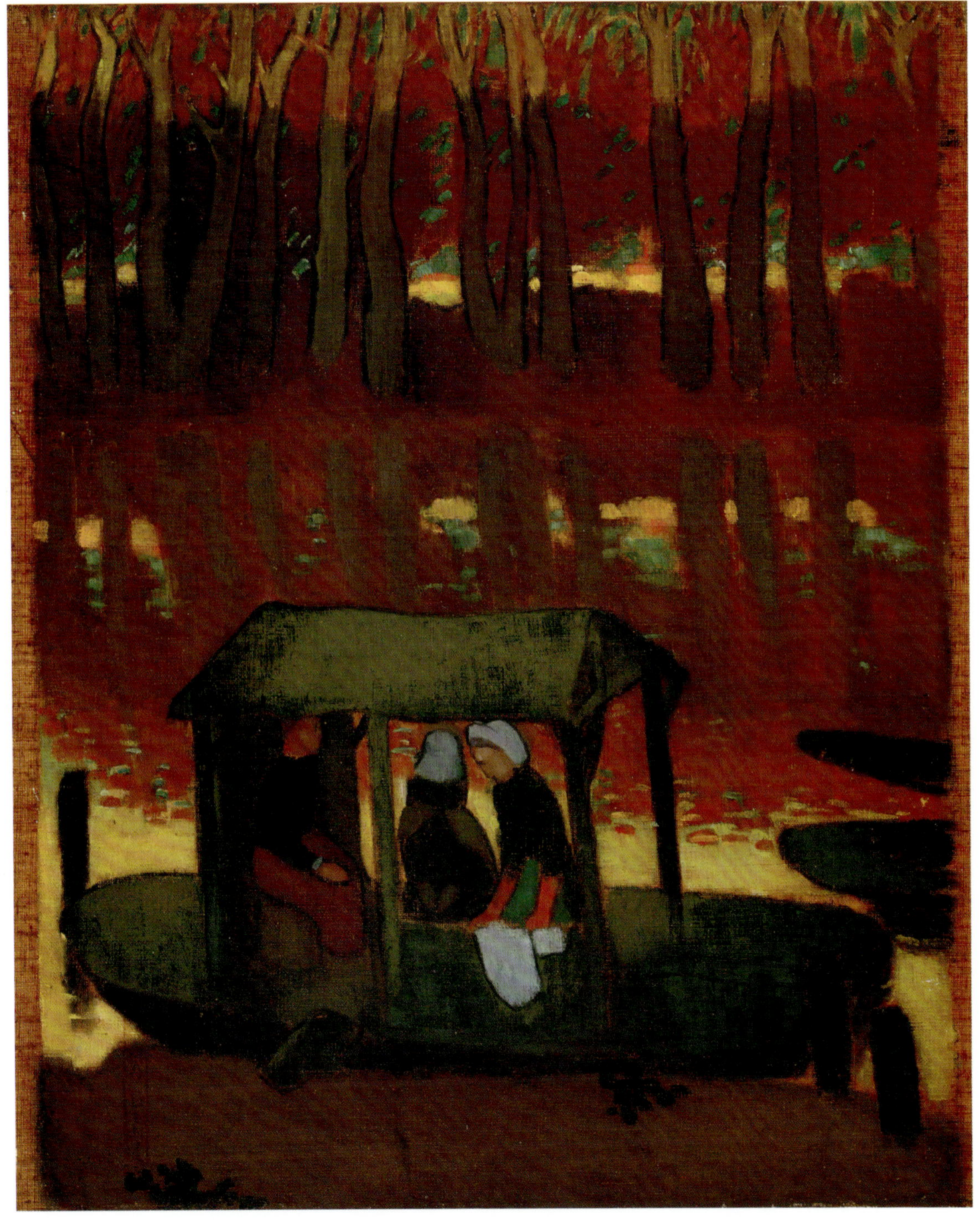

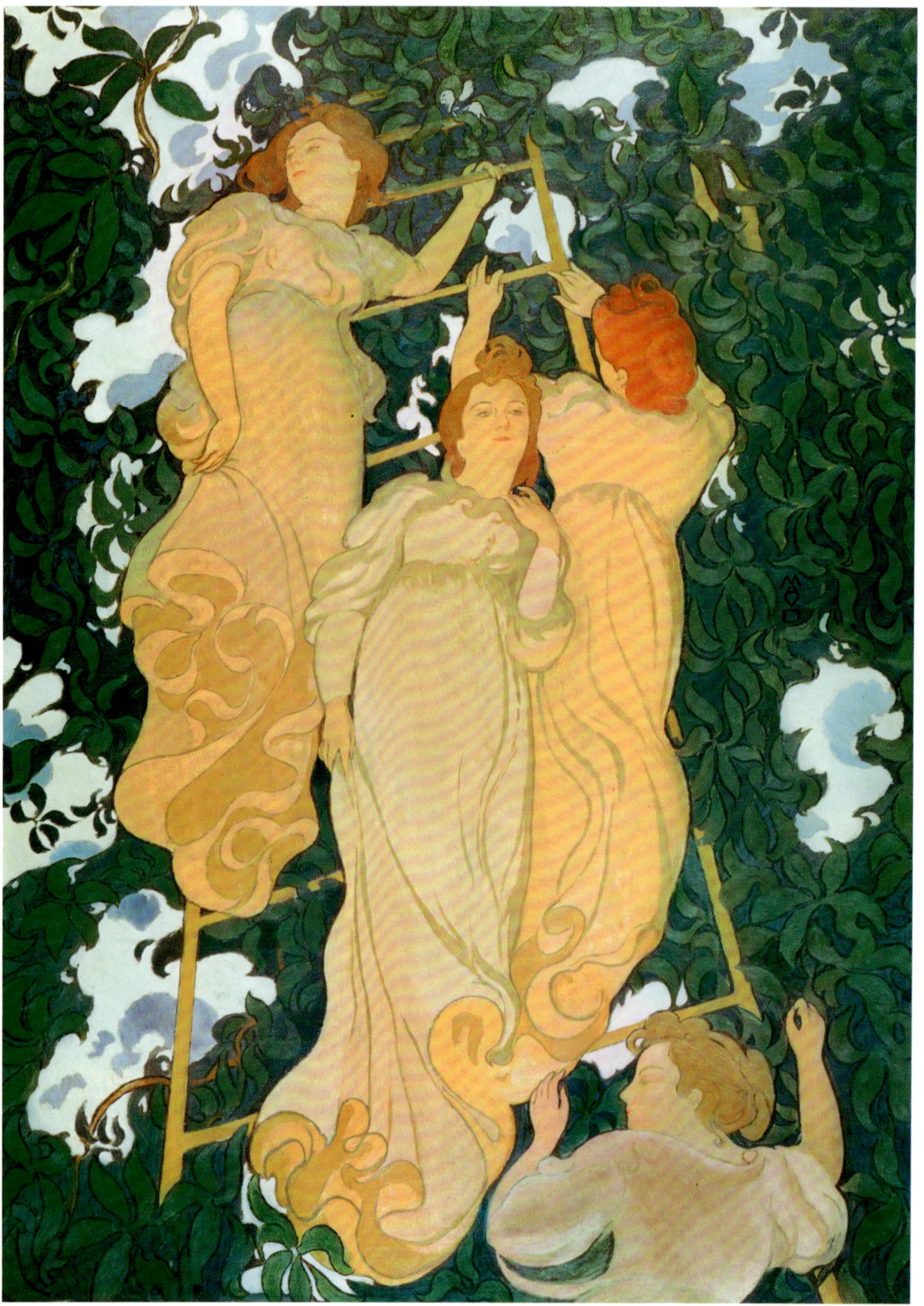

The Ladder in the Foliage

L'Échelle dans le feuillage

Die Leiter im Laub

La escalera en el follaje

A escada na folhagem

De ladder in het loof

MAURICE DENIS (1870-1943)
1892, Oil on canvas glued on cardboard/Huile sur toile collée sur carton, 235 × 172 cm, Musée Maurice Denis, Saint-Germain-en-Laye

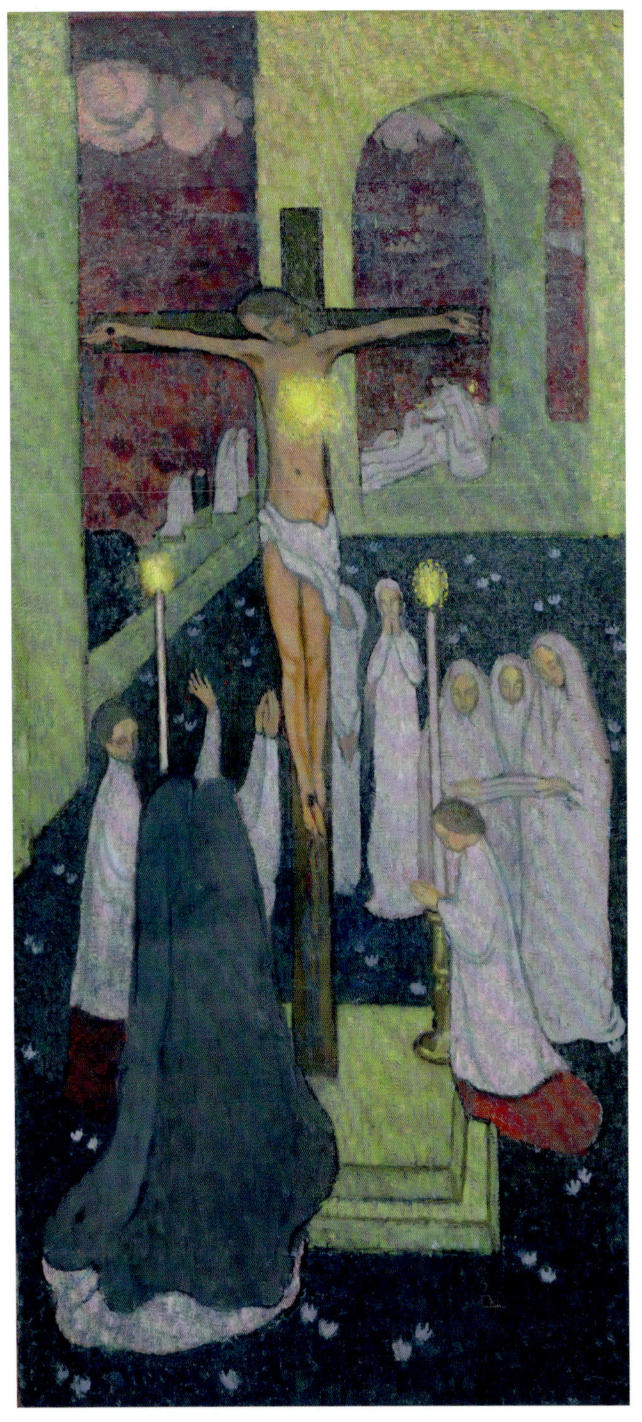

Crucified Sacred Heart

Sacré-Cœur crucifié

Kreuzigung Herz Jesu

Sagrado Corazón crucifijado

Crucificação Coração de Jesus

Kruisiging van het Heilige Hart

MAURICE DENIS (1870-1943)

1894, Oil on canvas/Huile sur toile,
131 × 61 cm, Private collection

8

Symbolism

Le symbolisme

Der Symbolismus

Símbolismo

Simbologia

Symbolisme

Symbolism

The world does not only consist of its surface - the credo of the Symbolists was to dive into the mysteries behind the beings and things. In painting, but also in literature, poetry (Stéphane Mallarmé, Arthur Rimbaud, Paul Verlaine) and music (Claude Debussy), the current opened up a space for "vision". Be it with pictures, words or notes - the inner world should be expressed by addressing the gaze and spirit of the viewer. The style of fantasy, delusions, dreams and nightmares flourished towards the end of the 19th century. Their followers rejected all rationalism. They broke away from realism and impressionism. Instead, they referred to romanticism - the art of passion and agony of the soul. But also influences of the Nazarenes and the Pre-Raphaelites characterize symbolism. French symbolists often found their subjects in poetry, literature and spiritual or profane texts, with a preference for the gods and heroes of Greek mythology. From the mystical depictions of biblical and mythological figures by Gustave Moreau, to

Le symbolisme

Le monde n'est pas seulement ce que l'on voit. Rendre visible l'invisible, plonger dans le mystère des êtres et des choses, telle est l'ambition des symbolistes. En peinture comme en littérature, en poésie (Stéphane Mallarmé, Arthur Rimbaud, Paul Verlaine…) ou en musique (Claude Debussy), le symbolisme donne naissance à des « visions ». Par les images, les mots ou les notes, il s'agit d'exprimer un monde intérieur, en sollicitant le regard, mais aussi l'esprit du spectateur. Art de l'imagination, du fantasme, du rêve ou du cauchemar, le symbolisme s'épanouit à la fin du xixᵉ siècle. Il fait fi de tout rationalisme, et tourne le dos au naturalisme, au réalisme, à l'impressionnisme. Il trouve sa source dans le romantisme – art des passions et des tourments de l'âme –, et témoigne d'influences européennes, celle des nazaréens en Allemagne, ou des préraphaélites en Angleterre. En France, le symbolisme puise principalement ses sujets dans la poésie, la littérature, les textes sacrés ou profanes, avec une prédilection pour les dieux et les héros de la Grèce antique (Apollon, Prométhée, Ulysse, Hélène,

Der Symbolismus

Die Welt besteht nicht nur aus ihrer Oberfläche – das Credo der Symbolisten war es, in die Mysterien hinter den Wesen und Dingen einzutauchen. In der Malerei, aber auch in der Literatur, der Poesie (Stéphane Mallarmé, Arthur Rimbaud, Paul Verlaine) und der Musik (Claude Debussy) eröffnete die Strömung einen Freiraum für die „Vision". Sei es mit Bildern, Wörtern oder Noten – die innere Welt sollte zum Ausdruck kommen, indem der Blick und der Geist des Betrachters angesprochen werden. Die Stilrichtung der Fantasie, der Wahnvorstellungen, der Träume und Albträume erlebt gegen Ende des 19. Jahrhunderts ihre Blütezeit. Ihre Anhänger lehnen jeglichen Rationalismus ab. Sie brechen mit dem Realismus und dem Impressionismus. Dafür beziehen sie sich auf die Romantik – die Kunst der Leidenschaft und der Seelenqualen. Aber auch Einflüsse der Nazarener und der Präraffaeliten prägen den Symbolismus. Die französischen Symbolisten finden ihre Sujets oft in der Lyrik, der Literatur und in geistlichen oder profanen Texten, mit einer Vorliebe für die Götter und Helden der griechischen Mythologie. Angefangen bei den

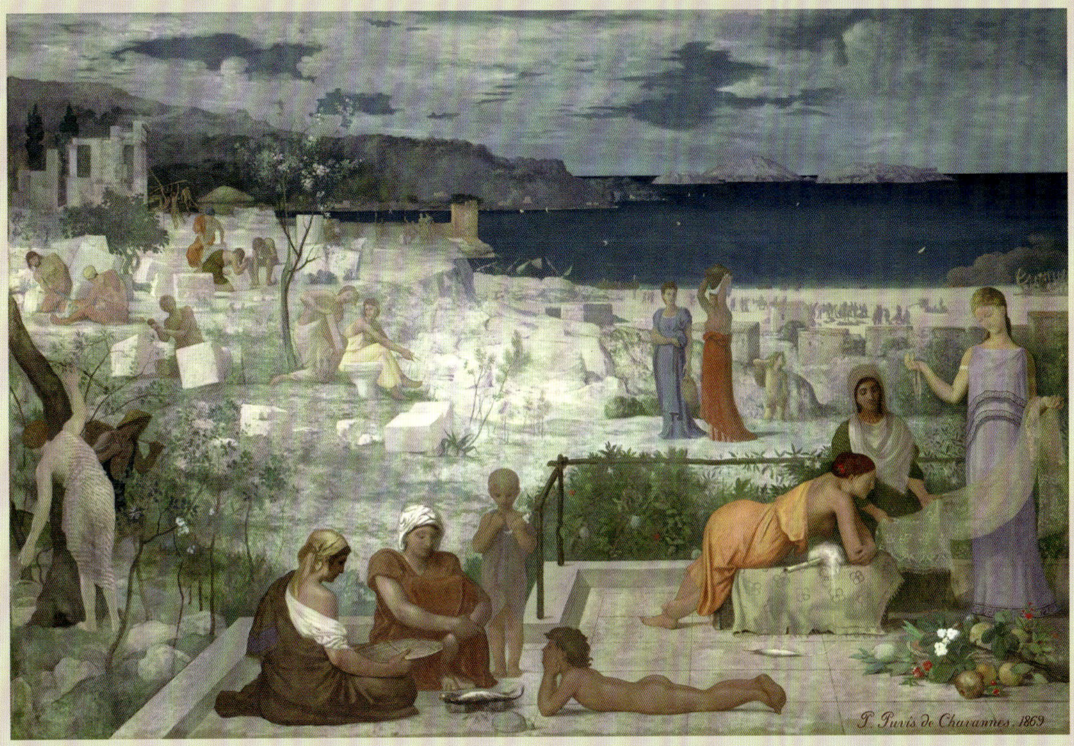

Símbolismo

el mundo no sólo consiste en su superficie - el credo de los Simbolistas era sumergirse en los misterios detrás de los seres y las cosas. En la pintura, pero también en la literatura, la poesía (Stéphane Mallarmé, Arthur Rimbaud, Paul Verlaine) y la música (Claude Debussy), la corriente abrió un espacio para la "visión". Ya sea con imágenes, palabras o notas, el mundo interior debe expresarse a través de la mirada y el espíritu del espectador. El estilo de fantasía, delirios, sueños y pesadillas floreció a finales del siglo XIX. Sus seguidores rechazan todo racionalismo. Rompen con el realismo y el impresionismo. A cambio, se refieren al romanticismo, el arte de la pasión y la agonía del alma. Pero también las influencias de los nazarenos y de los prerrafaelitas caracterizan el simbolismo. Los simbolistas franceses encuentran a menudo sus temas en la poesía, la literatura y los textos espirituales o profanos, con preferencia por los dioses y héroes de la mitología griega. Desde las representaciones místicas de figuras bíblicas y mitológicas de Gustave Moreau,

Simbologia

o mundo não consiste apenas em sua superfície - o credo dos simbolistas era mergulhar nos mistérios por trás dos seres e coisas. Na pintura, mas também na literatura, na poesia (Stéphane Mallarmé, Arthur Rimbaud, Paul Verlaine) e na música (Claude Debussy), a corrente abre espaço para a "visão". Seja com imagens, palavras ou notas - o mundo interior deve ser expresso através do olhar e do espírito do espectador. O estilo de fantasia, ilusões, sonhos e pesadelos floresceu no final do século XIX. Os seus seguidores rejeitam todo o racionalismo. Estás a romper com o realismo e o impressionismo. Em troca, eles se referem ao romantismo - a arte da paixão e da agonia da alma. Mas também as influências dos nazarenos e dos pré-rafaelitas caracterizam o simbolismo. Os simbolistas franceses encontram frequentemente os seus temas na poesia, na literatura e nos textos espirituais ou profanos, com preferência pelos deuses e heróis da mitologia grega. Das representações místicas de figuras bíblicas e mitológicas de Gustave Moreau, às pinturas poéticas

Symbolisme

De wereld bestaat niet alleen uit zijn oppervlak. Dat was het credo van de symbolisten. Zij wilden zich verdiepen in de mysteries achter de wezens en dingen. In de schilderkunst, maar ook in de literatuur, de dichtkunst (Stéphane Mallarmé, Arthur Rimbaud, Paul Verlaine) en de muziek (Claude Debussy), maakte de stroming ruimte vrij voor 'het visioen'. Of dat nu met beelden, woorden of noten gebeurde – de innerlijke wereld moest tot uitdrukking komen om de blik en de geest van de kijker aan te spreken. Deze stijl van de fantasie, waanideeën, dromen en nachtmerries bloeide aan het eind van de 19e eeuw. De aanhangers ervan verwierpen elke vorm van rationalisme. Ze braken met het realisme en impressionisme. In plaats daarvan verwezen ze naar de romantiek – de kunst van de hartstocht en kwelling van de ziel. Maar ook invloeden van de Nazareners en de prerafaëlieten drukten hun stempel op het symbolisme. Franse symbolisten vonden hun onderwerpen vaak in de dichtkunst, literatuur en spirituele of profane teksten, met een voorkeur voor de goden en helden

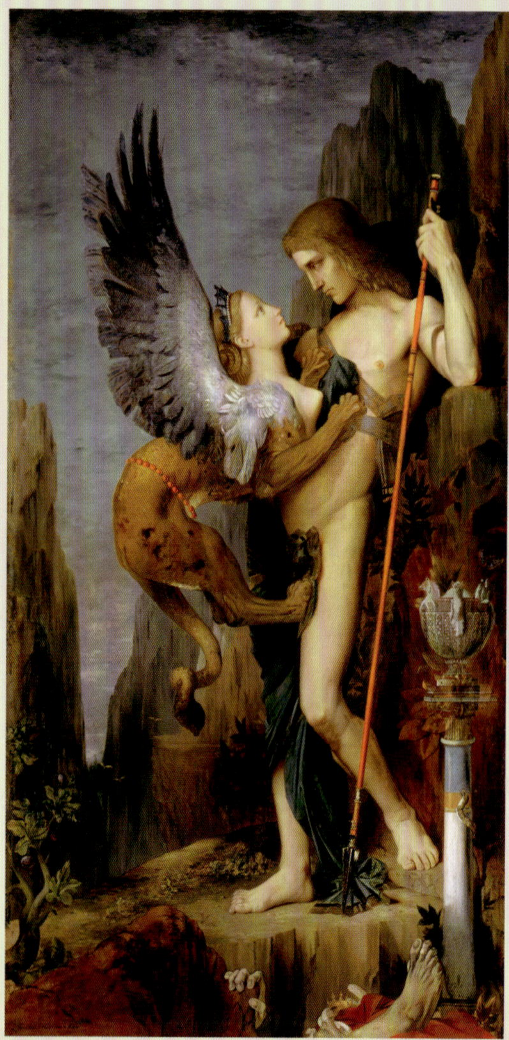

GUSTAVE MOREAU (1826-1898)
1864, Oil on canvas/Huile sur toile,
206,4 × 105 cm, Metropolitan
Museum of Art, New York

the poetic paintings by Alexandre Séon, to Odilon Redon's symphonies of color, to Gustave Doreau's fantastic imagery - the painters tried to lend form and color to the mysterious and fairytale-like. Some of them combined their spiritual quest with a decorative aesthetic, such as Pierre Puvis de Chavannes, one of the forerunners of the style. In his works, simplicity and balance prevail over mysterious strangeness. He developed into a master of peaceful allegories with figures in a motionless beauty.

Orphée, Œdipe et le Sphinx…). Des figures bibliques et mythologiques transcendées par le mysticisme de Gustave Moreau aux compositions poétiques d'Alexandre Séon, des symphonies colorées d'Odilon Redon à l'univers fantastique de Gustave Doré, les symbolistes s'appliquent à donner formes et couleurs au mystère et au merveilleux. Certains peintres, comme Pierre Puvis de Chavannes (considéré comme l'un des précurseurs du symbolisme en peinture), associent leur quête spirituelle à une esthétique plus décorative. Chez lui, la simplicité et l'équilibre l'emportent sur une quelconque étrangeté. Il est le maître des allégories paisibles, des figures silencieuses d'une beauté immobile.

mystischen Darstellungen biblischer und mythologischer Figuren eines Gustave Moreau über die poetischen Gemälde von Alexandre Séon bis hin zu Odilon Redons Farbsymphonien oder Gustave Dorés fantastischen Bilderwelten – die Maler versuchen, dem Mysteriösen und Märchenhaften Form und Farbe zu verleihen. Einige unter ihnen verbinden ihre spirituelle Suche mit einer dekorativen Ästhetik, wie Pierre Puvis de Chavannes, der als einer der Vorläufer der Stilrichtung gilt. In seinen Werken siegt die Schlichtheit und Ausgewogenheit über das mysteriöse Fremde. Er entwickelt sich zum Meister der friedvollen Allegorien mit Figuren in einer regungslosen Schönheit.

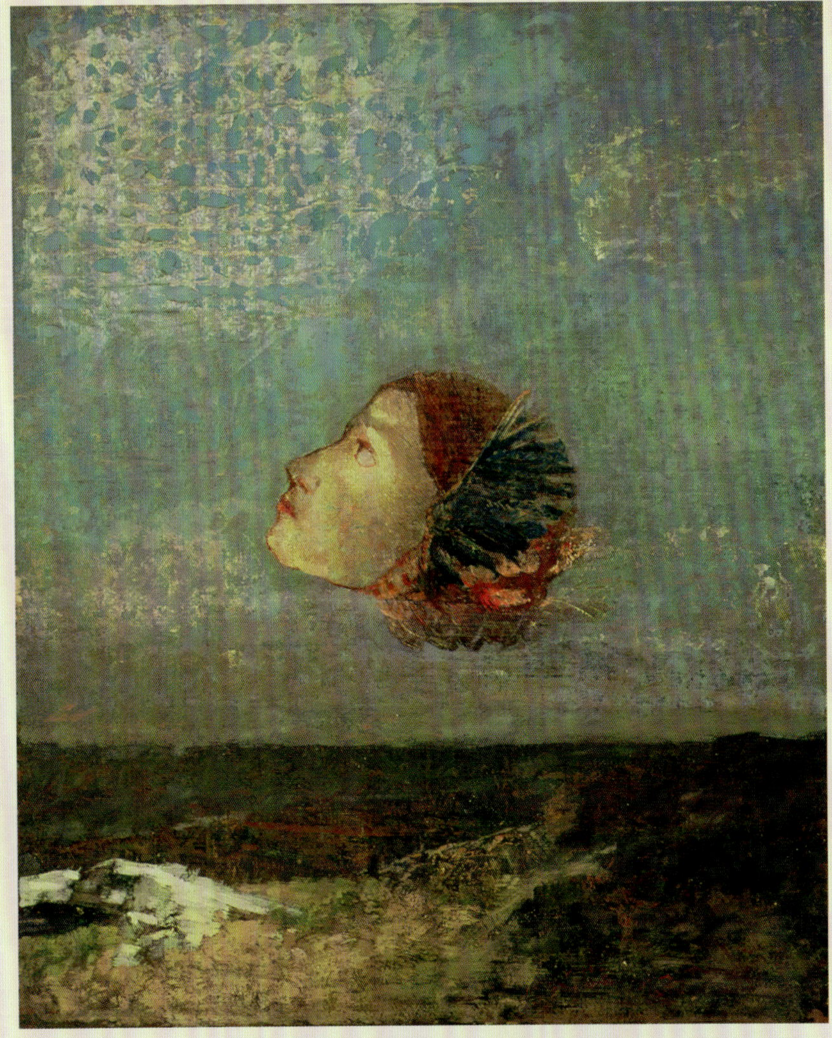

pasando por las pinturas poéticas de Alexandre Séon, hasta las sinfonías de color de Odilon Redon, pasando por la fantástica imaginería de Gustave Doreau, los pintores intentan dar forma y color a lo misterioso y de cuento de hadas. Algunos de ellos combinan su búsqueda espiritual con una estética decorativa, como Pierre Puvis de Chavannes, uno de los precursores del estilo. En sus obras, la sencillez y el equilibrio prevalecen sobre la extrañeza misteriosa. Se convirtió en un maestro de alegorías pacíficas con figuras de una belleza inmóvil.

de Alexandre Séon, às sinfonias de cor de Odilon Redon, às fantásticas imagens de Gustave Doreau - os pintores tentam dar forma e cor ao misterioso e fábilo-like. Alguns deles combinam sua busca espiritual com uma estética decorativa, como Pierre Puvis de Chavannes, um dos precursores do estilo. Nas suas obras, a simplicidade e o equilíbrio prevalecem sobre a estranheza misteriosa. Ele se tornou um mestre de alegorias pacíficas com figuras em uma beleza imóvel.

uit de Griekse mythologie. Begonnen met de mystieke voorstellingen van bijbelse en mythologische figuren van Gustave Moreau via de poëtische schilderijen van Alexandre Séon tot de kleurensymfonieën van Odilon Redon en de fantasievolle beeldenwerelden van Gustave Doreau – de schilders probeerden vorm en kleur te geven aan het mysterieuze en sprookjesachtige. Sommigen combineerden hun spirituele zoektocht met een decoratieve esthetiek, zoals Pierre Puvis de Chavannes, een van de voorlopers van de stijl. In zijn werk winnen eenvoud en evenwicht het van mysterieuze vreemdheid. Hij groeide uit tot een meester van vreedzame allegorieën met figuren in een roerloze schoonheid.

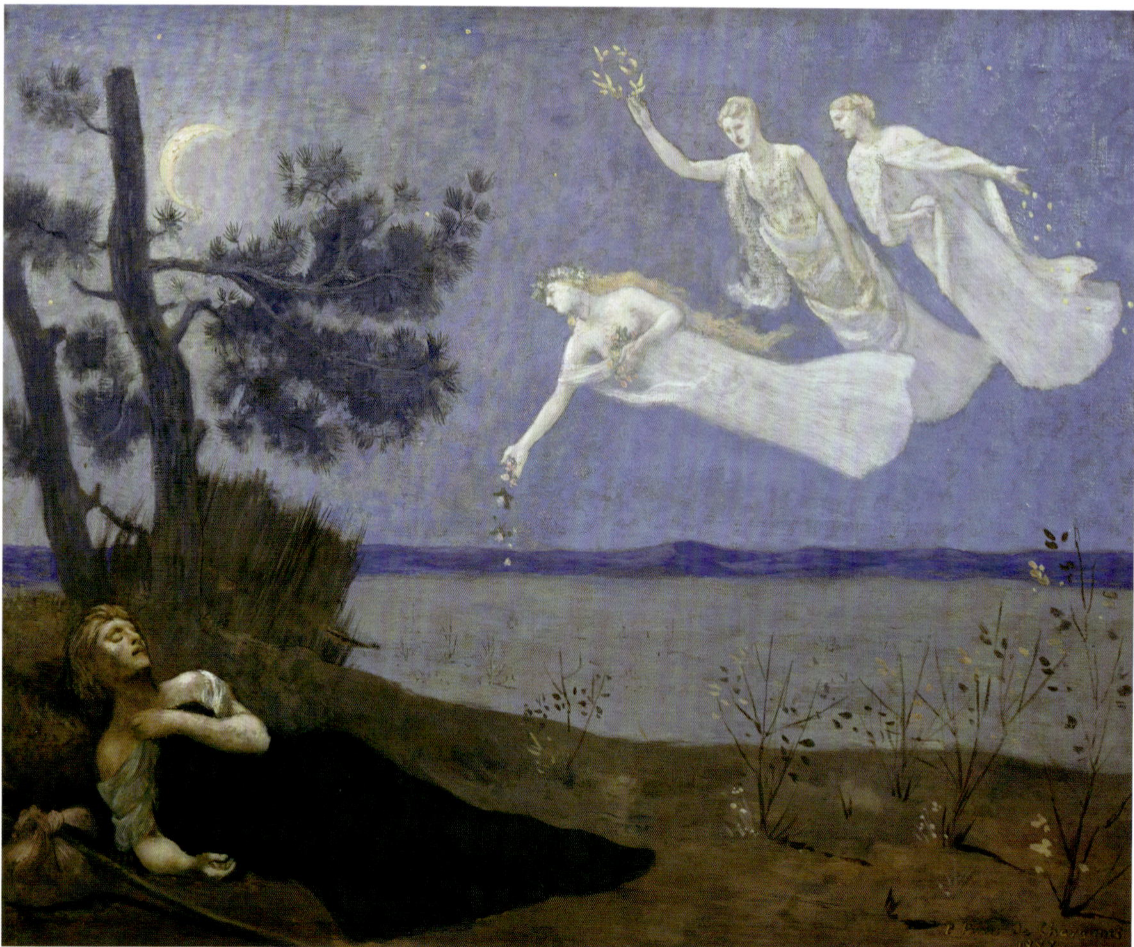

The Dream

«Love, Glory and Wealth appear to him in his sleep.»
During his sleep in the moonlight, the young man
dreams of love, fame and wealth - symbolized by the
three women holding roses, a laurel wreath and pieces
of gold in their hands.

Le Rêve

« Il voit, dans son sommeil, l'Amour, la Gloire
et la Richesse lui apparaître. » Au clair de lune,
un jeune homme endormi rêve d'amour, de gloire
et de richesse, que symbolisent trois femmes en blanc
tenant entre leurs doigts des roses, une couronne
de laurier et des pièces d'or.

Der Traum

„Im Schlaf erscheint ihm Liebe, Ruhm und Reichtum."
Während seines Schlafes träumt der junge Mann von
Liebe, Ruhm und Reichtum – symbolisiert durch
die drei Frauen, die in ihren Händen Rosen, einen
Lorbeerkranz und Goldstücke halten.

El sueño

«El amor, la gloria y la riqueza se le aparecen en su
sueño.» Durante su sueño a la luz de la luna, el joven
sueña con el amor, la fama y la riqueza - simbolizada
por las tres mujeres con rosas, una corona de laurel
y trozos de oro en sus manos.

O sonho

«Amor, glória e riqueza aparecem-lhe no seu sono.»
Durante seu sono ao luar, o jovem sonha com amor,
fama e riqueza - simbolizado pelas três mulheres
segurando rosas, uma coroa de louros e pedaços de
ouro em suas mãos.

De droom

'Liefde, roem en rijkdom verschijnen hem in zijn
slaap' Tijdens zijn slaap in het maanlicht droomt
de jongeman van liefde, roem en rijkdom -
gesymboliseerd door de drie vrouwen met rozen, een
lauwerkrans en goudstukken in hun handen.

PIERRE PUVIS DE CHAVANNES (1824-1898)

1883, Oil on canvas/Huile sur toile, 82 × 102 cm, Musée d'Orsay, Paris

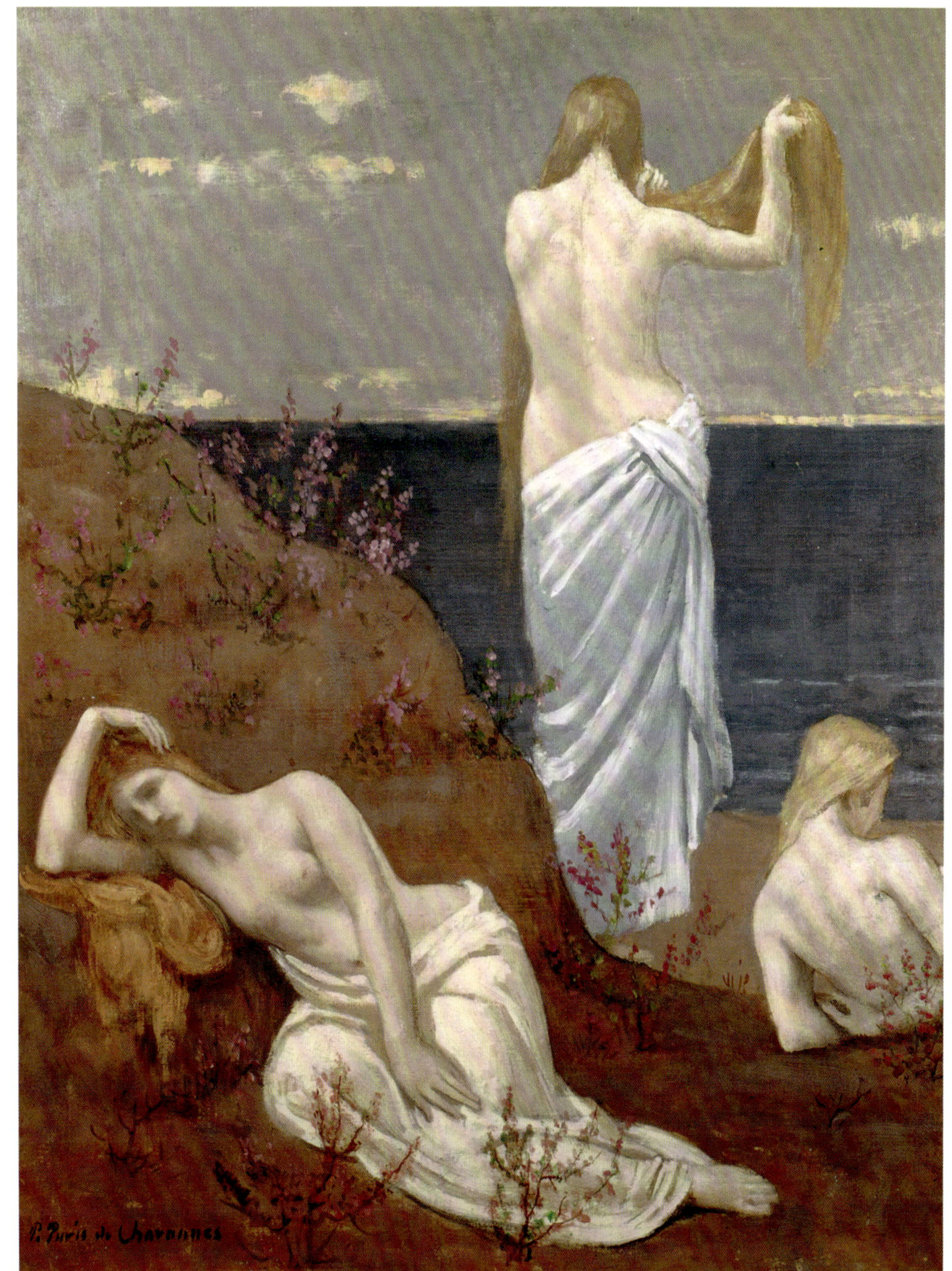

Young Girls by the Sea

Jeunes Filles au
bord de la mer

Mädchen am Meeresufer

Chica en la orilla del mar

Garota na praia

Jonge meisjes
aan de kust

**PIERRE PUVIS DE
CHAVANNES (1824-1898)**

1879, Oil on canvas/
Huile sur toile, 61 × 47 cm,
Musée d'Orsay, Paris

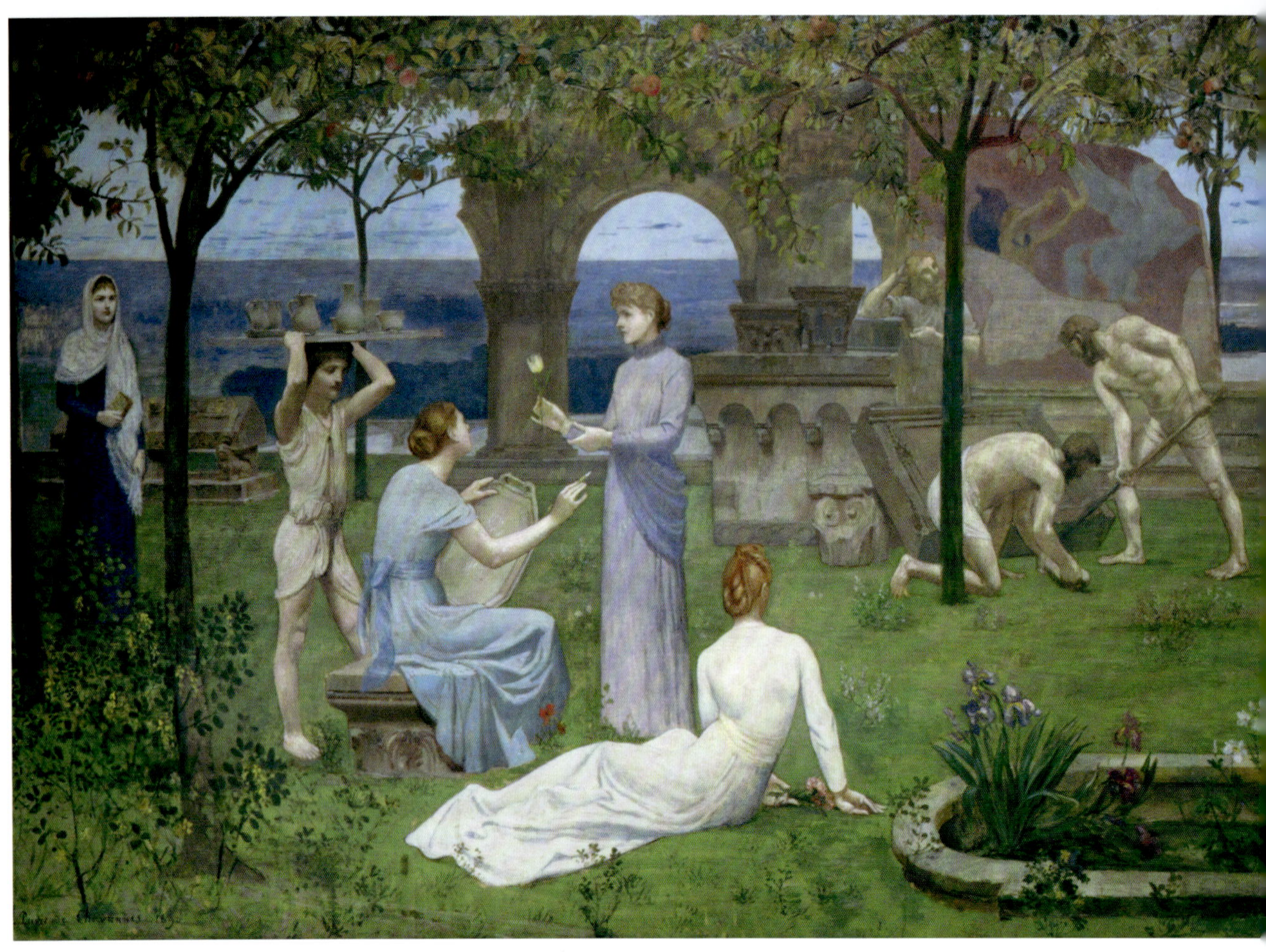

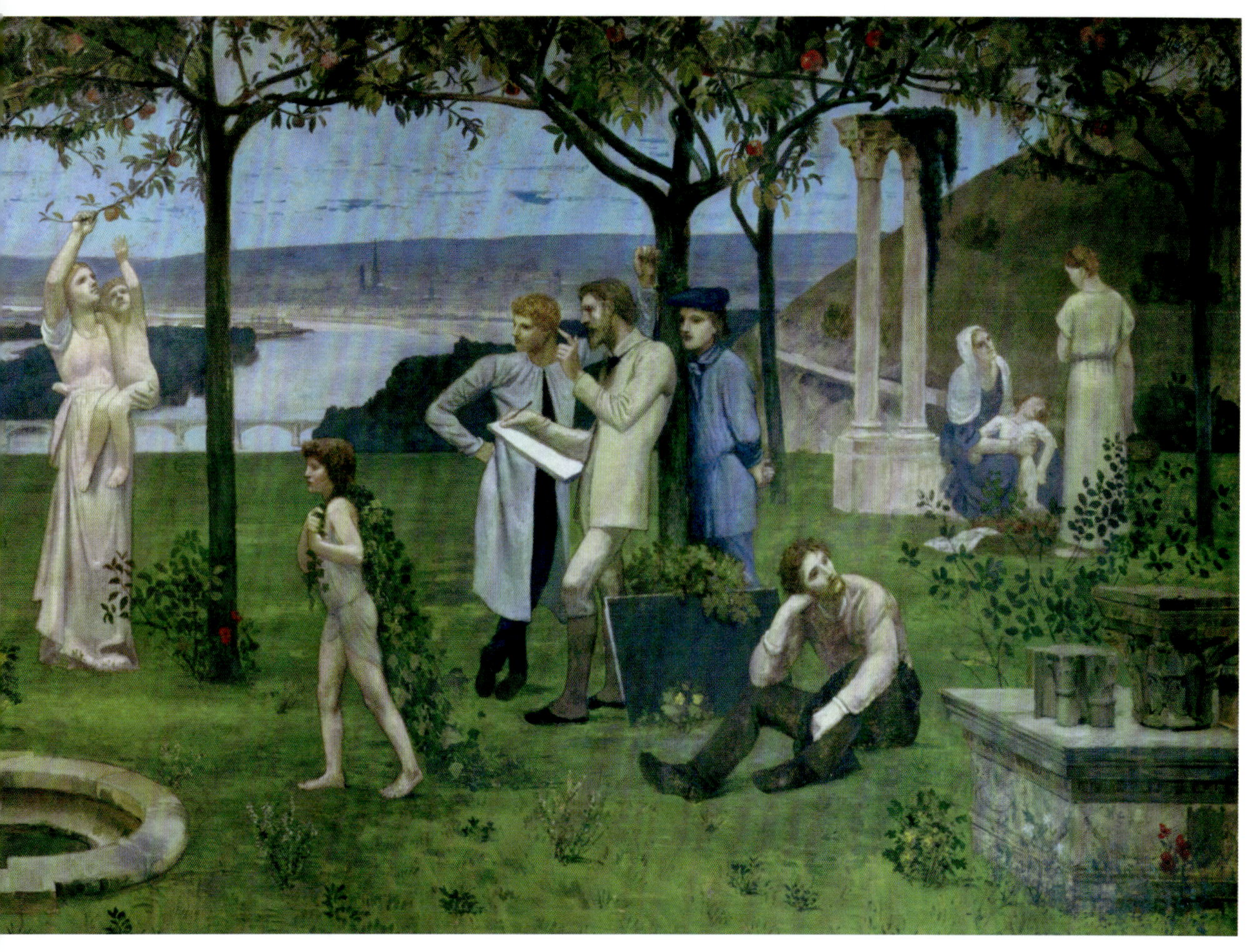

Inter artes et Naturam (Between Art and Nature)

Inter artes et Naturam (Entre Art et Nature)

Inter artes et Naturam (Zwischen Kunst und Natur)

Inter artes et Naturam (Entre arte y naturaleza)

Inter artes et Naturam (Entre Arte e Natureza)

Inter artes et naturam (Tussen kunst en natuur)

PIERRE PUVIS DE CHAVANNES (1824-1898)
1890, Oil on canvas/Huile sur toile, 295 × 165 cm, Musée des Beaux-Arts, Rouen

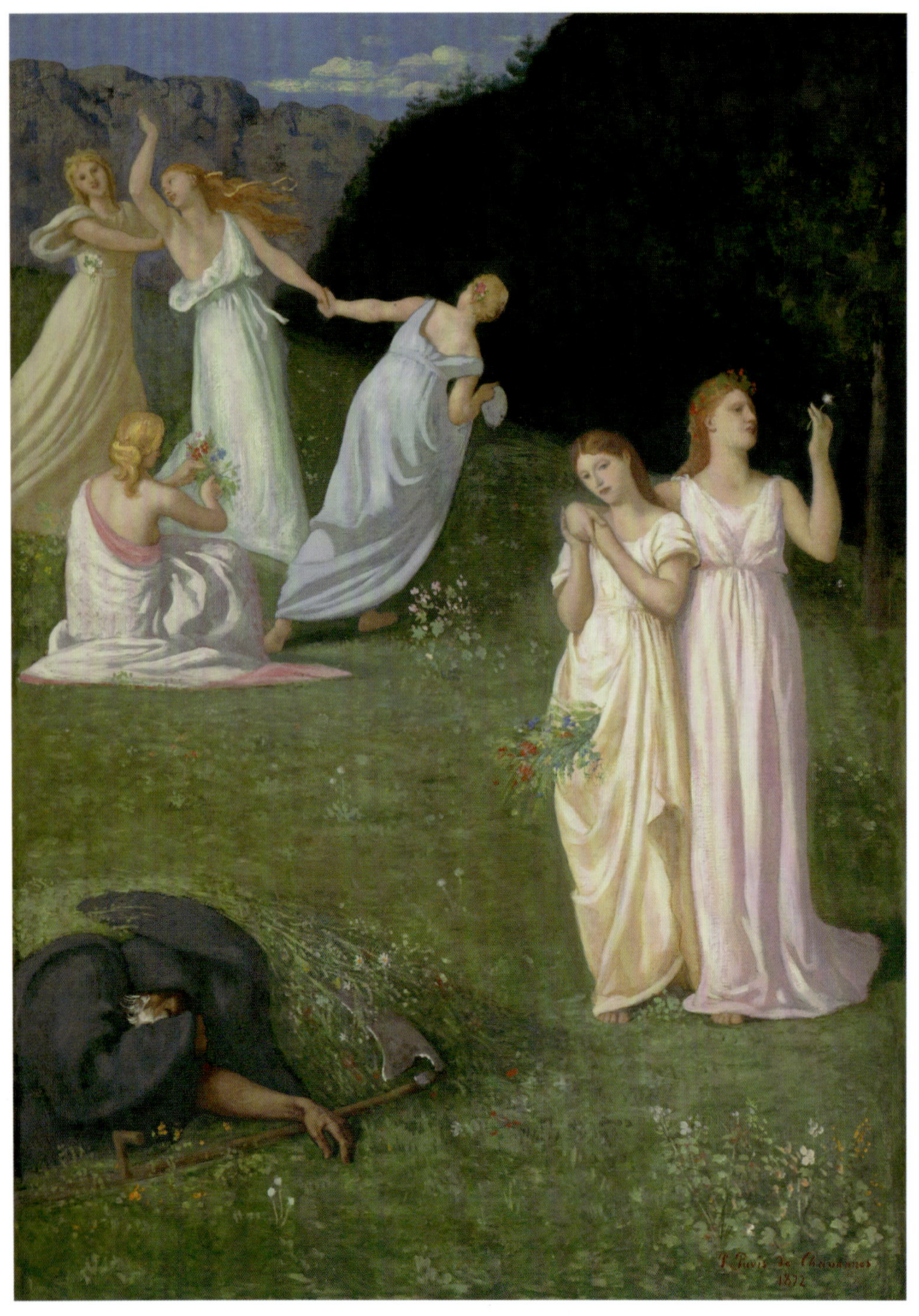

Death and the Maidens

La Mort et les Jeunes Filles

Die Mädchen und der Tod

Las chicas y la muerte

As meninas e a morte

De dood en de meisjes

**PIERRE PUVIS DE CHAVANNES
(1824-1898)**

1872, Oil on canvas/Huile sur toile,
146,1 × 107 cm, The Clark, Williamstown

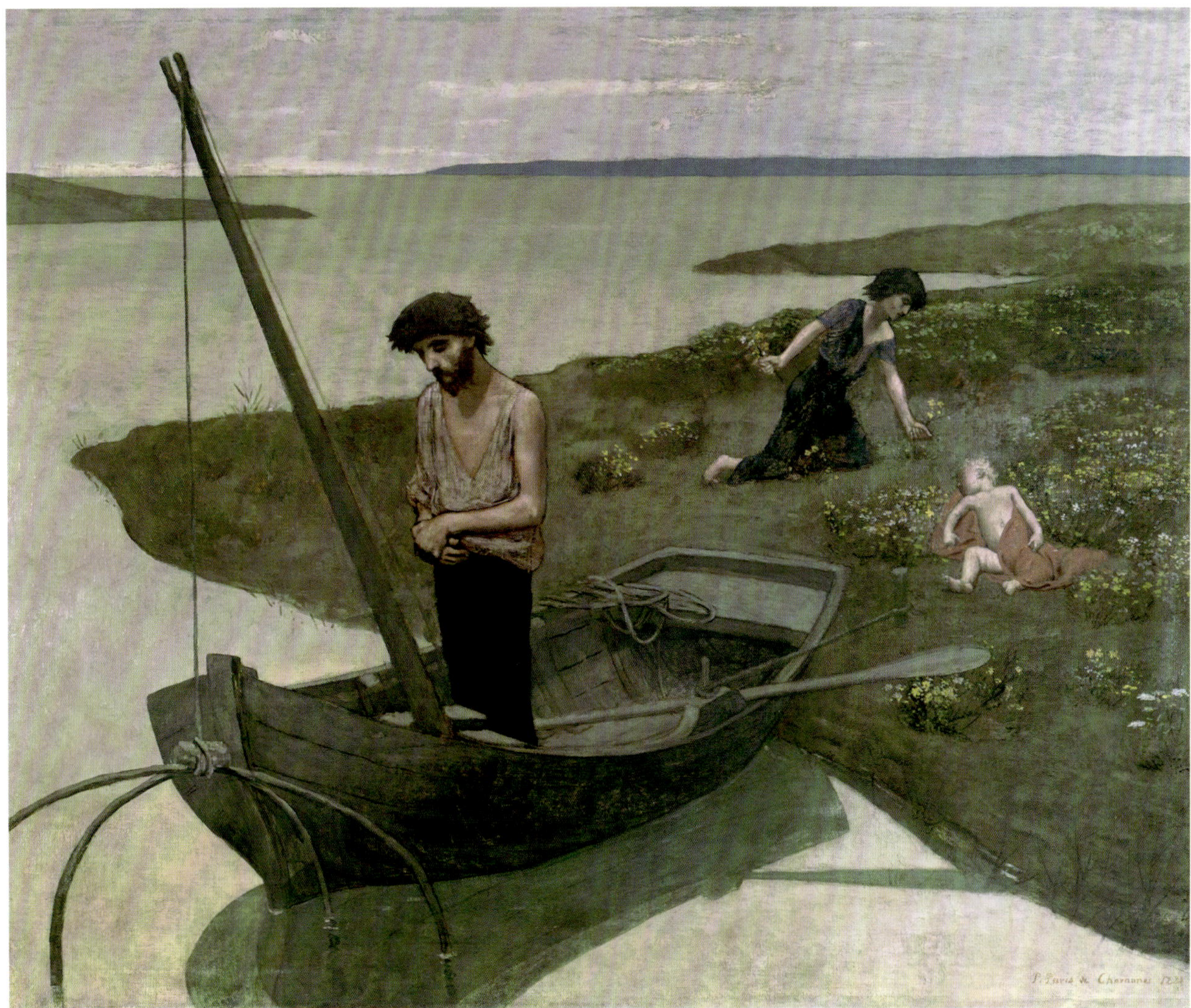

The Poor Fisherman

Silence and resignation characterize this portrait of a destitute, widowed fisherman with his two children. Feelings reinforced by the sobriety and subdued colors of the landscape.

Le Pauvre Pêcheur

Tristesse et désœuvrement caractérisent cette vision d'un pauvre pêcheur veuf, accompagné de ses deux enfants. Un sentiment que vient renforcer le dépouillement d'un paysage aux couleurs sans éclat.

Der arme Fischer

Stille und Resignation charakterisieren dieses Bildnis eines mittellosen, verwitweten Fischers mit seinen zwei Kindern. Gefühle, die durch die Nüchternheit und die gedämpften Farben der Landschaft verstärkt werden.

El pobre pescador

El silencio y la resignación caracterizan este retrato de un pescador indigente y viudo con sus dos hijos. Sentimientos reforzados por la sobriedad y los colores apagados del paisaje.

O pobre pescador

O silêncio e a resignação caracterizam este retrato de um pescador desamparado e viúvo com seus dois filhos. Sentimentos reforçados pela sobriedade e cores suaves da paisagem.

De arme visser

Stilte en berusting kenmerken dit portret van een arme, verweduwde visser met zijn twee kinderen. Gevoelens die worden versterkt door de soberheid en ingetogen kleuren van het landschap.

PIERRE PUVIS DE CHAVANNES (1824-1898)

1881, Oil on canvas/Huile sur toile, 155,5 × 192,5 cm, Musée d'Orsay, Paris

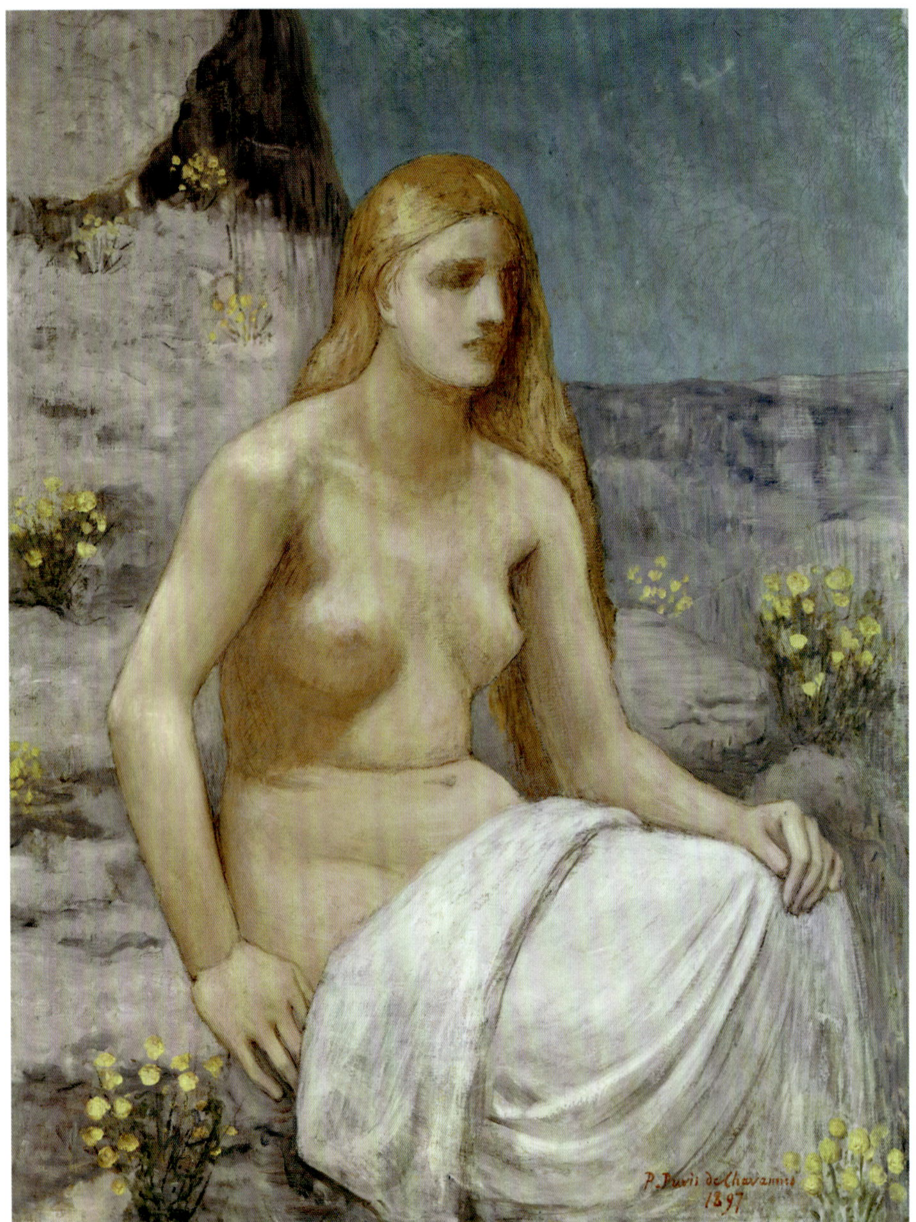

The Penitent Mary Magdalene

The representation is less known
than the work *Saint Mary Magdalene in
the Desert* (1869). Chavannes painted Mary
Magdalene in a contemporary way, and lets
the light shape her body.

Marie-Madeleine pénitente

Moins connue que sa *Marie-Madeleine
dans le désert* (1869), cette représentation du
personnage biblique est plus moderne.
Puvis de Chavannes en fait un être de chair,
au corps modelé par la lumière.

Die büßende Maria Magdalena

Die Darstellung ist weniger bekannt als
das Werk *Die heilige Maria Magdalena in
der Wüste* (1869). Chavannes malt Maria
Magdalena auf eine zeitgenössische Art,
und lässt das Licht ihren Körper formen.

La penitente María Magdalena

La representación es menos conocida que la
obra *Santa María Magdalena en el desierto*
(1869). Chavannes pinta a María Magdalena
de manera contemporánea, y deja que la luz
modele su cuerpo.

A penitente Maria Madalena

A representação é menos conhecida que
a obra *Santa Maria Madalena no Deserto*
(1869). Chavannes pinta Maria Madalena
de forma contemporânea, e deixa a luz
moldar seu corpo.

De boetvaardige Maria Magdalena

De voorstelling is minder bekend dan
Maria Magdalena in de woestijn (1869).
Puvis de Chavannes schilderde Maria
Magdalena op een eigentijdse manier en laat
het licht haar lichaam vormgeven.

PIERRE PUVIS DE CHAVANNES (1824-1898)
1897, Oil on canvas/
Huile sur toile, 116,5 × 89,5 cm,
Museum of Fine Arts, Budapest

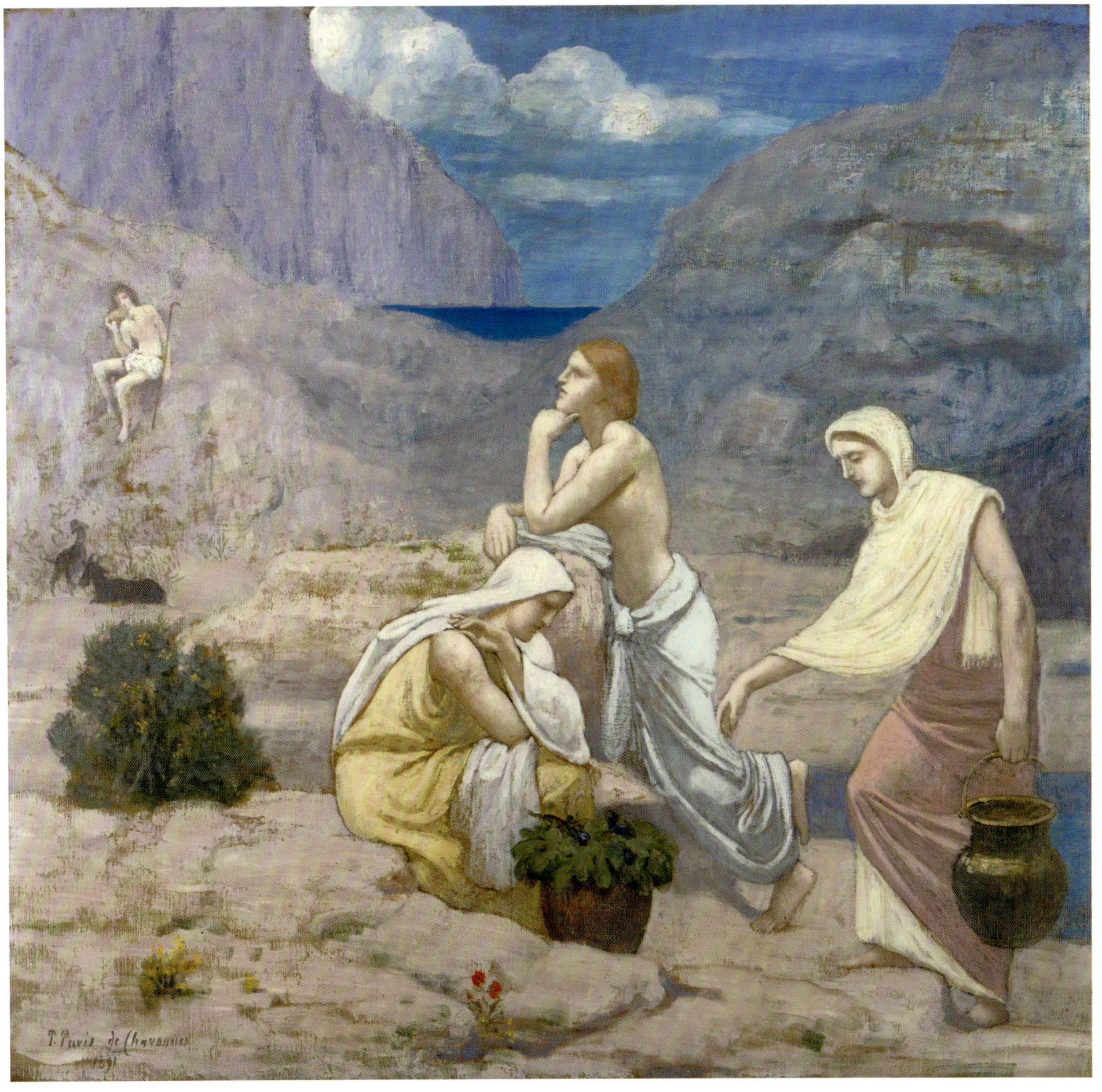

The Shepherd's Song

La Chanson du berger

Das Lied des Hirten

El canto del pastor

O Canto do Pastor

Het lied van de herder

PIERRE PUVIS DE CHAVANNES (1824-1898)

1891, Oil on canvas/Huile sur toile, 104,5 × 109,9 cm, Metropolitan Museum of Art, New York

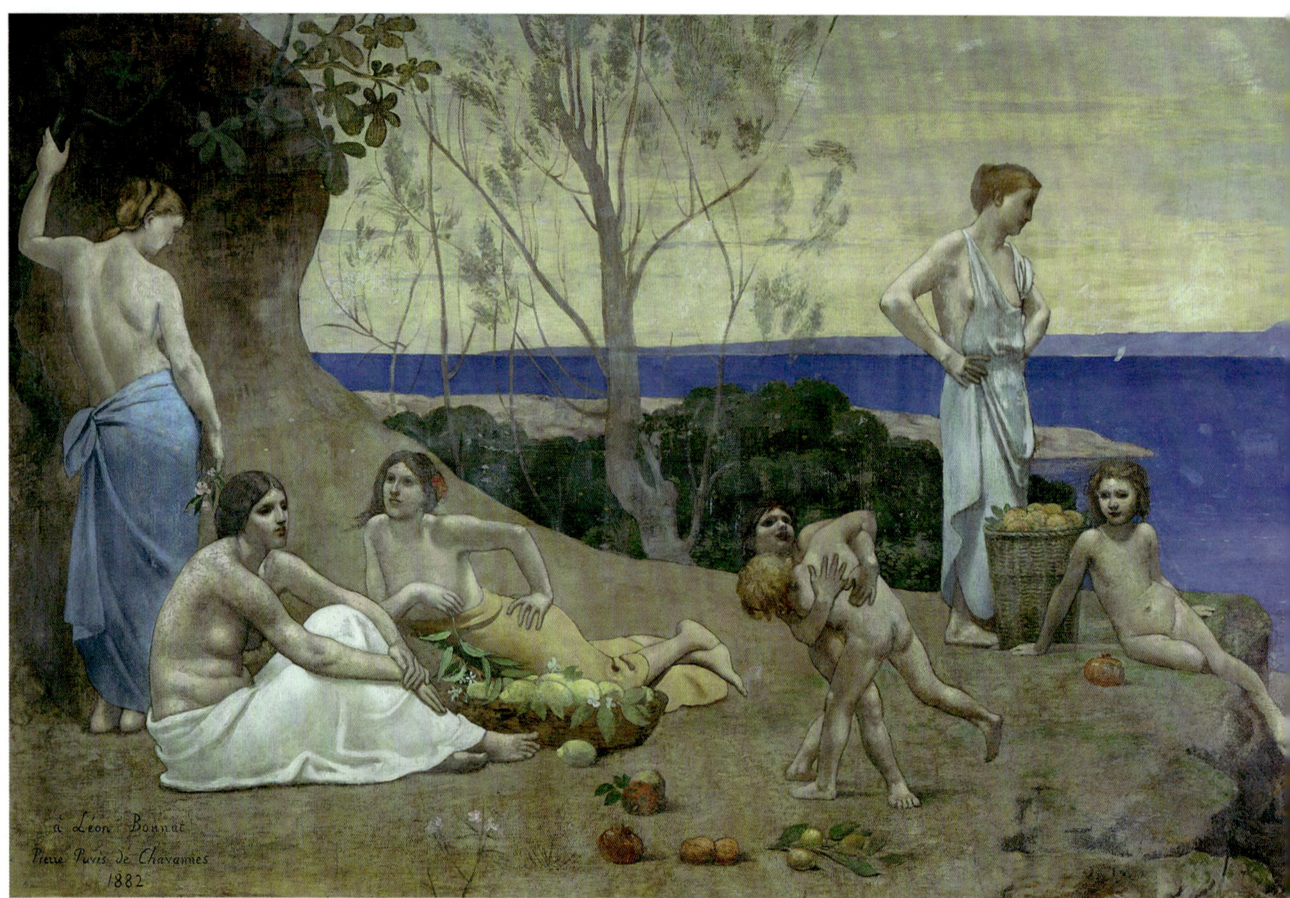

Sweet Country

Doux Pays

Süßes Land

Dulce país

Doce país

Zoet land

PIERRE PUVIS DE CHAVANNES (1824-1898)

1882, Oil on canvas/Huile sur toile, 230 × 300 cm, Musée Bonnat, Bayonne

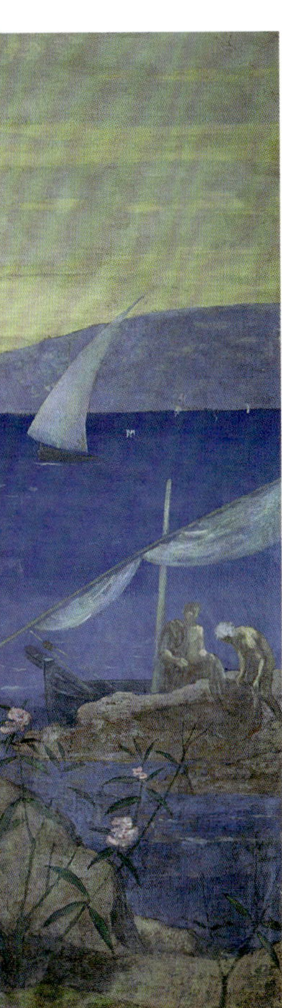

Saint Genoveva Watches over
the Sleeping City of Paris.

Sainte Geneviève
veillant sur Paris

Die heilige Genoveva wacht
über das schlafende Paris

Santa Genoveva
vela por París

Saint Genoveva vigia
Paris adormecida.

De heilige Genoveva waakt
over het slapende Parijs

PIERRE PUVIS DE CHAVANNES
(1824-1898)

1898, Oil on canvas/
Huile sur toile,
462 × 226 cm,
Panthéon, Paris

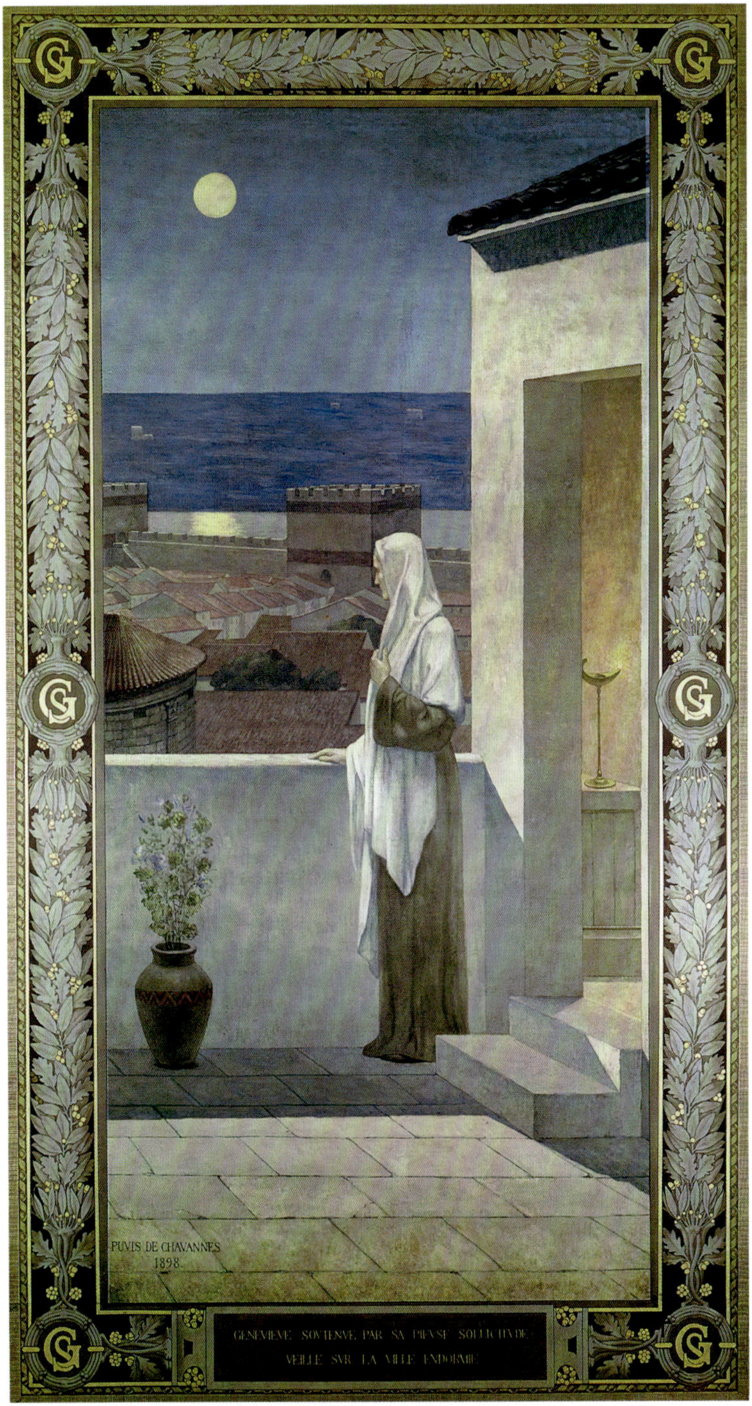

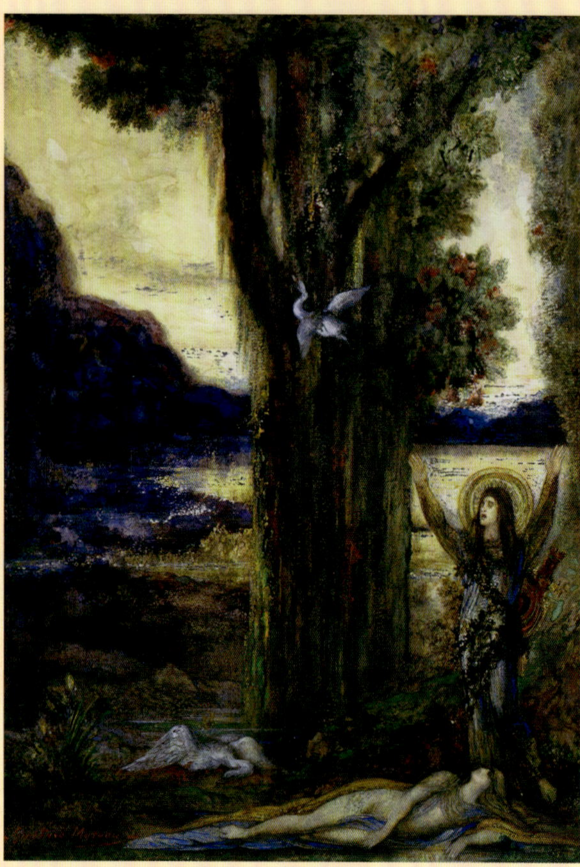

Gustave Moreau

Moreau's (1826-1898) paintings can be recognised at first glance. His stroke is restless, sometimes blurred, the colors radiant, almost phosphorescent. His motifs come from mythology or fables. At the age of eight he was already enthusiastic about drawing. In 1846 he entered the Académie des Beaux-Arts. Five years later he painted with Théodore Chassériau, whose influence was to shape his style. In 1852 he exhibited for the first time at the Salon, where in 1864 he presented his work *Oedipus and the Sphinx*, acquired by Napoleon III. In 1879 he painted a series of 64 watercolors to illustrate La Fontaine's *Fables*. From 1892 to 1898, Moreau taught at the Académie des Beaux-Arts. Georges Rouault, Albert Marquet and Henri Matisse were among his students there. His last masterpiece, *Jupiter and Semele*, was completed in 1895 and shortly afterwards he decided to transform his family's house on Rue de La Rochefoucauld in Paris into the museum that it still is today.

Gustave Moreau

Une peinture de Gustave Moreau (1826-1898) est immédiatement reconnaissable. La touche est fiévreuse, parfois brouillée, les couleurs éclatantes, presque phosphorescentes, les sujets traversés par la mythologie et les fables. Passionné de dessin dès l'âge de 8 ans, Moreau entre aux Beaux-Arts en 1846. Cinq ans plus tard, il se lie avec Théodore Chassériau, dont l'influence sera décisive sur son art. Il est repéré au Salon officiel en 1852. Il y présentera en 1864 *Œdipe et le Sphinx*, acquis par Napoléon III. En 1879, il entreprend une série de soixante-quatre aquarelles pour illustrer les *Fables* de La Fontaine. Entre 1892 et 1898, Gustave Moreau enseigne à l'École des beaux-arts, où il aura comme élèves Georges Rouault, Albert Marquet, Henri Matisse… L'artiste signe son dernier grand chef-d'œuvre en 1895, *Jupiter et Sémélé*, et décide alors de transformer la maison familiale de la rue de La Rochefoucauld, à Paris, pour qu'elle puisse devenir, après son décès, le musée que l'on connaît aujourd'hui.

Gustave Moreau

Moreaus (1826–1898) Gemälde lassen sich auf den ersten Blick zuordnen. Sein Strich ist unruhig, manchmal verschwommen, die Farben strahlend, fast phosphoreszierend. Seine Motive entstammen der Mythologie oder Fabeln. Im Alter von acht Jahren begeistert er sich bereits für das Zeichnen. 1846 tritt er in die Académie des Beaux-Arts ein. Fünf Jahre später malt er bei Théodore Chassériau, dessen Einfluss seinen Stil prägen wird. 1852 stellt er zum ersten Mal auf dem Salon aus, wo er 1864 sein Werk *Ödipus und die Sphinx* zeigt, das von Napoleon III. erworben wird. 1879 malt er eine Serie von 64 Aquarellen als Illustration für La Fontaines *Fabeln*. Von 1892 bis 1898 unterrichtet Moreau an der Académie des Beaux-Arts. Dort gehören Georges Rouault, Albert Marquet und Henri Matisse zu seinen Schülern. Sein letztes Meisterwerk *Jupiter und Semele* vollendet er 1895. Kurz danach beschließt er, das Haus seiner Familie in der Rue de La Rochefoucauld in Paris in ein Museum umzuwandeln, als das es bis heute fungiert.

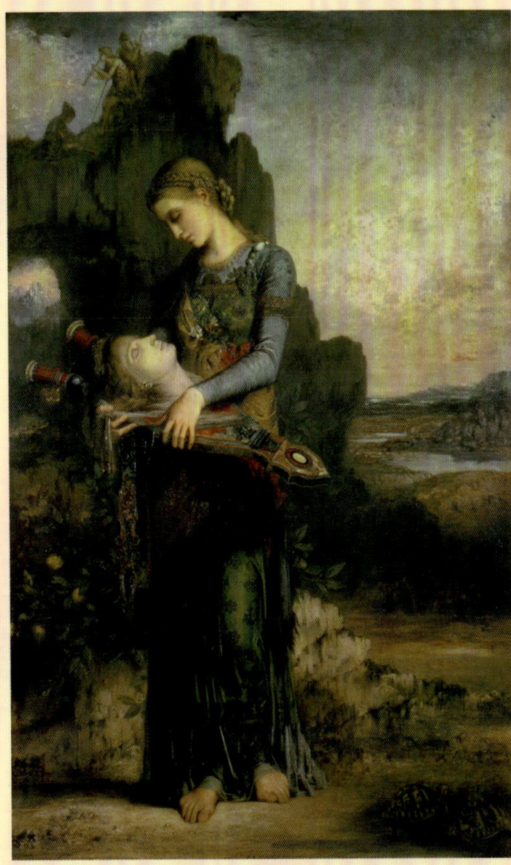

GUSTAVE MOREAU (1826-1898)
1865, Oil on wood/Huile sur bois, 155 × 99,5 cm, Musée d'Orsay, Paris

Gustave Moreau

Las pinturas de Moreau (1826-1898) se pueden asignar
a primera vista. Su trazo es inquieto, a veces borroso,
los colores radiantes, casi fosforescentes. Sus motivos
provienen de la mitología o de las fábulas. A los ocho
años ya estaba entusiasmado con el dibujo. En 1846
ingresó en la Academia de Bellas Artes. Cinco años más
tarde pintó con Théodore Chassériau, cuya influencia
dará forma a su estilo. En 1852 expone por primera vez
en el Salón, donde en 1864 presenta su obra *Edipo y
la Esfinge*, adquirida por Napoleón III. En 1879 pintó
una serie de 64 acuarelas para ilustrar *las fábulas de
La Fontaine*. De 1892 a 1898, Moreau enseñó en la
Academia de Bellas Artes. Georges Rouault,
Albert Marquet y Henri Matisse se encuentran
entre sus alumnos. Su última obra maestra, *Júpiter y
Semele*, fue terminada en 1895 y poco después decidió
transformar la casa de su familia en la calle de
La Rochefoucauld en París en un museo que aún
existe hoy en día.

Gustavo Moreau

As pinturas de Moreaus (1826-1898) podem ser
atribuídas à primeira vista. Seu traço é inquieto, às
vezes borrado, as cores radiantes, quase fosforescentes.
Os seus motivos vêm da mitologia ou de fábulas. Aos
oito anos já estava entusiasmado com o desenho. Em
1846 entrou na Académie des Beaux-Arts. Cinco anos
mais tarde pintou com Théodore Chassériau, cuja
influência irá moldar o seu estilo. Em 1852 expôs pela
primeira vez no Salão, onde em 1864 apresentou a sua
obra *Édipo e a Esfinge*, adquirida por Napoleão III. Em
1879, pintou uma série de 64 aquarelas para ilustrar as
fábulas de La Fontaine. De 1892 a 1898, Moreau ensinou
na Académie des Beaux-Arts. Georges Rouault,
Albert Marquet e Henri Matisse estão entre seus
alunos. Sua última obra-prima, *Júpiter e Semele*, foi
concluída em 1895 e, pouco depois, decidiu transformar
a casa de sua família na Rue de La Rochefoucauld, em
Paris, em um museu que ainda hoje funciona.

Gustave Moreau

Moreaus (1826-1898) schilderijen laten zich op het eerste
gezicht goed indelen. Zijn penseelstreken zijn onrustig,
soms wazig, de kleuren stralend, bijna fluorescerend.
Zijn onderwerpen komen uit de mythologie of uit fabels.
Op achtjarige leeftijd tekende hij al vol enthousiasme.
In 1846 trad hij toe tot de Académie des Beaux-Arts.
Vijf jaar later schilderde hij bij Théodore Chassériau,
wiens invloed een stempel zou drukken op zijn stijl. In
1852 exposeerde hij voor het eerst op de Salon, waar hij
in 1864 zijn werk *Oedipus en de sfinx* presenteerde, dat
door Napoleon III werd aangekocht. In 1879 schilderde
hij een serie van 64 aquarellen ter illustratie van de fabels
van La Fontaine. Van 1892 tot 1898 gaf Moreau les aan
de Académie des Beaux-Arts. Georges Rouault, Albert
Marquet en Henri Matisse behoorden tot zijn studenten.
Hij voltooide zijn laatste meesterwerk, *Jupiter en Semele*,
in 1895. Kort daarna besloot hij het huis van zijn familie
aan de Rue de La Rochefoucauld in Parijs te veranderen
in een museum. Dat is het nu nog steeds.

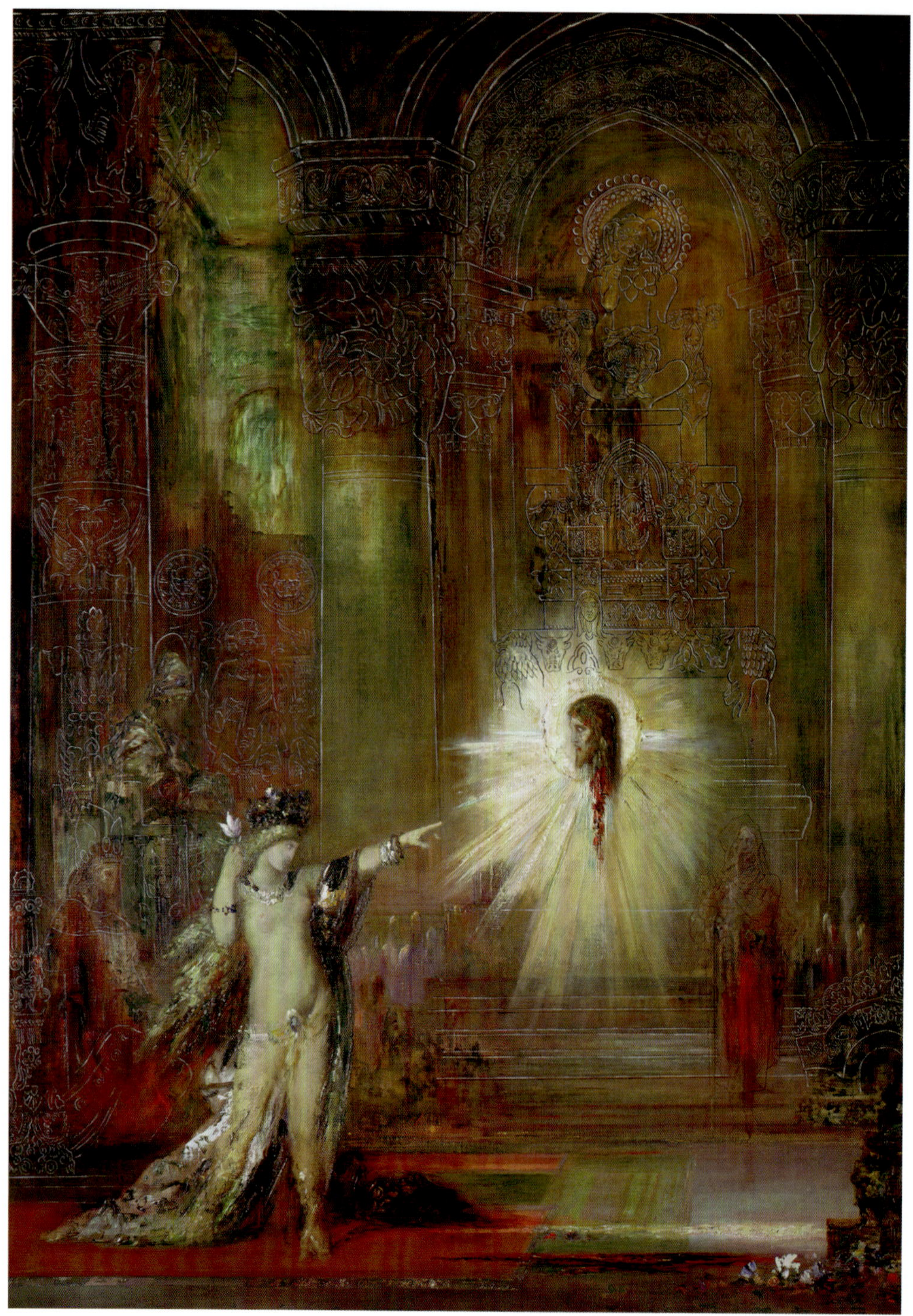

The Apparition

The painting shows the appearance of the head of John the Baptist. Salome had received it as a reward for her dance before Herod Antipas, who is depicted to the left of his wife Herodias.

L'Apparition

L'apparition en question est celle de la tête coupée de Jean-Baptiste. Salomé l'a demandée en récompense, après avoir dansé devant Hérode Antipas, représenté à gauche près de son épouse Hérodiade.

Die Erscheinung

Das Gemälde zeigt die Erscheinung des Kopfes von Johannes dem Täufer. Salome hatte ihn als Belohnung für ihren Tanz vor Herodes Antipas erhalten, der links neben seiner Gemahlin Herodias abgebildet ist.

La Aparición

La apariencia en cuestión es la de la cabeza cortada de Juan el Bautista. Salomé lo pidió como recompensa, después de bailar delante de Herodes Antipas, representado a la izquierda junto a su esposa Herodías.

A Aparição

A pintura mostra a aparência da cabeça de João Batista. Salomé a recebeu como recompensa por sua dança antes de Herodes Antipas, que é retratado à esquerda de sua esposa Herodíades.

De verschijning

Het schilderij toont de verschijning van het hoofd van Johannes de Doper. Salomé had het ontvangen als beloning voor haar dans voor Herodes Antipas, die links van zijn vrouw Herodias is afgebeeld.

GUSTAVE MOREAU (1826-1898)

n. d., Oil on canvas/Huile sur toile, 142 × 103 cm, Musée Gustave Moreau, Paris

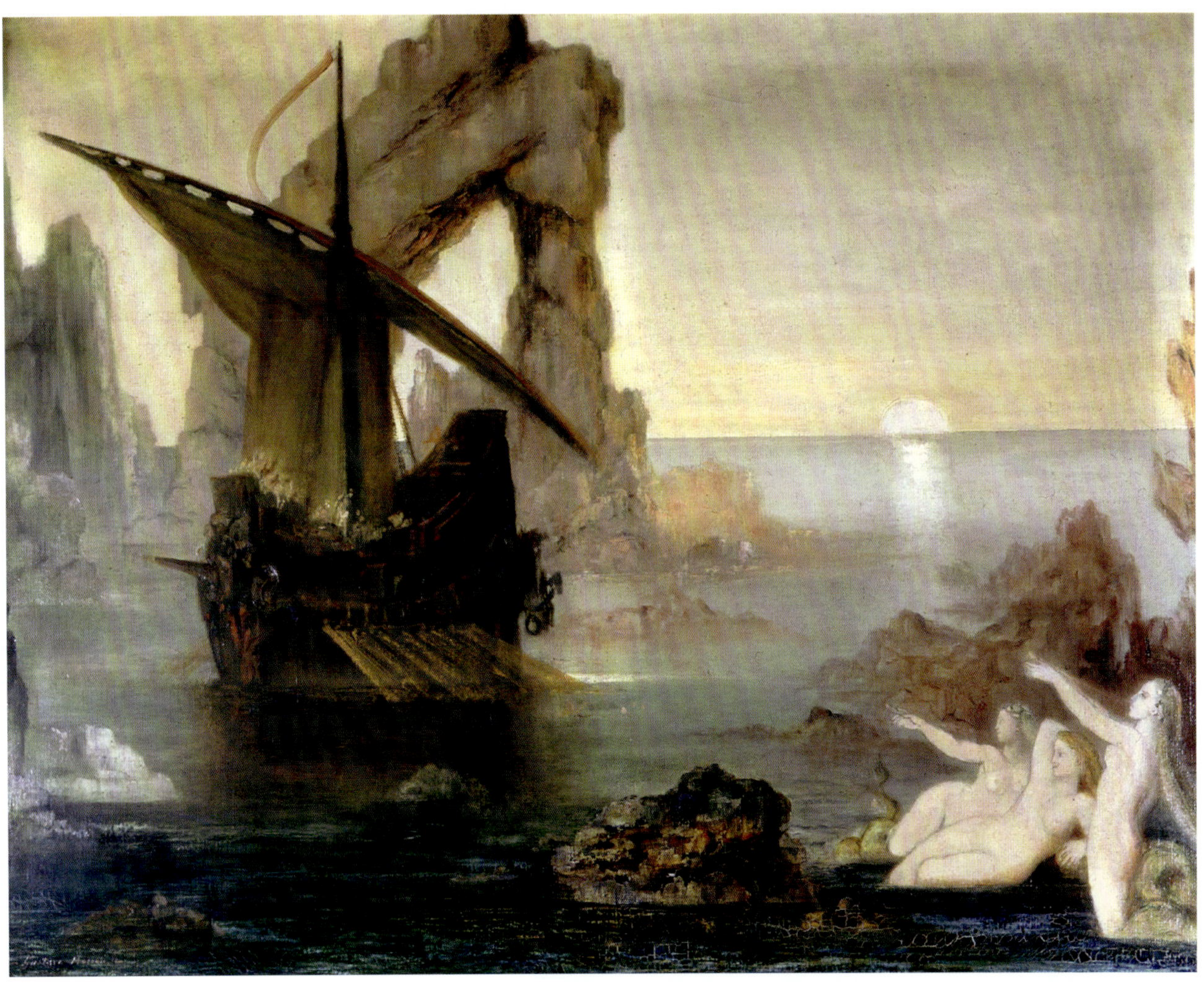

Ulysses and the Sirens

Ulysse et les Sirènes

Odysseus und die Sirenen

Odiseo y las sirenas

Odisseu e as Sirenes

Odysseus en de sirenes

GUSTAVE MOREAU (1826-1898)

c. 1875-80, Oil on canvas/Huile sur toile, 93,03 × 117 cm, Musée Gustave Moreau, Paris

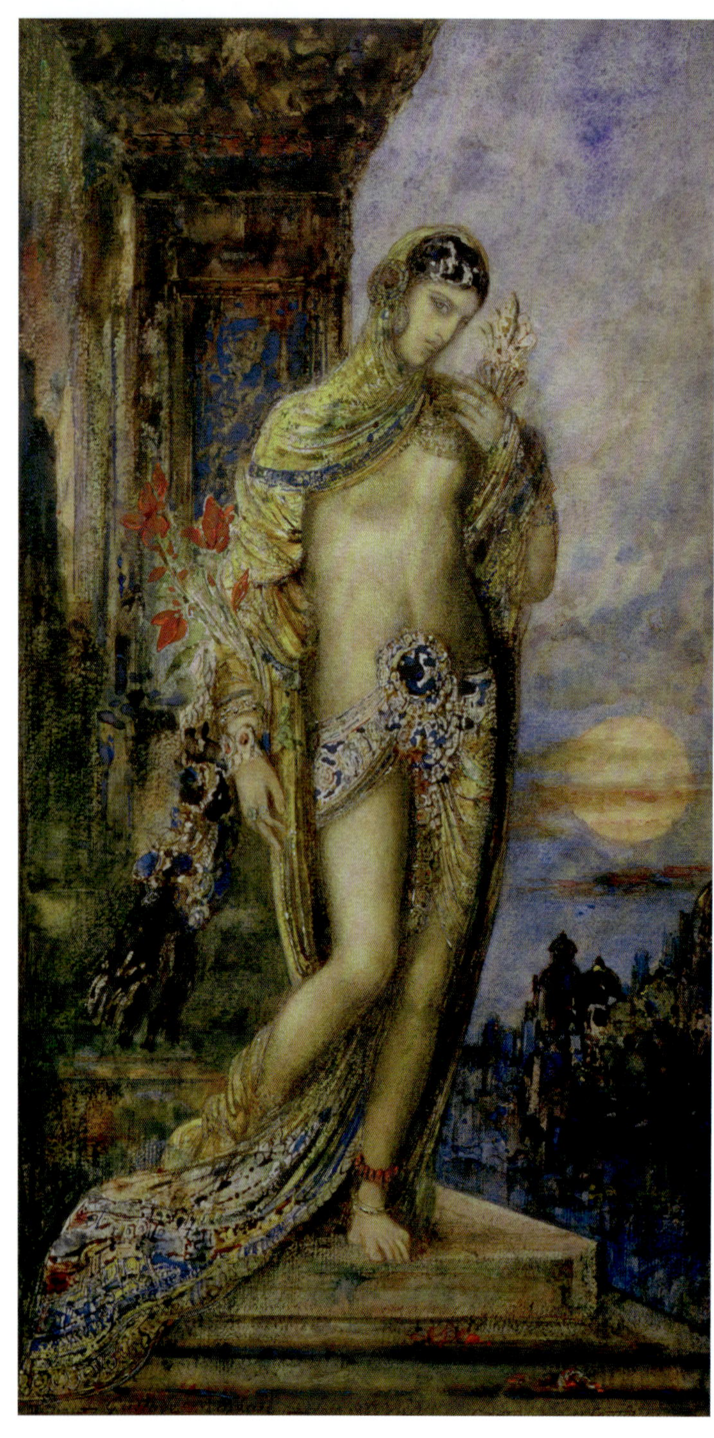

The Song of Songs: The Shulammite Maiden

Le Cantique des cantiques : la jeune fille sulamite

Das Hohelied Salomos: Die junge Sulamith

El Cantar de los Cantares: el joven Sulamith

O Cântico dos Cânticos de Salomão: O jovem Sulamith

Het Hooglied: de jonge Sulamitische vrouw

GUSTAVE MOREAU (1826-1898)

n. d., Watercolour/Aquarelle, 37 × 19 cm, Private collection

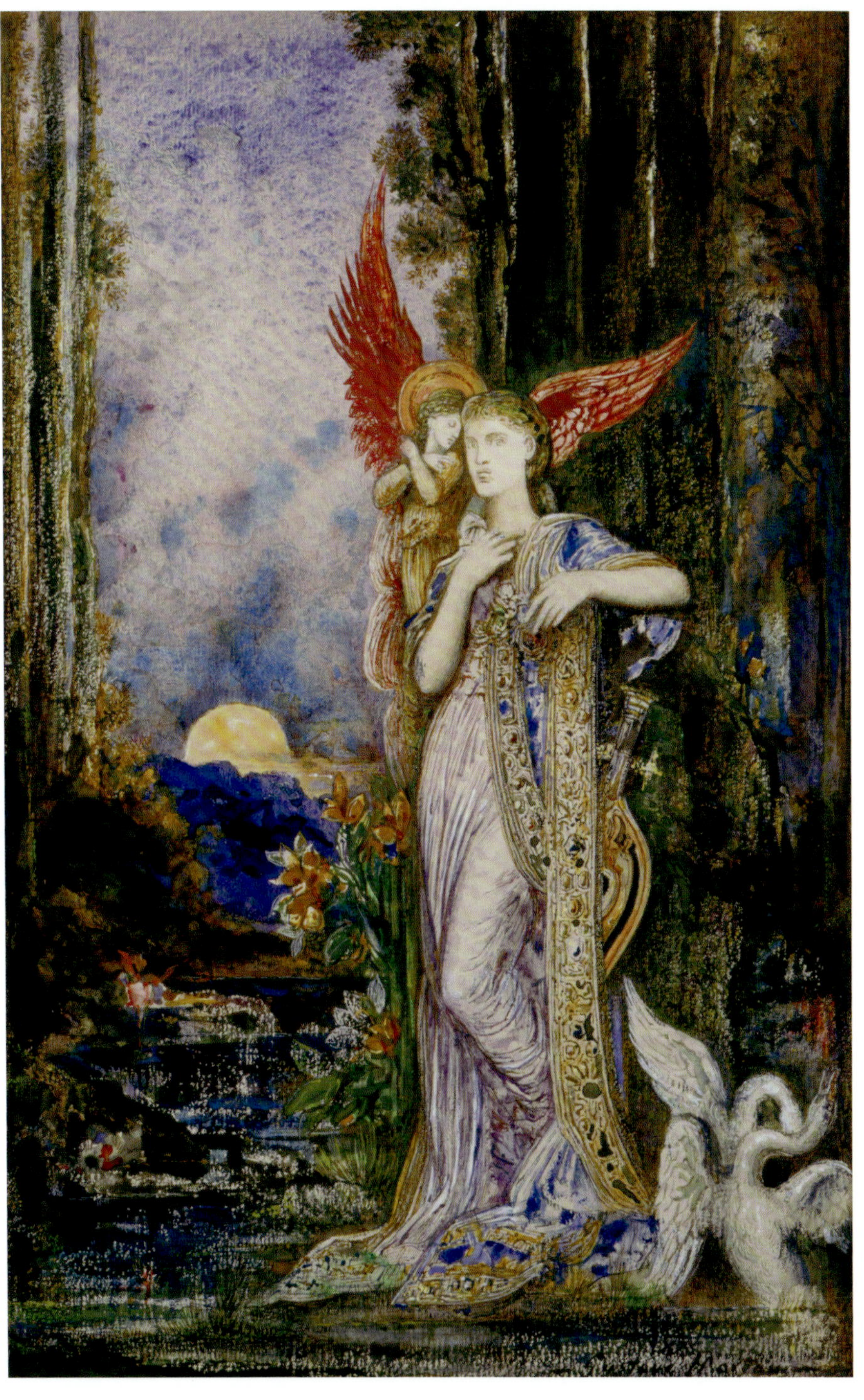

The Inspiration

L'Inspiration

Die Eingebung

La inspiración

A intuição

De inspiratie

GUSTAVE MOREAU (1826-1898)
1893, Watercolour and gouache, in pen and blue
ink, on traces of graphite, on ivory wove paper/
Aquarelle et gouache, à la plume et à l'encre
bleue, sur traces de mine de plomb, sur papier
vélin ivoire, 29,9 × 23 cm, Private collection

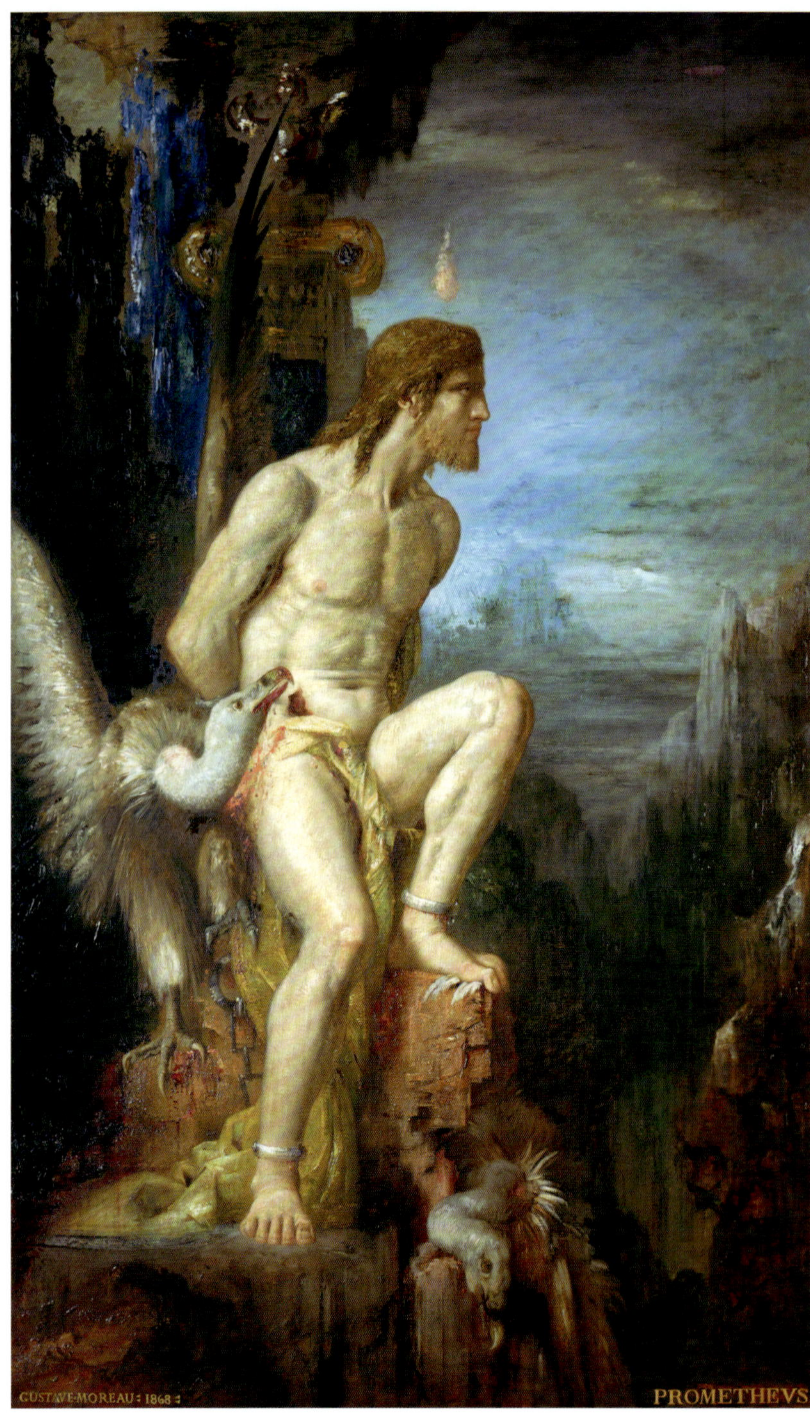

Prometheus

In Greek mythology, Prometheus stole the fire of Olympus. Angry Zeus had him chained to a rock in the Caucasus Mountains, where an eagle regularly ate his liver, which is constantly renewed.

Prométhée

Titan dans la mythologie grecque, Prométhée a volé le feu de l'Olympe, entraînant la colère de Zeus. Ce dernier le condamne à être attaché sur un rocher du mont Caucase, où un aigle vient dévorer son foie qui repousse sans cesse.

Prometheus

In der griechischen Mythologie stiehlt Prometheus das Feuer des Olymps. Der erzürnte Zeus lässt ihn an einen Felsen des Kaukasusgebirges ketten, wo ein Adler regelmäßig seine Leber frisst, die sich stets erneuert.

Prometeo

En la mitología griega, Prometeo roba el fuego del Olimpo. El enfadado Zeus lo tiene encadenado a una roca de las montañas del Cáucaso, donde un águila se come regularmente su hígado, que se renueva constantemente.

Prometeu

Na mitologia grega, Prometeu rouba o fogo do Olimpo. O zangado Zeus tem-no acorrentado a uma rocha das montanhas do Cáucaso, onde uma águia come regularmente o seu fígado, que é constantemente renovado.

Prometheus

In de Griekse mythologie steelt Prometheus het vuur van de Olympus. De boze Zeus laat hem vastketenen aan een rots in het Kaukasusgebergte, waar een adelaar regelmatig van zijn lever eet, die voortdurend weer aangroeit.

GUSTAVE MOREAU (1826-1898)

1868, Oil on canvas/Huile sur toile,
205 × 122 cm, Musée Gustave Moreau, Paris

Jason *or* Jason and Medea

Jason *ou* Jason et Médée

Iason *oder* Iason und Medea

Iason *o* Iason y Medea

Iason *ou* Iason y Medea

Jason *of* Jason en Medea

GUSTAVE MOREAU (1826-1898)

1865, Oil on canvas/Huile sur toile,
204 × 115,5 cm, Musée d'Orsay, Paris

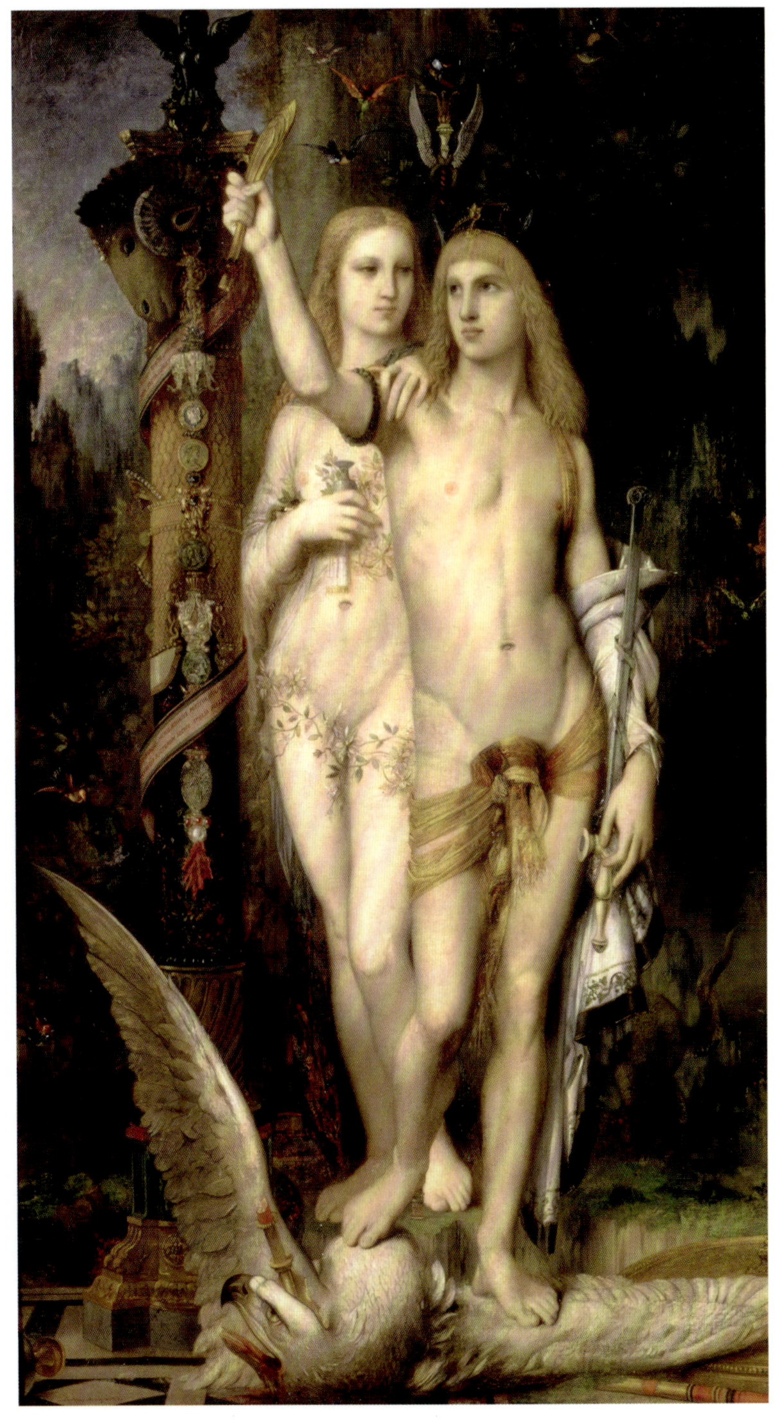

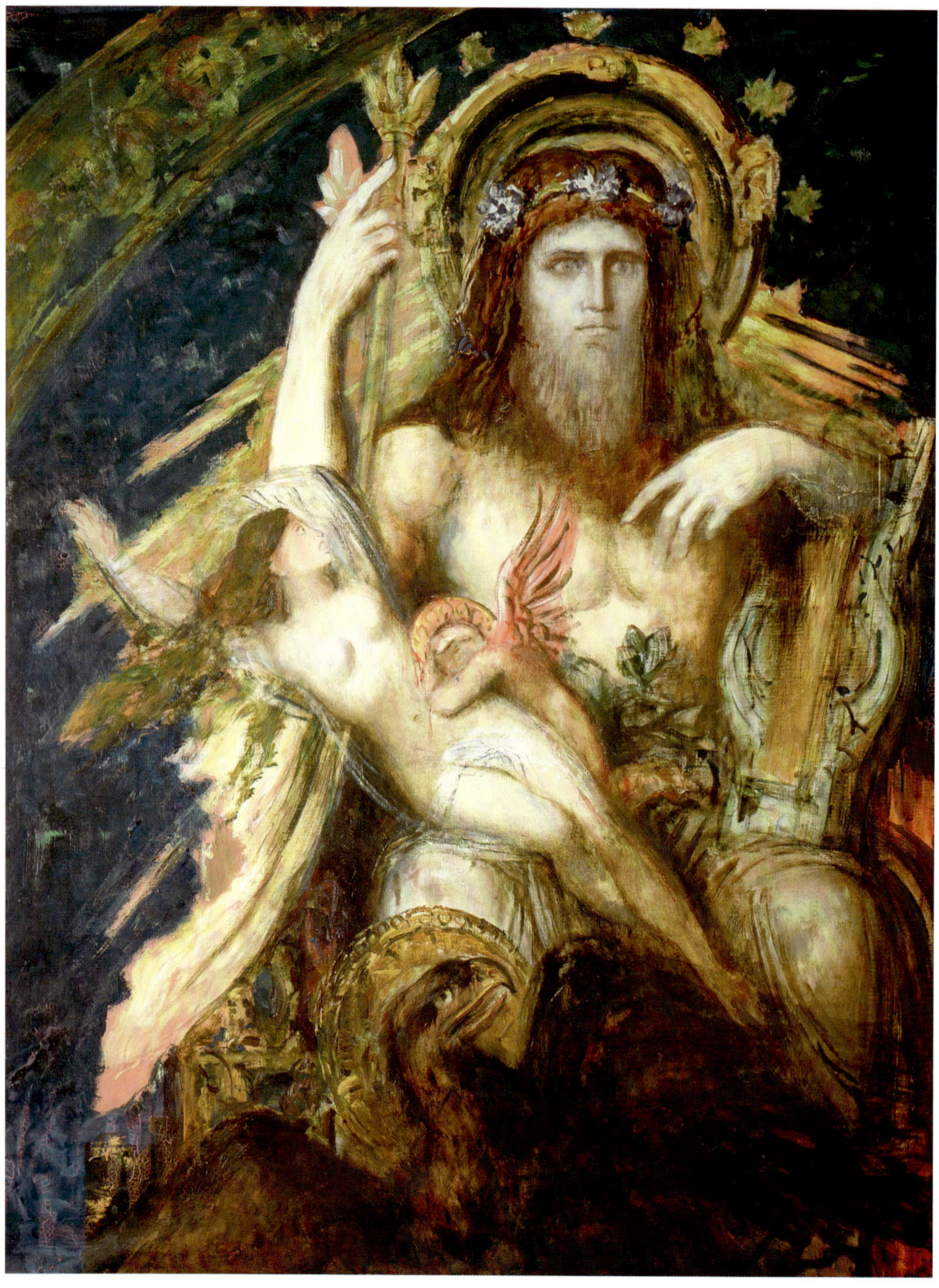

Jupiter and Semele

Jupiter et Sémélé

Jupiter und Semele

Júpiter y Semele

Júpiter e Semele

Jupiter en Semele

GUSTAVE MOREAU
(1826-1898)

c. 1894, Oil on canvas/
Huile sur toile, 149 × 110 cm,
Musée Gustave Moreau, Paris

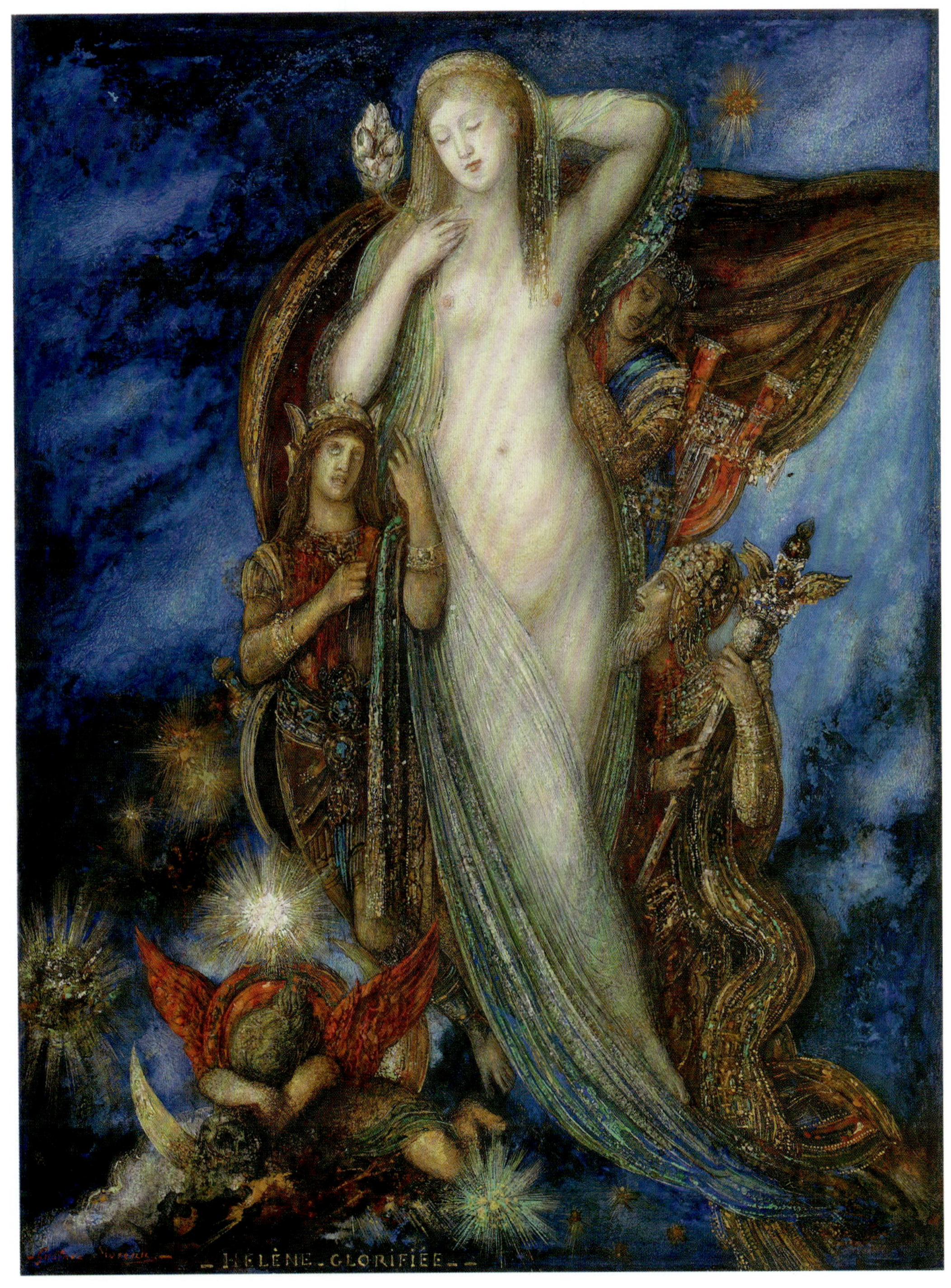

Helen Glorified

Hélène glorifiée

Verherrlichung Helenas

Helena glorificada

Glorificação Helenas

De verheerlijking
van Helena

GUSTAVE MOREAU
(1826-1898)

1896/97, Watercolour,
gouache and golden shell
on paper/Aquarelle, gouache
et coquillage doré sur papier,
30,5 × 23,2 cm,
Private collection

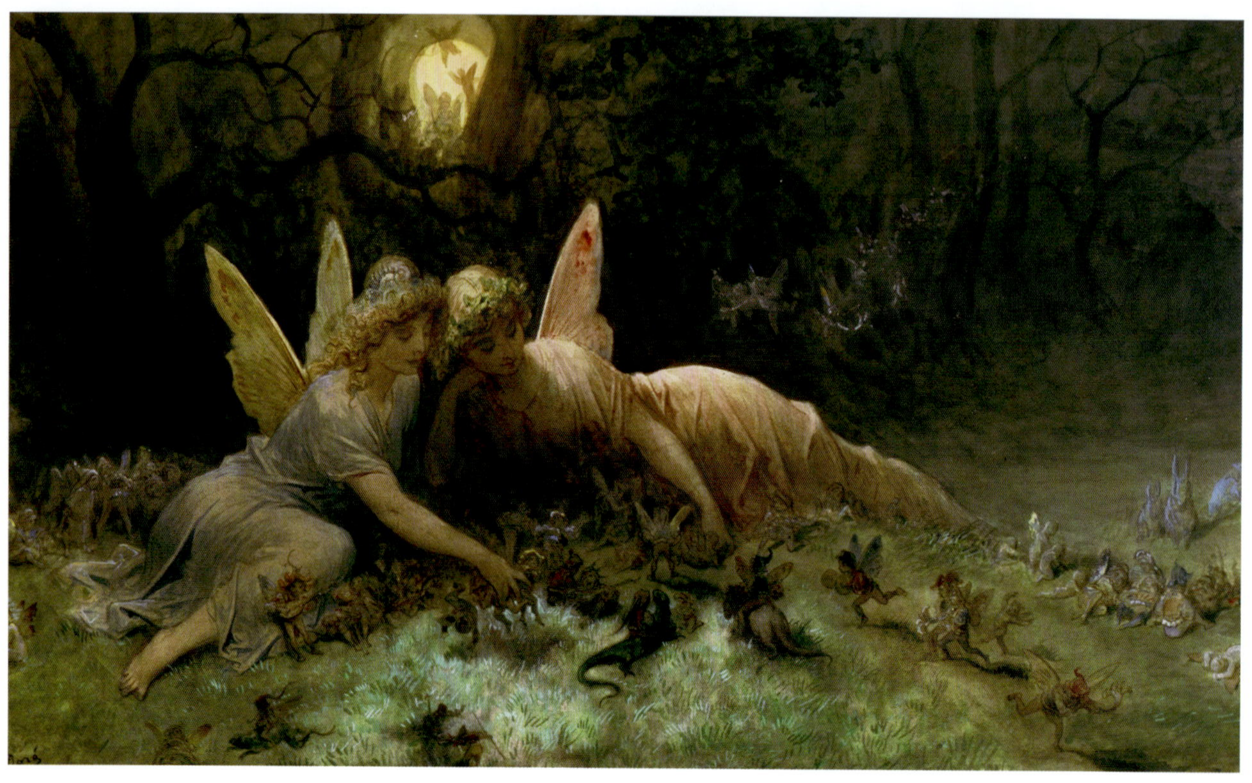

Faeries (from Shakespeare, *A Midsummer Night's Dream*)

Les Fées (de Shakespeare, *Le Songe d'une nuit d'été*)

Die Feen (aus Shakespeare, *Sommernachtstraum*)

Las hadas (de Shakespeare, *El sueño de una noche de verano*)

As Fadas (de Shakespeare, *Sonho de Noite de Verão*)

De Feeën (van Shakespeare, *Midzomernachtsdroom*)

GUSTAVE DORÉ (1832-1883)

1873, Watercolour/Aquarelle, 40,6 × 69,2 cm, Private collection

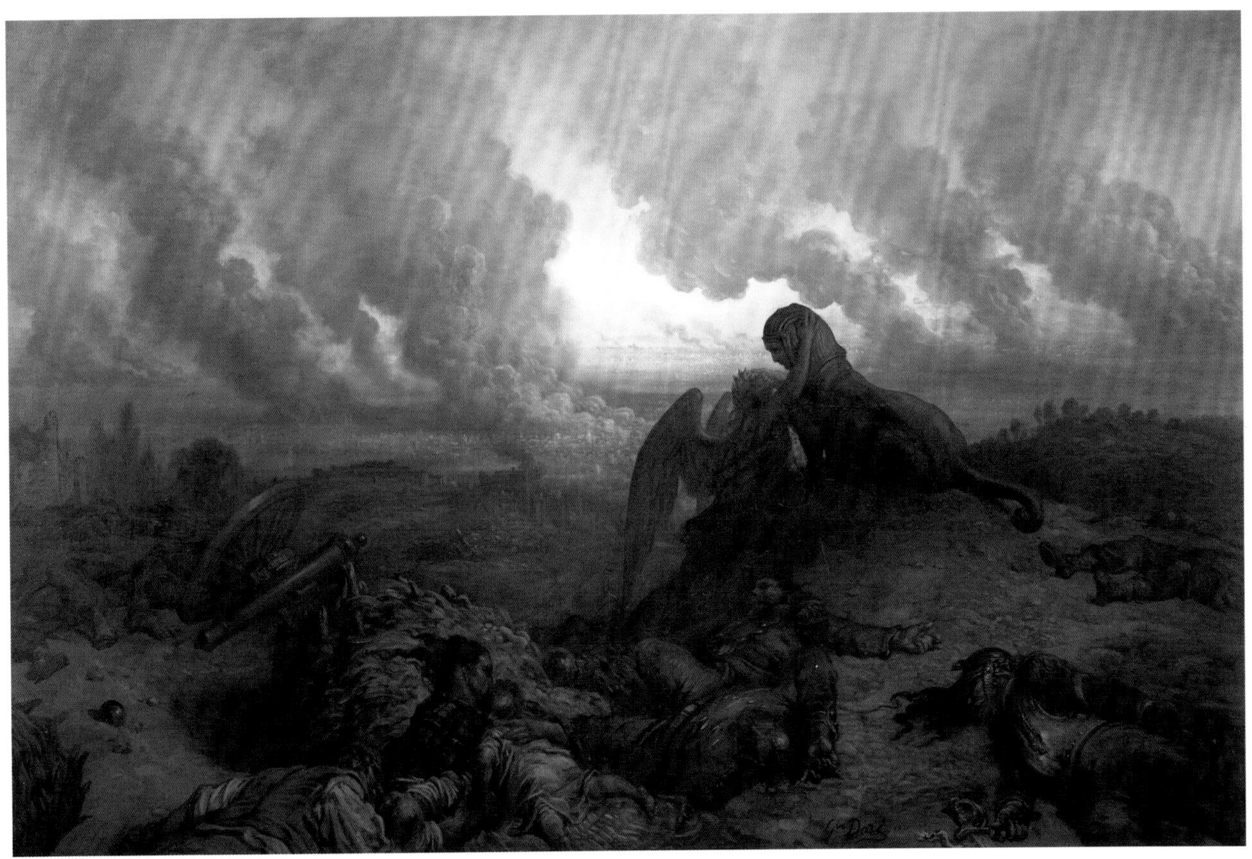

The Enigma

L'Énigme

Das Rätsel

El enigma

O enigma

Het raadsel

GUSTAVE DORÉ (1832-1883)

1871, Oil on canvas/Huile sur toile, 130 × 195,5 cm, Musée d'Orsay, Paris

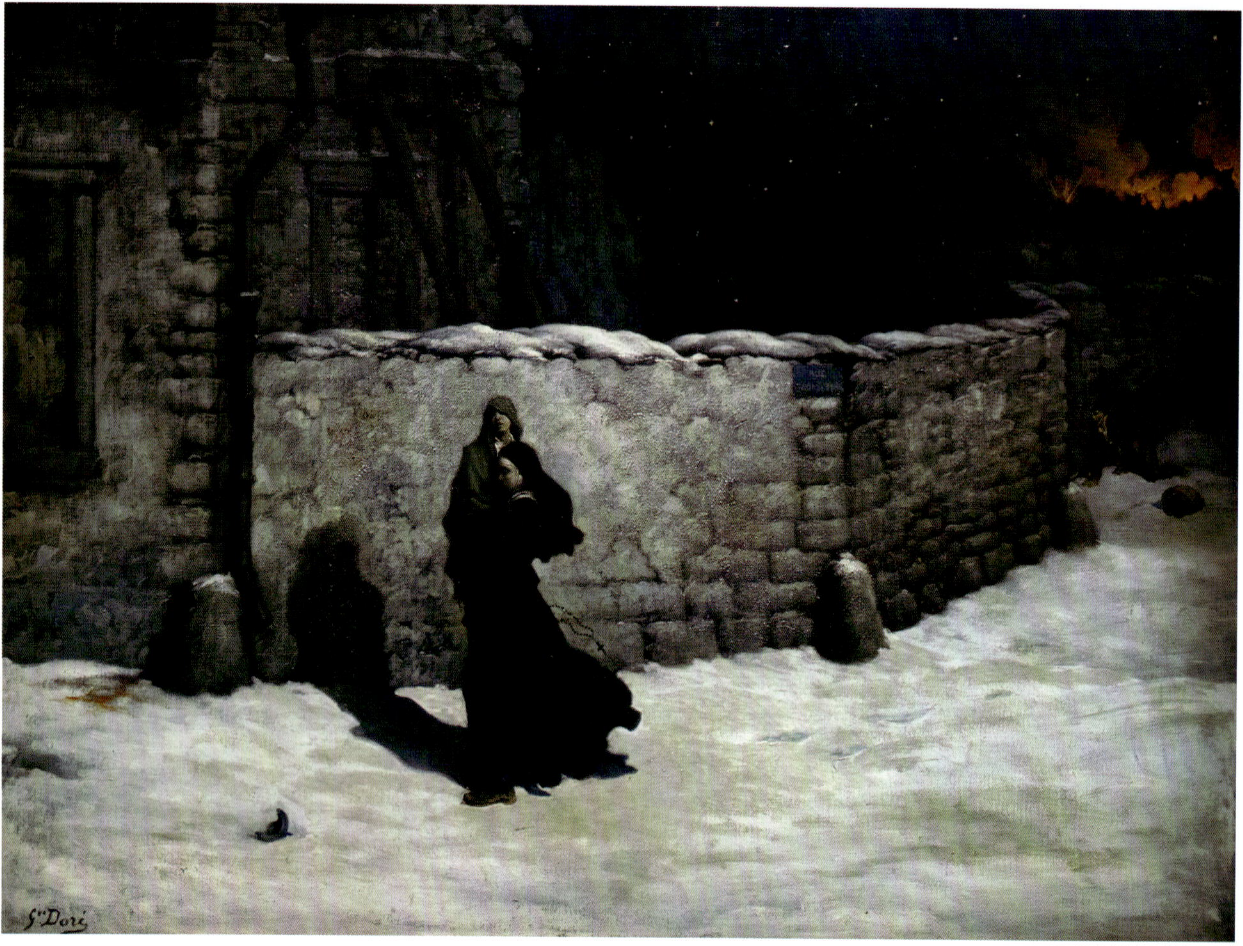

Sister of Charity Saving a Child *or*
Episode of the Siege of Paris

The Master of Symbolism also worked as a chronicler. In a dusky atmosphere, Doré depicted the rescue of a child by a nun during the siege and bombing of Paris.

Sœur de la Charité sauvant un enfant
Épisode du siège de Paris

Le maître du symbolisme se fait ici chroniqueur réaliste. Dans une ambiance crépusculaire, Gustave Doré dépeint le sauvetage d'un enfant par une sœur durant les bombardements du siège de Paris.

Eine Nonne rettet ein Kind *oder* **Episode der Belagerung von Paris**

Der Meister des Symbolismus betätigte sich auch als Chronist. In einer dämmrigen Atmosphäre stellt Doré die Rettung eines Kindes durch eine Nonne während der Belagerung und Bombardierung von Paris dar.

Una monja salvando a un niño *o* **un episodio del asedio de París**

El Maestro del Simbolismo también trabajó como cronista. En un ambiente oscuro, Doré representa el rescate de un niño por una monja durante el asedio y el bombardeo de París.

Uma freira salvando uma criança *ou* **episódio do cerco de Paris**

O Mestre do Simbolismo também trabalhou como cronista. Em uma atmosfera escura, Doré retrata o resgate de uma criança por uma freira durante o cerco e o bombardeio de Paris.

Een zuster van de liefdadigheid redt een kind *of* **Episode uit de belegering van Parijs**

De meester van het symbolisme werkte ook als chroniqueur. In een schemerige sfeer gaf Doré de redding van een kind door een non tijdens het beleg en de bombardementen op Parijs weer.

GUSTAVE DORÉ (1832–1883)

1870/71, Oil on canvas/Huile sur toile, 97 × 130 cm, Musée d'Art Moderne André Malraux, Le Havre

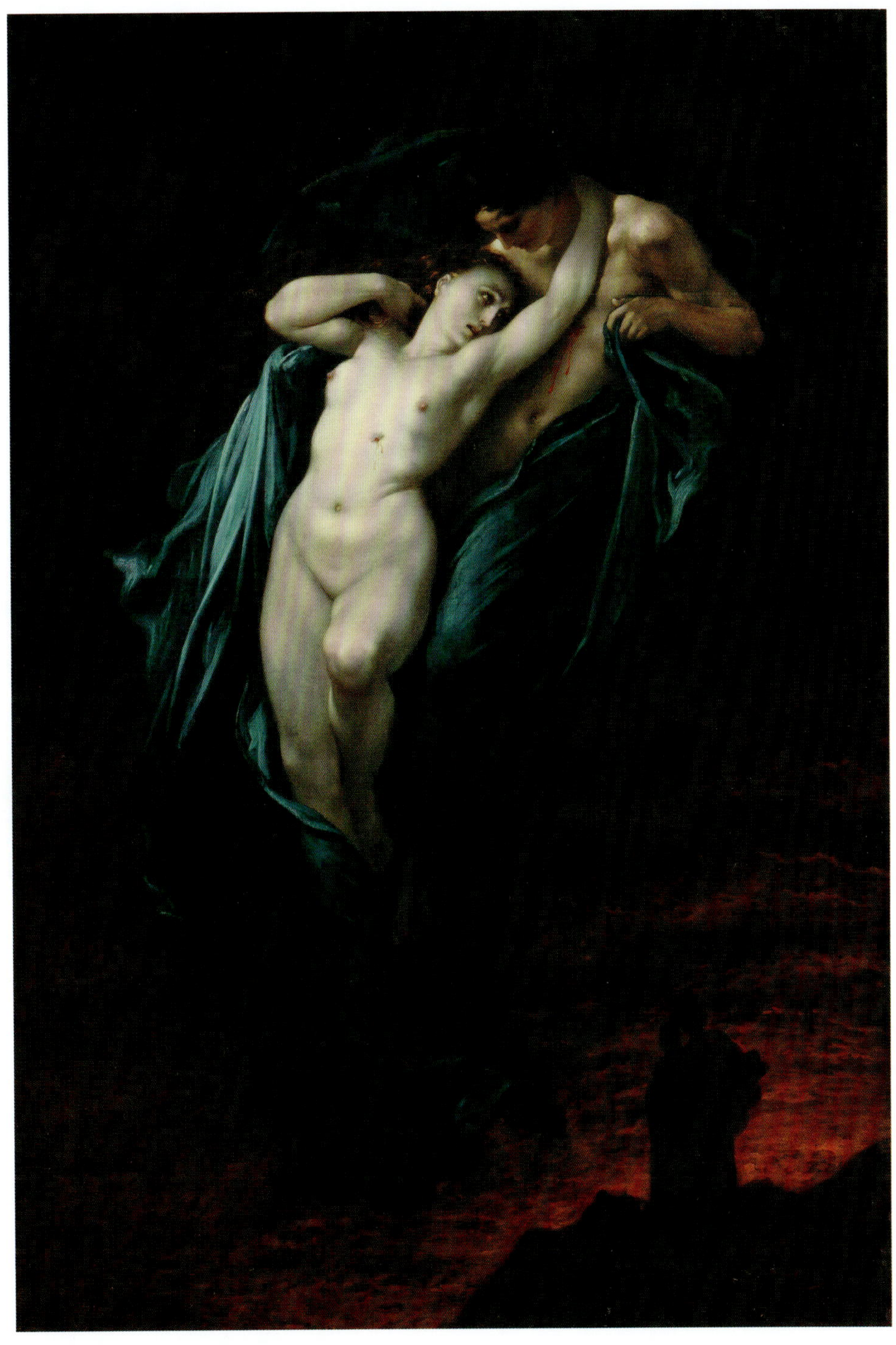

Paolo and Francesca da Rimini

Paolo et Francesca da Rimini

Paolo und Francesca da Rimini

Paolo y Francesca da Rimini

Paolo e Francesca da Rimini

Paolo en Francesca da Rimini

GUSTAVE DORÉ (1832-1883)
1863, Oil on canvas/Huile sur toile,
279,4 × 194,3 cm, Private collection

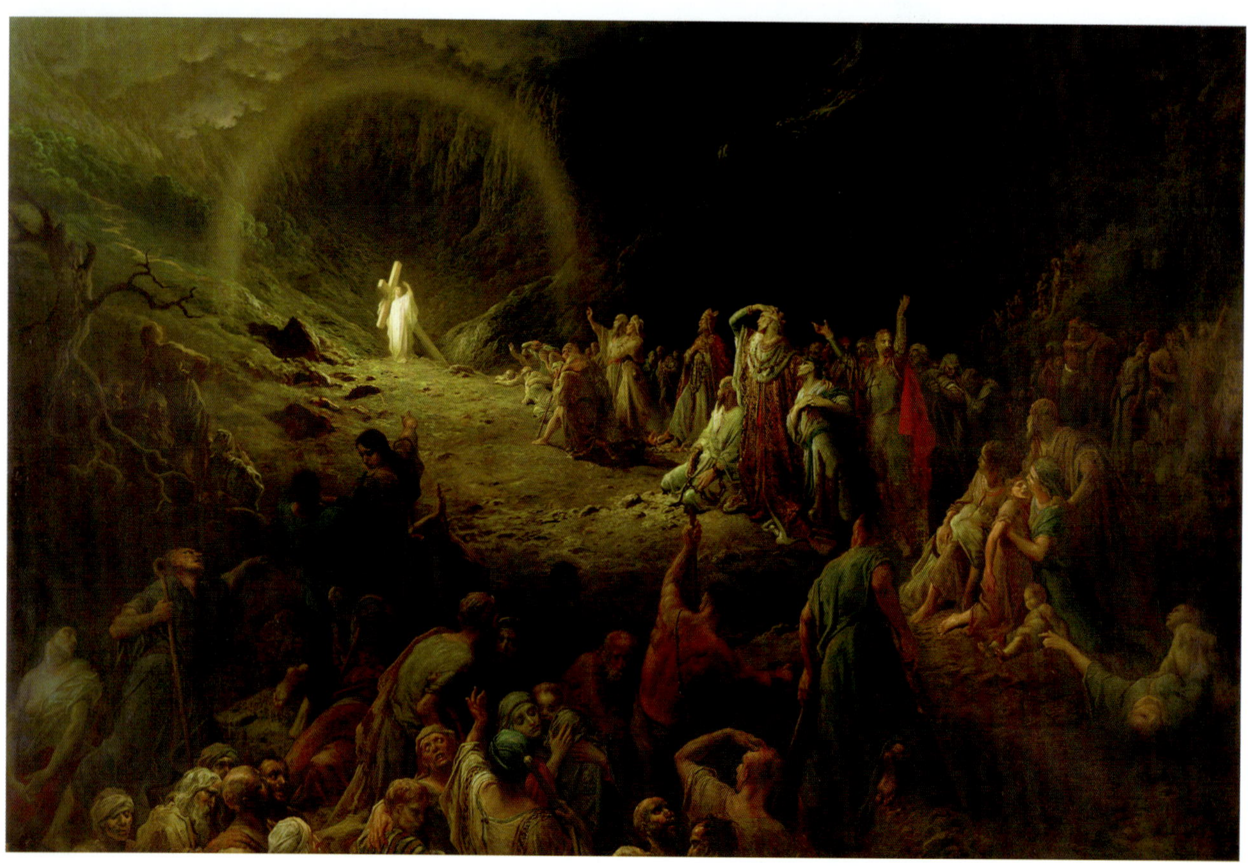

The Valley of Tears

La Vallée de larmes

Das Tal der Tränen

El valle de las lágrimas

O Vale das Lágrimas

Dal van tranen

GUSTAVE DORÉ (1832-1883)

1883, Oil on canvas/Huile sur toile, 413,5 x 627 cm, Petit Palais, Paris

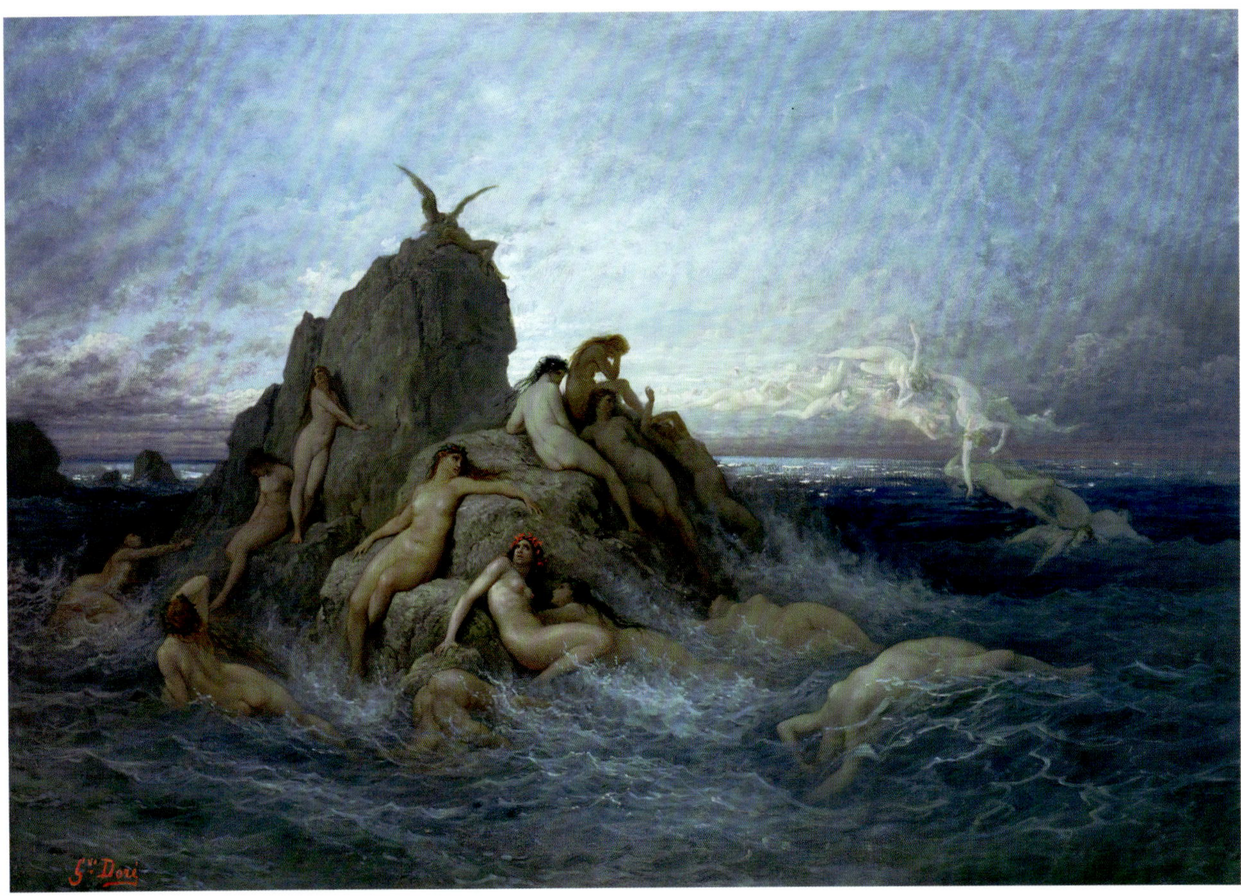

The Oceanids *or* The Naiads

The Oceanids, the daughters of Okeanos and Tethys, are
water nymphs from Greek mythology. Their 3,000 members
are the guardians of rivers, streams, lakes and the sea.

Les Océanides *ou* Les Naïades de la mer

Filles d'Océan et de Thétis, les Océanides sont des nymphes
aquatiques. Dans la mythologie grecque, elles sont les trois
mille gardiennes des fleuves, des rivières, des lacs
et des ruisseaux.

GUSTAVE DORÉ (1832-1883)

1878, Oil on canvas/Huile sur toile, 127 × 185,4 cm, Private collection

Die Okeaniden *oder* Die Najaden des Meeres

Die Okeaniden die Töchter des Okeanos und der Tethys,
sind Wassernymphen aus der griechischen Mythologie.
Ihre 3.000 Angehörigen sind die Wächterinnen der Flüsse,
Bäche, Seen und des Meeres.

Las Oceánides *o* las Náyades del Mar

Hijas del Océano y de Thetis, las Oceánidas son ninfas
acuáticas. En la mitología griega, son los tres mil guardianes
de los ríos, lagos y arroyos.

Os Okeanids *ou* os Najads do Mar

Os Okeanids, as filhas de Okeanos e Tétis, são ninfas
de água da mitologia grega. Seus 3.000 membros são os
guardiões dos rios, riachos, lagos e do mar.

De oceaniden *of* De najaden van de zee

De oceaniden, de dochters van Oceanos en Tethys, zijn
waternimfen uit de Griekse mythologie. Ze zijn met 3000
leden en bewaken rivieren, beken, meren en de zee.

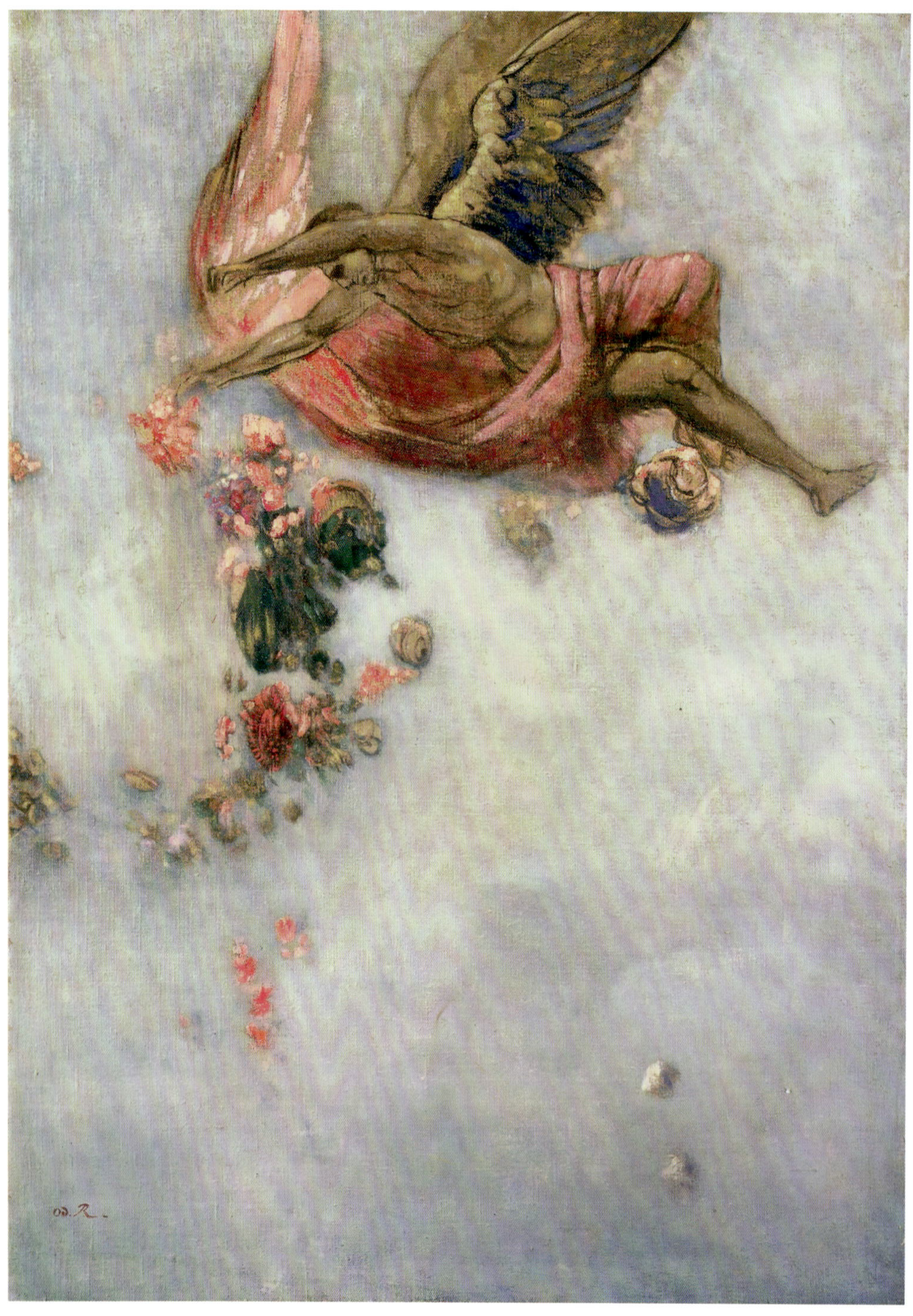

The Fall of Icarus

La Chute d'Icare

Der Sturz des Ikarus

La caída de Ícaro

A queda de Ícaro

De val van Icarus

ODILON REDON (1840-1916)
n.d., Oil on canvas/Huile sur toile,
66 × 47,5 cm, Private collection

Two Young Girls with Flowers

In his dreamlike portrayal, Redon has presented a harmonious connection between the two faces and the flowers that cover most of the canvas. He has created a firework of colors.

Deux jeunes filles parmi les fleurs

Dans cette composition onirique, Odilon Redon mêle harmonieusement deux visages féminins à des fleurs qui envahissent l'espace. Une œuvre placée sous le signe du rêve, dans un feu d'artifice de couleurs.

Zwei junge Mädchen zwischen Blumen

In seiner traumgleichen Darstellung schafft Redon eine harmonische Verbindung zwischen den zwei Gesichtern und den Blumen, die den Großteil der Leinwand bedecken. Er kreiert ein Feuerwerk der Farben.

Dos jovencitas entre flores

En su retrato onírico, Redon crea una conexión armoniosa entre las dos caras y las flores que cubren la mayor parte del lienzo. Crea un fuego artificial de colores.

Duas jovens raparigas entre flores

Em seu retrato sonhador, Redon cria uma conexão harmoniosa entre os dois rostos e as flores que cobrem a maior parte da tela. Ele cria um fogo de artifício de cores.

Twee jonge meisjes tussen bloemen

In zijn droomachtige voorstelling creëerde Redon een harmonieuze verbinding tussen de twee gezichten en de bloemen die het grootste deel van het doek beslaan. Hij schilderde een vuurwerk van kleuren.

ODILON REDON (1840-1916)
1912, Oil on canvas/Huile sur toile, 62,5 × 51,2 cm, Private collection

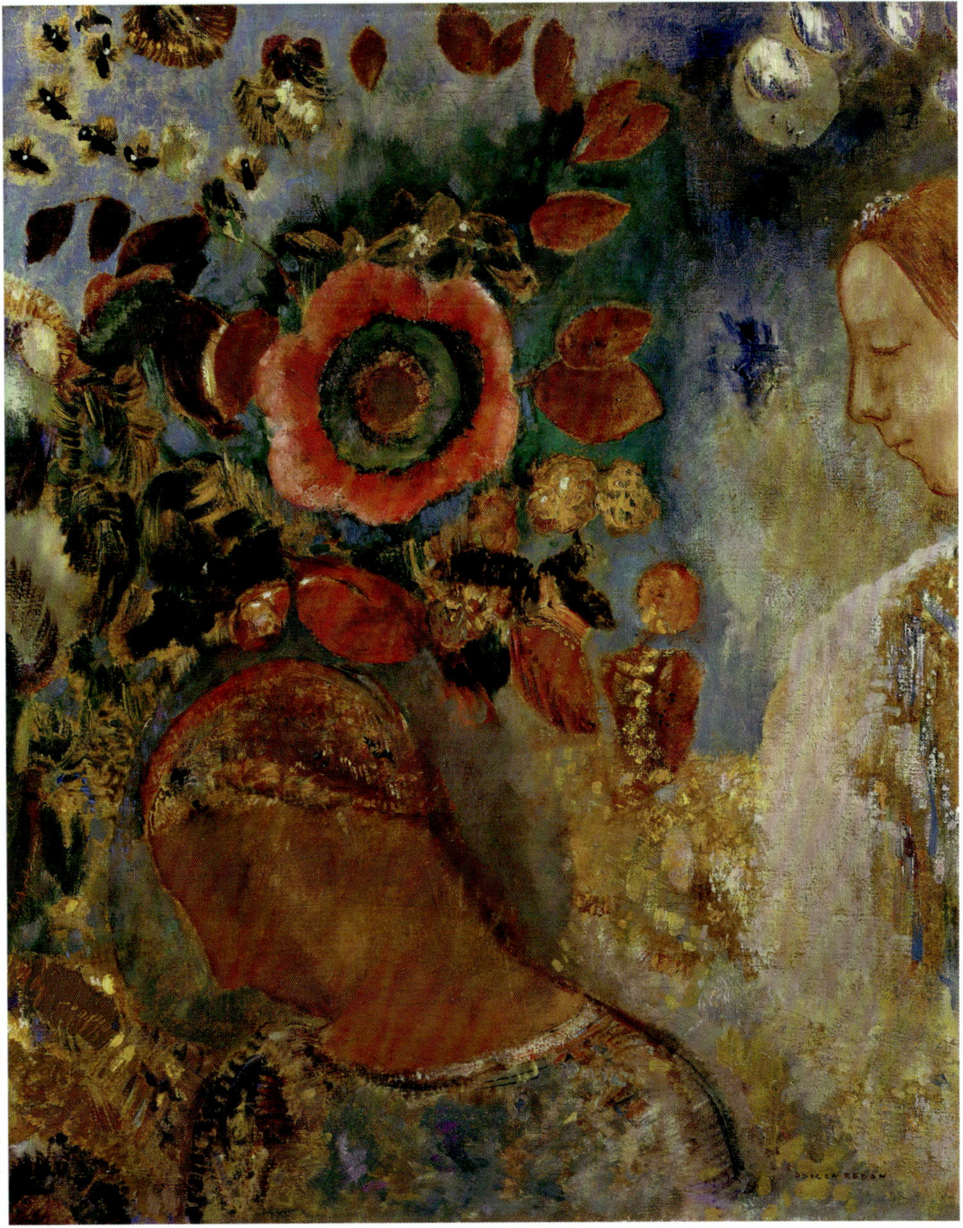

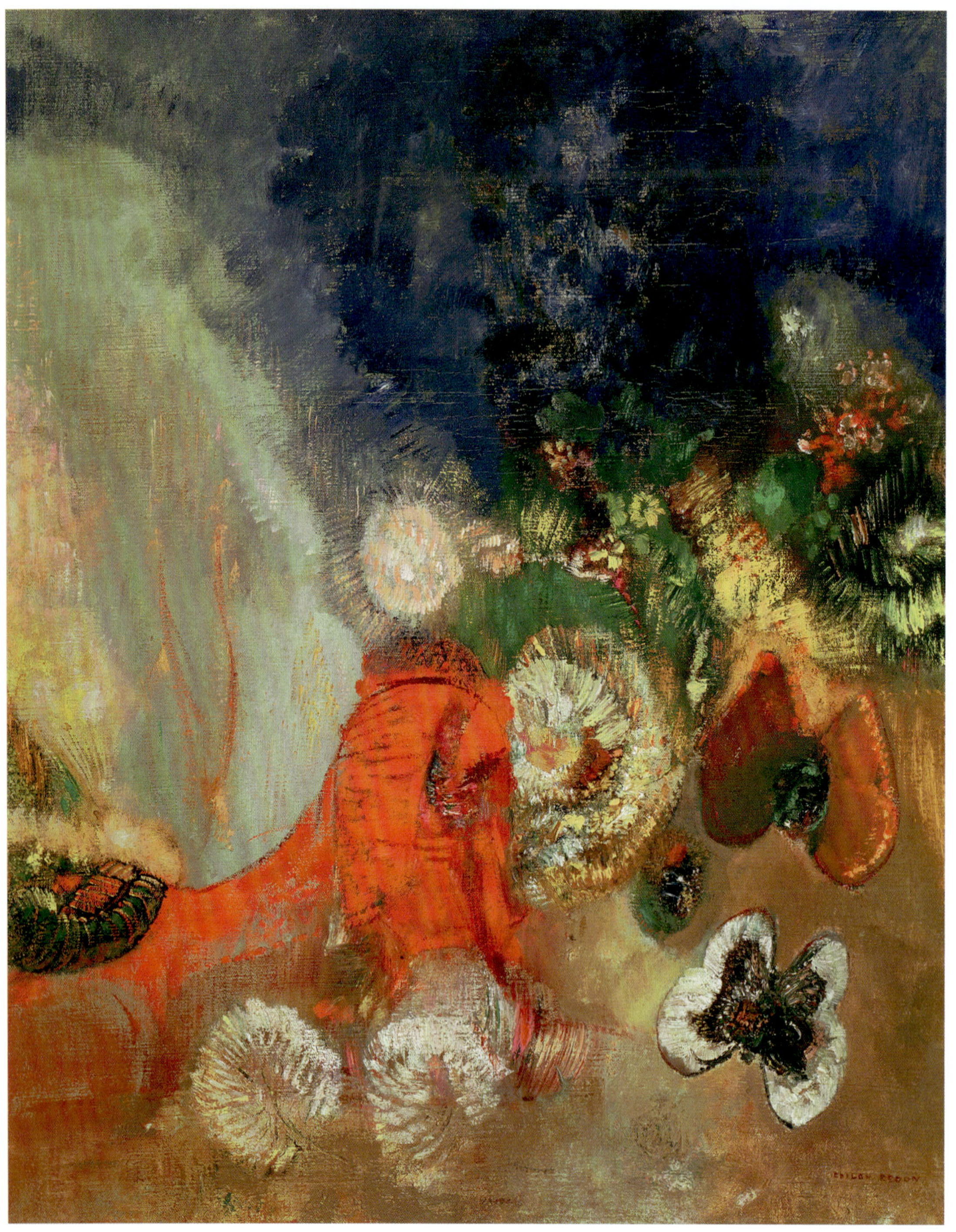

The Red Sphinx

Le Sphinx rouge

Die rote Sphinx

La esfinge roja

A Esfinge vermelha

De rode sfinx

ODILON REDON (1840-1916)

c. 1912, Oil on canvas/Huile sur toile, 61 × 49,5 cm, Private collection

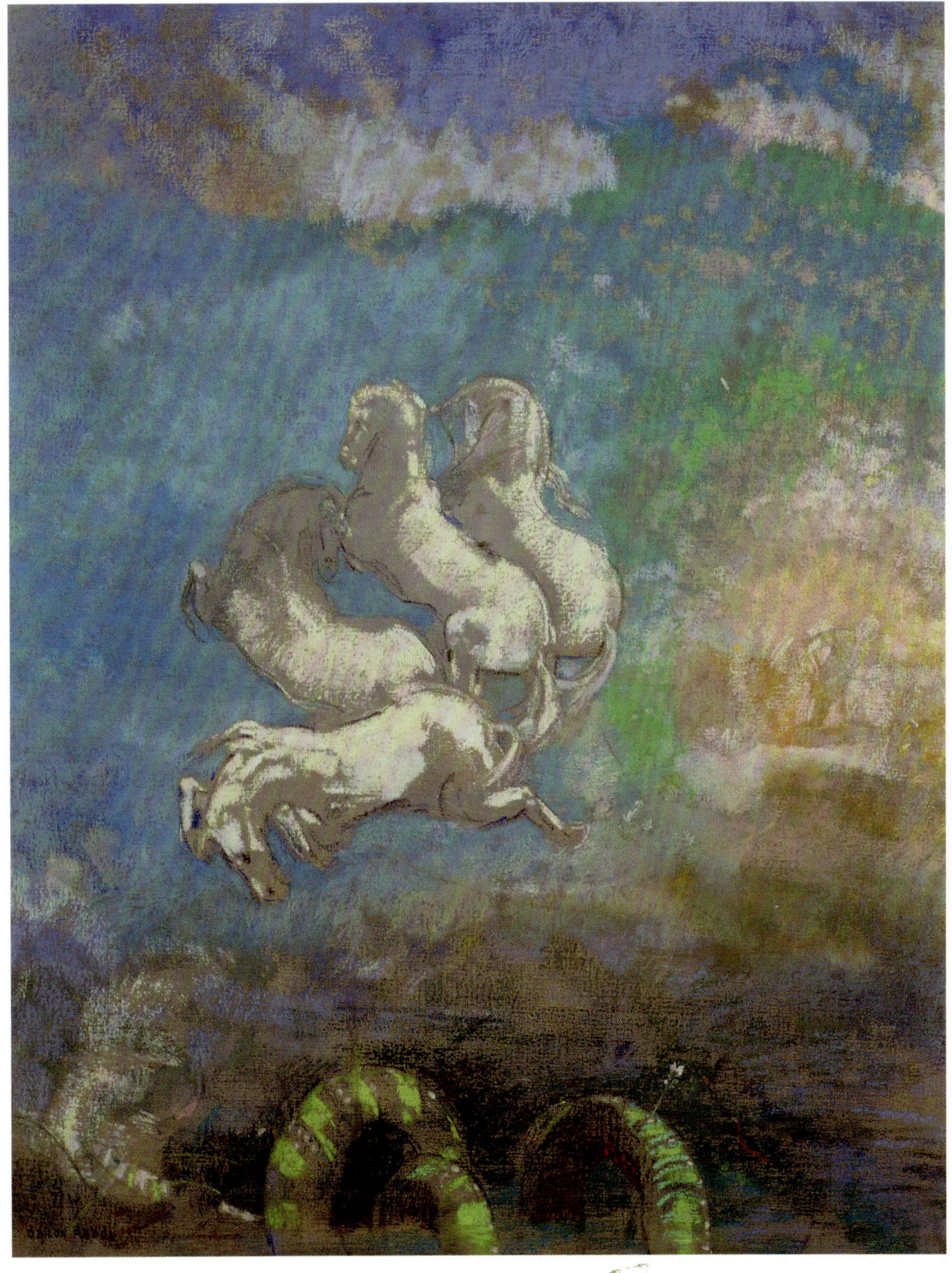

Apollo's Chariot

Redon painted several variations
of the motif. Apollo's silhouette
is only faintly visible in the light.
As if weightless, the horses move
freely through the infinity
of the sky.

Le Char d'Apollon

L'artiste a réalisé plusieurs
variations sur ce thème.
La silhouette d'Apollon se devine
à peine, noyée dans la lumière, et
les chevaux évoluent librement,
comme en apesanteur,
dans l'infini du ciel.

Der Wagen des Apoll

Redon malte mehrere Variationen
des Motivs. Apolls Silhouette
zeichnet sich nur schwach im
Licht ab. Die Pferde bewegen sich,
wie schwerelos, frei durch die
Unendlichkeit des Himmels.

El coche de Apolo

Redon pintó diferentes variaciones
del motivo. La silueta de Apolo
sólo es débilmente visible a la luz.
Los caballos se mueven, como si
fueran ingrávidos, libremente
por el infinito del cielo.

O carro de Apollo

Redon pintou várias variações do
motivo. A silhueta da Apollo é
apenas ligeiramente visível à luz.
Os cavalos movem-se, como que
sem peso, livremente através
do infinito do céu.

De wagen van Apollo

Redon schilderde verschillende
versies van het onderwerp.
Apollo's silhouet tekent zich
slechts zwak af in het licht. De
paarden bewegen zich, als waren
ze gewichtloos, vrij door de
oneindigheid van de lucht.

ODILON REDON (1840-1916)
c. 1910, Pastel and tempera on
canvas/Pastel et détrempe sur toile,
91,5 × 77 cm, Musée d'Orsay, Paris

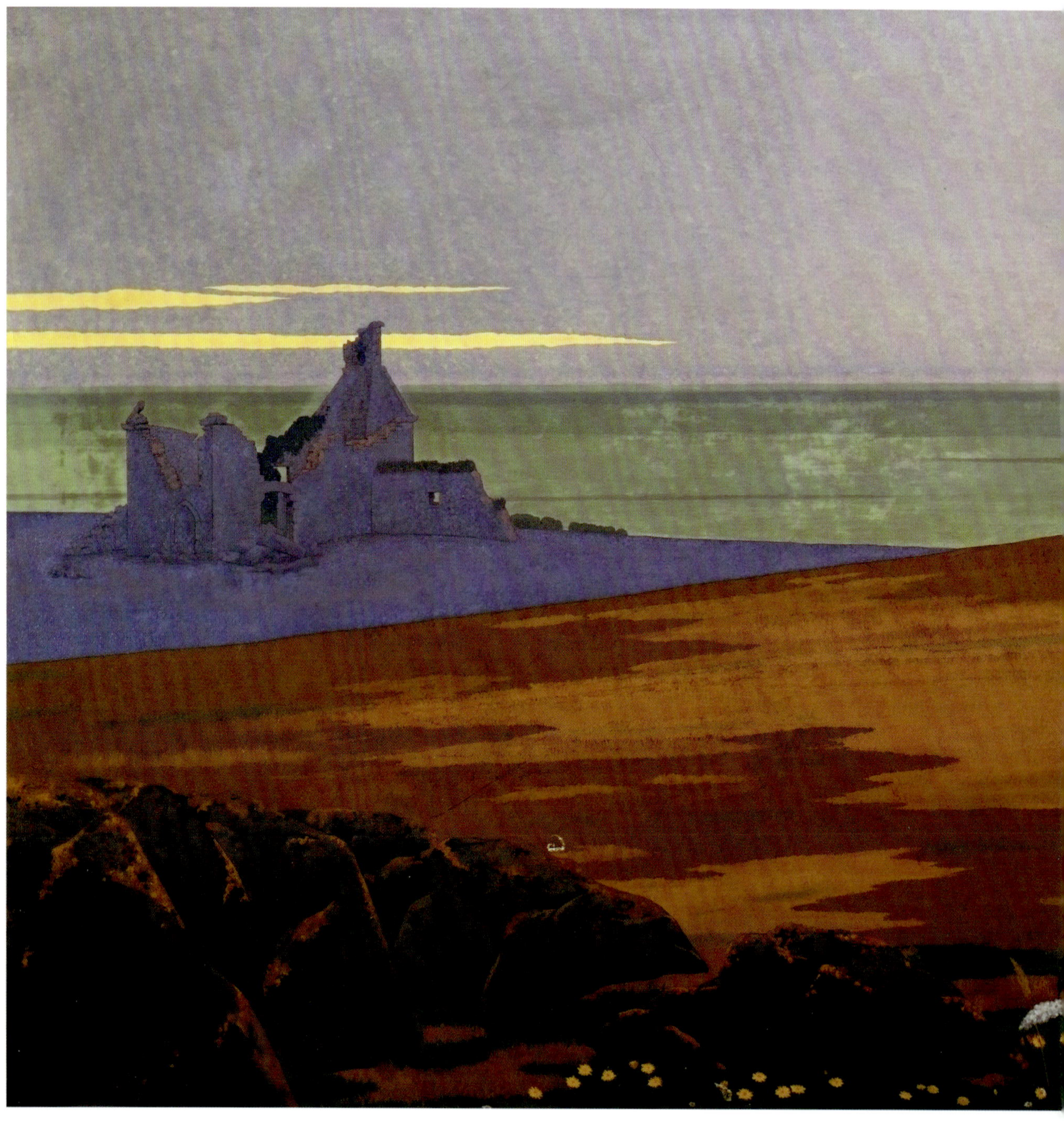

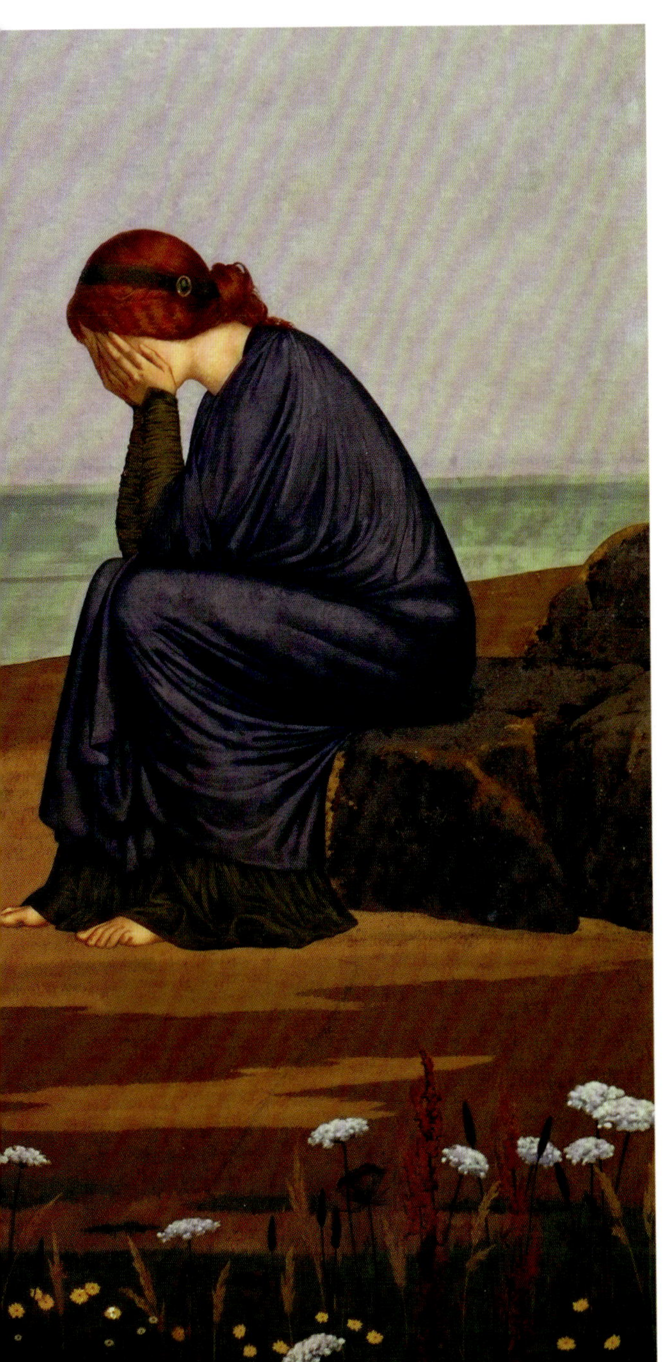

Return Home

Alexandre Séon was a pupil and assistant to Pierre Puvis de Chavannes. His style is close to that of his teacher. His often misunderstood work comprises silent and poetic paintings of great graphic clarity.

Le Retour au foyer

Stylistiquement proche de Pierre Puvis de Chavannes dont il fut l'élève puis l'assistant, Alexandre Séon est l'auteur méconnu d'une œuvre symboliste apaisante et poétique d'une grande pureté graphique.

Die Rückkehr nach Hause

Alexandre Séon war Schüler und Assistent von Pierre Puvis de Chavannes. Sein Stil steht dem seines Lehrers nahe. Sein oft verkanntes Werk umfasst stille und poetische Gemälde von einer großen grafischen Klarheit.

El regreso a casa

Alexandre Séon fue alumno y asistente de Pierre Puvis de Chavannes. Su estilo se acerca al de su maestro. Su obra, a menudo incomprendida, está formada por pinturas silenciosas y poéticas de gran claridad gráfica.

O regresso a casa

Alexandre Séon foi aluno e assistente de Pierre Puvis de Chavannes. O seu estilo é parecido com o do seu professor. Seu trabalho, muitas vezes mal entendido, compreende pinturas silenciosas e poéticas de grande clareza gráfica.

De terugkeer naar huis

Alexandre Séon was een leerling en assistent van Pierre Puvis de Chavannes. Zijn stijl ligt dicht bij die van zijn leraar. Zijn vaak verkeerd begrepen werk bestaat uit stille en poëtische schilderijen met een grote grafische helderheid.

ALEXANDRE SÉON (1855-1917)

c. 1912, Oil on canvas/Huile sur toile, 92,6 × 140,7 cm, Musée d'Art moderne et contemporain, Saint-Étienne

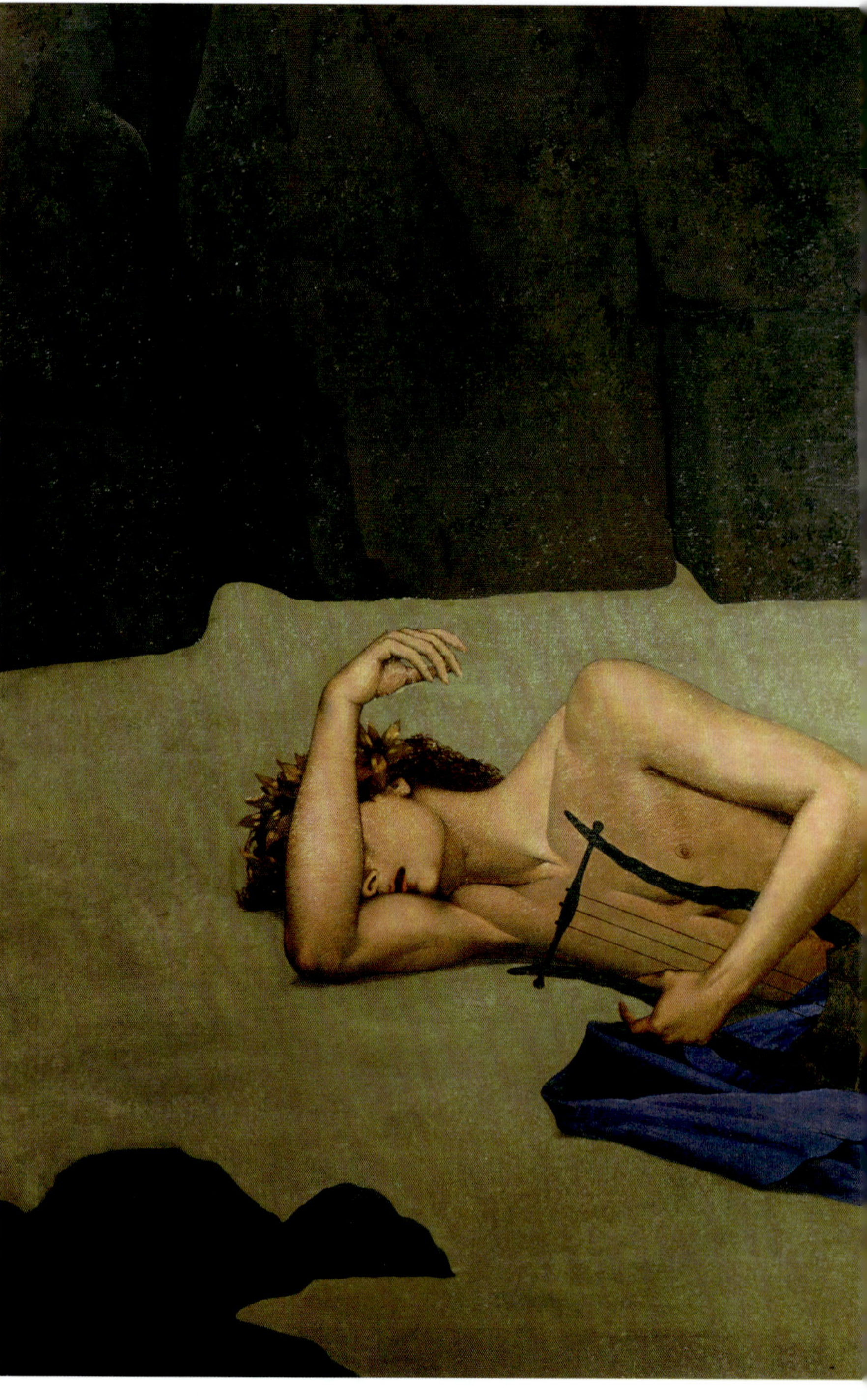

The Lamentation of Orpheus

Lamentation d'Orphée

Die Klage des Orpheus

El lamento de Orfeo

O lamento de Orfeu

De klaagzang van Orpheus

ALEXANDRE SÉON (1855-1917)

c. 1896, Oil on wood/Huile sur bois,
73 × 116 cm, Musée d'Orsay, Paris

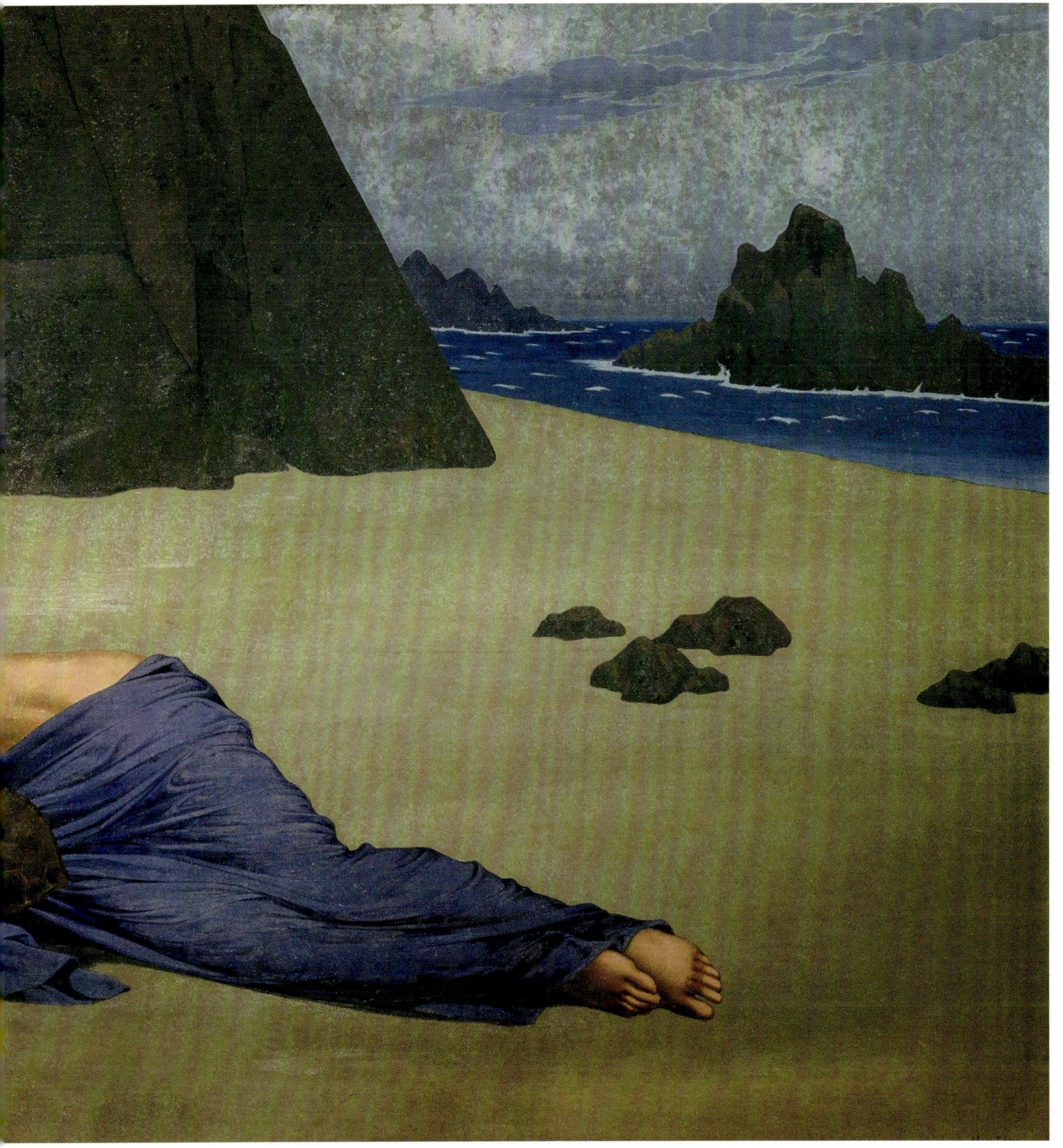

B

Bastien-Lepage, Jules (1848-1884) 148, 149
Bazille, Jean-Frédéric (1841-1870) 184, 185, 186, 187, 188-189, 190, 191, 192, 193
Béraud, Jean (1849-1935) 11, 26-27, 28, 29, 30, 31, 32, 33, 34, 35, 36-37, 38, 39, 40, 41, 42, 43, 44, 45
Bernard, Émile (1868-1941) 440, 441, 442, 443
Besnard, Albert (1849-1934) 46, 47
Blanche, Jacques-Émile (1861-1942) 54, 55
Bonheur, Rosa (1822-1899) 126, 127, 128, 129
Bonnard, Pierre (1867-1947) 371, 426, 427, 428, 429, 430, 431, 432, 433, 434, 435, 437, 438, 439
Boudin, Eugène (1824-1898) 156, 157, 158, 159, 160, 161, 162, 163, 164, 165
Breton, Jules (1827-1906) 135, 136, 137, 138, 139

C

Caillebotte, Gustave (1848-1894) 7, 286-287, 288, 289, 290, 291, 292, 293, 294, 295, 296, 297, 298, 299, 300-301, 302, 303, 304, 305, 306, 307
Cézanne, Paul (1839-1906) 8, 9, 309, 312, 313, 314, 315, 316, 317, 318, 319, 320, 321, 322, 323
Chaplin, Charles Joshua (1825-1891) 134
Corot, Jean-Baptiste Camille (1796-1875) 57, 60, 61, 62, 63, 64, 65, 66, 67, 68, 69, 70, 71, 72, 73, 74, 75
Courbet, Gustave (1819-1877) 99, 106, 107, 108-109, 110, 111, 112, 113, 114-115, 116, 117, 118, 119, 120, 121, 122, 123, 124, 125
Cross, Henri-Edmond (1856-1910) 329, 330, 331, 332, 333

D

Dagnan-Bouveret, Jean (1852-1929) 150, 151, 152
Daubigny, Charles-François (1817-1878) 59, 91, 92-93, 94-95, 96-97
Daumier, Honoré (1808-1879) 102, 103
Degas, Edgar (1834-1917) 197, 211, 212, 213, 214, 215, 216-217, 218, 219, 220, 221, 222, 223, 224, 225
Denis, Maurice (1870-1943) 373, 457, 458, 459, 460-461, 462-463
Diaz de la Peña, Narcisse (1807-1876) 76, 77
Doré, Gustave (1832-1883) 488, 489, 490, 491, 492, 493

F

Fantin-Latour, Henri (1836-1904) 100, 140, 141, 142, 143, 144, 145, 146
Filiger, Charles (1863-1928) 398, 399

G

Gauguin, Paul (1848-1903) 2, 374, 375, 376, 377, 378, 379, 380, 381, 382, 383, 384, 385, 386, 387, 388-389, 390, 391, 392, 393, 394, 395
Gervex, Henri (1852-1929) 48, 49, 50, 51, 52, 53
Guillaumin, Armand (1841-1927) 260, 261

L

Lacombe, Georges (1868-1916) 445, 446, 447
Lhermitte, Léon (1844-1925) 101, 147
Luce, Maximilien (1858-1941) 334, 335, 336, 337, 338, 339

M

Maillol, Aristide (1861-1944) 400, 401
Manet, Édouard (1832-1883) 155, 166-167, 168, 169, 170, 171, 172, 173, 174, 175, 176, 177, 178, 179, 180, 181, 182, 183
Maufra, Maxime (1861-1918) 402-403
Millet, Jean-François (1814-1875) 58, 84, 85, 86, 87, 88, 89, 90
Monet, Claude (1840-1926) 195, 226, 227, 228, 229, 230, 231, 232, 233, 234, 235, 236, 237, 238, 239, 240, 241, 242, 243, 244, 245, 246, 247, 248, 249, 250, 251, 252, 253, 254, 255, 256, 257, 258, 259
Moreau, Gustave (1826-1898) 466, 478, 479, 480, 481, 482, 483, 484, 485, 486, 487
Moret, Henry (1856-1913) 397
Morisot, Berthe (1841-1895) 262, 263, 264, 265, 266, 267, 268, 269

N

Noël, Jules (1810-1881) 104, 105

P

Petitjean, Hippolyte (1854-1929) 328
Pissarro, Camille (1830-1903) 196, 198, 199, 200, 201, 202, 203, 204, 205, 206, 207, 208, 209, 210
Puvis de Chavannes, Pierre (1824-1898) 465, 468, 469, 470-471, 472, 473, 474, 475, 476, 477

R

Ranson, Paul (1861-1909) 404, 405, 406, 407, 408, 409
Redon, Odilon (1840-1916) 467, 494, 495, 496, 497
Renoir, Auguste (1841-1919) 270, 271, 272, 273, 274, 275, 276, 277, 278, 279, 280, 281, 282, 283, 284, 285
Ribot, Théodule (1823-1891) 130, 131, 132, 133
Rousseau, Théodore (1812-1867) 78, 79, 80, 81, 82, 83
Rousseau, Henri (le Douanier Rousseau) (1844-1910) 324, 325, 326, 327
Royer, Henri (1869-1938) 153

S

Schuffenecker, Émile (1851-1934) 396
Seguin, Armand (1869-1903) 444
Séon, Alexandre (1855-1917) 498-499, 500-501
Sérusier, Paul (1864-1927) 410, 411, 412, 413, 414, 415, 416, 417
Seurat, Georges (1859-1891) 311, 340-341, 342, 343, 344, 345, 346
Signac, Paul (1863-1935) 310, 347, 348, 349, 350, 351, 352, 353, 354, 355

T

Tissot, James (1836-1902) 12, 13, 14, 15, 16-17, 18, 19, 20-21, 22, 23, 24, 25
Toulous-Lautrec, Henri de (1864-1901) 358, 359, 360, 361, 362, 363, 364, 365, 366, 367, 368, 369

V

Valadon, Suzanne (1865-1938) 356, 357
Vallotton, Félix (1865-1925) 418, 419, 420, 421, 422, 423, 424, 425
Vuillard, Édouard (1868-1940) 372, 448, 449, 450, 451, 452-453, 454, 455, 456

P. 2

And the Gold of their Bodies *(detail)*

Et l'or de leur corps *(détail)*

Und das Gold ihrer Körper *(Detail)*

Y el oro de sus cuerpos *(detalle)*

E o ouro de seus corpos *(detalhe)*

En het goud van hun lichamen *(detail)*

PAUL GAUGUIN (1848–1903)

1901, Oil on canvas/Huile sur toile, 67 × 76,5 cm, Musée d'Orsay, Paris

KÖNEMANN

© 2020 koenemann.com GmbH

www.koenemann.com

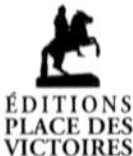

**ÉDITIONS
PLACE DES
VICTOIRES**

© Éditions Place des Victoires

6, rue du Mail – 75002 Paris

www.victoires.com

ISBN: 978-2-8099-1827-4

Dépôt légal : 2e trimestre 2020

Concept, project management: koenemann.com GmbH

Text: Valentin Grivet

Translations into English, German, Spanish, Portuguese
and Dutch by koenemann.com GmbH

Layout: Michelle Aflalo

Picture credits: Bridgeman images except pp. 34, 36–37, 45, 52, 82, 83, 88, 91, 140,
150, 152, 186, 188–189, 222, 225, 338–389, 400, 488, 489, 490:akg images gmbh

Colour separation: Nord Compo, Villeneuve-d'Ascq

ISBN: 978-3-7419-2929-8 (international)

Printed in China by Shyft Publishing/Hunan Tianwen Xinhua Printing Co., Ltd